THE PREACHER'S COMMENTARY

ON THE

BOOK OF LEVITICUS.

THE
Preacher's Complete Homiletical
COMMENTARY

ON THE

OLD TESTAMENT

(ON AN ORIGINAL PLAN).

With Critical and Explanatory Notes, Indices, &c., &c.

BY

VARIOUS AUTHORS.

New York
FUNK & WAGNALLS COMPANY
LONDON AND TORONTO
1892

THE PREACHER'S COMMENTARY

ON THE BOOK OF

LEVITICUS:

CONTAINING

SUGGESTIVE READINGS: Being comments on each chapter, Didactic and Experimental.
HOMILETICS: Consisting of three hundred and fifty Breviates and Outlines on *Sections, Topics,* or *Verses* of each chapter.
ILLUSTRATIONS: Furnishing apt incident or quotation on the Homiletic Themes.

BY THE

REV. W. HARVEY JELLIE,

Author of "The Preacher's Commentary on Jeremiah," etc.

Assisted in the Homiletics by

REV. FREDERICK W. BROWN.

New York
FUNK & WAGNALLS COMPANY
LONDON & TORONTO
1892

PREFACE.

HAVING regard to the Commentaries on Leviticus already in existence, ponderous with erudition and criticism, claiming also to be literary and exegetical, this "Homiletical Commentary" has deliberately shunned the profundities of scholarship, and works along practical and experimental lines. From first to last, distinctive in this intent, it has quietly kept to its homiletical aim. Perhaps it may be found, on that very account, none the less serviceable as a help towards pulpit preparations. In its Readings, Homilies, and Outlines it seeks throughout to be suggestive and didactic, searching amid Hebrew ordinances for universal obligations, and gospel teachings in the sacrifices and rites of the Wilderness.

To read the book of Leviticus in its rich significance, the Tabernacle Revelations must be pondered in connexion with the "Word made flesh who tabernacled among us"; its Altar Sacrifices be read in the light which radiates from the sacred Cross; its Priestly offices and sanctions be viewed as foreshadowing the Christian's privileges and ministries; and its Moral Enactments be regarded as affirming those virtues essential through every age in man's relation to man. The Levitical ceremonies and ritual are picturesque delineations of the doctrines and duties of Christianity.

A cursory survey of this book of the Decalogue might dispose preachers to conclude that it contains few themes suited to present day needs; this error may explain why sermons on texts in Leviticus are so strangely rare. Closer acquaintance with its contents, and the appliance of a steady interpretative faculty to its symbols, will reveal that scarcely a Doctrine of Grace is lacking in those sanctuary ceremonies, whilst a wealth of Ethical Instruction dwells in the regulations of the Israelitish Camp.

The endeavour to force a homily from any and every text has been honourably abandoned. Whatever verses or themes presented a natural basis for homiletic effort, there an outline or breviate has been furnished. If this Commentary were compacted of homiletics which no preacher could use and no congregation would hear, it would merit the rebuke—"To what purpose is this waste?" The age is greatly too earnest to greet or value mere dexterous products which can serve no practical end.

Each chapter opens with Suggestive Readings, which it is hoped will afford guidance to suitable expository comments in the services of the Sanctuary. They are, therefore, not critical and analytical, but didactic and experimental.

The Commentary contains three hundred and forty-nine Homilies and Outlines : of these, 35 have been condensed from printed sermons, a further 35 are homilies constructed from books on Leviticus which are not homiletical ; the remaining 247 are original contributions for this book. Those prepared by our co-labourer, the Rev. Frederick W. Brown, are subscribed with his initials. Where no name or initials appear, the reader may justly ascribe the homily to our own pen : this applies also to all the Suggestive Readings, as well as to the Illustrative Addenda. And in those instances, where a name is undersigned to a homily or outline, one of two processes must be credited to our account. Either the homily is a creation based upon some note book on Leviticus, in which the author's ideas and words are given as nearly as practicable, with addition of our own to complete the homily ; or it is a condensation of some published sermon on a text in Leviticus, which it has been our personal task to prepare for the pages of this Commentary.

Among the books specially suggestive of these homilies may be mentioned, " Jukes on the Offerings "; " Thoughts on Leviticus," by B. W. Newton ; " Notes on Leviticus," by C. H. M. ; " Christ is All," by Dean Law ; " The Doctrine of Sacrifice," by Maurice ; " The Levitical Priests," by Curtiss ; and Atwater's " The sacred Tabernacle of the Hebrews."

By summarizing or reconstructing sermons it has been possible to enrich this Commentary with the quickening thoughts of such preachers as Edward T. Atwood, A. Coquerel, Albert H. Currier, A. E. Dunning, James Fleming, D.D., H. M. Grant, D.D., D. C. Hughes, M.A., G. R. Leavitt, David O. Mears, C. H. Spurgeon, W. Stephenson, Samuel Thodey, Lewis O. Thompson, W. Wayland, Jno. Wesley, and others.

The Illustrative Addenda to each chapter will afford choice quotation or apt incident with which to enforce a truth.

Three Indices, with exact and detailed classifications of topics, analysis, and illustrations are supplied, by which access to the contents of this volume for every purpose is rendered simple and direct.

To the generous appreciation with which the larger and more laborious *Homiletical Commentary on Jeremiah* was received, we venture to commend this companion volume, with this testimony—that no joy so deep and true comes to any worker for Christ as that of knowing his labours are found helpful to others amid the stress of their public toils, and that the Word of God is opening its stores of truth more freely to students in consequence of his honest, though humble, endeavours to serve them in the Divine Master's name.

W. HARVEY-JELLIE.

A HOMILETIC COMMENTARY

ON THE BOOK OF

LEVITICUS.

INTRODUCTORY NOTES.

i. **Concerning the book itself.** Because it is occupied mainly with directions respecting the offerings and services of the sons of Levi, it is called the Book of Leviticus. Under the very shadow of Mount Sinai Jehovah gave these ecclesiastical enactments for Israel. The entire contents of the book are included within the brief term of about one month, viz., from the erection of the Tabernacle to the numbering of the people. The historical occurrences which it narrates are few; the consecration of the priesthood (chaps. viii., ix.), God's destruction of Nadab and Abihu for profanation (chap. ix.), and the magistrate's punishment of Shelomith's son for blasphemy (chap. xxiv.). Evidence the most valid connects Moses with the *authorship* of Leviticus, who most probably wrote these divinely given regulations during the fifty days preceding the starting of the Israelites from their encampment near Sinai upon their wilderness journeyings.

ii. **Its natural position in the Pentateuch.** Exodus closes with the record of the Tabernacle being completed; the shrine was ready for the worship of God. Leviticus follows with directions for that worship; gives Divine regulations for sacrifices and services, whereby man might acceptably and appropriately "come before the Lord." The sacred house being reared, now ensue the orders of that house. God Himself designed the holy fabric; He also prescribes the ordinances for approaching Him therein.

iii. **A general summary of its contents.** Minute institutions and regulations are given concerning the *altar sacrifices* in chaps. i. to vii., the consecration and conduct of the *priesthood* in chaps. viii. to x.; enactments respecting the *purification of uncleanness*—in chap. xi. of animals, and chaps. xii. to xv. of men; the *Day of Atonement*, ordained to propitiate for all omissions and faultiness in sacrifice during the year, is appointed in chap. xvi., and varied statutes are prescribed relating to the *rectitude of the people* among themselves (chaps. xvii. to xx.), the *purity of the priesthood* in their ministrations (chaps. xxi., xxii.), the hallowed observance of the sacred festivals (chaps. xxiii., xxiv.), supplemented with directions concerning the land, vows, etc. (chaps. xxv. to xxvii.).

iv. **The spiritual significance of its sacrifices and ceremonies.** Jehovah had erected His sanctuary in Israel's midst; His people must now understand and observe the solemn *sanctities essential to access and fellowship* with Him. A place for worship, and arrangements for altar sacrifices, were matters of inferior importance to the spiritual condition of those who should come before the Lord. Hence the sacrificial enactments of Leviticus show how acceptance with God and ceremonial purification should be sought by Israel. But additional to that immediate purpose of these Levitical arrangements, the appointed offerings presented on that altar were all made typical and suggestive of the Sacrifice of the Cross, and the sacred festivals ordained for the Tabernacle indicated the gracious ordinances of the future Gospel age. Thus, in its altar types and symbolic ceremonies, Leviticus prefigures the efficacy of the Redeemer's substitutionary death, and the spiritual privileges which should be enjoyed in the Christian Church.

CHAPTER I.

The Law of the Burnt Sacrifices.

SUGGESTIVE READINGS.

V. 1.—Lord called . . and spake. From within the Tabernacle: God's first habitation among men. Never before had He "dwelt with men on the earth"; He speaks now for the first time from His holy tent in Israel's midst. It foreshadowed the "*Word* tabernacling among us" (John i. 14). "The Lord *called*" is a phrase specially used when important communications were to follow; as from the burning bush (Ex. iii. 4), and from Sinai's heights (xix. 3-20). The law of *commandments* was given to Moses amid flames and thunder, as being condemnatory of man's sin. Now, the law of *sacrifice* is given in gracious communication through Moses, as revealing God's plan of mercy. For *us*, in these Christian times, the gentler teachings of the Mount of Beatitudes form our law of duty and of life.

V. 2.—If any man of you bring. God assumes—

(1) *That men would seek Him;* would draw near to Him in the sacred tent, wherein He had come so near to men. If so, surely more readily and gratefully we should seek Him in Jesus. "God was in Christ," etc. (2 Cor. v. 19). (2) That men will *seek Him, bringing offerings;* some presentation as a token of homage and gratitude for His gifts to them; or some propitiation as a lament over their sin and an appeal to His mercy. God still looks for offerings as we "come before His presence"; what shall we render? what worthiest presentation can we take?

V. 3.—A burnt sacrifice. This expressed the offerer's *surrender of himself* unto God as "a living sacrifice" (Rom. xii. 1). The victim must have *no blemish*, must be the choicest product of his pastures; for God asks, and will only receive, our *best* (Mal. i. 14). It must be offered "*of his own voluntary will*," or rather "for his own acceptance," expressing his great concern to win God's gracious regard; and indeed, we ought to concern ourselves supremely for this; "in Thy favour is life." And he must offer it "*at the door of the tabernacle*," as being unworthy to enter. With humility and reverence, and a lowly sense of demerit, we should venture near God.

(*a*) *Christ* is herein typified; our Sacrifice "without blemish," offered for man's "acceptance," ere He "entered the holy place" (Heb. ix. 12-24).

(*b*) *The Christian* is prefigured; "yielding himself alive unto God," "holy and acceptable," ere he is admitted into covenant privileges within the Church now, and finally into God's presence in heaven.

V. 4.—Put his hand upon the head. An act of transfer: threefold; signifying transference of his *right of possession* in the victim, his *sense of sin* to the victim, and his *substitution for suffering* of the victim. Thus the Christian gives up all rights of self-possession (" Ye are not your own "): thus also the sinner lays all his sin, and the believer all his hope, on Christ his sacrifice and substitute. It must be the individual's own act, none can do it for another; every one must himself lay *"his* hand" on Christ.

V. 5.—He shall kill the bullock. Thereby he identified himself with the victim designated to die, and thereby claimed the "atonement" effected by its sacrificial substitution. To be saved we must also be identified with Christ in His death, and thereby inherit His atonement. "*The priest* shall bring the blood," not the offerer; for the priestly offices of Christ are essential; man must let Jesus do all the work of propitiation. "*Sprinkle the blood round about upon the altar*"; attesting thereby that life had been given up in sacrificial suffering unto God. Christ's death is the sinner's death, and "the blood of sprinkling" testifies that "He made His soul an offering for sin." Diffused "round about upon the altar," the blood is the memorial of an accomplished atonement, the seal of an accepted sacrifice.

Vv. 6-9.—Fire upon the altar . . . an offering made by fire. Once lighted, that fire was never more to go out (ch. vi. 13). Yet every part of the victim must be "*washed*" faultlessly clean before being placed on the altar: only the absolutely clean can be acceptable to God. And then the entire victim, every part thereof, must ascend in sacrificial fire unto God. Thus (1) Christ our atonement-offering must Himself be "holy, harmless, undefiled"; and must also be completely sacrificed for man's sin. And (2) *Christian life* must likewise be both thoroughly sanctified and wholly devoted unto God. "Therefore glorify God in your body, and in your spirit, which are God's" (1 Cor. vi. 20).

A sweet savour unto the Lord. The very virtue and essence of the offering ascended by fire from the altar on earth to God in heaven. Duly offered by fire, the sacrifice was "a sweet savour" to the Lord. *Christ's* sacrifice was: " He gave Himself for us an offering and a *sacrifice to God for a sweet smelling savour* " (Eph. v. 2). Christian self-consecration is: "For we are unto God a *sweet savour of Christ*" (2 Cor. ii. 15). Christian life perpetuates on earth and yields continually to heaven the incense of a pure offering, "an odour of a sweet smell, a sacrifice acceptable, well-pleasing to God" (Phil. iv. 18).

Vv. 10-13.—A burnt sacrifice of the flocks. Only the wealthier offerers could bring the costlier sacrifice " of the herd " (v. 3). God equally provides for the less opulent among the people; gives directions for their sacrifices just as specific, denoting that He valued their presentation as much as the costlier offering. Our straitened lot does not release us from God's claims, neither is our humbler gift depreciated by God. But He requires entirety in all our sacrifices, that we devote to Him our utmost, our all. "Bring it *all* and burn it upon the altar."

Vv. 14-17.—A burnt sacrifice of fowls. Thus God, with minute care, arranges for the poorest, that none may feel God's requirements too heavy for them to meet, or deem their poverty a disqualification for approaching Him acceptably. In this instance, however, the *priest* was to bring the bird to the altar and slay it (v. 15), thereby giving peculiar importance to the poor man's offering as worthy special attention; for God has always put honour on the sacrifices of the poor, as our Lord did on the widow's mite. Yet insignificant as was the offering of the poor, it must as fully denote entire self-devotion to God. He prizes the love which shows itself in our casting in " all our living " (Mark xii. 44).

INTRODUCTORY HOMILIES.

(A). THE LEVITICAL RITUAL.

That Moses was the author of this Book is acknowledged by most competent scholars. The events of the Book cover only about a month of time, *i.e.*, from the erection of the tabernacle to the numbering of the people, and they relate to the establishment of sacrificial worship among the Hebrews in the wilderness of Sinai.

I. Although the words of Leviticus were written by Moses, they were dictated by the Lord.

The first verse of the Book decides this point, Moses records the utterances that proceeded from the tabernacle. So far then as Leviticus is concerned, we have the thoughts of God in the words of God, and, as such, they deserve our reverent attention, as indicating Jehovah's desire for our acceptable approach to Him.

Note that (1) *the pure ethical teaching of the Levitical ritual could not have been invented by a people so perverse and prone to corruption as Israel;* (2) *and they would not voluntarily have put themselves under such restrictions if they could.* The revelation of God to Israel, through His servant Moses, was the outcome of the Divine disposition to communicate to and commune with man, of His deep concern for human holiness and happiness; this the basis and spring of all revelation and blessing to our race. [See Illustrative Addenda, p. 18, *Revelation*.]

II. Although the rites of Leviticus have been superseded, its moral teaching has not been abrogated.

If read in connection with the Epistle to Hebrews (which is its best commentary) lessons upon Christian work, worship, witnessing may be gathered. Christ came not to destroy the law, but to give it a fuller and deeper significance, to exemplify and enforce the principles therein taught. The perfect ethics of the Gospel have their germs and roots in the law, both enjoin holiness to the Lord.

III. Although the sacrifices of Leviticus have been discontinued, the one offering of Christ abideth for ever.

We need no material *altar* or *sacrifice;* and, therefore, no human priest. Christ finished His atoning work upon the Cross—appears now as "Lamb in the midst of the throne," showing that while He was once a *victim* ("Lamb") He is now a *victor* ("throne"). The law is our schoolmaster to lead us to Christ. Except read in light of the New Testament, Leviticus becomes a form without power, shadow without substance. With joy we may draw water out of these wells of salvation. In its typical rites we may apprehend Him who hath obtained eternal redemption for us.—*Rev. F. W. Brown.*

(B). COMMUNION WITH GOD BY A REDEEMED PEOPLE THROUGH ALTAR OFFERINGS.

The *Exodus* sacrifices, those offered by the children of Israel while *in Egypt*, *i.e.*, the paschal lamb and unleavened bread, had reference and significance wholly to their *redemption:* deliverance from death and bondage. The *Levitical* sacrifices were those of a *saved people*, and were appointed for their *acceptable approaches to God* their Saviour. Instead, therefore, of seeing Christ as redeeming us, we see Him in His work for those already redeemed; bringing them into fellowship with God and restoring them when they fail or fall. To hold communion with God they need Christ both as Offering and Mediator, Sacrifice and Priest; thus He appears in the tabernacle services. Gathering all the tabernacle offerings into one view, remark that:

I. **Altar offerings and tabernacle ministries all reach their completion in Christ.**

He is the Burnt Offering, Meat Offering, Peace Offering, Sin Offering, Trespass Offering for His people. "When He said, sacrifice and offering and burnt offering and offering for sin Thou wouldst not, neither hadst pleasure therein, which are offered by the law; then said He, Lo I come to do Thy will, O God. He taketh away the first, that He may establish the second " (Heb. x. 8, 9). By the one oblation of Himself He has stood in all those relations; relations precious to God, needful to His Church.

1. In each offering *three distinct objects* are present: *the offering, the priest, the offerer.* Christ is each of and all these. So manifold are the relations in which Christ has stood for man and to man that all types are required to represent His fulness. First He comes as *Offerer;* but we cannot see the Offerer without the *offering;* and the Offerer is Himself the Offering; and He who is both Offerer and Offering is also the *Priest.* (1) As offerer, we see Him our *Substitute,* "fulfilling all righteousness." (2) As priest, we see Him our *Mediator,* ministering between God and Israel. (3) As offering, He is seen the *Innocent Victim,* a sweet savour to God, yet bearing the sin and dying for it. (1) The offerer sets forth Christ *in His Person;* who became *man* to meet God's requirements. (2) The offering presents Him *in His character and work,* as the victim by which atonement was ratified. (3) The priest shows Him *in His official relation* as the appointed intercessor.

2. The *difference in the several offerings* asks notice; the *Burnt,* the *Meat,* the *Peace* offerings, etc. They represent *different aspects* of Christ's offering. [For their different meaning compare Homilies on each.]

3. The *offerer* himself also reflects Christ *in His diverse aspects.* The faithful Israelite stands, in one instance, as a *sinless* offerer, presenting a "sweet smelling savour" for acceptance with God, not propitiating for sin; in another as a *convicted sinner,* offering an expiatory sacrifice which bears the pain and penalty of his transgressions.

The offering of Christ was but one, and but once offered; but as Christ's fulness and relations are so manifold, all aspects are needful to represent Him in those manifold relations and His various work for us.

4. The *different grades* in the various offerings is equally significant; the *bullock,* the *lamb,* the *dove.* And these denote the different *estimates and apprehensions* formed of Christ by His people. Christ's work is so complete that each aspect may be differently apprehended *according to the measure of light* in the believer. Some never go beyond the conception of Christ as their Paschal Offering, *securing their redemption* from Egyptian bondage and death. Others, however, see Him as their *Burnt* Offering, wholly *devoted to God* for them; while to others He is as the passive Lamb *silent and submissive in affliction;* and to others the mourning Dove *gentle and sorrowful in His innocency.*

II. *Altar offerings and tabernacle ministries* were **designed for Israel's acceptable communion with God.**

The types of Leviticus, in distinction from the types of redemption or deliverance from doom, give us the work of Christ in its bearing on worship and communion.

1. They meet the needs of a ransomed people *in providing for their access to God.* If they come for *consecration* they bring the burnt offerings: if for *grateful acknowledgment* of Divine bounty and graciousness, they bring the food offerings; if for *reconciliation* after ignorant misadventure or neglect of duty or temporary transgression, they bring their peace or trespass offering, &c. But they all provide a basis for *access* to and *acceptance with* God.

How thoroughly all these qualities unite in the one offering of Jesus is manifest; so that we, redeemed by Him, come before God with His merits and graces, and are accepted in Him. "Therefore, *being justified* by faith, we have peace with God, through our Lord Jesus Christ, by whom *also we have access* by faith into *this grace* wherein we stand . . . . and not only so, but we *also joy in God* through our Lord Jesus Christ, by whom we have now received the atonement" (Rom. v. 1, 2, 11).

2. Christ's work as connected with the communion of His people, *must be viewed under manifold representations.* The Offering first: for His one oblation

"Provides for those who come to God
An all-prevailing plea."

Yet how few believers enter earnestly into the manifold aspects and aims of Christ's one offering represented in the various victims and the arrangements for their sacrifice. They read of Him as the *Sin* Offering, the *Burnt* Offering, &c., but no corresponding thought is suggested to them by this distinction. It is enough for them that the blood of the Paschal Lamb has been sprinkled on their door post and they are saved: they inquire not more concerning Him. But they who would know *the joy of communion* must go from strength to strength in the knowledge of the grace and work of Jesus. Have they known Him as the Paschal Lamb? They will then seek to know Him as the offering *within the Tabernacle.* Have they learnt Him in His different relations as offering? They will then seek to know Him in His Offices as Priest: His ministrations for us within the Holy Place: His grace and acceptableness as our Mediator at the altar: His free entrance on our behalf into the presence of God.

Thus, redemption being known, the Levitical sacrifices relate to the access of a chosen people to God: and show Christ as He is discerned by one who already knows the certainty of redemption; Christ the Priest, the Offerer, the Offering: Christ as meeting all that a sinner saved needs in approaching to God: Christ for the believer, and all that Christ is to the believer as keeping up his daily communion with God, meeting his needs in his access to Jehovah.—Homiletically arranged by Editor from "*Jukes on the Offerings.*"

SECTIONAL HOMILIES.

Topic.—WORSHIP BY SACRIFICE (Vv. 1-9).

A great change had now occurred in the conditions of worship. God had hitherto declared His will amid terrible manifestations. The people had stood afar off in fear. Only through Moses, as a daysman betwixt them, had God spoken to men, or men approached Him. Now the Lord had commanded, "Build Me a tabernacle that I may dwell among them" (Ex. xxv. 8). Within their camp was a smoking altar, whose incense was a voiceless but constant prayer; and a Holy of Holies, in whose mysterious recesses dwelt the unseen Jehovah. To Him all the people were to approach, presenting their sacrificial offerings to Him for propitiation and consecration.

I. ACCEPTABLE WORSHIP MUST BE IN ACCORDANCE WITH DIVINE DIRECTION.

1. Many approach God with the feeling that He is glad to have the attention of men, *and will welcome them under any circumstances.* But He has made conditions for acceptable worship. It must be with

(*a*) *An obedient spirit.* "Not every one that saith, Lord, Lord, etc., but he that doeth the will of My Father."

(*b*) *A reverent spirit.* "Put thy shoes from off thy feet."

(*c*) *Faith.* "He that cometh to God must believe," etc.

The people who had been so awestricken by the voice from the Mount that "they entreated that the word should not be spoken to them any more" would not venture to approach Jehovah unless called, nor in any way than the appointed. *God has a right to prescribe the methods by which He shall be worshipped,* and it is a proof of His mercy that He entered into minute details.

2. In any way that God commands, *worship is a priceless privilege.*

Here He appoints approach through sacrifices. Origin of sacrifice seems to have been man's feeling of sin and need, and conviction of obligation to God. First recorded sacrifice is Abel's offering. From that time sacrifice became a common method of worship. God took this method of expressing religious feelings and thoughts, and taught the people to use it in approaching Him, but in elevated and refined forms. It was figurative and symbolic.

3. God's appointed way for the approach of men to Him has *always been by sacrifice.* The object of sacrifice was to awaken and maintain reverence for God, and express men's feelings towards Him. Not now by the blood of bulls and goats, but the blood of Christ is the sacrifice by which we come to God. "He taketh away the first that He may establish the second." But except through sacrifice no man may draw near. True religion is a revealed way of approach to God.

II. SACRIFICIAL WORSHIP WAS ORDAINED AS EXPRESSIVE OF THE WORSHIPPER'S VOLUNTARY AND ENTIRE DEDICATION TO GOD.

The burnt offering was the oldest symbol by which was sought communion with God. Its Hebrew name means "an ascending." They declared by it

(a) *Their aspiration after Him;* (b) *Their desire to do His will;* (c) *Their self-surrender to Him.*

It was this devotion of soul which made the offering a "sweet savour unto Him." Therefore the *worshipper took prominent part in the act of sacrifice.* Laid his hand on the victim to make it his representative. Then slew it. Priest dashed its blood against the altar, then cut it up and burned it. Blood signified the life, that by which life is supported. The word used for "blood" in earliest Old Testament times was "soul." Blood was "holy"; never to be taken as food; was symbol of the *immaterial* and *immortal.* It meant, when dashed against the altar, that the real inward life must be devoted entirely to God; that the sacrificer offered himself, soul and body, in submission to God's will.

III. SYMBOLIC WORSHIP BY SACRIFICE FINDS ITS FULL ELUCIDATION IN CHRISTIAN WORSHIP.

1. The burnt offering suggests *the holiness of God.* All Jewish sacrifices express the feeling from which a religious life flows as its source, the sense of sin and of the divine holiness. That ritual is pervaded with this recognition of holiness. The tabernacle, vessels, garments, the priests who minister and the people who worship, all must be holy. But in the burnt offering this was concentrated. Infinite holiness claims the life of men. Mounting upwards towards God by self-sacrifice; that is His will. That is the central idea of Christian living—" present your bodies a living sacrifice, holy," etc.

2. The burnt offering suggests the *spirit of acceptable Christian worship.* It must be *pure;* and we are not pure. It is sacrilege to offer a polluted object in sacrifice to a holy God. New purposes, good resolutions, good acts, do not fit one already stained by sin to offer himself as an acceptable sacrifice. The burnt offering was always *preceded by a sin offering.* And "Christ has offered Himself a *sacrifice for sins* for ever"; we may therefore offer ourselves as living sacrifices, acceptable to God.

3. The burnt offering suggests the *character of the acceptable Christian worshipper.* He is indebted to Christ for access to the throne of grace; he knows that all his hope is in the sacrifice of Jesus. His only return, therefore, is the offering of himself as the sign and expression of the love of his heart. This

offering of ourselves is (*a*) a *whole self-sacrifice*; (*b*) a *continual sacrifice*—breathing life out in voluntary consecration. Such a breathing forth of self to Christ requires a constant kindling of spirit in love and devotion; a strong faith, and a habit of regarding one's self, in all relations, as created to live for His glory.

All the solemnity of the temple, all the significance of its worship, and all the glory of the Divine presence in it, are realised in every consecrated life.

"For man the living temple is:—
The mercy-seat and cherubim
And all the holy mysteries,
He bears with him."—*Rev. Albert E. Dunning.*

Topic: A SWEET SAVOUR FOR ACCEPTANCE (Vv. 9, 13, 17).

Thrice reiterated: "*It is a burnt sacrifice, an offering made by fire, of a sweet savour unto the Lord.*"

Notable differences between the burnt offerings and the sin offerings: *Burnt offerings* were (*a*) *sweet savour* offerings (*b*) *for acceptance*; whereas *sin* offerings were (*a*) *not* of a sweet savour, and (*b*) were required as an expiation *for guilt*. (*a*) The sweet savour offerings, *i.e.*, the burnt, the meat, and the peace offerings, were offered *on the brazen altar*, which stood within the *court of the tabernacle*. (*b*) The unsavoury offerings, *i.e.*, the sin and trespass offerings, were *not* consumed on the altar, some being burnt on the earth without the camp, others were sprinkled by blood and ate by the priest. (*a*) In the "sweet savour" offerings *sin is not seen* or thought of; it is the *faithful Israelite* giving a *pleasant offering* to Jehovah. (*b*) In the sin offerings it is the reverse, it is a sacrifice *charged with the sin of the offerer.* Thus: in the "sweet savour" offerings the offerer comes for *acceptance as a worshipper;* whereas in the sin and trespass offerings he comes as a *sinner to pay the penalty of guilt.* Therein is suggested and pictured

I. A HOLY WORSHIPPER, PRESENTING BEFORE GOD A PERFECT AND PLEASANT OFFERING.

Not that the offerer himself is holy; but *his offering*, which God accepts in his stead, is a *representative of perfectness*, and its quality of perfection is transferred to the offerer. The act typifies a *perfect* man, in his approach to God, *standing the test of fire, i.e.*, God's searching holiness, *accepted* as *a fragrant savour;* the offering all ascending as a sweet offering to Jehovah.

1. The transaction represents *man giving to God what truly satisfies Him*. It is not a transaction symbolic of a sinner bearing his sin (that appears in the sin offering), but of man giving to God an offering so pleasing to Him that the "sweet savour" of it satisfies and delights Him. With our experience of what man is, it seems wondrous that he should ever perfectly perform his part. But *in Christ* man has so performed it; *His* offering was "a sweet savour unto the Lord." Hence we are in the burnt sacrifice brought to consider, not Christ as the Sin Bearer, but

2. *Christ*, as *man in perfectness, meeting God in holiness.* The work of Jesus here is not "God hath made Him to be *sin* for us"; but rather, "He loved us, and gave Himself for us, an offering and a sacrifice to God of a sweet-smelling savour" (Ephes. v. 2). He appears in the burnt offering for us as man offering to God something which is most precious and most pleasing to Him.

Here note:

(*a*) The *altar* is "*the table of the Lord*" (Mal. i. 12); whatever was put thereon was "the food of God." Here, therefore, God finds that which suffices His longings; an offering which satisfies Him.

(*b*) *The fire from heaven*, emblem of God's holiness, consumes the offering; and it all ascends as sweet incense before Him; betokening that all was worthy His acceptance, without fault.

(c) The victim was "*without blemish*"; and because of Christ's unblemished sacrifice, His perfect spotlessness and devotedness was a sweet feast to the God of heaven.

II. A PERFECT AND PLEASANT OFFERING OFFERED TO GOD FOR HIS GRACIOUS ACCEPTANCE.

In itself "a sweet savour," the burnt offering was presented "*for acceptance*" [the words in v. 3 "of his own voluntary will" should read "to be accepted"; and are so rendered in the Sept. Vulgate, Targum, etc.] It was offered to God to secure the acceptance of the offerer. Observe now *Christ's position as Offerer*. He stood as Man for man under the law; hence:

1. *His acceptance depended upon His perfectness.* God made man upright; he erred and fell. God gave him opportunities and aids, for age after age, that he might again *render himself acceptable* to God: but in vain his efforts. The law then came; it taught him the conditions of righteousness; but none could fulfil it, and "there was none righteous, no not one." How then could man be brought to meet God's requirements? One way only remained (Rom. viii, 3, 4): *the Son of God undertook it for us*. As man's representative, He took our place; and there offered a perfect obedience, "a sacrifice without blemish," for our "acceptance"; and thus answered the question and demand, Could Man bring an *offering so acceptable as to satisfy God?* He offered Himself; and His offering was accepted (Titus ii. 14).

2. *His complete acceptance guarantees His people's also.* And that it was *completely* accepted is assured by its being "*all burnt on the altar*"; nothing rejected, nothing left remaining. God gathered it all up in the incense of fire, as welcome and pleasant to Him; so that He received it all. All the virtue of that satisfactory offering is transferred *from the offering* to the *offerer*. And the *believer* is the offerer; his faith identifies him with Christ; he lays the hand of identifying trust on the Lord Jesus. Hence "by one offering He hath *perfected for ever* them that are sanctified" (Heb. x. 14). "We are sanctified by the offering of the body of Jesus once for all" (Heb. x. 10). Christ's "atonement" was the satisfaction God receives for the perfectness which the offerer presents to Him. Christ only ever did this perfectly, and was accepted for us; and we are "complete in Him."—Developed from "*Jukes on the Offerings.*"

Topic: SIGNIFICANCE OF THE BURNT OFFERING (Vv. 3-9).

Probably *we* see the meaning of the Mosaic ritual more clearly than Hebrews did, for we look at it in the light of New Testament elucidation. Those who offered the sacrifices in the tabernacle knew only in part, and saw as through a glass darkly; now that the Great Sacrifice has been offered, we look at those rites face to face.

Among the Jews the burnt offering was the oldest and most significant, and announced, every day, truths of transcendent importance. *Such sacrifices were symbolic of the kind of worship God requires of the human race.* Notice :

I. THE NATURE OF THE BURNT OFFERING. Neither valueless nor unclean creatures were to be presented, but living, wholesome, sound, and valuable gifts; the pride and prime of the flocks and herds, "a male without blemish." So God demands, as well as deserves, the first and best of all that we possess. He will not accept the refuse and dregs of our time and talents. Youth, strength, worth, and beauty are to be ungrudgingly, unreservedly given.

II. THE CHARACTER OF THE BURNT OFFERING.

(a) *Voluntary.* "He shall offer it of his own voluntary will." Though commanded, it was not extorted; obedience was to be willing, not compelled. God treated Israelites as men, not machines; as servants, not slaves. Men have always been allowed to "choose whom they would serve"; it is so still, we may accept or reject the Great Sacrifice ; we must present ourselves voluntarily to the Lord, none other is acceptable service.

(*b*) *Vicarious.* "And he shall put his hand upon the head of the burnt offering, and it shall be accepted for him, to make atonement for him." This act indicated the identification of the offerer with the offering, and the transference of his *guilt* to it. The perfect suffered for the imperfect, the guiltless for the guilty. So Christ suffered in our stead, and bore our sins, "the just for the unjust, to bring us to God." As we lay our hand, by faith, upon the spotless Lamb of God, we become identified with Him, and our guilt is transferred to Him. [See Addenda, p. 19, *Propitiation.*]

III. THE MANNER OF THE BURNT OFFERING. Not only strict injunction about what to be offered, and when, and where, but *how* the offering was to be presented.

(*a*) *Orderly.* "Order Heaven's first law." Minute directions given even to washing inwards and legs of victim, the plucking away of the crops of the pigeons and doves. Thus *obedience was enjoined, resignation taught*, and *respect paid to Divine sovereignty.* Voluntaryism was not to be latitudinarianism ; God still requires order in our worship ; forms may exist without frigid formality ; and method, without mechanical monotony. Unrestrained religious fervour is only fanaticism or "will worship" and "strange fire."

(*b*) *Openly.* "At the door of the tabernacle of the congregation," not secretly in the tent, not away from open gaze in some hidden place, but publicly. Thus the worshipper became a *witness* and *confessor* before God and man. Witnessing for God, confession of Christ still required of all who profess to believe and worship. Our light is to "shine before men," we are to be "living epistles known and read of all men."

(*c*) *Devoutly.* "Before the Lord." This expression repeated to remind the offerer he was observed and judged by the searching Eye that looks into the secrets of the heart. Consciousness of being "before the Lord" would beget *humility, sincerity, solemnity.* Let us remember that all we think and say and do is in the light of God. "All things are naked and opened unto the eyes of Him with whom we have to do."

(*d*) *Cheerfully.* "A sweet savour unto the Lord." As the fragrant flame ascended from the sacrifice, gladness and gratitude were symbolised, indicative of a joyful heart, and willing mind. God still requires sincerity and truth in the inward parts, and in the hidden parts we need to know wisdom. The holocaust thus taught the need of ardent love, aspiring desire, entire surrender, as the first essentials of real religion. In the self-sacrificing life and love of Christ those features meet in harmony and perfection. Though we are exempted from repeating the burnt offerings, we may present to God the sacrifice of a broken and contrite heart with the assurance it will not be despised.—*F. W. Brown.*

Topic: VARIETY IN SACRIFICES (Vv. 10-17).

He who had, in Egypt, appointed for every household the one sacrifice of the Passover, now directs sacrifices of a wider and various order, graduated to the personal ability, and spiritual condition of each worshipper. These sacrifices which are to be brought to the Lord to propitiate His graciousness to them, are themselves the appointment of His graciousness to them. So absolute are His decrees concerning what is to be presented, and how, when and by whom to be presented, that to vary them at any suggestion of priest or priests, under any impulse of devotion, gratitude or fear, or through sense of dread and distress, would be to commit one of these transgressions which the sacrifices themselves were provided to meet. [See Maurice, *Doctrine of Sacrifice.*]

I. THE CONSCIOUSNESS OF SIN AND NEED FOR PROPITIATION PERVADES THE VARIED RANKS OF HUMAN SOCIETY.

Guilt is universal. "Rich and poor meet together," in sense of personal transgression and necessity for a sacrifice. Hence the *wealthy* who could offer "sacrifice of the *herd*," the *middle class* who could only bring "offering of the *flocks*," and the *poorest* whose impecuniosity compelled them to bring an "offering to the Lord of *fowls*," are all provided for in God's arrangements for propitiatory sacrifices. [See Addenda, p. 19, *Sacrifices of the Poor.*]

1. The condition and history of *every people showed the desire for sacrifice;* that it could only be stifled when the strongest and deepest convictions of humanity were stifled. But where there was sense of guilt, dependence, obligation, thankfulness, there sacrifices were offered.

2. The *entire Jewish people,* irrespective of social gradation, *had experienced God's redeeming mercy,* which constrained them all to seek Him with offerings. The Lord had ransomed them all, and was now drawing them into privileged relationship with Himself. He was "no respecter of persons": all alike were within Divine grace. And equally "the grace of God which bringeth salvation hath appeared unto all men" (Tit. ii. 11).

3. In *every human heart* there dwells the *condemnation for sin and the promptings to seek propitiation with God.*

For though each man bears his own special sin, and each class in society carries its own distinctive transgression; yet all know that "all have sinned," and that God requires of every "wicked man that he forsake his way and return unto the Lord" (Isa. lv. 7).

II. DIVINE PROVISION FOR PROPITIATION IS VARIED TO SUIT ALL GRADATIONS OF HUMAN SOCIETY.

In no demand He makes does He "exact more than our iniquity deserveth." Nay, He relieves the weight of requirement that none should find the yoke other than easy, and the burden light.

1. *The resources and ability of the offerer* are considered. God is no "hard taskmaster." None can be discouraged by sense of inability.

2. *No one is exempted from the demand* of a propitiatory offering. The poorest are included in God's arrangement equally with the wealthiest.

3. *Liberty of choice is allowed that each may prove his sincerity* by bringing his utmost and best. God *tests* us thus.

4. *Humblest offerings were as acceptable with God as the costliest:* evidenced in the minuteness of God's directions for the poor man's offering of the fowls.

5. Supreme importance was attached to *the spirit in which the offering was brought* (v. 3). Thus "let us draw near with a pure heart" (Heb. x. 22).

III. AMID ALL VARIETY IN SACRIFICES THE ONE QUALITY OF PROPITIATION WAS CONSPICUOUS AND INHERENT.

1. *The quality of the offering,* as faultless, was specified, indicating that substitution could only be effective as giving to God a *sinless victim* in place of a sinful offerer.

2. *The identifying act of the offerer* denoted his sense of deserving the fate of the victim about to die.

3. *His being detained at the door of the tabernacle* until the sacrifice was offered impressed the truth that God was too holy for sinful man to approach until propitiated by sacrifice.

4. *By the process of cleansing, flaying, and burning,* a typical foreshadowing was enacted of the atoning sufferings of Christ, as the world's atonement, the "propitiation for our sins; and not for ours only, but also for the whole world" (1 John ii. 2). And in that all-inclusive sacrifice every variety of the human family has a share; none too poor to be excluded, none too wealthy to be exempted; for "all have sinned and come short of the glory of God."

OUTLINES ON VERSES.

V. 1.—*Theme:* GOD WITHIN THE TABERNACLE. "*And the Lord spake unto him out of the tabernacle of the congregation.*"

The tabernacle was erected in the midst of a people supernaturally separated from the rest of mankind to be the *recipients* and *mediators* of a revelation which Jehovah would make of Himself to the world. In it a constant worship was to be maintained by the priests in the name of the holy nation.

I. *Within the sanctuary* **God makes His presence known.**

He may do it by "*calling*" men to Him there, or by "*speaking*" to them in messages of truth and life. Many have found, who entered the sanctuary, "surely God is in this place." He is there—

1. *Invisible.* Moses saw not God; but "no man hath seen God at any time." He is the "King immortal, invisible." Yet there are solemn realities which eye hath not seen. The *material world* has in it many invisible facts: forces and agencies hidden from physical sight. *Life* also is crowded with invisible activities, energies of vast influence which elude vision. *Holy places* are not void scenes, an Unseen Presence is there.

2. *Recognised.* A solemn symbol dwelt in the tabernacle: the shekinah cloud. We have no visible sign; but none the less God makes His presence realised in His tabernacles now. He has spiritual resources for attesting that He is amidst "the congregation" still.

3. *Gracious.* Not as on Sinai, too awful for men to bear the sight; but gently dwelling above the mercy-seat. How graciously the Lord reveals Himself in His holy place now; to arouse the heedless, allure the sinful, heal the stricken, reveal His compassion, cleanse the contrite, save the trustful soul.

II. *Within the tabernacle* **God sends His messages of redemption to the congregation.**

Here the Lord sent directions for sacrifices which should be for an "atonement." The messages through Moses contained a system of religious truth answering all the spiritual necessities of Israel, revealing:

(1) *The nature and character of God.*
(2) *The covenant relation between Him and them.*
(3) *Provision for the pardon and restoration of the penitent transgressor.*
(4) *The condemnation of the wilfully and persistently disobedient.*

In these Christian times He sends tidings and offers of redemption unto His people; gracious messages of salvation in Christ to the congregations who gather.

1. *By His minister and representative:* as by Moses.
2. *Based upon the merits of atoning sacrifice.*
3. *Requiring man's response and co-operation.*

III. *Within the sanctuary* **God is willing to meet every soul who will seek Him.**

"*If any of you,*" etc. No restriction. True we may meet the Lord elsewhere than in His sanctuaries now; yet none but *may* find Him there. Only in order to meet Him acceptably, now as then, each must

1. *Come with sacrificial offering: i.e.,* resting on the atonement of Christ.
2. *With thorough earnestness of desire.* Not prefunctorily, not in alien mind, but "of his own voluntary will," *i.e.,* with personal effort to meet Him acceptably, and in His own way.
3. *With self-dedication.* Suggested in the burnt offering. Lay yourself before God, He will "receive you graciously."

V. 2.—*Theme:* REVELATION OF PROPITIATION. "*Speak unto the children of Israel, and say unto them, Ye shall bring your offering of the herd and of the flock.*"

I. The Author *of Divine Revelation* —*God.* "The Lord called unto Moses."

God *could* reveal: He *knew* what man needed: would not remain silent, and let man perish for want of *light* additional to that of Nature.

II. **The Medium** *of Divine Revelation—Man.* To a representative and brother of our race Divine communications came. Most *reasonable* and *appropriate* vehicle. Glorifying to God: dignifying to man.

III. **The Scene** *of Divine Revelation —Tabernacle.* Sacred place fitted to be audience chamber with Deity. Revelations given in sacred spots, as well as to select persons.

IV. **The Means** *of Divine Revelation—Speech.* The Lord "spake" unto Moses, used human speech, though imperfect; other language would have been unintelligible and useless.

V. **The Purpose** *of Divine Revelation—Redemption.* To sanctify from guilt, to save from consequences of sin, to recover holiness in man here and for ever. Such redemption (1) *Mediatorial*—through priest; (2) *Sacrificial*—through oblations.—F. W. B.

V. 2.—*Theme:* THE WAY OF ACCESS TO GOD. " If any man of you *bring an offering unto the Lord*, ye shall bring your offering of the cattle, even of the herd, and of the flock."

Human liberty is here recognised, but it is a liberty emphatically *restricted*. Any man *might* bring an offering if he desired; but if he did, he must bring it according to absolute directions. In our dealings with God there must be acceptance of a Will beyond our own will; obedience to commands; reverent and humble observance of Divine authority. "Who art thou that repliest against God?" "Hath not the potter power over the clay?" etc. "Whatsoever He saith unto thee, do it." " If ye be *willing* and *obedient*," etc.

I. *In our approach to God* **nothing is left to human invention.**

1. *There are conditions to our acceptable approach.* Therefore, he who would draw nigh should pause and ask solemnly: "Wherewith shall I come before the Lord, or bow before the high God?" Do not "rush in where angels fear to tread." Think Whom you approach, and inquire how to draw near aright.

2. There are *minutely revealed* conditions for our approach. Neither priest nor people might take one step except as directed (chap. viii. 36; ix. 6, 7). We may be sincere and even devout in spirit when adopting methods and ideas of our own in spiritual behaviour; but God will not have *our* way, but *His* way. It must be according to the revelation of God.

II. *For our* rightful *approach to Him* God has made full and gracious provision.

1. A *place* for meeting God (v. 1). Within the *sanctuary;* at the mercy-seat; in the "secret place of the tabernacle of the Most High." God asks us apart. "Having boldness to *enter into the holiest* by the blood of Jesus." Israel had a "worldly sanctuary," because then "the way into the holiest was not yet made manifest while as the first tabernacle was yet standing." Now there is no *outer court* for the people and *inner temple* for the priest; all may meet God in "heavenly places, in Christ Jesus"—drawing near God in blessed privacy.

2. *A sacrificial basis of acceptance.*

Being guilty man needs propitiatory sacrifice. "Without shedding of blood there is no remission." This basis of a propitiatory sacrifice constituted Israel an acceptable people with God. The atonement of Christ is the guarantee of our welcome also. "Through the offering of the body of Jesus Christ once for all" we may approach "in full assurance of faith."

3. *A mediatorial ministry.* "The priests shall bring the blood" (v. 5). "We have such a High Priest ... a minister of the sanctuary," etc (comp. Heb. viii. 1, 2). Jesus *represents* us there continually; " in the presence of God *for us*"; and He *presents* to God our sacrifices and gifts; "*by Him*, therefore, let us offer the sacrifice," etc. (Heb. xiii. 15)

III. *By such arrangements for our acceptable approach,* **God has laid us** under most solemn obligations to seek Him.

1. Shall God wait in vain within the holy place, and *none draw near?* He says, "Seek ye My face." Surely our "hearts shall say to Him, Thy face, O Lord, will I seek."

2. Can sinful man *despise the sacrifice of Jesus* offered for his propitiation? Nay! "My soul looks backs to see," etc.

3. With such a Priest within the Holy Place, have we *no mediation to ask,* no *sins to confess,* no *offerings to bring?*

V. 3.—*Theme:* NECESSITY OF SACRIFICE. "*If his offering be a burnt sacrifice.*"

The fall of man necessitated "the republication of the religion of Nature (as Butler says) with additional truths and additional proofs." Man required to be taught how depraved he had become, and how he might be delivered from the guilt and consequences of that fallen state. The burnt offering was eminently calculated to impress upon worshippers in the tabernacle services

I. *The heinous nature of sin.*
II. *The wickedness of idolatry.*
III. *The oneness of Israel's nationality.*
IV. *The duty and privilege of Divine worship.*
V. *The need of substitutionary sacrifice in order to salvation.*
VI. *The sovereign claim of Jehovah upon His people's life and love.*

The doctrine of mediation and vicarious sacrifice is taught in Nature, we get the principles there; but the eternal and spiritual truths, which those principles illustrate, are presented in the Levitical Ritual; and pre-eminently in the Redemption wrought by Jesus Christ. The directions concerning the burnt offering show *that the recognition of the existence of sin and the need of its removal in order to acceptable service lies at the foundation of the Mosaic and Christian economies.*—F. W. B.

V. 3.—*Theme:* VOLITION IN WORSHIP. "*He shall offer it of his own voluntary will.*"

As expressive of *our Saviour's act in devoting Himself* to be man's sacrifice, it accords with the grand statement, "Lo I come to do Thy will, O God; Thy law is within My heart." And as expressive of the *soul's act in coming before God* with his own offerings of love and service, or with the free exercise of trust in Jesus' atonement, it suggests the right state in which to seek God. The offering is not the chief thing in the transaction, but the spirit of the man occupied in it.

I. **True worship springs from the soul.** Should be—

1. *Spontaneous.* As a joy, not constrained, not reluctant.
2. *Grateful.* Recognising the privilege, seizing the gracious opportunity.
3. *Earnest.* With a whole heart in the act.

II. **Acceptable worship depends on the offerer's will.** On—

1. *The thoroughness of his purpose.* Christ asks, "What *wilt* thou?" and makes His answer wait upon our desire.
2. *The ardour of his approach.* Come with intensity of aim, ask large things, cry, "I will not let Thee go except Thou bless me."
3. *The individuality of his suit.* Every man must be himself in worship, not echo others' prayers, not repeat others' acts, but stand before God as a worshipper, having something which is "*his own*"—to repent of, to ask for, to offer.

III. **Sacrificial worship is the transgressor's personal transaction.**

1. The *victim* must be one which *the offerer himself brings.* We must "bring" our sacrifice now, come before God with the mention and merits of Christ.
2. *The offerer must exert his own faith in the act of substitution.* Claiming Christ's merit, identifying himself with the atonement of Calvary by his appropriating faith.
3. *The transaction must be wholly one of volition.* God does not force us unwilling. We must act with a prompt and earnest spirit, or miss the precious benefits of the Redeemer's sacrifice.

Note: *Faith,* when real, *acts eagerly. Love* is always swift in volition. *Misery* (as over sin) goes willingly to the Lord with its "sacrifice of a broken heart," or with trust in the redemption of the Cross.

IV. **Self dedicatory worship draws its virtues from the free will which prompts it.**

1. Only thus is it *sincere*. Yet some offer themselves to God moved by example, induced by companions, under transient excitement, agitated by alarm, but void of full, and earnest, and determined action of the will.

2. Only thus is it *pleasing to God*. He "loveth a cheerful giver." Whatever we bring, it should be with enentirety, resoluteness.

3. Only thus can it *gain us spiritual benefit*. "With what measure we mete it shall be measured to us." If we are heedless and heartless in going to God, He will return leanness to our souls. But He has "abundant pardon," "plenteous redemption," "abounding grace," for earnest souls.

They who give themselves *wholly* and *voluntarily* to the Lord, He "receives graciously and loves freely." [See Addenda, p. 19, *Consecration*.]

V. 4.—*Theme:* ACCEPTANCE WITH GOD. "*And he shall put his hand upon the head of the offering.*"

This book might be called the Gospel according to Leviticus, for it exhibits the gospel in its spirit, though under figurative rites. One of the fathers says that *every syllable of this book contains a mystery*, and Paul tells us that "*the law was a shadow of good things*," etc.

If a man happen to find a monument of antiquity with inscriptions of old letters and characters, how anxious is he to decipher the meaning and reveal the hidden mystery! Much more should we be anxious to examine and investigate the figures of this book. Every sacrifice was a kind of silent sermon presented to the eye, indicating the nature of Christ's office and the design of His death. And by such visible signs the gospel was preached, just as when John said, "*Behold the Lamb of God.*"

I. **That God alone is competent to reveal the nature of the sacrifice and the method of our acceptance.**

He strongly resents every neglect of His prescribed institutions and every invasion of His prerogative.

"*The Lord called to Moses and spake unto him,*" etc. In the setting up of the tabernacle, every particular is closed with "*As the Lord commanded Moses.*" Learn, then, how sweet *commanded obedience* is. "*In vain do ye worship by tradition.*"

If none of the *outward* offices were left to human invention, how much less able is man to originate the *terms of acceptance with God!* None but God knew the evil of sin, the value of the soul, the conditions of worthy approach, etc. God prescribes a method of acceptance and worship for all classes. All stand in equal need of an interest in the atonement; all must seek it on the same terms, by God's prescribed rule; all shall derive the same benefit. The rich were to present a bullock; but where the ability differed the offering differed. Those next in degree were to present a sheep or goat, and those poorer still were to present turtle doves or young pigeons.

It should be remembered that the offering of the Virgin Mary at the birth of our Lord was not a costly, but a simple, one—the humblest; no more than a turtle dove and two young pigeons. To put honour on humble poverty Jesus was born in a borrowed manger, and was buried in a borrowed grave. "*Foxes have holes.*" "God dwells with the poor in spirit."

II. **That God prescribes not only the offering itself but the spirit in which it should be presented.**

1. *It was to be a bullock*, to show that the *best* of our possessions are to be offered to the Lord; and *without blemish*. God condemns those who brought the blind and lame. And it intimates, too, the purity of the appointed sacrifice. "*Such an High Priest became us,*" etc. The excellency and perfection of Christ had much to do with the efficacy of His sacrifice. "*A lamb without blemish or spot.*" "Who through the Eternal Spirit," etc.

Some are desirous of *a cheap religion*, but when God provided a sacrifice it was the most costly; "*not silver and gold, but precious blood.*" As God deemed nothing too precious for us, we deem nothing too precious for Him.

2. *It was to be freely offered.* "Of His own voluntary will." To show that God does not accept constrained service. "*The people offered willingly.*" "*Thy people shall be willing in the day of Thy power.*" "*With my whole heart have I sought Thee.*" "*I beseech you,*" etc. (Rom. xii. 1).

3. *It was to be openly presented*—to show that we publicly confess Christ before men. "At the door of the congregation." "*I am not ashamed of the gospel.*" "*Whosoever is ashamed.*" A public avowal—for the good of others and for the glory of God.

4. *The offerer must take a distinct personal part in the transaction.* "He shall put his hand upon the head of the burnt offering," to show that he was deeply sensible of his need of mercy; to show that he fully concurred in the appointed sacrifice, that he was anxious to transfer all his guilt to the victim, and derived all his hope from it. "*My faith would lay her hand.*"

Our devout affections must centre in Christ; our only trust be reposed in Him. "We *receive* the atonement." Not merely driven by the stress of necessity, but a hearty concurrence.

5. *Not only was the victim slain, but the blood sprinkled.*

6. *The whole was to be presented by the priest.* Not only at the altar, but within the veil.

III. That God has left us in no doubt of our acceptance when thus approaching Him in faith and prayer. "It shall be accepted for him, to make an atonement for him."

1. *The substitutionary offering is allowed by God to stand in the sinner's stead*—" accepted *for* him."

2. The provision of the substitute is *even a more welcome arrangement* than that the sinner should bear his own punishment. "It shall be *accepted.*" God "desires not the death of a sinner," is well pleased that we find escape by laying our hand on the Sacrifice of Calvary.

3. *It effects a full "atonement"* for the soul, satisfies the Divine requirements, and secures the justification of the believer. "There is, therefore, now no condemnation to them which are in Christ Jesus."

4. *It makes the offerer himself an object of pleasure in God's regard.* Not merely is our substitutionary offering "*accepted*" by God, but we become *ourselves beloved* for the *sake of our* trust in the Sacrifice. "I will accept *you*, saith the Lord God" (Ezekiel xliii. 27).

V. 9.—*Theme:* THE ALTAR FIRE "*An Offering made by Fire.*"

The flame devours. The victim is consumed. Seek the truth reflected from the altar fire. The Cross flashes it out vividly. The fire consumes the sacrifice.

I. *That fire tells* what is sin's due.

It pourtrays what the guilty must bear. Look on the consuming blaze, and think how the "fire shall be ever burning, it shall never go out." Remember Christ's picture of the sinner's doom—"everlasting fire"; "where their worm dieth not and the fire is not quenched." Ponder, therefore, *sin's sure doom!*

II. *That fire suggests* the anguish of Christ.

Type of the Cross is that altar; and of the sufferings of Jesus, that burning fire. "He made His soul an offering for sin."

" O, the pangs His soul sustained! "

His anguish was as a "consuming fire," it raged within Him as a scorching blaze. It was as though God's wrath was hot and devastating upon Him. Mark, therefore, the *Saviour's redeeming grace!*

III. *That fire pourtrays* the fervour of Christian consecration.

With burning devotion, and flaming zeal, and self-consuming love, ardent, glowing, manifest. Shall *Christ's* "zeal consume Him," and *ours lack intens-*

ity? The entire life of a Christian should be one continuous blaze of flaming love and ardent devotion. [See Addenda: p. 19, *Consecration.*]

V. 9.—*Theme:* THE SPIRIT'S EFFICACY. "An offering made by fire, of a sweet savour unto the Lord."

The Holy Spirit is symbolised by fire. All the grace and virtue of sacrifices depend upon the Spirit

I. Altar sacrifices were consecrated by the element of Divinely kindled fire.

The fire came from heaven (comp. chap. ix. 24): and any fire not thus supernaturally originated was offensive (comp. chap. x. 1). That fire *coming "out from before the Lord"* symbolises the Holy Ghost, which came as *fire from God* on the Pentecost. Only through the Spirit's sanctifying could those offerings have become holy.

II. Christ's sacrifice was rendered efficacious through the energy of the Holy Spirit.

He suffered in the spirit. "Who *through the eternal Spirit* offered Himself without spot to God." That Divine fire burned within the soul of Jesus: the Spirit was given without measure unto Him; and His sacred unction consecrated the sufferings of Jesus to be a perfect atonement for human sin.

III. Spiritual sacrifices depend for their sanctity on the Spirit's grace.

Of Jesus it was declared "He shall baptise you with the Holy Ghost and *with fire.*" Is not that the "*Spirit of burning*" which rendered "holy" everyone "written among the living in Jerusalem"? [See Isa. iv. 3, 4.] This "manifestation of the Spirit" (1 Cor. xii. 7, 11) is the occasion of all Christian sanctity and of all acceptable sacrifice and service. His glowing grace and energy within the soul constrains and seals our devotions; and "the *unction* from the Holy One" (1 Jno. ii. 20) makes our lives and offerings "*a sweet savour* unto the Lord."

IV. All sacrifices sanctified by the Spirit rise as a delightful incense unto God.

When Noah, saved by the ark, burned his sacrifice of gratitude upon the altar he reared, "the Lord smelled a sweet savour" (Gen. viii. 21).

So from the holocaust in the tabernacle there arose "by fire a sweet savour unto the Lord." The ransomed Israelites, brought again from captivity to God's "holy mountain," should once more offer their oblations, and God would "*accept them with their sweet savour*" (Ezek. xx. 41). Supremely the *Lord Jesus Himself* was "an offering and a sacrifice to God for a sweet smelling savour" (Ephes. v. 2). And *we*, whom God "causeth to triumph in Christ," are "unto *God a sweet savour of Christ*" (2 Cor. ii. 15).

Every sacrifice which is the outflowing of our love and zeal for the Lord, becomes, through the virtue of the Spirit consecrating our gifts, "an *odour of a sweet smell, a sacrifice acceptable,* well pleasing to God" (Phil. iv.18).

The Holy Spirit is the sacred fire in the Christian life, by whose gracious influences our offerings ascend in sweetness and acceptableness "unto the Lord." "*Quench* not the Spirit." [See Addenda p. 19, *The Ascending Fire.*]

V. 11. *Theme:* A LIFE-OFFERING. "He shall *kill it on the side of the altar.*"

I Its substitutionary significance.

1 That the offerer *deserved to forfeit his life.*

2. That he *sought escape from the penalty of his sinfulness.*

3 That he *believed God would accept the victim* in lieu of himself.

4. That substitution not alone sufficed Jehovah, but was more acceptable to Him than the sinner's death.

II. Its practical interpretation.

1. *Life peculiarly belongs to God:* it is supremely His part in creation. Lower things He gives to man; but life is His.

2. Representing thus His claim on His creatures, it stands as *the emblem of what we owe Him.* What we owe we *ought* to pay. We should give our life to God. It is our *duty.*

3. It denotes that *what is most precious in us,* and forms the supremely

valuable element in our being, should all and *wholly be the Lord's*. Not the inferior part, not the less essential qualities, not "part of the price," but everything in us of worth : our *life*.

III. **Its Gospel foreshadowing.**

1. *The body of Jesus* is the offering pourtrayed. "A body hast Thou prepared Me."

2. He yielded to God *man's duty:* the *dutiful life* man had failed to surrender to Him.

3. He gave *life in its perfectness* to God. In Himself perfect, He offered Himself wholly and absolutely and perfectly to God : and the perfectly obedient *Man* then "seeing that all things were now accomplished, cried, It is finished, and gave up the ghost."

V. 13.—*Theme:* COMPLETENESS IN SELF DEVOTION. "The priest shall *bring it all*, and *burn it* on the altar."

1. In this particular the Burnt offering differed from the Meat offering and Peace offering ; for in these *only a part* was burnt with fire.

2. It differed also from the Sin offering, which though wholly burnt, was *not* burnt "*on the altar.*"

I. **Man's duty to God is the absolute surrender of all.**

Not of one faculty or several ; but the entirety.

1. This *accords with Christ's summary of the first commandment:* which demands all the *mind*, all the *soul*, all the *affection*, all the *strength.* "Thou shalt love the Lord thy God with *all,*" etc. (Matt xxii. 37).

2. The *minute and all-inclusive devotion of the victim* affirms the same truth. The "head," the "fat," the "legs," the "inwards" all are enumerated. Symbolic : "head" of *thoughts ;* "fat" of *vigour ;* "legs" of *walk, conduct ;* "inwards" of *affections and emotions.*

II. **Christ's performance of Man's** duty to God was characterised by *absolute surrender of all.*

1. *Jesus reserved nothing ;* He gave up all. Had there been but *one thought* in the mind of Christ not perfectly given to God, one *affection* in His heart not yielded to His Father's will, one *step* in the walk of Jesus not taken for God but for His own pleasure, then He would not have offered Himself, or been accepted, as "a whole burnt offering" to Jehovah. But all was *offered,* and all was *consumed* on the altar.

2. *From first to last, in Jesus, self had no place.* So entirely was His whole life devoted to His Father that it *almost seems He could have had no will of His own.* Everything He did or said was for God. His *first* recorded words were, "I must be about My Father's business"; His *last,* "It is finished." Yet as perfect man, He *had a human will,* and human *affections.* But no one hour was spent, nor act performed for His own advancement or gratification ; all was given in entire devotedness to God.

III. **Christian self devotion will attempt to reproduce Christ's absolute surrender of all.**

1. True, this is *a conception of life repudiated by the world.* "Men will praise thee when thou doest *well to thyself*" (Psa. xlix. 18).

2. *Few Christians exhibit such self devotion* to God. Our thoughts are for *self,* our ease, *our* interest, etc. But if *David* resolved "Neither will I offer burnt offerings unto the Lord of that which doth *cost me nothing*"*;* if *Ananias* was punished for grieving the Spirit by "*keeping back part of the price*"*;* surely we whom "*the love of Christ constraineth*" should rise to highest devotion of our all to God ; and, like our Lord who "gave Himself" (Ephes. v. 2) in all His perfectness, "*yield ourselves unto God.*"

ILLUSTRATIVE ADDENDA TO CHAPTER I.

Revelation. Varro, a Roman writer of the first century B.C., states, that in his day he had been at pains to collect the various opinions on the question "What is the true object of human life ?" and had reckoned up as many as *three hundred and twenty different answers.* How much we need "the wisdom which is from above," teaching from God! He reveals what we need to know for our truest good on earth, our acceptance with Him now, and our entrance at last into His presence. We are to listen to Him, and obey His word.

"'Tis revelation satisfies all doubts,
Explains all mysteries except her own,
And so illuminates the path of life
That fools discover it, and stray no more."
—*Cowper.*

Dr. Taylor of Norwich once said to me (wrote John Newton), "Sir, I have collated every word in the Hebrew Scriptures seventeen times, and it is very strange if the doctrine of the atonement you hold should not have been found by me." "I am not surprised at this" (John Newton answered); "I once went to light my candle, and could not, for the *extinguisher* was on it. Now prejudice, from education, learning, etc., often proves an extinguisher; it is not enough that you bring the candle, you must remove the extinguisher."

The Ascending Fire. "The symbolism of this combustion (upon the altar) is manifest. It was a *sending of the gift to God*. After arranging the divided or the selected portions of the carcase in the heaven-born fire, which had issued forth from the Divine presence at the consecration of the tabernacle, they were burned, that is to say, they were *etherialised* and they *rose to heaven* as 'a sweet savour.' To burn was to effectually present."—*Principal Cave.*

Sacrifices of the Poor. The Jews at Jassy still bring *offerings of the fowls.* "In one house" records those who were observers of the incident, "we came to the window of the house and saw distinctly what was going on within. A little boy was reading the prayers, and his widowed mother stood over him with a white hen in her hands. When he came to a certain place in the prayer, the mother lifted up the struggling fowl, and waving it round her head, repeated these words: '*This be my substitute, this be my exchange: this fowl shall go to death and I to a blessed life.*' This was done three times over, and then the door of the house was opened, and out ran the boy carrying the fowl to the shocket, or slayer, to be killed by him in the proper manner." This occurred on the eve of the Day of Atonement.

"Sacrifice is the first element of religion, and resolves itself in theological language into the love of God." —*Froude, "Short Stories."*

Propitiation. Cowper, the poet, speaking of his religious experiences, says, "But the happy period which was to shake off my fetters, and afford me a clear opening of the free mercy of God in Christ Jesus, was now arrived. I flung myself into a chair near the window, and seeing a Bible there, ventured once more to apply to it for comfort and instruction. The first verse I saw was the 25th of the 3rd of Romans: 'Whom God hath set forth *to be a propitiation* through faith in His blood, to declare His righteousness for the remission of sins that are past, through the forbearance of God.' Immediately I received strength to believe, and the full beams of the Sun of Righteousness shone upon me. I saw the *sufficiency of the Atonement* He had made, my pardon sealed in His blood, and all the fulness and completeness of His justification. In a moment I believed and received the Gospel."

Consecration. "And here we offer and present unto Thee, O Lord, ourselves, our souls and bodies, to be a reasonable, holy and lively sacrifice unto Thee," etc.—*Communion Service.*

"From henceforth thou shalt learn that there is love to long for, pureness to desire, a mount of consecration it were good to scale."—*Jean Ingelow.*

On the seal of the Baptist Missionary Society is the figure of an ox, standing patiently, with a *plough* on one side, and an *altar* on the other, with the inscription beneath: "*Ready for either,*" to *serve* or suffer.

Calvin's motto was: "*I give Thee all; I keep back nothing for myself.*"

CHAPTER II.

Bloodless Sacrifices: The Food-Offerings.

SUGGESTIVE READINGS.

V. 1. His offering shall be of fine flour.—Sacrifices for the "meat offering" were from the vegetable, not animal, kingdom. *Food offering* more expresses the idea. Prepared from wheat, and presented in various forms; fine flour, and cakes of four different kinds, and wheat in the grain. These were products of husbandry, not spontaneous growths entailing no anxiety in provision, or labour in preparation; they represent human labour; were the daily food of man, essential to his life; suggestive, therefore, of his *dependence* on God, to whom he offered them, his *gratitude* to God, from whom he received them, his *dedication* to God, whom he worshipped in the act of sacrifice. As typical of Christ: His *excellency* is indicated in the quality of the flour, "fine," and His *sufferings* in the disposal of it. God looks for grateful returns from those who share the gifts of His bounty in Providence: "What shall I render unto the Lord for all His benefits towards me?" How much more He should receive responses of our thankful love for His greatest Gift whose worth and virtue are prefigured in this "fine flour burned upon the altar" as "a thing *most holy* of the offerings of the Lord made by fire."

Oil and frankincense.—Symbolic of the Holy Spirit's grace, and the sacred joy of a consecrated life. If "flour" suggests the product of human labour, the "oil" points to the added sanctity of the Spirit, needful in order to our offering being worthy a place on God's altar; and "frankincense" denotes the devout gladness with which we should make fragrant every act of sacrifice and service to the Lord. Compass God's altar, enriched by the Spirit's unction, and inspired with holy fervour; thus our consecration becomes "a sweet savour unto the Lord."

V. 2. Burn the memorial of it.—As a heavenward appeal to God that He would *remember* both the offerer and His "word unto His servants on which He had caused them to hope." So David pleads—the Lord "remember all thy offerings, and accept thy burnt sacrifice" (Psa. xx. 3); and thus the prayers and alms of Cornelius rose up "for a memorial before God." We may send up to Heaven our "incense of a pure offering," and keep a memorial continually before God of our enduring hope in Him and of His covenant engagements for us.

V. 3 The remnant.—The priests of the tabernacle lived upon these consecrated gifts. As "priests unto God" (Rev. i. 6) we Christians have a share in all the provisions of God's house: the Bread of Life, the grace of the Spirit, the delights of Divine fellowship. This is "the feast of fat things" which they within the Church enjoy. "Eat ye that which is good, and let your soul delight itself in fatness" (Isa. lv. 2).

V. 8. Bring the Meat Offering.—Choose which kind of offering you prefer (three kinds are specified in vv. 4-7), then come with it "unto the Lord"; through the mediation of our *Divine* "Priest"; and He who prizes the "prayers of the saints" and loves the "sacrifices of joy," will seal our offerings with acceptance, and "hear from His holy heaven with the saving strength of His right hand" (Psa. xx. 6).

V. 11. No offering with leaven nor any honey.—They would produce fermentation. "Leaven" is symbolic of pride and hypocrisy, malice and wickedness; and "honey," though sweet to the taste, soon begets sickness, thus suggesting a soul quickly satiated and nauseated. God desires "truth in the inward parts," worship from a "honest heart," sacrifices from those whose delight in Him is not quickly reversed, whose love changes not. A mingling of corruption and insincerity spoils our finest offerings. What need to pray, "Create in me a clean heart," etc., and to examine ourselves and our motives when employed in sacred occupations, lest we offend with leaven and honey.

V. 13. Season with salt.—It preserves from putrefaction; renders food savoury; denotes uncorruptedness, durability, constancy; was and is an oriental symbol of hospitality and amity. "Every sacrifice shall be salted with salt," says Christ (Mark ix. 49): there must be no corruptness allowed in the individual Christian life; and all our services should be savoured with the precious qualities of enduring fidelity and constant love. Salt, too, betokens the perpetuity of the Spirit's grace; and because of His abiding presence (glad fact in the Christian's experience, "He *dwelleth* with you and shall be in you") the consecrated soul retains its sweetness with God and its healthful influence on men. "Ye are the salt of the earth."

SECTIONAL HOMILIES.

Topic: HOMAGE GRACED WITH EXCELLENCIES (Vv. 1-3).

In seeking God it should be our aim to press much into the act of adoration: not to approach Him with a poverty of graces, but with every virtue combined in the service; thought and feeling, desire and devotion all being of the highest, the finest and most fragrant. Not with one excellency alone beautifying our homage, but with manifold excellencies combined. "The *preparations* (plural) of the heart" are desirable; all our resources of devout feeling and intelligence; the soul's fulness of gracious yearnings and aspirations; so that our offerings are rich in excellent qualities of homage: these make worship and service "things most holy" unto the Lord.

I. EVERY ELEMENT OF WORTH AND ATTRACTIVENESS SHOULD CONCENTRATE IN OUR WORSHIP AND SERVICE OF GOD. "His offering shall be of *fine* flour; and he shall *pour oil* upon it, and put *frankincense* thereon." By all these combined ingredients a total result would be produced which constituted the offering one "of a sweet savour unto the Lord."

1. *Solitary graces are not despised* by Him we worship. We may take Him *gratitude*, as did Noah when he burnt his sacrifice upon quitting the Ark; our *appeasement* sacrifices, as did Balaam on Pisgah; our *penitential* oblation, as David did in the threshing-floor of Araunah; we may take Him our *look of faith*, as did the Israelites suffering from the serpent-bite; our *tears*, as did Peter when he "wept bitterly"; and none of these sacrifices are rejected. For he condescends to our low estate, and accepts the one ruling feeling or desire which prompts us to seek His face.

2. Yet worship should be *the outflow of all noble affections and aspirations* of the soul. "Fine flour, oil and frankincense," all should mingle, all should blend into an offering "of sweet savour." As when the woman "who was a sinner" brought her "alabaster *box of ointment*," and besides this, "washed His feet with *tears*," yea, and "*kissed* His feet," and then "anointed them with the ointment" (Luke vii. 37-8)—all passions of penitence, gratitude, adoration, trust, love, combining and concentrated on Jesus!

3. *Preparation for such a blending of graces in worship* is our evident duty. We ought not to enter God's presence with a poverty of homage, with hearts cold and heedless, with no affection astir, with no sacred graces alert; but with all holy emotions and desires awake, and intelligent perceptions quickened by *forethought* and *pre-vision*. God emphatically directs this preparatory arrangement

for a right offering: "When any will offer, etc., he shall take thereout the flour and the oil and the frankincense" (vv. 1 and 2). [See Addenda, p. 29, *Sweet Incense.*]

So David arouses and prepares himself: "Bless the Lord, O my soul; and *all that is within me,* bless His holy name." Having no occasion in this age of the Spirit to seek God with material presents, we may and should take Him the realities they symbolised; so that as from "golden vials *full of odours*" the prayers of saints might "ascend up before God" (Rev. v. 8; viii. 5). All this should enforce upon worshippers a deeply earnest concern to go in unto the King with their *purest, holiest, devoutest* feelings and thoughts. "Let not thine heart be hasty to utter *anything* before God" (Eccles. v. 1, 2). He asks of us "whatsoever things are true, venerable, just, pure, lovely," etc.

II. ADORABLE PRESENTATIONS TO GOD SECURE HIS GRACIOUS APPRECIATION AND LAVISH PRAISE.

What a richness of approving words we have here! "An offering . . . of a *sweet savour* unto the Lord." "It is a thing *most holy* of the offerings," etc. (Vv. 2, 3).

1. *No poverty of approval ever repels a fervent worshipper.*

Affection may be wasted upon the unappreciating; pearls cast before swine will be trodden under foot; Art's beauties are insipid to the unsympathetic soul. To the imbecile and the eye void of discernment,

> "A primrose by the river's brim
> A yellow primrose is to him,
> And it *is nothing more.*"

Much that is beautiful in the world, and in human life, misses recognition; eyes and hearts are closed to their preciousness. But "God *knoweth the heart*"; sees the motive of action, the meaning of sighs and tears, the graces of desire and design in our feeblest and frustrated efforts. "It is well that it was *in thine heart.*" "The Lord loveth a *cheerful* giver." "It is accepted according *to that a man hath.*" Nothing escapes Him. Jesus so *instantly saw the charm of Mary's act,* though against it the "disciples murmured" (Mark xiv. 6, 8, 9). God "*smelled a sweet savour*" when Noah sacrificed.

2. Offering such excellency of homage we *shall assuredly realise that God is well pleased.* If " the Lord had respect unto Abel and to his offering," because " by faith Abel offered a more excellent sacrifice than Cain, by which he obtained witness that he was righteous, *God testifying of his gift,*" will He fail to seal His favour upon the soul who "worships Him in spirit and in truth," seeing "the Father *seeketh* such to worship Him"? Did there not come transfiguration glories upon Jesus "*as He prayed*" (Luke ix. 29), followed by the inspiring testimony, "This is My beloved Son"? "In everything by *prayer* and *supplication* with *thanksgiving,* let your requests be made known unto God; and *the peace of God,* which passeth all understanding, *shall keep your hearts and minds* through Christ Jesus" (Phil. iv. 6, 7). God will make us glad, assured that we are "*accepted of Him.*"

III. *Excellences in typical offerings* FORESHADOWED THE BEAUTIES AND WORTHINESS OF JESUS.

1. The quality of the flour bespeaks the *intrinsic excellence of Christ.* He is the faultless One, "holy, harmless, undefiled"; God's most gracious Son; "fairer than the children of men." Inheriting His virtues by faith, we are beauteous in His beauty, faultless in His perfection, "accepted in the Beloved," "made the righteousness of God in Him," so as to stand at last " perfect before Him in love."

2. The pouring oil thereon denotes the *anointing of the Spirit.* For the Holy Ghost descended on Him; "baptised with the Holy Ghost," Jesus was enriched

with the Spirit's grace. And as "heirs of Christ" we also "have an unction from the Holy One"; and "the anointing which ye have received of Him abideth in you" (1 Jno. ii. 27).

3. The added frankincense, creating a pleasing odour through the tabernacle, tells *of the delightfulness of Christ;* His joy-inspiring grace. Is not His name " as ointment poured forth"? He gladdens all who share in His sacrifice. And He adds the beauty of spiritual delightfulness to the believer, so that God joys in us; and we are both to Him and among men as "the sweet savour of Christ."

Our approach to God *in the excellences of worship* becomes acceptable and well-pleasing to Him only because of *Jesus' merits and virtues*, which add all the worth to every accepted service men can render to the Lord. [See Addenda, p. 28, *The Beautiful in Worship.*]

Topic: MAINTENANCE OF PRIESTLY MINISTRATION (Vv. 8-10).

I. APPROACH TO GOD'S ALTAR THROUGH GOD'S PRIESTHOOD.

1. *Their office and ministers were Divinely ordained.* (*a*) **As to the** *office:* " No man taketh this honour to himself but he that is called of God" (Heb v. 4). Christian preachers must hear God's call to the ministry. " Christ glorified not Himself to be made an high priest, but He that said unto Him, Thou art My Son" (Heb. v. 5). (*b*) As to the *ministrations*: Every act of the priests is here minutely prescribed. So of *Christian ministers* (1 Cor. ix. 16-23). And our Lord's ministrations equally so. (See Heb. vii. 24. &c.)

2. *Without their mediation none could approach God.* Nor may any come nigh His presence now except through the priesthood of Jesus Christ (John xiv. 6), " No man cometh to the Father but by Me"; and (Heb. iv. 15, 16), " Having a High Priest, &c., let us therefore come boldly," &c. The Christian ministry does not reproduce and perpetuate a human priesthood. No sacrifices are now offered (Heb x. 11, 12); but " we are ambassadors for Christ, as though *God did beseech you by us . . . be ye reconciled to God.*"

II. MAINTENANCE OF GOD'S PRIESTS BY THE PEOPLES' GIFTS.

1. A *Divine ordinance* that they should be *generously supported while sacredly employed.* Not *supernaturally.* God did not feed them with angels' food, nor from the skies, nor from other than human resources, but by *the offerings of individual worshippers.* It *left them free* for their hallowed work. It *called out the generous thoughtfulness* of those whom they sacredly served. It knit priest and people together in *mutual dependence* and *mutual helpfulness.*

2. *Individual responsibility to support God's servants and maintain His sanctuary.* Not a single sacrifice could be laid on the altar, of any kind, without some part being assigned to the priests. This affirms our duty to give of our life and love *to Christ* while we approach His Sacrifice to draw atonement *from Christ.* It also *pronounces against a selfish spirit,* concerned only for personal gain, in seeking salvation. The offerer must consider others' wants as well as care for his own soul. And equally it teaches that they who enter God's house and *benefit by the ministration of the Christian pastor* should contribute to his comfort and support (1 Cor. ix. 11, 13, 14 ; Phil. iv. 18). [See Addenda, p. 29, *God's Ministers.*]

III. PRIESTLY MINISTRATIONS PROTECTED WITH UTMOST SANCTITY.

1. Closed within the sacred precincts of God's house, *they lived apart from the world.* God's witnesses to a *spiritual* life, and to a "life *hid with Christ in God.*" " Wherefore come out from among them, and be ye separate "

2. Ceaselessly employed in sacred services, they *summoned men to a self-surrendered career,* glorifying God in *their body and their spirit* which are His."

"Ye are a holy priesthood, a peculiar people" (1 Pet. ii. 5-9), "zealous of good works."

3. Living in the very scene where God dwelt, they *pledged to all sanctified souls a home with God.* "*These are not of the world.*" "I will that they be with Me where I am" (John xvii. 16-24). "Therefore are they before the throne of God and serve Him *day and night in His temple,*" &c. (Rev. vii. 15).

Topic: SUGGESTIVENESS OF THE MEAT OFFERING (Vv. 8-10)

I. ITS HUMAN ASPECT.

The Burnt Offering indicated consecration to, reconciliation with God; transferrence of guilt to victim slain. The meat offering points to *restoration* after reconciliation, the introduction of the worshipper to favour and friendship of the Lord. At the Lord's Table, we may remember, the associations are Eucharistic as well as Sacrificial. What did the meat offering teach the offerer concerning himself?

1. *That he was dependent upon God.* As he prepared and presented the finest of the wheat, made the pure white flour into cakes such as formed his daily meal, he would be reminded of his dependence upon God who makes the corn to grow, and crowns the year with His goodness. This offering, suggestive of the *social meal,* would remind the worshipper that he sat at the board of his heavenly Father who gave him daily food, and loaded him with life's bounteous blessings.

2. *That he was under obligation to God.* The offering acknowledged his duty and indebtedness. Though small, yet it was of the best. Not *chaff, husks,* or *bran,* but "fine flour." The obligation was to be discharged with (*a*) *Cheerfulness.* Oil was to mingle with offering, suggesting gladness in the worshipper, grace and favour in the worshipped. (*b*) *Devoutness.* "Frankincense," an emblem of prayer and praise ascending like sweet incense to the sky.

We are prone to forget the goodness of God as exercised and exhibited in our unceasing Providential supplies. He gives us necessaries and luxuries. Yet some (*a*) *forget Him* amid the excitements and enjoyments of life. Some (*b*) *ignore Him* in their exclusive attention to the laws and agencies of nature. Some (*c*) *insult Him,* by denying His existence, and attributing all phenomena and providence to chance. But some (*d*) *adore Him* by grateful hearts and obedient lives. We should thankfully partake of His temporal mercies, but with supreme gratitude accept "His unspeakable gift," the true Bread from heaven.

II. ITS SACERDOTAL ASPECT; or, What did the meat offering teach concerning the Priests?

1. *Their office was worthy of respect.* Selected by the Lord, they were His special servants, and were appointed to perform sacred duties which the people could not do for themselves. They were God's priests, and as such deserved the considerate regard of the people. Though Christian ministers are not priests, yet they are ambassadors for Christ, and stand, as it were, in His stead, beseeching men to be reconciled unto God; and, as such, are to be held in high esteem for their work's sake.

2. *Their services commanded recompense.* Being withdrawn from secular engagements, and giving their time and thoughts to sacerdotal duties, they had a cogent claim (*a*) *to live in the affections and sympathies of the people;* and (*b*) *to be supported by them* (Ezek. xliv. 27-30; 1. Cor. ix. 13). In connection with the sacrifices there was the priest's portion (v. 3), so that their physical wants might be supplied. The New Testament teaches that "the labourer is worthy of his hire," and "those who preach the Gospel should live by the Gospel."

3. *Their sacredness claimed for them no worship.* No sacrifice was offered to the priests. They had to seek forgiveness and offer sacrifices for themselves.

Till the worship had been completed they partook of nothing offered in sacrifice to God; then it was their privilege to share what remained. Under the New Testament dispensation ministers are not priests. They occupy no such unique position, and have no priestly functions to fulfil. Yet, the minister of the Cross —if he be true and faithful—is worthy of the highest esteem, as well as worthy of his hire, though unworthy of worship, as the Levitical priests. Through relationship to our Great High Priest the whole company of the faithful become "kings and priests unto God"; though not even "the glorious company of the apostles" would receive homage, but would exclaim with one voice, "Worship God."

III. ITS THEOLOGICAL ASPECT; or, What did the meat offering teach the offerer concerning God?

1. *That He greatly valued His own gifts to man.* "The earth is the Lord's, and the fulness thereof, the world, and they that dwell therein"; and yet He holds His smallest works and common gifts to man in great esteem. His directing the priests about their offerings with such minuteness of detail shows that the works His hands had made are worthy being presented with scrupulous care and order in His service.

2. *That He reclaims and accepts His own gifts from man.* He had the right to do so, and to have them offered and disposed of as He saw fit. All objections about waste and uselessness in the sacrifices vanish when we remember this. When the people offered of their flocks and crops they only gave back a small portion of what they had received in abundance; so that their offerings were (a) *provided by God;* (b) *belonged to Him;* and (c), *however great, were below His deserts.* We cannot offer to the Lord anything that is absolutely our own, for all we have and are belong to Him. "Not your own, bought with a price." God has a right to our service and sacrifice. If we present ourselves as living sacrifices He will accept and appreciate them as His own gifts restored.

3. *That He may be propitiated by such offerings of His gifts by man.* Offerings of the produce of the earth (such as Cain's), unassociated with substitutionary sacrifice, fall below what God requires of man. Hence the Deist leaves out of his worship the essential element to efficiency and acceptability. The hand of faith must first be laid upon the head of the burnt offering, and an atonement be accepted for him, before other services and sacrifices can be well pleasing to God. We cannot enrich the Lord by our gifts, yet He accepts them as expressions of our fealty and faith. Such offerings of our gratitude and trust will be unto Him a "sweet savour."—F. W. B.

Topic: CHARACTER AS QUALIFYING SACRIFICE (Vv. 1-3 and 11-13).

"*Fine* flour, *oil, frankincense,* it is a thing *most holy* unto the Lord. *No leaven* nor any *honey.* Every oblation season with *salt.*" Beyond all dispute the *frankincense* and *salt* indicate certain moral features of *good;* and *leaven, honey,* &c., certain moral features of *evil.* This specification of the excellent, this prohibition of the deleterious, denotes how the *qualities* which enter into our sacrifices and services are considered by God.

I. Symbolised here we behold THE GRACES AND FAULTLESSNESS WHICH DISTINGUISHED JESUS.

1. *His life was sacrificial.* Bruised corn suggests suffering, and our Redeemer knew such bruising from God and man "It pleased the Lord to bruise Him," &c. "Reproach hath broken My heart." But a crushed and suffering Jesus is man's salvation. "By His stripes we are healed."

2. *Yet His sacrifice was full of grace.* "*Fine* flour, *oil, frankincense, salt.*" (a) Highest qualities of person and character distinguished Jesus. No husk, no common quality in the flour; "that *Holy Thing* which shall be born of thee shall

be called the Son of God" (Luke i. 35). "It is a thing most holy." (*b*) The *sacred oil of the Spirit* enriched the character of Christ. "Pour oil" (v. 1). "Grace is *poured* into thy lips." "The Word became flesh, full of grace and truth." "The Father giveth not the Spirit by measure unto Him." "Jesus being full of the Holy Ghost," &c. [See Acts x. 38.] (*c*) The delightfulness of a *perfect willinghood*, the fragrance of a *zealous consecration* crowned His sacrifice: "Frankincense." "Thy law is within my heart." "His zeal it consumed me." "My beloved Son in whom I am *well pleased.*"

3. *In His character there was no fault.* (*a*) *No corruption tainted His sinless nature and sacrifice.* "No leaven." "Holy, harmless, undefiled, separate from sinners." "I find no fault in this man." (*b*) *No mere earthly sweetness* which might become sickly; no weak sentiments of feeling; no low or fitful affections of the heart; no private preferences or fleeting fantasies. His soul was moved alone by loyalty and love to God and His high work for man.

4. *Perpetuity and unchangeableness of excellence* distinguished Christ's character and sacrifice. "*Seasoned with salt.*" His devotion to man was an incorruptible and invariable principle. His saving grace is an enduring and inexhaustible quality in His sacrifice.

II. Indicated here we recognise THE QUALITIES OF CHARACTER GOD DESIRES IN SACRIFICIAL LIVES.

This offering was to present on the Lord's altar what would be grateful and savoury to Him. Such is the aim of the Christian life: to consecrate to Him a "sweet savour of Christ."

1. *An even devotion*, genuine and excellent throughout, like "fine flour."

2. An *anointed* character, beautified by the Spirit; for "if any man have not the Spirit of Christ, he is none of His."

3. *A sweet fervour of soul.* For as the *fire brought out the aroma* of frankincense, so should affliction exhibit Christian sweetness and grace. God desires, too, a *glad and grateful spirit* in service. "Giving thanks to His name." Also qualities *which spread pleasure around*, as did the frankincense. "To do good and communicate forget not, for with such sacrifices God is well pleased."

4. *Uncorruptedness of heart.* "No leaven, nor honey." Void of selfishness and guile; neither insincerity nor mere natural sweetness, which may decay: but the abiding graces of the Holy Spirit; having an "unction from the Holy One."

5. *Enduring integrity of heart and life.* "Salt." Counteracting the putrefactions of sin. Maintaining perpetuity of sacred love and consecration. "Showing forth the virtues of the Lord."

Holy and consecrated lives; the noblest qualities of heart; the incorruptible graces of the Spirit; these make our services and sacrifices "in the sight of God of great price." [See Addenda, p. 29, *Character*.]

Topic: RESURRECTION EMBLEMS. "*The oblation of the first-fruits*" (Vv. 12-16).

The order in which this offering came is given in chap. xxiii. First the *Passover*, then the *Wave-sheaf*, then the *Pentecost*. The "*sheaf* of the *first-fruits*" might be burnt as a sweet savour to the Lord, but the "*oblation* of the *first-fruits*" might *not* be burnt on the altar (chap. ii. 12). The reason for this being that the "*sheaf*" was unleavened, whereas the "*oblation*" was mixed and made with leaven (chap. xxiii. 17).

I. OUR LORD'S RESURRECTION presented the "*Sheaf* of the first-fruits" unto the Lord.

"Now is Christ risen from the dead, and become the first-fruits of them that sleep" (1 Cor. xv. 20).

1. "In Him was *no sin*"—no leaven. 2. He was Himself a "*sweet savour*" to God. 3. He therefore *rose to God* in His pure humanity as incense from the sacrifice.

II. THE CHURCH OF CHRIST was the "*oblation* of the first-fruits."

"We are a kind of first-fruits of His creatures" (Jas. i. 18).

1. This offering, *having sin in it*, "mixed with leaven," could *not stand the test of fire*, God's searching holiness.

2. Yet it was to be *consecrated to God*. "Ye shall offer it, but it shall not be burnt" (Lev. ii. 12).

3. And was *both offered* and *accepted*. For along "*with it*" was presented a burnt offering, a meat offering, a peace offering, and a sin offering: symbols of Christ's *propitiatory atonement*. The Church comes before God *with the merits of Christ;* and is offered with *all the value of His work associated with it*. Though in itself unable to stand the fire of God's holiness; yet, with Christ's virtue added, it is accepted even as the *Sheaf* was accepted.

4. All the *merits of the propitiatory sacrifices were needful* to secure the *acceptance* of the *leavened* oblation. All the *virtues of Christ's sacrifice* and *offices of His priesthood* are needful to ensure our acceptance with God, in consequence of the *sin intermixed* with our redeemed humanity. "The priests shall *wave them with* the bread of the first-fruits" (xxiii. 20). [Compare *Jukes on the Offerings*]

III. ALL THE OFFERINGS OF FIRST-FRUITS APPEARED BEFORE THE LORD.

1. *Christ Himself entered into the Holy Place* before the Lord. He ascended to the heavenly places.

2. *His redeemed Church also entered accepted* into the very presence of the Lord. "These were redeemed from among men, being the *first-fruits* unto God and to the Lamb" (Rev. xiv. 4).

3. Identified with Him in consecration to God, we shall be *united with Him in the temple of God*. "Where I am there also shall My servants be." "Father, I will that they also whom Thou hast given Me be with Me where I am." "By Man came also the *resurrection of the dead*." "So shall they be for ever *with the Lord*." [See Addenda, p. 29, *Resurrection Emblems*.]

OUTLINES ON VERSES OF CHAPTER II.

V. 1.—*Theme:* THE PERFECT SUBDUEDNESS AND MEEKNESS OF CHRIST. "*Fine flour*."

The types supply various aspects of Christ's one work. "The Holy Spirit takes truth in portions, and seems sometimes to turn our eyes away from one portion of truth to let us see better some other portion, by keeping our attention for a time fixed on that alone" (Bonar). The Burnt offering has shown us Christ as the *Devoted One*, dedicating Himself and all His powers always to God. Now the Meat offering will reveal to us *Christ in meek subduedness*.

I. CHRIST WAS HERE TO DEVELOP A CHARACTER OF PERFECT SUBJECTION TO GOD.

1. *Men* had through all their history been *marked by self will and arrogant insubordination* to God. "Cedars of Lebanon high and lifted up." "Pride compassed them about," &c.

2. Among such Christ came *to manifest implicit obedience and subjection*. "Lo I come to *do Thy will*, O God"

"Not My will but Thine be done." Cheerful subservience to Another's will, even through bitterness of suffering; meek submission to insult and reproach; gentle patience and kindness even to enemies—such were His characteristics.

II. CHRIST'S QUALITIES OF MEEKEST SUBDUEDNESS ARE TYPIFIED IN THE FOOD OFFERING. "*Fine flour*."

1. There is *no suggestion in the type of subduedness conferred*. No millstone is seen *grinding the corn* into its smoothness. The flour is brought perfected in its fineness. Such was Christ *as He came into the world*: perfect in meekness and lowliness and every quality of submission. Affliction and suffering found these qualities *in* Him, as the fire on the altar found them in the flour; it did not produce them.

2. *The invariable evenness of Christ's submission* is suggested. The meekness He manifested in the judgment hall and on the Cross was not more perfect than that which marked Him as He grew up in the home of Joseph and Mary, sharing their low estate. "He was subject unto them." The excellen-

cies of His character were intrinsic and essential. "*Fine flour.*"

(*a*) How *contrasted* is this excellency of Christ *with the variable spirit and behaviour of His followers.* John wished to call fire from heaven on others! Paul spake in anger, "God shall smite thee thou whited wall!" But the equability of Jesus never failed.

(*b*) Yet we *may cultivate* "*the meekness and gentleness of Christ.*" Guard against the hinderances to graciousness of character and the irritations which molest the spirit, and "learn of Him who was meek and lowly of heart." [Compare *Newton's Thoughts on Leviticus.*]

V. 3.—*Theme*: CHRIST THE FOOD OF PRIVILEGED SOULS. "*The remnant of the Meat offering shall be Aaron's and his sons.*"

Before any portion went to supply the necessities of the ministering priests, note—

I. IN THE OFFERING OF CHRIST WHICH IS DESIGNED TO SUSTAIN MAN'S LIFE, GOD HAD A PORTION. "A handful," "the memorial" of the offering was first burned upon the altar. Even in devoting Himself to meet the hunger and wants of humanity, Christ did it as "an offering *unto the Lord.*" He did all with His Father in first and highest thought.

II. IN THE OFFERING OF CHRIST PROVISION IS MADE FOR THE SPIRITUAL WANTS AND NEEDS OF MEN.

1. In Christ Jesus will be found *man's sufficiency.* The soul's wants are all supplied in Him. Whoever drew upon Him and went away unsatisfied? What need, what trial, what demand of our manifold life does Christ not meet? He will satisfy us in every condition: when poor to give us succour, when weary to give us strength, when sorrowful to give us joy. Christ is our Food.

2. Yet it is *limited to those who are in priestly relation to Him.* Those who are "priests unto God"; all *sanctified souls,* who live to God, they will find in Jesus every true need met. Others may wander elsewhere crying, "Who will show us any good?" but "they who *are Christ's* have crucified the flesh with its affections and lusts," and these find "Christ is all in all."

V. 9.—*Theme*: A MEMORIAL ON GOD'S ALTAR. "*The priest shall take of the meat offering a memorial thereof,* and shall burn it upon the altar.*" Consider—

I. ITS CONTRAST WITH A MEMORIAL OF INIQUITY.

In Numb. v. 11 we read of "an offering *of memorial,* bringing *iniquity to remembrance.*"

That was a food offering of barley meal, without *oil,* and without *frankincense.*

No intrinsic virtue, no sacred anointing, no pleasing grace.

The memorial was *associated with sin,* and the *forerunner of a curse* (Numb. v. 18).

How appalling if Christ's offering were to—

1. *Memorialise our guilt* before God; and
2. *Evoke a curse upon our conviction of wrong.*

II. THE GRACIOUS SIGNIFICANCE IN CHRIST'S MEMORIAL OFFERING.

In this instance of the "memorial"—

1. It was *rendered sweet to God* by admixture of oil, frankincense and salt. A pleasant offering to Him, therefore. And assuredly no memorial of iniquity could be pleasant to God; it was a remembrance of the *sacred grace of Christ for man.*

2. It was designed to *bring righteousness to remembrance.* Christ's precious merits. And going up before the Lord *for us* they represent the truth that *by imputation* those merits become ours, on whose behalf "the memorial" is burned on the altar.

V. 9.—*Theme*: THOROUGHNESS IN SERVICE FOR THE LORD. "It is an offering made by fire, of a sweet savour unto the Lord."

I. COMPLETE CONSECRATION. Fire *absorbs, transforms* all.

II. ARDENT ENTHUSIASM. Fire *intense, demonstrative, aggressive.*

III. DIVINE APPROBATION. "The Lord."

(*a*) *Recognises* such thorough service.

(*b*) *Rejoices* in such thorough service; "a sweet savour."—*F. W. B.*

V. 11.—*Theme*: PURITY IN SERVICE OF THE LORD. "Ye shall burn no leaven, nor any honey."

Service for the Lord to be—

I. *Unmixed with impure influences.* "Leaven" penetrates, and permeates, and transforms the meal into its own nature; evil spreads rapidly when entertained, has power to vitiate the heart, and corrupt religious work and worship.

II. *Unmixed with sensual indulgences.* "Honey" suggestive of self-gratification, of luxury to satiety. Appetites must be curbed, selfishness crucified; not the sweet and safe sought so much as the right and true. We need the *thoughts* of our hearts cleansed by the inspiration of the Holy Ghost, that *motives* and *desires* may be pure; for the outward act of service, however costly, is only an abomination if not offered from a sincere and sanctified heart.—*F. W. B.*

ILLUSTRATIVE ADDENDA TO CHAPTER II.

THE BEAUTIFUL IN WORSHIP.
No sacred lore, howe'er profound,
Nor all the long and varied round
Of sacred rites, can bliss procure
For worthless man, in heart impure.

Altho' a man with zeal and skill
Should all external rites fulfil,
He reaps no fruit of all his toil
If sin his inner man should soil.

E'en he his all in alms who spends,
With heart defiled, secures no meed;
The *disposition*, not the deed,
Has value—on it all depends.
Vayu Purana, viii. 190.
See *Bonar's*
"'Tis first the true and then the beautiful,
Not first the beautiful and then the true."

"Onward, onward may we press
  Thro' the path of duty;
Virtue is true happiness,
  Excellence true beauty.
Minds are of supernal birth,
Let us make a heaven of earth."
James Montgomery.

The *merely* beautiful, *external and æsthetic* in worship is not enough, and is perilous when, as expressed in *Aurora Leigh*,
"The beautiful seems right
By force of beauty."
"In the spirit of that significant Oriental usage which drops its sandals at the palace door, the decent worshipper will put off his travel-tarnished shoes, will try to divest himself of secular anxieties and worldly profits, when the place where he stands is converted into holy ground by the words, "Let us worship God!"—*Dr. Jas. Hamilton.*

SWEET INCENSE. Worship is the compound of many gracious ingredients—repentance, faith, contrition, desire, love, joy in God, and other graces. Offered daily and inspired by the Spirit, such worship is no intrusion, but welcome before the Eternal Throne, performed with all the precious sweetness of the meritorious grace of Christ.

GOD'S MINISTERS.
"The man who has adopted the Church as a profession, and goes through the routine of his duties with the coldness of a mere official—filled by him the pulpit seems filled by the ghastly form of a skeleton, which, in its cold and bony fingers, holds a burning lamp."—*Dr. Guthrie.*
"A minister's credentials as a pastor will be most readily accepted who shows himself the follower of One who turned and said to His disciples, 'But I have called you friends.'"—*Anon.*

"The Apostle saith that they are worthy of double honour, an honour of reverence and an honour of maintenance; and, doubtless, the very heathen shall rise up in judgment against many who profess the truth in this respect; for the heathen themselves did show such honour to their devilish priests that one of the Roman consuls seeing a priest and some vestal virgins going on foot, and he riding in his chariot, descended, and would not go into it again till those votaries were first placed."—*Bishop Reynolds.*

"The spirit and manner of a minister often affects more than the matter."—*Cecil.*

It is said of *Whitefield*, "So close was his communion with God before preaching, that he used to come down to the people *as if there were a rainbow about his head.*" And of the Rev. *J. H. Stewart*, "He was a precious box of ointment in a wounding world." And of the Rev. J. H. Forsyth, "He did what thousands do, but he did it *as not one in a thousand does.*"

RESURRECTION EMBLEMS. "The very first employment of Israel in *Canaan* was preparing the type of the Saviour's resurrection, and their first religious act was holding up that type of a risen Saviour."—*Bonar.*

"The wheat sheaf was an *earnest* that the whole field should be reaped, as well as a *sample* of the harvest. . . . The ideas of pagans respecting the dead are suggested by the *broken Corinthian pillar* or the *stringless harp*. . . . The word *cemetery*, which means a sleeping-place, gives us the Christian idea, for He 'giveth His beloved sleep.'"—*Pilkington.*

CHARACTER. "Character is higher than intellect."—*Emerson.*
"A soul of power, a well of lofty thought,
A chastened hope that ever points to heaven." *J. Hunter.*
"When character is lost all is lost."—*German Motto.*

CHAPTER III.

The Peace Offering of Thanksgiving.

SUGGESTIVE READINGS.

V. 1.—**A sacrifice of peace offering.** Happy are the truths made evident in this peace sacrifice; delightful to God, blessed for man. Peace is established between God and the soul, reconciliation is realised; and the offerer comes to the altar with festive gladness in his heart. Yes, and God also, and the priests, and the offerer's friends, all join in *the sacrificial banquet of joy over peace restored*. Its completeness was realised in Christ: "For *He is our Peace*, who hath made both one" (Ephes. ii. 14). The angels' carol has become translated into Christian experience—"On earth *peace*, goodwill toward men." He who would enter into and enjoy "peace with God," must bring the Redeemer's "sacrifice of peace offering" (Rom. v. 1)

Whether male or female. Unrestricted freedom in choice of the victim; as though God was so desirous of peace with man that every possible opportunity and convenience should be arranged for effecting conciliation. That is the lesson: and in the atonement of Calvary the plan of appeasement and acceptance is ready of access to every one. No difficulty, no embarrassment, is left by God in the way of our obtaining reconciliation and fellowship with Him.

V. 2.—Lay his hand on . . . and kill it. Here is the crowning act of the sinner: act of identification with the very death of the victim. Who slew the Sacrifice? even he who lays his hand on Him in order to be saved; yes, saved by the *death the sinner himself inflicted!* Jesus claims the victim's place; gives His life for man. Each altar sprinkled with blood proclaims the *peace* thus bought, peace bought by death. "The chastisement of our peace was upon Him."

V. 3.—All the fat that is upon the inwards. In the *burnt* offering it was the fat connected with the limbs and *external* parts of the victim which God required; but in the *peace* sacrifice He specifically asks the *inward* fat which covers the vitals. This denoted inward health; and typified the *inmost excellency of Christ*. And as this was to be *for God*, placed and consumed upon His altar, it bespeaks how all the virtue and grace of Jesus in His own essential perfectness and preciousness were necessary to a satisfactory peace between God and man. For what inferior sacrifice could suffice? The enmity and outrage wrought by our sin and sinfulness were such that the most absolute excellence was essential in our propitiatory offering. But Christ offered "*all*" His virtue to God for us.

V. 5.—On the altar upon the burnt sacrifice. *Peace* is not the first thing for man to seek with God, but *satisfaction*: that having been made in the burnt sacrifice, he may "burn" his peace offering "*upon* the burnt sacrifice." No basis for peace except the sufferings of Christ. He having been offered in substitution for guilt we may lay our peace offering *upon* that Sacrifice.

V. 11.—The food of the offering made by fire unto the Lord. God finds "*food*"—satisfaction, gratification—in the altar offering, in the excellencies of Christ devoted in sacrifice to win man's acceptance. Grand truth: the presentation of atonement by Jesus for man's peace yields to God a satisfying "food," a substantial joy, which both fills all the Divine desires and answers all the Divine demands. The Saviour's sacrifice was very precious to the holy God.

V. 17.—Eat neither fat nor blood. As the "fat" symbolised the inmost virtue, this law claimed the *best* as God's portion: and as the "blood" represented the life of the victim, this law claimed *life* as inalienably God's. You owe Him your inmost affections, the most precious qualities of your being; yea, your whole life. Jesus gave them *all* to His Father: and we should also yield our noblest, our all.

EXPLANATORY HOMILY.

i. The spiritual standing, or sacred qualification of the offerer. Peace offerings could be presented only by persons who had already *obtained forgiveness of sins* (by the sin and trespass offerings, comp. chap. vi. 7), and had *consecrated themselves* as on the altar *to Jehovah* (by the burnt offering, comp. vii. 12), and were thus at *peace with God*.

This sacrificial regulation indicates an enduring spiritual law: that he who would enter into a state of friendship with God must first have secured expiation of his sins (sin offering), and have consecrated himself (burnt offering) and his substance (meat offering) to the Lord.

ii. **Propitiation and self surrender are not absent even in presenting** *peace offerings.* The *blood* of the victim was sprinkled on the altar, and *portions* of the carcass were burnt in the fire. Whereas the *imposition of hands* and *slaughter of the substitute* by the offerer betokened sense of condemnation and appeal to sovereign grace.

We cannot acceptably offer even sacrifices of peace and praise apart from the meritorious death and substitutionary atonement of Jesus.

iii. **Peace offerings were various**, both in the *victims chosen* and in the *purpose for which they were offered.* (1) The *victims:* from the herds or flocks, male or female. (2) The *purpose:* thank offerings, votive offerings, free-will offerings. The first expressed gratitude for God's gracious favours; the second fulfilled a vow made on condition of receiving God's goodness; the third entreated a mercy, but without conditions, as in a vow, retaining freedom to make return to the Lord as occasion served.

Great variety may mark our thank offerings to God, but the liberty leaves us without excuse if we render nothing to the Lord for all His benefits towards us.

iv. In the *distribution of portions of the peace offering* a **sacrificial feast of fellowship was enacted.**

A part to Jehovah, other parts to the priests, and the remainder to the offerer, all meeting in amity and peace, and joyously sharing in the sweet savour offering.

For the reconciliation of man to God, and Divine fellowship with man, occasioned heart gladness to the Divine Father (see parable of Prodigal Son), to the reinstated worshipper, and to the Daysman betwixt them who laid His hand on them both—the mediating Priest.

v. *The part of the divided victims were specially apportioned*, establishing a **law of priority in sacred claims.** To *God* the choicest parts first. These were burned on the altar, and became a "sweet savour unto the Lord." To the *community of priests* ("the breast"), and to *the officiating priest* ("the right hind leg") next, indicating grateful recognition of Priesthood ministries, specially *Christ's*, and fellowship with the sacred priesthood of believers. The *sacrificer retained the rest*, but only that he, *with his friends,* might join the *sacred repast*, and thus emphasize the truth of the communion of saints; they and God's household, and God Himself, all partaking of the one offering, as a feast of friendship and communion.

Our first aim should be to offer the worthiest to the Lord; next to own grateful obligations to the mediatorial service of Christ; then to establish festal relationship with the household of God, the household of faith. Self last in fellowship, no man living to himself. Christian life joyously communing with the *Father,* the *Mediator,* and the *Church.*

SECTIONAL HOMILIES.

Topic: PEACE-OFFERING SACRIFICES (Vv. 1-5).

Consider—

I. HISTORIC INSTANCES OF PRESENTING THE PEACE OFFERING.

Scripture records of these occurrences are instructive. Some of the occasions when the offering was presented were *Divinely appointed.*

(*a*) At the consecration of priests for their holy office and ministry (Lev. vii. 30-34). (*b*) At the completion of the term of a Nazarite's vow (Numb. vi. 14). (*c*) At the dedication of the completed tabernacle (Numb. vii. 17). (*d*) At the feast of the first-fruits (Lev. xxiii. 19); and (e) At the joyful opening of Solomon's temple (1 Kings viii. 63).

Others were *spontaneous*—

1. *For signal experience of Providential deliverance.* Thus (a) David *in the hour of victory*, when " his head was lifted up above his enemies round about him," resolved to " sacrifice in God's tabernacle *sacrifices of joy* " (Psa. xxvii. 6). (b) Amid *merciful rescues from peril*, enumerated in Psalm cvii., as when guided through a lone wilderness (v. 4), or brought out of sore oppression (vv. 10-14), or upon recovery from wasting sickness (v. 18), or when the haven is reached after terrible voyage (v. 30), etc. Then " let them *sacrifice the sacrifice of thanksgiving* " (v. 22).

2. As the *fulfilment of vows* made in troublous circumstances. Thus *Jonah* " prayed unto the Lord his God out of the fish's belly " (Jonah ii. 1), and vowed, when " salvation came to him of the Lord " (v. 9), that he would *sacrifice unto Him* with the voice *of thanksgiving*, and pay that he had vowed " (v. 9). [See also Psa. cxvi. 3, 17-19.]

3. *As a seal of fervent and trustful prayer.* So did the confederate tribes before going to battle against the victorious Benjamites. They " went up and came to the house of God and wept, and sat there before the Lord, and fasted that day until even, and offered burnt offerings and *peace offerings* before the Lord " (Judges xx. 26). [See Addenda, p. 38, *Sacrifices of Peace.*] Consider again the—

II. SACRED SENTIMENTS PROMPTING TO THE OFFERING OF THE PEACE SACRIFICES.

Noting the attitude of thought, the feelings of heart, with which the sacrifices were presented, we shall realise the religious affections which found expression in this form of altar offering.

1. Prominent, as a motive to the peace offering, is *thanksgiving*. It presented a *sacrifice of praise to God;* it yielded an offering to Jehovah's glory. This implies a heart of gratitude in man; a reverent sense of the goodness of God; a desire to perform some act to His glory and praise. In chap. vii. 12 it is distinctly marked as intended *"for a thanksgiving."* The worshipper should seek God not alone with requests, and under sense of danger or need, but with the *homage of joy*. " I will sacrifice *sacrifices* of joy. I will sing," etc. (Psa. xxvii. 6). " God hath done great things for us, whereof we are glad." " What shall I shall render unto the Lord for all His benefits towards me ?" " Bless the Lord, O my soul," etc. *" Thanks be unto God* for His unspeakable gift." We are to *glorify God* with praises. Hence the exhortation, " By Him, therefore, let us offer the *sacrifice of praise* to God continually, that is the fruit of our lips giving thanks to His name " (Heb. xiii. 15). [See Addenda, p. 38, *Thanksgiving.*]

2. Equally manifest, as a motive to the peace offering, is *dedication*. Thus it is provided that " the sacrifice of his offering [may] be *a vow*" (Lev. vii. 16). This means a consecration to some *act of service* for God. As the " sweet savour" ascended to God it bore to Heaven a hostage and pledge of practical godliness and grateful obedience which should follow. " Praise waiteth for Thee, O God, in Zion, and *unto Thee shall the vow be performed*" (Psa. lxv. 1). " I will go into Thy house with *burnt offerings*, I will pay Thee *my vows which my lips have uttered*, etc. I will offer unto Thee burnt sacrifices of fatlings, with the incense of rams," etc. (Psa. lxvi. 13-15). Christian life should assuredly be yielded in devotion to the Lord in return for the grace we have received.

III. GOSPEL REALISATIONS OF THE TYPICAL SIGNIFICANCE OF THE PEACE OFFERINGS.

1. *The varieties in the victims* symbolise the *manifold aspects of Christ's gracious offering.* As in the burnt offering. [See on Chapter I.]

2. The *different motives prompting* the offering suggest the *various purposes*

Christ's sacrifice effected. His peace offering both was for *God's praise,* in sinners reconciled ; and for *man's dedication,* in Christian lives being vowed and devoted to His service. For when "made nigh" in Christ it is our joy to live unto God in loving, willing obedience. Christ's sacrificial life represented both significant aspects of the peace offering : it was an offering to *Divine praise and glory,* and an enactment of *man's grateful consecration* to God.

3. *The blessed reconciliation of God and man* was sealed in the peace offering of Jesus. "Having *made peace* through the blood of His cross, by Him to reconcile all things unto Himself," etc. (Colos. i. 20).

IV. PRESENT-DAY OBLIGATIONS IN THE LIGHT OF THE ANCIENT PEACE OFFERINGS.

1. He who would offer *praise* to God must *do so at the altar.* That was the place where the offering was made. Nothing, no grateful affection, no dedicatory vow, may go from man to God irrespective of the altar. Nothing can be accepted, nothing is permitted, apart from Christ's sacrifice. The peace offering must be "on the altar *upon* the burnt sacrifice " (v. 5) ; something additional to and following upon Christ's atoning merits. Gratitude is beautiful, dedication is right ; but God will have neither—from sinful man—apart from the Saviour's grace. These are lovely flowers which can only properly unfold and bloom under the radiance of the Cross.

2. Divine graciousness summons us to *the sacrifices of thankful devotion.* Not a moment but our hearts and lips should be pouring out streams of praise, the sweet savour of love, the homage of joy, the evidence that we are the Lord's : "wherefore glorify God in your body and in your spirit, which are God's."

3. *Peace with God in Christ is the basis of a joyful godly life.* Praise can only be where peace is realised and enjoyed. All our happiness rests on our being in Christ, partakers of "peace with God through Jesus." Then we can " also joy in God " (Rom. v. 1 and 11). And Christian life should " *show forth the praises* of Him who hath called us out of darkness," etc. (1 Pet. ii. 9). Blessed peace which imparts such joy and inspires such praise !

Topic : THE FEAST OF MAN'S FELLOWSHIP WITH GOD (Vv. 3, 9, 14, 16).

" He shall offer *of* the sacrifice of the peace offering unto the Lord." Not the whole, but *a part* was to be burnt on the altar fire, and " Aaron's sons shall burn it—*i.e.,* the specified portion which God required (see v. 4). And this *part participation* by God is further particularised in v. 16—"The priest shall burn them upon the altar ; it is the food of the offering made by fire for a sweet savour ; *all the fat is the Lord's.*"

The remaining parts (chap. vii.) were distributed to the *priests* who ministered and the *offerer* himself. Thus the peace offering was *shared* by God with man ; they *met together in a sacrificial feast,* and partook of the same altar oblation. To eat together is a sign of friendship and fellowship.

I. SUCH PRIVILEGED COMMUNION BETWEEN GOD AND MAN IS ESTABLISHED ON SPECIAL CONDITIONS.

Who is the man who thus is admitted to feast with God? May anyone adventure into such privilege ? Are there no restrictions or conditions regulating so wondrous an incident?

1. Fellowship between God and man must be *at the altar of sacrifice.* There, where sin is acknowledged, atoned and purged ; where substitution is accepted for the life of sinful man ; where "no condemnation" is attained by penalty having been laid upon the Victim. Only there can God meet man in friendship. *Sacrifice* must go first.

2. Fellowship proceeds on the recognition that *we yield our highest affections*

and virtues first to God. That victim being offered is in the offerer's stead, and represents man. What part of the man does God require? *The very choicest part;* just as He was to have the *inmost vitalities and fat* of the sacrifice. It means that *before* God can have blessed communion with man, man must give God his inmost affections and noblest powers in ready consecration; that, indeed, it is only *in the act of such dedication* of our highest qualities to Him God comes into fellowship with man at all. God would have refused to partake of the feast if any inferior part had been presented Him. We must bring our first energies, our purest love, if God is to "sup with us and we with Him" (Rev. iii. 20).

3. Fellowship can only be enjoyed in connection with *intervening priestly services.* "Aaron's sons," etc. (vv. 2-4). No communion, no acceptance with God apart from the mediation of Jesus.

4. Fellowship with God requires that we *associate His priests with us in the feast.* [Compare chap. vii. 14, 31-35.] The lessons of this enactment are (1) *Generous attention* to and support of those who *minister to us in holy things.* We "reap their spiritual things," and should show appreciation. (2) *Communion with the saints* who *unite with us in temple service.* All fellow Christians are "priests." (3) *Largeness of heart in sharing* with others the blessings we enjoy. Give a better portion to them than that we retain for ourselves. "Hospitality one to another without grudging" (1 Peter iv. 9). In a feast the host gives the best to his guests. The idea is *regal.* We entertain *the King and His courtiers,* and place the choicest part of the banquet first before the King; then the best remaining portions we serve to His attendant ministers; for ourselves, happy and honoured that we may sit down at such a banquet and entertain such guests. [See Addenda, p. 38, *Blessedness of Peace.*]

II SUCH PRIVILEGED COMMUNION POURTRAYS THE JOYOUS EXPERIENCE OPEN TO MAN IN CHRIST.

Felicity is the prevalent sentiment in such a feast. Joy with God; joy in Jesus; joy among fellow saints. But all this blessedness is in connection with a *sacrificed life.* As all our felicity springs from the redemption of Jesus.

1. *God's satisfaction and delight with the choice virtues of Jesus.* Christ, as our Representative, is here giving Himself to God for us, and He finds *sweet savoury food* in the offering (vv. 11, 16). "This is My beloved Son, in whom I am well pleased." For the *inmost affections* of Jesus were all supremely consecrated to His Father. Yet there was also another cause of God's delight in Jesus—that He offered Himself as the sacrifice for man's salvation: "*therefore* doth My Father love Me because I lay down My life." God looked on the altar, saw that to Him were yielded the best affections of His Son, and saw equally that His life was readily offered as a Peace Sacrifice for sinners, that the *Father and the family might be again at one.*

2. *Man's blessedness in the experiences of fellowship in Christ Jesus.* Peace is not all we find in Him, but happiness, "*joy unspeakable and full of glory*": "a feast of fat things." Christian life is a banquet. "Eat, O my friends." And it is a feast, not upon faulty and false diet, which mocks the cravings and hopes of men, but is upon an offering "*without blemish,*" the choicest of the flock. Christ Himself is the food of the believer.

"Yes. Thou art precious to my soul."

Happy they who are "partakers of Christ Jesus," and live upon Him. He "satisfies our mouth with good things," and so daintily feasts the heart's longings that "His joy remains in us, and our joy is full."

Note: This feast of fellowship was both an *expression of love* by the offerer of the sacrifice, and in turn *nourished that love* in him by communion with God and His Church.

3. *Christ's own happiness in the feast of man's fellowship with God.* The priest had a choice part in the sacrifice. He who is "Priest over the house of God" shares in this glad banquet. Himself the Victim sacrificed, He is also the mediating and partaking Priest. How does this open to view the heart of Christ: He as mediating Priest joins in the gladness of the event of communion reinstated between God and man: feasts with us as the intervening Friend, and is satisfied with the portion which is His. For can our Lord be other than satisfied with His part in the transaction? It is through His mediation that God and men feast together. And in the *delighted love of the Father* and the *grateful happiness of man* Jesus finds a rich satisfaction: it is "the joy set before Him" for which He "endured the cross, despising the shame."

(1) Into such a feast He asks to be admitted, as He appeals *at the sinner's heart*: "Behold I stand at the door and knock; if any man will hear My voice and open the door, I will come in and sup with him and he with Me."

(2) To such a feast He comes when His saints gather *at the sacramental table.* "With desire I have desired to eat this passover with you." "This do in remembrance of Me." "There am I in the midst of you."

(3) For such a feast He is preparing *in the Father's house.* That "supper of the Lamb" was often in His thoughts when on earth (Luke xiv. 15; xxii. 16, 18) "He saith unto me, Write, Blessed are they which are called unto the marriage supper of the Lamb" (Rev. xix. 9). Joy will indeed fill the Saviour's heart then; for "He shall see of the travail of His soul and shall be satisfied" (Isa. liii. 11).

Topic: PEACE BY FULFILLING DIVINE CONDITIONS (Vv. 2-5, etc.).

Temporal blessings God showers down alike upon the evil and the good. Unsolicited He loads mankind daily with His benefits. But for spiritual blessings He will be inquired of. Specified means must be employed that pardon and peace may be enjoyed. The first part of the peace offering was expiatory; then came the Eucharistic feast.

I. THE OFFERING WAS TO BE CAREFULLY CHOSEN. The strongest, best and purest parts were to be kept exclusively sacred to the Lord. Everything was to be done in order, and according to minute directions.

II. THE OFFERING WAS TO BE PERSONALLY APPROPRIATED. No offering by proxy; each offerer to offer for himself with his own hands. Not enough to purpose in the heart, to have sound views and clear knowledge of what required. The *act* must *promptly, personally* be performed.

III. THE OFFERING WAS TO BE CHEERFULLY PRESENTED. (This fully shown in chap. vii.) All not to be consumed as in holocaust; the offered had anticipation of partaking with priests of residue in joyful fellowship.

Our inestimable privilege is to have fellowship with the Father and with His Son Christ Jesus, who has left to the world through His Church the Divine legacy of Peace. He is our peace, and hath broken down the middle wall of partition between us and God.—*F. W. B.*

Topic: PEACE RESULTING FROM PROPITIATION (Vv. 1-17).

Reconciliation and restoration to God bring peace; hence the peace offering, so peculiarly significant of tranquil joy, follows the burnt and meat offerings. In this festival God, the priests, and the people partook together. It signified *to complete, to make whole,* and was therefore a symbol of *fulness, fellowship,* and *friendship.* In it God showed not only that He is to be ministered to *by* man, but also that He delights to minister *to* man. The great truth taught is, that reconciliation to God leads to intimate communion with Him.

I. *Great freedom was allowed in selection of the Offerings.* Any sacrificial animal of either sex, or of any age, might be offered, so long as it was without blemish. The worshipper could suit his own convenience, the demand made was in no way exacting or irksome. The commandments of God are not grievous: we are only expected to offer according to our ability, but what we offer must be the best we have, and offered in a right spirit. "Whether we eat or drink," etc.

II. *Great freedom was allowed in participation of the Offering.* Part was to be presented to the Lord, part eaten by the priests, and part by the people; so that God and man, Heaven and earth, would hold festival together, in one solemn covenant. Such a condition of peace was one of the great moral wants of man, for sin had estranged man from God and thrown discord into the human family. This offering proclaimed peace on earth, goodwill to men. Christ our Peace invites us to His table to hold communion with Him, and feed by faith on the sacrifice He has provided. This life of happy communion with God in Christ is the prelude of, and preparation for, the marriage supper of the Lamb.—F. W. B.

OUTLINES ON VERSES.

V. 1.—*Theme:* FAULTLESSNESS IN SACRIFICE. "He shall offer it *without* blemish unto the Lord."

I. AS REPRESENTING THE PURITY OF HIM TO WHOM THE OFFERING WAS PRESENTED.

II. AS PRESHADOWING THE PURITY OF HIM WHOM THE OFFERING TYPIFIED.

III. AS SYMBOLISING THE PURITY DESIDERATED BY THE OFFER OF THE SACRIFICE.

Our offerings to the Lord must be *complete and pure*—by association with the merits of Christ's perfect sacrifice, and prompted by motives made pure by the indwelling of the Holy Ghost.—F. W. B.

V. 2.—*Theme:* IDENTIFICATION OF THE OFFERER WITH THE OFFERING. "And he shall lay his hand upon the head of the offering, and kill it at the door of the tabernacle of the congregation" (v. 2).

I. ACTUAL CONTACT.

"Lay hand on," sig. (*a*) *apprehension*, (*b*) *appropriation*, (*c*) *identification*.

II. ACTUAL COMMITTAL.

"And kill it," offerer's *own act*, acknowledging he deserved to die as the victim, his substitute, died. This would (*a*) *teach the heinousness of sin* that it needed the sacrifice of life, (*b*) *beget hatred for sin* upon which Jehovah thus placed Divine displeasure.

By act of faith we must lay our hand upon the sacred head of Christ, and have a personal interest in His life and death.—F. W. B.

V. 3.—*Theme:* GOD'S POSITIVE COMMANDS. "And he shall," &c.

God's commands to Israel peremptory. How they were to worship, what they were to sacrifice, arbitrarily stated. Though commands are imperious, people are under moral obligations to obey. No room for option or exception when precept associated with unequivocal "*shall.*" Such commands—

I. EXHIBIT THE SOVEREIGNTY OF THE LORD. He has right to command without giving reasons or explanations. He has right to do what He pleases with His own.

II. EXERCISE THE FAITH AND PATIENCE OF THE WORSHIPPERS. To obey precepts the reasons for which were hidden would show greater confidence and resignation than were reasons seen.

III. EXALT THE OBEDIENCE OF THE LIFE. The people not required to offer that which cost them nothing, or they would have had mean ideas of worship. God demands large things of us, and "blessed are they that do His commandments."—F. W. B.

V. 8.—*Theme:* PEACE ASSOCIATED WITH PENITENCE AND PRAYER. "He shall lay his hand upon the head of his offering."

Until sin is pardoned there can be no real peace, no real enjoyment of the Divine presence. This truth comes out in all the offerings, for every sacrifice was to be the symbol of the broken and contrite heart of the offerer. God was pleased with the sufferings of the victims slain and the savour of their burning carcasses only as they represented the self-surrender of the worshipper, and the incense of holy prayer ascending from the penitent spirit.

I. *In the peace offering the offerer acknowledged his guilt.* As he laid his hand upon the head of the victim at the Tabernacle door he owned that he was guilty and deserved to die. It would be a public confession of guilt and the need of atonement for offences.

II. *In the peace offering the offerer transferred his guilt.* God accepted a substitute for the guilty one who deserved to die. Probable that the Hebrews felt more was included in their offerings than they could then see, that they pointed to a greater sacrifice yet to be offered in God's good time, upon whom would be laid the iniquity of us all.

The privileges associated with Peace offerings would awaken praise. The offerer would stand *in the attitude of prayer,* as with eyes lifted to Heaven he presented his oblation; *he would be filled with praise,* as in the house of the Lord he enjoyed peaceful communion. When we commune with God, let us blend *penitence, prayer,* and *praise,* remembering blessings received, anticipating blessings to come. With such sacrifices God is well pleased, and in association with them he imparts his own peace, which passeth all understanding.—F. W. B.

V. 5—*Theme:* SUCCESSION IN SACRIFICES. " Burn it on the altar *upon the burnt sacrifice,* which is upon the wood that is on the fire."

There is order established by God in—

I. THE SUCCESSIVE SACRIFICIAL OFFERINGS REQUIRED.

1. First on the altar must be laid the *burnt offering,* which must *"all"* be burnt, for God required complete consecration of Christ *in death* to satisfy the fire of His holiness, the demands of His righteous law.

2. Then follows the meat offering, which signifies the presentation of the *best and richest life* in substitution for man. It asserted His requirement of the first and finest qualities of humanity. Christ must offer His perfect manhood in living form as an obedience offering. Which means, that when God's holiness finds satisfaction in Christ's death, Jehovah still demands the full offering of the redeemed man's living obedience.

3. The peace sacrifice then may be presented, and the man who has *satisfied Justice in the death of Christ,* and yielded obedience *in the life of Christ,* may enter into *fellowship and peace through Christ.* [See Addenda, p. 38, *Terms of Peace.*]

II. THE SUCCESSIVE SPIRITUAL ATTAINMENTS REACHED.

1. Whole *surrender* to God. The burnt offering required and enforced that attainment. The redeemed soul lays itself wholly on the altar, is wholly consumed in dedication to God.

2. *Perfectness of character;* the excellencies of obedience; pure uncorruptness of heart; the submissiveness of will. These are reached in succession, and are suggested in the meat offering.

3. *Fellowship with God.* Feasting in the blessedness of peace and acceptance with Him in and through Christ Jesus. "O God I will praise Thee, for though Thou wast angry with me, Thine anger is turned away, *and Thou comfortest me.*"

III. THE SUCCESSIVE REALISATIONS OF CHRISTIAN PRIVILEGE.

1 *Acceptance.* That is assured as the fruit of the burnt offering. It is offered "for acceptance" (see on i. 5), and God does accept the entire sacrifice for atonement.

2. *Spiritual graces.* The beauties of Christ become ours; the charms of the anointing Spirit rest on us. "The frankincense, oil, salt," etc.

3. *Joyous communion with God.* Raised into blissful privilege, feasting with the Lord and His priests. "Truly our fellowship is with the Father and with His Son Jesus Christ."

IV. THE SUCCESSIVE RELIGIOUS OBLIGATIONS URGED.

Not fellowship and privilege first, but first *entire dedication.*

Then *cultivation of spiritual excellencies.*

Following these comes *glad fellowship with heaven.*

V. 16.—*Theme:* GOD DESERVES AND DEMANDS THE BEST. "All the fat is the Lord's."

I. Not the mere *bones* of rigid formalism.

II. Not the mere *sinews* of strenuous observances.

III. Not the mere *skin* of outward profession.

IV. Not the mere *blood* of ardent enthusiasm, but the—

V. "*Fat*"—the *richest, fullest, best* that we can offer: not lean, shrivelled work or worship, but "the fat for the Lord," the most prime and precious we can procure. Let us give our youth and strength, our richest love and fullest fervour to Him who is worthy of all.—F. W. B.

V. 17.—*Theme:* OBEDIENCE THE TEST OF FAITH. "It shall be a perpetual statute."

It would require *faith* to constantly obey, for the offerings would *seem* to be—

I. AN INFLICTION OF NEEDLESS PAIN.

II. A WASTE OF VALUABLE LIFE.

III. UNEQUAL TO THE END DESIGNED:— that there should be any correspondence between the physical suffering of brutes and atonement for moral guilt of man.

We cannot formulate a rationale of the great Peace offering presented in the Gospel. It is beset with formidable difficulties. *Faith,* not reason, must lead us to the Cross, the hand of simple trust must appropriate the blessings of salvation.

Note: The CULPABILITY OF DISOBEDIENCE.

To omit obedience to the statutes of Jehovah was sin, because of transgression of His law.

Omission would spring from (1) *indifference,* (2) *independence,* (3) *disloyalty,* (4) *rebellion.* So now to invitations and commands of Gospel. Christ taught that sins of omission were culpable and condemnatory. The rich man in the parable *omitted* to care for Lazarus. The man who *did not* use his talent was punished. The wicked in the day of judgment are represented as being punished for omissions (Matt. xxv. 31-46).—F. W. B.

ILLUSTRATIVE ADDENDA TO CHAPTER III.

SACRIFICES OF PEACE. "They were either intended to testify thankfulness for blessings already received, in which view they are called 'thank offerings' in Coverdale's translation; or were else votive, being offered with prayer for future blessings. No doubt they were sometimes both in one. . . . Only the fat parts were consumed on the altar. A small portion was appropriated to the priest, the rest being allowed to the offerer and his guests as an offering feast. Whence Dr. Boothroyd, following Michaelis, prefers to translate *Shelamim* by 'feast sacrifice' rather than 'peace offering.'"—*Kitto*.

PEACE OF THE GOSPEL. It is a great mercy to have the Gospel of peace, but it is far greater to have the peace of the Gospel.

BLESSEDNESS OF PEACE. "If joy be love exulting, peace is joy reposing. It is love in the green pastures and beside the still waters."—*Dr. James Hamilton*.

Father of life and light! Thou good Supreme!
. . . . .
Save me from folly, vanity and vice,
From every low pursuit; and feed my soul
With knowledge, conscious peace, and virtue pure,
Sacred, substantial, never-fading bliss!
THOMSON'S *Seasons*.

ON EARTH PEACE. "People are always expecting to get peace in heaven; but you know whatever peace they get there will be ready made. Whatever, of making peace they can be blest for, must be on the earth here."—RUSKIN, *Eagle's Nest*.

TERMS OF PEACE.
"The consciousness of faith of sins forgiven,
Of wrath appeased, of heavy guilt thrown off,
Sheds on my breast its long-forgotten peace."
L. J. HALL, *Miriam*.

THANKSGIVING. "Praise is the rent we owe to God, and the larger the farm the larger the rent. The Lord has many fine farms from which He receives little rent. Thanksgiving is a good thing; thanks-living is better."—P. HENRY.

Life work. "Let not thy praises be transient—a fit of music, and then the instrument hung by the wall till another gaudy day of some remarkable providence make thee take it down. God comes not guest-wise to His saints' house, but to dwell with them. David took this up for a life work: 'As long as I live I will praise thee.'"—*Gurnall*.

Constant. "There was a beautiful tradition among the Jews which Lancisius quotes from Philo. It is to this effect: When God had created the world, He asked the angels what they thought of the work of His hands. One of them replied that it was so vast and perfect that only one thing was wanting to it, namely that there should be created a clear, mighty and harmonious voice, which should fill all the quarters of the world incessantly with its sweet sound, thus day and night to offer thanksgiving to its Maker."—F. W. FABER.

"And touched their golden harps, and hymning praised
God and His works."
MILTON, *Paradise Lost*.

"Now God be praised, that to believing souls
Gives light in darkness, comfort in despair."
Henry VI. ii. 3, § 1.

CHAPTER IV.

Sacrifices for Sins.

SUGGESTIVE READINGS.

V. 2.—**If a soul shall sin.** Be it noted that the foregoing sacrifices are specified as sacrifices already *familiar* to the Hebrew people. In distinction from those, the sin and trespass offering are for *the first time mentioned*. The law only just given on Sinai created a new standard of obedience and righteousness; thus, "by the law is the knowledge of sin." It is here defined as "against the commandments of the Lord," etc.; and to meet this new disclosure of human frailty and guiltiness, God appointed the sin and trespass offerings. Shall we not welcome a full discovery of our sinfulness, since it both disposes the sinner to *despair* *of self-justification* and constrains him to *seek the redemption* divinely provided ? When God reveals sin it is to show its antidote ; and " with Him is plenteous redemption."

Through ignorance, *i.e.*, inadvertently, as distinguished from deliberate and defiant disobedience (comp. Numb. xv. 30), for which there was no expiation Are these of small import ? Shall we think them of such inferior consequence as compared with sins done wilfully ? Let it then be recalled that *Christ was crucified* by inadvertence ! That greatest act of human wrong was done "*through ignorance*" (Acts iii. 17) : " Had they *known it*, they would not have crucified the Lord of glory" (1 Cor. ii. 8). Hence, though great the crime it may be forgiven mankind ; as a wilful sin, done in the full light of knowledge, could not ; but man's guilt at the Cross was a vast sin of inadvertence : " Father, forgive them, *for* they know not what they do !" (Luke xxiii. 34). Alas ! for such as " sin wilfully after they have received the knowledge of the truth ! there remaineth for such no more sacrifice for sins" (Heb. x. 26).

Vv. 3-12.—The priest that is anointed, etc. Thus it is affirmed that even the highest personage in the priestly ranks is frail *and as liable to sin* as the commonest of the people ; he may " do according to the sin of the people" (v. 3). Shall Christ's ministers, then, dare assume to possess superior spiritual sanctity ? [See Heb. vi. 27, 28.] The "*anointed*" priest was the high priest (chap. viii. 12) ; other priests were only consecrated. Yet, though he was frail as ordinary persons, his sacred office and privileges made *his sin so much the greater* that he had to bring a far more costly sacrifice for his atonement. [See vv. 27, 28.] God distinguishes concerning the criminality of sins : they who live nearer the light have less excuse for " ignorance." So here, God requires most solemn arrangements for expiation : the blood is to be sprinkled "seven times before the Lord, before the veil of the sanctuary," *i.e.*, in front of the holy of holies, and even be smeared upon the golden altar itself ! thus setting his sin in the very light of God's countenance ! How would this fill the anointed priest with self-reproach and shame ! God cannot deal leniently with elevated souls. We shall be "judged according to that we have."

V. 7.—Pour all the blood at the bottom of the altar. By this rite the sinner acknowledged that he *deserved to have his blood thus poured out* like water. It likewise signified the pouring out of the soul before God *in true repentance ;* and typified our *Saviour's pouring out His soul* unto death.—Henry.

V. 12.—Without the camp. As being *accursed*, for it symbolically held the sinner's guilt, he having laid his hand (v. 4) thereon. So did our Sin-Bearer "suffer without the gate" (Heb. xi. 11-13). Thus, too, is *sin removed from God's presence* by expiation, carried into oblivion, and consumed out of existence. Jesus "*put away sin* by the sacrifice of Himself."

Vv. 13-21.—If the whole congregation, etc. Crime may spread itself throughout a community, a state, or a nation ; and equally, a congregation or a *church* may lapse into evil conduct and contract iniquity. When the sin becomes "*known*" to them (v. 14), an expiation must be made with a solemnity equal to the high priest's. Guilt is not less guilty because of its being prevalent in a community. God has declared against wrong-doers that " though hand join in hand they shall not be unpunished." Sanctioned wrongs, evils connived at, customary misdemeanours, immoralities and impieties which find currency, popular sins, all are hateful to Jehovah, and none the less hateful because the moral or spiritual distemper rages amid the multitudes rather than confines itself to individuals. Nations have suffered God's displeasure for unrepented sins ; and churches have been withered for cherishing impurities which have wounded Christ in the house of His friends. True *patriotism* should bemoan and seek to remove the evils which degrade the national life ; and earnest *piety* will show itself in endeavouring to arouse a lukewarm Church to "repent and do her first works."

Vv. 22-26.—**When a ruler hath sinned.** They who dispense laws are amenable to the Lawgiver; they who call others to account are themselves accountable to the Supreme Ruler. The word "ruler" is rendered "king" in 1 Kings xi. 34, Ezek. xxxiv. 24, etc.; but God is "King of kings, and Lord of lords"; and before His bar they must stand in judgment if before the Cross they do not bow in penitence and faith. "Be wise now, therefore, O ye kings; be instructed ye judges of the earth. Serve the Lord with fear, and rejoice with trembling. Kiss the Son, lest He be angry," etc. (Psa. ii. 10-12).

Vv. 27-35.—**One of the common people sin.** The lowest are not overlooked by the searching eye of God. Though in his humble station he may be less instructed, less responsible for error, less blameworthy for sin, yet God demands expiation. If none are exempted from the sinfulness of his deeds, surely each should *watch* against sin, never excusing himself that he "did it ignorantly," but seek to inform himself of God's requirements, and thus come to "understand his errors." Yes; and leaving his evil state, every one should seek the altar with his sin offering; go to Calvary with meek contrition and an upturned look of prayerful trust. "Behold the Lamb of God that taketh away the sin of the world."

SECTIONAL HOMILIES.

Topic: SINS COMMITTED IN IGNORANCE (Vv. 1-12).

Our evil nature does not slumber; it acts. "Dead" as regards all power of living to God, it is full of untiring energy in living "according to the prince of this world, the spirit which worketh in the children of disobedience." Cain and his children were "dead" towards God, yet full of activity in wrong, they builded cities and invented arts, living to Satan and themselves. So we are *committers* of sin, doers of iniquity. No remedy, therefore, would be commensurate with our need which failed to meet the consequences of committed sin. Accordingly the sin offering and the trespass offering were appointed.

Committed sin may be distributed into those committed *in ignorance* (and of these this chapter treats), and those committed *consciously* (which are dealt with in chapter v.).

I. MAN'S OWN DISPOSITION IS TO CONDONE INADVERTENT SINS.

In the heart of many there is readiness to think of sins of ignorance as if they were no sins; or if admitted to be sins and need mercy, such mercy is regarded rather as a right than as the unmerited gift of grace.

1. *Ignorance* is treated as if *synonymous* with *guiltlessness.* To act conscientiously, however dark or dead the conscience, is, in the esteem of many, to act blamelessly. Hence

2. The *responsibilities which attach to knowledge* become secretly a reason why *knowledge is eschewed.* "Darkness is loved rather than light," because darkness brings quiet; whereas light has an awakening and convicting power.

To these *errors of thought* the appointment of the sin offering is an answer: it is designed to meet sins committed in ignorance. No one who reverences the Word of God will speak lightly of sins of ignorance after reading, "If a soul shall sin through ignorance, etc. . . . let him bring for the sin that he hath sinned," etc. (vv. 4, 5).

II. WHEREIN THE GUILTINESS OF INADVERTENT SINS CONSISTS.

The heinousness of such sins depends not so much on the character of the deed done as on that *condition of heart* which is *capable* of committing sin without knowing that it is sin; and commits it, perhaps, *exultingly*, triumphing in it as good! What must angels think of the state of that soul which is so *thoroughly blinded*, so utterly *astray* from God, as to violate His commandments and resist His will in total unconsciousness that it is doing wrong!

1. *What such sinfulness has wrought.* It was thus that multitudes in Israel hated and persecuted the Lord Jesus, that Paul shed the blood of Stephen, resisting the testimony of the Holy Ghost from one whose face shone with heavenly brightness while he spake; that Paul again " verily thought he was doing God service" when persecuting the saints. All this argued thorough blindness of soul, thorough alienation of heart from God.

2. Sin in ignorance is *the embodiment in action of those dark principles of enmity against God* which lie embosomed in the human heart.

III. GOD'S EMPHATIC WITNESS AGAINST INADVERTENT SINS.

1. *Sources of Divine remonstrance* against such sins.

(1) In Nature. Throughout the heathen world the eternal power and Godhead are declared by the works of God's hands. "The heavens declare the glory of God," etc. (Psa. xix.) "He left not Himself without witness in that He gave them rain," etc. (Acts xiv. 17). "The invisible things of Him," etc. (Rom. i. 20).

(2) In Scripture. The Jews, in addition to the testimony of creation, had the written Word. "To them were committed the oracles of God" (Rom. iii. 2).

(3) By living preachers. From them came many a warning, "line upon line, precept upon precept."

(4) In conscience. The consciences both of Jews and Gentiles were often made to feel the appeals of God; as Paul made Felix tremble.

2. *Man's resistance* of the Divine remonstrance. Satan and man's own evil disposition quenched or obscured the light. As they turned from the light—

(1) Their conscience became more hardened. And as it hardened, sins of ignorance were multiplied, and

(2) Committed with a higher and more reckless hand.

3. Such daring ignorance, *how is it fostered ?*

(1) By the perversion of revealed truth. Truth had been revealed to, received by, Israel; but received to be betrayed. Their imposing systems of worship and sacrifice were constantly distorted, were false renderings of Divinely given truth.

(2) Erroneous teaching was welcomed. In vain, therefore, the Scriptures spake of Jesus; in vain John, His forerunner, testified; in vain the Lord Himself proved by His words, His character, His miracles, that He was indeed the Son of the living God. The light of holiness and grace shone fruitlessly upon their hearts, whose *natural darkness* was *deepened* by the systematic influence of a religious corruption which had sanctified error by holy titles, and had blessed wickedness in the name of God.

Nor has it been otherwise in *Christendom.* The history of the Church of God supplies countless instances of souls so *nourished from childhood in error* as to be deadened in every power of right discernment and apprehension. What wonder, seeing that our hearts naturally love darkness, that sins of ignorance should abound!

IV. GODLY SOULS ARE BETRAYED INTO THE COMMISSION OF INADVERTENT SINS.

It would be happy could we assert even of real Christians that they were free from these fearful sins of ignorance.

1. *How are Christians betrayed thereinto?* Whenever they give themselves up to *the guidance of any individual,* or of any *system not strictly accordant with God's revealed truth,* they will surely act against Christ and His commandments ignorantly. Hence nothing operates more terribly against the progress of truth than the misdirected energies of real *Christians ignorantly sustaining error,* ignorantly resisting light.

2. *Christians may therefore be beguiled.* Paul was keenly alive to their peril. He knew how easily the souls of believers can be bewitched. "O foolish Galatians, who hath bewitched you?" He knew how easily Satan can transform himself into an angel of light to deceive.

3. If *where there is most diligence and watchfulness* there may be sins of ignorance, how much more where there is negligence or slumber, or acquiescence in the prevailing evil of the age!

V. SINS IN THE GODLY ARE MOST HEINOUS IN GOD'S ESTEEM.

Addressed as is this chapter to those who were *ostensibly the separated people of God*, it teaches us especially respecting sins of ignorance committed by believers.

1. Sins are *greater in proportion to the spiritual status of those who commit them.* The loftier our privileges, the nearer we are brought to God, the more intimately we are connected with His service, the more terrible must be the consequences of transgression.

2. *God's name was more dishonoured.* The sins of an instructed Israelite threw discredit on the God he acknowledged.

3. *Sacred life was defamed.* With the priest or Israelite there should have been found understanding and the fear of the Lord.

Notes: (a) *God had a right to expect such sins to be avoided.* The priests were anointed that they might minister in the near presence of God: their employment was in holy things; their place the sanctuary. As instructed in the Word of the Lord, acquainted with the ways of His house, their lips were to keep knowledge; and others through them were to learn the ways of the Lord. Sins of ignorance were therefore the very sins that should have been absent from the priest.

(b) Sin is to be *estimated by a man's spiritual elevation.* As here; by the holiness of the things and places in which the priest ministered, and by the *disastrous consequences* to others, as well as to himself, that flowed from its commission.

VI. EXPIATION PROVIDED FOR SINS OF INADVERTENCE.

Sin, as in the priest, had invaded the holy place, had entered before the veil, had tainted the place of his ministration, had defiled the altar, had involved others in its consequences: *the stain must be effaced*, either by vengeance consuming the sinner, or be expiated by the blood of a substituted victim.

God, in the unsearchable riches of His grace, appointed the sin offering; on whose head the transgressor laid his hand, and whose blood was sprinkled before the Lord. Thus was denoted—

1. *Against Whom the sins were committed.* Seven times the blood was sprinkled "before the Lord." "Against Thee, Thee only, have I sinned," etc. (Psa. li. 4).

2. *The process of purging.* The ground on which the priest was accustomed to stand, the altar at which he ministered, were *covered with blood:* thus the taint was covered over, himself purchased back from destruction, the privileged place he had occupied preserved unforfeited.

3. *Its suggestion of death.* The remainder of the blood was poured out at the bottom of the altar, betokening that the just requisition of God's holiness had been met—met by death. It was the token of accomplished and accepted atoning death. It was blood *shed.*

4. *Its suggestion of wrath.* **On fire**, kindled not on the altar, not even within the camp, but "without the gate," the place of dishonour and reproach, like the fire of Gehenna, it was devoured as an accursed thing.

VII. TYPICAL INTIMATIONS OF CHRIST'S DEATH FOR MAN'S SINS.

1. *God's condemnation* of our Substitute. Faith, as it stands by the fire *without the camp,* and gazes on the devoted parts of the sin offering being consumed, beholds—

(1) The memorial of *what Christ became on account of His people.*

(2) Sees not only their sins, but *their sins judicially ended.*

(3) That their guilt is remembered no more as the subject of wrath—evidenced by the ashes; for ashes are the token of fire having burned itself out.

2. *God's acceptance* of our Substitute. The internal parts of the victim were *burned on the altar;* representing the inherent excellencies of Christ, and accepted as "a sweet savour" by God. Jehovah provided for us One whose excellencies are here presented for our vileness. In atonement Divine holiness requires in the Surety not only that He should bear every penalty, but that He should also present a substitutional perfectness for us. Thus, while *sins committed in ignorance* showed the inherent corruption of our inmost nature; the acceptance of the inmost parts of the sin-offering by God upon His holy altar declares the satisfaction made by Christ on our account.—Homiletically developed from *Thoughts on Leviticus*, by B. W. NEWTON.

Topic : SINAI'S LAW NECESSITATED THE ORIGIN OF THE SIN OFFERING (Vv. 2, 13, 14, 22, 27, etc.).

Revelation from God and religious feeling in man are not synonymous, are not synchronous. The religious feeling is *instinctive.* Revelation comes to inform and guide that instinct. Prior to any revelation, man was religious. Within himself, in the thoughts and fears and aspirations of his own soul, man possesses the incitements to religion, *i.e.*, to recognise and seek and propitiate God.

I. EARLIEST ANNALS OF HUMAN HISTORY SHOW MAN TO HAVE BEEN RELIGIOUS.

1. Touched by conscious *dependence,* man acknowledged it by *tributary gifts* to Deity.

2. *Grateful for enjoyed blessings* or providential deliverances, he brings to his altar a *thank offering.*

3. Troubled by *sense of error, wrong, guilt,* he rears an altar and offers some *propitiatory* presentation. Well nigh every ancient people thus expressed religious feeling, even where no revelation was given. Either these *votive* and *appeasement* offerings originated in—

(*a*) The outcry and *outlook of the human soul* for its unseen and unknown God; or—

(*b*) *An intimation, in some form, from Heaven* that men "should seek the Lord if haply they might feel after Him and find Him" (Acts xvii. 27).

But, whether by supernatural intimation or by spiritual intuition, man has always been religious.

Turning to the Hebrew scriptures we find offerings on some rude form of altar presented to God *by the children of the first human family,* Cain and Abel. And noteworthy: they bring their offerings not as if they were adventuring upon and originating a new mode of worship, but as if *in conformity with a custom already existing.*

Through the *antedeluvian period,* and following the dispersion of *Noah's descendants,* worship by altar offerings was preserved in all branches of the Semitic family. [Compare ATWATER on *Tabernacle of the Hebrews.*]

II. PRIOR TO THE SINAITIC LAW NEITHER SIN OR TRESPASS SACRIFICES WERE INSTITUTED.

The early patriarchs were familiar with burnt offerings and meat offerings; but, until the Exodus, sacrifices for expiation seem to have had no specific existence.

1. *Subordinately* every ancient sacrifice of victims on the altar *intimated conscious sin* and desire for *expiation.* But it was only subsidiary. The sacrifice was not offered with the single and supreme thought of atonement for sin. Those remoter sacrifices expressed *self-surrender and allegiance* rather than expiation.

No sacrifice is recorded as a distinct effort to *expiate for sin* prior to the Sinaitic law.

2. *Until the law was given sin was not clearly realised and felt.* There was doubtless a vague and indefinite sense of wrong in men, but "where there is *no law* there is no *transgression*" (Rom. iv. 15). So also "by the law is the knowledge of sin" (Rom. iii. 20); but "sin is not imputed where there is no law" (Rom. v. 13).

3. *The conviction of man of sin rendered the Sin-offering a necessity.* The law convicted man of sin; his inherent guiltiness had not been apprehended till it stood revealed in the light of God's holy commandments. Hence this provision of the sin offering has relation to a man "*sinning* against any of *the commandments*" (Lev. iv. 2, 13, 14, 22, 27, etc.). "The law entered that the offence might abound" (Rom. v. 20).

III. *In the Sin offering* ASSURANCE OF SALVATION MEETS THE AWAKENED CONSCIOUSNESS OF GUILT.

It seems evident that the sacrificial offerings of the Hebrews became modified and developed in order to meet the advancing consciousness of sin. With a nearer acquaintance with God came a keener sense of unworthiness and wrong. Hence their sacrifices became increasingly expiatory.

1. Sin, essential and inherent sin, was so pressed upon man's conscience by the standard of perfect and unattainable righteousness given in the law, as to render the *sin offering an absolutely necessary provision* of God's mercy.

2. Hence the *expiatory element in sacrifice*, which had been subordinate until the law, was *raised into eminence and vividness* in the newly and specially instituted offering of the sin sacrifice.

3. And in the sin sacrifice a prophecy of God's purpose was given to provide *the great expiatory sacrifice of Calvary*, in which all anticipatory sacrifices were to be completed and annulled.

Topic: IGNORANCE IN SINNING (Vv. 2, 13, 22, 27.)

"If a soul *sin through ignorance*"; but a soul should *not* be so ignorant as to inadvertently sin. Has not God plainly declared what "ought not to be done"? (v. 2). If therefore "they have done somewhat against any of the commandments of the Lord concerning things which should not be done," they "*are guilty*" (v. 13). Such ignorance must be either from *carelessness*, which shows culpable neglect; or through *blindness*, which argues wilful repudiation of light. A perverse will, an "evil heart of unbelief in departing from the living God," a refusal to "come to the light lest their deeds should be made manifest"; these are criminal, and are sternly condemned.

I. MAN'S PERCEPTION OF RIGHT AND WRONG CANNOT BE AN ALLOWED STANDARD. He may "*sin through ignorance.*"

1. Neither his *judgment* nor his *conscience* is *an adequate guide* in detecting sin. There are many wrong things which *escape man's cognizance*, many which *his conscience fails to condemn*, many which indeed "seem right unto a man" and *his heart approves*, which God cannot tolerate. [See Addenda, p. 57, *Ignorance v. Knowledge.*]

2. Hence the inquiry, What is sin? must be *determined from without a man*, and *not from within* him. God must be heard. "God is light, and in Him is *no darkness* at all." He knows what is sin; and He has *revealed it in* "*the commandments* of the Lord."

3. The presence of sin in man, sin even ignorantly contracted, *imperils man's relationship to God.* He cannot look upon sin. It must be cast out from His presence. "*Carry it forth* without the camp" (v. 12). Sin, therefore, interrupts

man's *approach* to God, prevents his acceptable *worship* of God, and alienates his *relationship* with God.

II. GOD'S ESTIMATE AND MEASUREMENT OF SIN REGULATED THE ATONEMENT. "Bring for the sin which he hath sinned," etc. (v. 3). All the depths and subtilties of sin were in God's thoughts when He arranged for its expiation.

1. Man's faulty apprehension of sin would have *narrowed the atonement*. We should then have found our guilt exceeding the provisions; an unexpiated sinfulness would have remained beyond the appeasement we had made.

2. Sin has been expiated *according to God's measurement of sin*. Hence a *full* atonement for the believer's sins of ignorance as well as for his recognised sins has been made in Christ.

(*a*) This, if apprehended, lays the ground of a *settled peace*. All may be left with Christ.

(*b*) This will exalt our conception of the *fulness and efficacy of the Saviour's sacrifice*.

(*c*) This will assure us of *acceptable and satisfactory fellowship* with God, since all sin is propitiated.

III. *Ignorance concerning sin* argues MAN'S REAL HELPLESSNESS IN DEALING WITH IT.

Even if he could, by any process, rid himself of sin, *what can he do with the sin of which he is not cognizant ?* There is guiltiness in man which never comes (until he is Divinely enlightened) within the range of his own consciousness or conscience.

1. Man's ignorance of sin proves his total *inability to put it away*. He is like a physician, when himself so sick as to become *delirious*, attempting to prescribe and apply remedies for his recovery. [See Addenda, p. 57, *Perils of Ignorance*.]

2. Even the most elevated human conscience is *inadequate to determine and depose sin*. "Who can understand his errors ?"

3. If there may be sin eluding our detection, how would the *dread of undetected and unexpiated guilt destroy all peace* were we left to deal with our sin ?

4. *No happy communion with God would be possible* were a misgiving over lurking sin troubling our hearts. An uneasy mind, anxious on the question of sin, would mar all worship and blessedness.

(*a*) A happy spiritual life rests upon an *assured peace*.

(*b*) Assured peace must rest on a *perfectly purged conscience*.

(*c*) A purged conscience must rest on the foundation of *a perfect remission of all our sins*, whether sins of knowledge or of ignorance.

"And He is the propitiation for *our sins*."

Topic: DEFILED SANCTITIES (Vv. 6, 7.)

"The *priest* shall dip his finger in the blood, and sprinkle of the blood seven times *before the Lord, before the veil of the sanctuary*. And the *priest* shall put some of the blood *upon the horns of the altar of sweet incense* before the Lord," etc.

The sin of a "priest" marks the wrong-doing of *exalted and privileged souls*, and the defamation wrought by one so eminent in sacred relationship and service. In his misdemeanour a defiled foot would taint the holy ground on which he stood; a defiled hand would taint the altar at which he ministered.

1. Christians *occupying exalted positions*, enjoying elevated privileges, rendering distinguished service for God, may *fall into sin*.

2. They know that the *dishonour done to God is commensurate* with the *dignity of their position* and the *holiness of their profession*.

3. So acutely is their guilt felt by them when thus brought under conscious-

ness of sin, that its burden and bitterness would overwhelm them were there not *adequate grace* in the sin offering for even such sin as theirs.

Here, therefore, it is clearly shown by the Holy Spirit—

I. That HOWEVER FAR SIN MAY HAVE PENETRATED, even though to the very "veil of the sanctuary," and WHATEVER SOLEMN AND SACRED THINGS SIN MAY HAVE DEFILED, even though it be the holy "altar" itself, thither THE ATONING BLOOD FOLLOWS, carrying full expiation where sin has carried defilement.

1. When sin enters *the inmost recesses of a Christian soul*, high in sacred relationship and godly service, into the *motives, thoughts*, affections of a holy man, it intrudes to the very "veil of the sanctuary" wherein God dwells. *Sin* thus invades scenes so hallowed, the very vestibule of the Divine indwelling.

2. When sin mars *the life and conduct and ministries of a consecrated servant of the Lord*, who had occupied high station in the church, and fulfilled prominent functions in the sanctuary, it profanes the very "altar" of Jehovah, for it casts a stain and defamation on the holiest solemnities of the Christian profession. In touching one who dwells so near God, and whose life is so devoted to Him, sin lays its defiling hand on that which on earth is most godly, which most represents God, and which is nearest God.

Can there be atonement and purifying for such desecration of most holy things?

Yes, the virtue of the Redeemer's blood penetrates to any shrine, to every object sin has reached.

And "where sin abounded grace doth much more abound." [See Addenda, p. 57, *Pardon*.]

II. That THE DISHONOUR DONE TO GOD, to the SANCTITIES OF A GODLY LIFE, and to the SOLEMNITIES OF SANCTUARY MINISTRIES was compensated for in offering upon that "altar of sweet incense" the symbols of the INHERENT AND INTRINSIC EXCELLENCY OF CHRIST.

1. The inward excellency of the victim (represented in "the fat that covereth the inwards," etc.) is laid on the sacred altar in lieu of, and as an appeasement for, the *inward impurity* of the sinner, whose *soul* had contracted defilement through ignorance And in that precious excellency of Jesus as our Substitute God receives a perfectly satisfactory compensation. The ill savour of our sin dishonoured God and defiled His holy altar; but on the "sweet incense altar" Christ offered so fragrant a presentation as to answer for all the fallibilities and faults of man.

2. Especially is this *perfectly acceptable* offering of *Christ's excellence* a consolatory fact in contrast with the imperfection which discredits the most consecrated and sacred human life. Even a *priest* "anointed" with the holy oil (v. 3), called to minister at the altar and before the veil of the sanctuary, may "sin according to the sin of the people." Alas! "there is none righteous, no, not one." Men may be now "anointed of the Holy Ghost," raised to a "holy priesthood" in Christ, elevated to loftiest spiritual privileges, made partakers of the heavenly gift, and yet may *defile all this sacred excellence* through sin. "The best of men are but men at the best." But Christ was "holy, harmless, undefiled." "In Him was no sin." And in Him God's "soul delighted." And in Him *God was honoured by a perfection so unsullied* as to obliterate the dishonour done to Him by man's faultiness and sin.

Topic:—SIN'S FEARFUL ASPECTS. "If a *soul* shall sin" (vv. 2); if a *priest* shall sin" (v. 3); if the *whole congregation* of Israel shall sin" (v. 13), etc.

Sin! The sound is brief. But it presents a dark abyss of thought.

I. Think much of sin: IT IS EARTH'S DEATH-BLOW

It marred the beauty of a beauteous world; stripped it of its lovely robe;

caused life to wither and decay, etc. It placed its foot upon a perfect workmanship, and left it a disordered wreck.

II. Think much of sin : IT IS MAN'S RUIN.

Its most tremendous blight fell on our inner life. It drove the soul from peaceful fellowship with God ; changed the loving child into a hardened rebel ; robbed the mind of light ; made the heart a whirlpool of tumultuous passions, a spring of impure streams. It is the malady, the misery, the shame of our whole race. It is the mother of—*death ;* it digs each grave ; every widow and orphan tastes its gall. It fills each hospital with sick ; strews the battle-field with slain. It is the core in every grief, the worm that gnaws the root of peace.

III. Think much of sin : ITS TERRIBLE DESTRUCTION DIES NOT IN THE GRAVE. There is a region where its full effects run revel. It kindled quenchless flames ; sharpened the undying sting of an upbraiding conscience ; bars the hopeless in that outer darkness, where weeping ever weeps, and wailing ever wails.

IV. Think much of sin : it works this bitter and eternal anguish *because* GOD'S CURSE ATTENDS IT.

It raised a rebel hand against His will ; dared to violate His holy law ; strove to lay His honour in the dust ; trampled on the statute book of Heaven. Therefore God's anger fiercely burns against it ; hence every misery follows in its rear. He must be wretched who has God against him.

V. Think much of sin : REGARD IT WITH AN EARNEST DREAD.

No power can over-paint the terrible reality of what *sin is*, what *sin has done*, what *penalties it evokes*. Those terrors of a human heart are the best prelude to the tidings of the sin offering. Tears magnify the Cross. Hell seen betimes is hell escaped for ever. Though sin is death, the sinner need not die. There is a way by which the vilest may stand pure. God's love decreed a plan. He willed a ransom, and His Son achieved it. Flee to the Sin Offering. Blessed are they whose curse descends on the Saviour's Cross.—From *" Christ is All,"* by Dean of Gloucester.

Topic: HOW THE SIN OFFERING MEETS MAN'S INMOST NEED (Vv. 27, 35).

The *trespass* offering provides expiation for specific *acts* of transgression, for what man does ; the *sin* offering provides expiation for the evil inherent *in* man, for what he *is*. Our error is to see sinfulness only as it breaks into expression in deeds ; God sees that there is in us a sinfulness which is essential, and which is the *source* whence the evil acts proceed ; that so tainted is man's moral nature as that he may sin without even recognising his conduct to be sinful. It is a mere peradventure whether, having sinned, his sin will even " *come to his knowledge*" (v. 28).

I. MOURNFUL RECOGNITION OF THE SINNER'S INHERENT CORRUPTION.

Sin is in our very nature. The institution of the law of " commandments" does not create us sinners, it only *reveals* us to be sinners. It holds the standard up which discloses how void man is of righteousness, of rightness. This inherent corruption is—

1. *Not realised by the unenlightened.* Unconverted persons only apprehend sin as it appears in actions ; they repudiate, or fail to recognise, the fact that they are essentially, and in all the springs of thought and life, sinful.

2. *Faintly discerned at first by the awakened.* The young convert perceives and bewails his *trespasses* more than his sin. He deplores that he has *done* evil, but scarcely sees how really he *is* evil.

3. *Supremely apprehended by the most godly.* Those highest in grace, with conscience most illumined and heart most instructed through fellowship with God, and realisation of the beauty of Christ, and enlightenment of the Holy

Ghost, "abhor *themselves*" and not their acts only. "*In me*, that is, in my flesh, dwelleth *no good thing*." Most keenly is this realised by holiest men. "The flesh lusteth against the spirit," so that "when we would do good evil is present." [See Rom. vii. and Gal. v. 17.]

II. JOYOUS SATISFACTION OVER THE INCLUSIVE ATONEMENT OF JESUS. "A sweet savour *unto the Lord*"; "an atonement *for him*" (v. 31).

When the painful fact is realised that *sin in us*, as well as *trespasses by us*, constitutes our condemnation, what consolation comes in the fact that an offering *for sin*, as well as offerings for trespasses, was appointed by God. Thus Christ was "made *sin* for us"; He "bore our *sin*"; as well as "was delivered for our *offences*."

1. *Because of our indwelling sinfulness* Christ was offered as our Sin Sacrifice (v. 29).

2. *Because Christ was offered as our Sin Sacrifice* we who trust in Him are saved from an indwelling sin (v. 35).

Note, therefore :

(1) When *the Spirit reveals to believers their deeper sinfulness* ("He shall convince *of sin*," John xvi. 8), it is not to destroy their peace in Christ, or rob them of joyful realisation of His full atonement; but to reveal how much Christ's salvation is needed, and to provoke to fuller gratitude and faith.

(2) To *doubt our justification and acceptance* because we see our "sin," betrays a low estimate of Christ's work for us, and reflects on the all-abounding graciousness of God in providing the sin offering. He "*put away sin* by the sacrifice of Himself." "He by Himself purged our sins" (Heb. i. 3).

Topic: THREE ASPECTS OF SIN OFFERING (Vv. 3, 13, 22, 27).

I. THREE DISTINCT CLASSES OF TRANSGRESSION ARE SPECIFIED.

1. "*The priest that is anointed*" and "*the whole congregation of Israel*" are classed together as if identified. For the priest represented all Israel, and all Israel suffered in the error of the priest, so that the individual and collective sin are to be atoned for on precisely the same conditions and by precisely the same methods. This points to those transgressors who had enjoyed sacred privileges, and were in covenant relation to Jehovah, representing *godly souls* who yet had erred from their integrity.

2. The "*ruler*" represents the *civil and secular life of a people*, men of state dignity, social eminence, and foremost in patriotic affairs rather than in the church; statesmen, legislators, magistrates, civil functionaries. These may err from their uprightness.

3. "*The common people*" gather in the multitudes, who are distinguished by no eminence, burdened by no public responsibility, holding no office in Church or State, simple ordinary persons exposed to none of the temptations and perils of an exalted station. Yet these may err and lapse into wrong.

II. THREE ALIENATIONS WROUGHT BY SIN are intimated.

1. *God's dwelling-place* in the tabernacle was rendered unsanctified. "Holiness becometh Thine house, O Lord, for ever." But instead of stainless sanctity sin had been carried by the priest "before the veil of the sanctuary." The holy place was sullied in God's sight.

2. *God's worship was marred.* The whole "congregation" had to pause in consecration and peace offerings, in the joy of adoration, and to assume the sad attitude of criminals suing escape from vengeance by bringing a victim which must be treated as "accursed" in order that sinful men might be spared. It turned aside the homage of a happy people from Jehovah, while they bowed in mournful prostration as a multitude of condemned transgressors.

3. *The individual conscience* was molested. Sin raised a barrier between the soul and God, separated the sinner from the Divine acceptance, and destroyed—so long as it lay on the conscience—all fellowship, all bliss.

III. THREEFOLD APPEASEMENTS WROUGHT BY THE BLOOD are suggested.

1. The blood being "sprinkled before the Lord, before the veil of the sanctuary," *secured Jehovah's relationship with His people* (which, but for this atonement, must have been severed) *and His continued dwelling in their midst.*

2. The blood being put upon "the golden altar" *preserved the basis of acceptable worship,* so that the flame of "the sweet incense" might acceptably ascend to God, He being propitiated by the atonement.

3. By pouring "all the blood" at "the bottom of the altar" the *claims of God on the individual soul* were met, for thereby substitutionary death was attested. [Compare *Notes on Leviticus*, by C. H. M.]

Topic: THE EMINENT SINFULNESS OF ERROR IN THE PRIEST (Vv. 1-12).

Contrition for sin must always have some proportion to its malignity and magnitude. In the gradations of the sin offering—as in all the other sacrifices—this truth is clearly taught. Not that any amount of contrition could really atone for any sin; but the contrition symbolised in the sacrifice was to bear some proportion to the character of the sin to be condoned. The same sin in the priest would be considered greater than in the people, from many considerations.

I. *From the superior position he occupied.* Placed in front of the people, and anointed to a conspicuous as well as dignified office, being mediator between God and man.

II. *From the superior privileges he enjoyed.* He had exemption from many secular anxieties that would irritate and embarrass others; was not exposed to many temptations that encompassed others; had more familiar and frequent fellowship with Jehovah than the common people; and was constantly coming in contact with influences in the discharge of his duties that would tend to render his falling into error inexcusable and very culpable.

III. *From the superior knowledge he possessed.* He would be intimately acquainted with the requirements of the law, having to expound and enforce it; and he would have ample means and opportunities for ascertaining the purpose of the precepts enjoined, and of avoiding omissions and mistakes.

IV. *From the superior influence he exerted.* The priest would be looked up to by the people as an example, and his influence would be very powerful upon Israel for good or for evil. The old saying, "Like priest, like people," has much truth in it; and if sin had been allowed in the priest to be passed over and healed up slightly, it would have been like offering a premium to sin and proclaiming an indulgence to transgression. The sin of the priests would not only taint all the holy places that they frequented in the prosecution of their sacerdotal work and worship, but it would contaminate the magnetic circle of moral influence by which they were enveloped, and which necessarily affected the minds and morals of the people among whom they daily ministered. *Sin grows heinous according to the rank and influence of the transgressors;* and God acknowledged the exalted position of the priests by exacting larger sacrifice from them in the sin offering than from the common people. Sins in the priests—who were regarded as the theocratic earthly head of Israel—would tend to debase the moral sense of the whole community. The sins of the priest were conspicuous, and the sacrifice, therefore, was conspicuous too; and, as the unintentional offender brought the young bullock for an offering, we read in his obedience—anxiety and willingness to be forgiven, as well as confession of his sin. The fact that the offering was equal to that required for the sin of the whole congregation, and more than was to be made for the sin of a ruler, showed how great the contrition and self-abasement were. There was no oil mixed with the sin offering to suggest gladness; no fragrance of frankincense; no festive joy or communion, as at the meat offering. Everything about it denoted sorrow and suffering on account of wrong-doing.—*F. W. Brown.*

Topic: THE SIN OFFERING OF IGNORANCE FOR THE CONGREGATION (Vv. 13-22).

The people were as liable to sin through ignorance as the priest, so provision was made for their forgiveness as had been mercifully made for his. The laws recently promulgated were so *many, minute,* and *complicated* that the people would be liable to misinterpret and misunderstand them. The Divine Lawgiver knew that; made provision to meet such liability by appointing an offering easily available and that would effectually atone. The people had mixed before their exodus with an idolatrous nation; their old propensities and practices would pursue them in the wilderness, as their old foes had pursued them even though they had been delivered from their final bondage. The offering for the sins of ignorance of the people teaches us—

I. *That error is so indigenous to, and insidious in man, that a whole community may become the victim of it.*

(a) A whole community may sin ignorantly when—
1. *It unwittingly obeys unrighteous human laws.*
2. *When it misinterprets a righteous Divine law.*
3. *When it is misled by the incorrect interpretations of its leaders.*
4. *When it is unaware of the existence of the law.*

In any of the above instances the persons committing sin do so ignorantly, and such wrong-doing, though unintentional, may incur guilt, *i.e.*, may entail evil consequences. Let us pray and strive to be saved from such delinquencies.

(b) A whole community may sin ignorantly—
1. *Even when it has anointed and authoritative leaders.*
2. *Even when it has ample means of ascertaining the truth.*
3. *Even when it is surrounded by helpful and hallowed associations.*

We see these facts exemplified in the history of Israel. How constantly they went wrong wilfully, and frequently ignorantly, although blessed with peculiar and pre-eminent advantages. Notwithstanding our light and knowledge we are in danger of falling into error; our high privileges may even prove a snare to us, put us off our guard, and render us an easy prey to sin.

No nation is exempt from this danger. If God's ancient people were not exempt, where He specially manifested His presence and power, where His will was openly made known, no people at any subsequent period of the world's history can be exempt.

No church is exempt, for although the Spirit takes of the things of Christ and shows them unto His people, and leads them into all truth, yet we only see as through a glass darkly, and "know in part." The Church has committed great errors in all ages, and no man, and no body of men, however saintly, are infallible. The larger the disc of light the greater the circumference of darkness.

No family is exempt. Where the best interests and welfare of each is sought there may be sins committed ignorantly, yet fraught with disastrous consequences. We may mislead by the advice we give, misjudge in the opinions we form; may omit to discharge our duty by neglecting judicious and necessary discipline and counsel.

II. *That when a whole community becomes the victim of inadvertent error nothing but a general expiation will atone for it.*

The elders of the congregation laid their hands upon the heads of the offering to be presented to the Lord to denote that the whole people confessed their sin and desired its removal, and the priest did with the bullock as with his own sin offering. Thus he made an atonement for the people, and their sin was forgiven. Such a service and sacrifice would be equivalent to *a season of national confession and humiliation*, and would be accepted as such in the sight of God. We are not under the law, but under grace, yet the principle that was underlying these old rites exists still, and though we are called upon to offer no bullock for our individual or national sins, yet we are expected to present the sacrifice of broken and contrite hearts to the God against whom we have wittingly or unwittingly sinned, and to expect that our sacrifice will be accepted through the atonement of our great Redeemer, who is at once our Sacrifice and Priest. When sin is participated in by a *nation*, or *church*, or *family*, the whole community and circle should participate in the contrition, acknowledging complicity in the commission of the sin, and deprecating the consequences which, but for forgiveness, would inevitably ensue.

In our united and public worship we should unitedly and publicly confess sin, for if we are not conscious of any flagrant and high-handed sins, we are sure to have upon us the stain of some inadvertent offence against the Divine laws. In many things—yea, in all things—we all offend. There is full and free forgiveness for all secret and unknown faults as well as for open, unmistakable sins. —F. W. B.

Topic: THE SIN OFFERING FOR THE RULER (Vv. 22-26).

By the sin offering of the ruler being inferior in quality to that of the priest, the Lord taught the people that no secular position was so high as that of the priest's, and that no influence was so potent and extensive as that which he, by virtue of his person and position, exerted. The humblest sacred office is higher than the highest secular position, and the sincere believer and true disciple in the Kingdom of Heaven, though poor and obscure in the world, is a king and a priest unto God. We learn from this rite—

I. *That persons in the highest positions of secular authority among men are held responsible to God.*

It has often been said that "a king can do no wrong"; but the teaching of the old economy shows us that kings could do wrong, and that rulers could do wrong through ignorance, and that their ignorant acts of wrong-doing were not connived at or condoned by the King of Heaven. When they committed error, even by mistake or in ignorance, the law could not be broken without the Lawgiver being slighted and insulted. The inculcation of this truth, and the institution of this rite, would arouse rulers to be circumspect in their conduct, and check them in the exercise of their regal authority, when tending to grow exacting and despotic.

II. *That persons in the highest positions of secular authority among men must humble themselves before God and men when they discover their public errors.*

The example of the ruler would influence the people injuriously. The atonement of his sin was therefore to be made in a public manner before the Lord, and in the presence of the people he must acknowledge his offences. Just as mercy adds lustre to crowned heads, so the acknowledgment of inadvertent errors or wilful sins will purify and dignify the conscience, and add to the glory of earth's mightiest potentates.

III. *That persons in the highest positions of secular authority among men—thus humbling themselves—obtain forgiveness of their sins and arrest the consequences of their guilt.*

God was just, and yet the justifier of the penitent sinner; He demanded atonement that His broken law might be vindicated, and His slighted authority satisfied. The people would see the exceeding heinousness of sin, how exacting and inevitable its penalty, that a priest or a ruler could not sin ignorantly without having to humble himself and seek forgiveness from Him whose laws he had broken. The guilt of such sins would be arrested, their moral consequences would be removed. Such sins would not likely be repeated, they could not be ignorantly by the same persons, and they probably would not be wilfully, when they had been shown to be so offensive in the sight of God, and when for them such sacrifices had to be made. When a course of sin is arrested a multitude of sins are hidden—not only blotted out, but prevented—sins of the past removed and sins of the future restrained. Guilt removed here, and consequences hereafter.—F. W. B.

Topic: THE SIN OFFERING OF ONE OF THE COMMON PEOPLE (Vv. 27-35).

The law of the sin offering of ignorance included all persons and positions. *The sanctity of the priest* did not shield him from its demands and scrutiny. *The dignity of the ruler* did not hedge him in from its surveillance. *The multitude of the congregation* did not hinder the action of its claims; and the obscurity of any one of the congregation did not excuse or exempt an offender from its requirements. So soon as the sin was discovered *to*, or *by* the offender, expiation according to Divine direction must be promptly and penitently made for *them*. The sin offering for one of the common people teaches us—

I. *That obscurity of social position does not shut men out from the cognizance of the great God.* The requirement of an offering from a common person who might inadvertently sin, showed that none were too obscure to be observed by the eye of the Lord. Each member of the congregation of Israel was a creature of God, each had a soul capable of sinning, and needing forgiveness, and each one was recognised by and known unto Him. The actions of all men are not only *seen*, but their moral quality *judged*.

II. *That obscurity of social position does not shut men out from the government of the great God.*

Laws were imposed upon and obedience expected from each and all. The poorest might look at the manifestation of God in the shekinah cloud, and recognise Him as their King.

III. *That obscurity of social position does not shut men out from the clemency of the great God.*

The offering required from a common person was not so great and costly as that required from a *priest* or *ruler;* it was adapted to the humbler circumstances of the offerer. This showed that the great God was not willing that even the poorest among the people should perish, not willing that they should sin on without an offering, and so become reprobates. He restored—though they might have sinned—to His fellowship and friendship. "The Lord is good to all, and His tender mercies are over all His works." In the nature and extent of the sin offering we see foreshadowed the fact that in the great sin offering of the Lamb of God provision is made for the forgiveness of all. "We have redemption through His blood, even the forgiveness of sins."—F. W. B.

OUTLINES ON VERSES OF CHAPTER IV.

V. 2.—*Theme:* SIN THROUGH IGNORANCE.
1. *The seat of sin.* "If a *soul*," etc.—body with organs only instruments of soul.
2. *The source of sin.* "Ignorance"—of God—His love, mercy, grace, etc.
3. *The strength of sin.* Law, "commandments."
4. *The stain of sin.* Deep—requires blood to wash it away.

Temptation in itself not sin; yielding is sin. Ignorance of Israel inexcusable. They had sacred memories, public directions, repeated remindings. The Judge of all the earth will do right with those who have never heard His name; but those who know His will and do it not shall be beaten with many stripes.—*F. W. B.*

V. 3.—*Theme:* SIN IN THE PRIESTHOOD. "If the priest that is anointed do sin."
I. A HOLY OFFICE DOES NOT ENSURE INFALLIBILITY.
II. Occupants of a holy office are SPECIALLY CALLED TO SANCTITY. "Be ye clean that bear the vessels of the Lord."
III. *Eminently privileged and enlightened*, they *who minister before God* SHOULD BE MOST VIGILANT LEST THEY SIN. To "sin through *ignorance*" should be impossible.
IV. Sin in God's priests had to be PURGED BY A GREAT SACRIFICIAL EXPIATION. Expressing—
1. The peculiar magnitude of sin in them.
2. The boundless sufficiency of redemption, even for them.

V. 6. *Note:* SEVENFOLD PURGING. "Sprinkle of the blood *seven times* before the Lord."

The different treatment of the blood is here to be noticed. Whilst in the case of the other sacrifices the priest threw the blood upon the walls of the altar of burnt offering (see chap. i. 5), in the sin offering the high priest is—
1. First, *to dip his finger seven times* in the blood, and sprinkle it before the Lord.

The finger, according to the rules which obtained during the second temple, was that of the right hand, as the blood was always taken and sprinkled with the right hand. [The right hand is the symbol of *strength*, as if denoting that the act was done with a resolute purpose to find purifying.—ED.]
2. Seven, being a complete number, is used for *the perfect finishing of a work.*

Hence, the seven days of creation (Gen. ii. 2, 3); seven branches in the golden candlestick (Exod. xxv. 37; xxxvii. 23); seven times the blood was sprinkled on the day of atonement (Lev. xvi. 14); seven times was the oil sprinkled upon the altar when it was consecrated (Lev. viii. 11); seven days were required for consecrating the priests (Lev. viii. 35); seven days were necessary for purifying the defiled (Lev. xii. 2; Numb. xix. 19); seven times Naaman washed in the Jordan (2 Kings v. 10-14); seven days Jericho was besieged, and seven priests with seven trumpets blew when the walls fell down (Josh. vi.); the Lamb had seven horns and seven eyes, which are the seven spirits of God (Rev. v. 6); seven seals are on God's book (Rev. v. 5), etc.—*Ellicott's Commentary.*

V. 6.—*Note:* EXPIATION WROUGHT IN THE GAZE OF HEAVEN. "Before the Lord, before the veil of the sanctuary."
1. The phrase "BEFORE THE LORD" indicates that the act of expiation was to be performed in the immediate presence of (1) Him *whom the sin had dishonoured;* (2) Him *whom the sprinkled blood was to propitiate;* and on the very spot where the priest had ministered, and which—

(1) *By priestly sin had been desecrated*, and
(2) *By expiatory blood was to be again sanctified.*

This twofold effort of expiation, reconciliation to God, and sanctification of sacred scenes, suggests *what the sinner has to secure through the blood of Christ*, viz.:—

(*a*) Jehovah propitiated, so that **man may** stand unrebuked in His presence.
(*b*) Defiled scenes reconsecrated, so that God may still dwell in the temple, in the human heart. *That* must be sanctified, for "*ye* are the temple of God."

2. The phrase "BEFORE THE VEIL OF THE SANCTUARY" indicates that the act of expiation was to be performed *in the gaze of the angel hosts.* That blue "veil" was all overwrought with cherubic and angel forms, typical of the firmament, the heavenly world, crowded with the angelic hosts.

1. *For angelic beholders watch and bewail man's sin.*
2. *They joy in the presence of God over the sinner's repentance.*
3. *They "desire to look into" the wonders of redemption.*
4. *They "minister unto those who are heirs of salvation."*
Hence—

(*a*) Having beheld God's holy place defiled, *they watch its re-hallowing*, and thus ponder how are justified the ways of God with men.

(*b*) Having witnessed the withdrawal of God from the defiled scenes (for "your iniquities have *separated* between you and God, and your sins have *hid His face* from you," Isa. lix. 2), they are eager observers of the *renewal of favour and fellowship* between God and the expiated soul. "The father ran and fell on his neck and kissed him"; and "the father said to *his servants* (comp. Psa. ciii. 20, 21; Zech. iii. 4, 5), Bring forth the best robe," etc.

V. 6.—*Theme:* SEVENFOLD SPRINKLING.

To denote completeness, perfection, to indicate how deeply dyed sin was, and impress the mind that it fully was forgiven: sprinkled "*before the Lord.*" To teach—

(1) That all sin is committed against Him.
(2) That all sin must be forgiven by Him.

Atonement and mediation the basis and means of pardon.—*F. W. B.*

V. 12.—*Theme:* SIN LOATHED BY GOD. "*Even the whole bullock shall he carry forth without the camp,*" etc.

If the law reveals sin in man, it is to drive the convicted and condemned sinner to the sacrifice for sin. The law was not given to make men holy, but to prove us sinners. Deluded souls, "blinded" by the deceiver, try to keep the law and thus become righteous: in vain! For "the law makes nothing perfect"; it unveils man's deformity that he may hide himself in the redeeming merits of Christ.

I SIN'S HATEFULNESS. "*Carry forth* without the camp."

Look at the sin offering, and see there how hateful sin is! See how the perfect Substitute, God's own beloved One, is cast out.

1. Our sin is repulsive, odious, *an offence to God.* He cannot bear it in His presence.
2. He in *whom sin centres* is repelled as loathsome, yes: be it Jesus, our Surety, on whom our sin is laid; or be it man himself, carrying his own unpardoned sins—the *sin-bearer is banished!*

II. SIN'S ANNIHILATION. "Shall he be *burnt.*" Nothing remaining.

1. *Sin consumed.* "Behold the Lamb of God which *taketh away* the sin of the world." Those dead "ashes" tell of sin's annihilation.
2. *Sins cancelled.* All our bewailing over our sins could never cancel one; if, therefore, they were not all cancelled when Christ "died for our sins" they cannot now be cancelled. "There remaineth no more offering for sin."

(*a*) If the sin offering has been sacrificed and accepted, we may joy in the fact of *sin for ever expiated.*

(*b*) We may rejoice, even when most convinced of sin, that *God asks no penalty beyond the death already borne.* [See Addenda, p. 57. *Pardon.*]

V. 12.—*Theme:* DISCIPLESHIP FOLLOWING CHRIST TO REPROACH. "The whole bullock shall he *carry forth without the camp.*"

This act is to be viewed as expressing—
a. The place which the Lord Jesus took for *us,* as bearing sin.
b. The place into which He was cast, by a world which had rejected Him.

The use which the Apostle, in Heb. xiii., makes of Christ's having "suffered without the gate" is deeply practical: "Let *us go forth,* therefore, *unto Him,* without the camp, *bearing His reproach.*"

1. The place where He suffered expresses *our rejection from earth.* Though His death has secured us a city on high, it has forfeited **for us a city below.**

2. In suffering "without the gate" He *set aside Jerusalem* as the present centre of Divine operations. There is no such thing now as a consecrated spot on earth.

3. Christ has taken His place as a suffering One, *outside the range of this world's religion* —its politics, and all that pertains to it. The world hated Him, and cast Him out.

Wherefore, the word is, "*Go forth.*"

I OUTSIDE EVERY RELIGIOUS CAMP.

You must "go forth" out of every "holy city," every religious system which men set up, to find the rejected Christ.

1. *From the gross absurdities of ignorant superstitions.*

Christ is not to be found amid the ruins of Jerusalem, amid the so-called sacred scenes and the relics of antiquity. A single ray of revelation shows that we must "go forth" from all such trifles to find communion with a rejected Christ.

2. So, when *men set up* "*a camp,*" and rally round a standard on which is emblazoned *some dogma of truth,* or some imposing institution, when they appeal to some orthodox creed or splendid ritual—it then requires much *spiritual discernment for the proper application* of the words "let us go forth," and much *spiritual energy* and decision to act upon them. Still, they should be discerned and acted upon, for the atmosphere of a camp is destructive of personal communion with a rejected Christ.

3. It is the tendency of our hearts to drop into *cold stereotyped forms.* These forms may have originated from real visitations of the Spirit. The temptation is to stereotype the form when the spirit and power have departed. This is, in principle, to set up a camp. The Jewish system could boast a Divine origin—its temple, splendid worship, priesthood, sacrifices, etc. Where is the system which could put forth such powerful and lofty pretentions to-day? And yet the command was to "go forth." It is our proneness to slip away from communion with Christ, and sink into a dead routine.

II. *Outside the Camp* TO THE LORD JESUS "*Unto Him.*"

Not glide from one system to another, from one set of opinions to another, from one company of people to another, but from all which merits the appellation of "a camp" *to Him* who "suffered without the gate."

1. *The Lord Jesus is as thoroughly outside the gate now.*

The religious world put Him outside eighteen centuries ago; and the religious world of that day is, in spirit and principle, the religious world of the present moment. The world has covered itself with the cloak of Christianity.

2. If we would walk with a rejected Christ *we must be a rejected people.*

Our Master " suffered *without* the gate," we cannot reign *within* the gate. If we walk in His footsteps whither will He lead us? Surely not to the high places of this Godless, Christless world.

"His path, uncheered by earthly smiles,
  Led only to the Cross."
He was a despised Christ, a rejected Christ, a Christ *outside the camp.*
3. *Bearing His reproach,* let us go forth *unto Him.*
Not bask in the sunshine of the world's favour Let us be faithful to a rejected Lord. While our consciences repose in His blood let our hearts' affections entwine themselves around His sacred Person. We ask a bold separateness from the world, a joyous, living attachment to Christ.—Arranged from *Notes on Leviticus,* by C. H.M.

V. 13.—*Theme:* HIDDEN SIN.
Sin may be hidden, undetected by the doer; may be concealed from others; but cannot from God. The genesis of sin—(*a*) *begins* in secret chambers of heart, (*b*) *proceeds* to, *exhibits* itself in, words and deeds. No sin so secret and subtle but known fully to God. Thought, feeling, intention, are known to Him. Sins of heart need pardon—unfulfilled evil purposes need forgiveness.—*F. W. B.*

V. 20.—*Theme:* GOOD NEWS.
I. *Of appointment of mediator* —" Priest."
II. *Of acceptance of sacrifice*—"Atonement."
III. *Of proclamation of pardon.* "Shall be forgiven them."
In the Gospel we have these glad tidings fully and freely proclaimed, and all centred in Christ.—*F. W. B.*

V. 27.—*Theme:* COMMON PEOPLE.
I. *No one so common as to be overlooked by God.*
II. *No sin so trivial as to be connived at by God.*
Life, then, is real, solemn earnest, even in humblest. *Venial* as well as mortal sins to be deprecated and avoided.—*F. W. B.*

V. 20.—*Theme:* FORGIVEN. "It shall *be forgiven them.*"
Based on the "atonement." No forgiveness otherwise. "The priest shall *make an atonement for them* and it shall be forgiven them." The *terms* of forgiveness are fixed : and the *order* in which forgiveness is gained is determined. Atonement first: then forgiveness.
I. THE CONSCIOUSNESS OF FORGIVENESS: *how is it gained?*
The mind of the Jewish offerer *was set at rest* by the presentation of his sin offering. How did he know that the sin for which he brought his sacrifice was forgiven ?
Because God had said "*It shall be forgiven him.*"
1. His peace of heart rested on the *testimony of God.*
2. His peace of heart rested on the *offered and accepted sacrifice.*
It was a *transaction* with a *covenant promise.* The transaction effected ("atonement made for him"), the promise was *believed* (" it shall be forgiven him "). Thus—

(*a*) FAITH in *God's Word* and in the *Saviour's atonement* imparts the peace and satisfaction of forgiveness to the sinner.
For an offerer of the sin offering *not to believe* that his sin was forgiven would have reflected on the truthfulness of God who had pledged forgiveness as the issue of atonement. To *doubt* is to "make God a liar." We must believe !
(*b*) *Christ's crucifixion* is a fact; as really so as the death of the victim for the sin offering. The blood of Christ is our satisfaction to justice : as the blood of the victim was. What then? *Sin is expiated.* That fact stands. The believer sees in Christ One who has been judged for his sin ; One who made himself responsible for his sin. And, as God sealed His acceptance of that sacrifice by Christ's resurrection, the *sinner's pardon and justification are truths* to be held with the joy of *faith*
II. THE REALISATION OF FORGIVENESS: *What it ensures?*
1. *All fear of judgment and wrath* is eternally set aside. God "made Him to be sin for us that we might be made the righteousness of God in Him" (2 Cor. v. 21). Our judgment, the wrath due to sin, these were settled, effected, on the accursed tree, between Divine holiness and the Spotless Victim. Justice has no charge to bring against the believer, because it has no charge to bring against Christ. If a charge *could* be brought against a soul identified with Christ by faith, it would deny the perfectness of Christ's work on his behalf.
2. *Eternal life* is inherited : for the *death* which sin brings is escaped by its falling on the Substitute. The sin is gone, because the life to which it was transferred is gone. There is no other death required. The sinner does not die: for Christ has died his death. It remains to the forgiven and justified soul that *he lives:* "he that believeth in Me shall *never die* " (John xi. 26). The *judgment* and *death* of Christ on the Cross were realities ; then the *righteousness* and *life* of the believer are also realities. Imputed *sin*—ours laid on Christ—was a reality ; imputed *righteousness* —Christ's transferred to us—is a reality. The death of Jesus satisfies all the demands made as to human sin, satisfies them *for ever.* [Comp. *Notes on Leviticus,* by C. H. M.] [See Addenda, p. 57, *Pardon.*]

V. 27. *Theme:* CULPABILITY OF IGNORANCE. "If any one *sin,*" etc.
The majesty of the law of God was exhibited, and declared, by the fact that it could not be broken inadvertently with impunity ; and the mercy of God was displayed in that, for any transgression, an offering would not only be accepted, but was commanded. It is an eternal law that the moral quality of an action lies in the intention. Sins, committed through ignorance, may be fraught with disastrous consequences, as in the case of those who rejected and crucified Christ "through ignorance," for

whom He prayed on the Cross saying "they know not what they do." Their ignorance was not wholly excusable; they shut their eyes to evidences of the Messiahship; through pride and prejudice they regarded Him as an impostor and usurper, and had, as Jesus said, "no cloak for their sins."

Saul of Tarsus, though "blameless, as touching the righteousness which is in the law," yet his legal blamelessness did not exempt him from errors of ignorance, nor did his scrupulous conscientiousness prevent him from doing wrong; for he persecuted the Christians, and thought he was doing God service. The Pharisee in the Temple thought himself better than other men, and seemed unaware of the heinous pride and wicked self righteousness that prevented him going down to his house justified as did the poor publican. Even conscience needs educating and enlightening; it has shared the fate of all the other faculties, and is liable to seriously mislead us.

We may commit sins of ignorance.—

I. *Through mere want of thought; through absolute neglect.*

II. *Through lack of knowledge that might have been acquired.*

III. *Through misapprehension of information, or direction given.*

IV. *Through defectiveness of memory, not retentive or ready at the needed juncture to prevent error.*

V. *Through not heeding protests and obstacles which God may have placed in the way, and presented against wrong-doing.*

The sacrifice provided for sins of ignorance shows that God does not connive at the errors and mistakes of any one; and, that for inadvertent wrong-doing, as well as for highhanded sins, pardon must be sought. We need to pray to be forgiven for unknown, as well as for known sins; and to be cleansed from secret faults, as well as to be kept back from presumptuous sins.—*F. W. B.*

V. 27.—*Theme:* Scripture the antidote for ignorance.

"Sin *through ignorance*, while he doeth somewhat *against any of the commandments* of the Lord."

Honest-hearted reception of the Word of God can alone preserve us from ignorance.

I. Acquaintance with Scripture: This alone is the *effectual remedy for the darkness of ignorance.*

1. Is not *the light of Scripture hidden* today, other lights being substituted instead?

(1) Think of the manner in which *ceremonial rites* (many of them mere inventions of man), ministered, too, by unholy hands, have supplanted the true and saving ministrations of the Gospel of the grace of God.

(2) Think of multitudes while yet in their sins, because unsanctified by faith in Jesus, being *taught falsely to say* to the great Shepherd of Israel, "We are Thy people, and the sheep of Thy pasture."

(3) Think how many, uncommissioned by God, unacquainted with His truth, untaught by His Spirit, have *usurped the place of ministers of Christ,* and are so owned and honoured.

(4) Think how *professed discipleship of Christ* has degenerated into seeking unholy place and gain, coveting the splendour of Solomon rather than the reproach of Jesus.

2. Is there *not a natural tendency in the heart of man* to bow to *perverted and falsely assumed authority?*

"The prophets prophesy falsely, and the priests bear rule by their means, and Thy people love to have it so."

(1) All such authority, neither based upon nor guided by truth, can *only lead into the darkness* to which itself belongs. What wonder, then, that ignorance should settle upon that soul which has made itself the slave of such authority! What wonder if it should welcome falsehood, and fight against truth, and congratulate itself most when furthest from the principles of Christ!

(2) *Individuals,* too, as well as collective bodies, may *claim an authority which God has never given.* And not unfrequently fear, or affection, or self interest, or a disposition to lean upon others, causes it to be gladly recognised. But such authority, seeing that it is not grounded upon truth, that it directs not to the Scriptures alone, can only lead towards, if not into, darkness.

II. Close adherence to Scripture: This alone will save us from the *false leadings and lights of our age.*

1. Is *that which we hear true or false?* Is it or is not *the Word of God?* Such are the great questions we have to ask ourselves now.

2. The faithful use of the Scripture will *expose many an error, detect many a sin of ignorance,* and show us much that we have not sufficient grace to attain.

3. Instruction and exhortation of the Scriptures is employed by the Lord to *free His people from the sins of ignorance* and their disastrous consequences.

III. The steady light of God's word: This is appointed to shine on in the darkness, until the day dawn.

The energies of Satan, and the impelling of evil in us, are active to resist the Scriptures and quench the sacred light of truth.

1. The delusions of Satan and of the human heart *struggle to increase darkness and confirm error.* And we cannot wonder that they prosper in their plans during a period marked by our Lord Himself as one wherein "iniquity shall abound."

2. Yet *the greater the darkness the more precious is any light* that is available in our midst. Amid all the dark and stifling scenes through which the fierce passions of men, under Satan, are hurrying alike the Church and the world, the *Word of God remains unchanged and unchangeable;* the *only one steady light.*

3. Happy they who stand most apart from the tumults, and *cleave most closely to the Scriptures,* and most *meditate therein.*

4. If, as the history of Christianity pecu-

liarly shows, the *perpetual effort of Satan be to hide, veil or distort* the light of Scripture, *let our effort be to unveil it*, and to give steady direction to its beams. He will not have lived in vain who shall have caused one ray of light from the Word of God to rest steadily on a heart that was dark to it before.

IV. SCRIPTURE LIGHT WILL SURELY MANIFEST SINS OF IGNORANCE: how, then, can we have courage to use, or to approach a light, so certain to reveal such sins both in ourselves and others, if there were no Sin Offering?

What hope could we have unless we were able to say that the whole family of faith are protected for ever under its efficacy? We have not again to offer it: it has been offered, once and for ever offered, every ceremony fulfilled, every ordinance obeyed.

Let us use it, not to nurture ignorance, listlessness and slumber, but to encourage ourselves to cleave to and maintain the light of revealed truth, which, however beset by evil, however much it may be for the time shrouded, shall never have its essential brightness marred by one element of darkness, on to the hour when it mingles with the light of the eternal day.—Developed from *Thoughts on Leviticus*, by B. W. Newton, Vol. I.—[See Addenda, p. 58, *Scripture Light*.]

ILLUSTRATIVE ADDENDA TO CHAPTER IV.

IGNORANCE. *Classical* quotations:—
Ignoratione rerum bonarum et malarum maxime hominum vita vexatur.—Cicero.
[Through ignorance of what is good and bad the life of man is greatly perplexed.]
O miseras hominum mentes! Oh pectora cœca!—Lucretius.
[How wretched are the minds of men, how blind their understandings.]
Quantum animis errois inest!—Ovid.
[What error there is in human minds!]

IGNORANCE *versus* KNOWLEDGE.
"When you know a thing, to hold that you know it; and when you do not know a thing, to allow that you do not know it—this is knowledge."—Confucius: *Analects*.
"Wisdom is humble that he knows no more."
—Cowper: *The Task*.
"The first step to self-knowledge is self-distrust. Nor can we attain to any kind of knowledge except by a like process."—J. C. and A. W. Hare: *Guesses at Truth*.
"All things I thought I knew; but now confess
The more I know I know, I know the less."
—Owen.
"Ignorance is the curse of God;
Knowledge the wing wherewith we fly to heaven."—Henry VI.
"By knowledge we do learn ourselves to know,
And what to man, and what to God we owe."—Spencer: *Tears of the Muses*.
"Conviction of ignorance is the door-step to the temple of wisdom."—Spurgeon.

PERILS OF IGNORANCE.
Modern science has shown that the seeds of epidemic and miasmatic diseases are generated and exert their activity *during the night*, and in places unvisited by the sun's beams—a true image of the evils developed from unillumined ignorance.
"So long as thou art ignorant be not ashamed to learn. Ignorance is the greatest of all infirmities, and when justified the greatest of all follies."—Isaak Walton.
"Ignorance is the night of the mind, but a night without moon or star."—Confucius.

"Ignorance, when voluntary, is criminal, and that man may be properly charged with that evil which he neglected or refused to learn how to prevent."—Johnson.

EXPLANATION OF MAN'S IGNORANCE.
"Ignorance of things very near to us, and in which we are nearly concerned, may be from two causes:
i. *From want of Light*. Nothing can be perceived in the dark. If you are in a dark room, though it be richly adorned and furnished, all is lost to you. If you stand in a dark night on the top of a hill that commands a fine prospect, still you are able to see no more than if you were in a valley. Though you were in a dangerous place, with pitfalls, precipices, thieves and murderers all around you, still you might imagine yourself in safety, if you had no light with you.
ii. It may be *from some ignorance or obstruction between you* and the object. Thus, your dearest friend or greatest enemy might be within a few yards of you, and you know nothing of it, if there were a wall between you.

These comparisons may in some measure represent our state by nature. *God* is near: "in Him we live and move and have our being! *Eternity* is near; we stand upon the brink of it. *Death* is near; advancing towards us with hasty strides. The *truths of God's Word* are most certain in themselves, and of the utmost consequence to us, but we perceive none of these things, we are not affected by them, because our *understandings are dark*, and because thick walls of *ignorance, prejudice and unbelief* stand before the eyes of our minds, and keep them from our view."

PARDON.
"*I believe in the forgiveness of sins*"—The article of the creed which brought peace to Luther's troubled mind when seeking the way of salvation. "Oh my sins! my sins!" was his cry, almost of despair; from which, however, he was greatly relieved by the good counsel and comforting advice of Staupitz. But the work was not yet finished. One day

all his fears and terrors had returned, when an old monk entered his cell, and Luther opened his heart to him. The venerable old man was unable to follow his soul in all its doubts as Staupitz had done, but he knew his *creed*, and found much consolation in it for his own heart; so he repeated to Luther the cheering article, "*I believe in the forgiveness of sins.*"

These simple words, pronounced with much sincerity in the decisive moment, diffused great consolation in Luther's mind. From that instant light sprang up in his rejoicing heart.

"I feel more sure than ever that the right thing is to take each sin the *moment the conscience feels it*, to the *blood of Jesus*, and there, having once purged it, to remember it no more. I don't think of one scriptural example of a sin once forgiven ever being charged upon the conscience again; and I suppose the yearly sins were never expected to be again brought to mind, after the scapegoat had borne them into the land of forgetfulness. Oh for grace to plunge into the ocean of Divine forgiveness."—A. L. Newton.

SCRIPTURE LIGHT.

At a missionary meeting in Mangaia, after the whole Bible had been received in their own language, an aged disciple rose up to exhort the people to read the whole Bible through. Lifting his own new Bible before the congregation, he exclaimed, "My brothers and sisters, this is my resolve: the dust shall never cover my new Bible, the moths shall never eat it, the mildew shall never rot it! my light, **my joy!**"

What ignorance of the Bible existed in Europe before printing was introduced! *Stephanus* relates of a certain doctor of Sorbonne, who, speaking of the Reformers, expressed his surprise at their mode of reasoning by exclaiming, " I wonder why these youths are constantly quoting the New Testament. I was *more than 50 years old before I knew anything of a New Testament.*" And *Albert*, Archbishop and Elector of Mentz, in the year 1530, accidentally meeting with a Bible, opened it, and having read some pages of it, observed, "I do not indeed know what this book is, but this I see, that *everything in it is against us.*" Even *Carolastadius*, who was afterwards one of the Reformers, acknowledged that he had never begun to read the Bible till eight years after he had taken his *highest degree in divinity.*

Dr. Samuel Johnson, distinguished as a writer on morals, and whose writings have seldom been excelled in energy of thought and beauty of expression, said to a young gentleman who visited him on his dying bed "young man, attend to the voice of one who has possessed a certain degree of fame in the world, and will shortly appear before his **Maker**: *read the Bible every day of your life.*"

Salmasius, one of the most consummate scholars of his time, saw cause to exclaim bitterly against himself: " O, I have lost a world of time—time, the most precious thing in the world! Had I but one year more, it should be spent in perusing David's Psalms and Paul's Epistles. O sirs"—addressing those about him—" mind the world less and God more!"

CHAPTER V.

𝔗𝔯𝔢𝔰𝔭𝔞𝔰𝔰𝔢𝔰 𝔥𝔢𝔢𝔡𝔩𝔢𝔰𝔰𝔩𝔶 𝔒𝔬𝔪𝔪𝔦𝔱𝔱𝔢𝔡.

SUGGESTIVE READINGS.

V. 1.—**If the soul . . .** hear the voice of swearing. Sins may be acted out consciously and defiantly; for such there was no expiation provided. But sins may be committed *without realising their sinfulness;* of these the preceding chapter deals, and for such there was expiatory sacrifice and assured forgiveness. Yet, also, sins may be *contracted* where *no volition or action* occurs, by passive non-resistance, by tacit connivance, by incautious heedlessness: and such are the sins this chapter interdicts while it also prescribes expiation. Sin may come in through the ear: "*hear* the voice of swearing"; albeit it is no sin in itself to hear, unless we shut it in wilfully and become accessory thereto. It should be let out through the lips: "*utter* it": give it no harbour, but prompt escape; for it defiles the soul which retains it as a secret. Let no evil thing find a quiet chamber in our thoughts; expose it, and thereby exorcise and condemn it. Impurity must ensue from entertaining secretly what God bids us renounce and denounce.

V. 2.—**Touch any unclean thing.** God would have His people untainted by uncleanness. With minute care He had defined what were unclean things. From every contagion they must keep free, if they were to remain ceremonially holy. Shall not we also shun contact with forbidden things? "For God hath not called us unto uncleanness, but unto holiness." There are institutions in society, companionships and friendships, indulgences and pastimes, recreations and books, which would defile a Christian life and lower the sanctities of existence. "Wherefore, come out from among them, and be ye separate, saith the Lord, and touch not the unclean thing" (2 Cor. vi. 17).

It be hidden from him. How often do we touch defilement unconsciously! And having by contact derived the contagion (in pure thoughts sullied, our sensitive recoil from evil blunted, elevated aims lowered, and Christward affections decoyed) how do we forget that we have touched! How constantly we argue with our own consciences that the tainted pleasures and pastimes we foster are outside the interdicted list. Yet this self-excusing is vain; "he also shall be *unclean* and *guilty*."

V. 4.—**Whatsoever a man shall pronounce with an oath.** Vows which bind us to lines of conduct should never be made in ignorance. It is perilous to society as well as to individual honour for a man to make himself subject to a vow whose issues are "*hid from him*." This reprehensible plan prevails in those "secret societies" and "brotherhoods" whose programme is the destruction of civil institutions and State stability. If a man blindly swears away his liberty, and binds himself by oath to any confederation, he is "*guilty*" of any and all the deeds done by the associates of such organisations. Oaths should only be taken when their issues are fully discerned; certainly no right-minded man will allow himself to become the dupe of bad associates, or the accomplice of evil designs, under the specious plea that the effects of his oath were "hid from him" when he bound himself thereby. Prudence and piety will warn us against being thus "rash with our mouth." [Compare Eccles. v. 2 and 6; Acts xxiii. 12-14.]

V. 5.—**He shall bring his trespass offering.** Rash oaths incurred guiltiness, and must be atoned for; the folly of taking an oath to "do evil" was an offence to be expiated; whereas the neglect of an oath to "do good" was equally a trespass. God's requirement of an expiatory offering for both misdemeanours acted beneficially on the community, by restraining persons from taking hasty and inconsiderate oaths. "This served very effectually (says Michaelis) to maintain the honour of oaths, inasmuch as every oath, however inconsiderate, or unlawful, or impossible, was regarded so far obligatory that it was necessary to expiate its non-fulfilment by an offering; and it was, at the same time, the best possible means of weaning the people from rash oaths, because a man who had grown addicted to the unbecoming practice would find himself too frequently obliged either to keep his oaths, how great soever the inconvenience, or else to make an offering for their atonement."

V. 15.—**Ignorance in the holy things of the Lord.** There were dues or debts to the sanctuary of God, and he who failed to bring his tithes and first-fruits, even though unintentionally and "through ignorance," was a transgressor. A costly "amends" (v. 16) was to be made for this oversight, if his trespass was to be forgiven him. Thus jealous is God that we withhold no duty from Him, that we "enter into His presence with thanksgiving," *i.e.*, with gifts as thank offerings. Every soul, spared in the land of the living, succoured by Divine goodness and grace, overshadowed by the Fatherhood of God, shepherded by the patient care of Christ, upheld by the energy of the Spirit, owes offerings to Heaven, and should enter the sanctuary with the acknowledgments of all the mercy received. Our grateful souls should seek to fulfil "something of the debt we owe." "What shall I render unto the Lord for all His benefits towards me?" God asks sanctuary presents from every one of His people.

V. 17.—Forbidden to be done. For the Lord had prohibited the profane use, or the appropriation to personal ends, of "holy things" dedicated to the sanctuary and its services. If a soul had reason only to *suspect* his misuse thereof, he must seek forgiveness by trespass offering. All such stern requirements tended to enforce a recognition of the supreme claims of Jehovah and the sanctity of religion. No trifling, no forgetfulness, no error was excusable. Shall not we "stand in awe and sin not," guarding ourselves from "presumptuous sins" and inadvertent negligence by "watching unto prayer" and by swift fulfilment of our obligations to Heaven?

SECTIONAL HOMILIES.

Topic: COMPLACENT IGNORANCE (Vv. 1-5).

Sins of ignorance differ greatly in kind and in degree. Transgression may ensue from *lack of knowledge* that such conduct is forbidden; or it may be that, knowing the prohibition, disobedience is *speciously excused* on some vague plea that circumstances warrant it or expediency condones it. In such cases ignorance, if it be really ignorance at all, is self-induced, and is therefore the more culpable. Amid such reprehensible forms of ignorance may be placed—

I. CARELESSNESS; the mind too placid to rouse itself to inquiry.

II. INDISCRIMINATION; the habit of ignoring vital principles and conniving at inconsistencies.

III. SELF-EXCUSING; finding exceptional circumstances which extenuate faults and condone misconduct.

IV. NEGLECT OF SCRIPTURE; not "coming to the light lest their deeds should be reproved" (John iii. 20).

V. SATISFACTION WITH A STATE OF CONSCIOUS DARKNESS; indifference to precise regulations of religion, indisposition of heart towards "perfect holiness"; a loose and easy content over failings and negligence. Ignorance is by some persons consciously *cherished:* it allows them a covert from the exactions of a lofty and honest piety.

VI. PLAUSIBLE SOPHISTRY; entertaining the delusion that because there is not determined wilfulness in sinning, or not fullest knowledge of God's prohibitions of sin, they are less responsible, less to be condemned.

Note: Many persons, trained from youth in a school of error, grow up with *false principles dominating their judgments and consciences,* or with ignorance of *the application of right principles to particular incidents and actions.* The perception of righteousness is vague and dim, the moral sense is feeble and faltering, "darkness in part" has happened to them. Thus *Luther,* trained amid the blinding theories of Romanism, groped on till manhood in delusions and dimness. Thus *Paul,* brought up amid the traditions of Judaism, found his soul clouded with wholly wrong thoughts concerning what was "doing God service."

It is *our duty to undeceive ourselves,* to inquire after knowledge, to seek full light, that our dimness may yield to discernment.

A complacent ignorance is as the softly gliding stream which flows onwards to the rapids. To be able to rest in such self-satisfied ignorance indicates that self-delusion has begun, portending doom. "Whom the gods would destroy they first dement." And such contentment, while in error of the very way of godly obedience and acceptance, betokens a demented state ominous of worst issues. Therefore :—

1. *Search the Scriptures.* 2. *Seek the Spirit's illumination.* 3. *Culture a pure and enlightened conscience.* 4. *Exercise the judgment and will* in efforts to " cease from evil and learn to do well."

Topic : The Sin of Conniving at Wrong-doings (V. 1).

The trespass offering atoned for voluntary offences, thus fitly supplementing the offerings for sins of ignorance. All crime—*i.e.*, wrong done to men—is *sin* in the sight of God, and needs to be followed by repentance as well as reparation. Here we are taught that a person committed sin in withholding knowledge when able and judicially commanded to divulge it.

The camp of Israel in the wilderness was not only a Church, but a Commonwealth ; the interests of the people were mutual, and their duties reciprocal. It was the duty of the rulers to defend and promote the right, and to expose and denounce the wrong. When an evil doer was arrested, a proclamation was made calling upon any who could furnish evidence (that the ends of justice might not be defeated) to present themselves as witnesses in the court. If any such person, through fear or neglect, failed to furnish the information in his possession he was a partaker in the sin. The safety and sanctity of society demanded that evidence should not wilfully be withheld. Jehovah here required His people to co-operate with Him in protesting against and exposing sin. Observe—

I. That the sins of men cannot evade witnesses.

An old writer has forcibly said " that to every sin there must be at least two witnesses," viz , "a man's own conscience and the great God." Wrong-doing so confuses and condemns a man, except he be very degraded and hardened, that even though he was not really observed in the act, he will so betray himself to others that evidence of a presumptive or positive kind, circumstantial or self-evident can be presented.

Living together as the Israelites did in the wilderness, they would be constantly under each other's eye, wrong-doing would be easily detected, its guilt easily proved.

We are all daily revealing ourselves more or less to each other, and persons who observe our conduct are tacitly gathering evidence to accuse or excuse, to commend or condemn our conduct and character. This world is a place of trial, a place of judgment. We are not only arraigned before the tribunal of our own consciences, but also before the bar of public observation and opinion.

II. That it is the duty of witnesses to give evidence when justice demands it.

When a witness heard the words of adjuration he was required at the proper place to give the needed information. It was his duty because (1) the law of the Lord commanded it, and (2) the purity of society demanded it. It would also be an injustice to a wrong-doer, for the sake of shielding him from present punishment, by conniving at his sin to encourage him in evil ways. Moreover, a witness owes the duty to himself to testify against sin, for if he does not expose it and bring it to condemnation, he may foster even in himself a careless unconcern about wrong. By bearing witness against evil doing we utter our protest against the wrong, and if we do it in the right spirit and "speak the whole truth, and nothing but the truth," we are serving righteously and faithfully our day and generation, and we therein discharge a duty we owe to God against whom all sin is a transgression, and who has appointed rulers to administer justice for the praise of those who do well, and to be a terror to evil doers.

III. That in concealing evidence against sin we involve ourselves in serious guilt.

By withholding evidence we may think to cover over sins, and so we may; but we do not *remove* them. We may prevent them coming to light and meeting their merited punishment, but the *sins* remain, and will take deeper root and throw out wider branches. It is a trespass, a breach of the Divine law, when we allow sin to go unaccused and unexposed; we thereby offer an inducement to sin, and tacitly encourage indulgence in transgression. The guilt of concealing evidence is seen, in that by so doing we—

1. *Dishonour God's voice, which speaks within us.*
2. *Disobey God's published laws.*
3. *Decrease our own antipathy to sin.*
4. *Encourage the trespasser in his wrong-doing.*

All sin ought to be acknowledged and expiated for the sake of the sinner and the wronged. A person refusing to give evidence makes himself an accessory to a wicked deed after its accomplishment, and becomes an accomplice in its guilt. Divine revelation teaches us that we have duties we owe to ourselves, to society, and to God.—F. W. B.

Topic: THE CONTAGIOUSNESS OF SIN (V. 2, 3).

The sin of touching an unclean person or thing is here described. The whole of the directions given respecting ceremonial defilement were to teach most emphatically the holiness of God, and His deep concern for the holiness of His creatures. The children of Israel were not only to obey Him, but also to worship Him, and as their service was to be a sacrament and their work worship, it was necessary that they should be taught the utmost scrupulousness in ceremonial, as well as inward, purity. These regulations and requirements would not only teach the people who were immediately affected by them the most salutary lessons, but would also teach (through them) the world valuable truths. We learn—

I. THE IMPORTANCE OF CIRCUMSPECTION IN OUR OUTWARD BEHAVIOUR.

The Israelites would feel that the greatest possible vigilance would be needed as they went in and out the camp and mixed with the congregation, lest they should become defiled by contact with some unclean thing. As we mingle with our fellow-men, and discharge our duties in the world, although we are not under the restrictions and regulations of the Levitical law, yet we are in a world where the moral atmosphere is tainted, and where we are in constant danger of being morally defiled. We are not only ourselves surrounded by a sympathetic moral influence, which affects all with whom we have contact, but we also in turn receive influence, good or ill, from others with whom we associate. We learn that the greatest possible circumspection is essential as we move amid the busy throngs.

II. THE POSSIBILITY OF CONTAMINATION, EVEN THOUGH WE PRACTISE CIRCUMSPECTION IN OUR OUTWARD CONDUCT.

The text shows that it was possible for people to become defiled and be unconscious of it. A man might find even that his extreme caution had ensnared him. He might not always be able to discriminate between the clean and the unclean, especially at first sight. So, as we pass through the world, we are so closely surrounded by morally contaminating influences that sometimes we may acquire infection before we are aware of it. Even the most innocent pleasures and pursuits may be perverted by us, becoming suggestive and ministrant of sin; in our ignorance or simplicity we may get a wrong bias, wicked thoughts may be awakened. For such defilement we shall need to make expiation; also seek forgiveness and cleansing, that the impurity of our heart and conscience may be removed, and the progress of moral depravity and deterioration be arrested.—F. W. B.

Topic: THE RESPONSIBILITY OF WORDS (V. 4, 5).

Here is taught the sin of a person making a rash oath. In their conversation with each other the people were to beware of uttering idle words, especially when calling upon God to witness what they said; also, they were to be careful how they committed themselves by solemn engagements to do evil or to do good. The people were at present rude and unpolished, and one of the objects of the ritual was to elevate and refine them. Words are often spoken as if they were of no importance, vows made and oaths uttered as if they were unnoticed by God; but this law shows us that He does take strict notice of them, and that though forgotten by us, they are not forgotten by Him. Though spoken heedlessly and easily forgotten, yet God would hold them responsible. The gospel has not repealed the law's condemnation of rash speaking, for Christ taught that "for every idle word that men speak they shall give an account at the day of judgment." And we are taught, moreover, to "swear not at all, neither by heaven, for it is God's throne, nor by earth, for it is His footstool, neither by our heads, for we cannot make one hair black or white." The influence of this Levitical injunction would be to lead the people to make an oath—

I. RARELY. There would be no need for oaths if they cultivated veracity, if their simple word was known to be their bond. To employ oaths frequently would be taking God's name in vain, and incurring danger of frequently transgressing one of the great commandments. God was in their midst as their Lawgiver and King; they must not use too frequently and familiarly His holy name in connection with their common, ordinary conversation and conduct.

II. DELIBERATELY. Even when circumstances seemed to require that they should call God to witness and confirm what they affirmed, the act was so solemn that they would need to do so with great caution and deliberateness, pondering what they were about to affirm or deny, and estimating the probability that they could promptly perform their purpose. An oath deliberately made would be *impressed upon the memory;* if not fulfilled, no excuse could be offered. The nature of an oath, of the pledge with which it is accompanied, should be thoroughly weighed before God is called upon to help and witness.

III. CONDITIONALLY. There may be some cases and instances where an unconditional oath may be safely pronounced; but it is more prudent to associate with it qualifying conditions. Such a course would not make the oath less binding for all reasonable intents, and ought to meet the requirements of any ordinary case. Our proneness to err, the impossibility of our meeting exorbitant demands, the probability of after-thought showing us that what we had engaged to do was impracticable or undesirable, ought to be taken into account. Conditions and circumstances may so change as to relieve us from promises which, at the time, we made in good faith. When wise men make oaths, they will make them cautiously.

1. *Cultivate transparency and veracity of speech,* so that our communications may require to be simply yea, and nay; for when more is required it indicates that we have become unreliable, so that our word cannot be trusted.

2. If *pledges made between man and man* are thus solemn and binding, and the breach of them so blameworthy, pledges to God in solemn sacrament must be more solemn and binding, and their non-fulfilment more culpable.—F. W. B.

Topic: THE WAY OF PARDON (Vv. 6-13).

In the fifth verse it is enjoined that when any person shall be guilty of any of the trespasses specified, he shall confess that he had thus sinned; from which we at once see that *confession* was to immediately follow *conviction*, and the next step—as we learn from the succeeding verse—would be *contrition*. The offender was to bring his trespass offering unto the Lord for his sin, and the priest would present it to the Lord as an atonement for the sin. The offering was to be one of the flock, or a fowl, or of flour. From this arrangement we learn that—

I. THE WAY OF PARDON WAS MADE EASY. The circumstances of the transgressor were mercifully considered. The gradation of the offerings from a bullock down to the tenth part of an ephah of fine flour showed that God would allow no difficulty to stand in the way of transgressors seeking expiation. For the various gradations of wrong-doing there was pardon on confession and contrition. The offerings could be easily obtained, and the priest and altar were close at hand, so that at any moment the needed confession and atonement could be made. In the Mosaic, as well as the Christian dispensation, the way of forgiveness is made easy.

II. THE WAY OF PARDON WAS MADE EXPLICIT. Full and clear directions are given, even to minute details, in the way the victim was to be slain, and its various parts disposed of, and each direction (meaningless and useless as some at first sight appeared) had some symbolical or typical import. In every instance assurance was given of forgiveness, if only the required conditions were complied with. The unsavouriness of the offering—from the absence of sweet oil and frankincense—suggests the *loathsomeness* of sin : that it is displeasing to God, ought to be offensive to man, and is to those truly humble and contrite.

(*a*) *The mercy of God displayed* in (1) *providing remedy to arrest the course of sin ;* (2) *providing remedy to arrest the consequences of sin.* Man's ignorance of sin proves his utter inability to put it away of himself.

(*b*) *The misery of sin discovered* in that it (1) *produces separation from God and all real good ;* (2) *necessitates suffering and atonement before it can be forgiven.* In the rites and ceremonies of the Levitical economy we get God's provision for man's need—*a sacrifice* appointed for man's sin ; *a priest* to present the sacrifice for man's sin ; and *a place of worship* where the sacrifice may be offered and accepted.—F. W. B.

OUTLINES ON VERSES OF CHAPTER V. 1—13.

V. 2.—*Theme :* CONTRACTION OF DEFILEMENT. "*If a soul touch an unclean thing ... he also shall be unclean,* and guilty."

Human depravity, inherent—universal—"Out of the heart proceed evil thoughts," etc. Depravity may be *deepened* and *developed* by outward influences and circumstances. The body and mind may generate or acquire disease; so, with the soul. We are surrounded by a magnetic circle of influence which affects us, and through it we affect others for good or evil. Hence importance of guarding our sympathies, susceptibilities, senses, and every avenue and vehicle of our being. "Touch not the unclean thing."

We learn the importance—

I. OF ABSENCE FROM EVIL ASSOCIATIONS. "Enter not into the path of the wicked, and walk not in the way of evil men." [See Ps. i.]

II. OF ABSTINENCE FROM APPEARANCE OF EVIL. Beware of every infectious interdicted thing. "Taste not, touch not, handle not."

Christ could mix with sinners, could touch lepers and the dead without defilement, because there was nothing in Him to respond to, or to be laid hold on, by temptation or corruption. As the needle leaps to the loadstone, so our hearts leap to meet temptation by the law of attractive affinities. For every stain of defilement we contract, even though as deep as crimson or scarlet, there is a remedy : " The blood of Jesus Christ cleanses from all sin," and can make our souls as white as snow.—*F. W. B.*

V. 7.—*Theme :* WHAT GOD EXPECTS OF US. " If he be not able to bring a lamb, then he shall bring for his trespass two turtle doves, or two young pigeons, unto the Lord."

There is nothing exacting or exorbitant in the claims of God upon His creatures. He expects of us only what we can render according to talents, circumstances, opportunity, claims. He regards our purposes, and accepts them as acts performed when performance is impossible, e.g , He said of David's purpose to erect the Temple, " It was well that it was in thine heart." Christ commended the act of the woman in the gospels because " she had done what she could."

If God expects of us only what we can render—

I. THEN NONE ARE EXEMPT FROM HIS SERVICE. Doves and pigeons were accepted where lambs could not be furnished. The widow's two mites were as acceptable as the box of precious ointment and Solomon's Temple.

II. THEN HIS SERVICE IS PERFECT FREEDOM. The offerer had to judge and choose what he would offer. God expects voluntary cheerful gifts, not simply from a sense of duty but from impulses of a generous love. If we give *ourselves* to the Lord, all we have will be laid upon the altar that sanctifies both the giver and the gift.—*F. W. B.*

V. 8.—*Theme:* MEDIATION. "He shall bring them unto *the priest, who shall offer,*" etc.

The sin offering taught that guilt separated between the sinner and his Sovereign Lord:— Priest came between to connect, and be medium of communication. Such an arrangement would (a) *inspire courage*, and (b) *impart comfort* to the offerer.

The offerer brought his offering to the priest, yet—

I. THE VALUE OF THE OBLATION WAS NOT ENHANCED BY ANY MERIT OF THE PRIEST. But the infinite dignity of our High Priest gave infinite dignity to His sacrifice.

II. THE PRIEST OFFERED SACRIFICE PROVIDED BY ANOTHER: our High Priest offered Himself, once for all.

In the hands of the priest the sinner's sacrifice was acceptable: through Christ our offerings are well-pleasing to God. The only thing that God hates, and that can separate between Jehovah and His creatures is *sin*. Its removal restores harmony, holiness, happiness in man, and the universe — *F. W. B.*

V. 10.—*Theme:* DIVINE FORGIVENESS. "The priest shall make atonement for him for his sin which he hath sinned, and *it shall be forgiven him.*"

Nature is unable to show how sin may be forgiven. By an inevitable and almost universal law reaping follows sowing, both in quality and quantity. Retribution follows wrong-doing. Nature is stern, unrelenting; only in revealed religion can we learn how God can be just and yet forgive the sinner. The Bible alone teaches that there is forgiveness with God that He may be feared. The offerer was assured that if he presented the prescribed oblation, his sin would " *be forgiven him.*" This arrangement teaches –

I. THAT SATISFACTION MUST BE OFFERED BY THE SINNER HIMSELF, OR BY HIS ACCREDITED SUBSTITUTE. Pardon costs something both to God and man.

II. THAT THE SINNER MUST BE SINCERELY SORRY FOR HIS SINS. The offerings were to be presented in a manner which would denote *reverence* and *repentance*. Only forsaken sin is forgiven.

III. THAT IN THE FORGIVENESS OF SIN THE RIGHTEOUSNESS OF GOD IS VINDICATED. The demands of His justice were met—His broken law honoured—atonement sufficient and satisfactory made.

In the Gospels all these points are *exemplified* and *enforced.*—*F. W. B.*

SECTIONAL HOMILIES.

Topic: TRESPASSES, DONE IGNORANTLY, AGAINST THE LORD (Vv. 14-19).

Scarcely is it possible to accredit absolute ignorance to trespassers in these "holy things of the Lord": for God's declarations respecting His rights were neither unintelligible nor obscure. They ought to have been known thoroughly, they must have been known to some degree. The ignorance was, therefore, in some sense wilful; certainly it was conscious, and was even preferred to knowledge.

Still, it is noteworthy that ignorance is predicated of these trespassers *against the Lord*, whereas there is no allowance of ignorance in the trespasses done against *men*. [Compare chap. vi.] This marks a melancholy fact in the conduct of wrong-doers. We *defraud God* of His due *carelessly and without giving it a thought;* whereas we are *too cautious* to trespass against *a neighbour* without knowing it. For the fear of man is more operative over us than the fear of God.

I. FRAUDULENT CONDUCT AGAINST THE LORD.

1. *Israel's history for ages* illustrates the ready ease with which men could "rob God" (Mal. iii. 8-10). Commanded to appear repeatedly every year before the Lord and celebrate His feasts, yet era upon era passed without their keeping those sacred feasts at all—until, in the times of Ezra and Nehemiah,

they read the Scriptures (long closed and neglected) and discovered their omissions to have been so numerous, so grievous, so long continued, that the people all lifted up their voices and wept.

Fifty years later, again Israel is described as habitually defrauding God of His due, and even justifying themselves in their "robbery," asking with effrontery, "Wherein have we robbed Thee?" (Mal. iii. 8).

Such warning incidents should have aroused the Church of Christ to greater watchfulness in later days. Yet—

2. *The present conduct of Christians* repeats the trespass of the ancient Church. Is there not a defrauding "of the holy things of the Lord" still rampant? Consider—

(*a*) *Doctrines suppressed and truths silenced* which ought to be "sounded out" clearly.

(*b*) *Worship rendered perfunctorily*, and void of "spirit and truth"; "the form of godliness without the power thereof."

(*c*) *Open allegiance to Christ withheld*; a careless and compromising profession supplanting whole consecration.

(*d*) *The selfish retention of our gains and possessions*, spending so freely upon ourselves that we have little or nothing to give God.

II. RESTITUTION DEMANDED AS THE CONDITION OF PARDON.

Unlike the sin offering, the "trespass offering" must not be presented until reparation had been made.

1. *Satisfaction was to precede sacrifice.* Man is a debtor, having withheld dues from the Lord. Those dues were not to be set aside by substituting contrition or expiatory offerings. It were easy to trespass if all could be righted by penitential confessions. But God says "Behold, to obey is better than sacrifice." "*He shall make amends*": such is Jehovah's fiat (v. 16).

2. *In Christ's obedient life satisfaction did precede sacrifice.* Man "had nothing to pay"; but Jesus paid the debt. In His own career He "fulfilled all righteousness" on man's behalf. Then, having perfectly satisfied the Divine requirements in His life, He bore man's merited punishment for long disobedience.

3. *Divine forgiveness differs essentially from connivance at man's sin.* God can pardon all manner of trespasses, but can gloss over not one jot or tittle of iniquity. "His grace is perfect, and therefore He can forgive *all*: His holiness is perfect, and therefore he cannot pass over anything. He cannot sanction iniquity, but He can blot it out."—C. H. M.

4. *Restitution by obedience* is a law which still incites believers to a diligent piety. Not by the merit of their acts to justify themselves with God, but to make such "amends" as a soul reclaimed from disloyalty naturally desires to make to its gracious Lord and King. "The love of Christ constrains us"; and by every act of sacrifice and service we aim to set right all wrong we have done, to counteract the follies of past years, to benefit those whom we may have harmed, to redeem the time by diligent use of opportunities remaining, and "henceforth to live not unto ourselves, but unto Him who loved us and gave Himself for us." By such earnest efforts to "do good as he has opportunity" does the Christian seal his salvation, and enjoy the "Well done" of his Lord. [See Addenda, p. 71, *Reparation.*]

Topic: "AMENDS" MADE BY CHRIST FOR MAN'S FAULTS (Vv. 15, 16).

Think of all the wrong and all the trespass which have been done against the Lord.

I. GOD HAS BEEN WRONGED OF HIS RIGHTS IN THIS WICKED WORLD.

1. What are the *just rights of Jehovah* in His creature, man?

2. What are man's returns to Jehovah in *actual obedience and righteousness ?*
3. What amazing *outrage and transgression have defrauded God* of His due!
4. What shortcomings and blemishes have marred even *the best lives of His redeemed people!*

II. GOD HAS GAINED MORE BY CHRIST'S REDEMPTION THAN HE LOST BY MAN'S FALL.

The trespass offerer *adds a surplus!* But who can weigh the surplus Christ brings?

1. Jehovah reaps a *richer harvest of glory, honour and praise* in the fields of redemption than ever He could have reaped in those of creation.
2. The "sons of God" would raise a loftier song of praise *around the empty tomb of Jesus* than ever they raised in view of the Creator's accomplished work.
3. The wrong has not only been perfectly atoned for, but an *eternal advantage* has been gained by the work of the Cross. God is gainer by the work of Calvary.

III. ALL HONOUR TO JESUS, IN WHOSE CROSS SUCH VAST "AMENDS" WERE MADE.

1. No wonder that around the Crucified One the *affections* of patriarchs, prophets, apostles, martyrs, and *saints have ever entwined themselves.*
2. No marvel that the Holy Ghost should have given forth that solemn but just decree, "If any man *love not our Lord Jesus Christ*, let him be anathema, maranatha" (1 Cor. xvi. 22). Heaven and earth shall echo forth a loud and eternal amen to this anathema.
3. No marvel that it should be the fixed and immutable purpose of the Divine mind that "at the name of Jesus every knee should bow of things in heaven and things on earth, and things under the earth, and that every tongue should confess that Jesus Christ is Lord, to the glory of God the Father" (Phil. ii. 10, 11). [Compare *Notes on Leviticus*, by C. H. M.]

Topic : TRESPASSERS AND THE TRESPASS PENALTY (Vv. 15, 16).

(*a*) Sin has many forms : breaks out into *trespasses.*
(*b*) The trespass offerings are manifold : meet with penalty and satisfaction all wrongs done.

I. THE DUES OF HEAVEN ARE WITHHELD : God's will is transgressed, His law infringed.

1. Creation's law makes *man God's sole possession.* No faculty of mind or frame, no power of intellect or thought, no talent of influence or time, no opportunity, no gift, no grace, is property of our own. All, then, should serve the cause of one Sovereign Lord. Reason should plan, and eyes should see, and hands should work, and feet should run, to do Him honour and augment His praise. Our every energy should fly abroad with morning light to gather fruits of glory for His name. Each night should prove that faith and love have laboured to advance His Kingdom upon earth.
2. Instead of this, *self mounts the great Creator's throne.* We rise, enter on the day, journey on, as if self-seeking were legitimate employ. Whether we rest or toil it is "unto ourselves." Is not this trespass? It robs our God; wastes His dues. It brands us as purloining from a Father's and a Benefactor's store.
3. *Judgment must follow upon such trespasses.* The fire must consume. **Life** must be laid on the altar. **Blood must flow. Trespass brings death.** No **soul** can sin and escape wrath.

II. MAN CAN MAKE NO TRUE AMENDS.

1. *Devotedness cannot repay the debt.* That is a vast conceit. If not one thought of any moment ever swerved from a pure effort for the Lord, it would but be *that moment's due.*

2. *Surplus of merit* there is none. That is a papist's dream. Our best acts are only increase of our debt. Hence all our works make bankruptcy more deep. When Justice calls to the white throne, the fairest reckoning is one huge debt. Who, then, can stay arrest?

III. THE TRESPASS OFFERING PRESENTS RELIEF.

1. *Jesus is satisfaction to the full.* Hence *death for sin* is not the whole of His grand work. That decks us with no merit; it fills no hand with fruits of righteousness. He pays then a *whole life's homage* to the law. He gives compliance to its largest rule. It asked for one undeviating course of love. Jesus was love without one straying step.

2. This pure fulfilment is *for those who are Christ's.* For such Christ wrought it; to their account he puts it. Unsullied righteousness by Him avails for believers.

Such is the Gospel which pervades this rite. It declares in emphatic terms that—

(1) *Trespass stains your life*, your heart, soul, and mind, every day, every hour.

(2) It warns that *trespass strengthens Satan's claims*, places a vast barrier between you and God.

(3) *Shows a full recovery.* Christ's cross and life are both pictured. You see Him dying to pay the trespass penalty: you see His righteousness supplying trespass wrongs.—Homiletically arranged from the Dean of Gloucester's *Christ is all.*

Topic: SACRILEGE (Vv. 14-19).

The former offerings may be regarded as both sin and trespass offerings; these in the closing verses of this fifth chapter, and in the opening seven verses of the sixth, are particularly and exclusively trespass offerings. Wrong has been done to God and man; and for that trespass contrition must be shown, an offering made, and restitution given. The trespass here indicated is sacrilege—mistake and misappropriation in the use of sacred things: a *culpable* trespass, whether done wittingly or unwittingly. From this rite we are taught—

I. THE JEALOUSY OF JEHOVAH FOR THE HONOUR OF HIS WORSHIP IN THE TABERNACLE.

By the Levitical ritual the people were taught that worship was only rendered acceptable when associated with Divinely prescribed sacrifices. There would be danger of the people becoming formal in their worship; that they would fall short of the full requirements of the ritual. The holy things here spoken of were the tithes, first-fruits, gifts, etc., demanded of the Lord. Such things were His before they were devoted as sacrifices, but they were doubly His when He claimed them as offerings unto Himself in connection with the worship of the tabernacle. To withhold would be to rob and wrong God; the honour of His worship would be insulted, His law outraged. Whether the sacrilege was committed knowingly or unknowingly it mattered not: the worship was marred, and for the trespass an offering must be presented. The trespasser was to bring a ram without blemish out of his flocks, and the priest was to make an atonement for him. Restitution was to accompany his contrition. He must make amends for the wrong he had done in the holy thing; and then his trespass was to be forgiven him.

Worship is a privilege we are permitted to enjoy, a duty we are bound to discharge. When we draw near to God to pay our vows and commune with Him in prayer and praise, we draw near to give to Him the glory that is *due* to His name. Under the gospel dispensation we have not to erect a material altar and present offerings such as the Israelites did under the law. No definitely prescribed portion of our substance is required of us, as was required under the old economy, but we are expected to give unto the Lord of our means in proportion as He hath prospered us. Yet, however liberal we may be, and conscientious in discharging our trust as stewards of the Kingdom, we constantly fall short of our duty as indicated in the gospel; we trespass, wittingly and unwittingly, and need constantly to seek, in confession and contrition, the pardon of our religious defalcations, and to make, in so far as we are able, some restitution to God, some humble amends, by bringing "forth fruits meet for repentance."

II. THE INFLUENCE THIS JEALOUSY WAS CALCULATED TO EXERT UPON THE WORSHIPPERS IN THE TABERNACLE.

Such scrupulous concern on the part of Jehovah about the sanctity of His service would teach the people to cultivate—

(1) *Sensitiveness of feeling.* It would be evident that indifference or carelessness would render the worshipper liable to a breach of trust, to make mistake or misapply the things devoted to the Lord.

(2) *Tenderness of conscience.* It would be easy for conscience to become perverted and hardened in the midst of so many privileges and in the abundance of blessings.

(3) *Scrupulousness of conduct.* The worshipper would find that merely good intentions would not suffice; contrition and confession would not be enough: there was to be implicit and complete obedience—nothing wanting of all that the Lord commanded. None of the sacrifice kept back, none of the holy things be employed or used for their own gain. If they did, even though they wist it not, they were guilty, and should bear their iniquity.

Watch that we trespass not against God as Achan did, and as Ananias and Sapphira did in the early Christian Church. Beware of trespassing through contempt, carelessness, or presumption. Aim to be suspiciously, as well as scrupulously, sensitive of doing wrong. Pray for pardon of inadvertent and unknown sins. God does not pass over, but forgives trespasses for the sake of our great Trespass Offering. This is the gospel order of blessing to the penitent: *repentance, reformation, restitution,* then *reconciliation* to God's favour, and *restoration* to His family, here and hereafter.—F. W. B.

OUTLINES ON VERSES, CHAPTER V. 14-19.

V. 16.—*Theme:* REPARATION. "And he shall *make amends* for *the harm that he hath done* in the holy thing," etc.

In forgiving sins God does not teach that transgression of His law is a trivial matter; for, atonement not only *expiates* but *makes amends.* Amends must be made, for—

I. SIN IS A WRONG DONE TO GOD.
II. SIN IS A WRONG DONE TO MAN.

Amends must be made by—
(1) *Appropriate contrition.*
(2) *Personal sacrifice.*
(3) *Unreserved consecration:*—evincing itself in a holy, useful, *Christly* life.—*F. W. B.*
[See Addenda, p. 71, *Reparation.*]

V. 17.—*Theme:* ERROR, THOUGH INADVERTENT, IS GUILTY. "If a soul sin, and commit things forbidden, though he wist it not, yet is he guilty, and shall bear his iniquity."

God required a trespass offering for the smallest error in relation to any of His ordinances, however unwittingly that error was committed.

Yet so multitudinous were the rights of the ceremonial law, that its requirements wore heavily and anxiously upon the lives and consciences of God's people. Righteousness by the law, therefore, became a weary, a fruitless hope.

By this very weariness and failure, Israel was led to crave and look for release from this "yoke," which was promised when Messiah brought in the "better covenant."

The gospel age promised release from the oppression of a ritual righteousness, and freedom for a more spiritual service.

I. A SOPHISTRY NEEDING CORRECTION.

This: that *intention constitutes the quality of an action*; whether conduct is criminal or not. But this declaration of "guilt," though in the action he "wist it not," testifies against a sweeping and all-inclusive application of that principle, viz., that intention qualifies action.

1. Ignorance may and does *extenuate* the guilt of an action. Knowledge deepens guilt (John ix. 41; xv. 22). Ignorance alleviates it (Luke xxiii 34; Acts iii. 17; 1 Tim. i. 13).

2. Yet ignorance cannot *excuse* guilt.

A man is not excused for breaking the laws of the land because he was ignorant of them. Nor is a servant's ignorance of his master's will, when he might and ought to have known it, a sufficient plea.

Nor is he innocent who trespasses, through error, against any ordinance of the Lord. And, if so in respect of *ceremonial* observances, much more so in relation to *moral* duties. Hence the curse stands against "*every* one that *continueth* not in *all* things written in the book of the law to do them" (Gal. iii. 10).

3. God Himself *refuses to condone* such ignorance. His Word declares that men "*perish* for lack of knowledge" (Hos. iv. 6); and that though "a people be of *no understanding*, He will not have mercy on them, and will show them no favour" (Isa. xxvii. 11). [Comp. *Simeon's* Sermons].

II. MAN'S UNCOMPUTED GUILT.

1. Reckon up our *remembered* sins. "They are more in number than the hairs of our head."

2. Add the sins *realised* at the time but *now forgotten*. Memory lets slip multitudinous trespasses.

3. Yet what can represent the number of our *unrecognised* sins, done in ignorance, done in error?

4. *Deviations and defects* also, which God's eye alone detected, and which we too self-indulgently condoned.

Eliphaz charges the inquiry on Job, and on us, "Is not thy wickedness *great*, and thine iniquities *infinite*?" (Job xxii. 5).

God's Word declares, "There is not a just man upon earth that doeth good and sinneth not" (Eccles. vii. 20), that "in many things we all offend" (Jas. iii. 2; Prov. xxiv. 16).

In estimating our guiltiness we fail: "Who can understand his *errors*?" (Psa. xix. 12).

To *extenuate guilt* by saying "*It is an error*" (Eccles. v. 6), is to add to sin: rather let us humble ourselves in shame before God.

III. VAST VIRTUE NEEDED IN ATONEMENT.

1. Under the ceremonial arrangements for expiation, how *manifold and minute and numerous* were the regulations and provisions necessary to make atonement for sin! "Without shedding of blood there was no remission." And to that were added costly offerings and exacting observances.

2. When all sin had to be expiated by Christ's *one offering, what value it must needs possess!* Yet "by *one* offering" the Saviour "purged our sins."

(*a*) It summons us to *faith*. "Look unto Me and be ye saved." "Behold the Lamb of God which taketh away the sin of the world."

(*b*) It incites us to *grateful adoration*. "Unto Him that loved us and *washed us from our sin* in His own blood," etc. (Rev. i. 5, 6).

(*c*) It assures us of *perfect redemption*. "There remaineth no more offering for sin," for "the blood of Jesus Christ, God's Son, cleanseth us from all sin" (1 John i. 7). [See Addenda, p. 71, *Redemption*].

ILLUSTRATIVE ADDENDA TO CHAPTER V.

TAKING OATHS.

The judicial oaths taken in courts of justice are administered variously: "The usual practice in England and Ireland is, for the witness, after hearing the oath repeated by the officer of the court, to kiss the four gospels by way of assent: and in Scotland, the witness repeats similar words after the judge, standing and holding up his right hand, 'swearing by Almighty God, as he shall answer to God at the great day of judgment,' but without kissing the book. Jews are sworn on the Pentateuch, keeping on their hats, and the oath ends with the words, 'So help you, Jehovah.' A Mohammedan is sworn on the Koran. A Chinese witness has been sworn by kneeling and breaking a china saucer against the witness-box. Thus, the mere form of taking the oath is immaterial; the witness is allowed to take it in whatever form he considers most binding upon his own conscience —the essential thing being, however, that the witness acknowledge some binding effect derived from his belief in a God and a future state.... The objections of Quakers, Moravians, and Separatists to taking an oath have long been respected as not being fundamentally at variance with a due sense of religious feeling, and hence they have been allowed to make an affirmation instead of taking the oath. In 1854 another concession was made to those who, not being Quakers, yet refuse to take the oath for sincere conscientious motives; and these are now also allowed to affirm instead of to swear. But the law remains as before, that atheists and persons who admit that they have no religious belief whatever, are excluded from giving evidence in courts of justice."—*Chamber's Ency.*

"UNLAWFUL OATHS generally mean oaths taken by members of secret and illegal societies of a treasonable description: and statutes long ago were passed to inflict penalties on all who took or administered such oaths."—*Ibid*.

PROFANE OATHS.—Louis the French king was taken prisoner by Meletisaka the Sultan and conditions of peace being concluded between them, for more assurance thereof the Sultan offered to swear, " if he failed in performance of anything, to *renounce his Mohammed*," requiring likewise of the king to swear, if he failed in anything he had promised, to *deny his Christ to be God:* which profane oath the king detesting, and wishing rather to die than to give the same, the Sultan, wondering at his constancy, took his word without an oath at all, and so published the league.

As, on the other side, King John of England, being overlaid in his barons' wars, when he sent ambassadors to the monarch of Morocco for aid, offered to swear fealty to him and to *receive the law of Mohammed;* and thereby the monarch grew into such dislike of the king that ever after he abhorred the mention of him.—*Trapp*.

" It is a great sin to swear unto a sin ;
But greater sin to keep a sinful oath."
Henry VI., II. v. 1.

SINCERE OATHS.
" His words are bonds, his oaths are oracles ;
His love sincere, his thoughts immaculate ;
His heart as far from fraud as heaven from earth."—*Two Gentlemen of Verona*, II. 7.

" An oath, an oath, I have an oath in heaven :
Shall I lay perjury upon my soul ?
No, not for Venice."
Merchant of Venice, IV. 1.

" Tis not the many oaths that make the truth :
But the plain single vow, that is vow'd true."
All's well that ends well, IV. 2.

" Unheedful vows may heedfully be broken."
Shakespeare.

INDIFFERENCE.—Idle swimmers who go floating carelessly down the stream, reckless of the nearing peril until they get beyond reach of the bank.

" I asked a young man, ' Are you in anxiety about yourself and your salvation ? ' He replied, ' I have little concern or feeling on the subject.'

" ' Are you not trying to do what God commands you as well as you are able, and with such light as you have ? '

" ' Oh no; it would seem absurd for one who feels so little as I do to attempt any religious duty ! '

" ' Yet, you admit that God does require of you repentance, and faith, and worship, and a holy life ; do you not? '

" ' Yes, I admit all this, but do not feel interested, or troubled, or concerned, respecting it.'

" ' What would you advise a customer to do who had contracted a debt with you, who admits his debt, and that he ought to pay it, but says he knows it all, yet is so void of interest or feeling about it ? '

" In an instant he replied, ' I would advise him to *pay it, not waiting for feeling.*' "

REDEMPTION.
" Heavenly powers where shall we find such love ?
Which of ye will be mortal to redeem
Man's mortal crime ; and just th' unjust to save ? " *Paradise Lost, III.* 213.

" The Cross,
There, and there only (tho' the deist rave,
And atheist, if earth bears so base a slave),
There, and there only, is the power to save."
COWPER, *Progress of Error*, 613.

" Why, all the souls that were, were forfeit once;
And he that might the vantage best have took
Found out the remedy."
Measure for Measure, II. 2.

REPARATION.
" Restore to God His due, in tithe and time;
A tithe purloined cankers the whole estate."
G. HERBERT, *The Temple*.

" God is much displeased
That you take with unthankfulness His doing :
In common worldly things 'tis called ungrateful,
With dull unwillingness to repay a debt
Which with a bounteous hand was kindly lent ;
Much more to be thus opposite with heaven :
For it requires the royal debt it lent you."
Richard III., II. 2.

CHAPTER VI.

Trespass Offerings: and Priestly Consecration Offerings.

SUGGESTIVE READINGS.

V. 2.—Trespass against the Lord and lie unto his neighbour. Wrong done to man is done to God. To deceive and defraud our neighbour is an insult to Jehovah. To harm man is to inflict injury on God; as to touch His people is to "touch the apple of His eye"; and as Saul's persecution of the saints was persecution of Christ Himself (Acts ix. 5). Take heed, lest acts of injustice to others so affect heaven as to evoke remonstrance and rebuke.

Vv. 2, 3.—Violence, or hath deceived, or sweareth falsely. Evil is fruitful in forms of development. Two distinct classes of wrong are here indicated: embezzlement of things placed confidingly by a neighbour in his hand, "*that which was delivered him to keep, or in fellowship*" [Lit. "something placed in his hand," a deposit]; and now, plunder and fraud, a neighbour's property being possessed with violence and seizure. When Adam revolted from obedience to God it introduced a fraudulent principle into human life which soon wrought wrong between man and man. He who can sin against the Lord will be found equally capable of sinning against man. Dishonesty heavenward is likely to be confirmed by dishonesty in transaction with neighbours. There is no guarantee of integrity where there is impiety. *Righteousness* before God means *rightness* towards man.

V. 5.—Restore it in the principal. Reparation should follow repentance, and precede propitiation. First, set right the evil done to your neighbour, then come to the Lord for acceptance. It is an easy and delusive repentance of sin—sin done to men on every hand, sin continued for years, sin working sorrow in homes and in social circles—if the penitent may leave unremedied all this woful wrong among men, and free himself from further concern by simply on his knees lamenting all before God. No! if convinced of guilt, go and do right where your selfishness, and greed, and fraudulence have wrought havoc and misery; wipe out the blots of crime on human pathways, then come for appeasement and acceptance to the Lord. "Bring forth fruit meet for repentance" (Matt. iii. 7-10).

Add a fifth part more. Let there be an overflow of generosity to compensate for former selfishness. And let Christian life be distinguished by a liberal diffusion of your possessions, in order both to lessen the cares of neighbours and attest the reality of your conversion. "Freely ye have received, freely give."

V. 6.—Bring his trespass offering. Zacchæus might pledge himself "if he had taken anything from any man by false accusation to *restore him fourfold*"; but to lavish reparation on man could not obliterate the guilt of his actions as concerns the law and holiness of God. There must be atonement. Good deeds and generous benefactions cannot expunge guiltiness of soul. And besides the actual trespasses, which reparation may in part requite, there remains the criminality of conscience, the impurity of soul, the impiety towards God. And "it is *blood* that maketh atonement for the *soul*."

Vv. 8-13.—The burnt offering, because of the burning upon the altar, etc. Every evening a lamb was sacrificed (Exod. xxix. 38), and these directions refer to the ritual; the burning was to be "*all night until the morning.*" And the altar fire was ceaselessly to be maintained; symbolic of (1) *the perpetual atonement needed* by men; (2) *the continuous acceptance of worship by God*: (3) the *uninterrupted relationship of Jehovah with Israel.* In this Christian epoch we maintain no ceaseless fire, but we enjoy a ceaseless atonement, which assures us of undoubted acceptance and unbroken fellowship with God. Instead of the daily feeding of the altar fire with wood, we may devote afresh daily our love and obedience, for these should "*never go out*" in Christian lives.

Vv. 14-18.—The meat offering This section adds directions for the priests, supplementing the regulation given in chap. ii. 1-3.

V. 18.—**Every one that toucheth them shall be holy.** Either this contact with holy things *claimed* that the person so "touched" should be set apart for God, or the contact *communicated* a sanctity which henceforth secured his consecration. Derived sanctity: it is a law in continuous operation: many souls having been drawn to Christ through the influence of such contact with "holy *things*" as *e.g.* the Bible, the Sanctuary, etc.; or with holy *persons*, as godly parents, Christian friends, ministers of the Lord Jesus. Grace goes forth from them, as virtue went out from Jesus to heal. Seek such contact, if yet in your sins. Send out such sanctifying energy, if the sacred grace is in you.

Vv. 19-23.—*Consecration offerings for the priest* "**in the day when he is anointed**" With glad thank offerings the priest was to seal his dedication to the sacerdotal office. No tone or aspect of despondency would be proper to such an incident. It was to high privilege and honour the young priest was set apart: entire separation for the Divine service. And to what joyous life can we aspire comparable to this? "Yield yourselves unto God as those that are alive from the dead." The entrance upon a sacred life is a blissful incident, and should be marked with festive dedications.

Vv. 24-30.—**The sin offering killed before the Lord.** Supplementary directions are supplied to chap. iv. 1-5. So specially sacred was the blood of the sin offering that, if perchance a spray of the blood of the victim spurted out upon the priest's garments, the stain must be dealt with as of solemn consequence, and even the vessel in which the stained garment was washed (vv. 27, 28). Thus specific were Jehovah's regulations that the atoning blood might not be profaned. How much more should "the *precious* blood of Christ" be cherished as "a holy thing," and guarded from profanation! (Heb. x. 29). From within that ancient temple a voice of appeal comes to us to this day that we solemnly regard the blood of atonement, and so value it that we prize its sanctifying virtue and honour its efficacy by a blameless life.

SECTIONAL HOMILIES, CHAPTER VI. 1-12.

Topic: DISTINCTIONS BETWEEN TRESPASSES AGAINST GOD AND AGAINST MEN.
(Connect Chap. v. 15-19 with vi. 1-7.)

The trespasses in ch. v. relate to misconduct "in the holy things of the Lord"; the trespasses in ch. vi. refer to misdeeds in the common transactions and relations of life.

Distinction A: Note that the expression, "if a soul *sin through ignorance*," which occurs in the former, is omitted in the latter. The reason for this is obvious—

I. The claims which stand connected with "the holy things of the Lord" must *pass infinitely* BEYOND THE REACH OF THE MOST ELEVATED HUMAN SENSIBILITY. Those claims may be continually interfered with, continually trespassed upon, and the trespassers be *not aware* of the fact.

1. *Man's conscience can never be the regulator in the sanctuary of God.* How often may we have wronged God "in His holy things" without ever taking a note of it in the tablet of conscience, yea, without having the competency to detect it! [See Mal. iii. 8.]

2. *God's holiness alone must fix the standard* when *God's rights* are in question. That higher light must shine on man's conscience, therefore, to correct his "ignorance" of the laws which governed the sanctuary.

II. On the other hand, the HUMAN CONSCIENCE CAN READILY GRASP THE FULL AMOUNT OF THE HUMAN CLAIM, and can readily take cognizance of any interference with such claim.

1. When *man's rights* are in question, *conscience acts as a prompt and efficient standard.* The wrong which the human eye can see and the human heart feel, the human conscience can judge. A man could not, "through ignorance," tell a lie, swear falsely, act violently, deceive his neighbour, or find a lost thing and deny it. These were all plain and palpable acts, lying within the range of the most sluggish sensibility.

2. "Ignorance" is, therefore, *not allowed as qualifying and condoning men's conduct* in the common affairs of life.

How blessed it is to know that the precious blood of Christ has settled all questions with respect to God or man, our sins of ignorance or our known sins! Here lies the deep and settled foundation of the believer's peace. The Cross has divinely met *all*.

Distinction B: Note that when it was a question of trespass "in the holy things of the Lord," the unblemished sacrifice was *first* introduced, and *afterward* "the principal" and "the fifth." This order was *reversed* when it was a question of the common affairs of life. [Compare ch. v. 15, 16, with ch. vi. 4-7.] The reason of this is equally obvious—

I. When the *Divine rights were infringed* the BLOOD OF ATONEMENT *was the prominent requirement.*

If an Israelite had, by an act of trespass, deranged his relation *with Jehovah,* the order was *sacrifice* and restitution.

II. When *human rights* were infringed, RESTITUTION *would naturally assume the leading place* in the mind.

If an Israelite, by an act of trespass, had deranged his relation *with his neighbour,* the order was *restitution* and then sacrifice.

1. To *wrong a fellow-man interferes with communion with God.* And that communion can only be restored on the ground of atonement. Mere restitution would not avail. It might satisfy the injured man, but could form no basis of restored communion with God. To restore "the principal" and add "the fifth" would still leave the *sin* remaining; and "without shedding of blood is no remission."

2. To *set right the wrong to the injured man, restitution is efficacious.* "If thou bring thy gift to the altar, and there remember that thy brother hast aught against thee, leave there thy gift before the altar and go thy way; first be reconciled to thy brother, and then come and offer thy gift" (Matt. v. 23, 24).

The claims which arise out of our human relations must not be disregarded. They must ever get their proper place in the heart. [Compare *C. H. M.*]

Topic: HARM DONE BY TRESPASS (Vv. 2-4).

In the trespass *against* "*the Lord,*" considered in ch. v., there was specific declaration as to "the *harm* done" by that trespass; and for that "harm" the trespasser had to "make amends" (ch. v. 15, 16). In this chapter trespasses *against a* "*neighbour*" are under consideration, and these trespasses are explained as being deeds of actual wrong. Not imaginary or sentimental trespasses, but *acts.* Which statement shows how truly the greatest enemy of mankind is man. Or, as *Robert Burns* declares it:

> " Man's inhumanity to man
> Makes countless thousands mourn."

In the same vein writes *Young*, in his " Night Thoughts":

> " *Inhumanity* is caught from *man*,
> From smiling man."

[See Addenda, p. 86, *Injury.*]

I. THE INJURY WROUGHT BY TRESPASS.

Ample terms are employed here to describe the forms of wrong-doing. We read of " *violently taking*," " *deceitfully getting*," and " *swearing falsely about that which is found.*"

1. *Trespass defined.* In every act of trespass *practical* and *positive wrong* was done; there was an *act of evil* by which another was injured. " Trespass " differed from "sin" in this: *sin* marked what man *was in himself, trespass* described what man *had done.* Deeds of wrong, therefore, are here under consideration; actual wrong and robbery.

2. *Trespass conditioned.* It might be wrought " *in ignorance* " (ch. v. 15, 17, 19) when done against " the Lord"; and it is implied even in these acts of wrong against man that the trespasser did not deliberately, and "of malice aforethought" do these acts, but under impulse or through connivance, or simply from inattention. For it comes to be recognised as trespass *afterwards*, not at the time of the act. God has harsher names and heavier judgments for wrong-doing wrought in full consciousness and full light. Still, recognised or unrecognised, it is "trespass."

3. *Trespass weighed.* Neither our conscience, nor our knowledge, nor our ability are allowed to be the standard by which our actions are measured, weighed, judged; but *God's truth.* " Though he *wist it not*, yet is he *guilty; * he hath certainly *trespassed against the Lord*" (ch v. 17-19). Man's judgment of his own acts is not to be trusted. If a man's conscience or his light were the standard, every man would weigh his conduct by a different rule; there would be no absolute standard of right and wrong. Evil then would consist, not in the act itself, but in man's estimate or perception thereof. Sin has blinded our perceptions to the " sinfulness of sin "; but that does not alter the fact. God measures and weighs our trespasses by His Word.

4. *Trespass recognised.* Light comes in at last, and the wrong-doer discovers that he has committed a trespass. " *When he knoweth of it* " (chap. v. 4); and in due course transgression makes itself known to the transgressor. Light shines in the darkness, and its beams fall about every life, and will ultimately " bring to light the hidden things of darkness." Conscience in man will awake, and memory will convict the sinner of his long-forgotten sin.

> "Conscience . . mutinies in a man's bosom;
> It fills one full of obstacles."—*Shakespeare.*

> " There is no future pang
> Can deal that justice on the self-condemned
> He deals on his own soul."—*Byron.*

> " Conscience is harder than our enemies,
> Knows more, accuses with more nicety."—*George Eliot.*

> " Yet still there whispers the small voice within,
> Heard thro' gain's silence, and o'er glory's din;
> Whatever creed be taught or land be trod,
> Man's conscience is the oracle of God."—*Byron.*

II. THE REPARATION MADE FOR TRESPASS.

When the trespass was realised, it had to be *expiated by sacrifice*, and *amends had to be made* to the injured neighbour.

1. *Trespass atoned.* Blessed be God (whose *voice within us*, whose *inspired Word*, whose *convincing Spirit* brings home to us our trespass), that His grace has "found a Ransom." "He shall bring his *trespass offering* unto the Lord," etc. (v. 6). He that sees Jesus in the trespass offering, sees trespass expiated, annihilated; for Christ has assumed its guiltiness, borne its judgment, paid its penalty. Not alone was "His soul made an offering for *sin*," but "He was wounded for our *transgressions*" (Isa. liii. 5-10).

2. *Trespass compensated.* For the wrongs the trespasser has done to his neighbour *restitution* must be made: "He shall even restore it in the principal" (v. 5). Our Lord has made full reparation for the wrong we had done—to God and man; *satisfying God* by His own merits given for our demerits, and *blessing man* by ensuring to him richer advantages than those which sin forfeited.

Wherefore this *reparation* after *expiation?* Thus: for a victim merely to die would leave the injured neighbour a loser still. Though the trespasser were punished, the injury would remain. The death of the wrong-doer would not restore defrauded rights. Yet until this was done satisfaction could not be regarded as perfect; nor could justice be said to have righted the wrong. Therefore, punishment fell upon the victim, and the wrong was also repaired. So that in the atonement for trespass we find—

1. *Judgment inflicted.* The victim's life is forfeited, as was the sinner's for his sin. And Christ gave His life as man's substituted victim.

2. *Injury compensated.* The evil had to be remedied. Having wrought evil in time past of our lives (comp. Ephes. ii. 2, 3), we, saved by Christ Jesus, now give ourselves to earnest effort to repair the wrong done; to *glorify God*, whom we had wronged by disobedience and dishonour; to *benefit men*, whom we had harmed by sinful influence and example. To these are to be added:

3. *Dues exceeded.* More than the original loss had to be repaid; the wrong more than remedied. A "*fifth part more*" had to be "added thereto." For there was in *Christ's obedience and virtue* a surplus, an excess of merit *presented to God*, passing beyond man's demerit. And in *Christian devotedness and ministry* there are blessings brought *to men by man* far more sacred, and tender, and consolatory, and helpful, which more than outweigh all the injury done to men by man. "Let him know that he which converteth the sinner from the error of his way, shall save a soul from death, and shall *hide a multitude of sins*" (Jas. v. 20). [See Addenda p. 87, *Faithlessness.*]

Topic: RESTITUTION MADE FOR WRONG (Vv. 4, 5).

Besides the original due was added a "fifth." Consider—

i. *How this was fulfilled for us in Christ.* At His hands God received *more* than all whereof man had robbed Him.

ii. *The consequence of this to those "in Christ."* They are "complete in Him" through whom we have received the atonement.

But the practical bearing of that transaction commands attention. Enquire in what way, and how far, this view of *Christ's act of reparation* should prove an *incentive* and an *example* to us.

I. RESTITUTION MADE *by those who are in fellowship with Christ.*

By standing in behalf of man Christ makes full restitution for man's wrong and trespass; "not with corruptible things, as silver and gold" (1 Pet i. 18, 19); but by the value of His own offering and obedience He repays our trespasses.

1. In this sense, of satisfying God for our trespasses, we *can make no restitution.*

If Christ has not made it we are lost. The rest of our lives, if wholly spent for God, could never atone for our acts of trespass. Each day would bring its own proper claim. Works of supererogation, therefore, we could have none.

2. Yet there is a sense in which the soul in fellowship with Christ *will make restitution*. Not, indeed, to win acceptance, but as showing how, according to his measure, through the Spirit, he sympathises with Christ. As he has, in days past, "as the servant of sin," robbed God and man of their rights, so now, as " having been made free from sin," he will "become the servant of righteousness" (Rom. vi. 22).

II. AMENDS SUPERADDED *to the restitution offered*.

In consequence of trespass, against God or man, more than their *original claim* was due to them.

1. Under the law, the claim on man *was righteousness*. If man dealt justly toward God and man nothing further could be claimed of him. But it became different when he had trespassed. Then, by God's appointment—

2. *Right was no longer the measure of man's debt*. The trespasser now is in no condition to attempt to deal out righteousness, either to God or man. The fact of our having become trespassers—

(1) Gives *God a claim upon us* which is *not the bare claim of right*. Above and beyond this, the trespasser is a debtor. He requires more than the righteousness which sinless souls could have rendered; additional "amends" have to be made; something more than an equivalent for man's sin; this—Christ's bounteous virtues; yea, and also—that we *love* Him for His grace to us.

The law did not ask *love;* it asked of man rectitude! But God now asks **more than** rectitude; He desires and expects *gratitude, affection, consecration*.

> " For souls redeemed, for sins forgiven,
> For means of grace, for hopes of heaven,
> Father, what can to Thee be given,
> Who givest all?"

(2) *Calls us to unselfish devotion to others*. As the recipients of *grace* we are called to exhibit grace in all our transactions with others. Not dealing out justice to men, but generosity, and kindness, and unselfishness. " Ye have heard that it hath been said, an eye for an eye; but I say unto you, *resist not evil:* do good to them that hate you; pray for them that despitefully use you" (Matt. v. 38-44).

"And when ye stand praying, *forgive* if ye have ought *against* any; that your Father also in heaven may forgive *you* your *trespasses*. But if you do not forgive, neither will your heavenly Father forgive you your trespasses " (Mark xi. 25, 26). [Comp. also Luke vi. 32-35.]

Yet how far is this principle of *grace exceeding justice* the rule of Christian lives? If we are *just*, how little concern have we as to being *gracious* in our dealings with fellow-men! We go to law (1 Cor. vi. 1-7); we claim our rights, little thinking of the added " fifth " of the trespass offering.

Grace, not right, must be the law, as it is the *hope*, of the trespasser. [Comp. *Jukes on the Offerings*.]

OUTLINES ON VERSES OF CHAPTER VI. 1-7.

V. 2. *Theme:* THE DUTY OF HONESTY.

History and civilisation began with promulgation of law from Sinai, which would regulate man's conduct towards God and his neighbour. Israel in wilderness, not only a *church*, but *commonwealth;* hence, laws to govern civil and social relationships, as well as religious life. Society could not exist without respect to rights of property, and restraint of liberty. Israel in wilderness without laws would have been a horde of savages, where only the strongest would have survived. The Lord's freemen were not to be out-laws and freebooters, but obedient servants of the most High. He would dwell with them, they were to dwell in peace with each other, and hold each other in mutual esteem. Every breach of trust, every species of dishonesty, strictly prohibited; when committed, amends to be made, and forgiveness sought. From the trespass offering we learn—

I. THAT PROPERTY—THOUGH NOT INTEGRALLY A HUMAN RIGHT—MAY BE LAWFULLY POSSESSED BY MAN.

Though the earth is the Lord's and the fulness thereof, yet He hath given it to the children of men. Though a man absolutely possesses nothing but *what he is*, he may acquire the right to call worldly possessions lawfully his own. No community of goods among Israelites. Communism is Utopian; infringement upon the due interests of others, and therefore robbery. As trustees and stewards, in holding and using possessions, we must have respect (*a*) *to the good of others*, and (*b*) *the claims of God*.

II. THAT PROPERTY UNLAWFULLY POSSESSED, IS NOT ONLY A CRIME AGAINST MAN, BUT ALSO A SIN AGAINST GOD.

Every breach of trust, dishonest act, or fraudulent transaction, displeased Jehovah, and required atonement at the hands of the offender. Guilt was contracted when the law was dishonoured, and no circumstances were to be pleaded *in extenuation of the guilt* or *in mitigation of the sacrifice demanded*. The principle of this law has never been repealed; it is *morally*, as well as legally, criminal, to obtain property of any sort by any wrong means, either from individuals or societies. Revealed religion lies at the basis of all *political, commercial* and *social* morality. —F.W.B.

V. 2. *Theme:* BREACH OF CONFIDENCE. "Lie unto his neighbour, or hath *deceived his neighbour*."

I. Note some EXAMPLES OF THIS SIN.
1. Injury to. or loss of, borrowed goods. [See Kings vi. 5.]
2. Retaining a found article, knowing, not seeking, the owner.
3 Obtaining property under false pretences.

II. EFFECTS OF THIS SIN.
1. Diminishes the trust men should have in each other.
2 Lessens the stock of general kindness. [See Matt. v. 42.]
3. Fosters a spirit of dishonesty.

III THE DIVINE VIEW OF THIS SIN.
1. Reparation to be made to man.
2. Confession and atonement to be made to God.—Rev. J. Comper Gray, *Biblical Museum*.

Theme: DEPOSITING PROPERTY.

I. A NEIGHBOURLY CONVENIENCE. To deposit valuable property with a neighbour was. and still is, a common practice in the East, where no establishments exist for the storing of private treasure.
1. How *helpful a neighbour* may become.
2. How *grand is this confidence* in another.
3. How *mutually dependent we are* one upon another.
4. How *honourable we should be* in all transactions.
5. How *jealously we should strive to merit implicit trust*. [See Addenda, p. 86, *Injury*.]

II. A HAZARDOUS TRANSACTION.
1. *Man's reliableness is sorely discredited* by continuous breaches of faith.
2 *Treasure becomes often a serious anxiety* to its possessor.
3. *No security can be guaranteed* in any earthly confidence. [See Addenda, p. 87, *Faithlessness*.]

III. A DOUBTFUL ALTERNATIVE.

There was another method adopted, when a man was about to journey, if he could not trust his neighbour: he would conceal his treasures under ground.

1. *What light this throws on Scripture phraseology*.

The Hebrew word for treasure denotes *hidden*: and explains such phrases as "*hidden riches of secret places*" (Isa., xlv. 3) and "search for her *hid treasure*" (Prov. ii. 4; Job iii. 24).

2. *What light this throws on Christ's parables*.

There was danger of a man *forgetting the spot* where he had long ago buried his treasure. Hence our Lord's language concerning "treasure hid in the field" and "*searching*" "*digging*" to find it.

IV. A SPIRITUAL ANALOGY.

This committing treasure to a neighbour suggests Paul's imagery of

The soul committed to Christ: "I know whom I *have trusted* and am persuaded that He is able to *keep that which I have committed unto him* against that day" (2 Tim. i. 12). [See also v. 14 and Tim, vi. 20].
1. Christ is faithful to our trust.
2. We *cannot safely risk our souls in other keeping*.

V. 5. *Theme:* THE BENEFICENCE OF A REDEEMED LIFE.

The same law in reference to "the fifth part" obtained in the case of a trespass *against a man*, as in a trespass against the Lord. The application of this regulation to the work of Christ indicates that man, as well as God, is a positive gainer by the Cross. The believer can say, as he gazes upon that Cross, "However I have been wronged, trespassed against, deceived, whatever ills have been done to me, *I am a gainer by the Cross*. I have not merely received back all that was lost, but much more beside."

Thus, whether we think of the injured or the injurer, we are equally struck with the glorious triumphs of redemption, and the mighty practical results which flow from that gospel, which fills the soul with the happy assurance that "all trepasses" are "forgiven," and that the root from whence those trespasses have sprung has been judged.

I. A TRESPASSER IS TRANSFORMED INTO A BENEFACTOR *by the law of Divine grace*.

He carries blessings—
1. *Into the scenes* which have been the

witness of a man's sins, his trespasses, and his injurious ways.

2. *Among persons who have suffered* in consequence of his evil doings, his deceits, and his transgressions.

3. *The renewing grace of God having worked in him*, he is sent back to those *scenes* and among those sufferers furnished with grace, in order that he should—

4. Not only *repair the wrongs*, but to allow the full tide *of practical benevolence* to flow forth in all his ways, yea, to "love his enemies, and do good to them that hate him, and to pray for them that despitefully use and persecute him." Such are the rich, rare, and refreshing fruits of the grace of God that act in connection with our great Trespass Offering.

II. A GRACIOUS LIFE WILL ATTEST ITSELF IN GENEROUS CONDUCT.

Sinfulness and selfishness can have no licence in a redeemed life. Instead of the caviller against godliness being able to show that God's people allow sin "that grace may abound," sin is cut up by the roots; the sinner is turned from a curse into a blessing, from a moral plague into a channel of Divine mercy, from an emissary of Satan into a messenger of God, from a child of darkness into a son of the light, from a self-indulgent pleasure-seeker into a self-denying lover of God, from a slave of vile lusts into a willing-hearted servant of Christ, from a narrow-hearted miser into a benevolent minister to the needs of his fellow-men. The thief, the defrauder, is transformed into a generous donor; giving the "fifth" of his possessions.

2. *Practical righteousness is the crowning witness of that life whose sin is expiated and forgiven.* Away, then, with the oft repeated taunts, "Are we to do nothing?" "According to this gospel we may live as we list!" They who utter such language know not what grace means: have never felt its sanctifying and elevating influences. They forget that, while the blood of the trespass offering cleanses the conscience, the law of the offering sends the trespasser back to him whom he has wronged with "the principal" and "the fifth" in his hand. Noble testimony, this, both to the grace and righteousness of the God of Israel!

If the *conscience* has been set to rights, by the *blood* of the Cross, in reference to the claims of God, the *conduct* also must be set to rights by the *holiness* of the Cross in reference to the claims of practical righteousness. This hallowed union will never be dissolved by any mind which is governed by pure gospel morality. "He that doth not righteousness is not of God" (1 John iii 10).

III. DIVINE GRACE IS DISHONOURED *in those whose conduct and character exhibit not the fair traces* OF PRACTICAL HOLINESS.

1. God has given us in His Word those evidences by which *we can discern those that belong to Him.* "The Lord knoweth them that are His; and let every one that nameth the name of Christ depart from iniquity" (2 Tim. iii. 19).

(*a*) We *have no right to suppose that an evil-doer belongs to God.* The holy instincts of the Divine nature are shocked by such a thought. Difficulty is felt in accounting for evil practices in those who are regarded as Christians. But the Word of God settles the matter clearly and authoritatively :—" In this the children of God are manifest, and the children of the devil : whoever doeth not righteousness is not of God," etc. (1 John iii. 9, 10).

(*b*) *Laxity and self-indulgence*, specially the perils of our times, must be severely and sternly shunned.

2. *An accommodating, easy profession of Christianity is rebuked* by this law of the trespass offering. Every genuine Christian is called upon to give a clear testimony, a testimony resulting from the steady exhibition of "the fruits of righteousness which are by Jesus Christ unto the glory and praise of God." Most deplorable is it to see such faulty manifestation abroad of the *love and holiness* which should distinguish Christian conduct.

Let us rebuke, by *a life of self-denial and genuine benevolence*, the culpable inactivity of professors. Christian life should abound in large and generous ministries. [Comp. C. H. M. on *Leviticus.*]

V. 6, 7. *Theme:* THE SIN OF DISHONESTY.

In the natural government of the world God has made the laws of nature on the side of goodness and virtue ; and in the moral government of the universe the Divine favour is on the side of honesty, integrity and righteousness. The enactments of Sinai, and those from the door of the tabernacle, were a transcript of the holiness of the Divine character, fixing approval upon the right, and stigma upon the wrong. Men were to do to others as they would others should do to them, remembering that the eye of the Lord was upon them. Thus Israel was taught—

I. THAT THE SIN OF DISHONESTY INCURS THE JUST INDIGNATION OF HEAVEN.

Moses and others, who administered the laws among the people, would feel the sacredness and responsibility of their office, in that they were Jehovah's deputies, and punished offenders in His name. Earthly rulers and governments should—

(*a*) *Base their statutes upon Divine enactments ;* and

(*b*) *Seek the reformation, as well as punishment, of the offender.*

The appointed offering, and the appearance of the trespassers before the Lord, denoted that sin had been committed, that guilt had been incurred. All sin is hateful in the eyes of Him with whom we have to do.

II. THAT THE SIN OF DISHONESTY MAY NEVERTHELESS BE FORGIVEN.

Specific directions were given respecting the offering required, that the offerer might have no doubt as to the way of forgiveness. Obedience would show that the trespasser—

(*a*) *Acknowledged his offence ;*

(*b*) *Was sorry for it ;*

(c) *Was ready to make amends;*
(d) *Desired absolution.*

The root and essence of sin is that *it is committed against God;* hence, only God can forgive it. In the gospel the law is not destroyed, but fulfilled; For Christ, our Sin, or Trespass Offering, procures complete and free pardon for all sin. Fools make a mock at the sin offering, but with the righteous it is in esteem.—F. W. B.

SECTIONAL HOMILIES CHAP. VI. 8-13.

THE LAW OF THE BURNT OFFERING (resumed).

Topic.—DIGNITY LINKED TO DUTY (Vv. 8-12).

With the eighth verse of this chapter we traverse ground already gone over. Directions having been given for the institution of the burnt offering, Aaron and his sons now receive particulars as to their parts in the service. The burnt offering was the first and most important of all the ordinary oblations, pointing as it did to *unreserved* personal consecration, and *universal Divine redemption.* In the directions given to Aaron and his sons, we learn—

I. HOW APPARENTLY UNDIGNIFIED DUTIES MAY BE ASSOCIATED WITH THE MOST EXALTED SERVICE.

The Divine work to which the priests were appointed would distinguish them from the common people; ensure them reverent recognition; be their passports to social, as well as sacred eminence. Their spotless vestments were a symbol of their official purity. How undignified it would *seem* for the priest to be busy removing the ashes of the consumed sacrifice with his own hands to a clean place without the camp. But no work, however lowly, if done for God and at His command, can bring real degradation. Men always go up when they go to duty. David felt he would "rather be a door-keeper in the house of the Lord than," etc. The priests were as great and dignified when removing the ashes of the offering as when they ascended to their loftiest sacerdotal duties. Let us think nothing mean or low that we can do in the service of our risen and loving Lord.

II. HOW THE ASSOCIATION OF LOWLY DUTIES WITH EXALTED SERVICE MAY BE A SALUTARY DISCIPLINE TO THE WORSHIPPER.

That the reasons for the sacrifices, and the laws relating to them, were only partially given; and that in matters of precision and detail so much seemed mysterious and even unnecessary, would—

(a) *Test the faith,* (b) *quicken vigilance,* (c) *stimulate energy,* and (d) *prepare for higher and more spiritual service.* He that is faithful in the least will be in that which is greatest. Fidelity in what the world may deem small and meaningless will receive the recognition of heaven, and promotion to higher and holier service.—*F. W. Brown.*

OUTLINES ON VERSES, CHAPTER VI. 8-13.

V. 9. *Theme:* SACRED ATTIRE.

These directions concerning offering the burnt sacrifice relate to the priests; and denote the divinely acceptable method of their ministrations. In all these specific ceremonial regulations there lay couched important spiritual suggestions.

I. IN HOLY ATTIRE *they serve at the altar.*

1. Suggestive of *the essential holiness of Christ.* By His grace all offerings were rendered a sweet savour to God.

2. Symbolic of *their derived purity and righteousness.* [Comp. Exod. xxviii. 40-43 with Psa. cxxxii. 9; Rev. iii. 4; vii. 13, 14; xix. 8.]

3. *Indicative of the spirit of service.* Bring to God services and sacrifices with clean hands, and pure hearts, and holy lives. The *state of the offerer* affects the character of the offering. [See Heb. x. 22.]

II. IN ALTERED GARMENTS *they bear the ashes from the sanctuary.*

1. The *changed tone of feeling* in the minis-

trant. He no longer serves in delight at God's altar, but takes part in the act of outcasting the sin sacrifice. A saddened mood is upon him as he becomes for the moment associated with the *repulsiveness of sin* in carrying the ashes " without the camp." There are two aspects of Christian ministry—*joyous privilege*, when clothed in the garments of salvation, and *saddened reflection* when realising the offensiveness of sin.

2. *The altered scenes which a Christian frequents.* He is not always within "the holy place of the tabernacle of the Most High," he has to *go forth* to outside scenes: the rougher, less hallowed scenes of life and human society. Yet, though laying aside the holiest priestly garb when he left the most sacred scenes, as a Christian soul necessarily *laves behind him the sublimer thoughts and feelings* he wore when in the very secret of God's presence: still *his changed garments were consecrated garments.* The Christian must *never lay aside his sanctity*, nor his *priestly profession.* Everywhere, whether apart with God or busy amongst men, he must wear the consecrated attire.

V. 12. *Theme:* DIVINE FIRE HUMANLY MAINTAINED.

"The fire upon the altar shall be burning in it; it shall not be put out; and *the priest shall burn wood on it every morning*," etc.

It might have been supposed that this "fire," having been Divine in its origin, would have been Divinely maintained. That fire, so given, suggests—

I. DIVINE ENDOWMENTS COMMITTED TO THE CONTROL OF MEN.

As in the instances of that "fire," supernaturally originated on that altar, and then *left in man's hands*, so with—

1. *Pure sympathies implanted within man.*
2. *Revelation in the Scriptures.*
3. *Quickened life in the regenerated soul.*
4. *Spiritual endowments to the believer.*
5. *Sacred affections in the Christian heart.*
6. *Holy enthusiasm firing an earnest nature.*

From God they come: but man has them in his hands.

II. DIVINE ENDOWMENTS ENTRUSTED TO THE PRESERVATION OF MEN.

The priests had to keep that "fire" alive, or it would expire.

1. *Having received the gifts of God we are responsible for their maintenance.* God holds us as in trust with them.
2. *How solemn the priestly office*, which all are called to perform: feeding the Divine "fire" in our souls continually!

III. DIVINE ENDOWMENTS REQUIRING THE CO-OPERATIVE WATCHFULNESS OF MEN.

The priest's eye would need to be often turned to the altar fire: "*every morning*" it needed care.

1. *A watchful life is imperative* if we would maintain godliness within.
2. *Neglect* will allow the *extinction* of the divinest gift. It needs scarcely that positive effort be made to "*put* out" the fire: it will go out of itself if not attended to.

Only *neglect*
(*a*) *Daily prayer;*
(*b*) *Daily reading of the Scriptures;*
(*c*) *Daily fellowship with Christ;*
(*d*) *Daily watching against temptation.*

Fail in these duties, and the "fire" will expire.

"*Every morning*" bring wood to the fire!

IV. DIVINE ENDOWMENTS ENDURING ONLY WHERE ACTIVELY MAINTAINED.

That fire *did* expire! At the destruction o the temple by Nebuchadnezzar.

1. May the *Divine life in a soul* go out?
2. May the *Christian's* "*first love*" become extinct?
3. May the *holy aspirations* of a child of God droop?
4. May *all sacred ardour*, in prayer, in consecration, die away?

"*Work out* your salvation with *fear and trembling.*"

"See that ye *make your calling* and election sure."

V. 13. *Theme:* FIRE NOT TO GO OUT.

I. Its *typical* import, as *relating to the* GOSPEL.

1. That we all *constantly need the atonement.* This fire was given for the use of all Israel without exception: all needed to offer atonement; Aaron as well as the people. We must all bring our offering to the altar. The fire, too, was for daily use. And daily we need to come to God through the atonement.

2. That the *Levitical sacrifices are insufficient* for us. Thousands of victims were consumed on God's altar, yet the fire continued to burn; indicating that full atonement had not been offered (Heb x. 1-4, 11, and ix. 9).

3. That *God intended to supply a satisfactory sacrifice.* The continuous fire, and the daily supply of wood, seemed to repeat Isaac's inquiry, " Behold *the fire and the wood,* but *where is the lamb* for a burnt offering ?" (Gen. xxii. 7, 8). God kept up the expectation of the Great Sacrifice.

4. That *all who repudiated that Great Sacrifice* must expect *severest judgments.* The victims consumed by that fire betokened the sinner's deserts (Mark ix. 43, 44, 45, etc.). " Who can dwell with the devouring fire? who can dwell with *everlasting burnings?* " (Isa. xxxiii. 14).

II. Its *mystical* import, as *relating to the* CHURCH.

That altar represents the *heart of man*, from whence offerings of every kind go up to God (Heb. xiii. 15, 16).

1. That no offering can be accepted of God *unless it be inflamed with heavenly fire.*

Compare Nadab and Abihu's doom (Lev. x. 1, 2); and the remonstrance of Isaiah (l. 11).

2. That if God have kindled in our hearts a fire, *we must keep it alive by our own vigilance*: " Stir up the gift of God that is in thee " (2 Tim i. 6); " Be watchful, and strengthen the things which remain, that are ready to die " (Rev. iii. 2).

3. That every sacrifice, offered in God's appointed way, *will be accepted.* Though unable to bring a kid or lamb or young pigeons, yet

bring a small measure of flour (Lev. v. 5-13). The sigh, tear, groan, will be accepted equally with the most fluent prayer; the widow's mite equally with the offerings of the wealthy.

III. *Its personal* suggestion, indicating OUR DUTY.

1. *Look to the Great Atonement* as your only hope.

2. *Surrender up yourselves* as living sacrifices unto God.—*C. Simeon.* [See Addenda, p. 86, *Enduring Fire.*]

V. 13. *Theme:* THE ALTAR FIRE.

"The fire shall ever be burning upon the altar; it shall never go out."

A. This fire is *typical* of HOLY DESIRES, *and of* DIVINE LOVE; to which it bears an exact parallel in a variety of instances, in its various operations:—

i. Fire is an *illuminating* quality.
ii. It is a *warming and heating* quality.
iii. It will *burn any combustible matter;* separating metal from dross and rust.
iv. It is an *ascending* quality; greedily mounting to its proper seat, and will not rest till it incorporates with its own element.
v. It is a *melting and softening* quality. Iron and other metals are made pliable by it.
vi. It is a *comforting and consoling* quality.
vii. It is of an *assimilating* quality. It changes materials into its own nature, and sets them on fire.
viii. Without fire business would be arrested; nor could we exist. Parallel: "Man lives not by bread alone," etc. "His Word was in mine heart as a burning fire."

B. *How may we* QUENCH THE FIRE *of holy desires and Divine love?*

i. By *inconsideration* or unwatchfulness.
ii. By a *trifling spirit*, or permitting levity to prevail.
iii. Not keeping our eye single, our *heart sincere.*
iv. *Fond conceits of ourselves;* being wise above what is written.
v. Not harmonising our lives by the rule of God's Word.—*Methodist Plans*, by Rev. Wm. Stephens, A.D. 1786.

V. 13. *Theme:* THE ALTAR FIRE A SYMBOL OF REGENERATING GRACE.

The ANALOGY between this fire and regenerating grace appears—

I. In its *source and origin.*
II. In its *tendency.*
III. In its *nature and properties.*
IV. In its *permanency.*
V. In its *perpetuity.*

The PRACTICAL LESSON gathered from the subject, is diligence in the use of means:—

1. *Prayer:* secret, family, social.
2. *Study of God's Word.*
3. *Meditation* (Ps cxix.; Mal iii. 16; Heb. x. 25).
4. *Attendance on the means of grace.*
5. *Faithful labour* for the glory of God and the salvation of souls.—From *Homiletic Monthly*, by Rev. G. F. Love. [See Addenda, page 86, *Enduring Fire.*]

V. 18. *Theme:* THE UNEXTINGUISHABLE FIRE.

The Divine injunction to keep the fire upon the altar ever burning has been thought by some Biblical scholars to imply, *that the wrath of God against sin will never expire; that the Divine punishment for sin is interminable.* But we must remember that the fire on the altar consumed *not the sinner but the sacrifice* offered in the sinner's stead And *the fire did ultimately go out.*

It seems more consistent with the moral teaching of the rite (and certainly beset with fewer difficulties) to take the fire (*a*) *as symbolic of the fact* that the constantly offered sacrifices met with abiding approval of the Lord; and (*b*) *as an emblem* of the deep devotion and constant love of the heart necessary to secure unbroken communion with heaven.

Our bodies are temples of the Holy Ghost; and, as priests unto God, "we are to offer up ourselves living sacrifices, holy and acceptable unto Him." Fire is a Divine emblem by which God is represented *to* us; and by which God is manifested *in* us. Enthusiasm means God in us. The fire of consecration must be—

I. DIVINELY KINDLED. It must come from the presence of Jehovah, or we shall offer strange fire on the altar. The baptism of fire, like that of the Holy Ghost, is from above.

II. CONSTANTLY REPLENISHED. The altar fire was every day fed by the repeated sacrifices. Enthusiastic consecration can be sustained only by repeated supplies of appropriate fuel. We must *pile up grateful memories, holy resolutions, self-denying services,* etc. The flash of religious excitement will not suffice, God will not accept the white ashes of a former fire.

III. FREQUENTLY REVIVED. The fire must not be choked, or damped, it would need fresh air, and stirring: the fire in our hearts *needs the fresh air from heaven—to be stirred by renewed efforts*—we need to *beware of extinguishing influences*, such as unholy lusts, undue anxieties, unbelief in God, inattention to public and private devotions, etc.

IV. JUDICIOUSLY CONTROLLED. The fire upon the altar was kept within reasonable bounds, or it might have spread disaster through the whole camp. Zeal and consecration must be governed by intelligence, or they will degenerate into fanaticism and lead to bigotry and persecution. Let us seek to be clad with zeal as with a garment, and to possess holy fire in our souls.

The fire of consecration may be known by—
(*a*) *Intense heat of love.*
(*b*) *Twofold flame of devotion*—prayer and praise.
(*c*) *Clear light of knowledge.*

Such a fire within will be *comforting, purifying, aggressive, ascending.* Take fire, hold fire, spread fire; then when death comes we shall be translated to the land where we shall be as seraphs before the sapphire throne.—F. W. B.

SECTIONAL HOMILIES, CHAPTER VI. 14-30.

THE PRIESTS' MEAT OFFERING.

Topic: PRIESTLY SERVICES AND PRIVILEGES (Vv. 14-16).

"The sons of Aaron *shall offer it before* the Lord . . the remainder shall *Aaron and his sons eat.*"
I. FULFILMENT OF SACRED FUNCTIONS.
Christ was typified in "Aaron," *Christians* in "his sons."
1. Consider the *priestly ministrations of Jesus Christ within the sanctuary.* (*a*) Within *His Church on earth,* in maintaining the love, and devotion, and piety which there are offered to God. (*b*) Within the *heavenly sanctuary,* in gathering up the prayers of His saints, adding His own virtues to human offerings, and interceding in the presence of God for us.
2. *The subsidiary ministries of the Christian priesthood.* (*a*) *In consecrated lives.* (*b*) *In loving gifts.* (*c*) *In prayerful fellowship.* (*d*) *In useful agencies.*
II. ENJOYMENT OF SPECIAL PRIVILEGES.
1. *Christ feasts with His followers.* "Aaron and his sons shall eat." For our Lord appeals to us, "Eat, My friends; yea, eat and drink, O My beloved." We have "fellowship with Jesus Christ" (1 John i. 4). Thus our Lord ate "the passover *with His disciples.*" Thus He "*sups with us*" (Rev. iii. 20). Thus He will eat *with His Church at the heavenly feast.*
2. *A repast reserved for the priesthood.* None but "Aaron and his sons" might eat. There is a joy the world knows not of, a hidden life in Christ to which all but Christians are strangers, there are lofty fellowships with God which none but priestly souls can approach. Note, this feast was to be "*in the holy place*"—not the innermost court, type of "heaven itself," but in "the court of the tabernacle of the congregation"—symbolic of *the Church on earth.* It thus points to the sacred favours enjoyed *now* in *the spiritual life* and in *Christian communion.*

Topic: DIVINE FRIENDSHIP (Vv. 14-18).

The leading idea of this offering is *communion with Jehovah.* In the sacrifice presented the Divine and the human meet in hallowed fellowship and banquet together with great rejoicing. We learn:
I. THAT THE ALMIGHTY DEIGNS TO COMMUNE FAMILIARLY WITH MAN. At Sinai the people were commanded to keep distant; in the burnt offering, the whole of the sacrifice was consumed, indicating that the offerer deserved to be consumed for his iniquity; here a small portion only was consumed, the greater part was taken by the priests, and the meal was peculiarly sacred. "I have given it them for their portion of My offerings made by fire." Thus Jehovah partook with the priests, and entered into intimate fellowship. Under the new dispensation we are all made priests unto God, through faith in His dear Son—we become partakers of the Divine nature; we enter His banqueting house, and His banner over us is love. He calls us not servants, but friends; sups with us in our hearts, at His table in the Church, and will, with us, hereafter at the marriage feast in heaven.
II. THAT MAN MUST NOT TAKE UNDUE ADVANTAGE OF SUCH DIVINE FAMILIARITY.

The meat offering was to be solemnly and carefully presented : strict attention to be paid to dress and deportment : no ceremonial or personal impurity to be allowed : no leaven of any kind used. A sacred circle was drawn around the altar, the service invested with great importance, even the priests placed under restrictions. We may come with holy boldness and childlike confidence to God; but we must do so with becoming reverence. "God is a spirit," etc. Where the Spirit of the Lord is there is liberty, but not levity and irreverence. *Sincerity, thankfulness,* and a *sense of deep responsibility* will give the right tone to our religious exercises.

III. THAT SUCH HALLOWED FELLOWSHIP IS ACCEPTABLE TO GOD AND PROFITABLE TO MAN. The people offered their flour, oil, and frankincense; the priests took their portion and ate it in the court of the tabernacle; the fragrant incense perfumed the air; Jehovah accepted all as a sweet savour, having respect to the obedience and reverence represented in the offering. The worshipper was taught his relation to the Lord, acceptance of Him, friendship with Him. Christ has not only become our Sin Offering, but our Meat Offering, in that He invites us to partake of His love : "My flesh is meat indeed, and My blood is drink indeed." Only by *personal, spiritual participation of Christ,* can we have fellowship with Him here, and companionship with Him in eternity. "If any man have not the Spirit of Christ he is none of His."—F. W. B.

Topic : MINISTERIAL DEDICATION : THE PRIEST'S CONSECRATION OFFERING
(Vv. 19-23).

Here can be found suggestions concerning dedication and devotion to the ministerial office.

I. *Consecration to the ministry : an event to be* MARKED BY IMPRESSIVE SOLEMNITIES. "The *day when he is anointed*." What a day that is to a young minister! His entrance upon so solemn and responsible a work as that of becoming "a minister of the sanctuary" should be specially signalised.

"*This is the offering unto the Lord* in the day when he is anointed." God asks that the consecration solemnities should be "unto" Him. For it signifies the setting apart of a life "unto the Lord," and the placing upon His altar of every *energy, faculty, affection, and aspiration.*

"O Lord, Thy heavenly grace impart,
And fill my frail, inconstant heart :
Henceforth my chief desire shall be
To dedicate myself to Thee—
To Thee, my God, to Thee."

II. *Consecration to the ministry : an act to be* CHARACTERISED BY COMPLETE SELF-DEVOTION.

1. *Perpetuity* is to mark the offering. "For a meat offering *perpetual.*" It is to be no temporary dedication, but a whole life-long devotion.

2. *Continuity* is to mark the offering. "Half of it in *the morning,* and half thereof *at night*"; *i.e.,* it was to be a day-by-day dedication; the offering was to go on *every morning and night.* God asks not one demonstrative act of consecration at the outset of our official life, or our Christian life, but a ceaseless repetition, a daily reproduction of that act of devotion; "the love of our *espousals*" is to be daily enacted.

3. *Entirety* is to mark the offering. "It is a *statute for ever;* it shall be *wholly burnt*" (v. 22). "Every meat offering *for the priest* shall be *wholly burnt*" (v. 23). In the offering for the people God required only a "handful of flour" as a "memorial of it unto the Lord" (v. 15); but He required the complete offering

from a priest. No part of the price might be withheld : time, talents, all the man is and has—"*wholly.*"

> "How can I, Lord, withhold
> Life's brightest hour
> From Thee ; or gathered gold,
> Or any power ?
> Why should I keep one precious thing from Thee
> When Thou hast given Thine own dear Self for me ?"

III. *Consecration to the ministry: a service to be* ASSOCIATED WITH GRATITUDE AND JOY.

1. *Emblems of thankfulness* were to be laid on the altar. " Fine flour, and oil." For it should be that the young minister, laying himself out for his high calling, should realise *how much he owes his Lord,* and ask : " *What shall I render unto the Lord for all His benefits towards me ?*" To His grace we must ascribe all we have received of endowments, gifts, holy affections, enjoyment of His redemption, enlightenment by His Spirit, the call to ministerial work.

> " To Thee, Thou bleeding Lamb,
> I all things owe ;
> All that I have and am,
> And all I know ;
> All that I have is now no longer mine,
> And I am not my own ; Lord, I am Thine."

2. *Such joyous self-devotion is peculiarly fragrant to the Lord.* " For a *sweet savour unto the Lord*" (v. 21). There is so much that charms even the glorious Jehovah in a young life fully consecrated: the ardour and bloom of opening manhood laid wholly on His altar ; the aspirations and affections of the heart withdrawn entirely from secular attractions and pursuits, and fixed on Christ and His service ; the fervour of being dedicated to the sublime mission of winning souls for the Saviour and ministering in His courts.

> "Accept these hands to labour,
> These hearts to trust and love,
> And deign with them to hasten
> Thy kingdom from above."

Topic: THE SIN OFFERING A SHADOW OF GOOD THINGS TO COME
(Vv. 24-30).

The sin offering was presented on the north side of the altar : in the fulness of time the world's Great Sacrifice was offered on the north side of Jerusalem. *How,* as well as *what* to be presented clearly indicated in this, as in previous offerings. In directions given we learn :

I. HOW COMPLETE THE SIN OFFERING WAS. Though parts of the sacrifice were to be eaten by the priests when the oblation was made for the people, the whole was to be consumed by fire when presented for the priests. The sin offering atoned for every kind of sin, thus showing great completeness, and adaptation for priests and people, who in the sight of God need forgiveness and restoration to His favour. When a part of the offering was eaten by the priests it was shown how God and man were reconciled ; when the offering was wholly burned it was shown how complete the atonement was, how fully pardon was secured.

II. HOW TRANSITORY THE SIN OFFERING WAS. Frequently repeated, it was only of temporary virtue. It borrowed all its efficacy from the great Sin Offering which it typified. " It was not possible for the blood of bulls and goats to take away sin" ; without the sacrifice of Christ they would have been of no avail.

Altars and offerings have passed away, but Jesus hath procured "eternal redemption for us."

III. How SACRED THE SIN OFFERING WAS. It was called "most holy," great precaution was taken that it should not be desecrated, even the implements and vessels used in its observance were scrupulously guarded from ceremonial impurity. Priests were not allowed to partake if ceremonially defiled: showing that sin and holiness are alike contagious—may be communicated, intentionally or unintentionally, to *persons, places, offices, things*. How complete and sacred the sin offering of the Redeemer! If contempt for, and neglect of, Levitical rites was heinous in the sight of God, how much more so similar conduct when shown to what they foreshadowed!

Conclusion. The sin offering showed (*a*) *the exceeding sinfulness of sin;* (*b*) *the absolute necessity of atonement being made for it;* (*c*) *the transcendant importance of deliverance from every taint of it.* These truths fully taught and actually embodied in the glorious gospel of the blessed God.—F. W. B.

ILLUSTRATIVE ADDENDA TO CHAPTER VI.

INJURY.

"Of all the things that have had record in the world, of the many sources of violence, injustice and cruelty, I do not know of anything else that is so cruel as man. It is only man that studies cruelty, and makes it exquisite, and prolongs it, and carries it out with appliances and art. From the despot on the throne to the despot of the household, all men alike carry vengeance, bitterness, wrath, hurtfulness, as characteristics of the race."—*H. W. Beecher.*

"How should you feel if you were to enter the room where your child is sleeping, and find upon it a stealthy cat, stationed at the portal of life, and stopping its very breath? How should you feel were you to find upon your child a vampire that had fastened into its flesh its blood-sucking bill, and was fast consuming its vitality? How do you feel when one of your children tramples upon another? or when your neighbour's children crush yours? or when ruffian violence strikes against those whose hearts for ever carry the core of your heart? Judge from your own feelings *how God, with His infinite sensibility*, must feel when He sees men rising up against their fellow-men: performing gross deeds of cruelty on every hand . . . devastating society by every infernal mischief that their ingenuity can invent."—*H. W. Beecher.*

"Justice consists in doing no injury to men; decency, in giving them no offence."—*Cicero.*

"Recompense injury with justice, and kindness with kindness."—*Confucius.*

"He threatens many that hath injured one."
—*Ben. Jonson.*

"Brutus hath riv'd my heart;
A friend should bear his friend's infirmities,
But Brutus makes mine greater than they are."—*Shakespeare.*

"Virtue is not left to stand alone. He who practises it will have neighbours.—*Confucius.*

"Be as just and gracious unto me
As I am confident and kind to thee.
—*Titus Andronicus.*

ENDURING FIRE.

The perpetual fire of the Persian Magi and modern Parsees; the eternal fire, as it was called at Rome, kept perpetually burning by the Vestal virgins; and the *Pur Asbeston* "unextinguishable fire," of the Greeks at Delphi, were evident imitations of this sacred fire.

"It was one of the distinguishing marks of the chieftainship of one of the Samoan nobility that his fire never went out. His attendants had a peculiar name for their special business of keeping his fire blazing all night long while he was asleep."—*Turner's Polynesia.*

"During the second temple this perpetual fire consisted of three parts or separate piles of wood on the same altar; on the largest one the daily sacrifice was burnt; the second, called the pile of incense, supplied the fire for the censers to burn the morning and evening incense; and the third was the perpetual fire from which the other two portions were fed. It never was quenched till the destruction of the temple by Nebuchadnezzar. Indeed we are positively assured that the pious priests who were carried captives into Persia, concealed it in a pit, where it remained till the time of Nehemiah, when it was restored to the altar (2 Macc. i. 19-22). The authorities in the time of Christ, however, assure us that the perpetual fire was one of the five things wanting in the sacred temple.'—*Elliott's Commentary.*

"Wake in our breasts the living fires,
The holy faith that warmed our sires."
—*Holmes. Army Hymn.*

FAITHLESSNESS.

"Treason is there in its most horrid shape
Where trust is greatest! and the soul re-
    sign'd
Is stabbed by her own guards!"—*Dryden.*

"He who does not respect confidence will never find happiness in his path. The belief in virtue vanishes from his heart, the source of nobler actions becomes extinct in him."—*Auffenberg.*

"Faith and unfaith can ne'er be equal powers;
Unfaith in aught is want of faith in all."
                        —*Tennyson.*

"O what a goodly outside falsehood hath!"
                —*Merchant of Venice.*

"Trust that man in nothing who hath not a conscience in everything."—*Sterne.*

"A slender acquaintance with the world must convince every man that actions, not words, are the true criterion of the attachment of friends; and that the most liberal professions of goodwill are very far from being the surest marks of it."—*Geo. Washington.*

"A foe to God was ne'er true friend to man,
Some sinister intent taints all he does."
        —YOUNG'S *Night Thoughts.*

"The highest compact we can make with our fellow is: Let there be truth between us two for evermore. It is sublime to feel and say of another: I never need meet, or speak, or write to him; we need not reinforce ourselves, or send tokens of remembrance; I rely on him as on myself; if he did this or thus I know it was right."—*Emerson.*

CHAPTER VII.

Ritual of the Sacrifices: the Peace Offering.

SUGGESTIVE READINGS.

V. 1.—Likewise this is the law of the trespass offering. More precise instructions are now added to those given in chap. v. 1-13, expressly for the guidance of the priest. Every minute detail is of Divine regulation; God rules within the sanctuary, directs every particular of worship and service therein; for altar sacrifice is "*most holy*," and man must scrupulously refrain from adding, omitting, or altering aught when he approaches Jehovah with expiation. Neither, in the Christian dispensation, is license, or caprice, or self-assertion allowed to sinful man who would propitiate God; he must implicitly follow instructions. "He hath showed thee, O man, what is good."

V. 7.—As the sin offering, so is the trespass offering. If any item of regulation was given for one offering which was not given in the other, then it was to be applied as equally binding in both cases. The priest was entrusted with the duty of searching out each particular and fulfilling it sedulously. It should be our study to "*know* the Holy Scriptures," and therefore we should "compare spiritual things with spiritual," "*searching* the Scriptures daily," as did the Bereans, in order that nothing be left undiscovered, nothing unfulfilled. How careful should be our endeavour to make the written will of God our law in every particular of worship and of habit, of life and conduct.

V. 10.—One as much as another [literally, *a man as his brother*]. In the "*meat* offering" "all the sons of Aaron" were to share, and the dividing was to be equal. And this law assures us, who in Christ are of the "priesthood," that there is an equal participation in the *merits* of the sacrifice and the *privileges* of the Christian life for all who are sacredly related. The gracious rule of *brotherhood* is to be illustrated in our enjoyment of the sacramental feast at the Lord's table, "All ye are brethren." No assumption of superiority is permissible, no exclusive appropriation of the sacred provisions; in the Gospel feast, and at the

Lord's Supper, "*a man is as his brother.*" How, then, dare the Romish celebrant assume the sole right of participating? or where is the warrant for "priestly" superiority in the "household of faith"?

V. 12.—Offer it for a thanksgiving. These "*peace* offerings" are of three kinds—*thank* offerings (vv. 12-15), *votive* offerings (v. 16), and *voluntary* offerings (vv. 16-18). [Comp. on chap. iii.]

V. 18.—Neither shall it be imputed unto him that offereth it. The offerer was expected to see that the entire votive or voluntary offering was "*eaten the same day*" as it was offered; a regulation this which compelled him to hospitality, to invite together a sufficient number of neighbours or poor persons to the festal board. And if through inattention to this duty of considerate and generous hospitality any part remained uneaten that "same day," it must be completely consumed "on the morrow," or the offerer was liable to a serious risk—the part not consumed might fall into some person's hands after the limited time; and then the efficacy of the sacrifice would be entirely disannulled and the offerer must bring another votive offering and go through the regulations of lavish hospitality again, but with more promptitude and precision. A Christian must "not live to himself"; his care for others must be generous; he must be hospitable to the needy; and in his enjoyment of sacred privileges he must bring in others to share with himself the "feast of fat things," or his own *selfish religious life* becomes "an abomination."

V. 20.—Having his uncleanness upon him. The penalty of legal defilement was excision from the Lord's people. "Ye are a *holy* nation." Such was Jehovah's reiterated declaration; and every infringement of ceremonial sanctity was immediately stamped with disapprobation and disfranchisement. Shall not the *Church of Christ* be equally guarded from the presence of the unclean? Wherefore "let a man examine himself," and let those charged with the care of the Church preserve her fellowship from contamination by "trying the spirits." As for ourselves, this is the injunction for us to heed : "Wherefore come out from among them, be ye separate, and touch not the unclean thing."

Vv. 22-27.—Ye shall eat no manner of fat. . . no manner of blood. [Comp. on chap. iii. 17]. That which was the *Lord's* man must not appropriate. "What shall I render unto the Lord?" Our aim should be rather to exceed His specified requirements by offering something beyond, "some very precious" alabastron, some free-will sacrifice of love "for the great love wherewith He has loved us."

V. 30.—His own hand shall bring the offerings of the Lord. Divine service could not be done by proxy. Just as at the judgment "every one shall give account of *himself* to God," so in now seeking appeasement and acceptance every soul must come to the Lord on his own behalf. "The Master calleth for *thee.*"

V. 34.—The wave breast and the heave shoulder. The spectacular movements of parts of the sacrificial victim before the altar intimated their consecration to Jehovah, and their performance was justified by the necessity of impressing on the people the supreme claims of God upon them when they brought their offerings. It was an uplifting of the sacrifice to Him who dwelt between the cherubim; a recognition of His unseen presence, a response to His solemn demands. A vivid realization of *God within the sanctuary* would constrain to more reverence in our offerings and actions. "Who hath required this at your hands to *tread My* courts?" (Isa. i. 12).

V. 37.—This is the law of the burnt offering, etc. An enumeration of the various kinds of sacrifices, which carries the suggestion that Jehovah could omit no one from the list, that all were essential to His continued favour towards and fellowship with man, that the religious life could not be thorough if one were withheld—self-consecration, fellowship, atonement, reconciliation, peace.

SECTIONAL HOMILIES.

Topic: INVARIABLE LAWS REGULATING SACRIFICIAL WORSHIP (Vv. 1-10).

With minute precision God reiterates His requirements in sacrificial worship Thus emphasizing the conditions of man's propitiation, and his acceptance with Him. "There is *one law* for them" (v. 7). Though some diversity existed in the details, *e.g.*, as to the disposal of the blood of the victim by the priest [comp. ch. iv. 6, 7, with v. 2], and the sharing of the different parts of the animal; yet amid all diversity in details, *an invariable law* ruled in the arrangements, and this God again emphasizes. What was that invariable law? In chap. vi. 27, etc., the stress of Divine injunctions is laid on the *quality of the sanctity* distinguishing the sin offering: and here it is reaffirmed (vii. 1) "it is *most holy*," and (v. 6) "it shall be eaten *in the holy place*, it is *most holy*." Ponder that inflexible requirement and consider that there are still inevitable laws and fixed conditions of acceptable approach to God.

I. METHODS OF WORSHIP MAY VARY, BUT HOLINESS IS INEVITABLE IN ALL.

1. *Moral qualities* are essentially more valuable than outward rituals.
2. Modes of approaching God, though important, *fail to win Divine favour*, if the inmost state is alien to His will.
3. *Sanctity is the most precious quality in man.* Not grandeur, not punctiliousness, but holiness.
4. This holiness indicates not so much moral faultlessness and absolute perfectness in the offerer, as *sincerity, humility*, "a right spirit," a reverence of God, and a trustfulness in His grace. [See Addenda, p. 100, *True Worship.*]

II. *All propitiatory acts are secondary to* THE SUPREME FACT—DEATH FOR SIN.

1. First in *order of time*: the offering was to *be slain* (v. 2). After that was done, then began the ritual. Any attempt to draw near God until the atonement death is a realised fact is an intrusion, an anachronism.
2. First in *order of consequence*: the worshipper must *substitute a victim's life*. Or he himself must die! Shielded from death by substitution, he may then seek God by propitiatory ritual or reconciliatory worship.
3. *Calvary* was thus the consummation of all types: *Death for sin* making possible man's approach to God.

III. *Offerings to God must always be* THE CHOICEST IN OUR POWER TO PRESENT.

1. *Vast variety was allowed and ordained* in the sacrificial offerings. God permits and approves our various gifts; every one bringing his distinctive offering; every life presenting its special and peculiar quality. Considerable freedom in choice is granted.
2. Yet the invariable law rules—*God must have the finest, the very best.* The vital parts, the choicest of the inwards of the victim were claimed for Him (vv. 3-5).
3. *Each worshipper has to bring something of peculiar preciousness* to God, something *additional to atonement.* Yes; beyond Christ's death, God asks the *very choicest qualities of the life* of all who seek Him. [See Addenda, p. 100 *Offerings for God.*]

IV. ABSOLUTE CONSECRATION MARKED WHATEVER WAS PRESENTED TO THE LORD. "It is most holy."

1. There might be *no taking back* that which had been offered. Think on Ananias and Sapphira.
2. *No one might share* that which "pertained unto the Lord." [Comp. v. 20.]
Hence: once dedicated to the Lord we are *His absolutely and always.* And whatever is dedicated to the Lord none may partake with Him—it is *His only.*

Topic: THE SACRIFICE OF PEACE OFFERING (Vv. 11-18).

"And this is the law of the sacrifice of peace offerings, which he shall offer unto the Lord," etc.

In the ritual of the Hebrews there were three great classes of offerings: the burnt offering, the sin offering, and the peace offering. The meat and drink offerings were secondary, and usually were offered in connection with other sacrifices.

The burnt offering and the peace offering were *known before the giving of the law*. The sin offering was instituted in connection with the law, as made necessary by it.

The law of the peace offering is *given last* in publication of the sacrificial arrangements, as if to declare that it naturally follows the others as a sacrifice of *completeness* (as expressive of restored fellowship between God and man); and also that *every view of Christ is gathered into it*.

I. *The peace offering is a* SACRIFICE OF THANKSGIVING.

Three forms of it are specified:

(1) The offering of thanksgiving, *i.e.*, for some special blessing.

(2) The vow, the fulfilment of a promise to God.

(3) The voluntary offering made from a *principle* of gratitude, when, with no special occasion, the worshipper *called* upon his soul and all within him to bless and praise God's holy name.

It was a peace offering, a *national thanksgiving*, which Solomon made at the dedication of the temple. It is this sacrifice so frequently referred to in the Psalms.

In connection with the *Passover celebration* there were two peace offerings: the former of these is *continued in the Pascal supper*, which is a sacrifice of peace offering, a feast of thanksgiving for God's greatest gift to men, a service by the Church to be joyously observed. At the *sacramental table* we should (1) *thank God for all special exhibition of Divine goodness;* (2) should *joyfully fulfil our promises* to Him, those sacred covenants into which, in trial or difficulty, we have entered with Him; (3) should *make our voluntary offerings*, in view of the *constant* mercies of God, the daily and hourly grace; not the freshet water in the stream of Divine providence, but the constant flow from the inexhaustible "upper springs." How well do these befit all our approaches to God, how well, of all places, do they befit the sacrifice of the Communion!

II. *The peace offering is a* SACRIFICE OF FELLOWSHIP.

This idea lies at its centre. The peculiar feature of it was the sacrificial meal; the *priests shared* in what was offered; the *offerer* also partook; the offering was presented *to God*, and part thereof consumed, *as if by Him*, upon His altar.

1. It was an act of *communion with God*. He gives us back a portion from the altar. Christ is our sacrifice. At the Communion we partake of the Paschal Lamb. God gives us His flesh to eat, His blood to drink. When we came home as returning prodigals the Father set the table *for* us, and sat down *with* us: "Let *us* eat and be merry," He said. At the Communion Christ says, "Let *us* eat: let *us* drink." He sits at the table with us.

2. So also the sacred meal was an act of *mutual communion*. It was a social meal: the priest, the worshipper, his family, and other friends shared with him. So was it in the peace offering of the Passover; so in Solomon's great feast of dedication; so it is at the Communion table. We partake of Christ *together*. Holy fellowship, of loftiest, tenderest experience.

What a beautiful *relation of Christian to fellow Christian* is here exhibited. How the fact of our having sat at Christ's table together, partaken of the Lamb of God, commits us to purest brotherly love, most free from all self-seeking, alienation, suspicion, bitterness ; charges us, " Ye are members one of another."

How much is meant when we are exhorted to " *be at peace among yourselves.*" It is to be in fellowship in the sacrament, in offering together our offering of peace, partaking together our joyous supper at which the Father, Son, and Holy Ghost unite with us. Is true communion anything less than this?

III. *The basis of communion in the peace offering is* SACRIFICE : *and, in the sacrifice,* THE SHEDDING OF BLOOD.

The shedding of blood in this particular sacrifice does not represent, as in the sin offering, the act of atoning for sin. 1. *The bleeding Christ, as our Peace Offering, is not our Sin Bearer.* But His blood in this offering also declares that an atonement has been made, and that the *sole ground of fellowship* with God is *in the reconciling blood* of the Lamb. " But now in Christ Jesus," etc. (Eph. ii. 13, 14).

2. We *follow* our sin offering *with the peace offering of the sacrament,* and we constantly renew our sacrament to express *our joy in redemption,* and our recognition of the *sole ground of it,* the blood of the Redeemer. The sacrament is only an act of communion with him whose sins have been washed away in the " fountain filled with blood." We must make our peace offering on the basis of a previous sin offering of atonement for our soul.

3. *Communion with God* is impossible, on any natural basis, *without the blood of Christ.* You speak of enjoying communion with God and with good people ; is it in the blood of the Son of God? Certain tribes in Africa have a custom which they call *blood-brotherhood,* the most sacred of all relationships. By the mutual transference from the veins of each to the other of their blood, two become in the most binding and inevitable manner brothers. Ours is a *blood-brotherhood,* fellow Christians ; only with us the seal of the covenant is the blood of Christ.

IV. *The peace offering* REQUIRES HOLINESS IN THE WORSHIPPER.

This fact is expressed in the provision that "*unleavened* bread" should be offered as a part of the sacrifice. Yeast or leaven was a symbol of corruption. The absence of leaven suggested the absence, therefore the *removal,* of sin.

If *in your heart* there is *a preference for sin* let it concern you. Ask yourself, how can this be, if you are a new man. [See Addenda, p. 100, *True Worship.*]

V. *In the peace offering* THE SINFULNESS OF A NATURE PARTIALLY SANCTIFIED *is confessed.*

With the offering of unleavened bread *one of leavened bread* was also to be made. This was not a part of the sacrifice, but a meat offering accompanying the sacrifice. It is particularly stated that the bread was leavened ; *i.e.,* the principle of corruption was within, and working in it.

Since our conversion we are not sinners as before ; but *sin is in us.* We cannot make God an absolutely holy offering.

Some claim that they have no sin. They are deceived. " If we say we have no sin we deceive ourselves, and the truth is not in us." We need cry to God with pangs of conscience ever keener :

"Break off the yoke of inbred sin
And fully set my spirit free."

VI. *In the peace offering* THE WORSHIPPER WAS TO KEEP NEAR THE SACRIFICE.

1. This is suggested in the regulation that the offering was to be " eaten the same day." If the offerer had been allowed to keep the offering over day after day he would be tempted to make his communion meal off unwholesome meat, less than the freshest and best. Do not let the sacrifice be abandoned, allowed to suffer neglect. Keep near God. Renew your sacrifice daily. Think not you can live on past devotions—of yesterday, of last Sabbath.

2. We tend to make religion consist of other elements *to the exclusion of sacrifices*. We conceal from ourselves, in attention to externals, that the life of religion is devotion, and that the life of devotion is the element of sacrifice. The early Church kept near the Sacrifice. They *communed daily*. The freshest offering is best. The near place is the place of fellowship; keep near Christ.

3. The suggestions of the peace offering are most practical for any one who seeks to live close to God.

(*a*) It is the *complete* offering: expressing the idea of the burnt offering, *entire consecration*; of the sin and trespass offerings, *atonement for sin*; and it expresses its own characteristic idea, *the joyous communion* of the soul with God and all saints.

(*b*) It suggests all *the possible relations of Christ to the soul* which sacrifice can embody Keep we Christ ever before us in all His offices.

(*c*) Daily we should remember that *the condition of daily communion* is *a daily offering*.

Whosoever so approaches God, Christ is his peace. However far away sometime, daily he is now brought nigh by the blood of Christ, daily he finds the middle wall of partition broken down, and the way into the holiest place opened. —*Rev. Geo. R. Leavitt.* [Compare Homilies on *the Peace Offering*, pp. 30-37 *infra.*]

Topic: THE BELIEVER'S PEACE AND PORTION (Vv. 29-31).

(1) There is nothing that men more require in their natural and restless condition than *peace*, a composed and assured state of mind. The need is, however, to be met; the amplest provision has been made for its being met; and we have only to appropriate to enjoy it. (2) Yet there are but *few who avail themselves of the provision*. Instead of being restful, men are disquieted; dissatisfied instead of contented; apprehensive instead of assured. A broad gulf separates them from the Centre of their being, and from all that is serene and satisfying.

I. TO HAVE GOD IS TO HAVE PEACE: for He is the God of peace; especially as revealed and given us in Christ. But what is given may be enjoyed, as what is offered may be received. Then let the gift be accepted, and the peace you desire will "keep your heart and mind," and this in all circumstances. The winds of adversity may smite you, and the waters of affliction overwhelm you; but as God is greater than these, He keeps in the perfectness of peace the minds that are stayed upon Him.

II. Such peace is FOUND IN CHRIST ALONE; not in anything *done* by Him, or *given* by Him, but in His personal indwelling. The apostle's declaration is, that "*He* is our peace" (Ephes. ii. 14). [See Addenda, p. 100, *Sacred Peace.*]

The *knowledge* of Him will illuminate, and the *faith* of Him will impart security; but you must *have Himself* to have the portion that will satisfy, and the peace you need.

III. But not only is Christ our peace, but from being the ATONER, OUR PEACE OFFERING, He gives Himself *to God* an offering and a sweet smelling savour, and then *to us* who trust in Him for deliverance and satisfaction.

The ancient Jewish sacrifice of the peace offering illustrates this. (1) The *material* of which it consisted was either a bullock, heifer, lamb, or goat; but in all cases it was to be "without blemish." God is entitled to the best, and will receive nothing less. Yet how often is less than what He asks offered Him! That they who so act by Him should have few answers to their prayers, and little satisfaction in their religion, can be wondered at by no one.

(2) Peace offerings were offered by persons who, *having obtained forgiveness of sins, and given themselves to God*, were at peace with Him. Friendship with God was the principal idea represented therein.

(3) Only *a part* of the peace offering was given to God; but that was the *best*, the part to which He was entitled, and which He claimed. And it was accepted, as was shown by its consumption by fire. Offer Him your best, and though in itself small and poor, He will receive it, and make liberal acknowledgement of His approval of it.

(4) The Israelite was not at liberty to lay the fat of his offering *at random*, any way, or any where, on the altar. He had to lay it "*upon the sacrifice* that was upon the wood on the altar fire." But that sacrifice was the lamb of the daily offering, which typified atonement in its fulness. There, God's portion of the peace offering was laid, and accepted according to the value of that on which it was offered.

(5) *Apart from Christ nothing is acceptable to Him.* What you bring to Him may be *your best*, that which He *asks* for, and what is in *itself valuable;* but unless offered on the ground of atonement it is not received by Him.

(6) But that is the ground *within everyone's reach*, and on which everything that is offered to God may be presented. There is no one by whom the name of Jesus may not be used as a plea, and His sacrifice urged as a reason for acceptance.

IV. The peace offering expressed the thought of COMMUNION AND SATISFACTION. It supplied God with a portion, and man also. It furnished a table at which both met, and where they had fellowship with one another. God fed on the fat, and man on the shoulder and breast (v. 31); and both were satisfied.

(1) But we have *Christ* here; and we know what *the Father ever found in Him;* with what pleasure He ever regarded Him, in His righteousness of walk, perfection of obedience, and beauty of character. God was supremely pleased with all that Jesus was and did, as the *representative of Himself to men,* and *the ideal Man to the world,* the indicator of holiness and the honourer of the law. Christ was, and is still, His well-beloved and His joy.

(2) But not God alone fed on the peace offering, *man did that also;* he ate of the breast and the shoulder. In the anti-type these typified *love* and *strength.* These, believer, are *your portion in Christ.* You have His heart of love and His shoulder of might—His unchanging affection and His all-sustaining power. Enfolded in His embrace and enthroned on His shoulder of strength, you occupy a position where evil cannot harm you, nor want remain unmet.

V. *No Israelite who was ceremonially* UNCLEAN *was permitted to partake of the peace offering,* or share with God in the provision it supplied. And without holiness no man is now allowed to see God. But provision is made both for man's expiation and for his sanctifying from all impurity. The cross that separates from the guilt of sin also separates from its defilement. Christ is thus Sanctifier as well as Justifier. He "gave Himself for us, that He might redeem us from all iniquity, and purify unto Himself a peculiar people" (Tit ii. 14).

Thus beautified with His salvation, you will find a place in His banqueting house of love, a guest at the Lord's table, and satisfied with the food of which you partake (John vi. 57, 55, 35).

Are you *satisfied with Christ?* Does He appease all your yearnings, fulfil your every desire, give you rest, and prove your peace? "My beloved is mine, and I am His" (Song of Sol. ii. 16). His resources are inexhaustible, His communications are continuous, and His glory is divine.—Arranged from "*The Gospel in Leviticus,*" by *James Fleming, D.D.*

Topic: THE LAW OF THE PEACE OFFERING (Vv. 11-35).

A halo of gladness surrounds this sacrifice. Persons grateful for deliverances wrought and mercies received, desirous of paying vows previously made, or pledging themselves voluntarily to some new obligation, were to offer before the Lord their sacrifice of thanksgiving and praise. In this law we see:

I. THAT PEACE FOLLOWS FORGIVENESS.

The expiatory sacrifices removed guilt, which is the only barrier that can exist between God and man. The peace offering admitted man into the reconciled presence of God. The offerer came not as a culprit seeking pardon, but as a forgiven child drawing near to a loving Father. Pardon is the door into the chamber of Peace. So, in the Gospel, "Being justified by faith we have peace with God, through our Lord Jesus Christ." Peace is the Divine legacy Christ has left to all who come to Him for rest from the burden of the ceremonial law, and guilt of sin.

II. THAT RESTORATION FOLLOWS PEACE.

In presenting the peace offerings, and feasting on the same, the worshippers would feel they were admitted into the family of God. They sat in His banqueting house, and His banner over them was love. The priests and people joined with the Lord in the divinely appointed eucharistic feast. This privilege is taught in the parable of the Prodigal Son. It would not have been enough for him to be pardoned for his rebellion and sin, he needed restoration to his father's house and favour. Christ is our peace, He has broken down the middle wall of partition, and made us one with God.

III. THAT GRATITUDE FOLLOWS RESTORATION.

The pardoned and restored worshipper would be constrained to render to the Lord the glory due to His name. Brought into a right relationship with God, there would be the expression of right feelings towards Him. The offering waved to and fro, and heaved toward heaven, would denote the offerer's gratitude to Jehovah; recognising Him as the Proprietor of all things, and as worthy of the warmest and strongest love. The gratitude was—

(a) *Prompt.* The offering was to be made at once, none of the things provided were to be kept until the third day, all to be partaken of while memory of the blessings acknowledged was fresh.

(b) *Large hearted.* The priests and people were to invite their families to join them in the feast, and to eat unsparingly.

(c) *Perpetual.* The statute was never to be repealed while the economy continued. The people were under obligation to be thankful, and they knew how their thankfulness might be acceptably expressed. The injunction of the Gospel is "In everything give thanks: for this is the will of God in Christ Jesus concerning you."

IV. THAT DEVOTION FOLLOWS GRATITUDE.

The waving of the breast, the heaving of the shoulder, symbolised *consecration of strength, and affection to the Lord.* Everything offered was to be *clean,* and even the inward parts, obviously teaching the necessity of moral purity in character of those who presented the offerings. Those who dared to transgress by omitting the directions, or were in any way hypocritical, exposed themselves to the penalty of *excommunication,* as well as to severe reproof.

(a) The peace offering was partaken of in *tents* of the people. Religion is for the tent as well as the altar, for the *home* as well as the *sanctuary.* Christ expects our service to spring from love, not from fear; from gratitude to Him for what He has done for us. "We love Him, because He first loved us."—*F. W. Brown.*

Topic: RECAPITULATION OF SACRIFICIAL RITUAL (Vv. 35-38).

Here the directions respecting sacrifices are solemnly emphasised: "This is the portion," etc. Offerings and the priesthood were inseparably connected; when, and in the fulness of time, the offerings ceased, the priesthood ended. All priestly assumption under the Christian dispensation is out of place *chronologically,* and presumptuous *religiously.* Israel, by the Mosaic economy, was to become the repository of the Word of God, and the reflector of His glory. The offerings taught that man is a guilty sinner in the sight of God, that his sinfulness separates him from God, that removal of sin restores man to God. The Jewish economy was perfectly unique; the Hebrew nation stood out in distinct relief among surrounding idolatrous nations. In this recapitulation of the Levitical ritual we are taught—

I. THAT GOD DOES NOT ENJOIN OBEDIENCE UPON MAN WITHOUT AT THE SAME TIME FURNISHING DIRECTIONS FOR RENDERING IT.

Had directions been given that certain offerings were to be presented, and no specifications added as to how they were to be offered, the people would have been in constant uncertainty whether or not they were doing the thing that was required. As it was, the priests and people entered upon their religious observances with a full knowledge of their duties and how to discharge them In the Gospel we are told what God requires of us under the Christian dispensation. Christ has taught us in His royal law what all the law and the prophets taught. In our worship we may observe and present all that the offerings of the Levitical economy signified. We may receive, in answer to believing prayer, the influences of the Holy Ghost, whose office it is to guide us into all truth and to take of the things of Christ and show them unto us.

II. THAT GOD DOES NOT PRESENT ALTERNATIVES TO MAN WHEN HE FURNISHES DIRECTIONS FOR OBEDIENCE.

The laws of the offerings were as emphatic as they were clear; there was no margin left for human invention, no zone of uncertainty about the things to be presented. In some offerings there were gradations, but it was in specified things; the offerer was to bring no substitute for what was divinely ordained. This exclusiveness would give assurance to the offerer that what he presented God would accept, and would prevent oscillation between rival claims. The straight line of the law was laid down, and clearly indicating finger-posts set up; the commands were unmistakable, "This is the way, walk ye in it." So under the Gospel we have no alternatives in the way of salvation. "No other name given," etc. The Christian religion excludes all others.

III. THAT GOD DOES NOT WITHHOLD FROM MAN INDUCEMENTS TO RENDER OBEDIENCE TO DIVINE COMMANDS.

The promulgation of the law from Sinai, and the enunciation of the ritual from the tabernacle, were associated with the most solemn sanctions. The Hebrews could have no reasonable doubt about the *Divine origin* and *binding obligation* of those enactments. With equal solemnity our duties toward the Gospel have been inculcated. Not from Sinai, but from the Mount of Beatitudes; not from Moses, but from Christ. Evidences of the Messiahship of Christ, of the supremacy of His claims, of the truth of His religion, are many and conclusive. His life was public, His miracles were not done in a corner. "He that despised Moses' law died," etc. (Heb. x. 28, 29). In the Gospel, as on the Mount of Transfiguration, Moses and Elias meet to bear witness to His character and mission; all the rays of spread light that gave guidance to the Hebrews centre in the cross, focus on Calvary. "Before Messiah's coming the ceremonies of the Jewish economy were as the swaddling bands in which He was wrapped, but after it they resembled the linen clothes which He left in the grave. Christ was in the one, but not in the other."—*F. W. B.*

Topic: SURVEY OF THE ENTIRE ALTAR SACRIFICES; WITH THEIR PRACTICAL SIGNIFICANCES (Vv. 37, 8).

"*This is the law* of the *burnt* offering, of the *meat* offering, and of the *sin* offering, and of the *trespass* offering, and of the *consecrations*, and of the sacrifice of the *peace* offerings," etc.

The offerings set forth Christ. We see in them how man in Christ has made atonement. We look at the sin and trespass offerings and see that the sin of man has been fully borne : at the burnt and meat offerings, and see all God's requirements satisfied. And this is our confidence, that as Christ " for us " has been " without the camp," as " for us " He has been laid on the altar, so truly do we stand in Him, even as He is; "for by one offering He hath perfected for ever them that are sanctified."

We are one with Christ. In this view His offering, as our Example, sets before us the model and standard of our self-sacrifice. And, just as Christ's sacrifice for us had varied aspects, as satisfying God, and as satisfying man, and as bearing sin; so will our sacrifice, in a lower sense, have these same aspects. In this way the typical offerings have an application to Christians. Thus we also are offerers; "present your bodies a living sacrifice" (Rom. xii. 1). Between Christ's sacrifice and ours there will, of course, be dissimilarities neither few nor small, arising from the fact that He was sinless and we are sinners. Yet the saint will "be made conformable unto His death" (Phil. iii. 10), and his rule in sacrifice will be "the offering of the body of Jesus Christ."

Trace, therefore, how far the various aspects of the offering of the body of Christ may be applicable to those, who, being members of His mystical body, are called to " walk even as He walked."

I. THE BURNT OFFERING. This was man *satisfying* GOD; man in Christ *giving himself to God as His portion*. We have seen how far *for us* [comp. pp. 8, 9 *infra.*] this was fulfilled in Christ : we now inquire how far *in us* it may be fulfilled by the Spirit.

The burnt offering stands as a witness how we should "*yield ourselves*" (Rom. vi. 13).

1. As to *its measure*. It was "wholly burnt." No part was withheld from God. Entire self-surrender. It must "cost us something" (2 Sam. xxiv. 24). The burnt offering was *God's claim*: the fulfilment of this required the life of Christ. It will demand our lives—"Thou shalt love the Lord with *all* thine heart, *all* thy soul, *all* thy mind and *all* thy strength."

Our path after Christ must be still a sacrifice. Can we "present our bodies a living sacrifice" without cost, without feeling that sacrifice is still sacrifice? Christ felt *His* sacrifice.

2. As to *its character*. In the varieties of the burnt sacrifice, of bullock, lamb, and turtle dove, each brought out some distinct particular in the character of our blessed Lord. Would to God that in *active, yet patient service* (as the bullock), *in silent, unmurmuring submission* (as the lamb), in *gentleness and innocency of life* (as the dove), we might be conformed to Him who went before us.

Service, submission, meekness, will *gain no crown for us here;* nor did they for Christ. We cannot seize greatness, or secure honour in this world, by offering ourselves to God in the character these emblems signify. Christ was despised and rejected of man, as a lamb slain and none to pity. May He give us grace gladly to acquiesce in the likeness.

II. THE MEAT OFFERING. This was Christ *satisfying* MAN ; offering *Himself as man's meat*. In doing this He met man's claim on Him as man. Man had a claim on man; God had ratified that claim, saying, "Thou shalt love thy neighbour as thyself." In the meat offering, Christ met and satisfied this claim, by giving Himself to God as man's portion.

1. For the *measure* of it it is enough to say, the type shows us the whole consumed. Such is our standard.

2. For its *character*, the "bruised corn," the "oil," the "salt," and the "frankincense," are sufficiently explicit.

How far may we be conformed to it? To answer this question let us look to other days, and see how men have conformed to it. Time was when the Church, though but "a leavened cake" (Lev. xxiii. 17), was so far filled with the anointing of the Holy Ghost that "the multitude of them which believed were of one heart and of one soul, neither *said any of them that aught of the things which he possessed was his own*. But they had all things common ; *neither was there any that lacked ;* for as many as were possessors of lands or houses, sold them, etc., and *distribution was made to every man as he had need*" (Act viii. 31-35). Here was a *meat offering ;* and costly ; yet not a rare one.

In that day there were living men, who for the Gospel had "lost all things" (Phil. iii. 8), yet were willing to suffer more : " Yea, if I *be poured out* (alluding to the *drink* offering which was an adjunct to the meat offering), on the sacrifice and service of your faith, I joy and rejoice with you" (Phil. iii. 17). See also concerning Onesiphorus, Epaphroditus, Philemon, Phebe.

There is yet a Church. There must yet be offerings ; and we hear of sacrifices, but what is their measure, their character ? Let each judge himself. But this stands, that just in measure as we are like our Master, just as we accept His words as the rule of our devotion, just so far shall we find our path a sacrifice.

III. THE PEACE OFFERING. This view of the offering shows us the *offerer fed ;* for he, with the priest and God, partook of, *i.e*, found *satisfaction* in, the offering. The peace offering has a fulfilment, not only in Christ, but in His members.

1. Does *God* find satisfaction in our offerings ? The answer is clear : " To do good and to communicate forget not, *for with such sacrifices God is well pleased*" (Heb. xiii. 16). So the offering sent by the Philippians to Paul was " an odour of a sweet smell, *a sacrifice acceptable, well pleasing to God* " (Phil. iv. 18). God puts value on, finds satisfaction in, the offerings of His Church. He "loveth a cheerful giver" (2 Cor. ix 7) ; and as our greatest gift is " to give ourselves " (2 Cor. viii. 5), so the presentation of our bodies as living sacrifices is "acceptable unto the Lord" (Rom. xii. 1).

2. The *priest* also fed in the peace offering. Our Priest finds joy in our offerings, poor though they be ; so that even in a cup of cold water and in bread to the hungry He is refreshed and fed. " I was an hungered, and *ye gave Me meat ;* I was thirsty and *ye gave Me drink* " (Matt. xxv. 35). Did we but know His joy in seeing us yield ourselves an offering to Him ; did we realise His gladness of soul in each work of faith and labour of love in ministering to His saints, we could not give with narrow, grudging, selfish hearts. " Ye did it *unto Me !"*

3. The peace offering fed *the offerer*. And surely we have been strangers to self-sacrifice if we need to be told the joy it imparts to him who sacrifices. Paul says, " Yea if I be sacrificed *I joy and rejoice with you* " (Phil. ii. 17) ; " *I rejoice* in my sufferings for you," etc. (Col. i 24) ; "I count not my life dear unto me, so that I might finish my course *with joy* " (Acts xx. 24).

The very costliness of our sacrifice increases our joy when we know that He, to whom we offer, rejoices with us.

IV. THE SIN AND TRESPASS OFFERINGS. And first as to the *sin* offering.

1. There is a sense in which *the Christian may bear sin and suffer its judgment in his mortal flesh*. For lack of knowing this, many are sparing that flesh which the cross of Christ was given to crucify. Is there, then, anything to be wrought in us by the Spirit answering to the dying for sin of the sin offering ? Yes ; Christ's death *in the flesh for sin* is made our example: " Forasmuch, then, as Christ hath suffered for us in the flesh, arm yourselves with the same mind ; for he that hath suffered in the flesh hath ceased from sin" (1 Pet. iv. 1). The Christian, as having been judged in the person of Christ, and knowing that for him Christ has borne the cross, follows on by that cross to judge and mortify all that he finds in himself still contrary to his Lord. The flesh in him is contrary ; the flesh, therefore, must die (Gal. vi. 14 ; v. 24 ; Rom. vi. 6).

2. In the trespass offering *restitution was made for wrong*. And the saint in

H

fellowship with Christ will make restitution; in acts of generosity and kindness to men; and will "add the fifth," going beyond bare justice, in dealing graciously and mercifully with others.

Such is "THE LAW OF THE OFFERINGS." It gives but one view of Christ; yet how much is involved in it both as to our standing and walk in Him. His offering witnesses of *sacrifice even to the cross.* [Comp. *Jukes on the Offerings.*]

OUTLINES ON VERSES OF CHAPTER VII.

Vv. 1-10.—*Theme:* THE TRESPASS OFFERING. This law similar to that of sin offering, with additional directions respecting the blood of the sacrifice, which was to be sprinkled round about the altar. The shedding and sprinkling of so much blood in the worship of God was doubtless intended to impress the worshipper with *the repulsiveness of sin; the enormity of guilt, the absolute necessity of pardon,* in order to acceptance and peace. In this law we see—

I. *God's jealous regard for the strictest order in His service.* The directions given in the ritual were emphatically Divine; He, to whom belong the silver and the gold, and the cattle upon a thousand hills, condescended to give minute directions about slaying a "bullock," "ram," and "pigeon," to teach that no part of His service is beneath His notice, or may be performed carelessly. Everything we do for God is worthy of being done well, or it should not be done at all. Mankind should aim at perfectly doing God's will, as it is done in heaven.

II. *God's generous concern for the temporal wants of His servants.* All the parts of the sacrifice not burnt upon the altar were the perquisite of the priests. The offering not only provided for the spiritual needs of the people, but for the physical requirements of those who had surrendered themselves to the service of the tabernacle. The provision was suitable, liberal, and constant. As the priests with their sons partook of their ample provisions, gratitude to Jehovah and mutual good feeling would be cultivated. No one can serve God for nought. He cares for all His creatures, especially for those who trust Him; "no good thing will He withhold from them that walk uprightly."

We are not under the law but under grace yet, we are not to conduct our religious services lawlessly. We do not obey because commanded, and from fear, but from *constraint* and *love.* One of the first questions a true believer will ask, is: "Lord what wilt Thou have me to do?" Duties to ourselves, our fellow-men, and God, run parallel with every privilege we enjoy and every blessing we receive. We are saved by faith in Christ, and not by works of the law; but "faith without works is dead."—*F. W. B.*

Vv. 1, 11, 37.—*Theme:* RIGIDITY OF THE LAW. "This is the law," etc.

Reiteration employed to indelibly impress the statutes upon the minds of priests and people; to show their pressing and transcendant importance. The worshipper would thus be impressed with—

I. THE MAJESTY OF JEHOVAH. He, God over all, exercised in all royal supremacy. From His word there was no appeal.

II. THE PRIVILEGE, AS WELL AS DUTY, OF WORSHIPPING HIM.

They were not to draw near as slaves, but as servants and friends, and obtain the favour of the King of kings.

III. THE NECESSITY OF PREPARATION FOR WORSHIPPING HIM.

It would need *personal,* as well as *ceremonial* purity to approach acceptably one so *august* and *holy.*

IV. THE BLESSEDNESS OF OBEDIENCE TO HIS COMMANDS.

(*a*) *By obedience they would bless the Lord.*
(*b*) *By obedience they would be blessed themselves.*

Carelessness in preparation for service might not only lead to *useless,* but *offensive* worship. The heart needed to be in full accord with the purposes for which the offerings were instituted. Surely obedience to the commands of Christ are as binding as was obedience to the laws of Moses. The ordinances of the Christian religion are the *invariable accompaniments,* as well as the *external badges,* of membership in the Christian Church.—*F. W. B.*

V. 12.—*Theme:* THANKSGIVING. "If he offer it for a thanksgiving."

Even brutes are capable of gratitude. Israel was often rebuked by the prophets for thanklessness, and reminded that the dumb creation put them to shame. Gratitude rises naturally in our hearts towards human benefactors; shall we not be thankful to Him, in whom we live and move and have our being? Concerning thanksgiving, we observe—

I. IT IS UNIVERSALLY OBLIGATORY, for—
(*a*) *We are dependent creatures,*
(*b*) *Recipient,*
(*c*) *Unworthy,*
(*d*) *Responsible.*

III. IT MAY BE OCCASIONALLY VOLUNTARY. When no particular command calls for it; when no special mercy suggests or prompts it. It may rise out of a full and gladsome heart. It may be adoration for what God *is* in Himself, and has promised to bestow; as well as for gifts received. The *Giver* is above and better than His gifts. Let us bless Him, and forget not all His benefits, especially "*His unspeakable gift.*"

III. IT SHOULD BE PRESENTED BECOMINGLY.

(*a*) *Without delay,* for life is short; duty demands; God deserves; opportunity favours; delay is a slight; we are liable to forget altogether what we postpone.

(*b*) *With freshness:* nothing deteriorated, or exhausted. Beauty, vigour, sweetness, fragrance, virtue, soundness, all should be laid at His feet, offered at His throne.

(*c*) *With generosity:* Let us not *withhold;* and having given, let us not *withdraw;* The Lord loves a cheerful, an ungrudging giver. "Whoso offereth such praise glorifieth God." —*F. W. B.*

Vv. 20, 21.—*Theme:* EXCOMMUNICATION. "That soul shall be cut off from his people." Precaution against laxity in service, carelessness in offering. Failure to comply *minutely* with directions, would incur Jehovah's righteous displeasure.

I. THE OFFERING WOULD BE REJECTED.

II. THE OFFERER WOULD BE EXCOMMUNICATED.

The strength of the strongest chain is the weakest link, if that breaks, all fails. So, if the offerer omitted one requirement, broke one link in the chain of law, he was guilty of violating the whole. We have *analogies of similar exactness in nature.* There perversions, excesses, shortcomings, violations, miscarriages, etc., entail forfeiture of blessing; indeed, they convert the blessing into a bane. Men are constantly cutting themselves off from good by placing themselves voluntarily under the ban of heaven. Rigid discipline is especially needed in the infancy of the affairs connected with *State, Church, Society, Family.* Law is intended to be a terror to evil doers, and an encouragement to those who do well. Under the Gospel Christ is able to save to the uttermost.—*F. W. B.*

Vv. 23, 26.—*Theme:* RESERVED THINGS.

"Ye shall eat no manner of fat."
"Ye shall eat no manner of blood."

I. *To beget reverence for God's altar.*

II. *To preserve a sense of the sacredness of life.*

III. *To show that the best and richest things can be claimed righteously by God.*

IV. *To cultivate delicacy of feeling; check gross and savage passions.*

Thus the hearts and minds of men were cultured in the elementary education of the wilderness; preparatory to the higher culture; which after ages would *demand* and *develop.* —*F. W. B.*

V. 36.—*Theme:* THE WHOLE DUTY OF MAN. "Which the Lord commanded to be given unto the children of Israel."

In heathen sacrifices, man is seeking after God; in the Hebrew sacrifices, God was seeking after man. The *fixing* of *times, places, offerings* for sacrifice, showed that the Lord was anxious and ready to bless. The things which the law enjoined showed—

I. THE TRANSCENDENT IMPORTANCE OF TRUE RELIGION.

Nature, conscience, convenience, choice were not sufficient. True religion must be revealed. Offerings did not explain *the origin of evil,* but what was more important, *how it might be removed.* That which God has specially revealed, in addition to His revelation in nature, must be specially important for us to know and obey.

II. THE PARAMOUNT CLAIMS OF TRUE RELIGION. The Jewish religion, promulgated from Sinai, put in the forefront of all other claim. Christ commands us to "seek first the kingdom of God and His righteousness." Religion is "the one thing needful."—*F. W. B.*

Vv. 37, 38.—*Theme:* SUMMARY OF THE OFFERINGS.

The laws given from the tabernacle are an expansion and enforcement of those given from Sinai. They *symbolised* essential spiritual truths for the Hebrew, and *typified* the same for the Christian Church, viz., the necessity of mental, moral, and spiritual purity in drawing near to God. Thus the foundation of true religion was laid for all ages. These laws were *a protest against idolatry; a witness to the sovereignty of Jehovah; a badge of distinction for Israel; a training for further and higher service, and fuller revelation.* Looking at the offerings as a whole they taught—

I. THAT MAN IS A SINNER, AND NEEDS TO ACKNOWLEDGE HIMSELF AS SUCH IN THE SIGHT OF GOD.

A sinner by nature; by transgression of Divine law; deserving punishment—death; a sinner absolutely at the mercy of Him against whom the sin had been committed.

II. THAT MAN REQUIRED TO MAKE AN ATONEMENT FOR HIS SIN IN ORDER TO APPROACH GOD ACCEPTABLY.

He must not come to God empty-handed, there must be the divinely appointed gift, *the substitute,* for whose sake, *in some way,* sin should be forgiven. Vicarious sacrifice in harmony with the law of nature.

III. THAT MAN REQUIRED PERSONAL FAITH IN THE ATONEMENT MADE ON HIS BEHALF, TO RENDER IT EFFICACIOUS FOR HIM.

Neither *offering* or *act* of any avail except representing faith and obedience of offerer. The fire that consumed the sacrifice represented *the ascending consecration of the worshipper's spirit.*

IV. THAT MAN REQUIRED COMPLETE CONFORMITY TO GOD'S WILL, AND RESTORATION TO HIS FAVOUR.

The perpetual offering of sacrifices would necessitate constant remembrance of the Divine precepts; the frequent coming to God would keep alive a sense of His presence and sovereignty. Thus the chief end of man would be secured—"To glorify God, and enjoy Him for ever."—*F. W. B.*

ILLUSTRATIVE ADDENDA TO CHAPTER VII.

TRUE WORSHIP.

"*Deos placatos pietas efficiet et sanctitas.*"—CICERO.
[Piety and sanctity will propitiate the gods.]

"*Res sacros non modo manibus attingi, se ne cogitatione quidem violari fas fuit.*"—CICERO.
[Things sacred should not only not be touched with hands, they should not be violated even in thought].

"When once thy foot enters the Church, be bare:
God is more there than thou; for thou art there
Only by His permission. Then beware,
And make thyself all reverence and fear."
—*Geo. Herbert.*

"In the temple every little ornament, even of the mighty structure that crowned the cliffs of Zion, was "holy" to the Lord. Not the great courts and inner shrines and pillared halls merely, but all. Not a carven pomegranate, not a bell, silver or gold, but was "holy." The table and its lamps, with flowers of silver light, tent and staves, fluttering curtains and ascending incense, altar and sacrifice, breastplate and ephod, mitre and gem-clasped girdle, wreathen chain and jewelled hangings—over all was inscribed *Holy*, while within, in the innermost shrine, where God manifested Himself above the mercy seat, was THE HOLIEST. Thus the utter holiness of that God with whom they had to do was by every detail impressed upon the heart and conscience of ancient Israel."
—*Grosart.*

OFFERINGS TO GOD.

"Just as a thing looks green which is looked at through green glass, or red through a red glass, so is everything most pleasing and acceptable to God the Father which is offered through His Only Begotten Son."—*F. W. Faber.*

SACRED PEACE.

"Peace is greater than all other treasures, but no philosophy can bestow it: for how can it cleanse from sin? Nor can any works: for how are they able to justify? Descend into whatever mine, shake whatever tree, knock at whatever door in the world thou wilt, the poor world cannot offer it thee. Peace is but one; One only has peace; One only can give it: know ye Him who says: "These things have I spoken unto you that in Me ye might have peace"? His name is "the Prince of Peace."
—*Krummacher.*

"As on the Sea of Galilee,
The Christ is whispering 'Peace.'"—*Whittier.*

"Happy the heart that keeps its twilight hour,
And, in the depths of heavenly peace reclined,
Loves to commune with thoughts of tender power,
Thoughts that ascend, like angels beautiful,
A shining Jacob's ladder of the mind!"
—*Paul H. Hayne.*

"Years ago a Christian friend had experienced a heavy and most unexpected loss, a loss which to most men in his circumstances would have been crushing. The moment the announcement of what had happened was made to him his mind turned to the believer's all-sufficient and never failing portion in God, and the certainty of the unsearchable riches of Christ; and the calm of his spirit continued. The next day was the Sabbath: and he was seen in his place in the sanctuary, joining in worship with the people of God as if nothing of misfortune had overtaken him. It was a regret to him that his means of doing good were diminished, but his own peace of heart remained unbroken."—*Dr. Jas. Fleming.*

CHAPTER VIII.

The Priesthood Initiated and Consecrated.

SUGGESTIVE READINGS.

V. 2.—**Take Aaron and his sons and the garments, etc.** All that was to be now done by Moses had previously been specifically enjoined (Exod. xxviii., xxix., xxx.). The office of the priesthood was now to be formally instituted, that office being necessary to the maintenance and performance of the sacrificial system ordained in the preceding chapters. Hitherto, Moses had fulfilled the priestly functions; from this time he ceases such ministries. It is for him a valediction, for Aaron an inauguration. Thus do sacred ministries become transferred, familiar human forms pass away from the services by which God's people have been aided and blessed; but the work ceases not, for God never fails His Church nor overlooks her needs; while for us in Christ, who has "an unchangeable priesthood," and is Himself "the same yesterday, and to-day, and for ever," an abiding provision is assured. "He ever liveth to make intercession for us."

Vv. 6-9.—Washed them with water, etc. Washing is the first stage in the process of priestly consecration. As cleansing from all unrighteousnes is inevitable ere we can enter spiritual privilege. "Who shall ascend the hill of the Lord, or who shall stand in His holy place? He that hath clean hands and a pure heart" (Psa. xxiv. 3, 4). The priestly washing was by bathing, the whole body being thus cleansed; for entire purifying was required and was symbolised. And "he that is bathed . . . is clean every whit" (John xiii. 10). Only they who have experienced this "cleansing from all sin" can stand within God's sanctuary; but we have "boldness to enter into the holiest by the blood of Jesus . . . having our hearts sprinkled from an evil conscience, and our bodies washed with pure water" (Heb. x. 19-22).

Vv. 7, 8.—Put upon him the coat, and girded him, etc. The "*coat*" was a close-fitting garment of white linen, covering the entire body; this was bound about the body with a linen "*girdle,*" or sash, embroidered with figures, and fringed at its ends; over this was placed the "*robe,*" called "the robe of the ephod" (Exod. xxviii. 31-35), which was all blue, and was woven without seam; above the robe was the "*ephod,*" which fell one part over the front, and another part over the back of the shoulders; this compound and ornate upper garment was wrought of blue, purple, scarlet, and fine twined linen, interwoven with threads of gold. The "*curious girdle of the ephod*" was of the same costly material as the ephod itself, and fastened the ephod below. The "*breastplate*" was a square pocket, suspended by gold chains from the onyx and gold epaulettes on the shoulders; around its four sides were set twelve precious stones, each stone bearing the name of a tribe of Israel. Within this breast-pocket—open on the upper side to receive them—were placed "*the Urim and the Thummim,*" the oracular stones by which the priest learned the mind of God on questions of judgment. Then the head-dress or turban of linen, the "*mitre,*" was placed on his head, across which was tied "*the golden plate, the holy crown,*" bearing the awful inscription, "HOLINESS TO THE LORD."

This solemn robing suggested—

1. The installation of the high priest in his pontifical office, as the supreme minister in the sanctuary, and as God's representative amid Israel.

2. His personal adornment with righteousness and sanctity, the qualities which alone fitted man to dwell in near communion with the Lord.

3. The mediatorial glory and beauty of the coming Messiah, whose graces all these symbolic adornments typified and prefigured.

Surely if Jehovah attached to such minute symbols so great significance and importance, He must value the realities of which they were but signs: *the mediatorial graces of Jesus*, with which God was "well pleased"; *the sanctities of a priestly character* in us who, in the Gospel, have become "priests unto God"; and the *beauties of the perfect righteousness* with which all believers in Christ are adorned.

Vv. 10-13.—Anointed the tabernacle, etc., including the ark of the covenant, the altar of incense, the candlestick, the table of shewbread, the veil, and sacred utensils. Then the anointing oil was "seven times" sprinkled upon "the *altar and its vessels,*" and "the *laver and its foot.*" By their anointing they were "*sanctified*" for sanctuary uses, and as symbols of gracious truths to worshippers.

He poured the anointing oil upon Aaron's head: not sprinkled it, but in such quantity as that it "ran down unto the beard, and went down to the skirts of his garments" (Psa. cxxxiii. 2), suggesting the plenteous grace of the Holy Spirit which covered over the entire manhood of God's consecrated priest, "baptised with the Holy Ghost," "endued with power from on high," "receiving an unction from the Holy One." The Spirit was "given without measure" to Christ, and we may also be richly anointed with His energy and grace. But they who are so *"anointed"* are consecrated to a holy ministry, sealed for a sacred life on earth.

Vv. 14-17.—The bullock for the sin offering. For the *first time* in all history, as a new incident on earth, full of interest to all the hosts of heaven, instinct with significance for all humanity, suggesting new conceptions of man's guilt and Christ's atonement—the sin offering was now offered. Jehovah Himself must have viewed with peculiar regard the *first sin offering ever presented*. Calvary witnessed the *last* ever to be offered! "There remaineth no more offering for sin." The order of the sacrifices is noticeable:

1. The *sin offering* first: for substitution is the basis of the sinner's justification with God.
2. Next the *burnt offering* (v. 18): as declaring complete self-surrender of life, in its highest qualities and complete devotion, unto God.
3. Then the *ram of consecration* (v. 22), which was the thank offering and the peace offering: representing the grateful joy of those whom God honoured with the privileges of priesthood, and as initiating a career of festal fellowship with the Lord.

V. 23.—The tip of Aaron's right ear, etc. The "right" member conveys the meaning of entirety, thoroughness, fulness, and strength. Every sense and every member, all avenues of feeling, and all life's active powers, were to be used for God. See here the standard of life's dedication for all Christians, who owe to their Lord so great a debt of love as should constrain them to most fervent and absolute devotion.

V. 30.—Anointing oil, and of the blood. The Spirit's grace mingles with the Redeemer's virtue: both are imperative. Salvation must be sealed with sanctification, and the good work of renewing is in no case complete where there is not the blended application of both the "blood" and the "anointing oil."

Vv. 33-36.—Seven days shall he consecrate you. Within the sacred enclosure they were to tarry during that period. Consecration must not be hurried. Zeal to be engaged in Christian work may lead to rash and reckless haste; let the young convert pause amid the Divine sanctities, and get his soul filled with reverence, nourished into strength, enriched with grace, such as can only be secured by *"waiting* on the Lord." Ardour is good, alacrity is often needed, for opportunities summon us to activity; but the young life needs first the sacred fostering, and a "quiet resting place," or ever it is equipped for the duties of the Christian priesthood. Moreover, God asks for Himself this consecration interlude. Each day of the seven these priests were to "*fill the hand*," *i.e.*, were to repeat the same sacrifices. God must be served first, then man. Dwell much and restfully "in the secret places of the Most High," give Him leisurely your homage, wait on Him in meditation and prayer; you will be more endowed for gracious ministries to men by such solemn seclusion with the Lord. "Wait on the Lord and He shall strengthen your heart; *wait*, I say, on the Lord."

SECTIONAL HOMILIES.

Topic: PRIESTS *versus* PRIESTISM (Vv. 1-5).

So great have been the abuses of the priestly office, so enormous its pretensions, so offensive its intrusions, that it requires an effort of thought in order to entertain, in these times, pleasant and grateful ideas respecting "priests" and the functions of priesthood. The modern assumptions of priestism are so painful an outrage on Christianity as to start the intelligent mind into revulsion and move the devout heart to grief. Yet—

I. PRIESTS MINISTERED IN ISRAEL WITH THE HIGH SANCTION OF GOD. He—

1. *Created the office*, and defined its solemn functions, which were of the loftiest character.

2. *Invested the person* of the priest with splendour, majesty, and beauty, to command admiration and awe.

3. *Determined the mediatorial intervention* of the priest between man and God; set one man in this august and solemn supremacy among his fellows.

4. *Refused any other than the priest* to come direct to His altar and stand in His most holy presence.

II. THE PRIESTHOOD WAS A PROVISIONAL ARRANGEMENT ANTICIPATORY OF CHRIST'S GLORIOUS OFFICES.

1. In the personal excellence and piety of individual priests, the faultless being always chosen, Christ's *perfect humanity* was foreshadowed.

2. In the splendid attire with which the priests were adorned, *Christ's majestic attributes* and *Divine qualities* were represented.

3. In the imposing ministries before and within the veil, Christ's offices as *atoning and mediating Priest* were pourtrayed.

4. In the sacred and exclusive privileges the priests enjoyed, *Christ's entire acceptableness* and *God's great delight in Him* were impressively and constantly intimated.

III. CHRISTIAN MINISTERS INHERIT MANY OF THE MOST AUGUST AND RESPONSIBLE SPIRITUAL FUNCTIONS OF THE PRIESTHOOD.

1. They have no priestly calling, yet are as distinctly commissioned and *divinely consecrated to their work*.

2. Their solemn trust places them in highest ministries and responsibilites as *mediators between God and human souls*.

3. The Christian Church is *commanded to maintain* them in their ministry and *esteem them very highly* in the discharge of their sacred commission.

4. As bishops and shepherds of Christ's flock, they are put in *trust with the souls of their people;* "they watch for souls."

IV. MODERN PRIESTLINESS PERVERTS AND PROSTITUTES THE SACRED OFFICE OF THE MINISTRY IN THE CHRISTIAN CHURCH.

1. Its *offensive assumption of spiritual supremacy* is in defiance of Christ's law of equality and brotherhood among believers.

2. Its *officious intrusion between God and men* is an affront to the unfettered liberty and right of every one to seek God for himself, and is an infringement upon the mediatorship of Jesus which always avails for all.

3. Its *daring pretensions of altar ministries* is a perversion of New Covenant doctrines; neither altar nor sacrificial rites remaining now within the Church.

4. Its *appalling misleading of seduced souls*, who rest on such beguiling priestliness for spiritual safety, instead of wholly trusting Christ, is sufficient to fill Christian hearts with indignation and to cover the very name of "priest" with anathemas. [See Addenda, p. 114, *Priestism.*]

(*a*) There is now *no priest but Jesus Christ*.

(*b*) His ministers falsify their trust if they *thrust the shadow of a human presence between* the soul and Jesus.

(*c*) The Christian Church will rightly *value the ministry as it elevates Christ's offices before men.*

(*d*) *Every believer*, though not called to the ministry of the Word, *is entrusted with priestly functions,* as a pleader with men for God, a pleader with God for men.

Topic: THE CALLING OF THE PRIESTS (Vv. 1-13).

Notable in this record is the *exclusive agency of God* in placing on His people the blessings of redemption. It recounts the consecration of His priests, those whom He was pleased to call into His sanctuary to *know* and *serve* Him: a calling now granted to all the family of faith. Former chapters of Leviticus have revealed the arrangements of God's mercy in providing the satisfaction due to His own holy government, and in securing the pardon and acceptance of His people. But pardon and acceptance are not the only blessings God has provided through redemption.

I. THE PRIESTLY CALLING.

To what does God summon and set them apart?

1. *Intimate access* with Him; coming into special nearness to His presence, His altar, and His holy place.

2. *Fullest knowledge* of Him; learning His secret will, enjoying freest communion with Him.

3. *Holy service* for Him. "His servants shall serve Him."

II. A CALLING OF HIGHEST HAPPINESS AND PRIVILEGE.

1. The fact of His being what He is as God, perfect in all goodness and in all blessing, must necessarily make *admission into His service, joy;* and exclusion from it, woe. [See Addenda, p. 114, *Sanctity.*]

2. What higher *honour* than to be employed in carrying out the designs of One who is perfect in wisdom and love, and all powerful likewise, so as surely to accomplish the contemplated end.

III. A CALLING HARMONIOUS WITH A CHRISTIAN'S SACRED INSTINCTS AND ENERGIES.

1. God's saints have energies, imperishable energies which, *if unoccupied, must cause them unceasing sorrow;* and how could they be *fitly occupied* except in His service?

2. But they are not to be unoccupied. He who gave those energies *intends that they should be fully occupied,* and that not in distance from Himself, but *in His own near presence.*

IV. A CALLING INTO A WONDROUS LIFE.

Israel was now in the midst of a waste and howling wilderness; and God might have assigned to their priests that they should serve and commune with Him amid those wild and ungenial scenes.

1. But they were called to *enter beneath the shelter of the tabernacle of God.* Its golden boards enclosed them, its mystic curtains covered them. They were shut in with God, encompassed within the sacred and hallowing seclusion.

2. Amid what *solemn experiences they daily dwelt!* There they found *incense* ascending for them, and shrouding them with its fragrance; *light* shining for them and encompassing them with its brightness; and *bread* prepared for them as food, even on the table of God. There, in the presence of God's own goodness, they learned His lessons, and when they went back into the wilderness, they never again entered *it as their home,* but as those *whose dwelling place was with God* in the peace of redemption. They might go in or they might go out; but still they were His priests always. [Comp. B. W. Newton's *Thoughts on Leviticus.*]

Topic: THE MINISTRY OF THE PRIESTHOOD (Vv. 1, 2).

I. DEFINITION OF THE PRIESTHOOD. *A priest is one who mediates between God and man.* He presents the gifts and sacrifices which the worshipper may not, or does not, or dare not offer in person ; and brings back from God the assurance of acceptance and favour.

II. DEVELOPMENT OF THE PRIESTLY OFFICE. Among the Hebrews, as among kindred nations, priestly functions were discharged by the head of each family till the institution of the covenant at Sinai. This, by consecrating one family as priests for the nation, and requiring all sacrifices to be presented in front of the tabernacle of meeting, put an end to the ancient practice.

The transition from the *family* priesthood to the Levitical—the *national* priesthood was indicated when Moses was entrusted to conduct the sacrifices of Israel, as the mediator of the covenant ; and the closing of the old régime was marked by his choosing young men as his assistants in the offering of national sacrifices. As the mediator of the covenant, divinely authorised to communicate God's messages to the people, and the people's messages to God, Moses would be the first person thought of for the priesthood. But his hands being already sufficiently occupied, the office was conferred on his brother, as the person nearest to him in consanguinity and harmony of feeling.

III. THE UNIFYING VALUE OF A NATIONAL PRIESTHOOD. It would help to consolidate the families which had before worshipped at different altars. The union of all Hebrews, of whatever parentage, in the worship of the tabernacle, was an important element of national life. The families were henceforth, at least so far as concerns the rites of religion, united together as a nation ; and the family of Aaron were, by the appointment of Jehovah, mediators between the nation and Himself.

IV. SELECTION OF THE AARONIC FAMILY. The nation being constituted especially Jehovah's, by virtue of their election as His covenant people, the family of Aaron were elected to a corresponding eminence above their kindred ; not only belonging to Jehovah as all Hebrews did, but being in a peculiar sense His for the service of mediation. As the entire nation was holy, or separate from other nations, so this family was called to be holy, for the office and ministrations of the priesthood. As this separation of the Hebrews from the rest of mankind did not begin with any act of their own, but they were chosen by the Lord to be His ; so Aaron and his sons did not take the prerogatives of the priesthood spontaneously, but were called to the office by the election of Jehovah Himself.

V. BENEFICENCE OF THE PRIESTLY OFFICE. The people were not qualified to draw near to God in person ; and though, by virtue of their election, they were entitled to dwell in His habitation, their consciousness of sin made them afraid of Him ; therefore, in condescension to their inability to understand the greatness of His love, He provided a class of persons who, as representatives of His elect, might in their stead enter the tabernacle. To draw near to God, to be a priest, are equivalent expressions. Aaron drew near in behalf of those who were elected to have spiritual communion with God, but were not yet delivered from the bondage of fear ; and his admission within the habitation signified that they were entitled to a corresponding access in spirit, that they were called " a kingdom of priests " for the reason that they might thus draw near God in spiritual fellowship. By his office he was qualified to do outwardly and symbolically what all might do in spirit and in truth.

VI. EXPIATORY MINISTRY OF THE PRIESTHOOD. Before Aaron could enter the holy habitation in behalf of the people, he must officiate at the altar of sacrifice, and expiate sin ; for his constituents were sinful, and the representation of their approach to God as members of His household must be preceded by signs that their sin was taken away; otherwise it might be inferred that Jehovah was indifferent whether His people were holy or unholy. The Hebrew priesthood therefore symbolised in general the expiation of sin, and the admission to filial intercourse with God effected thereby. [Comp. Atwater, *Sacred Tabernacle*].

Topic: QUALIFICATIONS AND MINISTRIES OF GOD'S PRIESTS (Vv. 6-30).

All now done to the tabernacle priests symbolises the experiences of the sanctified soul.

I. *Consecration* WHOLLY THE WORK OF ANOTHER.

Moses, acting for and representing God, *did everything* needful to complete their consecration; whilst they, the *subjects of consecration,* stood as passive recipients of blessings which were placed upon them by another's hand. Moses washed them, clothed them, anointed them, slew the appointed sacrifices, sprinkled the blood, etc. He ceased not from his ministrations until he left them at the door of the tabernacle *fully consecrated* as the priests of God.

A lesson this to those who *desire to be established in grace.* We have not properly learned the typical lesson if we trust to either our power of appreciation, or the applicatory power of faith. The garments brought to us and placed upon us by God become the spring of joy, steadfast and abiding, only as we realise that our possession of them rests not in powers connected with the creature, but in God alone.

II. PERFECT CLEANNESS THE INITIAL REQUIREMENT.

Their cleansing was received *as a gift from God.* They washed not themselves, the hand of another did it. Even as Jesus says to His disciples, "If I wash thee not, thou hast no part with Me" (Jno. xiii. 8).

III. INVESTITURE IN HOLY ATTIRE.

To Moses it had before been said, "Thou shalt make holy garments for Aaron thy brother, for glory and beauty." Those garments had been made.

1. All the adornments of grace have been *prepared for us;* wait in readiness for us.

2. *A moment of intensest joy to Moses* when he brought forth those prepared garments for adornment. Nor less to Christ when He clothes the soul "with the garments of salvation."

3. *Attire symbolic of sacred qualities.* They were of blue, purple, scarlet, finetwined linen, with connecting chains and ouches or settings of gold, indicating:

(*a*) Heavenliness of character (typified by the *blue*).
(*b*) Purity (typified by the *white* linen).
(*c*) Official dignity (typified by the *scarlet and purple*).
(*d*) Divine power of sustaining others (typified by the chains and ouches of *gold*); gold being used in the tabernacle as a symbol of Deity.

IV. ADORNED WITH THE CROWN OF HOLINESS.

On his head was placed "the holy crown, the golden plate."

(*a*) A "crown" is the symbol of *kingship*; it declares the *royalty of consecrated souls,* "kings unto God."
(*b*) *Holiness* inscribed on the crown: it declares that the *highest dignity of man* is *moral rectitude, spiritual sanctity.*

That plate bore the inscription "HOLINESS TO THE LORD." It implied that—

1. *The vindication of that "holiness"* was the avowed object of his priestly service.

2. Bearing that inscription on his brow among the people, during his priestly ministries, asserted that *God's holiness had been and was being adequately maintained.*

3. Entering into God's presence with that inscription was evidence that *God acknowledged the fact of His holiness being maintained.* It was so with the temple priests; so with our glorious High Priest; is so with every soul who fulfils on earth the ministry of Christian devotion.

V. THE BADGE OF MEDIATORSHIP.

1. From the high priest's shoulders (the place of *endurance and strength*), suspended by chains of gold (symbol of *Divine sustaining power*), hung the "breastplate." And that badge of his office, to intercede for others, *lay upon his heart.*

2. It bore upon it the *names of those for whom he was appointed to minister,* and whose high priest he was. Every one who had a place within that cluster of names had a claim on his ministry and mediatorship.

3. Besides being suspended from the shoulders, the place of strength, it was firmly bound to the pontifical ephod, the distinguishing garment of the *mediatorial office* of high priest.

The most glorious function of the high priest was the bearing *others' names,* not his own; and mediating *for others,* not for himself, before the Lord. It is certainly the crowning glory of the Lord Jesus. And the Christian soul has a priestly mission, supreme above all others, to "look not every man on his own things but the things of others"; to *bring others before the Lord in prayer,* and to *win souls into blessed reconciliation with God* by his gracious interventions and Christly ministries.

VI. SPIRITUAL ANOINTING.

That "holy oil" is the "unction from the Holy One." (1) The *plenitude* of the Spirit; and (2) the *graces* of the Spirit; and (3) the *efficient power* of the Spirit, are essential to a priestly life of sanctity and service.

VII. QUALIFICATION BASED ON SACRIFICE.

1. The scene suddenly changes; and the gloriously attired and anointed priest stands *as a sinner* by the sin offering. For sin must be expiated even for the most privileged souls.

(1) Its blood sprinkled upon the altar indicated that *appeasement was demanded* or ever they could approach that altar in ministry.

(2) Its body being consumed without the camp declared *what their doom would be* did justice exact its due.

(3) But the blood on the altar *and accepted,* announced complete propitiation and acceptance.

(4) While the *choice inward parts* consumed on the altar fire, testified that God's claim of *inward perfectness* was satisfied.

2. The burnt sacrifice summoned them to *absolute self-devotion;* for God will receive no less in any who avowedly become His. "His zeal must *consume* us".

3. But in the *consecration offering* they yielded themselves up to God with *gratitude* and *gladness:* as those who reach towards the self-devotion of Jesus—"I delight to do Thy will; yea, Thy law is within my heart."

In every sacrifice the merits of Christ and His atonement are primarily set forth: but there is a subsidiary relevancy to the self-denials of a Christian career.

VIII. APPLIED SACRIFICIAL GRACE.

"Moses took the blood of it, and put it upon the tip of Aaron's ear," etc.

1. The *value* of sacrifice, which had before been accepted *for* them, was now *applied to* them.

2. The *meaning* of sacrifice, also, was now *urged upon them:* all life laid out for God, and in His service.

IX. SYMBOLIC OFFERINGS PRESENTED TO GOD.

This was their first act of personal presentation within God's sanctuary of consecrated sacrifices. Moses took offerings and "put all upon Aaron's hands, and upon his sons' hands, and waved them for a wave offering before the Lord,' etc.

The sacrifices which thus filled their hands were those which signified:

1. *Inward perfectness:* perfectness in the reins, and in the heart; indicating the bringing, on their part, into God's employ of their purest affections, and highest virtues, and noblest intelligence.

2. *Outward developed perfectness* of character; represented in the unleavened anointed bread that constituted the meat offering.

It is only in Christ's perfectness, a perfectness to be appropriated by us, that we can present such offerings before God.

X. SIGN OF DIVINE ACCEPTANCE.

1. *Being sprinkled by the blood* which first had been sprinkled and *accepted upon the altar*, conveyed the fact that God received their consecration: that themselves, their office, and all its various functions were placed under the sanction and the acceptableness of the blood.

2. The sprinkling of the *holy anointing oil* symbolically connected the Holy Spirit's grace with those offices into which God was, and is pleased to call His people. Without this, by whatever dignity or beauty they might be clothed, they would remain inefficient and powerless to minister aright before the Lord. But He who calls into holy office bestows the needed grace and power.

3. Their *feeding upon* the sacrifice signified the *communication of strength*, for we are nourished by food; and suggested the *fellowship now established between them and God.* They fed on part of that on which the holy fire of the altar had fed. There was communion, therefore, with God in the sacrifice.

Thus consecrated, they were to abide within the tabernacle, and "keep the charge" of Jehovah. And "blessed is the man whom Thou choosest, and causeth to approach unto Thee." [See Addenda, p. 114, *Sanctity.*]

Topic: CONSECRATION OF THE PRIESTS.—A.: THE PUBLICITY OF THE CEREMONY (Vv. 1-5).

Among the Hebrews, previous to the promulgation of the law from Sinai, the priesthood was not confined to particular individuals; though, as a rule, the head of the family discharged duties at the altar of the household associated with divine worship. The Levitical priesthood corresponds, in many of its features, with most of the religions of antiquity, in their sacerdotal institutions. In them, we read of *priests, altars, and sacrifices;* supposed to be mediums of communication between the worshippers and worshipped, and the means of propitiation.

The institution of the priesthood followed the request of the people that Jehovah would not speak to them except through some mediator. The priests became servants of the Lord, and of the people for His sake. The consecration services, by which Aaron and his sons were inducted to their offices, were calculated to humble as well as exalt them. They were to be free from personal blemish, sanctified from all ceremonial defilement, and were to exercise self-denial by abstaining from wine during the performance of their duties. In this chapter we have the performance of ceremonies directed in Exodus xxix., and they were not repeated subsequently, except in the succession of the high priest. The ceremony was *public*—

I. TO CONFIRM ITS GREAT IMPORTANCE. Among a people so prone to be rebellious and jealous, it was necessary that conclusive evidence should be furnished to leave no room for the shadow of a reasonable doubt respecting the persons selected for so distinguished a position. The purposes for which the priesthood was instituted were the most solemn and important; upon the rightful discharge of the duties the most momentous issues hung. Aaron and his sons were to stand in the breach which sin had made between man and God, and be dispensers of life and death.

II. To CONFIRM ITS DIVINE APPOINTMENT. Had they been consecrated in a private way, suspicions that the offices had been assumed from personal ambition, or for selfish ends, might have been suggested; but the ceremony being performed in the presence of the whole congregation, "at the door of the tabernacle," *the open approval of Jehovah was proclaimed*. The congregation would thus be deeply impressed with the sacredness of the priesthood, as selected and anointed of the Lord.

III. To CONFIRM ITS GENERAL ACCEPTANCE. The people had asked for the intervention of a priest, their request had been granted, and they were now required to show at a public ceremony that they *approved* and *accepted* what was done. At the door of the tabernacle they would recognise the divine appointment, and unitedly engage to accord with the arrangements made. They were the subjects of, and witnesses to, the covenant made with Moses and Aaron; and pledged themselves ready to render implicit obedience.

Read in the light of the New Testament, these considerations may be applied to the public consecration of our blessed Lord, when baptised in the Jordan by John. Heaven opened, the divine voice, the descent of the Spirit in the presence of many witnesses, indicated the great importance of the mission He was beginning; showed that He was beloved of God, and possessed His unqualified approval. Such facts place upon all to whom the tidings come binding obligations to accept the Messiah as the Atoning Priest of the world, for all men, for all time.—*F. W. Brown.*

B.: THE SOLEMNITY OF THE CEREMONY (Vv. 6-17).

Commanded to draw near to Jehovah at the door of the tabernacle, and to observe the ceremony under direct Divine superintendence, the Israelites would be at once impressed with a sense of deep solemnity in the service; they would feel they were standing on holy ground. The solemnity seen—

I. BY THE PREPARATORY ABLUTIONS ENJOINED. Appointed to come nigh to a God spotlessly pure and holy, Aaron and his sons must adopt means fitting to suggest the need of inward holiness and official blamelessness.

II. BY THE SACERDOTAL VESTMENTS REQUIRED. Garments so beautiful and elaborate, rendering the priests (especially the High Priest) imposing in their appearance, would not only adorn the person, but convey the idea that Jehovah's worship required the presentation of things *pure* and *excellent*. The priests' attire was chosen by the Lord, and each part suggested some solemn lesson. The mind is impressed through the eye, the spirit may be made devout through the senses.

III. BY THE APPROPRIATE SACRIFICES OFFERED. Their "sin" "burnt" and "peace" offerings symbolised *death to sin, fulness of consecration, acceptance with God*. Every act in connection with sacrifices was calculated to prepare the priests for their holy work, to beget reverence in the people towards them.

IV. BY THE GENERAL ANOINTING OBSERVED. The tabernacle, as well as the priests, was anointed with oil. Israel was to entertain reverence for the place where the priests would officiate, where oblations would be presented; everything associated with divine worship was to be regarded as peculiarly sacred.

When, "in the fulness of time," Christ came, He was pointed out as "the Lamb of God," denoting the solemn *sacrificial character* of His work, as well as the *exemplary character* of His life. Through Him we have access into the holiest of all by a new and living way.—*F. W. B.*

C.: THE COMPLETENESS OF THE CEREMONY (Vv. 17-36).

In the consecration observances every place where the priests would officiate, and every faculty of the priest, was impressively dedicated. The *head*, the seat of intelligence; the *shoulders*, the repository of strength; the *breast*, the home of love; all were clothed appropriately to indicate *purity, energy, excellence*. Beauty in appearance, efficiency in service, comfort for the worshippers, benedictions for the whole congregation, all were arranged for, and guaranteed. As the hands of the priests were lifted towards heaven, and waved to and fro, they were reminded that their ministry would reach to heaven; and at the same time bless the children of men. The completeness of the ceremony is seen in that—

I. THERE WAS NO MARGIN LEFT FOR HUMAN INVENTION.

Every thing was done *fully* and *exactly* as Jehovah commanded; the pattern of the tabernacle was given to Moses on the mount, and every minute arrangement in the series of sacrifices, and consecration of the priests, *finally fixed*. Had the people been left to add, or subtract, there would have been room for manifold innovations and absurdities.

II. THERE WOULD BE NO AFTER NEED FOR DIVINE REVISION.

Jehovah never makes mistakes; what He does stands fast, His plans are perfect, His purposes immutable. The priesthood met the moral needs of the Hebrews; was perfectly adapted to requirements of the age. When the prophetical age dawned, and clearer light shone upon divine revelation, the things instituted in connection with the tabernacle service developed into more spiritual significance; what they *taught* remained unimpaired. These things continued till they were lost in the substance of which they were only shadows. Christ *embraced all* the divine teaching, and *embodied all* the excellencies to be found in Moses and the law. Christianity is not so much a new, as a perfected religion, as the first verse of the Epistle to the Hebrews teaches. The whole of revelation, from first to last, is a development; every stage complete in itself, each growing out of its predecessor, and merging into something better. *The completion of redemption* will be when we are made kings and priests unto God, and reign with Christ for ever and ever.—F. W. B.

D.: THE SIGNIFICANCE OF THE CEREMONY (Vv. 17-36).

The institution of sacrificial worship, through an ordained priesthood, would deepen in the hearts of the Hebrews impressions of Divine truth already there as the outcome of the patriarchal teaching. They were now very clearly taught—

I. *That there can be no acceptable service rendered to God without purity in the worshipper.*

II. *That the imperfection of purity in the worshipper demands an atonement in the sight of God to make up for that defect.*

III. *That the distance between God and man, produced by sin, can be removed only by a divinely-appointed mediator.*

The priests were the *channels*, not the sources, of blessing to the people; they had no power of their own to dispense pardon, nor could they exempt from blame, or furnish indulgences. They existed *for the people*, not the people for them. They wielded deputed and responsible power. Medieval priestly assumption, papal arrogance, find no sanction in these Levitical rites.

The Epistle to the Hebrews teaches that in the Gospel dispensation we, as priests to God, are, (*a*) *cleansed by the washing of regeneration;* (*b*) *clothed with the garments of Christ's righteousness;* (c) *offer sacrifices of praise and prayer;* (d) *surrender ourselves wholly to the Lord;* (e) *receive the unction of the Holy One.*

To seek position and succession in such a spiritual priesthood is the duty and privilege of all.—*F. W. B.*

OUTLINES ON VERSES OF CHAPTER VIII.

V. 2.—*Theme:* GOD'S ELECTED PRIESTS.

i. "It is not only historically true that Aaron and his descendants were PRIESTS BY THE ELECTION OF JEHOVAH declared through Moses, the mediator of the covenant, and confirmed by the sign of the almond rod, but *such a calling of God is essential to the idea of the office;* for a priest is one who comes near to God, dwells with Him in His home as a companion in behalf of others, because more acceptable than they. The priest is preferred before those he represents; therefore no man may take this honour to himself, or be exalted to it by his fellows. 'Blessed is the man whom *Thou chooseth,* and causest to approach unto Thee, that he may dwell in Thy courts; we shall be satisfied with the goodness of Thy house, even of Thy holy temple' (Psa. lxv. 4). Only those thus chosen by God were priests.

ii. "This divine election of the family of Aaron out of Israel signifies that those who had been admitted to filial fellowship with the Holy One of Israel were called thereto by the SOVEREIGN CHOICE OF GOD. As Jehovah chose the family of Aaron out of the tribe of Levi, the Levites out of the twelve tribes of Israel, and the Hebrews out of all the nations, so has He chosen His spiritual seed out of every kindred, and tongue, and people, and nation. Without such election they would have remained, like the rest of mankind, strangers to the covenant, instead of becoming 'a holy priesthood to offer up spiritual sacrifices.' The New Testament writers make this Divine election very prominent, declaring that those who, by receiving Christ became sons of God, were 'born not of the will of man, but of God' (Jno. i. 13), were 'called to be saints' (Rom. i. 17), were 'chosen before the foundation of the world that they should be holy' (Eph. i. 4), were 'predestinated to the adoption of children' (Eph. i. 5), were 'elect unto obedience and sprinkling of the blood of Jesus Christ' (1 Pet. i. 2).

iii. "*The priesthood were* ELECTED TO HOLINESS. The whole people, as a kingdom of priests, were to be a holy nation; but the family of Aaron were chosen to a still higher ceremonial purity than was required of their brethren. When Korah and his companions claimed the right to officiate as priests, they did so on the ground that all the congregation were holy; and the reply of the mutineers was, 'To-morrow Jehovah will show who are His, and who is holy; and will cause him to come near unto Him; even him whom He hath chosen will He cause to come near unto him' (Numb. xvi. 5). The budding of Aaron's rod decided the question between him and those who claimed the office on the ground that all were holy. It was a sign that Aaron was elected to a superiority of holiness among the Hebrews, as the nation was to a similar eminence among the nations of the earth.

"The election of the Hebrews to be a holy nation set forth before the eyes of men the truth that Jehovah is holy, and that the true Israel who in spirit and in truth have access to Him must be holy; the calling of *the priests to a greater strictness of life* than was required of the common people, and the requirements of a *still higher degree of holiness in the head of the sacerdotal order,* were concurrent and cumulative testimonies to the same truth. —Atwater, *Sacred Tabernacle.*

V. 3.—*Theme:* AN ELECT PEOPLE. "And gather them," etc.

The circumstances amid which Divine directions were given to the people, as well as the directions themselves, were calculated to impress the fact upon all Israel that they were *an elect nation,* brought out from Egypt to inaugurate a new era for the world. Every other nation was sunken in idolatry, and Israel had proneness to it, as evinced in the worship of the calf at the foot of the Mount. All idolatry debases and degrades; has never been known to develop into civilisation, much less into pure and undefiled religion. Man could not develop from his innate wisdom or inner consciousness such ideas of *God, holiness, duty* and *worship,* as those which were promulgated and established around Sinai. The institution and consecration of the priesthood taught that God is holy, and that "holiness becometh His house for ever." Man, without supernatural aid, has always transferred and affixed his own sinful passions to priests and gods; and, has sought to become like them, to avoid their anger, and secure their benediction. In Israel, Jehovah showed who He was; and *how* His favour might be secured. Consider:

I. THE CONGREGATION ASSEMBLED. All the people were to meet, they had been prepared for united service. In Egypt they had become bound together by strong and tender ties—they had no prejudices or predilections in respect to government, were ready to take directions from their Divine king. Had Jehovah revealed Himself equally, and at once, to all men, revelation would have seemed the spontaneous and simultaneous growth of human inquiry; and the plan by which God governs our race would have been thwarted.

Israel was chosen to high honour, but onerous duties were associated with their privileges; they were called to self-denying service, and to the attainment of holiness, requiring constant self-mortification. The priesth .ould convey knowledge of God *through the medium of the senses;* thus. the revelation in the wilderness was adapted to the infancy of the Jewish Church.

II. THE PLACE OF ASSEMBLY. " The door of the tabernacle." Everything done in order to beget devoutness and solemnity. There was no image of Jehovah before which the people would bow; but they were to remember that God had taken up His abode among them, and revealed His will from the tabernacle. What a contrast the place would be to the heathen temples in Egypt, with which Israel had been familiar. *They* were places where revolting abominations were practised; *here,* all would impress the mind with purity. The priests who were to officiate in the holy place must be sanctified, to denote how spotlessly pure the God of Israel was. The gathering of the congregation at the door of the tabernacle, and the consecration of the priesthood would meet the great wants of man's moral nature. He has something in him that compels him to recognise and worship a superior Being; he becomes like the Being he worships; he seeks to commune with and receive communications from, the Being he worships; he desires a mediator between him and his God.

All the light and purity that gathered around the Levitical priesthood was *symbolic* of the purity of character required in those who draw near to God; and *typical* of the perfect purity of Him who was "holy, harmless, undefiled, and separate from sinners."—*F. W. B.*

V. 8.—*Theme:* ISRAEL'S GLORY.
" And he put the breastplate," etc.

To outward seeming at this time the people, in themselves and their circumstances, did not present a very dignified appearance. With no visible means of subsistence, a horde of emancipated slaves, and before them as their new arena for enterprise a waste, howling wilderness. Yet they were the Lord's freemen; He was their Deliverer and King. Through and *with* their priests, consecrated in their presence, they would draw very near to God. They had not been permitted to engrave their names upon tablets of fame in the land of bondage, but now their names are engraved upon the breastplate of the high priest, and presented before the Lord. This denoted—

I. THAT THEY WOULD BE EVER REMEMBERED IN THE DIVINE PRESENCE.

Their names *uncovered; plainly immediately* seen.

II. THAT THEY HAD A PLACE NEAR THE HEART OF THEIR REPRESENTATIVE.

Not behind his back, or beneath his feet, but on his breast.

III. THAT THEY WERE REGARDED AS VERY PRECIOUS BY THE LORD.

Their names not written in the sands of the desert, which would be soon obliterated, nor on raw and rough material, but on precious stones. The Lord esteems those as His "*jewels*" who become His people.

IV. THAT THEY MIGHT RECEIVE LIGHT AND DIRECTION IN ALL THEIR JOURNEYINGS.

The Urim and Thummim in the breastplate would, in some way unknown to us, indicate the Divine will to priests and people. The precious stones of the breastplate may suggest *the paradise lost by the fall,* where there were gold and precious stones; and *paradise regained by the redemption of Christ,* where precious stones abound. Our great High Priest carries us, not only on His breast, but *in His heart.* He remembers, represents us, pleads for us. Through His righteousness we may hereafter be admitted into the holiest of all. —*F. W. B.*

V. 9.—*Theme:* THE HOLY CROWN.
" Upon his forefront did he put the golden plate, the holy crown; as the Lord commanded Moses."

Man is the only creature whose forehead fronts the temple of the sky. Fitting that the head of High Priest, "the human face divine," should be crowned with gold when approaching the King of kings, and representing Him among the people. The gold band upon the mitre shone like a diadem, caught and reflected the glory of heaven. On it in letters patent to all: " Holiness to the Lord." Gold denotes *preciousness* and *incorruptibility.* Such ever are the *nature* and *character* of Jehovah. The holy crown upon the head of the High Priest implied—

I. THAT HE HAD REGAL DUTIES TO DISCHARGE. He was in the service of the King, immortal, invisible, the only wise God. Nothing he commanded to be performed could therefore be mean or unimportant.

II. THAT HE HAD REGAL POWER TO EXERCISE. Weak, like other men, in himself, he was a plenipotentiary, full of power, because of the authority by which He was commissioned and sustained. Ambassadors in councils and courts are powerful on account of the *Sovereign* and *Realm* they represent: so here.

III. THAT HE HAD REGAL DIGNITY TO SUSTAIN. He, a kingly priest, would need to magnify his office. He was under necessity to keep the glory of the crown unsullied. The people would look up to Aaron as their exemplar, as well as mediator. Every thought, word, deed to be " Holiness to the Lord."

Here we have a significant *Type of Christ* our High Priest. He was anointed with the oil of gladness above His fellows. He is *King* and *Priest.* Our great Intercessor was seen by John (Rev. xiv. 14.) " having on His head a golden crown." Holiness is the crown and glory of the universe; constitutes the *nature* and *blessedness* of God; is the ultimatum of human redemption. Holiness and blessedness are wedded together by indissoluble bonds.—*F. W. B.*

V. 12.—*Theme:* SANCTIFICATION. "To sanctify him."

Aaron was set apart to his grand work, not only by lavations and lustrations, but by annointings. This would show—

I. THAT HE WAS ENTIRELY DEDICATED TO GOD'S SERVICE. As the oil was poured profusely upon his head, it symbolised the fact that so *readily* and *cheerfully* would he pour out his life's best and brightest energies in Jehovah's service.

II. THAT HE WAS COMPLETELY SANCTIFIED IN GOD'S PRESENCE.

As the oil made the face of Aaron shine, and he submitted to every preliminary in connection with his entry upon his office, he would have the inward witness, and give ocular proof, that the needed preparation was complete.

Christ, as our great High Priest, "*sanctified Himself*," not for His office simply, but for the sake of His disciples; and His will is that we should be "sanctified through the truth." We all need the "unction of the Holy One," sanctification by the grace of Christ, and the influences of the Holy Ghost to fit us for sacred service and communion with the Lord.—*F. W. B.*

V. 21.—*Theme:* PERFECT SERVICE. "And he washed the inwards," etc.

The minute and strict directions given respecting the offerings presented at the consecration of the priests showed—

I. THE NEED OF INWARD PURITY. Man looks only on the outward appearance; the Lord looks upon the inward parts, and in the hidden parts He would have us to know wisdom. The inwards, as well as the legs of offering were to be cleansed before being presented.

II. THE NEED OF UNRESERVED SURRENDER. *The whole ram* was to be offered. This same truth fully taught in the holocaust. The new dispensation demands that we present our bodies living sacrifices holy and acceptable unto God. Let us seek, then, to please the Lord and to be accepted of Him.—*F. W. B.*

V. 23.—*Theme:* LIVING SACRIFICES.

"And he slew it; and Moses took," etc.

Aaron and his sons laying their hands upon the ram of consecration, identified them with it; denoted their unqualified surrender to Jehovah. The blood of the victim being put upon the priests' ears, hands, and feet, must have been intended to teach important lessons. The blood sprinkled upon the right ear, suggests—

I. THAT THE PRIESTS WERE TO ATTENTIVELY LISTEN TO THE COMMANDS OF THE LORD. They were not to exercise their own ingenuity in forming precepts, they were not to listen to anything that would border on collusion, or conspiracy. Ear-gate was ever to be open and ready to receive the communications from heaven; was to be kept sacred to the Lord. The sprinkling of blood upon the thumb of the right hand suggests—

II. THAT THE PRIESTS WERE TO READILY RECEIVE THE COMMANDS OF THE LORD. The hand is an emblem of *receptivity*, as well as *energy*; represents *capacity* and *will*. By it, we *distribute* and *receive*. The hands of priests would be busy in offering sacrifices, in waving incense, in presenting prayer. They must be therefore clean and consecrated, ever ready to present gifts to God from the people, and to convey blessings to them from God. The sprinkling of blood upon the great toe of the right foot suggests—

III. THAT THE PRIESTS WERE TO IMMEDIATELY OBEY THE COMMANDS OF THE LORD. By our feet we move in the direction our hearts prompt and lean. The feet of the priests would stand in the holy place, it was fitting they should be sanctified.

Our great High Priest gave the words to His disciples that He received from His Father; His holy hands were ever busy doing good; His "holy feet, trod the sacred fields of Palestine for our advantage." Let us seek that all our powers may be sanctified by and consecrated to the Lord.—*F. W. B.*

V. 27.—*Theme:* HEARTY SERVICE.

"And he put all upon Aaron's hands," etc. Moses had the honour of inducting Aaron to his office, as well as robing him for it. *Placing the offering upon the hands of Aaron and his sons*—

I. CLEARLY INDICATED THEIR WORK. Gave them practical knowledge of the duties to be prepared.

II. FULLY DEDICATED THEM TO THEIR WORK. Not only were they sanctified and attired in sacerdotal vestments, but really began their work.

Waving the offering in their hands, showed—

I. THE SUBORDINACY OF THE PRIESTHOOD. They were only servants, with hands full of obligations; they held gifts which already belonged to Jehovah: of His own they would offer at the altar.

II. THE SUPREMACY OF THE LORD. Themselves, as well as the offering, belonged to God; they stood before the Lord acknowledging His sovereign claims.

Let us do the work of the Lord with both hands earnestly. Our work is (*a*) *important*—requires both hands; (*b*) *great*—fills both hands; (*c*) *urgent*—prompts both hands. Thus our Redeemer toiled for us, so let us labour for Him.—*F. W. B.*

V. 33.—*Theme:* SEVEN DAYS' CONSECRATION. "Seven days shall he consecrate you."

The protracted period of consecration within the tabernacle would suggest—

I. *The deep dyed character of sin.*
II. *The immaculate purity of God.*
III. *The need of patient preparation for sacred work.*
IV. *The conditions of success in sacred work.*—*F. W. B.*

V. 36.—*Theme:* EXEMPLARY OBEDIENCE. "So Aaron and his sons did all," etc.

Though many things commanded to be

I

done seemed strange and unimportant, yet "*all things*" were done by Aaron and his sons that the Lord directed. Indicating—

I. WILLINGNESS FOR THE SERVICES *to which they were called.* Thus they enjoyed—

II. GUARANTEE OF SUCCESS IN THE WORK *to which they were called.*

Fulfilling their part of the covenant, the Lord would fulfil His part. Those who honour the Lord He will honour. Through the priesthood priceless blessings would be vouchsafed to Israel; through our Great Prophet, Priest, and King, innumerable and inestimable blessings came to the world.—*F. W. B.*

ILLUSTRATIVE ADDENDA TO CHAPTER VIII.

PRIESTISM.
"Go forth and preach impostures to the world,
But give them truth to build upon."
—*Dante.*

"The power to bind and loose to Truth is given,
The mouth that speaks it is the mouth of Heaven;
The power which in a sense belongs to none,
Thus understood, belongs to every one.
. . . . . .
It owes its high prerogatives to none,
It shines *for* all, as shines the blessed sun;
It shines *in* all who do not shut it out
By dungeon doors of unbelief and doubt.
To shine, it *does not ask*—O, far from it—
For hierarchal privilege and permit!
Rabbi and priest may be chained down to lies,
And babes and sucklings winged to mount the skies."
—Abraham Coles: *The Evangel.*

"Led so grossly by *this meddling priest,*
Dreading the curse that money may buy out."
—*King John*, III., i.

"Hateful to me, as are the gates of hell,
Is he who, hiding one thing in his heart,
Utters another."—Bryant's *Homer's Iliad.*

"O what a godly outside falsehood hath!"
Merchant of Venice, I., 3.

"Priest, beware your beard;
I mean to tug it, and to cuff you soundly;
Under my feet I stamp thy cardinal's hat;
In spite of pomp, or dignities of Church,
Here by thy cheek I drag thee up and down."—*Henry VI.*, i., 3.

SANCTITY.

"Holiness—as I then wrote down some of my contemplations on it—appeared to me to be of a sweet, calm, pleasant, charming, serene nature, which brought an inexpressible purity, brightness, peacefulness, ravishment to the soul; in other words, that it made the soul like a field or garden of God, with all manner of pleasant fruits and flowers, all delightful and undisturbed, enjoying a sweet calm and the gentle vivifying beams of the sun. The soul of a true Christian—as I then wrote my meditations—appeared like such a little white flower as we see in the spring of the year, low and humble on the ground, opening its bosom to receive the pleasant beams of the sun's glory; rejoicing, as it were, in a calm rapture, diffusing around a sweet fragrance, standing peacefully and lovingly in the midst of other flowers round about, all in like manner opening their bosoms to drink in the light of the sun."—*Jonathan Edwards.*

"A Christian should let us see his graces walking abroad in his daily conversation; and, if such guests are in the house, they will often look out of the window, and be publicly seen abroad in all duties and holy actions.'—*Gurner.*

"When courtiers come down into the country, the common home-bred people possibly think their habits strange; but they care not for that. 'It is the fashion at Court.' What need, then, have the godly to be so tender-foreheaded, to be out of countenance because the world looks on holiness as a singularity? It is the only fashion in the highest Court, yea, of the King of kings Himself."—*Salter.*

"Inward holiness and eternal glory are the crown with which God dignifies His elect. But they are not the cause of the election. A king is not made a king by the royal robe he wears and the crown that encircles his brow; but he therefore wears his robes and puts on his crown because he is a king."—*Salter.*

"True ornaments to know a holy man."
—*Richard III.*, iii., 7.

"Our holy lives must win a new world's crown."—*Richard II.*, v., 1.

"Holiness and happiness are always an indissoluble connection; yea, holiness is felicity itself."—*Alex. Macworter.*

"He's honourable;
And, doubling that, most holy."
—*Cymbeline*, III., 4.

CHAPTER IX.

Inaugural Ministries of Aaron.

SUGGESTIVE READINGS.

V. 1.—**On the eighth day.** It was the dawn of their Sabbath, and followed a week of seclusion within the tabernacle, where they had daily presented their consecration offerings. With what solemn eagerness they must have anticipated this day: the day of their inauguration into their public ministry as God's priests for Israel. Moreover, the day was to be distinguished by a sublime manifestation of "the glory of Jehovah" unto them and before the people. Such privileged days enter into all saintly careers, fervently desired, surpassingly blessed: when the soul is led into hallowed spiritual experiences, and when "the Lord suddenly comes to His temple." It intimates the truths that—

1. Preparation for sacred service ought to be made in seclusion with thoroughness and utmost solemnity.
2. Devout waiting for the Lord will in due season be sealed with glad realisations of Him.
3. Entrance upon any sacred project or pursuit should be stayed until God has been sought in patient communion.
4. A ministry for God will only be acceptable and effective as the minister is himself fully and spiritually in readiness for his "high calling."

That "life hid with God" is symbolic of the sacred separateness to which the Christian is called, and summons us to like retirement from the world, that we may become meet to render true service as "priests unto God."

V. 2.—**Take thee a young calf.** Was there in this a calling Aaron's sin to remembrance? Jesus, as He commissioned Peter to his apostolic ministry, called his sin (of denying Him thrice) back to memory by His thrice repeated inquiry, "Lovest thou Me?" And here Jehovah recalls the *calf-idolatry* at the base of Sinai; for on no other occasion was "a calf" appointed for a sin offering. But surely, in now entering upon his high-priesthood, that great occasion of sin should be in his mind to humble his soul in the hour of his exaltation, and teach him how wholly unmerited was the sacred honour into which Jehovah now admitted him. It is well that we, in hours of exalted privilege, "look to the hole from which we were digged," and have our sins in mind, "lest we be exalted above measure." Paul needed a like restraint. Human nature is apt to become self-satisfied and arrogant; the remedy is to see our frailty in the light of past follies.

V. 4.—**To-day the Lord will appear unto you.** When an appointment is made to an exalted office in the State, it is accompanied by presentation in person to the Sovereign of the realm. This was Aaron's introduction, in his high official status, to the very presence of Jehovah, whose priest he was henceforth to be, and in whose Regal presence he was henceforth to minister. The Shekinah, which had dwelt in the secresy of the holy place, would that day "shine forth" in brightness. God's elect servants should behold His glory. It would teach them to serve with awe, and impress on them the grandeur of their office; thus fostering reverence and circumspection in their ministry. When the like incident occurred to Isaiah, his spirit was utterly overwhelmed (Isa. vi. 5); and even John the beloved fell as one dead at the feet of the glorified Jesus (Rev. i. 17). Blessed are they who have had Paul's glad yet gentler experience: "It pleased God to reveal His Son *in* me" (Gal. i. 16). It was then he was designated to his apostolic work; and such a vision calls us also to a sacred life and service.

V. 7.—Go unto the altar . . . make atonement for thyself. Installed though Aaron was as high priest, he yet waited the command to act; and Moses stood to him as God. Hence the words, "No man taketh this honour unto himself, but he that is called of God, as was Aaron" (Heb. v. 4, 5). Yet it is well that we heed God's will in the call addressed to us from the demands and opportunities around us. "Go *unto the altar*": for there is frequent occasion that we approach the altar in service for man and sacrifice to God.

Atonement for thyself, and for the people. The "people" were concerned in Aaron's sin of idolatry: "They made the calf which Aaron made" (Exod. xxxii. 25); hence there was to be an inclusive sacrificial offering for both Aaron and the people. But "such an High Priest became us who is holy, harmless, undefiled, separate from sinners . . . who needeth not to offer up sacrifice first for His own sins" (Heb. vii. 26, 27).

V. 15.—The people's offering. This consisted of the sin offering, burnt offering, meat offering, and peace offering. It was Aaron's first mediatorial service, standing between God and the people, and propitiating on their behalf. From that hour there never has ceased to be an intercessory priest; nor shall the priesthood fail henceforth; for "the word of the oath has consecrated Christ *for evermore*" (Heb vii. 28). How consolatory and assuring the truth, that within "the holy place made without hands" our Lord unceasingly presents the merits of His mighty sacrifice, and intercedes for all who come to God by Him. None need fear neglect, since Jesus assumes the gracious ministry of mediation; it is the office to which He devotes Himself now in heaven: "He ever liveth to make intercession for us." And as His sacrificial death on the cross was not for Himself, but for mankind, He still presents "the people's offering." But He "needeth not daily" to renew the sacrifice Aaron's duty was to maintain with undeviating regularity and recurrence the burnt sacrifice of the morning (verse 17); type of the enduring virtue of Jesus' atonement day unto day, till time shall be no more.

V. 22.—Aaron lifted up his hand toward the people. Sacrifices completed, Aaron now, with hands upraised, pronounced his first priestly blessing upon Israel. The very words of the blessing were ordered by Jehovah: "Speak unto Aaron, and unto his sons, saying, On this wise ye shall bless the children of Israel, saying unto them: The Lord bless thee and keep thee: the Lord make His face shine upon thee, and be gracious unto thee: the Lord lift up His countenance upon thee, and give thee peace" (Numb. vi. 23-26).

So Jesus, His sacrifice finished, "lifted up His hands and blessed" His Church; and "it came to pass, while He blessed them, He was parted from them, and carried up into heaven" (Luke xxiv. 50, 51); whence still and unceasingly that unfinished act of blessing goes on, and its sacred gladness and peace come down perpetually upon an adoring Church.

V. 23.—Moses and Aaron went into the tabernacle. The *last* entrance for Moses, the *first* for Aaron; and it marked the moment for transmitting the priestly duties from the younger to the elder brother. Surely they bowed the knee together when within that "secret place of the tabernacle of the Most High," and sought on each other's behalf the succour and grace of God for the onerous responsibilities of their Divine service. Beautiful the thought of such hidden prayer by two brothers, ere they "came out" to their high and holy ministries.

V. 24.—There came a fire out from before the Lord. Forth from the effulgent "glory" cloud (verse 23) sprang living flames on to the altar, and the smouldering sacrifice was quickly consumed by miraculous fire. This fire was jealously maintained; it went not out by day or night: it burned always as the symbol of Jehovah's sanction upon the altar presentations, and His acceptance of those who offered them.

When the people saw, they fell on their faces. "Blessed are they who have *not seen*, and yet have believed"; for still "the Lord is in His holy temple," though the shekinah is not visible. " O come, let us worship and bow down ; let us kneel before the Lord our Maker : for He is our God " (Psa. xcv. 6, 7).

SECTIONAL HOMILIES.

Topic: ENTERING UPON PRIESTLY WORK (Vv. 1, 2).

"On the eighth day Moses called Aaron and his sons, and said unto Aaron, Take thee a young calf for a sin offering, and a ram for a burnt offering, and offer them before the Lord."

A train of solemn rites preceded the priests' admission to their functions. The entrance-path was long and holy. None might draw near *uncalled, uncleansed*— without atonement made through blood, without the sprinklings of anointing oil (chap. viii. 6, 24, 30).

Through a whole week the victims died, and consecrating services went on. During those days the sacred tent enclosed the devoted band. They might not pass its separating gate. The world was left. A barrier parted them from common life. They dwelt, shut out from man, shut in with God.

I. THERE IS A RIGHTFUL PATH BY WHICH GOD'S MINISTERS REACH THEIR SACRED OFFICE.

Called ; cleansed ; consecrated.

II. PREPARATION COMPLETED : THE HOLY OFFICE IS ASSUMED.

"On the eighth day " service commenced in fulness. Life is now one cloud of incense to the Lord. From morn till night the willing priests discharge foreshadowing forms.

III. IN THE CHRISTIAN MINISTRY THE PRIESTLY SYMBOLS ARE REALISED.

Altars no more are raised : victims no longer die : all vanished in the Cross. No lights now are lighted, no incense burns : twilight ordinances fled when the Sun of Righteousness arose. Yet still wide fields of labour open : and grand facts are to be set forth by your ministry. Your life is to proclaim the Lamb of God, the blood once and for ever shed. Your voice must never cease the cry— Behold this truth ; bathe in this stream ; trust in this death ; plead this atoning Cross.

Shame would it be if legal priests relaxed not typifying work, and your hands wearied in uplifting the grand substance—CHRIST. [Compare " *Christ is all.*" By Dean of Gloucester.]

[See Addenda, p. 127, *Ministerial Dedication.*]

Topic: SACRIFICIAL PREPARATION FOR JEHOVAH'S APPEARING (Vv. 2-4)

"Take thee a sin offering, a burnt offering, peace offerings, to sacrifice before the Lord ; and a meat offering ; *for to-day* the Lord *will appear unto you.*"

Who would see God ? Let the soul make ready. To whom will God show Himself ? They who make ready by sacrifices.

I. TO SEE THE LORD DEMANDS SPIRITUAL PREPAREDNESS IN MAN.

1. For man to *meet God without readiness* would entail on him terror and death.
2. But man *may meet God with readiness*, prepared even to behold His glory.
3. When man *meets God thus prepared*, the meeting is propitious and privileged.

II. SACRIFICIAL MERITS PREPARE MAN FOR SEARCHING MANIFESTATIONS OF GOD.

1. By effecting the *complete removal of his sin* (by Sin offering) and therefore cancelling his condemnation.

2. By presenting *an offering of self-devotion* (Burnt offering), and thereby appeasing the Divine favour.

3. By conciliatory acts of propitiation (Peace offering), thus removing all estrangement.

4. By *covenanted communion with God* (Meat offering); fellowship with God in the sacrificial feast.

When Jehovah meets a soul thus "made nigh" by sacrificial merit, not only is there "no condemnation," but "access unto grace" is assured, and even "joy in God." [Compare Rom. v. 1, 2, 11.]

III. AMID MOST GLORIOUS DIVINE MANIFESTATION THE SOUL PREPARED BY SACRIFICE STANDS FEARLESS AND BLEST.

1. Revelations of God come now to privileged souls: and are "*times of refreshing.*"

2. The unveilings of death, which will bring the soul to God's clear presence, will not terrify the believer: it will be "*far better.*"

3. The Lord's appearance "in great glory" at the judgment will be welcomed *with joyous acclaim* by those who "look for His appearing."

4. And in the splendour of heaven, the ransomed hosts will stand without rebuke; realising in God's presence "fulness of joy." [See Addenda, p. 128, *Nearness to God.*]

Topic: CONSECRATION A QUALIFICATION FOR ACTION (Vv. 7-22).

Between the records of this and the preceding chapter there is a striking contrast.

(*a*) The cleansing and adornment of the priests—in which the priests themselves took no active part—represent the truth that the soul, in being made ready for sacred office and sanctuary privilege, is a *passive recipient* of grace which flows from God through Christ our mediator.

As with Aaron and his sons, so with Joshua (Zach. iii. 3-5); all investiture with purity and dignity was wrought *for* them not *by* them. We do not make ourselves clean, do not consecrate ourselves priests. All is of grace, derived from Christ.

(*b*) Our complete consecration and equipment for privileged relationship and a life of near access with God, are *preparatory for a career of service.* [See Addenda p. 128, *Spiritual Benefactors.*]

I. *Consecrated souls are called* TO SERVE IN THE POWER OF THE GRACE THEY HAVE RECEIVED.

1. *New energies* are imparted to the soul on which the grace of Christ rests. "We are His workmanship, created in Christ Jesus *unto good works*" (Eph. ii. 10).

2. *New qualifications are* bestown upon the soul for a life of sacred service. "When thou art converted, strengthen thy brethren" (Luke xxii. 32). "Go stand and speak in the temple to the people all the words of this life" (Act v. 20). "Let him that heareth say come" (Rev. xxii. 17). "Maketh manifest the savour of His knowledge by us in every place" (2 Cor. ii. 14).

3. *New inspirations* animate the life thus divinely enriched. "The love of Christ constraineth us" (2 Cor. v. 14). "They which live should not henceforth live unto themselves, but unto Him who died for them and rose again" (2 Cor. v. 15).

II. *They who have received grace are* REQUIRED TO EXPEND THEIR REDEEMED LIVES IN SACRED MINISTRIES FOR OTHERS.

1. The *virtue of sacrifice is not exhausted* in consecrating us who are made priests in Christ.

2. Sacrificial merits *avail for the people among whom we are to serve* as priests in offices helpful to their salvation.

3. The peculiar sphere of Christian thought and action is defined—carrying to others the blessings of altar sacrifice. For priestly service now, as with Aaron, is all associated with *the* SACRIFICE.

III. CONSECRATION AND SERVICE ARE THE TWO SACRED SEALS AND GUARANTEES OF A PRIVILEGED CHRISTIAN LIFE.

1. Merely to *dwell apart from men as being ourselves consecrated souls*, of a higher sanctity and more heavenly calling than the people, is to *miss the end* for which we were "called of God as was Aaron."

2. Equally so, to *toil in service thereby to gain assurance of our acceptance with God*, is to fulfil the duties and carry the burdens of the priesthood *forgetful of the derived and sufficient grace of Christ for ourselves.*

3. *Sanctity and service ;* sanctity *derived* and service *rendered ;* these form the blended *credentials* of our hallowed priestly life, our blessed relationship to God, and they afford us the full *guarantee* of sufficiency for and success in our ministries for man.

Topic : A SOLEMN BENEDICTION (V. 22).

"And Aaron lifted up his hand towards the people and blessed them."

It would be an act of presumption in a man to assume the part of blessing others if he were not himself occupying a superior spiritual altitude to those he blessed.

I. *In the relations of men to Jehovah there are those who* ATTAIN A HIGHER LIFE OF PRIVILEGE AND OF POWER.

The *high* priest alone was empowered to bless. His was a spiritual elevation above the priests.

1. *Conscious nearness to God* is not equally attained by all.

2. *Sacred power from God* is not equally derived by all.

II. HIDDEN FELLOWSHIP WITH JEHOVAH *is the* SOURCE OF EXALTED QUALIFICATION, *the spring of* BENEFICENT SPIRITUAL POWER.

Aaron had spent solemn seasons during the seven days *enclosed within the tabernacle.* It nerved his heart for his high task, it gave him assurance as he assumed the high function of blessing the people in Jehovah's name. But *after* that official act, he went into more intimate fellowship and prayer with God (v. 23); and when he came forth, he again "blessed the people." It was the act of one whose soul was full of conscious power, to whom it was no longer *an official trust and duty to bless,* but a *delight and privilege;* it was the outflowing of a soul all ardent and adoring.

1. Blessings can only flow from a soul *itself rich in the affluence of blessedness.*

2. Affluence of blessedness can only be won by *the most intimate communion with the Lord.*

III. THEY WHO LIVE AN ELEVATED SPIRITUAL LIFE ARE RICH BENEFACTORS TO A SINFUL WORLD.

1. They draw power from God which does not rest unused, but *goes forth in blessing others.*

2. They exert salutary and saving energy among men, by which earthly life is sweetened, and spiritual health is imparted, and Christian peace is bestown.

3. Their very prayers, unheeded as factors of good, win daily benediction from heaven on many hearts and homes.

4. As a *daily influence in society* such elevated souls shed a benign grace, making social circles purer, kinder, less selfish and sinful, more gentle, peaceful, and Christian.

5. In all their *active ministries for Christ* they are potent for good. They cannot "lift up their hands towards the people" but gracious results ensue.

Thus should every Christian seek to be a "*light* of the world," "*salt* in the earth." Therefore let each (*a*) live a life of *nearest intercourse* with the Lord; a "life hid with Christ in God"; (*b*) fulfil the solemn office of *gracious intercessors* for men; winning blessings by secret prayers.

> "But that from us aught should ascend to heaven
> So prevalent as to concern the mind
> Of God high blest, or to incline His will,
> Hard to belief may seem: Yet *this will prayer.*"—*Milton.*

> "More things are wrought by prayer
> Than this world dreams of. Wherefore, let thy voice
> Rise like a fountain for me night and day."—*Tennyson.*

> "Prayer ardent opens heaven, lets down a stream
> Of glory on the consecrated hour
> Of man, in audience with the Deity."—*Young.*

[See Addenda, p. 128, *Spiritual Benefactors.*]

Topic: WITHIN THE SECRET OF GOD'S TABERNACLE (Vv. 23, 24.).

"And Moses and Aaron *went into the tabernacle* of the congregation," etc.

In this first day of priestly work a fact of significance occurs. When all the offerings had been duly made, Moses and Aaron seek the holy tent. For a short season they retire. They leave the busy scene. It is their wish in stillness to seek God's clearer face. He was before them in the public rite; but calm retreat would give them more calm approach.

I. THE CHRISTIAN SERVANT LABOURS IN OPEN SCENES.

In busy haunts of busy men he strains the toiling nerve. The world is the wide field. There are the precious souls which need the wholesome warning and the faithful word. There sin abounds, and misery dwells, and ignorance spreads its blinding veil. There Satan rules with dreadful sway. In this wild waste the good seed must be sown. Amid graceless crowds grace must be manfully displayed. But—

II. PRIVATE HOURS GAIN STRENGTH FOR PUBLIC ZEAL.

When all is still the opening heavens pour down their dew. In quietude the soul draws nearer to Christ's arms. Then tender whispers testify of love; then truth unfolds the wondrous page; then promises assume substantial form; then distant prospects brighten to the view. It is when apart from men that grace takes deeper root, temptations wither, the world's false glitter fades, the inner man is strengthened to resist, and loins are girded for the battle field. The soldier of the cross goes forth from solitude to fight his fight. He who seeks God alone has God in public by his side.

III. COMMUNION WITH GOD ENRICHES THE SOUL WITH PRECIOUS GRACE.

Grace for *others.* Moses and Aaron soon return; but they come not with empty hands; they are enriched with the best gifts. Here is beautiful evidence of gainful commerce with the Lord. Laden with good, they haste to scatter good around. Their souls are redolent of heaven; "they *blessed the people.*"

The *blessed of the Lord bless earth.* And they are the most blessed who seek the mercy-seat. The wise, the rich, the learned, and the strong, are tools employed by God to move the world's machine, but it is *piety* which strews real weal on men. They who descend from Zion's heights are as the clouds which drop refreshing rain.—"*Christ is all.*" [See Addenda, p. 128, *Nearer to God.*]

Topic: THE PRIESTS' ENTRANCE UPON THEIR OFFICE (Vv. 1-7).

At the close of the seven days' consecration service in the court of the tabernacle, the priests entered publicly upon their office, began their holy and solemn work. On the eighth day, Moses called Aaron and his sons, and the elders of Israel, and gave directions how the sacrifical services of the tabernacle were to be inaugurated. The rites of consecration were to culminate in a public declaration and recognition, in the presence of Israel and the Lord. On this occasion Aaron and his four sons were to slay the victims to be offered; and the ceremony was of the most imposing character. As Aaron and his sons came forth from their seclusion at the call of Moses, they appeared in vestments which were a visible expression of the offices they held, and an outward sign of the power and authority with which they had been invested. Moses here transfers the office he had held to Aaron, and declares that he does so at the command of the Lord. Aaron was now to speak to the people as the oracle of God to man, and the mouthpiece of man to God. As the people saw the high priest ascend the altar steps for the first time, they would recognise the person through whom henceforth they would draw near to heaven. We notice:

I. *That the installation of Aaron and his sons to the office of the priesthood, was* SOLEMNIZED BY THE PRESENTATION OF SYMBOLIC SACRIFICES TO THE LORD.

Although the consecration service had extended over seven days, and had been most searching and complete, though the high priest had been washed, anointed and clothed with gorgeous and spotless apparel, crowned with the mitre which displayed in pure gold the words, "Holiness unto the Lord"; although appointed sacrifices had been presented during those seven secluded days; yet, when the consecrated priest and his sons came forth to begin their duties, it is necessary that additional sacrifices be offered before they can perform any acceptable service for the people.

This showed that the priests, after all consecrating ceremenies, were (1) *not perfect men*, that they were compassed about with infirmity, and that for them as with the rest of the people forgiveness and cleansing from sin must be sought of God. False religions lift the priesthood above human faultiness and infirmity, and invest those who officiate at the altar with superhuman privilege and power. In the Levitical economy this error was not committed, and it is one of the distinguishing works of the divinity of the old dispensation that the imperfections of the best of men are acknowledged as demanding repentance and forgiveness.

(2) The priests of the Levitical economy were *not perfect types of Christ;* for He was "holy, harmless, undefiled, and separate from sinners."

The *order* of the sacrifices offered on the first day of the official service of the priests, shows the progressive steps by which we approach unto, and find acceptance with God. (*a*) *The sin offering* suggests that first there must be *forgiveness of sin*, the barrier must be removed which separates between the soul and its Maker. (*b*) *The burnt offering* suggests that pardon having been procured, *there must be complete consecration* to Him who has mercifully forgiven. (*c*) *The peace offering* suggests *devotion of the life to the Lord*, the enjoyment of union and communion with Him, and constant communications from Him. These sacrifices were to be presented in the presence of the people, at the command of, and unto the Lord. Though set apart to the holiest service, no man is perfectly pure. No acceptable service can be rendered to God except by persons who have been pardoned and prepared. The clear statements in the New Testament of the perfect purity of Christ, and the evidence we have that those statements are correct, furnish conclusive proofs that He was *infinitely superior to the Aaronic priesthood;* that—unlike them—He was not even "the best of men," but was *God-man* "God manifest in the flesh."

II. *That the installation of Aaron and his sons to the office of the priesthood was* SIGNALISED BY THE MANIFESTATION OF THE PRESENCE OF THE LORD.

What Moses had done and commanded with respect to the tabernacle and its services, had been by the authority of the Lord. He had received authority not only respecting the sacrifices to be offered, but also to announce that following the presentation, the Lord Himself would make Himself known, and reveal His glory. The offerings were to be presented "before the Lord," and He would give open demonstration that He both saw and approved. He would show His regard for their obedient worship, by manifesting His glorious presence. In all our acts of worship, in every service we present to the Lord, we shall derive inspiration and stimulus by remembering (*a*) *His commandments;* (*b*) *His presence;* (*c*) *His promises.* He crowns the well doing of earth with His own eternal " well done !" But those who are faithless and despise His Word shall be covered with shame and everlasting contempt.—*F. W. B.*

Topic: AARON'S FIRST OFFERING FOR HIMSELF (Vv. 7-14).

What unquestioning obedience Aaron yielded to the will of the Lord, as made known through Moses ! for we read, " Aaron went *therefore* unto the altar, and slew the calf of the sin offering, which was for himself." The ritual is the same as that in chap. iv., except that the blood is not brought into the sanctuary. Holiness without which no man can see the Lord, could only be *typically* attained by the Levitical priesthood.

I. *The offerings presented by Aaron for himself show that* HIS PRIESTHOOD WOULD BE ACCEPTED He could not have drawn near to God acceptably for others, had there been any unforgiven guilt resting upon him. The three offerings he presented fully satisfied the Divine claims, and placed him in a position of acceptance and communion ; so that he could represent the interests of the people in the presence of Jehovah. God would be well pleased with arrangements He had Himself made.

II. *The offerings presented by Aaron for himself showed that* HE WAS COMPASSED BY INFIRMITIES. This lesson respecting the servants of the Lord, chosen and appointed to wait upon Him for His own glory and the best interests of men, is continually presenting itself through the sacred scriptures. Aaron had sin that needed to be forgiven, there was natural enmity in his mind that needed to be slain. It was a humbling thing for Aaron to proceed, arrayed in his splendid sacerdotal garments, upon which the people looked with awe and wonder, to slay the calf that was appointed for sacrifice, and to offer it for his own sins. The calf would probably remind him of his great sin in making a golden calf for the people to worship while Moses was up in the mount. Any pride of heart, or presumption of mind, would now be checked by a public acknowledgment of his sins and need of pardon, though chosen and lifted to so high and holy an office.

III. *The offerings presented by Aaron for himself show that* A GREATER OFFERING MUST HAVE BEEN TYPIFIED, BY VIRTUE OF WHICH THESE WERE ACCEPTED. All the washings, anointings, offerings, and attirings of the seven consecration days had not sufficed to make the priests pure and holy ; and one offering now is not enough to make the ceremony complete ; nor are the three that are now offered final. None of these could make the comers thereunto perfect, they had only *temporary* and *typical* value. *Our High Priest's offering of Himself* was accepted, He is therefore able to save all who come unto God by Him. He made no offering *for* Himself, for He had no sins to own, no guilt to atone for. His sacrifice is final, for by one offering He hath perfected for ever them that are sanctified. Tasting death for every man, no other offering is needed by man, and no other can be accepted by God.—*F. W. B.*

Topic: AARON'S OFFERINGS FOR THE PEOPLE (Vv. 15-21).

In these offerings for the people, the people were led to express their desire for forgiveness and their complete consecration to the service of Jehovah. They had asked for some one to go propitiously between them and God; their request had been granted, their offerings are taken by Aaron and presented to the Lord for them. By such an arrangement, both priests and people were taught—

I. THAT THEY STOOD ON A COMMON MORAL EQUALITY BEFORE GOD. The election of persons to eminent positions and distinguished service did not imply that they were the favourites of heaven, exempted from responsibility, or from moral blame. The priests were under the same moral obligations with those for whom they officiated at the altar; and had to seek acceptance *in the same way*, of the God who alone can forgive sins.

II. THAT THEY BOTH NEEDED PARDON FROM, BEFORE THEY COULD HAVE PEACE WITH, GOD. A condition of sinfulness unrepented and unforgiven is a condition of rebellion and hostility. And, as two cannot walk together except they agree, so God and man cannot commune together except strife and variance cease. Both people and priests, after acknowledgment of, and atonement for sin, could draw near to God, and enjoy friendship and fellowship with Him.

III. THAT THEY WERE BOTH EXPECTED TO RENDER IMPLICIT AND COMPLETE OBEDIENCE TO GOD. Priests and people had to do what Moses commanded, and he only commanded what God enjoined. Jehovah alone was the source of authority and power in the commonwealth and theocracy of Israel. The way by which God comes to man is by the blood of sprinkling, and the blood must be applied according to His own will and pleasure. The most minute details had to be carried out, which would test the *faith*, as well as the *obedience* of the worshippers. The Word of the Lord was, "*Do and live.*"

Under the Gospel dispensation, and around the cross of Christ, all men meet on a level *morally;* and none are saved except through faith in His Name. Being pardoned and justified by faith, we have peace with God through our Lord Jesus Christ. But, "no cross no crown." Faith and works must go together, we are saved by faith, but faith without works is dead. What God hath joined together let no man put asunder. Christ enjoins obedience to His commandments, as well as faith in His Name.—*F. W. B.*

Topic: BLESSING THE PEOPLE (Vv. 22, 23).

How earnestly Aaron entered upon his solemn and responsible work! Having presented the required sacrifices, prompted by the Spirit of the Lord he pronounced his benediction upon the people. Descending the sloping side of the altar Moses conducted him into the tabernacle of the congregation to finally instruct him in his duties. On returning, Aaron blessed the people, for this was to be the outcome of all the rites and ceremonies of the Levitical economy: blessing from the Lord.

The people were not only prepared for a holy and lofty mission by the strict and searching discipline of the Levitical ritual, but they were initiated unto elementary knowledge of spiritual truths, and introduced into the possession of priceless spiritual blessings. The sacrifices themselves had no virtue or power to bless, but they were the tests of the people's faith and obedience; appointed and approved means by which the demands of God's law were, for that age of the world, satisfactorily met. God favourably regarded the relation into which Israel had been brought, and His blessing descended upon the people when Aaron outspread his hands. Aaron's act foreshadowed the work of Him who was to come, and in whom all nations would be blessed. When the sacrifices had been offered the blessing fell on the people, denoting that God was satisfied with obedience to His commandments; and typifying the greater benediction of our High Priest, as from the most holy place He dispenses His blessings upon the hearts of men.

In the act of Aaron blessing the people we observe—

I. *The recognition of* MAN'S GREATEST NEED, *viz.,* GOD'S BLESSING. By sin man had incurred the Divine displeasure; had fled from the Divine presence; his mind had become carnal and alienated from God. The mercy of God could not let man perish; His justice demanded an atonement, in order that reconciliation and restoration might be effected. Divinely appointed substitutionary sacrifices satisfied the claims of Divine justice for the time being; and, through them, friendship and communion with God were enjoyed. Man, as the offspring of God, could not be happy without God, without his reconciled presence, and paternal benediction. The needed blessing was promised, if only the needed conditions for its bestowment were observed. In these incidents, the preliminaries were completed; and Aaron, with the sanction and smile of Heaven, came forth and blessed the people. Probably, the formulary employed was that recorded in Num. vi., 23-27, or Ps. xc., 17; words which the Lord commanded Aaron and his sons to use, "The Lord bless thee, and keep thee; the Lord make His face to shine upon thee and be gracious unto thee; the Lord lift up His countenance upon thee, and give thee peace." "And let the beauty of the Lord our God be upon us; and establish the work of our hands upon us: yea, the work of our hands establish Thou it." What a complete and comprehensive blessing! Some have thought that the mention of the name of Jehovah three times in the words to be used by Aaron have reference to the triune nature of God, according with the threefold apostolic blessing of the new Testament, and the formulary pronounced at the ordinance of baptism. Man needed the blessing, good will, and aid of the Lord, His friendship and smile. Needed to be kept from all evil within, and from the Evil One. Man needed the face of God to shine upon him, God's reconciled, cheering, transforming face, the face of his Father and King. The peace of God alone could remove remorse for the past and dread apprehensions for the future. Here, then, was the bestowment of all needed grace, the earnest as well as preparation for final glory. These blessings centre in, and flow from Christ with (*a*) *infinite fulness;* (*b*) *inestimable graciousness;* for all men and all time. Observe—

II. THE DECLARATION OF GOD'S GREATEST JOY, *viz.,* BLESSING MEN.

How quickly the mercy of God whispered blessing in the ears of the first offending pair ere they were expelled from the blissful bowers of Eden! How He sanctioned the erection of altars and accepted their offerings wherever the patriarchs pitched their tents! How faithfully He now fulfilled the promises made to Moses, to meet with and bless His people if they erected an altar to His name and offered sacrifices thereon. His greatest joy is in blessing man. He is slow to anger, and delights in mercy. Aaron, standing with outspread hands, was the representative of God as well as of the people; and in the words of the Lord, as well as in His name, he pronounced the blessing. God blessed man; (*a*) *in equity*: He had not connived at iniquity, had not accepted man into His confidence and communion without obedience and satisfaction. He was just, and yet the justifier of those who came to Him in sacrifices, which typified the one sacrifice of Jesus. (*b*) *Out of the sanctuary.* The high priest came out of the tabernacle and blessed the people; and God still pronounces His best and brightest blessing out of Zion, where His name is recorded, His worship observed. (*c*) *In connection with human means.* It was the blessing of God, but it passed through the lips of Aaron. God employed and honoured human agency. Man could not bless himself; Aaron, of himself, could not bless the people. He could be, and was, the *channel* to convey the Divine benediction. Moses inducted Aaron to his office, and then Aaron conveyed blessings to men. We cannot be sources, but we can be *means* of blessing to others; we may glorify God by co-working with Him in His plans and purposes for blessing men. The Gospel, which blesses men, is the Gospel of God's glory.

Aaron blessing men from the holy place where the sacrifices were completed may be regarded as a type of Him who, when on earth, opened His lips and pronounced His benedictions upon men, not only in the beatitudes but all through His life as He went about doing good, when He descended from Olivet with hands outspread, blessing His disciples. He has His hands full of blessing now, since He has led captivity captive and received gifts for men.—*F. W. B.*

Topic: THE MIRACULOUS FIRE (Vv. 23, 24).

According to the word of Moses, when all was completed that the Lord had commanded, the Divine glory was displayed in the presence of the congregation. There was no delay on the part of Israel to comply with the Divine requirements, and there was no delay on the part of the Lord to signify He had accepted their sacrifices. There was a sudden flash of mysterious flame from the resplendent light that filled the holy place. It lighted upon the brazen altar, and *consumed* the sacrifice which was already on fire ; thus, the altar fire was consecrated. Look

I. AT SOME OF THE FACTS WHICH THE FLASHING FIRE CONFIRMED.

(*a*) *That the sacrifices were divinely accepted.* The priests had kindled a fire, had done all needed to render their offering complete and acceptable ; Aaron had been into the tabernacle, returned, and blessed the people ; it needed **only** now the baptism of fire, the smile of the Lord to be seen beaming forth from the holy place. That radiant and effulgent smile came, took possession of the sacrifice upon the altar, compassed and consumed it. The *ascending* flame symbolizes that heaven received it.

(*b*) *That the priests were divinely accredited.* What Aaron and his sons had done pleased the Lord ; He inspected their work, saw that it was good ; and, to show to priests and people that the order of the priesthood was confirmed, the fire came leaping forth to crown the fire the priests had lighted. Thus the Lord owned the priests as co-workers with Himself, as mediators between the human and Divine. Henceforth, they would be His accredited servants.

(*c*) *That the tabernacle was divinely appropriated.* God had already taken possession of it and had filled it with His glory ; but the eyes of the common people were not permitted to see the glory that dwelt within. It was well, therefore, for them to witness the glory manifested from within ; to see the fire of the Lord leap forth, giving them ocular demonstration that Jehovah had really appropriated the tabernacle as His earthly, local, temporary dwelling place. Jehovah has never ceased to answer by fire. The Scriptures record many instances where, by cloud and flame, the Divine Presence has been manifested to men, *e.g.*, the dedication of the temple ; the nativity of Christ ; the descent of the Holy Ghost at Pentecost. At the end of the world, by clouds and fire the great assizes will be inaugurated. Let us seek to present acceptable sacrifices to Him in the sanctuaries of our hearts, let us seek for the descent of the fire of His love to consume all selfishness and sin, and make our bodies temples of the Holy Ghost. Consider also :

II. SOME OF THE EFFECTS WHICH THE FLASHING FIRE PRODUCED.

The people, having been told beforehand by Moses that at the completion of their offerings the glory of the Lord would appear, were anticipating the manifestation which took place. There had been *atonement,* and *mediation,* sin had been forgiven and removed ; all had been declared " holiness unto the Lord," there was nothing now to dread. The people were filled with *holy rapture.* A loud simultaneous shout of joy arose. They could not restrain their gladness ; adoration blended with praise ; they were *grateful* as well as *glad.* They felt that God was propitiated by what had been done. They were filled with *sacred awe.* They fell upon their faces ; the glory was so resplendent, or they may have felt how great the disparity existing between them and God, how unworthy they were of His favour. They were not prostrate with dread and terror, but from feelings of reverence and worship. The people had no doubt about the reality of the fire—about its miraculous character—they were satisfied as to its origin and meaning. *All the manifestations of God's glory to men, in nature, and in revelation, are calculated and designed to awaken rapture and beget reverence.* The Gospel brings glad tidings of great joy, even a joy unspeakable and full of glory; it begets reverence for it shows us how great our sins and how holy our God. We see God as a consuming fire to consume sin, and to purify from all defilement. Let us so live that hereafter we may enter into the glory unchanging and eternal. Rapture and reverence will characterise the delight and worship of heaven.—*F. W. B.*

OUTLINES ON VERSES OF CHAPTER IX.

V. 6.—*Theme:* CONDITIONS OF BLESSING.

Inanimate nature governed by fixed laws; brute creation by instinct; man by reason. These facts asserted in scripture, obvious to experience and analogy. Man can exercise intelligent and deliberate choice. God compels where law and instinct rule, but commands where reason reigns. Animals submitted unconsciously to their fate, but the worshippers voluntarily slayed and intelligently presented them in sacrifice. The people were told to obey the Lord, and then His glory would appear unto them. Thus, a promise was given to inspire, reward held out to stimulate and sustain. Thus the people were taught—

I. THE DUTY OF OBEDIENCE TO DIVINE COMMANDMENTS.

Implying—

(*a*) *That God has the right to command.*

(*b*) *That man has ability to obey.*

(*c*) *That man is under obligation to obey.*

II. THE BLESSING OF OBEDIENCE TO DIVINE COMMANDMENTS.

(*a*) *It pleases God.* He is satisfied—glorified.

(*b*) *It blesses man.* Exercises and honours his noblest faculties, awakens keenest delight, secures manifestation of Divine glory. Those who obey increase in knowledge of the Divine will, and become transformed into the Divine likeness. God's highest delight to exercise mercy, to purify, and save.—*F. W. B.*

V. 12.—*Theme:* THE BLOOD OF SPRINKLING.

In tabernacle service and furniture almost everything sprinkled with blood. There must have been something peculiarly significant in the fact. Among other things it—

I. INDICATED THAT LIFE HAD BEEN REALLY SACRIFICED.

II. AWAKED FEELINGS OF AWE IN THE WORSHIPPERS.

III. INVESTED THINGS WITH PECULIAR SACREDNESS.

IV. PROCLAIMED THAT PROPITIATION HAD BEEN EFFECTED.

The precious blood of Christ teaches these things, and more; for the blood sprinkled round about the altar had no virtue in itself to wash away sin, whereas Christ's blood cleanses from all sin. (See Heb. xii. 24; 1 Peter i. 2.) The robes of the glorified are made white in the blood of the Lamb. The new song of heaven extols the efficacy of the blood that was shed on Calvary.—*F. W. B.*

V. 24.—*Theme:* THE ANSWER BY FIRE.

The flame that leaped out of the tabernacle and consumed the burnt offering, and the fat upon the altar—

I. DEMONSTRATED THE FACT OF THE DIVINE PRESENCE.

II. EXHIBITED THE AWFULNESS OF THE DIVINE POWER.

III. PROVED THE FIDELITY OF THE DIVINE WORD.

IV. TAUGHT THE TENDERNESS OF THE DIVINE MERCY.

The fire might have consumed the sinners instead of the sacrifice, but God is a consuming fire against sin, He loves the sinner, is not willing that any should perish.—*F. W. B.*

Vv. 23, 24.—*Theme:* GOD'S ACCEPTANCE OF THE SACRIFICES.

When we see the variety of ordinances and multitude of sacrifices, we are ready to ask, What compensation could be made to the people for all the expense and trouble to which they were put? Here we have a sufficient answer: God would not withhold from them communication such as would abundantly recompense all they did for His sake. He gave them such testimonies of His acceptance as made their hearts overflow. Consider—

I. THE TESTIMONIES OF GOD'S ACCEPTANCE. These were of different kinds:

1. *Ministerial.* Moses and Aaron having finished all they had to do within the tabernacle, came forth and "blessed the people." In this they were—

(1) *Types of Christ:* Showing what He would do as soon as He had finished His sacrifice: He blessed His disciples (Luke xxiv 50, 51) as He was taken up to heaven; and He sent the promised blessing of the Holy Spirit quickly thence (Acts ii. 33; iii. 26).

(2) *Examples to ministers:* Showing what all ministers are authorised and empowered to declare to those who rely on the Great Sacrifice. They are to stand forth in the very name of God, and proclaim pardon and peace to all (Acts xiii. 38, 39).

2. *Personal.* In two ways did *God Himself by direct testimonies,* apart from all indirect human agency, manifest His acceptance.

(1) *He displayed His glory* before all the people. Now we have no such visible manifestation, but we have instead, as direct testimonies from God, " the Spirit of God witnessing with our spirit"; and "the love of God shed abroad in our hearts."

(2) *He sent fire upon the sacrifice:* Showing what fiery indignation they deserved, but that he had turned it aside from them, and caused it to fall on the altar.

II. EFFECTS PRODUCED BY THESE TESTIMONIES OF GOD'S ACCEPTANCE.

Visible objects affect us strongly; the people now were deeply impressed with what they saw. They were filled—

1. *With exalted joy.* Had they not been taught to expect this manifestation they would have been terrified thereby, as Gideon and Manoah (Judges vi. 21, 22; xiii. 19-22); but being prepared, they rent the air with their shouts.

The inward triumph of Paul seems more suited to our dispensation (Romans viii. 31-39), and that is both the privilege and duty of every one of us to enjoy.

2. *With profound reverence.* Humility united with joy. Even the seraphim cover their faces and feet before the throne; glorified saints cast their crowns at the feet of Him who sitteth thereon. Exalted joys should be tempered with adoration. Illustrations will be found in Gen. xvii. 3; Exod. iii. 6.

Learn:—

(*a*) *To lay no stress on transient affections.* Such a state of feeling in the people ought to have issued well, but soon passed away when temptation arose.

(*b*) *To be thankful for the advantages we enjoy.* We are apt to envy the Jews their privileges: they walked by sight, we walk by faith. But our High Priest "blesses us with all spiritual blessings." *Chas. Simeon, M.A.*

V. 24.—*Theme:* GRACIOUS FIRE.

A sudden marvel fills all minds with awe.

While blessings fall from blessing saints (Moses and Aaron) heaven brightens with resplendent signs. Glory shines around. Fire is sent forth.

I. FIRE SEALS WITH HEAVEN'S OWN SEAL THE ATONING RITES.

Wherefore comes the fire forth? Is it to seize the guilty sons of men? Is it to hurl on them deserved wrath? Far otherwise. It comes with olive branch of peace. It settles on the altar. It feeds on the victim as its feast. Then it brings evidence of God's delight. Then it fills hearts with tranquil peace. The flame with blazing tongue proclaims: Here is the sacrifice which God selects, approves, calls men to bring, and never will refuse.

II. THE ATTESTING FIRE SPEAKS GOD'S ACCEPTANCE OF SUBSTITUTION.

The altar victims were the foreshadowing of Christ. Faith therefore loves this scene. It is one of the wells from which it gladly draws new joy. It is one of the meadows of its richest food.

But *what is the antitype of the descending flame?* The clear Gospel page. There, distinct testimonies answer to this approving sign:—

(1) The angelic host, a shining train, which swept down from heaven at Jesus' birth.

(2) The baptismal seal (Luke iii. 21, 22).

(3) Transfiguration glories rest on Him: and a voice from the cloud proclaims, "This is My beloved Son."

(4) The opened grave, guarded by the angels, for in the resurrection of Christ we have the fiery seal of an accepted sacrifice

When Israel's host beheld the fire of God, what were their feelings? "They shouted and fell on their faces." Sweet joy was theirs. Deep *adoration* warmed each heart. Exulting praise burst forth. Profoundest *worship* was their instant act.

Shall we not do the like? God sent His Son to seek, to save. He lays on Him our every sin; gives us every pledge that He approves, attests, receives, delights in the accepted offering. Witness after witness from His courts assures that pardon, acquittal, release from every woe, admission to the home of heaven, may be ours. Oh, then, let every breath praise God! Let every hour of every day be inward worship.—*Dean Law.*

ILLUSTRATIVE ADDENDA TO CHAPTER IX.

MINISTERIAL DEDICATION.

"If so poor a worm as I may to Thy great glory live,
All my actions sanctify, all my words and thoughts receive;
Claim for Thy service, claim all I have and all I am.

"Take my soul and body's powers; take my memory, mind, and will;

All my goods and all my hours; all I know and all I feel;
All I think, or speak, or do—take my heart, but make it new.

"Now, O God, Thine own I am; now I give Thee back Thine own;
Freedom, friends, and health and fame, consecrate to Thee alone;
Thine I live, thrice happy I! Happier still if Thine to die."—*Charles Wesley.*

"I thank Thee, Lord, for using me for Thee
  to work and speak;
However trembling is the hand, the voice
  however weak.

"For those to whom, through me, Thou hast
  some heavenly guidance given;
For some, it may be, saved from death,
  and some brought nearer heaven.

" Oh, honour higher, truer far, than earthly
  fame could bring,
Thus to be used in work like this, so long,
  by such a King!

" A blunted sword, a rusted spear, which only
  He could wield;
A broken sickle in His hand to reap His
  harvest field."—*Bonar.*

NEARNESS TO GOD.

Favoured *places* :—Eden, Peniel, Sinai, Temple, Transfiguration Mount, Olivet, etc.

Favoured *persons:* — Enoch, Abraham, Jacob, Moses, Aaron, David, Elijah, Daniel, Stephen, Paul, John.

SPIRITUAL BENEFACTORS. Our power to benefit others will just be in proportion to our personal holiness. " Speak for eternity," says Mr. Cheyne, " but above all, cultivate your own spirit. A word spoken by you when your conscience is clear, when your heart is full of God's Spirit, is worth two thousand words spoken in unbelief and sin. This was my great fault in the ministry. Remember it is not man but God that must have the glory. It is not so much speaking as faith that is heard."

" The vertical power of religion in the heart is the truest measure of its horizontal power in the world."—*Bowes.*

" When one that holds communion with the
  skies,
Has filled his urn where those pure waters
  rise,
And once more mingles with us meaner
  things—
'Tis e'en as if an angel shook his wings;
Immortal fragrance fills the circuit wide,
That tells us whence his treasures are
  supplied."—*Cowper.*

CHAPTER X.

Reckless Ministry Sternly Rebuked.

SUGGESTIVE READINGS.

V. 1.—Nahab and Abihu offered strange fire. Whether they were prompted by impetuous religious feeling, or were confused with wine, the act was reckless; they offered before the Lord incense on fire which was unsanctified. Probably, instead of holy fire taken from the altar, they lit their censers from the fire burning " at the door of the tabernacle," used for " boiling the flesh." [See chap. viii. 31.] To act in God's service from heated *impulse* is as blameworthy as to act under *intoxication.* Strong feeling makes a man as confused in thought and rash in conduct as does strong drink. When God commands what should be done, that and that only should be done : and done in the manner He prescribes. Self-will, heedlessness, impetuosity, must be absolutely arrested on the very threshold of sacred service. God asks obedience: literal and absolute : and " behold to obey is better than sacrifice; and to hearken than the fat of rams."

V. 2.—Went out fire from the Lord. That fire had only just before fallen upon the altar victim instead of falling on the sinner : God thus expressed His pleasure in sparing man and accepting the substituted atonement offering. And " He is not willing that any should perish." But if man will act disobediently, notwithstanding God's desire to spare him, man must bear his penalty. And now the fire falls direct on the sinner and devours him. " For our God is a consuming fire." The cross of Jesus shelters all who will hide beneath its grace, but on the presumptuous the wrath of God must surely fall. " *They died before the Lord.*"

V. 3.—This is it that the Lord spake. Moses appeals to a well-known divine utterance, which, however, is not to be found in the written Scriptures. Just so, the apostle Paul quotes a saying of the Lord Jesus, which nowhere appears in the Gospels (Acts xx. 35). There were sayings of Jehovah living in the people's memory which the pen had not transcribed to the sacred page. There is an unwritten Bible : for God's messages, in which He "spake in times past unto the fathers by the prophets," were so numerous that all could not be gathered into the written Bible.

In this sense must be understood John's statement that much of our Lord's life—His words and deeds—is left unrecorded in the pages of the evangelists (John xx. 30 ; xxi. 35). Yet, lest any should use this fact as a warrant for *adding* aught "to the words of the book of this prophecy" (Rev. xxii. 18) John declares that the written Gospels are sufficient for our faith, "that ye might believe that Jesus is the Christ, the Son of God : and that believing ye might have life through His name " (John xx. 31).

I will be sanctified in them that come nigh Me. Aaron and His sons had been most solemnly consecrated for their ministries : and, because of their perfected sanctification (ceremonially), were to be allowed near access to Jehovah's awful presence. Should they presume upon their privilege and act heedlessly, violating their sanctity by thoughtless and irreverent conduct? God would not have it so. The presumptuous soul is offensive to Jehovah. [See Num. xx. 30.] If we do not honour Him by our reverence, He will get honour to Himself in our punishment.

Aaron held his peace—bowing to the appalling judgment of God with acquiescence : recognising that his sons had summoned upon themselves the doom which befel them. It was the silence of a soul overwhelmed with grief, but grief regulated by the sense that "the Judge of all the earth doeth right."

V. 5.—Carried them in their coats out of the camp. Their priestly tunics were not burned by the fire which had struck the wearers with death. The garments were symbols of the sanctity God approved : they remained unharmed. What a hush of awe must have gone through "the camp," as the crowds of Israel watched the carrying of the blanched corpses through their midst. It told the warning truth that God was so jealous for His holiness that He would not spare even the young priests so newly consecrated if they failed to sanctify Him. "Let us have grace, whereby we may serve God acceptably, with reverence and godly fear : for our God is a consuming fire."

V. 6.—Uncover not your heads. To let the hair fall dishevelled was the custom of mourners, the sign of bereavement. For them to express open and violent grief would appear like casting blame upon God, like strife against His providence. They must submit. "I was dumb, I opened not my mouth, because Thou didst it." Hard indeed it is not to complain and rebel when the hand of God lays bitter strokes upon us : but piety will manifest itself best in meek submission and quiet endurance.

Much grace will be needed, however, in mourners if they are to yield up their treasures of affection thus uncomplainingly to the Lord. Yet let it be remembered that Jesus had no rebuke for the tears shed over Lazarus' death ; yea, more, that as He stood by the grave and beheld the scene of weepers, "*Jesus wept*" (John xi. 35). The case was exceptional with these young priests, and God's prohibition of mourning for them must not be regarded as a divine interdict of the tears of love.

V. 7.—For the anointing oil of the Lord is upon you. They who are dedicated to God's service must let that be supreme ; its claims subordinate all private duties ; even the burial of their dead was insufficient as a warrant for them however briefly to desert their sacred offices. "Let the dead bury their dead," said Jesus ; "and come, follow me" (Matt. viii. 21, 22). For religious claims are superlative, and our human affections (in themselves becoming) may prove a snare if permitted to assert themselves against divine claims.

Vv. 8-11.—Do not drink wine, etc. Certainly such a possible cause for excited action, confused thought, or ungoverned feeling must be scrupulously shunned by all when occupied in sanctuary ministrations and sacred employ. Jesus "would not drink" (Matt. xxvii. 34) when the narcotic drug was offered Him at Calvary; for He was at that moment engaged in divinest employ—offering Himself unto God as man's atonement. Paul's admonitions to bishops and deacons (1 Tim. iii. 2, 3) not to be "given to wine," is in the same direction; any cause of false excitement or possible rashness must be sedulously avoided by those occupied in God's service. The prohibition is, however, not all-inclusive; it only applies to specified persons, and to specified occasions—"when ye go into the tabernacle of the congregation."

Vv. 12-15.—Take the meat offering, etc. Moses pressed upon the priests to turn to their spiritual functions and ministries without delay. For the best solace in grief is activity. Sit not in repining because of God's stroke, turn to Him in holy service. Possibly the dread of God, "lest He be angry," urged all to quick attention to duty. Sad it is that we need often the startling visitation of God to awaken us to vigilance in religion. "When thy judgments are in the earth, the inhabitants of the world will learn righteousness" (Isa. xxvi. 9).

Vv. 16-20.—Moses diligently sought the goat of the sin offering. The flesh of this sacrificial offering should have been eaten by the priests; and Moses grew "angry" with the surviving sons of Aaron that they had neglected this part of the prescribed ritual. But Aaron produced an explanation of the omission: that all the sacred regulations for the sin offering had been observed by them, except the festive part which was an obligation upon the priest and his family; and that the calamity which had befallen them unfitted them for this social repast or rendered the festivity inappropriate. This was an error; express commands should not be evaded even by plea of untimeliness or impropriety; duty must be first: but Moses was touched by his brother's great grief, and "was content." For is it not written, "I desired mercy and not sacrifice, and the knowledge of God more than burnt offerings" (Hosea vi. 6)? Where the "spirit" is right the "letter" is less important.

SECTIONAL HOMILIES.

Topic: REPULSIVE INCENSE (Vv. 1, 2).

"*Nadab and Abihu offered strange fire before the Lord.*"

Nadab and Abihu were priests, ministers of the tabernacle; therefore lessons from their example possess a special fitness to *ministers of Christ.* To preach to others, forgetting admonitions to ourselves, were deplorable, fulfilling the lament, "They made me the keeper of the vineyards, but mine own vineyard have I not kept" (Cant. i. 6). Yet, though the lesson of this incident is special to ministers of the sanctuary, it is not exclusive; for "*ye* are a holy priesthood, to offer spiritual sacrifices" (1 Pet. ii. 5). Every redeemed soul is consecrated by grace to be God's priest in His great universe. Christ "hath made us kings and priests unto God."

From every priest God looks for incense; of affection, influence, service, possessions, praises, prayers. God called us into the temple of His grace that we might "offer living sacrifices; holy and acceptable, our reasonable service." This is our mission on earth, the design of our conversion; for this the Spirit works in us: we must be priests.

And each of us, as a priest, *does take his censer*, and the fire ascends to the Lord. Each is doing something in work, or worship, or ministry, to fill the temple of earth with offerings to the Lord. But it is for us solemnly to ask in presence of this incident—

WHAT INCENSE ARE WE OFFERING ? Even priests may err here: burn "strange fire," offer what God will abhor, and imperil their souls in the action. Consider therefore—

I. THEIR OFFENSIVE OFFERING. "Offered *strange fire.*"

1. *What rendered their incense odious to God?* "The fire was *strange.*" It lacked two essential and acceptable qualities—

(*a*) It had *not been kindled by God.* The fire on the altar was kindled from heaven. The divine origin of that fire changed human offerings laid on that altar into atoning sacrifices. They became thereby sanctified. Without this divine element the human offerings were not acceptable (chap. ix. 24). But these priests "took their censers and put fire therein"; and thus the fire had nothing of divinity in it; the offering was altogether earthly and human; "strange fire."

(*b*) It had *not been mingled with blood.* Sacrificial victims were being continuously offered on that altar ; that fire never went out ; the fire was never free, therefore, from the blood. This rendered the fire sacred. Consecrated by blood. Nothing came to God pleasing Him except mingled with blood. But their fire had nothing of the savour of blood in it : it was, therefore, " strange," offensive to God.

2. *What corresponding offensiveness may mar our offerings?*

In the Christian church to-day, not a little "strange fire" is burned before the Lord. The *motive* that prompts what we do is *not divine;* the fire is earthly, human. The incense is not sanctified by blood ; for much we do is done *without associating it with the atonement of Christ,* and resting on the merits of His blood for acceptableness and worth. Thus, the fire is " strange " when our religion or work is the outcome of—

(*a*) *Mere emotional fervour.* The "wild fire" of hot sensationalism, the religion of boisterous emotion and animal tumult, the raging vulgarity of noise, these are no acceptable substitute to offer before the Lord, in place of calm devoutness and holy earnestness. There may be the noisiness of the "crackling of thorns," without fervid glow or quiet heat. Emotional people are not the most devotional. Sensation is no test or measure of sincerity.

(*b*) *Mere intellectual excitement.* Public prayers which are voluble and boisterous, lacking thoughtful reverence, how are they rebuked by the homage of the veiled cherubim, repudiated by the emphatic command : " Be not rash with thy mouth, for God is in heaven and thou upon earth ; therefore let thy words be few" (Eccles. v. 2). Preaching which abandons itself to the mere "fire of oratory," though rousing an audience, may be more human than divine ; souls are never converted by "excellency of speech" (1 Cor. ii. 1, 4, 5).

(*c*) *Mere feverish activity.* There is an evil under the sun into which very young converts are betrayed. Before becoming themselves enriched in the Christian life, before they have nourished and fortified their minds in divine truth, without giving any one opportunity of " instructing them in the way of the Lord more perfectly," as Paul did Aquila and Priscilla (Acts xviii. 26), they seize their censer, and with restless eagerness rush out to wave their incense forth. "Not a novice," says Paul, "lest, being lifted up with pride, he fall into the condemnation of the devil" (1 Tim. iii. 6).

(*d*) *Mere self glorifying religious effort.* He who rejects Christ's righteousness, but labours, by diligent efforts, " to establish his own righteousness," offers strange fire. The Christian who is active for love of eminence or observation, zealous or liberal for the sake of praise or distinction, offers " strange fire."

(*e*) *Mere spiritual rhapsody.* Spiritual moods and "frames of feeling" which are elevated, ardent, rapturous, are not the divinest in which a child of God may be found. God does not intend that we live in the cloud-land of ecstasy, for elation of feeling may be but self-elevation. God brought even Paul down from "the third heaven" by a "thorn in his flesh," that he might "rather glory in his infirmities"; for much of that lofty sentiment of piety is "strange fire." [See Addenda, p. 151, *Sensationalism.*]

II. THEIR RASH IMPIETY. "Offered strange fire *before the Lord.*"

To ordinary observers that fire looked like altar fire, as prayers which are sensational, and services which are self-seeking, look like ardent piety; but " God seeth not as man seeth, he looketh at the heart." Their act was one of—

1. *Fearless presumption.* Even amid the solemnities of the sanctuary they were reckless, frivolous. They "took fire" and swung their censers, as if it mattered not how they ministered; as if God deserved no special reverence. To enter God's awful presence without awe, to engage in His worship without adoration, seems a repetition of this careless swinging of censers. It is as though God still addressed the trifler: "When ye come to appear before me, who hath required this at your hands that ye should tread my courts" (Isa. i. 12).

"Lo, God is here; let us adore,
And own how dreadful is this place."

Their conduct seems to have resulted from *festive indulgence.* The command of v. 9 indicates that in a state of intoxicated excitement they rushed into the holy place. But indulgence of any sort, if it unfits us for God's presence or service, should be shunned. Human nature is likely to be overbalanced when the senses are gratified; therefore Paul "kept his body in subjection," and "crucified the flesh." We may come "before the Lord" "drunk, but *not* with wine" (Isa. xxix. 9); intoxicated with worldly thoughts, with foolish vanity; the mind excited with delirious readings; and whatever takes solemnity from us must be shunned as we come before the Holy One of Israel. [See Addenda, p. 151, *Intemperance*].

2. *Wilful disobedience.* By lighting their own fire, and by assuming an office strictly assigned to the *high* priest, they violated God's commands.

Analogy of their conduct:—Refusing divine provisions made for us in the sacrifice of Christ, and *making a religion of our own.* When God has "given a name under heaven whereby we must be saved," and said : "Neither is there salvation in any other" (Acts iv. 12), what is it but wilful disobedience to set up other trusts? Pitiful the wrongly directed efforts of mistaken souls, whether of those who, not animated with the love of Christ, are yet doing Christian work in their own strength; or those who, seeking salvation, are relying on other merits than those of the blood poured out on the altar.

III. THEIR ALARMING DESTRUCTION.

They offered offensive fire; God sent out devouring fire. "Before the Lord" they burned their fire; "before the Lord" they were burned with fire. "With what measure ye mete it shall be measured to you again." Let this admonish us to remember—

1. *The God with whom we have to do.* Hitherto, in the tabernacle service, God had not asserted indignation against the sinful, so much as provided for pardon and redemption. But He who is *gracious* can also show Himself *just*, as he who presumes upon His mercy will prove. [See Addenda, p. 150, *Presumption.*]

2. *The rebuke which presumption will receive.*

(*a*) *The complete overthrow of their rash efforts.* For what is not of God shall not stand. He will put every human thing to confusion. "The fire shall try every man's work." Much "work" which is thought the outcome of zeal for

God, will prove but " wood, hay, stubble," merely human; and, therefore, " if the work be burned he shall suffer loss."

(b) *More terrible rebuke* may be given than the frustration of our work : the *fire may fall upon ourselves.* " For the Lord Jesus shall be revealed from heaven *in flaming fire,* taking vengeance on them that know not God and obey not the gospel of our Lord Jesus Christ" (2 Thess. i. 7). And "if judgment begin at the house of God, *what shall the end be of them that obey not the gospel of God?*" (1 Pet. iv. 17). [See Addenda, p. 151, *Punishment.*]

Topic: YOUTHFUL PROFANATION OF A SACRED OFFICE (Vv. 1, 2).

Special grace is indeed needed by those occupying highest offices in the Church of God.

Nadab and Abihu were *the first young men* called into the ancient priesthood; and in their career a *warning is offered to the young* who think it easy to bear, and covet precipitately to secure, the dignity and gravity of a sacred office.

Paul gives warning against calling out *the young to prominent positions in the Church;* and commanded " not a novice, lest," etc. (1 Tim. iii. 6).

If only the foe of the Church can secure that a *young and incautious spirit be placed in the forefront of God's people* then he will bring all his artifices for his overthrow; and in the fall of a leader there will be great cause for " the enemy to blaspheme."

God grant that many young men may be led out into usefulness in the Church, and, if He will, into high stations in the Church of Christ; into the ministry of the gospel, into influential scenes of witness for truth; but God also grant to such the measure of special grace they will need, lest they *stumble on the high places,* and enable them to bear the standard of the Lord with steady hand to victory !

I. SOLEMN PREPARATION FOR A SACRED CAREER.

Nadab and Abihu "*saw the God of Israel*" (Exod. xxiv. 1, 9, 10). This was Jehovah's method of *preparing a man for a sacred career, e.g.,* Moses at the burning bush (Exod. iii. 3, 6); Isaiah and Ezekiel for prophetic work (Isa. vi. 1, 6, 8; Ezek. i. 1); Saul of Tarsus for apostleship (Acts ix. 27).

That sight gave them qualification. It taught them who God was; how glorious and holy (Exod. xxiv. 10). As also saith Isaiah, " I have seen the King the Lord of Hosts." They would surely be reverent and solemn hereafter in all their service within the tabernacle in presence of resplendent Deity.

Have you seen God for yourselves? It is your qualification for serving Him. You cannot minister before the Lord unless. Hold back from all sacred work until you have " seen the King." But if God has revealed Himself to you it is both a qualification and call to His service. For He wants those who have seen Him to " tell the vision," to go from that secresy of blessed experience, saying, " That which our eyes have seen, which we have looked upon, declare we unto you, that ye may have fellowship with us " (1 John i. 1-3).

II. ENTIRE SEPARATION TO SANCTUARY MINISTRY (Exod. xxviii. 1).

1. Their designation to this office was to be accompanied *by most solemn rites of consecration* (Exod. xxix.). Washing (v. 4); clothing with priestly robes (vv. 5, 8, 9); reconciliation offerings (vv. 10-18); sanctifying unction (vv. 20, 21). Note: that *a year intervened* between the directions given for their dedication and the event. An interval of serious thought, meditation on their high calling, forming of resolves and prayerful preparation for their future.

2. Obeying these minute directions, Moses did then *consecrate them* (Levit. viii. 4, 30) *in the sight of all Israel.* They were thus *publicly* set apart to the holy office.

From all this it appears *how careful God is* that they who are to engage in His service should be *spiritually prepared.* It was God's idea, God's work, wrought through Moses. And ye are "God's workmanship, created in Christ Jesus unto good works, which God hath before ordained that ye should walk in them."

God wants you, who are called to sacred service and high trust in His Church, not less hallowed and consecrated than Nadab and Abihu. "Be ye clean that bear the vessels of the Lord." God must have holiness in those who serve Him.

III. STARTLING MISDEMEANOUR AND PROFANITY.

O how great a fall is here! (Lev. x. 1, 2).

1. *For awhile they maintained a reverent demeanour.* They gave good promise (chap. viii. 36); were observant and obedient to God's word; and attended to the duties of their office (ix. 8, 9, 12, 13). Not instantaneously did they fall from their eminence. The castle must first be undermined before it crumbles into ruins.

"Ye *did* run well." Young Christians began their spiritual life with every promise of "adorning the doctrine of God their Saviour in all things," *conversion seemed thorough;* and Christian service was entered on with seriousness and earnestness, consecration seemed real. But a vast difference exists between a hopeful beginning and "continuing therein with all perseverance": "holding fast the beginning of our confidence steadfast unto the end."

Many a ship made a good start—wrecked! Many a well formed bud—blighted! Many a promising youth—destroyed!

2. *What explains and accounts for their fall?*

Was it a *mere mistake*, an act of ignorance? No; "the Lord commanded them not." Emphatic prohibition: "Ye shall burn no strange incense thereon," etc. (Exod. xxx. 9). It arose from *recklessness*. They may have thought their own fire as good as that on the altar; but they had no right to think on such a matter; God had commanded.

When God has made the way of obedience, the way of salvation, the way of holiness plain, to substitute anything is an act of daring presumption and a horrible offence to God.

What could have led them to this act of presumption? With God's express command, how dared they disobey? In a festive moment they seemed to have lost sobriety; and their act was done under the confusion of drink. How fearful the act! What bitter woes and wrongs has not the baneful indulgence wrought! O what homes desolated, what characters destroyed, what souls ruined! True, indeed of intemperance—

> When once the demon enters,
> Stands within the door,
> Peace and hope and gladness
> Dwell there nevermore.

Alas for the *young* who have fallen thereby!

Put away from you all indulgence which imperils your character and piety. Have a just fear of yourselves. Do not think you stand, lest you fall. [See Addenda p. 151, *Intemperance.*]

IV. PUNISHMENT OF YOUTHFUL PROFANITY. "They died before the Lord."

1. *Though exalted in religious privileges:* how terrible their doom. "Thou Capernaum, exalted unto heaven, shalt be cast down to hell."

Yes: the divine *grace* with which men trifle will invoke most fearful retribution. "Of how *much sorer punishment*, suppose ye, shall he be thought worthy who hath trampled under foot the Son of God." "Therefore, kiss the Son lest he be angry, and ye perish from the way when his wrath is kindled but a little."

> That high All-Seer which I *dallied* with
> Hath turned my *feigned* prayer upon my head,
> And given in earnest what I begged in jest.
> Thus doth He force the swords of wicked men
> To turn their own points on their master's bosom.

2. In the beauty and fulness of youth, how *instant their destruction !* Dread the possibility of being thus arrested : life arrested in an act of sin ! Leave the way of godliness but for a moment ; you may never return ! Adventure upon one rash step of impiety : it may be your last. There is but one step between you and death !

"God is angry with the wicked *every* day" : but He holds back judgment ; yet it may leap forth *any* day. "Wherefore, let us have grace, whereby we may *serve God acceptably with reverence* and godly fear : for our God is a consuming fire." [See Addenda p. 151, *Rashness.*]

Topic : THE SIN OF AARON'S SONS (Vv. 1, 2).

Not many hours had elapsed since Nadab and Abihu were consecrated to the sacred office of the priesthood. They knew that only the high priest was to officiate with the holy incense, and that the fire to be employed must be taken from the brazen, and put upon the golden altar. Yet they usurped the functions of the high priest, kindled common fire, and offered it on the golden altar, "which the Lord had not commanded." Such an act was a flagrant exhibition of insubordination, and a direct insult to Jehovah. In their heinous sin we see—

I. HOW ELEVATION TO HIGH AND HOLY POSITIONS DOES NOT PLACE MEN BEYOND THE TEMPTATION AND LIABILITY TO COMMIT SIN.

Consecrated to the priestly office, they were henceforth expected to be examples to the people of purity, and piety. They would be amid scenes, and engage in services, calculated to restrain them from wrong-doing, and to stimulate them to good works. It was reasonable to expect that, while the solemn ceremony of consecration and inauguration was fresh in their memories, they would be conscientious, circumspect, and magnify their office ; but a day did not elapse without a strong temptation to desecrate their office ; a day did not elapse before they yielded to the temptation. They were proud and presumptuous ; intoxicated with the elevation they had received to the priestly office (if not with drink), and snatching up common fire, went unbidden into the holy place before the Lord, and insulted Him to His face. The temptation was peculiar to their position ; flatterered their vanity ; promised them equality with Moses and Aaron in authority and power ; they yielded to it and fell. By unholy ambition fell the angels and our first parents—no position, however exalted, seems to be exempt from temptation to pride and presumption. We learn that (i.) *having pious parents ;* (ii.) *being in holy places ;* (iii.) *holding sacred offices ;* (iv.) *seeing divine manifestations,* will not place us beyond the reach of temptation to commit sin, or screen us from punishment if we commit it. Even Jesus Christ was assailed by the shafts and insinuations of the wicked one. Being a servant, and even a son of God, does not exempt from temptation, but temptation is not in itself sin, yielding is sin.

II. HOW THE COMMITTAL OF SIN MERITS, AND MAY MEET WITH SUDDEN CORRESPONDING RETRIBUTION.

Their punishment may seem severe, but it must be remembered that the sin was committed (*a*) *by persons in high position,* (*b*) *enjoying great privilege,* (*c*) *possessing great light and knowledge,* (*d*) *deliberately,* and (*e*) *daringly,* on the floor of the holy place, and before the face of the holy God. It was a sin, which, if not signally and immediately punished, would have been a precedent for presumption of the highest kind. Had they sinned ignorantly, they would have been allowed the privilege of the sin offering. We may not always be able to trace resemblance between sin and its punishment, in kind or degree, but the Judge of all the earth is equitable, and allots His punishments according to the deeds done, and in the end will render unto every man according to his works. *Position, circumstances, knowledge, intention, ability*—all will be taken into account in adjusting penalty and awarding bliss.

III. HOW SUCH RETRIBUTION, WHILE IT CONDEMNS THE SINNER, VINDICATES THE BROKEN LAW AND GLORIFIES THE LAWGIVER.

We may note that the punishment they received (1) *condemned them here in the eyes of all Israel;* (2) *showed the exceeding sinfulness of sin;* and (3) *the exacting demands and exalted dignity of the law.* The Lord had said to Moses that He would be sanctified in them who drew near Him, and glorified by all the people; and He would make even the wrath, or wickedness of man, to praise Him. Nadab and Abihu treated the law and the Lawgiver with contempt, and the Lord showed, by visiting them with immediate retribution, that such sins deserve death, and that He is able to vindicate His own glory. God thus manifesting Himself as a consuming fire, showed (1) *His jealousy*, that He could not be openly and grossly insulted; (2) *His power*, that the fire which glowed in the cloud, which had kindly led them out of Egypt, protected them from their foes, and which consumed the burnt offering on the day of consecration, had power to destroy, and, unless held in check, would consume all sinners; (3) *His mercy*, that while sin deserved punishment, and God had the right and power to destroy, He made judgment His strange work, and such retribution—as that which visited Aaron's sons—an exceptional thing. Let us learn that, though worship must be voluntary, yet it must be according to God's own appointed way. Liberty is not to be perverted into lawlessness. Knowledge of God will be good or ill to us according as we use or abuse it. The law set before men life and death, and left them to choose. The gospel is a savour of life unto life, or of death unto death, according as men accept or reject it. Sacred fire renders divine worship acceptable, strange fire renders divine worship abominable; the former God longs for, the latter God loathes. Strange fire is offered upon God's altar when worship is presented with (1) *unsolicited materials*, or from (2) *unsanctified motives*. Enthusiasm is holy ardour—literally, *God in us*—His own fire ascending to Himself.—*F. W. B.*

Topic: MAN'S DEGRADATION OF WHAT IS HOLY (Vv. 1-3).

The page of human history has ever been a sadly blotted one. It is a record of failure from first to last. Amid all the delights of Eden man hearkened to the tempter's lie (Gen. iii.). When preserved from judgment by the hand of electing Love and introduced into a restored earth, he was guilty of the sin of intemperance (Gen. ix.). When conducted by Jehovah's outstretched arm into the land of Canaan, he "forsook the Lord, and served Baal and Ashtaroth" (Judges ii. 13). When placed at the very summit of earthly power and glory, with untold wealth at his feet, and all the resources of the world at his command, he gave his heart to the uncircumcised stranger (1 Kings xi.). No sooner had the blessings of the gospel been promulgated, than it became needful for the Holy Ghost to prophecy concerning "grievous wolves," "apostasy," and all manner of failure (Acts xx. 29; 1 Tim. iv. 1-3; 2 Tim. iii. 1-5; 2 Peter, ii.; Jude). And, to crown all, we have the prophetic record of human apostasy from amid all the splendours of millenial glory (Rev. xx. 7-10). Thus:

I. MAN SPOILS EVERYTHING. Place him in position of highest dignity, and he will degrade himself. Endow him with most ample privileges, and he will abuse them. Scatter blessings around him in richest profusion, and he will corrupt them. Such is man! Such is nature in its fairest forms, and under the most favourable circumstances. Here, with Nadab and Abihu—

1. Hardly had the *divine position been assumed* ere it was *deliberately abandoned*, through neglect of the divine commandment. Hardly had the echo of the shout of victory died away ere the elements of a spurious worship are prepared.

2. Man has always proved himself ill-disposed to walk in the narrow path of strict adherence to the plain word of God. The by-path has ever seemed to present resistless charms to the poor human heart. "Stolen waters are sweet" (Prov. ix. 17); such is the enemy's language.

3. Nadab and Abihu *took their own way :* they should have acted according to the word of the Lord.

II. DIVINE HOLINESS REJECTS THAT WHICH IS THE FRUIT OF MAN'S CORRUPT WILL. "There went out fire from the Lord and devoured them." How deeply solemn.

1. By the outgoing of fire Jehovah had signified *His acceptance of a true sacrifice* (chap. ix.).

2. By the outgoing of fire He sends *His judgment upon erring priests* (chap. x.). The "strange fire" was rejected as an abomination. The Lord was glorified in the former; but it would have been a dishonour to accept the latter.

Men's corrupt will is never more hideous and abominable than when active in the things of God. But—

III. MAN CANNOT BE PERMITTED TO DESECRATE THE SANCTUARY OF THE DIVINE PRESENCE. "I will be sanctified in them that come *nigh* me," etc.

1. The *dignity and glory of the entire economy* depended on Jehovah's maintenance of His righteous claims. If these were to be trifled with all was forfeited. If men were allowed to defile the sanctuary by "strange fire" there was an end to everything.

2. Nothing could be permitted to ascend from *the priestly censer* but the pure fire, kindled from off the altar of God, and fed by the "pure incense beaten small."

3. Man *must not be allowed to introduce his devices into the worship of God.* All his efforts can only issue in the presentation of "strange fire," unhallowed incense, false worship. His very best attempts are an absolute abomination in the sight of God.—C. H. M.

Topic: THE LAW OF WORSHIP (Vv. 1-11).

Religious history is a continuous series of revelations of God : every incident freighted with significance and suggestiveness. The gleam of the seraph's sword at the gates of Eden declares *the sinner's banishment from God :* the roar of the deluge is the voice of many waters attesting the *terrible might of Divine judgments :* the lightnings of Sinai write out in letters of fire the *sovereignty of the decalogue.* And so in the doom of Nadab and Abihu we have announced in tongues of flame *the law of worship.* What answer does the incident give us to the vital question, How can men worship God acceptably?

I. THE CHARACTER OF THE WORSHIPPER *is a factor of importance.*

While the people were yet trembling at the judgments sent upon the offending priests, God ordained certain restrictions to be observed by those who ministered at His altars, as a "statute for ever throughout your generations, that ye may put differences between holy and unholy, and between unclean and clean."

1. The numerous directions in the Jewish ritual relating to *personal purity*, were all significant of the *value of character* in the office of worship.

2. Yet the *soundness of the inward life as pre-requisite to a real approach to God*

is seldom considered. This material age exalts the form above the spirit. If a man observe the formalities of public worship his spiritual condition is assumed to be correct.

3. But *character*, the style and stamp of the man, is the one thing needful. " Blessed are the pure in heart, for *they* shall see God."

II. THE PURPOSE OF THE WORSHIPPER *is the element of which God makes account.*

Nadab and Abihu offered "strange fire" in obedience to some selfish end. Their proper offices in the ministry were subordinate; the adoption of a new method would secure them reputation. Egotism, vanity, prompted them.

1. When a minister at God's altar now *cultivates eccentricities and extravagances of manner* to attract a crowd and become famous, he is offering " strange fire." A singleness of purpose to honour God should be the sovereign motive in every minister's heart.

2. *Attendance in God's house* is not proof of true worship. *Why* are they there ? Coming to be charmed with eloquence is not worship. Attendance from force of habit is not worship. Ceremony is easier than consecration; so men satisfy themselves with the outward observance, while the essential need of the inward aspiration is overlooked.

It is averred that the offices of public worship are waning in interest and influence. The reason is not far. It is not from lack of facilities and appliances. There are wheels enough, but not enough of "the living spirit within the wheels." Abolish the intellectual and æsthetic theory of worship, and restore the spiritual, and the evil is corrected. Let every man feel that only the outgo of His heart to God is worship, and our places of prayer will become true temples where the glory of the Shekinah burns, and where hushed assemblies gather to sun themselves in the light of the Divine Presence.

III. THE PREPARATION FOR WORSHIP *is a matter to which God attaches great importance.*

1. *Men should be at their best* when they approach the place and hour of worship. In the house of God things suffered elsewhere were forbidden (vv. 8, 9). Every faculty should be in highest exercise; every barrier to God's freest access to the soul should be broken down.

2. Now, as then, *true worship requires preparation*. It cannot be extemporised. We cannot turn to it at a moment's notice, and realise it while our ears are full of the babble of the market and our hands are clenched in the grip of gain. As Moses in sight of the flaming bush must put off his shoes because he was standing on holy ground, so those who would meet God in their worship must prepare themselves. A hushed season of reverence is a pre-requisite; a ready soul, and no other, finds a waiting God.

IV. THE MODE OF WORSHIP *has its limits of importance.*

Nadab and Abihu were punished for departing from the divinely established order of service. Under the Christian dispensation larger liberty is allowed. Men are free to adopt such methods of worship as are most affluent in ministries to their spiritual life. But the old underlying principle is still in force.

1. *Forms of worship are only to help men to get to God.* All claims to antiquity, or beauty of diction, or appeal to the sensuous in men, are barred out; the one question is, Do they help us to push open the doors of the invisible world, and make our way to the presence of our Lord ?

2. *In the nature of the case there is no one set method for reaching this end.* The ritual which gives wings to the soul in Christian lands may prove a drag weight to the Zulu.

3. *The soul owes no loyalty to ceremonials of human contriving.* Along which way it can quickest find God it is bound to travel. There is no best way for the whole world.

Right character, earnest purpose, due preparation, helpful method, these are the essentials to acceptable worship. These will open a door through which the divine Spirit shall come in, until the soul of the worshipper is "filled with all the fulness of God."—Rev. Edward S. Atwood, in *Sermons on the International S. S. Lessons*.

Topic: SPURIOUS WORSHIPPERS: THEIR DARING AND DOOM (Vv. 2-5).

I. GOD DISCRIMINATES BETWEEN TRUE AND SPURIOUS WORSHIP.

1. Earnest spirits, honest in their struggles in searching after peace with God, *may make mistakes in coming nigh Him*. They may bring what He cannot receive; *self-reliant efforts*. "If I wash myself in snow-water, and make my hands never so clean" (Job. ix. 30); *repentant tears*, hoping to appease by contrition; *generous acts*, endeavouring to win by deeds of mercy. Such efforts, though erroneous, may be sincere endeavours of upright, but unenlightened consciences to attain a knowledge of sins forgiven. Hence eager souls are seeking God by works of the law, or the ordinances of systematic religion.

2. All such will doubtless issue through the exceeding goodness of God, *in the clear light of a known and enjoyed salvation*. There never yet was one who followed the faintest glimmerings of light which fell upon his understanding, who did not, in due time, receive more. "To him that hath shall be given." "The path of the just is as the shining light, which *shineth more and more* unto the perfect day." All this is as plain as it is encouraging.

3. Yet they who *bring their own impious wills* into the worship and service of God can expect no graciousness from God; on them, sooner or later, the solemn judgments of a righteous God, who cannot allow His claims to be trifled with, must fall. "I will be sanctified in them that come nigh me."

II. GOD DEALS WITH WORSHIPPERS ON THE TERMS OF THEIR OWN PROFESSION.

1. If men come near Him, *honestly seeking Him*, He will meet them *as seekers*, and they shall surely find Him.

2. But when men approach *as priests*, He will demand from them *such worship and incense* as priests should offer.

3. They who come before God as *worshippers* are regarded by Him as no longer seekers, enquirers, asking the right way to Him, but as *those who believe they know* and *profess to have found*. From such He requires the true worship, the acceptable offering. If their censer smokes with unhallowed fire, if they offer unto God the elements of a spurious worship, if they essay to tread His courts unwashed, unsanctified, unsubdued, if they place on His altar the workings of their own corrupt will, *judgment must be the result*. There will be (*a*) the *immediate* rejection of all worship which has not the Father for its goal, Christ for its substance and hope, the Holy Spirit for its sanctity and acceptableness; and there will be (*b*) the *fearful judgment at the last*, when all folly and wrong will be accursed.

4. God's *holiness* is as quick to reject all "strange fire," as His *grace* is quick to accept the faintest, feeblest breathings of a true heart. He must pour out His righteous judgment upon all false worship, though He will never "quench the smoking flax, or break the bruised reed."

III. YET WHAT AN ENORMITY OF SPURIOUS WORSHIP GOES UP BEFORE GOD.

1. Very much of that which *passes among men for worship of God* is but "strange fire" after all. There is neither the pure fire nor the pure incense, and therefore heaven accepts it not.

2. *Attainment to the true qualities of hallowed worship* is a result of divine grace in the soul. He who knows through grace the pardon which the blood of Christ

brings, he who has received the illumination of the Holy Ghost, can worship the Father in spirit and in truth.

3. It is consolatory to turn our thoughts from the vain worship which within so many shrines is burned before the Lord, to consider the *true worship which from so many honest and Christian hearts is ascending to God's sanctuary.*

IV. THE JUST JUDGMENT, WHICH FALSITY OF WORSHIP EVOKES, CANNOT FAIL TO COME.

1. It tarries *now, because of the interposing grace of Christ,* staying the plague, arresting the doom. *During this age of grace,* "God is in Christ *reconciling* the world unto Himself, *not imputing their trespasses unto them.*" Therefore the judgment falls not direct, as on Nadab and Abihu it did, on spurious worshippers.

2. Yet the throne of God cannot ever *continue to be insulted by clouds of impure incense* ascending from unpurged worshippers. "Strange fire" will ultimately be quenched for ever, and all that is spurious be abolished, and the whole universe become as one hallowed temple wherein the true God, Father, Son, and Holy Ghost, shall be adored in acceptable and reverent worship throughout the everlasting ages.

Topic: A WARNING TO WORSHIPPERS (V. 1, 2).

There are three circumstances in which the Old Testament dispensation deserves our notice. (1) *As it prefigured the times of the gospel and the sacrifice of Christ—* "the law a shadow." (2) *As it showed the true requisites of acceptable worship.* (3) *As it plainly marks the solemnity which God attaches to all the institutions of His own appointment.* Everything was marked by severity. The Sabbath breaker was punished with death, disobedience to parents with death, the slightest infraction of a solemn ordinance was punished with death. Instance before us, Nadab and Abihu. Say not we have no concern. The dispensation differs, but the Lawgiver is still the same (Heb. xii. 28, 29). Tabernacle typified Christ (Heb. ix. 8).

Consider the *circumstances, warnings, inferences.* Necessary to mark these.

I. THE CHIEF CIRCUMSTANCES WHICH THE HISTORY RECORDS.

1. *The setting up of the tabernacle.* This had been erected at a great expense, and was truly a national work, and the completion of it was a subject of universal congratulation. No labour was withheld, no cost spared, no difficulty considered; all ages, all classes, all ranks, almost all hands were employed in forwarding it (Ex. xxxv. 20). It had been framed after the pattern in the mount, by God's express appointment, "as the Lord commanded." The most consummate skill had been employed in its erection; and as they saw its hallowed curtains finished, they rejoiced with an elevated and a reasonable joy. They felt that they were no longer aliens; they had the visible symbol of God's presence; they were raised to the dignity of moral life; they had a sanctuary to which they might repair, and, amidst the toils of the wilderness, there was one object on which the eye might rest, one sacred enclosure which formed the link between earth and heaven. It was their refuge in danger, their guide in perplexity, their solace in weariness, and their hope when every other hope failed them.

2. *The acceptance of their sacrifices.* At length the expected day arrived when the tabernacle should be publicly consecrated and the first services performed. Ten thousand hearts beat with warm devotion when the solemnities began. Moses and Aaron, the elders of Israel, the Levitical priesthood, the great congregation—all were assembled. And now the sin offering for Aaron was to be presented. The beasts were slain, the ceremonies performed, the blood was sprinkled, the wave offering was offered; Aaron, in the ardour of devotion and with a heart overflowing with love, blessed the people (23, 24). The sacrifice was accepted.

3. *The death of Nadab and Abihu.* " And Nadab and Abihu took each a censer and put fire." This had been distinctly prohibited—*went beyond God's ordinance.* It was a virtual contempt of the authority of God, a dishonour to the spiritual nature of that institution. They were, probably, over-elated with the honour of their new function, and perhaps, with the headstrong vanity of irreligious youth, anxious to overstep the ordinary forms and show their independence of the example and authority of Aaron. The Jewish doctors suppose that these young men were intoxicated with wine, and had also neglected to make the proper distinctions in the sacrifices (from 8 and 9).

Their sin was compounded of impiety, presumption, and sacrilege. *"And there went out fire from the Lord."* Fire was their sin, fire their punishment. God saw that fire was the fittest vengeance for a sin of fire—his own fire for their strange fire; the same fire which consumed the sacrifice now consumed the sacrificers. *" It is a fearful thing to fall into the hands of the living God."* They had to do with one who was *wise* to prescribe His own worship, *just* to require what He hath prescribed, and *powerful* to avenge what was in opposition to His command.

There is something inexpressibly awful in the thought that the service of the sanctuary began with death and judgment *" before the mercy-seat"* (4-6).

II. THE WARNINGS WHICH THE TEXT PERPETUATES.

Lay it to heart, and remember that it is as effectual to all the purposes of solemn caution as though it had occurred but yesterday and had taken place within the precincts of a Christian temple. Is is recorded for your instruction. God is the same, religion is the same, worship is the same, and the sanctions of Gospel ordinances are the same; the only difference is that the *punishment* is *deferred* till death, and that instead of earthly and material fire, those who mock God in His ordinances will be exposed to a fire *never quenched,* " *suffering the vengeance of eternal fire.*"

1. *The awful solemnity which God attaches to the ordinances of religion.* " *I will be sanctified in them that come nigh me.*" This law has never been repealed, but it has been renewed and perpetuated by Christ Himself. " *God is a spirit.*" Ex. x. 22. Sanctified God will be, either in the spirituality of men's worship, or the severity of their condemnation. Let us beware of falling into their sin. When we come with prayerless and unsanctified hearts, with worldly affections, with profane imaginations, when we worship without spirituality of mind, without imploring the grace of the Holy Spirit, and without a lively faith in the sacrifice and intercession of Christ, we bring common fire, " strange fire," to the altar. *These flames were never of His kindling.* He hates both altar and fire, priest and sacrifice. Who can calculate our guilt ?

Remember this, ye who only come to trifle, who never pray before you come, who make no conscience of spiritual worship—remember, you never leave His house as you enter it. You leave it with a heavier weight of guilt. " Keep thy foot," etc. (Eccles. v. 1).

2. *No outward profession, no forms of religion, however specious, will avail without internal piety.* Nadab and Abihu had been anointed with holy oil, set apart by God Himself, clad with beautiful garments, *had taken part in a sacrifice which had been accepted* (ix. 9). But all this was as nothing. What a lesson to *ministers !* Well may we tremble, answerable for the spirit we diffuse in prayer, etc.

3. *The piety of parents will form no shield for the iniquity of children* Aaron's sacrifice had been accepted, his *sons* were smitten instantly. We might have pleaded their youth and inexperience, a *first* offence, their relation to Aaron. Even Aaron had not a word.

III. THE INFERENCES WHICH THIS EVENT SUPPLIES.

1. *Bless God for the more gracious age in which you live,* that " mercy now rejoices against judgment."

2. *Mourn the iniquity of your holy things.* Even our very approaches to God,

our prayers, hymns, services, are all marred by our sad defects, in spirit, manner, and aim.

3. *Implore the divine Spirit* to "help your infirmities, for we know not what to pray for as *we ought;* but the Spirit himself maketh intercession for us with groanings which cannot be uttered, and maketh intercession for the saints according to the will of God" (Rom. viii. 26, 27).—*Rev. Samuel Thodey*, A.D. 1822.

Topic: THE SILENCE OF AARON'S SORROW (V. 3).

The sudden and awful destruction of Nadab and Abihu filled the heart of their father with unutterable grief. It must have been a most appalling sight to see two young men clad in priestly vestments smitten dead before the Lord in the midst of an iniquitous act of innovation. But "Aaron held his peace." Let us notice—

I. THE POIGNANT CHARACTER OF AARON'S SORROW. The blow came and smote (i.) his *patriotism*—he would feel that Israel as a nation was disgraced; (ii.) his *piety*—religion was dishonoured and God insulted; (iii.) his *paternity*. As a man, he would have felt deeply had any two men of Israel met with such a doom; but for the victims to be HIS SONS, the flower and promise of his family, this would make his grief exceedingly great. He may have looked upon them with pardonable pride the day before, when they stood by his side and received the commendation of the Lord; now he stands beside them with unutterable shame, as well as sorrow, as he sees them lying lifeless under the condemnation of the Lord. (1) It is a great grief for parents to watch their children die when they have *seen the end approaching*, and have prepared their hearts to meet the bereavement by its slow approach; but in Aaron's case the bereavement was sudden, there were no premonitions to prepare the father's heart to meet it. (2) It is a great grief for parents to surrender their children even when they feel *sure they die in the Lord*, and that God gently takes their life away; but, in Aaron's case, his sons died under the frown of the Lord, and concerning their future he could have no sure and certain hope. To lose two sons under such circumstances was sorrow of the most poignant kind.

II. THE PATIENT CONDUCT OF AARON UNDER SUCH SORROW.

The catastrophe struck him dumb. He restrained himself, and refrained from uttering any comment on the event, any complaint against God. It was not the silence of *stoicism*, or *sullenness*, or *obstinacy*; but of *devout and reticent submission*. He heard what Moses had to say upon the event; he felt his sons had grossly insulted the Lord; that God's glory must be vindicated; that the punishment was merited; so, he "*held his peace.*" He offered no objection, asked for no explanation; knew he could not reverse the verdict, could not restore the victims; it was *an irreparable loss!* He "held his peace"; no language of his could have described his grief, or conveyed a fair idea of his sorrow. He "held his peace" with men, but by thought, which is inarticulate speech, he could tell his grief to God. Out of the abundance of the heart the mouth sometimes cannot speak; at such a time as this, in the hidden depths of the spirit, the heart only knows its own bitterness. This incident of Aaron silently and meekly bearing his great grief teaches us that one of the most consistent and expressive ways to show our sincere sorrow in the hour of any great calamity, is by holding our peace. Silence at such a time is (*a*) *safe*, (*b*) *devout*, (*c*) *consistent*. The silence must be holy and resigned; for there may be rebellion and anger in the heart when the lips are dumb.—*F. W. B.*

Topic: PRIESTLY ELEVATION ABOVE PRIVATE SORROW (Vv. 6, 7).

Aaron, Eleazar and Ithamar were to remain unmoved in their elevated place, their holy dignity, their position of priestly sanctity. Neither the failure, nor the judgment consequent thereon, was to be allowed to interfere with those who wore the priestly robes and were anointed with "the oil of the Lord." Those outside might "bewail the burning," but as for Aaron and his sons, they were to go on in the discharge of their hallowed ministries.

I. WORSHIP, NOT LAMENTATION, IS THE SOLEMN FUNCTION OF PRIESTS.

Priests in the sanctuary were not to bewail but to adore; not to weep as in the presence of death, but to bow their anointed heads as in the presence of the divine visitation. The fire of the Lord might act and do its solemn work of judgment, but to a true priest it mattered not what that "fire" came to do—to express divine approval by consuming the sacrifice, or divine displeasure by smiting sin; that "fire" was the known *manifestation of God*, and whether it acted in mercy or judgment the business of all true priests was to worship. "I will sing of mercy and of judgment; unto thee, O Lord, will I sing."

II. *They who have the anointing of the Holy Ghost must* MAINTAIN AN ELEVATION OF SOUL ABOVE NATURE'S WEAKNESSES.

1. *Priestly nearness to God gives the soul an insight into all God's ways,* and such a sense of the *rightness* of all His dispensations that one is *enabled* to worship in His presence, even though the stroke of His hand has removed from us the object of tender affection.

2. Though godly souls *feel* as men, they *worship* as *priests*. They are not stoics; but an elevated spiritual life opens up a region to the soul brought "nigh to God" of thought, feeling, experience, in which nature can never move; a region in which, with all its boasted refinement and self-sufficiency, nature (unhallowed by God's grace and unsustained by the Lord's sufficiency) knows nothing. We must tread the sanctuary of God with *true priestly energy,* in order to enter into the depth, the meaning, and power of such holy mysteries.

The prophet Ezekiel was called, in his day, to sit down to this difficult lesson (Ezek. xxiv. 16-18); and it proves that in *prophetic* testimony, as well as in *priestly* worship, we must rise superior to all the claims and influences of nature and of earth.

III. OUR HIGH PRIESTLY PRIVILEGES MAY BE FORFEITED BY THE ASSERTION OF NATURE'S FRAILTIES.

Too often sanctified and hallowed souls fall below their divine elevation.

1. Nothing save *realised priestly nearness to God* can preserve the heart from the power of evil or maintain its spiritual tone.

2. All believers are priests unto God, and nothing can deprive them of their position as such. But though they cannot lose their position they may *grievously fail in the discharge of their functions.* While looking at the precious truth of the believer's security we may forget the possibility of our failing to discharge our sacred duties.

3. There is continual need of watchfulness and prayer, *that the hallowed elevation of priests unto God be preserved*. His heavenly grace alone will preserve us from every species of failure, whether it be personal defilement, or the presentation of any of the varied forms of "strange fire," which abound so in the professing Church, or in the yielding to personal weakness of grief and complaint of our frail human nature.—Developed from *Notes on Leviticus,* by C. H. M.

Topic: EXCITATIONS PERILOUS TO COMMUNION (Vv. 8-11).

The effect of wine is to excite nature; and all natural excitement hinders that calm, well-balanced condition of soul which is essential to the proper discharge of the priestly office.

I. *Each should discover for himself* WHAT ACTS UPON HIM AS A DELETERIOUS EXCITEMENT.

1. The *causes which excite are manifold* indeed; wealth, ambition, politics, the varied objects of emulation around us in the world, as well as " wine and strong drink."

2. Acting upon us with exciting power, they entirely unfit us from every department of priestly service. If the heart be swollen with (*a*) *feelings of pride, covetousness or emulation*, it is utterly impossible that the pure air of the sanctuary can be enjoyed, or the sacred functions of priestly ministry discharged. Men speak of the versatility of genius, or a capacity of turning quickly from one thing to another; but the most versatile genius ever possessed could not enable a man to pass from (*b*) *an unhallowed arena* of literary, commercial or political competition, into the holy retirement of the sanctuary of the divine presence; nor could it so adjust the eye that has become dimmed by the influence of such scenes as to enable it to discern, with priestly accuracy, the difference " between holy and unholy, and between unclean and clean."

II. GOD'S PRIESTS MUST KEEP THEMSELVES APART FROM UNHALLOWED EXCITATIONS.

1. Theirs is *a path of holy separation and abstraction.* They are called aside from and raised far above the influence of merely earthly joy as well as earthly sorrow. In other words, the joy of God's priests is not the joy of earth, but the joy of heaven, the joy of the sanctuary. "The joy of the Lord is their strength."

2. Hence, everything that incapacitates us for our priestly function, *that tends to derange our priestly relation or dim our priestly vision*, must unfit us for the service we are called to render. The heart must be kept right, the conscience pure, the eye single, the spiritual vision undimmed.

3. *The soul's business in the holy place must be faithfully and diligently attended to*, else all will go wrong. Private communion with God must be kept up, else we shall be fruitless as servants, and defeated as men of war. It is vain for us to bustle about, and run hither and thither in what we call service, or indulge in vapid words about Christian valour and warfare. If we are not keeping our priestly garments unspotted, if we are not keeping ourselves free from all that would excite nature, we shall assuredly fail and be defeated. Our success in every department depends on our cultivating a spirit of worship.

(*a*) Let us then *exercise a spirit of self-judgment* over our habits, our ways, our associations. It is the business of each one to be fully aware of what is to him as " wine and strong drink," what blunts his spiritual perceptions. It may be the auction mart, a cattle show, a newspaper—the merest trifle. But if it tends to excite, it will disqualify us for future ministry.

(*b*) When by grace we discern aught that in the slightest degree unfits us for the elevated exercises of the sanctuary, let us *put it away*, cost what it may. Let us not suffer ourselves to become slaves of a habit.

(*c*) Communion with God should be dearer to our hearts than all besides; and just in proportion as we prize that communion shall we watch and pray against everything that would rob us of it, against everything that would excite, ruffle or unhinge.

(*d*) The more we live in the presence of God, the *less we can bear to be out of it ;* and no one who knows the deep joy of being there could lightly indulge in aught that would take or keep him thence. There is not that object within the compass of earth which would, in the judgment of a spiritual mind, be an equivalent for one hour's fellowship with God.

By abiding in the secret retirement of His holy presence, and keeping implicitly to His truth, we shall be kept from false worship of every kind, and fleshly excitement in all its forms ; so shall we be enabled to carry ourselves aright in every department of priestly ministration, and to enjoy all the privileges of our priestly position. The communion of a Christian is easily hurt by the rude influences of an evil world ; within the sacred precincts of the divine presence all is pure, safe, and happy.

Far from a world of grief and sin,
With God eternally shut in.

[See Addenda, p. 151, *Sensationalism.*]—*Vide,* C. H. M.

Topic: THE UNRELAXING STRICTNESS OF THE RITUAL (Vv. 12-20).

The Lord having spoken unto Aaron (v. 8), showing that he was not dismissed from service on account of the sins of his sons—Moses now addresses him and his two surviving sons upon the law of eating the holy things ; showing they were still as priests to draw near to the Lord, and mediate for the people.

Workers may sin and die, but God's work must go on. The reiteration of the law of the meat offering was useful and timely, as Aaron and his sons may have forgotten it in alarm and confusion at the calamity just occurred. They were to partake of their portion according to the law of the Lord, as their due, according to the commandment of the Lord.

Then having given these directions concerning the offerings, Moses betrays some misgivings respecting the full observance of the sin-offering ritual : and " Moses diligently sought the goat of the sin offering, and, behold it was burnt " ; this made him angry, he questioned the sons of Aaron upon their delinquency, and assured them that they might and ought to have eaten what was appointed them as their share of the sacrifice in the holy place. [See chap. vi. 26-29.] Aaron offered an apology for the omission, and Moses accepted it. Let us look—

I. AT THE FAILURE OF THE PRIESTS TO FULFIL THE REQUIRED RITUAL.

Moses reminded them that he had enjoined it upon them ; that what he enjoined he received from the Lord ; the portion allotted them was the gift of God, and given in connection with the privilege of acting as typical sin-bearers of the congregation. How jealous Moses was for the honour and strict observance of the ritual : he would not have any part of it neglected under any circumstances or pretext. They were to be performed in the right *time, place,* and *manner,* as well as in the right *spirit.* Neither priests nor people were at liberty to innovate upon the details of the offerings.

II. AT THE CAUSES OF THE FAILURE. (*a*) *An overwhelming feeling of sorrow.* Aaron said : " Such things have befallen me," and they were "*such things*" of sorrow as no language could describe ; he had held his peace under the stroke of a double simultaneous bereavement, but " *such things* " had not been known by him before, nor had he heard of any " *such things* " occurring in connection with any other family. He had been overwhelmed, and that had contributed to the failure to comply with what was required of him and his sons. (*b*) *An overawing fear of sin.* He feared that if he had eaten of the sin-offering it might not have been accepted of the Lord, that too much sin clung to him and his sons, and he would rather leave the rite uncompleted than perform it in a wrong spirit. Aaron apprehended the great truth that " God is a Spirit, and that those who worship Him must worship Him in spirit and in truth." Aaron felt that with such feelings as pervaded his breast, to have eaten his portion of the sin-offering would have been a mere empty and meaningless form. Such a full and frank acknowledgment of deviation and unworthiness satisfied Moses, and he said no more.

III. AT THE FORGIVENESS OF THE FAILURE. It is not directly stated that Aaron and his sons were forgiven, but doubtless they were. The Lord allowed the omission to pass unnoticed; and evidently, Moses—although he was angry at first—saw that, in the exceptional circumstances under which the failure occurred, no dishonour was intended, and no offence was offered to the Lord. The sin of Aaron's sons in offering strange fire was a positive outrage. The sin of Aaron and his two surviving sons was a simple failure. Forgiveness was granted on the ground (*a*) *of human infirmity.* Aaron and his sons must have been physically, as well as mentally and morally, exhausted by the sorrow into which they were so suddenly plunged; they felt constrained to fast as well as to weep. The flesh was weak, though the spirit may have been willing. (*b*) *Of spiritual sincerity.* Aaron declared he was afraid that if he ate he might do so unworthily and unacceptably; that he shrank from a forced and false compliance with the letter of the law. (*c*) *Of Divine clemency.* Moses knew that God was a jealous God, that the ritual was very rigid and exacting; and yet he knew that the Lord was merciful and ready to forgive. He pointed out the error and failing to his brother, then held his peace, content with what Aaron had to say in his defence. In all our service and worship we have to do with a God who pities those who fear Him, even as a father pities his children; who knows our frame, and remembers that we are dust. All errors and failings, yea, all sin, may now be forgiven through Christ's one great atonement, if only the penitent ask in faith and sincerity.—*F. W. B.*

Topic: NO JOY BEFORE GOD'S ALTAR (Vv. 18, 19).

Origen (A. D. 185-254) in his Commentary on Leviticus (*In Levit.*, *Hom.* viii.) supplies suggestions based on Aaron's grief amid his priestly ministrations which may be headed—

CHRIST'S GRIEF AT GOD'S HEAVENLY ALTAR:

And reflects thus : " My Saviour even now is mourning for my sin. How can He, who is the Advocate for my sins, drink the wine of gladness when I am grieving Him with my transgressions ? He is therefore in sorrow as long as we remain in error. . . For we cannot think that while Paul mourned for sinners and wept for the guilty, my Lord Jesus abstains from weeping when He approaches the Father, when He stands near the Altar and offers the propitiation for us. And this is the meaning of *the prohibition against drinking the wine of gladness* when coming near the altar, for Christ suffers still the bitterness for our sins."

In the *Benedictine Breviary* this passage from Origen formed one of the "lectures" or readings, and its teaching became thus diffused over the whole Catholic Church.

St. Bernard (A.D. 1091-1153) recognising the erroneousness of doctrinal teaching in this comment of Origen, wrote a special discourse [*S. Bernardi Serm.* xxxiv. *de verbis Origenis,* see Canon Jenkin's *Devotion to the Sacred Heart*] pointing out the error and danger of *extending the sufferings of Christ,* either in *body* or *mind,* into the reign of His glory. " On earth " he exclaims, "Jesus truly wept, was truly sorrowful, truly suffered, truly died, was truly buried. But now that He is risen again, old things are passed away. Seek not then thy Beloved on His bed ; He is risen, He is not here. . . Now He is no longer among the dead, but is taken from the midst of them, changed in body, changed in heart, He hath entered into the majesty of the Lord. . . Though our Lord wept over Jerusalem, now He weeps no more for ever (even as raised from the dead He dieth no more); and as rising from His bed He is no more found therein. Yet He hath now an unspeakably larger and more effectual feeling than they have who mourn for sinners, or lay down their lives for their brethren; although He who hath finished His work can no longer do either of these acts of mercy."

OUTLINES ON VERSES OF CHAPTER X.

V. 1.—*Theme*: SELF-EXALTING ZEAL.

Sounds of high joy had first been swelling through the holy court: sure tokens of approving love had rested on the altar.

But a vile foe is always near. Satan sees the sacred hour, and flies to mar. He sees the gospel of that heaven-sent fire, and will strive to quench.

I. NO STATION IS TOO HIGH FOR TEMPTATION TO ASSAIL.

The foe has keys for every gate. Though the place is sacred and the office holy, no consecrated functions scare him back. He seeks the side of Aaron's first-born sons. Their calling to be priests is no protecting shield. He can ascend the altar steps. He knows the fit temptation for the holiest place. So now he fosters *self-exalting* zeal. He leads to worship, but the worship must be "strange." Such was his bait: mark its success.

II. SELF-WILL OFFERINGS HAVE NO PLACE IN GOD'S WORSHIP.

1. Their *first step strays*. Each takes his censer. God did not require this act: it was not His will.

2. The next act *errs more*. They add fire. Whence was it brought? God has provided what alone He would receive. An outstretched hand might instantly obtain the divinely sanctioned fire.

3. Was there *defiant reasoning* on their part? What, will no other flame avail? Will His altar fire alone cause incense to ascend? Impious self-will thus reasons unto ruin.

4. A "strange" *service* is acted Their hands feign holy work, but *rebel feet tread down God's ordinance*.

III. TO DESPISE GOD IS RAPID DOWNFALL.

1. *His frown is withering blight*: it arms each creature with destructive sting. Behold a proof. The pledge of *favour*, "fire," inflicts sudden *death!* The symbol of accepted service now hurls the disobedient into ruin's gulf.

2. The fire thus *scorned*, puts forth its mighty strength; *acts out God's indignation*. It vindicates its sacred import. They who rejected the fire of God cannot now cast it off. It wraps them in its burning arms, and lays their blackened corpses in the dust. Thus Nadab and Abihu perish from the earth.

IV. THE JUDGMENT OF GOD STILL LIVES FOR TRANSGRESSORS.

This story stands as a dark beacon on a rocky coast. It cries, beware! to all despisers of the gospel scheme. It shows that—

1. *They who stray from God's appointed path*, fall into quicksands of tremendous wrath. It declares that—

2. If men *despise, reject, neglect the atonement* God has provided, death without a remedy is near.—*The Very Rev. Henry Law, D.D.*

V. 2.—*Theme*: DESPISING GOD'S ALTAR.

I. ON THAT ALTAR BURNED THE SYMBOL OF GOD'S GRACE FOR MEN.

"Fire" given by Him, as—

1. *A seal of His acceptance of human offerings*.

2. *A sanctifying element rendering sacrifice efficacious*.

II. FROM THAT ALTAR SCORNERS TURN IN WILFUL PRESUMPTION.

They despise the grace, they reject the provisions of God. There are Nadabs and Abihus still. Who are they?

1. They hear of Christ and *refuse His sufferings* and merits for their own salvation.

2. They see the cross and *reject it as the symbol of faith*. They rather choose a self-created fire: merits of their own. They develop an obedience of their own contriving.

III. ALL SUBSTITUTED MERITS ARE HATEFUL TO A GRACIOUS GOD.

The sin of Nadab and Abihu, therefore, re-appears to-day in the—

1. *Self-righteous*. A round of duties towards God, of charity towards men: and they ask, what lack we more? But what is man's *best*? Rags and pollution. Yet for these, God's well-beloved Son is scorned, His righteousness put aside.

2. *Self-reformation*. Flagrant faults are shunned. Foul transgressions have soiled their lives. These they own and flee. But they bring self-reformation fruits, Cain-like, and lay them on fire for offerings. Self-amendments are their incense. But outward changes are not inward grace; a painted surface will not purify a tomb.

3. *Contrition* is offered. Feelings are stirred, tears flow. The tempter whispers— there is merit in tears. The mourning spirit

fondly hopes that mourning can bring peace. Sorrow when brought as the price of pardon is "strange."

4. *Formalists* crowd God's courts in studied reverence. Their lips drop holiest words, their hands touch holiest symbols. If rites and outward decorum were devotion, they worship indeed. But such worshippers reject the substance and rest on signs. They stay no wrath, purge no sins.

(*a*) What does your censer contain?
(*b*) Christ's merits alone are delightful incense to God.

V. 3.—*Theme:* VIOLATION OF SANCTITY. "I *will be sanctified*," etc.

I. THE ESSENCE OF THEIR SIN in their conduct before the Lord.

1. The emphasis is to be placed on the word "I." "*I* will be sanctified." *God* must be served with sanctity: and *He* must be alone considered in our worship, and not ourselves or others.

2. This implies that when *deviations from divine and clearly defined instructions* occur, the Lord charges that such deviations do *not enhance His glory*: neither is He sanctified in those who are guilty of such deviations.

II. THE REQUISITES IN WORSHIP which are hereby enforced.

1. The *only acceptable manner of administering the ordinances of God's house*—strict observance of the prescribed order. Not with the "strange fire" of will worship.

2. The *unfitness of those who minister* in holy things who *neglect* the proper observance of the ordinances, and *teach* men so to do.

3. Avoid everything which would disqualify us for acceptable worship.—*D. C. Hughes, A.M.*

V. 3.—*Theme:* THE SILENCE OF AARON.

Of the silence of grief there is no example more renowned than that of Aaron. This was *truly* the *silence of grief*, and no reproach of *insensibility* can be attached to him.

I. THE CONDUCT OF AARON MUST BE EXPLAINED IN THE LIGHT OF THE WHOLE EVENTS.

1. The slaying of his sons was a *necessity*, in order to arrest further presumption and profanity spreading throughout all Israel.

2. God's holy ordinances had *been outraged*, whose penalty was death.

II. It is the *case of* GODLY HUMILITY to be thus silent in the bosom of an irreparable loss, of a profound affliction.

III. In this mute sorrow, there is also more than wise humility; as we must see there also ACQUIESCENCE.

Aaron cannot hide from himself that his sons *merited* their fate.

IV. It is just to recognise in this conduct LOWLY AND FIRM RESIGNATION.

1. *Rebellion* speaks.
2. *Resignation* holds its peace.—*A. Coquerel.*

V. 3.—*Theme:* MUTE SUFFERING.

I. HOW GREAT THE GRACE NEEDED FOR THIS.

II. *How exemplary* THE USE OF NEEDED GRACE *in such a trial as this.*

Let us learn to submit to God's judgments however severe.—*D. C. Hughes, A.M.* [See Addenda p. 151, *Submission.*]

V. 3.—*Theme:* SUBMISSION TO GOD IN AFFLICTION. "*And Aaron held* his peace."

The becoming behaviour of a servant of God under very great and sore affliction: who, through divine assistance, stilled the murmurings of nature and replied nothing against God. Observe—

I. That the CHILDREN OF GOD ARE SOMETIMES LIABLE TO SEVERE AFFLICTION, both personal and relative. David complains (Psa. xxxviii. 2). *Job* also (Job ix. 27). Paul's testimony (2 Cor. v. 4). And it is in heaven only where all tears shall be wiped from their eyes (Rev. vii. 17). The blessed God *intends* by his afflictions their advantage in time and eternity.

1. He never afflicts till there is a *real necessity* (1 Peter iv. 16).
2. He afflicts *in wisdom* (Heb. xii. 9, 10).
3. *In measure* (1 Cor. x. 13).
4. *In love and tenderness* (Prov. iii. 12; Heb. xii. 5, 6; Rev. iii. 19).
5. To *sanctify our hearts and affections* (Heb. xii. 10).
6. To *save us from condemnation* (2 Cor iv. 17).
7. They are but *light and momentary* (Psa. xxx. 5; Isa. liv. 7, 8; 2 Cor. iv. 17).

II. *What is implied in being* SILENT IN TRIALS AND AFFLICTIONS?

Not a careless indifference (Heb. xii. 5).
Not a sullen, daring obstinacy (Jer. v. 3).
Not a restraint of prayer before God, nor a restraint of communication before a real friend (Job xix. 22). But—

1. A deep *sense of God's hand in what we suffer* (Psa. xxxix. 9; Isa. xxxviii. 15; 1 Sam. ii. 6).
2. An *humble acquiesence in the justice* of His proceedings.
3. A *resigning ourselves* to His pleasure (Matt xxvi. 39).
4. Acknowledging *His right in us*, to do as He thinks best (Job i. 21).

III. *Considerations by which* TO INDUCE SUCH A GRACIOUS TEMPER OF MIND.

1. *God has an unquestionable right* to dispose of us and ours as He pleases (Rom. ix. 21, 22).
2. He grants many daily mercies which *we do not deserve.*
3. We have *sinned* against Him (Mic. vii. 9).
4. The *sufferings of Christ* for us were infinitely greater than are ours (Isa. liii. 4, 5; Heb. ii. 10).
5. We shall be adjudged *unworthy to reign with Him* if we do not suffer with HIM (Matt. x. 38, 39).
6. In afflicting His people God has a *view to His own* glory (Lev. x. 3).

Improvement—

1. To be impatient under affliction is unbecoming in a child of God, considered as a new creature.

2. To oppose our wills to the will of God is high presumption (Isa. vi. 9).

3. It is inconsistent with our prayers.

4. It would subject us to the charge of ingratitude to our best Friend and Benefactor, who has drawn us to Christ, pardoned our sins, given us the spirit of adoption, and made us heirs of a glorious immortality, and who is, by these very afflictions, preparing us for our heavenly state (2 Cor. iv. 17).—*Hannum.*

V. 6.—*Theme:* PUBLIC LAMENTATION.

Aaron and his sons, Eleazar and Ithamar, were to refrain from exhibiting outward signs of grief; were not to uncover their heads so that their hair might not become dishevelled; nor rend their clothes, as was the custom at such times of sorrow. They were to suppress their grief, lest they seemed to rebel against the retributive providence of God and unfit themselves for their duties; lest they die, and wrath come upon all the people. They were to show in the presence of the people supreme love to the Lord, and unmoved, exalted devotion to His service. Although Aaron and his two sons were not to disengage themselves from their duties nor exhibit outward signs of grief there was to be a general lamentation, evincing:

I. PUBLIC RECOGNITION OF A SIGNAL JUDGMENT. The sin was too great to be passed unnoticed by the people, and the judgment was too solemn to be hushed up and treated as of transient moment; the whole house of Israel was to bewail the burning which the Lord had kindled. They were to lament *the sin* that had caused the judgment, and the sudden transformation of a joyful ceremony into a scene of lamentation and woe. Such a public and sorrowful recognition of the divine judgment would impress the people with the exceeding sinfulness of sin, and be calculated to deter them from repeating a similar offence; would teach them the dignity of the Law, and jealousy of the Lawgiver for His own glory. The people were to show, by an act of national humiliation and sorrow, that they deplored the sin, and deprecated the divine anger. The general lamentation also evinced—

II. PUBLIC SYMPATHY WITH A SIGNAL SORROW. "Slight sorrows are loquacious, deep anguish has no voice." The sight of the whole congregation mourning, weeping, and wailing, would help Aaron and his sons to bear their griefs; especially when they knew that the Lord had commanded the public lamentation. The expressed grief of the sympathising people would be the counterpart of the suppressed grief of the sorrowing priests. Similar judgments following flagrant sins are recorded in 2 Sam. vi. 7; 1 Chron. xiii. 10; Num. xv. 32-36. We further learn—

(*a*) That when the leaders of a people sin, the whole community shares in the blame.

(*b*) That when the leaders of a people are signally punished, the whole community shares in the sorrow.

(*c*) That bereavement, even of the most painful kind, must not prevent us discharging sacred duties.

(*d*) That sympathy with the bereaved is in keeping with the instincts of our nature, and in harmony with the will of God.

(*e*) That when God's righteous wrath is made manifest against sin, penitential grief should be prompt and general.—*F. W. B.*

V. 9.—*Theme:* HELP TO TEMPERANCE

Combine with this verse, Jer. xxxv. 6; Ephes. v. 18; 1. Thess v. 7.

Intemperance, one of the giant evils of the land, is self imposed This is its saddest feature. All the evils connected with it might be swept away if men so willed.

I. THE NATURAL. Use no intoxicants: and thus never acquire a passion for them.

II THE MEDICAL. Some treat drunkenness as a disease: and by medicine seek to destroy the appetite for alcohol.

III. THE SANITARY. Asylums for inebriates have been opened, which combine physical and moral means to effect a cure: and with success.

IV. THE LEGAL. Its object is to control or arrest the evil; and by prohibition of its manufacture and sale, to remove it from the land.

V. THE VOLUNTARY. This involves the pledge and membership in societies banded together for mutual help and safety. Earnest work for others is a good preventative, so long as it is actively continued.

VI. THE SPIRITUAL. Grace, wherever received, casts out the demon of drink.

VII. THE PHILANTHROPIC. Here is a reform in which to engage. Intemperance is the fruitful source of crime, misery and ruin. The resources it wastes are enormous. Its results on the individual, the family, friends, and country, are appalling.

Dark as is the picture of its ravages, yet the progress made towards sobriety within this century has been considerable. Sidney Smith said that at the beginning of his life, "even in the best society, one third of the gentlemen, at least, were always drunk." To-day the use of liquors at public tables is the exception, not the rule.

This beneficent change in public sentiment demands devout thankfulness, and is prophetic of what shall be achieved.—*Rev. Lewis O. Thompson.* [See Addenda p. 151, *Intemperance*]

V. 9.—*Theme:* A DIVINE PROHIBITION.

The prohibition, occurring here, seems to indicate the secret of the rashness and rebellion of Nadab and Abihu; that they offered the strange fire before the Lord when under the unhallowed excitement of intoxicating drink. Let us regard the prohibition—

I AS A PRECAUTION AGAINST IMPIOUS PRESUMPTION. The position the priests occupied and the duties they performed would be calculated to excite them. They would require no artificial stimulants to inflame their passions. Participation of wine and strong drink may lead to indulgence and excess, which are the sources of many evils; such as (*a*) *Offensive carelessness;* persons become careless about the promises they have made and the duties they have to discharge, heedless of the smiles or frowns of those they profess to please and obey. (*b*) *Offensive independence;* persons get puffed up with a vain notion of their dignity and importance, assume absurd airs, and forget their position in, and relation to society around them. (*c*) *Offensive arrogance;* persons become overbearing and disrespectful, employ words and perform actions most insulting, and of which they would feel ashamed in their sober hours. (*d*) *Offensive indolence;* persons become paralyzed for useful and holy employment; although, frequently they become infuriated and enthusiastic in useless and unholy engagements. None of these things could be tolerated in the service of Jehovah in the tabernacle, for the priests were to be *devout, careful, vigilant,* were to exercise self-restraint and control; with concentration of strength, and consecration of spirit give themselves up wholly to the Lord. Such a prohibition was therefore necessary and merciful. We may also regard it—

II. AS A SAFEGUARD AGAINST SINFUL INDULGENCE. Tarrying in wine and strong drink is directly opposed to reasonable and acceptable religious service; it perverts the powers of body, mind, and soul. It leads to the perversion (*a*) *of personal endowments.* Bodily strength becomes abused, health deteriorated and undermined; mental faculties weakened and frequently deranged; natural geniality and amiability soured. (*b*) *Of Providential bestowments.* Princes have been brought to pauperism, fortunes have been wasted at the shrine of Bacchus; homes and friends have been brought to a common ruin by its degraded devotees. (*c*) *Of reasonable enjoyment.* The priests were not commanded to abstain from wine and strong drink, except when they were in the tabernacle officiating at the services. They might partake at other seasons, but were to use and not abuse what they were allowed. (*d*) *Of religious ordinances.* The various directions of the ritual were so *minute* and *numerous,* that except the head was kept clear, the nerves calm, there was a great risk of mistakes being made, of some parts of the ceremonies being omitted. The memories of the priests were to be kept unclouded, their imaginations unexcited, their animal passions uninflamed. Ancient historians speak with great ardour and decision upon the fact, that in connection with heathen worship, the priests were prohibited taking wine during their attendance upon the gods and the performance of their worship. The reasons given are, that indulgence in wine and strong drink induces *hesitation, forgetfulness, sleep, folly,* and *insanity*. The prohibiton under consideration subserved divine purposes during the Levitical economy, conduced to the safety and well-being of the priests and the glory of Jehovah. "Where the Spirit of the Lord is there is liberty;" we may under the gospel abstain from meat as well as wine, if thereby we can be the means of saving a soul from death, and hiding a multitude of sins.—*F. W. B.*

ILLUSTRATIVE ADDENDA TO CHAPTER X.

PRIDE.

"In general pride is at the bottom of all great mistakes."—RUSKIN, *True and Beautiful.*

"But man, proud man!
Drest in a little brief authority,
Most ignorant of what he's most assur'd,
His glassy essence—like an angry ape,
Plays such fantastic tricks before high heaven
As makes the angels weep."
—*Measure for Measure, II.* 2.

'Pride in their port, defiance in their eye."
—GOLDSMITH, *The Traveller.*

"It thrust proud Nebuchadnezzar out of men's society; proud Saul out of his kingdom; proud Adam out of paradise; proud Haman out of court; proud Lucifer out of heaven."—Henry Smith.

"What is pride? A whizzing rocket
That would emulate a star."
—*Wordsworth.*

PRESUMPTION.

"Presumption is a firework made up of pride and foolhardiness. It is indeed like a heavy house built upon slender crutches. Like dust, which men throw against the wind, it flies back in their faces and makes them blind. Wise men presume nothing but hope the best; presumption is hope out of her wits."—*T. Adams.*

"*Sequitur superbos ultor a tergo Deus.*"
—SENECA.
[An avenging God closely follows the haughty.]

"*Omne animi vitium tanto conspectius in se Crimen habet, quarto major, qui peccat habetur.*"—JUVENAL.
[Every vice makes its guilt the more conspicuous in proportion to the rank of the offender.]

"It is a dangerous thing in the service of God to decline from His own institutions. We have to do with a Being who is wise to prescribe His own worship, just to require what

He hath prescribed, and powerful to revenge that which He hath not required."—*Bishop Hall.*

RASHNESS.
"*Audax omnia perpeti*
Gens humana ruit per vetitum nefas"
—HORACE.
[The human race, afraid of nothing, rushes on through every crime.]

"*Paucis temeritas est bono, multis malo.*"
—PHAEDRUS.
[Rashness brings advantage to few, misfortune to many.]

"*Juvenile vitium regere non posse impetum.*"
SENECA.
[It is the fault of youth that it cannot control its own impetuosity.]

SUBMISSION.
"Calamity is man's true touch-stone."
—*Fletcher.*
"All are not taken! there are left behind
Living beloveds, tender looks to bring
And make the daylight still a happy thing,
And tender voices to make soft the wind.
But if it were not so—if I could find
No love in all the world for comforting,
Nor any path but hollowly did ring:
Where 'Dust to dust' the love from life disjoined—
And if before these sepulchres unmoving
I stood alone (as some forsaken lamb
Goes bleating up the moors in weary dearth)
Crying, 'Where are ye, O, my loved and loving?'
I know a voice would sound, 'Daughter, I AM;
Can I suffice for heaven and not for earth?'"—*Mrs. Browning.*

During the siege of Barcelona by the Spaniards and English, in 1705, an affecting incident occurred, which is thus related by Captain Carleton in his Memoirs : " ' I remember I saw an old officer, having his only son with him, a fine young man, about twenty years of age, going into the tent to dine. While they were at dinner a shot from the bastion of St. Antonio took off the head of his son. The father immediately rose up, first looking down upon his headless child, and then lifting up his eyes to heaven, while the tears ran down his cheeks, only said, ' Thy will be done!' "

SENSATIONALISM.
" Violent fires soon burn out themselves :
Small showers last long, but sudden storms are short :
He tires betimes that spurs too fast betimes :
With eager feeding, food doth choke the feeder :
Light vanity, insatiate cormorant,
Consuming means, soon preys upon itself."
—*Shakespeare.*

INTEMPERANCE.
"*Bonarum rerum consuetudo pessima est.*"
[The too constant use even of good things is hurtful.]

"Touch the goblet no more!
It will make thy heart sore
To its very core!"—LONGFELLOW, *Cristus.*

"Drunkenness is an immoderate affection and use of drink That I call immoderate that is besides or beyond that order of good things for which God hath given us the use of drink.—JEREMY TAYLOR, *Holy Living* II. 2.

PUNISHMENT.
"Punishment is the recoil of crime, and the strength of the back-stroke is in proportion to the original blow."—*Trench.*

CHAPTER XI.

Food: Permitted and Prohibited.

SUGGESTIVE READINGS.

V. 2.—**These are the beasts which ye shall eat.** [For scientific and sanitary information respecting the animals, reptiles, birds, and fishes specified, valuable information will be found in *Whitlaw's Code of Health;* also in *Calmet;* and a useful summary in the *Critical and Explanatory Commentary* on this chapter].

How noteworthy the fact that the glorious Jehovah should extend his oversight of Israel to such minute dietic and sanitary regulations. But the minute is not less within God's thought than the majestic; the "hairs of your head" are guarded (Matt. x. 30) with a providence which equally controls dynasties and kings (Matt. x. 18). There is nothing unimportant with Him " whose we are "

He careth for you with a care which gathers all into consideration—each single step, "lest we dash our foot against a stone"; each moment of life, lest "sudden destruction" come upon us; each item which makes for health, for happiness, for holiness; for God thinks of us in every particular.

The special purposes effected by these dietic regulations for the Hebrew people were :—

1. *Sanitary :* to effect health and cleanliness in the individual and the family. And beyond question the classification of meats is founded upon the wholesomeness of the creatures as man's food, while the stringent laws respecting the "dead" were of emphatic importance in an Oriental country and climate. It is Bacon's testimony that "*cleanliness of body* was ever esteemed to proceed from a due reverence of God"; and Thomson affirms that "*health* is the vital principle of bliss."

2. *Political:* to enforce a distinction between the Hebrew and surrounding nations, restricting them, by minute prohibitions in diet, from mingling with other people in the usages and indulgences of social life; enforcing on them a constant necessity of avoiding all close familiarity with "strangers." This distinction, in habits at the table, and in all festivities, rendered them "a peculiar people," and restrained them from a perilous intermingling with idolatrous neighbours; thus conserving the Theocracy, and marking out Israel as a nation selected and governed by Jehovah.

3. *Religious :* The distinction of meats rested on a moral, a religious, a theological basis. The creatures here classified were images of virtues and vices, suggestive to the Oriental mind of moral and sacred truths; were a pictorial delineation, therefore, of theological instructions. Certainly those creatures pronounced "clean" have been acknowledged most wholesome as man's meat in all after times; and this enforced limitation on Israel that only "clean" food should pass their lips carried the important lesson to every man, woman, and child, that "God had called them not to uncleanness but unto holiness" (1 Thess. iv. 7).

Every enactment of the old dispensation aimed at cultivating virtue, purity, sanctity in God's people; and equally, even more solemnly, every requirement of the gospel and all the provisions of our Lord's atonement summon us to be "clean every whit." "Be ye holy," saith God, "for I am holy."

SECTIONAL HOMILIES.

Topic: Distinguishing the Precious from the Vile (Vv. 4, 5, 6, 7).

"*He is unclean unto you.*"

God's charge, through Ezekiel, against the faithless priests was that "they put no difference between the holy and profane, neither showed difference between the unclean and the clean" (Ezek. xxii. 26). It was also His requirement from Jeremiah in order to his being dignified as God's acknowledged messenger : "If thou take forth the precious from the vile, thou shalt be as My mouth" (Jer. xv. 19).

The emphasis with which Jehovah insists upon this habitual and minute distinguishing the unclean from the clean proclaims therefore *a foremost law in godly conduct.* Consider—

I. *That God's people,* the spiritual Israel, *move in a* SCENE OF MINGLED GOOD AND EVIL.

Man coveted in Eden to "know good and evil." From that hour the "clean and unclean" have been around him in every path of life.

1. In the *sphere of daily life we have contact with both*. The world around us—earth, air, and sea—all elements, all scenes, are occupied with these physical and moral opposites, "clean and unclean." A character, a quality, is upon all that lives. And this fact in the lower orders of creatures forcibly indicates the like realities of moral and spiritual contrasts in the human lives which throng our sphere.

2. Our contact with them *entails the danger of contamination.* Taste the unclean and we thereby become defiled. God has marked specifically and minutely the things which are to be accounted "an abomination" (vv. 12, 20, etc.). So in the human sphere, there are interdicted pleasures, companionships, alliances. The ban of heaven is upon much which the world sanctions. We cannot "have fellowship with the unfruitful works of darkness" without being made "unclean" (v. 26). "Every one that toucheth them shall be unclean."

3. In such a defiling sphere *our duty is to separate the precious from the vile.* God has separated them for us by His prohibitions and permissions; by His "thou shalt" and "thou shalt not." We are to act out His commands, work along the line of His directions. Ignorance is inexcusable when God hath "shown us what is good, and what the Lord requires of us" (Micah vi. 8).

II. That *in life's mingled scene the godly* MUST EXERCISE CONTINUOUS VIGILANCE.

People who knew not the Lord put no difference between things clean and unclean. But the "Israel of God" would need to hourly walk as amid treachery and hazard; they could not eat of the dish of an alien without possibility of tasting the condemned food. This enforced a divided life upon the Israelite, as Christianity still does, leading us to "abhor that which is evil and cleave to that which is good," and maintain a "separation from sinners."

1. We enter, by relationship with Christ, into *a separated life.* As Israel was by these dietic ordinances severed from intimacy and festivity with the heathen, so are Christians called aside, led out from near intercourse with unsanctified society, to "put a difference between the unclean and the clean" (vv. 43-47). We are separated unto God in Christ : "They are not of the world, even as I am not of the world" (John xvii. 16).

2. Such a separated life must *assert itself in habitual avoidance of prohibited things.* The "unclean" is to be marked, repudiated, shunned, as "an abomination." It entails an hourly watchfulness, a quick habit of penetrating into the moral differences which underlie society, men, and manners, pastimes and pursuits. Things must be looked at, not from their popularity, their advantages, their attractions, but faced with a challenge as to their moral quality and tendency. Will this defile? Is it "clean or unclean"? We must "take the precious from the vile."

3. *Minute distinctions are forced upon us* by this principle of conduct. The "unclean" things are not glaringly so; the "clean" are not manifestly different from the "abominable." These creatures—beasts, reptiles, fishes, etc.—are so similar that the lines seem almost to converge and intersect. We may easily avoid sinful men, shun their society, hide from their power; and yet men throw out their influence where they themselves are invisible and unsuspected. We might loathe the company of a vile man, and yet think it no risk to *read* his thoughts as they appear on the printed page. "Thereby many are defiled." Thoughts read enter our minds, are within us to soil and fret us. The sentiments, maxims, and ideas of worldly-wise men gain currency as motives to common conduct, as rules of life. They may act as decoys. Let us challenge their "cleanness" in God's sight, and estimate them by His truth. Our age is charmed with the specious plea of "expediency," "tolerance," "utilitarianism." Let us separate the "precious from the vile."

III. *That by strictest adherence to divine directions* SANCTITY OF LIFE SHOULD BE

MAINTAINED. "Ye shall not make yourselves abominable, etc.; ye shall sanctify yourselves" (vv. 43, 44).

1. Every godly soul is, to a degree, *put in trust with the imparted sanctity.* All Israel's peculiar and distinguishing holiness was the bestowment of Jehovah's grace; as all our Christian purity and piety are derived from Christ. Yet sanctity is not a passive condition of the soul, but a cultivated quality of temperament and behaviour. "Ye shall therefore sanctify yourselves, and ye shall be holy; for I am holy: neither shall ye defile yourselves with any manner of creeping thing" (v. 44). Godliness is to be wrought out into life, shunning the "corruptions which are in the world," and cultivating the holiness which assimilates us to God.

2. *Derived sanctity is no assurance against defilement* if we forsake God's commands. The Israelite only maintained his spiritual status as he held by his sacred separateness from the heathen; repudiating their festivities, broadening rather than obliterating the line of demarcation which distinguished him from the godless world. The admonitory word to us is this: "As obedient children, not fashioning yourselves according to your former lusts in your ignorance; but as he which hath called you is holy, so be ye holy in all manner of conversation" (1 Pet. i. 14, 15). It is our covenant privilege to be as God's sanctified household amid alienated peoples; with His sanctuary amongst us, admitted through a High Priesthood into the holiest of all; accepted by sacrifice, sanctified by the Spirit. It therefore behoves us to shun the vile, touch not and eat not " the unclean," but live in delightful observance of His commands, and thus " perfect holiness in the fear of the Lord" (2 Cor. vii. 1). [See Addenda to chap. xi., *Separate from Sinners.*]

Topic: FORBIDDEN FOODS.

" *Neither shall ye defile yourselves* " (V. 44).

The details of these ceremonial restrictions are unimportant to us. They had their meaning and purpose for the Jew. But the suggestiveness of these prohibitions comes powerfully upon us who are not under Jewish ceremonialism.

> "Govern well thy appetite, lest Sin
> Surprise thee, and her black-attendant Death."
> *Paradise Lost*, Bk. vii. line 546.

I. Man's *duty* is—That his PHYSICAL HEALTH AND PURITY BE SEDULOUSLY MAINTAINED.

The lust of the eye, the caprices of appetite, are not to rule him. He may give no license to cravings whose indulgence would violate the health and sanctity of his physical frame. Every fitful fancy, every low desire, can find gratification in the varieties of meats and drinks which are within man's reach. Yet that is no justification for his indiscriminate and unrestricted indulgence. His self-respect, his intelligence, his sense of propriety, his regard for purity, his recoil from vicious and vitiating habits, and his recognition of responsibility to God, should restrain him from any gratification which is low and degrading, which will inflame the blood, intoxicate the brain, disease the body, defile the conscience.

"*Keep thyself pure*" (1 Tim. v. 22). Such is man's duty. If he trifle with his health, and defile his flesh, he mars the work of God's hands. [Addenda to chapter xi., *Feasting.*]

"All philosophy," says Epictetus, "lies in two words—'Sustain' and Abstain'"

II Man's *dignity* is—THAT HIS ENTIRE NATURE BE HALLOWED AND SANCTIFIED.

"For I am the Lord your God: ye shall therefore sanctify yourselves, and ye shall be holy, for I am holy; neither shall ye defile yourselves" (v. 44).

All God's solicitous care for Israel's physical health and purity was but the index to His supreme desire for their moral rectitude and spiritual holiness. He does not interdict delights, but He requires that no defilement be admitted into the temple of the human life, sensuous, intellectual, or spiritual.

"Religion does not censure or exclude
Unnumbered pleasures, harmlessly pursued" (COWPER'S *Retirement*),

but it lays prohibition on all that would demoralise us and offend God. "Unless the vessel be pure," says *Horace*, "whatever is put in will turn sour." [*Sincerum est nisi vas, quodcunque infundis acescit.*] The first requirement, therefore, to a hallowed life is a *purified body;* its passions subdued, its vile affections extinguished, its immoral tendencies arrested. Conversion proves itself by the renunciation of all sins of the flesh. From the *mental nature* must then be excluded all "evil thoughts"; the intellectual citadel of man must be purged of impure imaginations, decoying fallacies, fitful reasonings, and "every thought be brought into the obedience of Christ" (2 Cor. x. 5). The *spiritual life* can only be perfected in holiness, dignified with sanctity, as the tabernacle in which it dwells is preserved inviolate. Hence the appeal, "Come out from among them, and be ye separate, and touch not the unclean thing; and I will receive you, and will be a Father unto you, and ye shall be my sons and daughters, saith the Lord Almighty" (2 Cor. vi. 17, 18).

Note: The word "*holy*" has its root in the ancient Saxon word *halig*, hale, sound, whole; and *health* is therefore the primal idea of holiness—an unblemished, unimpaired, perfect physique. It glides into the higher application—perfect in a moral sense; pure in heart, pious in thought and life.

Inferentially: All Jehovah's regulations for Israel's physical cleanness and health carried with them the higher demand—"a clean heart and a right spirit." For only he that is "clean every whit" has attained to the divine ideal of man's true dignity—"*Holiness unto the Lord.*"

Topic: A RESTRAINT UPON FESTIVITIES.

The design of God's directions concerning food was not guidance to nutritious diet. The palate suffices man to discern between the luscious and the harmful. And the classification is not into salubrious and insalubrious, tasteful and tasteless, but *clean* and *unclean.* The results of these distinctions and directions are:

I. REMOVAL FROM ALL SOCIAL CONTACT AND FELLOWSHIP WITH THE HEATHEN.

God's chosen tribes could hold no intimacy, share no festivity with idol worshippers. The tables of the nations were unclean. The Jew could have no seat at impure boards.

The principle is divine. The need of separateness remains, for the world is still the world. Its baits, its indulgences, its corruptions are unchanged. It extends its nets for unwary souls. Hence Scripture's voice still cries, Beware. Beacons still show a coast bestrewed with wrecks, and wisdom calls the holy pilgrim from the treacherous path.

A clear precept interdicts the world. Believers must not cross the line. They must dwell apart, avoid intimacies, share no vile festivities.

1. Mark the *divine goodness* in this separating law. The climate of the world checks growth in grace. A coiling serpent sucks the life blood. Rough contact blunts the edge. Solomon's lustre becomes clouded with shame because his heart declined to pleasure's charms. All indulgent intimacies with the

world cause holiness to sicken and wane. Therefore Mercy warns, "Be not conformed to this world" (Rom. xii. 2). [See Addenda to chap. xi. *Separate from Sinners.*]

2. Consider that the *world wars incessantly against Christ and His honour.* It declares itself Christ's open foe: it proclaims hostility against sacred truth. Is it not, then, a traitor's part to feast with the enemy? The true believer shows himself on the Lord's side, in company, act and step. We are the "salt of the earth": but, mixed with corruption, the salt loses its savour.

3. *Usefulness is neutralised where godliness is accommodating.* Suspicion fastens on the faltering steps, on the compromising profession. Society will heed no warning words from one who courts to share its vanities. Therefore Jesus says, "They are not of the world, even as I am not of the world" (Jno. xvii. 14). Tread down the barrier line, stray out beyond the limits of Israel's fellowship, and you wrong your own soul, shadow the glory of Christianity, and enfeeble the witness of gospel truth. The second result is—

II. UNCEASING VIGILANCE WAS ENFORCED UPON GOD'S PEOPLE.

God's dividing line was drawn everywhere, on all scenes, on every hour, between clean and unclean. Its lesson is to us—

1. That at every step we inquire *Is this a lawful path?* The quality of cleanness or uncleanness stamps every movement of every mind, every act throughout each day. Each minutest thing is the seed of some result. We may contract defilement from veriest trifles. This law enforces us to apply a constant test.

2. *No act is neutral*—void of quality, good or ill. We always stand in a path which is right or wrong. Ask continuously, Am I in a "clean" path? and it will be found often impossible to tarry. Examine *thoughts* by this test: dispel those found to be "unclean." Put *words* before this criterion, and "set a watch upon the door of thy lips." Place *books* at this bar of judgment; and how many trifling offsprings of a worldly pen will be consigned to oblivion! Bring *employ* to this light; and flee from what stands rebuked in the light of gospel truth.

Is your *soul* clean or unclean? By nature it is vile. But there is a Saviour's blood and a purifying Spirit. Jesus can cleanse, the Spirit can sanctify.—Compare Dean Law's "*Christ is All.*"

Topic: LEGAL PROHIBITIONS ABROGATED BY CHRISTIANITY (Vv. 44-47).

The *ceremonial* dispensation made righteousness and sanctity dependant on external observances and habits. Judaism "stood only in meats and drinks, and divers washings, and carnal ordinances, imposed until the time of reformation."

The *spiritual* dispensation institutes an inward life of holiness, the Christian being "sanctified in Christ Jesus." Hence for us the Levitical restrictions and regulations are set aside. "Every creature of God is good and nothing to be refused, if it be received with thanksgiving" (1 Tim. iv. 4).

Peter received a special revelation upon this matter (Acts x.), which at once and for ever swept away the distinctions between clean and unclean creatures; and with it abrogated that righteousness of moral life and religious feeling, which consisted in attendance to mere details of ceremonialism. The vision to Peter was especially intended to abolish the distinction between the Jewish and Gentile nations: since the gospel offered cleansing to all people, and Christ, by His atonement as the Lamb of God, took away the sin of the whole world (John i. 29; 1 John ii. 2).

Paul likewise received instruction direct from Christ on this same truth: "I know, and am persuaded by the Lord Jesus, that *there is nothing unclean of itself.*"

So that we are under an economy based upon grand principles rather than punctilious rites.

I. CHRISTIANITY REGARDS NOTHING AS IRREMEDIABLY UNCLEAN.

Its message is that the unclean may be made clean : that what was before forbidden and "cast away" may now find acceptance, and be placed among the sanctified. Nothing is so impure but it may be purified : the *human heart*, the *godless will*, the *evil imaginations*, the *defiled habits*, the *guilty conscience*, the degraded soul. "Lord, if thou wilt, thou canst make *me* clean." Christianity declares that none, nothing, is unchangeably impure : defilement may be removed ; God's prohibition is withdrawn : the "handwriting against us" is abolished ; the sinner may be "washed, sanctified, justified in the name of the Lord Jesus, and by the Spirit of our God" (1 Cor. vi. 2).

II. CHRISTIANITY DENOUNCES NOTHING BECAUSE OF ITS BEING UNCLEAN.

The law had denounced much. Not foods only, but *people*. The Gentiles were excluded from spiritual fellowship with Israel. But the doom has been revoked : the "middle wall of partition" has been broken down (Ephes. ii. 14) ; all may enter the sacred enclosure and become accepted in Christ.

Every sin-defiled soul is in its sinfulness a separated and forbidden thing ; in its uncleanness it is put aside, it has no place among the pure, no part in the heritage of them who are sanctified through faith in Jesus. But *not denounced !* Guilt renders it necessary that the sinner should be thus excluded so long as guilt remains ; "without holiness no man shall see the Lord ;" for "the unclean can not stand in His sight." Yet Christianity offers, opens "salvation even to the uttermost ;' declares that "where sin abounded grace doth much more abound."

Men who missed the large and loving truth denounced the "publican and the harlot"; Jesus Christ set the door open wide to them and became their Friend. "Behold a friend of publicans and sinners."

III. CHRISTIANITY ABANDONS NOTHING HOWEVER UNCLEAN.

No ! it goes down to the depths. The *leper* was abandoned—socially and ceremonially—left to perish ; his plaintive cry "Unclean ! unclean !" winning no help till Christ "touched the leper" and healed his leprosy and restored him to society again. Until the possibility and potency of Christ's redemption and sanctity came to our souls, we were thus *outcasts*. The kingdom of God on earth was closed upon the unclean ; and heaven too : "Nothing entereth that defileth."

No more now ; a "new and living way" affords us entrance even "into the holiest of all." The grace of the Lord Jesus avails for each ; and "him that cometh unto me I will in no wise cast out." Not a soul need remain unclean. Christ can cleanse. There is hope for the vilest.

"The Cross ! it takes our guilt away
It holds the fainting spirit up."

Topic : SYMBOLS OF CLEANNESS IN THE LOWER FORMS OF LIFE.

"*To make a difference between the unclean and the clean*" (V. 41).

i. With regard to "BEASTS," two distinctive marks point out those which are clean and may be eaten ; they should chew the cud and divide the hoof. Either of itself would be insufficient to constitute ceremonial cleanness. What spiritual truth may we learn from such marks being given ? The chewing of the cud expresses the natural process of "inwardly digesting" that which one eats ; while the divided hoof sets forth the character of one's outward walk. He who feeds upon the green pastures of the Word of God, and inwardly digests what he takes in, combines *calm meditation with prayerful* study, will manifest the *character of outward walk* which should distinguish him who obeys the Word.

The one without the other was insufficient (vv. 4-8). A man may profess to love and feed upon the Word of God as the pasture of his soul; but, if his footprints along the pathway of life are not such as the Word requires, he is not clean. And also, though a man walk blamelessly, if his walk be not the result of the hidden life it is worthless. The impression of the foot is of no avail without the divine principle within which feeds upon and digests the rich pasture of God's Word.

ii. With respect to "*all that are* IN THE WATERS," the double mark of cleanness again is given. Two distinctions were necessary, "fins and scales" (vv. 9, 10). A fish needs the "fin" to enable it to *move through the water*, and "scales" to *resist their penetrating action*. And so does the believer require that spiritual capacity which enables him to move onward through the elements surrounding him, and at the same time to resist their penetrating influence. Both are essential. Encased against the action upon us of the evil world, yet endowed with the energy to pass onward through it.

iii. The law with respect to BIRDS was that the carnivorous, the omnivorous, the grovelling, were unclean (vv. 13-24). A striking exhibition is therein given of what must be strenuously shunned by every Christian. He must refuse everything of a "*carnal*" nature. Nor may he feed promiscuously upon everything which comes before him; he must "make a difference between unclean and clean"; must exercise a *discerning mind*, a spiritual judgment, a heavenly taste. Finally, he must use his wings : *rise on the pinions of faith*, and find his place in the celestial sphere to which he belongs. Nothing grovelling, nothing promiscuous, nothing unclean for the Christian.

iv. As to "CREEPING THINGS" there was entire prohibition (vv. 41-43). Jehovah would have his people free from the defilement consequent upon contact with, touching or tasting anything unclean. They were not their own; they belonged to Jehovah : His name was called upon them. Other nations might eat what they pleased : but Israel enjoyed the high distinction of being regulated by the Lord in every detail of life.

(*a*) Their entire separation from all manner of uncleanness flows out of *their relationship to Him*. It is not the principle of "stand by thyself, I am holier than thou"; but simply this, "God is holy," and therefore all who are brought into association with Him must be holy likewise. If a Christian be now asked why he walks apart from the ten thousand things in which men of the world participate, his answer is simply "My Father is holy." This is the true foundation of personal holiness.

(*b*) They are *bound to aim at the maintenance of the character* which He prescribes. If God, in His exceeding grace, stoops down to our low estate, and lifts us in association with Christ, has He not a right to prescribe what our character should be? And a true Israelite will maintain that "difference between the unclean and the clean."

(*c*) How strange to one who had scrupulously observed these ceremonial distinctions all his days, must have been that vision of the vessel containing "*all manner* of four-footed beasts, and wild beasts, and *creeping things*, and fowls of the air" (Acts x. 11-16) let down from heaven, and to have heard the voice say, "Rise, Peter, kill and eat." No examination of hoofs and habits; no need now of this. The soul was now to rise above all ceremonial barriers into the magnificence of heaven's grace. True cleanness, the cleanness God required, was no longer outward and ceremonial, but should consist in being washed in the blood of the Lamb, which cleanseth from all sin, and renders the believer clean enough to tread the sapphire pavement of the heavenly courts.

The door of the kingdom is thrown open by the hand of Sovereign grace; but *not to admit aught that is unclean*. Nothing unclean could enter heaven. But a "cloven hoof" was no longer to be the criterion : but this—"*what God hath cleansed*."

The standard by which true cleanses must be regulated is no longer carnal, ceremonial, earthly; but spiritual, moral, and heavenly. We are no longer hemmed round about by "touch not, taste not, handle not"; but the divine Word assures us that "every creature of God is good and nothing to be refused, if it be received with thanksgiving; for it is sanctified by the Word of God and prayer" (1 Tim iv. 4, 5).—*C. H. M.*

Topic: JEHOVAH'S CONCERN FOR ISRAEL'S WELL-BEING (Vv. 1-43).

Doubtless the laws concerning clean and unclean animals were *symbolic*, conveying lessons specially adapted to Israel at the time; they were also *typical* of moral truths to be observed by worshippers of Jehovah through all time. So far as regards the animals themselves they were all on the same moral level in the sight of God; each followed the instincts implanted by the great Creator, acquired the habits, and exercised the passions peculiar to its nature. Some were more repulsive to man than others, of less service when alive, less utility when dead.

Animals had been classified by the patriarchs and among heathen nations; some animals had been considered more sacred than others. But these laws definitely fixed the line of demarcation to be drawn, the main distinction being twofold: All animals were unclean except those which divided the hoof and chewed the cud. The directions for determining the difference were numerous and minute, entailing careful and constant discrimination. Origen and other allegorical writers have found symbol and type in every permitted or prohibited thing; but the course is dangerous, and likely to lead to most erroneous conclusions. General truths are suggested, such as—

I. DIVINE CONCERN FOR THE TEMPORAL WELFARE OF ISRAEL.

Laws of purity enjoined would obviously conduce to their physical comfort. Cleanliness is a safeguard against many bodily ills. Nothing was interdicted in these restrictions that would tend to health and longevity. Caring for Israel as a father for his children, Jehovah would have them partake only of food that was nutritious. Nothing is beneath His notice that affects the welfare of the children of men.

II. DIVINE CONCERN FOR THE NATIONAL UNITY OF ISRAEL.

Elected to special privileges and responsibilities, the Hebrew nation was to be clearly distinguished from all other nations on the earth. The laws would keep the people from joining with the heathen in their ordinary meals and sacred feasts; would be a barrier against every intruder; for the Canaanites ate some of the animals these laws prohibited, and offered others in sacrifice to heathen gods. Nothing tends to obliterate national differences and to throw social distinctions into oblivion more than sitting together at the same table and partaking of common food. Israel's observance of the directions given in this chapter would set a hedge around the family life, and indicate a peculiar people.

III. DIVINE CONCERN FOR THE EXCLUSIVE WORSHIP OF ISRAEL.

Rites and ceremonies had already been instituted that would exclude other nations from mingling with the Hebrew in the worship of the tabernacle; now a guard is put around the *social* as well as sacred table. *Tent*, as well as tabernacle, to be consecrated to the Lord. Here we see Jehovah's *sovereignty* exercised, His *jealousy* for the exclusive worship of His people. Whether the people ate or drank, they were to do all to the glory of God. They were to come out from the ungodly and be separate, and touch not the unclean thing, and thus become the sons and daughters of the Lord God Almighty. Nothing less than cheerful obedience to divine regulations for private and public life would satisfy the claims Jehovah made upon the loyalty and worship of His people.

IV. DIVINE CONCERN FOR THE COMPLETE PURITY OF ISRAEL.

While purity of heart and mind were of the first importance, the body also was to be kept pure. Nothing to be eaten that would make it gross, or vitiate the blood. Even the dwellings of the people, their garments, and every article for use or ornament, to be ceremonially clean. These minute and exact requirements would impress Israel with the holiness of the Lord with whom they had to do. In avoiding the proscribed animals—the habits and appearance of which in many cases would beget natural disgust—the people would be reminded (a) *of the vileness and loathsomeness of sin;* (b) *of the need of constant circumspection to avoid contamination with evil;* (c) *of the necessity of complete purity in the sight of Jehovah.* Attention thus called to the body and physical things would show that the human frame is not the vile product (as the Gnostics contended) of a malevolent deity, but created and cared for by Him who breathed into it at first the breath of life, and made man a living soul.

V. DIVINE CONCERN FOR THE EXALTED PIETY OF ISRAEL.

Selfishness is the root of all sin, pride of all impiety. These laws would tend to humble the people, teach them self-denial. Having to abstain from eating animals savage and voracious in their nature, unattractive in their form, repulsive in their habits, would remind Israel that the most scrupulous sanctity of heart was required by Him who *demanded* such purity in meaner things. These unclean animals may be regarded as types of persons it is always well to avoid. Thus the brute creation is a book full of useful lessons upon what we may with advantage adopt, and what we ought to shun. In all these things we see the wisdom and goodness of the Lord, conducing to well-being here, and furnishing stepping-stones to blessedness hereafter.—*F. W. B.*

Topic: JEHOVAH'S CONCERN FOR HIS OWN GLORY (Vv. 44-49).

The regulations taught Israel that Jehovah was their—

I. SUPREME RULER. "For I am the Lord your God." All authority resided in Him. He had sovereign right to command and restrain. The people were not to study their own preferences, or conveniences, but obey the mandates that issued from the King of kings.

II. SPOTLESS KING. "For I am holy." The constant reiteration of this truth must have engraved it deeply in the consciences of the congregation, and impressed them most solemnly with the purity of the divine nature. Israel could never have conceived of so holy a Being, surrounded as they had been, and were still, by hideous and degrading idolatry.

III. GREAT DELIVERER. "For I am the Lord that bringeth you up out of the land of Egypt." The people were under vast obligation to the Almighty. He had wrought signal deliverances for them They were His by redemption. He had a right to expect obedience from them. He had brought them out of Egypt for the specific purpose of making them a people for Himself. These laws would test their *faith, gratitude,* and *obedience*; teach them self-denial, and restraint. Their spiritual nature was to be in ascendancy over everything carnal and temporal.

In the New Testament a new interpretation is given to these Levitical laws; we are shown that, not what we eat or drink defiles the soul, but what comes out of it. The root and seat of evil are within; yet, care needs to be exercised against temptation and contamination. Touching the unclean thing, such as *pernicious literature, places of ill-fame, sinful companionship,* may lead to moral defilement, to spiritual degeneracy. In the gospel—

(1) *Special emphasis is laid upon spiritual purity;*
(2) *With spiritual purity is associated our highest joy.*

Our *bodies* are temples of the Holy Ghost; they ought, therefore, to be kept pure. The *Church* is the Body of Christ: from it, therefore, everything should be excluded that is unclean. Into the *celestial city* " there shall in no wise enter anything that defileth, neither whatsoever worketh abomination"; all there shall be for ever, "Holiness unto the Lord."—*F.W.B.*

Topic: THE CLEAN AND THE UNCLEAN.

"*Speak unto the children of Israel, saying, These are the beasts which ye shall eat among all the beasts that are on the earth. Whatsoever parteth the hoof, and is cloven-footed, and cheweth the cud, among the beasts, that shall ye eat*" (Lev. xi. 2, 3).

As the Mosaic was peculiarly a typical dispensation, we shall not exaggerate the uses of the text if we show that there was something instructive to us and something typical of the better covenant in the command given that the people were to eat no creatures but those which divided the hoof and those which chewed the cud.

I. These distinctions of meat were laid down TO KEEP THE JEWS AS A DISTINCT PEOPLE, and that herein they might be a type of the people of God, who are also, throughout all ages, to be a distinct and separate people—not of the world, even as Christ was not of the world.

With this Levitical rule it was quite impossible for the Hebrews to mix with any other nation without violating the statutes they were commanded to keep. Their food was so restricted that they could not possibly enter into social intercourse with any of the neighbouring peoples. The Canaanites, for instance, ate everything, even the flesh that had been torn by dogs, and the dogs themselves. Now, a Jew could never sit at a Canaanite's table, because he could never be sure that there would not be the flesh of some unclean and accursed thing upon it. The Jews could not even eat with the Arabs, who were near akin to them, for they frequently partook of the flesh forbidden to the Jew. This command made them a distinct and isolated republic so long as they were obedient to the law. Just so the Mohammedan regulations, less strict than those of the Jew, prevent their becoming socially intermingled either with the idolators or with Christians. Now, what is the use of this to us? *It is the earthly type of a heavenly mystery.* Thus all who name the name of Christ are solemnly bound to be for ever separated from the world. Our Saviour " was holy, harmless, undefiled, and separate from sinners." He was with them, but He was never of them; among them, but always distinct and separate from them. He hath set us an example. Be among men as a light in the midst of darkness, as salt scattered over putridity, as heavenly angels in the midst of fallen men; a distinct people, a chosen generation.

But *in what respects are we to be distinguished?*

1. In *a pure consistency* always, in vain eccentricity never. Not in our garments; not by any peculiar jargon in speech; such artificial separations we leave to the people whose vanity feeds on its own conceit. Not trying to make ourselves look like Christians. Heavenly realities within do not always need to be labelled outside, so that everybody may say, "There goes a saint." There are other modes of being distinguished from the world than any of these.

2. We ought ever to be distinguished from the world *in the great object of our life.* Our main and principal motive as Christians should always be to live for Christ. You can make the commonest calling become really sacred. You may take the highest orders by dedicating your daily life wholly to the service of Jesus. There is such a thing—and let those that deny the possibility stand

self-convicted that they obey not the precept—"Whether ye eat or drink, or whatsoever ye do, do all to the glory of God."

3. By *our spirit* as well as our aim we should likewise be distinguished; a spirit which watcheth humbly before God, and seeketh to know His will and to do it through the grace of God given.

4. *Our maxims* and rules which regulate us should be very different from those of others. A Christian never considers what is usual, but what is right. The believer reads things, not in man's light, in the obscurity of which so many blind bats are willing to fly, but he reads things in the sunlight of heaven. If a thing be right, though he lose by it, it is done; if it be wrong, though he should become as rich as Crœsus by allowing it, he scorns the sin for his Master's sake.

3. *Our actions* should be distinctive. Let your conduct talk out your soul. Let the main sermon of your life be illustrated by all your conduct, and it shall not fail to be illustrious. This will furnish the best proof that you have been with Jesus.

4. A Christian is distinguished *by his conversation*. If he would have a jest, he picks the mirth but leaves the sin; his conversation is not used to levity; it is not mere froth, but it ministereth grace unto the hearers. Oh! commend me to the man who talks like Jesus; who will not for the world suffer corrupt communications to come out of his mouth. You know the value of the gold of heaven too well to pawn it away for the counterfeits of earth. "Come ye out from among them; be ye separate, and touch not the unclean thing." By a holiness which merely moral men cannot equal, stand as on a pedestal aloft above the world. Thus men may know you to be of the seed of Jesus, even as they knew the Jew to be the seed of Israel.

II. The distinction drawn between clean and unclean animals was intended by God TO KEEP HIS PEOPLE ALWAYS CONSCIOUS THAT THEY WERE IN THE NEIGHBOURHOOD OF SIN.

An oriental Jew, sensible and intelligent, walks out in the fields. He walks along close by the side of the high-road, and what should he see but a string of camels going along? "Ah!" he says to himself "those are unclean animals." Sin, you see, is brought at once before his mind's eye. He turns away from the road and walks down one of his own fields, and as he goes along a hare starts across his path. "Ah!" says he, "an unclean animal again; there is sin in my path." He gets into a more retired place; he walks on the mountains; surely he shall be alone there. But he sees a coney burrowing among the rocks; "Ah!" says he, "unclean; there is sin there!" He lifts his eye up to heaven; he sees the osprey, the bald eagle, flying along through the air, and he says, "Ah! there is an emblem of sin there!" A dragon-fly has just flitted by him—there is sin there. There are insects among the flowers; now every creeping thing, and every insect, except the locust, was unclean to the Jew. Everywhere he would be reminded that this world, however beautiful, still has sin in it. Even the fish, in sea, or river, or inland lake, had their divisions; those that had no scales or fins were unclean to the Jew, so the little Hebrew boys could not even fish for minnows in the brook but they would know that the minnow was unclean, and so their young hearts were made to dread little wrongs and little sins, for there were little sins in the little pools, even as there were leviathan sins floating in the deep and rude sea. We want to have this more before our minds. Not a spot is there in the universe where the curse of sin has never inflicted a blight, or where the hope of redemption should not inspire a prayer. See that you put on the whole panoply of God, and watch and pray lest ye enter into temptation. Every morning we ought to ask the Lord to keep us from unknown sins, to preserve us from temptation that we cannot foresee, to check us in every path of life if we are about to go wrong, and hold us up every hour that we sin not. May the Lord set sin straight before your eyes, and then set the cross of Christ there too, and so you will be saved.

III. This injunction was also intended to be A RULE OF DISCRIMINATION BY WHICH WE MAY JUDGE WHO ARE CLEAN AND WHO ARE UNCLEAN, that is, WHO ARE SAINTS AND WHO ARE NOT.

There are two tests, but they must both be united. The beast that was clean was to chew the cud, here is *the inner life;* every true-hearted man must know how to read, mark, learn, and inwardly digest the sacred Word. The man who does not feed upon gospel truth, and so feed upon it, too, that he knows the sweetness and relish of it, and seeks out its marrow and fatness, that man is no heir of heaven. You must know a Christian by that which supports his life and sustains his frame. But then the clean creatures were also known by *their walk.* The Jew at once discovered the unclean animal by its having an undivided hoof; but if the hoof was thoroughly divided, then it was clean, provided that it also chewed the cud. So there must be in the true Christian a peculiar walk such as God requires. You cannot tell a man by either of these tests alone, you must have them both. But while you use them upon others apply them to yourselves. You may profess the faith within, but if you do not walk aright without, you belong to the unclean. On the other hand, you may walk aright without, but unless there is a real feeding upon precious truth in the heart, all the right walking in the world will not prove you to be a Christian. That holiness which is only outward is moral not spiritual; it does not save the soul. That religion which is only inward is but fancy; it cannot save the soul either. But the two together, the inwards parts made capable of knowing the lusciousness, the sweetness, the fatness of Christ's truth; and the outward parts conformed to Christ's image and character; these conjoined point out the true and clean Christian with whom it is blessed to associate here, and for whom a better portion is prepared hereafter.—*C. H. Spurgeon, in " Metro. Tab. Pulpit."*

ILLUSTRATIVE ADDENDA TO CHAPTER XI.

SEPARATE FROM SINNERS :—
This was Christ's distinction: it should distinguish all who are Christ's.

" The friendships of the world are oft
Confederacies in vice, or leagues of pleasure.
Ours has severest virtue for its basis,
And such a friendship ends not but with life."—ADDISON : *Cato* iii. 1.

" There are three friendships which are advantageous, and three which are injurious. Friendship with the upright, friendship with the sincere, and friendship with the man of observation; these are advantageous. Friendship with the men of specious airs, friendship with the insinuatingly soft, and friendship with the glib-tongued; these are injurious." —CONFUCIUS : *Analects* iii.

" Nature and religion are the bands of friendship; excellency and usefulness are its great endearments. But as all cannot actually be of our society, so neither can all be admitted to a special, actual friendship."
— JEREMY TAYLOR.

" Not with the light and vain,
    The man of idle feet and wanton eyes;
Not with the world's gay, ever smiling train;
    My lot be with the grave and wise.

" Not with the trifler gay,
    To whom life seems but sunshine on the wave;
Not with the empty idler of the day;
    My lot be with the wise and grave.

" Not with the jesting fool,
    Who knows not what to sober truth is due;
Whose words fly out without an aim rule;
    My lot be with the wise and true.

" With them I'd walk each day,
    From them time's solemn lessons would learn,
That false from true and true from false I may
    Each hour more patiently discern."
— BONAR.

FEASTING:—
"Simple diet is best; for many dishes bring many diseases."—PLINY.

"They eat, they drink, and in communion secret
Quaff immortality and joy."—MILTON.

"Health and liberty
Attend on those bare meals: if all were blest

With such a temperance
There would be no slaves, no sycophants
At great men's tables.—MAY.

"Fatal effects of luxury and ease!
We drink our poison, and we eat disease,
Indulge our senses at our reason's cost,
Till sense is pain, and reason hurt or lost.
—CHANDLER.

CHAPTER XII.

Maternity.

SUGGESTIVE READINGS.

V. 2.—If a woman hath conceived . . she shall be unclean. Thus at the very entrance into life uncleanness clings to us. Not a child is born without defilement surrounding its birth. "Behold, I was shapen in iniquity, and in sin did my mother conceive me" (Psa. li. 5). "How can he be clean that is born of a woman?" (Job xxv. 4). How humbling is this Scripture presentation of our case. From the cradle to the grave man's life is pronounced unclean. Surely it should arrest all self-elation and boasting. Pitiable indeed sounds the vain panegyric upon the dignity of human nature; melancholy is the haughty assumption of excellence and worthiness, in the light of this vision of man's defilement from birth till death. He should rather "abhor himself, and repent in dust and ashes" (Job xlii. 6). Instead of the too common flattery of human nature, be this mirror of his humiliating impurity held up to the face of the self-satisfied sinner, that he may see the "hole of the pit whence he was digged" (Isa. li. 1), and cry in penitential lowliness, "We are all as an unclean thing, and all our righteousnesses are as filthy rags" (Isa. lxiv. 6).

V. 6.—She shall bring a lamb. Always, in God's graciousness, the remedy rises for the malady. Defilement has its antidote in atonement. The two grand aspects of the sacrificial death of Christ stood out here in the "lamb for a *burnt offering*," in which He offered Himself without spot *to God;* and in the "*sin offering*," in which He substituted Himself as the victim *for men*. From the humbling spectacle of human helplessness and defilement here given what can be more assuring and consolatory than to gain a view, in type, of the perfect merits of Jesus—who in Himself concentrated the unsullied grace and dignity of humanity, and in His sacrifice effectually atoned for the guiltiness and degredation of our fallen race. "Behold the Lamb of God, which taketh away the sin of the world."

Vv. 2, 5.—If the woman have born a man child. . . If she bear a maid child. The mother's defilement was ceremoniously less for the male child than for the female. Is not this a perpetuated memorial of the fact that sin entered the world through the woman, she being the first transgressor? Certainly this is the basis of Paul's argument for her inferior position in the Christian Church (1 Tim. ii. 11-14) Or, in this shorter banishment from sanctuary privileges when her child was a male, there may be found an intimation of the blessed privilege coveted by all Hebrew mothers, of giving birth to THE "MAN CHILD," who was to be "born of a woman," to redress the woes of the fall. Every suggestion of the coming Emmanuel was cherished as the soft radiance of that promised "Morning Star." And so the heavier penalty fell on the birth of the female child, since woman was a remembrance of sin, whereas the ameliorated penalty was attached to the birth of a male, since the Man Child was the herald of the promised Saviour.

V. 8.—**If she be not able to bring a lamb.** However poor the woman might be, there could be no exemption from the presentation of an atonement offering. Poverty must come, though with meek aspect, trusting in reconciling blood. And the "poor in spirit," whose faith is tremulous, whose apprehension is feeble, must, nevertheless, lay hope on the merits of sacrifice. None can be allowed, through lowliness of station or poverty of soul, to evade the propitiatory atonement. All must place trust in Christ whatever our lot in life, whatever our spiritual mood. Yet how tender is God's consideration! He will allow the turtle dove to suffice for the poor, and regard it as equally efficacious as the richer offerer's lamb, so that the humblest Israelite should be harassed by no fear lest she forfeit privilege by her lowlier gift. God's perfect grace comes to the very condition in which the "poor and needy" are to be found. And so, in this Christian dispensation, the lowest and the feeblest have the atoning blood brought within their reach, and through its merits may recover all the privileges from which "uncleanness" excludes them. "To the poor the gospel is preached."

HOMILIES.

Topic: MOTHERHOOD.

Scripture shows that God *thinks much of mothers*. Allusions to a mother's sufferings, perils, relationship, affection, are very numerous. She passes through no experience which has not been noticed, described, and used by the Lord as a simile of spiritual truth. Motherhood, in all its aspects, is the reiterated theme of God's Word. This must afford a wealth of consolation and support to a believing mother in her trials and solicitudes; her watchful Father has shown that He minutely considers all her various cares, her mysterious pangs, her heart struggles between dread and delight, her yearnings and her love.

The *birth of a child* is also an event which constantly engages inspiration. The Word makes frequent reference to the incident. A new life ushered into the world, is a fact which touches the heart of God. Another being launched upon the floods of possibility; another factor in the intricate sum of human existence, whose results must affect the ultimate reckoning; another soul added to the millions whose destiny is bliss or woe. There is no room for doubting that the divine Father is concerned for each human offspring. He notes the child's entrance, gives directions concerning it, sends counsels for its career, desires its salvation and sanctification, calls it to the immortal Home made ready by Christ. "It is not the will of your Father in heaven that one of these little ones should perish" (Matt. xviii. 14).

I. *How observant is Scripture* of the HUMILIATIONS *incident to* MOTHERHOOD. This chapter is a witness.

1. Scripture has *sanctioned and sanctified wifely relationship* (Psa. cxiii. 9).
2. Scripture recognises *every stage of physical suffering* which motherhood entails (Jer. iv. 31).
3. Scripture forewarns of the tender *sorrows and distresses incident to maternity* (Jno. xvi. 21; Isa. xxvi. 17).
4. Scripture contains special *messages of compassion and hope* for mothers in their period of solicitude (Isa. xl. 11).

II. *How emphatically does Scripture pay tribute* to the HONOURS *of* MOTHERHOOD.

In making a *mother* the *symbol of the Church of God* (Gal. iv. 6; Ephes. v. 32).
In comparing *Jehovah's consolatory ministries* to those of a mother (Isa. lxvi. 13).
In using *motherhood as the channel of Christ's advent* (Luke i. 35).
In the *tender consideration for His mother manifested by Jesus* (Luke ii. 52; Jno. xix 26, 27).
In the *command given to children* to pay their mothers reverence (Matt. xv. 4, etc.). [See Addenda to chap. xii., *Maternity*]

III. *How watchfully does Scripture guard the* HAPPINESS *which should be the crown of* MOTHERHOOD.

1. *Conjugal loyalty is scrupulously demanded* (Mal. ii. 15, 16; Ephes. v. 25, 28).
2. *A mother's place in the family is carefully indicated* (Ephes. vi. 1, 2).
3. *The grace which flows through mothers to their children* is recognised with emphatic approval (2 Tim. i. 5).
4. *The blessedness of a mother's privilege* is indicated in Christ's welcome of the mothers who brought their children to Him (Luke xviii. 15-17).

> "And say to mothers, What a holy charge
> Is theirs; with what a kingly power their love
> Might rule the fountains of the new-born mind;
> Warn them to wake at early dawn, and sow
> Good seed before the world has sown its tares."—*Mrs. Sigourney.*

Though her child is "born in sin," and she is humiliated by her own "uncleanness," yet can a mother retrieve her humiliation by uplifting her child in prayer to God, by training her offspring in the faith of Christ, and at last, with her children saved in the Lord, appearing in the glory of the Eternal Presence with the glad cry, "Behold me, and the children which thou hast given me!" [See Addenda, *Childhood.*]

Topic: BIRTH.

I. In its *pangs* there survives the MEMORIES OF THE WOEFUL FALL.

Our ancestress Eve sinned, therefore, "unto the woman God said, I will greatly multiply thy sorrow and thy conception; in sorrow thou shalt bring forth children" (Gen. iii. 16).

II. In its "*uncleanness*" there arise SUGGESTIONS OF OUR TRANSMITTED DEFILEMENT.

Physical impurity, amid which a babe is ushered into the world, is but a sign of that corruption, moral and spiritual, which parents pass on to their offspring: "Altogether born in sin" (Jno. ix. 34).

III. In its *transports* there reappears the JOYOUSNESS OF THE MESSIAH'S INCARNATION.

Sang the angels, "Unto you is born a Saviour, which is Christ the Lord" (Luke ii. 11). A woman, "as soon as she is delivered of the child, remembereth no more the anguish for joy that a man-child is born into the world" (Jno. xvi. 21).

Topic: POLLUTION AND PURIFYING.

The birth of a child should be an event of gratitude and delight. It is never wholly so; for a shadow falls on every new-born life.

(*a*) It is "born in sin," and, therefore *may* perish in sin!
(*b*) It is born amid travail, and may—dread possibility that!—*occasion death* through the anguish of birth.

(c) It is an event marked by God as qualified with "uncleanness." For He sees in every birth, since Eve's fall, the *perpetuation* of sin, the *propagation of a sinning race.*

I. UNCLEAN : such is the VERDICT OF HEAVEN UPON HUMAN LIFE.
God has here written the word pollution upon the very entrance of a babe into existence.

1. It brands *the mother as* "*unclean,*" and excludes her from social fellowship and sanctuary privileges. We are not now judged by this ceremonial standard; but a principle underlies this banishment of the mother. It declares that there is taint in the blood. There has never been a sinless mother on this earth. Certainly not Eve; nor even the Virgin Mary—for she had equally to observe "the days of her purification" (Luke ii. 22). Womanhood is defiled; therefore maternity is not pure.

2. It brands the *child as defiled.* The tender babe holds in its physical form the germs of foul disease, of corrupt affections and passions. "Who can bring a clean thing out of an unclean ?" From a poisoned fountain there can flow only vitiated streams. Leave that babe to follow its inbred desires and it will degenerate into evil. Goodness is never self-evolved, but only badness. "They go astray as soon as they be born" (Psalm lviii. 2).

II. CLEANSING : such is THE DEMAND OF GOD UPON EVERY ONE DEFILED.
Here upon the mother only, because the ceremonial directions deal with the mother. But the demand is equally enforced upon all; each sex, every life. The male child was unclean till " circumcised" (v. 3).

1. Until cleansing is effected there is *banishment :* the door is closed upon social life, for she must be separate : and closed upon sacred scenes, for she must "not come into the sanctuary." Defilement excludes us from all that is happiest, purest, best.

2. Until cleansing is effected there is *degradation :* the woman forfeited her place of dignity in her own home and in God's temple. Impurity *is* a degradation. We sink thereby from our honoured place in creation; we grovel instead of triumph ; we are bowed into shame before God instead of joying in His favour; and we are refused the blessedness which is the right of sinless man, of treading God's courts with acceptance, and abiding in the delights of holy privilege.

III. PURIFIED : such is the POSSIBILITY OPENED BY GOD TO ALL WHO ARE UNCLEAN.

1. *Womanhood sanctified* (v. 7). In the Christian dispensation there is a richer purifying than the ceremonial; it " cleanses from all sin." Look in upon the Bethany home—" Mary sat at Jesus' feet." See the apostles' list of consecrated women in the Christian church at Rome (Romans xvi.). Lift your eyes to the pure souls, "an hundred and forty and four thousand" with the Lamb on Mount Sion : virgin saints, all undefiled (Rev. xiv. 1, 4).

2. *Childhood consecrated* (v. 3), thereby enrolled as a member of the Israel of God : and now placed in the hands of Jesus who, blessing the children, declares, " of such is the kingdom of heaven."

There is merit in Christ's " atonement" which purges all sin's stains. There is grace in His heart by which all may be rejoiced. There is beauty in His righteousness with which all may be clothed in sacred comeliness.

Topic: THE STATUTE RELATING TO MATERNITY.

This chapter records the rites to be observed by Hebrew women in connection with their new experiences of maternity. The period of ceremonial restrictions would differ according to the sex of the child ; but, in both cases, the mother would be permitted to present her offering before the Lord, and, eventually, be restored to her former status among the people. The statute suggests the following reflections :

I. THAT ANGUISH IS ASSOCIATED WITH MATERNITY.

Through the Fall the sorrows of conception were greatly multiplied, and the pangs of childbirth became intensified. The whole period of conception, with many, is a burden; and the time of travail one of most excruciating pain. Though the mother experiences one of nature's keenest joys when she knows that to her a child is born, yet there are accompanying sorrows which only the feelings of maternity can know, as no stranger can intermendle with the joy.

II. THAT PRIVACY IS ASSOCIATED WITH MATERNITY.

Although the procreation of children is normal and of divine ordination, yet, where there is virtuous womanly modesty, there is always a sense of shyness and reserve during period of preparation for advent of the little stranger, especially at the season of delivery. The instincts of nature suggest withdrawal from public observation and general familiar intercourse even with friends. Hence, even among heathen nations, special rites and customs have always been associated with the experiences under consideration. Such restraints and reserve do not degrade the gentler sex in the sight of God or the eyes of right-minded men; woman rather rises thereby in honour and esteem.

III. THAT DEPRAVITY IS ASSOCIATED WITH MATERNITY.

Maternity, under honourable conditions, is no sin: yet, by it, depravity is communicated; as the Psalmist expresses the fact, "Behold I was shapen in iniquity, and in sin did my mother conceive me." There is a hereditary tendency in human nature to sin; so that giving birth to a child is the propagation of sinfulness, and an extension of the consequences of transgression, entailing *moral*, as well as ceremonial defilement. The rite of purification, under these circumstances, is both symbol and type of purification of the children of men by atonement of our great High Priest on Calvary. Responsibilities, commensurate with the honour of maternity, suggested by the statute. Imperative, that children born in sin, with inherent depraved propensities, should be taught the law of the Lord, and trained in holiness and righteousness all their days.

IV. THAT SALVATION IS ASSOCIATED WITH MATERNITY.

Though for a while the mother was kept secluded from society, the restrictions were only of a temporary character. She was soon seen presenting her appointed offerings before the Lord at the door of the tabernacle of the congregation. The burnt offering was the basis of all other offerings; and signified, not only the sovereign claim of Jehovah upon all we have and are; but, also the disposition of the worshipper to become a living sacrifice, holy and acceptable unto God. Behold the *goodness of God* in promising to accept "two turtles, or two young pigeons" if the offerer were not able to present a lamb; *one for the burnt offering, the other for the sin offering.* The intention and frame of mind were of more importance than the offering itself, as the Scriptures elsewhere declare, "Behold! to obey is better than sacrifice, and to hearken than the fat of rams." This rite—being for the Jews, and associated with the Levitical economy—is abrogated now; *a more minute examination, therefore, would not minister to edification—is not necessary.* Some moral teachings have been indicated, and they may, when convenient, be reiterated in public as part of the didactic function of preaching; for principles, gathered from divine laws, have undying roots, and inexhaustible meanings. This, as well as other rights, was observed down to the advent of our blessed Lord; for Mary, the mother of Jesus, offered in the Temple the least offering allowed at thanksgiving and sacrifice after child-birth; an irrefutable proof of the abject poverty of her worldly circumstances. On national, as well as on religious grounds, no objection can be offered under the gospel to women, having been delivered in the time of maternal solicitude and sorrow, publicly paying their vows in the courts of the

Lord, and with grateful hearts re-dedicating themselves to the service of the Most High. If womankind reflect with sorrow upon the fact that it was through Eve's seduction that Adam fell and sin entered our world, they may reflect with joy upon the fact that *it was through their own sex that the second Adam came*, who has reversed the curse of sin and redeemed the human race. If in connection with the first man shame seems to cover womanhood, the second man, the Lord from heaven, placed a wreath of undying glory on her brow, as we see lying in the arms of Mary at Bethlehem, "*the holy child Jesus.*" Paul asserts, in his first Epistle to Timothy (v. 15), that women shall be saved through the child-bearing; salvation has come through its ordinance, and if women abide in *faith, love, sanctification,* and *holy self-control,* they shall be cleansed from all moral impurity, shall be not only sanctified, but saved, through the Child born, the Son given.—*F. W. B.*

ILLUSTRATIVE ADDENDA TO CHAPTER XII.

MOTHERHOOD:
"There is no mother like the mother that bore us."—*Spanish Proverb.*

"A mother is a mother still,
 The holiest thing alive."—COLERIDGE.

". . . . . A mother's love
 Is an undying feeling. Earth may chill
And sever other sympathies, and prove
 How weak all human bonds are; it may kill
 Friendship, and crush hearts with them; but the thrill
Of the maternal breast must ever move
 In blest communion with her child, and fill
Even heaven itself with prayers and hymns of love.—PATTERSON.

Monica, Augustine's mother. Never did mother struggle more earnestly than she. From her son's nineteenth to his twenty-eighth year, while he was revelling in all sin's foulness, she persisted in resolute hope and fervent prayer. In his twenty-ninth year she was still "instant in prayer," when he left her and journeyed to Rome. From Rome he went to Milan, and thither the praying mother followed him. And there the answer to her prayer and reward of her Christian influence came. In Ambrose's preaching contrition came to Augustine, and that event made Monica's happiness complete.

CHILDHOOD:
"Children are what their mothers are.
 No fondest father's fondest care
 Can fashion so the infant's heart
 As those creative beams that dart,
 With all their hopes and fears, upon
 The cradle of a sleeping son."—LANDER.

"The mother's heart is the child's school-room."—BEECHER.

Cecil, who had adopted infidel sentiment in his youth, and prided himself upon his strong arguments against religion, said, long afterwards: "There was one argument I could never get over, the influence and life of a holy mother."

CHAPTER XIII.

Leprosy: its Discovery and Treatment.

SUGGESTIVE READINGS.

Gathering into view the circumstantial and concise description of the malady here given; the directions concerning leprosy may be thus analysed and arranged:
Symptoms of leprosy:
 1. Their *minuteness:* small in their beginnings, trifling skin blemishes or hair defects, scarcely distinguishable at the outset, evasive therefore, and subtle.

2. Their *intricacy:* so resembling other ailments, in some cases rising out of other blemishes and wounds; complicate and interblending.

3. Their *repulsiveness:* all the descriptions are loathsome.

Discrimination of the symptoms. The investigation had to be—

1. *Cautious:* lest that should be pronounced leprosy which was not; or that which was, be exempted.

2. *Patient:* the sufferer must be repeatedly examined where the signs were uncertain: no haste, no summary decision.

3. *Thorough:* searching to the very root: watching a wound to note its developments, shaving the hair that no symptom escape notice.

Treatment of the leper. When the malady was beyond doubt, the doom was—

1. *Absolute:* he was banished, there might be no concessions; he was excluded the camp.

2. *Mournful:* garments to be torn, the hair dishevelled, the lips covered, as for the dead.

3. *Proclaimed:* from the outlawed leper must rise the cry of warning to others, which was also the death knell of his own fate—" Unclean !"

Six various aspects under which leprosy may develop itself in man are here specified:

1. *First appearance* of the plague: the victim manifesting symptoms which excite suspicion (vv. 1-9.)

2. *Return of* the distemper (vv. 9-11). But two features of the malady are here exempted from the ban of uncleanness.

(1). The plague has exhausted itself upon the *entire body* of the sufferer (vv. 12, 13).

(2). The *plague spots* have lost their virulence (vv. 16, 17).

3. Leprosy *developing* from other sores or accidental wounds: seizing these blemishes in which to root itself (vv. 18-28).

4. The plague *burying itself amid the hair:* called the "dry scall" (vv. 29-37).

5. *Harmless* leprosy (vv. 38, 39). It is still accounted harmless by the Arabs: causes no inconvenience, and lasts variously from two months to two years.

6. The *baldness* distemper: leading to the falling off of the hair from the back of the head (vv. 40-44).

Vv. 45, 46.—The leper in whom the plague is, etc. As the victim of a grievous calamity the poor leper must assume the melancholy aspects of mourning, he must tell out his woe in the doleful cry " Unclean," and his doom must be to wander as an outcast from the society of Israel and from the sanctuary of God. This foul distemper has always been a parable of the loathsomeness of sin, and its dismal punishment vividly pourtrays the grievous penalties of moral and spiritual defilement—" a castaway."

Vv. 47-59.—The garment also that the plague of leprosy is in, etc. Equal minuteness of inspection, discrimination of taint were to be exercised upon garments affected with the plague, and if judged to be really contagious they were to be burned. Clothes were scarce, and not easily to be replaced in the desert, hence care that nothing be needlessly destroyed. But no unclean thing, nor "anything that defileth" could be allowed to abide within the camp. Evil must be rooted from our own persons, or we become outcasts; and evil must be shunned, contact therewith be scrupulously avoided, or the malady may return. Therefore, like leprous garments, we must " lay aside every weight and the sin that doth so easily beset us." Within the fellowship of the redeemed Church on earth, and amid the blessedness of the ransomed society of heaven, God will allow no place for any unclean thing, " neither whatsoever worketh abomination or maketh a lie, but they which are written in the Lamb's book of life" (Rev. xxi. 27).

SECTIONAL HOMILIES.

Topic: MAN PHYSICALLY A VICTIM OF CRUEL MALADIES.

How appalling this picture of physical misery! To what sickening and wearying distempers has the human frame become a prey! How humiliating to contemplate

"the thousand natural shocks
That flesh is heir to!"

I. *Fashioned after the divine image,* HOW GRACEFUL AND DIGNIFIED IS THE HUMAN FORM!

Moving among all products of God's creating skill, man is His " noblest work."

1. As a *tenement of the mind and spirit,* the body is endowed with a natural comeliness.

It is no unfit abode for the higher nature within. Physically we are "fearfully and wonderfully made." Mark its symmetry, its erectness, its agility. Well says *Hamlet,* "What a piece of work is a man! How noble in reason! how infinite in faculty! in form and moving how express and admirable! in action how like an angel! in apprehension how like a god! the beauty of the world! the paragon of animals!"

2. As an *intrustment of the mind and spirit,* the body possesses finest aptitudes.

Its motions, its senses, its abilities, afford admirable outlets for the impulses and aims of the inner being. The eyes for vision, the lips for speech, the hands for ministry and work, the limbs for movement—the physical form is a thing of marvellous suitableness to the necessities of intellectual life and spiritual sympathies. It is in itself no grim prison, no harsh machine, but a supple instrument, ready to all the requirements of the indwelling soul.

II. *Assailed by foul diseases,* HOW DESECRATED AND PITIABLE IS THE HUMAN FORM!

Look upon the mighty fallen! writhing in anguish, wasted by disease, distorted by maladies!

1. In bodily diseases we *mark the traces of calamitous experiences* having befallen man.

As in the geological strata the torn and disordered upheavals declare that violence has wrought harm, so in the sufferings and maladies of the human frame. Some dire disaster has come upon the serene world of human life. Diseases are evidences of ruinous activities having invaded man's history. God made his noble creature for something better than to be the victim of sufferings and maladies. A foul hand has been laid upon his beauteous form. "An enemy hath done this." Sin has done dire work. Every pang, disorder, disease, is therefore a warning cry against sin which brought death into the world and all our woes.

2. In our physical maladies we may note the *inducements to watchfulness and virtue.*

If diseases point to a historic disaster in man's career—his fall through sin, they also quicken man to carefulness against repeating the follies and vices which engender physical maladies. They are a call—Beware! It is not altogether a melancholy fact that illnesses and sufferings assail us, if they warn us from indulgences and defilements which develop physical misery. The evil heart of man would urge him to unlimited vices if this penalty did not confront and restrain him.

"Just disease to luxury succeeds,
And every death its own avenger breeds" (*Pope*).

3. Amid all distresses of the body *there are ameliorations and consolations* offered in religion.

(1). A patient and devout spirit may "draw honey out of the rock," and find solace in anguish; for those who love God have had to testify, "It was good for me to be afflicted."

"Affliction is not sent in vain
From that good God who chastens whom He loves" (*Southey*).

(2). In suffering also there comes the consolation of Christ to those who are His. He knew affliction in bitterest degree, and is a "brother born for adversity."

(3). And there opens in prospect to the child of God the blissful life of heaven, where "the inhabitants never say they are sick," etc. (Rev. xxi. 4).

Topic: DISEASE—DEVELOPMENT—DOOM.

Trace the career of the malady: it does not complete itself at a stride: it has its outset and its goal. A pestilence in the land does not expand into its fatal proportions without antecedent incitements and advancing developments. In its germinal stage the peril may have been unsuspected or ignored, but its fructification proves that active energies have long and effectively operated. Harvest fields swept by the scythe once lay bare in ploughed furrows; the seed was sown, it grew, ripened, till the reapers entered, and the garners were filled. Good and bad products alike have their history of outset, advance and fruition. In man's physical and moral life there are equally traceable the beginnings and progressions of evil, till the fatal end is reached. No fact for contemplation in the moral realm is more melancholy than this—*the progress of corruption*. Consider the—

I. SUBTLE HISTORY OF ITS ORIGIN.

Transmitted; mysteriously passed on from parent to child: or *acquired* by contact with the leper, or things infected with leprosy 1. For awhile the distemper lies *concealed* in the blood, assumes no visible symptoms; is latent, passive. Thus sin long secretes itself in the nature as a subtle tendency, slumbers in the heart as a hidden taint. Whence the beginnings of evil in a human life? Came it from parentage, a moral tendency in the affections, the will, the habits? Was it imparted by early whisperings, faulty examples, harmful influences?

2. Its first *appearance* was in a form of uncertainty, not manifestly leprous, a swelling, a spot. Wrong when beginning in a child is not glaringly wrong, there is a something suggestive of possible deviation from right, but it is not certainly so, not manifestly and determinately so. It startles *suspicion* in the observer: the word, though not false, was hardly true; the secret act was scarcely deceitful, yet lacking in thorough honesty; it is scarcely a "rift in the lute"; not yet a rot on the fruit, only a "little pitted speck."

3. Thus starting, as evil does, in a kind of incertitude, as a slight dereliction, a wavering which creates suspicion, but is not yet sufficiently pronounced to be condemned, it only needs time in order to unfold and *declare itself*. Leave it to work its way out, and it quickly assumes more positive forms, and it becomes too manifest that the leprosy has a firm hold on the blood, the life. [Addenda to chap. xiii. *Developments.*]

II. APPALLING RAPIDITY OF ITS PROGRESS.

Having gained hold on its victim, and diffused itself through the blood, the infection hastens to spread over the system. Thought of sin, suggested from without, or awaking from within, grows into desire; desire into intention: intention into act.

Vital energy decays, good resolves droop, moral force and rectitude of purpose decline; then succeed estranged affections, a defiant will, an "evil heart of unbelief," character corrupted, till "sin reigns in our mortal body that we obey it in the lusts thereof" (Rom. vi. 12).

III. LOATHSOME ASPECTS OF ITS DEVELOPMENT.

Whether looked at in its incipient stage (vv. 2. 3), or in further advance (v. 7), or full outburst (v. 10), or in an inflamed state (v. 24), etc., it is always repulsive.

Of all forms and degrees of sin God pleads, "O do not the *abominable* thing which I *hate!*"

IV. CONTAGIOUS PROPERTIES OF THE MALADY.

One leper could spread infection through a community; all who came near him, all he touched, became contaminated.

"By one man sin entered the world, and death by sin: and so death passed upon all men." "One sinner destroyeth much good."

"*No man liveth to himself.*" One sin suggests sin to others. The contagion of evil example! The destructive influence of impurity. "Evil communications corrupt good manners." [Addenda to chap. xiii., *Transmitted Effects.*]

V. FATAL TERMINATION OF THE PLAGUE.

Disease, unless arrested, soon completes its ravages; and the victim sinks to death. And what are the issues of sin? "Wages of sin is death."

"When lust is conceived it bringeth forth sin; and sin, when it is finished, bringeth forth death."

1. Outcast for his uncleanness, *all his days* (v. 46).
2. If he "*die in his sins,*" rejected for evermore from the Heavenly Sanctuary and the Family of God. [Addenda to chap., *Unclean*].

Topic: THE LEPER BEFORE THE PRIEST (Vv. 12, 13).

"*And if a leprosy break out abroad in the skin, and the leprosy cover all the skin of him that hath the plague from his head even to his foot, wheresoever the priest looketh; then the priest shall consider: and, behold, if the leprosy have covered all his flesh, he shall pronounce him clean that hath the plague; it is all turned white; he is clean.*"

This is a singular paradox, but not to him who understands the gospel. Carry in your thoughts the one key, namely, that leprosy is the type of sin; and, first of all, *see the leper,* and *in the leper the sinner.* Then *bring him before the priest and watch while the priest examines him.*

I. Turn your eyes to the LOATHSOME AND GHASTLY SPECTACLE OF A LEPER.

1. A leper was extremely *loathsome in his person.* The leprosy broke out, at first almost imperceptibly, in certain red spots which appeared in the skin. The withering of the skin followed, and was an index of what was going on within; for in the very marrow of the bones there was a most frightful rottenness, which in due time would utterly consume the victim. When it came to its very worst phase the whole house of manhood would become a horrible mass of animated rubbish rather than the stately temple which God originally made it. It is a very poor portrait of the loathsomeness of sin. When once taught of God the Holy Ghost, we see that we are vile and full of sin, that there is no good thing whatsoever in us. Loathsome as was the leper, it was not more so in the type than is sin in the estimation of every enlightened mind.

2. The leper was *defiled in all his acts.* If he drank out of a vessel, the vessel was defiled. If he lay upon a bed, the bed became unclean, and whosoever sat upon the bed afterwards became unclean too. If he touched but the wall of a house the wall became unclean and must be purged. Wherever he went he tainted the atmosphere; his breath was as dangerous as the pestilence. He

shot baneful glances from his eyes. All that he did was full of the same loathsomeness as was himself. The actions of the "natural man" are tainted with sin. Whether he eats or drinks, or whatsoever he does, he continues to sin against his God. Nay, if he should come up to God's house and sing and pray, there is sin in his songs, for they are but hypocrisy; there is guilt in his prayers, for the prayers of the wicked are an abomination unto the Lord. Let him attempt to perform holy actions, he is like Uzziah who laid hold upon the censer of the priest while the leprosy was on his brow, till he was glad to retire from the sacred place lest he should be struck dead. If thou dost not confess that all thy actions before thou wast regenerate were full of sin and abominable in the sight of God, thou hast not yet learned what thou art, and it is not likely that thou wilt wish to know what a Saviour is.

3. Being thus the medium of contagion and defilement wherever he went, the Lord demanded that he should be *shut out from the society of Israel*. There was a spot outside the camp, barren, solitary, where lepers are confined. They were commanded to wear a covering over the mouth and upon the upper lip, and if any passed by they were compelled to cry "Unclean! unclean! unclean!" Some of the Rabbi translate the cry "Avoid! avoid! avoid!" One of the American poets has put it, "Room for the leper! room!" They were required never to drink of a running stream of water of which others might drink; nor might they sit down on any stone by the roadside upon which it was probable any other person might rest. They were dead to all the enjoyments of life, dead to all the endearments and society of their friends. Such is the case with the sinner with regard to the people of God. He can go and find such mirth as the company of his fellow-lepers can afford, but where God's people are he is out of place, shut out from the communion of saints, cannot pray their prayer nor sing their hymns, know not their joys, never taste their perfect peace, never enter into the rest which remaineth for them.

4. The leper was *wholly unable to come up to the house of God*. Other men might offer sacrifices but not the leper; others had a share in the great high priest's sacrifice, and when he went within the vail he appeared for all others, but the leper had neither part nor lot in this matter. He was shut out from God as well as shut out from man. He was no partaker of the sacred things of Israel, and all the ordinances of the tabernacle were as nothing to him. Think of that, sinner! As a sinner full of guilt, thou art shut out from all communion with God. Thou canst not stand in His presence, for He is a devouring fire and would consume thee. Thy prayers are shut out from Him, thy words are unheard; shut out utterly and entirely by sin from the presence and acceptance of God.

II. Now BRING THE LEPER UP TO THE HIGH PRIEST.

Whenever a leper was cleansed under the Jewish law *the leper did nothing, the priest did all*. Previous to his being pronounced clean, the leper was passive—the priest did everything. The priest comes out from the sanctuary, comes to the place of the lepers, where no other man might go but he in his priestly office. He calls up one leper before him; he looks at him and there is a spot on that leper which is not leprous—quick, raw, healthy flesh. The priest puts him aside; he is an unclean leper. Here is another, and he has but one or two red spots appearing beneath the skin, all the rest of his body is perfectly sound; the priest puts him aside, he is an unclean leper. Here is another; he is from head to foot covered with a scaly whiteness of the filthy disease, the hair is all turned white, owing to the decay of the powers of nature which are unable now to nourish the roots of the hair. There is not a single speck of health in him from the crown of his head to the soul of his foot, but all is pollution and filth. But hark! the high priest says to him, "Thou art clean." And after certain necessary ceremonies he is admitted into the camp, and afterwards into the very sanctuary of God. "If there was found any sound place in him, he was unclean." But when the leprosy had covered him, wheresoever the priest looked, then the man became by sacrificial rights a clean leper.

Bring up the sinner before the Great High Priest. How many there are ready to confess that they have done many things which are wrong, but they say, "Though we have done much which we cannot justify, yet there have been many good actions which might almost counterbalance the sin; been charitable to the poor, sought to instruct the ignorant, to help those that are out of the way. We have some sins we do confess; but there is much which is still right and good, and we therefore hope that we shall be delivered." I put you aside, in God's name, by His authority, as unclean lepers. For you there is no hope and no promise of salvation whatever. A second comes. He admits a very great measure of guilt; not open immorality, but his thoughts and the imaginations of his heart have been evil, and evil frequently. "But still," saith he, "though I have not one good work of which to boast, nor any righteousness in which to glory, yet I do hope that by repentance I may amend; I trust that by a resolute persistence in good works I may yet blot out my past life, and so may enter heaven." I set him aside again, as being an unclean leper, for whom cleansing rites are not provided. He is one who must still be kept without the camp; he has not arrived at that stage in which it is possible for him to be made clean. But another comes. Probably he is a really better man than either of the other two, but not in his own opinion. With many a sigh and tear he confesses that he is utterly ruined and undone. "A month or two ago I would have claimed a righteousness with the very best, could have boasted of what I have done; but now I see my righteousness to be as filthy rags, and all my goodness is as an unclean thing. I count all these things but dross and dung. I tread upon them and despise them. I have done no good thing. I have sinned and come short of the glory of God. Lord, at Thy feet I fall, full of leprosy from head to foot; nothing have I to boast of, nothing to trust to except Thy mercy." He is a clean leper; sins forgiven, iniquities put away. Through the blood of Jesus Christ, who died upon the tree, saved! As soon as ever the leprosy had come right out the man was clean, and as soon as ever your sin is fully manifest, so that in your conscience you feel yourself to be really a sinner, there is a way of salvation for you. As long as a man has anything to boast of, there is no Christ for him; but the moment he has nothing of his own, Christ is his.—*C. H. Spurgeon*, A.D. 1860.

Topic: "UNCLEAN, UNCLEAN" (V. 45).

God's *mercy* paints malady in hideous tints, that the sufferer may see his plague and hasten to the healer.

Leprosy showed, by a long train of emblem, the complex loathsomeness of sin, that evil might be the more abhorred.

I. THIS MALADY CREPT IN WITH STEALTHY STEPS.

Not easily discerned. Human skill was blind. Wisdom from on high was needed. The anointed priest must search.

Sin lurks within the veins. The world has no detecting eye. The self-pleased fancy boasts of health. Death is begun when all seems life. The plague devours, but ignorance sees not.

Only the Spirit can "convince of sin": He only can reveal the inborn defilement. He sets the soul before the mirror of God's Word; opens sightless eyes; and the sinner beholds a hideous mass of polluted self. The light from heaven shows leprosy throughout. [See Job xlii. 6; and Isa. vi. 5. Compare also Paul's testimony, Rom. vii. 24.]

Sinners, bring heart, and thought, and ways, and life to the revealing Word. Consult not the world's counsel. Call in the Faithful Witness. Shrink not. Self-knowledge is a step towards Christ. The malady perceived leads to the malady relieved.

II. THE SUFFERER HEARS THE PRIEST'S CODEMNING VOICE.

He is pronounced "Unclean."

He goes forth; tastes no more the joys of social scenes; shunning and shunned he hides himself in solitude. His whole mien proclaims the misery of his dejected soul. Clothes rent, head bare, mouth covered; and when the hollow voice must speak it sounds the plaintive knell, "Unclean, unclean!"

1. The *wretchedness* of sin: The "clothes are rent"—symbol of bitterest grief (2 Sam. iii. 31; Job i. 20). There is no woe like that of sin.

2 *Lowly shame* also: "Head uncovered." [See Job xix. 9.] In the leper thus despoiled we see how sin inflicts an ignominious brand. [Compare Ezra ix. 6.]

3. *Utterance stifled:* "upper lip covered." The sorrowful and shameful sinner finds speech muffled and choked. When God withdrew, "Then were the seers ashamed," etc. (Micah iii. 7). Sin should be mute. While faithful lips abound in prayer, and send forth songs of praise, and tell of redeeming grace; a sinner's "throat is an open sepulchre."

4. *Pollution is bemoaned.* If a passing step draws near, a piteous warning must be raised—"Unclean, unclean!" (Zech. iii. 3; Isa. lxiv. 6).

5. *Outcast from social life.* No home may welcome him. In loneliness he pines. No station gains exemption. Miriam (Numb. xii. 14); King Uzziah (2 Kings xv. 5).

What has sin done? Driven angels from heaven's light. Excluded multitudes of men from communion with God, holy fellowship, the consecrated board: makes sinners exiles from the heaven bound host, lone "off-scourings" amid the miseries of desert life.

6. *Shut without the gates.* God and His people *within*, he "without." The saved within heaven's gates—barred; the lost "without" for ever. Thus the leper stands an emblem of sin's dreadful plague.

Why this picture of horror? That [you may sink in despair? Far otherwise.

III. THE GREAT HIGH PRIEST IS NEAR.

1. He *comes to the leper.* With healing grace, He draws nigh the foulest, the hopeless.

2. *His remedy is ready and sure.* "Lord, if thou wilt, thou canst make me clean!" was a leper's cry. Hear His reply, "I *will*, be *thou clean.*"

3. *None need be an outcast* from His fold. He opens grace and glory to the penitent and trustful soul. [Comp. "*Christ is all.*"]

Topic: LEPROSY, A PARABLE OF HUMAN DEPRAVITY.

A. As it affects the Moral Constitution of Man (Vv. 1-45).

Leprosy has always been regarded as a mysterious as well as a malignant disease. Unlike other diseases, it was to be detected and treated by the priests. Probably the disease was acquired by the Hebrews while badly fed and hardly worked in Egypt. Their skin would become liable to cutaneous diseases on account of exposure to the dust of brickfields and heat of the burning sun. In the whole range of Scripture is no other malady so fully described. Invested with such prominence and importance, the Hebrews would be (*a*) *put on their guard against ceremonial defilement:* (*b*) *filled with the spirit of religious fear:* (*c*) *stimulated to desire spiritual purity.* The patient, as he repaired to the priest, convicted of pollution, would be humbled, and have thoughts suggested to his mind of unworthiness and sin.

I. LEPROSY WAS MYSTERIOUS IN ITS ORIGIN. Neither the patient nor the priest could tell exactly how or when the disease originated; they had to attend to the symptoms, and concern themselves about the reality and *removal*. The priest could not look into the springs of life and analyse the seeds of the evil. So, moral evil, that affects our race, is mysterious in its origin; we can detect and trace its symptoms, prove its presence; it corrupts the springs of our moral nature, vitiates all the faculties of the soul. We know by *history, observation,* especially by *experience,* that we are children of a sin-smitten race, the taint is in our blood, and only requires favourable circumstances to assert its malignity and power.

II. LEPROSY WAS INSIDIOUS IN ITS PROGRESS. For a while the person affected might be unconscious of its presence; and even the priest might find difficulty in passing judgment after careful examination. It was liable to break out at any time, and assume various aspects. So, with depravity having its seat within, at any time, and under any circumstances, it may reveal its presence and power—develop the most alarming symptoms. Little spots, so-called sins of inadvertency, slight infirmities, may secretly develop into morally corrupt habits, and disfigure the whole life.

III. LEPROSY WAS DETESTABLE IN ITS SYMPTOMS. Every phase of it was associated with uncleanness. The patient not only became loathsome to himself, but offensive to society. Mental and moral anguish would accompany physical pain. The disease would disfigure and deform the frame, rendering life almost intolerable. So, sin produces moral disfigurement, induces all kinds of sorrow. Holiness is beautiful, but wickedness is hideous. Our moral sense puts its stigma upon vice. Moral impurity God loathes, and will ultimately destroy. Society has its lazar-houses, where depravity may not only be checked, but where its hideous symptoms may be hidden from beholders. Such sins as those spoken of in Rom. i. 21-32 justify the statement of Isaiah i. 5, 6, concerning the offensive features of moral corruption.

IV. LEPROSY WAS INVETERATE IN ITS TENACITY. When once it asserted itself, the sufferer would have to be prompt and persevering in his efforts to get it eradicated. The priest had to make very close scrutiny, to re-examine, and put the leper under repeated probation. Any contact with contagion would suffice to revive the old evil in all its virulence. There was the pre-disposition in the blood, *the secret of the trouble was there* So, with moral depravity, it has been transmitted in our blood, the springs of life are vitiated. Sin is indigenous, and defies complete eradiction in this life. Only one sinless Being has lived on our earth, He was immaculately conceived; *we,* are "born in sin, and shapen in iniquity." Leprosy defied all human means to remove it; through the instrumentality of the divinely appointed priest alone it succumbed. *Education, reform,* etc., cannot cure the depravity of the heart, nothing short of "the fountain opened in the house of David for sin and for uncleanness." Through the mercy of God we can be "abundantly pardoned" here, and become "without spot" hereafter.—*F. W. B.*

Topic: B. AS IT AFFECTS THE EARTHLY CIRCUMSTANCES OF MAN (Vv. 45-59).

One of the first penalties the leper suffered was *excommunication.* No sooner did the priest detect disease, than he commanded withdrawal on the part of the sufferer from healthy society, in order that the infection might not spread.

I. HE WOULD BE SHUT OUT FROM THE DOMESTIC CIRCLE. So sin unsocializes, unfits men for the joys and purity of hearth and home; frequently the morally impure have to be excluded from the company of the virtuous.

II. HE WOULD BE SHUT OUT FROM THE SECULAR CIRCLE. Not permitted to return to his tent, he would be unfit to take his place in society, and fulfil his duties in the world. So wrong-doing and moral turpitude will render men unfit for society, and necessitate their incarceration for reformation and restraint.

III. HE WOULD BE SHUT OUT FROM THE SACRED CIRCLE. Although allowed to repair to the priest, he would not be allowed to mingle and take part in the services of the house of God, the priest shut him up in seclusion. So evil shuts men out from communion with God and His people. Those composing the Church are persons who become separate, and who touch not the unclean thing. The saddest aspect of sin is that *it separates the soul from God;* and, but for the intervention of our great High Priest, would shut us out from His presence for ever.

How circumspect, therefore, we ought to be! How anxious that the leprosy of our souls may be cleansed!—F. W. B.

Topic: SINFUL SURROUNDINGS (Vv. 47-57).

Notice was to be taken of leprous garments and houses; and, no matter what their texture or value, if found to be incurably diseased, were to be unscrupulously destroyed. By these things we are taught—

I. THAT GREAT CARE SHOULD BE EXERCISED IN THE SELECTION OF OUR SURROUNDINGS.

We are not *absolutely* creatures of circumstances, but are marvellously affected by them. We are not responsible for our parentage, nor the early environments which give bias and tone to after life. These are circumstances unforeseen and uncontrollable, to which we are compelled resignedly to submit. But we have to make many of the influences that enwrap us like garments, as we go through life.

(a) *The clothes we wear.*
(b) *The books we read.*
(c) *The company we keep.*
(d) *The places we frequent.*
(e) *The scenes we visit.*

All these may have a pernicious and demoralising tendency; they may be leprous, and introduce sin through the *gateways of the town* of man's soul. How suitable, then, the advice in Psa. i. and in Proverbs of Solomon.

II. THAT PROMPT AND DECISIVE ACTION SHOULD BE TAKEN WHEN OUR SURROUNDINGS AWAKEN SUSPICION.

(a) *Avail ourselves of judicious advice.* The leper took anything he suspected to priest for scrutiny. Let us test our surroundings by the teaching of our Great High Priest; for there can be no high morality without His religion.

(b) *Suspend the suspected thing till scrutiny has been made.* Suspected garments were shut up seven days; and repeated if needed. Let us be shy of suspicious books, places, etc. Have them fairly investigated.

(c) *If the suspected thing be righteously condemned, let unconditional destruction of it immediately ensue.*

The leprous garment was to be consumed with fire. So let us break off at once from bad company or vicious books. The converts at Ephesus burnt their wicked books; that ensured—

(1) *That they should do the owners no more harm;*
(2) *That they should not corrupt others, and—*
(3) *Showed the reality of conversion.*

Things that will not wash, that will not improve by washing, are not to be relied on. Sin is not *an external deformity, a trifling irregularity, infirmity,* or *failing;* but in the soul, degrading all its powers, which, if not cleansed, will ultimately get its desert, in everlasting destruction from the presence of the Lord.—*F. W. B.*

Topic: THE WONDROUS WORKING OF GOD'S GRACE (Vv. 12, 13, 45, 46).

The God of Israel could bear with infirmity, blemish, failure, but the moment it became a case of defilement—in head, beard, forehead, or any part—it could not be tolerated in the holy assembly (vv. 45, 46). Here was the leper's *condition*, the leper's *occupation*, the leper's *place*. What more humiliating than this! Excluded from the only spot in all the world in which Jehovah's presence was known or enjoyed. In that poor, solitary leper behold—

I. A VIVID TYPE OF ONE IN WHOM SIN IS WORKING.

It is not a helpless, *convicted* sinner who is here pourtrayed, whose guilt and misery have thoroughly come out—a fit subject, therefore, for God's love and the Saviour's blood—but one in whom sin is actually working, one in whom there is the positive energy of evil.

1. *So long as sin is working* there can be *no fellowship* with God or with His people. "He shall dwell alone; without the camp shall his habitation be." How long? "All the days wherein the *plague* shall be *in* him." This is a great practical truth: the energy of evil is the death blow to communion. It matters not what the amount of the evil be, if it were but a foolish thought, so long as it *continues to work* it must cause suspension of fellowship.

2. *A suggestive paradox in God's dealing with sinners.* When the plague "*break out abroad* in the skin, and the leprosy *cover all* the skin of him," etc., "he is clean" (vv. 12, 13). The moment a sinner is in his true place before God, the matter is settled. Directly his real character is fully out, no difficulty remains. When the soul is before Him with the cry, "*Just as I am!*" the free grace of God flows down to him. "When I kept silence," etc. (Psa. xxxii. 3, 4); but when "I acknowledged my sin," etc. (v. 5), "*thou forgavest.*" The moment a sinner takes his true place *as one thoroughly lost*, guilty, and undone, as one in whom there is not a single spot on which the eye of Infinite Holiness can rest with complacency, so bad that he cannot possibly be worse, that moment there is a perfect settlement of the entire matter.

II. THE GRACE OF GOD DEALS WITH ACKNOWLEDGED SINNERS.

1. The *more evidently a man is a sinner* the *more clearly is established* his title *to the grace of God*, and to the work of Christ, "for Christ also hath suffered for sins, the just for the unjust," etc. (1 Pet. iii 8). The gospel applies itself to all who are on the ground of being lost. It is there, and there alone, that grace can meet the guilty. "Where sin abounded, grace did much more abound."

2. *To have a hopeless view of one's self is the beginning of salvation.* So long as a sinner thinks there is a single spot which is not covered with the direful disease, he has not come to the *end of himself.* It is when his true condition is fully disclosed to view, and he sees himself "wretched, and poor, and miserable," that there opens to him the meaning of *salvation* BY GRACE.—*Evolved from* "*Notes on Leviticus*" *by C. H. M.*

OUTLINES ON VERSES OF CHAPTER XIII.

V. 2.—*Theme:* FIRST SYMPTOMS OF DEPRAVITY TO BE SUSPECTED.

As soon as a person had suspicion that leprosy was in the blood, before he was certain, or society had branded him, he was to repair to the appointed priest, and submit to a careful examination. If the priest pronounced the presence of disease, the sufferer was to acquiesce uncomplainingly to the decison. We have suggested—

I. BY WHAT SIGNS INDWELLING DEPRAVITY MAY BE DETECTED.

(*a*) *Uprising of evil desire.* "When a man shall have in the skin of his flesh a rising." Inordinate cravings, sensual promptings, etc.

(*b*) *Uprising of inflamed passions.* "A scab or bright spot." Evil, like leaven, soon spreads, and demonstrates its existence ; though secret at first, it reveals its vitality and virulence in a palpable manner. Sin has its roots in lust, evil desire ; and, when hidden lust hath conceived it bringeth forth sin; and sin, when it is finished, bringeth forth death. In first transgression, the lustful looking preceded the tasting and fatal eating of the forbidden fruit. Let us check the looking and inward longing, and seek to arrest the uprisings of inward depravity, thus nip sin in the bud.

Indwelling depravity cannot always be detected by (*a*) *personal feelings ;* or (*b*) *personal inconvenience.* Many diseases, at their beginning, are insidious and flattering : do not occasion pain, or seem to impair the strength.

II. BY WHAT TESTS THE EXISTENCE OF INDWELLING DEPRAVITY MAY BE PROVED.

(*a*) *By comparing ourselves with divine descriptions of sin.* Probably the Hebrews were furnished with directions to guide them in self-examination, to indicate when they had need to have recourse to the priest. God, in His great mercy, has given a description of sin in the Holy Scriptures ; and, by comparing ourselves with the mirror of the Word, we may detect the uprisings of depravity, and see what ravages sin commits in our moral nature.

(*b*) *By repairing to persons competent to guide us in our investigation.*

The leper was to be brought to the priest; who, under divine guidance and authority, would give needed counsel. So now—although there are no priests after the Aaronic pattern—persons anxious about their souls and the removal of sin, do well to confer with the ambassadors of Christ, who have obtained healing of the plague of their own hearts, and seek help from heaven to direct anxious inquirers who ask, " What must I do to be saved ?"—*F. W. B.*

V. 5.—*Theme :* SCRUPULOUS CARE IN DEALING WITH DEPRAVITY.

The priest exercised great patience in examining every case brought before him; he did not cloak or cover, or seek only to slightly heal; the course adopted was searching and thorough; Sin is not to be treated as a slight moral indisposition, but as a *serious radical disease.*

I. DEPRAVITY, LIKE LEPROSY, MAY SOMETIMES APPEAR " AT A STAY." This might be the outcome of—

(*a*) *Heredity.* Life healthy transmitted by parentage—ability to resist inroads of infection, development of disease. So, though piety does not run in the blood, yet propensities and dispositions are inherited, and check or quicken depravity.

(*b*) *Organisation.* The fires of lust will kindle quicker in some natures than in others. Some persons have animality so preponderating that Satan seems able easily to get the advantage over them.

(*c*) *Environment.* Pure surroundings help to repress tendencies to go wrong, to develop dispositions to virtue. The restraints of *a godly home,* refining influences of *a good education* may stay the tide of depravity that otherwise would break forth with great volume and power.

II. THOUGH APPARENTLY " AT A STAY," DEPRAVITY, LIKE LEPROSY, MAY BE UNABATED IN ITS VIRULENCE.

Though the priest did not at first detect signs of disease, yet it may have been lurking dormant in the system, and waiting only for a favourable occasion to awaken into activity. This might occur from

(*a*) *Inward irritation,* or

(*b*) *Outward influences.*

We do not know what depths of depravity are within us, till some unexpected temptation stirs them, till the enemy comes in upon us as a flood.

III. THE ARREST OF SYMPTOMS OF DEPRAVITY MAY ISSUE IN THE REMOVAL OF THEIR CAUSE.

(*a*) *When sinful habits are stayed, their fires may burn out.*

(*b*) *When sinful habits are stayed a new life is to be exhibited.*

The healed leper was to " wash his clothes and be clean." He was to appear among society as a new creature, both in conduct and character. The life of recovered lepers would be (1) *beautiful,* (2) *holy,* (3) *useful,* (4) *happy.* So of every *saved* and *sanctified* soul.—*F. W. B.*

V. 9.—*Theme :* SIN NOT TO BE CONNIVED AT.

It was the *duty* of the leper to go to the priest; of society, to see that he went : " he shall be brought unto the priest."

I. A MAN WITH LEPROSY NOT TO BE LEFT TO HIS MORBID FEELINGS.

He not at liberty to neglect means of recovery. No excuse, no willingness to commit his case to fate or chance to exonerate him from obligation to own his malady. Liberty in society is only lawful as it is compatible with the general good. The leper must go to priest, for—

(*a*) *His own sake.*

(*b*) *Sake of others.*

So sinners ought to repair to great High Priest for similar reasons.

II. A MAN WITH LEPROSY TO BE DIRECTED TO MEANS OF CURE.

Friends would take and introduce him to priest, especially those who had obtained healing themselves. We have a right to interfere with the liberty of our fellows when it is for their real and unmistakable good. Let us take sinners to Christ, the Great Physician. He is *able* and *willing* to heal, as He healed the lepers in the days of His flesh. He removes leprosy of sin.

The leper was not to puzzle his brains about such questions as—
(*a*) Why was leprosy permitted?
(*b*) How is it generated?
(*c*) How is it cured?

Enough for him *to own it; avail himself of means of recovery.* Useless, *absurd, dangerous* to hide or disown it. So with leprosy of sin, it is a good sign when it is acknowledged, sorrowed over, taken to Him who alone can remove depravity, and make our souls as clean as spotless wool, as white as virgin snow.—*F. W. B.*

Vv. 2, 10 18, 24, 29, 44.—*Theme*: DEGREES OF DEPRAVITY.

Obviously, in leprosy there were varieties in kind, as well as symptoms. So in depravity it assumes various forms, manifests itself in different ways, though all may be grouped under the denomination, *sin.* We have suggested—

I. INHERENT DEPRAVITY. "In the skin of the flesh a rising" (v. 2).
II. QUICKENED DEPRAVITY. "Quick raw flesh in the rising" (v. 10).
III. AGGRAVATED DEPRAVITY. "In sight, lower than the skin" (v. 20).
IV. VIRULENT DEPRAVITY. "The quick flesh that burneth" (v. 24).
V. HIDEOUS DEPRAVITY. "Plague upon the head, or the beard" (v. 29).
VI. TOTAL DEPRAVITY. "The priest shall pronounce him utterly unclean; his plague is in his head" (v. 44).

Thus depravity culminates in disfigurement of "the human face divine," suggesting the fact that sin has marred the image of God in man, and deranged the whole of his intellectual and moral powers.

What an evidence of spiritual blindness, that men do not see the hideous nature of sin. No wonder that God—who sees every secret sin—should hate it, and provide for its removal. Those who voluntarily close their eyes to their sinful state, and die impenitent will be moral suicides.—*F. W. B.*

Vv. 45-47.—*Theme*: RESULTS OF UNREMOVED DEPRAVITY.

When the leper was pronounced "utterly unclean" by the priest, the case was regarded as desperate and hopeless. So, when sinners become exceedingly vile, and defy every effort made for their amendment, the following things ensue:

I. CHARACTER DESTROYED. The leper's clothes were rent; so, sin ruins the character of its victims.
II. INTELLECT DETHRONED. The leper's head was bare; so, the mind of the abandoned sinner becomes *neglected, deformed,* and *unprotected.*
III. INFLUENCE PERNICIOUS. The leper's upper lip covered, to indicate that the breath had become exceedingly corrupt. So, sin changes the tongue from being a wholesome tree, to a pestilential stream of polluting influences.
IV. LIFE CORRUPTED. "He is unclean." All the springs of life become impure, the whole man is corrupt. So, sin defiles the body, soul, and spirit; pollutes *thought, word,* and *deed.*
V. CONDITION SOLITARY. "He shall dwell alone." Sin cuts men off from society with each other, from holy angels, from God. Religion unites men with the divine Father; and with each other, in the bonds of holy brotherhood.
VI. SELF-CONDEMNED. The poor leper cried "Unclean, unclean!" Wherever he went he proclaimed his complaint. So sinners—whether they know it or not - proclaim, wherever they go (by their character), the depravity that debases them; and, if at last excluded from the place of the holy, they will own the justice of the sentence that excludes them.—*F. W. B.*

ILLUSTRATIVE ADDENDA TO CHAPTER XIII.

DEVELOPMENTS.
"The Present is the living sum-total of the whole Past."—CARLYLE, *Characteristics.*

"Consequences are unpitying. Our deeds carry their terrible consequences, quite apart from any fluctuations that went before, consequences that are hardly ever confined to ourselves."—GEORGE ELIOT, *Adam Bede.*

"Large streams from little fountains flow
Tall oaks from little acorns grow."
—DAVID EVERETT.

"From little sparks may burst a mighty flame."—DANTE.

"Things bad begun make strong themselves by ill."—*Macbeth, III.* 2.

TRANSMITTED EFFECTS:
"And out of darkness came the hands
That reach through nature, moulding men."
—TENNYSON, *In Memoriam.*

"The seed we sow another reaps;
The wealth we find another keeps;
The robes we weave another wears;
The arms we forge another bears."
—SHELLEY.

"The evil that men do lives after them."
—*Julius Cæsar, III.* 2.

"No act of man, nothing (how much less the man himself!) is extinguished when it disappears; through considerable time it still works, though done and vanished."—CARLYLE.

"No action, whether foul or fair,
Is ever done, but it leaves somewhere
A record, written by fingers ghostly,
As a blessing or curse, and mostly
In the greater weakness or greater strength
Of the acts which follow it."
—LONGFELLOW, *Christus*.

UNCLEAN.
"The seeds of all my sins are in my heart, and perhaps the more dangerous that I do not see them."—M'CHEYNE.

"Great sins make great sufferers."—ANNA K. GREEN.

CHAPTER XIV

Leprosy Cleansed.

SUGGESTIVE READINGS.

V. 2.—In the day of his cleansing. Remedy and respite came to the pitiable leper. Although his case seemed forlorn and dismal—unclean, and an outcast—yet the hope was left to him that the plague might be healed, and he be again restored to society and the sanctuary. The darkest lot of human life is illumined by hope; faint may be its ray, yet it breaks the dreariest gloom. Weary indeed were "*all the days* wherein the plague was in him" (chap. xiii. 46), but after long waiting there might come in due season "*the day* of his cleansing." Yes, the possibilities of better things cheer us in every adverse case; the promises of God alleviate the desolation of all who wait for Him, even as the outlook for "the accepted time and the day of salvation" cheers the languishing soul in its conscious misery and sin. To every plague-bound soul this solace remains—"the day of his cleansing" may perchance come.

V. 3.—The priest shall go forth out of the camp. No restoration from banishment to God, no removal of the bane of uncleanness, except through priestly mediation. Between the soul and salvation comes the priest. And the whole work of reinstating the outcast in his lost privileges begins in this act of the priest going forth to the place of the leper's banishment. The coming forth of Christ Jesus to us, to where we were in our banishment, that was the initial incident in our restoration to God. No one but the priest could come nigh a leper without contracting defilement; no one but the sacred person of our divine Priest could approach us "in our sins" and both Himself remain "holy, harmless, undefiled," and also bring the unclean life back to purity and privilege.

V. 4.—Two birds, cedar wood, scarlet and hyssop. Symbols of ceremonial and sacrificial cleansing. The one bird was killed, the other set at liberty. The one bird *dead*, symbolising that the leprous life of the victim was now also dead; the other bird *free*, symbolising that henceforth a new life of liberty was set before the restored leper. Or the evangelical symbolism may suggest to us in the slain bird the *death*, and in the soaring bird the *resurrection* of Christ—two aspects of His perfected redemption for the sinner.

The "*cedar*" in Scripture is the symbol of loftiness and pride, and leprosy was regarded as God's rebuke for arrogance and haughtiness. "*Hyssop*" symbolised lowliness. Tradition affirms, "Pride was the cause of the distemper, which cannot be cured till man becomes humble, and keeps himself as low as hyssop."

"*Scarlet*," a binding of crimson wool, by which the cedar and hyssop were connected; suggestive of "sins as scarlet," and equally of the blood of atonement; or it may symbolise the now purified and healthy blood flowing in the cleansed leper's veins.

V. 7.—Sprinkle upon him seven times. Welcome to the leper those sprinklings of the blood; each one being a testimony of his deliverance. And to a sin-burdened life how welcome "the blood of sprinkling." There is no impatience while the sign of cleansing is "seven times" repeated. Naaman might resent the requirement of the seven washings in Jordan; but it was in ignorance of the fact that "seven" is the sign of perfectness. The life which craves emancipation from uncleanness and banishment, frets not under the repeated application of the purifying blood; it is to him "precious blood," and his outcry is "Wash me throughly from mine iniquity." They who have experienced the bitterness of sin, weary not under the process of cleansing.

Vv. 8, 9.—He that is to be cleansed. The first process of personal purifying restored the leper to the camp, the place of acknowledged relationship to Jehovah; he entered the society of Israel. Even so does the repentant sinner, who has been recalled from his outcast life, seeks to cleanse himself from evil ways and outward defilements, and then takes his place amid the congregations of God's people. It is the beginning of his new and better life. He ventures not yet into "his tent," nor treads the floors of the sanctuary; for these nearer and more sacred felicities require a fuller sanctifying. He must be "clean" who would dwell in "the *camp*"; doubly cleansed who could enter the *family* of God's people in happy "tent" fellowship; supremely sanctified if he would tread the sanctuary of holy privilege, accepted within the very presence of the Lord.

Vv. 10-20.—He shall take two lambs, etc. For now, at the end of seven days the soul is to come "before the Lord" (v. 11); and who will venture near Him without sacrifice? The priest leads him to the very "door of the tabernacle," waves the "trespass offering" in God's presence, slays the "sin offering and burnt offering in the holy place," then applies the trespass-offering blood, to the person of the suppliant together with the oil of consecration, making atonement for him, that he may be clean. The priestly ministries, and the sacrificial offerings reveal to us the works of Jesus; the applied blood and oil suggest the gracious offices of the Holy Spirit. All the most effective methods of purifying are called into requisition if a leper is to be made acceptable to God. True types of the needs of guilty men. It is not by easy and superficial processes they can be reinstated in grace. The priestly offices and sacrificial merits of Christ, the direct ministries of the Holy Spirit in applying the healing virtues of redemption, are imperative for their acceptance with the Lord. The sinner needs *all* that Christ and the Spirit can do for him if he is to stand without spot or rebuke before God.

Vv. 21-32.—If he be poor. Poverty is left without plea of inability by such concessions; and equally is saved from fear of rejection by such evidence that God thinks specially of the poor.

Vv. 33-53.—Leprosy in a house. A law given in the desert which was applicable to their future lot in the Land of Promise. It is thus a hostage that they *would* "come into the land of Canaan." God sees the end from the beginning. He knows the way we take, and He arranges the goal we shall reach. It is so in our earthly movements; it is certainly so in our spiritual pilgrimage.

God would have our homes pure. No care could be too minute, no toil too heavy, no sacrifice too serious, in order to keep the house clean from plague. The habitations of the righteous should be free from all impurities; the walls bared of all suggestions of wrong thoughts and passions; the house free from every enticement to indulgence and sin. Modern Art is responsible for many a plague spot on the walls of our houses; and Luxury is to-day laying decoys on our tables which allure to habits whose issue is sin. Christian houses should be free from all occasions to such defilement. At all costs, though it mean the parting with ideal pictures and valued sculpture in the adornment of our rooms, or the removing of indulgences from our board, which may encourage in our children impure thoughts or perilous habits, let us show ourselves to be God's people by keeping our homes clean. For a Christian home is earth's best type of the beauteous and blissful heaven.

SECTIONAL HOMILIES.

Topic: THE LAW OF CLEANSING (Vv. 1-3).

The "*law of cleansing*" is clearly and emphatically shown at the outset; man's part in his own purifying is to "stand still, and see the salvation of God." All is to be done for him, nothing done by him. The leper must make no advances, could effect no purifying; he must for ever remain unclean and an outcast if help and deliverance are not brought him. And in the redemption, in the re-creation of the sinner, all must be of God, all of grace; "not of works, lest any man should boast." [Addenda to chap. xiv., *Helplessness*.]

I. GUILTY MAN'S ABSOLUTE HELPLESSNESS.

1. His *position*. The leper's place was outside the camp, in the place of (symbolical) banishment from God. He was consigned to solitude, dreary isolation, beyond the reach of human aid. Doubly outlawed, from God and man; all help divorced from him; far off from the agencies of healing and amelioration; shut out from divine and human regard. In the ranks of sinful men and women to-day, there are thousands equally outlawed from help; living far off from God, apparently untouched by gracious influences of heaven, never hearing of Christ, unarrested and unawakened, living as outcasts. Nor do their fellow men come to their aid; "no man careth for their soul;" they are shunned as criminals, abandoned as hopeless. Let not this be supposed true only of the lower classes of society; in the *highest* stations there are those of whom, so far as sacred agencies reaching them, God seems to say, "Let them alone!" and to whom no delivering help or saving word ever appears to come from those who know the way of salvation.

2. His *condition*. Beyond human aid, certainly the leper was beyond *self*-aid. How could he act to secure his own cleansing? He could only communicate defilement to everything and every one he touched. He was a defiled and a defiling leper; could make nothing clean, only unclean. Without any helper, he was absolutely helpless. Are sinners thus? Can we minimise or escape our guilt? If it were possible for us to do "works of righteousness," they would not diminish the guilt to our past account or obliterate present sinfulness. All our righteousnesses are as filthy rags; "there is none that doeth good and sinneth not." It is mournfully true that the unclean cannot act any single part for the removal of their uncleanness.

Add to this the fact that *one leper could not cleanse another*, and the sum of his helplessness is complete. Neither in himself nor in his fellow-men, clean or unclean, could deliverance or healing be found.

When shut out from men we are shut up to God. Grace meets us in our extremity. Jesus finds him whom men "cast out" (John ix. 35), and receives sinners whom society rejects (Matt. ix. 11, 12).

<blockquote>
When penitence has wept in vain
Over some foul dark spot,
One only stream, a stream of blood,
Can wash away the blot.
</blockquote>

II. GOD'S ABOUNDING HELPFULNESS.

Since his *only* resource was in God, He alone devised and accomplished the plan of his cleansing.

1. The *outgoing of divine help.* " The priest shall go forth out of the camp." He was in this the "minister of God," acting out God's purpose. In the priest God approached the leper. Later in time, to guilty men there came the Supreme Priest; man could not, in his sin, come to God, but God came to man in Christ. And still He comes, by mediatorial agencies, to the lone spirit in the misery of sin. The first step in a sinner's salvation is taken by God. He does not shrink from leprous scenes. Where sinners are the Saviour comes. " In this was manifested the love of God toward us " (1 John iv. 9, 10).

2. The *process of divine cleansing.* Having " began a good work," God carries it on to completion (vv. 5, 7). Sacrificial bloodshedding follows (v. 6), then the blood of sprinkling is applied (v. 7) in token of redeeming merits communicated; followed by the soaring bird (v. 7), symbolic of the *risen life* into which God's grace calls the soul whose death is both symbolised and substituted in the offering slain.

3. *Cleanness proclaimed.* The priest " shall pronounce him clean," that it may convey glad assurance to the sufferer, that he may fearlessly claim the privileges now his. A wondrous hour to the stricken spirit is that when God pronounces him clean; it brings with it the "peace of God which passeth all understanding," it imparts strong confidence and acceptance to the long outcast life. For as truly as the leper heard, and heard with eagerness, the priest's voice of acquittal, so to the sinner entering into the Saviour's grace comes the " witness in himself," the voice of blessed testimony for the Lord, " Thy sins are forgiven thee, go in peace."

One only hand, a piercèd hand,
Can salve the sinner's wound.

" *I am the Lord that healeth thee.*" [Addenda to chap. xiv., *Cleansed.*]

Topic: ANXIETY FOR RECOVERY (Vv. 1-3).

Medicinal remedies were not prescribed for leprosy; it was treated more as *an uncleanness* than as a disease, and the sufferer repaired not to the physician, but *the priest.* From the decision of the priest there was no appeal. In the leper was expected—

I. WILLINGNESS TO BE HEALED. There was anxiety in the congregation that the diseased should submit to the required regulations, and become quickly healed. The leper must not, through feelings of shame, hide his complaint, or keep from the necessary scrutiny. He must be willing to submit frequently, if needed, and follow closely the directions given. The first step towards *moral recovery* is to know, and *acknowledge* the plague of sin in the heart; to have *anxiety* to be searched by the candle of the Lord, and have every evil way rooted out. It is good when an anxious inquirer exclaims from solemn conviction: " I am altogether as an unclean thing, and my righteousness is as filthy rags."

II. CONFIDENCE IN HIS HEALER. Faith in the priest would lie at the basis of the leper's obedience to the requirements of the Ceremonial Law; abandoning all dependence in any other means. The priest was to confirm the cure God had wrought by directing a process of cleansing, which would exercise and prove the offerer's faith. The priest was the representative of Jehovah; the directions he gave were to be regarded as the commands of the Lord; confidence in him, and implicit obedience to his directions, were accepted as compliance with the expressed purposes of God.

To be completely recovered from the leprosy of sin, unshaken confidence must be reposed in Him who alone has power to heal, who alone can give us the inward witness that we have passed from death unto life. Meeting the priest outside the camp, as mediator between God and His people, would give comfort and composure to the suppliant for mercy; so, God coming to meet us in the likeness of man, and unattended by overawing manifestations, awakens confidence in the earnest seeker after salvation. Willingness to be saved, belief in the Saviour, personal appropriation of the blessings of redemption, are the *sole* and *indispensible* requisites for deliverance from sin and death.—*F. W. B.*

Topic: REMEDIAL MEASURES (Vv. 4-9).

Leprosy, next to death, was regarded as a symbol of the pollution and loathsomeness of sin. The care taken in the purification of the leper may be regarded as peculiarly referring to the fact that sin separates man from all pure and holy beings, or the whole family of God, and as setting forth the restoration of the penitent to the company of all faithful people, by means of the great appointed sacrifice. The ceremony to be observed would impress the mind of the restored, not only with the fact that he had become whole, but that a fresh tide of life had started in his veins; and, as he saw the live bird escape and soar towards heaven, he would probably have suggested to his mind that, henceforth, he was to rise superior to earthly things, and seek those that are above.

I. RESTORATION TO THE DIVINE FAVOUR IS THROUGH DIVINELY APPOINTED SACRIFICES.

The leper may have wondered what connection there was between the sacrifices and the cleansing he desired; yet it was not for him to question but to obey, and accept gratefully the blessing conferred. So, in what *we* are commanded to do for our cleansing and sanctifying the reason may not be apparent, but, since God has enjoined obligations upon us, exceptions and questionings are excluded. These offerings certainly suggest that only by the sacrifice of the life of a substitute can we be cleansed from defilements, only by compliance with divine directions can we obtain restoration to divine favour.

II. WHEN RESTORED TO DIVINE FAVOUR, THE FACT SHOULD HAVE PUBLIC DECLARATION.

The leper was to be cleansed at the door of the tabernacle, "before the Lord," and *there* he was to be pronounced whole when the rites of purification were completed. Thus the whole camp would know that the man who had been unclean and excommunicated was now recovered, and re-admitted into the society of his friends. His ear, hand, and foot having been consecrated by the priest, a pledge was given that henceforth a new life would be lived before Israel. So, when persons are restored from the plague of sin, and cleansed by the influences of the Holy Ghost, public confession is *expected* and *becoming* to the honour of God, and for the encouragement of goodness. Christ has enjoined the duty of confessing Him publicly upon all His disciples, and declared that He will be ashamed of those in the last day who are now ashamed of Him.—*F. W. B.*

Topic: PROGRESSIVE CLEANSING (Vv. 8-20).

Until a change came upon the leper's state which was both (*a*) a *conscious* change to himself, and (*b*) an *evident* change to the priest, nothing could be done towards his admission to God's fold. So long as a sinner remains dead in his sin, without feeling or desire towards salvation, destitute of penitence and faith, the way of his reception to the community of Christ's redeemed is barred: **he must, in contact with the priest, prove his awakened state.**

This initial movement accomplished, there follows the application of the merits of sacrificial blood, and the liberation of the soul for a freed and a resurrection life, as one "alive from the dead," alive unto God through Jesus Christ our Lord. These are all the *basis incidents* of the Christian life, upon which are superadded the fuller cleansings, the advancing experiences, the higher privileges.

I. FULLER CLEANSINGS.

The seven-fold sprinklings (v. 7) declare the reiterated application and the abounding virtues of the atonement of Christ. But there is yet more to come. Note:

1. *Human co-operation with God's working.* The priest's acts stand for the divine operations in the sinner's cleansing; but the man himself has to "co-work together with God"; he must shave himself and wash himself. The sinner must "put off, concerning the former conversation, the old man which is corrupt according to the deceitful lust" (Ephes. iv. 22; comp. Colos. iii. 8-10), rid himself of all sinful excrescences, and taints, and indulgences, and habits. He must also apply the pure water of the Word, the truths and precepts of religion, enforcing upon himself the sacred teachings and requirements of the gospel. "Ye are my friends if ye do whatsoever I command you." (Jno. xv. 14). "Sanctify them through thy truth" (Jno. xvii. 17). " Now ye are *clean through the word* which I have spoken unto you" (Jno. xv. 3).

2. *Repeated efforts after perfect cleansing.* What was done at first before he could be admitted to the camp, the congregation of Israel (v. 8), must be repeated seven days after, even more scrupulously and minutely (v. 9), as a preparation for his entering his own "tent" (v. 8) and the "tabernacle" of the Lord (v. 11). It is needful that he who has been living in sin reform his life and cleanse his ways before he becomes even an attendant on sacred scenes, entering into the *camp and society* of Christians; but if he is to come into the *more intimate fellowship of the saints* ("tent" nearness, and family intimacy), and into personal *communion with the Lord* ("tabernacle" access to God), he must purge himself of every relic of his former life of impurity, get rid of his old self, and seek a more thorough cleanness by most sedulous use of sanctifying gospel aids. The sources of spiritual cleansing are Scripture, prayer, self-mortification, cross-bearing after Jesus, the Holy Spirit's energies, the culture of a godly mind and a pure heart. [Addenda to chap. xiv., *Sanctification.*]

II. ADVANCING EXPERIENCES.

That soaring bird was emblematic of the freed and aspiring career now set before him. The whole of the new life came not to him at a bound: he had to "go from strength to strength," to move forward by intervals and stages.

1. *Time intervals* separated his experiences. Though allowed to come into the camp at once he had to put "seven days," a slow space of time, between that event and the next,—entrance into his tent; and "on the eighth day" followed his presentation before the Lord in the tabernacle of the congregation. The soul being "made nigh," translated "from the power of darkness into "the kingdom of God's dear Son," moves onward by time stages; and sometimes the intervals are wide, years coming between the successive incidents of his progress. Human nature is *sluggish,* cannot move rapidly into new conditions of life; and so also it is *slow to apprehend* the transformations of grace. They must come by deliberate advances upon the renewed life, or the soul is overwhelmed and confounded; " we are changed into the same image *from glory to* glory, as by the Spirit of the Lord" (2 Cor. iii. 18).

2. *Attainments* follow successively. To the *priest,* the *camp,* the *tent,* the tabernacle. Is there any of us who can "count himself to have attained, or already perfect"? Much advance has through divine love and help been made; but there are further possibilities. "To the *mark* for the *prize* of our high calling of God." [Addenda to chap. xiv., *Progress.*]

III. HIGHER PRIVILEGES.

Blessed the initial incident to the long outcast soul which brought him to the priest, in living contact with one who could declare him clean. Glad the experience of his cleansing which gave him qualification again for the fellowship with Israel.

1. *According to fitness* so is *privilege regulated*. The first cleansing only gave him access to the camp (v. 8); the seven days' waiting qualified him to enter his tent (v. 8); the after purging fitted him for the tabernacle. More grace for those who aspire higher. But the successive advancements in the divine life come according to our preparedness to enter into them.

2. *Spiritual favours increase as we go forward.* The longer we live in Christ and press forward in the culture of Christian virtues and habits, the more blessed becomes our state; more intimate and assured enjoyments, richer delights and loftier elevations. Piety gives not its most precious fruits at the outset. The luxuries are more entrancing, the triumphs are more splendid, the satisfaction is more complete, the virtues are more Christ-like the longer we abide in grace and seek the things that are above. The most blissful sanctuary life has yet only began to "taste" how gracious the Lord is. The most ample application of the "blood" and "oil"—graces of redemption and consecration—may be exceeded by the still richer realizations; for "He giveth *more grace.*" So may we advance nearer yet, till we "appear in Zion before God," and gain the highest sanctity and the loftiest bliss."

Topic: GRACE FOR THE POOR (Vv. 21-32).

"The law of him in whom is the plague of leprosy, whose *hand is not able to get* that which pertaineth to his cleansing."

"If he be poor": thus opens the gentle message of Heaven to the needy. "And *cannot get so much.*" What then? Let him bring the lesser offering, and it shall be accepted for his atonement as readily as the larger offerings (v. 8) of the rich man who *is able* to get "that which pertaineth to his cleansing."

I. POVERTY IS NO BARRIER TO GOD'S CLEANSING GRACE.

1. Grace meets the needy one just *where* he is, and *as* he is. The atoning blood is brought within reach of the very lowest, the very feeblest. All who need it can have it. "*He that hath no money,*" etc. (Isa. lv. 1).

2. *The lowly need fear no heedless disregard.* Man may despise them, put them aside: not so our gracious Saviour. Within those whose lot is hard there may be beauteous souls, "rich in faith."

> Let us be very tender;
> The lowliest soul may be
> A temple of priceless treasure
> That only God can see.

II. POVERTY HAS NO INFLUENCE ON THE MERITS OF ATONING SACRIFICE.

1. The *value of atonement lies*, not in the offerer's social status and resources, but *in the sacrificial blood.* It is not what we are, but what Christ is and has done for us, that forms the sure basis of our acceptance. The sacrifice of the cross has the same efficiency to every soul that brings it before God as his offering, whether lowly or wealthy. And in the smaller offering, equally with the richer, there was exhibited the full value of the atoning work, "precious blood," a spotless victim, a perfect substitute for man's uncleanness.

2. *The acceptance of the poor is guaranteed* by this sacrifice. There need be no trepidation in the breast of the lowly, the feeble, the needy, the misgiving; all are welcomed on the ground of an offering such as they are "*able* to get." Nothing beyond. Jesus said of the woman, "She hath done *what she could.*"

III. Poverty affords no excuse for failing to seek God's mercy.
1. *Without the presentation of sacrificial offering none could be readmitted* to divine favour and fellowship. God would not dispense with atonement, however straightened the individual's case. Every one, the poorest, must come with sacrifice. Christ Jesus must be every one's trust and hope. And there is grace in His meritorious cross for each. God will allow none to excuse themselves. Sacrifice or rejection!
2. The *terms of admission to the divine life* are that we bring our utmost. " *Such as he be able* to get." Not pleading poverty as a reason for doing poorly, offering a meaner presentation than is justifiable. The poor may not cover themselves from God's requirements by their penury: but must bring "such as they are able to get," their *very best*. None may "offer to God that which *costs him nothing*." God would reject it as a "vain oblation." The widow's mite was pleasing to Christ as being "*all her* living."
"*Little* faith" is but a poor offering to bring to Christ: but if the trembling and anxious soul can *only* bring that, " it is accepted *according to what a man hath*, and not according to what he hath not."
Our *treasury offerings* to the sanctuary, our *working energies* in Christian service, our talents for *speaking to others* for Christ, or in *prayers* to God for blessing on sacred work; all stand on this divine principle, "such as he be able." Then the sacrifices will be welcomed, and the soul admitted into all the fellowship and felicities of grace. [Addenda to chap. xiv., *Poverty*.]

Topic: Purity in the House (Vv. 34-53).

It awakes wonder that leprosy could cling to the walls, could fix itself upon the very stones of a house, in some cases defying purgation, necessitating, therefore, the demolition of the structure and the casting out of all its fouled materials into an unclean place. The precautions here so expressly given show the *danger*, and denote that *God abhorred house defilement* equally with uncleanness in the human person. It is not alone that "*sinners* shall not dwell in His sight " (Psa. v. 4, 5), but unclean *things* were revolting to Him—"*whatsoever* (as well as *who*soever) worketh abomination or maketh a lie " (Rev. xxi. 27) is hateful to Him. So God is *emphatic in condemnation* of any *defiling thing in His people's abodes*. Themselves clean, their *homes must be pure*.
1. Household cleanliness should distinguish the abodes of the good.
1. Surely a *pure mind will express itself in scrupulous cleanliness in its surroundings*. Virtue and piety are as sensitive plants, recoiling from every physical uncleanness.
Burns speaks of the devout Cotter's return to
His *clean hearth-stane*, his thrifty wifie's smile.
Goldsmith marks the Traveller's delight as
His loved partner, boastful of her hoard,
Displays her *cleanly platter* on the board.
It would prove a pleasing study to note how *character may be tested* by such minute domestic purities.
2. Certainly the *cleanliness of a home reflects its influence upon those who dwell therein*. If the occupants' purity stamps itself on the house, the condition of the house casts back impressions of the occupant.
Thomson says:
Even from the body's purity, the mind
Receives a secret sympathetic aid.
And not less so from the purity of home scenes.
3. The *motive to such cleanliness* will be with the Christian a *regard for God's*

approval. What care would not Martha feel that every spot and article in her Bethany home should be spotless and bright, knowing that the Lord Jesus might be there any hour as a Guest. Cleanliness is fostered by a spirit of reverence.

> A servant with this clause,
> Makes drudgery divine;
> Who sweeps a room as *for Thy laws,*
> Makes that and th' action fine.—*Geo. Herbert.*

4. *Such care for simple home satisfactions* renders the dwellings *delightful* to its inmates. It is the sense of the purity and the carefulness which we find at home that leads us to rest so confidingly there. Suspicion and detraction may disturb thought and spoil enjoyment when in scenes which love and piety have not made sweet for us; but all is good and genial at home. "No little room so warm and bright" (Tennyson) anywhere in the great world, as that where gentle hands have made all so satisfactory for us.

And though, as the French proverb affirms, "to every bird its nest is fair," yet it is not easy to believe it fair if the nest be fouled.

> The sober comfort, all the peace which springs
> From the large aggregate of little things;
> On these small cares of daughter, wife, or friend,
> The almost sacred joys of home depend.—HANNAH MORE.

II. HOME SANCTITIES WILL BE SCRUPULOUSLY MAINTAINED BY THE GODLY.

1. *Impurities would force entrance into the homes of God's people still.* Not leprous spots cleaving to the structure, but *moral* plague spots and *intellectual* defilements. Nude *art,* and sensuous pictures, and indecent drawings, by which incautious parents adorn their rooms; *books* and magazines, containing articles and stories in which there is a taint upon virtue, or a sneer against truth, are recklessly laid upon the table, because it is fashionable to subscribe for such literature. *Companionships* press into our family enclosure, which it is difficult to refuse; friendships which are desirable for wordly ends are allowed in Christian households, but whereby is fulfilled the warning, "evil communications corrupt good manners." Verily in all such cases "it seemeth to me there is, as it were, a plague in the house" (v. 25).

2. *Devout minds will resolutely cleanse from the family all such defilements.* It would not be easy or pleasant work to "*empty* the house" (v. 36), to "*take away the stones in which the plague is*" (v. 40), to "have the house scraped within round about" (v. 41); but the work has to be rigorously done in the name of God! "*Abhor that which is evil!*" giving no assent or connivance to what may defile. *Duty,* not agreeableness, is the Christian's law. Parents are home-guardians. The husband is the *house band.* There may be no looseness in the keeping of the home. "If any provide not for his own house, he hath denied the faith, and is worse than an infidel" (1 Tim. v. 8).

Home has been designated "Heaven's fallen sister"; and it is—where pure and hallowed—the nearest similitude to Heaven. To Adam, paradise was home; to the Christian, home should be paradise. Let there be unsullied purity in the house.

> Around each pure, domestic shrine,
> Bright flowers of Eden bloom and twine,
> Our hearths are altars all.—KEBLE.

III. HABITATIONS INCURABLY DEFILED ARE DESTINED TO DESTRUCTION.

There is no alternative. If the plague cannot be arrested and removed, the habitation must be demolished; "he shall *break down the house*" (v. 45).

1. *Destroyed habitations;* let them warn against the faintest beginnings of error and sin, against the connivance of the slightest dereliction from sanctity. Wrong works ruin! Purest homes have become devastated by incautious inattention to small impieties. If a house is to be saved, sin must be out-barred.

2 *Sanctified homes.* Evil may be purged (v. 49). Ask *holy visitants* to come

in; not "priests" now, but the presence of the good, the virtuous, the Christian, and let the *atoning blood* (v. 50) have application, and "the *running water*" of God's word, the living stream of sacred truth, be used. There is remedy for home defects and defilements; and the doom of a family may be averted, the "salvation of a house" (Luke xix. 9) may be secured, by the admission therein of the Saviour Himself, and the graces of His kingdom, the agencies of religion, and the sanctifying influence of family prayer and Scripture reading; for so the plague shall be expelled, and the house "shall be clean" (v. 53). [Addenda to chap. xiv., *Home.*]

OUTLINES OF VERSES ON CHAPTER XIV.

V. 2.—*Theme:* CLEANSING THE LEPER. "This is the law of the leper in the day of his cleansing: he shall be brought unto the priest."

Consider—

I. THE DISEASE.

1. *Its peculiar designation.* Leprosy the "plague of boils" (Deut. xxviii.), which applies very forcibly to sin.

2. *Its distinguishing characteristics.* Small in appearance; so in a vicious course of life. It *gradually spread,* as does sin spread over all the powers and faculties of a man.

3. *Its pernicious consequences.* The malady was injurious to *society,* as being infectious and pernicious; to the *person himself,* excluding him from all society, civil and religious. So sinners corrupt others, while their abominable ways shut them from the communion of the faithful.

II. THE CURE OF THE DISEASE.

1. *No human means could be availing.* The leper would gladly have cured himself. No art of man was effectual (2 Kings v. 7). We have no remedy of man's devising for sin (Rom. vii. 19, 24).

2. If the leper was cured, it was *by God alone, without the intervention of human means.* Comp. Luke xvii. 14; Isa. li. 7. Nothing was prescribed or attempted for the removal of this distemper. And none but God can remove sin, etc. Rom. vii. 10, 18; Ephes. v. 9; 1 Pet. ii. 2.

3. *But the cure was associated with blood and water.* And to be cleansed from the leprosy of sin we must have applied the blood and spirit of Christ (1 John i. 7; Ezek. xxxvi. 25).

II. THE CONFIRMATION OF THE CURE BY THE PRIEST.

1. A person was *not to be pronounced clean on a sudden.* The priest was to use much caution and deliberation. *Caution* should be exercised by ministers and office bearers in the church towards those who are candidates for fellowship.

2. *When it evidently appeared that soundness had been imparted* to his disordered body, this was *declared with due solemnity.* Here we see the pre-eminence of our High Priest; for while the priest merely *declared* the leper healed He most effectually heals.

Let those *infected* with the leprosy apply to their souls the divinely appointed remedy; and—

Let those who have been *cleansed* from it carefully discharge the duty enjoined on them (v. 10, etc.).—*W. Sleigh.*

V. 3 *Theme:* DIVINE COMPASSION EXHIBITED.

The lonely leper, desiring an audience with the priest, would go towards the camp, and wait for the opportunity to present his case. The priest, ascertaining that his services were required, would go forth out of the camp, and discharge his duty. This would indicate that the condition of the leper—

I. THOUGH HELPLESS WAS NOT HOPELESS.

He could not cure himself—no mortal man could cure him, but the priest, as *medium* of communication from heaven, could be the *channel* of cleansing. Helpless in the presence of men, he was hopeful in the presence of the Lord. So, sinners, reprobated by their fellows, are renewed and restored by their Maker. The condition of the leper—

II. THOUGH REPULSIVE WAS NOT IRRECOVERABLE.

He was shunned by society, and branded as unclean; but the priest came out of the camp and met him, showing that Jehovah had not given him up, was not unwilling to heal him. God, by sending His dear Son into our world, has come forth to meet us, not to speak from a distance, and treat us as reprobates, but He has come *close to us, touched us, worn* our humanity, that we may be healed. Here, indeed, is divine compassion; meeting us, not in disdain or to destroy, but to sanctify and save.—*F. W. B*

V. 4.—*Theme:* A TYPE OF REDEMPTION.

Though the rite prescribed here was to be observed *after* the leper was cured, yet it may be regarded as typical of the offering made for the removal of sin from the soul of man.

I. THE LEPER'S CLEANSING WAS PROCURED BY—

(*a*) *Infliction of death.* Two live, clean birds brought to priest; one of them killed, its blood sprinkled on leper to be cleansed, seven times. Through sacrifice of life of

Christ, through His blood, we have forgiveness of sins.

(*b*) *Victory over death.* The living bird after being dipped in the blood of the slain bird was let loose in the open field. Here we get, if not type—yet illustration, of conquest *over* the grave by Him who bare our sins in His own body on the tree.

II. THE LEPER'S CLEANSING WAS COMMUNICATED BY—

(*a*) *Personal application.* The blood was sprinkled *upon* the person to be cleansed. So, nothing short of actual contact with virtue of Christ's death will cleanse from sin.

(*b*) *Repeated application.* The blood was sprinkled *seven* times, to denote that the cure was thorough and complete. We need the constant application of the merits of Christ's sacrifice to remove the guilt we are constantly contracting from contact with a sinful world, and the uprising of remaining depravity in our hearts.

Thus, coming to the priest, and submitting to the ordinance of cleansing, the leper would be taught—

(1) *Humility.* He would be deeply impressed with his corruption and unworthiness.

(2) *Gratitude.* That God had devised means whereby so helpless a condition might be met, so miserable a state be changed.

(3) *Responsibility.* If cleansed thus he would be a new creature; expected to live a new life; under lasting obligation to Him who had given the healing. So, in redemption; those who are saved are taught humility, gratitude, consecration. "Ye are not your own," etc.—*F. W. B.*

Vv. 8, 9.—*Theme:* SANCTIFICATION.

Personal efforts of the leper for himself to follow services performed for him by the priest. He to co-operate with the divine means employed. In directions given, means of sanctification are suggested, such as—

I. PURIFICATION OF ASSOCIATIONS. Leper to "wash his clothes."

II. MORTIFICATION OF SELF. "Shave off all his hair."

III. MEASURES OF REFORM. "Wash his flesh in water."

IV. SCRUPULOUS SELF-EXAMINATION. "Tarry out of his tent seven days."

V. CONGENIAL SOCIETY. When cleansed, the leper was restored to the worship of the tabernacle, publicly presented at the door before the Lord. He was then allowed to mingle with the sacred and social life of the nation.

Sanctification, a *progressive* work. We are "*being saved*" in this life. Our complete purification hinges on perseverance in use of divinely appointed means. Constant circumspection and introspection essential. Sanctification on earth culminates in presentation before the presence of the Lord in heaven, without spot or wrinkle or any such thing.—*F. W. B.*

Vv. 21, 22.—*Theme:* NO EXCUSE FOR NEGLECTING MEANS OF CLEANSING.

As in other rites, provision is here made, so that even the poorest were not shut out from ordinance of healing, so that none could make excuse in justification of neglect. There was—

I. GRADATION IN THE OFFERINGS. The leper was to offer "such as he could get." God does not expect more than we can do. He demands the best we can offer; if we offer our best He accepts it.

II. EQUALITY IN THE OFFERERS. Whatever they brought they all stood upon a moral level before Jehovah. He makes no distinctions, in the bestowment of His mercy, between rich and poor.

III. COMPLETENESS IN THE RECOVERY. The smallness and poverty of the offering did not hinder a full blessing coming on the leper; all alike pronounced clean when conditions complied with. The merits of Christ's sacrifice more than make up for any defects and deficiencies in our services. Though we and our works are less than nothing, He is all and in all.—*F. W. B.*

Vv. 17, 25, 28, 29.—*Theme:* COMPLETENESS OF CLEANSING.

The leper was not only cleansed from defilement, delivered from past disabilities, but introduced to a new life. He is now the servant of Jehovah, and expected to enter into solemn covenant with Him. There was to be henceforth—

I. DEVOUT ATTENTION TO DIVINE COMMANDS. The "right ear" of the cleansed leper touched with blood and oil.

II. ENERGETIC SERVICE. The "right hand" touched, etc.

III. READY OBEDIENCE. The "right foot" touched, etc.

IV. INTELLIGENT CONSECRATION. "Oil poured upon the head." Thus all our powers should be set apart for the service and glory of Him who has interposed to save us, and who sets us apart as His peculiar people by the washing of regeneration and renewing of the Holy Ghost.—*F. W. B.*

Vv. 33, 34.—*Theme:* LEPROUS HOUSES.

Material things not evil in themselves, yet, since the Fall, they have often become vehicles of contamination, incentives to depravity. Man has disfigured the world and made it like a leprous house, so that "the whole creation groans and travails" on account of sin, syren songs are sung to beguile the unwary, and wrecking lights are held out from scenes which appear both beautiful and safe. The leprosy of lewdness, licentiousness, cling to many a dwelling in the midst even of civilised Christian society. Thus—

I. THE WORLD—AS THE HOUSE OF OUR RACE—HAS BECOME LEPROUS. Let us beware of its tempting, tainting influences.

II. THE BODY—AS THE HOUSE OF THE SOUL—HAS BECOME LEPROUS. It contains not only seeds of mortality, but of depravity. Corruption clings to all its issues and powers. The world will be purified by the final wrecking fires; the vile body of our mortality is to be changed by our risen Lord, if we live and die to Him.—*F. W. B*

Vv. 45-49.—*Theme:* DEPRAVED SURROUNDINGS TO BE DEMOLISHED.

Every effort was to be made to effect the complete cleansing of leprous houses; such efforts failing, the houses were to be pulled down and the materials carried to an unclean place without the city. So—

I. STRENUOUS EFFORTS SHOULD BE MADE TO PURIFY CORRUPT SURROUNDINGS. In the *world;* our own *homes;* in our *bodies;* in our *hearts.*

II. COMPLETE DESTRUCTION MUST ENSUE WHERE CORRUPTION IS INCURABLE. At length the house was demolished, to prevent spread of infection, to show hatefulness of corruption. So, in the end, when period of probation is over, all uncured depravity will be removed to an unclean place; the finally impure, even in surroundings, will be destroyed. Purity shall ultimately triumph over corruption, and happiness over misery.—*F. W. B.*

ILLUSTRATIVE ADDENDA TO CHAPTER XIV.

HELPLESSNESS.

A physician, attending a Christian patient, became concerned to gain such spiritual assurance and joy in Christ as the sufferer manifested, and asked how it might be secured. He replied:
"Doctor, I have felt that I could *do nothing*, and so I have put my case in your hands; I am *trusting in you.*"

He saw the simplicity of the way, absolute helplessness, but absolute trust in Christ; and he found peace therein.

"Lord, save me from my sin;
Thine is the work alone;
Come to this erring soul of mine
And make that power known."
—OFFORD.

CLEANSED.

"His garb was simple, and his sandals worn;
His stature modelled with a perfect grace;
His countenance the impress of a God.
. . . .
He looked on Helon earnestly awhile,
As if His heart were moved; and stooping down
He took a little water in His hand
And laved the sufferer's brow, and said,
'Be clean!'
And lo! the scales fell from him, and his blood
Coursed with delicious coolness through his veins,
And his dry palms grew moist, and on his lips
The dewy softness of an infant's stole.
His *leprosy was cleansed;* and he fell down
Prostrate at Jesus' feet, and worshipp'd Him."
—WILLIS: *Room for the Leper.*

SANCTIFICATION.

"Justification regards something done *for* us; *sanctification*, something done *in* us. The one is a change in our state, the other in our nature. The one is perfect, the other gradual. The one is derived from obedience to the Saviour, the other from His Spirit. The one gives a title to heaven, the other a meetness for it. Suppose you had a son; you forbade him to enter a place of contagion on pain of losing all you could leave him. He goes, and is seized with the infection. He is guilty, for he had transgressed your command; but he is also *diseased.* Do you not perceive that your *forgiving* him does not *heal him?* He wants not only the father's pardon, but the physician's aid. In vain is he freed from the forfeiture of his estate, if he be left under the force of the disorder."—JAY.

"Who would be cleansed from every sin
Must to God's holy altar bring
The whole of life—its joys, its tears,
Its hopes, its loves, its powers, its years,
The will, and every cherished thing."
—ALLIE.

PROGRESS.

"Flying birds are never taken in the fowler's snare."—SECKER.

"He never was so good as he should be, who does not strive to be better than he is."—WARWICK.

"It is so with all climbing: Every upward step makes another needful; and so we must go on until we reach heaven, the summit of the aspiration of time."—H. W. BEECHER

"All growth that is not growth towards God
Is growing to decay."—GEO. MACDONALD.

POVERTY: THE SAINTLY POOR.

"The shell may be coarse which encloses the pearl. An iron safe may hold treasures of gold. A broken frame may contain the most beautiful picture. Poor believers may be rich Christians."—BOWES.

"There was no part of creature-holiness that I had so great a sense of the loveliness of as humility, brokenness of heart, and poverty of spirit; and there was nothing that I so earnestly longed for. My heart panted after this—to be before God as in the dust; that I might be as nothing, and that God might be *All;* that I might become a little child.'"—EDWARDS.

"The Emperor heard that the *treasures of the Church* had been confided to St. Laurence; he was brought before the tribunal and required to confess where those treasures were concealed. He answered that in three days he would show them. On the third day St. Laurence gathered together the sick and the poor, to whom he had dispensed alms, and placing them before the tribunal said, "Behold! here are the *treasures of Christ's Church*."

"God's riches to my soul be given,
And 'tis enough for earth and heaven!"
—HANS SACHS.

"That life on earth may be the best
In which by want the soul is tried;
For He whose word is ever sure,
Hath said that 'Blessed are the poor.'"
—WELD.

HOME.
"A man's house should be on the hill-top of cherfulness and serenity; so high that no shadows rest upon it; and where the morning comes so early and the evening tarries so late that the day has twice as many golden hours as those of other scenes Home should be the centre of joy."—BEECHER.

"Oh, happy home! oh, home supremely blest,
Where Thou, Lord Jesus Christ, art entertained
As the most welcome and beloved guest,
With true devotion and with love unfeigned;
Where all hearts beat in unison with Thine,
Where eyes grow brighter as they look on Thee,
Where all are ready at the slightest sign
To do Thy will, and do it heartily."

CHAPTER XV.

Secret Physical Impurities.

SUGGESTIVE READINGS.

Secret impurities, whether of men or women, are carefully discriminated here as resulting from guilty sexual intercourse, and as the effect of natural infirmity. God has stern thoughts for the licentious, He brands him as polluted and polluting, and interdicts from all privileges those who have become basely defiled.

Yet even where no moral vileness attaches to the uncleanness, where the impurity is the consequence of physical weakness and natural processes, God enforces exclusion. For although the Lord is very pitiful to our weaknesses, "knows our frame, and remembers that we are dust," commiserates our secret maladies, and "breaks not the bruised reed," nevertheless, only the clean can be allowed free enjoyment of social and spiritual favours within the camp and congregation of His "holy nation."

Considering even the sanitary value of these prohibitions and laws we discern God's wisdom and benignity, for they placed the ban on self-destroying indulgences and arrested contamination of loathsome diseases. But as a witness to the necessity of moral and spiritual purity in the person and habits of God's people these restrictions are full of significance. "Cleanse thou me from *secret faults*."

HOMILETIC HINTS.

I **The distressing vileness of fallen human nature.** An ever-flowing stream of uncleanness. While unsanctified by grace, not only is it true concerning the "vile body" that "in us, that is in our flesh, dwelleth no good thing," but all its habits and infirmities are corrupt and corrupting. What occasion is left for "glorying in the flesh"? Let those who vaunt the dignity of human nature see its revolting side in this chapter. Then "every mouth shall be stopped, and all become guilty before God."

II. **The stainless sanctity required in God's presence.** Any soil, stain, or mark of impurity must close the unclean from coming near where He dwells. Jehovah had associated Himself with this people, was in their midst; and as He could not bear defilement He insists on the most rigorous sanctity, in their persons, their privacy, their homes, their worship. It carries its appeal to us that we "perfect holiness in the fear of God." "Wash you, make you clean, put away your evil from before mine eyes."

III. **The bounteous provisions made for the sinner's cleansing.** The redeeming blood and purifying water are again available · *atonement* through Christ, and *sanctification* through the Spirit and the Word; these are efficacious for even vilest stains and most loathsome impurities.

Thus, while "in the body," whose every habit and infirmity affirms its natural corruptness, we can hope for renewing grace through the redemption and washing which the gospel offers to all who will "wash and be clean."

"*We have the blood of Christ!*" said Schliermacher, and so passed away to glory.

NOTES.

i. *Indecencies* both shock a virtuous mind, and are signally offensive to Divine Holiness.

ii. *The human frame*, formed for noble uses, may be most basely degraded by forbidden indulgences.

iii. *Low passions*, if allowed sway, inflict miseries on others, entailing them in the humiliation of communicated uncleanness.

iv. *Hidden* physical impurities are as minutely marked by the Omniscient Eye as are the flagrant leprous taints.

v. A more emphatic *loathing* is noticeable in God's denunciation of these secret sexual uncleannesses than of any other forms of human defilement.

vi. Our *Lord's healing* of the woman's secret malady (Mark v. 25 27) may be allowed to denote the *Source of help* to all who ask deliverance from corrupting weaknesses and vicious tendencies.

vii. Infinite pity has provided expiation for, and cleansing from, even our basest sins, equally as for our natural infirmities.

SECTIONAL HOMILIES.

Topic: THE ODIOUSNESS OF PERSONAL IMPURITY (Vv. 1-14, 19-27).

These regulations, which at first sight may appear *indelicate* and *unnecessary*, were "holy, just and true." Among the licentious idolatrous Egyptians Israel was to become a model for purity; no secret sin of any kind tolerated among them. Laws necessary to the physical and moral well-being of the whole nation ought not to be considered offensive. A vast multitude was to be conducted through the wilderness with a crowded encampment of tents. Nothing, in such a case, would keep them pure and make social life tolerable but such rigid legislation as the Mosaic regulations enjoined. These regulations:

I. ASSERTED THE NEED OF SCRUPULOUS PERSONAL PURITY.

Not only were the people to be on their guard against diseases such as leprosy, which revealed itself by outward manifestations, but against *secret impurities* which might be known only to the persons suffering therefrom.

Thus the encampment of the wilderness would be kept from degenerating into a hotbed of impurity and disease. Into whatever flagrant sins the Jews as a nation fell, they never became notorious for impurity or immorality, and, to this day, the ranks of the licentious are conspicuously free from members of the family of Abraham. The gospel is not less rigid in its demands for personal purity; indeed, it probes the moral nature of man more deeply, and demands purity of thought and desire as well as of word and deed. *Unaccomplished vicious purposes* are regarded as performed. The gospel condemns every species of impurity that would defile the body, and teaches higher morality than the ceremonial law ever reached.

II. SUGGESTED THE NEED OF COMPLETE MORAL SPOTLESSNESS.

Having to *repair to the priest;* and, when cleansed, *to appear before the Lord*, would naturally suggest to the mind the necessity of absolute purity of heart in the service of Jehovah. He who demanded the complete removal of all pollution from the physical frame, must require truth and purity in the human heart. All sin is a diseased and wasteful outflowing of the vitality of the soul. As none were too impure to apply to the priest, no case so desperate but might be cured, so the vilest of the vile may repair to our Great High Priest, who is able and willing to save to *the uttermost of human need, in all the world, through all time.—F. W. B.*

Topic: THE CONSEQUENCES OF PERSONAL IMPURITY (Vv. 13-18, 28-33).

The laws of nature cannot be set aside, or perverted, without the infliction of penalties upon the delinquent. This world is *a* place, though not *the* place of punishment for sin. Impurity of life entails *weakness, suffering, shame;* disgrace and deprivation were the penalty borne by those ceremonially defiled, teaching us—

I. THAT PERSONAL IMPURITY NATURALLY ENTAILS DISASTROUS CONSEQUENCES.

The body becomes deteriorated, the stamina reduced, when vices of a secret character work in the dark at the basis of life. *The mind* becomes enfeebled, *the soul* debased. The sensualist and impure carry the brand of their iniquity upon their countenance, signs of their immoral character in their gait. Personal impurity bars the gate to heaven! for there nothing that defileth or worketh abomination can enter. Its consequences extend to others; for morally unclean persons carry contamination wherever they go, as the law declared the unclean did in the cases before us. The Jews were taught that the slightest touch conveyed defilement; so, sinful influences, however apparently slight, vitiate and convey moral infection. Blessed be God we are taught—

II. THAT THE CONSEQUENCES OF PERSONAL IMPURITY MAY BE ARRESTED AND REMOVED.

Persons and *things* defiled by contact with the unclean could be cleansed by being bathed in water, and the presentation of two clean live birds for an atonement. Thus, not only the unclean persons could obtain cleansing, but the entail of their corrupt influences could be stayed. The stains of guilt, the course of sin, can only be arrested and removed by the intervention of the Lord. The consequences of sin in our *world* can only be counteracted by the sanctifying influences of the Holy Ghost, and the sacrificial life of the spotless Lamb of God.

Note 1: The Laws respecting *uncleanness* could *not have been invented by man;* for human nature does not voluntarily inflict penalties upon itself, does not bring its vices into the light of day, and arraign them at the bar of public opinion; for, "men love darkness rather than light because their deeds are evil."

Note 2: Instead of sin flowing secretly from our words and deeds, corrupting ourselves, and contaminating others, "*light*" *is to shine from us*, pure, cheerful, penetrating, divine. Thus shall our lives redound to the glory of God, and contribute towards the moral regeneration of our race.—*F. W. B.*

OUTLINES ON VERSES OF CHAPTER XV.

V. 2.—*Theme*: THE SECRET FLOW OF SIN. "When any man hath a running issue out of his flesh, because of his issue he is unclean."

Jehovah demands *purity of body*, as well as of *mind* and *heart*, in those who profess to be His people, and draw near to Him in sacred worship. Our bodies, not to be despised or neglected, but kept pure, *as the handiwork of God*, and *as the dwelling-place of the human soul*. The uncleanness here spoken of, probably the outcome of secret wantonness, or open licentiousness, or self-pollution. Secret sins, witnessed by no one but ourselves and God, vitiate the springs of life, and waste the substance of which our bodies are composed. Thus the Moral Governor of the universe has set His inevitable stigma upon all wrong-doing. By this statute we have suggested—

I. THAT SIN IS AN IMMORAL ISSUE FROM WITHIN MAN. *Not a complexion*, that may easily be changed; *not an excrescence*, that clings to the surface only; *but a radical defilement* issuing from the heart, which is the fountain of life. How disgusting and injurious sin is! How inveterate its hold upon our nature! Flowing from within, it often escapes detection, and defies all merely human remedies for its removal. "In us, that is in our flesh, there dwelleth no good thing;" when we would do good evil is present with us. Sin is not to be got rid of by change of scenery or society. Those who retreat from the world—*hermits, monks, nuns*, etc.—carry their evil propensities with them, and the secret flow of sin does not cease. However moral the *outward* life may be, out of the heart will flow *secret pride, unbelief, lust, evil thoughts*, which defile the soul and burden the conscience with guilt.

II. THAT SIN THUS POLLUTES EVERY THING IT COMES IN CONTACT WITH. Whatever the persons mentioned in this chapter touched became unclean; showing how exceedingly contagious the defilement was. So sin pollutes and transmits itself. Like a serpent, its trail is left wherever it goes. The *beauty* of the world, its *bounties* and *pleasures*, have been distorted and abused by the contaminating touch of sin. Let us pray to be kept from secret sins. Suggestions to evil come up the corridors of memory, flash from pictures in the chambers of imagination. Indulgence in secret impure desires will induce and excite the flow of moral evil from the heart, wasting the powers of the soul, corrupting every circle that it touches. Sin *indisposes* and *incapacitates* men for pure society and holy service.

If not stayed, consequence death. Blessed be God! sin has been atoned for, may be removed: death has been abolished, life and immortality brought to light by the gospel.—*F. W. B.*

V. 13.—*Theme*: THE RADICAL CURE OF SIN. "And when he that hath an issue is cleansed of his issue," etc.

Though the uncleanness here mentioned was so deeply rooted and virulent, yet it was curable; the persons cured were restored to their former positions in society, and declared whole in the presence of the Lord. We learn here—

I. THAT SIN CAN BE REMOVED ONLY THROUGH ATONEMENT. "The priest shall make an atonement for him before the Lord." The water and the blood that flowed seem to typify the fountain opened upon the cross in the Saviour's side. In every instance under the law where sin was to be forgiven some pure life had to be offered as an atonement, the innocent suffered as a substitute for the guilty. Thus the *roots* and *principles* of the gospel of Christ are found in the economy of Moses.

II. THAT THE REMOVAL OF SIN CAN ONLY BE COMPLETED BY SANCTIFICATION. The ablutions of the candidate for cleansing indicated that only by persistence in the means of grace, and thoroughness of dedication to the conditions of mercy, can we become sanctified. *At eventide* the cleansed person became clean; so, when life's day is over, and the shadows of death close upon the believer, the work of sanctification, which has progressed through the whole period of probation, will become complete; the "*vile body*" will be laid aside, the emancipated and immaculate spirit be "*present with the Lord*"

Obviously, contaminating influences may be communicated *unexpectedly* and *unintentionally*. What need to pray, as David did (Ps. li.), "Wash me throughly," etc. The writer of the Epistle to the Hebrews urged them to seek to have their "bodies washed with pure water, and their hearts sprinkled from an evil conscience." Christ can arrest the flow of sinful influences, as He stayed the issue of the poor sufferer, recorded Mark v. 29. The gospel dispenses with the burdensome ceremonials of the Law; but, all they pointed to is *preserved* and *fulfilled*, for "the blood of Jesus Christ cleanseth from all sin."—*F. W. B.*

ILLUSTRATIVE ADDENDA TO CHAPTER XV.

SECRESY.
" Go to your own bosom
Knock there: and ask your heart what it doth
know."—SHAKESPEARE.

SELF MASTERY.
" I will be lord over myself. No one who
cannot master himself is worthy to rule."—
GOETHE.

" A little fire is quickly trodden out:
Which, being suffered, rivers cannot quench."
—*Henry VI.*

PASSIONS.
' The passions may be humoured till they
become our master, as a horse may be pampered till he gets the better of his rider; but
early discipline will prevent mutiny and keep
the helm in the hands of reason."
—CUMBERLAND.

"His soul, like bark with rudder lost,
On passions' changeful tide was tost;
Nor vice, nor virtue, had the power
Beyond the impression of the hour;
And O! when passion rules, how rare
The hour that falls to Virtue's share!"
—SCOTT.

" No man's body is as strong as his appetite: but heaven has corrected the boundlessness of his voluptuous desires by stinting
his strength and contracting his capacities."
—TILLOTSON.

" What profits us that we from Heaven derive
A soul immortal; and with looks erect
Survey the stars; if, like the brutal kind,
We follow where our passions lead the way ?"
—CLAUDIAN.

VICE.
" Vice stings us even in our pleasures; but
virtue consoles us even in our pains "—COLTON

" Why is there no man who *confesses* his
vices? It is because he has not yet laid them
aside. It is a *waking* man only who can tell
his dreams."—SENECA.

" Men only feel the *smart*, but not the vice."
—POPE.

VIRTUE.
" Virtue that transgresses, is but patched
with sin;
But sin that amends, is but patched with virtue."—SHAKESPEARE, *Twelfth Night*, I, 3.

" Wisdom and virtue require a tutor;
though we can easily learn to be vicious without a master."—SENECA.

" God sure esteems the growth and completing of one virtuous person more than the
restraint of ten vicious."—MILTON.

" The soul's calm sunshine, and the heartfelt
joy,
Is virtue's prize."—*Essay on Man*, POPE.

CHAPTER XVI

The Great Day of Atonement.

SUGGESTIVE READINGS.

V. 2.—Come not at all times into the holy place within the veil. It was but natural that the solemn judgment which befel Nadab and Abihu " when they offered before the Lord and *died* " (v 1) should have rendered Aaron apprehensive lest he also might err in his ministries before Jehovah. God's message of direction, therefore, came to guide him in his sacred duties; for He will show the good and the right way to such as desire to do His will, albeit He is swift to rebuke those who adventure to act presumptuously in His sacred presence.

For I will appear in the cloud upon the mercy seat. Shall we not " stand in awe and sin not " where we know that God is present ? That " cloud " softened His exceeding glory, so as to allow the eye of mortal man to look and yet live;

and that "mercy-seat" suggested the divine pitifulness towards the sinner who desired to approach Him in reconciliation. Nevertheless, there might be no trifling, no profanity in His holy light; for God is severe as well as gracious. Man should fear before Him. And since there is no scene where God is not present, should we not cultivate reverence, and live as in readiness to meet Him? Within His house still there should be solemnity; His worship demands homage; "the Lord is in His holy temple." He will be gracious to the lowly and devout wherever they approach Him, shielding His great glory from them as with a "cloud" while they seek with supplications and offerings His "mercy seat."

V. 3.—Thus shall Aaron come into the holy place. Only "*once a year*"; on the august *Day of Atonement*. This restriction carried a pensive lesson: "that the way into the holiest of all was not yet made manifest"; that the hindrances to man's free approach to God had been only partially removed; that no provision was in existence for his abiding in the holy presence. Man might, by special arrangements of grace, enter where God dwelt, but he could not tarry there. Because atonement was not then complete; for types could not "take away sins" so satisfactorily as to qualify man for continuous nearness to God. Only in the perfect work of Jesus Christ can sinners gain abiding fitness for this highest privilege.

Sin offering and a burnt offering. These again meeting the twofold aspects of atonement (*vide* chaps. iv. and vi.); meeting every requirement of God's holiness and of man's guilt.

V. 4.—He shall put on the holy linen coat. Attired "in fine linen, clean and white" (Rev. xiv. 7, 8), symbolic of a blameless righteousness:—the inherent perfection and purity of Christ our High Priest, and the derived sanctity of His redeemed and priestly followers. Being divested of His glorious robes, and appearing simply in these "garments of righteousness," suggests to us our Lord's condition while He was engaged in making "atonement"; His majesty and splendour laid aside, but adorned with faultless sanctity and grace. Such meek purity became Him most while engaged in the sad work of atoning for human transgression and wrong.

Vv. 5-10.—Two kids of the goats: the one lot for the Lord and the other lot for the scapegoat. The two goats formed *one* sin offering God takes His share and is well pleased therewith; for there was a portion in Christ's sacrifice which was specially welcome to His Father, the perfect worthiness, the sweet subjection, the willing suffering of His Son—that was "*the Lord's lot*." The other part was for the sinner's release, removing from the transgressor the guilt and penalty of sin; and in the virtue of Christ's work through which we have "remission of sins" we find *the sinner's* "*lot*." "As far as the east is from the west so far hath he removed our transgressions from us" (Psa. ciii. 12).

Vv. 11-19.—The sin offering for priest, people, and sanctuary. The incidents were as follows; the young bullock was slain; while its blood was being gathered into a vessel Aaron entered within the veil carrying a censer of burning coals in his right hand and a platter of fragrant incense in his left; placing the burning coals at the foot of the Ark he cast the incense thereon and thus filled the Most Holy shrine with a soft cloud, thereby veiling the Ark from open vision: he then returned for the vessel of blood, and going again within the veil he sprinkled the Mercy Seat therewith, thus making atonement for his own sin and for his priestly associates; for the "sweet savour of Christ" and the "blood of sprinkling" are needed even for consecrated and priestly souls. Leaving the Holy of Holies, where the incense still burned, he offered on the altar the goat which had been allotted as the sacrifice for the *people's* sin, afterwards re-entering the veil to sprinkle also its blood of atonement upon and before the Ark. Thus three entrances were made that day into the Most Holy of All. No other priest was allowed within the tabernacle (v. 17) during these solemn incidents ; for unworthiness excluded every one, since " none doeth good and sinneth not." The faultlessly Divine Priest alone—typified in Aaron—might have access to where the Glory dwelt. With the sprinkling of blood Aaron also made atonement for the defilement of the sanctuary and the altar ; symbolically purifying them from all defilements which had incidentally accumulated through neglect or misdemeanour during the year. For uncleanness clings to our holiest things and our best deeds, and "almost all things are by the law purged with blood."

Vv. 20-22.—**The live goat.** Propitiation by *death* has been enacted in these first regulations. The *release of the living* is signified by the second typical arrangement. It pictorially shows us the *taking away of sin from the sinner* by his Substitute ; " behold the Lamb of God, which taketh away the sin of the world," but it also expresses the *removal from the believer's conscience* of the burden and grief of his transgressions—the confession of iniquities leading to their being carried into oblivion ; "the goat shall bear upon him all their iniquities into a land not inhabited." Glad remission indeed ! " Thou hast cast all my sins behind thy back " (Isa. xxxviii. 17) ; they are annulled by God ; and as for ourselves, " the worshippers once purged have no more conscience of sins " (Heb. x. 2) ; they are obliterated for the believer. And is *every* iniquity and transgression thus borne into forgetfulness ? Yes. " *All* their iniquities " (vv. 21, 22). This is remission of sins to the full ! Hence the " peace which passeth all understanding " ; for, " being justified by faith we have peace with God through our Lord Jesus Christ " (Rom. v. 1).

Vv. 23, 24.—**Aaron shall put off the linen garments.** The magnificent attire re-assumed by Aaron when the sin offerings were completed may remind us of the glory which did follow when our Lord had finished atonement ; He re-assumed His majesty ; though still, as High Priest for man in the heavenly sanctuary, He perpetuates sacrificial merits for His people. " **The fat of the sin offering,**" etc. (comp. iv. 10), the choicest virtues of our Redeemer's atonement still go up from the altar as a delightsome offering unto the Lord.

Vv. 29-34.—**A statute for ever unto you.** Every year the Day of Atonement should be solemnly set apart, and its ordinances devoutly observed. Such seasons for self-mortification, for severance from the affairs of this life, for concentrated attention to the needs of our souls and the claims of God, foster humility and reverence, bring eternal realities powerfully before our thoughts, and impress us with the preciousness of the Redeemer's work. Our peril is in habitual heedlessness ; we are borne on in the rush of secular concerns. The Lord's Day ought to bring us a healthful pause, enough to correct our worldliness and awaken to spiritual attention. But it is for our good that we check life's ensnaring routine, and secure an interlude in which to give supreme consideration to the wonders of God's redeeming grace and the urgency of our spiritual interests : " that ye may be clean from all your sins before the Lord " (v. 30) : "*it shall be a sabbath of rest unto you.*"

EXPLANATORY ARTICLE.

Concerning the Meaning of "Azazel," or the "Scapegoat" (V. 8).

"*And Aaron shall cast lots upon the two goats : one lot for the Lord (Heb. La-Jehovah), and the other lot for the scapegoat (Heb. La-Azazel).*"

In the eastern part of the Court of Priests in the Temple, *i.e.*, close to the worshippers, stood an urn, called *Calphi*, in which were two lots of the same shape, size, and material ; (in the second temple these were of gold) ; the one bore the inscription " la-Jehovah," for Jehovah,; the other " la-Azazel," for

Azazel. The two goats were placed with their backs to the people, and the faces toward the sanctuary (westward). The high priest now faced the people, shook the urn, thurst his two hands into it, drew out the two lots, laying one on the head of each goat. Popularly it was considered a good augury if the right hand lot had fallen "for Jehovah." The two goats must be altogether alike in appearance, size, and value. The lot having designated each of the two goats, the high priest tied a tongue-shaped piece of scarlet cloth to the horn of the goat "for Azazel," and around the throat of the goat "for Jehovah." The goat that was to be sent into the wilderness was now turned round face to the people, waiting, as it were, till their sins should be laid on him to carry them forth " to a land not inhabited." Afterwards the high priest, laying both his hands on the head of this goat, confessed and pleaded as follows :

"O Lord, the house of Israel Thy people have trespassed, rebelled, and sinned before Thee. I beseech thee, O Lord, forgive now their trespasses and sins which Thy people have committed, as it is written in the law of Moses, Thy servant, saying that in that day there shall be 'an atonement for you, to cleanse you, that you may be clean from all your sins before the Lord.'"

While the prostrate multitude worshipped at the name of JEHOVAH, the high priest turned his face towards them as he uttered the words " *Ye shall be cleansed,*" as if declaring to them the absolution and remission of their sins.

A strange scene was then witnessed; the priests led the sin burdened goat through " Solomon's porch," and, as tradition has it, through the eastern gate which opened upon the Mount of Olives. Here an arched bridge spanned the intervening valley, and over it they brought the goat to the Mount of Olives, where one, specially appointed for the purpose, took him in charge. Tradition enjoins that he should be a stranger, a non-Israelite. Scripture tells us no more of the destiny of the goat that bore upon him all the iniquity of the children of Israel than that they " shall send him away by the hand of a fit man into the wilderness " (v. 22), but tradition supplements this information.

The distance between Jerusalem and the beginning of " the wilderness " is computed at nearly 90 *stadia*, making precisely ten intervals, each half a Sabbath-day's journey from the other. At the end of each of these intervals there was a station, occupied by one or more persons detailed for the purpose, who offered refreshment to the man leading the goat, and then accompanied him to the next station. By this arrangement two results were secured : some trusted persons accompanied the goat all along his journey, and yet none of them walked more than a Sabbath day's journey. At last they reached the edge of the wilderness ; here they halted, and the attendant, viewing afar off, while the man led the goat forward, tore off half the scarlet tongue and stuck it on a projecting cliff; then, leading the animal backwards, he pushed it over the projecting ledge of rock.

If tradition be correct on this point it must have been a modern innovation, for originally the goat was set free.

There was a moment's pause, and the man, now defiled by contact with the sin-bearer, retraced his steps to the last of the ten stations, where he spent the rest of the day and night. But the arrival of the goat in the wilderness was immediately telegraphed by the waving of flags from station to station, so that in a few minutes after its occurence it was known in the temple.

In a subject so obscure great difference of opinion exists as to the significance of the word " Azazel " Those opinions most worthy of notice are : It is to be taken—

1. *As a designation of the goal itself.* Most old interpreters hold this view : regarding it as meaning the goat sent away, or let loose. In accordance with this the Vulgate renders it *Caper emissarius;* Luther, *der ledige Bock*; the Septuagint uses the term ὁ ἀποπομπαῖς applied to the goat itself. Theodoreb

and Cyril of Alexandria, consider the meaning of the Hebrew to be *the goat sent away*, and regard that as the sense of the word used in the Septuagint.

2. *As the name of the place to which the goat was sent.* Thus Vatlabus, Deyling, Kimchi, Abenezra, and others regard it as the desolate spot in the wilderness; Bochart and Carpvoz as any lonely place; and the Arabian version, some Rabbins, LeClerc and others, as " Mount Azaz," or the cliff down which the goat was thrown.

3. *As a personal being to whom the goat was sent.* They, Gesenius, Ewald, Rosenmüller, Dr. Wette, Knobel, and many of the Rabbins think that " Azazel " was an evil demon. Origen considers it was Satan. Spencer supposes the goat was given up to the devil, and committed to his disposal. Hengstenberg affirms very confidently that " Azazel " cannot possibly be anything but another name for Satan. He repudiates the notion that the goat was in any sense a sacrifice to Satan, but urges that it was *sent away laden with the sins of God's people*, now forgiven, in order *to mock their spiritual enemy* in the desert, his proper abode, and to symbolize by its free gambols *their exalting triumph*. He argues that the origin of the rite was Egyptian, and that the Jews substituted Satan for Typhon, whose dwelling was the desert.

4. The interpretation most harmonious with the scope of Scripture and with the nature of the service is that " Azazel " denotes " *a free going away*," or " *an entire and utter removal*." Michaelis and Jahn give the former rendering of the word, and Tholuck, Thompson, Bähr and Winer the latter.

Dr. Eudersheim (in his work, "*The Temple, its Ministry and Service*"), says, " The word *Azazel* is, by universal consent, derived from a root which means 'wholly to put aside,' or 'wholly to go away.' Whether, therefore, we render the la-Azazel by 'for him who is wholly put aside,' that is *the sin-bearing Christ*, or 'for being wholly separated,' or 'put wholly away, or aside,' that is, the putting away of sin, the truth is still the same, as pointing (1) to the *temporary and provisional removal of* sin by the goat 'let go' into 'the land not inhabited,' and (2) to the *final, real, and complete removal of sin* by the Lord Jesus Christ (Isa. liii. 6)."

And, as if to add to the significance of the rite, tradition has it that when the sacrifice was fully accepted, the scarlet mark which the scapegoat had borne became *white* (Isa. i. 18), but adds that this miracle did not take place for forty years before the destruction of Jerusalem.

" Smith's Dictionary " (see Day of Atonement) suggests that " the *slain goat* " should be viewed as setting forth the *act of sacrifice*, in giving up its own life for others " to Jehovah," in accordance with the requirements of divine law: and the *goat which carried off its load of sin* for " complete removal," as signifying the *cleansing influence of faith* in the sacrifice. . . . But for us the whole spiritual truth has been revealed in historic fact, in the life, death, and resurrection of Him who was made sin for us, who died for us, and rose again for our justification. This Mediator it was necessary should in some unspeakable manner unite death and life.

SECTIONAL HOMILIES.

Topic: A UNIQUE DAY IN ISRAEL (Vv. 2, 3).

I. A LAW OF SEPARATION: *Hindrances to abiding nearness to God.* " That he come not at all times into the holy place within the veil."

1. *God was enclosed from man* within that veil; man excluded from God: *sin's effect.*

2. *No permanent abiding place had been secured* for even the most privileged within God's presence; *atonement was not perfect* (Heb. x. 1-4).

3. *Perfection for man could not come of Levitical priesthood or sacrifices*: and the faulty, the unclean, could not abide in God's sight.

II. A LAW OF RECONCILIATION: *Atonement removing obstructions from between man and God.* Access within the veil effected, through—

1. *A spotless priest.* "These are holy garments" (v. 4). "Thus shall Aaron come into the holy place" (v. 3).

2. *The ample atonement.* "With *sin*-offering, and *burnt*-offering" (v. 3); satisfying all God's claims against the sinner; and sufficing for all man's guilt and requirements.

3. *Privileged recipients.* "Make atonement for himself and his house" (v. 6); representing the *Church* (Heb. iii. 6).

III. A LAW OF FELLOWSHIP: *Admission into the most sacred Presence.*

1. *By blood of sprinkling:* Evidence of substitutionary death. "Seven times" applied (v. 14): perfect redemption.

2. *By merits of the Saviour's grace;* sweet incense burned before the Lord (v. 12, 13): "*sweet savour of Christ.*" By the fragrant merits, by the precious blood of Christ, we may "*enter into the holiest.*" [See Addenda to chap. xvi., *Mercy Seat.*]

Topic: TYPICAL ENACTMENT OF ATONEMENT (V. 3, *seq.*).

Both the day and the observances were authorised of God (vv. 1, 2); both, therefore, divinely important. (1) In regard to the definiteness of the day. (2) In regard to the meaning and order of its ceremonies.

I. THE TYPICAL MEANING OF THE JEWISH ATONEMENT DAY.

1. The *divinely stated reason for its appointment* (v. 16).

(1) The fact of sin and the necessity for its expiation by blood, both unmistakeably and divinely declared. This is significant, as it bears upon the atonement of which this was only a type.

(2) Sin necessitates atonement if it is to be pardoned: "without shedding of blood there is no remission" (Heb. ix. 22).

 (*a*) Aaron's personal preparations typical of the purity and holiness of our Lord (v. 4: Heb. vii. 26).

 (*b*) Aaron's typical work (vv. 17, 18).

i. Our Lord was absolutely alone in His great atoning work.

ii. Though Aaron here typifies Christ, he must not himself forget that he is a sinner, and therefore must atone for his own sins. In this he was *not* a type of Christ (Heb. vii. 27).

(3) This fact bespeaks the antagonism of sin against the divine will, and the holiness and righteousness of the divine character.

2. *The divinely appointed measures for its observance.*

(1) In respect to the agent to carry out the measure.

 (*a*) It was not anyone who volunteered, but Aaron the priest (vv. 2-6).

 (*b*) So is the case of our Lord (Heb. v. 4, 5).

(2) In respect to the measures themselves.

iii. The blood of the sacrifice was sprinkled first upon the mercy seat eastward, and then before the mercy seat (v. 14), and then in the "holy place," and lastly upon "the altar that is before the Lord." Thus the atoning blood was sprinkled everywhere, from the throne of God within the veil to the altar which stood in the court of the tabernacle of the congregation (comp. Heb ix. 23-28).

iv. Now follows the typical act of releasing the live goat (vv. 20-22).

The two goats were designed to represent the two aspects of Christ's atonement: First, that on which "the Lord's lot" fell being doomed to death showed that the DEATH of Christ alone could vindicate the majesty, truth and holiness of the character of God. Secondly, the live goat over which Aaron confessed the people's sins, and thus typically was ordained to "bear upon him all their iniquities into a land not inhabited" (v. 22), signified the completeness of the divine act in the remission of the sins of him who, by confession and faith in Christ, transfers them to Him.

v. An instructive and significant scene follows (vv. 27, 28). The burnt offering represents consecration. Here, first, of our Lord; having atoned for our sins, He has consecrated Himself to His Father for His Church, to protect, guide, sympathise with, intercede for, and ultimately present her without spot unto the Father (Eph. v. 25-27; Jno. xiv. 3; Rom. viii. 34). Secondly, we have here represented the consecration of the believer.

vi. The perpetuity of this memorial.

PRACTICAL LESSONS.

1. The hatefulness, heinousness, and guiltiness of sin are here shown.
2. God's desire to provide for the removal of its guilt, and the prevention of its consequences demonstrated.
3. The comprehensiveness of the provision in the atonement.—*Rev. D. C. Hughes.*

Topic: THE SLAIN GOAT AND THE SCAPEGOAT (Vv. 8-10, 15, 16, 21, 22).

On this day many victims died. Each holy altar, each holy place received the reconciling sign of blood. Each sacrifice proclaims that substituted sufferings avail.

Christ, their full truth, has once laid down His life. That once is all-sufficient for all the sins of all His people.

But in the service of the atoning day one part stands singularly forth. Two goats are brought for a sin offering. The priest receives them at the tabernacle door. Lots are cast. Man's mind may not select. Some unseen hand takes one for death and bids the other live. This scene reveals the council of eternal love. Before the worlds, God's will called Jesus to the saving work. Each portion of the scheme was pre-resolved. Each was consigned to His receiving hands.

I. THE SENTENCED GOAT DIED; and mark the *uses of its blood.*

With this the high priest ventures within the mystic veil; the mercy seat receives the drops; the holy tent is strewn throughout; seven times the golden altar's horns are touched.

1. Blood is our peace. The wounded conscience writhes; sin is deepest misery. But when the Spirit shows the blood, all dread forebodings cease. It proves that peace is signed in heaven.
2. Blood has a sin-expelling power. How can that be loved which pierced the Lord?
3. Blood drives Satan back. Nothing can daunt him, no place exclude him, but this blood of Christ.
4. Blood bars the entrance to doom. A Christ-washed soul may not enter there.
5. Blood removes the hindrances to heaven. Behold the countless multitudes before the throne. "They have washed their robes and made them white in the blood of the Lamb."
6. The blood fills paradise with songs. This is the substance of their mighty anthem: "Thou wast slain," etc. They cannot sing above who have not washed on earth.

II. The laden goat is led away.

1. On its head is transmitted all Israel's guilt. The substitute receives the whole. The scapegoat takes the burden on its head.

2. It is borne by him afar; beyond the camp, beyond all sight, beyond the track of man. Unseen, unknown, forgotten, it departs from mortal view; buried in oblivion's land.

Faith knows this scapegoat well; there is no brighter picture of full pardon of all sin in Christ. Daily the soul tells out all its sin upon the head of Christ, who waits to bear it, and carry it far away. Christ hastens away with the accursed load, and God's all-searching eye finds it no more.

Is the east distant from the west? Can we move through the intervening space? As we advance the horizon still recedes; infinite separation divides. Thus far the scapegoat bears our guilt away (Psa. ciii. 12).

Can we recover what is buried in ocean depths? Such is the grave of sin (Micah vii. 19).

Are objects visible upon which the back is turned? Thus sins are hidden from God (Isa. xxxviii. 17).

How does a *mass of blackening clouds wrap the sky in a pall of impenetrable night!* Heed the voice of pardoning grace: "I have blotted out, as a thick cloud, thy transgression," etc. (Isa. xliv. 22).

No search finds His people's sins. A land of infinite forgetfulness conceals them (Jer. l. 20).

God's pledge stands. "I will remember their sin no more" (Jer. xxxi. 34). The scapegoat ordinance confirms the truth.

Ponder this ordinance. Sins, many, vile and hateful, pass to our Scapegoat, and so pass away. Faith transfers them; Christ removes them; God forgets them.

Have your hands touched the Scapegoat's head? If not, your loathsome load remains.—*Dean Law.*

Topic: Intercession of Christ (Vv. 12-14).

"*And he shall take a censer full of burning coals from off the altar, and his hands full of sweet incense and bring it within the veil.*"

We derive great advantage from being able to compare the Old Testament with the New. Since we see religion is essentially the same thing in all times and ages.

There are not two ways of acceptance with God: one under the law and another under the gospel—but one way for Jew and Gentile: "Jesus Christ the same yesterday, etc."

The fault of the Jews who entered not into the proper spirit of their own religion: that they valued the shell of their religion, but saw not the Pearl of great price. They fully estimated, perhaps over estimated the adornments of the casket, but certainly overlooked the bright Jewel within. They rejoiced in the pomp of their worship, the splendour of their ritual, the imposing grandeur of their sacrifices and the miraculous attestation that their religion came from God, but were strangely remiss in not discovering its real spirituality of design, and its intimate connection with the person and work of Christ. They cried "*The Temple of the Lord are we,*" but when the Lord of the Temple came, they treated Him with opposition and contempt. Had they been *good Jews,* they would have been good Christians. Our Lord implies this—"*If ye believed his writing* (marg.) *ye would have believed my words.*" If they had been true disciples of Moses they would have been of Christ.

Let us be warned, and pray that we may see the spiritual design both of their dispensation and of our own.

1. THE DOCTRINE OF THE INTERCESSION OF CHRIST.

i. *As typically exhibited under the law.*

Here Moses describes the ceremony of the great day of expiation and atonement. Aaron went into the most holy place to sprinkle the blood of the sacrifice before the mercy seat. No human being was permitted to accompany him. All the worshippers remained without (Luke i. 8, 9, 12). Aaron was to enter on behalf of the children of Israel—so that what he did within the veil was not merely on his own account but on theirs, all of which was a great type of Christ (Heb. ix. 11). He used *no words,* but what he did was significant enough. He appeared there that the virtue of the blood shed on the altar might be applied to the acceptance of the tribes he represented in the forgiveness of their sins, and the answer of their prayers. Herein a type of Christ.

2. *As actually fulfilled in Christ.* He not only suffered on the cross, but ascended. Not on His own account but ours.

It mainly consists in His presenting Himself before God in our nature, and in the merit of His finished atonement as the ground of our acceptance, and in the intimation of His will (in thought if not in words), that the purchased blessing of His salvation may be theirs, and that all law-charges and accusations against them may be hushed and cancelled.

"*To appear in the presence of God.*" Not for Himself but for us. Teaching us that His state of transcendant happiness has not removed Him to an inaccessible distance, and has neither dissolved nor impaired His gracious connection with us, but maintains, without any detraction from His own perfect bliss, the most generous sympathy with our interests and wants.

It puts a glory on His atonement—that everything is to pass through His hands. A shining testimony of the holiness of God, and the efficacy of Christ's work. No wonder if, having finished His work, He should appear above with large accessions of splendour to repossess the glory He had before all worlds. But here is the point of admiration, He does not appear for His benefit but *for ours.* Illustrated by common analogies:—as an advocate appears on behalf of his clients; a king on behalf of his subjects; a general as representative of his troops; a priest at the altar as representative of whole body of worshippers; so Christ appears as the representative of all His believing people. As our King He appears in beauty; as Captain of salvation appears victorious; as Elder Brother; as Priest, Counsellor, Advocate.

Grand expression of His *love.* Not *content* to offer one life on the Cross. He consecrates His new existence. Though raised to the throne of reverence, does not overlook His little flock (John xvii.).

II. THE BENEFITS WE DERIVE FROM IT.

i. *The forgiveness of our sins.* "If any man sin." After all done for us, we are guilty and undeserving. But while our sins are crying out against us on earth, Christ is pleading in heaven.

Every contrite sinner has liberty to apply by faith the merits of the atoning sacrifice. Nay, every sinner is condemned for not doing this. "*Whosoever cometh.*" But for this, our state would be less safe than under the law. Every Jew, to whatsoever tribe he belonged, might carry his sacrifice to the priest, and as he saw him enter the veil might say, "He is gone thither for me, sprinkled the Holy Place for me." So every Christian now.

ii. *Relief of our sorrows.* Christ possesses a capacity of sympathy, especially in mental distresses, tenderness of conscience, etc. Hannah prayed, but Eli's heart was not touched with feeling of her infirmity.

iii. *The acceptance of our duties.* These are maimed and imperfect. Enough evil in them to render them offensive and displeasing to God. But Christ presents them (Rev. viii. 2).

Your tears of penitence, labours of faith, songs of gratitude, vows of obedience,

He presents. Amid worship of angels, saints, and martyrs He disdains not to present the sighings of the prisoner, the tears of contrite, the prayers of the child whose mind is opening to devotion, and ejaculation of dying.

iv. *The frustration of spiritual enemies.* Satan is the avenger, but Christ is our advocate. " Peter, I have prayed for thee."—S. THODEY, A.D. 1840.

Topic: THE WORTH OF SACRIFICES (Vv. 16-30).

Of all the days of the Jewish year this was *The Day*, the meeting-time of God and man.

The priestly tribe could minister on all other days; none but the High Priest on this. No foot but his should press the floor of the sacred tent. Dressed in purest white, repeatedly cleansed with pure water, he entered—*one man for the nation*, into the holy of holies.

What did the elaborate ritual of the day mean? If divine forgiveness depended upon such a day, then why did the world wait for twenty-five hundred years before the Day's appointment? If absolutely necessary, why was not the day and its ritual enjoined upon Abraham, and even upon Adam in Paradise? What is the meaning of sacrifice? Observe—

1. *God's character is not changed by sacrifice.* He neither regards sin with less hatred, nor loves the sinner less in consequence. The burnt offerings and sacrifices of the centuries have not added jot or tittle to His immeasurable love. The sacrifice of Calvary was the natural outcome of the divine nature, rather than the means of changing that nature. This sacrifice, like all others, expressed His *change of attitude.*

2. *These mere sacrifices possessed no intrinsic value.* In themselves considered, sacrifices are a "vain oblation" (Isa. i. 13 ; comp. Mic. vi. 7 ; Psa. li. 16 ; Heb. x. 6). So, though thousands stood by the altar with their offerings, with a multitude of sacrifices, " It is not possible that the blood of bulls and of goats should take away sins."

Bearing these facts in mind, that the divine nature is unchanged by them, also that mere sacrifices are unpleasing to Him and powerless to take away sin ; what is their nature and history, and why commanded?

Of the 4,000 years ending with the Sacrifice of Calvary, 2,500 had passed ere sacrifices were instituted. God says by Jeremiah, " I spake not unto your fathers concerning burnt offerings and sacrifices" (Jer. vii. 22). They were instituted after the sinful worship of the golden calf at Sinai.

But the fact is evident that they were instituted because *there was a necessity:* yet since, as we have seen, it was *not a necessity on God's part*, it must have been for man's sake.

In the sacrifices of the Day of Atonement God proclaims eternal truths.

I. THE DIVINE TESTIMONY AGAINST SIN.

These were the chosen people whose God alone was holy. Yet behold the people all in abasement: it is the cry, "We have sinned!"

1. *Not one of all the people could offer a sacrifice:* not one was sinless: the high priest alone was allowed to act for them.

2. *One spot alone was sacred*, curtained with richest fabrics : and this one spot thus curtained was the divine rebuke against sin.

II. THE BASIS OF ATONEMENT.

Our sinfulness cannot change God's nature, although it changes His attitude towards us.

1. The whole sacrificial order of the Day of Atonement was *given for the cleansing from sin.* Just as Christ afterwards came to "save His people from their sins."

2. *Every sacrifice was one of blood*, from Abel's downward. Why? "The life of the flesh is in the blood, and I have given it you upon the altar to make an atonement for your soul."

3. This affirms that the *God of love must respect His holy law* even at the expense of death. These sacrifices were the elementary lessons declaring that by-and-by the law would be made honourable by the costliest of all sacrifices.

III. THE NECESSITY FOR A PERFECT HIGH PRIEST.

In silence, on that great silent Day, stood priests and people while the high priest entered the holy place and fulfilled his task.

1. *His unworthiness for such deeds* was impressed upon him every moment. He must offer sacrifices "for himself": then five times he washed his whole body, and ten times his hands and feet. He must lay aside his own garments and wear the whitest linen.

No imperfect man could become a perfect priest, any more than an imperfect sacrifice could give a perfect conscience. Salvation depends on a more perfect High Priest than Aaron.

2. *Our Great High Priest needed no such cleansing.* "He offered himself *without spot* to God."

Verily the Day of Atonement was the culminating day of Jewish history. Its sunrise was upon Sinai, its sunset upon Calvary. In the morning the people said to Moses, "Let not God speak to us lest we die!" but in the evening the surging crowd heard the sacred lips proclaim to a world longing for salvation, "IT IS FINISHED!"—*Rev. David O. Mears.*

Topic: FULL ATONEMENT.

"*This shall be an everlasting statute unto you, to make an atonement for the children of Israel for all their sins once a year*" (Levi. xvi. 34).

The day of atonement was pre-eminenently intended to typify that great day of vengeance of our God, which was also the great day of acceptance of our souls, when Jesus Christ "died, the just for the unjust, to bring us to God." That day of atonement happened only *once a year*, to teach us that only once should Jesus Christ die; and at a set and *appointed time*; not left to choice of Moses, or convenience of Aaron, but on a peculiar set day (v. 29), to show that God's great day of atonement was appointed and predestinated by Himself. Christ's expiation occurred but once, and then not by any chance; God had settled it from before the foundation of the world; and at that hour when God had predestinated, on the very day that God had decreed Christ should die, was He led like a lamb to the slaughter, and as a sheep before her shearers He was dumb.

I. THE PERSON WHO WAS TO MAKE THE ATONEMENT. *Aaron the high priest* did it. "Thus shall Aaron come into the holy place; with a young bullock for a sin offering and a lamb for a burnt offering." Inferior priests slaughtered lambs; other priests at other times did almost all the work of the sanctuary; but on this day nothing was done by any one, as a part of the business of the great day of atonement, except by the high priest. Old rabbinical traditions tell us that everything on that day was done by him, even the lighting of the candles, and the fires, and the incense, and all the offices that were required, and that, for a fortnight beforehand, he was obliged to go into the tabernacle to slaughter the bullocks and assist in the work of the priests and Levites, that he might be prepared to do the work which was unusual to him. All the labour was left to him. So Jesus Christ, the High Priest, and He only, works the atonement. There are other priests, for "he hath made *us* priests and kings unto God." Every Christian is a priest to offer sacrifice of prayer and praise unto God, but none save the high priest must offer atonement, go within the veil, slaughter the goat, and sprinkle the blood.

2. The high priest on this day was *a humbled priest*. "He shall put on the holy *linen* coat, and he shall have the linen breeches upon his flesh, and shall be girded with a linen girdle, and with the linen mitre shall he be attired ; these are holy garments" (v. 4). On other days he wore the golden garments ; the mitre with a plate of pure gold around his brow, tied with brillian blue ; the splendid breastplate, studded with gems, adorned with pure gold and set with precious stones ; the glorious ephod, the tinkling bells, and all the other ornaments wherewith he came before the people as the accepted high priest. But on this day he had none of them. On that day he humbled himself just as the people humbled themselves. Jesus Christ, when He made atonement, was a humbled priest. He did not make atonement arrayed in all the glories of His ancient throne in heaven. Upon His brow there was no diadem save the crown of thorns ; around Him was cast no purple robe, save that which He wore for a time in mockery ; on His head was no sceptre, save the reed which they thrust in cruel contempt upon Him. But oh ! adore Him, for it was the simple clean linen of His own humanity, in which He made atonement for your sins.

3. *A spotless high priest ;* and because there were none such to be found, Aaron had to sanctify himself and make atonement for his own sin before he could go in to make an atonement for the sins of the people (v. 3). Yea, more, before he went within the veil with the blood of the goat which was the atonement for the people, he had to go within the veil to make atonement there for himself (vv. 11-13). Aaron must not go within the veil until his sins had been typically expiated, nor even then without the burning smoking incense before his face, lest God should look on him and he should die, being an impure mortal. Moreover, it is said, that he had to wash himself many times that day (vv. 4, 24). So you see it was strictly provided for that Aaron on that day should be a spotless priest ; not so as to nature, but, ceremonially, care was taken that he should be clean. But we have a spotless High Priest, who needed no washing, needed no atonement for Himself ; needed no incense to wave before the mercy seat to hide the angry face of justice ; needed nothing to hide and shelter Him ; He was all pure and clean. Adore and love Him, the spotless High Priest, who, on the day of atonement, took away guilt.

4. The atonement was made by *a solitary high priest*—alone and unassisted. "And there shall be no man in the tabernacle of the congregation when he goeth in to make an atonement in the holy place" (v. 17). Matthew Henry observes, that no disciple died with Christ : when He was put to death His disciples forsook Him and fled ; they crucified none of His followers with Him, lest any should suppose that the disciple shared the honour of atonement. Thieves were crucified with Him because none would suspect that they could assist Him: but if a disciple had died, it might have been imagined that he had shared the atonement. God kept that holy circle of Calvary select to Christ. O glorious High Priest, Thou hast done it all alone. "I have trodden the wine-press alone, and of the people there was none with me." Then give all the glory unto His holy name, for alone and unassisted He made atonement for your guilt.

5. Again, it was a *laborious high priest* who did the work on that day. There were fifteen beasts which he slaughtered at different times, besides the other offices, which were all left to him. He who was ordained priest in Jeshurun, for that day toiled like a common Levite, worked as laboriously as priest could do, and far more so than on any ordinary day. Just so with our Lord Jesus Christ. Oh, what a labour the atonement was to Him ! It was a work that all the hands of the universe could not have accomplished ; yet He completed it alone. There was the bloody sweat in Gethsemane, the watching all night, then came the shame, the spitting, the cruel flagellations in Pilate's hall ; then there was the

via dolorosa through Jerusalem's sad streets; then came the hanging on the cross, with the weight of His people's sins on His shoulders. Ay, it was a divine labour that our great High Priest did on that day—a labour mightier than the making of the world: it was the new making of a world, the taking of its sins upon His almighty shoulders and casting them into the depths of the sea. Jesus, though He had toiled before, yet never worked as He did on that wondrous day of atonement.

II. THE MEANS WHEREBY THIS ATONEMENT WAS MADE.

"And he shall take of the congregation of the children of Israel two kids of the goats for a sin offering, and one ram for a burnt offering" (v. 5; see also vv. 7-10). The first is the type of the means whereby the atonement was made.

1. It answered all the pre-requisites of every other thing sacrificed; it must be *a perfect, unblemished goat of the first year*. Even so was our Lord a perfect man, in the prime and vigour of his manhood. And further, this goat was an eminent type of Christ from the fact that *it was taken of the congregation of the children of Israel* (v. 5). The public treasury furnished the goat. So Jesus Christ was, first of all, purchased by the public treasury of the Jewish people before He died. Thirty pieces of silver they had valued Him at, a goodly price; and as they had been accustomed to bring the goat, so they brought Him to be offered; not with the intention that He should be their sacrifice, but unwittingly they fulfilled this when they cried " Crucify Him!"

2. Though this goat, like the scapegoat, was brought by the people, *God's decision* was in it still. Mark, it is said, "Aaron shall cast lots upon the two goats; one lot for the Lord, and the other lot for the scapegoat." This mention of lots is to teach that although the Jews brought Jesus Christ of their own will to die, yet, Christ had been appointed to die. Christ's death was fore-ordained, and there was not only man's hand in it, but God's. "The lot is cast into the lap, but the whole disposing thereof is of the Lord." So it is true that man put Christ to death, but it was of the Lord's disposal that Jesus Christ was slaughtered, " the just for the unjust, to bring us to God."

3. Behold the goat marked out to make the atonement, and *see it die*. The priest stabs it. Mark it in its agonies; behold it struggling; observe the blood. Ye have here your Saviour. See His Father's vengeful sword sheathed in His heart; behold His death agonies. Mark the blood from His open side. As the blood of the goat made the atonement typically, so thy dying Saviour made the great atonement for thy sins.

4. That blood was *taken within the veil*, and there sprinkled. So with Jesus's blood, " Sprinkled now with blood the throne." The Saviour's blood has made atonement within the veil; He has taken it there himself. By this one offering atonement was made for ever.

III. We now come to the EFFECTS.

1. One of the first effects of the death of this goat was *the sanctification of the holy things which had been made unholy*. " He shall sprinkle it upon the mercy seat: and he shall make an atonement for the holy place," etc. (v. 15). Where God dwelt should be holy, but where man comes there must be some degree of unholiness. This blood of the goat made the unholy place holy. So of this sanctuary, our praises and our prayers, there is blood on them all; our holy Sabbath services have been sprinkled with the blood of the great Jesus, and as such they will be accepted through Him. Is it not sweet to reflect that our holy things are now really holy; that though sin is mixed with them all, and we think them defiled, yet the blood has washed out every stain: and our Sanctuary service is as holy in God's sight as the service of the cherubim, and is acceptable as the psalms of the glorified; we have washed our worship in the blood of the Lamb, and it is accepted through Him.

2. The second great fact was that *their sins were taken away*. This was set forth by the scapegoat. The first goat was a type of the atonement; the second is the type of the effect of the atonement. The second goat went away, after the first was slaughtered, carrying the sins of the people on its head, and so it sets forth, as a scapegoat, how our sins are carried away into the depths of the wilderness. But mark, this goat did not sacrificially make the atonement: it is the fruit of the atonement; but the sacrifice is the means of making it. So by the death of Christ there was full, free, perfect remission for all those whose sins are laid upon His head. For on this day all sins were laid on the scapegoat's head—sins of presumption, ignorance, uncleanness, sins little and sins great, sins against the law, morality, ceremonies, sins of all kinds were taken away on that great day of atonement.

3. An interesting fact is here worth mentioning. Turn to chap. xxv. 9, and you will read: "Then shalt thou cause the trumpet of *the jubilee* to sound on the tenth day of the seventh month, in the day of atonement shall ye make the trumpet sound throughout all your land." So one of the effects of the atonement was set forth to us, the scapegoat is gone and the sins are gone; and no sooner are they gone than the silver trumpet sounds.

> The year of jubilee is come,
> Return, ye ransomed sinners, home.

On that day sinners go free; on that day our poor mortgaged lands are liberated, and our poor estates which have been forfeited by our spiritual bankruptcy are all returned to us. So when Jesus dies, slaves win their liberty, and lost ones receive spiritual life again; when He dies, heaven, the long lost inheritance, is ours. Blessed day! Atonement and jubilee ought to go together. Have you ever had a jubilee in your hearts? If you have not, it is because you have not had a day of atonement.

4. One more effect of this great day of atonement: *entrance within the veil*. Only on one day in the year might the high priest enter within the veil, and then it must be for the great purposes of the atonement. Now, the atonement is finished, and you may enter within the veil; "Having boldness, therefore, to enter into the holiest, let us come with boldness unto the throne of the heavenly grace."

IV. What is OUR PROPER BEHAVIOUR WHEN WE CONSIDER THE DAY OF ATONEMENT.

1. "This shall be a statute for ever unto you: that in the seventh month, on the tenth day of the month, ye shall *afflict your souls*" (v. 29). That is one thing that we ought to do when we remember the atonement. Sure, sinner, there is nothing that should move thee to repentance like the thought of that great sacrifice of Christ which is necessary to wash away thy guilt. "Law and terrors do but harden," but methinks, the thought that Jesus died is enough to make us melt. It is well, when we hear the name of Calvary, always to shed a tear, for there is nothing that ought to make a sinner weep like the mention of the death of Jesus. On that day "ye shall afflict your souls." And even you, Christians, when you think that your Saviour died, should afflict your souls: ye should say,

> Alas! and did my Saviour bleed?
> And did my Sov'reign die?
> Would He devote that sacred head
> For such a worm as I?

Drops of grief ought to flow, to show our grief for what we did to pierce the Saviour. "Afflict your souls," weep for Him that died; weep for Him who was murdered by your sins.

2. Then, we are to "*do no work at all*" (v. 29). When we consider the atonement, we should rest, and "do no work at all." Rest from your works as God did from His on the great Sabbath of the world; rest from your own righteous-

ness; rest from your toilsome duties; rest in Him. "We that believe do enter into rest." No longer seek to save thyself; it is done, it is done for aye!

3. When the priest had made the atonement, after he had washed himself, he came *out again in his glorious garments* When the people saw him they attended him to his house with joy, and they offered burnt offerings of praise on that day: he being thankful that his life was spared, and they being thankful that the atonement was accepted; both of them offering burnt offerings as a type that they desired now to be "a living sacrifice, holy and acceptable unto God." Let us go into our houses with joy. The atonement is finished; the High Priest has laid aside the linen garments, and He stands before you with His breastplate, and His mitre, and His embroidered vest, in all His glory. How He rejoices over us, for He hath redeemed His people, and ransomed them out of the hands of His enemies. Come, let us go home with the High Priest; the atonement is accepted, and we are accepted too; the scapegoat is gone, our sins are gone with it. He hath given unto us a day of atonement, and a day of acceptance, and a year of jubilee.—*C. H. Spurgeon*, A.D. 1856 : *Abbreviated*.

Topic: THE DAY OF ATONEMENT (Vv. 1-5).

The Mosaic ritual here reaches a climacteric point. On this annual day of national expiation every kind of sin was confessed and atoned for, which might have escaped notice before. Propitiation being offered for the whole nation, all the people received forgiveness. The day gave all other days a deeper meaning, its rites interpreted and intensified all other ceremonies. Notice—

I. THE TIME; *when the day of atonement was instituted.* "After the death of the two sons of Aaron." (*a*) *It was just after a great catastrophe.* The fire of the Lord had flashed out, revealing the divine indignation against the reckless priests. Thus the Lord showed, that, though the workers may sin and die, the work must go on; that in the midst of deserved wrath He remembers mercy. (*b*) *It was just at a great crisis.* The Jewish theocracy was being consolidated, and those rites and ceremonies completed that would distinguish the Jews for ever from all other nations. The basis was being laid, broad and deep, for the operations of God to bless the world. All the light of nature and revelation, of the patriarchial dispensation and the human conscience, was centred in the day of atonement. (*c*) *It was just before a great career.* Israel had before them a great mission, they had been miraculously delivered from Egyptian bondage, were to pass the wilderness and enter the promised land. They were to be the custodians of the Word of God, and the representatives of real religion. Through them all the nations of the earth were to be blessed; with them Jehovah would dwell; by them, make Himself known to the world; and eventually through their posterity He would come, and in very deed would dwell with man on the earth.

II. THE PERSON *by whom the atonement was to be made.* "The Lord said unto Moses, speak unto Aaron thy brother," etc. Any of the priests could offer the daily sacrifices; but, the annual one could be offered by the high priest alone. For so great and distinguished an office (*a*) *a human agent was selected.* A man—feeble, sinful, sorrowful, and dying—Moses' brother, and a brother of the whole race. What dignity God puts on man! How He selects feeble agents to accomplish mighty results, and makes men co-workers with Himself in the most solemn and sublime engagements. (*b*) *A human agent was directed.* Moses—to convey directions about the duties Aaron should perform in connection with his high office. The Lord never calls men to work for Him without giving them, at the same time, *ability* to do it, and *directions* how to do it. Aaron but faintly foreshadowed our great High Priest; for Christ was God, as well as man, and needed not to be instructed. He knew the Father's will completely, and did it perfectly; and knew also what was in man, and needed for man.

III. THE SPIRIT *in which the person was to officiate.* Aaron was not to come at all times unto the holy place; so, he was to possess (*a*) *a reticent spirit.* His sons, who were slain before the Lord, had not restrained themselves, but rushed unbidden into the holy place; Aaron was to take warning by their fate, hold himself under restraint, not be too free and familiar with sacred things, even though he might be tempted to go into the holy of holies more than once a year. (*b*) *A devout spirit.* The most holy place was calculated to inspire the priests with reverent feelings. That it was to be entered but once a year would impress the mind of Aaron with religious awe, as well as the fact that, on entering, he had to attire himself in special vestments and offer specified sacrifices. The holy of holies was the audience chamber of the theocratic King, the seat and throne of the divine kingdom among men. The peculiar privilege of meeting God face to face once a year demanded the deepest solemnity and profoundest reverence. (*c*) *A sanctified spirit.* Not only was Aaron to feel becomingly reverent, when he offered the atonement, but he was also to possess a suitable disposition in other respects. He was commanded to lay aside his splendid pontifical robes, and attire himself in the simple sacerdotal garments of an ordinary Levite He did not appear now as the representative of the people simply, but as a sinful man seeking pardon for himself and the whole nation. The clean white linen in which he officiated would symbolise *purity;* and the complete washing before putting it on would represent *sanctity of character.*

When Christ came to our world to atone for men, He laid aside His glory and took upon Him the clean white garment of the virgin's nature; He came in a spirit that pleased God, that met all the requirements of the divine law, thereby securing a perfect and everlasting righteousness, which is unto all and upon all who believe.

IV. THE RESULTS *the officiator was to expect.* The Lord, always present in the cloud upon the mercy seat, had promised the people that on the day of atonement He would "*appear*" unto them. (*a*) *There would be the special manifestation of the divine presence.* Not in the cloud of incense ascending from the swinging censer in Aaron's hand, but in the supernatural cloud that did not waste away—did not change like other clouds; that was lighted up, not with rays of the natural sun, but with beams of divine brightness. The divine appearance was supernatural. (*b*) *There would be the mysterious manifestation of the divine presence.* The Lord would appear, but it would be in the cloud, His glory would be veiled; for no man could literally see His face and live. The Deity was to be seen "through a glass darkly." He was to be apprehended, but not comprehended. (*c*) *There would be the gracious manifestation of the divine presence.* It was upon "*the mercy seat*" that the Lord promised to appear. Had the Deity erected a judgment seat, instead, among the people, they would all, not only have been condemned, but speedily consumed. But the day of atonement would work propitiation, and win both pardon and peace.

If the gospel is in any part of the book of Leviticus, we have it here; and, read in the light of the ninth chapter of Hebrews we see the great atonement of the Redeemer foreshadowed in the ceremonies connected with this national day of expiation. Through Christ's atonement the veil has been rent in twain; we may now draw *near* to God, and *know* Him as our Father; for Christ was "the brightness of His glory, and the express image of His person." Through Him we have now received *the atonement.*—*F. W. B.*

Topic: AARON'S SIN OFFERING FOR HIMSELF (Vv. 5-14).

The holiness communicated and imputed to the high priest at his consecration, did not free him from liability to commit sin and incur guilt. Hence, **previous** to presenting an atonement for the sins of the whole nation Aaron was commanded to present a sin offering for himself and his house. He needed clean hands and a pure heart when entering into the most holy place. According to the word of the Lord so Aaron did. Observe—

I. *It was* AN OBEDIENT ACT. The bullock was to be taken and slain by the high priest's own hands, indicating ready and unquestioning acquiescence with the divine will. Such obedience is still indispensible to acceptable worship and sacrifice.

II. *It was* A FRAGRANT ACT. A censer full of burning coals, of the fire from off the altar of the Lord, was taken within the veil, and sweet incense, beaten small, put upon the fire, that its fragrance might fill the holy place.

III. *It was* A REVERENT ACT. The cloud of the incense was to cover the mercy-seat, that the offerer die not. He was not to gaze with unclouded eyes upon the place where God made Himself specially known. He was to be reminded of the infinite and unapproachable majesty, as well of the infinite meekness and mercy of Jehovah; and, that though privileged to draw near the mercy seat, he must worship with profound reverence.

IV. *It was* A SUPPLIANT ACT. The blood of the bullock was to be sprinkled upon the mercy seat, eastward, and before it, with his finger seven times. The incense would not only denote *cheerful* but also *expectant* worship, for it suggests the sweet and ascending nature of prayer. The blood sprinkled on and before the mercy seat would seem to cry for mercy; and indicate, not only *prayer*, but *propitiation*.—*F. W. B.*

Topic: AARON'S SACRIFICE COMPARED AND CONTRASTED WITH CHRIST'S.

I. ANALOGY.

(1) *Both were divinely appointed.* Aaron was chosen and anointed to be the high priest of Israel. Christ was set apart, and ordained as the High Priest of man, and " anointed with the oil of gladness above his fellows."

(2) *Both atoned " alone" on the great day of atonement.* No one was allowed to enter the most holy place with Aaron; and Christ " trod the winepress alone"; neither man, nor angels shared with Him the suffering and oblation of the cross.

(3) *Both were divinely accepted.* Assurances were given that the great oblation would be accepted; and, when offered, indications were vouchsafed that Jehovah was well pleased. Aaron's return from the solemn seclusion of the most holy place was proof he had pleased Jehovah; for unacceptable sacrifice would have been visited with death to the offerer. So, when Christ came from the darkness of the grave after His atonement it showed He was accepted, and Jehovah satisfied.

(4). *The blessings of both were discriminately dispensed.* The atoning blood only bedewed those who felt and confessed their guilt. So, while the atonement of Christ is sufficient for all, it is only efficient and applied where hearts are truly broken and contrite.

II. DISPARITY.

(1). *Aaron had to make the atonement once a year;* showing how imperfect and temporary the efficacy of his offering was; but *Christ offered His atonement once for ever*, never to be repealed or repeated.

(2). *Aaron atoned for himself,* needed to obtain pardon before he could atone for the people; but *Christ was " holy, harmless, undefiled, and separate from sinners,"* and *needed not to atone for Himself;* He " did no sin, neither was any deceit found in his mouth."

(3). *Aaron offered a sacrifice that was provided for him;* but Christ offered Him-

self; was both priest and victim; and it was the infinite dignity of His nature that gave infinite value to His sacrifice.

(4). *Aaron offered a material sacrifice, but Christ* ' *poured out his soul unto death.*" He gave His blood, *i.e.*, His life and love to reconcile the world unto God.

(5). *Aaron offered for* HIMSELF *and the sins of* ISRAEL ONLY. Christ did not offer for Himself but *He offered "for the sins of the whole world."*

(6) *Aaron's offering only atoned for inadvertant sins, for faults and failings of men;* for high-handed sins, and wilful transgressions there was no remedy; when those were discovered, they were met with the penalty of death. *But the sacrifice of Christ atones for* ALL SIN, even the most flagrant and heinous (see Heb. x.).—*F. W. B.*

Topic: RATIFICATION OF THE STATUTE OF THE ATONEMENT (Vv. 29-34).

Special significance was given to the day of atonement by directions concerning it being reiterated, by freedom from all ceremonial defilement being insisted upon. The priests burnt incense every day on the golden altar *without* the veil, but the high priest alone was permitted to enter into the holy of holies *within* the veil once a year. This statute would awaken solemn reflection, and be an abiding precaution against undue familiarity with the visible symbolic presence of Jehovah. The day of atonement was to be observed—

I. ANNUALLY. "And it shall be a statute for ever unto you." The tenth day of the seventh month (Tisri) in every year was to be observed down to the time when the great antitype would render the annual repetition of the rite unnecessary. The day gave a rounded completeness to the oblations of the year; the ceremony would be perpetually needed, for each succeeding generation would require the blessings of propitiation and forgiveness.

II. PUBLICLY. The whole nation was commanded to join in celebration with great unanimity. "Whether it be one of your own country, or of a stranger that sojourneth among you." The blood of the sacrifice was to be taken by the high priest within the veil, and sprinkled secretly upon the mercy seat, but he was to reappear among the people, pronounce publicly his benediction, and show openly that the sacrifice had been completed, the end of the ceremony secured. The service included, because it was intended for, all.

III. TRANQUILLY. "It shall be a sabbath of rest to you." No manner of work to be done by any who were in the camp. Thus disengaged from all secular toil, the people could concentrate their thoughts upon the solemn engagements of the day, with undistracted minds and undivided hearts. The exercises of the day were not sanguinary struggles with the Almighty for victory over His wrath against sin, but an exhibition of His mercy in opening a way of propitiation for all who would embrace opportunity. The tranquillity of the day of atonement was symbolic of the rest of soul Israel might enjoy under a consciousness of sin forgiven and restoration to the divine favour; suggestive of the peace of God which passeth all understanding, and which those enjoy who are made one with Him by sacrifice.

IV. CONTRITELY. "Ye shall afflict your souls." According to many Jewish writers, the children of Israel submitted to manifold deep humiliations on that day, observed it as a solemn fast. They were not commanded to afflict their bodies or rend their garments, but to present the sacrifice of broken and contrite hearts, which God will never despise. This would necessitate the suppression of worldliness, the repression of every sinful passion. When the hands of the high priest were placed upon the head of the scapegoat, and the sins of the people confessed, faith and repentance were to be exercised or the ceremony would be a mere farce, and offensive to Him who expects worshippers to draw near in spirit and in truth.

Many objections have been alleged against the doctrine of atonement by vicarious sacrifice, against propitiation by "blood." Those difficulties dwindle away as the light of the New Testament is thrown upon them. The Epistle to the Hebrews shows that "blood" represented life, which is symbolic of (*a*) *priceless worth;* (*b*) *highest sanctity;* (*c*) *choicest gift.* Thus the blood of Jesus Christ cleanseth from all sin, because it represents and means that His *life* and *love* were poured out for the sake of the world's redemption.

Against the doctrine of divine mediation reason can bring *no valid objection;* for nature, by abundant analogies and illustrations, suggests its probability in the realm of grace. The sacrifice of Christ was (*a*) *universal;* (*b*) *efficacious;* (*c*) *voluntary;* (*d*) *final.* Our duty and privilege to accept the blessings typified by the day of atonement. Our only hope for time and eternity is in Christ. The music that will hush all the discords of earth swells from the new song of Moses and the Lamb.—F. W. B.

OUTLINES ON VERSES OF CHAPTER XVI.

V. 2.—*Theme:* UNDUE FAMILIARITY IN DIVINE THINGS CHECKED.

" He shall come not at all times into the holy place within the veil before the *mercy seat.*"

The day of atonement, the most solemn day in the Jewish Calender. Everything about it calculated to awaken interest and solemnity. Other offerings had respect to particular persons and sins, *this* to the whole nation and all sin. Thus was prefigured the great sacrifice of Calvary, which atoned for sins of whole world. Nadab and Abihu had displayed presumption and irreverence in drawing near to the Lord, and for their wicked conduct had been slain; now, Aaron is commanded not to go into the holy of holies but once a year, lest he should also die. Notice—

I. THAT ACCESS INTO JEHOVAH'S PRESENCE WAS RESTRICTED. Every day ordinary offerings could be presented, and divine favour secured; but, lest the people should become unduly familiar, and therefore irreverent, restraint was put upon their communion, they were not allowed to enter the most holy place at all, and the high priest only on the day of atonement. Access into God's special presence could only be—

1. *In a special place.* The holy of holies; within the veil, where was the mercy seat crowned with the shekinah cloud. God is everywhere, His favour may be secured in every place; but, His full presence and glory are only beheld in heaven, within the veil.

2. *At special times.* On the day of atonement special revelations were made of divine mercy, special benedictions were bestowed upon the people. God's love was signally displayed when Christ effected the atonement upon the cross; special blessings come upon man on the days of rest that remind us of the seal of the atonement, of the resurrection of Jesus on the morning of the third day.

3. *By special persons.* Only the high priest could enter within the veil, thus teaching Israel how great and worshipful Jehovah was. There was only One in the whole universe who could offer atonement for the sins of the world, and appear in the presence of God for us, the Son of God, the man Christ Jesus.

4. *After special preparation.* Aaron had to present offerings for himself, and become cleansed from all ceremonial uncleanness, the preparation very thorough and complete. Christ, our Great High Priest, needed not to sacrifice for Himself, nor to seek purification; but He was made perfect through sufferings, and passed through the baptism of Gethsemane on the way to Calvary.

5. *For special purposes.* Aaron went in to atone and intercede, to fulfil the will and purposes of Jehovah in relation to Israel. Christ died to remove sin, to open gate of heaven to all believers for the regeneration and redemption of humanity.

II. THAT SUCH RESTRICTION WAS MERCIFUL AND BENEFICIAL.

(*a*) *Impressed the people with the deep solemnity of the ceremony.*

(*b*) *Produced profound reverence in their hearts for the worship of Jehovah.*

(*c*) *Awakened expectations of special blessings.*

The veil of the Temple has been rent in twain; we may go with holy boldness to the throne of grace; yet reverence ought to be cultivated, worship is to be associated with godly fear, for our God is a consuming fire.—F. W. B.

Vv. 10-12.—*Theme:* SIN REMOVED.

The two goats, presented at the door of the tabernacle before the Lord, were but one offering, though one was allowed to escape into the wilderness. The goat slain would indicate that atonement could be effected only by the shedding of blood; the scapegoat would teach that in atonement sin is not only forgiven, but *completely taken away*. The gospel and the law agree here.

I. THAT SIN TO BE FORGIVEN MUST BE CONFESSED. The people could not atone for their sins, but they must offer the sacrifice of broken and contrite hearts. As Aaron laid his hands on the goat and confessed the sins of the people he would be showing in the most emphatic way that *personal faith and repentance* were needed in order that guilt might be forgiven. So God requires still that those who seek His pardoning mercy shall feel sorry for their sins and confess them with humble, lowly, and believing hearts.

II. THAT SIN TO BE FORGIVEN MUST BE REMOVED. Not connived at or covered up, not clung to and repeated when the pardon is secured, but taken away for ever; not only the guilt, but *the love and practice of sin gone*. Christ atoned for, and *removed* sin. Redemption is to produce *sanctification* and *righteousness*. Holiness is the outcome of propitiation, the end of the law and the gospel Christ has secured by His atonement pardon for the guilt of sin and the annihilation of its existence when His kingdom shall be complete, and He "all and in all."—*F. W B.*

V. 13—*Theme:* INTERCESSION

The incense may be regarded as symbolic of the merits of the atonement and intercession of the high priest. Sweet ascending fragrance from live coals off altar of sacrifice suggests concerning intercession—

I. ITS BASIS. Sacrifice, mercy-seat: the cloud covered the place where God met propitiously with man.

II. ITS SANCTION. God commanded it; had it before Him. Aaron could swing the censer with holy boldness *when* and *where* divinely directed.

III. ITS EFFICACY. Saved life of the priest, "that He die not"; showed that the ceremony had been acceptably observed; gave Aaron warrant to complete the rite and bless the people. Our great High Priest presents the merits of His own sacrifice within the veil; the fragrance of His life and death avail for all who come to God by Him Our prayers and praises may rise mingled with the merits of His intercession, and find acceptance in the holiest of all.—*F. W. B.*

V 24.—*Theme:* SUPREME DEMAND FOR HOLINESS.

Aaron, having offered the appointed sacrifice, laid aside his linen garments, washed his person in pure water, arrayed himself in his gorgeous vestments, and stood before the people as their earthly representative and head. Every act in the service pointed to the holiness of God, to His disapproval of every form of sin Sanctification from the stains of guilt, and assumption of the beautiful garments of holiness, essential to acceptable fellowship with the Lord; for—

I. DEFILEMENT CANNOT APPEAR IN THE PRESENCE OF THE LORD. Only sin can separate between God and man, but sin, producing defilement of the soul, withdraws the sinner far from God, renders him unfit for the divine presence. When our first parents sinned they fled from the presence of the Lord; the atonement heals the breach, effects righteousness within a man, and shows how the perfect righteousness of another may be set over to his account; and this because—

II PROVISION HAS BEEN MADE FOR THE REMOVAL OF DEFILEMENT. Aaron's ablutions of his flesh were symbolic of moral cleansing, and suggest to us how guilt may now be removed. In the fountain opened for sin and uncleanness we may have every stain removed, by the washing of regeneration and renewing of the Holy Ghost. The old man, with the lusts of the flesh, must be put off, and the new man put on transforming the worshippers into new creatures in Christ Jesus.—*F. W. B.*

V. 30 —*Theme:* THE ATONING SACRIFICE

Israel was taught both helplessness and need, in that atonement had to be made for the nation by one who stood as mediator in its stead. Atonement was made in Jehovah's own way, the people were to reverently submit to the arrangements, and by repentance and faith avail themselves of the blessings presented Observe—

I. THE ATONEMENT WAS OF A VICARIOUS CHARACTER The innocent suffered for the guilty, the priest atoned for the people.

II. THE ATONEMENT SECURED SPIRITUAL PURITY. "That ye may be clean from all your sins"

(*a*) *The moral depravity of man needed it.*
(*b*) *The holy nature of Jehovah demanded it.*

Once, in the fulness of time, atonement has been made for the sins of the world; a way has been opened for the removal of guilt here, for admission unto perfect holiness and blessedness hereafter.—*F. W. B.*

ILLUSTRATIVE ADDENDA TO CHAPTER XVI.

THE MERCY SEAT.

"Propitiation," or *mercy seat* (the same word as in Heb. ix 5) If we would have mercy it must be through Christ; out of Christ no mercy is to be had. We read in the old law—

First: None might come into the holy of holies, where the mercy seat stood, but the high priest; signifying that we have nothing to do with mercy but through Christ our High Priest.

Secondly: The high priest might not come

near the mercy seat without blood (Lev. xvi. 14), to show that we have no right to mercy but through the expiatory sacrifice of Christ's blood.

Thirdly: The high priest might not, upon pain of death, come near the mercy seat without incense (Lev. xvi. 13), indicating that there could be no mercy from God without the incense of Christ's intercession.

So that, if we would have mercy, we must get a part in Christ.—*Watson.*

THE SCAPEGOAT.

There was in the year 1856 exhibited in the Art Union a fine picture of the scapegoat dying in the wilderness: it was represented with a burning sky above it, its feet sticking in the mire, surrounded by hundreds of skeletons, and there dying a doleful and miserable death. Now, that was just a piece of gratuitous nonsense, for there is nothing in the Scripture that warrants it in the least degree. The rabbis tell us that this goat was taken by a man into the wilderness and there tumbled down a high rock to die; but, as an excellent commentator says, if the man did push it down the rock he did more than God ever told him to do. God told him to take a goat and let it go: as to what became of it neither you nor I know anything; that is purposely left. Our Lord Jesus Christ has taken away our sins upon His head, just as the scapegoat, and He is gone from us—that is all: the goat was not a type in its dying, or in regard to its subsequent fate. God has only told us that it should be taken by the hand of a fit man into the wilderness. The most correct account seems to be that of one Rabbi Jarchi, who says that they generally took the goat twelve miles out of Jerusalem, and at each mile there was a booth provided where the man who took it might refresh himself till he came to the tenth mile, when there was no more rest for him till he had seen the goat go. When he had come to the last mile he stood and looked at the goat till it was gone, and he could see it no more. Then the people's sins were all gone too. Now, what a fine type that is if you do not enquire any further! But if you will get meddling where God intended you to be in ignorance, you will get nothing by it. This scapegoat was not designed to show us the victim or the sacrifice, but simply what became of the sins. The sins of the people are confessed upon that head; the goat is going; the people lose sight of it; a fit man goes with it; the sins are going from them, and now the man has arrived at his destination; the man sees the goat in the distance skipping here and there over the mountains, glad of its liberty; it is not quite gone; a little farther, and now it is lost to sight. The man returns, and says he can no longer see it; then the people clap their hands, for their sins are all gone too. Oh! soul; canst thou see thy sins all gone? We may have to take a long journey, and carry our sins with us; but oh! how we watch and watch till they are utterly cast into the depths of the wilderness of forgetfulness, where they shall never more be found against us for ever.—*C. H. Spurgeon.*

CHAPTER XVII.

The Sanctity of the Blood.

SUGGESTIVE READINGS.

V. 4.—*And bringeth it not unto the door of the tabernacle.* A captious mind will ask, Why is not sacrifice acceptable to God wherever offered? Surely it is in the spirit of the offerer, rather than in the circumstances of the offering, that piety consists. Wherefore, then, this insistance on mere conditions, and importance attached to the place of sacrifice? But God meets such contention of thought with absolute interdict; *He* is the authority in human life and sacred regulations; and "who art thou that repliest against God?" Even when "your ways are not my ways" (Isa. lv. 8), the LORD must be obeyed, and *His terms of dealing with sinful creatures* be observed as absolute. Yet more. There was *wisdom* in those requirements; for the Israelites had been so trained to superstitious and heathenish ideas in Egypt as to need this fencing about in order to restrain them from lapsing, all but unconsciously, into the snares of familiar idolatrous practices. Our God is gracious in all His ways; His commandments are not grievous; but, knowing our tendencies to err, He arrests us at the first symptoms of erring, and shows us the path of safety. the plan of acceptance.

V. 5.—**The sacrifices which they offer in the open field.** [See Addenda to chap., *Sacrifices unto devils*.] They had learned this from the Egyptians, who peopled the scenes of nature with deities (v. 7), and Israel continually fell into this old habit, and sacrificed in groves and on high places; it was the snare of their whole after history. We may be redeemed from our spiritual bondage. and become pilgrims to Canaan, yet all the journey through the *power of old habits pursues us*, and would reassert itself up on us. Therefore the urgency with which God's Word prohibits any and every concession to "the former lusts in our ignorance." We must shun lurking perils.

V. 8.—**Whatsoever men there be.** It was an inflexible regulation, binding upon "the house of Israel," and also upon "*strangers that sojourn among you.*" For evil may be introduced by the society we entertain, the guests who visit us. And hospitality was to be restricted by divine laws. How ensnaring often becomes the courtesy which we think due to "strangers"! There is a tendency to relax from steadfast principles of righteousness and lofty habits of piety at such times as guests are staying in our homes. This is to lower God's standard in accommodation to men. It must not be; strangers in godly homes must conform to the godly laws which are there supreme; the children of God must never yield to unhallowed customs of their guests; hospitality must be no excuse for impiety.

V. 10.—**I will set my face against that soul that eateth blood.** God claimed the blood as being "the *life*" of the creature. He has ownership in all His creatures, and we should acknowledge Him therein. But this law has emphasized the value of blood as the symbol also of *atonement* (v. 11). And He would have every act, even of eating and drinking, testify of the atonement required by sinners. The table could not be spread for "strangers" (v. 12), nor could any one, Israelite or stranger, seek recreation and pleasure in "*hunting*" even, but the significance and sacredness of "the blood" must be recognised. We have reason, indeed, to regard as most suggestive and precious the blood of atonement. It leads our thoughts to Him whose death has gathered into itself all virtue for redemption. How dreadful the consequences of counting that "blood of the covenant an unholy thing!" (Heb. x. 29).

SECTIONAL HOMILIES.

Topic: The Solemnity of Sacrifice Publicly Recognised (**Vv. 1-10**).

Jehovah's concern for solemnity and **purity in** apparently trifling things revealed His intense hatred for sin, His supreme love for holiness. The demand for purity extended to private individual acts no less than to public national observances. The blood of all beasts slain for food or sacrifice was to be presented at the door of the tabernacle, to check the people from wanton destruction of animal life; to remind them that all life is from the Lord; its destruction under His cognizance. This injunction would—

I. Prevent idolatry. The idolatrous practices of the Egyptians, among whom Israel had lived, would have implanted a tendency in the people to relapse into heathenish superstitions during their encampment in the wilderness. The Egyptians sacrificed to the goats, or field devils—supposed to inhabit the wilderness —to avert their wrath, and secure their favour. To ensure that no idolatrous sacrifice should be offered in the camp the blood of every slain animal was to be presented before the Lord, as an acknowledgement that Jehovah was the sovereign King in Israel. God is the proprietor of all life, to Him all ought to be solemnly dedicated.

II. STIMULATE OBEDIENCE. Probably the Hebrews could not see the reason for so rigid a command, it was for them to render unquestioning obedience believing in the wisdom of their great Lawgiver, in the righteousness of His precepts. When enactments seemed meaningless, and ceremonies superfluous, the human was always and in every case to be subordinated to the divine will. Thus the discipline of the Jewish economy educated loyal and implicit surrender of all the faculties of heart and mind. Under the gospel dispensation we are saved by faith, which is the gift of God; yet, "faith without works is dead." Faith and love must prove their *existence* and *genuineness* by obedience to the commands of Christ.

III. PERPETUATE ALLEGIANCE. These arrangements were to continue in force through succeeding generations. In coming constantly to the door of the tabernacle, and making its services the constant theme of attention, the Israelites would be carrying out the first great injunction of the decalogue, "Thou shalt have none other gods but me." Identifying the tabernacle with the domestic acts of life, with acts performed to provide material food, would tend to keep in vivid remembrance the fact that everything was to be done to the glory of God. It is still so; every meal should become a sacrament, all we do should be done devoutly and heartily as unto the Lord.

IV. AWAKEN GRATITUDE. Coming so frequently to the door of the tabernacle with the blood of animals slain for food or sacrifice would remind the Hebrews how constantly they were indebted to Jehovah for all the temporal and spiritual blessings they enjoyed. They would thus trace their mercies to the Source from which all good and perfect gifts flow to man.

V. PROMOTE HOLINESS. Such constant reference to the tabernacle would keep the Lord perpetually before the people, and act as a solemn restraint upon their conduct. In common as well as sacred meals, in the tent as well as in the tabernacle, "Holiness to the Lord" was to be inscribed above all. As the Israelites presented the blood at the door of the tabernacle they would be reminded of the sacredness of life; have suggested to their minds the necessity of complete self-surrender to Jehovah. The New Testament has no diviner injunction than this, "Be ye holy, for I am holy."

VI. BEGET REVERENCE. As the people drew nigh to the door of the tabernacle they would be reminded of the august authority of God in demanding such obedience and annexing such penalties to disobedience. The justice and jealousy of God would fill every devout worshipper with profound religious awe. In all Christian worship godly fear should have its place, "for our God is a consuming fire."

VII. INDICATE RECONCILIATION. The fact that the people were permitted thus frequently to approach the tabernacle proved that Jehovah was propitious, and delighted in mercy. He had come to dwell with men because He delighted in their company and fellowship. If those who drew near to God only fulfilled the conditions He saw fit to lay down, there was no need for slavish fear or apprehensions of disapproval. That God expects us to live in His favour and fear denotes the fact that He is reconciled to us, and that the only thing that hinders our bliss here and hereafter is unwillingness to be reconciled to Him.—F. W. B.

Topic: THE PLACE OF SACRIFICE (Vv. 8, 9).

1. God has a right to say where and how He will be worshipped, and He has exercised the right. He has told us the way in which He will be approached.

2. The way to life may be narrow, but there is no one, with the Word of Truth in his hand, who may not discover it and follow it.

3. Of old God gave minute and ample instruction to His people; they were to approach Him by *sacrifice*, and that sacrifice was to be offered *on the altar* of burnt offering: "there shalt thou offer" (Deut. xii. 13, 14). It mattered not in what the offering consisted, expiatory or eucharistic, the requirements as to *the place of presentation* was the same—the place which the Lord had chosen and made His habitation.

"Even those animals which were slain for food in the wilderness were brought to the door of the tabernacle, and *there killed,* and their blood sprinkled on the altar. If an Israelite did not bring the animal which he intended for food to the door of the tabernacle, but killed it elsewhere, God declared that blood should be imputed to him" (*Bonar* on Leviticus, chap xvii.).

A. WHAT ADMONITORY PURPOSE WAS THEREBY SERVED.

1. The people were *indellibly impressed with their need of atonement.* Every time an intelligent Israelite took away life he must have felt his own life was forfeited to God, and that by the blood of sacrifice only could it be redeemed. The very preparation of his food impressed him with the truth that life is the gift of God. But if this is Old Testament truth, it is New Testament truth also (see Jno. vi. 51; iii. 36).

ii. *Idolatry was the root sin of the ancient nations;* and the head of every family, as priest in his own house, might sacrifice to whatever god he pleased. To correct this in Israel was one of the admonitory purposes of this enactment that all sacrifices should be offered at the house of God.

B. WHAT SACRED AND EVANGELICAL DOCTRINE UNDERLAYS THIS REGULATION.

i. *The tabernacle was a type of the Lord Jesus;* and just as the Israelite could only worship God by sacrifice at His own dwelling, so we can only present our offerings to Him through Christ. "By Him, therefore, let us offer the sacrifice of praise coutinually," etc. (Heb. xiii. 15; Col. iii. 17).

ii. The altar of brass was the place of sacrifice (v. 6), *on which burned the inextinguishable fire,* symbol of divine holiness and endless propitiation. It stood *between* the door of the tabernacle and the Shekinah within the veil. An interposing sacrificial altar, the Cross of Jesus stands between the human offerer and the Holy God. Had not Christ, our Atonement, put Himself between us and what we deserved wrath had fallen upon us.

C. WHAT PRACTICAL OBLIGATION THIS RESTRICTED SCENE OF SACRIFICE ENJOINS ON US NOW.

i. The altar was the *one way of approach;* even so, Christ is the one way to the Father (Jno. xiv. 6).

ii. *Excellencies* in the offerer or the offering *could not neutralize the necessity* for coming in this only way to God. The Jew's sacrifice might be, in itself, all that was required, but offered elsewhere than at the door of the tabernacle of the congregation it was refused. Though we be generous in disposition, upright in walk, reverent in manner, not for these, but for Christ's sake, can we be accepted.

iii. But *contact with that altar imparted sanctity.* Whatsoever toucheth the altar shall be holy (Exod. xxix. 37). The first touch of Christ by faith delivers from guilt.

iv. *At the cross* God is to be found and enjoyed. Only at the cross will He be merciful to our unrighteousness, and only in Christ meet us in grace. [Comp., *The Gospel in Leviticus.*—J. FLEMING, D.D.].

Topic: BLOOD PROHIBITED AS FOOD (Vv. 10-12).

This divine enactment forbidding blood as food was much older than the tabernacle ordinances: was given to Noah directly after the flood (Gen. ix. 4). Reiterated now to the Israelites (chap. iii. 17; vii. 26); and the *reason* for the statute is now assigned : "the blood is the life of the flesh, and is given to man to make an atonement for his soul." [See Addenda to chap., *Life in the Blood*]

1. BLOOD SACREDNESS : *solemnly appointed by God* for a *most gracious purpose*. Instances from the *Old Testament:*

Abel's offering of "the firstlings of his flock" (Gen. iv. 3-5), securing emphatic approbation over Cain's fruits of the ground.

Noah's altar sacrifices after the flood (Gen. viii. 20, 21).

Job's patriarchial offerings of sacrifices for propitiation and thanksgiving (Job i. 5).

Moses' entire system was atoning and sacrificial by means of blood. "No remission of sins without the shedding of blood."

The blood was to be *used for no other purpose*.

The *New Testament* testimony.

Prophecy had foretold that Messiah would " redeem Israel " (Psa. cxxx. 8), and "make an end of sins" (Dan. ix. 24); and it should be *done by blood:* "wounded for our transgressions" (Isa. liii. 5, 10).

At the Eucharistic Supper Jesus took the cup and said, "This is my blood of the New Testament which is shed for many for the remission of sins" (Matt. xxvi. 28).

The apostles testify to the same truth : "We have redemption through his blood" (Col. i. 14, 20).

The cry of the Church on earth and in heaven tells the sacred truth, "Unto him that loved us and washed us from our sins in his own blood" (Rev. i. 5, v. 9).

God has "given *to us the blood for the atonement of the soul*."

II. BLOOD APPROPRIATION : *emphatically restricted by God* for this one sacred purpose.

It is refused for food, and its mal-appropriation protected by penalties of a very appalling nature.

1. It would *lower the dignity and defile the sanctity of blood* if allowed for common uses. All serious regard for the "atonement" virtue which lay in the blood would have left their minds had it not been thus exclusively reserved. There is no less danger of irreverent minds "counting the blood of the covenant an unholy thing and doing despite to the Spirit of grace" (Heb. x. 29). In this prohibition of a familiar use of solemn things God sought to fence His people from a sin easily besetting them. God would have us touch sanctities with awe.

2. It would *perpetuate in their thoughts their need of "atonement"* to have blood thus interdicted for all other purposes. "Atonement" would confront them as their daily necessity, even at their meals. And it should be "ever before us" that we are sinners needing the atonement of Christ ; it is gracious for God to make us daily see and realise our case and the urgency of our need of that "precious blood of Christ."

3. It would *lead on their hopes to the effectual and final sacrifice which Messiah would present*. The very weariness of this continual presentation of blood in sacrifice would deepen the longing for Messiah's sacrifice ; which should end all provisional offerings. A tired traveller hails sight of each sign-post as it tells him *home is near*.

All the ancient types *pointed men onwards:* God would concentrate human desire on the promised Saviour.

Now He makes all teaching and experience of man *point human hope and faith backwards*, on the finished work of redemption, on the One Sacrifice of Jesus— "Whom God hath set forth to be a propitiation for sin through faith in his blood" (Rom. iii. 25).

A WARNING : *Christ* must be used as *an Atonement*. His "blood" must be recognised as of infinite urgency and value for sinful men. Whoso dares take

Christ as his food, refusing His sacrificial work, seeking to appropriate and enjoy Jesus as a Teacher, Example, Friend, but repudiating him as a Sin Offering, a Redeemer of the ruined soul, he falls under the menaces of these words of God, Christ's blood must be realised as a supreme necessity for man, as an "atonement for his soul."

Topic: HOLY BLOOD (Vv. 10, 11).

With stern command God sets a fence around all blood. All reverence enshrines it. An awful sanctity exempts it from the food of man.

What if offence occur, if rash hands bring it to the board for food? Then penalty frowns terribly, wrath darkens, excluding judgments follow.

But why is blood thus sanctified?

I. IS NOT BLOOD THE ALTAR'S FOOD?

Yes : there is its constant flow : it is the stream from expiring victims. It reminds of *death* as the *desert of sin,* and bears witness that *remission of sin* is prepared. Then it is linked with *expiating grace.* Thus :

II. IT POINTS TO CALVARY'S CROSS

It shadows forth the wrath-sustaining death of God's co-equal Son. It introduces Jesus bleeding that souls may live. It is the symbol of *redemption's price;* emblem of the one atoning Lamb.

Hence till Jesus came the same forbidding voice was heard : Touch not the blood! It is devoted to God. It is most holy unto Him. It pictures out *redeeming suffering.* It is "atonement for the soul."

We live in gospel light ; the wondrous death is no more veiled in mystic types. We gaze with open vision on the blood-stained cross ; may approach the fountain opened in the Saviour's side ; may there wash our every sin away.

Shall we, thus privileged, *fall short in reverence?* Think of the grand antitype, Christ's blood ; ponder its *worth,* its *use,* its *mighty power,* its *unspeakable results.*

i. Its glorious *worth.* Enter the Garden. The Sufferer seems a lowly man. Man verily He is, or He could possess no human blood. But in that lowly body Deity dwells. He is the Mighty God. It is the "blood of God" (Acts xx. 28).

ii. Its gracious *use.* The sinner is justly sentenced to woe. Nothing but boundless substitution can release. Jesus is God, and He brings blood divinely efficacious. He is an able Saviour, for blood flows in the channel of omnipotence.

iii. Its effectual *power.* It is the ransom price of all the saved. Their number baffles number. Each was defiled with darkest stains of guilt. But now behold them. Robes white ; not one stain spoils ; penalties all paid. The blood has saved.

iv. Its precious *results.*

1. It is the *peace* of all believing souls. The day of awakened conscience was one of bitter woe. The thundering law denounced, the wrath of God menaced. But the Spirit led the trembler to the cross. Faith heard the assurance, "Though your sins," etc. (Isaiah i. 18) ; faith gazed, and found full repose.

2. It is the source of *sanctifying grace.* He must flee sin whose eye is fixed on the blood. Can he love that which gave those wounds to Christ? The sight of calvary slays the love of sin.

(*a*) Make it *your study.* For every thought here is food. Angels gaze and they adore. But they glean no advantage from it. To you it is salvation's price ; the gate of heaven.

(*b*) *Love* it. It is proof of God's love, that Jesus loves you better than Himself. That mind is rock which is not melted by such flame.

(*c*) *Praise* it. All lips commend the charms of beauty and heroic deeds. But what so beauteous as grace leading Jesus to the cross? Where is noble act like His surrender of Himself for you?

(*d*) *Use* it. Every hour, when *temptation's darts* are flying round; it will "quench the fiery darts." When you *seek light* from scripture's pages; those lines are brightest in which blood is seen. Use it in *prayer;* it is the plea of pleas. In *sanctuary rites:* the service is cast out which is not hallowed with blood. Use it in *all holy work* for God: it consecrates the motive, way, end; and harvests grow from seeds sown in blood. And *when death draws near* use it: it ensures heaven, where it may be the eternal theme.—DEAN LAW.

Topic: A DIVINE PROHIBITION (Vv. 10-16).

Of all the sacrifices offered in the Tabernacle, the expiatory were the most important; that offered on the Day of Atonement the climax of all. The virtue and worth of the offering were symbolised in the blood of the victims; to *it*, therefore, peculiar solemnity and sanctity were attached. Noah and his descendants were forbidden to partake of flesh with the blood: thus, the way was prepared for the strict prohibition of this chapter. In putting a guard around the seat of animal life Jehovah taught the Hebrews—

I. THAT BLOOD WAS TO BE REGARDED AS A SACRED THING. Not because it was unwholesome, or unclean, or repulsive, was blood not to be partaken of, but because by *it* atonement was made for the sins of the soul. From the earliest history of our race God had taught that life must be given for life; and that without shedding of blood there could be no remission of sins. Thus blood became—

(*a*) *The means of expiation.*
(*b*) *The symbol of reconciliation.*
(*c*) *The type of the one great vicarious sacrifice;* by virtue of which all the Mosaic offerings were efficacious and accepted.

There was nothing so precious on earth, in the estimation of God, as life; upon it, therefore, He set His most solemn seal; to it He attached rigid regulations; and around it He erected His righteous restraint.

II. THAT, BEING A SACRED THING, BLOOD WAS NOT TO BE SHED HEEDLESSLY; *or to be, under any circumstances, partaken of.*

Acting under such prohibitions, Israel would be distinguished from the heathen nations, who recklessly shed blood, and who not only offered it to their gods but partook of it themselves. Jehovah, as the sovereign Lord of all life, reserved the symbol of it to Himself; it was to be in no way degraded, not left anywhere carelessly exposed, but treated with profound deference. A check was thus put upon indiscriminate slaughter, and in every creature slain for food, or sacrifice, the operator, by the divine restriction he was under, would be reminded of the absolute sovereignty of the Lord.

III. THAT DISREGARD TO THESE PROHIBITIONS WOULD INCUR THE RIGHTEOUS DISPLEASURE OF THE PROPRIETOR OF ALL LIFE.

Disobedience would not only displease God but incur excommunication from His presence. The enactments may seem severe, but they were needed under the circumstances of the wilderness, and taught lessons of circumspection and moral purity, calculated to lift the people from depraved and degrading practices. The guilt of taking life could only be atoned for by the sacrifice of life. Thus, in the fulness of time, Christ, by shedding His precious blood, by offering His divine infinite life a ransom for the souls of men, satisfied the claims of divine justice, opened the way to heaven for every man. Figuratively, and by faith, we are to eat the flesh and drink the blood of the Son of God, but care must be taken that the acts are not performed unworthily, nor must the blood of the covenant be trampled under foot and counted an unholy thing. Those who persist in abusing or despising the precious blood of Christ will wonder and perish in the day when the secrets of all hearts shall be disclosed.—*F. W. B.*

ILLUSTRATIVE ADDENDA TO CHAPTER XVII.

Sacrifices unto Devils (v. 7).
The word *Seirim*, here translated "devils," literally means *hairy or shaggy goats*, and then *goat-like deities*, or *demons*.

The *Egyptians*, and other nations of antiquity, worshipped goats as gods. Not only was there a celebrated temple in Thmuis, the capital of the Mendesian Nomos in Lower Egypt, dedicated to the goat image Pan, whom they called Mendes, and worshipped as an oracle and as the fertilising principle in nature, but they erected statues to him everywhere. Hence the Pan Silenus, satyrs, fawns, and woodland gods found among the *Greeks* and *Romans*; and hence, too, the *goat-like forms of the devil*, with a tail, horns, and cloven feet, which obtain in Medieval Christianity, and which may still be seen in some European cities.

The terror in which the devil, appearing in this Pan-like form, created in those who were thought to have seen him, has given rise to our expression *panic*.—*Ellicott's Commentary*.

Life in the Blood.
This statement (v. 14) that "*the life of the flesh is in the blood*" had stood in the Mosaic Scriptures for 3,600 years before philosophers, scientists, and anatomists had found their way to this physical truism.

That the blood holds the vitality of the entire bodily structure is given here as a fact of *revelation*; and it lay in the Bible for nearly 4,000 years before anatomists discovered the fact by their research. Now it is acknowledged as a principle confirmed by elaborate and accurate experiments.

CHAPTER XVIII.

Incestuous Marriages: Domestic Purity.

SUGGESTIVE READINGS.

V. 2.—**Speak unto them and say, I am the Lord your God.** Jehovah is the sole lawgiver, His word the one law to His people: ungodly customs and usages claim no heed from them: what He wills is absolute. Relationship to, and fellowship with God are based upon implicit obedience. There must be cheerful acceptance of His authority in all the details of life. Ethics are to be decided by the word divine, for who but "the Lord" should erect the standard of rectitude for man?

V. 3.—**After the doings of the land of Egypt.** The Israelites dwelt amid a people of corrupt and debasing habits for so long a period that it was with difficulty they purged themselves from sympathy with familiar evils. They who enter upon the new life of grace in Christ Jesus find that their "old sins" follow close upon their steps and exert seductive influence. To "cast out the old leaven" is a necessity still, if we would enjoy the favours of our redeemed lot and our new-covenant relationships. What "Egypt" approved or "Canaan" practised may no longer regulate the godly life; but, What saith the Lord?

V. 5.—**He shall live in them.** Social health and spiritual blessedness will always attend obedience to God's just and benign "statutes." Violation of the laws of humanity, the laws of rectitude and purity, bring physical decrepitude and social disaster.

Here note that these words form the basis of the Old Testament doctrine of *salvation by works*. Obedience secures life—sacred and eternal life. These words are quoted by the prophet Ezekiel (xx. 11, 13, 21), and by the Apostle Paul

(Rom. x. 5; Gal. iii. 12.), as summarizing the teachings of Moses' dispensation—*the merits of works, justification by obedience.* We, in gospel times, realise life through faith; salvation in Christ's merits, and not in our own. Yet the beneficent law stands for ever: that observance of God's law is salutory; for "life" is most truly realised now by those whose conduct is godly, and blessed rewards are assured hereafter to those who do those things which please the Lord.

Vv. 6-18.—**None of you shall approach to any that is near of kin.** The prohibited cases of intercourse or marriage are: the son's own mother, and consequently, by inference, the daughter's own father (v. 7); a stepmother, and, by inference, a stepfather (v. 8); a full sister or half-sister (v. 9); a granddaughter (v. 10); a half-sister (v. 11); an aunt (v. 12); an aunt by marriage (vv. 13, 14); a daughter-in-law (v. 15); a brother's wife (v. 16); a step-daughter, and a step-granddaughter (v, 17); polygamy is interdicted (v. 18), the adding "a wife to her sister," and this during the wife's "lifetime." The inference in each case carries prohibition also to the corresponding relationship: as *e.g.*, half-brother (v. 9); uncle (v. 12); son-in-law (v. 15), and so on throughout. Every marriage alliance is to be ruled by the initiatory definition (v. 6), "Near of kin"; and the instances specified show this near kinship to include cases of consanguinity and also equally of marriage relationship. Let this interpretation be applied to the question of the "deceased wife's sister."

The important law running through all these regulations is: Fidelity in wedlock; scrupulous honour in the marriage relationship; the door is to be closed on all occasion of jealousy or illicit love. Home bonds are to be cherished as all too sacred and precious for passion or caprice to trifle with. God will have family obligations loyally and vigorously maintained.

Vv. 19-23 **Crimes against Purity.** How shamefully vile humanity may become! What a gross being is he whom God pities and would save; and how low has he fallen whom Christ would lift up to sanctity and bliss!

Vv. 24-30. **The land is defiled.** The well-being of a land depends on the morality of its inhabitants. National decay sets in when the people become abandoned. The records of national life, from ancient times till now, emphasise the precept, "Righteousness exalteth a nation, but sin is a reproach to any people" (Prov. xiv. 34).

SECTIONAL AND TOPICAL HOMILIES.

Topic: UNACCOMMODATING GODLINESS (Vv. 1-5).

"*After the doings of the land of Egypt, wherein ye dwelt, shall ye not do; and after the doings of the land of Canaan, whither I bring you, shall ye not do,*" etc.

Danger lurks in example; customs lure us from strict integrity; easy to fall in with prevailing habits, sentiments, ideas. With "men of *this* world" who have no disposition to "come out from among them, be separate, and touch not the unclean thing," the current maxims and methods are accepted without challenge, they stream along with the flow of social life; they yield themselves unresistingly to the popular course.

Herein lies the distinction, the distinguishing element of piety; it refuses to allow *custom* to dominate either *conscience* or *conduct.*

1. WORLDLY SEDUCTIONS EVERYWHERE ENVIRON THE GODLY LIFE.

"After the doings of the *land of Egypt,* and after the doings of the *land of Canaan.*"

1. Ensnarements are not escaped *by change of place*. He who thinks to flee the world by exchanging "Egypt" for "Canaan," will find the world still at his heels. To quit your gentle home for the cloister or the nunnery; to forsake one sphere of business for another in hope of fleeing the sanctioned malpractices of trade; to attempt to be "not of the world" by any process of mere exclusion and avoidance of places and people, is a fallacy; for evil is everywhere, in some guise or disguise; and from the snares of sin and the sanctions of impiety there is no hiding-place in "this present evil world."

2. Ensnarements are not left behind with the *advance of years* Forty years were spent by the Israelites in the desert, between "Egypt" and "Canaan"; yet that distance of time would not liberate them from the seductions of worldliness. What they left behind them in "Egypt" they would meet again, in altered forms, in "Canaan," when at length they reached that land. No Christian ever advances beyond the reach of evil and the subtleties of the world. What he had to fight with during his Egyptian life he will have to fight with all his career through. Time does not rid the godly of this seductive peril.

3. Ensnarements are not absent from *coveted scenes of privilege*. "Canaan" was the hope and desire of every Israelite. It was a "goodly land," the inheritance of faith, the goal of pilgrimage. "Egypt" was a scene of bondage and grief, *type of a sinner's lot ere redeemed*. But "Canaan" was suggestive of liberty, prosperity, privilege, *symbol of the Christian life of sacred rest, freedom, and joy in the Lord*. Yet even within "Canaan" the snares of sin would be encountered; no release from danger, a stern necessity to "watch and pray, lest ye enter into temptation"; and this in most delightful and hallowed hours, amid spiritual favours and privileges. Even the happiest Christian life is encompassed about with "the sins that so easily beset us." [See Addenda to chapter xviii., *Custom*.]

II. SANCTIONED IMPIETIES MUST BE EVERYWHEREE SHUNNED BY THE GODLY LIFE.

The *Egyptians* were the most civilised and majestic people of the age; and their "doings" and "ordinances" may represent the usages of society and culture: the customs of refinement and respectability. The *Canaanites* were a rude and unpolished people, easy and free; and their "doings" and "ordinances" answer to the popular maxims and habits, the pleasures and practices current among the less educated, the customs of the masses.

1. *Wherever our place, whatever our station*, godliness repudiates and renounces sin.

Yes: and every form of sin; personal or social; secret or open; sanctioned or unpopular. The man of God loathes impurity, shuns impiety. Not fashioning himself to the standard of morals around him, he has "no fellowship with the unfaithful works of darkness, but rather reproves them."

2. *An accommodating conscience*, and *an obliging disposition*, must be allowed no sanction in commerce with the world. "After their doings ye shall *not* do!" "Neither shall ye walk in their ordinances."

      And to my mind, tho' I am a native here,
      And to the manner born, it is a custom
      More honoured in the breach than in the observance.—*Hamlet*.

3. Amid prevailing error it is *the business of godliness to show the right and good*. What else is the significance of our Lord's words: "Ye are *the light* of the world"; "ye are *the salt* of the earth"? It is neither convenient or advantageous to assume this attitude of resistance against the cherished "ordinances" of *social, literary*, or *professedly religious* life. But the Christian is among men with a divine business, to put wrong to the blush; to pronounce by his virtues against all vice, by his spirituality against all earthliness of soul, by his self-denials against all low indulgence, by his lofty worship against all dead formality or careless irreverence. Religion is the fearless yet beautiful exhibition of the

      Piety, whose soul sincere,
      Fears God, and knows no other fear.

III. AN INFLEXIBLE DIVINE STANDARD EVERYWHERE REGULATES THE GODLY LIFE.

1. The standard of *divine relationship*. "I am the Lord your God" (v. 2). Israel's "doings" were to take tone and character from this fact—their God was the Lord; He was *theirs*, and they *His*. Living under the influence of that solemn relationship, their conduct should harmonise with His perfections—"holy as He is holy." It is the hourly obligation of the Christian, to "*walk worthy of the Lord*," to "walk *so as also He walked*."

2. The standard of *divine teachings*. God has told us His will; in precept and commandment we have our directory of conduct. His word is to be "a lamp to our feet and a light to our path." None can err through lack of instruction. "Wherewithal shall a young man cleanse his way? By taking heed thereto according to thy word." This is the law for Israel everywhere: "Ye shall do *my* judgments, and keep *mine* ordinances, to walk therein" (v. 4).

3. The standard of *divine claims*. God's ordinances were not imperious exactions; He deserved all He asked of Israel in return for His grace and love to them. Already they were, by His almighty arm, redeemed from "Egypt," and they were journeying to "Canaan, whither I bring you." They owed Him loyal obedience, loving regard, cheerful acquiescence. "What shall I render unto the Lord for all His benefits towards me?" "How much owest thou unto my Lord?" What claim on your life comes from His cross?

4. The standard of *divine promise*. "Keep my statutes, which if a man do he shall live in them" (v. 5). *Present* gains and comforts, *eternal* life and bliss. For "godliness is profitable unto all things, having the promise of the life which now is, and of that which is to come." [See Addenda to chap. xviii., *Religion*.]

Topic: NONCONFORMITY TO THE WORLD.

"*After the doings of the land of Egypt, wherein ye dwelt, shall ye not do*" (v. 3).

Israel now under the drill and discipline of Jehovah. The pilgrimage through the wilderness to be a period of moral probation. Moral precepts now associated with positive commands. The need of this injunction seen from—

I. THE INHERENT PROPENSITY OF HUMAN NATURE TO WORLDLINESS. Indulgence of animal appetites, exclusive concern for present enjoyment, inclination to conform to prevailing customs, worldliness congenial, and therefore easy to our fallen nature; these things show the need for the call to nonconformity to the world.

II. THE EXALTED MISSION TO WHICH ISRAEL WAS CALLED. The nation was selected to be the repository of divine truth, the community among which Jehovah would specially display His goodness and glory. Israel was not to move with the evil stream of tendency making for unrighteousness, but to become singular, come out from the ungodly, and touch not the unclean thing. This, the true idea of a Church—drawn out, separated from the world. Christ taught that those who escape a worse than Egyptian bondage are to be known by the nonconformity to the world, separation from sin, "light of the world," "salt of the earth," "city set on a hill."

To become thus peculiar and distinguished for holiness would require, on the part of Israel—as it does of Christians—(*a*) *Deep rooted repugnance to sin;* (*b*) *resolute resistance of temptation;* (*c*) *prayer for divine assistance;* (*d*) *heroic struggles after self-conquest.* To achieve victory over the world is life, to sustain defeat is death. While in the world, let us seek not to be *of* it. While not praying to be taken out of the world, we should pray to be kept from the evil.
—*F. W. B.*

Topic: THE BLESSEDNESS OF OBEDIENCE.

"If a man do, he shall live in them" (v. 5).

The legislation to which Israel was expected to submit was not an arbitrary and despotic code of laws imposed to humble them and force them into subjection; but a government of righteousness that would secure the glory of God and, at the same time, the salvation of man. Jehovah entered into covenant with His people, and engaged to fulfil all His gracious promises, if only the conditions were secured upon which their fulfilment was made to hinge. The way of life and the way of death were set before the people; they were exhorted to embrace the former, warned to escape the latter. Punishment was annexed to disobedience, reward to doing well. Thus the world was taught through the Mosaic legislation—

I. THAT LIFE IS NOT AN IDLE DREAM. Time was not to be spent in self-gratification, or wasted in wanton wickedness. Life, though brief, and like a vapour, to be turned to something real, spent in doing the will of God. Life not a period for lounging or loitering, but for *service, conflict, progress.* It is the morning, the seed time of eternity; let us improve each golden opportunity, and remember whatsoever we sow that shall we reap,

> We live in thoughts, not breath; in deeds, not years;
> In feelings, not in figures on the dial:
> We must count time by heart-throbs,
> He most lives, who thinks most, feels the noblest,
> Acts the best.

II. THAT MAN IS NOT A CREATURE OF CIRCUMSTANCES. Israel was not to be the victim of the environments of Egypt, from which they had just emerged; nor of the influences that would encircle them in the land towards which they were journeying. They were not to drift but to *live*—not to be moulded by circumstances, but conquer them, and leave the stamp of their piety and loyalty wherever they went. They had the faculty of reason, the prerogative of choice, were responsible for the use they made of the privileges they enjoyed. Though Jehovah commanded, He did not coerce, the people were left free to obey or rebel. With *life* attached to obedience, surely the people would be led to (*a*) *resist every seduction to disobedience;* (*b*) *avoid every place, person, and thing that would suggest sin and incite to wrong doing;* (*c*) *covet above everything else the favour of the great king,* who declared Himself, "I am the Lord your God." Concerning the commandments of the gospel, in the language of its glorious Author, "If ye know these things, happy are ye if ye do them."—F. W. B.

Topic: GOD'S HOLY NAME.

"Neither shalt thou profane the Name of thy God" (v. 21).

Peculiar solemnity attached to the divine name; it conveyed to the minds of the Hebrews ideas of the infinite greatness and glory of Jehovah's nature. It was hedged in by special sanctity, and gave infinite importance and power to everything to which it was attached. The sacredness of the name of the Lord, and the command to keep it holy—

I. SHOWED HOW CLOSELY HE IDENTIFIED HIMSELF WITH HIS PEOPLE. He was one with them, called them into close fellowship, and His honour was bound up with their character and conduct. If Israel fell into sin and shame, Jehovah's name was profaned.

II. Showed how immaculately pure Jehovah is. His name was emphatically holy and distinguished from all other names known in earth and heaven. The nature of Jehovah so transparently pure that every kind of evil, however trivial in appearance, was to be scrupulously avoided for His sake.

III. Showed how heinous all sin is. Sin is odious and repulsive when we remember (a) *Its brutish and fiendish influences;* (b) *how it defiles the perpetrator, and contaminates society;* (c) *how it brings punishment here and torment hereafter.* But sin appears most abominable in its nature and awful in its consequences when regarded as *an insult to the Almighty, a profanation of His holy name.* Let us hate and forsake sin because God hates it; let us view it in the light of Gethsemane and Calvary. The love of Christ will not only conquer our selfishness, and constrain us to holy consecration, but make us hate and forsake every form of iniquity in thought, word, and deed. Life will not be the dragging out of a miserable existence, but a triumphant march to the heavenly Canaan, if we seek to become cleansed from all unrighteousness, and to "perfect holiness in the fear of the Lord."—*F. W. B.*

Topic: Conjugal Chastity; or, Holiness in the Home (Vv. 1-30).

In this chapter *moral* precepts are associated with ceremonial observances. The home life of Israel was to be kept pure, sexual intercourse to be righteously restricted. The people among whom Jehovah would dwell must be clean in their domestic habits, pure in their social relationship. The natives of Canaan became so addicted to the vices here interdicted that by a retributive providence they became exterminated. These statutes, being moral, are of perpetual obligation; were not destroyed, but fulfilled in the ethical teaching of Christ and His Apostles. The fire of divine anger against impurity burns with greater intensity in the New Testament than in the Old. Observe—

I. That the social affections of human nature are prone to become wicked and wild.

Man was made at first with social instinct and affections; therefore, it is "not good for him to be alone." In the one help-meet made for him would be found congenial society, conjugal bliss. In the first family marriage relationships were entered upon among its own members, but as the race multiplied it was to the general advantage of families to marry out of their own circles, that the purity and unity of the race might be preserved. Bounds within which the affections might be indulged were divinely revealed, and the displeasure of the Almighty unmistakably announced against every infringement or perversion. The natural propensity to inordinate affection is confirmed (a) *By history.* Nations and individuals, mentioned in sacred and profane history, present sad proofs of the excesses into which social love will run when the reins are thrown upon the neck of lust. (b) *By observation.* In our own land and age, amid abounding religious advantages, and restraining influences of civilisation, what vice, immorality, conjugal unfaithfulness, and domestic impurity, abound! Deeds of infamy are done that the powers of darkness may blush to look upon, which the stern hand of the law and the sweet influence of the gospel are aiming to prevent and remove. (c) *By experience.* "When *we* would do good evil is present with us," and the most invincible enemy we have to contend with in our hearts is the *Goliath of lust.* Our animal passions are our "body of death," that often wrings from us the doleful exclamation, "O wretched man that I am." Pure Platonic love is a splendid but Utopian idea. The best of men have found it necessary to watch carefully the issues of life, to keep the body under subjection, lest passions intended to play honourably become prolific sources of corruption and misery.

II. THAT GOD HAS THEREFORE PROMULGATED SUITABLE LAWS TO RESTRICT THE SOCIAL AFFECTIONS OF HUMAN NATURE.

The springs of national purity are in the homes of the people; when the home life is corrupt the knell of a nation's greatness is tolled by the hand of doom. *Expediency, conscience,* and *self-love* might, in some instances, suggest restrictions in the indulgence of sensuous affection; but nothing short of such regulations as those here enjoined could effect the desirable end. And these regulations were enforced with great authority—on the ground of Jehovah's sovereignty and holiness, " I am the Lord your God." From such an authority there could be no appeal, for it respect and obedience would be demanded. Thus, all incest and unchastity were (*a*) *detestable to Jehovah;* (*b*) *an outrage upon human nature;* (*c*) *incompatible with man's physical, mental, and moral well-being;* (*d*) *in antagonism to the laws and forces of the universe* These statutes exhibit the *wisdom* and *goodness* of our great Creator; that as a holy and righteous Father He cares for the best interests of His children by wedding holiness and happiness in indissoluble union. Having made man, He knew what was in him, what was best for him; being his natural and moral governor He could justly impose what prohibitions He saw fit.

III. THAT THOSE LAWS DEMAND IMPLICIT OBEDIENCE FROM ALL WHO KNOW THEM.

Whether *positive* or *moral,* divine precepts ought to be obeyed, for (*a*) *they are all sovereign.* Emanate from the King of kings, from the Source of all authority and power. God has *absolute right* to command or restrain. (*b*) *They are all humane.* Everything interdicted would be good for man to shun, for vice is *cruel, degrading* and *filthy.* (*c*) *They are all salutary.* The *Individual,* the *Family,* the *Church,* the *State,* all made healthy, pure and strong by avoidance of every species of immorality, by the practice of moral virtues. (1) *To keep these divine commandments was life.* They tended to prolong his life, make it worth living, secure the favour of the Almighty, which is better than life. (2) *To break them was death.* Those who indulged in corrupt heathenish habits would be cut off from among the people. Immorality debases, deteriorates, and entails death. Let but the divine laws regarding purity be rigidly observed, the social fabric of a nation will rest upon a rock; neglected, it will sink into the mire of corruption, into the pit of oblivion. To go on in sin that grace may abound *is a foul heresy, injurious to man, detestable to God.* The gospel gathers up the teachings of the law and the prophets, and shows that " to obey is better than sacrifice, and to hearken than the fat of rams."—F. W. B.

ILLUSTRATIVE ADDENDA TO CHAPTER XVIII.

CUSTOM:
" Man yields to custom, as he bows to fate,
In all things ruled—mind, body, and estate."
—CRABBE.

" Custom calls me to't :—
What custom wills, in all things should we do it ?"—*Coriolanus,* II. 3.

" New customs
Tho' they be never so ridiculous,
Nay, let them be unmanly, yet are followed."
—*Henry VIII.,* I. 3.

RELIGION:
" The body of all true religion consists, to be true, in *obedience to the will* of the Sovereign of the world, in a *confidence in His declarations,* and in *imitation of His perfections.*"—BURKE.

" Piety, like wisdom, consists in the discovery of the rules under which we are actually placed, and in faithfully obeying them."
—FROUDE.

" Life and Religion are one, or neither is anything. I will not say neither is going to be anything. Religion is no way of life, no show of life, no observances of any sort. It is neither the food nor medicine of being. It is life essential."—GEO. MACDONALD.

" A religious life is a struggle and not a hymn."—MADAME DE STAEL.

CHAPTER XIX.

Practical Piety: Religion in all Relationships.

SUGGESTIVE READINGS.

V. 2.—Speak unto all the congregation of the children of Israel, and say: Nowhere else in the whole of Leviticus does this direction to address "*all* the *congregation*" occur; a fact which indicates the importance of this section of the decalogue. And in the precepts of this chapter, traversing the entire range of personal, social, and religious life, we have the law summarized—"the whole duty of man" in epitome.

Reverence for *parents* (v. 3); *sabbath* observance (v. 3); repudiation of *idolatry* (v. 4); the conditions of acceptable *sacrifice* (vv. 5 8); regard for the *poor* in harvest *gleanings* (vv. 9, 10); *honesty* in act and speech (v. 11); fidelity to *oaths* (v. 12); *commercial* integrity (v. 13); consideration for sufferers, the *deaf* and *blind* (v. 14); *impartiality* in justice (v. 15); avoidance of *slander* (v. 16); care for one's *neighbour* (v. 16); *gentleness* yet *faithfulness* to other's faults (v. 17); *malice* to be shunned (v. 18); *hybrid products* forbidden (v. 19); the crime of *seduction* (vv. 20-22); regulations concerning *fruit growths* (vv. 22-25); *blood* to be put aside as food (v. 26); and *sorceries and superstitious practices* avoided (v. 26); prohibition of *heathenish manners and rites of mourning* (vv. 27, 28); *traffic in vice* condemned (v. 29); regard for the *sabbath and sanctuary* (v. 30); *necromancy* denounced (v. 31); respect for the *aged* commanded (v. 32); courtesy to *strangers* (vv. 33, 34); honesty, in *trade* (vv. 35. 36): and all based on the grand requirement that the "*statutes and judgments*" of "the Lord" were to be the rule of their conduct in all relationships and all transactions.

The righteousness which God delights in pervades our whole life, purifies all habits, ennobles all actions, stamps character with rectitude and conduct with integrity. Religion is for daily life; not for sacred scenes and solemn hours, but for every place, every moment; sanctifying the full manhood, elevating all action, dignifying all aims. There is not a plan or project, not a fault or foible, not a vice or misdemeanour, not a social or sacred duty, but the thought of God is upon it, and He has a word in condemnation or sanction respecting it. He "with whom we have to do" overlooks nothing in our behaviour, "neither is there any creature that is not manifest in His sight, but all things are open and naked to the eyes of Him" (Heb. iv. 13).

How scrupulously should we, therefore, speak and act; not in reluctant submission but in cheerful obedience; His "laws within our heart"; His "statutes our song"; delighting to do His will. For He who requires such minute dutifulness shows concern *that none should suffer at our hands*, and therefore that we should suffer nought from others. Divine benevolence regulates these requirements, and all are detailed indications of His fatherly eagerness for His children's comfort. Only in right doing is there happiness, whether in the family, in society, or in the church, hence God requires the right to be maintained in all relationships; and when His "will is done on earth" earth will be a reflection of heaven.

HOMILIES ON CHAPTER XIX.

Topic: THE RELIGION OF MORALITY.

i. Piety is not to be all *ecstatic*. Tabor heights, Beulah rhapsodies, third-heaven visions—these are not the whole of religion, nor indeed the standard of a sacred life. There is the piety of daily work, of common things. Easier to be religious when we are on the *wing* soaring, than when we are on our *feet* struggling.

ii. Piety may not become *eclectic*. There are divine precepts and laws congenial to us, others the reverse. Yet we may not select. Directions concerning the "Sabbath and sanctuary" are easier and more pleasant to heed than those against tale-bearing, fraud in business, gleaning on the fields, etc. But "these ought ye to have done, and not to have left the others undone."

iii. Piety should not be narrowly *egotistic*. God's laws and directions call us out of ourselves, give no room for selfishness, self-assertion, individualism. Think of *others first*, care for the "poor" (v. 9), your "neighbours" (vv. 13, 17), bearing no malice (v. 18), etc. Let self give place; "look not every man on his own things, but every man also on the things of others" (Phil. ii. 4).

iv. Piety must never become *elastic*. There is a peril of the godly man relaxing and relapsing from strict and severe rectitude; stretching his convictions, and accommodating himself to prevailing tastes or personal fancies. Here is rigid law; to that he must bring all conduct; by this standard all his behaviour must be ruled. Avoid an easily adjusting religion, straining and shaping itself to the conveniences of the hour, and the inducements of temptation, and the impulses of the carnal heart.

I. RELIGION REQUIRES THE MORALITIES OF FAMILY LIFE.

God asks that there be "first *piety* at home." [See Addenda to chapter, *Morality*.]

1. *Family dutifulness among children*. "Ye shall fear every man his mother and his father" (v. 3). This is the "first commandment with promise" (Ephes. vi. 2). The word "fear" enjoins *respect, felt* and *shown;* generous *succour* and attention to their comfort; *obedience* to their rule and desires.

2. *Purity in conjugal relationships*. Between *husband and wife* there should be strictest fidelity. Any departure from morality is severely denounced as the violation of the sanctities of family bonds (vv. 20 22). "No man should go beyond or defraud his brother" in this matter (1 Thess. iv. 4-6). And equally, with sternest reprobation, God marks the *traffic in vice* (v. 29). There have been parents sufficiently "earthly, sensual, devilish," to be capable of this foul crime against a child. Jehovah would have the home *clean* and *loving* and *hallowed*.

3. *Homage for the aged* (v. 32). Venerating the "hoary head," and caring for the "old man" gently in his drooping years, and paying him the courtesies and attentions due to one who has lived a lengthened life and is nearing eternity.

II. RELIGION REQUIRES THE MORALITIES OF NEIGHBOURLY RELATIONSHIP.

In the *narrowest circle of our neighbours*, near residents, there should be the cultivation of rectitude and goodwill. The *yet larger range of neighbourliness* is taught us in our Lord's parable of the Good Samaritan—care for anyone in need.

1. Every device of *deceitfulness* is to be abhorred (vv. 11, 12). No advantage to be taken, no trickery practised, no falsity condoned

2. All *oppression and injustice* is to be shunned (v. 13). Straightforwardness in dealings, considerateness in payment of his dues.

3. *Slander* and *whispering* are denounced (v. 16). How disastrous this pernicious habit has proved! (see 1 Sam xxii. 9, 18; Ezk xxii. 9, etc.). Yes: and as harm may come to a neighbour from *doing nothing* equally as from our slandering him, God denounces our "standing," *i.e.*, standing still, when inactivity might let a neighbour's blood be shed, either in *accident from which we could rescue him*, or from the *stroke of justice when we could prove him innocent*.

4. *Generous concern* for a neighbour is inculcated. "*Hate*" to be closed from thine "*heart*"; then venturing to "*rebuke*" him if he be going into "sin" (v. 17); yet never allowing malice to urge thee to "*avenge* or *bear grudge*"; but to "*love* thy neighbour as thyself" (v. 18). In this last precept is summed up all the moral aspects, the *human side of religion*.

III. Religion requires the moralities of civic benevolence.

A man of God is not less a member of society, of the state, or of the nation because he is religious. He has duties *towards his fellow-citizens* as such.

1. *The prosperous are to care for the "poor."* When the harvest is being reaped (v. 9) there is to be a generous dropping of ears for the poor : and so with the vine gathering (v. 10).

2. The *healthy are to be pitiful to the afflicted.* Instead of despising and maltreating "the deaf" and "the blind" (v. 14), all the instincts of philanthropy —which is piety humanized—prompt "the strong to bear the infirmities of the weak."

3. *Hospitality for the stranger* (vv. 33, 34). A willing asylum should be offered to any fugitive or sojourner : there might be no national exclusiveness or selfishness : the generous hand should be outstretched to any one who would find a home amid the people of God.

IV. Religion requires the moralities of honest transactions.

1. *Impartiality in the administration of justice* (v. 15). If the high courts of judgment should be demoralized by no cupidity, certainly our personal conduct should be swayed by no servility. The "poor" and the "mighty" should have equal justice at our hands : not one law for the rich and another for the poor.

2. *Fairness in the transactions of trade* (vv. 35, 36). Honesty in commerce; in forming *estimate* of articles of purchase ("in judgment"), not saying "It is nought, it is nought," etc. (Prov. xx. 14) ; as well as in *serving* and *selling* these articles.

V. Religion requires all moralities to be joined with the elevated sanctities of worship.

Just as that religion is wrong which consists in *serving God to the neglect of man;* so is that as surely wrong which fulfils duties to man but *neglects God's claims.* Week-day righteousness needs to be crowned by sacred solemnities on the sabbath and in the sanctuary.

1. Family life should be *hallowed with Sabbath sanctities.* "Keep my Sabbaths" (v. 3); for that is the day of days in which to instruct the household in sacred duties. When God is revered in the home family reverence will not wane.

2. *Delusive idolatries will be escaped by homage for Jehovah on His day.* Keeping His Sabbaths will correct the perils of "turning unto idols" (connect v. 3 thus with v. 4).

3. *Worship of the Lord should be with sacrificial offerings* (v. 5-8); for man is a sinner, and must come with propitiation to God's altar.

4. *God's sanctuary should be held in reverence* (v. 30) ; "not forsaking the assembling of yourselves together" (Heb. x. 25) ; but coming with solemn thought and prayer.

5. *All superstition to be sedulously shunned.* Heathenish delusions (v. 26-28), and "familiar spirits" (v. 31). God should fill the spiritual life of man; and Him only should we serve.

Topic: The Genius of the Mosaic Laws.

"And the Lord spake unto Moses, saying," etc. How repeatedly these words occur previous to enunciation of statutes to Israel, to indicate that Moses was only the amanuensis, or mouthpiece of Jehovah, and that the statutes demanded devout attention and implicit obedience. The repetition of sundry laws recorded in this chapter furnishes a fair specimen of the whole economy, embraces principles and doctrines exhibited in the realms of *Nature, Providence,* and *Grace.* Looked at as a whole, they suggest the following trains of thought :—

I. THEIR STRIKING ANALOGY WITH THE CONSTITUTION OF NATURE This accords with what might have been expected *à priori* viz., that God would govern men by *similar* laws to those by which He governs the world, that between physical and spiritual laws there would be close correspondence. The laws here promulgated were:

(*a*) *Unsystematic in their arrangement.* Like the glorious diffuseness in nature, where the geologist and botanist can make their scientific arrangements from world-wide materials, scattered here and there in great profusion ; so, in the Mosaic economy, running through Leviticus—and through the whole Bible—are sundry precepts unformulated, unscientifically arranged, leaving scope for the sanctified soul of man to arrange in a course of systematic theology.

(*b*) *Disciplinary in their character.* Nature's laws teach man that he is a probationer; that if he obeys, safety and happiness will ensue ; if he disobeys, danger and death will await him. The Mosaic laws taught that whatsoever a man sows that shall he reap, that retribution follows closely on the heels of the wrong-doer. Thus, the law was a schoolmaster, teaching self-restraint, and enforcing lessons upon human conduct that have been the basis of all good government in the world, the germs of all pure morality among men.

(*c*) *Merciful in their tendency.* The law put no embargo upon anything that would minister to the real welfare of the human race, only pernicious habits were condemned. The *weak,* the *poor,* the *aged, parents* and *strangers,* all were to be treated with kindness ; sympathy and aid were to be extended to them. Even towards the brute creation care and kindness were to be exercised, nothing was to be wantonly or unmercifully treated. Nature's laws exhibit kindness and mercy in their operations ; even in their sternest moods they work for good, and in the end produce happiness.

(*d*) *Mysterious in their operations.* Many of nature's laws perplex and puzzle the greatest minds, *seem* inconsistent with the perfect wisdom and goodness of the Infinite Author of the universe. And in the Levitical code many of the sacrificial rites and ceremonial observances *seem* strange and ambiguous. These facts teach us (i.) *how comprehensive God's laws are;* (ii.) *how limited our knowledge is;* (iii.) *how incumbent faith, humility, and resignation are upon all who would know the will of the Lord and do it.*

II. THEIR BENEFICENT INFLUENCE UPON THE NATIONAL LIFE OF ISRAEL. The people were in great danger of becoming corrupt, from their recollections of their surroundings in Egypt, from their inherent tendency to depart from the living God ; the system of sacrifices instituted among them, the ceremonial laws to which they were expected rigidly to submit, would keep them distinct from the surrounding nations, lift them to a high standard of national greatness. The prohibition of all *false swearing, fraud, deception, tale-bearing, selfishness, revenge,* and every kind of private and public immorality, would conduce to the safety and stability of the Hebrew Commonwealth. The Levitical laws, while they taught the people that they were *one as a nation,* also enjoined upon each *individual responsibility.* The whole nation was one great family, mutually related to each other, all amenable to Jehovah, their Father and King. The religion of the Bible exalts the life of any nation that follows its precepts. Those —where the Holy Scriptures are regarded as the foundation of national greatness —will be found in the van of the civilisation of the world.

III. THEIR SPECIAL ADAPTATION TO ELEVATE THE WHOLE NATURE OF MAN. The laws respecting uncleanness, restraining the animal passions and appetites, securing rest one day in seven, would conduce to man's physical well being. Powers of the mind would be awakened and expanded by efforts required to apprehend and obey the elaborate ritual of the tabernacle. The moral powers would be cultivated by everything having reference to purity of heart, and the spotless supremacy of Jehovah. Thus Israel were shown that God took special interest in them, that they were not like the brutes which perish, but servants of the Lord, children of the great King, being educated for higher future employment. They had access to the *house of the Lord;* listened to the *Word of the Lord;* were led by *chosen servants of the Lord.* These facts would lead them to look onward and upward, present to them the way to pardon and peace, to fellowship with God and meetness for Heaven.

IV. THEIR ELEMENTARY FORESHADOWINGS OF THE TEACHINGS OF THE GOSPEL. (*a*) *In the supremacy of their claims.* Everything was to be subordinated to the demands of Jehovah ; so, Christ said, "seek ye first the kingdom of God," etc. (*b*) *In the object of their observances.* Holiness was the end of everything in the law; so, the gospel—in the precepts of Christ and His apostles—demands purity of heart, sets holiness as the mark of our high calling, to which is attached the prize of heaven. (*c*) *In the substitutionary character of their sacrifices.* The Hebrews were taught to consider their guilt transferred to the victim offered for them; through it, in some way, they were forgiven, accepted of the Lord; so, in the gospel, through the one great sin offering guilt is removed, the favour of God secured, heaven opened. The services of the tabernacle, the statutes of the Levitical law, were calculated to suggest the priceless value of the human soul, the existence for it of a life beyond, of which the present is introductory and preparatory. In the gospel all these *foreshadowings* are presented as *substantial realities,* just as indefinite twilight merges into revealing distinguishing day. —F. W. B.

OUTLINES ON VERSES OF CHAPTER XIX.

V. 2.—*Theme :* PERSONAL HOLINESS.
" *Ye shall be holy, for I, the Lord your God, am holy.*"

The glorious end for which the law was given, every ceremonial precept enforced, was that the people should become holy. The holy *nature, name, will* and *purpose* of Jehovah demanded that those who would be constantly drawing near to Him in the tabernacle services should come out from the heathen world, forsake their sinful customs, and become conformed to His commandments, which were—

I. WORTHY OF JEHOVAH. Not one can be characterised as mean or unmerciful; some of them may *seem beyond,* but not one against, reason. The unreaped corners of the field, the gleanings of the harvest, the grapes left upon the vine for the poor and the stranger in the land, would speak of the *considerateness* of Jehovah for the physical wants of the people; and the injunctions against fraud, against hating in the heart, against impurity in social life; the command, " thou shalt love thy neighbour as thyself "; all these injunctions *pointed to the heart* as the seat of all holiness, and demanded that the *motives* by which the Hebrews would be actuated should be pure. Such a code of laws, with such humane and holy ends, reflected glory upon the supreme Lawgiver, proving that He is holy, that His nature is on the side of righteousness.

II. BENEFICIAL TO ISRAEL. Everything was to be avoided that would work detoriation in the physical constitution, for vice and impurity produce feebleness and decay. Want of reverence for parents and the aged; lack of sympathy for the suffering and infirm, bring ruin into the domestic and social circle. Greed, dishonesty, unrighteousness, work disintegration and disaster in the commercial world. The holy laws of God were a barrier against all these terrible evils by demanding personal holiness in everyone who heard these injunctions.

The disposition of the heart and mind was to be brought into conformity with the will of Jehovah, " ye shall offer at your own will." The people were not slaves, to do reluctantly the will of God, or perform services and offer sacrifices in a mechanical manner; they were the Lord's free men, and from wills in harmony with Him were to obey His statutes. Thus inward, personal holiness would be secured, Jehovah's glory displayed. The great end of the gospel is holiness of heart and life The Christian Church is a community of " saints." The redeemed in heaven are those who are faultless, without spot in the presence of God's unsullied glory.—*F. W. B.*

V. 3.—*Theme :* FAMILY PIETY.
" *Ye shall fear every man his mother and his father, and keep my Sabbaths ; I am the Lord your God.*"

I. *In home life the* SPIRIT OF FEAR DEMANDS CULTURE.

1. *No dutiful submission to parents* where "fear" has no place in children's hearts. This "fear" not slavish but respectful, leading to an unresisting spirit, and obedient behaviour.

2. No proper basis of obedience where duty is *not made forceful by the requirements of religion.* "Keep my sabbaths," making piety an integral part of home-life; thus fortifying the claims of parentage by the teachings of God's Word and His house.

II. *In children, both their* HUMAN AND DIVINE RELATIONSHIPS SHOULD BE FOSTERED

1. This requires *piety in the parents.* How else can they show their children the ways of the Lord? Parents are to their children God's representatives and vicegerents on earth.

2 This will cultivate *piety in the children.* "Keep God's Sabbath" in the home : bring upon young hearts and minds the graces of religion, the delight of "holy psalm and song," the teachings of Jesus, the bliss of adoption through Christ; and "bringing them up in the nurture and admonition of the Lord."

III. IN SABBATH HABITS *the family needs be devoutly educated.*

1. *Sabbath leisure* gives opportunity for parental attention to the religious interests of the family.

2. *The Sabbath solemnity* is helpful to the effort of leading children's thoughts to godly instruction.

3. *Sanctuary services and ordinances* should form themes of teaching and interest in the home on sabbath days

Children, thus trained in early recognition of God by parents who link themselves with God in holy life and word, and who "make the Sabbath a delight" in their homes, assuredly will not depart from the ways of religion, but tread early the path after Jesus. [See Addenda to chapter, *Family Piety* and *Sabbath and Sanctuary*]

V 3 — *Theme:* FILIAL OBLIGATIONS.

"*Ye shall fear every man his mother and his father.*"

Under the patriarchal dispensation the father was to be revered not only as the head of the family, but as the priest in the home circle The tent and the altar were reared together, children were expected to honour their parents by becoming attention to social and sacred duties. In the decalogue the claims of parental authority were enforced; and, being here reiterated, the Hebrews would be taught those duties which, disregarded, bring discord and misery into the home. Natural instincts prompt filial fear, but undutifulness to parents will often spring up with other moral delinquencies to which our fallen nature is prone. Want of reverence for parenthood—

I. EXHIBITS BASENESS OF HEART. The affections must have become corrupt, the feelings hardened, when parents are dishonoured

II INCURS THE DIVINE DISPLEASURE. It is God's will that children should reverence their parents ; to disobey His will is to dishonour and displease Him.

III ENTAILS DISASTROUS CONSEQUENCES. A special promise was made to those who would obey in these particulars, and in several parts of Scripture threatenings of punishment are annexed to disobedience. Obedience should be *reverent affectionate, cheerful* and *constant.* "Children obey your parents in the Lord, for this is right."— *F. W. B.*

V. 5.—*Theme:* WILLING OFFERINGS OF PEACE.

See homilies on Chapters iii and vii. Compare specially Outline, Chapter i, v. 3, p. 14, VOLITION IN WORSHIP.

V. 9.—*Theme:* HARVEST GLEANINGS

How notable are the provisions made in the Mosaic law for the poor.

The Sabbatical year (Exodus xxiii. 10, 11 ; compare Deut xv. 12, 15)

The equalization of the atonement money for poor and rich, thus establishing the value of the poor as equal to the rich (Exodus xxx. 12).

The same minute directions for the poor man's offerings, showing God's equal interest in his sacrifice (Levit. ii., etc.).

And here the command that the harvest and vintage gleanings should be left (vv. 9, 10).

Notice—

I. THAT THE HUMANE LAWS OF MODERN TIMES, *respecting gleaning privileges, are all based upon this Mosaic command*

Everywhere there is a popular feeling that the farmer should allow, and was not entitled to prevent the poor from gathering what the reaper left behind.

In England the custom of gleaning had very nearly passed into a *legal right,* for there is an extra judicial dictum of Lord Hall, in which he says that those who enter a field for this purpose are not guilty of trespass ; and Blackstone (iii. 12) seems to adopt his opinion. But that has since been twice tried, and decided in the negative in the Court of Common Pleas ; the Court finding it to be a practice incompatible with the exclusive enjoyment of property, and productive of vagrancy and many mischievous consequences.

"It is still, however, the *custom* all over England to allow the poor to glean, at least after the harvest is carried " (Chambers).

The law of Moses directed a liberal consideration for the poor at the seasons of harvest and ingathering. The corners of the field were not to be reaped; the owner was not to glean his own fields; and a sheaf accidentally left in a field was not to be fetched away, but to be the possession of the poor gleaners.

Although the permission to glean was a favour, it required no special influence to secure it; for Ruth secured this liberty without any recommendation (Ruth ii 2, 3).

II. *That a benevolent helpfulness in respect of the poor* IS A SPECIAL OBLIGATION OF THOSE WHO ENJOY PLENTY.

1. *With God in thought*, the rich will *spare of their abundance* that the poor may be fed. And this is the meaning of this sealing sentence, "I am the Lord your God" (v. 10). You *owe all to Him*, especially in harvest; and, therefore, share with the needy His gifts to you.

2. *Amid harvest rejoicings, gratitude should incite to generosity*. What render to God? "As ye have received, give!" Seek occasion to gladden others—those in need. Gladness which has no kindly outlet and expression makes men selfish and hard. God is lavish; let your "hands be open" also (Psa. cxlv. 16).

3. Kindness to the poor has *especial assurances of divine approval*. "He that giveth to the poor lendeth to the Lord." "The liberal soul shall be made full." But He will requite those who neglect the poor (Psa. ix. 18; xii. 5).

III. *That this generous consideration for the poor is* A TOKEN OF GOD'S REGARD FOR THE LOWLY.

1 *Their maintenance* engaged the divine attention. For them "the corner" of the field was claimed from the reapers, and to them was assigned the right to clear the ground. It was their part in the national soil, the poor had this heritage in the land. And God enjoins on His Church now to "care for the poor." They are Christ's bequeathment to His disciples. "The poor always ye have with you."

2. Their *salvation* is prominently sought in the gospel. "To the poor the gospel is preached." And "God hath chosen the poor rich in faith." He who showed concern for their *physical supply* and maintenance, as emphatically manifests His desire that they be "blessed with all *spiritual* blessings" in Christ. Therefore—

(*a*) The poor should cherish a grateful and trustful hope in their God.

(*b*) They should value the high mercies of redemption in Christ beyond all the kindnesses of His providence. For the favours of providence only affect them temporally, but "the riches of His grace" are of eternal consequence. Therefore, "seek ye first the kingdom of God and his righteousness, and all these things shall be added unto you."

(*c*) Let none, because of lowliness or poverty, despond of God's favour. All His regulations prove that "he careth for you." Look unto Him with assurance. "This poor man cried and the Lord heard him, and saved him out of all his troubles" (Psa. xxxiv. 6).

"His love ordained the seasons,
By Him are all things fed,
He for the sparrow careth,
He gives the poor their bread:

Every bounteous blessing
His faithful love bestows:
Then magnify His glorious Name
From Whom all goodness flows."

V. 10.—*Theme*: JEHOVAH'S RIGHTEOUS DEMANDS.

"*I am the Lord your God.*"

Though the record of divine revelation contains no argument to *prove* the existence of God, it repeatedly asserts *the fact*; all the forces of nature, all positive and moral statutes, are traced to the sovereign will and absolute authority of Jehovah. The Hebrews were taught that their obedience was not to be governed by the customs of society, their own preferences or prejudices, but by the declared will of Him Who had sovereign claim to them and theirs. Thus they were emphatically taught—

I. *The absolute supremacy of Jehovah*. No imaginary deity was to be brought into competition, or comparison with Him. *He*, the Eternal, Infinite, Almighty, Creator, and Governor of all things. He had right to assert His claim to universal homage; to settle the question of the human mind about the divine existence. God has spoken, declared His existence, and character; to doubt that word, deny that existence, impeach that character, indicate derangement of the mental powers, and debasement of the heart.

II. *The absolute character of their obligations*. They belonged to the Lord, He claimed them as His own peculiar people. All idols were to be forsaken (v. 4), the worship of Israel was not to have its basis in ignorance, or origin in fear, but in the recognition of the obligations under which Jehovah's relationship and dealings had placed them. He was a jealous God, and would not share worship with another. Having received such a revelation of the divine character and claims, Israel was under obligation to render *intelligent, cheerful, devout, constant, implicit, willing* obedience. The divine claims to obedience are unrelaxing, declarations of our obligations unrepealed. "Ye are not your own," etc. "I beseech you, brethren, by the mercies of God," etc. The divine supremacy of Christ places us under binding obligation to *serve Him loyally*; His self-sacrificing love constrains us to *serve Him lovingly*.—F. W. B.

V. 12—*Theme:* FALSE SWEARING.

All nations have severely *punished* perjury. The *Egyptians* with death or mutilation; the *Greeks* with heavy fines and ultimate loss of all civil rights; the *Romans* visited it with the penalty of death.

These ancient nations all held that the gods were especially incensed by this crime, and that a divine Nemesis pursued the perjurer. [See Addenda to chapter, *Perjury*].

I. WHAT SWEARING BY GOD'S NAME ENTAILS.

1. *Acknowledgment of His Omniscience*. It calls Him to *witness*, and imprecates Him as the avenger of falsehood.

2. *Acknowledgment of His Righteousness.* He is to be the umpire and arbitrator. We call in as a witness to our fidelity only such a one as is himself faithful and true, and will act a right part. Such is God. Man's use of His name is an appeal to the certainty that He will judge aright.

II. WHAT PERJURY IN GOD'S NAME ENTAILS.

1. *An insolent affront upon God's character.* It is infamy, daring insolence, the degradation of His most holy name for unholy ends. It invokes Him to act as a witness that a lie is true Yet He loathes falsity. It is defiant trifling, an affront to the God of truth. It "*profanes* his name."

2. *A certain visitation of judgment.* He "will not hold him guiltless that taketh his name in vain" (Exod. xx. 7) Certainly, therefore, He will punish lying and profanity. Having been called in as a witness to a lie He will prove that He witnessed it. Thus to insult His love of truth and defy His power to vindicate it, and trail the purity of His character in the mire—before whom the very angels veil their faces as they adore Him—will ensure a just requital (Heb. x 30). And "there shall in no wise enter the heavenly city any who loveth and maketh a lie " (Rev. xxi. 27).

V. 13— *Theme:* FAIRNESS TO HIRED LABOURERS.

I. WORK IS A JUST BASIS FOR AN EQUITABLE CLAIM.

Therefore it should be paid for, not *patron isingly*, nor *grudgingly*, but as a due. The labourer has given you his *time, strength, ability*, and *ingenuity ;* he has a *right* to an equivalent from you, and should not be treated ignominiously, but respectfully in asking a just return

II. WAGES CANNOT RIGHTEOUSLY BE DEFERRED AFTER WORK IS DONE.

During a day of toil the labourer has put his capital into your service, spent his life for that period for your advantage and gain. You are to that extent his debtor; to detain his wages is to make yourself more his debtor, and delay in payment should be compensated with increment. "Short reckonings make long friends."

III. MASTERS SHOULD STUDY THE POSITION AND COMFORT OF THOSE THEY EMPLOY.

A poor man has no capital, wants prompt settlement ; he lives day by day upon his hard earnings. His strength—expended by the day's toil—must be replenished for the morrow's work. To hold back the means for his nourishment is to rob him of the morrow's capital, his replenished energy. And he may have dependents in his lowly home waiting to share in the earnings of the day. Hold not back his dues "all night until the morning," lest your inconsiderateness inflict privation and embitter poverty. Comp. Deut. xxiv. 14, 15 ; Jer. xxxii. 13 ; Mal iii. 5 ; James v. 4. [See Addenda to chapter, *Business and Work.*]

V. 14.— *Theme :* DEAF AND BLIND.

i. *As witnesses to* AFFLICTIONS POSSIBLE TO ALL, they call for our commiseration.

ii. As sufferers of DIREFUL INFIRMITIES, they should enlist our gentle care and generous helpfulness. " Eyes to the blind."

iii. As pensive illustrations of MAN'S FRAILTY they should incite our gratitude that God made us to differ.

Consider—

1. How *mean the act of ridiculing those* who carry the grief of such bodily infirmities. " But fear thy God," for He will requite.

2. How *swift was the compassion of Jesus* towards those sad children of infirmity.

3. How glad the outlook of the heavenly life for such as suffer here—if they have hope in Christ. For "there shall be no more sorrow, nor crying, neither any more pain."

V. 15.— *Theme :* IMPARTIAL JUSTICE.

I. JUSTICE PERVERTED.

In every nation and age wealth and influence have effectively distorted the administration of justice.

Poverty and weakness have borne cruel and basest wrongs by reason of their very helplessness.

II. JUSTICE INFLEXIBLE.

Poverty may not be pleaded in arrest of justice. He, who being poor, acts wrongly, may not make poverty his screen; he must bear his guilt. A *sentimental pity* for the poor would thwart the ends of righteousness. Sin is sin whether committed in rags or in ermine. [Comp. Exod. xxiii. 3.]

A *servile courtesy* to the " mighty "is equally subversive of righteousness. A perfidious king is as guilty a traitor to his country as a perfidious subject. Neither station nor purse should sway the balances of justice.

As in the *sanctuary*, so at the bar, there should be " no respect of persons." [Comp. Jas. ii. 6, 19, with verses 2-4.]

III. JUSTICE CERTAIN.

God will judge those who now administer or pervert judgment. " Every man shall give account of himself to God."

The " *supreme Judge* of all the earth " will do right. He " *discerns judgment* " now, and will *dispense justice* at the last day. [See Addenda to chapter, *Justice.*]

V. 16.— *Theme:* TALE-BEARING AND SLANDER.

I. CHARACTER IS IN THE KEEPING, and *therefore at the mercy of acquaintances.*

1. Therefore *supremely value* each other's good name.

2. *Jealously defend* a worthy reputation.

3. *Scornfully silence the unproved rumours* of evils [See Addenda to chapter, *Slander.*]

II. CHARACTER MAY BE RUTHLESSLY SHATTERED *by sinister whisperings.*

1. For *listeners are ready to entertain* and repeat slander.

"Man's inhumanity to man !"

2. *Aspersions feed on the inventiveness of malice.*

Proof not asked; nothing therefore to check or refute the slander. And "lying lips" find delight in adding to the lie as they pass it on.

3. *Reputation is easily damaged.* That which only a lifetime can build an hour may defame.

III. CHARACTER IS SO PRECIOUS *that its traducers should be loathed.*

1. *Dread a tale bearer as a destroying pestilence.*

2. *He who wrongs another's reputation may next wrong yours.* By heeding his slanders you encourage his vile trade, and slander must find *new* victims!

3. *Put to shame all tale-bearers* with ruthless severity.

Note—

i. There is *enough of woe abroad* without increasing it.

ii. As we *need our many evils to be pitied* by man and pardoned by God, let us with "charity hide sins," not expose them.

iii. There is *grace in Christ*, and energy in the Holy Spirit, by which to perfect a good life and win a good name, which even enemies of religion shall be unable to defame or destroy.

iv. The *light of the final judgment* will refute all slander, and bring every secret thing to the open gaze of the world.

V. 18 —*Theme:* NEIGHBOURLY LOVE.

"*Thou shalt love thy neighbour as thyself.*"

Disinterested love is difficult to cherish, and is all too rare.

The contraries of love are everywhere rife: jealousy, rivalry, cruelty, selfishness, greed, hate.

An unloving spirit is an ungodly one; for a malicious man is as unlike God as an immoral man is; the slanderer is as cruel as the murderer.

I. ALL TRUE HUMAN LOVE HAS ITS ROOT AND ORIGIN IN GOD.

It is a ray of His glory, a breath of His Spirit. A *mother's* love is a divinely-implanted instinct. So the love of *friendship* is heaven-born. And *neighbourly* love is an inspiration from God. The fine feelings of *benevolence*, of *philanthrophy*, of *charity*—all aspects of the divine spirit of love are of Him. And *Christian love*, the love of God, love for Christ, the *brotherly love* of saints, all come from our drinking in the spirit of Jesus.

II. EVERY EXPRESSION OF TRUE HUMAN LOVE HAS HEAVEN'S HIGHEST APPROVAL.

Our love *Godward* is the rising of the flame towards its Source, and is as a "sweet savour of Christ" to Him.

Our love for *man* is the outbreathing of the mind of Christ in us, the diffusion of the very spirit of Jesus.

Love for God and for man, let it prevail, and it brings *heaven's blessedness within the human breast*, and will make our bleared and distracted earth again like heaven

III. NEIGHBOURLY LOVE HAS AMPLE OPPORTUNITIES FOR ILLUSTRATION.

1. In seeking to *turn him aside from sin* (v. 17). [See Addenda to chapter, *Neighbourliness*.]

2. In *bearing patiently any wrong* received from him (v. 18).

3 In *praying and working for his conversion* to God.

4. In *leading him to the Saviour* you have yourself found; as did the woman of Samaria her neighbours.

A *Cultivate kindness and generosity by communion with Jesus*; and that will so fill your soul with *pity for the erring*, and *yearning for their deliverance* as will make it easy to love your neighbour.

B. *Consider how many evils you have wrought*, which *men have had to condone* and *God to forgive*, and then you will take meekly the wrongs others have done you.

C. *Live with eternity in view*, and act towards others more as you will wish you had done in the Day of Account, and through the everlasting ages.

D. And *as opportunity goes by swiftly*, do at once what love prompts, and "do it with thy might." There are wounds waiting to be healed, hearts to be comforted, estrangements to be conciliated, errors to be forgiven.

"*Love thy neighbour*," with like depth and thoroughness as thou lovest "thyself."

V. 19.—*Theme:* THE RESPONSIBILITY OF STEWARDSHIP.

"*Ye shall keep my statutes.*"

The Israelites knew that the land towards which they were moving was given them for their inheritance, they were to possess it, and enjoy its abundant resources. But they had to remember that it was Jehovah who had delivered them from Egypt, who would conduct them through the wilderness, and to whom they would be responsible when they would get to the end of their wanderings, and enter upon the land flowing with milk and honey. In Canaan they would be the Lord's husbandmen, and stewards, to farm the land according to His will. "Ye shall keep my statutes." They would be reminded of their stewardship in—

I. THE SACRIFICES THEY OFFERED TO THE LORD (see preceding Homilies on offerings). As the Hebrews brought the best of their substance and offered it to the Lord, they would recognise the claims of the Highest and Holiest to themselves and all they possessed.

II. IN THE PORTIONS THEY RESERVED FOR THE POOR. They were the almoners of the Lord, and at His command must see that the needy did not perish from want. Coveteousness and selfishness were alike condemned; they could not do as they pleased with the grapes and corn.

III. IN THE NON-PARTICIPATION OF UNCIRCUMCISED FRUIT The young trees were to be left for four years, the fifth year they might partake thereof. Thus a curb was put upon their appetites, and the first-fruits were to be wholly devoted to the Lord. Thus the earth would be to Israel God's banqueting house, and the people were to partake only of those things which the divine host considered good for them and the land.

IV. IN THE PRESERVATION OF PRODUCE AND STOCK FROM ADULTERATION. There was to be no breeding between diverse kinds of cattle, no mingling of seed in sowing a field, no mixing of materials in fabrics for garments. These injunctions would not only be in harmony with Jehovah's requirement of purity in heart and life, but would keep before the minds of the people the fact that corn and cattle, food and clothing were all under His surveillance. He was the proprietor of all; to Him account must be rendered for all.

V. IN THE RIGHTEOUSNESS OF THEIR COMMERCIAL TRANSACTIONS. Here we see (vv. 35, 36) how thorough and searching the morality of the Mosaic law was. The Hebrews were to avoid every kind of wrong-doing. Religion was to affect their business transactions, cover the whole of their secular life. In everything they did they were to remember that the eye of the Lord was on them, they were His servants, under obligation to do all to His glory, according to the principles of righteousness.

Under the new dispensation we are stewards in the kingdom of Christ. We are responsible for the use we make of the talents entrusted to us. The gospel does not exempt us from responsibility to live righteously all our days; all the precepts of the moral law are summed up in the golden law, as enunciated by Christ, "Thou shalt love," etc. Christianity demands a holy, righteous life, as well as a sound scriptural belief.—*F. W. B.*

Theme: THE DUTY OF REPROVING OUR NEIGHBOUR. "Thou shalt not hate thy brother in thy heart: thou shalt in anywise rebuke thy neighbour, and not suffer sin upon him."

The ritual or ceremonial law was such "a yoke as neither our fathers nor we (says Peter) were able to bear." Yet many excellent moral precepts are interspersed among those laws. Several in this chapter (vv. 10, 11, 13, 14, 15, 16). In this injunction consider—

I. WHAT DUTY IS ENJOINED, AND WHAT SHOULD BE REBUKED.

1. *To tell anyone of his fault,* "Thou shalt not suffer sin upon him." *Sin,* therefore, is the thing we are called to reprove, or rather him that commits sin. Do all we can to convince him of his fault, and lead him in the right way.

2. Love requires that we also *warn him of error* which would naturally *lead to sin.* If we do "not hate him in our heart," but love our neighbour, we shall generously warn him of mistakes likely to end in evil.

3. *Avoid reproving for anything that is disputable.* A thing appears evil to me, therefore if I do it I am a sinner before God. But another is not to be judged by my conscience. So I must only reprove for what is clearly and undeniably evil, *e.g.,* profanity, insobriety. Few who are guilty of these will defend them, when appeal is made to their conscience in the sight of God.

II. WHO THEY ARE WE ARE CALLED TO REPROVE.

1 There are *some sinners we are forbidden to rebuke.* "Cast not pearl before swine," *i.e.,* brutish men, known to be immersed in sins, having no fear of God before their eyes. Do not expose the precious pearls, *i.e,* the sublime doctrines of the gospel, to their contempt, and yourself to injurious treatment. Yet if we saw *such* persons speak or do what they themselves know to be evil we ought to reprove them.

1. Our "neighbour" *is every child of man,* all that have souls to be saved. If we refrain because some are sinners above other men they may perish in their iniquity, but God will require their blood at our hands.

3. Else, in the lower world there might be *upraiding of us for our neglect of duty,* through which souls, *left unwarned,* failed to "flee from the wrath to come."

4. Yet, the reproving is *not to be done in the same degree to everyone* First it is particularly due to our *parents,* if needing it; then to *brothers and sisters;* then to *relatives;* then to our *servants;* to our *fellow citizens;* members of the same *religious society;* watch over each other that we may not suffer sin upon our brother. To neglect this is to "hate our brother in our heart"; and "he that hateth his brother is a murderer." It imperils *our own salvation* to neglect this duty.

III. WHAT SPIRIT AND MANNER SHOULD MARK OUR PERFORMANCE OF THIS DUTY.

1. There is *considerable difficulty in doing it aright.* Although some are specially qualified to do it *by grace,* and skilful *by practice.* But, though difficult, we must do it; and God will aid us.

2. How most *effectual?* When done in "the spirit of *love,*" of tender goodwill for our neighbour, as for one who is the son of our common Father, as for one for whom Christ died, that he might be a partaker of salvation.

3. Yet speak in the spirit of *humility* "Not think of yourself more highly than you ought to think." Not feeling or showing the least contempt of those whom you reprove; disclaiming all self superiority; owning the good there is in him

4. In the spirit of *meekness.* "For the wrath of man worketh not the righteousness of God." Anger begets anger, not holiness.

5. Put *no trust* in *yourself;* in you wisdom or abilities; speak in the spirit of *prayer.*

6. And as for the *outward manner,* as well as the spirit, in which it should be done; let there be a *frank outspokenness,* a plain and artless declaration of *disinterested love.* It will pierce like lightning.

7. With *great seriousness,* showing that you

are really in earnest. A ludicrous reproof makes little impression, or is taken ill.

8. Yet there are exceptions when a little *well placed raillery* will pierce deeper than solid argument. "*Ridiculum acri fortius.*" "Answer a fool according to his folly, lest he be wise in his own eyes."

9. *Adapt the manner to the occasion.* By few or many words as the situation determines; or by no words at all, but a look, a gesture, a sigh. Such *silent* reproof may be attended by the power of God.

10. *Watch for a fair occasion.* "A word spoken in season, how good it is." Catch the "*Mollia tempora fandi,*" the time when his mind is soft and mild.

11. But should a man be left alone *when intoxicated?* I dare not say so; for instances are forthcoming of its having had good effects. Despise not the poor drunkard. Many of them are self-condemned, but they despair. He that tells a man there is no help for him is a liar from the beginning. "Behold the Lamb of God that taketh away the sins of the world."

12. You that are diligent in this labour of love *be not discouraged.* You have need of patience. That "you reap, if you faint not."

When a *religious movement* is abroad it will be *accompanied with a spirit of reproving.* All who are awakened by God's Spirit will be reprovers of outward sin.—*John Wesley, M.A.,* Sermons lxv.

Vv. 26, 31.—*Theme:* WICKED SUPERSTITIONS.

I. A PROOF OF MAN'S ARRANT ALIENATION FROM GOD.

He will create oracles, consult devils, anything rather than seek unto God.

II. A RECOGNITION OF DARK SPIRITUAL AGENCIES OPPOSED TO GOD.

Scripture does not declare these "familiar spirits" to be unreal; it acknowledges them, and records man's dealings with them: Samuel and Witch of Endor. [Compare Acts xvi. 16.]

III. A REPROBATION OF SUCH PERSONS AS CLAIM TO BE "MEDIUMS" OF INTERCOURSE WITH SPIRITS.

"Regard not them." God disowns them. A fearful case they are in who make this their trade. Heaven denounces them, and will exclude them. Spiritualists are in no favour or league with Deity.

IV. A PROHIBITION OF ALL USE OF THESE WICKED MYSTERIES.

Man is to deal alone with Deity, with God in Christ, with the Holy Spirit. They who "seek after wizards," and "use enchantments," are *offending God,* and are "*defiled by them.*"

Prayer brings us direct to Him who is the "Father of lights"; and He giveth liberally to "any who *lack wisdom* and will *ask of God*" (James i. 17. and 5).

Jesus Christ is the one Mediator, and "ever liveth to make intercession for us." There should be no intercourse with the spirit world but *through Jesus,* and through Him *with the Father alone.* [See Addenda to chapter, *Superstitions.*]

Vv. 3 and 30.—*Theme:* SACREDNESS OF THE SABBATHS.

"*Ye shall keep my Sabbaths.*"

All days belong to God, and should therefore be kept sacred, but He has seen fit to anoint one day in seven with the oil of gladness above its fellows. The Sabbath is a divine institution dating from Eden, is associated with the completion of the great work of creation It was heaven's antidote to the curse of labour. Let us consider:

I. FOR WHAT PURPOSE WAS THE SABBATH ORIGINALLY INSTITUTED?

Certainly not because God *needed* it: though on it He rested from His labours and sanctified it. It was made for man, that in it he might enjoy; (*a*) *physical repose;* (*b*) *mental recreation;* (*c*) *spiritual profit;* (*d*) *uninterrupted opportunities for divine worship.* Godlessness has ignored its claims, selfishness has begrudged its weekly advent and call from secular engagements. The observance of one day in seven for the repose and refreshment of body, mind and heart brings blessings to man and glory to God.

II. FOR WHAT PURPOSES THE SABBATH HAS BEEN PERPETUATED UNDER THE NEW DISPENSATION.

The change of day, the less rigid demand for its ceremonial observance, have not lessened its importance and necessity, It is still to be observed as a day of rest from secular toil, and specially devoted to the work and worship of Jehovah. The Christian Sabbath is associated with the completion of the great work of redemption. Christ set His *appropriation* and *approval* upon it by making special posthumous appearances to His disciples on the *first day* of the week. The conduct of the apostles gives authoritative sanction to the observance of the first day instead of the seventh; and the Holy Spirit has set His seal of approval upon the change, not only by the descent at Pentecost, but by exerting His saving power, as Christians have met for worship and extending the Redeemer's Kingdom on *the Lord's Day.—F. W. B.*

V. 32.—*Theme:* HOMAGE FOR AGE.

That is, *when* and—

i. *Because the aged* REPRESENT MATURE WISDOM.

ii. *Because the aged record* LONG YEARS SPENT IN OUR SERVICE.

iii. *Because the aged demonstrate* GOD'S PROVIDENTIAL CARE.

iv. *Because the aged are* SOLEMN ADMONITIONS OF LIFE'S DECAY.

v. *Because the aged suggest* NEARNESS TO ETERNITY.

vi. *Because the aged exhibit the* RICHEST FRUITS OF GRACE.

vii. *Because the aged mark the* LINE OF GOD'S COVENANT BLESSINGS *for descendants.*
viii. *Because the aged* REPRESENT ON EARTH HIM WHO IS THE "ANCIENT OF DAYS."
(*a*) Youth should *venerate* the aged (Job xxx. i. 12; Isa. iii. 4, 5).
(*b*) Age should *influence and hallow the young* (2 Tim. i. 5).
[See Addenda to chapter, *Old Age.*]

V. 33.—*Theme:* COURTESY TO STRANGERS.
I. WE OURSELVES ARE STRANGERS ON THE EARTH.
"For ye were strangers in the land" (v. 34).
1. *Dependent* on other care than our own; human and divine.
2. *Transient,* soon to leave, resting but a little while on earth.
Observe: it is good to see in the case of others an analogy with our own; it will foster *sympathy*, and *helpfulness.*
II. COURTESY SHOULD ROOT ITSELF IN GENEROUS LOVE.
"Thou shalt *love him* as *thyself.*"
1. Acting to the stranger as *if the service were being rendered to us.* This will teach us *what* to do, and *how* to show kindness.
2. Recognising that *we may perchance be in the stranger's position.* As thus needing kindness, let us now exhibit it.
3. Opening our hearts in *ungrudging benevolence.* "Love" gives lavishly. Courtesy should not be meagre and superficial.
III. GRATITUDE TO HEAVEN PROMPTS US TO GENEROUS KINDNESS.
"Ye were strangers in the land of Egypt; I am the Lord your God."

1. *Memory of God's rescue* should constrain us to care for others.
2. *God's relationship to us* requires that we illustrate *His lovingkindness.*
3. *His commands to courtesy cannot be evaded with impunity.*
"I was a stranger and ye took me *not* in: Depart!"

Vv. 35, 36—*Theme:* BUSINESS HONESTY.
i. SOCIAL LIFE IS BASED UPON COMMERCIAL CONTRACTS.
Each bringing to the other some product of skill or toil. We cannot supply a fraction of our own wants, we must buy; and we have also, in turn, something to sell. Business is the outcome of this *reciprocal dependence* Each *can*, each *must* help the other; or social and civic life would be impossible
ii. DISHONESTY IS SUBVERSIVE OF THE VERY BASIS OF SOCIAL LIFE
It breaks *confidence,* alienates *intercourse;* closes friendly relationships, substitutes roguery for righteousness, and wrecks all goodwill.
Pleasant to reflect—
1. How much *trade honour* there is among men.
2. How surely *trickery brings discovery*, and therefore penalty, on rogues.
3. How *honesty is ever winning respect and reward.*
iii. JUSTICE SITS OBSERVANT OF ALL DECEITFUL DEEDS.
"I am the Lord"
He *sees* all secresies; *weighs* all balances; *hates* all dishonesties; *will requite* all deceits.

ILLUSTRATIVE ADDENDA TO CHAPTER XIX.

MORALITY.
Morality is the object of government. We want a state of things in which crime will not pay, a state of things which allows every man the largest liberty compatible with the liberty of every other man."—EMERSON, *Fortune of the Republic.*

"O let us still the secret joy partake
To follow virtue even for virtue's sake."
—POPE.

FAMILY PIETY.
Where Abraham pitched his tent, there he built an altar.
"We are really what we are relatively."
—P. HENRY.
"Children are what their mothers are."
—LANDOR.

SABBATH AND SANCTUARY.
"O day of rest! How beautiful, how fair, How welcome to the weary and the old! Day of the Lord! and truce to earthy care!"
— LONGFELLOW, *Christus.*

Sin keeps no Sabbaths.
Of a well spent Sabbath Philip Henry used to say: "If this be not the way to heaven, I know not what is."

POOR.
"This mournful truth is everywhere confessed,
Slow rises worth by poverty depressed."
—SAMUEL JOHNSON.

"Poverty is the only load which is the heavier the more loved ones there are to assist in supporting it."—RICHTER.

CHARITY.
"They serve God well,
Who serve His creatures."
—MRS. NORTON.

"He is truly great, that is great in charity."
—THOMAS A. KEMPIS.

"To pity distress is but human; to relieve it is Godlike."—HORACE MANN.

PERJURY.
"Sworn on every slight pretence,
Till perjuries are common as bad pence,
While thousands, careless of the damning sin,
Kiss the Book outside, who ne'er looked within."— COWPER.

BUSINESS AND WORK.
"Business dispatched is business well done, but business hurried is business ill done."— BULWER LYTTON.

"All true work is sacred; in all the work, were it but true hand labour, there is something of divineness."—CARLYLE.

"In every rank, or great or small,
'Tis industry supports us all."—GAY.

"For men must work, and women must weep,
And the sooner it's over, the sooner to sleep."
—KINGSLEY.

JUSTICE.
"Heaven is above all yet; there sits a Judge
That no king can corrupt."
—*Henry VIII.* iii., 1.

"He who the sword of Heaven would bear,
Should be as holy as severe;
Pattern in himself, to know
Grace to stand, and virtue go;
More nor less to others paying
Than by self-offences weighing."
—*Measure for Measure.*

"Four things belong to a judge: to hear courteously, to answer wisely, to consider soberly, and to decide impartially."
—SOCRATES.

"The virtue of justice consists in moderation, as regulated by wisdom."—ARISTOTLE.

SLANDER.
"One evil tongue," say the Jews, "hurts three persons, the speaker, the hearer, and the person spoken of."

"A lost good name is ne'er retrieved."
—GAY.

"I hate the man who builds his name
On ruins of another's fame."—GAY.

"'Twas slander filled her mouth with lying words:
Slander, the foulest whelp of sin."
— POLLOCK.

"Low breathed talkers, minion lispers
Cutting honest throats by whispers."
—SCOTT.

"Be thou as chaste as ice, as pure as
Snow, thou shalt not escape slander."
—*Hamlet.*

"Convey a libel in a frown,
And wink a reputation down."
—SWIFT.

NEIGHBOURLINESS.
"We cannot show ourselves more friendly to any man than by an early reproof of his error, or, as it is here expressed, *by not suffering sin upon him.* 'Tis a mercy to meet with reproof (though late) from others; but to be *soon* reproved is much mercy. Every good, the sooner it comes to us, the better it is."— CARYL.

SUPERSTITIONS.
"Superstition is related to this life, religion to the next; superstition is allied to fatality, religion to virtue: it is by the vivacity of earthly devices that we become superstitious: it is, on the contrary, by the sacrifice of these devices that we become religious."—MADAME DE STAEL.

OLD AGE.
"Life's shadows are meeting Eternity's day."—JAS. G CLARKE.

"Age is not all decay: it is the ripening, the swelling, of the fresh life within, that withers and bursts the husk."—GEO. MACDONALD.

"Thus fares it still in our decay,
And yet the wiser mind
Mourns less for what age takes away,
Than what it leaves behind."
—WORDSWORTH.

CHAPTER XX.

Social and Moral Crimes.

SUGGESTIVE READINGS.

V. 2.—*Again thou shalt say to the children of Israel.* These denunciations of sin (already denounced in ch. xviii.) are to be *repeated* in the hearing of the nation. The holy God would have these social and moral commands reiterated that they may be emphasised upon the people's attention. When sins are pleasant to us, when inclination leads us towards them, it is scarcely in human nature to halt at the first command to desist. Evil indulgence deadens sensibility to God's voice. Although the law of heaven denounces iniquities, yet when the sins are cherished, we are very slow to "turn at God's reproof." Therefore, God speaks once more, "*Again* thou shalt say." "For God speaketh once, yea, *twice*, yet man perceiveth it not" (Job xxxiii. 14). He knows our disposition to lurk in the enjoyment of our sins, therefore pursues us with His voice, reiterating the warning words.

Vv. 3 and 5.—**I will set My face against that man** Penalty is now attached to prohibition. God emphasises His denunciations by affixing terrible punishments to corrupt deeds. For a sinner will find he has to do with something more than divine expostulations and commands; "God is *angry* with the wicked," and to crimes against righteousness He has attached doom. They who will not pause at persuasions will be overtaken with punishments.

V. 4.—**If the people hide their eyes.** Connivance at wrong entails joint-guiltiness in the deed, and joint-penalty. Affection and friendship often lead us to wink at errors and misdemeanours in those we love, but we thereby become "partakers of their sins" (Rev. xviii. 4), and shall "receive of their plagues."

*** Compare foregoing chapters for suggestive readings on the verses following.

It is specially noticeable that the *penalty* rather than the *sin* of all misdemeanour is distinctive of this chapter. If men are not restrained from evil practices which the law has denounced as *sin*, it may be they will shun them when the law annexes to them *death!* How gracious is this act of God: making it so clear to us that transgression of the law is not only *repulsive to Him*—as being sin, but also *destructive to us*—as entailing death. There are minds less startled by the heinousness of wrong as God sees it than with the disastrous consequences which wrong brings on themselves. Yet God appeals even to the selfishness of sinners as a motive to shun sin.

Vv. 22-27.—**A separated and sanctified people.** God had separated Israel from all the nations of the earth, to *exhibit His holy character* in their purity and to *illustrate the reward of holiness* by possessing "the land flowing with milk and honey"; thus connecting purity with privilege, as cause and consequence. Being thus "separated" by God (v. 24), they were to separate themselves by distinctive conduct (v. 25), and show themselves before the less favoured nations as "holy unto the Lord" (v. 26).

If thus it behoved the Jewish people to maintain sanctity, surely we, who are chosen in Christ Jesus and called to be saints, should show forth the virtues of the Lord, and thus connect holiness of life with our **enjoyment of the inheritance** which is made ours by grace.

HOMILIES.

Topic: THE AXE LAID AT THE ROOT OF MORAL EVIL.

Here, commandments already given are repeated and enforced with renewed authority and power. Repetition essential to inculcation of knowledge, and fixing indelibly the truths taught. The vices into which Israel was liable to fall are odiously repulsive to the virtuous human mind; how inexpressibly abominable they must have been to the nature of the immaculately holy God! *Inward* as well as *ceremonial* purity demanded of the Hebrews, hence the constant call to *circumspection* and *consecration.* One great purpose running through the whole economy—the recovery of man from the practice, guilt, and penalty of sin. Looking at this chapter in the light of the circumstances under which it was given we learn—

I. CONSTANT VIGILANCE ENJOINED AGAINST ENSNARING SIN. The people of Israel were not elected to divine advantages unconditionally, exempted from responsibility for the use they made of their privileges. The elaborate and searching character of the laws by which they were governed denoted (*a*) *that the people were very depraved by nature, and ever prone to sin;* (*b*) *that they were liable to yield to temptations arising from remembrances of the sinful habits of the Eyptians;* (*c*) *that they would be ever coming in contact with seductions to wrong-doing* (v. 22). Every vice—condemned in this chapter—is an outrage upon decency and the moral sense. Nature sets her face against all such iniquity, sets her burning stigma upon immorality. Filthy practices entail retributive consequences. As a great family of which Jehovah was the head, Israel was to guard against everything indecent and indelicate. Nothing could destroy them but inward corruption, every weapon formed against them would be futile if they kept pure in character, faithful in allegiance to the Lord. Abandonment to the abominations of the heathen would bring down the indignation of heaven, and the land whither they were going would cast them out as apostates and reprobates.

II. TREMENDOUS RETRIBUTIONS ATTACHED TO WRONG-DOING. Expressions of divine displeasure against sin (in this chapter) are very strong, punishments threatened very awful. It mattered not who the person might be upon whom the guilt of idolatry and licentiousness might be brought, the sentence was to be executed. The penalties seemed severe, but they showed (i.) *the holiness of the divine law;* (ii.) *the detestable nature of sin;* (iii.) *the retributive character of guilt.* The fate of sinful nations was to be a warning to the Hebrews. The revealed indignation of Jehovah against every kind of moral evil, was to lead the people to avoid the approach and appearance of evil. These righteous statutes calculated to awaken devout reflection, rigid self-examination.

Under grace in Jesus Christ we are elected to privileges, predestinated to be conformed to the image of God's Son. The world is to see the purity of the divine nature reflected in the light of our Christly lives. We are expected, by Him who has called us out of nature's darkness, to represent and thus recommend the religion which, like its Author, is pure and undefiled. Unfaithfulness to our sacred trust, unholiness in our lives, will forfeit the favour of our Master, destroy peace, produce spiritual ruin. The grand object of redemption is not mere salvation from sin's consequences, but its complete removal from the human soul and the universe of God. Nowhere as in the gospel of Christ does the fire of indignation burn so fiercely against unrighteousness and impurity, its intensest heat is centred in the mysteries and sufferings of the cross.—*F. W. B.*

Topic: CAPITAL OFFENCES.

"*And I will set my face against that man, and will cut him off from among his people.*" (v. 3).

How frequently we read in this chapter of excommunication and death. The words "he shall surely be put to death" occur again and again; flash after flash of the lightning of divine wrath, peal after peal of the thunder of divine condemnation startle us, as the various crimes are indicated towards which such judgments are directed. As we reverently gaze and listen, we learn—

I. TO WHAT DIABOLICAL DEPTHS HUMAN DEPRAVITY CAN SINK. Those who indulged in Molech worship, committed murder of the most horrible kind, and in the heathen temples immoralities of the most degrading and disgusting character were practised. Vice was not confined to public places, but its pollutions cursed the most sacred and delicate relationships in life. Human nature can sink into a condition of degradation, compared with which the natural habits of the brute creation are pure and noble.

II. TO WHAT A FEARFUL EXTENT THE DIVINE ANGER CAN TURN. "God is Love," and it is equally clear from nature and revelation He is also holy, just, and true. He is angry with sin, and with the sinner while He loves and indulges in sin, and such announcements of anger against the guilty as this chapter contains, show God is a consuming fire against evil; He sets His face against it, visits its perpetrators with death. Only by infliction of death upon the sinner's Substitute, can the claims of divine justice be met, the divine anger against sin be averted.

III. TO WHAT FATAL ISSUES TRANSGRESSION OF THE DIVINE LAWS CONDUCTS. (*a*) *The loss of divine favour.* "I will set my face against that man." Nothing can be more awful than to incur the antagonism of the Almighty. (*b*) *The loss o; congenial society.* "And will cut him off from among his people." He shall be excommunicated, an exile and outcast for ever. The loss of the favour of God, banishment from the society of the blessed, will constitute the punishment of the finally impenitent.

IV. TO WHAT SOLEMN FACTS THESE DIVINE DECLARATIONS POINT. Unquestionably: (*a*) *To the heinousness of sin.* That it required atonement, to be forgiven; that unforgiven it entailed death. (*b*) *To the righteousness of God's law.* That it denounced every kind of iniquity, could not be broken in the smallest point with impunity. (*c*) *To the holinsss of God's name.* Jehovah's nature arrayed against even secret sins; where He dwelt, where His name is recorded, nothing impure must be allowed.

CONCLUSION. Human nature is still the same, prone to depart from the living God, liable to sink to the lowest depths of sensuality and guilt. The anger of God still burns against evil, His face set against evil-doers. Sin, if unrepented, unremoved, brings death, destruction from the presence of the Lord. As of old, so now, but *with greater freeness and fulness*, a way is open for pardon, purity, peace. In the Christian Church, proclaimed in the glad tidings of the gospel, we have—

1. *Higher examples of holiness.* Especially in our Exemplar, Christ Jesus.
2. *Loftier precepts to guide us.* Ethics of the gospel transcend those of the law.
3. *Stronger inducements to urge us.* Not fear but *love*, the gospel motive.
4. *Superior prospects to cheer us.* Life and immortality have been brought to light by the gospel; we may look forward to an eternity of rest in the Canaan above.—*F. W. B.*

Topic: CONNIVANCE AT INIQUITY.

"*If the people of the land do any ways hide their eyes from the man when he giveth his seed to Molech,*" *etc* (v. 4).

(*a*) *Evils are allowed to pass unrebuked.* From *indifference*: a total unconcern about either right or wrong, piety or sin. Or from *indolence*: habitual inertia, unwillingness to take any trouble to set wrong-doers right, or rescue the debased from their degradations.

(*b*) *Errors are permitted to flourish unmolested.* From *contempt of truth*: caring nothing for sacred knowledge, content to let others dwell and to dwell themselves in ignorance or delusion, serving Molech or any other fallacy, as they may prefer. Or from *false charitableness*: pleading that if men but be loyal to the light they had, or faithful to convictions they cherish, as their standard of duty and code of religion, it matters little what errors thrive. But consider—

I. Appalling inhumanities wrought under sanction of religion.

"*Giveth his seed unto Molech.*" Tender infants offered up to devouring fires. *Heathenism* has its frightful records: the car of Juggernauth; the funereal fires for widows: the abandonment of aged parents; children cast into the Ganges; etc.

Romanism has its catalogue of enormities; prison tortures; inquisitorial horrors, faggot fires of martyrdom, etc.

II. Pathetic unconcern over the enormities of sin.

Superstition is but one of the many foul products of sin; and the barbarities wrought through superstition are but a fraction of the cruelties developed by sin.

1. There is a *common callousness* respecting the miseries rampant. The victims of sin are everywhere—in debased homes, in asylums, in prisons: poverty, brutality, villainy: yet society connives at it all, and avowed Christians lift not the burdens with one of their fingers.

2. *A willing ignorance* of existing woes prevails. The people of the land *hide their eyes.* How different this from—

> The keen spirit, which
> Seizes the prompt occasion, makes the thought
> Start into instant action, and at once
> Plans and performs, resolves and executes!

A true *grief for* sin, and *pity for the sinner*, and hatred of what degrades the soul of man and dishonours God, would stir us to generous activity.

III. Delusive self satisfaction amid prevailing wrong.

It is not enough that we "hide our eyes." When men err and sin around us—

1. *Not to know* may be criminal ignorance. Each man is set in charge with the other; and we owe it to him that we inform ourselves of his condition and conduct. To pass by on the other side "is no excuse for letting the sufferer die."

2. *Not to share in his deed* does not exonerate us from his sins. If we connive at his deed we to a degree both sanction and encourage it. We ought to "rebuke the unfruitful works of darkness." But instead of that we give consent by our silence, by our ignoring them.

3. *Not to stay the inhumanities* which are being inflicted renders us chargeable with complicity. What brutality to stand inactive while children were being sacrificed to Molech! What cruelty to let the helpless suffer, the deceived perish, the sinner be lost!

IV Connivance at iniquities severely adjudged by God.

"Then I will set my face against that man" (v. 8)

1. The *watchman's duty* is to raise the sound of warning. [Comp. Ezekiel xxxiii.]

2. Yet every man *who will keep his eyes open* sees the occasion and necessity for this ministry of protest, and warning, and rescue. He who sees not is guilty of "hiding his eyes from the man." *Sinners* are everywhere; *sufferers* are everywhere.

3. Judgment will be based on *our actions to others.* "Inasmuch as ye *did it* unto me"; or, "inasmuch as ye *did it not*" (Matt. xxv. 41, 45).

Note: Our urgent duty in the world is to—

(*a*) Rebuke sin and wrong-doing, and seek to check its ravages.

(*b*) Be alert amid opportunities to rescue the victims of iniquity from their woes.

(*c*) Our own salvation is without guarantee unless we also seek "by all means to save some." For we may inherit judgment for neglect of those "ready to perish."

(*d*) The very spirit of Christianity incites to eager and loving endeavour to "convert the sinner from the error of his ways, save his soul from death, and hide the multitude of his sins."

Topic: THE POSSIBILITIES OF SANCTITY (Vv. 7, 8).

Certainly "this present world" (Titus ii. 12) is not very friendly or favourable to active sanctity.
Yet it is the only world in which the human character and life can rise out of sin into active sanctity. Death closes the door on opportunity. "As the tree falleth so shall it lie."
Hence the urgency and repetition of this call of God, pleading with men to "sanctify yourselves." Is it possible to effect this? How may we thus attain to sanctity? By

I. ABSTINENCE: A STEADFAST NEGATION OF ALL TENDENCIES AND INDUCEMENTS TO IMPURITY.

There must be diligent, strenuous and minute regard to every "Thou shalt *not*" of God's Word. Assuredly, all sinful propensity in us must be *repressed;* all habits of evil *denied;* all indulgence of impure imaginations and desires *refused.* "Taste *not,* touch *not,* handle *not.*" "Put *off* the works of darkness." "Crucify the flesh with its affections and lusts." This chapter shows us how in many sinful ways and works of the flesh we must "*deny ourselves.*"
In order to this negation of all unholy dispositions and practices we shall need that "grace may abound." For sinful man is "weak through the flesh." But this grace is available to us in Jesus Christ.

II. OBEDIENCE: THE DILIGENT PRACTICE OF ALL THE DUTIES AND REQUIREMENTS OF HOLINESS.

The *affirmative* side of sanctity is certainly not less important than the negative. "*Do* this and thou shalt live." "Ye shall *keep my statutes* and *do* them" (v. 8).
A practical piety is imperative. To secure that the "house be empty and swept" is something; iniquities cast out of the heart and life: but the good, the true, the devout, the lovely must also be brought in. To have the vine pruned and purged of all dead and fruitless boughs is necessary; but equally it is desiderated that what remains should "bring forth much fruit."
He who would "sanctify himself" must therefore cultivate pure affections, thoughts and desires; practise the duties and obligations of religion, maintain habits of rectitude and godliness: "perfecting holiness in the fear of the Lord." He who is "watchful unto prayer," "alive unto God," quick to heed and obey His word, will not fail to attain to these affirmative qualities of sanctity.

III. ASSISTANCE: DIVINE CO-OPERATION SUSTAINING AND SUCCEEDING HUMAN EFFORTS TOWARDS SANCTITY.

"Sanctify yourselves" (v. 7), for "I am the Lord which sanctify you" (v. 8).
All His (1) *disciplinary corrections and afflictions;* (2) *Scripture teachings and promises;* (3) *spiritual communications and religious privileges;* (4) *gifts and comfort of His Holy Spirit;* (5) *purifying power of the indwelling love of Christ,* are resources of God's sanctifying, with which He seals our earnest endeavours after holiness.
"*Work out your own salvation* with fear and trembling, for it is *God which worketh in you* both to will and to do of His good pleasure" (Phil. ii. 12, 13).

Topic: THE GRIEF OF UNDUTIFUL CHILDREN.

"*Every one that curseth his father or his mother shall surely be put to death,*" etc. (v. 9).
Family life should be a source and centre of consolation, affection and delight;

parents proving a comfort and benediction to their children, and children bringing gladness and honour to their parents.

Home is the sphere of harmony and peace.

Fearful is the conception of an accursed family: abusive children, agonized parents! It is the most dreadful perversion which earth contains; love changed into cursing; duty into rebellion; purity into foulness; rest into hateful strife and war. It is clearly true of such children that they are—

I. A GRIEF TO THEIR PARENTS. Bitter the very thought—" he hath *cursed* his father or his mother."

1. The grief of *blighted hopes*. What tender and bright expectations were centred in the little one as parents first looked upon their cherished child!

They are idols of hearts and of households,
They are angels of God in disguise.—*Chas. M. Dickenson.*

Terrible the grief when all glad hopes are desolated, and what promised joy and love only yields a " curse."

2. The grief of *outraged affection*. No stint of fond thought and care is lavished on the child.

How sharper than a serpent's tooth it is
To have a thankless child.—*Shakespeare.*

3. The grief of *frustrated prayer*. Over the children's heads parents have bowed in supplication to God, and pleadings full of heartfelt fervour have been poured. Yet is this what results—a "curse" in the home, a terror to the parental heart!

4. The grief of *ruined happiness*. How can joy ever again dwell in the parent's soul against whom his own child has risen with "cursings"? It must darken all the light of earthly gladness; and it must deeply shade even the anticipations of heaven—for no place in " the Father's house " will be found for a child who brought a curse into his earthly home.

II. A GRIEF TO THEMSELVES. Dreadful the penalties which are threatened —" he shall surely be put to *death;* his *blood is upon him.*"

1. *God's anger* will be upon him. A wicked son or daughter knows this awful fact before the judgment day arrives; God loathes the child who curses a parent. It is a terrible thought to carry through life.

2. *Human contempt* will be won. For all respect and trust is forfeited by a child whose behaviour is so cruel; society shuns the unnatural creature where his or her conduct is known.

3. *Conscience* can never have peace. Children who have outraged home and left the parental roof have been harrowed through years with the woes of an "accusing conscience," and traversed lands and seas to weep over a parent's grave.

4. A *retributive justice* pursues them. Their own crime re-appears against them: for the very quality in themselves that rendered them capable of " cursing " their parents will betray itself in all relationships in after years, making them *hateful* and *hated*, and lay them open to the consequences. And this vile quality will *re-appear in their offspring*, and win back from their own children's lips like "curses" which they once uttered themselves. God follows such cruelty to parents with relentless rigour. Penalty overtakes this crime in this life and doom awaits it hereafter.

III. A GRIEF TO GOD.

1. *Undutifulness to parents* is inseparable from *impiety towards God*. Such sons and daughters are always godless, alien from all sacred duties and claims: "a smoke in God's nostrils," a dishonour to His laws.

2. *Outrage to parental relationship* and feeling is felt by God as an *outrage on His own Fatherly love and grace*. He feels a parent's grief; and wrong done to so tender a relationship is a wound to the divine Father's heart.

3. In His "*beloved Son*" and "*holy child Jesus*" God shows the fulness of

affection which should mark a child: and it degrades the very name of a "*son*" and a "*child*," the relationship which Jesus assumed, when it brings a *curse* upon human parents instead of love.

4. *Home is God's earthly type of heaven:* and a home filled with "cursing" is a peculiar abomination to Him who designed our earthly homes to be a foretaste here of "the Father's house" above. It is a most offensive and sorrowful evidence of the ravages which sin—"the abominable thing God hates"—has wrought in His world. How different this delineation of a "cursing" child from the *poetic* and the *divine* idea of a child.

A sweet new blossom of humanity
Fresh fallen from God's own home to flower on earth.

Let parents, with diligent prayer and training, bring their children to Jesus; who alone can cast out the evil spirit from a child. [Compare Matt. xviii. 14, 21.]

Topic: THE HEBREW CHURCH.

"*And ye shall be holy unto me: for I the Lord am holy, and have severed you from other people that ye should be mine*" (v. 26).

The Hebrews were not only *a royal nation*, with Jehovah for their King, but they constituted *an established church*, not by the edict of any earthly monarch or political assembly, but by a royal proclamation from the Court of Heaven. That the people might know and ever remember the high dignity thus conferred upon them, Moses was directed to proclaim the fact in association with the promulgation of laws demanding holiness of heart and life. The Hebrew Church was composed of persons—

I. SEPARATED FROM THE WORLD, "have severed you from other people." They had been delivered from Egypt, protected, preserved, guided, exceeding great and precious promises vouchsafed to them, beside laws for the regulation of their lives. They had been severed from other nations that they might become distinguished for purity, and be the means of blessing the world.

II. SEPARATED FROM SIN. "Ye shall be holy unto me." All the rites and ceremonies imposed upon them were to this end. The divine image, lost by the fall, was to be restored. Holiness, to which the people were called, would not only produce happiness in the restored, but yield pleasure to Jehovah, whose name is holy.

III. CONSECRATED TO THE LORD. "Holy unto me." The people were not to live for self-gratification, they were not their own or at their own disposal, their wills were to fall in with the divine will, they were to be holy for Jehovah's sake. All the services of the tabernacle, every sacrifice offered, would remind the worshippers of their duty to surrender themselves unreservedly to Him who had set them apart for His own service and glory.

IV. OWNED OF THE LORD. "That ye should be mine." Herein we see the *condescension* of Jehovah, to take into His possession, as His intimate friends, such unworthy creatures as the Hebrews were. We see His infinite *goodness* in providing for their wants and educating them for a sublime position among the nations of the earth. He owned them, they were therefore to feel themselves at His disposal, and to act implicitly under His direction.

The same things hold good in the Christian Church. Believers are to come out from the ungodly, be distinct from the world. They are to be separate from sin and touch not the unclean thing. They are to be consecrated to the Lord, their motto "For me to live is Christ, and to die is gain." They are not their own, but bought with a price, even the precious blood of Christ. Let us warn others against sin; watch over our own hearts; pray for help to resist every temptation; avoid everything likely to contaminate; avail ourselves of every aid to growth in grace and progress in holiness.—*F. W. B.*

Topic: GODLY DISTINCTIVENESS (Vv. 22-26).

It manifests itself in, and results from :—
I. A UNIQUE CODE OF MORAL AND SACRED LAWS.
"Ye shall keep all *My* statutes and all *My* judgments, and do them" (v. 22).
No other people had a *standard of morals*, or a *directory of religious regulations* comparable to these.
II. A STUDIOUS AVOIDANCE OF THE CUSTOMS OF UNGODLINESS.
"Ye shall *not walk* in the manners of the nations," etc (v. 23).
Conformity to the world was prohibited. However sanctioned, or desirable, or seemingly harmless, the customs of the ungodly were to be shunned.
III. A CAUTIOUS SELECTION OF SOCIAL ENJOYMENTS AND INDULGENCES.
"Ye shall put difference between clean and unclean," etc. (v. 25).
Palate not to be gratified, tables not to be spread with promiscuous viands. God's wish and word were to rule them in every *enjoyment*; and *self restraint* was to mark them in every gratification.
IV. A HERITAGE OF SPECIAL PRIVILEGES AS GOD'S PEOPLE.
"Ye shall inherit their land, a land that floweth with milk and honey," etc (v. 24).
Sinners *lose* earthly felicities, as the penalty of their impiety : "therefore I abhorred them" (v. 23).
The godly *possess* rich heritage of good as the mark of God's favour : "I will give it unto you to possess" (v. 24).
V. A SEAL OF DIVINE SANCTITY RESTING UPON THEM.
They show themselves to be—
1. *Divinely "separated"* (v. 24) from other people. Their history and career attest God's dealing with them as with no other people.
2. *Divinely sanctified.* ("Ye shall be holy unto me : for I the Lord am holy, and have severed you from other people" (v. 26). For the very "beauty of the Lord" rests upon the character and conduct of those He redeems.
Note :
(*a*) God *claims* His people : they are not their own; may not follow their own desires and delights, He is their law, they must surrender to Him. "That ye should *be mine*" (v. 26). It is a blessed fact to *belong to God:* but it carries its obligations.
(*b*) *Priviliges are conditioned upon fidelity* (v. 22). The inheritance would be forfeited if obedience were withheld. All God's covenant promises to us wait upon our loyalty to Him. "Ye are my friends *if ye do*," etc.

CHAPTER XXI.

Purity of the Priesthood.

SUGGESTIVE READINGS.

V. 1.—*Speak unto the priests . . there shall none be defiled.* If it was important that the whole community of Israel should maintain ceremonial and moral purity, it was certainly not less urgent for "the priests, the sons of Aaron." Through the past ten chapters the laws have had reference to the "congregation of Israel"; the divine word now comes to His ministers within the sanctuary.

These priests were types of *Christ*, and also of the sacred character and sacerdotal ministry of *believers:* their life and service should therefore be inviolate, consecrated, worthy. For Christ was "holy, harmless, separate from sinners"; and His followers, who maintain His witness in the world, are also to be "holy and unblamable." This sanctity is now to be typically enacted and foreshadowed in the conduct and ministry of these priests.

Vv 2-4.—**Contact with the dead** entailed ceremonial uncleanness, and excluded from the sanctuary for a week. For a priest to be disqualified for his functions was both derogatory to his sacred office and a most serious interruption of his duties. In Christians who are "priests unto God" there may be neither disqualification for, nor interruption of, their ministry. Human claims, and even domestic sorrows, may not intercept the Christian life: that must be maintained unchecked whatever befalls us. Happy we that the succour of our Lord so supports us in our griefs and bereavements that, instead of checking us in our Christian life and work, they qualify us for even a richer ministry for Christ among men.

Vv. 5, 6.—**Marks of mourning** prohibited. For they who live near God's presence, in the joy of His favour, both have such consolations in Him as to temper grief over bereavement, and also realise the world beyond the dark veil which has fallen between them and their loved ones. Therefore, by moderating their distress, they would teach us how to "sorrow not as others who have no hope." Even in our darkest sorrow let us never "profane the name" which we are to glorify; remembering our high office and privileged standing in Christ.

Vv. 7-9.—**They shall not take a wife**, etc. Called himself to a hallowed life, the priest must preserve himself from faulty alliances. Marriage should be regulated by fitness. There should be moral harmony, spiritual sympathy, between man and wife; emphatically so with all who profess Christ. "Be ye not unequally yoked together."

Vv. 10-15.—**He that is the high priest**, etc. The ordinary priests were allowed, when death fell on their nearest relationships, to relax their ministries awhile; but not so the *high* priest; for his absence from the tabernacle would arrest all the services of the sanctuary, while his contact with the dead would disqualify him to intercede for the people before God.

Vv. 16-24.—**He that hath any blemish, let him not approach**, etc. Physical malformations necessarily unfit men for solemn public offices when they attract observation, disturb reverence, and induce ridicule. Yet, although bodily infirmities still offer a natural obstruction to any one so afflicted entering the ministry of the Christian Church, they create no barrier to usefulness in many other honourable and hallowed paths of service. Within a deformed body may dwell a beautiful soul; and "our feeble frame" need not disqualify us for gracious and loving work in the Church of our Lord.

Our Divine Priest was in all points perfect—"without blemish"; in Him God was "well pleased." No defect mars His acceptance as He appears in the presence of God for us, and no infirmity in person or character exposes Him to the depreciation of men. He is the faultless Jesus; "fairest among ten thousand, and altogether lovely."

SECTIONAL HOMILIES.

Topic: SACRED RELATIONSHIP DEMANDS SANCTITY OF LIFE.

"*Speak unto the priests, There shall none be defiled; the bread of their God do they offer, therefore they shall be holy*" (vv. 1-6).

If there is one fact more notably emphasised than another in this address to *priests*, it is this: their

I. Absolute and Indestructible Relationship.

Every son of Aaron was a "priest." Of this union with Aaron it is observable that—

1. It results from *a living relationship.* By *birth* he was connected with Aaron, a lineal descendant of God's High Priest. And no truth is more a truism than that every Christian is by birth-relationship connected with Christ—born a priest, entering the spiritual life a "priest"; not rising later into the priestly relationship, but the moment he is quickened and becomes a believing and a living soul, he is a "priest unto God."

By no process of *spiritual development* or *self-culture* or *studied effort* does the convert to Christ become a "priest"; he is that by virtue of his living relationship to the High Priest: for as all the sons of Aaron were priests, so are all the sons of God through their connection with Christ. The spiritual priesthood is the appendage of our spiritual birth.

2. The relationship is *inalienable and indestructible.* *Conduct* is not the basis of relationship with Christ, but *life.* A son of Aaron might be defiled " for the dead" (v. 2), yet he did not thereby cease to be related to Aaron. If we were only priests to God as our conduct was faultless, who could stand? If none remained a "priest" longer than he preserved himself undefiled, who would hold the spiritual office an hour? We are all unclean; defile ourselves continuously with "the dead," the guilty and contaminating things of earth. But "our *life is hid* with Christ in God"; and by virtue of that life-union we remain priests.

3. *Imperfections of nature and character* do not sever relationship. A "blemish," deformity of body, proved a disqualification for ministry, but did not destroy association with Aaron. Yes; there is *exclusion from high and honoured services* in consequence of *irremediable defect and fault;* and Christians with incurable weakness of disposition, worldliness of sympathy, infirmities of character, vacillation of purpose, are thereby set aside from honour in the Church and highest ministries for their Lord; yet still the relationship to Christ continues, for it is a birth-relationship, based upon a life-union with Jesus. Christ is our life, and Christ liveth in us. We are therefore in priestly connection with our High Priest.

But though relationship is absolute and indestructible—

II. Privilege is dependent and conditional.

1. *Defilement is a disqualification* for near fellowship and highest enjoyment of the priestly relationship. Contact with "the dead" was forbidden; it excluded the priest from the service of God until cleansed anew and so reinstated. All contamination works disqualification, therefore "touch not, taste not, handle not." A priestly life should be pure. "Keep thyself pure." "The temple of God is holy." "Unspotted from the world." Spiritual favours are surrendered by the Christian the moment he *defiles himself.* Privilege is connected with purity. Near fellowship is for the uncorrupt.

2. *Defect is a disqualification* for highest service for our Lord. [See v. 17, etc.] *Physical* deformities even now form a natural barrier to the loftiest offices in the Church of Christ. Not unfitting the sufferer for many lowlier and less public ministries; for sacred grace is not dependent upon physical "form and comeliness." [See Addenda to chapter, *Bodily Infirmities.*]

Defects of character, of mental and moral constitution, also exclude from loftiest stations and services in the Christian kingdom. They are a barrier to such positions in the church as require noblest qualities of character: for eminence gives influence; and he who moves in the public gaze must be free from such weaknesses of will, or principle, or conduct as would lay him open to inconstancy. For such infirmities would bring reproach and derision on the Holy Name we bear. There is still 'll for the weak and defective a relationship with Christ "for by grace are they saved"; but not eminent position in the Church. "He shall eat the bread of his God: only he shall not go in unto the veil, nor come nigh unto the altar, because he hath a blemish" (vv. 22, 23). [See Addenda to chapter, *Bodily Appearance.*]

A. *All imperfections* in Christians *work deprivation.*
   (*a*) Loss of *near fellowship* with God in most privileged secrecy.
   (*b*) Forfeiture of rights to *most sacred services* in connection with the sanctuary.
   (*c*) Refusal to *represent God* before men, exclusion from the solemnities of priestly station and function.

B. *Sacred relationship* summons to *exalted sanctity.*
   (*a*) Avoidance of all forms and causes of *contamination* (v. 1).
   (*b*) *Customs,* harmless in themselves and not forbidden to others, must be shunned by priestly souls (vv. 5, 6).
   (*c*) *Indulgences and relationships* are to be regulated by our exalted standing in Christ (v. 9).
   (*d*) Life must be lived under the *power of the "annointing"* (v. 10), the "unction of the Holy Ghost."

Only thus can we maintain ourselves as "a spiritual priesthood to offer up spiritual sacrifices, acceptable to God by Jesus Christ" (1 Pet. ii. 5).

Topic: DIGNITY OF THE PRIESTHOOD TO BE KEPT INVIOLATE.

That the Levitical priests were to be blameless and without blemish, indicated the peculiar sanctity of their office, and the holiness of Jehovah, whom they represented among the people. The priesthood filled the gap between the Holy God and sinful man, the offerings they presented were the means of securing fellowship at the mercy seat, pardon for national and individual offences. The directions to the priests respecting their qualifications for the service of the tabernacle were repeated before all Israel, that the people might recognise the office and dignity of those who were solemnly set apart for sacerdotal duties. The directions of this chapter taught the priests—

I. THAT THEIR PATRIOTISM WAS TO BE SUBORDINATE TO THEIR SUPERIOR SAINTLY OFFICE.

When tidings came to the priests of any great sorrow in the camp of Israel, of suffering and death, human sympathy would prompt them to repair to the spot and condole with the bereaved; but they were not to "be defiled for the dead among the people," nor surround the dead body, nor join in the necessary obsequies. However patriotic they might feel, and however much they loved their people, the claims of their office were paramount; they had a great work to do, and could not turn aside to mourn for the dead, except under very special circumstances. Even natural, as well as national sympathy, was to be suppressed, nothing was to be done that would in any way produce ceremonial defilement. These restrictions would be for the best interests of the people, as in obeying them the priests would not neglect those duties in the discharge of which priceless blessings came from the presence of Jehovah to Israel.

II. THAT THEIR PERSONAL APPEARANCE WAS TO BE APPROPRIATE TO THEIR SAINTLY OFFICE.

Directions had already been given respecting vestments. [See former Homilies.] The heathen priests mutilated their bodies, disfigured their features, corrupted themselves with vicious habits; the Hebrew hierarchy were not to practise such things, their bodies, as well as their hearts and minds, were to be kept whole and pure. The exquisite beauty of nature—even in the minutest things—betokens the tastefulness of the great Creator. He loves the lovely, is pleased with the beautiful; the unsightly and discordant are incompatible with His glorious purposes. It is a serious deficiency in the equipment for efficient service, when the physical powers are feeble, or bodily appearance repellent. Those who minister before the Lord should be free as possible from all physical defects, mental obliquity, and moral obtuseness, as well as from flagrant wrongdoing.

III. THAT THEIR CONJUGAL ALLIANCES WERE TO BE HELPFUL TO THEIR SAINTLY OFFICE.

Celibacy was not imposed upon the Levitical priesthood, but full and strict directions given respecting their matrimonial engagements. They were not to marry persons beneath them in dignity, or concerning whose chastity and morality anything detrimental was known to exist. For a priest to take an unsuitable wife would be to beset his office with insuperable embarrassments. By her evil communications his good manners would become corrupted. None of his family could act wrongly without some unfavourable reflection being cast on him. This ancient statute has a good lesson for modern days. Too much care cannot be exercised by Christian ministers in the selection of help-meets for life; the Church, as well as the home, will be affected for good or evil as the wife and children of the minister of Christ conduct themselves before the people.

As the ages progress, less importance will become attached to physical blemishes than to mental and moral defects. The moral standard of human measurement is divine, and will outlive all other authority. The cause of Christ has often been injured by its members yoking themselves with unsuitable partners; the purity and harmony of home life will conduce to the light and sweetness of church life. The house of the Lord must not be profaned, nor must anything be allowed in the character of its ministers calculated to bring its hallowed services into ridicule or contempt. Ministers of Christ should aim *to live above suspicion*, to be renowned for moral worth, and to be highly esteemed for their work's sake. Such favour will be the foreshadowing of the approval of the Master in the last great day.—*F. W. B.*

Topic: QUALIFICATIONS FOR SACRED SERVICE (V. 4).

Impossible that the ceremonial rites and observances, and the elevated spiritual teachings of Leviticus could have been the inventions of the Hebrew priesthood. Uninspired men, under the sway of human passions, would have exempted themselves from disabilities and censures and accorded to themselves unrestrained license. Though the priests were peculiarly honoured, and permitted to draw very near to God, yet they needed to observe ceremonies for spiritual cleansing, they needed to resist temptation, and seek forgiveness the same as ordinary men. The priests—

I. WERE TO BE FREE FROM PHYSICAL BLEMISHES arising from heredity, accident, acquired malformation, or self infliction.

II. WERE TO AVOID ALL CONTACT WITH EVIL. Everything that would disqualify and detain them from regular consecrated service was to be sedulously avoided, (*a*) all contact with things ceremonially unclean, (*b*) all unholy alliances of a social and domestic character. These directions needed because the priests—

III. WERE THE REPRESENTATIVES OF THE LORD. Bore His name, reflected His nature, executed His laws. He sanctified them, set them specially apart to be mediators between Himself and the people.

IV. WERE THE EXEMPLARS OF THE PEOPLE. Possessing special advantages, called to exalted duties, exempted largely from other cares, the priests were expected to exhibit conspicuous holiness, to become examples to Israel in all things that Jehovah commanded.

V. WERE TYPES OF THE PREDICTED REDEEMER. Especially was this so in the character and work of the high priest. His sanctification from all defilement, admission into the holiest of all, presentation of the blood of the atonement before the mercy seat, etc.; all were, as the epistle to the Hebrews teaches, typical of Him, who, in the fulness of time, would abrogate the ceremonial law of Moses.

In the Christian dispensation, where all believers are kings and priests unto God, spiritual qualifications are required for sacred services. Freedom from physical blemishes, avoidance of contact with contaminating influences, non-association with uncongenial companions, will tend to make service for Christ more efficient. Every physical, mental, and spiritual excellence is necessary to adequate equipment for the work of the ministry, for the service of the sanctuary. Persons may serve God well who are encumbered with various deficiencies, but they can serve Him better who have few, and could serve Him best if they had none. We are called upon to be imitators of God; the world is to see the divine likeness in us. The Christliness of our lives is to be so unmistakable that men shall recognise us as having been with Jesus. "Let your light so shine before men," etc.—*F. W. B.*

Topic: ALLOWANCE FOR HUMAN INFIRMITY (Vv. 22, 23).

How fitting that the priests who were commanded to offer spotless sacrifices should themselves be without blemish. How fitting, also, that in a dispensation of types and symbols, respect should be paid to the purity and perfection of the body, which would naturally be regarded as mirroring the faculties of the soul. Impressions are produced upon the spirit through the corporeal senses, the physical *appearance* of the priests, therefore, as they officiated at the altar, would affect the tone of devotion in the people. It would be for the best interests of Israel, as well as for the glory of Jehovah, that no one with a blemish should take a prominent part in the services of the tabernacle. Consider—

I. THE INFLUENCE PHYSICAL INFIRMITIES OUGHT TO EXERT UPON THE HUMAN MIND.

They are often the cause of perplexity and pain, but they should always awaken (*a*) *Reflection:* Why has disease invaded the frame so "fearfully and wonderfully made"? Why such malformations and imperfections in organs originally designed for healthy and harmonious activities? The reply comes—Sin has done all the mischief, caused all the infirmities and pains. (*b*) *Caution:* If the body is so liable to disease and injury, to many disqualifications for fulfilling the great purposes of life, surely we cannot exercise too much vigilance in warding off injury, in avoiding everything that would vitiate the springs of life, or disorganize and corrupt our mortal bodies. (*c*) *Humility:* A body so liable to disease, weakness and death, so marred by sin, is not a thing to be proud of and idolised; at the best it is a body of death, only the feeble vehicle of the soul, a muddy vestment of decay grossly shutting us in from hearing and seeing the beauties and harmonies of heaven. The soul demands our *first, constant, supreme* care.

II. THE HINDRANCE PHYSICAL INFIRMITIES MAY PROVE IN THE DISCHARGE OF SACRED DUTIES.

Though the heart might be consecrated, the mind willing, priests with physical defects were not allowed to perform sacerdotal duties. Though no such exclusive regulations are in force in the Christian Church, yet physical defects are serious drawbacks to efficient service; *lameness, deafness, blindness, loss of*

s

voice, general debility, deformity, deficiency, etc., not only make the appearance unattractive, but unfit the person for complete and thorough service. There may be full and acceptable service rendered in the heart, the frail body disqualified for outward service may become a temple of the Holy Ghost. "They also serve who wait."

III. THE CONSIDERATION PHYSICAL INFIRMITIES RECEIVE FROM HIM WHO MADE US. Those disqualified to serve at the altar of the tabernacle were not wholly excommunicated, were not expelled from the precincts of the sanctuary or deprived of its sacred provisions. They might eat the priest's portions of the *meat, sin,* and *trespass* offerings, of the shewbread, and other priestly perquisites; probably also they aided the officiating priests by performing various subordinate duties. Thus we get an illustration of the fact mentioned by David, "He knoweth our frame, He remembereth that we are dust." Evidently (*a*) *physical features are not an invariable index to the qualities of the soul*. Some of the most lovely looking creatures are the most ferocious and deadly—tigers, serpents, etc. Some of the most uncomely frames have been known to possess exquisite minds, sublime spirits; and *vice versa*. (*b*) *Physical features are not the signs by which Jehovah judges of real worth*. Priests with blemishes were simply excluded from prominent conspicuous duties, the Lord owned them, "He shall eat the bread of *his God*." The Lord looketh not upon the outward appearauce (as a rule, and never when judging of real worth) but upon the heart. To Him, *character*, not circumstances or appearances, is the criterion by which the favour is bestowed. All through the Bible, election and promotion are based upon character. (*c*) *Physical features will neither distort nor disqualify in the future life*. The believer's body of humiliation is to be fashioned like unto the Saviour's glorious body; no imperfection of any kind in the perfect state of the purified. Those who suffer from physical infirmities may gather comfort from foregoing considerations; those who are largely exempt from them shall bear the infirmities of the weak. Our blessed Master will not break the bruised reed or quench the smoking flax. He can make us strong in weakness, we may glory in infirmities that the power of Christ may rest upon us.—*F.W.B.*

ILLUSTRATIVE ADDENDA TO CHAPTER XXI.

CELIBACY:
"Lust may be in the heart though it be not seen by others; as guests may be in the house though they look not out of the window."—BOWES.

BODILY INFIRMITIES:
"Our bodily infirmities, blessed be God, cannot exclude us from His heavenly glory. And they who, on many accounts, may be disqualified for the work of the ministry, may serve God with comfort in other stations in His Church."— SCOTT.

"Though such blemishes do not disable men from the ministry of the gospel, such remarkable deformities as apparently procure contempt should discourage any from undertaking that work, except where such persons feel irresistibly called to it. But that which in the Evangelical ministry is most liable to exception is such blemishes in the *mind* or *manners* as render such men incompetent to teach others and unfit to be public examples."—*Assembly's Annotation.*

BODILY APPEARANCE:
Auxilium non leve vultus habet.
[A pleasing countenance is no slight advantage].—OVID.

"'Tis not a lip, or eye, we beauty call,
But the joint force and full result of all."
—POPE.

'I pray Thee, O God, that I may be beautiful within."—SOCRATES.

"Let none presume
To wear an undeserved dignity."
—*Merchant of Venice,* II. 9.

"Though nature with a beauteous wall
Doth oft close in pollution, yet of thee
I will believe, that thou hast a mind to suit
With this thy fair and outward character."
—SHAKESPEARE.

"Handsome is that handsome does."
—GOLDSMITH, *Vicar of Wakefield,* I.

"Charms strike the sight, but merit wins the soul."—POPE.

Gratior ac pulchro veniens in corpore virtus.
[Even virtue is fairer when it appears in a beautiful person.]—VIRGIL.

"How this grace
Speaks his own standing! What a mental power
This eye shoots forth! How big imagination
Moves in this lip! To the dumbness of the gesture
One might interpret."—*Timon of Athens,* I. 1.

"What tender force, what dignity divine;
What virtue consecrating every feature!"
—YOUNG.

CHAPTER XXII.

Priestly Privileges Forfeited by Uncleanness.

SUGGESTIVE READINGS.

V. 1.—*Profane not My holy name in those things which they hallow unto Me.* Holy things must not be touched with unclean hands. What God hallows should be revered. To treat heedlessly any sacred thing profanes that *Name* with which it has become associated. If this applied to the altar offerings of the ancient tabernacle, surely it applies to our holy things—the Scriptures, the Sanctuary, the Lord's Day; for the Divine Name is linked to them, they are hallowed unto Him, and must not be profaned. More forcibly this requirement applies to lives hallowed in consecration to Christ; they must not be profaned by fellowship with evil, lest it lead to "that holy name by which they are called being blasphemed."

V. 2.—*That soul shall be cut off from My presence.* Did not the devouring fire consume Nadab and Abihu? Infliction of such severe penalties was a measure necessary in that age for the enforcement of duty, for inculcating correct ideas of Jehovah's sanctity and authority. Priests, by their privileged access to His "presence," might lapse into incaution; and as their favours were special, so their warnings were emphatic. If we dwell "in the light," how appalling the possibility of being thrust into outer darkness! Having preached to others, how fearful to think of becoming a castaway! Such possibilities should arouse privileged souls to "take heed lest they fall."

V. 10.—*There shall no stranger eat of the holy thing.* Hospitality is everywhere in Scripture commended; we should be "careful to entertain strangers." But guests in our homes do not, on that account, become qualified to share the covenant privileges of religion, which are reserved to those who are Christ's. Relation to God as a priest is a personal matter; and as a spiritual priest each believer is entitled to sit at the sacred table—yes, to feast in the very banqueting house of sovereign love—but we have no authority to extend these divine favours to others who have no priestly relationship to God, even though they have domestic or friendly relationship to us. Courtesy or magnanimity may not obliterate the spiritual distinctions with which God separates men.

V. 11.—*But if the priest buy any soul with his money, he shall eat.* So that when a soul becomes a priest's possession, he shares the priest's privileges. Its counterpart is in those we win to Christ—not by "money," but by the energies of Christian persuasion and influence; bound to us in the obligations of love. Our converts enter into our sacred enjoyments: "Ye are all partakers of my grace" (Phil. i. 7).

V. 14.—*If a man eat of the holy thing unwittingly.* Intruding where he ought not; taking advantages for which he had no qualification; enjoying sacred food for which he had done no sacred service. This is "trespass" (v. 16). Yet all assumption of religion without being in heart religious, all church offices and emoluments held by unchristian men for the sake more of "gain than godliness"—this is profanation, and these "bear the iniquity of trespass."

Vv. 17-24.—*Physical perfectness required in animals sacrificed.* For they were suggestive of the *perfect Christ*, and must therefore have no defect; and they betokened the *perfect life* which believers are called to devote to God: "Be ye therefore perfect, even as your Father in heaven is perfect."

V. 25.—*Neither from a stranger's hand*, etc. Offerings must be faultless, and the offerer must be qualified. Precious gifts from unhallowed hands God cannot accept. Leave the gift on the altar, and enter first into sacred relationship with God through Christ. Our standing "in Him" is of supreme importance; until we are thus "*made* nigh," we cannot acceptably "*draw* nigh."

V. 32.—*I will be hallowed . . . I am the Lord which hallow you.* It is for that sublime end we are sanctified. Men seek their own salvation, God seeks their sanctity; because salvation is a selfish goal, while sanctity is a testimony for God to men and angels. The work of divine grace in us is not merely for our gain, but to "adorn the doctrine of God our Saviour," to show the holy character of God to those who "take knowledge of us," and thus help to fulfilment the prayer, "Hallowed be thy name."

HOMILIES ON CHAPTER XXII.

Topic: A SOLEMN REGARD FOR HALLOWED THINGS.

"*That they profane not my holy name in those things which they hallow unto me*" (V. 2).

Religion is a sacred inward life. It consists not in outward things, such as symbols and ceremonies, which it uses and calls to its aid, but in the soul's acceptance with God, in its homage of Him, and in its glad resignation to Him and service for Him.

Yet *religion has its outward expression* in material things which it "*hallows.*" It does this by their consecration to God's service and honour. What in itself may be common and worldly becomes sacred when dedicated to religious purposes. And in this act of hallowing worldly things, religious men show their difference from the ungodly, who merely keep all earthly things for worldly and human ends, devoting none to God. But the children of God will have "things which they hallow unto me."

I. MAN'S ABILITY TO RENDER THINGS HALLOWED.

1. *Places:* As *sanctuaries* devoted to God's worship. *Homes* consecrated by piety and prayer. Select *scenes of retirement,* as some secret glen where a devout soul goes apart for meditation, etc., like Isaac at the well Lahai-roi. A *lowly room or shed,* used for gathering two or three in Christ's name for reading and exhortation.

2. *Seasons:* As the "Lord's day"; or appointed days, as "holy days"; or a fixed hour for bending the knee with some distant friend; or times in which to commemorate God's work in history.

3. *Possessions:* As *wealth* set apart for Christ; or *time* deliberately determined to be spent in Christian work; or some *particular object* we dedicate to the

Master's use—as Peter's boat, which he lent to Christ from which to preach to the multitudes on the shore.

4. *Persons:* Our *own* lives with all their talents and affections, "they gave *themselves* unto the Lord"; or a *child*, as Hannah dedicated Samuel; or a *band of Christian workers* sent forth on a specific mission.

II. MAN'S TENDENCY TO PROFANE THINGS HALLOWED.

1. As when regard for the sanctity of *holy scenes* ceases; the *sanctuary* fails to be in thought "none other but the house of God and the gate of heaven"; or *home* piety and prayer are discouraged by neglect.

2. Regard for the solemnity of *sacred seasons* declines; the *Sabbath* is not cherished as "a delight, the holy of the Lord, honourable"; *prayer times* are let slip disregarded.

3. Regard for the *divine claim on our possessions* abates; we "keep back some part of the price"; we recall from its dedicated purpose some consecrated object.

4. Regard for *true spirituality* in ourselves and others wanes; the "first love" waxes cold; the eagerness for our child or families to become Christian abates in the presence of their worldly interests and prospects.

III. MAN'S RESPONSIBILITY TO RESPECT THINGS HALLOWED.

1. They are *no longer ours*, either to recall from consecration or to divert to ourselves. *Money* was not Ananias's after he had professedly given it to Christ. And "*Ye* are not your own." Vowed to the Lord, our appropriation of it, or diversion from its sacred purpose, is profanation.

2. *God's name becomes identified* with "things hallowed unto Him." What a dishonour and derision to God and religion if, *e.g*, a *church* should be debased and turned into a tavern or a theatre: if a *Christian home* be degraded into a habitation of libertines and revilers: if a *sanctified life* returns again to the vileness of iniquity. Scoffers then will "blaspheme that holy name by which we are called."

3. When anything is "hallowed" it is *a witness amid ungodliness for religion and the unseen*. The tendency of man is to grow absorbed in material things, to attend merely to his physical and earthly interests. "Things hallowed" to God speak to men of what is divine, spiritual, eternal, and they cannot be removed from amongst us without danger of men sinking lower into dark materialism, and so forfeiting all the benefits which Christianity has brought into our national, social, and individual life.

(*a*) The *Bible* deserves to be cherished as a hallowed book, yet how many *neglect* it: how many deride it: how many read it only to disobey it.

(*b*) The *cross* is a symbol of a most pathetic, solemn, yet precious fact—the death of Jesus. Yet to how many Protestants has it become a mere *trinket* for adornment: while to many Romanists it has become an object of idolatrous *superstition*.

(*c*) The *bread and wine* are tokens of a finished redemption and our fellowship with Christ by faith. Yet they may be "eaten and drunk unworthily, not discerning the Lord's body," as if they had no solemn meaning: or they may be travestied on the "altar" of Ritualists, and in the Papal "mass."

"Then beware,
And make thyself all reverence and fear."

"*Speak, that they profane not my holy name in those things which they hallow unto me.*"

Topic: DEFILING HOLY THINGS.

"*Whosoever goeth unto the holy things, which the children of Israel hallow unto the Lord, having his uncleanness upon him, that soul shall be cut off from my presence: I am the Lord*" (V. 3).

Caryl says, "The very heathen had this notion, they would not admit any to their religious services unless they were prepared: therefore one cried out to the people when they came to sacrifice, 'All you that are unclean and profane go far away from these sacrifices.' Not only the word of God but the very light of nature taught them not to meddle with holy things till they were themselves sanctified."

In proof of this stands that saying of *Æneas* to his father when he came from the war, "*In genitor*," etc. "Father, do you meddle with the sacrifices: but as for me it is a sinful thing to touch them till I have washed myself at the fountain."

Cicero teaches a noble reverence for things hallowed: *Res sacros non modo manibus attingi, se ne cogitatione quidem violari fas fuit.* "Things sacred should not only not be touched with the hands, but not violated even in thought."

Yet there have been priests of our holy religion—yes, ministers of the gospel of Christ—and men in sacred eminence, who have defamed Christianity by their levity and sacrilege, until verily—

Religion, blushing, veils her sacred fires.—POPE.

ADMONITORY INCIDENTS:

Belshazzar converted the consecrated *vessels of the temple* into instruments of luxury and intemperance, touching holy things while himself unclean; but the hand of indignant judgment wrote in flaming letters upon his banqueting hall his sentence of doom.

Herod polluted the *sepulchres of the saints* with a sacrilegious search for treasures supposed to be hidden there, when God made fire rise from the earth to devour the infamous men who touched holy things with their uncleanness upon them.

Antiochus ransacked the very temple of God; *Heliodorus* emptied the treasures of their consecrated moneys; *Pompey* defiled the Sabbath and the sanctuary; *Crassus* despoiled the house of God of ten thousand talents; but their careers all tell the story of scathing judgment for defiling holy things, that ruin is ever the avenger of sacrilege.

Judas dared to touch with foul hands the sacred person of Christ, and sell Him for money; but the curse fell upon him, and he perished in his iniquity.

"*That soul shall be cut off from my presence; I am the Lord.*"

Topic: IRREVERENCE AMID SANCTITIES (Vv. 1-16).

The heathen hierarchy practised and exemplified the *debasing vices of* the idols they represented and professed to propitiate. Jehovah declared holiness indispensable to acceptable service in His presence. The Hebrews were taught by symbol, by ceremonies which appealed to their senses—truths concerning holiness which, under the gospel, are more fully enforced by the teachings of the Holy Ghost. In order that undue familiarity with holy things might be prevented—

I. A LINE OF DEMARCATION WAS TO BE DRAWN BETWEEN SACRED AND SECULAR THINGS.

For the performance of sacred duties there were fixed places and set times; no priest was to officiate when physically, ceremonially, or morally impure. "Speak unto Aaron and his sons, that they separate themselves from the holy things of the children of Israel." Why such strictness? (*a*) *Because sacred things enshrined the name of the Lord.* "That they profane not my holy name." (*b*) *Because sacred things honoured the name of the Lord.* "These things which they hallow unto me." Still required that those who bear the vessels of the Lord shall be holy, and make a difference between sacred and secular things.

II. A LINE OF DEMARCATION WAS TO BE DRAWN BETWEEN PURITY AND IMPURITY FOCHARACTER.

No priest was to officiate at the altar in a state of unfitness, under penalty of excommunication. "That soul shall be cut off from my presence: I am the Lord." This declares the priest to be fallible and frail; need for constant watchfulness lest the altar become polluted. Under the new dispensation a fountain full and free is open for sin and uncleanness. As kings and priests unto God, believers are expected to exhibit in their lives the fruits of the Spirit. Christianity has not relaxed the demands of the law for holiness of character, the standard is even higher, for "If any man have not the spirit of Christ, he is none of his."—*F.W.B.*

Topic: THE BEST FOR THE HIGHEST (Vv. 17-30)

The sacrifice—not the officiating priest—was the centre of the Levitical economy. He existed for the altar, not it for him. If absolutely necessary that priests should be holy, equally so that the offerings should be perfect, especially when regarded in the light of the epistle to the Hebrews as of typical import, as shadows of good things to come. Every offering was to be presented—

I. WITH A WILLING MIND. "Freewill offerings, which they will offer unto the Lord for a burnt offering." The authoritative commands of Jehovah did not interfere with free agency; the judgment and moral sense of offerers were appealed to, they were to choose what God had chosen. Unless voluntarily, there could have been no moral quality in the services they rendered. No virtue, where no possibility of vice, at least *in a probationary state.* At the erection of the Temple the same willingness was required. In the service of Christ we are to present ourselves *willing,* as well as *living* sacrifices.

II. WITH PERFECT OBEDIENCE. "Whatsoever hath a blemish shall he not offer." No unwholesome or unsightly thing was to be laid on the altar. The Highest *deserved,* as He demanded, the best. Obedience in the offerer thus required to be complete; no withholding, or withdrawing. (*a*) That the holy harmony of the economy might not be broken. (*b*) That the spotless antitype might be clearly foreshadowed.

God still demands *the best* we can offer, *the vigour and vivacity of youth ; the most wakeful and valuable portions of our time; the choicest and richest fruits of our substance.*

III. WITH A GRATEFUL HEART. "Neither from a stranger's hand shall ye offer the bread of your God." Offerings were to be presented by those who knew the Lord and would be actuated by devoted love. Acquaintance with God, reconciliation with Him, must precede offerings on His altar. The *character* of the giver, more than the nature of the gift, determines the divine estimate of offerings.

IV. WITH A LOYAL SPIRIT. The constant reiteration of the declaration, "I am the Lord," rendered obvious that all ought to be done with the profoundest reverence for the divine majesty. The Hebrews were to acknowledge Jehovah as their sovereign king. Time has not altered these conditions of acceptable offering. *Energy, time, means,* etc., all to be cheerfully surrendered to Him who is our Prophet, Priest and King. We owe Him the best of everything; He sacrificed the best—His life—for us; how irresistible the words of the apostle, "For ye are not your own," etc.—*F.W.B.*

Topic: BLEMISHES IN OUR SACRIFICES

"*Whatsoever hath a blemish, that shall ye not offer; for it shall not be acceptable for you*" (V. 20).

Reference is to sacrifices. All religious service is of the nature of sacrifice. "Whatsoever, etc." (Text).

I. Read this requirement of perfect sacrifices, and by it let us *test our regard for the* SABBATH SERVICES.

God has once, at least, read us a very solemn lesson of the manner in which He regards lost Sabbaths. Seventy Sabbatical years the Jews allowed to drop out of their calendar. Seventy years were spent by them in captivity. A fearful presage to us of what might be the national judgment, if, as a church and people, we went on to blot out from amongst us our day of rest. And yet, is that fear groundless? Are we not already gone far towards such a state of things? Is not the Sunday, to a fearful extent, an omitted day? The fourth commandment an omitted commandment? Such as the Sunday is, so is the week. It is the keystone of the arch of our secular life. The folly and sin of most men is, they begin by making the Sunday a blank day. And as a blank becomes intolerable, therefore the day proves to them listless, weary, worldly, profane. A taste for spiritual things needs to be cultivated and prayed for. A vague mind, a dull feeling, the sense of its being a long day each time the Sunday comes round—these afford proof that to us heaven is still very far off, that the bright and beautiful world is not " *our own place*." To pass a little more into detail, ordinarily everyone will agree that if the Sabbath be obligatory, then it is assuredly obligatory thus far—

1. That there be *regular attendance* upon *public service.*
2. Of the other hours of the day, that a part be spent in *private devotional exercises*, a part in *religious reading;* that a higher and more sacred *tone of conversation* be maintained; that some work of piety and love be performed.

These are but *some* of the most obvious and necessary Sunday duties and Sunday enjoyments. How do many of us acquit ourselves in this matter? Has the sacrifice of the seventh portion of our time, which we profess to offer week by week, any "blemish"? An unoccupied day must prove an unpleasant day. We omit duty, therefore God omits blessing. Need we look further than our Sundays, idle, &c., for many a disappointment and discontent and bitterness of life?

II. By this test let us *judge our* SANCTUARY WORSHIP.

Examine ourselves in the house of God. Difficulty of keeping the mind collected and devout results from want of due *preparation.*

1. Something may be said respecting the *posture of body* we assume in the sanctuary. Position of body re-acts upon the mind. Indolence is associated with, and leads to, irreverence. Kneeling is required equally by the dignity of God and the weakness of our nature.

2. So with the *voice.* Difficult to over-estimate how much is lost (*a*) To the beauty of our services; (*b*) To the glory of God; (*c*) To our own souls, by the silence so many of us maintain, both in the responses and in the service of song. But there are more serious "blemishes" in our sanctuary sacrifices than these. Where is—

(1) The *constant mental* effort essential to true worship, and proper in the presence of God?
(2) The *self-distrust* due from such sinful creatures as we?
(4) The *self-discipline* to bring ourselves into responsiveness to God's Spirit?
(3) The *inward up-looking* for divine light and grace?
(5) The frequent reminding ourselves of *what we are and what God is*
(6) The *simple spirit of self-application?*
(7) The *faith* to give wings to prayer?

Well might St. James say "Ye have not because ye ask not, or ask amiss." "Blemish on sacrifice" drives the flame down again.

III. By this test let us *examine our observance of* THE SACRAMENT OF THE LORD'S SUPPER.

A word in solemn affection to some. You never *attend* the sacrament to celebrate the Lord's death at all. Others, if at all, so *irregularly* as almost to turn the attendance into a mockery. Do you consider that that with which you so deal is none other than the dying command of the Lord and Saviour: the highest and best of all the means of grace? And yet you habitually pass it by. Can there be any limit to the evil which such an omission may be entailing upon your soul? Your religion is barren of joy if your soul fails to realise peace; if your prayers work no effect; if your faith seems to rest on no reality; if you gain no sense of forgiveness. Well, there is a chain of cause and consequences here; we must divide its links. The soul's losses all fasten themselves into the soul's omissions. Note:

1. Happy for us that we can turn from all our poor "*blemished*" *sacrifices* to that *pure and perfect sacrifice of Christ*, which has been offered "without blemish and without spot" for us.

2. Only let us never forget that he who would *safely trust in the power of that* "*Sacrifice*" for his salvation, must take the spotlessness of that Sacrifice for his *daily pattern.*—*Anon.*

Topic: UNQUESTIONING OBEDIENCE PEREMPTORILY ENFORCED (Vv. 31-33).

The pilgrimage of Israel through the wilderness was of a probationary character, affording a suggestive emblem of all human life. The natural tendency of the human will to rebellion required imperative commands to subdue and bend it to the obedience of the just. The minute and exacting requirements of the Mosaic ritual would train the people to humble obedience. Such peremptory statutes were based upon:

I. WHAT JEHOVAH WAS IN ISRAEL. "I am the Lord." The Lord had perfect right to enjoin what obedience He chose upon His subjects. In the midst of Israel Jehovah was King, His word went forth with power. Let all the inhabitants of the earth stand in awe of Him, and obey His voice, for it is still universally true, "The Lord reigneth."

II. WHAT JEHOVAH WAS TO ISRAEL. "Your God." To carry out His wise and benevolent designs towards the race, God saw fit to make Israel His chosen people, custodians of His written word, channels of blessing to the whole world. Israel was under the most solemn obligations to obey divine statutes, to conform to the divine will. Under the new dispensation no stronger motive can prompt to Christian consecration and obedience than the declaration of the apostle to the Gentiles, "Whose I am, and whom I serve."

III. WHAT JEHOVAH HAD DONE FOR ISRAEL. "That brought you out of the land of Egypt." The Exodus had exhibited the goodness of the Lord. Wonders had been performed, unexpected channels of deliverance had been opened, abundant supplies had been vouchsafed to them. Obligations to obedience were many and weighty. The goodness of God calleth us to repentance. Redemption from the slavery of Satan and sin should constrain to obedience. Translated into the kingdom of God's dear Son, this the becoming question of the soul, "Lord, what wilt thou have me to do?"

IV. WHAT JEHOVAH WOULD DO WITH ISRAEL. "I am the Lord which hallow you." The Lord's purpose in selecting Israel as His peculiar people, was not only that His name might be hallowed among them, but that their hearts might become sanctified by His presence. *Holiness* was the supreme end of the Mosaic ritual. Ceremonially and symbolically priests and people were made holy by (*a*) *the rites they observed;* (*b*) *the sacrifices they offered;* (*c*) *the manifested presence of the Lord.*—*F.W.B.*

OUTLINES ON VERSES OF CHAPTER XXII.

Vv. 1, 2.—*Theme:* THE JEALOUSY OF JEHOVAH.

Human nature inherently prone to presumption and irreverence. Upon the priests was enjoined the most scrupulous care, lest in any way they disgraced themselves and dishonoured Jehovah. Small gifts were not excluded from the altar of the Lord, but all blemished offerings were; to teach Israel (*a*) *The supremacy of the divine will*. What He required, not what they might feel disposed to offer, must be presented. (*b*) *The necessity of unquestioning obedience.* " I am the Lord." Enough for Israel to know that the Lord required it at their hands. The jealousy of Jehovah for His name and glory would inculcate the need of—

I. CONSTANT CIRCUMSPECTION. Sacerdotal duties so intricate and various, the priests would require to exercise unrelaxing vigilance.

II. CAREFUL DISCRIMINATION. Offerings to be unmixed; in strict accordance with minutely prescribed directions.

III. COMPLETE CONSECRATION. Everything to be done to the full; no reserve, shortcoming, or withdrawal. No imperfection in servant or service tolerated in the tabernacle worship.

Inherited and unavoidable disabilities for public service form no barrier in the way of divine favour. *A willing heart* is accepted when the accomplishment of its sincere purpose is impossible. *Willingness* and *ability* characterise the service of the Upper Temple. Scrupulous care still to be exercised, that there be no profanation of God's *Name, Day, Book, House, Ordinances.—F.W.B.*

V. 10.—*Theme:* HOLY FEASTS FORBIDDEN TO STRANGERS.

" *There shall no stranger eat of the holy thing*."

Salvation is common, open to all; but privileges are special, reserved to consecrated souls. [See " Suggestive Readings " on the verse.]

These " strangers " in the priest's house represent persons near the Kingdom of Grace but not within it.

I. FRIENDSHIP *with the godly does not confer qualification for religious privileges.* Not though we be *guests* in the home of a minister of Christ's sanctuary; not though we enjoy Christian *intimacy* and *affection*, do we on that account become qualified to share the covenant blessings of religion.

Personal alliances and family intimacies with God's people do not render us partakers of their grace.

II. *Enjoyment of* RELIGIOUS INTERCOURSE *does not create qualification for sacred privileges.*

Within the priest's home there would be much religious *converse*, and acquaintance with the meaning of religious truths and duties; but *knowledge* of divine things, and the advantage of *holy conversation*, do not necessarily lead to spiritual life.

" Having all knowledge and understanding all mysteries profit nothing " if there be not inward life and personal love.

III. Residence in HOLY DWELLINGS *does not confer qualifications for saintly privileges.*

Though resident in the priest's home, " strangers " might not partake of the priest's food.

Attendance on the sanctuary; frequenting holy places; being continually *near God's servant* in sacred scenes; all this may be without personal piety.

Being a doorkeeper in the house of God; a persistent attendant at sacred services; maintaining a constant connexion with the sanctuary; these do not ensure and guarantee a state of grace, a qualification for the privilege of sanctified souls.

Apply :—

1. *Better be* " *strangers*," near though not in the kingdom, *than aliens* far off from all the allurements and opportunities of religion.

2. Though " strangers," the way is possible in the gospel for such to *become partakers* of the feasts of redemption and of grace. " At that time ye were without Christ, being aliens from the commonwealth of Israel, and strangers," etc. (Ephes. ii. 12).

Nearness to those who are sanctified in Christ Jesus, and spiritually " priests unto God," should help forward a religious life until those once " *strangers*," *yet guests*, become *welcomed to the feasts* of sacred love. [See outline on v. 25, *Holy Ministries refused from Strangers*.]

V. 20.—*Theme:* UNBLEMISHED SACRIFICES. " But whatsoever hath a blemish, that shall ye not offer; for it shall not be acceptable for you."

Everything laid on the altar to be free from (*a*) *bodily disease*, (*b*) *national deformity*, (*c*) *acquired defects*. These defects, emblems of moral blemishes, which disqualify for service under the gospel—*depraved passions, crooked conduct, deflection from duty, indulgence in any kind of sin*—will render the most costly offering obnoxious to the divine mind.

Men present blemished sacrifices to the Lord—

I. WHEN THEIR GIFTS ARE NOT PROPORTIONATE TO THEIR MEANS. Many profess to give to the utmost of their ability, when they only give a pitiable fraction from the abundance with which God has prospered them. Such blemished sacrifices God rejects.

II. WHEN THEIR GIFTS ARE NOT THE SYMBOLS OF SELF-SACRIFICE. No offering is accepted except presented in a willing and devout spirit; God expects living sacrifices, the wealth of human love—all the heart mind, soul, strength; then other gifts as evidences of complete self-consecration.

III. WHEN THEIR GIFTS ARE PRESENTED TO PROCURE SALVATION. Sensuous worship, ritualistic observances are valueless; only the merits of the one all-atoning sacrifice of Christ can render the most perfect gifts acceptable.

Let but the heart be wholly given to the Lord, then not the deceased or decayed, the refuse or leavings, the chaff or dregs, but the best, costliest, and brightest will be consecrated to the Lord.

These things read in the light of the New Testament teach—(*a*) *How completely the spotlessness of Christ fulfilled the rigid requirements for perfection in Jewish sacrifices.* (*b*) *How the material offerings of the tabernacle were adapted to prepare the way for the proclamation of what they foreshadowed.* (*c*) *How the constant demand for holiness in offerings and offerers reiterated the abiding facts, that Jehovah is spotlessly holy; and that "without holiness no man can see the Lord."*—F.W.B.

V. 25.—*Theme:* HOLY MINISTRIES REFUSED FROM STRANGERS.

If "strangers" might not eat the feast reserved for priestly souls (comp. on v. 10) so neither would God allow them to minister at the altar of His sanctuary.

This interdict demands—

I. That MINISTERS OF THE GOSPEL be themselves *true-born sons of God.*

II. That WORKERS IN THE CHURCH be chosen exclusively from those *in spiritual fellowship with God's people.*

III. That SACRED OFFERINGS, gifts laid on the altar of religion, are *only acceptable as the giver is a sincere Christian.*

IV. That A SPIRITUAL STATE is the *supremely precious thing* in God's esteem; not *what* we bring, but *what we are* ourselves who bring the offering.

NOTES:—

1. God abhors *hallowed services* by *unhallowed souls.* "They shall be not accepted for you."

2. *A gracious relationship* to God in Christ must *precede* all attempts to please Him by service or gifts.

3. From saintly souls *every offering, however lowly,* is a "sacrifice well pleasing unto God," as a token of sonship and love.

CHAPTER XXIII.

Israel's Holy Festivals.

SUGGESTIVE READINGS.

V. 2.—Concerning the feasts of the Lord. Religion has its joy seasons, its festive aspects. Israel's sacred feasts symbolised the festivals of the Christian soul, those holy delights which believers now realise in their life of faith and fellowship.

(*a*) *Sacred festivals*, breaking in upon the monotony of the year, and arresting society amidst its common worldly employ, confer valued benefits on humanity; they are a temporary reprieve from the clamour of secular toils, and set men free for refreshment and rest; while they also incite to some degree of religious interest and gratitude, for they witness to gracious events in God's redeeming purposes for the world, and summon the multitudes to gladness in commemoration.

(*b*) *Spiritual joyousness*, that sacred gladness we inherit in Christ, and of which those festivals were but suggestions and scintillations, has its special and more emphatic seasons within the experience of the Christian; for although religion brings into the soul an enduring happiness and a perennial feast of love, there are times when richer enjoyment of divine fellowship and privilege delights the godly man, and his holy relationship to Christ and the Church fills him with profounder satisfaction and bliss. The sun's light shines steadily on throughout the entire day, but there are occasional intervals when his beams burst forth in more resplendant glory.

V. 2.—Holy convocations, even these are my feasts. Heathenism had its wild, licentious orgies; Christianity claims sanctity for all its festivities. On all pleasures and delights it inscribes "Holiness to the Lord." Happiness must be holy. God sends gladness into the soul He redeems, and its joy must be always kept pure.

Yet, in this arrangement that the feasts should be "*convocations*," emphasis is placed on the fact that our joy should be sympathetic and communicative, not isolate and selfish. Redeemed men have common reasons for happiness and praise; God would have them meet together in grateful celebration, fostering a sacred friendship, entering into each other's joy. Sin has drawn society together in the sympathy of sorrow and degradation; religion re-unites those it blesses in the fellowship of sacred gladness.

V. 3.—The sabbath of rest. As the oldest of all sacred festivals, and the most frequent in recurrence, God places the sabbath in the front; it brings to toil-worn lives a day of "rest," it announces to weary souls that sacred rest which Jesus gives, it foreshadows to life's pilgrims Zionwards the "rest which remaineth" when heaven is reached.

The sabbath rest is to be enjoyed, not in selfish ease, but as a time for meeting with God's people in *sacred assembly*, "a holy convocation," and as a season for devout *social fellowship;* "it is the sabbath of the Lord in all your dwellings."

V. 5.—The Lord's passover. A commemoration of grand events: spared from the angel's stroke of death, freed from the cruelty of oppressive slavery. Redemption and emancipation—such truths are proclaimed now to man through the "sacrifice of Christ our Passover." Christians who have experienced the deliverance, and escaped into the "glorious liberty" of faith, should celebrate with joy this work of God's salvation; for if Israel kept holy festival in memory of the Egyptian rescue, surely we should "keep the feast" (1 Cor. v. 7, 8).

Vv. 7, 8.—Ye shall do no servile work; but ye shall offer an offering made by fire. They who are gathered under the merits of the Paschal Atonement are set free from "servile" toils. No more "servile work" now for the sinner; no weary efforts, no fruitless endeavours, no degrading labours; for the "offering made by fire," the sweet incense offering of Christ, has gone up to God, and it is enough. The soul is set free from legal "work," and now stands an observer of the meritorious offering which rises to heaven as "by fire." Not the labours of our hands but the offering on Calvary: with that "sweet savour of Christ" God is well pleased; and sinners stand acquitted with their trust fixed on the accepted sacrifice.

V. 10.—Bring a sheaf of the first-fruits of your harvest. The paschal offering foreshadowed the death of Christ, the "sheaf of first-fruits" His resurrection. And equally is symbolised the risen and renewed life into which all Christians emerge from their death in sin, under the quickening of God's Spirit. Further, it predicts the final resurrection of those who "sleep in Christ." "Christ the first-fruits, afterwards they that are Christ's at His coming." And as our resurrection *body* at the last day will be "fashioned like unto his own glorious body," so, meanwhile, should our resurrection *life* be graced with all the perfections of His character. "If ye then be risen with Christ, seek those things which are above." Surely every soul called from sin to grace, raised from death unto life, should seal the outset (see v. 14) of His spiritual career by an act of "first-fruits" consecration, which should be the pledge of an after "harvest" of devoted service to the Lord.

V. 16.—Number fifty days, and offer a new meat offering. This was the feast of Pentecost, which opened with the presentation of the first-fruits barley sheaf, and was to be closed with the offering of a loaf made from the ingathered wheat harvest. It celebrated the completion of the harvest season. It thus testified that God had given an abundant ingathering, and had blessed His people with bread. In the Christian Church the "first-fruits" were the foretoken of harvest abundance; for Christ's resurrection guaranteed a great ingathering of souls; and on the day of Pentecost the spiritual harvest was brought in unto the Lord. It was exactly "fifty days" after Christ arose from the dead that the Holy Ghost was given, and the bountiful ingathering of converts was secured for the church (Acts ii.).

V. 24.—**A memorial of blowing of trumpets** It was the rallying note amid the camp and throughout Israel, making known the opening of a new era. The "Feast of Trumpets" proclaimed the arrival of "New Year's Day," for the civil year began on "the first day of the seventh month." With a great outburst of joy-strains the new epoch opened. Suggestive of the new era upon which a redeemed soul enters, the Christian convert starts forth as with music and gladness upon a holy career. The trumpet notes are typical of the *Gospel call*, by which men are aroused to regard and seize the first opportunity presented them. It prefigures also that mighty trumpeting at the end of time, which will summon living and dead to the day of God, to which those in Christ will first respond (1 Thess. iv. 16), but which will awaken all who sleep to a new era for universal humanity (1 Cor. xv. 51, 52).

V. 27.—**A day of atonement.** In chap. xvi. the ritual of the great day is elaborately given; here the spirit and temper of the people is described, the whole congregation was to bow before God abased and penitential. It is well if only once every year we chasten "and afflict" our souls with humiliating thought of our sin, and bend before Jehovah with contrite hearts. Alas, there is need that we bemoan our demerit, and thus contemplate the "Atonement." Yet how precious the fact that, while like a penitent we stand in shame for our sin, the "Day of Atonement" proclaims redeeming efficacy and grace for all who lay their hand and hope on the sacrificial Lamb.

V. 34.—**The Feast of Tabernacles.** It is minutely directed in v. 40 that they were to take "boughs of goodly trees," affording shade and shelter and suggestive of God's overshadowing care and covenant; "branches of palm trees," emblematic of victory (Rev. vii. 9), for they were the triumphant host of God marching onward to possess Canaan; and "willows of the brook," symbols of plenitude and prosperity (Isa. xliv. 4). This dwelling in booths seven days every year (v. 42) would perpetuate the memory of their pilgrim career, their dependence on divine care and providence, and God's unfailing sufficiency for them from the outset to the close of their journey to Zion. And shall not we also keep in remembrance the years in which we have been "strangers and pilgrims on the earth," through which the Lord has surely led us, never failing in the watchfulness of His providence or the sufficiency of His grace? "Thou shalt remember all the ways the Lord thy God has led thee these forty years in the wilderness, to humble thee, and to prove thee, to know what is in thine heart" (Deut. viii. 2).

SECTIONAL HOMILIES.

Topic: THE SABBATH OF REST (V. 3).

Levitical enactments, its rites and regulations, its festivals and solemnities, were all transient and Jewish. The Sabbath is not to be classified with these: it is not one of many institutes of Israel. It preceded the wilderness encampment, was anterior to the enactments of Sinai. The Sabbath dates with man's creation, it began in Eden. It is primeval law. Its origin preceded sin.

If thus *remote its origin*, what of its *permanency?*

It was recognised through Antediluvian times. Noah kept it within the ark, sending forth his dove after seven days' interval. Moses urges its observance, and this, not after its promulgation on Sinai, but at the outset of the encamping of the Israelites in the desert (Exo. xvi. 23), as being an institute well understood; it had, therefore, been known to them through their Egyptian bondage. It was no novel statute, therefore, when incorporated in the decalogue on Sinai.

In Jewish history it became re-inforced with all the solemnities of the giving of the law, the Sabbath's sanctity was inscribed on stone with the finger of God.

The line of prophets in succession urged its solemnity, and denounced its neglect and violation.

Our Lord re-asserted its authority, " The Sabbath was made for man " (Mark ii. 27), for all men, for all ages. And now—

> Sabbaths are threefold, as St. Austin says:
> The first of time, or Sabbath here of days;
> The second is a conscience trespass free;
> The last a Sabbath of eternity.—*Herrick.*

I. THE WEARY LIFE OF MAN CALLS FOR THIS INTERVAL OF SABBATH REST.

1. *Each individual life requires it.* Toil wastes our physical fabric, the strain on nerve and brain wears away the energy of life. The rush of daily duties consumes all leisure, allows no pause for bodily rest, no repose for thought, or attention to the soul's great concerns.

2. *Family life* demands it. Amid the eagerness of worldly work parents and children are scattered, each to a separate scene and diverse tasks. Yet home is a unity; family life is a blended harmony. There is need for a lull in the clamour; a truce for the rallying together of the scattered ones; that home might quietly re-construct itself, and family life be realised.

3. *Moral life* calls for it. A worn and spent state of body, nerve, and brain, brings with it a relaxed will, an enfeebled moral purpose. With recouped physical energy comes reaffirmed force of mind and character. A pause for bodily rest is essential for this moral resuscitation.

4. *Spiritual life* cries out for it. Amid the arid scenes of the world the soul droops and thirsts. It pants for the living streams And as Christ called His disciples apart to rest awhile, so does the Sabbath; giving to overtaxed lives the sacred joy of going apart with Jesus.

Enquire: *Is this inflexible command of God necessary in order to conserve the Sabbath?*

If man so greatly needs it, would not his need assert itself, and lead men to perpetuate the beneficent institute without a divine command?

Answer: (*a*) Man's *greed* would lead him to *deny a Sabbath to himself.* His lust of gain, and clamour for success, would drive him on to ruinous absorption in earthly schemes and lucrative pursuits. " The love of money " urges on to suicidal indifference to all higher interests. He would never let a day go each week from his eager life. " Time is money "; and if a Sabbath brings no gain to his grasping hands it is a day lost.

(*b*) *Nor would selfish men concede the Sabbath's rest* to weary toilers. Already the oppressed and overwrought workers find it difficult to arrest the encroachments of trade on the sanctities of the Lord's Day. Heartless employers would snatch precious hours from the Sabbath, and force their servants to labour. Men would not give the holy day to their fellows if no divine law interposed to check such infringements.

Every interest, therefore, of human life, is bound up with the maintenance of the Sabbath as a day of rest. [See *Addenda* to chapter; SABBATH.]

II. The sin-worn spirit of man sighs for the consolations of sabbatic sacred rest.

The Sabbath is but typical of the rest of faith which the gospel brings to burdened souls.

1. *All trials cease* when the spirit enters into the Sabbatic rest which Jesus gives. The sinner "ceases from his own works" (Heb. iv. 10). Worn with labour, and heavy laden with the burdens of conscious unrighteousness, the toiling soul comes to the Saviour (Matt. xi. 28). A heavenly day, a serene Sabbatic life, dawns upon him at once, and in the restfulness of faith, trusting all to Jesus, he desists from fruitless efforts to " establish his own righteousness," and sits down at the feet of Jesus. It is the Sabbath rest of his life begun.

2. *Our daily conflicts and crosses* render the Sabbath privilege a precious consolation to the believer. Resting in Jesus does not render the world a restful scene to the Christian. Nor does human life cease to know the common griefs and struggles of existence. Whereas also, the keen longings of the soul for fellowship with Christ finds few occasions for gratification amid the busy hours of the week. How welcome, therefore, to the believer is the day of rest! By "still waters" and amid "green pastures" he roams, in all the solemn delights of leisurely meditation: and his soul is "restored" (Psa. xxiv.). To his troubled heart comes the solace of the "peace" which only Jesus gives (Jno. xiv. 1, 27). Within the sanctuary, "soothed with holy hymn and psalm," quickened by fellowship with saints, and renewed through waiting upon God, he gains "times of refreshing" and strengthening of soul. He drinks of the brook by the way and lifts the head with freshened vigour for life's journey. Full oft the rejoicing soul, glad in Christ, and refreshed by the Sabbath privileges, has to say,

> Thou art a cooling fountain
> In life's dry, dreary sand;
> From thee, like Pisgah's mountain,
> We view the promised land;
> A day of sweet reflection
> Thou art, a day of love—
> A day of resurrection
> From earth to things above.

III. The life-tired soul of man longs for the sabbath of heavenly rest.

All sabbath repose and refreshing on earth; all realisations of the rest of soul Christ gives to the believer, all sanctuary consolations enjoyed on the Lord's day, are but foretastes and foreshadowings of heaven's eternal peace, and joy, and love.

1. *As the sabbath day dawns after the night is spent,* so *heaven's sabbath follows death's dark night.*

We have to live our life's day of duty and service to confront the responsibilities of worldly trusts and opportunities to "work while it is called day." "This is not our rest." But the shadows at length fall; a hush spreads over the tumult of existence; the hand slackens its hold on the instruments of labour; darkness comes gently down upon earthly scenes. But a "lively hope" fills the Christian soul; a vision of a glorious dawn sweeps across the dimming human gaze.

> And a voice, while earth cares fly,
> With the closing hours is blending—
> "Rest is coming, rest is nigh!"

Night wraps itself around the life: the day of eternity breaks upon the spirit: Heaven's rest is gained. And "there shall be no night there," "neither sorrow, nor crying, neither any more pain; for the former things are passed away." "Blessed are the dead who die in the Lord: yea, from henceforth, saith the Spirit, for they *rest*"

2. *As the sacred rest of faith is gained by the sinner only when he comes unto Jesu*

so the heavenly rest is gained only when the Christian reaches the very presence of his Lord.

"Come *unto me*," says Jesus, " and I will give you rest!" Blessed the experience of reaching Him now by faith : but when the soul bursts through the barrier of death and passes the gates of the heavenly city, and finds itself within the " Everlasting Arms," leaning on Jesus' bosom, never more to leave the radiant presence of his Lord, then, indeed, will the full rest of heaven be known.

No rough billows heave on the serene ocean of life eternal. No shadow falls on the bright sky of heaven's bliss. No distance ever more divides the redeemed soul from the rapture of Christ's presence. " For ever with the Lord ": and therefore there remaineth a keeping of sabbaths for the people of God

> Rest, spirit free!
> In the green pastures of the heavenly shore,
> Where sin and sorrow can approach no more,
> With all the flock by the Good Shepherd fed,
> Beside the streams of life eternal led,
> For ever with thy God and Saviour blest,
> Rest, sweetly rest!

Topic: THE SABBATH (V. 3).

Placed first among the Hebrew festivals, the sabbath becomes invested with peculiar honour and importance. It *claimed* priority, dating back to the completion of creation, and reaching forward throughout all time, to be consummated in eternity. The institution and perpetuation of the sabbath secured time for the full observance of sacred duties ; and, by its weekly advent, called attention to them. No institution of the Hebrew economy was more frequently referred to, or its observance more strictly enforced. Part of the badge that distinguished Israel from surrounding nations was cessation from worldly toil and complete consecration to sacred service one day in seven. The Hebrew Sabbath was—

I. A SACRED MEMORIAL, of the original institution of a special season for rest and undisturbed attention to divine things. It would be a perpetual reminder of the fact that " in six days the Lord made heaven and earth," therefore, a constant rebuke to every form of heathenism, where the true God was ignored or unknown. Under the Christian dispensation observance of " the Lord's Day " is a perpetual memorial of the fundamental fact of Christianity, that the Redeemer's atoning work was completed on earth when He rose from the grave on the morning of the third day.

II. A SACRED FESTIVAL.

In it God took special delight. He demanded it as *a sacrifice of time* from those whose days really all belonged to Him. Though all *secular* work was to be discontinued, works of mercy, piety, and necessity were to be performed. The Hebrews were to gather together for divine worship and the cultivation of personal holiness. Though God did not *need* the rest—for He never grows weary - yet man needed it; and God rejoiced in it, as its claims were recognised, its duties discharged. It was *a festival*, not a fast ; for man to use, not abuse ; to be made a delight, not a burden ; for, in sanctifying time and strength to the Lord according to His gracious will, man finds his highest and truest joy.

The transfer of the sabbath from the seventh to the first day of the week has not diminished its sacredness, or relaxed its claims. It is still a feast of the Lord, to be devoted to sacred purposes. It proclaims to all the right of freedom from exacting toil, and places all upon a level as the Lord's free men.

III. A SACRED TYPE.

The law of the sabbath, re-published in the wilderness, pointed to the time when Israel would be able fully to observe it in the land of Canaan. The peculiar sanctity and blessedness of the day may fitly be regarded as typical of the perfect rest of heaven, where all the toils and trials of time will—for those who keep His commandments—issue in the rest and recompense of eternity. In observing the sabbath, we not only obey the divine command, but we follow the divine example (Gen. ii. 2, 3). Thus God is pleased and man is blessed. Thus time becomes hallowed, life worth living, and heaven won. [See also preceding Homily on chap. xix. v. 3.]—*F.W.B.*

Topic: SIGNIFICANCE OF THE PASSOVER (Vv. 5-8).

"The first Passover was the commencement of the special privileges of the chosen nation, every subsequent Passover became a pledge of the continuance of those privileges" (Cave).

(*a*) The feast was RETROSPECTIVE and *commemorative*.

Israel's deliverance from the *destroying angel*, and from *Egyptian bondage*, was an event unparalleled in human history. God would perpetuate the memory of so wondrous an incident as a testimony for all time that "salvation is of the Lord," and that mightiest deliverances can be wrought for His people by our Redeemer.

Thus the *Lord's Supper*, as a commemorative feast, also "shows forth the Lord's death," leading back our thoughts and faith to "Christ our Passover, sacrificed for us," and the wondrous redemption wrought for an enslaved Church and a death-doomed world.

(*b*) The feast was PROSPECTIVE and *typical*.

The lamb of the paschal feast foreshadowed "the *Lamb of God*, which taketh away the sins of the world." For the lamb employed at this commemorative feast was more than a symbol of the victim whose blood was sprinkled on the doorposts in Egypt, it was a *sacrifice*. It meant substitution. It typically "put away sin."

At the Lord's Supper, Christ said to His followers, "My body is *broken for you*, my blood is *shed for you*." And Paul adds the testimony that "our Passover is *sacrificed* for us."

The Identification of the Paschal Victim with Jesus Christ :—

I. *With regard to the* SELECTED VICTIM.

1. Was it a *lamb*? Christ is often so called on account of His innocence, meekness, and resignation (Isa. liii. 7 ; Jno. i. 29 ; 1 Pet. i. 19 ; Rev. v. 6).

2. Was it *taken from the flock*? Christ was chosen from among His brethren, was one of us (Acts iii. 22, 23).

3. Was it a *male of the first year*? (Exod. xii. 5). Because the "male," being the stronger, symbolised energy and excellence ; and in "its first year" was at its fullest and most perfect development; so was Christ all "comely," in the fulness and perfection of His days.

4. Was it *without blemish*? Christ was altogether spotless and faultless (1 Pet. i. 10 ; Heb. vii. 25).

II. *With regard to its* SACRIFICIAL OBLATION.

1. As the lamb was *set apart four days* before it was slain, so Christ was, during the last four days of His life, under examination, preparatory to His death (Matt. xxi. 1).

2. As the lamb was *eventually slain*, so was Christ (Rev. v. 9).

3. As its death was *witnessed by the entire assembly*, so was Christ publicly crucified (Luke xxiii. 18).

4. As the time of the sacrifice was "*at even*" (v. 5), so was our Saviour's death (Matt. xxvii. 45; Luke xxiii. 44-46). [Comp. Sleigh's *Aids to Reflection*.]

III. *With regard to the* PASCHAL FEAST.

1. The *eating* of the passover typified that *we find in Christ our life, our nourishment, and sufficiency* (Jno. vi. 35, 53-56).

2. The *spirit* in which the feast was to be partaken is indicated in the significance of the "bitter herbs," suggesting a penitential spirit and bitter mourning, in remembrance of our sin (Zech. xii. 10).

3. The *regulations* for partakers of the feast are significant. Eaten "*with haste*," indicates the *urgency* with which we should receive Christ; with "*loins girded*," denotes our willingness to *quit the past for a pilgrim life of faith;* with "*feet shod*," suggestive of rough ways to be resolutely trod; "staff in hand," declares our defence and support.

4. The feast being *eaten in companies*, teaches the Christian law of union in Church fellowship, that religion may not be isolate. Christ gathers His disciples together at the feast of His Supper, and says, "Eat ye *all* of it, drink ye *all* of it."

> O wondrous emblems! setting forth His death from whom our life doth flow;
> Never can finite reason sound such depths of love, such depths of woe.

Topic: THE PASSOVER (Vv. 5-8).

The Exodus of Israel from Egypt, one of the most prominent landmarks in the history of the nation. The feast of the Passover was the significant memorial by which the memory of that event was perpetuated (Exod. xii.). Not only individual, but national deliverance ought to be remembered.

I. THE HALLOWED MEMORIES IT EMBALMED.

The final plague with which Pharaoh and his people were visited led to the emancipation of Israel, and their departure from Egypt. The miraculous preservation of Israel, the destruction of the firstborn of Egypt, and the means employed to accomplish both were brought to mind when the Passover was observed as the anniversary of the solemn night of death that gave birth to the Hebrew nation.

II. THE SACRED DUTIES IT INCULCATED.

(*a*) *Humility*. Their own arm had not gotten them the victory, they had been redeemed from abject poverty and slavery. They had nothing in themselves to boast of when they remembered the hole of the pit from which they had been digged. (*b*) *Thankfulness:* seeing Jehovah had interposed in such a critical juncture for their race, He deserved their heartfelt gratitude, jubilant as the song of Moses, bright as the beautiful sea. (*c*) *Gladness* that they had escaped exacting toil, cruel oppression, bitter bondage; before them was a career of honour and blessedness, well might their hearts leap for gladness and their feet move with joyful steps. (*d*) *Consecration*. At the Exodus, Israel started on a new life. Henceforth the people were to be known as the servants of Jehovah, set apart and sanctified for His glory. They were not their own; to them His divine will would be communicated, and through them made known to the world.

In the Gospels the Passover is identified with the feast of unleavened bread, which began and closed with a Sabbath, suggesting the idea of a complete consecrated life. Only unleavened bread was to be eaten at the feast; in all our Christian service the leaven of evil is to be scrupulously avoided. Christ our passover is sacrificed for us, let us keep the feast with *humility, solemnity, thankfulness, gladness, devoutness,* and *consecration.*

III. THE GLORIOUS EVENT IT FORESHADOWED.

About the typical character of the feast there is no room for doubt (see

1 Cor. v. 7, 8). (*a*) *In the deliverance it affected;* from slavery, degradation misery, death. (*b*) *In the means employed for deliverance;* sacrifice of appointed lamb, sprinkling of its blood, etc. (*c*) *In the co-operation the means demanded;* the people were to believe, obey, fulfil the conditions laid down. (*d*) *All who embraced the opportunity, and adopted the means, were saved.* Not one house was visited by death where the blood had been sprinkled upon the doorposts and lintel. The above considerations may all be applied to what Christ has done and is for us, and to our duty in relation to His great atonement.

Conclusion. (*a*) *There was but one way of deliverance.* (*b*) *It was not invented or suggested by man, but by God.* (*c*) *Only practical faith availed.* So in relation to the Gospel. The *excellence* of Christ our Passover is seen in that while many victims were slain in Egypt and they were only efficacious for a select people and one period of time, the Lamb of God by one offering atoned for the *whole world* and *all time*. *Indifference*, as well as unbelief in, and rejection of the world's Redeemer, will be visited with sore punishment, for "how can we escape if we *neglect* so great salvation ?"—*F. W. B.*

Topic: THE SHEAF OF THE FIRST FRUITS (Vv. 10, 11).

The book of nature is a fruitful study. In all God's works He strives to fix attention on Himself. In feeding the body He would show Himself to the soul.

Harvest time nears. The early promise is fulfilled (Gen. viii. 22). The firstlings of the grain are ripe. The fields of barley wave their golden heads. But shall the gatherers heedlessly reap, and thoughtless hands store the garner? No. On the altar the first sheaf must be laid.

I. THE ACKNOWLEDGMENT OF GOD MUST PRECEDE EVERY WORK.

The first act of harvest adores the harvest's Lord. The first sickle cuts an offering for God.

1. *Thought of God* should precede all. Let morning dawn with Him. Let adoration introduce each task. Nothing is well done unless begun with God. All is disorder except the First be first.

2. The priest *uplifts the sheaf on high*. The first-fruits represent the entire produce of the fields. The act is a confession that all earth yields is *from* God, and belongs *to* God. Man's toil and care may be employed, but all results are divine.

3. The offering of the sheaf is but *small*. He who might justly claim the harvest, takes but one sheaf. The large abundance remains for man's supply. Thus, while a bounteous Hand fills our garners, while valleys bend with corn and clouds distil their fatness, the Giver makes His small demand. But the little God asks is an acknowledgment of His claim. He is no hard task master; but He requires that He be first in our thoughts: He then gives abundantly into our lives and hearts.

4. But in this demand He shows that all must not be consumed on *self*. We cannot take a sheaf to God now: but the poor need food: famished souls cry for the Word; the heathen perish for the bread of life. Such are the claims on our first fruits.

II. IN THIS HARVEST SHEAF CHRIST IS SET BEFORE THE SEEKING HEART.

1. The *name* of "first fruits" leads by a straight path to Him. The Spirit's voice is very clear: "Now is Christ risen from the dead, and become the first fruits of them that slept"; "Christ the first fruits: afterwards they that are Christ's at His coming" (1 Cor. xv. 20, 23).

2. The *day of offering* next seals this truth. On the *morning which succeeds the Paschal Sabbath* the sheaf is waved. On this same dawn *Jesus arose.*

Following this clue, let us gaze on this type. That sheaf—

(a) Brings back thought of the *seed cast into the ground*. Buried in the earth: the frost imprisoned it: storms sealed its interment: but at last it rose into life: victory over death.

Thus Christ descended to the grave : life seemed extinct : the grave made fast its bars : but in vain. He came forth—the First fruit from the dead.

(b) That sheaf relates a tale of *triumph*. It symbolises success. Death fails to hold Him. He is "declared the Son of God with power by His resurrection." Raise high before God, therefore, your sheaf. It is the exultation of the believer. "Christ being raised from the dead dieth no more": and "because I live, ye shall live also."

Though that sheaf is alone before God, yet it predicts and guarantees the after harvest.

III. THE HARVEST INGATHERING IS SURE TO FOLLOW THE FIRST FRUITS.

1. Already it is fulfilled in *the harvest of upraised souls*. Believers have been "raised up together, and made to sit together in heavenly places in Christ Jesus."

2. *The rising dead as they quit their graves* shall perfect the fulfilment of this sign. How changed shall they come forth! Decay will bloom into unfading youth: the mortal will be robed in immortality. "We shall be like Him!" The first sheaf predicts your resurrection.

3. A *world-wide harvest*, a glorious prospect is promised; when the whole mass of sanctified and ripened souls shall be reaped from earth's fields and garnered in glory.—Based on *Dean Law's* "CHRIST IS ALL." [See Addenda to Chapter *Harvest First fruits*].

Topic: PENTECOST AND THE SPIRIT (Vv. 15, 16).

The feast of Pentecost was celebrated on the fiftieth day after that in the Passover week on which the wave sheaf was presented to the Lord, and was marked by offering to Jehovah two loaves. It was also known by the name of the "Feast of Harvest," from its coming at the close of the wheat harvest.

It was attended by *vast multitudes* (comp. Acts ii.), was "a holy convocation," and it was a day of *gladness and joy* (Deut. xvi. 14).

I. GRATITUDE EXPRESSING ITSELF IN JOYOUS DEDICATION.

1. Of *themselves;* 2. Of their *property*. For Israel not only renewed their self-consecration in worship and sacrifices laid on God's altar, but also their possessions in the harvest reaped, as expressed by the waving of the baked loaves before Him.

(a) Pentecost thus reminded Israel of their *dependance* on God for the *produce of their fields*, as well as for *higher good*. God is the God of *providence* as well as of *grace*. He is supreme alike in the natural and spiritual worlds. Laws are everywhere the action of His power. "He giveth to all life, and breath, and all things" (Acts xvii. 25).

(b) But *God will be acknowledged* in His gifts and doings. Pentecost, therefore, excited a spirit of *thankfulness;* it kept alive in Israel the feeling of being God's in what they possessed as well as in what they were. Yet what belongs to Him *He claims*. It is not only ourselves, therefore, that we are to yield to Him, but what we *have*. The burnt offering must not only be laid on the altar, but the baked loaves waved before Him as alike His property.

II. SACRED ASSOCIATIONS CONNECTED WITH THE PENTECOST FESTIVAL.

1. *Historic*. It was commemorative on the *giving of the law on Sinai*. With the chronological data of Exod. xix. before us, it is clear that it was on the fiftieth day after the departure of Israel from Egypt, *i.e.*, after the first Passover, that the law was given, and the national existence of the Hebrews was in-

augurated. Thus *God's manifestation of Himself* to Israel on Sinai, and *His words* to Moses, effected for His wilderness Church what *His Spirit's advent* and the *gift of new tongues* effected for the Christian Church at Jerusalem.

2. *Typical.* It looked forward as well as backward. As the Passover foreshadowed the death of Christ, so did the Pentecost the Spirit's descent. At the Feast of Pentecost the Holy Ghost, who writes the law of God, not on tables of stone, but on "the fleshy tables of the heart," was poured out.

III. THE HARVEST BOUNTY SUGGESTS THE FULNESS OF THE SPIRIT WHICH MARKED THE CHRISTIAN PENTECOST.

1. The endowments of the Christian Pentecost were first *for the apostles*, giving them *qualification for their life-work*, and ensuring the maintenance of their joy of faith. For "the promise of the Father" they were bidden by Christ to wait at Jerusalem. Until the Holy Ghost came upon them they were not "endowed with power," not prepared to be "witnesses for Christ in Jerusalem and all Judea," etc.

2. But this baptism of power is what *every child of grace needs and may possess*. Discipleship is not of itself sufficient for all that we are required to be in *character* and *service*. For these we want the *fulness of the Spirit's indwelling*.

What the Spirit was, in the fulness of His indwelling presence, to the first disciples, He is, in a very real and blessed sense, to all so possessed by Him now: "*strengthened with might in the inner man*," and *equipped for a life-work of witness* for Christ Jesus.

The bountiful harvest shows *God's plenitude*, and *His joy in enriching man*. Certainly He is as willing to bestow the abundance of His Spirit. We receive Him by faith, and according to the degree of such faith. The promise of the Spirit, and the bestowment, are both Christ's, and He will never allow the desire for Him to remain unmet. He is too anxious to see us what the Spirit's indwelling alone will make us, to delay or refuse the answer to prayer for this holy gift.

Then will come into our souls grace in increasing supplies, fulness of assurance of faith and hope, and strength added to strength. So endowed and enriched, we shall "yield ourselves unto God, and our members instruments for righteousness." "The fruit of the Spirit is love, joy, peace, long-suffering, gentleness, goodness, and faith" (Gal. v. 22).—Outlined from "*Gospel in Leviticus*," by Jas. Fleming, D.D.

Topic: "A MEMORIAL OF BLOWING OF TRUMPETS" (Vv. 23-25).

With reverberating tones of joy this blast of trumpets ushered in Israel's civil year. At earliest dawn of the "first day of the month" the exhilarating notes sounded forth throughout the camp, or the land, of Israel. The music strains were continued all day. It was "a Sabbath," for rest from work, for "an holy convocation," but it was a Sabbath of praise, of music, of delight.

I. TRUMPET TONES AWAKEN ATTENTION.

Sleepers would start from their slumbers at that early blast of the trumpets. What need is there that sleepers should awake! Drowsiness is on the souls of multitudes. They dream on heedlessly, letting life glide away, and salvation lie in neglect. Thought sleeps, interest sleeps, spiritual claims and gospel realities are ignored. Eyes are closed from the "Day Dawn," they see not that the Sun of Righteousness has arisen. "It is high time to awake out of sleep."

Clarion notes startle drowsy souls. *Providence* sends out trumpet blasts. The *preacher's words* may startle sleeping consciences. *God's Spirit* may sound the note of arousing in the soul. "Awake, O sleeper: arise and call upon thy God!"

II. This "*blowing of trumpets*" ANNOUNCED THE END OF A YEAR.

1. A year gone! A cause for *joy*, for *glad trumpet tones*. Yes! if the year has been spent well. Yes! if God has been known by us as a Refuge and a Faithful Friend; having kept us by His grace, and magnified His sufficiency for us. Yes! if we have escaped perils and conquered foes, and in review can cry, "O my soul, thou hast trodden down strength; now thanks be to God who always causeth us to triumph in Christ." Yes! if our "salvation is nearer," heaven nearer, the reward of faithful service nearer, the goal at hand.

2. A year gone! A *startling* fact; shrill trumpet notes should stir us to alarm. If *not* saved, if time has run to waste, if we have let slip from us the opportunities of grace, if we are yet in the bonds of iniquity, if still the door of our hearts is closed upon the knocking Christ, if we are without hope and without God in the world, "redeem the time."

III. *The Feast of Trumpets proclaimed* A NEW YEAR OPENED.

The past is past. Opportunities unused are gone beyond recall. Penitential tears cannot bring back the misspent year. Verily God might "cut us down as cumberers of the ground."

1. But a *respite is announced*. Another year opens. The Intercessor has pleaded "Let be this year also." It is an extension of opportunity to seek the Lord, for sinners to forsake their ways, and unrighteous men their thoughts, to "flee from the wrath to come," to haste to the "hope set before us," to claim the salvation in Christ offered to the penitent and believing. O use the precious respite mercy gives. The trumpets sound; they tell of hope prolonged: seize the precious hour "while it is called *to-day*."

2. *A new era is set before Israel*. Gratitude for past mercies, the memory of God's great goodness, the experiences of redeeming and sustaining grace, incite to service, to consecration. "How much owest thou unto thy Lord? Take thy bill and *write quickly*." "Whatsoever thy hand findeth to do, do it with thy might." Let love and thankfulness urge to more diligence, more self-sacrifice, more eagerness in use of privileges, more fervent culture of holiness. "Go up higher." "Press to the mark." "Repent, and do thy first works." The trumpet sounds; it rallies the hosts of the Lord to their ranks, to the battle, to brave achievements, to victories for the King.

IV. *Those trumpet blasts were* A MEMORIAL OF SINAI.

When God came down on the cloud-robed peak of the mount, it was a scene of appalling splendour and solemnity. The myriad observers below trembled, "so terrible was the sight." When suddenly a weird trumpet note swelled out on the air, filling all hearts with amaze: and "the voice of the Trumpet sounded long, and waxed louder and louder" (Exod. xix. 19). This "blowing of trumpets" was "a memorial."

1. It *led them back to solemn thoughts of God*. Because Jehovah was now more graciously dwelling among them in the Holy place, He was still the God of Sinai. We must not presume on His grace. How august and dreadful is He with whom we have to do. "Fear before Him, all ye saints."

2. It *recalled the law*, as the basis of their covenant relationship. "Do this and live." Such were the terms on which they stood to Jehovah. Transgress, and you die. "Cursed is every one that continueth not in all things written in the book of the law to do them." But who can? Is the trumpet blast, therefore, a summons to judgment? It need not be. It declares the standard for righteousness, only to emphasize the mercy which has provided sacrifice that the sinner might propitiate and live.

V. *Assuredly the trumpet is* A SYMBOL OF THE GOSPEL.

"Blessed are the people that know the joyful sound" (Psa. lxxxix. 15). "I was in the Spirit on the Lord's day, and heard behind me a great voice, as of a **trumpet**, saying, I am Alpha and Omega" (Rev. i. 10).

1. *Christ's voice should be heard* in that "blowing of trumpets." It sounds forth in the announcements of the gospel through the Scriptures, through all who tell the message of hope and grace. Jesus speaks to the heart affrighted by the clamour of Sinai's awful peals. The Gospel is the silvery note sending a thrill of comfort and gladness into condemned souls. It is as " music in our ears."

2. *Christianity is a trumpet-toned herald:* hastening through the heavens with the calls of grace to all mankind. "I saw an angel flying in the midst of heaven, having the everlasting gospel to preach" (Rev. xiv. 6). All who know the good news should take up the trumpet of Truth and send out the tidings over all the earth.

3. *The Gospel is a joy note* to the world. Not " a voice of thunder," but of sweet melody. It brings " good tidings of great joy"; salvation to the uttermost; cleansing of all sin; a precious Saviour; an upraised cross; a " new covenant " of redemption; of an opened door in heaven for all who cleave to Jesus. Glad indeed are these trumpet tones; they calm the sinner's fears; allure the troubled to peace, win the anxious to faith.

All around us are sad notes: O sorrow, O oppression, O anguished prayer, O dark despair. Earth is a scene of Babel discord. The air clangs with confusion.

But let the Gospel trumpet blow. Its sweet harmonies float, as did the songs of angels over Bethlehem fields, soothing unrest, heralding " peace and good will," thrilling hearts with joy.

And still its heavenly music floats
Oe'r all this weary world.

VI. A prophetic thought is stirred by those trumpets: *they foretell* THE RESURRECTION SCENE

The close of time will arrive; the great white throne will be set; the mighty angel will set his foot on the sea and another on the land, and declare that time shall be no more. And then "the Lord Himself shall descend from heaven with a shout, with the voice of the archangel, and with the trump of God" (1 Thess. iv. 16). From opened graves the dead shall arise; and you with them.

Listen expectantly for that trumpet blast. At such an hour as ye think not it will sound. Sleepers were awoke when at early dawn the priests blew their trumpets on this Hebrew festival. And *sleepers will awake* at the judgment blast. And " all that are in their graves shall come forth." Be ye therefore ready, so that that day should not overtake you unawares.

Fill the interval with a wise use of life. The Gospel trumpet offers you a perfect righteousness; the judgment trumpet will demand it. The Gospel trumpet bids you robe yourself in spotless garments: the judgment trump will call to condemnation those who are not " white and clean," covered with the robe of salvation. Such will arise from death's sleep glad " to meet the Lord in the air, and so to be for ever with the Lord." [See Addenda to chapter " BLOWING OF TRUMPETS."]

Topic: THE FEAST OF TRUMPETS (Vv. 24, 25).

The feast of trumpets is mentioned here for the first time. It was kept on the first day of Tisri, with which the civil year began. It was a time of holy rest, and communion with the Lord through an offering made by fire unto Him. The feast was kept by Israel when they took possession of Canaan, and was characterised by great joy and gladness. The feast was suggestive of—

I. THE COMPLETION OF THE WORK OF CREATION.

The earth (fitted to be the abode of man) was clad in beautiful garments; presented an aspect of great fertility and richness. The Lord pronounced it good; "the morning stars sang together, and all the sons of God shouted for joy." The beginning of the civil year, when the harvest was ripe, and the air was ringing with the shouts of harvest home, would seem suggestive of the beginning of human history, which began amid scenes of plenty, as the first human pair came through the gate Beautiful.

II. THE PROMULGATION OF THE LAW FROM SINAI.

The sounding of the trumpet from morning to evening would remind Israel of the time when the sound of the trumpet called attention to the promulgation of those statutes, in the observance of which they would please Jehovah, and show to the world that they were His people. The feast would call attention to the divine voice, the trumpets would proclaim His right to be heard, the imperative duty of the listeners to hearken and obey.

III. THE BLESSINGS OF THE DEPARTED YEAR.

Israel had been spared through another year. God had been faithful to His promises, all their wants had been supplied. It became them to let their voices be heard in loud and joyful notes; the music of their hearts echoed in vocal praise.

IV. THE BOUNTY OF THE DAWNING YEAR.

As their storehouses were filled with plenty, and their presses burst forth with new wine, anxieties about the future would be allayed, provision would be abundant for man and beast. Israel would have wherewith to satisfy their physical necessities, and to offer the various sacrifices in connection with the tabernacle services. The trumpets would call to thankfulness and cheerful acknowledgment of indebtedness. However rich and abundant the oblations might be, they ought to be presented in the willing and gladsome spirit such words as these inspire, "Of thine own have we given thee; thine is all the glory."

V. THE NEED OF WAKEFUL ALACRITY IN THE SERVICE OF JEHOVAH.

Trumpet peals rousing and stimulating; and, when blown by the priests, loud calls to hearty service. Though no servile work was to be done, yet sacred services were to be performed, solemn sacrifices offered. Israel was to awake and put on strength, enter with special enthusiasm upon the work of the Lord. External material aid may be consistently used to awaken attention and quicken devotion. Illustrative also of—

VI. THE INAUGURATION OF THE GOSPEL AGE.

At the day of Pentecost, when the Holy Ghost was given, and the first fruits of the Gospel harvest were gathered in, the apostles went forth lifting up their voices like trumpets, preaching Jesus and the resurrection. Isaiah in predicting the Gospel age said, "In that day the trumpet shall be blown"; and verily the sound of the Gospel trumpet went speedily through all the earth. John in apocalyptic vision heard the divine voice as the sound of a trumpet; and the voice of God as of a trumpet shall, in the last great day, awake the dead to judgment. Let us begin each year with a feast of trumpets, and each day with a loud call to privilege and duty, that our lives may be one continuous litany and psalm. Then when the morn of eternity dawns, and the shadows of earth flee away, we shall join in singing the song of Moses and the Lamb.—*F.W.B.*

Topic: THE FEAST OF TABERNACLES (Vv. 33-44).

On the fifteenth day of the seventh month, five days after the Day of Atonement, the Feast of Tabernacles began, and (according to additional information gathered from Numbers and Nehemiah) the sacrifices, which were many, gradually decreased in number to the eighth day. Israel was very remiss in observing the feast on entrance upon Canaan; for, from the time of Joshua to Nehemiah, it was unobserved. Obviously, the object of the feast was to keep alive the spiritual life of the nation, to perpetually renew its youth. The feast was calculated—

I. TO PERPETUATE AMONG THE PEOPLE THE MEMORY OF MIRACULOUS EVENTS CONNECTED WITH THEIR NATIONAL HISTORY.

"That your generations may know that I made the children of Israel to dwell in booths, when I brought them out of the land of Egypt." *Emancipation, protection, preservation,* all the miraculous events connected with the exodus from Egypt and the pilgrimage through the wilderness, exhibited the faithfulness and goodness of the Lord. It would be well for Israel to be put in constant remembrance of these things. Such interpositions suggested their *dignity* and *duty* as a people, and their *destiny* among the nations of the earth. It is good for all peoples, in all time, to remember great national deliverers and deliverances. Surely, *He* should be lovingly remembered who has redeemed us from the bondage of sin and death!

II. TO AWAKEN IN THE PEOPLE GRATEFUL JOY FOR THE COMPLETED FRUITFUL SEASONS OF THE YEAR.

This the crowning, most joyous feast of the year. What a glad picture the people would present, as they sat under their booths rejoicing with the joy of harvest, the roads and fields vocal with the sound of happy voices, and the courts of the Lord resounding with sacred praise.

Permission to indulge in such innocent pleasures taught the people that Jehovah delighted in their happiness as well as in their holiness. "God (as Cowper puts it) made the country, man the town." The verdure of the grass, the hues and fragrance of the flowers, the abundant foliage of the trees, the luscious fruits and golden corn, remind us that God would have us experience many joys in our earthly pilgrimage, while we look forward to the Canaan of ineffable beauty and undisturbed repose. In the gospel we have provision for all our spiritual wants, *rich, full, free.*

III. TO ENJOIN UPON THE PEOPLE CONSTANT OBEDIENCE TO THE REVEALED COMMANDMENTS OF THE LORD.

The large number of sacrifices connected with the feast, and the septennial public reading of the whole law, would train and exercise the people in obedience, revive their knowledge of the Lord and acknowledgment of His sovereignty. In later times there was the additional custom of a solemn libation of water fetched from the pool of Siloam every day at the time of morning sacrifice. The whole ceremony was characterised by great enjoyment and delight. The feast may be regarded as illustrative, if not typical, of (*a*) *The pilgrim character of the believer's life.* Here we dwell in frail tenements, and have no continuing city. (*b*) *The advent of the Messiah;* when "God in very deed dwelt with man on the earth." At one of the celebrations of this feast, Jesus said, "If any man thirst, let him come unto me and drink." (*c*) *The latter-day glory of the Church militant.* (*d*) *The glorious state of the Church triumphant;* where the redeemed are represented as waving palm branches, indicative of peace, conquest, and joy. The Feast of Tabernacles followed closely on the Day of Atonement, thus joy sprang out of sorrow. Blessedness that flows from mediation and sacrifice is incomparable joy. Let sin be atoned for and removed, holiness and happiness inevitably ensue.—*F. W. B.*

Topic: FESTIVAL OF TABERNACLES AND INGATHERING (Vv. 33-44).

It is a mistake to suppose that the Old Testament religion was only stern and repressive. It had its side of restraint and self-denial, and thence sprang much of all that was best in the character and happiness of the people. But it had also its side of cheer and hope, indeed of festivity. Its weekly Sabbaths were intended to be days of delight; so were its New Moons. Then each season had its great festival, save winter; the spring its Passover; the summer its Pentecost; the autumn its Feast of Tabernacles. Each was a joyful feast; but the last, falling on a time of the year when all hearts would naturally be glad, was the most joyful of all.

Note some of its more instructive features.

I. IT WAS A PROTRACTED RELIGIOUS MEETING.

As a "feast unto the Lord" it began and ended with a "holy convocation," a coming together for religious ends.

1. These were held *in the central sanctuary of the nation*. All male Israelites were required to attend.

2. The *highly religious character of this feast* appears in the unusual number of its gifts and sacrifices.

3. All the Hebrew festivals were intended *to inspire patriotism*, and promote *the separation of Israel* from other nations; to remind the people of their covenant relations to God, and bind them in loyal piety to Him.

We should value occasions for holy convocation; and use them for such religiously joyous ends.

II. IT WAS A THANKSGIVING FOR GOD'S BOUNTY IN A COMPLETE HARVEST.

It came at the end of the year, when they had "gathered in the fruit of the land" (v. 39), and was therefore—

1. *A public recognition of divine faithfulness* in giving rain in due season, causing the earth to yield her increase. Hence it was called the "Feast of Ingatherings" (Exod. xxiii. 16).

2. *A feast of grateful gladness.* The sixty-first Psalm, supposed to be sung at this feast, well expresses the thought supreme in devout minds. This expressed itself in—

3. *A profusion of gifts and sacrifices.* Multiplied and great mercies demanded the more abounding recognition. [See *Addenda* to chapter, HARVEST FIRST-FRUITS.]

III. IT WAS A COMMEMORATION FOR MERCIES ATTEMPERING HARDSHIPS AND DANGERS.

A part of the command ran thus: "All that are Israelites born shall dwell in booths, that your generations may know that I made the children of Israel to dwell in booths, when I brought them out of the land of Egypt" (43, 44).

In such a sight—a whole people deserting their homes, and lodging in temporary arbours, decorated with foliage and fruit-laden boughs—there was something picturesque and inspiriting. But—

1. It was also *an impressive memorial.* Israel was again "abiding in tents according to their tribes," as he did when Balaam looked from the heights of Moab, and said, "How goodly are thy tents, O Jacob, and thy tabernacles, O Israel," etc.

2. The celebration commemorated *all the diverse experiences of the wilderness.* Not its trials alone, but its triumphs and blessings. Doubtless the materials of the booths were reminders of the different stages of their wilderness journey; the "branches of palm trees," of the valleys and the plains; the "boughs of thick trees" of the bushy mountain heights; the "willows," of the refreshing water brooks.

3. For all times *commemoration has its uses.* To fire the patriotism of a nation, it is helpful to rehearse the memories of its founders and defenders. To rekindle enthusiasm in a noble cause, it is a good thing to recall its early struggles and victories. Stimulus is often found in keeping great days in personal history.

The manner of modern times is to foster pride by celebrating human exploits; that of ancient Israel was to kindle gratitude and stir obedience by recalling the goodness of God.

IV. *In every aspect this festival was* AN EXPRESSION OF THE JOYFUL SIDE OF RELIGION.

A feast. The people were to "rejoice before the Lord their God" (v. 40). Comp. also Deut. xvi. 14, 15. There was a grand illumination of the court of the Temple; an evening procession in holiday attire, and with branches of myrtle and palm and willow; and a going in *mass* for water, which was poured out at the foot of the altar, while there arose the chant—accompanied with glad music—" Therefore with joy shall ye draw water out of the wells of salvation."

It was concerning this ceremony that there sprang up the proverb : " *Whosoever hath not seen the rejoicing at the drawing of this water, hath never seen rejoicing at all.*"

1. This joy had its root in the *sense of inward peace which comes from the pardon of sin.* This feast followed close upon the Day of Atonement.

2. The joy was *neither selfish nor lawless.* Gifts for the poor designated it; intimating that life has no true delight that can be separated from either love or duty.

3. How *false the theory that religion,* if earnest, *is joyless !* It has indeed its restraints and obligations, its laws and duties; but this is a beneficent arrangement, giving zeal to our gladness. Between religion that knows how to be steadfast, self-denying, and heroic, and that

Mirth that after no repenting draws

there can be no quarrel. They go often and well together.

V. *This feast was a type of* A GREATER FEAST NOW PREPARING FOR GOD'S PEOPLE.

Archbishop Trench has reminded us that " on this rests the possibility of a real and not merely arbitrary teaching by parables, that the world of nature is throughout a witness for a world of spirit, proceeding from the same hand, growing out of the same root, and constituted for that very end. All lovers of truth readily admit these mysterious harmonies, to them the things of earth are copies of things of heaven." In this feast there is—

1. *A prophecy of the latter-day rest and joy of the earthly church* (Zec. xiv. 16, 20; and also Isa. xxv. 6, 8). Under the abundant outpouring of God's Spirit, closer fellowship with God and fuller bliss.

2. *The heavenly feast following* " *the harvest which is the end of the world.*" John beheld the scene : " I looked, and behold a great multitude, palms in their hand," etc. (Rev. vii. 9, 10).

Evermore they shall drink of God's river of pleasure. They shall be satisfied with delight.

What assurance have you that, when that bright day dawns, *you* will witness its rising beam ; that when that great feast is spread, *you* will share in its delights ? —*Rev. H. M. Grant, D.D.*

OUTLINES ON VERSES OF CHAPTER XXIII.

V. 2.—*Theme :* "FEASTS OF THE LORD."
I. SACRED LIFE IS ITSELF A FESTIVAL.
1. Divine in its *origin.* " Feasts of the Lord."
2. Blissful in its quality. " *Feasts.*"
3 Enriched with *frequent* delights.
" Feasts; " plural, for God breaks in upon he Christain career, itself a festival, with times of refreshing and incidents of gladness giving " days of heaven on the earth."
II. THE CHRISTIAN YEAR HAS ITS FESTIVITIES.

1. *Time is interrupted by sacred seasons.*
A pause in the rush and absorption of earthly affairs, that God and His doings may have attention and commemoration.
2. *Human life is refreshed by the blessings of religion.*
Even the godless share in the relief and rest which our holy-days, " holidays," bring them.
3. *A witness to what is God's will for man.*
That all should have a joyous life even here.

That heaven should make earth glad; for happiness has its spring in the Lord.

III. GRACIOUS SEASONS ARE APPOINTED FOR THE CHURCH.

God would fill His people with blessedness; so there comes to them:

1. *Days of rest and gladness.* The Sabbath, the anniversaries of great gospel incidents.

2. *Special times of revival.* For quickened life; renewed power; aroused earnestness; rekindled love; awakened prayerfulness; enlarged prosperity.

3. *Foretaste of heaven's joy.* He feasts His saints with felicities at gracious seasons, and the fulness of His favour satiates their souls. In such wondrous seasons, " whether in the body or out of the body, God knoweth," they rise into " third heavens," they find a " feast of fat things" provided, and enter the very " banquetting house " of heaven's bliss.

V. 10.—*Theme:* FIRST FRUITS SHEAF. " *Then shall ye bring a sheaf of firstfruits.*"

The celebration of this feast could not take place till Israel entered Canaan; for during the pilgrimage through the wilderness there was neither sowing nor reaping, the daily descent of manna from Heaven being adequate to supply daily bread. The first sheaf presented before the Lord *hallowed* and *guaranteed* the complete harvest. It exhibited—

I. THE DEPENDENCE OF ISRAEL UPON THE LORD. The Holy Land was the Lord's. Israel could not claim it by right of inheritance, purchase, or conquest. Being a free gift, reaping a harvest they had not sown, it was fitting the first-reaped sheaf should be presented in a solemn act of worship, acknowledging that the harvest was the outcome of divine goodness and power. Israel would be as much dependent upon divine supply in Canaan as in the wilderness. Israel was to think of themselves last, God was to be owned and honoured first. Though selfishness would reverse the order, the command is, to honour the Lord with our substance, and the firstfruits of all our increase.

II. THE DELIGHT OF ISRAEL IN THE LORD. A meat offering accompanying the waving of the barley sheaf constituted the service a *feast,* not a fast. The fine flour, wine, and oil indicated that the feast was eucharistic, a season of social and sacred joy. " The Lord loveth a cheerful giver." Offerings should be presented ungrudgingly to Him who loads us with His benefits. The acceptability of offerings depend upon *what* and *how,* as well as upon *what* and *when* presented. The cheerful and loyal heart will devise liberal things.

III. THE DEDICATION OF ISRAEL TO THE LORD. The waving sheaf would excite the people to *gratitude,* and symbolise their devotion to the glory of Jehovah. The thankoffering was accepted through the burntoffering, denoting that all service must have its basis in complete self-surrender. The sheaf of first fruits, was an earnest that the whole harvest would be gathered in, and it consecrated the whole. Christ is the " First fruits of them that slept." He rose on the day of the offering of first fruits of Jewish harvest, as an earnest that all who are one with Him, shall be safely gathered in at the harvest home of the world. All our gifts to the Lord must be preceded by complete self-consecration, through the mediation and merits of our Great High Priest.—*F. W. B.*

V. 14.—*Theme:* SELF IN ABEYANCE. " *Ye shall eat neither bread, nor parched corn, nor green ears, until the selfsame day that ye have brought an offering unto your God.*"

I. MAN'S SINFUL TENDENCY IS TO INTRUDE SELF BEFORE THE LORD.

1. Through *impatient self-will.*
2. Through a *weak craving after visible enticements.*
3. Through a *habit of ignoring God* in his life.
4. Through the infatuation which *places material gains above spiritual interests.*

II. SUBORDINATION OF SELF IS THE LAW OF RELIGION.

1. God is to be *first* in our *affections.*
2. Our gratitude should prompt us to *quick recognition of what we owe Him.*
3. Saved by Him, and enriched by His gifts, how natural that He be *adored with alacrity and served with delight!*
4. Christ Jesus *sacrificed self* for us: and has left us an example to make Him *our first thought.*

III. SELF-REPRESSION IS REWARDED WITH RICH BESTOWMENTS.

1. We deny ourselves but for a *brief season.* " *Until the selfsame day* that ye have brought an offering."
2. God gives us a *present reward* for every denial of self for His pleasure: in the approval of conscience, and the witness of His Spirit, and the happiness of a hallowed life.
3. *Earthly denials and crosses* for Christ's sake and God's service, quickly yield to the rich feasts of the heavenly world.

(*a*) If it become true of any in this *self-indulgence,* " Remember that thou *in thy lifetime* receiveth thy good things," the loss will come in the future.

(*b*) Every subjection of self for God now is a pledge of coming bliss. For "he that *abaseth himself shall be exalted.*"

V. 15.—*Theme:* THE FEAST OF PENTECOST; HARVEST HOME.

There were three divinely appointed harvest festivals among the Jews. The Pentecost feast followed the Passover feast, and the presentation of two loaves before the Lord was a token that the corn had been safely gathered in, and an expression of gratitude and acknowledgment of obligation to Jehovah. If Pentecost did not commemorate the giving of law from Sinai fifty days after exodus from Egypt, or typify the day when the Spirit would be given, symbolized by rushing wind and forks of flame; it certainly signified to the Hebrews:

I. THAT TEMPORAL BLESSINGS OUGHT TO BE GRATEFULLY ACKNOWLEDGED. Ingratitude is a besetting sin. Among the sins for which Israel was rebuked by the prophets, unthankfulness was the blackest. It led to forgetfulness of the Lord, to sensuousness and idolatry. Rain from heaven, and fruitful seasons come from God. He fills our hearts with good and gladness.

II. THAT SUCH ACKNOWLEDGMENTS OUGHT TO BE MADE WITH BECOMING SOLEMNITY.

The observance of the day as a holy convocation, the abstinence from all servile work, and the presentation of various sacrifices, would invest the feast with great solemnity. The burnt offering would remind the people of the sovereign claim of Jehovah to their complete consecration to His service; the sin offering, of their entire unworthiness of the blessings received. Their festivities were not to be marked by frivolity and levity like Bacchanalian orgies, but by sacred devotion and becoming reverence. All seasons of individual and national rejoicing should be free from sinful indulgences and in harmony with a sanctified conscience enlightened by the word of God.

III. THAT BECOMING SOLEMNITY IN SACRED WORSHIP DOES NOT EXCLUDE THE HIGHEST POSSIBLE JOY.

Such a festival would sanctify and sweeten the blessing of the year, induce the people to feel, as they sat at their daily board, that they were in God's banquetting house, and that His banner over them was love. In remembering the poor, Israel would have the exquisite joy that benevolence brings, and exemplify Him who is good to all. The fountain of joy springs up close by the altar of sacrifice and unselfishness. Let us not allow the gifts of Providence to stagnate in the Dead Sea of selfishness, but send them forth to gladden weary hearts and desolate homes. The joy of the Lord is the joy of giving; it is more blessed to give than to receive. Love to God and man sums up the whole law, is the new commandment of the Gospel.—*F. W. B.*

V. 17.—*Theme:* BEGINNING THE REAPING. " *They are the firstfruits.*"

No sickle moved in Israel's land before the sheaf had been brought. God's bounteous hand must be revered before man's taking hand may work. Such was the ordinance. This was more than *due worship*, it was *pure delight*.

There is no joy like gratitude. They most enjoy who most perceive and bless the Giver. Earthly comforts should give wings to praise. But this holy service discharged—

I. ALACRITY PERVADES THE FIELD OF SERVICE.

With cheerful heart, animated look, and rapid step, the crowding reapers hasten forth.

1. *Rich abundance* meets them on all hands.
2. All is *busy* joy. No hand is idle. Life is brisk with work.

II. TOIL WHEN HALLOWED BY GOD'S SMILE IS SWEET.

1. Labour is delight when *God calls toil*.
2. *Every willing hand* finds occasion. And every religious heart will see occasion to be from God.

III. LIFE IS OUR INGATHERING DAY.

1. All about us is *the harvest*.
2. *Every morning calls us to reap*.
3. God's blessing is on the diligent life.
4. The day is gone too quickly for loitering.

IV. EACH WORKER MAY FIND HIS OWN FIELD OF INGATHERING.

1. Ask, "*Lord, what wilt Thou have me to do?*" and He will show where we should go work.
2. The fields *are various:*
1. The *Scripture field* is ever ready. What have you gathered this day from the Bible page?
2. *Duties are individual*, and always close to hand. Not a day but some finished obligation should be gathered in. An empty hand proclaims a graceless heart.
3. The world is a wide-spread scene, *thick with precious souls*. These call for ingathering. Here every grain is priceless.

V. THE REAPING *methods and appliances* ARE MANIFOLD.

1. *Personal effort* in the hot day of opportunity.
2. *Direction and inspiration of others* in Christian work.
3. *Prayer for gracious hours*.

VI. HARVEST SEASONS QUICKLY GO.

1. *Scenes of eager toil are soon cleared.* Then no more work can be done. They *die around us;* and are gone! How should we hasten.
3. The *hours of work* glide past. Evening comes on. Life is rapid. Opportunity is swift winged.

Woe to the man whose life is not a reaping day. No idler enters the heavenly rest. DEAN LAW.

V. 22.—*Theme:* HARVEST GLEANINGS FOR THE POOR.

Compare on Chap. xix., 9.

V. 27.—*Theme:* THE GREAT DAY OF ATONEMENT.

The day of Atonement is here introduced as a Hebrew fast. It was a solemn preparation for seasons of rejoicing before the Lord at ensuing feasts. As this great day of expiation has been considered in Homilies on chap. xvi., remarks here upon it may be limited. The day was a call to—

I. REPENTANCE. " Ye shall afflict your souls." Not simply the observance of outward rites indicative of penitence, the mortification of the body; but *thorough, sincere, public* acknowledgment of guilt, *heartfelt sorrow* for sin. The call was *peremptory*, for the soul was to be cut off from the people that did not truly repent. Sin was to be felt, acknowledged, mourned for, and forsaken, in order that it might be forgiven through the atonement. The same call and conditions obtain in the new dispensation. The day was also a call to—

II. RECONCILIATION. Sin excluded man from God, and necessitated restraint and restriction being imposed on the worshippers. On the day of Atonement, as the contrite Hebrews saw their representative enter the most holy place to offer incense before Jehovah, they would see that the distance had been removed, that God was pleased with, and reconciled to them, as they were reconciled to Him. The day was a Sabbath of rest in all their dwellings, so that their piety and purity were to be known in their homes as well as at the holy altar. Blessed be God, through the one offering on Calvary, all who repent towards God and exercise faith in Jesus Christ, may enter into the most holy place and enjoy Divine fellowship and peace. Thus God reconciles the world unto Himself, and repentance culminates in life —*F. W. B.*

V. 42.—*Theme:* SOJOURNING IN BOOTHS. "Ye shall dwell in booths seven days: all that are Israelites born shall dwell in booths."

It was commemorative: see v. 43.

It was *significant:* of

I. CHRIST TABERNACLING IN THE FLESH.

Three facts are suggestive here of Christ's incarnation being foreshadowed in this feast:

1. *John's use of the idea,* "The Word dwelt (tabernacled) among us, full of grace and truth" (Jno. i. 14).

2. The people's gathering of *palm branches* when persuaded of His Messiahship (Matt. xxi. 8, 9).

3. Christ chose "*the great day of the feast,*" of this very feast of tabernacles, to identify Himself with one of its incidents. While the waters of Siloam were being, on that eighth day, poured on the altar steps, "Jesus stood and cried, If any man thirst let him come unto me and drink" (Jno vii 37, 38).

4. Yet *His tabernacle life was not permanent.* Booths are for pilgrims, not residents. And Jesus was here but for a season. "Yet a little while I am with you."

II. MAN'S INSECURE TENURE ON THE EARTH.

1. A booth of boughs and palms *would quickly wither:* so does our frail tabernacle. What are these bodies but tents of drooping flesh?

2. It was, moreover, *occupied but a few days;* and we are resident in this body only a brief season. Think not to stay long here.

3. The materials of the booths were *of the earth and returned to the earth:* mere growths from the soil, soon to decay and go back to the soil. Even so, " dust thou art," etc., " of the earth earthy."

III. A CHRISTIAN'S PILGRIM CAREER.

Israel dwelt in booths through their journey from Egypt to Canaan (see v. 43).

1. Christ's redeemed are *pressing through a wilderness.* It is not their goal.

2. *Rest and content* are not to be sought here. A temporary accommodation is enough.

3. Earth's discomfort gives *zest to desire for the "city of habitation."* And as Israel, weary with their booth-life, craved the sure abodes of Canaan, so we " earnestly desire to be clothed upon with our house which is from heaven; for in this we groan, being burdened."

4. God's ordinance of a booth life was *a pledge of the certainty of Canaan.* It assured them that He desired them to journey forward to the goodly land. And He would have us "set our face Zionward."

[See Addenda to Chapter. FRAIL HABITATIONS.]

ILLUSTRATIVE ADDENDA TO CHAPTER XXIII

SABBATH:

"As if a segment of the eternal Sabbath had been inserted in the days of earth, and men wondered at their own happiness."
—HAMILTON.

Called by the Jews the 'Day of Light,' by the Africans 'Ossa-day,' the day of silence; by the Cree Indians the 'Praying day;' by the early Christians the 'Queen of days.'
—BOWES.

"How still the morning of the hallowed day! Mute is the voice of rural labour, hushed The ploughboy's whistle and the milkmaid's song."—GRAHAM.

Of a well-spent Sunday, Philip Henry used to say: "If this be not the way to heaven I know not what is."

"O, day of rest! How beautiful and fair How welcome to the weary and the old! Day of the Lord! And truce to earthly care!
Day of the Lord, as all our days should be."
—LONGFELLOW—*Christus.*

"Oh, what a blessing is Sunday, interposed between the waves of worldly business like the Divine path of the Israelites through Jordan. There is nothing in which I would advise you to be more strictly conscientious than in keeping the Sabbath holy. I can truly declare that to me the Sabbath has been invaluable."—WILBERFORCE.

"I feel as if God had, in giving the Sabbath, given fifty-two Springs in every year."
—S. T. COLERIDGE.

"Sir," said a man addressing a minister returning from church on Sabbath morning, "did you meet a lad on the road driving a cart with instruments for harvesting in it?"

"I think I did," replied the minister, "a boy with a short memory, wasn't he?"

"What makes you think he had a short memory, sir?" was the surprised answer.

"I think he has," answered the minister, "and belongs to a family who have short memories."

"What in the world makes you think so?" asked the man, greatly puzzled.

"Because," replied the minister in a serious tone, " the Great God has proclaimed from Mount Sinai, ' Remember the Sabbath day to keep it holy ;' and that boy has forgotten all about it."—*Christian Treasury*.

"Now let us repose from our care and our sorrow,
Let all that is anxious and sad pass away :
The rough cares of life lay aside till to-morrow,
And let us be tranquil and happy to-day.

"Let us say to the world, should it tempt us to wander,
As Abraham said to his men on the plain :
"There's the mountain of prayer, I am going up yonder,
And tarry you here till I seek you again.'

"To-day, on the mount we would seek for thy blessing :
O, Spirit of holiness meet with us there ;
Our hearts then will feel thine influence possessing,
The sweetness of praise, and the fervour of prayer."—EDMERTON.

HARVEST FIRST FRUITS :

The Hindoos, when gathering in their harvest, before it is removed for the threshing floor, always put aside a part for their gods.

"Lord of the harvest ! all is Thine !
The rains that fall, the suns that shine,
The seed once hidden in the ground,
The skill that makes our fruits abound!
New every year,
Thy gifts appear,
New praises from our lips shall bound !"
—GURNEY.

"BLOWING OF TRUMPETS":
"The trumpet ! the trumpet ! the dead all have heard,
Lo the depths of the stone-covered charnels are stirred ;
From the sea, from the land, from the south, from the north,
The vast generations of men are come forth."
—MILMAN.

FRAIL HABITATIONS.

On a house near Tretsey, in Cheshire, built in 1636, of thick oak framework filled in with brick, was this inscription:—"*Fleres si scires unum tua tempora mensem ; ridis cum non scis si sit forsitan una dies.*" [" You would weep if you knew that your life was limited to one month ; yet you laugh while you know not but that it may be restricted to a day"].

"*When I get settled, I'll*—"; so people are always planning ; but how little they think of the uncertainty that lies in the first word "*when!*"—BOWES.

A father with his little son is journeying overland to California, and when at night he pitches his tent in some pleasant valley, the child is charmed with the spot, and begs his father to rear a house and remain there ; and he begins to make a little fence about the tent, and digs up the wild flowers and plants them within the enclosure. But the father says, "No, my son, our home is far distant, let these things go, for to-morrow we must depart." Now God is taking us, His children, as pilgrims and strangers homeward ; but we desire to build here, and must be often overthrown before we can learn to seek "the city that hath foundation, whose Builder and Maker is God."—H. W. BEECHER.

CHAPTER XXIV.

Sanctuary Light; The Shewbread; Blasphemy Punished.

SUGGESTIVE READINGS.

Vv. 1-4.—Cause the lamps to burn continually. There is a Light whose radiance never dims, whose glow never pales—self-luminous and eternally lustrous ; "that is the True Light which lighteth every man that cometh into the world" (Jno. i. 9). But our illumined lives, made by grace to shine even amid the beauty of God's sanctuary, these need constant fostering and care, or their glory would wane. Because the virgins slept, neglecting to trim their lamps, their lights faded; and their sudden cry on awakening was, " Our lamps are *going out !*" (Matt. xxv. 8). There is a human responsibility in this matter of keeping our "lights burning" (Luke xii. 35), and we must "bring the pure oil" by which the flame is fed. Self-watchfulness and prayer for grace are inevitable if Christian character is to shine "*continually.*"

Vv. 5—9.—Bake twelve cakes and set them upon the pure table before the Lord. Every tribe was to be represented in this sacred food laid before the Lord, none exempted. Jehovah asks from the Church in its entirety, from all within His Church, that His table be spread with the sacrificial offerings of their love, that He may feast thereupon with satisfaction and delight. If *He* gives riches of salvation to man, *we* may return Him the offerings of our sanctified lives: " they gave their own selves unto the Lord " (2 Cor. viii. 5). Nor may these sacrifices of righteousness be fitful and intermittent; the loaves must be "set in order before the Lord continually" (v. 8), even as the devotion of our affections and services must be unceasing, a life-long consecration. Such fulness and constancy in our piety renders it "most holy unto Him of all the offerings."

Vv. 10-16.—The Israelitish woman's son blasphemed the Name of the Lord, and cursed. An unwise marriage issued in an evil result. This youth of half blood, in a quarrel with " a man of Israel," vented his malignity in uttering some vile blasphemy against the Holy Name which the Israelite so solemnly revered. A special revelation of " the mind of the Lord " was sought, in order that this new sin in Israel's midst might be judged aright, and every one who heard the blasphemy was summoned to join in the administration of punishment (v. 14). Surely, " if he that despised Moses' law died without mercy," terrible must be the doom of those who insult the grace of God in Jesus, and slight His redemption! (Heb. x. 28, 29). If words of impiety were sufficient to bring death upon an offender, what shall be the consequence of a life of disobedience and of persistent ungodliness! See Rom. ii. 8, 9. Let us guard against anger; it impels to outbursts of wickedness. And let our souls guard jealously the majesty of the Divine Name.

Vv. 17-22.—Breach for breach, eye for eye, tooth for tooth. This was the Mosaic rule of equity: a wrong was punished by demanding its equivalent. Our Lord gave a more gracious law to His followers, whose mission in the world was to expound and foster the spirit—not of revenge, nor even of exact justice, but of forgiveness and love. " But I say unto you, that ye resist not evil" (Matt. v. 38, 39). " Dearly beloved, avenge not yourselves."

SECTIONAL HOMILIES.

Topic: CONTINUOUS LUSTRE OF A GODLY LIFE (Vv. 1-4).

Darkness might brood over the outer world, but light must continuously glow within the sanctuary. Outside of the Church of Christ there may spread the gloom of error, the night dreariness of delusion; but *within the sanctuary* " the light of the knowledge of the glory of God " must shine undimmed. Even so, though men in sin dwell in darkness and love darkness rather than light, *within the Christian soul* there must always shine the marvellous light of the Spirit's illumination and of the Gospel truth.

I. A BEAUTIFUL LIGHT-BEARER: what an ideal picture of the Christian!

" He shall order *the lamps upon the pure candlestick*" (v. 4). A golden candlestick hung with burning lamps! [See Addenda to chapter, *Light-bearers.*] Here note—

1. *A Christian's intrinsic worth.* The candlestick was of "pure" gold. God thus images the preciousness of a redeemed and sanctified life. Worth of character, individual nobleness, must be the basis of a beneficent ministry for others.

2. *A lustrous mission.* On every branch was hung a lamp. Christians live not for themselves, not even to exhibit their own graces. A candlestick, however precious its metal and exquisite its workmanship, is intended to—not hold attention to itself, but to hold up the light, to show light.

3. *Ceaseless luminosity.* There are lights, set up for mariners, which gleam and wane; their stream of lustre is not perennial. But the lamps in the sanctuary burned on with ceaseless glow, with unvarying radiance. Piety should maintain its steadiness, not flicker, not burst into splendour at favoured seasons and then wane. "Your *light burning.*"

4. *Every grace aglow.* In some Christians only one beautiful quality is conspicuous, while all other graces are obscure. But every branch of the candlestick should bear a lamp, and *each lamp* should be *alight.*

II. SANCTITY REQUISITE FOR A CLEAR LIGHT.

"They shall bring *pure* oil olive, beaten for the light."

1. *Christian grace is divinely "pure."* It is the work of the Holy Spirit. "Oil" is the Scripture symbol of the Spirit, and "pure oil" marks the essential sanctity of each endowment of the Spirit of God. No other source exists whence man can derive what is unalloyed. This is the only "pure" spring of good; all others are unclean. How "pure" is every bestowment which God's Spirit imparts: *knowledge, feeling, energy, enjoyment, aspiration, hope*—all unalloyed, unmixed with ingredients of evil!

2. *Christian life emits clear lustre.* As we are, so we produce. A clean fountain yields clean waters. Pure oil produces clear burning lamps. If our minds are spiritually illumined there will be no emission of error: error indicates a human admixture with the Divine enlightenment. So with emotion; "the fruit of the Spirit is *love.*" If we shed forth an unlovely and unloving spirit it intimates the presence of deleterious intermixtures. We need to close the lamps, into which the Spirit's "pure oil" is poured, against all impurities, or our light will not be clear.

III. THE STEADY LIGHT OF TESTIMONY.

"From the *evening unto the morning*, before the Lord *continually.*" The golden lamp diffused its light without intermission, clear and constant.

1. *The High Priest's responsibility.* "Aaron shall order it, etc." No secondary hands had charge of the light. It was not left to inferior priests. Ministers of the sanctuary may wish and endeavour to keep Christian life alive and Christian lustre radiant in the Church, in the souls of believers; but they fail. Man's work is full of peradventures and frustrations. And there must be no risk in the maintenance of the Sanctuary light. If left to one of the minor priests, or assigned as a trust to many, neglect might ensue. Aaron himself, therefore, was charged with this office of keeping the light continually burning. He typified Christ; and our Lord "*walketh amid the golden candlesticks,*" ever nourishing the life and lustre of His Church.

2. *The continuous testimony of the Church.* Every age has seen the "True Light" shining amid the darkness of error and the delusions of the world. Though virgins slumber who should watch, though indifference to Truth mark the guardians of the sacred light, yet on, age after age, the light has shone, increasingly clear; for Christ keeps the lamps nourished, and will not let the lustre expire. "He shall order the lamps upon the pure candlestick before the Lord *continually.*"

(*a*) Here is the *guarantee of the Church fulfilling her Lord's design.* "Ye are the light of the world;" "holding forth the word of life."

(*b*) In this lies *the hope of the constancy of the Christian life.* Christ nourishes the flame.

▼

Topic: THE BREAD OF THE PRESENCE (Vv. 5—9).

In the Tabernacle we have a type of the "more perfect Tabernacle," in which Deity sojourned during the Incarnation—"God manifested in the flesh." For the physical form of Christ was what the Mosaic Tabernacle was, a shrine of the Divine indwelling, in which He came in nearness and grace to men, holding communion with us.

The table on which the loaves of shewbread were laid was made of acacia wood overlaid with plates of pure gold, symbolic of those sacred and divine qualities of Christ's person and character, which form the basis of all accepted offerings. Only as ourselves or our gifts are *laid upon Christ* can they be allowed a place "before the Lord." Here, then, we have the key to the meaning and suggestiveness of the shewbread: *a consecrated people resting on the perfections of Christ.*

I. CONSECRATION MUST DEPEND FOR ITS ACCEPTANCE UPON THE PERFECTIONS OF CHRIST.

These loaves represented the twelve tribes of Israel, all *dedicated to the Lord*; laid "before the Lord"; surrendered entirely to Him. Every one should be *devoted* to Him, fully and absolutely His.

Is consecration *sufficient of itself* to ensure Jehovah's acceptance? Far from it. It is "the altar that sanctifieth the gift"; and it was the golden *Table*, Christ's pure and glorious perfections, which—becoming the basis on which the consecrated offerings rested—rendered these loaves an accepted presentation.

No acceptance apart from Christ. Full acceptance for all who *place themselves upon Christ.*

II. CONSECRATED OFFERINGS MUST BE ALWAYS OUR CHOICEST AND BEST.

On the Golden Table no common bread might be placed. The profanity that presumes on Christ's perfections, and presents before the Lord faulty things, will ensure rebuke. Christ's grace adds all the element of acceptableness to what we bring; but God will not accept aught that we bring which is not the purest and noblest we can present. "Thou shalt take *fine flour*." These loaves represented, therefore,

1. *The dedication of what was choicest.* Are any powers too noble, any attainments too exalted, any affections too pure to be yielded to Him?

2. *A generous largeness* in the act of consecration. The loaves were of *double* size: "Two-tenth deals shall be in one cake" (v. 5). Ananias and Sapphira offered "*part* of the price," and were rejected for their cupidity and grudging. Lay lavishly on God's altar of your best.

III. CONSECRATION REQUIRES TO BE PERPETUALLY RENEWED.

Every Sabbath fresh loaves were to be substituted.

1. There is *no finality* in our devotion. It must be repeated, continued; perennially *fresh*.

2. *Sabbath obligations are as imperious* as Sabbath privileges are precious. We may not greet the holy day for what bliss we can gain or enjoy, without greeting the day by attempting the re-consecration of ourselves and our services to the Lord. Leave "the things which are behind"; come with renewed zeal and love and devotion before the Lord.

3. Each renewal must be *sanctified by our prayers*, and the *merits of Christ Jesus*. That burning of incense symbolises *prayer rising from the offerer*—for prayer hallows our gifts: but it also betokens "*the sweet savour of Christ*," without which nothing rises as a fragrant offering to the Lord.

Topic: THE LAMPS OF THE TABERNACLE (Vv. 1-4).

Israel had to constantly appear in the Tabernacle to present sacrifices and observe ceremonies; it was essential, therefore, that light should be supplied by which divine service might be conducted. The golden candlestick was hung with its seven lamps.

I. THEY WERE SYMBOLICAL OF THE POSITION AND PRIVILEGES OF THE HEBREW NATION.

(a) *The light shone in the midst of darkness.* However dense the night might be around the Tabernacle, light was within shining upon the altar, lighting up the holy place. So, where the darkness of moral night enwrapped surrounding nations, Israel had the light of the knowledge of God.

(b) *The light was derived from a divine source.* The lamps were lighted from the sacred fire upon the altar. Israel did not obtain knowledge of divine things from surrounding nations, but direct from Jehovah. Their light was supernatural divine revelation, a lamp unto the feet, light unto the path in the probation and pilgrimage of life.

(c) *The light of the best and purest kind.* Candlestick was of pure gold. Oil was the finest, even good for food. The light of the knowledge of the glory of God incomparable, inestimable.

II. THEY WERE TYPICAL OF THE CHARACTER AND WORK OF THE CHRISTIAN CHURCH.

(a) In their *Purity,* (b) *Preciousness,* (c) *Manifoldness,* (d) *Unity.* The Priests had to keep their lamps supplied, for churches need constantly the unction of the Holy One supplied by the Great Head of the Church. Churches are to give light, and save life. Christians are to be lights in the world.

The lamps were *outside the veil* that enclosed the Holy of holies; so the Church is outside the veil of Heaven, but near and preparatory for it.

No nobler ambition of position than this to live and walk in the light of God. Those who refuse the light, and walk in darkness, secure for themselves despair and death. For the righteous there is reserved light for the eventide, in eternity they shall shine as the brightness of the firmament, and as the stars for ever and ever.—F.W.B.

Topic: THE TABLE OF SHEWBREAD (Vv. 5-9).

Directions, for the construction of the table upon which the shewbread was to be placed, are recorded in the xxv. of Exodus. In this chapter we have directions given for making the shewbread, which was to be placed before the Lord continually. The shewbread, being the "Bread of the presence of the Lord," was a memorial—

I. OF THE NEARNESS OF ISRAEL TO THE LORD.

The twelve loaves, made of fine flour, and placed in two rows upon the *pure table, outside the veil* of the testimony in the Tabernacle, corresponded with the twelve stones in the breastplate of the High Priest, which contained the names of the twelve tribes of Israel; and showed, when he went into the most holy place, not only how near the people were to his own heart, but also how near they were to the presence and power of Jehovah. The bread, brought by the people, represented the staff of their life, their strength, and stay; and the Lord, by admitting and adopting those representations, showed how near He allowed Israel to draw to Him. Bread, representing their life, was perpetually in the Divine presence, and the weekly renewal of the loaves denoted that God permitted the perpetual enjoyment of His presence.

II. OF THE UNITY OF ISRAEL BEFORE THE LORD.

The bread was of one kind and size, and placed on one table, though divided into twelve cakes. So, though Israel was divided into twelve tribes, they were one in the presence of the Lord; and not one of them would ever be despised, so long as they obeyed His commandments, and drew near to Him at His appointed meeting-place. The Lord had set apart the nation for Himself; they were, therefore, one great family, a special religious community, of which He was sole and supreme Head.

III. OF THE DEPENDENCE OF ISRAEL UPON THE LORD.

Some have suggested that the constantly replenished bread upon the table was a memorial of the manna, to remind Israel how mercifully and miraculously they were fed in the wilderness. Doubtless, the loaves would tend to remind them of that great fact; but they would also remind them how, in Canaan, they were constantly dependent upon the Lord, who crowned the year with His goodness, and gave them the finest of the wheat. The loaves were a slight return and acknowledgment of their constant obligation to the Divine bounty. The shewbread may be regarded as an emblem of the *pure, sufficient,* and *satisfying* bread of heaven, which, if a man eat, he shall live for ever.

IV. OF THE DEDICATION OF ISRAEL TO THE LORD.

Pure frankincense was put upon each row of loaves; two vessels of wine were also placed beside them, as an accessory to the service, to be poured out withal, when the incense was offered. Under the old dispensation, bread and wine are always spoken of as means and emblems of bodily strength and cheerful service; and those elements on the table before the Lord denoted the complete dedication of the tribes to His service, while the ascending incense would represent the prayers of the people, the rising of their grateful and gladsome hearts to Heaven. The perpetual presence of the bread symbolized perpetual consecration to the Theocratic King.

V. OF THE ACCESSIBILITY OF ISRAEL TO THE LORD.

The Tabernacle was the Divine dwelling-place, and the acceptance of twelve loaves from the people to lie before the Lord, and to be called "*the Bread of His presence,*" showed that He took the people into His friendship and favour. Sabbath after Sabbath, as the incense ascended, the people would rejoice, that through mediation and intercession their offerings were accepted. God is not only pleased with the faith and love, the praises and prayers of His people, but also with their almsdeeds. Let us present an offering to the Lord, *pure, wholesome, valuable,* and *constant, perfumed* with the merits of the sacrifice of our Great High Priest; thus shall we enjoy the presence of the Lord, and pass the days of our pilgrimage in His favour and fear.—*F. W. B.*

Topic: BLASPHEMY AGAINST GOD'S HOLY NAME (Vv. 10—16).

This is the earliest Scripture record of blasphemy; and, as a newly-developed form of sin, it is treated with rigour for its complete suppression. Yet notwithstanding the swift judgment which overtook this first blasphemer, this is *not the last* Scripture instance of blasphemy.

The provocation or motive to this act of "the Israelitish woman's son" seems to have been mere malignity of thought against God and His people, a wish to wound reverent minds by reviling the Name they revered.

"Swearing is a sin that hath more malignancy in it against God, by how much the less is the temptation to it," says *Burroughs*; and adds, "I verily believe that if God had never made the Third Commandment, there could never have been so many oaths in the world; but it springs from a mere *malignancy of spirit in man against God* because He has forbidden, for no profit can arise from the practice."

Yet, while "no profit" comes to the blasphemer, *great ill and grief are thereby caused to others.* Dr. Scudder was returning from India with his son, and the lad was shocked to hear from an English passenger on the steamboat God's name used in dreadful blasphemy. Accosting him, the doctor said, "This boy has been born and reared *in a heathen country* and a land of idolatry; but, in all his life, he never heard a man blaspheme his Maker until now." (See Addenda to Chapter, *Profanity*).

I. THE HISTORIC INTEREST OF THIS INCIDENT.

This act of blasphemy, and the judgment which it called forth on the sinner,

1. Brought out clearly that the *Name of the Lord* was *Israel's most solemn trust*. The people evidently felt this, by the horror which the reviler's conduct awakened throughout the whole camp; and by their anxiety to learn how Jehovah regarded the indignity. And this was emphasized by God's sentence of doom upon the blasphemer. A crime must be great which evokes such condign punishment. That Holy Name was to be guarded with jealous awe. The event showed, therefore, how emphatically God will " not hold him guiltless that taketh His name in vain."

2. Introduced the significant custom of *avoiding the very use* of *the Name of the Lord*. The Jews interpreted this command (v. 16) as prohibiting the utterance of the divine Name under any circumstances, and consequently they never after pronounced the word JEHOVAH. When blasphemy was uttered, the person hearing it laid his hand on the head of the transgressor, to indicate his sole responsibility for the guilty act; and then tore his own robe as a symbol of his shame and alarm. Certainly this may admonish us against an undue freeness in the use of the august Name either in pious speech or effusive prayer.

II. THE HEINOUS QUALITY OF THE CRIME.

1. *The crime defined.* Blasphemy is calumny and insult against the holy God, uttered with the *intention* to defame Him. It not only expresses the hatred of Him in the speaker's own heart, but *aims* at awakening in his hearer's mind an equal loathing of Jehovah and all His claims. It is held up in Scripture as an assault upon the dignity and sanctity of God's name: Psa. lxxiv. 18; Isa. lii. 5; Rom. ii. 24.

Real blasphemy consists in *intended and direct insult* upon God's honour and holiness. But *relative* blasphemy consists in the *unconscious* and *indirect effect* of a man's words or acts, as, *e.g.* the uttering opinions or sentiments which dishonour God's name and discredit His word. To allow one's lips to utter with irreverence and familiarity the august Name is near akin to the sin of wilfully maligning Him.

2. *The root of the sin.* This must be traced to the vileness of the human heart, and its natural enmity to God (Comp. Matt. xv. 19). It should be noticed also as being the outgrowth of folly and pride (see 2 Kings xix. 22; Psa. lxxiv. 18). Of all sins, blasphemy is an indication of a mind mad with impiety.

3. Its *great offensiveness* to God and man. How *hateful to God* is evident from the penalties inflicted—[see v. 16 and comp. Isa. lxv. 7; Ezek. xx. 27-32., xxxv. 11, 12; Matt. xii. 31, 32]—how *hurtful to man* is manifest from Psa. xliv. 15, 16; lxxiv. 10, 18, 22. They who revere "*this glorious and fearful Name*, THE LORD THY GOD" (Deut. xxviii. 58) are distressed at its profanation.

Louis IX. of France branded swearers' lips with a hot iron for this offence, and when some complained that the punishment was too severe, he replied, "I could wish that by searing my own lips I could banish all profanity from my realm."

III. FACTS EXPLANATORY OF SUCH BLASPHEMOUS SPEECH.

The sin of profanity points to :—

1. *An ungoverned tongue.* Speech should be held under control. The tongue may be "set on fire of hell." Allow unbridled speech, and profanity easily grows. "Set a watch, O Lord, before my mouth."

2. *Passionate contention and strife.* Little do men anticipate to what extremes passion will carry them when they enter upon controversy or strife (Prov. xvii. 14).

3. *An unsanctified heart.* This man was not a true Israelite: not by birth, not by sentiment. He did not share in the nation's solemn fear of God. Unless a "clean heart and right spirit" is in us, evil may easily get dominion over us.

a. How *beautiful the assurance* of Solomon—"He that loveth pureness of heart, for the grace of his lips, the king shall be his friend"! If such purity of heart and grace of speech win an earthly monarch's favour, certainly the King divine will seal with favour now and eternally such qualities of character and conduct.

b. How *winning is that Name* which in our Christian dispensation we are called to cherish! It is the name of Jesus. And the Father gave it His Son to be "a Name above every name, that at the name of Jesus every knee should bow" (Phil. ii. 9, 10); and it is "given under heaven among men" (Acts iv. 12) to be loved as the "sweetest sound on mortal tongue," and the pledge of grace and bliss.

Topic: BLASPHEMY OF SHELOMITH'S SON (Vv. 10-15).

This incident in the career of Israel is similar in character to that of the two sons of Aaron, who offered strange fire upon the altar, thereby insulting the name of the Lord, degrading His sanctuary, and meeting with sore retribution. When Israel left Egypt, a mixed multitude of camp followers proceeded with them into the wilderness. They encamped outside the tents of Israel, and only occasionally entered the sacred enclosure. A son of an Israelitish woman, whose father was an Egyptian, had an altercation with a man of Israel, and when striving with him in the camp blasphemed the name of the Lord, and cursed. Moses at once sought to learn the mind of the Lord concerning such an offence; and the offender was stoned. The sentence was strictly and solemnly carried out, for "the children of Israel did as the Lord commanded Moses." From this incident we learn—

I. THAT THE NAME OF JEHOVAH COULD NOT BE BLASPHEMED WITH IMPUNITY. In all the oldest MSS. "the Name" stands alone, without the words "of Jehovah." The Hebrew name of God was peculiarly solemn; the Jews, afraid to pronounce it, employed the word "Lord" instead. "Jehovah" meant the underived, infinite, and eternal existence of deity, and was the incommunicable name by which He made His august might and majesty known. It was enthroned above all the names of heathen deities, and enshrined the Divine Glory. Around it was set a sacred fence. To blaspheme it was a sin of the deepest dye. The Jews have always been marked, even in their most degenerate days, by reverence for the great name of Jehovah. Alas! how the name of the Lord is profaned and blasphemed to-day. Because of swearing the land mourneth. Though blasphemers are not now stoned, yet over their heads hangs the sword of His righteous retribution, threatening them with everlasting shame and contempt.

II. THAT THE SANCTITY OF THE CAMP COULD NOT REMAIN DEGRADED BY THE PRESENCE OF A BLASPHEMER.

It is evident that blaspheming in the camp was a very rare thing, for no sooner had the son of Shelomith uttered his oaths than the people arrested him, and demanded that he might be appropriately punished. This shows their jealousy for the honour of the divine name, and for the moral safety and purity of society. Let us beware, lest the name of the Lord Jesus be profaned, lest He be crucified afresh and put to an open shame. The camp of Israel and the Church of the living God, cannot be profaned without incurring the divine displeasure.

III. THAT THE SIGNAL AND SEVERE PUNISHMENT COULD NOT BE INFLICTED UPON THE BLASPHEMER WITHOUT ACCOMPANYING APPROPRIATE SOLEMNITY.

The sentence was to be executed outside the camp, in the presence of witnesses who heard the words spoken; they were to lay their hands upon the head of the doomed man, to show that he bore his own guilt, and was devoted to expiate it. As we see him publicly and solemnly stoned, we learn how fearful a thing sin is, and how fearful it is to fall into the hands of the living God, except we do so in penitence and prayer. We also learn—(*a*) *The danger of anger.* (*b*) *How one sin leads to another.*—F. W. B.

OUTLINES ON VERSES OF CHAPTER XXIV.

V. 2.—*Theme:* THE GOLDEN CANDLESTICK.
That part of the temple exclusively claimed by Jehovah was lighted by a candlestick with seven lamps, which were kept continually burning. This candlestick might possibly be intended to represent Christ as "the light of the world," but certainly shadowed forth *his church* in—

I. ITS PRIVILEGES.
1. Christ declared that *the candlestick represented His church* (Rev. i. 20). Consider—
(1.) *Of what it was composed.* Pure gold (Exod. xxv. 31-38). Symbol of the "divine nature" of which saints are made partakers (2 Pet. i. 4).
(2.) *How it was supplied.* With purest oil; symbol of the "unction of the Holy One which we have received" (1 John ii. 20, 27), for the enlightenment of our minds and sanctifying of our souls.
(3.) *For what purpose it was used.* To shine in darkness, that all who were engaged in God's service might fulfil their duties aright, and that God might be glorified in them (Rev. i. 12, 13).
2. *The priestly attendant prefigured Christ.* This is affirmed on Christ's own authority (Heb. iv. 14, 15).
(1.) He is *constantly employed* in inspecting and trimming the lamps.
(2.) *Not a saint escapes His watchfulness;* He sees all our declensions and needs.
(3.) He *interposes to correct their dulness,* and to restore them to their wonted splendour (John xv. 2).

II. ITS DUTIES.
The duties of the saints are—
1. To *shine;* that God's power and grace may be magnified among men, and that their fellow-creatures may be benefitted by their instructions, example, and influence (Matt. v. 14-16).
2. To *be receiving more grace from Christ,* in order to their *shining with yet brighter lustre.*
He has "the residue of the Spirit" (Mal ii. 15); and "of that fulness we must all receive even grace for grace" (John i. 16). Comp. Zech iv. 2-4, 11-14.
(*a*) *An important inquiry.* Are you as lights shining in a dark place? Judge yourselves.
(*b*) *A solemn admonition.* If we would not have "our candlestick removed" we must repent every known defect and seek to be pure as He is pure.
(*c*) *An encouraging reflection.* He "will not quench the smoking flax" (Matt. xii. 20). "Thou wilt light my candle, etc." (Psa. xviii. 28.)—*C. Simeon.*

V. 4.—*Theme:* THE GLORY OF THE CHURCH.
"*He shall order the lamps upon the pure candlestick before the Lord continually.*"

The high priest caring for the golden candlestick, a type of Christ in His care for the churches (Zech. iv. 2-6; Rev. i. 12-20). God is Light. Light, the firstborn of creation. Light, the beginning of work of grace in soul of man. Christ the Light of the world, a light to lighten the Gentiles, glory of Israel. The lamps before the Lord continually, so churches ever under His eye and care. Consider—(*a*) *how the light of the lamps was derived;* (*b*) *it was cheering;* (*c*) *it was revealing;* (*d*) *it was beautiful;* (*e*) *it was constant;* (*f*) *it was precious;* (*g*) *it was essential.* Trace analogy in light vouchsafed to Christian church and Christly souls.—*F.W.B.*

V. 5.—*Theme:* THE SHEWBREAD.
The mystery of the shewbread is applied by some to Christ, who called Himself "the true bread." But the circumstance of the flour "being taken from all the children of Israel," and made into "twelve cakes," denotes that those loaves represented the twelve tribes *i.e.*, the Church of God.

I. THEIR SOLEMN DEDICATION TO GOD.
"For a memorial, as an offering made by fire unto the Lord." As such, His eyes are upon them continually; and as the frankincense was to God an odour of a sweet smell, so they are accepted by Him.

II THEIR PERIODICAL RENEWAL.
While one generation is passing away another comes in to supply their place. Never shall God's people be removed but others shall be ready to succeed them. There are always souls prepared to be "baptised from the dead."

III. THEIR ULTIMATE DESTINATION.
The saints, when *their appointed period here is fulfilled, pass into the possession of Christ,* the Great High Priest. "The Lord's portion is his people" (Deut. xxxiii. 9). Christ will claim His people as His "peculiar treasure."
It is the duty of God's people, therefore:—
1. *To consecrate themselves entirely to God,* as being made and "set apart" absolutely for Him (Isa. xliii. 21).
2. *To occupy themselves in prayer and intercession.*
As the loaves represented "before the Lord" all Israel, so Christians should regard themselves as required to "make supplications, prayers, intercession, and thanksgiving for all men."
3. *To wait patiently their removal hence.*
"All the days of my appointed time will I wait, till my charge come."—*C. Simeon.*

V. 8.—*Theme:* SPECIAL TIME FOR SERVICE.
"*Every Sabbath he shall set it in order before the Lord.*"
Forms may exist without formality. Continuous worship does not preclude special

seasons for service. The Sabbath a peculiarly holy and consecrated day. The house of God a specially consecrated place. Special seasons for attention to divine things, (*a*) *prevent forgetfulness*, (*b*) *arrest attention*, (*c*) *secure freshness*, (*d*) *awaken inquiry*. The bread was never allowed to get mouldy or stale. The frankincense upon each row upon the golden table symbolic of prayer, purity, and praise. In Christian service and worship renewal of strength, refreshment in service, replenishment of sacrifice essential to acceptable worship and spiritual profit. At all times, especially on the Lord's day, there must be renewed consecration to Him before whose presence we bow.—*F. W. B.*

Vv. 13-15.—*Theme:* EVIL CONNEXIONS.
I. THE DANGER OF UNGODLY CONNEXIONS. As a caution against *intimacy with the ungodly* we are told that "evil communications corrupt good manners," and "the companion of fools shall be destroyed." Whereas in the marriage union such connexion is peculiarly dangerous, because its influence is incessant.
1. *Injurious to the person himself.* It cannot be productive of happiness, or piety. Comp. 2 Cor. vi. 14, 15.
2. *Injurious to their offspring.* It sorrowfully happens that when parents are divided in relation to religion the children yield most to the influence of the ungodly parent.
II. THE DANGER OF UNGODLY HABITS.
1. The *habits of this young man were bad*, a son of *wrathful* nature and *reviling* habits.
2. *The consequences proved fatal* to him. Little did he anticipate the issues of his evil habits. "Sin bringeth forth *death*."
(*a*) *Check strife* and anger *in ourselves*.
(*b*) *Arrest blasphemy in others*.
—*C. Simeon, M.A.*

Vv. 10-16.—*Theme:* SLAYING THE BLASPHEMER.
The narrative shows
I. THE EVIL RESULTING FROM CONNEXION WITH THE UNGODLY, "whose father was an Egyptian"—said by the Rabbins to be the man whom Moses killed.
II. *The danger* ARISING FROM INDULGENCE IN PASSIONATE ANGER: "strove"; the blasphemy was uttered in a quarrelsome passion.
III. THE BLASPHEMY *which, in this case*, RESULTED FROM SUCH INDULGENCE.
"Cursed" the Holy Name of Jehovah; which, the Israelite claimed, belonged to none but Israelites.
IV. THE PUNISHMENT WHICH ALL LIKE SIN MERITS.—*W. Wayland, B.A.*

V. 16.—*Theme:* BLASPHEMY.
"*And he that blasphemeth the name of the Lord, he shall surely be put to death.*"
A flaming sword here guards the sacred name of Jehovah. Not only were holy services to be rendered to Him, but reverent thoughts entertained of Him, whether uttered or unexpressed. Why were contemptuous or irreverent words uttered impiously against God's name considered as heinous?
I. *Because God's Name reveals and represents Him.* As the Eternal, Infinite, Self-existent, Almighty, Only God.
II. *Because to blaspheme God's Name, indicates the lowest depths of human sinfulness.* The blasphemer is capable of doing every other kind of evil without compunction.
III. *Because such wickedness exerts a most baneful influence upon others.* When contempt is thrown upon the divine name, obedience to divine laws is discouraged, the seeds of rebellion to divine authority are sown.
IV. *Because the Divine Name is worthy of all honour and blessing.*
V. *Because God has justly branded the sin with intensest hatred; and attached to it hopeless doom.*
No sin had denounced upon it a severer judgment by the Son of God. How needful that we constantly offer the prayer, "Hallowed be thy name."—*F. W. B.*

V. 22.—*Theme:* THE INEXORABLENESS OF THE LAW.
"*Ye shall have one manner of Law.*"
To maintain order in the wilderness among the tribes of Israel, it was essential that punishment should not be tardy in its movements, but summary in its infliction. The people needed to be held with a tight rein, chastised with a strong hand. The law of retaliation was,
I. *Strictly just.* Only fair that punishment should be of the kind and extent of the crime, for crime is an offence against man and society, the sin of the crime is taken cognizance of by God, He only can forgive it.
II. *Highly salutary.* It would check tendencies to oppression, robbery, and cruelty. Self-love and fear, where principle was absent, would deter from wrong doing for which severe retaliating punishment would ensue.
The law anticipated and foreshadowed the golden rule, "Whatsoever ye would that men should" etc., for the people would seek to do only such things as they would, should retaliation be done to them.
Under the Gospel, magnanimity supplants retaliation. The beau-ideal of Christian manhood is, lamblike innocence, and dovelike gentleness, patience, love.—*F. W. B.*

ILLUSTRATIVE ADDENDA TO CHAPTER XXIV.

LIGHT BEARERS.—The ancient Insignia of the Waldensian Church was a candlestick, with a light radiating its rays across the surrounding darkness, and encircled with seven stars; with the motto, "*Lux lucet in tenebris.*" Anything more appropriately descriptive of the position and history of the Church, it would be impossible to conceive.

PROFANITY. A good old man was once in company with a gentleman, who occasionally introduced into conversation the words, "devil, deuce," etc., and who, at last, took the name of God in vain, "Stop, sir," said the old man, "I said nothing while you only used freedoms with the name of your own master, but I insist upon it that you shall use no freedoms with the Name of mine."

CHAPTER XXV.

The Year of Jubilee.

SUGGESTIVE READINGS.

Vv. 1-7.—Then shall the land keep a Sabbath unto the Lord. For a whole year the land ceased to be the property of the owner; he might not till the soil, neither gather its spontaneous produce; God asserted *His* ownership by this enactment, and manifested His providential sufficiency for His people by the guarantee of plenty in the harvest preceding. The fallow land acquired new productive powers by this year of rest, as man and beast gather fresh energy by the weekly sabbath. The sabbatic law is a boon to the whole word. They who would secularise the holy day are "madmen, casting firebrands, arrows, and death." The Heaven-given day's rest is a solace to man's fretting life: a quiet interval amid earth's clamour for thought of his sacred interests; and a gentle admonition of his need of that spiritual rest which burdened souls should seek in Christ Jesus.

Vv. 8-22.—Thou shalt number seven sabbaths of years. On the great day of Atonement, the tenth day of the seventh month, the sound of trumpets proclaimed the dawn of a Jubilee year of universal restitution and redemption. Prisoners were liberated, slaves were set free, debtors were absolved, ancestral heritages were restored, the land enjoyed rest from tillage, and its produce was the common lot of all. Beautiful symbolism: of *the joyous proclamation of the gospel liberty* and salvation following upon the sacrifice of the Redeemer; and of man's emancipation by Christ from the tyranny of sin and Satan, and restoration to the glad liberty of a spiritual life. The restoration of inheritances effected the sharp distinction of the tribes, keeping the families intact. It also neutralised over-reaching and land greed. God's *promise of abundance* (Vv 22, 23) to compensate for the Jubilee year's cessation of agricultural processes carries with it still the lesson that none are losers who serve God even in the face of seeming sacrifice: for "the blessing of the Lord it maketh rich" "'Tis mine to obey, 'tis His to provide." The *questioning spirit of distrust* (v. 20) is arrested by God's assurance of prosperity following upon obedience. We may dismiss fear if intent on duty. The path of righteousness is always safe to tread, and none that trust in the Lord shall be desolate.

Let *this supernatural fact in history* be pondered. A miraculous year of super-abundance was guaranteed every fiftieth year, as a provision for the Jubilee Sabbath. If it had failed, what would have ensued? Moses would have been proved a deceiver. Pretending to divine inspiration as Israel's legislator, the Jewish religion would have received utter refutation. The pledge of verses 22 and 23 were a supernatural attestation every fifty years—easily verified or refuted—of the reality of the true religion, and of Jehovah's personal superintendence over the order of nature and the experiences of man.

A whole nation, age after age, acted on the command to keep Jubilee because satisfied by the preceding sign that the ordinance was indeed divine.

Vv. 23-34.—**The land shall not be sold for ever,** &c. The twelve tribes held the land of Canaan of Jehovah as His tenants at will, having no right or permission to barter with the soil, which was not their's but *His*. It were well if all dwellers on the earth would consider that no sure or extended tenancy can be maintained by man in this transient abode. Though it is true "that the earth hath He given to the children of men," yet "the earth is the Lord's": even as He gave Canaan by lots to the tribes, yet declared "the land is Mine" (v. 23). Here we have no continuing city; men can call nothing their own; the day of restitution will reverse our possessions; the hour of relinquishment hastens for us all. Death will end all occupancy here. But there is "a better and more enduring substance" for us to inherit, by faith in Christ: and he only is truly rich in heritages who "lays up for himself treasures in Heaven."

Vv. 35-38.—**If thy brother be waxen poor.** The poor always ye have with you: and the near of kin who have been unfortunate, "fallen in decay," claim special commiseration and leniency. What have we that we have not received? Should we not, therefore, show generosity and kindness?

Vv. 39-55.—**Not compel him to serve as a bondman.** An Israelite must be treated as became his dignity, however penurious and helpless he might be, for he was God's ransomed and chosen child, a "son of Abraham." Full redemption came with the Jubilee, from every contract and claim. And the day of our redemption draweth nigh: when "the creature itself shall be delivered from the bondage of corruption into the glorious liberty of the children of God" (Rom. viii. 21).

SECTIONAL HOMILIES.

Topic: A SABBATH OF REST UNTO THE LAND (Vv. 1-7).

Agriculturists still recognize the value of this law of one year's rest in seven for the land. Violation of this regulation will exhaust the richest soil, and bring sterility. [See Addenda to chapter, *Sabbath*.] This law proclaimed,

I. DIVINE OWNERSHIP IN THE SOIL.

Just as the reservation of the "seventh day" as a Sabbath asserted God's claim upon man's *time*, so this law affirmed His right to the *soil* man occupies and utilizes.

II. MAN'S HIGHEST INTERESTS ARE NOT MATERIAL AND EARTHLY.

He is here for nobler pursuits and more solemn concerns than to dig and toil, to buy and sell and get gain. For a man's life consisteth not in the abundance of the things which he possesseth.

III. NEIGHBOURLINESS AND BENEVOLENCE SHOULD BE CULTIVATED.

A common interest in all relationships of life (Vv. 6-7), and a helpful regard one for another would be promoted. Release from the stern occupancies of life would also awaken those social instincts and foster those healthy friendships which render intercourse cheering and elevating. Men were designed for fellowship and affection; not for exacting from each other what each can be forced to produce. Cultivate brotherliness. [See Addenda to chapter, *Benevolence*.]

IV. RELIANCE ON GOD, IN IMPLICIT OBEDIENCE TO HIS WILL.

To desist from effort to provide for their own maintenance would

1. *Elicit their faith in the fatherly* care of God.

2. Summon them to a *religious use of the time* which God had set free from secular toils.

3. Incite them to *grateful thoughts* of God's dealings with them as His people,

and win them to a renewed recognition that they were "not their own," but His, who had redeemed and still cared for them.

V. SABBATIC REST: HEAVEN'S GRACIOUS LAW FOR EARTHLY TOILERS.

Human life becomes a toilsome drudgery, unless God interposes restraints. He would save men from grinding degradation, from absorbing labours; and give them respite and rest. Man needs the Sabbath pause, in order to realise—

1. That higher *possibilities* are opened to him by God's grace than to be a servant of the soil on which he dwells. He may live for a "better country, even a heavenly."

2. That God desires of men the *devotion of fixed seasons*, and leisurely hours for sacred meditation and fellowship with the skies.

Topic: THE JUBILEE YEAR: ITS FOURFOLD SIGNIFICANCE (Vv. 8-13).

To the Hebrew the blessings of the jubilee year were local and literal; it was a year of *rest* and of *restitution* for the land; a year of *release* and *rejoicing* to every inhabitant. Liberty was regained by the slave; possessions in the soil reverted to their owners; agricultural toils were suspended that a whole year of relaxation and repose might be enjoyed. Every home was in enjoyment of plenty, every hand ceased from weary labours, and both man and beast dwelt in quietude and peace.

Glad, indeed, was the hour when the silver trumpet tones announced the arrival of the year of rest. It was like the prelude to a joyous anthem, and that anthem was the angels' song over Bethlehem fields—"Peace on earth, goodwill among men."

It was a richly symbolic institute, that Year of Jubilee, whose suggestiveness finds fulfilment in three distinct directions. It points to

I. THE CHRISTIAN DISPENSATION OF GOSPEL LIBERTY AND REST. [See Luke iv. 18-21].

II. THE BELIEVER'S PRIVILEGED LIFE OF SACRED RELEASE AND JOY. [Comp. Ephes. i. 13, 14; Heb. iv. 9; viii. 12].

III. THE MILLENNIAL AGE, OF ESTABLISHED RIGHTEOUSNESS AND PEACE. [See Isa. lxvi. 18-23; Rev. xx. 2-4].

IV. THE HEAVENLY STATE OF ETERNAL SECURITY AND SERENITY. [See 2 Pet. iii. 13; Rev. xiv. 13; xxi. 4].

In the application of the Jubilee incidents to each of these grand fulfilments of its symbolism, the following facts stand out clearly:—

i. BOUNTY. God gave a supernatural abundance the year preceding the Jubilee, that in the enjoyment of vast supplies there should be *no necessity for toil, no occasion for care*—[See v. 21]. And assuredly there is
    1. *Bounty in the provisions of the Gospel* (1 Tim. i. 14).
    2. *Fulness of grace for the believer in Jesus* (2 Cor. iv. 15; Titus iii. 6).
    3. *Abundance of good to be enjoyed in the Millennial Age* (Psa. lxxii. 7).
    4. *Limitless bliss in the Heavenly land* (Psa. xvi. ii).

ii. REST. That Sabbatic year was to be consecrated to repose; the land was to be allowed to rest; the toiler was to cease from toil. Every want was supplied without the weariness of labour. Equally true of the
    1. *Gospel rest* which Christianity announces (Matt. xi. 29).
    2. *Believer's rest* which faith secures (Heb. iv. 3).
    3. *Millennial rest* for a wearied Church (Rev. xx. 2, 3).
    4. *Heavenly rest* for Christ's redeemed followers (Rev. xiv. 13). [See Addenda to chapter, *Rest*].

iii. LIBERTY. All bondservants were set free the moment the Jubilee trumpet sounded (Vv. 39-44). And assuredly, this finds verification in the

1. *Liberty which Christ proclaimed* to souls enslaved in sin and fear (Luke iv. 18 ; Heb. ii. 15).
2. *Spiritual freedom realized by faith* (Rom. viii. 15 ; Jno. viii. 36).
3. *Emancipation from thraldom* which shall distinguish the *Millennial* reign (Isa. xlix. 8, 9).
4. *Glorious liberty of the children of God in Heaven* (Rom. viii. 21 ; Rev. xxi. 24, 25). [See Addenda to chapter, *Liberty*].

iv. RESTITUTION. If the Israelite had parted with his inheritance, its possession was restored to him in the Year of Jubilee, and that without payment (Vv. 25-37). So

1. The redemption of Christ recovers for man all that sin had forfeited.
2. Believers in Jesus regain all the virtue, happiness, and hopes which the fall had ruined.
3. The weary and wronged world would enjoy paradisal gladness through Christ's millennial sway.
4. Heaven will realize all which on earth had been desired, and restore all which death had desolated. [See Addenda to chapter, *Possessions*].

V. Let it be marked that *the Jubilee*, with all its blessings, was CONSQUENT UPON ATONEMENT. Not till the blood of Expiation had been shed, and the living goat had borne into the land of oblivion the sins which (ceremonially) had been transferred to it, did the silver trumpets peal forth their exultant notes, proclaiming liberty and rest, restitution and rectitude for the people. And it is *because of Christ's atonement* that

1. *Christianity has come to sinful man*, with all its tidings of good and wealth of salvation (John i. 29 ; Ephes. i. 6).
2. *Spiritual blessings are inherited by the believer in Jesus* (Rom. v. 11).
3. *The Church will enjoy the Sabbatic millennial glory* (Rev. xix. 11-14).
4. *Heaven will be the eternal possession of the redeemed* (Rev. viii. 14-17).

The cross is the source of all human good. All things are ours, because Christ has died. As the blood on the doorposts freed Israel from the plague of death in Egypt, so it is to us now and for ever the *Blood of Christ* which ensures all sacred good (Rev. i. 5, 6 ; v. 9, 10).

Topic: GLAD FACTS OF THE JUBILEE.

I. GOD'S SOVEREIGN RIGHT TO THE EARTH. He determines when and whether its fields should be tilled and reaped. Man, in his pride, calls the lands his own ; thinks and acts as if he were Creation's lord. His fancy rears a throne and crowns himself the king. But this decree establishes God's rule. We are dependant tenants of His fields. "The earth is the Lord's, and the fulness thereof."

II. GOD'S POWER TO PROVIDE. He wills, and crops abound. Thus through this year of rest no want is known. The marvel grows when it is considered that the Jubilee Year succeeds a Sabbath Year, in which no seeding or reaping had gone on. But God gave forth a treble harvest in each forty-eighth year. And, as the poor widow's meal and oil, it proved an unexhausted feast. As Joseph's well-replenished store, it fed the hungry and never failed.

None can succeed without the Lord, and none shall want who truly follow Him. Faith works when God says, Work ; it rests when God says, Rest ; and thrives in obedience.

III. UNIVERSAL REST ENJOINED AND ENJOYED. No hand should toil. Tillage and harvest sleeps. Repese is the one law—for man, beast, and soil. A Year long Sabbath reigns.

Emblem of soul rest in Christ.

IV. ATONEMENT USHERS IN THIS CONSECRATED YEAR. When the scapegoat has borne sins out of sight, when the High Priest has sprinkled the mercy-seat, this holy season begins. A light here shines upon the path which leads to rest—through penitence for sin, and reliance on the Victim.

V. THE TRUMPET SOUNDS THROUGHOUT THE LAND. In every place, by every ear, the long-expected notes are heard. They tell no doubtful tale. "Glad tidings" are yours to proclaim, ye ministers of Christ. O, see that your lips publish rest in Christ. "Comfort ye, comfort ye, my people, saith your God."

VI. CAUSES FOR ISRAEL'S DELIGHT. The downcast debtor was now free. The bondman cast away his yoke. All forfeited estates returned. The oppressor might no more oppress. No servant trembled at his stern lord's voice. The former owner claimed his father's fields. The ancient landmarks were rebuilt, and liberty resumed its sway. In every house and heart there was consciousness of relief. Sorrow and mourning fled away. So there is *all-deliverance in Christ*.

1. We are poor *debtors*. Our debts exceed the moments of our lives. But Justice must have reckoning. There is no trifling with God. But hark! the Jubilee is come! Christ avails to pay. His ransomed ones are all free. No debt remains.

2. The Jubilee relaxes the *ties of bondage*. Each soul, apart from Christ, is a poor slave. Tyrants are many, and their yoke is hard. But Christ liberates from fetters (Jno. viii. 36).

(*a*) *Satan enchains the soul*. But Jesus vanquishes this despot, and the Jubilee sets free from Satan's power.

(*b*) *Sin rules the captive race of men*. Till expelled by Christ, it must reign. But a new passion gains the throne when Christ comes in, and shews His dying love, His blood to attone.

(*c*) This *world* is a foul tyrant. Its smiles allure, its frowns deter, its fashions force compliance, its laws exact submission: it drives its millions to a slavish toil. But the grace of Christ emancipates from the world's enthralling snares.

(*d*) *Death*, too, is a fearful tyrant. Its chilly features terrify. The stoutest quails. None can relieve but Christ.

3. *The Jubilee restores inheritance*. Sin drove man from a fair abode; forced him to a wilderness of desolation. God's smile was lost; the blessing of communion ceased. But Christ re-instates with more than Eden heritage. He places us in a land of peace, where God is our joy for ever. More is found than was lost by sin.

Christ came, lived, died, reigns, *to grant this Jubilee to souls*. Hear His own words (Luke iv., 18, 19). He becomes His people's life, their liberty, their ransom, their peace, their joy, their hope, their glory. The trustful soul reposes in a jubilee of joy. (Arranged from Dean Law's "Christ is All").

Topic: THE YEAR OF JUBILEE (Vv. 8-14.)

This was the last and most remarkable of the Hebrew festivals. It bears unmistakeable marks of Divine origin, of wise and benevolent design. The trumpet of jubilee sounded on the tenth day of Tisri, immediately after the great atonement had been made by the High Priest, and the sound of it went forth throughout the whole land. Every valley and mountain resounded with the soul-stirring notes, and the people knew that the acceptable year of the Lord had come. The Jubilee taught—(*a*) *The dependence of Israel upon the bounty of Heaven* (*b*) *The duty of mutual kindness, forbearance, and forgiveness*. (*c*) *The unique position Israel occupied among the nations*. (*d*) *The unity of their race*. By its advent was proclaimed—

I. REST FROM MANUAL LABOUR.

The ordinary law with respect to physical subsistence was, "In the sweat of thy brow thou shalt eat bread," but in the eighth and fiftieth years the law was suspended, for no agricultural work of any kind was to be performed, the land was to lie fallow, and have perfect rest. Labour suspended for such a protracted period would restore the wasted energies of man, and secure renewed vitality to the soil. Such an arrest of the tide of busy life would suggest to the Hebrews the necessity of seeking the meat that endureth to everlasting life.

II. DELIVERANCE FROM CIVIL BONDAGE.

Liberty was to be proclaimed throughout the land, every slave was to be set free. In exceptional cases, where full freedom was not given, the condition of the most abject was ameliorated. Thus the common brotherhood of man was emphatically proclaimed, during the period of the jubilee all were on a level. This was an invaluable boon to men, and gave the dependent and downtrodden a fair and new start in secular life.

III. FORGIVENESS OF DEBTS.

Pecuniary liabilities that had been contracted in the transaction of business, and which debtors were unable to discharge, were remitted. No usury or increase was to be taken from the poor, the millstone of debt was to be removed from their necks. Thus the inequalities of social and secular life were readjusted, and society started afresh upon a reformed and revived basis.

IV. RESTITUTION OF LOST PROPERTY.

Of course, there would necessarily be inequalities in the social circumstances of the people; some would accumulate property that others would lose through misfortune or negligence, and wide gaps would be thus created between classes of the community. Those gaps would be filled up at the Jubilee, where all wicked or undue accumulation of possessions would be rectified, and a period put to boundless ambition and lawless aggression. Selfishness and greed would thus be cut up root and branch, and all men taught to be reasonable in their aims and claims.

V. REJOICING FOR THE PEOPLE.

The sounding of the trumpet, immediately upon the atonement being made, would inform the people that an acceptable offering had been presented for their sins; and that all the blessings promised in connection with the Jubilee might be enjoyed. A full tide of gladness would flow through the land, for the great national holiday had begun, and innumerable and inestimable blessings were available for all. The trumpet sound would set the joy bells in every devout Hebrew heart ringing with gladsome melody.

VI. EXEMPTION FROM CARE.

During the previous year the horn of plenty, with twofold richness, was poured into the nation's lap, and as the people beheld the super-abundant stores provided in anticipation of their manifold wants, they would be relieved from care and anxiety while the land had the long rest. They would not need to watch the clouds, their well-filled barns and overflowing presses would calm all their anxieties and fears. In these arrangements would be seen the kind thoughtfulness of Israel's gracious Father, the sovereignty of their eternal King.

VII. HOMECOMING OF FAMILIES.

However scattered through adverse circumstances from the old homestead, or exiled through debt, all could now return, domestic devotion and social love could now be completely restored. All this would tend to socialize and humanize the people, and foster home and national piety.

VIII. REGENERATION OF THE NATION.

Every Jubilee year the people started afresh with a renewed consciousness of the presence of the Lord in their midst, and of their intimate relationship to Him. He brought them out of Egypt, gave them the goodly fertile land; and every Jubilee they were reminded that the land was His, that it was not to be impoverished and exhausted, that the nation was not to decay or become disintegrated. The divinely appointed conditions upon which the people took possession of the land were restored, and they looked up to Jehovah as their merciful and bountiful Benefactor.

Regarding the year of Jubilee as a type of the gospel age which Christ came to proclaim, and of the latter day glory such reflections as these are suggested:— The gospel brings *rest of heart* for all who hear and obey its joyful sound. *Deliverance from bondage* of Satan, sin, and self. *Recovery of our lost inheritance. Forgiveness* of the debt we owe to God. *Rejoicing* because of good news and glad tidings of reconciliation and peace. *Exemption from care* about guilt of past, events of present, revelations of the future. *Complete restoration to God.*

It is man's highest honour and joy to proclaim the acceptable year of the Lord. The day shall come when a weary world and longing Church shall be fully blest in enjoyment a Jubilee universal and perpetual.—*F. W. B.*

Topic: IMPORTANT PRINCIPLES CONTAINED IN THE JUBILEE REGULATIONS (Vv. 8-28).

Not till God uttered His voice in Christ could men understand the Jewish institutions. We who have heard the voice of Christ and His apostles have come plainly to see that "the acceptable year of the Lord," and "the times for the restitution of all things"—by which terms, and others, the year of Jubilee was described—have their *fulfilment in the Gospel.*

(1). The Jubilee began on the Day of Atonement, announced by trumpet blasts. Following upon the expiatory services of the day, the *gladness occasioned* by the "joyful sound" was *in accord with the truths symbolized in those expiatory services.*

(2). The Jubilee was marked by a complete suspension of agricultural labour. Fear was quieted by God's promise (v. 21). *God's blessing upon the obedient* is better than the sowing of the disobedient.

(3). The spontaneous fruits that grew during the suspension of agricultural operations were open to all. No man had the right to appropriate them. Thus *the common dependence* of all classes upon God's bounty, and *His equal regard for all* was declared.

(4). The Jubilee restored to men their lost liberties (v. 10). Every Hebrew whom poverty, or misfortune, or misconduct had deprived of freedom, regained all the rights and privileges of a free man.

(5). It brought back to their original or hereditary owners the family estates which had been alienated from them (v. 10). Thus *the consolation of misfortune,* or *the joy of old age,* might be that one recovered at the Jubilee *the home of his childhood* from which he had been driven by sore stress of poverty.

Macaulay tells how Warren Hastings, "when under a tropical sun he ruled fifty millions of Asiatics," was haunted with the wish to recover the ancestral manor of Daylesford. "He would be Hastings of Daylesford." This purpose, formed in infancy and poverty, was steadfastly cherished. "And when his long public life, so chequered with good and evil, with glory and obloquy, had at length closed for ever, it was to Daylesford that he retired to die."

The Jubilee recalled to the remembrance of the nation the fact that *the land was God's,* and they but "strangers and sojourners" therein (v. 23); and that institution gave back, as with the hand of God, to every man from whom it had been alienated the inheritance of his fathers. By the two great blessings it gave him—the *recovery of his freedom* and of *his family inheritance*—every one was given *a new start in life,* and the nation as a whole made a fresh beginning on an equal footing, as if they entered anew the promised land, and experienced afresh in all their fulness the privilege of the original covenant of grace.

Important principles, in their germs, were contained in this institution:—

I. MAN'S NEED OF OCCASIONAL REST FROM TOIL.

By the emphasis given to rest, God hallowed it as being a duty and a privilege. Man was not to give himself to a ceaseless course of grinding toil, or to unrelaxing endeavours to keep up riches. Such confinement to labour is deadening to the best faculties of the soul. It destroys the elasticity of the heart and the sweetness of the spirit.

Christianity repeats the old lesson. Mary *pausing from her work to listen to Jesus* is a better model than Martha ceaselessly toiling. "Come ye apart and rest awhile."

II. ALL MEN ARE ENTITLED TO A SHARE OF GOD'S BOUNTY.

What grew in the fields in the Jubilee year was God's harvest, free to all. It was to be distributed, like other pure bounties of His hand, the rain and sunshine, to all alike. This happened every Sabbatic year as well as in the Jubilee. It asserted that man's share in producing any harvests is very small, that God is its chief agent, and therefore that it rightly belongs in great part to Him, and ought to be *largely employed for the general weal.*

Christianity endorses it. The early believers "had all things common." Christian charity urges that we contribute to the happiness of the community.

III. THE WELFARE OF SOCIETY IS IMPERILLED BY THE ACQUISITION OF LANDED ESTATES.

The operation of the Jubilee was to prevent the accumulation of land in the hands of a few. The public good demanded its general division among the people. Great Britain may be said to be suffering because of the absence of such a rule. Ireland is rocking as with an earthquake because the land is held in the grasp of a few rich landowners, while the mass of the people, stripped of their ancestral fields, are sunken in extreme poverty. Because of a similar evil the French Revolution overturned the government of France.

The doctrines of Communism find no support in the reasonings of a wise statesmanship, or in the teachings of Christianity. But Christianity suggests a remedy for the evil. Let property be held and administered on Christian principles: "Be rich in good works, ready to distribute, willing to communicate."

IV. THE DIGNITY OF MAN VIEWED AS A RANSOMED CHILD OF GOD.

The Jubilee proclaimed the *equality of men* in the sight of Jehovah, and forbade their tyrannizing over or holding another in slavery. The ground of the prohibition was the same as that which forbade the absolute sale of land—*God's ownership of them.* "They are My servants," etc. (v. 42). The Jubilee made the slave a freeman, and the poor man a property owner.

How Christianity emphasizes this truth! It forbids contempt or oppression of any man for whom Christ died. He may be poor, ignorant, or even wicked. But for him also the scheme of redemption was planned. For his sake Christ laid aside the regalia of heaven and came down to earth. For him He made atonement for sin. For his regeneration He shed forth His Holy Spirit. There is joy in heaven when he repents; and when he dies, if he dies in faith and submission to God, he is carried by angels to the realm of the blessed.

By these things the dignity of man as man is proclaimed. He is to be treated, therefore, with consideration and kindness, with love and forbearance; and in the judgment Christ will say, "Inasmuch as ye did it to one of the least of these my brethren, ye did it unto me."—ALBERT H. CURRIER.

Topic: CANAAN, THE LORD'S LAND FOR EVER (Vv. 23-24).

"The land is *mine!*" How decisive this claim by Jehovah on the soil, to the possessions which He secured for Israel and settled upon His people for ever! It is to be marked that the land is never called *theirs*; always called *His*; for though God gave it into their occupancy He claimed it as His peculiar possession. "He will be merciful unto *His* land" (Deut. xxxiii. 43); "I will pluck them (Israel) up by the roots out of *My* land" (2 Chron. vii. 20); "Lord, Thou hast been favourable unto (*well pleased with*; margin) *Thy* land" (Psa. lxxxv. 1); "Then will the Lord be jealous for *His* land, and pity His people" (Joel ii. 18; Psa. iii. 2).

I. IN THE LAND OF CANAAN JEHOVAH'S MOST WONDROUS DEEDS ALL CENTRED.

"There He set up His throne and sanctuary; there His priests stood to minister continually before Him. There the voices of His prophets were heard testifying of present ruin and future restoration and glory; there the Baptist began, continued, and ended his career as the forerunner of the Messiah; there the Blessed One was born of a woman; there He was baptised; there He preached and taught; there He laboured and died; and thence He ascended in triumph to the right hand of God; thither God the Holy Ghost descended, in Pentecostal power; and thence the overflowing tide of gospel testimony emanated to the ends of the earth; thither the Lord of glory will descend, ere long, and plant His feet "on the Mount of Olives"; there "His throne will be re-established and His worship restored."—*C. H. M.*

II. OVER THE LAND OF CANAAN JEHOVAH'S MOST JEALOUS WATCHFULNESS IS EXTENDED.

There is no spot in all the earth like unto the land of Canaan in the divine estimation. His eyes and His heart are there continually; it's dust is precious in His sight; it is the centre of all His thoughts and operations, as touching the earth; and it is His purpose to make it an eternal excellency, the joy of many generations.

III. UPON THE LAND OF CANAAN JEHOVAH'S MOST EMPHATIC CLAIM IS SEALED.

"The land *is Mine*." It might not be sold for ever. It dwells in the keeping of the Omnipotent. It has been a coveted object through many ages, and by many earthly dynasties; and will yet be, if prophecy is rightly read, the scene of cruel war and sanguinary strife. But Jehovah maintains, and will perpetuate His claim. Inalienably, "the land is Mine."

For what purpose, and *for whom*, does God claim and keep that land? It is to be the inheritance of His covenant people; to be re occupied by those to whom He entrusted it by an everlasting covenant; and when "the fulness of the Gentiles" ends, and its present era of downtrodden abuse, which symbolises also the oppressed and outlawed lot of "lost" Israel and "dispersed" Judah is closed, then He who hath "*not* cast away His people" will require the land for Israel's re-possession. [See Isa. lxvi. 12-23.].

Topic: EXALTED PHILANTHROPY.

"Ye shall not oppress one another," etc."—(Vv. 14, 35-38).

In the Jubilee year the ambitious and affluent among the Israelites were to surrender their possessions on terms that would lift up the unfortunate, and better the condition of the poor. All overreaching and oppression were to be abandoned. What faith in God, obedience to His commands, time for thoughtful meditations, incentives to human kindness, etc., the year of Jubilee would inspire! The spontaneous produce of the land became public property, the poorest Israelite, even the stranger and the slave, enjoyed liberty and fared liberally. The poor have always been the objects of divine concern, and attention has been called to the amelioration of their condition. Let us consider.

I. SOME OF THE CAUSES OF POVERTY. Hereditary or acquired weakness, obscure origin, ignorance, extravagance, idleness, incompetencey, misfortune, calamity, or sometimes divine chastisement, as in case of Job.

II. SOME OF THE MISERIES OF POVERTY. Exacting, unremunerative labour; degrading surroundings; deficiencies in necessaries of life; indisposition for physical, mental, and moral improvement. Poverty has a bitter cry, hunger a sharp thorn. Under such circumstances life scarcely seems worth living.

III. SOME OF THE AMELIORATIONS OF POVERTY. Industry; economy; cleanliness; sobriety; sympathy; charity; above all, the uplifting, cheering influences of the gospel, which are peculiarly adapted and specially intended for the poor. The gospel will fire men with a laudable ambition, which will lift them in the social scale, or will make them happy in their unavoidable, lowly circumstances. On the basis of common brotherhood, and the universal Fatherhood of God, the temporal as well as spiritual interests of the poor should be cared for and ministered unto, not by patronising indiscriminate charity which fosters idleness and begets hypocrisy, but under the guidance of sanctified intelligence and Christly charity.—*F. W. B.*

OUTLINES ON VERSES OF CHAPTER XXV.

V. 3.—*Theme:* THE SABBATICAL YEAR.

The institution of the sabbath of the seventh year taught that the Lord was the sovereign King of the people, and the sole Proprietor of the land; very appropriate that the law concerning it should be pronounced amid all the solemn scenes and sanctions of Sinai. The Sabbatic year inculcated the lessons:

I. THAT THE LORD WAS THE SOLE PROPRIETOR OF THE LAND.

In all the promises made respecting Canaan, it was constantly kept before the people that the land was the Lord's; and that He would give it to the people—give it as He gives all His other gifts, to be used according to His good pleasure and revealed will. The people were tenants, and must obey the Lord of the land; for, while "the earth is the Lord's and the fulness thereof," Canaan was to Him the most holy place. The land would be as His most gracious land, which He would open or shut as He saw fit; and the people would see that they were in His land, and dependent upon Him, as the seasons rolled in their annual round.

II. THAT THE LAND HAD RESTING UPON IT, CONTINUALLY, THE FAVOUR OF THE LORD.

The land was to be ordinarily fertile every year; but, the sixth year was to be *exceptionally fruitful*, yielding enough for the seventh; so that, in it, the land, as well as the people, might repose. Each sixth year would exhibit in an extraordinary manner the unfailing and inexhaustible resources of God, and show how His smile and blessing rested on the soil. Canaan would look like a second Eden, as she appeared decked in her rich and beautiful garments. When the waters of the flood subsided, God said to Noah, "I will no more curse the ground for man's sake," and the fertile earth shows that the Almighty crowns the year with His goodness and that His paths drop fatness.

III. THAT THE DIVINE FAVOUR PROVIDES FOR THE WELL-BEING OF EVERY LIVING THING.

This is a general and world-wide truth; but it was especially seen in the Sabbatic year. During its months, every stranger in the land, and every beast, had abundant provision in the stores laid up, and the spontaneous growth of the soil. The great God of Nature pays respect to the wants of the minutest creatures His hands have made; and the directions given about brute creation would show that He was kind to them, and would suggest to men to treat them kindly. He "is good to all and His tender mercies are over all His works."

IV. THAT OF EVERY LIVING THING, MAN IS THE NEAREST AND DEAREST TO THE GREAT CREATOR.

During the seventh year the poor were to be fed, and the bound set at liberty; thus lessons of *kindness* and *forgiveness* were taught. The year was not to be passed in luxury and idleness, but time was to be spent in reading the whole Law; it was a Sabbath to the Lord, when He could be pleased and glorified with the prayers and praises of His people. To man alone are directions given for worship—He is the offspring of God, made in His image, and capable of worshipping Him. Not only one day in seven, but one year in seven, was to be kept as a sabbath, showing how God looked for man's devoted service.

V. THAT THE GREAT CREATOR TEACHES MORAL TRUTHS TO MAN BY MEANS OF WORKS OF NATURE.

All the processes and phenomena of nature are intended to illustrate and enforce spiritual things. Hence the Bible is full of references to correspondences and analogies between the kingdoms of nature and grace. The extraordinary provision made for the Sabbatic year would inculcate lessons of *faith*, obedience, reverence, love. In the fulness of time the great Teacher by His inimitable parables threw a flood of light upon similitudes between the outer and inner courts of divine revelation. To devoutly study and practice these lessons will ensure exquisite pleasure and eternal profit. —*F. W. B.*

V. 9.—*Theme:* LESSONS OF THE JUBILEE.
I. ITS PECULIAR FEATURES.
1. *It was a great boon to all sorrowing ones.*
(1.) Every captive was liberated.
(2.) The exiled wanderer returned.
(3.) The oppressed debtor was released from his debts.
(4.) The unfortunate poor were restored to their ancestral heritage.

(5.) Families that had been separated were now re-united.

(6.) Every estate reverted to the families to whom they were originally allotted in the conquest of Canaan.

2. *All this was intimately connected with the* DAY OF ATONEMENT. It was on the day of atonement, every year, that the trumpet was sounded in every corner of the land, reminding the people of the year of Jubilee (v. 9).

3. *It was to be a year of perfect freedom from toil* (Vv. 11, 12).

4. *Every business transaction had reference to the* year of jubilee (v. 16). Prices were regulated by its nearness or distance.

II. ITS TYPICAL MEANING.

I. *It had special reference to the millennial glory of Israel* in the land which Jehovah keeps for them through all generations.

(1.) God *claims* Canaan as He does no other.

(2.) God has *honoured* Canaan as He has no other.

2. *It is a beautiful and correct type of heaven.*

(1.) Where every believer will enter upon his inheritance, and enter into his rest.

(2.) Where all exile, captivity, separation, poverty and oppression will for ever cease, and God will wipe away all tears from our eyes.

III. ITS PRACTICAL LESSONS.

1. That which the Jubilee year restores, and the rest and joy and plenty it brings, *prove the graciousness of God.*

(1). The sorrow, poverty, oppression, exile, etc., which occurred between two Jubilee years *show the workings of human selfishness and sin.*

(2). That which the Jubilee restores *shows the workings of divine grace.*

2. The unspeakable blessedness of *the world's Jubilee in the millennial period* (Isa. xxv. 6-12; xxxiii. 23 24; xxxv. 1-10; lv. 13; Rom. xi. 25; viii. 18-22.).

3. *The more glorious and more enduring bliss of heaven* (Rev. xxi. 1-27; xxii. 1-15).
—*D. C. Hughes.*

Vv. 9, 10, 11.—*Theme:* THE JUBILEE A TYPE OF THE GOSPEL.

I. ITS PRIMARY PURPOSE.

1. *It was kind and benevolent*: showing that, by remedying the evils the Israelites entailed on themselves, God took an interest in their welfare.

2. It was *wise and politic.* A people thus regulated would be kept distinct as to their various tribes and families, while an affectionate and dependant spirit would be promoted.

3. It was *good and beneficial.* The insolvent debtor delivered, &c.

II. ITS TYPICAL REFERENCE.

1. The Jubilee of *grace.* This finds us deeply in *arrears* to divine justice, and fully remits all our debt. It reverses our state of spiritual *bondage*, restoring to us the rights and blessings of freedom. And it invests us with a new title to our forfeited *inheritance*, opening to us the kingdom of heaven (Acts x. 43; Rom. vi. 14; Jno. viii. 36; Ephe. ii. 12).

2. The Jubilee of *glory.*

III. ITS JOYFUL COMMENCEMENT.

This was announced by *the sound of trumpets* throughout the land *on the day of atonement.* Our jubilee also, which begins in the great atonement, is now proclaimed among us, and is the joyful season of God's grace, mercy, and salvation.

" Blessed are the people that know the joyful sound " (Psa. lxxxix. 15).—*Wm. Sleigh.*

V. 18. *Theme:* THE DUTY OF OBEDIENCE.

"Wherefore ye shall do My statutes, and keep My judgments, and do them; and ye shall dwell on the land in safety."

Man not a machine, but a responsible, free agent; therefore conditioned on obedience. Herein, seen the dignity of man, the righteousness and holiness of God. God had right to command Israel under obligation to obey, for

I. HE WAS THEIR SOVEREIGN RULER. Lord, King, Almighty, Absolute, Eternal.

II. THEY WERE HIS DEPENDENT CREATURES. They derived all from Him, were defended, delivered, by Him.

III. THE PATH OF OBEDIENCE WAS SAFE. Whatever might befal them when doing the will of God would be overruled for their real good. No weapon formed against them could prosper, while they enjoyed the approving smile of the Lord.

IV. THE ONLY CRITERION OF CHARACTER IS OBEDIENCE. Faith, love, loyalty, sincerity, consecration, evinced and vindicated by unquestioning, cheerful, self-forgetful, constant obedience. The law of Christ confirms this test, "If ye love me, keep my commandments." Revelation closes with declaration of same truth. "Blessed are they that do His commandments, that they may have right to the tree of life, and may enter in through the gates into the city."—*F. W. B.*

V. 25.—*Theme:* THE KINSMAN'S RIGHTS.

The tale is simple. One of Israel's sons is destitute. His goods, his lands are torn away. The creditor demands, the claim is just, all must be yielded.

But is there some kinsman whose heart feels pity, and whose means abound? Then he has right to pay the price and buy back the forfeited estate. He may not be denied. Redeeming privilege is his.

Such is the statute of the Jewish realm. But it shows far more than *civil remedy for helpless debt.* It is a bright transcript of the work of Christ.

I. NO ONE BUT A KINSMAN COULD REDEEM US.

The needy ones are *offspring of earth;* dust is their origin, the worm their brother, the clod their home.

But to redeem requires *a kindred birth.*

Yet Jesus is God; an infinite distance divides Him from men. One sits enthroned in highest glory, the other grovels in earth's lowest mire. Jesus may *love*, but, as God, He cannot *redeem*, cannot claim a kinsman's right. Are then the destitute beyond relief?

Since the *Redeemer must be Man*, Jesus connects Himself with human ties. A human form is marvellously framed; and the virgin mother bears the heavenly child. The *God-Man* becomes a *kinsman to redeem*.

II. THE KINSMAN ALSO NEEDS WEALTH BY WHICH TO PAY THE PRICE.

Family ties are not enough. Much is required for the redemption of souls. But His deity imparts sufficiency. The price is boundless; the payment far exceeds. "In whom we have redemption through His blood, the forgiveness of sins, according to the *riches of His grace*" (Ephes. i 7).

The sinner, appalled at his debts, may approach the Saviour, and *plead His near kindred*, may tell Him that He is one of our family, and remind Him that He alone has the redeeming *right* and redeeming *might*.

Then, being redeemed, let your life proclaim that you are no more your own but "bought with a price." The kinsman claims your heart, your love, your all.—*Dean Law.*

V. 55.—*Theme:* ROYAL SERVICE.

"For unto me the children of Israel are servants."

All things serve the Lord, but there are gradations of service. Man occupies a sphere only second to angels. Israel chosen to co-operate with Jehovah in communicating His will to the world, in winning back a prodigal race to Himself.

I. THE SERVICE HE EXPECTS. (*a*) *Intelligent*, higher than that rendered by inanimate and irrational things. Thoughtful, reasonable, conscientious. (*b*) *Spontaneous*. The outcome of free and deliberate choice, of preference for Him above all others. (*c*) *Grateful*. Remembering deliverances vouchsafed, benedictions bestowed. (*d*) *Lifelong*. Not spasmodic service, nor a course marked by withholdings, backslidings, shortcomings, or apostacy. He demands fidelity unto death.

II. THE REWARD HE BESTOWS. (*a*) *His gracious approval;* (*b*) *improvement in holiness;* (*c*) *promotion to higher service here;* (*d*) *admission to perfect blessed service hereafter.* In heaven His servants shall see and serve Him. Service there will be ineffable rapture and rest, because not beyond the strength, nor against the will, but in complete harmony with the renewed and immortal faculties.—*F. W. B.*

ILLUSTRATIVE ADDENDA TO CHAPTER XXV.

BENEVOLENCE.
"Then none was for a party;
 Then all were for the state;
Then the great man helped the poor,
 And the poor man loved the great.
Then lands were fairly portioned;
 Then spoils were fairly sold;
The Romans were like brothers
 In the brave days of old."
—*Macaulay.*

"Beneficence is a duty. He who frequently practises it, and sees his benevolent intentions realised, at length comes to love him to whom he has done good. When, therefore, it is said, 'Thou shalt love thy neighbour as thyself,' it is not meant, Thou shalt *love him first* and do good in consequence of that love, but thou shalt do good to thy neighbour, and this thy beneficence will engender in thee that love to mankind which is the fullness and consummation of the inclination to do good."—*Kant.*

SABBATH. "Sin keeps no Sabbaths."—*Brooks.*

"Yes, child of suffering, thou might well be sure,
He who ordained the Sabbath loves the poor.'
—*Holmes, Urania.*

"A world without a Sabbath would be like a man without a smile, like a summer without flowers, and like a homestead without a garden. It is the joyous day of the whole week."—*H. W. Beecher.*

"We never knew a man work seven days in a week who did not kill himself or kill his mind."—*Anon.*

REST:
"No lamkin by its shepherd borne,
 No dove its mate caressing,
No bondman freed, no pilgrim worn
 The grateful shade possessing;
No child clasped to its mother's heart,
 No sick man when his pains depart,
 No warrior home returning;
No man can know such perfect rest
As that which ends our weary quest,
 Our gracious Lord discerning."
—*Hillier*

LIBERTY.
"A man, till he be in Christ, is a slave; and the more free a man thinks himself to be and labours to be, the more slave he is. Why? Because the more he sins the more he is enthralled to sin."—*Sibbes.*

"The end of Christian liberty is, that being delivered from the hands of our enemies, we might serve the Lord without fear."—*Westminster Catechism.*

"He is the freeman, whom the truth makes free,
And all are slaves besides."
—*Cowper.*

POSSESSIONS.
"How shocking must thy summons be, O Death!
To him that is at ease in his possessions;
Who, counting on long years of pleasure here,
Is quite unfurnished for that world to come."
—*Blair.*

CHAPTER XXVI.

Religion as determining a Nation's Destiny.

SUGGESTIVE READINGS.

Vv. 1-13.—If ye walk in My statutes, etc. The Lord engaged to enrich them as a nation with temporal blessings and religious advantages, if, and so long as, Israel maintained allegiance to God's worship and statutes, His Sabbaths and sanctuary. He crowns the enumeration of favours relating to this life with higher assurance that He would dwell among them in all the spiritual nearness ensured by His "covenant." Our fidelity to God is the measure of our prosperity and happiness. They who fear the Lord shall not lack any good thing. Human life is so dependant, in nothing sufficient of itself, either to provide the necessities of physical being, or to ensure for the soul fitness for Divine acceptance and favour; that we may well prize the "exceeding great and precious promises," which are all ours in Christ, if we but maintain a true relationship with Him by obedience and faith. God does not ask a hard thing in what He requires: how gratefully we should yield Him our utmost in return for the riches of His grace!

Vv. 14-39.—But if ye will not hearken unto Me. A happy people, honoured and privileged so long as they were religious, could sink to lowest degradation and misery by revolt against the Lord their God. The picture of Israel's pitiable desolation and anguish delineates the awful spoliation which now sin inflicts on transgressors, and the dark terrors which will follow in the world beyond. These terrible denunciations show how aggrieved God is with human wrong doing, how He regards with abhorrence man's impious rebellion against His goodness and grace, and how heavily He will avenge it. Let sinners "fear before Him," and "kiss the Son, lest He be angry." A brilliant light casts the blackest shadows. God's great grace for unworthy men throws on those who maltreat it the darkest gloom of His indignation and wrath (Rom. ii. 8-9.)

Vv. 40-46.—If they shall confess their iniquity. Though having deeply sinned, yet, if by their miseries they return in contrition, infinite mercy would receive them again. Wondrous pity: grace abounding! "Who is a God like unto thee, that pardoneth iniquity?" It is the glory of the gospel to proclaim salvation "even unto the uttermost," and our comfort to know that "if we confess our sins, God is faithful and just to forgive us our sins, and to *cleanse us from all unrighteousness*" (1 Jno. i. 9.)

PECULIARITIES OF CHAPTER XXVI.

i. Ceremonial institutions, social regulations, and moral injunctions, have hitherto constituted the substance of the book of Leviticus. Now they yield place to PROPHETIC PROMISES AND WARNINGS concerning the nation (which extend over all after ages of Israel's career, sketching the national apostacy and overthrow, its disappearance through long centuries, and its ultimate repentance and restoration.

ii. The camp of Israel has hitherto been regarded as a sacred community surrounding the Shekinah within the Holy of Holies, with whom Jehovah was maintaining gracious relationship and hallowed fellowship, through priests and sacrifices. Now Israel is viewed as a NATION TO BE RULED BY DIVINE GOVERNMENT, with material rewards and secular blessings, affixed to loyal obedience to Jehovah's laws, and likewise secular punishment threatened in the event of revolt from the Divine sway.

iii. Although the aspect of Israel as a sacred community passes into that of a nation under Divine government, yet THE BOND OF SPECIAL AND SPIRITUAL UNION BETWEEN JEHOVAH AND ISRAEL is forcefully emphasized, and Israel's national security and prosperity are bound up with the maintenance of the Theocracy: Religion being the secret of her life and continuance.

iv. The predictions of this chapter form THE BASIS OF ALL AFTER PROPHECIES concerning the future of Israel, the very phraseology of these promises and threatenings reappearing almost literally in the messages of God's prophets in successive ages—*E.g.*,

V. 4.—" Then will I give you *rain in due season*, and the *land shall yield her increase*, and the *trees of the field shall yield their fruit*;" v. 5.—And your *threshing shall reach unto the vintage*, and the vintage shall reach unto the sowing time; and ye shall eat your bread to the full, and *dwell in your land safely*;" v. 6.—" And I will give *peace in the land*, and ye shall lie down, and none shall make you afraid; and I will rid *evil beasts out of the land*, neither shall the sword go through your land."

Compare Ezekiel xxxiv., v. 26, "I will cause the *shower to come down in his season*, there shall be showers of blessing;" v. 27.—" And the *tree of the field shall yield her fruit*, and the earth shall *yield her increase*, and they shall be *safe in their land*;" v. 25.—"I will make with them a *convenant of peace*, and will cause the *evil beasts to cease out of the land*."

Compare with v. 5, Amos ix. 13, "Behold the days come, saith the Lord, that the *ploughman shall overtake the reaper*, and the treader of grapes him that soweth seed."

Notably, let Joel ii. 19-27, be read with these verses under view. Thus v. 23, "He will cause to come down for you the *rain*, the former rain, and the latter rain in the first month;" and v. 24.—" And the floors shall be *full of wheat*, and the vats shall overflow with *wine* and oil."

v. The *providential sway of Jehovah is claimed as* ORIGINATING, AND ORDERING THESE MATERIAL FAVOURS *or distresses*, making them consequent upon the religion or irreligion of Israel, although they may be naturally accounted for as results ensuing from certain physical conditions in the land or in the nation's social development. But behind natural incidents lies the supernatural hand of God, physical laws have an invisible legislator administering them, and all the occurrences in Israel's career, bright or dark, are traced directly to Jehovah's personal dealings with His people. "If ye walk in my statutes, then *I will give you rain*" (Vv. 3-4). "*I* will have respect unto you, and make you fruitful, and multiply you, and establish my convenant with you" (v. 9), etc.

SECTIONAL HOMILIES.

Topic: THE ADVANTAGES OF RELIGION IN A NATION'S LIFE (Vv. 1-12).

"We know," says Burke (in his *Reflections on the Revolution in France*), "and, what is better, we feel inwardly, that religion is the basis of civil society, and the source of all good, and of all comfort."

To this may be added the famous testimony of Josiah Quincy (Boston, 1830): "Human happiness has no perfect security but freedom; freedom none but virtue; virtue none but knowledge; and neither freedom, nor virtue, nor knowledge has any vigour, or immortal hope, except in the principles of the Christian faith, and in the sanctities of the Christian religion" (see Addenda to chapter, *National Irreligion*).

I. WHEREIN A NATION'S RELIGIOUS LIFE CONSISTS.

The recognised presence of God in the midst of the people (Vv. 11, 12): "I will set my tabernacle among you; and I will walk among you, and will be your God, and ye shall be my people." This may be realized—

1. In *sanctuaries* consecrated to Divine worship throughout the land, and in assembled *congregations* gathering to adore Him (v. 2).
2. In *sacred literature* diffusing religious knowledge among the people.
3. In benevolent and elevating *institutions* diffusing Christianity in its practical forms.
4. In *educational* agencies for the training of children early in moral and religious truth.
5. In *homes* and *family life* sweetened by the influence of piety.
6. In a *legislature* ruled by the fear of God and observant of Scripture precepts.
7. In *wealth*, gathered righteously, being expended for evangelical and Christian ends.
8. In the *happy relationship of all social classes*, based upon goodwill and respect.
9. In the stores of *harvest* and gains of *commerce* being acknowledged as God's providential gifts and generous benefactions (Vv. 4, 5). All such public recognitions of the *authority* and the *claims* of religion, emphasize and declare that within this nation's life God dwells—known, revered, and served.

II. ADVANTAGES WHICH RESULT TO A NATION FROM RELIGION.

1. Religion impels to *industry, intelligence, self-respect,* and *social improvement*; and these will affect every branch of labour and enterprise, resulting in *material prosperity* (Vv. 4, 5).
2. Religion leads to avoidance of *agitation and conflict*, checks *greed, ambition, and vainglory*, and thus promotes a *wise content* among the people, and *peaceful relationships* with surrounding nations (v. 6).
3. Religion fosters *sobriety, energy, and courage*, and these qualities will assert themselves on the *fields of war* when sad occasion arises, and will ensure the overthrow of tyranny and the defeat of invasion (v. 8).
4. Religion nurtures the *wise oversight of homes and families*, the preservation of *domestic purity*, the development of *healthful and intelligent children*, and these will work out in a strong and increasing population (v. 9).
5. Religion corrects the intrigues of self-destructive commerce, and teaches *honesty, forethought, and justice* in business arrangements; thus checking waste, extravagance and insolence, and these issue in the *enjoyment of plenty* (v. 10).
6. Religion enjoins *Sabbath observance and sanctuary services* (v. 2) which nourish holiness in thought and life, sweeten character, purify the springs of action, incite to righteous and noble deeds, to social good will, to mutual regard, to sacred ministries, to reverence for Scripture, to recognition of the claims of the unseen world, and thus bring down upon all people the *blessings of God*, the Father, the Son, and the Holy Spirit (Vv. 11, 12).

How can religion fail to convey benefits of every valuable order to society and the whole nation when it makes the individual a nobler, kinder, purer, Godlier man? That land is enriched in which dwells a people whose individual character may be sketched thus:

> I venerate a man whose heart is warm,
> Whose hands are pure, whose doctrines and whose life
> Coincident, exhibit lucid proof
> That he is honest in the Sacred Cause.—*Cowper.*

III. WITHIN A RELIGIOUS NATION GOD PLEDGES HIMSELF TO DWELL.
And where He makes His tabernacle (v. 11) there—
1. *Happiness* will be realised, the joy of the Lord will be known, " His loving kindness, which is more than life," will be enjoyed.
2. *Security* will be assured. "None make you afraid" (v. 6), for He will be as a " defence to His people."
3. *Sanctity* will flourish. Intercourse with God (v. 12) will elevate, refine, and grace a people's character and life. "Happy the people in such a case, yea, happy the people whose God is the Lord."

Topic: THE BLESSING AND THE CURSE (Vv. 3-14).

Throughout Leviticus the voice of mercy sounds; for what is mercy but a remedy for woe? At Sinai's base grace sweetly smiles; for what is grace but safety for the lost? These final words from God have an awakening import. There is a seriousness in parting words. Last admonitions usually sink deep.

Ere the tribes advance to Canaan, God seeks to admonish and impress. Truly when sinners rush to ruin they *strive against a warning God*, they stop their ears, they set their faces like flint, they harden their necks. Here God adjoins paternal counsels to a Sovereign's command. He shows what blessings crown obedient paths, what miseries beset the rebel-way.

I. ALLURING PROMISES.

Unfold the roll (vv. 3-13). It is a picture in which plenteousness abounds:—
The earth in season yields luxuriant stores. Peace waves her gentle sceptre. No invading hosts scare the quiet vales. No ravening beasts watch for prey. If assailing armies dare make attack, they advance to sure defeat. A little band puts multitudes to flight. A happy progeny rejoices in each house. These are external gifts.

Spiritual delights are scattered with copious hand. God's presence is assured. His near abode is among His people. He claims them as His own (v. 12). He gives Himself to them.

Such are the blessings pledged if His statutes are observed. Could any hear, yet choose the rebel path?

II. TREMENDOUS THREATS.

The scene now changes. Peal follows peal of terrifying awe (vv. 14—39). The disobedient must prepare for appalling miseries:—

Health shall wither: pining malady, sore disease, and racking pain shall prey upon the tortured frame.

Famine shall raise its ghastly form: penury shall sit at every hearth.

Nature shall not yield increase: no crops shall spring from sown seed, the trees shall mock with fruitless boughs.

Savage life shall ravage: children and cattle shall be mangled in the roads, and the homesteads become solitary.

War shall rage: the hostile banner deride the fallen city.

The holy *sanctuary* should be no refuge: its offerings God would refuse.

Such is the heritage if God's covenant be not kept.

III. FORESHADOWED DOOM REALISED.

God's word is sure. Performance follows.

1. Israel madly scorned His sway. They rashly followed their own hearts desire.

2. Threatened vengeance fell. Witness the desolation of their bounteous land and the tribes scattered through the world's breadth. The sterile plains at home, the outcast wanderers abroad, bear witness that the doom predicted comes.

IV. A SPIRITUAL ALLEGORY.

1. A picture is given of the *fair land of grace.* The obedience of faith wins the full possession of that beauteous inheritance which Christ purchased for His redeemed. And faith finds *abundance* in the land of grace. Surely that life is blessed which gains all-sufficiency in Christ's perfect righteousness, renewing power, plenteous redemption, unspeakable peace. "All things are yours, for ye are Christ's." Supplies of grace are lavishly given; the heavens come down in showers of goodness.

2. But *a fearful contrast* appears. Crowds upon crowds refuse to obey; slight the Saviour's charms. Therefore sins remain. The world enslaves. Troubles abound. Misery steeps your life. If you look upward the heavens are barred; God frowns; each attribute condemns. Friends bring no peace; foes wound, and no balm heals. Life is a misery, death plunges into deeper woe, eternity is hell.

When God's grace is scorned, when His precious Son is crucified afresh, Mercy can show no mercy, pardon cannot release. The heritage of unbelief is one unmitigated curse.

The blessing and the curse are set side by side. So sweetly *point the blessing* that eager souls will grasp it. So awfully *pronounce the curse* that alarmed sinners may dread it. Happy souls are they, who, yielding obedience to the persuasions of Almighty goodness, inherit the blessing.

Partly evolved from Dean Law's " Christ is All."

Topic : NATIONAL TRANSGRESSION AND DISASTER (Vv. 14-19).

For 770 years before they were literally fulfilled in their bitter experience, these appalling warnings, graphic and minute in their details, were in the hands of the Hebrew nation, were continuously read in their hearing as a voice of entreaty that they would cleave to the Lord their God. But "because sentence is not executed speedily, therefore the heart of the sons of men is fully set in them to do evil" (Eccles. viii. 12).

Yet *deferred sentence,* both
1. *Manifests the Divine patience* and His unwillingness to smite; and
2. *Prolongs man's opportunity* to forsake evil and find mercy.

Nevertheless: "The Lord is not slack concerning His promise"; He does not relax because He delays. The storm only gathers greater violence when long pent up. Here is vividly delineated

I. A NATION'S PROGRESSIVE APOSTASY.

1. *Passive indifference* to divine teachings and appeals (v. 14). Mental obliquity or wilful inattention to the known will of God. This mere listlessness is commonly the first downward step: "Ye will *not hearken* unto *Me.*" To this non-attention next succeeds,

2. *Non-compliance* with divine calls and claims (v. 14). "Will *not do all* these commandments." Practical resistance of God's authority: "We will not have this man to reign over us." Not as yet profane rebellion, but settled unconcern and neglect. This leads forward to,

3. *Contemptuous rejection* of God's statutes. "Ye shall *despise* My statutes" (v. 15). Pride lifts the heart into dislike and derision of sacred regulations and requirements. "Who is the Lord that I should serve Him?" "It is vain to serve God," etc. (Malachi iii. 14, 15).

4. *Spiritual revolt* from all sacred demands. "Your *soul abhor* my judgments" (v. 15). "For every one that doeth evil *hateth* the light," etc. (Jno. iii. 20). "These are they that rebel against the light" (Job xxiv. 13). It is the soul's loathing of all holy rule and heavenly allurement. It argues a fearful departure from God. How great a fall was that!

5. Violation of all covenant relationship. "Ye break my covenant" (v. 15). It severs all bonds between the soul and God; denies His right to command; rejects Him utterly—in atheistic scorn, in wilful rebellion. The "thing made" disowns Him who made it.

Notes: (a) Such decline from God, whether by communities or individuals, only occurs by *progressive stages.* The wreck is not instantaneous. The castle falls not a ruin by one stroke; it wastes by the process of dilapidation—stone from stone; crumbles to decay.

(b) This decline from God is not allowed to proceed without *gracious efforts* made to arrest its course. God sent His prophets to plead and warn, His judgments to awaken, His providential mercies to win, His sanctuary privileges to allure. A sinner goes from God amid pathetic pleadings and arresting importunities: "Turn ye, turn ye from your evil ways; for why will ye die?"

II. AN APOSTATE NATION'S CALAMITIES.

1. Sin brings *disease* and *physical suffering* in its train (v. 16): "Terror, consumption, and the burning ague, that shall consume the eyes and cause sorrow of heart." Impiety inevitably drifts into *impurity*. When God is rejected, the "lusts of the flesh and the eyes and the mind" dominate. And in physical degradation, defilement, and decay the fruits of sin are reaped. "Destruction and misery are in their way." These are the *natural* consequences of sin; but God smote Israel with *supernatural* afflictions.

2. *Failure and penury* follow quickly upon habits of indulgence and impurity. "Sow your seed in vain, for your enemies shall eat it" (v. 16). Nothing succeeds in the hands of a dissipated and dissolute man; and he becomes a prey to his hated scorners and rivals. There was a peculiar fulfilment to Israel of this threat; for God laid their land open to the incursions of predatory tribes and despotic spoilers, by which the people were continually wasted.

3. A godless life invites the *ravages of the enemy* (v. 17). God withdrew His protection, and adversaries swept down upon Israel. They who repudiate Divine government are "taken captive by the devil at his will," and serve their enemies. *Sin is very cruel.* It "*slays*" its victims; slaughters their virtue, peace, happiness, hopes; detroys precious souls.

4. Sin also *fills the life of wrong-doers with terrors*: they "flee when none pursueth." Even in *nations* there is "strong confidence" and "a sound mind" only when conscious of rectitude and the enjoyment of God's approval. It paralyses a people's heart to feel that Heaven is alienated and Divine favour lost. *Armies*, too, have gone with assurance into battles when convinced that God is with them; as Cromwell's "Ironsides": while enemies have *fled with panic*, as did the Spanish Armada, when possessed with alarm that God was against them.

5. There are the yet darker calamities of *abject overthrow and Divine desertion*: "I will break the pride of your power, and I will make your heaven as iron, and your earth as brass" (v. 19)—a picture of *prostration and helplessness* which finds verification in

(a) *Babylon's fall*: now lying buried amid bleaching sands, emblem of rebuked pride.

(b) *The desolation of Jerusalem:* now a waste scene, and her children the "tribes of the wandering foot and weary breast."

(c) *The buried cities of Pompeii and Herculaneum:* interred beneath volcanic ashes, a monument of sudden wrath on a voluptuous people.

Such historic admonitions—*Warn against National Impiety*, and *Call mankind to seriousness and prayer.* For even in the solemn threatenings of God, there lies an overt assurance of mercy, that "if a nation or individual will cease from apostacy and sin and *hearken unto Him*" (v. 18), He will turn aside the "seven times more" punishment for sins, and show the forgiveness in which He delights, and the salvation which the glorious gospel of His grace proclaims. (See Addenda to chapter, *National Irreligion*).

Topic: DESOLATION UPON ISRAEL (Vv. 29-39).

Though chosen in grace, and pledged in covenant, as God's people ; though being led miraculously to Canaan, to be settled in the goodly land ; yet an alarming picture of woe and ruin is outspread whose realisation seemed incredible.

I. HOW HORRIFYING THE MISERIES WHICH MAY BEFALL A PRIVILEGED PEOPLE.
The miseries of *penury and siege* (v. 29) ; of *captivity and slaughter* (v. 33) ; of *anguish and derision* (v. 36) ; of pitiless *misery and disaster* (v. 39).

1. None are so *secure* in grace and privilege that they can disregard the possibility of a fall.
2. None are so *rich* in sacred favours as to be beyond danger of their total loss.
3. None are so *honoured* by God's selecting and distinguishing grace but they may lapse into alienation and desolation.

II. HOW AMAZING THE DISASTERS WHICH MAY DEVASTATE A BEAUTIFUL COUNTRY.
Canaan was a wealthy land, a scene of loveliness, abundance and delight. Yet on it came the disasters of *depopulation* (v. 31) : *sterility* (v. 32) ; *desertion* (v 35)—even enemies abandoning it.

1. National *plenty and prosperity* are conditional upon national righteousness and piety.
2. National *greatness and glory* have been withered by the anger of an insulted God.
3. National *strength and safety* are only guaranteed as religion is fostered by the laws of a country, and in the habits and lives of its people.

III. HOW PITEOUS THE PROFANATION WHICH MAY DESPOIL A NATION'S SANCTITIES !
Canaan was the scene of Jehovah's sanctuary : the Temple rose on Zion ; and the land sent up her tribes to the celebration of sacred feasts and to the holy worship of God. Yet all her "*sanctuaries*" were brought "*unto desolation*" (v. 31), all the fragrance of *her sacrifices became loathsome* to Jehovah (v. 31), and her *desecrated Sabbaths* were avenged in the bleak silence and loneliness which fell on hallowed scenes (v. 34).

1. Religious favours, if abused, may be utterly withdrawn from us.
2. God loathes the offerings once delightful to Him : when the offerer's love is estranged.
3. Holy scenes and holy days become a barren mockery if a trifling spirit alienate the sacred Presence :—" Ichabod !"

Topic: THE LOST TRIBES OF ISRAEL (Vv. 38-39).

" Ye shall perish among the heathen, and the land of your enemies shall eat you up. And they that are left of you shall pine away in their iniquity in your enemies' land : and also in the iniquities of their fathers shall they pine away with them."

Does this threat import the *complete extermination* of the outcast Israel ? Are the exiles from Palestine literally "*eaten up*" in the land of their enemies ? What are the rival theories ?

1. THAT THE OUTCAST TRIBES OF ISRAEL ABSOLUTELY PERISHED IN THE LANDS OF THEIR CAPTIVITY : that they have ceased to be a distinct people ; that they or their descendants are not to be discovered in any portion of the globe ; and that, therefore, there is no possibility or hope of their recovery.

Against this theory it is to be urged that,
1. This threat applies equally to Judah and Israel ; and that as certainly *Judah is not exterminated,* so equally it is probable that *Israel,* though not discovered, is *still existing.*

2. That as *nineteen centuries have not sufficed to extinguish* the Jewish part of the original Hebrew nation, so neither can it be thought that the *preceding eight centuries,* from the Assyrian captivity till the Christian age, would effect the obliteration of the Israelitish tribes.

3. That as it was predicted of the Israelitish tribes that they should be "*lost*" *from sight* (2 Kings xviii. 18), whereas the Jewish tribes were to be preserved as a *visible witness* among the nations, the *non-discovery of the lost ten tribes* is as literal a part of God's plan as the distinctive preservation of the Jew.

4. That there are promises of God which *absolutely affirm Israel's ultimate discovery and restoration* equally with Judah's.

Therefore this threat must be *equally applied to all the twelve tribes,* and can only mean their *destruction as a distinct nation.*

ii. *That the* LONG AND MOURNFUL OBLITERATION OF THE HEBREW NATION, AS A JUDGMENT, WILL ISSUE IN ITS FINAL MIRACULOUS RE-GATHERING. For,

1. The *covenant of God with the whole nation ensures their imperishableness.*

2. The threat of obliteration is qualified by the *promise of recovery and restoration, if they should repent* (Vv. 41, 42). [Compare Deut. iv. 27, 31].

3. It is *pledged here absolutely* that, though driven away in exile, *God would not* Himself "cast them away," "*nor utterly destroy them*" (v. 44); because His "*covenant*" with them must stand (Rom. xi. 2).

Topic: FUNDAMENTALS IN TRUE RELIGION (Vv. 1, 2).

Israel was ever prone to depart from the living God, to forget His commandments. Hence the need of frequent reiteration of the divine precepts. The inculcation of statutes respecting fundamentals in religion comes very suitably here, enforcing Jehovah's claim to sole and supreme worship. Thus Israel was solemnly reminded —

I. OF THE PERSON *to whom alone religious worhip should be presented.*

The light of nature and our inner consciousness suggest that the author of all things, our Creator and King, ought to be reverently worshipped; but they do not teach us whether or not He will accept our worship, nor what kind of worship He requires. In Levitical ritual the needed information was given, not only as to what He would accept, but what He righteously demanded. No idol of any kind was to be set up in Canaan. No material object could fairly represent the invisible and eternal Lord. Idolatry degrades and brutalises men; men never rise above their ideals. Idolatry is an insult to the only true and living God. The only image of the invisible God ever presented to the world was the Man Christ Jesus. "Great is the mystery of godliness; God was manifest in the flesh," etc. Nothing short of the living God can satisfy the longing of the human heart. All his needs are fully met in the person and work of Christ.

II. OF THE TIME *most favourable for the presentation of religious worship.*

Worship is the *duty, privilege,* and *prerogative* of man at all times. His very work should be done in such a fervent and devout spirit that it may be worship, and all worldly service so performed that it may partake of the character of sacrament. But there are times when worship may be more full and devout: such are the divinely-appointed and weekly-occurring Sabbaths. They arrest the rush and roar of secular life. The hallowed associations of the day, the opportunity for public communion and fellowship suggest and foster reverence. The Sabbath reminds man that he has a soul to care for; and divine life in the individual and nation is generally concurrent with the extent to which the day of holy convocation is observed. Let the Sabbath be neglected and desecrated and at once the way is open for all kinds of irreligion and iniquity. The people were also reminded,

III. OF THE PLACE *where religious worship is the most acceptable to the Lord.*

Under the old dispensation God appointed certain spots and localities, where He would meet His people, and consecrated certain buildings as His audience chambers: among such places were the Tabernacle and Temple. "He loved the gates of Zion more than all the dwellings of Jacob," and spake glorious things of his own favourite city. The devout heart, nevertheless, could find any place a "house of God" and "gate of heaven" when God saw fit to make Himself known, as he did to the Patriarchs, especially to Jacob at Bethel. It aided men in worship, and gave them courage and confidence in seeking the Lord to know that He was to be found "*always at home,*" as it were, in some places, and ready to manifest Himself, as He did, not *to the world* or *out in the world*. Reverence for special sacred places among the Jews was not superstition; Christ paid respect to the Temple, and twice showed His indignation at its profanation by expelling the unholy traders. Though under the new dispensation we have no Tabernacle or Temple, as of old, yet our meeting-places for prayer and praise are sanctuaries of the Lord, for He has promised to meet with those who gather together in His name, even though there be but two or three. The Divine presence consecrates the house where believers meet, and earthly worship may become preparatory to the worship of heaven, where "the Lord God Almighty and the Lamb are the Temple of it."—*F. W. B.*

Topic: INCENTIVES TO TRUE RELIGION (Vv. 3, 42).

The injunctions of this chapter are contemporaneous with, and confirmatory of, the laws contained in the Book of Exodus, especially of the Ten Commandments given on the tables of stone. The people were evidently not elected to unconditional favours and salvation; they are addressed as free and accountable agents, in a state of trial, and passing through a period of probation. It was merciful and just to acquaint Israel of the conditions of service and stewardship, to warn them from evil doing, to excite them to holy living. Notice,

I. THE BLESSINGS PROMISED TO OBEDIENCE.

To those who would walk in the statutes of the Lord and keep His commandments, there would be vouchsafed,

1. *Temporal blessings.* (*a*) *Seasons of plenty*; (*b*) *Times of tranquility*; (*c*) *Joys of society.* Thus their physical and social wants would be met, their minds kept in peace, their hearts and homes filled with joy.

2. *Spiritual blessings.* (*a*) *The Lord would own them;* be their Friend and King; (*b*) *The Lord would dwell among them.* These were blessings and honours enjoyed by no other nations, and which laid upon Israel commensurate responsibility. The Lord would be with them, and bless them abundantly, if only they would walk in His statutes. The Gospel does not destroy the moral teaching of the law; Antinomianism is not taught in the New Testament. Christ comes to and blesses those who love His commandments and do them, and will pronounce His final approval upon those who have in this life, not simply believed, but "*well done.*"

II. THE PUNISHMENT THREATENED TO DISOBEDIENCE.

Here we have held out the red danger-light, the warning beacon, that the people might be deterred from breaking the divine laws. When the Lord entered into judgment with His people, they could plead no excuse, they had His mind and will made known repeatedly. In this chapter to the disobedient are threatened—(*a*) *Physical and mental sufferings*; (*b*) *Useless labour*; (*c*) *Ignominious defeat*; (*d*) *Aggravated sorrows*; (*e*) *Degradation*; (*f*) *Desolation*; (*g*) *Destruction.* Thus they would be chastised, and almost exterminated, if they turned from God and gave themselves up to iniquity.

We are here taught the doctrine of a *righteous retributive Providence*. The world is under, not only the natural, but the moral government of God. In this world God visits the sins of nations, and sometimes the sins of individuals— this is *a* place, though it is not *the* place of punishment. The covenants of the Lord with men have always been *conditional;* to obey has been to live; to disobey has been to die. While Israel obeyed, as in the days of Solomon, the blessing of this chapter came upon them; but when they forsook the Lord and gave themselves up to every kind of iniquity, the judgments denounced here were literally fulfilled. To-day the land of Canaan lies waste; and the Jews are scattered to the four winds of heaven. Blessing and curse are set before us in the gospel. Life or death depend on our choice. "The wages of sin is death, but the gift," etc.—*F. W. B.*

Topic: The Bow in the Cloud (Vv. 42-45).

In the hope held out to the rebellious, and the mercy promised to the penitent at the end of this chapter, we see how the Lord delighteth in mercy, how slow He is to anger, and plenteous in goodness and truth. For though the people should rebel and bring upon themselves all the threatened punishments; yet if they would repent and confess humbly their sins, the blessings promised to obedience should come upon them to replace the punishments, as they again took delight in the commandments of the Lord. On the black cloud that hung threateningly over the land, there fell rays of hope, a bow of promise arched the darkest sky. "The Lord was not willing that any should perish, but that all should come to repentance." These verses show,

I. That the way was left open for the rebellious to return.

1. *It was the way of reflection.* They were to look back upon the wrong doing of their lives, and see how far they had deflected from the good old way, how they had been guilty of dereliction of duty.

2. *It was the way of confession.* They were to feel sorry for their sins, and confess and acknowledge their iniquity.

3. *It was the way of humiliation.* They were not to return proudly, feeling they had not been rewarded according to their iniquities. The way is still open for the vilest to return; for, the New Testament teaches that these are the steps in the ladder of life, out of sin to holiness, from earth to heaven, from self to God, viz.: *Repentance, conversion, consecration.*

II. That if the rebellious returned to the Lord in His own appointed way, He would graciously receive them.

1. *He would do so for the sake of their fathers.* He would remember His covenant with Abraham, Isaac, and Jacob.

2. *He would do so for the sake of His name.* "For I am the Lord." He had purposed, as well as promised, to deal mercifully with them.

3. *He would do so for the sake of the land.* He had selected Canaan as the arena where He would specially display His glory to men, and He would not allow it to lie waste for ever.

4. *He would do it for the sake of His covenant.* "I will remember my covenant." The Lord does not make a covenant and then tear it rashly to pieces; if broken by man He will speedily renew, nor allow the irregularities and irreligion of men to thwart His beneficent arrangements. Here, indeed, was a resplendent bow of many colours, beaming with the beautiful light of the mild and merciful countenance of the Most High.

What encouragement for sinful men to return to the Lord, "for He will have mercy upon them, and abundantly pardon." The Levitical Law closes with offers of mercy, the last words of the Law are words of entreaty and promise.

Glad tidings reached the ears of Israel in the desert. The object of the Law was to restrain from sin and restore from its practice and power. Design of Law and Gospel identical; the tree of life has its roots deep down in the soil of the old economy. God's written word *is natural religion vocalised*, and Christianity is Judaism fulfilled, in the final declaration of how sins may be forgiven. This truth could not be learned from Nature, and was only symbolically and typically taught by Moses. Whosoever will, may come now and take of the water of life freely.—*F. W. B.*

OUTLINES ON VERSES OF CHAPTER XXVI.

V. 1.—*Theme:* IDOLATRY INTERDICTED.

The Israelites, having been surrounded by idolators during their sojourn in Egypt, would be in danger of yielding to the influence such surroundings would exert upon them, even when in the presence of circumstances calculated to keep alive constant recognition of the only true and living God. Hence the repetition needed of injunctions against all idol worship; indeed, the whole system of Judaism rests upon the sublime truth, there is but one God. Let us inquire—

I. WHAT THE PRONENESS OF HUMAN NATURE TO IDOLATRY SUGGESTS.

It shows both the dignity and depravity of man; that—

(*a*) *He is endowed with religious instincts.* Capable of worship, of exercising faith, hope, love, reverence, fear, etc.

(*b*) *He is conscious of amenability to some supreme power.* Seeks to propitiate, secure favour, and aid.

(*c*) *He is apprehensive of a future state of existence.* Ideas vague, indefinite, absurd, yet the outcome of inward presentiment, etc.

(*d*) *He is unable by light of nature to discover God.* His knowledge is so faded, light so dim. How low the soul must have fallen to substitute "nothings" for the Eternal One! *Heathenism has never of itself emerged into the light of the knowledge of the glory of God,* as seen in the voice that has spoken from heaven, and has been recorded by holy men moved by the Holy Ghost.

II. WHAT INDULGENCE IN IDOLATRY ENTAILS.

(*a*) *Degradation.* Worship of heathen deities demoralising. In their temples, at their services, the rites observed are grovelling, and, in some instances, *demoniacal.*

(*b*) *Superstition.* Devotees are duped by priests, enslaved by torturing ritualism, subject and victims of absurd delusions.

(*c*) *Misery.* Fear the ruling passion, not love. Nothing ennobling, inspiring, quickening, comforting. Idol worship mocks the longings of the human soul, cannot appease its hunger, satisfy its thirst.

III. HOW IDOLATRY MAY BE ABOLISHED.

Darkness can only be dispersed by the letting in of light. The folly of idolatry must be shown, its helplessness, misery, sin by the spread of the written revelation of heaven, the preaching of the glorious Gospel. Israel, by its worship of Jehovah, was a living protest against all idolatry; and the Christian Church is commissioned to proclaim the gospel among all nations, that the kingdoms of this world may become the kingdoms of our God and of His Christ. *No person, place, or thing* must come between our souls and God, or have the faith, hope, love, trust that are due only to Him. We are guilty of idolatry if we regard anything as a *representative of,* or *substitute for Him.* What we supremely love and live for *is our God.* Christ is God, we ought, therefore, to live to Him.—*F. W. B.*

Vv. 3, 14.—*Theme:* THE EQUITY OF GOD'S WAYS. "*If ye walk in my statutes*....... *then,*" etc. (v. 3). "*But if ye will not*..... *I will,*" etc. (v. 14).

Natural religion teaches us that the government of the author of nature is retributive. Revealed religion teaches analogous truth in other realms of the divine procedure. Penal consequences of wrong-doing act as warnings against sin, and awaken regret for transgression. Retribution is—

I. UNIVERSAL. Everywhere, and in all time, the transgression of God's laws entails, in some way, penalty.

II. REMEDIAL.

Intended to prevent defiance of heaven, usurpation of divine sovereignty. Pain has a merciful ministry. The peace and satisfaction virtue and obedience bring are a proof that God is holy and on the side of goodness. Israel was shown not only that God demanded worship and loyalty on account of what He is in Himself, but because of what they would secure for all who lived in harmony with His revealed will. Hence the *positive commands* in connection with the Levitical ritual were supplemented by *persuasives* to a holy life. Inducements were held out to win obedience, threatenings pronounced to deter from transgression. Thus the people were taught that Jehovah was not arbitrary and despotic, but merciful as well as just, unconditionally excluding none from the blessing of the covenant made to their fathers.

Not only was *the sovereignty of God* revealed to Israel, but *the prerogative of choice in man,* by which he is distinguished from all inanimate things and irrational creatures. In the gospel these truths are republished with additional clearness and power. Christ invites to supreme blessedness; those who remain unblest are those who will not come unto Him that they may have life, who destroy themselves, reap what they sow. Thus the ways of God are just and right, and will so be acknowledged at last before an assembled universe.—F. W. B.

V. 8.—*Theme*: VALOUR AND VICTORY THROUGH GODLINESS.

"Five of you shall chase an hundred, and an hundred of you shall put ten thousand to flight; and your enemies shall fall before you by the sword."

[See addenda to chapter, *Valour*].

I. *Religion begets a* DAUNTLESS ARDOUR.

A fervent enthusiasm is awakened, which defies obstacles, perils, foes.

Proved by the heroes of faith (Heb. xi.); by the sufferings of Huguenots Puritans, and Covenanters; by the records of martyrdom.

II. *Religion imparts an* INTREPID CONFIDENCE.

They who have God on their side, see armies of horses and chariots fighting with them (2 Kings vi. 17.); so as to realize that "they that be with us are more than they that be against us." And John Wesley's strong boast becomes their motto: "The best of all is, *God is for us*."

III *Religion animates with* STRONG CONSOLATION.

Foes may be many, and life may be beset with devices of evil; yet this is the stay of the believer, "No weapon that is formed against thee shall prosper" (Is. liv. 17).

IV. *Religion ensures a* GLORIOUS VICTORY.

Adversaries, however numerous, shall flee. Peace shall be realized, not by complicity with the world, nor compromise with enemies, but by their vanquishment. "We are more than conquerors through Him that loveth us:" and even *now* our pæon shout is this, "Thanks be unto God who always causeth us to triumph in Christ"; while *beyond death* this shall be our record: "They overcome by the blood of the Lamb."

V. 10.—*Theme*: EMMANUEL AMID HIS PEOPLE.

"*I will set my tabernacle among you.*"

I. AMID THE NATION ON ZION rested the SHEKINAH.

"In Salem is His tabernacle, and His dwelling place in Zion" (Psa. lxxvi. 2).

II. INCARNATE ON EARTH dwelt the *Lord Jesus.*

"The Word was made flesh and dwelt among us" (John i 14).

III. ENSHRINED IN LOWLY HEARTS abides the *Holy Spirit.*

"He shall abide with you for ever" (John xiv. 17).

IV. ETERNALLY AMID THE GLORIFIED is manifested the glad presence of GOD.

"I heard a great voice out of heaven, saying, Behold the tabernacle of God is with men, and He will dwell with them, and they shall be His people, and God Himself shall be with them, and be their God" (Rev. xxi. 3).

V 13.—*Theme*: EMANCIPATED AND ELEVATED.

"*I have broken the bands of your yoke, and made you go upright.*"

I. FREED FROM OLD ENSLAVEMENTS: such is the initial act of redeeming grace, "Being made free from sin," "Christ hath made us free," "The Lord's free men."

II. DELIVERANCE THE PREPARATION FOR RIGHTEOUSNESS.

The "yoke broken" is not the end; it sets the life free that it may "*go upright*"; in rectitude of conduct, in elevation of desire and aim; in uplifted longings and affections; in righteousness and holiness of spirit.

III. DIVINE SOURCE OF MAN'S REDEMPTION.

"Old things have passed away; behold all things are become new: *and all things are of God.* *He* is the emancipator from old sins, He our sufficiency for an "upright" walk.

"I am the Lord *your God*, which brought you forth out of the land of Egypt, that ye should not be their bondmen: and *I have broken* the bands of your yoke, and *made you go* upright." (See 1 Cor. i. 30.) "But *of Him* are ye in Christ Jesus," etc.

V. 17.—*Theme*: THE COWARDICE OF GUILT.

"Ye shall flee when none pursue you."

I. GOODNESS DESPISES SUCH SERVILITY.

A righteous soul scorns cringing, and counts fear a degradation of soul and a dishonour to his avowed faith in God. It is weak and unmanly.

"There is," says Montaigne, "but one thing of which I am afraid, and that is fear."

And most truly.

"To fear the foe, since fear oppresseth strength.
Gives, in your weakness, strength unto your foe."—*Richard II.*, iii 2.

II. GODLINESS RECTIFIES SUCH COWARDICE.

By showing what *resources* the soul has in God, and by embracing the *promises*, which assure him of all grace and strength equal to his day. "Who is he that shall harm you, if ye be followers of that which is good?"

Froude says, "Courage is, on all hands, considered as an essential of high character."

"The *righteous* are bold as a lion." In God's favour the soul dwells confident.

III. GUILT RENDERS SOULS CRAVEN.

Fear is the black spectre ever before the ungodly.

"Cowards die many times before their deaths."—*Julius Cæsar*, ii. 2.

Sinners "*flee*" from purity, salvation, Heaven; driven by their lusts, their folly, and their guilt to sin, to danger and to doom.

V. 17.—*Theme*: PRIDE CRUSHED.

"I will break the pride of your power."

I. *Carnal pride* BASES ITSELF ON FALSE TRUSTS.

The "*power*" of these Hebrews, what was

it? They beguiled and deluded themselves by imagining themselves strong and secure.

So sinners rest elate on satisfaction with their *health*, their *possessions*, their *self esteem*.

II. *Carnal pride* OFFENDS AGAINST ALL DIVINE TEACHINGS.

Every dealing of Jehovah with this people taught that they were nought in themselves; all they were God had made them.

Pride is *despicable* in those who owe everything to Divine pity and grace. It is specially *offensive* to Him who has "wrought all our works in us"; for "what have we that we have not *received?*"

III *Carnal pride* LEADS TO MOST RASH IMPIETY.

It led Israel to disregard Divine warnings, to indulge their own wayward inclinations, to disbelieve God and substitute idols after their own vain conceits; and thus to sever themselves from God's covenant of protection and peace.

Pride still rejects Christ; grieves the Holy Spirit; and "goeth before destruction."

IV. *Carnal pride* ASSUREDLY MUST BE CONTEMNED.

God will put it to shame. "I will break the pride of your power."

By sickness—laying us even with the dust. *By losses*—desolating us of all our boasted gains.

By terrors—filling the soul with horror and forebodings.

By death—stripping us of earth's frivolous glory, and brings us face to face with the realities of righteousness and judgment.

[See Addenda to chapter, *Pride crushed*].

Vv. 23, 24.—*Theme*: OBSTINACY PUNISHED.
I. THE CHARACTER DESCRIBED.

One who persists obstinately in evil courses: "*will not be reformed.*" This may apply to 1. A nation; 2. An individual.

Such obstinacy may be the effect of

(1). A proud confidence in human wisdom and resources.

(2) A rooted love of sin.

It betrays

(1). Great blindness of mind.

(2). Great hardness of heart.

II. THE DIVINE PROCEDURE *in relation thereto.*

1. *Opposition*. "I will walk contrary," etc. Nature and Providence armed against the rebellious.

2. *Punishment:* which will be,

(1) Severe; (2) Proportionate; (3) Increasing.—*J. Comper Gray.*

*** Compare also Outline on Vv. 27, 28 below.

Vv. 27-28.—*Theme*: GOD'S DETERMINATION TO PUNISH SINNERS.

"And if ye will not for all this hearken unto Me, but walk contrary unto Me, then will I walk contrary unto you also in fury."

I. AN AFFECTING SUPPOSITION STATED.

The Lord here supposes that His people may commit *three* grevious sins:

1. The sin of *disobedience*. "If *ye will not hearken* unto Me." Hence observe—

(*a*) That the Lord in His word *speaks to us* (Heb. viii. 12).

(*b*) That whatever the Lord says in His Word it is our bounden duty to hear (Heb. iii. 7; 1 Thess. v. 20; James i. 19).

(*c*) That we are too apt to turn a deaf ear to Him (Exod. v. 2; Psa. xii. 4).

2. The sin of *incorrigibleness*. "If *for all this* ye will not hearken." Note here—

(*a*) That afflictions sometimes have the nature of punishments (Jer. xiii 21).

(*b*) That punishment is the natural and necessary consequence of transgression.

(*c*) That in the punishment which God inflicts He seeks our reformation (2 Chron. xviii. 22).

(*d*) That our depravity in too many cases frustrates His designs (Zeph. iii. 2).

3. The sin of *perverseness*. "If ye walk *contrary* to Me." Observe again—

(*a*) That the Lord's pleasure is, we should walk with Him (Mic. vi. 8).

(*b*) That we walk with the Lord when we walk in His way (2 Kgs. xx. 3; Eccles. xii. 13).

(*c*) That walking otherwise than He has commanded is to show a perverse and untoward heart.

II. AN AWFUL CONSEQUENCE DECLARED.

"I will walk contrary also to you in fury." Thus we see that

1. *Conformable to our character will be our end.*

If God should deal thus with us

(*a*) We shall lose the blessing which He imparts to His obedient followers (vv. 4-12).

(*b*) Our expectations will issue in disappointment and vexation (Hos. vii. 7); and

(*c*) Like chaff before the wind we shall speedily be carried to destruction (Psa. i. 4, 5).

2. Enforcement of these considerations: We see

(*a*) That a religion consisting of mere notions will never save a man.

(*b*) That men are not at liberty, as some suppose, to live as they please.

(*c*) That God takes notice of the ways of all.

(*d*) That if He displays His anger we should be anxious to find out the cause; and

(*e*) That if anyone perish he will have no one to *blame for it but himself* (Isa. iii. 11).— *Wm. Sleigh.*

V. 34.—*Theme*: SABBATH BARRENNESS.

"Then shall the land *enjoy her Sabbaths*, as long as it *lieth desolate*, and *ye be in your enemies' land;* even then shall the land rest, and enjoy her Sabbaths."

God had required that Sabbatical years should be observed, during which the land should rest; no tillage or harvest work being done. Owners of the soil would disregard this enactment, thinking they would benefit by making the land yield its produce through these Sabbath years. For this sin against God's ordinance, the people would forfeit occupancy of the land, and pine in exile. " *Then* shall the land enjoy her Sabbaths."

1. SABBATH ABUSE.

This abuse consisted in turning God's sabbath into a time of selfish gain.

1. The *interval of rest* is not only *genial* but *essential.*

2. To *invade that interval* by exacting toils is to *violate a benignant ordinance* and to *outrage God's right of control.*

3. All *infringement of Sabbatic rest* is both a *folly* and a *profanation ;* for greed defeats itself in this undue exaction of return, whether from man or soil.

4. The Sabbath repose was designed to give *leisure for sacred interests* and the service of God. Man's spiritual life needs the pause.

5. The intrusion of selfish and covetous schemes into the holy period is the assertion of *self-will* to the rejection of God's will ; the enthronement of self in the supremacy claimed by God ; thus " serving the creature more than the Creator."

II. SABBATH DESOLATION.

God will refute such impious greed, such selfish effrontery. In the experience of these Israelites He *cast off from the soil* those who robbed it of the Sabbatic rest, and He *gave full requital* to the land in the years of depopulation.

1. *Desolate Sabbaths are still requited* upon transgressors.

Men neglect the holy day, in scorn of Heaven's blest law ; and do their own work and think their own thoughts through its sacred hours. As a fact *in human experience now,* God requites this wrong upon sinners in a *restless life*, a *weary heart*, a *troubled conscience*, a *shadowed happiness.*

2. Even *God's children suffer exile* from sacred scenes and Sabbath privileges.

In days of health they trifled with their Sabbaths ; spent them in indulgence rather than in earnest zeal and hallowed communion ; even desecrating in part the sacred hours by selfish enjoyments or worldly concerns. This sin lies at the door of professedly Christian people to-day ; *God's day is misused.* There will come afflictions—the exile time, when the soul will cry out for the living God, to " appear before God ;" and in *Sabbaths spent in pain and banishment, in restless discomfort of soul,* God will requite the wrong.

3. *Unblest Sabbaths* have their explanation in this law of requital. The sanctuary services bring to the hearer, when he went with eager longing, *no relief or help.* But it is the requital for those Sabbaths of *indifference and undevoutness* in which the sanctuary services have been contemned and marred. " Take heed how ye hear." " Call the Sabbath a *delight ;* the holy of the Lord, honourable."

Vv. 40-42.—*Theme :* GOD'S PROMISES TO PENITENTS.

Though God foreknew and foretold that His people would bring upon themselves His heavy judgments, He yet assured them that, if even in their lowest misery they should return to Him with humiliation and contrition, He would restore them to His favour, and to the land from whence they had been expelled. What consolation Nehemiah derived from these declarations (Nehem. i. 5-9.) !

I. WHAT IS THAT REPENTANCE WHICH GOD REQUIRES ?

1. That we *acknowledge our guilt.* Our father's sins as well as our own are first grounds of *national* humiliation. Our own sins are the chief burden of *personal* contrition. But sin should be viewed in its true light, as " walking contrary to God " (Psa. li. 4).

2. That we *justify God in His judgments.* If we have dared to walk contrary to Him, is not He justified in " walking contrary to us "? Whatever inflictions He imposes we have reason to own it as *less than our deserts* (Ezra. ix. 13), and that *His judgments are just* (Rev. xvi. 7).

3. That we *be thankful for His dealings* by which He has " humbled our uncircumcised hearts."

Only real contrition can produce this. It realises mercy in judgment, and love in affliction.

II. THE CONNEXION BETWEEN OUR REPENTANCE AND GOD'S MERCY.

Repentance is void of *merit.* Even obedience is destitute of merit ; " when we have done all we could we are unprofitable servants." *The acknowledgment of a debt* is a very different thing from a *discharge of that debt.* A condemned criminal may be sorry for his offences, but that sorrow does not obliterate his crime, still less entitle him to rewards. Yet there is connection between repentance and pardon, and meekness in the exercise of mercy towards the penitent—

1. *On God's part.* For repentance glorifies God. [See Joshua vii. 19].

2. On the part of *the penitents.* It incites to *loathing of the sin,* and to *adoration of Divine grace.*

So God insists on the condition, " If they be humbled, *then* will I pardon." For then God can do it consistently with His honour, and they will make a suitable improvement of the mercy vouchsafed them.

III. THE GROUND AND MEASURE OF THAT MERCY WHICH PENITENTS MAY EXPECT.

God's covenant with their ancestors was the basis and warrant for His mercy to Israel (Vv. 42, 44, and 45).

His *covenant with us in Christ* is our hope and guarantee.

1. Be thankful that you are *yet within reach of mercy.*

2. Have especial respect unto *the covenant of grace.* It is to that God looks, and to that should we look also. It is the only basis

in which mercy and redemption are now possible.—*C. Simeon, M.A.*

V. 45.—*Theme:* GAINS OF A GOOD ANCESTRY.

"I will for their sake remember the covenant of their ancestors."

I. THE VOWS AND PRAYERS OF A GOODLY PARENTAGE EXERCISE INFLUENCE UPON THE DIVINE PLANS.

That "*covenant*" is thrice referred to as determining God's arrangements (Vv. 42, 44, 45).

Note *Job's prayers* for his children (Job i. 5); comp. with v. 10, "Made a hedge about Job and *about his house.*"

II. OVER LONG INTERVALS THE INFLUENCE OF PARENTAL COVENANTS EXTEND.

This "covenant" with Abraham was made 1900 years B.C. (Gen. xv. 13, 14). It is now 1900 years A.D., yet the word stands. "They are *beloved for the fathers' sakes.* For the gifts and calling of God are without repentance" (Rom. xi. 28, 29).

God is at work, though He seems to wait. "In due season ye shall reap if ye faint not." *Praying soul, anxious heart,* clinging to the promises—

"Hope, and be undismayed;
God hears thy cries, and counts thy tears,
God shall lift up thy head."

III. HOW GRAND THE LINK BETWEEN A PARENT'S PIETY AND THE CHILDREN'S DESTINY!

1. *Live and pray for your descendants.*
2. *Value the sacred benefits* even though as yet unrealised, *of a godly ancestry.*
3. *Rest in the unfailing pledge* of God to reward piety and prayer. [See Addenda to Chapter, *Ancestors.*]

ILLUSTRATIVE ADDENDA TO CHAPTER XXVI.

NATIONAL IRRELIGION.

"Men come to think that the guilt of sins committed in concert is distributed; and that, if there be a thousand men banded and handed together in wickedness, each shall have but one-thousandth part of guilt. If a firm succeeds, the gain is *distributed* to each partner; but, if it fails, each one may be held for the *whole loss*. Whoever commits a sin will bear the sins, whether alone or with a thousand; whoever commits or connives at public sin will bear the blame. *Public* guilt always has *private* endorsement; and each man is liable for the whole note."—*H. W. Beecher.*

"Sail on, O Ship of State!
Humanity, with all its fears,
With all the hopes of future years,
Is hanging breathless on thy fate!"
—*Longfellow.*

"To make us love our country, our country ought to be lovely."—*Burke.*

"Our heart, our hopes are all with thee,
Our hearts, our hopes, our prayers, our tears,
Our faith triumphant o'er our fears,
Are all with thee, are all with thee."
—*Longfellow.*

VALOUR.
It was said by a nobleman at the grave of John Knox: "Here lies one who never feared the face of men."

"The brave man is not he who feels no fear,
For that were stupid and irrational;
But he whose noble soul its fear subdues,
And bravely dares the danger nature shrinks from."
—*Joanna Bailie.*

PRIDE CRUSHED.

"Remember what thou wert before thy birth—*nothing*; what thou wert for many years after—*weakness*; what in all thy life—*a great sinner*; what in all thy excellencies—a *mere debtor* to God, to thy parents, to the earth, and to all creatures. Upon these or the like meditations, if we dwell, we shall see nothing more reasonable than to be humble, and nothing more foolish than to be proud."—*Jeremy Taylor.*

"Pride thrust proud Nebuchadnezzar out of men's society, proud Saul out of his kingdom, proud Adam out of paradise, proud Hamaan out of court, and proud Lucifer out of heaven."—*Henry Smith.*

ANCESTORS.
"My chastity's the jewel of our house,
Bequeathed down from my ancestors."
—*Shakespeare.*

CHAPTER XXVII.

Votive Offerings to the Lord.

SUGGESTIVE READINGS.

V. 2.—**Shall make a singular vow.** The Rabbins interpreted the phrase as meaning to "pronounce a vow," and the Chaldee version renders the words, "shall distinctly pronounce a vow." From this followed the subtle and misleading theory that no vow, unless pronounced audibly, was binding: ignoring the solemn truth that "Our thoughts are heard in heaven"; that "there is not a word *in* our tongue but the Lord knoweth it altogether" (Psa. cxxxix. 4). Thus they made void the law by their traditions. Surely, if iniquity, which secretely is "regarded in our hearts" (Psa. lxvi. 18), offends God, so that He will not hear our prayers, the formation of a solemn resolve in the privacy of thought is "regarded" by Him as equal to an uttered vow. He values a purpose when it is as yet only "in thy heart" (1 Kings viii. 18).

Vv. 1-13.—**The persons shall be for the Lord by thy estimation.** Gratitude impels to dedication; and it led individual Israelites to dedicate themselves or their children to God's service in His house for life. Hannah thus devoted Samuel. But while this was right, and it is well for the zeal and love of the soul to find outlet in such acts of surrender, vows made rashly are harmful in themselves and displeasing to God, whereas hesitancy in fulfilling right vows, will equally wound our own conscience and dishonour the Lord (Eccles. v. 2-5).

Vv. 14-25.—**Sanctify his house to be holy to the Lord.** Just as "persons" (v. 2) might be devoted to Jehovah, so might possessions—houses, lands, cattle, and all worldly substance. Yet God, while valuing the piety which led to such consecration, gently arrested excess of zeal which might carry persons beyond prudence in their act of dedication. In verse 16 the words "some part of a field" hold the suggestion, which afterwards became a recognized regulation in Israel, that no man should vow the whole of his estates to sacred purposes, since that would reduce him and his family to penury. God values a zeal ruled by prudence. In this Christian age of spiritual obligations it rises into a privilege to be permitted to *use* all we possess for the glory of our Lord and His kingdom rather than to consign it by vows to any ecclesiastical order or priestly control. Each is a steward, and must "spend and be spent" for his Lord: the right fulfilment of our stewardship may not be entrusted to another. [See Rom. xvi. 6-8]. Every man must bear his own burden, and give account of himself to God, for all are now priests unto God" (Rev. i. 6), each having his ministry to fulfil and his sacrifices to present (1 Pet. ii. 4).

Vv. 26-27.—**The Lord's firstling: no man should sanctify it.** Those firstlings belonged to Jehovah already; were His property by express enactment (Exod. xiii. 2), and therefore were not free for the possessor to dedicate. A vow implies something beyond defined duty. God has made some sacred demands upon His people so emphatic as to necessitate implicit obedience; but beyond these absolute duties there is a realm of liberty in which each may obey the incitements of gratitude and the spontaneity of love.

Vv. 28-29—**Every devoted thing is most holy unto the Lord.** It was allowed to the Israelite to transfer to God complete and irrevocable possession of his living treasures as children or servants, and also his material substance, cattle and estates. Once so devoted, it could never be redeemed. So Hannah devoted Samuel, and Jephtha his daughter. And we, who have surrendered ourselves to Christ, and devoted our children in baptismal covenant to the faith, may not "draw back" under penalty of death. The Lord's possessions may not be recalled from their sacred purpose and aim. "Therefore glorify God in your body and spirit, which are His."

Vv. 30-34.—The tithe of the land. [See "*History of Tithes*," homily on this section of chapter].

SECTIONAL HOMILIES.

Topic: LAWS CONCERNING VOWS.

Reasonable to suppose that pious Hebrews, anxious to obey the laws of the Lord, would resolve upon devoting themselves and their substance to His service. Some of them might make vows under sudden excitement or ecstatic feeling, which, upon calm reflection, they would devoutly wish commuted or remitted. Moses, and his successors, would need to know how to deal with such cases, with equity to worshippers, and the approval of Jehovah. Hence, necessity and blessing of such directions contained in this appendix to the book of Leviticus, which teach,

I. THAT VOLUNTARY AND SPECIAL VOWS WERE PERMITTED BY THE LORD.

The people were *commanded,* but never compelled to obey. In the strictest injunctions respecting ritual, a margin was left for voluntary service, free will offerings. Special vows were optional. "If thou shalt forbear to vow, it shall be no sin to thee" (Deut. xxiii. 22). Circumstances would be frequently occurring to prompt the formation and utterance of special dedication of persons or property to the Lord, *e.g.*, special blessing, signal deliverances, etc. Gratitude would suggest and duty demand exceptional service. Enthusiastic love, always inventive and ready to lavish, is ready to offer what unsympathetic spectators rashly denominate "*waste*" (Mark xiv. 4). Jehovah accepts unaccomplished purposes, if unavoidable circumstances or personal inability prevent their fulfilment. Vows should be made *cautiously, deliberately,* and in most instances, *conditionally* ; because further enlightenment, or changed conditions may render their fulfilment *undesirable, unnecessary,* or even *impossible.*

II. THAT VOWS WERE ACCEPTABLE TO THE LORD ACCORDING TO THE SPIRIT WHICH PROMPTED THEM, AND IN WHICH THEY WERE PAID.

When circumstances justified an Israelite repenting of his vow, it could be commutated or remitted, or some compensation offered in its stead. Jehovah would accept nothing that was recklessly or reluctantly presented. All adjustments and decisions were to be made according to the standards of the sanctuary, not according to human fallibility and caprice. Though a vow should not be *literally* performed, it must be *perfectly* fulfilled in respect to honourable intention, and sacred fidelity. The state of heart, in the presentation of sacrifice, determined the value of the gift. This law has never been repealed. Through the vail of the Levitical economy beam the rays of the Gospel, which do not destroy the law, but fulfil it.

III. THAT FREEDOM OF CHOICE GIVEN IN THE FULFILMENT OF VOWS DID NOT CONTRAVENE THE PURPOSES OF THE LORD CONCERNING HIS WORK AND WORSHIP.

The compensation paid in lieu of the original vow went to sustain the sanctuary services, and the Lord reserved to Himself some unalienable rights. Some things when devoted could not be withheld or withdrawn under any circumstances

He demanded a tenth of the produce of the land, and enforced His claim with righteous and unrelaxing rigour. Thus the preservation and perpetuation of Jehovah's worship were secured, and not left contingent upon the fickleness and uncertainty of human devotedness. Righteousness lies at the foundation of the Levitical economy ; is the basis of natural and revealed religion.

Though in the gospel, Moses and Elias withdrew, and we see "Jesus only"; though under the new dispensation the yoke of service is easy, the burden of sacrifice light; yet obedience is the divine test of love, and Christly works are the essential proofs of saving faith. Leviticus is a witness to Christ and His gospel. In Him we have combined all that the law embodied,—*Altar, Sacrifice, Priest.*

Simplicity, and purity of aims, loftiest motives, deepest meanings, and incomparable excellence, lift the law and the gospel infinitely above all other religions of the world. The superiority to Jewish narrowness and bigotry, to human sinfulness and shortsightedness, demonstrate *their divinity of origin, mutual dependence, absolute authority, undying vigour,* and *inestimable worth.*—F. W. B.

Topic : COMPARATIVE ABILITY (Vv. 1-8).

1. It is distinctly stated that *no obligation enforces individuals to make a vow* to the Lord (Deut. xxiii. 22).
2. But the stringency of *fulfilling a vow when once made* is emphatically laid down (Deut. xxiii. 21 ; Eccles. v. 4, 5).
3. The *practice of making vows largely prevailed* during the Mosaic dispensation (1 Chron. xxix. 9; Judges xi. 30 ; Num. xxx. 2, etc.).
4. *Voluntary vows* had recognition or place in the *Christian Economy* (Acts xviii. 18, etc.). Yet in the act of devoting ourselves or our possessions, it must be considered that

I. ABILITY IS NO STANDARD FOR OUR PERSONAL ACCEPTANCE WITH GOD.

It was obviously a question of capacity or resources, when a man was making his vow, *what that vow* should be ; but ability or resources had no place in God's acceptance of the individual himself. The rule of personal acceptance appears in Exod. xxx. 15.

1. Atonement and acceptance stand on the *common basis of guilt.* And there is no difference between rich and poor in this.
2. Redemption requires *an equal price for every human soul.* Christ's full merits are needed for and by each one.
3. No votive offering is accepted unless and until t*he atonement price has been paid.*

Then we may come with our vows. But *Christ's preciousness* must proceed. Personal merits or possessions have no regard with God until Christ has atoned for our souls. Into the relationship of *acceptance with* God we can only enter —and "we have boldness to enter"—by "the blood of Jesus."

II. ABILITY WILL BE ESTIMATED AS REGULATING OUR OFFERINGS TO GOD.

When atonement is made for our souls, and which are accepted on that ground, then we may bring our offerings.

1. The *differences which separate us* are reckoned in the "estimation" of our gifts. It is thus: "According to that a man hath."
2. The righteousness of God requires that *we offer according to what He has bestowed on us.* If *riches,* then a large gift, etc.
3. Our *own judgment is not sufficient to decide our obligation.* "The shekel of the sanctuary is to weigh every offering. All this disposes of fitfulness and caprice in the performances of religion ; God looks to our *bringing our utmost ;* and He *weighs what we bring.*

III. Ability, when below the measure of obligation, is determined by the priest of God.

There was a rigid rule by which the votive offerings were estimated: but to this standard some were *too poor* to attain (v. 8). "If he be poorer than thy estimation then shall he present himself to *the priest.*" Note: he turns from *Moses* to the *priest:* from the embodiment of *righteous exaction* to the representative of *gracious mediation.*

1. *A sense of insufficiency for righteous requirements* is here provided for. "We have a High Priest over the house of God."

From the righteousness of the law we may turn to the graciousness of the Priest.

2. Our poverty only serves to unfold *the resources of divine compassion and grace.* God does not burden the weak; He meets our penury with gentleness. His grace is magnified by our inability to rise to the standard of righteousness.

3. Yet every sinner is certainly *found by the lawgiver "poorer than his estimation."* What then? "Where sin abounded grace doth much more abound." "It is of grace that it might not be of works." "To the *poor* the gospel is preached."

Topic: Redemption of votive offerings (Vv. 14-35).

(*a*) Vows were sometimes made *erroneously* and with faulty motives; for it is human to err. In God's pity, arrangements were sanctioned for releasing devotees from these solemn obligations and bonds.

(*b*) By the imposition of a ransom price, which was in the nature of a fine, *rashness* was punished, and thus checked.

(*c*) This insistance upon an *equivalent* for the withdrawal of votive offerings, enforced the fact that inconsiderate action or impetuosity could not be neutralised by the mere feeling of regret for what had been done: God exacted His dues, and bound them to a reverence for His righteous claims.

I. Spontaneity in religious offerings.

Into every career come such manifest mercies or gracious deliverances as to constrain the thought, "What shall I render unto the Lord for all His benefits towards me?"

1. *A grateful recognition of God in our life* impels to acts of devotion: The glad heart would "bring an offering."

2. The *outgoing of our gratitude* is arrested by no strict imposts or demands. The offering may be a *person* or his *possessions.* God allows freedom where He can.

3. *Exceptional causes for gratitude* should find outlet in exceptional consecration. This "singular vow" was something in *excess* of the usual religious gifts and services; it was something besides the continual burnt offering.

Ask (*a*) Is there *one* of God's children to whom God, in providence or grace, has *not extended exceptional proofs of loving kindness* or deliverance? "What hath God wrought!" What abounding grace has He shown!

(*b*) Is there *one* of God's children from whom God has received *no return of dedication* or devotion for His wondrous goodness and love? Have our hearts been sepulchres in which to bury the records of His love?

(*c*) Is there *one* of God's children in whom awakes a sense of "how mucch he owes his Lord," ready *now* to lay self, heart, powers on the consecrating altar? "I will pay my vows unto the Lord now in the presene of all His people." God values a willing offering, and waits to receive what we earnestly bring.

II. ENFORCEMENT OF ESPOUSED OBLIGATIONS.

It is our melancholy tendency to lapse from vows made in times of mercy.

1. *God holds us to our vows.* In some covenants and consecrations He allows no recall (Vv. 28, 29); while in every instance some substitution or commutation is required. This is an enforcement of the law of *fidelity.* Between God and man there must be the fulfilment of rights. Never does *He* violate an obligation to which He has pledged Himself. He *fulfils all* that He covenants to regard—precious promises, supplies of grace, riches, provisions of mercy, plenteous redemption. There is *no withdrawal from His word*, on "that which He has caused us to hope:" "faithfulness is the girdle of His loins."

Neither may there be *fickleness in our obligations to Him.* Jacob might forget Bethel amid his successes in Padan-aran; but God did not: "Arise, go up to Bethel, and make there an altar unto God that appeared unto thee," etc. (Gen. xxxv. 1).

2. *God concedes to our weaknesses.* "He is very pitiful and of tender mercy," not a hard task-master. While maintaining the law of righteousness, and requiring our fidelity, He yet provides for our short-sightedness and variability. Vows made in an earnest moment might prove most burdensome and inexpedient to fulfil. We see only the moment; fuller reflexion may show us that the pledge we made was not wise, or that it would overtax us. Therefore, God allows commutation. Vows were redeemable on terms here defined.

a. A gracious principle of *considerateness* and *concession* runs through all God's requirements of us. He looks for the *spirit* of fidelity, the *wish to act aright;* and then He relaxes the literal bond. For He sees our frailty. "Know then that the Lord exacteth of thee less than thine iniquity requireth" (Job xi. 6).

b. The gentle law of *substitution* is here unveiled. God accepts *something else*, something *less*, in the place of that we owe Him. We owe Him perfect obedience. He accepts the *wish and effort* to obey. We owe Him all we are and have: He accepts a *portion* of our time, substance, and energies. We owe Him our complete ruin, for "the soul that sinneth shall die"; but He says, "Let the wicked *forsake* his way, and the unrighteous man his thoughts, and let him *return*," etc., and He will accept this, and stay the doom.

In the Person and Sacrifice of Christ, *substitution reaches its climax.* But it was not something *less* when He stood for the human race: it was infinitely *more!* A *perfect Son* for rebellious children; a *spotless Sacrifice* for a sinful world. "Thanks be unto God for His unspeakable gift." See Addenda, *Vows.*

Topic: THE HISTORY OF TITHES (Vv. 30-33).

I. THE SCRIPTURE RECORDS concerning the *law* of tithes.

1. *Antecedent to the Mosaic legislation.* The principle of dedicating a tenth to God was recognised in the act of *Abraham,* who paid tithes of his spoils to Melchizedek in his sacerdotal rather than his sovereign capacity (Gen xiv. 20; Heb. vii. 6). Later, in *Jacob's* vow (Gen. xxviii. 22), the dedication of a "tenth" presupposes a sacred enactment, or a custom in existence which fixed that proportion rather than any other proportion, such as a seventh, or twelfth.

2. *The Mosaic statutes.* These given in this section lay claim in God's name to the tenth of produce and cattle. An after enactment fixed that these tithes were to be paid to the Levites for their services (Numb. xviii. 21-24), who were to give a tithe of what they received to the priests (Vv. 26-28). The sacred festivals were later made occasion for a further tithe (Deut. xii. 5, 6, 11, 17; xiv. 22, 23); which was allowed to come in money-value rather than in kind (Deut. xiv. 24-26).

3. *Hezekiah's reformation.* This was signalized by the eagerness with which the people came with their tithes (2 Chron. xxxi. 5, 6).

4. *After the Captivity.* Nehemiah made marked and emphatic arrangements concerning the tithing (Nehem. x. 37; xii. 44).

5. *Prophets' teachings.* Both Amos (iv. 4) and Malachi (iii. 10) enforce this as a duty, by severely rebuking the nation for its neglect—as robbing God.

6. *In Christ's day.* Our Lord exposed and denounced the ostentatious punctiliousness of the Pharisees over their tithing (Matt. xxiii. 23).

7. *Teaching of the New Testament.* The fact of the existence of ministers as a distinct class, assumes provision made for their maintenance. The necessity for such provision, and the right on which it is founded, are recognized in such texts as Matt. x. 10; Lk. x. 7; Rom. xv. 27; 1 Cor. ix. 7-14.

II. THE ECCLESIASTICAL DEVELOPMENT OF THE *demand* FOR TITHES.

1. The *Fathers* urged the obligation of tithing on the earliest Christians. The "Apostolical Canons," the "Apostolical Constitutions," St. Cyprian on "*The Unity of the Church,*" and the writings of Ambrose, Chrysostom, Augustine, and other Fathers of both divisions of the early Church, abound with allusions to this as a duty; and the response was made, not in enforced tithing, but by *voluntary offerings.*

2. The *legislation of the first Christian Emperors* recognised the obligation of maintaining the ministers of Christ. But while they assigned lands and other property to their support, they enacted no general payment of the tenth of the produce of the lands.

3. *Ancient Church councils* favoured tithings of land and produce, *e.g.*, the Councils of Tours, A.D., 567; the second Council of Macon, A.D., 585; the Council of Rouen, A.D., 650; of Nantes, A.D., 660; of Metz, 756.

4. Its *first imperial enactment.* Charlemagne (king of the Franks, A.D. 768-814; and Roman Emperor, A.D. 800-814) originated the enactment of tithes as a public law, and by his capitularies formally established the practice over the Roman Empire which his rule swayed. From this start it extended itself over Western Christiandom; and it became general for a tenth to be paid to the Church.

5. *Introduction of tithes into England.* Offa, king of Mercia, is credited with its assertion here, at the close of the eighth century. It spread over other divisions of Saxon England, until Ethelwulf made it a law for the whole English realm. It remained optional with those who were compelled to pay tithes to determine to what Church they should be devoted; until Innocent III. addressed to the Archbishop of Canterbury, A.D. 1200, a decretal requiring tithes to be paid to the clergy of the parish to which payees belonged. About this time also, tithes, which had originally been confined to those called prædial, or the fruits of the earth, was extended to every species of profit and to the wages of every kind of labour.

6. The *great* and *small* tithe. The *great* tithe was made upon the main products of the soil, corn, hay, wood, etc.; the *small* on the less important growths. To the *rector* the great tithes of a parish are assigned, and to the *vicar* the small.

7. Tithes paid "*in kind.*" These claim the tenth portion of the product itself (Vv. 30-33). This is varied by a payment of an annual valuation; or an average taken over seven years; or by a composition, which, in a bulk sum, redeems the land from all future impost, rendering it henceforth "tithe free."

III. THE ARGUMENTS FOR REJECTING THE MODERN *impost* OF TITHES.

1. The rule of *Equity* is infringed. When every man belonged to the one Church of the realm, all inhabitants might, with some show of rectitude, be called to support it. In Ireland the larger part of the nation was antagonistic to the Church, for which tithes were, through many generations, levied, and the impost was resented as an affront and injustice. In England a half of the

population dissents from the Established Church, and both rears and maintains its own sanctuaries, and also sustains Noncomformist worship; on these adherents of English Free Churches the tithe is an oppression made in unrighteousness. In Wales, where the tithe-sustained Church has a vastly smaller proportional attachment, the enforcement of the law is even a greater breach of equity. The *only law of equity* in such ecclesiastical questions is—they who use a Church should pay for its support.

2. The *genius and teaching of Christianity* is violated. Christianity enforces no demand by *law*, it makes appeal to *love*. It asks willinghood. It states this principle: "That as there was a *readiness to will*, so there may be a *performance*" (2 Cor. viii. 11). And it limits the *acceptableness* of what is offered by this law: "If there be *first* a *willing mind*, it is accepted according to that a man hath," etc. (2 Cor. viii. 12). If exaction and impost were to cease, there would be good hope that all sections of Christ's Church in our land would combine to maintain the historic sanctuaries of Episcopalianism, and prove that charity and willinghood have yet a deep root in the Christian heart of England.

3. The *sacred persuasives* to generosity in Church maintenance are:

(*a*) That as the gospel is superior to the law, and Christ to Moses, so should *Christian generosity surpass Jewish.*

(*b*) That as to Jews Zion was dear, and for her they lavished vast wealth, so should *Christians bring, with yet grander bouutifulness*, of their substance to the *cause* and *Church* of their blessed Lord.

(*c*) That it is beyond question a *New Testament obligation on all believers* to support the ministry and maintain the ordinances of the gospel (1 Cor. ix. 13, 14).

(*d*) That while the *Gospel supplies motives to love and consecration and sacrifice*, it leaves Christians to apply these to themselves, and work out sacred principles in beautiful performances.

Note.—The *Jew* devoted nearly one-third of his income to religious purposes, by the command of the law; a tenth for the Levites, in *property* (Numb. xviii. 20, etc.); another tenth for the Sanctuary, chiefly in *cattle and grain* (Deut. xiv. 22, etc.); and every third year a tenth to the poor.

Christian: "How much *owest thou* unto my Lord? Take thy bill and write down quickly."

Topic: EPILOGUE.—THE LAW AND THE GOSPEL.

Leviticus, like the Tabernacle, may present to the cursory observer, a rough and uninviting exterior; but within are found priceless blessings for those who devoutly draw near, and reverently worship. The Law may *seem* cumbrously elaborate, needlessly exacting; but sanctified intelligence and patient investigation will discover mercy in its purposes, and evangelical doctrines in its statutes. The letter may sometimes kill, but the spirit invariably gives life. In their sublime ends, the old and the new dispensations are indissolubly linked together, thus suggesting—

I. THE POINTS UPON WHICH THE LAW AND THE GOSPEL ESSENTIALLY AGREE.

1. *Both proclaim the spotless holiness and inflexible justice of Jehovah.* The law allows no connivance at, or compromise with sin; so the gospel shows no weakness or flaw in the inflexibility of justice, for Christ fulfilled the law and satisfied the utmost claims of Divine justice. Perfect holiness is exhibited in His blameless life, enforced in His immaculate example.

2. *Both proclaim the extent and heinousness of sin.* For all sins, even those of ignorance, sacrifices were provided. The high priest, with the whole nation, needed forgiveness. Many and costly oblations taught how universal, inveterate,

and deep-dyed is sin. The Cross teaches that the sins of the world can only be washed away by the precious blood of Christ.

3. *Both proclaimed the necessity of mediation and vicarious sacrifice in order to reconciliation to God.* Priests introduced men to God, interceded for them. The sacrifices offered were in the offerer's stead. The gospel reveals one Mediator between God and man, one offering of the sins of the whole world.

4. *Both proclaimed the necessity of faith and obedience in order to salvation.* The offererof Jewish sacrifices identified himself with the victim, and appropriated the promised blessing. Sanctification and consecration were to accompany the application for forgiveness. Sacrifices were only efficacious when associated with holiness, the adoption of a new life. So, in the gospel believers are saved *from*, not *in*, their sins. Without holiness no man can see the Lord. All who bear the name of Christ and believe on Him must depart from iniquity.

II. THE POINTS UPON WHICH THE LAW AND THE GOSPEL PROGRESSIVELY DIFFER.

1. *The Law enforced authoritative commands; the Gospel exhibits gracious constraints.* The former appealed to fear, the latter appeals to love. Thunders peal from Sinai, music rings from Calvary.

2. *The Law seemed to limit its legislation to time; the Gospel discloses immortality, and points to eternity.* The Israelites met with retribution at the hands of Moses, wrong-doers are now reminded of the final account, "the judgment seat of Christ."

3. *The Law revealed God as man's Sovereign King; the Gospel reveals Him as man's loving Father.* Revelations at Sinia were *august, awe-inspiring*: made God known as Sovereign and Governor. Christ revealed the Fatherhood of God; that man, though fallen and profligate, is His child; that for him there are many mansions and unfading joys.

4. *The Law took main cognizance of overt acts; the Gospel has primary respect to motives and intentions of the heart.* Thus, the morality of the New Testament is *exceedingly pure* and *absolutely perfect*; a transcript of the holiness of the Divine nature.

5. *The Law was to be supplanted by some better thing; the Gospel is final, conclusive, and complete.* We look back to the law and see the foregleaming of the gospel; we look forward through Apocalyptic visions to the glorious consummation, when the redeemed universe will echo with the song of Moses and the Lamb, "Hallelujah! For the Lord God Omnipotent reigneth."—*F. W. B.*

Topic: "COMMANDMENTS WHICH THE LORD COMMANDED MOSES" (V. 34).

The Divine regulations and requirements of Leviticus are to be classified as—

1. *Ceremonial*: and consequently special to the Jewish nation; not binding upon or applicable to this Christian age.

2. *Moral*: for precepts and teachings intermingle with the ceremonies, whose relevancy and urgency are not to be restricted to any nation or period; there are Divine directions for us as for Israel.

3. *Spiritual*: A foreshadowing of gospel doctrines and of the better covenant of grace, and of the privileges of the Christian life, runs through the Levitical institutes. In these types and premonitions Christ and His work are prefigured; and, therefore, we read our inheritance in these Jewish signs.

I. SACRIFICE AND INCENSE. These have found their verification in the substitutionary death of Jesus.

II. TABERNACLE SANCTITIES AND SOLEMNITIES. These have become glorified in the incarnation of Christ which they predicted, and the indwelling of the Spirit in the believer which they pourtrayed.

III. CAMP DUTIES AND PURIFYINGS These find their sacred realization in those obligations, responsibilities, and services, which now distinguish believers who form the community of Christ's living Church.

IV. HOLY FEASTS AND CONVOCATIONS. These proclaim the spiritual fulness and delights with which the redeemed in Christ are now enriched; and those "times of refreshing" with which the Spirit gladdens humble hearts in which Emmanuel dwells.

V. ALTAR OFFERINGS AND VOWS. These mark that consecration of life and love which all who know the Lord should yield to Him, and which both distinguish the Christian character and dignify the Christian name.

"Unto Him that loved us, and washed us from our sins in His own blood, and hath made us kings and priests unto God and His Father; to Him be glory and dominion for ever and ever, Amen."

ILLUSTRATIVE ADDENDA TO CHAPTER XXVII.

VOWS UNPAID.

"Praise should always follow answered prayer. It was thus with one man; he was very ill; a great, strong man in his day; yet disease shrivelled him up, laid him upon a lowly bed, made him pray to the humblest creature in his house for favours hour by hour. As he lay there, in his lowliness and weakness, he said, "If God would raise me up I would be a new man, I would be a devout worshipper in the sanctuary, I would live to His glory." And God gathered him up again; didn't break the bruised reed; did not quench the smoking flax, but permitted the man to regain his faculties. And he was not well one month till he became as worldly as he was before his affliction. He prayed as if his heart loved God; and when he got his health back again he was a practical atheist, he was virtually the basest of blasphemers."
Joseph Parker, D.D.

"Call to thy God for grace to keep
Thy vows; and if thou break them weep;
Weep for thy broken vows, and vow again;
Vows made with tears cannot be made in vain.
 Then once again
I vow to mend my ways;
 Lord, say Amen,
And Thine be all the praise."
G. Herbert.

"It is the purpose that makes strong the vow;
But vows to every purpose must not hold."
Shakespeare.

"Unheedful vows may heedfully be broken."
Ibid.

TITHES.

"I know of two men who started business with this view: 'We will give to God one-tenth of our profits.' The first year the profits were considerable; the tithe was consequently considerable. The next year there was increase in the profits, and, of course, increase in the tithe. In a few years the profits became very, very large indeed, so that the partners said one to another: 'Is not a tenth of this rather too much to give away? Suppose we say now we will give a twentieth?' And they gave a twentieth; and the next year the profits had fallen down; the year after they fell down again, and the men said to one another as Christians should say in such a case, 'Have not we broken our vow? Have we not robbed God?' And in no spirit of selfish calculation, but with humility of soul, self-reproach and bitter contrition they went back to God and told Him how the matter stood, prayed His forgiveness, renewed their vow, and God opened the windows of heaven and came back to them and all the old prosperity."—*Joseph Parker, D.D.*

"Restore to God His due in tithe and time;
A tithe purloined cankers the whole estate."
G. Herbert.

"I cannot love Thee as I would,
 Yet pardon me, O Highest God!
My life, and all I call my own,
 I lay before Thy mercy throne:
And if a thousand lives were mine,
O sweetest Lord, they should be Thine,
And scanty would the offering be,
So richly hast Thou loved me."
From the German.

TOPICAL INDEX.

	PAGE.
Introductory Notes	1
Chapter I: THE LAW OF THE BURNT SACRIFICES	2
Suggestive Readings	3
The Levitical Ritual	4
Communion through Altar Offerings	4
Worship by Sacrifice	6
A Sweet Savour for Acceptance	8
Significance of the Burnt Offering	9
Variety in Sacrifices	10
God within the Tabernacle	12
Revelation of Propitiation	12
Way of Access to God	13
Necessity of Sacrifice	14
Volition in Worship	14
Acceptance with God	15
The Altar Fire	16
The Spirit's Efficacy	17
A Life Offering	17
Completeness in Self Devotion	18
Illustrated Addenda	18, 19

	PAGE.
Chapter II: BLOODLESS SACRIFICES: THE FOOD OFFERINGS	20
Suggestive Readings	20, 21
Homage Graced with Excellencies	21
Maintenance of Priestly Ministrations	23
Suggestiveness of the Meat Offering	24
Character as Qualifying Service	25
Resurrection Emblems	26
Subduedness and Meekness of Christ	27
Christ the Food of Privileged Souls	28
A Memorial on God's Altar	28
Purity in Service of the Lord	28
Illustrative Addenda	28, 29

	PAGE.
Chapter III: THE PEACE OFFERING OF THANKSGIVING	29
Suggestive Readings	29, 30
Explanatory Homily	30
Peace-Offering Sacrifices	31
Feast of Man's Fellowship with God	33
Peace by Fulfilling Divine Conditions	35
Peace Resulting from Propitiation	35
Faultlessness in Sacrifice	36
Identification of Offerer with Offering	36
God's Positive Commands	36
Peace Associated with Penitence	36
Succession in Sacrifices	37
The Best Deserved by God	37
Obedience the Test of Faith	37
Illustrative Addenda	38

	PAGE.
Chapter IV: SACRIFICES FOR SINS	38
Suggestive Readings	38, 39, 40
Sins Committed in Ignorance	40
Sinai's Law occasioned the Sin-Offering	43
Ignorance in Sinning	44
Defiled Sanctities	45
Sin's Fearful Aspects	46
Sin-Offering Meets Man's Need	47
Three Aspects of the Sin-Offering	48
Eminent Sinfulness of Error in the Priest	49
Sin-Offering for the Congregation	50
,, ,, Ruler	51
,, ,, Common People	52
Sins through Ignorance	53
,, in the Priesthood	53
Sevenfold Purging	53
Expiation in the Gaze of Heaven	53
Sin Loathed by God	54
Discipleship following Christ to Reproach	54
Hidden Sin	55
Good News	55
Common People	55
Forgiven	55
Culpability of Ignorance	55
Scripture the Antidote for Ignorance	56
Illustrative Addenda	57, 58

	PAGE.
Chapter V: TRESPASSES HEEDLESSLY COMMITTED	58
Suggestive Readings	58, 59, 60
Complacent Ignorance	60
Conniving at Wrong-doing	61
Contagiousness of Sin	62
Responsibility of Words	63
Way of Pardon	63
Contraction of Defilement	64
What God expects of Us	64
Mediation	65
Divine Forgiveness	65
Trespasses done Ignorantly	65
"Amends" by Christ for Man's Faults	66
Trespass Penalty	67
Sacrilege	68
Reparation	69
Error Through Inadvertence	69
Illustrative Addenda	70, 71

	PAGE.
Chapter VI: TRESPASS OFFERINGS; AND PRIESTLY CONSECRATION	72
Suggestive Readings	72, 73
Distinctions between Trespasses against God and Man	73

TOPICAL INDEX.

	PAGE.
Harm done by Trespass	75
Restitution made for Wrong	76
Duty of Honesty	77
Breach of Confidence	78
Depositing Property	78
Beneficence of a Redeemed Life	78
Dishonesty	79
Dignity Linked to Duty	80
Sacred Attire	80
Divine Fire Humanly Maintained	81
Fire not to Go Out	81
The Altar Fire	82
,, ,, A Symbol of Regenerating Grace	82
Inextinguishable Fire	82
Priestly Services and Privileges	83
Divine Friendship	83
Ministerial Dedication	84
Sin-offering a Shadow of the Gospel	85
Illustrative Addenda	86, 87

Chapter VII: Ritual of the Sacrifices: The Peace Offering   87

Suggestive Readings	87, 88
Invariable Laws for Sacrifice	89
Peace-offering Sacrifice	90
Believers' Peace and Portion	92
Law of the Peace-offerings	93
Ritual of Sacrifice	94
Practical Significance of Sacrifices	95
Trespass Offering	98
Rigidity of the Law	98
Thanksgiving	98
Excommunication	99
Reserved Things	99
Whole Duty of Man	99
Summary of the Offerings	99
Illustrative Addenda	100

Chapter VIII: Priesthood Initiated and Consecrated   100

Suggestive Readings	100, 101, 102
Priests versus Priestism	103
Calling of the Priests	104
Ministry of the Priesthood	105
Qualifications of God's Ministers	106
Consecration of the Priests	108
Solemnity of the Ceremony of Consecration	109
Completeness, etc. ,,	110
Significance, etc. ,,	111
God's Elected Priests	111
An Elect People	111
Israel's Glory	112
The Holy Crown	112
Sanctification	113
Perfect Service	113
Living Sacrifices	113
Hearty Service	113
Seven Days' Consecration	113
Exemplary Obedience	113
Illustrative Addenda	114

Chapter IX: Inaugural Ministries of Aaron   115

	PAGE.
Suggestive Readings	115, 116
Entering upon Priestly Work	117
Sacrificial Preparation for God's Appearing	117
Consecration Qualifying for Work	118
A Solemn Benediction	119
Within the Secret of God's Tabernacle	120
Priests' Entrance upon Office	120
Aaron's First Offering for Himself	122
,, Offering for the People	122
Blessing the People	123
Miraculous Fire	125
Conditions of Blessing	126
Blood of Sprinkling	126
God's Acceptance of Sacrifices	126
Gracious Fire	127
Illustrative Addenda	127, 128

Chapter X: Reckless Ministry Rebuked   128

Suggestive Readings	128, 129, 130
Repulsive Incense	130
Youthful Profanity	133
Sin of Aaron's Sons	135
Degradation of what is Holy	136
The Law of Worship	137
Spurious Worshippers: Daring and Doom	139
Warning to Worshippers	140
Silence of Aaron's Sorrow	142
Priestly Elevation above Private Sorrow	143
Excitations Perilous to Communion	144
Unrelaxing Strictness of the Ritual	145
No Joy before God's Altar	146
Self-exalting Zeal	147
Despising God's Altar	147
Violation of Sanctity	148
Silence of Aaron	148
Mute Suffering	148
Submission to God in Affliction	148
Public Lamentation	149
Help to Temperance	149
A Divine Prohibition	149
Illustrative Addenda	150, 151

Chapter XI: Food Permitted and Prohibited   151

Suggestive Readings	151, 152
Distinguishing the Precious from the Vile	152
Forbidden Foods	154
Restraint upon Festivities	155
Legal Prohibition Abrogated by Christianity	156
Symbols of Cleanness in Animal Life	157
Jehovah's Concern for Israel's Well-being	159
Jehovah's Concern for His own Glory	160
The Clean and Unclean	161
Illustrative Addenda	163, 164

Chapter XII: Maternity   164

Suggestive Readings	164, 165
Motherhood	165

TOPICAL INDEX. iii

	PAGE.
Birth	166
Pollution and Purifying	166
Statute Relating to Maternity	167
Illustrative Addenda	169

Chapter XIII: LEPROSY: ITS DISCOVERY AND TREATMENT 169
Suggestive Readings 169, 170
  Man Physically a Victim of Maladies 171
  Disease, Development, Doom 172
  The Leper before the Priest 173
  "Unclean! Uuclean!" 175
  Leprosy, a Parable of Human Depravity 176
  Sinful Surroundings 178
  Wondrous Workings of God's Grace 179
  First Symptoms of Depravity 179
  Scrupulous Care in Dealing with Depravity 180
  Sin not to be Connived at 180
  Degrees of Depravity 181
  Results of Unremoved Depravity 181
  Illustrative Addenda 181, 182

Chapter XIV: LEPROSY CLEANSED 182
Suggestive Readings 182, 183
  The Law of Cleansing 184
  Anxiety for Recovery 185
  Remedial Measures 186
  Progressive Cleansing 186
  Grace for the Poor 188
  Purity in the House 189
  Cleansing the Leper 191
  Divine Compassion Exhibited 191
  A Type of Redemption 191
  Sanctification 192
  No Excuse for Neglecting Cleansing 192
  Completeness of Cleansing 192
  Leprous Houses 192
  Depraved Surroundings 193
  Illustrative Addenda 193, 194

Chapter XV: SECRET PHYSICAL IMPURITIES 194
Suggestive Readings 194
  Vileness of Fallen Human Nature 194
  Indecencies 195
  Odiousness of Personal Impurity 195
  Consequences ,, ,, ... 196
  Secret flow of Sin 197
  Radical Cure of Sin 197
  Illustrative Addenda 198

Chapter XVI: THE GREAT DAY OF ATONEMENT 198
Suggestive Readings 198, 199, 200
  Explanatory Article on "Azazel" 200
  A Unique Day in Israel 202
  Typical Enactment of Atonement 203
  Slain Goat and Scapegoat 204
  Intercession of Christ 205
  Worth of Sacrifices 207
  Full Atonement 208
  Day of Atonement 212
  Aaron's Sin Offering for Himself 213

	PAGE.
Aaron's Sacrifice Compared with Christ's	214
Ratification of the Statute of Atonement	215
Undue Familiarity in Divine Things	216
Sin Removed	216
Intercession	217
Supreme Demand for Holiness	217
The Atoning Sacrifice	217
Illustrative Addenda	217, 218

Chapter XVII: THE SANCTITY OF THE BLOOD 218
Suggestive Readings 218, 219
  Solemnity of Sacrifice 219
  Place of Sacrifice 220
  Blood Prohibited as Food 221
  Holy Blood 223
  A Divine Prohibition 224
  Illustrative Addenda 225

Chapter XVIII: INCESTUOUS MARRIAGES: DOMESTIC PURITY 225
Suggestive Readings 225, 226
  Unaccommodating Godliness 226
  Nonconformity to the World 228
  Blessedness of Obedience 229
  God's Holy Name 229
  Conjugal Chastity, Holiness in the Home 230
  Illustrative Addenda 231

Chapter XIX: PRACTICAL PIETY: RELIGION IN ALL RELATIONSHIPS 232
Suggestive Readings 232
  Religion of Morality 232
  Genius of the Mosaic Laws 234
  Personal Holiness 236
  Family Piety 236
  Filial Obligations 237
  Willing Offerings of Peace 237
  Harvest Gleanings 237
  Jehovah's Righteous Demands 238
  Fairness to Hired Labourers 239
  Impartial Justice 239
  Tale-bearing and Slander 239
  Neighbourly Love 240
  Responsibility of Stewardship 240
  Reproving our Neighbour 241
  Wicked Superstitions 242
  Sacredness of the Sabbath 242
  Homage for Age 242
  Courtesy to Strangers 243
  Business Honesty 243
  Illustrative Addenda 243, 244

Chapter XX: SOCIAL AND MORAL CRIMES 244
Suggestive Readings 245
  Axe Laid at Root of Moral Evil 245
  Capital Offences 246
  Connivance at Iniquity 247
  Possibilities of Sanctity 249
  Grief of Undutiful Children 249
  The Hebrew Church 251
  Godly Distinctiveness 252

TOPICAL INDEX.

	PAGE.
Chapter XXI. Purity in the Priesthood	252
Suggestive Readings	253
Sacred Relationships	253
Dignity of the Priesthood Inviolate	255
Qualifications for Sacred Service	256
Allowance for Human Infirmity	257
Illustrative Addenda	258, 259
Chapter XXII: Priestly Privileges Forfeited by Uncleanness	259
Suggestive Readings	259, 260
Solemn Regard for Hallowed Things	260
Defiling Holy Things	261
Irreverence amid Sanctities	262
The Best for the Highest	263
Blemishes in our Sacrifices	263
Unquestioning Obedience Peremptory	265
The Jealousy of Jehovah	266
Holy Feasts Forbidden to Strangers	266
Unblemished Sacrifices	266
Holy Ministries Refused from Strangers	267
Chapter XXIII: Israel's Holy Festivals	267
Suggestive Readings	267, 268, 269
Sabbath of Rest	269
The Sabbath	272
Significance of the Passover	273
The Passover	274
Sheaf of the First Fruits	275
Pentecost and the Spirit	276
Memorial of Blowing of Trumpets	277
Feast of Trumpets	279
Feast of Tabernacles	280
Festival of Tabernacles and Ingathering	281
Feasts of the Lord	283
First Fruits Sheaf	284
Self in Abeyance	284
Feast of Pentecost: Harvest Home	284
Beginning the Reaping	285
Harvest Gleanings	285
Great Day of Atonement	285
Sojourning in Booths	286
Illustrative Addenda	286, 287
Chapter XXIV: Sanctuary Light: Shewbread: Blasphemy	287
Suggestive Readings	288
Continuous Lustre of a Godly Life	288
The Bread of the Presence	290
Lamps of the Tabernacle	290
Table of Shewbread	291
Blasphemy of God's Holy Name	292
„ of Shelomith's Son	294
Golden Candlestick	295
Glory of the Church	295
Shewbread	295
Special Time for Service	**295**

	PAGE.
Evil Connections	296
Slaying the Blasphemer	296
Blasphemy	296
Inexorableness of the Law	296
Illustrative Addenda	296, 297
Chapter XXV: The Year of Jubilee	297
Suggestive Readings	297, 298
Sabbath of Rest unto the Lord	298
Jubilee Year: its Fourfold Significance	299
Glad Facts of the Jubilee	300
Year of Jubilee	301
Principles Contained in Jubilee Regulations	303
Canaan: the Lord's Land for Ever	304
Exalted Philanthropy	305
Sabbatical Year	306
Lessons of the Jubilee	306
Jubilee a Type of the Gospel	307
Kinsman's Rights	307
Royal Service	308
Illustrative Addenda	308
Chapter XXVI: Religion as Determining a Nation's Destiny	309
Suggestive Readings	309
Peculiarities of the Chapter	309
Advantages of Religion in Nation's Life	310
Blessing or Curse	311
National Transgression and Disaster	313
Desolation upon Israel	315
Lost Tribes of Israel	315
Fundamentals in True Religion	316
Incentives to True Religion	317
The Bow in the Clouds	318
Idolatry Interdicted	319
Equity of God's Ways	319
Valour and Victory through Godliness	320
Emmanuel amid His People	320
Emancipated and Elevated	320
Cowardice of Guilt	320
Pride Crushed	320
Obstinacy Punished	321
God's Determination to Punish Sinners	321
Sabbath Barrenness	322
God's Promises to Penitents	322
Gains of a Good Ancestry	323
Illustrative Addenda	323
Chapter XXVII: Votive Offerings to the Lord	324
Suggestive Readings	324
Laws Concerning Vows	325
Comparative Ability	326
Redemption of Votive Offerings	327
History of Tithes	328
Law and Gospel	330
Commandments of the Lord	331
Illustrative Addenda	**332**

ANALYTICAL INDEX.

A

	PAGE.
Aaron, Grief for his Sons	129, 142, 145
" His First Offering "for Himself."	122, 213
" Inaugural Ministries of	115, 117, 121
" Makes the Atonement	212
" Offerings for the People	122
" Sorrow	146, 148
" Submission	142, 148
Aaron's Sacrifice Compared with Christ's	214
" Sons, The Son of	135
Ability, Comparative	326
" Determined by the Priest	327
" No Standard of our Acceptance	326
" to Hallow, Man's	260
Abihu and Nadab	128, 132, 135, 141
Absolute Consecration	89
Abstinence from Sin	249
Acceptable Worship	5, 8, 126
Acceptance with God	15, 108
Access to God	13, 216
Accommodating Conscience	227
Acquiesence in Affliction	148
Adoration in Worship	22
Aged, Homage for	233, 244
Agricultural Labours	298, 303
Allowance for Human Infirmity	257
Altar, Despising God's	147
" Fire	16
" Inextinguishable	82
" No Joy before God's	146
" Offerings, Communion through	4, 221
" Symbol of Regenerating Grace	82
"Amends" made by Christ	66
" Man Cannot Make	67, 77
Anger, Danger of	294
" Divine	247
Ancestry: Gains of a Good	323
Anointing	107, 109, 131
Anxiety for Recovery	185
Ascending Fire	19, 82
Associations, Evil	64
Atonement, Measured by Man's Sin	45
" Great Day of	198, 203, 212, 285
" Basis of	207, 210
" Typical Enactment of	203
" Full	208, 210
" Statute of, Ratification of the	215
" Vast Virtue Needed in	70
Attainments, Progressive	187
Attire, Sacred	80, 109, 199
Authorship of Leviticus	1
Awakened Conscience	44
"Azazel"	200

B

	PAGE.
Beauties of Jesus Foreshadowed	22
Beautiful Country Devastated	315
Beautiful in Worship	28
Beguiled into Sin	42
Benediction, A Solemn	119, 123, 126
Benefactor, The Christian a	78, 119
Beneficence of a Redeemed Life	78
Benevolence	308
Best, The: God Demands	37, 263
Birth	166, 168
Blasphemy	287
Blasphemer, Slaying the	296
Blasphemy against God's Holy Name	292, 296
" Real and Relative	293
" of Shelomith's Son	294
Blessing and Curse	312
Blemish, Christ without	2
Blemishes in Sacrifice	263, 266
Blind, The	239
Bloodless Sacrifices	20
Blood of Sprinkling	126
" Life in the	225
" Not to be Shed Heedlessly	224
" Prohibited as Food	221
" Sanctity of	218, 222, 223, 224
Bodily Appearance	258
" Deformities	171, 172
" Infirmities	258
Body, the House of the Soul	192
Bondage, Deliverance from	302
Bondmen, Redeeming the	298
Booths. See TABERNACLES.	
Bounty, God's	299, 304
Bow in the Cloud	318
Bread of God's Presence	290
Breastplate	112
Burnt Offering. See SACRIFICES.	
" Its Significance	9
Business Honesty	243, 244
" See TRADE.	

C

Cakes. See SHEWBREAD	
Calling, The Priestly	104
Camp, Without the	39
Canaan, God Claims the Soil	298, 304, 306
" Pilgrims to	286
" The Land Never to be Sold	298
Candlesticks, Golden	288, 295
" Christ amid the	289
Capital Offences	246
Celibacy	258
Church Glory of the	295

ANALYTICAL INDEX.

	PAGE.
Church : its Privileges and Duties	295
,, The Hebrew	251
,, Workers must be Godly	267
Character as Qualifying Sacrifices	25, 29
,, Defects of	254
,, Imperilled by Slander	239
Charity	243
Chastity	230
Childhood. See MATERNITY ; also	169
Children, Dutifulness of	233, 237
,, Grief of Undutiful	249
Christ amid the Golden Candlesticks	280
,, as Peace Offering	93
,, Giver of Rest	271
,, His Meekness	27
,, His Self-devotedness	18
,, Intercession of	205
,, our Passover	268
,, our Priest	67, 103, 208
,, Tabernacling in the Flesh	286
,, the Food of His People	28
,, the Lamb	273
,, the Lamb Slain	273
,, without Blemish	2
Christian Purity	253
Civic Benevolence	234
Clean and Unclean	157, 161, 167
Cleanliness in the House	189
Cleansed, Leprosy	182, 191, 193
Cleansing, Progressive	186
,, The Law of	184, 191
,, The Sinner's	195
Commandments of the Lord to Moses	331
Commerce. See BUSINESS	
Common People	52, 55
Communion with God	120, 144
Communion with God through Sacrifice	5
Communities, Sins of	50
Community, Sin in a	50
Companions, Evil	296
Compassion, Divine	191
Complacent Ignorance	60
Completeness in Self-Devotion	18
Confidence, Violated	78
Conformity to the World	228
Congregations. See CONVOCATIONS	
Conjugal Chastity	230, 256
Conniving at Wrong	61, 227, 247
Consecration 19, 84, 89, 100, 108, 113, 118, 290
Consequences of Personal Impurity	196
Contagiousness of Sin	62, 64
Contents of Leviticus Summarized	331
Contrition	215
Convocations, Holy	282, 332
Corruption, Man's Inherent	47
,, See DEPRAVITY	
Courage. See COWARDICE	
Courtesy to Strangers	243
Cowardice of Guilt	320
Craven. See COWARDICE	
Creation, Completed	279
Creator—God, of Everything	306
Crown, The Holy	106, 112
Cure of Sin	197
Custom	231

D.

Daring and Doom	139

	PAGE.
Day of Atonement	198
Deaf, The	239
Debts, Cancelling	302
Deceitfulness	233
Dedication	15, 18, 32, 127, 284
Defects of Character	254
Defiled Sanctities	45, 137, 148
Defilement	217
Defiling Holy Things	261
Degradation of Holy Things	136
Delight, God's in Christ	34
Depraved Surroundings	193
Depravity	176, 179, 180, 194, 217
,, Degrees of	181, 246
,, Results of Unremoved	181
Developments	181
Dignity Linked to Duty	80, 255
Dignity of Man	304
Discipleship, Following Christ to Reproach	54
Diseases	171, 172
Disease, Development, Doom	172
Dishonesty	79
Disobedience, Punishment of	317
Distinctness, Godly	252
Domestic Purity. See HOUSEHOLD, FAMILY	
Dread of Sin	47
Drunkenness. See INTOXICATION	
Duty of Man	99

E.

Early Annals of Man	43
Elect People	111
Elevated	320
Emancipated and Elevated	320
Emmanuel amid His People	320
Emotion in Worship	131
Employers	239
Endowments, Divine, to Man	81
Enslavement, Freed from	320
Ensnarements	227, 246
Equity of God's Ways	319
Evidence, Giving, against Wrong	61
Excellencies in Jesus	25, 46
Excellencies in Worship	21, 25
Excitement in Worship	131, 144
Excommunication	99
Excuse, No	192
Excusing Sins	60
Experiences, Advancing	187
Expiation	53, 105

F.

Fairness in Trade	234, 239
Faith, The Sacred Rest of	271
Faithlessness	87
False Swearing	238
Familiarity in Divine Things Checked	216
Family Connections	296
Family Piety	235, 237, 243
Family Purity	190, 225, 233
Faultlessness in Sacrifice	36
Feast of Blowing the Trumpets	277
,, First Fruits	275, 284, 287
,, Harvest	276
,, Paschal	274
,, Pentecost	276, 284
Feasts of the Lord	283
Fellowship, A Law of	203

ANALYTICAL INDEX.

	PAGE.
Fellowships, Christ's Happiness in	35
„ God's Feast of	31, 33, 83
„ in Christ, Man's Blessed	34
Fervour, Christian	16, 26
Festivities, Restrained	155, 164
Festivals, Israel's Holy	267
Festival, Sacred Life a	283
Filial Obligations	237
Fire, "Strange"	128, 131, 147
„ upon the Altar	3, 16, 81, 82, 147
„ not to go out	81
„ Miraculous	125, 126
„ Gracious	127
First Fruits. See FEASTS	
Food	151, 154
„ Unclean	152, 154
Forgiveness	55, 57, 65
Formalists	148
Fowls as Sacrificial Offerings	3
Fragrant Sacrifice	214
Frail Habitations	287
Frankincense	20
„ Symbolizes Christ's Delightfulness	23
Freedom in Offerings	36, 263
Friendship, Divine	83

G.

Garments. See ATTIRE	
Gifts to Priests	23
Gleanings, Harvest	237, 285
God, Creator	306
„ Equity of His Ways	319
„ His Holy Name	229
„ His wondrous Grace	179
„ Place for Meeting Him	13, 120
„ within the Tabernacle	12, 120
Godliness, Unaccommodating	226
„ Valour and Victory through	320
Godly Distinctiveness	252
„ Life, Lustre of a	288
„ Sin in the	46
God's Righteous Demands	238
Good News	55
Gratitude to God	94, 220, 263
Guilty Man's Helplessness	184
Gospel and Law Compared	330
„ Age Inaugurated	280
„ Foreshadowings	236
„ Joy	279
„ Trumpet	278
Government, Divine	310
Grace for the Poor	188
„ Transformations of	78
„ Wondrous	179

H.

Habits, Ungodly	296
Harm. See INJURY	
Harvest Home	284
Harvest	237, 281, 282, 284, 285, 286
„ Ingatherings	276, 281
„ Sheaf of First Fruits	275, 286
Heavenly Feast	283
„ Rest asked by the Soul	271
Hebrew Church	251
Healer, Confidence in	185
Helpfulness, God's Abounding	184

	PAGE.
Helplessness, Guilty Man's	184, 193
Helpless, not Hopeless	191
Hidden Sin	55
High Priest	208
Higher Privileges	188
Holiness Demanded	217, 236
„ to the Lord	101, 106
Holy Blood	223
„ Dwellings	266
„ Feasts Forbidden to Strangers	266
„ Ministries Refused from Strangers	267
„ Spirit's Energy	17
Home	194, 230, 302
„ Sanctities	190
„ Type of Heaven	251
Home. See FAMILY	
Homage	21
Honesty	77, 79
Honey	20
Hospitality	234
Household Purity	189, 230
Houses, Leprous	192

I.

Idolatry Interdicted	319
„ Prevented	219
Ignorance	57
„ Complacent	60
„ Sins of	39, 40, 44, 50, 53, 55
„ Trespasses done in	58, 65, 69
Immanuel. See EMMANUEL	
Impiety	136
Impure Service	28
Impurity	195
Inadvertent Sins. See IGNORANCE	
Incense Repulsive	130
Incestuous Marriages	225
Incorrigibleness	321
Indecencies	195
Indifference	71
Indulgence. See TEMPERANCE	
Inextinguishable Fire	82, 86
Infection	192
Infirmities a Hindrance	257
Inherent Corruption of the Sinner	47
Inhumanities in the Name of Religion	248
Initiation. See MINISTERS, PRIESTS	
Injury to Man	74, 85
Injustice	233
Intemperance. See INTOXICATION	
Intercession	217
„ of Christ	206
Intoxication	134, 144, 149, 151
Irreverence amid Sanctities	262
Israel, Desolation upon	315
„ Lost Ten Tribes of	315
Israel's Wellbeing	159

J.

Jealousy, God's, Concerning Worship	63, 160
„ of Jehovah	266
JEHOVAH, Name Disused by Jews	293
„ Jealousy of	266
Joy in Worship	285
„ of the Gospel	279
„ Heavenly	284
Joyful side of Religion	282
Joyous Privileges open to us in Christ	34

viii   ANALYTICAL INDEX.

	PAGE
Jubilee: a Type of the Gospel	307
" Blessings Consequent on Atonement	300
" Glad Facts of the	300
" Lessons of the	306
" Regulations of the	303
" Year of	297, 299, 301
Justice	234, 244
" Impartial	239

K.
Kinsman Needs Wealth	308
Kinsman's Rights	307
Knowledge v. Ignorance. See IGNORANCE.	

L.
Labourers, Fairness to Hired	239
Landed Estates	304
Lamps on the Candlestick	288
Law and Gospel	330
" Inexorableness of the	296
" of the Tabernacle	290
Leaven	20
Leper	173, 191
Leprosy	169, 176, 179
" loathsome	172
" a type of Redemption	191
Leprous houses	192
Liberty, Christian	299, 308
" a preparation for Elevation	320
Life Offering, A	17
" in the Blood	225
Lightbearers, Christian's	288, 296
Light, Sanctity requisite for	289
" of Testimony	289
Lips, Grace of	294
Loaves. See SHEWBREAD.	
Love to our Neighbour	240
Lowly. See POOR.	
" yal Spirit	263
Lustre of a godly life	288, 289

M.
Maladies	171
Maternity	164, 165, 167, 169
Marriages	225
Masters, Consideration from to Servants	239
Maintenance of the Priests	23, 24
Manifestation of God	117, 121
Man's Ability to Render Things Hallowed	260
" Earliest History	43
" Frail Body	286
" Inherent Corruption	47
" Insecure Life	286
" Physical Defilements	171
" Tendency to profane things hallowed	260
" Weary Life asks the Sabbath of rest	270
Meat Offering	20, 24
Meditation	23, 65, 107
Mediatorship	107
Meetings, Religious. See CONGREGATIONS.	
Memorial	20, 28
Mercy Seat	217
Merits, Hateful to God	147
Millennial Blessings	299, 300
Ministers	23, 24, 29

	PAGE
Ministers, Dedication of	84, 103, 108, 127
" Must be True-born Sons of God	267
" Not Priests	103
" Purity of	253
" Qualifications of	106, 133, 256
" Reckless	128, 139, 150
" Temptations of	135, 144
Moral Evil	244, 245
Morality	195, 196, 233, 243
" the Religion of	232
Mosaic Laws, Genesis of	234
Motherhood. See MATERNITY.	
Mute Suffering	148

N.
Nadab and Abihu. See ABIHU.	
National Priesthood	105
" Transgressions and Disaster	313
Name of God Blasphemed	292, 294
" JEHOVAH disused	293
Nation, Advantages of Religion to a	310
" Calamities on	314
" Profanation of Nation's Sanctities	315
" Progressive Apostasy of	313
Nearness to God	128
Neighbour, Duty to our	241
" Trespasses Against	72
Neighbourliness	78, 233, 239, 244, 298
New Year	278
Nonconformity to the World	228

O.
Oaths	63, 70
Obedience	95, 113, 220, 249, 263, 281, 307
" Blessings Promised to	317
" Blindness of	229
" Duty of	307
" Test of Faith	37
" Unquestioning	265
Obstinacy Punished	321
Odiousness of Sin	195, 230
Offensive Offerings	131
Offerings	99, 100
Offerings. See SACRIFICES.	
Offerer Identified with his Offering	36
Oil and Frankincense	20
Old. See AGED.	
Oppression	233

P
Parentage, A Godly	323
Parents	237
" Grief from Children	250
Pardon	57, 63
Paschal Victim. See PASSOVER.	
Passionate Strife	293
Passions, Low	195, 198
Passover, Feast of	268, 274
" Significance of	273
Peace, Divine Conditions of	35, 38
" -offering	29, 32, 87, 93
" The Believer's	92, 100
" Historic Instances of	31
Penitence	36, 65
Penitents, God's Promises to	332
Pentecost and the Spirit	276
Perfect Offerer, A	8
" Sacrifices	264

	PAGE.
Perjury	238
Personal Holiness	236
Poor	19
" Care for	234, 238, 298
" Gleanings of Harvest for the	285
" Grace for	188
Philanthropy	305
Physical Impurities	195
" Infirmities a Hindrance	257
Piety, Family	236, 243
" in all Relationships	232
Pilgrimage	286
Pleasant Offering	8
Pollution and Purifying	166
Possessions	309
Possibilities of Sanctity	249
Poverty. (See POOR).	193
" Causes of	305
Practical Piety	232
Prayer	36
Presumption	134, 147, 149, 150
Pride	150
" Crushed	320, 323
" Leads to Impiety	321
Priest, High, Necessity of	208
Priesthood, Approach to God, through	23
" Consecrated	100, 117, 120, 127
" Definition of	105
" Purity of the	252
Priestism	103, 114
Priestly Elevation above Private Sorrow	143
" Services	83
" Privileges	259
" Profanity	133, 147
Priests	103, 111
" Calling of	104, 111
" Conjugal Relationships	256
" Dedication of	108, 121
" Dignity of	255
" Errors in	49, 53
" Initiation of	120
" Qualifications of	106, 118, 133, 256
" Representatives of the Lord	256
" Their Failure in Service	145
" " Maintenance	23
" " Ministry	105
" Witnesses to a Spiritual Life	23
Privilege, Conditional	254
Privileged People, Miseries Befalling a	315
Privileges, Higher	188
Profanity	133, 147, 297
Progress	193
Progressive Cleansing	186
Prohibitions Abrogated by Christianity	156
Promises and Warnings	312
Property	78
Property, Ancestral	303
Prophetic Promises and Warnings	309
Propitiation	11, 12, 19, 31, 35, 49, 217
Public Lamentation	149
Punishment	151
" of Pride	321
" of Sinners	321
Purifying	53, 54, 167, 217
Purity and Impurity Distinguished	262
" in the House	189, 225, 230, 233
" in Service	28, 137
" of the Priesthood	252
" Personal	195, 196

	PAGE.
R	
Rashness	128, 139, 150
Reaping, Beginning Harvest	285
Rebellious, Way Open to Return	313
Reconciliation	203
" with God	88, 220, 286
Recovery, Anxiety for	185
" Complete	192
Regenerating Grace, Like Fire	82
Relationship Inseparable, Christian	254
Reliance on God	298
Religion	231
" Determining Nation's Destiny	309
" Incentives to True	317
Remedial Measures	186
Reparation. See RESTITUTION.	
Repentance	285, 322
Reproach for Christ	54
Reproving our Neighbour, Duty of	241
Repulsive Incense	130
Reserved Things	99
Resignation. See also SUBMISSION.	148
Rest, Christian Dispensation of	299
" From Toils	301, 303
" in Finding Christ	308
" Sabbatic Year a Symbol of	299
Restitution	65, 76, 97, 300, 302
Restoration	186
Resurrection, Christ's	26, 275
" Emblems	26, 29
" Final, of the Dead	276, 279
" First Fruits a Symbol of	275
" Scene	279
Retribution	135
Revelation: Its Author, etc.	13, 18, 56
Reverence	220
Ritual, The Levitical	4
" Sacrificial	94
Robbing God	66
Royal Service	308
Ruler, His Sin	40, 51
S	
Sabbath	286, 308
" Abuse	322
" Barrenness	321
" for the land	297, 298
" in the Family	237
" of rest	215, 243, 269, 299
" perfectly consecrated	264
" sanctity of	234, 242
Sabbatical Year	306
Sacrament of Lord's Supper	264, 273
Sacred life a Festival	283
" Office	133
" Seasons	283
Sacrifice, Bloodless	20
" Burnt	2, 9, 80, 96
" Meat	96
" necessity for	14, 89, 207
" Peace	29, 31, 35, 87, 90, 93
" Sin and Trespass	38, 85, 97, 98, 102
" Solemnity of, Publicly Recognised	219
" The Atoning	2, 7
" The Place of	220
" to Devils	225
Sacrifices, Living	113
" of Peace	83

ANALYTICAL INDEX.

	PAGE.
Sacrifices, The Worth of	207
Sacrilege	45, 68, 137, 148
Salt, Sacrifice Seasoned with	21
Sanctification	113, 154, 192, 193, 197
Sanctity, Possibilities of	249
Sanctuary Ministry	133
„ reverenced	224, 237, 243
Satisfaction to God. See RESTITUTION.	
Scapegoat	199, 200, 204, 218
Scripture, The Antidote for Ignorance	56, 58
Secresy	198
Secret Flow of Sin	197
„ Impurities	194
Secular and Sacred Things	262
Self-dedication	15, 18
„ excuse	60
„ glorying	131, 174
„ in abeyance	284
„ mastery	198
„ satisfaction	249
„ surrender	31, 284
„ will in Service	147
Sensationalism	144
Separation	202
„ between Good and Evil	153, 155, 163
Separateness, Godly	252
Service, Perfect	113, 119
„ Royal	308
„ Special Times for	295
Seven Days' Consecration	113
Sevenfold Purging	53
Sheaf of Firstfruits	26, 275, 284
Shewbread	290, 291, 295
Sin, Contagious	62, 179, 180
„ Heinous	230
„ Removed	216
Sinai's Law	43, 278, 280
Sinner's Vileness	195
Sins, Annihilation of	54
„ Fearful Aspect of	47, 246, 248
„ Loathed by God	54, 207
„ not Connived at	180
„ of Ignorance	40
„ Sacrifice for	38, 85
Sin-worn Spirit of Man Asks Rest	271
Slander	233, 239, 244
Social. See FAMILY, HOUSEHOLD.	
„ Crimes	244
„ Obscurity	52
Solemn Regard for Holy Things	260
Solitary, the High Priest	209
„ the Leper	181
Sorrow, Elevation Above	143
„ in God's presence	145
Sovereignty, God's	36
Spirit's Efficacy	17
„ Fulness	276
„ Grace	17
Spiritual Anointing	107
„ Benefactors	128
„ Significance of the Sacrifices	1
„ Union	310
Spotless High Priest	209
Sprinkling	54
Stewardship	240
Strangers, Hospitality to	234, 243, 259
Strife	293
Submission	148, 151

	PAGE.
Substitution of Victim for the Offerer	3, 17
Succession in Sacrifice	37
Summary of Contents of Leviticus	1, 321
Superstitions	234, 242, 244
Supper, The Lord's	273
Surroundings, Sinful	178, 226, 229
Swearing. See BLASPHEMY.	
„ False	238
Sweet Savour Sacrifices	3, 29
Sympathy	149

T

Tabernacle, Man's Frail	286
Tabernacles, Feast of	280, 281, 282, 286
Table, Golden	290
„ of Shewbread	291
Talebearers	239
Temperance	149, 150, 151
„ See INTOXICATION.	
Temptations of Ministers	135
Thanksgiving	29, 32, 38, 98
Thoroughness	28
Tithes: Arguments Against	330
„ Ecclesiastical	329
„ Great and Small	329
„ History of	328
„ Introduction into England of	329
„ Scripture Records of	328
„ Withholding	332
Tongue, Ungoverned	293
Trade, Fairness in	234, 243
Transmitted Effects	181
Trespasses. See SINS, IGNORANCE.	
Trumpets, Blowing of	277, 287
„ Feast of	279
„ Gospel	278
„ Memorial of Sinai	278

U.

Unblemished Sacrifices	266
"Unclean"	175
Unclean Foods	156
„ „ may be Cleansed	157
Uncleanness forfeits Priestly Privilege	259
Uncorruptness	26
Undignified Duties	80
Union, Spiritual, between God and Israel	310

V.

Valour and Victory through Godliness	320
Variety in Worship	10
Veil of the Sanctuary	53
Vicarious Sacrifice	10
Vice	198
Victory through Godliness	320
Vigilance. See WATCHFULNESS.	
Vile distinguished from the Precious	153
Vileness, Man's	195
Violation of Sanctity	148
Violation. See DEFILED, SACRILEGE.	
Virtue	198
Volition in Worship	14
Voluntary act of Offering	2, 9
„ Dedication	7
Votive Offerings to the Lord	324
„ Redemption of	327
Vows, Acceptable according to the motive	325
„ God holds us to our	328

ANALYTICAL INDEX.

	PAGE.
Vows Laws Concerning	325
„ the Singular vow	324
„ Unpaid	332

W.

	PAGE.
Wages	239
Warnings and Promises	312
Watchfulness	156
Way to God	13
Weaknesses forfeit privileges	143
Weary life of Man asks rest	270
What God expects of us	64
Whisperings	233, 239
Wilderness Pilgrims through the	286
Within the Veil	120
Witnesses against wrong	61
Words, Responsibility for	63
Workers in the Church must be godly	267
Worldliness	228
Worship acceptable	6, 137

	PAGE.
Worship, affections in	21
„ as a privilege	7
„ as Dedication	7
„ Christian	7
„ excellencies n	21, 138
„ excitable	131, 137, 144
„ preparation for	21, 138
„ spurious	139
„ symbolic	7
„ The Law of	137
„ true	100, 139
Worshippers, true and False	137, 138, 139
„ warning to	140
Worthiness of Jesus foreshadowed	22

Y.

Year, A new year begun	278, 280
„ gone	278
Youthful Profanity	188

ILLUSTRATIONS & QUOTATIONS.

A.

	PAGE.
Abraham's Tent and Altar	243
"Action, leaves somewhere a record"	182
„ "Keen spirit, starts into instant action"	248
Afraid of nothing but Fear	320
"Affliction is not sent in vain" (Southey)	172
"Angels of God in Disguise"	250
"Appetite, Govern well thy"	154
„ "No man's body is as strong as his" (Tillotson)	198
Ancestors	323
Ancestral Heritages	303
Antiochus' Sacrilege	262
Ascending Fire	19
Atonement not found in Bible. By Dr. Taylor.	19

B.

Beautiful in Worship	28
Beautiful, "'Tis first the Pure, and then the"	29

	PAGE
Beautiful, "Virtue is Fairer in a Person"	259
Beauty—"Excellence true Beauty"	29
„ "'Tis not a lip, an eye, we beauty call"	258
Beecher, H. W., concerning Injury	86
Belshazzar's Sacrilege	262
Benefactors, Spiritual	128
Beneficence a Duty	308
Benevolence	308
Bible, Ignorance of	58
„ Salmasius' advice	58
„ Samuel Johnson's daily reading of	58
Blasphemy, Incident of	292
„ Louis IX. concerning	293
Blood, Life in the ; A Modern Discovery	225
Blood—"We have the Blood of Christ" (Schliermacher)	195
Bodily Appearance	258
„ Infirmities	258
Bonar. "I thank Thee, Lord, for using me"	128
Bravery ; "Brave man feels no fear"	323

ILLUSTRATIONS AND QUOTATIONS.

	PAGE.
"Brutus hath riv'd my Heart"	86
Business and Work	244
Byron concerning Conscience	75

C.

"Calamity is Man's True Touchstone"	151
Calvin: Crest of, with Motto	19
Caryl, on Heathen Regard for Solemnities	262
Cave, Principal, on Altar Fire	19
Cecil Respecting Ministers	29
Celibacy	258
Character	29
„ "A Mind to Suit Thine Outward"	258
„ German Motto Concerning	29
Charity	243
„ "He Truly Great that is Great in Charity"	243
"Charms Strike the Sight"	259
Child, A Spoilt New Blossom of Humanity"	251
„ a Thankless	250
Childhood	169
"Children are what their Mothers are"	169
Christian Graces shown	114
„ Man: "Whose Doctrine and Life Coincident"	311
Cicero, concerning Error	58
„ Things hallowed	262
Cleanliness	189
"Cleanly platter on the board" (Goldsmith)	189
Cleansed	193
„ "Who would be cleansed from every sin"	193
"Comfort in Despair"	28
Communion. "With God eternally shut in"	145
Companions. "Not with the light and vain"	163
Confucius concerning Friendship	163
„ „ Ignorance	57
„ „ Justice	86
„ „ Virtue	86
Conscience—Mutinies in Bosom	75
„ "Harder than our Enemies"	75
„ "The Oracle of God"	75
„ in everything"	87
Consecration	19
„ Baptist Missionary Society's Motto	19
"Consequences are unpitying"	181
Country, love of	323
"Courage, essential to Character" (Froude)	320
"Cowards die many times," etc.	320
Cross, Cowper concerning the	71
"Cross, It takes our Guilt away"	157
Custom	231
„ calls me to it"	231
„ "Man yields to, as he bows to Fate"	231
„ more honoured in the breach"	227
„ New customs, though ridiculous, are followed	231

D.

Decay	244

	PAGE.
Dedication: "I cannot love Thee," etc.	330
Deeds. "We live in deeds not years" (Bailey)	229
Developments	181
"Disease to luxury succeeds"	171
"Disposition, not the deed"	29
Distress. "To pity distress is human"	243
Drink.— "We drink our poison," etc.	164
„ "When once the demon enters"	134
Drunkenness	151

E.

Eliot, George, Concerning "Conscience"	75
„ „ "Consequences"	181
"Evils that men do live after them"	181

F.

"Faith and unfaith can ne'er be equal powers"	87
Faithlessness	87
Falsehood a Goodly Outside	87
Family Piety	243
„ Abraham's Tent	243
Fear, Afraid of fear, *Montaigne*	320
„ "To fear the foe, since fear oppresseth strength"	320
Feasting	164
Fire, Enduring	86
Fires, Living	86
"Flesh is heir to"	171
Forgiveness, Luther Concerning	58
Frail Habitations	287
"Freeman whom truth makes free"	309
Friendships, Confucius Concerning	163
„ of the world are oft confederacies in vice"	163
„ "Nature and religion are the bands of"	163
Froude's View of Sacrifice	19
„ Testimony concerning Courage	320

G.

God's Name Blasphemed	292
Goethe Concerning "Self-Mastery"	198
Goldsmith Concerning Pride	150
Graces, a Christian should show his	114
Guthrie, Dr., on Ministers	29

H.

Hamilton, Dr. James, on Worship	29
„ „ on Peace	28
"Handsome is that handsome does"	259
Happiness, Virtue is True	29
Harvest Custom of Hindoos	287
„ First Fruits	287
„ "Lord of the harvest all is Thine"	287
Hare, A. W., Concerning Knowledge	
Hastings, Warren, his yearnings for Daylesford	302
Haughty, "An Avenging God follows"	150
"Hearths and altars"	190
Hearts. "Idols of Hearts and of Households"	250
Herbert, George, "Make thyself all reverence and fear"	100
„ „ "Restore to God His due"	71
Herod's Pollution of Sepulchres	263

	PAGE.		PAGE.
Helplessness	193	Milton, on Redemption	71
,, Medical Incident Illustrating the Soul's... ...	193	Ministers, Credentials of	29
Holiness, Inward	114	,, Dedication of	127
,, Jonathan Edwards on Personal	114	,, Dr. Guthrie concerning ...	29
Home and Happiness Connected ...	114	,, maintenance of	29
,, Cleanliness	189	,, used by God	128
,, Creature Holiness. *Edwards* ...	193	Morality	243
,, "Home should be the centre of joy"	194	Motherhood	169
,, "O happy home, O home supremely blest"	194	Mother. Monica, Augustine's mother ...	169
,, "The almost sacred joys of home depend"	190	,, Cecil's mother	169
Human Life, its True Object	18	Mothers: "A Mother is a Mother still"...	169
		,, "A Mother's love is an undying feeling"	169
		,, Say to Mothers, "What a holy charge!"	166
		,, "The Mother's heart is the child's school"	169

I.

Ignorance, Classical quotations concerning	57		
,, Conviction of	57	### N.	
,, Explanation of	57	Name: "A lost good name is ne'er retrieved."—*Gay*. ...	244
,, "is the curse of God" ...	57	,, God's Name blasphemed ...	292
,, Perils of	57	Nation, Advantage of Religion to.—*Burke*.	310
Imposture—Quotations under Priestism	114	,, ,, Testimony of Quincy	311
Incense, Sweet, in Worship	29	National Irreligion	323
"Industry supports us all"	244	Nearness to God	128
Indifference	71	Neighbours, Virtue wins	86
"Inhumanity to Man"	75	Neighbourliness	244
Injury	86	Newton, A. L., concerning "Forgiveness"	58
Intemperance 134,	151	,, John, concerning "Atonement"	19
Isaac Walton concerning Ignorance ...	57		

J.

		### O.	
Johnson, Dr., concerning Ignorance ...	57	"Oath. I had an oath in heaven" ...	71
,, ,, the Bible ...	58	Oaths, "Not many that make the truth"	71
Judge: "A Judge whom no king can corrupt"	244	,, Profane	71
,, "Four things belong to a Judge," etc. (Socrates)	244	,, Sincere	71
,, "He who the Sword of Heaven would bear"	244	,, Taking	70
Justice	86	,, Unlawful	70
,, The virtue of Justice is moderation," etc.	244	Occasion, Keen spirit seizes the prompt	248
		Offerings to God	100
		Old Age	244
		,, "is not all decay	244
### K.		,, "Mourns less for what age takes away"	244
Kitto, on Sacrifices of peace ...	38		

L.

		### P.	
"Lands were fairly portioned" ...	308	Pagan Images of Death	29
Large streams from little fountains flow	181	Pardon	57
Leper. "Room for the leper, room!" (Willis)	193	Passions	198
Liberty, in Christ	308	,, "Follow where our passions lead the way," *Claudian* ...	198
Libel. "Convey a libel in a frown" ...	244	,, "When passion rules," *Scott* ...	198
"Life's shadows are meeting Eternity's day"	244	Peace, Blessedness of	38
Life, insecurity of	287	,, Christ Whispering	100
"Light in darkness, comfort in despair"	38	,, Incidents of one finding Peace, *Fleming*	100
Light bearers	296	,, of the Gospel	38
"Little sparks may burst into a mighty flame"	181	,, on Earth	38
Louis, king of France, concerning profanity	71	,, Sacred	100
,, ,, blasphemy etc.	293	,, terms of	38
"Lowliest soul may be a temple" ...	188	"Penitence has wept in vain" ...	184
		Perjury. "Perjuries are common as bad pence"	215
### M.		"Piety, whose soul sincere, fears God," etc.	227
Macaulay concerning Ancestral property	303	"Pleasures, harmlessly pursued," *Cowper*	155
Mercy-seat	217	Pompey's Sacrilege	262
		"Poor man loved the great" ...	308

ILLUSTRATIONS AND QUOTATIONS.

	PAGE
Poor, Sacrifices of	19
Poor, the Church's Treasures	194
,, "Blessed are the poor"	194
Possessions	309
Poverty: the Saintly Poor	193
,, of Spirit	193
,, "Slow rises worth by poverty depressed"	243
,, "Poverty a load which is heavier the more share it"	243
Prayer: Opens Heaven	120
,, "More things wrought by," etc.	120
,, "Hath turned my feigned prayer upon my head"	135
"Preach impostures to the world"	114
Presumption	151
Pride	151
,, Crushed	323
Priestism	114
Priest, Meddling	114
"Primrose by the river's brim"	22
Profane Oaths	71
Profanity. (See also SWEARING, BLASPHEMY	297
Progress	193
,, "Every upward step makes another needful"	193
,, "Flying birds not taken"	193
Propitiation	217
"Punishment is the recoil of crime"	151
"Pure domestic shrine"	190

R.

Rashness, Classical Quotations	151
Redemption	71
,, Shakespeare, concerning	71
Relatively. "We are really what we are relatively"	243
Religious Men: "I Venerate a Man whose Heart" &c.	311
Religion	231
,, "Blushing, veils her sacred fires" *Pope*	262
,, "Consists in Obedience"	231
,, Faithfully Obeying God's Laws	231
,, "is a Struggle, not a Hymn," *Stael*	231
,, "is Life Essential," *Macdonald*	231
Reparation	71
Resurrection Emblems	29
Rest, Found in Christ	303
"Rest is coming, rest is nigh"	271
"Rest, Spirit, free, in the green pastures"	272
Ruskin, concerning Peace on Earth	38
,, ,, Pride	158
Revelation	19
,, Satisfies all Doubts	10

S.

Sabbath to the Poor	308
,, "A Segment of the Eternal Sabbath"	286
,, and Sanctuary	243
,, Called by Jews "Day of Light"	286
,, "Day of the Lord, and truce to Earthly care," *Longfellow*	243

	PAGE
Sabbath, "Fifty-two Springs in every Year," *Coleridge*	286
,, Forgetting the	287
,, "How Still the Morning of the Hallowed Day"	286
,, Philip Henry's Sabbaths	243
,, Sin keeps no	243
,, "Thou art a Cooling Fountain"	271
,, "Tranquil and Happy To-day"	287
,, *Wilberforce's* Testimony to its Value	286
"Sabbaths are Threefold, as St. Austin says"	270
Sacrifices of the Poor	19
Sacrifice, Froude's View	19
,, of Peace	38
,, to Devils	225
Sacred Peace	100
"Sail on, thou Ship of State"	323
Sanctuary, worship in the	100
,, All holy there	100
Sanctity	144
Sanctification	193
,, *v.* Justification, *Jay*	193
Scapegoat	218
Schliermacher's Dying Words, "We have the Blood!"	195
Scripture Light	58
Seasons: "His love ordained the seasons"	238
Secresy	198
,, "Go to your our bosom, knock there."	198
"Seeds of all my sins are in my Heart"	182
"Seed we sow another reaps"	181
Self-knowledge. Guesses at truth	57
Self mastery	198
,, "I will be lord over myself," *Goethe*	198
Sensationalism	151
Separate from sinners	163
Sincere Oaths	71
Sinners, Separate from	163
Sins. "Great sins make great sufferers"	182
"Slander filled her mouth with lying words"	244
Sleep, Death as a	29
Staupitz and Luther concerning Forgiveness	57
,, "Tho' pure as snow, not escape"	244
Submission	151
,, Mrs. Browing concerning	151
,, A father's submission	151
Superstitions	244
Swearing: Burroughs on	292
,, Louis, IX. Concerning	293

T.

Temperance in Diet	164
Tennyson, "More things are wrought by prayer"	120
,, "Hands moulding man"	181
Thanksgiving	38
,, Constant	38
,, Life's work	38
"'Tis not a lip, an eye, we beauty call"	250
Tithe, Incidents of lapsing from	332
Tithes, George Herbert's words	71

ILLUSTRATIONS AND QUOTATIONS.

	PAGE.
Tongue, "One evil tongue hurts three persons"	244
"Touch the Goblet no more"	151
Transmitted Effects	181
"Treason, where trust is greatest"	87
Trifler, "Not with the trifler gay"	163
True friend to man, ne'er a foe to God	87
Trust, Sterne concerning	87
" Emerson	87
Trumpets, Blowing of	287
" "The dead all have heard"	287

U

Unclean	182
Unlawful Oaths	71

V

Valour: John Knox	323
Varro, B.C. 100, Collects Opinions on Human Life	18
"Vice stings us even in our pleasures," Colton	198
" "Men only feel the smart," Pope	198
" "No man confesses his vices," Seneca	198
"Violent fires soon burn out themselves"	151
"Virtue that transgresses is but patched," &c.	198
" "consecrating every feature," Young	259
" "Follow virtue even for virtue's sake," Pope	243

	PAGE.
Virtue "is the soul's calm sunshine" Pope	198
,, "One virtuous person more than ten vicious"	198
,, "requires a tutor," Seneca	198
Vows: "Unheedful vows may heedfully be broken"	71
" "Grace to keep thy vows"	332
" "to every purpose must not hold"	332
" Unpaid	332

W

Wesley's Boast: "God is for us"	320
'When once the demon enters"	134
"When one that holds communion with the skies"	128
"Whispers, Cutting honest throats by"	244
"Words are bonds, his oaths are oracles"	71
Working Seven Days a Week	308
Work: "All true work is sacred," Carlyle	244
" "Men must work, and women must weep"	244
Worship, The Beautiful in	29
" Oriental usage in	29
,, Sweet Incense Worship	29
,, True	100

Y

"Yoke of inbred sin"	19
"Youth cannot control its impetuosity"	151

A HOMILETICAL COMMENTARY

ON THE BOOK OF

NUMBERS

(CHAPTERS I. TO XV.)

WITH CRITICAL AND EXPLANATORY NOTES, INDICES, Etc., Etc.

BY

REV. WILLIAM JONES.

New York
FUNK & WAGNALLS COMPANY
LONDON & TORONTO
1892

HOMILETIC COMMENTARY

ON

THE BOOK OF NUMBERS,

BY

WILLIAM JONES.

Introduction.

TITLE.

THE word *Numbers* is a translation of the title given to this book in the LXX, Ἀριθμοί, in the Vulgate *Numeri*, and was evidently applied to it because it contains the record of the two numberings of the people. The Jews sometimes call it וַיְדַבֵּר, *Vayedabber*, which is its first word in the Heb.; but more frequently בְּמִדְבַּר, *Bemidbar*, *in the desert*, which is its fifth word, and more accurately characterises the book.

CONTENTS.

"The book narrates the history of the Israelites during their sojourn in the wilderness from the completion of the law-giving at Sinai (Lev. xxvii. 34) to their mustering in the plains of Moab for actual entry into the Land of Promise" —or, from "the first day of the second month, in the second year after they were come out of the land of Egypt" (chap. i. 1) to the end of the tenth month of the fortieth year (Deut. i. 3), or a period of thirty-eight years and nine months. The events of the history are generally given in their chronological order, except in chapters xv.-xix., inclusive. These "chapters appear to deal with a long period, from which only isolated episodes are given; and of these the dates can only be conjectured."

AUTHORSHIP.

From the earliest times the book has been generally regarded as, in substance, at least, the work of Moses. In support of this view, the following reasons are given in the "Speaker's Commentary:"—"(1) The catalogue of the stations or encampments during the journeyings is assigned to Moses in xxxiii. 2. (2) The intermixture in this book of narrative and legislative matter is one of its characteristic features .... This feature is exactly one which belongs to the work of a contemporary annalist. (3) That the author had an intimate acquaintance with Egypt may be strikingly illustrated from Numbers. Compare viii. 7 *sqq.*; v. 11-35; xix. 1-10; xi. 5, 6; xiii. 22. (4) The statements of this book abound in evidences that the writer and those with whom he lived were still in the desert. Compare xix. 14; ii.; ix. 16 *sqq.*; x. 1-28, 35, 36. (5) There are topographical statements in the book which could hardly have been written after the days of Moses. Compare xxi. 13 with xxxii. (6) The various communications purporting to be from God to Moses are so worded and often of such a nature (cf. *e.g.* xiv. 11-26), that unless we go the length of denying their historical character altogether, we must admit them to have been recorded by the very person who received them. (7) No other person than Moses has been or can be named with anything like probability, or even plausibility, as the author .... We conclude then, with confidence, that nothing has been as yet alleged which disturbs the generally-accepted views respecting the authorship of this book. It is, in substance, the work of Moses; and whilst many portions of it were probably committed to writing for years before the whole was completed, yet the concluding chapters were not written until towards the close of the fortieth year after the exodus."

As to our work on this book, very few words are necessary. In accordance with a leading principle of this series of Commentaries, we have endeavoured to present the largest number of things in the smallest number of words. To this principle, literary finish and grace have been subordinated. Some of the records contained in this book are not well adapted to homiletic treatment or fruitful in homiletic suggestion. In dealing with these, we have endeavoured to suggest homiletic methods without any straining of the text or unworthy handling of the Sacred Word; and we venture to hope that we have not been altogether unsuccessful in this respect. The illustrations which are given are (by Mr. Dickinson's request) numerous. They are drawn from a wide range of literature, and very few of them are taken from "Storehouses," "Treasuries," or "Dictionaries of Illustration." Each one will be found to be well suited to illumine or impress the point to which it is attached. In our work we have consulted the best authors who have written on this book; and are under considerable obligations to "A Commentarie upon the Fourth Booke of Moses, called Numbers, by William Attersoll, Minister of the Word" (1618); "Comfortable Notes upon the Booke of Numbers, by Bishop Gervase Babington" (1637); "Keil and Delitzsch's Commentary on the Pentateuch;" and to the "Speaker's Commentary."

HOMILETIC COMMENTARY ON THE BOOK OF NUMBERS.

CHAPTER I.

The Numbering of the People.

(*Verses* 1–3.)

"The object of the encampment at Sinai," says Perowne, "has been accomplished. The Covenant has been made, the Law given, the Sanctuary set up, the Priests consecrated, the service of God appointed, and Jehovah dwells in the midst of His chosen people. It is now time to depart in order that the object may be achieved for which Israel has been sanctified. That object is the occupation of the Promised Land. But this is not to be accomplished by peaceable means, but by the forcible expulsion of its present inhabitants; for 'the iniquity of the Amorites is full,' they are ripe for judgment, and this judgment Israel is to execute. Therefore Israel must be organised as Jehovah's army; and to this end a mustering of all who are capable of bearing arms is necessary. Hence the book opens with the numbering of the people."

Thrice were the people numbered in the wilderness. Nine months previous they were numbered for the purpose of collecting atonement-money from every male of twenty years old and upward (Comp. Exod. xxx. 11-16 with xxxviii. 25, 26). On this occasion they were numbered with a view to war. And thirty-eight years afterwards, in the plains of Moab, they were again numbered, for the division of the Promised Land among the tribes, according to the number of their families (Comp. xxvi. and xxxiii. 54).

Our text sets forth:—

I. The Authority for this Numbering.

It was commanded by God. "The Lord spake unto Moses . . . Take ye the sum of all the congregation of the children of Israel." Contrast this with the numbering of the people by David (1 Sam. xxiv., and 1 Chron. xxi). This was expressly commanded by the Lord: that was utterly devoid of Divine authority. This was done for wise and worthy reasons (as we shall see); that, from pride and vain reliance. Moses numbered the people to see the number of God's subjects able to fight in the Lord's battles. David seems to have desired to know the number of the people as his own subjects, and to display the extent of his own dominion and power. As the result of David's sin, the Lord, by pestilence, slew seventy thousand men. It is of the utmost importance that the leaders of men should be well assured of two things in the movements which they inaugurate:—

1. *That they have the Divine approval of their undertakings.* The movement which is approved by God, and well prosecuted, shall advance to splendid triumph. But that which He approves

not must end in failure and disaster. Apply this test to our undertakings.

2. *That they are actuated by worthy motives in their undertakings.* A sinful, selfish, or mean motive will vitiate our enterprises and mar our works. "The Lord looketh at the heart." Let us scrutinize our motives.

II. **The Place of this Numbering.** "In the wilderness of Sinai."

1. *In a desert.* The wilderness suggests (1) the ideas of a life of *Privation.* Little or no food grows in the desert. There are no homes in the desert. Pleasant streams and refreshing shades are seldom found there. (2) *Peril.* This would arise from the scorching heat of the sun; from the furious violence of the storm, and from the fierce attacks of savage beasts. (3) *Perplexity.* The desert has no well-defined roads made through it. The traveller is very liable to lose his track, grow bewildered, and sink into utter perplexity. We have in this an illustration of the life of the good in this world. The world cannot supply the soul's needs. We have needs and yearnings that the best things of this world are utterly inadequate to satisfy. We cannot find a home for the soul in anything here. This is not our rest. There are perils many and great in this present life and world. We, too, are "in the desert."

2. *In a desert where the tabernacle of God was.* "In the wilderness of Sinai, in the tabernacle of the congregation." They were in the desert; but the Lord also was there. His presence was a guarantee of (1) *Provision.* He fed them with bread from heaven. His presence and power transformed the desert into a banquet hall. In obedience to His will the solid rock became a fountain, and the desert rejoiced in pleasant streams. In Him the homeless wanderers found a home and rest. (2) *Protection.* He guarded them from the scorching heat of the sun by day by the pillar of cloud, and from the attacks of savage beasts by night by the pillar of fire. In the day of battle He was their shield and fortress. (3) *Direction.* He "led His people like a flock by the hand of Moses and Aaron." He "guided them in the wilderness like a flock." "He led them forth by the right way, that they might go to a city of habitation." It matters not that this world is like a desert to the godly soul, if God be with us here. His presence will afford the most adequate and delightful supplies, the divinest satisfaction, the most impregnable defence, and the most infallible guidance.

" Though in a bare and rugged way,
Through devious, lonely wilds I stray,
Thy presence shall my pains beguile;
The barren wilderness shall smile,
With sudden green and herbage crowned,
And streams shall murmur all around."
Addison.

III. **The Time of this Numbering.** "On the first of the second month, in the second year after they were come out of the land of Egypt." That is, exactly one month after the setting up of the tabernacle (Exod. xl. 2, 17) and about eleven months from the time of their arrival in the desert of Sinai. The people abode in this desert nearly a whole year (Comp. Exod. xix. 1, with Num. i. 1, and x. 11). What was the reason of this protracted halt? With so great and inspiriting a destiny before them as the taking possession of the Promised Land, why did they not advance at once with eager resolution to their task? The design of this long stay was, that they might be instructed in their relations to God and to each other; that they might learn lessons of duty and worship; that they might be taught to reverence and obey God. The pause was for the purpose of promoting progress. There are times and circumstances in which standing still is the truest and speediest advance. It is well that the declaration of war should not be made until plans of operation are formed, equipments prepared, soldiers drilled and disciplined, etc. What a terrible reminder of this truth France received in her recent war with Prussia! It was well that the Apostles, with the commission to the most glorious task, and the world sorely needing their message, should, notwithstanding, tarry at Jerusalem in silence, until they were baptized with the Holy Ghost.

Let us learn the wisdom of waiting until circumstances, events, and agents are ripe for action ; and while we wait, make diligent preparation, etc. (*a*)

IV. **The Manner of this Numbering.**

"Take ye the sum of all the congregation of the children of Israel, after their families, by the house of their fathers, with the number of their names, every male by their polls, from twenty years old and upward, all that are able to go forth to war in Israel." They were to take account of—

1. *Only the males.* All females were excluded from the reckoning.

2. Only the males *above twenty years old.* Those who were under that age were not taken into the account, being regarded as too young to endure the strain of military service.

3. Only the males above twenty years old *who were in vigorous health,*—"able to go forth to war." The sick, the aged, the infirm, the maimed were exempted from this census, as unfit for war.

4. They were to be numbered "*after their families*," that it might be known of what tribe, and of what particular house every able man was.

5. The numbering was to be *individual, and by name.* "With the number of their names, every male by their polls." The census was particular and minute. From these directions as to the numbering we learn:—

First: *That the Lord chooses fit instruments for the accomplishment of His purposes.* He here selects for war not women, or boys, or old men, or the infirm ; but able men. He can use any instrumentality, even the feeblest, for the most arduous tasks. But such is not His method. He employs means adapted to the ends to be attained. Illustrations of this abound. Joseph, Moses, Joshua, David, Paul.

Second : *That the Lord is perfectly acquainted with every one who is fitted for His work.* He knows the tribe, the family, the name of every one who is " able to go forth to war " against ignorance, sin and misery. Ponder this ye able men who are at ease in Zion.

V. **The Design of this Numbering.**

1. The primary design was, *the organization of the army.* God had promised to give them the land of Canaan. He will certainly bestow it upon them ; but not without their effort. Innumerable foes must be vanquished before they enter upon the land. They must do battle with the heathen nations that are now in possession, and conquer them. And to do this, they must organise an army, employing the fittest men for soldiers, making the wisest arrangements for marching, encamping, etc. Where ordinary means are adequate to accomplish the desired end, God never uses extraordinary. What man can do for himself, God never does for him. God has promised to us the victory over our spiritual foes, the possession of the inheritance of spiritual perfection and privileges, and heaven as the goal of our earthly pilgrimage. He will not fail to fulfil His promise. But we, too, must use the means. If we would enter into the restful activities of heaven, we must live the life of faith and of Divine service on earth. If we would gain the victory we must be valiant and persistent in the fight. If we would win the prize we must " run with patience the race," etc. (*b*). But this numbering would serve other important purposes. It would tend—

2. *To manifest the Divine faithfulness.* God had promised Abraham that his seed should be as the stars for multitude. This census shows how God was fulfilling that promise. Seventy-five souls went down into Egypt. And how wonderfully are they increased in 215 years ! Now there are six hundred thousand men able to bear arms. And the whole population could not have been less than two millions, and this despite the oppression and persecutions of the Egyptians. " He is faithful that promised." *

---

* For a critical examination of the numbers recorded in this book see Keil and Delitzsch *in loco.*

3. *To show forth the Divine power.* We see this in His feeding and sustaining so immense a number in the desert, "without harvest or husbandry, without planting or tilling, without sowing of corn, or without feeding and breeding of cattle."

4. *To the promotion of order.* "It is a rout and a rabble, not an army, that is not mustered and put in order."

5. *To exhibit, on the coming of the Messiah, the correspondence of the event with the predictions concerning it.* He was predicted as to come of the seed of Abraham, of the tribe of Judah, of the house of David. Hence the importance of an accurate register of tribes and families.

6. *To illustrate the care of God for His people generally and particularly.* They were numbered individually and by name. The Lord's care over His people is most minute and constant and tender. "He calleth His own sheep by name, and leadeth them out. The good Shepherd giveth His life for the sheep." "The Lord knoweth them that are His." "The very hairs of your head are all numbered."

ILLUSTRATIONS.

(*a*) I warn those who have only lately found their Saviour from rushing before their fellow-men, and attempting to fill those posts in the service of Christ which demand a deeper experience and a more tried and tested Christianhood. The Lord's retirement to the wilderness after He had been baptised and announced as the Messiah, after He was in a peculiar manner "full of the Holy Ghost," gives to all of us not less humbling than profitable guidance as to the deliberation with which solemn work ought to be undertaken. . . . . Not up to Jerusalem, but away to the wilderness; not out to the multitude, but back to the solitude; not forth to the world to conquer, but away from it, "impelled" by the Spirit, "to be tempted." Nor does this stand solitary in the history of the Church. You remember that strange, half-involuntary forty years of Moses in the wilderness of Midian, when he had fled from Egypt. You remember, too, the almost equally strange years of retirement in Arabia by Paul when, if ever, humanly speaking, instant action was needed. And pre-eminently you remember the amazing charge of the ascending Lord to the disciples: "Tarry at Jerusalem." Speaking after the manner of men, one could not have wondered if out-spoken Peter, or fervid James, had said: "Tarry, Lord! How long? Tarry, Lord! Is there not a perishing world groaning for the 'good news'? Tarry! did we hear Thee aright, Lord? Was not the word, haste?" Nay: "Being assembled together with them, He *commanded* them that they should not depart from Jerusalem, but *wait* for the promise of the Father."—*Grosart.*

(*b*) We are here in every sense on a stage of probation; so that, having been once recovered from apostasy, we are candidates for a prize and wrestlers for a crown. It is not the mere admission into the kingdom for which we contend. When justified, there is open before us the widest field for a righteous ambition—and portions heightening in majesty, and deepening in brilliancy, rise on our vision to incite to unwearied endeavour. For I count it one of the glories of Christianity that, in place of repressing, it gives full scope to all the ardours of the spirit of man. . . . . Christianity tells her subjects that the rewards in eternity, though all purchased by Christ, and none merited by men, shall be rigidly apportioned to their works. She tells them that there are places of dignity, and stations of eminence, and crowns with more jewellery, and sceptres with more sway, in that glorious empire which Christ shall set up at His second appearing. And she bids them strive for a loftier recompense; she would not have them content with a lesser portion, though it infinitely outgrew human imagination as well as human desert. She sends them to wrestle for the loftiest, though unworthy of the lowest. She does not allow the believer to imagine that everything is done when a title to the kingdom is obtained. She shows him that the trials of the last great assize shall proceed most accurately by measure of works. There is no swerving in the Bible from this representation. And if one man become a ruler over ten cities, and another over five, and another over two, each receiving in exact proportion to his improvement of talents, then it is clear as demonstration can make it that our strivings will have a vast influence on our recompense—that there shall be no particle in the portion of the righteous which is not altogether an undeserved gift; still, in the arrangements of judgment there will be an accurate balancing of what is bestowed and what is performed. Oh! it shall not be said that because he is secure of admission to heaven, the Christian has nothing further to excite him to toil. He is to wrestle for a place amongst spirits of chief renown; he is to propose to himself a station close to the throne. —*H. Melvill, B.D.*

IN THE DESERT: AN ILLUSTRATION OF THE LIFE OF THE GOOD IN THIS WORLD.

(*Verse* 1.)

"And the Lord spake unto Moses in the wilderness of Sinai, in the tabernacle of the congregation."

In the Hebrew Bible this book is called בְּמִדְבַּר = in the desert. By this name also the Jews generally speak of it. The title is most appropriate for the book which records the history of Israel during the long wandering in the wilderness.

Consider:

I. **The natural trials of the desert.** Deserts are generally characterised by—

1. *Barrenness.* "The general character of the wâdys, as well as of the mountains of Sinai," says Dean Stanley, "is entire desolation. If the mountains are naked Alps, the valleys are dry rivers.... The Israelites were brought into contact with a desolation to them the more remarkable by its contrast with the green valley of the Nile." And in another place he speaks of "the whole wilderness" as having "a doubly dry and thirsty aspect." The world, with its wealth and pleasures, its honours and power, cannot afford satisfaction to the longing souls of men. It is clear from their very nature that temporal and material things cannot satisfy spiritual beings. (*a*)

2. *Homelessness.* Men do not as a rule establish homes in the desert. They may pitch their tent there for a little while, but they speedily move on to other scenes. The home of the soul is not here. Its rest is not here. If any man attempt to find the home of his soul in anything here he will find, sooner or later, that great has been his mistake, and sore will be his disappointment. Only in the *spiritual,* the *personal,* the *perfect,* and the *permanent* is the true home of the soul.

3. *Pathlessness.* There were no well-defined roads in the desert. And the Israelites were strangers in it. Left to themselves they were liable and likely to go astray. And man if left to himself now, or to the world's guidance, will not find the true path of life. And even when by Divine direction he has found it, the world presents many enticements to lure him from it.

4. *Perilousness.* They were exposed to danger from the scorching sun, from violent storms, from savage beasts, and from desperate bands of robbers. The perils to which the good are exposed in this world are many and great. They spring from "the wiles of the devil," "the depths of Satan," the seductions of the world, and the lusts of the flesh.

And in the case of Israel in the desert there seemed to be,—

5. *Aimlessness.* How aimless and fruitless must the thirty-eight years of wandering, to which they were con-

condemned for their unbelief and rebellion, have seemed to them! Inexpressibly weary and dreary must those years have been to the young generation. There are times in the spiritual life of good men when they pass through somewhat analogous experiences. The years pass, opportunities come and go, life hastens on towards its close; and so little seems accomplished, so little progress made in our character, so little true work done. We have toiled and struggled long, and at times painfully, and yet we have not attained, the goal of our ambition seems still so far off that the heart is prone to grow weary and despondent. Such are some of the trials of the desert.

II. **The Divine Presence in the desert.**

"The Lord spake unto Moses in the wilderness of Sinai, in the tabernacle of the congregation." They were in the desert; but God was with them there. We have here,—

1. *Divine communication in the desert.* "The Lord spake unto Moses," etc. And God is in constant communication with His people now. His voice is never silent; for in silence some of His most precious communications are made. The thoughtful and reverent spirit hears His voice in the sounds and silences of nature, and can say,

"Cleon hears no anthem ringing in the sea and sky:
Nature sings to me for ever—earnest listener, I." (*b*)

God is also ever speaking through the Sacred Scriptures, and by His Holy Spirit.

2. *Divine provision in the desert.* The Lord fed the vast host of Israel with manna from heaven, and with water from the rock He supplied them. They were in the desert, but the resources of God never failed them. So now, "The Lord will give grace and glory; no good will he withhold from them that walk uprightly." "Your heavenly Father knoweth that ye have need of all these things." "My God shall supply all your need according to His riches in glory by Christ Jesus."

3. *Divine shelter and rest in the desert.* The people of Israel for forty years were homeless wanderers; but they found their rest and home in God. "Lord, Thou hast been our dwelling-place in all generations." God is the only true home and rest of souls.

3. *Divine direction in the desert.* The Lord went before them in the pillar of cloud by day and in the pillar of fire by night. Thus the desert was not really pathless, their tedious wanderings were not really aimless. And still the Lord directs His people He does so,—(1) By the leadings of His providence. (2) By the teachings of the sacred Scriptures. (3) By the influences of the Holy Spirit.

5. *Divine protection in the desert.* The Lord protected the Israelites from the heat of the sun by day by means of the pillar of cloud; and from the attacks of savage beasts by night by means of the pillar of fire. He also guarded them from the assaults of neighbouring nations, except in those instances in which they disregarded His counsel, and rebelled against Him. God is still the sure defence of all who put their trust in Him. "No weapon that is formed against thee shall prosper." "If God be for us, who can be against us?" "Who is he that will harm you, if ye be followers of that which is good?" God is with us in our march through the desert; and His presence assures us of all good.

III. **The Divine uses of the desert.**

Why this wandering to and fro for thirty-eight years? What is the meaning of this tedious and painful delay? Of what use was it? To prepare a people for the inheritance of Canaan. God has not only to give them the inheritance, but to fit them for it—for its privileges, duties, etc. Time was needed for two things :—

1. *That the generation of slaves might pass away.* Were the people that left Egypt fit to enter upon the privileges and duties connected with the independent possession of the Promised Land? Slavery had robbed them of their manhood. They were most persistent and provoking unbelievers, contemptible cowards, shrinking from any difficulty,

quailing in the presence of any danger. They were the creatures of carnal appetites, preferring the fish, the cucumbers, the onions, and the melons of Egypt with slavery, rather than the manna of heaven and freedom. Emancipated in body, they are yet slaves in soul. And by reason of this, and of their murmurings and rebellions against God, they must live and die in the desert (see xiv. 26-35). In this we have an illustration of God's dealings with His people now. There is much in us that must die and be buried before we can enter upon the inheritance of spiritual perfection. Our craven-hearted fears, our carnal lusts, our miserable unbelief, must be buried in the desert. The slave nature must be put to death, etc. There are godly persons in this world who are past service, whose strength and health have long departed, whose life is one of constant weariness and pain, who long for the summons hence, and wonder why it is so long delayed. May it not be because the discipline of the desert is not yet ended? There is something of the old nature that is not yet dead and buried.

2. *That a generation of free men might be educated.* In the desert God was training the children into true manhood, —into fitness for the place, the duties, and the privileges designed for them. And the education was remarkably successful. The generation that was trained in the wilderness and entered the Promised Land, was honourably distinguished for faithfulness, etc. (comp. Josh. xxiv. 31; Jer. ii. 2, 3). So in this world God is educating us into calm, far-seeing faith, into high-souled courage, into reverent and hearty obedience, etc. This life, when truly lived, is not fruitless, aimless, or vain. Even its trials are designed to bless us. Its storms and strifes are intended to invigorate and nerve us. In the desert we are being trained by God into spiritual perfection and power, and educated for service and blessedness.

Conclusion:

Let us ponder well the Divine design of our life in this world. By the help of God let us seek its realization in ourselves.

ILLUSTRATIONS.

(*a*) We might ask the statesman, and as we wished him a happy new year, Lord Dundas would answer, "It had need to be happier than the last, for I never knew one happy day in it." We might ask the successful lawyer, and the wariest, luckiest, most self-complacent of them all would answer, as Lord Eldon was privately recording when the whole bar envied the Chancellor, "A few weeks will send me to dear Encomb, as a short resting-place between vexation and the grave." You might say to the golden millionaire, "You must be a happy man, Mr. Rothschild." "Happy! me happy! What! happy! when just as you are going to dine you have a letter placed in your hand, saying, 'If you do not send me £500, I will blow your brains out!' Happy! when you have to sleep with pistols at your pillow!" We might ask the clever artist (David Scott), and our gifted countryman would answer, of whose latter days a brother writes, "In the studio all the pictures seemed to stand up like enemies to receive me." This joy in labour, this desire for fame, what have they done for him? The walls of this gaunt sounding place, the frames, even some of the canvases, are furred with damp. In the little library where he painted last was the word "*Nepenthe*," written interrogatively with white chalk on the wall. We might ask the world-famed warrior, and get for an answer the "*Miserere*" of the Emperor Monk, or the sigh of a broken heart from St. Helena. We might ask the brilliant courtier, and Lord Chesterfield would tell us, "I have enjoyed all the pleasures of the world, and I do not regret their loss. I have been behind the scenes; I have seen all the coarse pulleys and dirty ropes which move the gaudy machines; and I have seen and smelt the tallow candles which illuminate the whole decorations to the astonishment of an ignorant audience." We might ask the dazzling wit, and faint with a glut of glory, yet disgusted with the creatures who adored him, Voltaire would condense the essence of his existence into one word "*Ennui*." And we might ask the world's poet, and we should be answered with an imprecation by that splendid genius, who—

"Drank every cup of joy, heard every trump
Of fame; drank early, deeply drank;
drank draughts
That common millions might have quenched, then died
Of thirst, because there was no more to drink."—*Pollok*.
—Dr. James Hamilton.

(*b*) God hath a voice that ever is heard,
In the peal of the thunder, the chirp of the bird;
It comes in the torrent, all rapid and strong,
In the streamlet's soft gush as it ripples along;
It breathes in the zephyr, just kissing the bloom;
It lives in the rush of the sweeping simoom;
Let the hurricane whistle or warblers rejoice,
What do they tell thee, but God hath a voice?
God hath a presence, and that ye may see
In the fold of the flower, the leaf of the tree;
In the sun of the noon-day, the star of the night;
In the storm-cloud of darkness, the rainbow of light;
In the waves of the ocean, the furrows of land;
In the mountains of granite, the atoms of sand;
Turn where ye may, from the sky to the sod,
Where can ye gaze that ye see not a God?
Eliza Cook.

The Numbered People.

(*Verses* 2, 3.)

These annals are an historic mirror. They image out a heavenly Father's special dealings with each child of faith. The parallel is quickly drawn. They once groaned bitterly in cruel bondage. But Mercy set them free. Believer, you too were once a slave at Satan's will. But now the chain is broken, etc. Israel's tribes are journeying, as strangers, through a desert waste. And is not yours a wilderness career? But they are conveyed by a heavenly guide. So, too, a beckoning hand marks out your wanderings by day—by night, etc. They had heard "the voice of words"—the fiery law. This law has also pierced the deep recesses of your inner man. You have thus learned the glorious righteousness of God, etc. Was Israel God's special portion? You, too, are not your own. You are a purchased property, etc. There is no novel thought in this. But common truths—like common blessings—soon lose their point. Colours soon fade without a renewing touch.

And now, before the people move, God speaks again. He gives command to register the number of each tribe. . . . . New instruction meets us here.

In common matters, men count possessions, which are choice, and dear, and prized. They whose mean joys are fixed on this world's pelf—thus calculate their gold. See, too, the watchful shepherd's care. Do we, then, stray beyond sound limits when in God's numbering we read God's love? Do not clear characters here write, that His people are thus numbered, because loved—counted, because prized? My God loves me: my name is in his heart. The knowledge of this fact is reached by happy steps. They are all Scripturally firm. Review them. Wherefore was Jesus sent to bear your sins, and deck you in his robe of rightteousness? Why was Christ slain? Why are you spared? .... Wherefore did the Spirit speed to arouse your sleeping conscience—to show self's ruin and the remedy of the Cross? .... How is it that your tottering feet are still upheld along the slippery hill, which leads to Zion's heights? The strength is not your own. There can be only one reply, God loves you. Would that the eye of Faith for ever rested on this glorious truth. God loves you! What an amazing impulse to bear the willing servant over all mountains of doubt, and fear, and hindrance! What a strong shield to ward off Satan's darts! It is victory, before one blow is struck! It is light in the dark day of trial! It is the holy wing to lift above the world!

Who are numbered? None are enrolled, but they whose age and strength enable them for war. Christ's service is a mighty work—a determined fight. Satan disputes each onward step. The world presents its countless troops, etc. The flesh is an internal foe, etc. Believer, yours is this warrior's life. Fight, as one fighting for eternity. Strive, as one striving for a kingdom. Jesus commands, etc. Follow him boldly. No one will triumph who has never fought. No one who truly fights, will fail.

Each numbered soldier paid a ransom price (Ex. xxx. 12). The rich—the poor—were equally assessed. All in Christ's camp are ransomed by his blood. All plead one sacrifice.

Next comes the register. It presents a vast array of numbered warriors. Beyond six hundred thousand men (Num. i. 46). Whence is this marvellous increase? One family had entered Egypt. Hardship, and cruelty, and toil had done their worst to keep them low. But God's early promise was their portion (Gen. xii. 2). The numbered people prove that our God is Truth as well as Love.

Behold, again, this multitude. It is an emblem of a far larger host (Rev. vii. 9). The fight is a prelude to the crown.

About a year has passed since the last numbering. The Levites then formed part of the collected mass. They are not now included. But the number then and now amounts exactly to the same. Israel has surrendered Levi's tribe, but Israel's forces are not thereby less. Here is a profitable lesson. We never lose by giving to the Lord. Selfishness is penury. Christian benevolence is wealth.

Once more survey the Numbered People. You are inclined to say, this band will safely reach the promised land. Alas! two only steadfastly adhere. The multitude distrusts the Lord. Their corpses strew the desert. An awful proof that outward privileges alone save not (Heb. iii. 19). Unbelief is the bar which shuts out Christ. Unbelief rejects the Gospel, and so perishes.—*Henry Law, D.D.*

RANK AND SERVICE.

(Verses 4-16.)

In these verses we have an illustration of—

I. Co-operation in Divine Service.

One man of every tribe, being head of the house of his fathers, was to be associated with Moses and Aaron in numbering the people. By this arrangement—

1. *The toil of Moses and Aaron would be lessened.* There is urgent need for the lessening of the labours of many overwrought Christian ministers to-day. And there are many things in which others may render them valuable assistance.

2. *The accomplishment of the task would be facilitated.* The cause of God in this world will advance with rapid strides when co-operation in Christian work shall become constant and universal amongst His people.

3. *The envy of the princes would be prevented.* We know that on a subsequent occasion certain "princes of the

assembly" arose against Moses and Aaron, saying, "Ye take too much upon you, seeing all the congregation are holy, every one of them, and the Lord is among them; wherefore then lift ye up yourselves above the congregation of the Lord?" "Sore eyes," say Babington, "cannot abide the clearness of the sun, and an evil stomach turneth the best nutriment to hurt. The greener the leaf is, the sooner the worms bite it." Probably, moved by envy, they would have murmured against Moses and Aaron at this time; but, being united with them in the business, all occasion thereof is removed. Co-operation in service is the best antidote to envy and complaint and carping criticism. Grumblers are seldom found among the workers of the Church.

We have in the text an illustration of—

II. Society's need of leaders.

1. *Because they are at present indispensable to social order and progress.* These men were representatives of the people. Instead of "the renowned," we should translate, "the called of the congregation."—Keil and Del.: "In verse 16 they are designated as 'called men of the congregation,' because they were called to diets of the congregation, as representatives of the tribes, to regulate the affairs of the nation." And society in this age must have its leaders and representatives in politics, in military affairs and enterprises, in science, in religion, etc. Moreover, it is essential that some persons should be entrusted with the reins of government. Rulers are indispensable to order. Leaders are necessary also to secure unity in the pursuit of any great and comprehensive aim. Certain objects of utmost importance to society cannot possibly be attained without cohesion of purpose and effort on the part of a large number of men, and such cohesion is impossible without leaders. "Amongst the masses," says Guizot, "even in revolutions, aristocracy must ever exist; destroy it in nobility, and it becomes centred in the rich and powerful Houses of the Commons. Pull them down, and it still survives in the master and foreman of the workshop."

2. *Because of the differences in the faculties of men.* These men were "princes" from the nobility of their birth: and they were probably men distinguished also for their abilities. Speaker's Comm.: "The selection of the Princes of the Tribes appears from v. 4 to have been made under Divine direction; but probably, as v. 16 seems to suggest, they were for the most part the same persons as those chosen a few months previously at the counsel of Jethro (Exod. xviii. 21-26.) Of those here named Naashon, prince of Judah, was brother-in-law of Aaron (Exod. vi. 23), and ancestor of King David. Elishama, prince of Ephraim, was grandfather of Joshua (1 Chron. vii. 26, 27). The peers of men like these, though nothing has been in fact preserved to us respecting them, were no doubt entitled, amongst their fellows, to the epithet 'renowned,' v. 16." Some men are born rulers. The governing faculty is innate in them. They have the extensive mental vision, the calmness of judgment, the promptitude in action, the love of order, the power of arrangement, the acquaintance with human nature, the skill in managing affairs, etc., which mark them off for leaders of men. But in others the qualifications of leadership are conspicuous by reason of their absence. And amongst those in whom the ruling faculty is innate it exists in different degrees of power. So they are fitted for different degrees of dominion. "We must have kings," says Emerson, "we must have nobles; nature is always providing such in every society; only let us have the real instead of the titular. In every society, some are born to rule, and some to advise. The chief is the chief all the world over, only not his cap and plume. It is only this dislike of the pretender which makes men sometimes unjust to the true and finished man." (*a*)

We have in the text an illustration of—

III. The grand characteristic of true leaders.

They are pre-eminent in service. These "princes of the tribes" were to serve the tribes in this numbering of the people. "Those that are honourable should study to be serviceable." "Whosoever will be great among you," said our Lord, "let him be your minister; and whosoever will be chief among you, let him be your servant; even as the Son of Man came not to be ministered unto, but to minister, and to give His life a ransom for many." "I am among you as He that serveth." The great God who is supreme over all is servant of all. And from the ministering of the archangel to the labour of the insect, the true rank and glory of a creature consist in the service which it renders in God's universe. *(b)*

ILLUSTRATIONS.

(*a*) Greatness is not a teachable nor gainable thing, but *the expression of the mind of a God-made great man;* teach or preach, or labour as you will, everlasting difference is set between one man's capacity and another's, and this God-given supremacy is the priceless thing, always just as rare in the world at one time as another. What you can manufacture or communicate, you can lower the price of, but this mental supremacy is incommunicable: you will never multiply its quantity, nor lower its price; and nearly the best thing that men can generally do, is to set themselves not to the attainment, but the discovery of this: learning to know gold when we see it from iron-glance, and diamonds from flint-sand, being for most of us a more profitable employment than trying to make diamonds out of our own charcoal.—*John Ruskin.*

(*b*) There is no dignity but of service. How different the whole notion of training is now from what it was in the middle ages. Service was honourable then. The first thing taught then was how to serve. No man could rise to the honour of knighthood without service. A nobleman's son even had to wait on his father, or to go into the family of another nobleman, and wait upon him as a page, standing behind his chair at dinner. This was an honour. No notion of degradation was in it; it was a necessary step to higher honour. And what was the next higher honour? To be free from service? No. To serve in the harder service of the field; to be a squire to some noble knight, to tend his horse, to clean his armour, to see that every rivet was sound, every buckle true, every strap strong, to ride behind him and carry his spear, and if more than one attacked him to rush to his aid. This service was the more honourable because it was harder, and was the next step to higher honour yet. And what was this higher honour? That of knighthood. Wherein did this knighthood consist? The very word means simply *service.* And for what was the knight thus waited on by his squire? That he might be free to do as he pleased? No, but that he might be free to be the servant of all. By being a squire first, the servant of one, he learned to rise to the higher rank, that of servant of all. His horse was tended, his armour observed, his sword and spear and shield held to his hand, that he might have no trouble looking after himself, but might be free, strong, unwearied, to shoot like an arrow to the rescue of any and every one who needed his ready aid. There was a grand heart of Christianity in that old chivalry.—*George Macdonald.*

God's Knowledge of His People.

(Verse 5.)

"These are the names of the men that shall stand with you."

The text teaches that the Lord knew these "princes of the tribes of their fathers"—their names, their parentage, their fitness for the work in which they were to take part, etc. We infer that *God is perfectly acquainted with His people.*

Consider:

I. The great truth here implied.

God knows His people individually and altogether.

1. *This is philosophical.* If God is infinite, He must know all things. Nothing can be so great as to surpass His comprehension; nothing so small as to escape His notice. Great and small, generally and particularly, He knows all things and everything. "The relation God holds to objects of knowledge," says Bushnell, "is different in all respects, from that which is held by us. Our general terms, *man, tree, insect, flower,* are the names of particular or single specimens, extended, on the ground of a perceived similarity, to kinds or species. They come, in this manner, to stand for millions of particular men, trees, insects, flowers, that we do not and never can know. But God does not generalise in this manner, getting up general terms under which to handle particulars, which, as particulars, He does not know. His knowledge of wholes is a real and complete knowledge. It is a knowledge of wholes as being a distinct knowledge of particulars. He knows the wholes in the particulars, the particulars in the wholes." "History acquaints us, that Cyrus had so vast a memory, that he knew the name of every particular soldier in his army, which consisted of divers nations; shall it be too hard for an infinite understanding to know every one of that host that march under His banners?" (a)

2. *This is Scriptural.* See 1 Kings xix. 14-18; Psalms i. 6; lvi. 8; cxlvii. 3, 4; Isa. xl. 26-31; Mal. iii. 16, 17; Matt. vi. 25-34; x. 29, 30; John x. 3, 14, 27; Phil. iv. 3; 2 Tim. ii. 19; Rev. iii. 5; xxi. 27. "No doubt but He that calls the stars of heaven by their names, knows the number of these living stars that sparkle in the firmament of His Church. He cannot be ignorant of their persons, when He numbers the hairs of their heads, and hath registered their names in the book of life. .... He knows them as a general to employ them, as a shepherd to preserve them." God's knowledge of His people involves His favour towards them. It is a knowledge not of apprehension merely, but of approbation also. It implies affection for them, the exercise of care over them, etc., as in Amos iii. 2.

II. The practical bearings of this great truth.

The realization of this truth will tend,—

1. *To restrain from sin.* The consideration of God's perfect acquaintance with us is fitted to check any rising inclination to evil. "The ways of man are before the eyes of the Lord, and He pondereth all His goings."

2. *To promote sincerity of life.* He cannot be imposed upon by any empty forms or hollow pretences. Our thoughts and feelings are known to Him. And simulation and dissimulation are an abomination in His sight.

3. *To promote humility.* The consideration of God's knowledge makes manifest the greatness of our ignorance. "We are but of yesterday, and know nothing." God knows all our secret sins,—all unholy desires, etc. Surely this should humble us.

4. *To quicken reverence towards God.* Great intelligence is a thing to command respect and admiration. But He in whom infinite intelligence is joined with infinite holiness should be admired and adored.

5. *To comfort the godly under re*

proaches. So it proved to Job when misunderstood and falsely accused by his friends (Job xvi. 19 ; xxiii. 10).

6. *To sustain the godly in affliction and trial.* He who thoroughly knows each and every one of His people will certainly support them in their afflictions, give them patience in their trials, and in His own time deliver them from all troubles.

7. *To incite to hearty obedience.* If He knows us always and altogether, shall we not endeavour to do those things which He approves? If He regards us with favour, shall we not seek to love and honour Him?

8. *To strengthen trust in God.* No plans that are formed against His people are unknown to Him. His own designs are formed in infinite wisdom. He knows all our temptation and weakness, all our danger and need. And His power to help is as great as His intelligence. "My sheep hear My voice, and I know them, and they follow Me ; and I give unto them eternal life; and they shall never perish, neither shall any one pluck them out of my hands.

ILLUSTRATIONS.

(a) A little child sits on the verandah and watches the worm. He is a voyager for his food on the leaf of the mulberry tree, and he goes eating, eating, eating. Let us suppose that some Divine Power enables that worm to be so far intelligent as to say, "It is said that there are beings who can understand this whole tree; but it does not seem to me possible. I can comprehend how there might be beings that should understand this leaf, and the next three or four; but to take in all the million leaves on this tree is a thing that transcends my conception. I do not believe it possible for any magnified worm to understand so much." It is *not* possible for any worm. But there is a little Sunday-school child sitting on the verandah, who looks on the tree and sees the whole of it; and not only sees the whole of it, but can individualize the leaves at its pleasure. How easy it is for that little child to take in that whole tree ! and how hard it is for that worm to take in more than three leaves ! And let that child grow up, and be educated, and trained in landscape-gardening, and it will take in, not merely a tree, but a whole forest. If one leaf is coloured, if one twig is broken, if there is a dry branch, it does not escape his notice. Differences of hue, light, and shadow, the infinite diversities that come in forest life—he takes them all in, and has a kind of omnipresence in his consciousness of the facts of this whole matter. What could a worm understand or imagine of a being that is competent to take in the realm of philosophy, and that makes himself the measure of creation? He says, "It does not seem reasonable to me that anybody can understand more than twenty leaves. I cannot; and I do not see how anybody else can." And yet, do not you understand how a person can take in sections, and gradations, and ranks, and degrees infinitely above what a worm could understand? And have you anything more to do than to carry on that idea to imagine a Being before whom all eternity passes, and to whom all the infinite treasures of this eternity shall be just as simple as to you the leaves on the individual tree are? It only requires magnitude of being, infinity.—*H. W. Beecher.*

The sun is a natural image of God ; if the sun had an eye, it would see; if it had an understanding, it would know all visible things ; it would see what it shines upon, and understand what it influenceth, in the most obscure bowels of the earth. Doth God excel His creature, the sun, in excellency and beauty, and not in light and understanding? certainly more than the sun excels an atom or grain of dust. We may yet make some representation of this knowledge of God by a lower thing, a picture, which seems to look upon every one, though there be never so great a multitude in the room where it hangs; no man can cast his eye upon it, but it seems to behold him in particular; and so exactly, as if there were none but him upon whom the eye of it were fixed; and every man finds the same cast of it: shall art frame a thing of that nature, and shall not the God of art and all knowledge, be much more in reality than that is in imagination? Shall not God have a far greater capacity to behold everything in the world, which is infinitely less to Him than a wide room to a picture?—*Charnocke.*

The Census and its Teachings.
(*Verses* 17-19.)

This census was taken as they were formed into a nation. In Egypt they were not a nation, but hordes of slaves. Now begins their national existence. God reduces them to order, consolidates them, that they might undertake the responsibilities and enjoy the privileges of nationhood.

Why did God give us this record? Paul writes that "all Scripture is given by inspiration of God, and is profitable," etc. The Bible is a practical book; it is inspired for our *profit—all* of it. True, some portions are more esteemed by us than others are. Look at the well-used Bible of an aged Christian. Some parts are more soiled than others. Is this right? Yes. It is compatible with reverence for the whole Bible, just as Christ, while loving all the disciples, had his *three* best-loved among them. But we ought not to neglect any part of the Bible. There is a blessing in all of it. In places we least expect it, we find it to be inspired for our profit. This chapter seems dry and profitless, but it is not so. Like some of the glens in South Wales,—sterile, barren, unattractive, and, to the outward look, valueless; but underneath are coal mines and untold wealth. So with this chapter. Let us inquire, what this numbering was calculated to teach the people at the time, and in like manner to teach us at the present day?

I. It was calculated to teach them the grand fact that God was personally interested in and well acquainted with each one of them individually.

The object of the census was to individualize them, to separate each from the mass, to register each name that the record might be kept before God. He wanted them all to feel, that He knew them and was interested in them. There is a tendency in man to think that he is lost in the mass, and that the great God is not interested in *him*. This tendency is very pernicious; it leads to sin, and then to despair. The Bible all through combats it; and there is no doubt that it was one great design of this census. This chapter is to us like the microscope in nature—revealing to us God's greatness by the interest He takes in the individual. It is a grand truth to feel, God sees *me*, knows all about *me*, cares for *me*. He is not some cold abstraction, indifferent, inaccessible, and unmindful of us. Far from it. The Bible and Christ bring Him near to us, showing Him to be full of interest in us. He feeds the fowls, clothes the lilies, knows the varying market-price of sparrows, numbers the hairs of our heads, knew the street, house, and person where Peter lodged. Struggling, anxious, suffering one, single yourself from the crowd. God knows, loves, cares for thee.

II. It was a vivid illustration of the faithfulness of God to His word.

He had said to Abraham that his seed should be numerous, that they should go to Egypt, etc. The figures of this chapter show how well He kept His word. To faith a fact is better than a hundred arguments. And anything that strengthens our faith in God's Word is a great blessing to us. The worth of the Bible and its promises in a suffering, sinful world no one can tell. To shake one's faith in the promises is like going through a hospital and rudely tearing the pillows from under the heads of the sufferers. It is faithfulness that makes the promises precious.

What a comfort to Israel to have confidence in the Word of God, to feel that they could trust Him! Nothing would impress His faithfulness more than this census, showing how well He Had kept His promise to Abraham. It also speaks to us, etc.

III. It afforded them striking proof of God's power to keep His word.

God is not only true, but His arm is almighty. It was by this census that the people knew how many they were. God led them out of Egypt, rescued them at the Red Sea, protected and fed them thus far in the wilderness. Was there anything too hard for the Lord? Would not all this encourage them to lean on His arm? He had proved His power to keep His word. God is equal to all our wants. His word is true; His arm is strong. With such a God for our Friend we have nothing to fear, etc. "Among the gods there is none like unto Thee, O Lord." "Happy is he that hath the God of Jacob for his help."

"This God is the God we adore,
Our faithful unchangeable Friend;
Whose love is as great as His power,
And knows neither measure nor end.
'Tis Jesus, the First and the Last,
Whose Spirit shall guide us safe home:
We'll praise Him for all that is past,
And trust Him for all that's to come."
Hart.

These figures then are eloquent. Let them lead us to trust more fully in God. The ungodly! what say they to you? They certify your doom, if ye repent not. The threatenings as well as the promises of the Bible rest on the word of the faithful and almighty God.—*David Lloyd.*

THE FIRST ARMY OF ISRAEL, AN ILLUSTRATION OF THE CHURCH MILITANT.

(Verses 20-46.)

In these verses we have the record of the number of men "from twenty years old and upwards that were able to go forth to war" in the respective tribes, and in the whole of the tribes united, with the exception of that of Levi. A consideration of the numbers of the respective tribes will be found in other commentaries. We propose to consider this first army of Israel as an illustration of the Church Militant.

Consider:

I. The necessity of this army.

Before the Children of Israel can take possession of the Promised Land the idolatrous Canaanitish nations must be dispossessed. To expel them from the country Israel must encounter them in battle and vanquish them. And to do this a large and brave army was necessary. It is necessary that the Christian Church should be militant. The individual Christian cannot attain the inheritance or spiritual perfection without conflict. And the Church cannot take its true place or fulfil its Divinely appointed mission without doing vigorous battle.

1. *Internal foes have to be conquered.* In ourselves there are carnal appetites which must be subdued, evil passions which must be quelled by the power and principles of Divine grace, etc. The Christian has to achieve self-conquest. "He that is slow to anger is better than the mighty, and he that ruleth his spirit than he that taketh a city." "The battle in which thoughts are the only swords, and purposes are the only spears, and tears are the only shots—the inward struggles of men's souls—these are, after all, the mightiest battles; and in the sight of God they are the most sublime."

2. *External foes have to be conquered.* God summons us to do battle with ignorance and superstition, with dirt and disease, with immorality and irreligion, with vice and crime. We need to guard against Satanic subtlety, and to resist Satanic influence. It is madness to make light of the adversaries with which the Church of Jesus Christ has to contend. It is to invite defeat, etc.

II. The authority for organising this army.

"The Lord spake unto Moses," expressly commanding him to take the number of men able to do military duty. The first army of Israel was organised under Divine direction. May we not infer from this that there are possible circumstances in which war is justifiable? In itself war is unquestionably a terrible evil. (*a*). But it certainly appears to us that circumstances may arise in which a nation would be justified in having recourse to war. "The arms are fair," says Shakspeare, "when the intent of bearing them is just."

"War is honourable
In those who do their native rights maintain;
In those whose swords an iron barrier are
Between the lawless spoiler and the weak;
But is, in those who draw the offensive blade
For added power or gain, sorded and despicable
As meanest office of the worldly churl."
Joanna Baillie. (*b*.)

III. The Composition of this Army.

1. *It was composed of Israelites only.* None of the "mixed multitude" were included. The warriors were men who could "declare their pedigrees after their families, by the house of their fathers." In fighting the battles of the Lord in this age thorough decision is required. "Who is on the Lord's side?" The victorious Church must be composed of true Christians. Victories for truth and right demand the prowess of true and righteous men.

2. *It was composed of able men only.* "Every male from twenty years old and upward, all that were able to go forth to war." In accomplishing His purposes God uses fit instruments. He employs means adapted to the attainment of His ends. In the conflicts of the spiritual life and work every Christian may through Jesus Christ be an able warrior. Weak and timid in ourselves, we may be courageous and "strong in the grace that is in Christ Jesus."

3. *It comprised all the able men.* "Every male from twenty years old and upward, all that were able to go forth to war." No excuses were allowed. None were exempted. Altogether the army was very large: it consisted of six hundred and three thousand five hundred and fifty men. Every Christian is called to be a soldier. The continuance and growth of the Christian life are impossible apart from vigorous conflict. We must either vanquish our spiritual enemies, or they will vanquish us. Neutrality is out of the question here. And no thought of truce can be entertained without loss and injury. Neither can we do our fighting by proxy. Every Christian must be a personal combatant in the great conflict.

IV. The conquering spirit of this Army.

Their leaders constantly endeavoured to inspire the soldiers with the spirit of intelligent trust in God. When this spirit animated them they achieved splendid triumphs: when it failed them they turned their backs to their enemies and fled in dismay. Victory in our spiritual conflicts is attainable only through faith. When our faith in God is strong, we are invincible. When it fails, we are overthrown by the first assault of the enemy. "This is the victory that overcometh the world, even our faith." "Above all, taking the shield of faith, wherewith ye shall be able to quench all the fiery darts of the wicked." True faith gives glorious visions to the spirit, inspires us with heroic courage, girds us with all-sufficient strength, makes us more than conquerors through the Captain of our salvation. (*c*.)

Conclusion:—1. *A call to decision.* "Who is on the Lord's side?" 2. *A call to courage.* Our arms are tried and true; our great Leader is invincible; let us then "be strong and of a good courage." 3. *A call to confidence.* Our courage, to be true, must spring from faith. By trust we triumph.

"Strong in the Lord of Hosts,
And in His mighty power;
Who in the strength of Jesus trusts
Is more than conqueror."
C. Wesley.

ILLUSTRATIONS.

(*a*) Wherever there is war, there *must* be injustice on one side or the other, or on both. There have been wars which were little more than trials of strength between friendly nations, and in which the injustice was not to each other, but to the God who gave them life. But in a malignant war of these present ages there is injustice of ignobler kind, at once to God and man, which *must* be stemmed for both their sakes. It may, indeed, be so involved with national prejudices, or ignorances, that neither of the contending nations can conceive it as attaching to their cause; nay, the constitution of their governments, and the clumsy crookedness of their political dealings with each other, may be such as to prevent either of them from knowing the actual cause for which they have gone to war.

John Ruskin.

(*b*) You may, perhaps, be surprised at my implying that war itself can be right, or necessary, or noble at all. Nor do I speak of all war as necessary, nor of all war as noble. Both peace and war are noble or ignoble according to their kind and occasion. No man has a profounder sense of the horror and guilt of ignoble war than I have. I have personally seen its effects upon nations, of unmitigated evil on soul and body, with perhaps as much pity and as much bitterness of indignation as any of those whom you will hear continually declaiming in the cause of peace. But peace may be sought in two ways. One way is as Gideon sought it, when he built his altar in Ophrah, naming it, 'God send peace,' yet sought this peace that he loved as he was ordered to seek it and the peace was sent in God's way:—"The country was in quietness forty years in the days of Gideon." And the other way of seeking peace is as Menahem sought it, when he gave the King of Assyria a thousand talents of silver, "that his hand might be with him." That is, you may either win your peace or buy it:—win it, by resistance to evil; buy it, by compromise with evil. You may buy your peace with silenced consciences; you may buy it with broken vows, buy it with lying words, buy it with base connivances, buy it with the blood of the slain, and the cry of the captive, and the silence of lost souls— over hemispheres of the earth, while you sit smiling at your serene hearths, lisping comfortable prayers evening and morning, and counting your pretty Protestant beads (which are flat, and of gold, instead of round, and of ebony, as the monks' ones were), and so mutter continually to yourselves, "Peace! peace!" when there is no peace, but only captivity and death for you, as well as for those you leave unsaved— and yours darker than theirs.—*Ibid.*

I believe in war. I believe there are times when it must be taken. I believe in it as a medicine. Medicine is not good to eat, but when you are sick it is good to take. War is not a part of the Gospel; but while men and the world are travelling on a plain where they are not capable of comprehending the Gospel, a rude form of justice is indispensable, though it is very low down. If you go to a plain still higher, war seems to be a very poor instrumentality. And if you go yet higher and higher till you reach that sphere where the crowned Sufferer stands, how hateful and hideous war seems! In the earlier periods of society it is recognised as having a certain value; but its value is the very lowest, and at every step upward, till you come to this central Divine exhibition, it loses in value. Always it is a rude and uncertain police of nations. It is never good. It is simply better than something worse. Physical force is the alternative of moral influence; if you have not one, you must have the other. —*H. W. Beecher.*

Few religious men could justify most of the wars of history. On one side or other war must be the greatest of all crimes, and the instances in which either side is right are but few. But this does not affect the principle. If but one can be instanced in which a people simply resisted aggression, conquest, violation of liberties, or wrong, it would suffice. If England were invaded by an unprovoked aggressor; if London were assailed, its homes in imminent peril of violation, the property of its merchants, the honour of its women, the lives of its children and citizens imperilled, what should I do? Go out and reason with the invader? appeal to to his sense of righteousness? Yes, it would be right to do that if it were practicable. Crowd into churches to pray? Yes, it would be eminently right to do that. But suppose the invader to be as ambitious, as false, and as conscienceless as Napoleon, to be sunk below any possible appeal to moral feeling, am I passively to let him work his devilry—to burn my house, murder my children, and do worse to my wife and daughters? Am I to pray, and passively expect God to work a moral miracle? I think not. I am to employ righteous means to resist wrong, and to ask God to bless them. If only the magistrate's sword will deter the robber and the murderer, I am to use that sword; and an army in its only lawful capacity is simply a power of magistracy. Some of the greatest deliverances that God wrought for His people were through armies. The most precious liberties of the world and the Church have been won by armed revolution and defence. From Marathon to the Armada, from the destruction of Sennacherib to that of Napoleon, from the revolt from under Pharaoh to that from under the Stuarts, or the King of Naples, the moral and religious sense of the world has approved the resistance of wrong by force. So long as force and the magistrate and the police are necessary to preserve righteousness and justice and liberty, they must be employed. The ideal of Christianity is peace and universal brotherhood, but it is not to be attained by permitting the ruffian and the robber and the tyrant to work their will unresisted—that would be to leave society to lawlessness and brutality.—*H. Allon, D.D.*

(c) How often, through the world's literature and history, have we heard some ambitious commander or emperor babbling, in his vain waking dreams, of a world's conquest! We turn from these poor visions of cruelty and blood to the meek army of the living God; from the false victories of force to the true victories of faith. Here, on a lowly bed, in an English village by the sea,—as I was lately reading,—fades out the earthly life of one of God's humblest, but noblest servants. Worn with the patient care of deserted prisoners and malefactors in the town jail for twenty-four years of unthanked service, earning her bread with her hands, and putting songs of worship on the lips of these penitent criminals—she is dying; and as the night falls some friend asks, "What shall I read?" The answer of the short breath is one firm syllable, "Praise!" To the question, "Are there no clouds?" "None; He never hides His face. It is our sins which form the clouds between us and Him. He is all love, all light." And when the hour of her departure was fully come, "Thank God, thank God!" And there,—as I read again—in his princely residence, surrounded with the insignia of power, but in equal weakness before God, expired a guileless statesman, nobleman by rank and character, calmly resigning back all his power into the Giver's hands, spending his last days of pain, like many hours of all his days before it, with the Bible and Prayer-book in his feeble hand, saying, at the end, "I have been the happiest of men, yet I feel that death will be gain to me, through Christ who died for me." Blessed be God for the manifold features of triumphant faith!—that He suffers His children to walk towards Him through ways so various in their outward look;—Sarah Martin from her cottage bed, Earl Spencer from his gorgeous couch, little children in their innocence, unpretending women in the quiet ministrations of faithful love, strong and useful and honoured men, whom suffering households and institutions and churches mourn. All bending their faces towards the Everlasting Light, in one faith, one cheering hope, called by one Lord, who has overcome the world, and dieth no more!

"One army of the living God,
To His command we bow:
Part of His host have crossed the flood,
And part are crossing now."

The sun sets; the autumn fades; life hastens with us all. But we stand yet in our Master's vineyard. All the day of our appointed time, let us labour righteously, and pray and wait, till our change come, that we may change only from virtue to virtue, from faith to faith, and thus from glory to glory.—*F. D. Huntington, D.D.*

The Levites and their Service an Illustration of the Christian Ministry.

(*Verses* 47-54.)

The tribe of Levi was not numbered with the other tribes. The Levites were exempted from military service, and set apart for the service of the tabernacle. In any wise and proper arrangement of the affairs of human society, provision will be made for the requirements of the spiritual nature of man. The chief features of the service of the Levites as here indicated may properly be regarded as illustrative of the work of the Christian ministry.

I. **The true Christian minister should manifest some fitness for the work before he is designated thereto.**

The Levites had manifested their zeal for the worship of God by slaying the worshippers of the golden calf at the command of Moses (Exod. xxxii. 26-29). And, as a reward, the honour of this sacred calling is conferred upon them. They had already acted as assistants to the priests (Exod. xxxviii. 21), being of the same tribe as Moses and Aaron. And now they are expressly appointed to the charge of the tabernacle. "But the Levites after the tribe of their fathers were not numbered among them. For the Lord spake" (not "had spoken") "unto Moses, saying," etc. "Singular services shall be recompensed with singular honours." That a person should manifest some fitness for the work of the Christian ministry before he is set apart to it seems so obvious and indisputable that it would be superfluous to call attention to it, were it not that in practice it is so often disregarded. There seems to be in some quarters an impression that almost anyone is competent for the sacred office of the ministry. In determining the trade which their sons shall learn, wise parents will consider their respective inclinations and aptitudes. An artist would, perhaps, make a poor minister; a successful merchant might utterly fail as a barrister. Is there less aptitude required in the work of the Gospel ministry than in the other pursuits of life? Unfitness should be tolerated in any sphere of life and activity rather than in this. There should be adaptation of *voice*, of *mind*, of *character*, etc.

II. **That the true Christian minister is called of God to his work.**

"The Lord spake unto Moses, saying, . . . Thou shalt appoint the Levites over the tabernacle of testimony," etc. In addition to fitness for the office, the true minister will feel a conviction of moral obligation to enter upon the holy work: the impulsions of the Divine Spirit will urge him in the same direction, until the words of St. Paul truly express his condition, "Necessity is laid upon me; yea, woe is unto me, if I preach not the Gospel." "True ministers," says Hugh Miller, "cannot be manufactured out of ordinary men—men ordinary in talent and character—in a given number of years, and then passed by the imposition of hands into the sacred office; ministers, when real, are all special creations of the grace of God." The Christian ministry is not a profession into which a man may or may not enter as he pleases; but a Divine vocation, which is solemnly binding upon those to whom it is addressed, and without which no

21

man can enter upon it without sin.—*(a)*

III. *That the work of the Christian minister demands his entire devotion thereto.*

The Levites were to be free from all other service, that they might give themselves unreservedly to the ministry of the tabernacle. There are men who are rendering (in preaching and otherwise) most useful and self-denying service to the Church of Christ, whose time and energy are not entirely devoted to it. They are worthy of high honour. But the work of the stated minister and pastor demands all his time and energy, if it is to be done well. His duties are so many, so great, and so unspeakably important, as to challenge all his powers. M. Henry:— "Those that minister about holy things should neither entangle themselves, nor be entangled, in secular affairs. The ministry is itself work enough for a whole man, and all little enough to be employed in it." The Apostle Paul, in writing to the Christians at Rome, specifies their respective duties, and urges each one to diligence in the discharge of his own (Rom. xii. 6, 8). And to Timothy he writes: "No man that warreth entangleth himself with the affairs of this life," etc. (2 Tim. ii. 3, 4). And considering the solemn issues of his work, in conscious weakness he cries, "Who is sufficient for these things?"

"'Tis not a cause of small import
The pastor's care demands;
But what might fill an angel's heart,
And filled a Saviour's hands."
Doddridge.

IV. *That a faithful discharge of the duties of the Christian minister is essential to the well-being of society.*

The duties of the Levites are briefly stated in verses 50, 51, and 53. No one who was not of their tribe was in any way to intermeddle with their duties or encroach upon their position. If a stranger drew near to the tabernacle he was to be put to death. If the functions of the Levites were not properly discharged, wrath would be upon Israel. What was the intention of these strict regulations?

We suggest—

1. *That the sacred things might be decently kept and ordered.* The Levites had charge "over all the vessels of the tabernacle, and over all things that pertained to it." It is most important that everything which is used in connection with the worship and service of God should be appropriate to its sacred uses, and be well preserved. God's service hallows even the meanest things which are employed in it; but we should devote our best things to it.

2. *That the people might be inspired with reverence for sacred things.* This to us, to a large extent, accounts for the stern penalty annexed to any intrusion upon the function of the Levites. Reverence is one of the highest attributes of mind. The Lord seeks to enkindle or increase it in Israel.

3. *That the people might be impressed with the unworthiness of sinful man to approach unto the Most High.* We sinners are utterly unfit to draw near unto Him who is "glorious in holiness." The Levites were called to the charge of the sacred things. They alone could draw near to the tabernacle. Through the mediation of Jesus Christ all men may now draw near to God. (See Heb. x. 19-22.)

Now, these things are needful at the present time. Becoming worship, reverence for sacred things, and humility towards God are ever obligatory and beneficial to us. The true Christian minister in the faithful discharge of his duties confers the greatest benefit upon society.—*(b)*

V. *That personal holiness of heart and life are essential to the faithful discharge of the duties of the Christian Ministry.*

The Levites were separated from the other tribes for their sacred work. Their outward separation was intended to show forth the separation from worldliness and sin which the Lord required of them. They who have to do with holy things should themselves be holy. "Be ye clean that bear the vessels of the Lord." (See Rom. ii. 21-24; 1 Tim. iv. 16; Tit. ii. 7.) Thus

Goldsmith describes the Christian minister—

"In his duty prompt at every call,
He watched and wept, he prayed and felt for all;
And, as a bird each fond endearment tries
To tempt its new-fledged offspring to the skies,
He tried each art, reproved each dull delay,
Allured to brighter worlds, and led the way."

(c)

ILLUSTRATIONS.

(a) The minister without a vocation is not only unhappy, he is guilty,—he occupies a place, he exercises a right which does not belong to him. He is, as Jesus Christ said, "a thief and a robber," who has not entered in through the gate, but climbed up some other way. The word *vocation* has, in other applications (that is to say, as applied to professions of a secular order), only a figurative significance,—at least only a figurative significance is attributed to it. It is equivalent to *aptitude, talent, taste.* It is natural to represent these qualifications as voices, as appeals. But when applied to the ministry, the word returns to its proper sense. When conscience authorises and compels us to the discharge of a certain duty, we have that which, although out of the sphere of miracle, deserves most fully the name of vocation. In order to exercise the ministry legitimately, a man must be called to it.—*A Vinet.*

(b) That a man stand and speak of spiritual things to men. It is beautiful,—even in its great obscuration and decadence, it is among the beautifullest, most touching objects one sees on the earth. This Speaking Man has indeed, in these times, wandered terribly from the point; has, alas! as it were, totally lost sight of the point; yet, at bottom, whom have we to compare with him? Of all public functionaries boarded and lodged on the Industry of Modern Europe, is there one worthier of the board he has? A man even professing, and never so languidly making still some endeavour, to save the souls of men: contrast him with a man professing to do little but shoot the partridges of men! I wish he could find the point again, this Speaking One, and stick to it with tenacity, with deadly energy; for there is need of him yet! The Speaking Function—this of Truth coming to us with a living voice, nay, in a living shape, and as a concrete practical exemplar: this, with all our Writings and Printing Functions, has a perennial place. Could he but find the point again,—take the old spectacles off his nose, and looking up discover, almost in contact with him, what the *real* Satanas, and soul-devouring, world-devouring *Devil*, Now is.—*Thomas Carlyle.*

(c) Beloved in our Lord and Saviour Jesus Christ, it is a very monstrous thing that any man should have more tongues than hands; for God hath given us two hands and but one tongue, that we might do much and say but little. Yet many say so much and do so little, as though they had two tongues and but one hand: nay, three tongues and never a hand. Insomuch as that may be aptly applied to them which *Pandulphus* said to some in his time: "You say much, but you do little; you say well, but you do ill. Again, you do little, but you say much; you do ill, but you say well." Such as these (which do either worse than they teach, or else less than they teach; teaching others to do well and to do much, but doing no whit themselves) may be resembled to diverse things. To a whetstone, which being blunt itself, makes a knife sharp; to a painter, which being deformed himself, makes a picture fair; to a sign, which being weather-beaten, and hanging without itself, directs passengers into the inn; to a bell, which being deaf and hearing not itself, calls the people into the church to hear; to a nightingale, which being restless and sitting upon a thorn herself, brings others by her singing into a sweet sleep; to a goldsmith, which being beggarly and having not one piece of plate to use himself, hath store for others which he shows and sells in his shop. Lastly, to a ridiculous actor in the city of Smyrna, which pronouncing "*O cœlum!*—O heaven!"—pointed with his finger toward the ground; which when *Polemo*, the chiefest man in the place, saw, he could abide to stay no longer, but went from the company in a chafe, saying, "This fool hath made a solecism with his hand; he hath spoken false Latin with his hand." Such are all they which teach one thing and do another; which teach well and do ill.—*Thomas Playfere.*

The faithful minister is strict in ordering his conversation. As for those who cleanse blurs with blotted fingers they make it the worse. It was said of one who preached very well, and lived very ill, that when he was out of the pulpit it was a pity he should ever go into it; and when he was in the pulpit, it was a pity he should ever come out of it. But our minister *lives* sermons. And yet I deny not but dissolute men, like unskilful horsemen who open a gate on the wrong side, may, by the virtue of their office, open heaven for others, and shut themselves out.—*Thomas Fuller.*

EVERY MAN BY HIS OWN STANDARD.

(Verse 52.)

The various tribes of Israel had to be placed in order, and the whole to be put under a strict regulation. This was needful for encampment, for march, for worship, for battle: without this, confusion, etc. Israel in many things typical of the Christian Church. We see it in this also,—

I. The One Israel.

Observe:

1. *Their real oneness of descent.* The children of Abraham.

2. *Their original condition.* All bondsmen.

3. *Their Divine deliverance.* Brought out of Egypt, etc.

4. *In one Divine covenant.* Promises, etc.

5. *Journeying to the one inheritance.*

6. *Under one command.* See how this all applies to the Church of the Saviour. All the children of God by faith, all heirs, all pilgrims, all of one covenant, one Saviour, etc.—essentially one; one in Christ Jesus.

II. The various Tribes.

Observe:

1. *Their different names.* Necessary for distinction—recognition.

2. *Their different positions in the camp.* See next chapter. East side, v. 3; south side, v. 10; west, v. 18; north, v. 25.

3. *The various tribes were in one general accord and union.* All one religious confederacy, absolutely one, worship one, etc.; in perils one, in warfare one, in prospects one.

III. The Special Directions to the different Tribes.

1. *Each tribe had their own standard or banner to distinguish it from the rest.* No order without.

2. *Each man was to be by his own standard.* Not a wanderer; not a visitor to all; but his own fixed, legitimate position.

3. *Thus the duties of every tribe would be regarded and fulfilled.*

4. *Thus the interests of all would be sustained.* Now, if this was important and necessary in the camp of Israel, how much more in the Church of the Lord Jesus! The thousands there: millions here. But let us see,—

IV. The Spiritual Lessons the subject presents to us.

1. *We see now the denominational tribes in the Kingdom of Christ.* Christians of different conditions, education, training, leaders, etc.

2. *Christians have a special interest in their own camp.*

3. *To devote themselves to these is the first duty and privilege.* Just as families are constituted, so churches.

4. *All the various denominational camps constitute the one Church of the Saviour.* Only one Israel, one body, one army, etc. For particular purposes, every man by his own camp; for general purposes, all acting in conjunction and harmony. How absurd jealousies and envyings! How ridiculous isolation! How oppressive assumptions and priestly dictations! How suicidal strifes and contentions! How monstrous exclusions and anathemas! The great tabernacle of God is built four-square, and includes all the tribes. Christian denominations have special standards, and serve the whole best by every man being by his own standard. The glory of God is identified with the unity of the whole. Christ's prayer to Him, etc.—*Jabez Burns, D.D.*

CHAPTER II.

The Marshalling of the People.

(Verses 1 and 2.)

In this chapter we have the order of the twelve tribes in the camp and on the march. And in these verses we have the general directions which the Lord gave unto Moses for marshalling the tribes. Keil and Del.: "The twelve tribes were to encamp each one by his standard, by the signs of their fathers' houses, opposite to the tabernacle (at some distance) round about, and, according to the more precise directions given afterwards, in such order that on every side of the tabernacle three tribes were encamped side by side and united under one banner, so that the twelve tribes formed four large camps or divisions of an army. Between these camps and the court surrounding the tabernacle, the three leading *mishpachoth* (*i.e.*, families or clans) of the Levites were to be encamped on three sides, and Moses and Aaron with the sons of Aaron (*i. e.*, the priests) upon the fourth, *i.e.*, the front or eastern side, before the entrance (chap. iii. 21-38). דֶּגֶל, a standard, banner, or flag, denotes primarily the larger *field sign*, possessed by every division composed of three tribes, which was also the banner of the tribe at the head of each division; and secondarily, in a derivative signification, it denotes the *army* united under one standard, like σημεία, or *vexillum*. It is used thus, for example, in verses 17, 31, 34, and in combination with מַחֲנֶה in verses 3, 10, 18, and 25, where 'standard of the camp of Judah, Reuben, Ephraim, and Dan' signifies the hosts of the tribes arranged under these banners. אֹתֹת, the *signs* (ensigns) were the smaller flags or banners which were carried at the heads of the different tribes and subdivisions of the tribes (the fathers' houses). Neither the Mosaic law, nor the Old Testament generally, gives us any intimation as to the form or character of the standard (*degel*). According to rabbinical tradition, the standard of Judah bore the figure of a lion, that of Reuben the likeness of a man, or of a man's head, that of Ephraim the figure of an ox, and that of Dan the figure of an eagle; so that the four living creatures united in the cherubic forms described by Ezekiel were represented upon these four standards."

In these verses we have four homiletic points.

I. Order.

The Lord here gives directions to Moses concerning the order that was to be observed amongst them. The great importance of a clear and well understood arrangement amongst so large a number of men will be obvious upon the slightest consideration. But notice:—

1. *God Himself delights in order.* This is clearly manifest in His works,—in the rising and setting of the sun and moon, in the sublime march of the stars, in the ebbing and flowing of the tides, in the regular succession of the seasons. Even comets, those apparently erratic wanderers in space, are not erratic; but move with perfect precision both as regards space and time.

2. *The importance of order is recognised in human affairs.* In the Christian Church, in national government, in military affairs, in the family and home, and in the individual life, order is of the utmost importance, and is fraught with the greatest advantages. "Order," says Southey, "is the sanity of the mind, the health of the body, the peace of the city, the security of the state. As the beams to a house, as the bones to the microcosm of man, so is order to all things." "Let all things," says St. Paul, "be done decently, and in order."

3. *This order was probably Divinely instituted as a means to peace and unity.*

It is probable that if God had not determined the order which should be observed among them, there would have been strife and contention for priority and precedence. Thus the tribe of Reuben might have claimed the pre-eminence as a birth-right, and refused to fall in with the arrangement by which Judah held the post of honour and headed the march. While Judah might have refused to concede the position to Reuben, because of their own vast numerical superiority. Again, the tribe of Simeon, for the same reason, might have refused to occupy a position subordinate to that of Reuben; for the former tribe numbered 59,300, while the latter only 46,500. Other causes of dissatisfaction and dispute would also, probably, have been discovered. And the issue would have been strife, divisions, and we know not what evils. But the Lord prevents this by himself determining the arrangement of the tribes. Order is ever conducive to peace and unity. Let us cultivate order. (*a*)

II. Variety.

There were different standards. Each camp had its own characteristic standard. And each tribe and each father's house had its own distinctive ensign. Their order was not monotonous. Monotony is not a mark of divinity. Variety characterises the works of God. Countries differ in their climates, conformations, productions, etc. The features of landscapes differ. "Star differeth from star." Trees, flowers, faces, minds differ. Hence it seems reasonable that we should find different ensigns in the Church of Christ. With one spirit there may be many forms. With unity of the inner life there may be great variety of outward development. There are many denominations in the Christian Church because there are differences of mind, temperament, degrees of education and culture, etc., in those who compose the Church. This variety is promotive of health, activity, usefulness. (*b*)

III. Unity.

All the tribes were gathered "about the tabernacle of the congregation," as around a common centre. They had different standards and ensigns, but constituted one nation. Their position in relation to the tabernacle illustrates—

1. *The dependence of all on God.* All the tribes looked to Him for support, provision, protection, direction, etc.

2. *The access of all to God.* The tabernacle was the sign of the presence of God with them. It was in their midst; not very far from any of them. All of them in the appointed way might approach Him in worship. Through Christ we both (Jews and Gentiles) "have access by one Spirit unto the Father." (See Ephes. ii. 18-22.)

3. *The reverence of all towards God.* They were to pitch "over against the tabernacle." Probably the tribes were 2,000 cubits distant from it. Compare Joshua iii. 4. They were thus to encamp around the sacred place, that no stranger might draw near to it; and the Levites were to encamp near the tabernacle on every side, that the people themselves might not draw too near to it, but might be taught to regard it with respect and reverence. "God is greatly to be feared in the assembly of the saints, and to be had in reverence of all them that are about Him." Now, all Christians are one in their relation to the Lord Jesus Christ. All depend upon God as revealed in Him; all approach unto God through Him; all reverence God in Him. The various denominations of Christians constitute the one Church of the Lord Jesus Christ. He is the centre of unity. As Christians draw nearer to Him they will draw nearer to each other; not in uniformity, but in increasing nearness to Jesus Christ will the increase of true unity be found. "Uniformity is the creation of man; unity is the inspiration of God. The first can be made by a mask; the latter must be created or imparted by the Spirit of God. Uniformity is compatible with death; unity is inseparable from real and conscious life. Uniformity is the churchyard; unity is the church itself of the living God. All may be uniform, yet all may be dead; none can have real, inner, spiritual, vital

unity, without having that truth which God inspires, and that life of which Christ is the Giver."

IV. Security.

The tabernacle of God in the midst of the camp was a guarantee of their safety. We may apply to them the words of one of their poets of a subsequent age: "God is in the midst of her; she shall not be moved," etc.

His presence in their midst would tend to—

1. *Quell their fears.* He had wrought marvellous things on their behalf in the past; He was ever doing great things for them. Then why should they quail before any danger or enemy?

2. *Inspire their confidence and courage.* It should have given to them the assurance of victory in conflict, etc. This seems to have been the idea of Moses:

"When the ark set forward, Moses said, Rise up, Lord, and let Thine enemies be scattered, and let them that hate Thee flee before Thee." Distance from God is weakness and peril to His Church. Nearness to Him is safety and power. Living in vital union with Him all-conquering might is ours.

Conclusion—

1. Let us learn sincerely and heartily to recognise as members of the Christian Israel all who have the Christian spirit, however widely they may differ from us in forms and opinions.

2. Let us think less of our *isms*, and more of Christ's Church; less of theological and ecclesiastical systems, and more of Christ's Gospel; less of human authority and patronage, and more of the Lord Jesus Christ.

ILLUSTRATIONS.

(*a*) Order is Heaven's first law—a glorious law,
Seen in those pure and beauteous isles of light
That come and go, as circling months fulfil
Their high behest. Nor less on earth discern'd,
'Mid rocks snow-clad, or wastes of herbless sand,
Throughout all climes, beneath all varying skies,
Fixing for e'en the smallest flower that blooms
Its place of growth.   *Milton.*

(*b*) Let us go down and stand by the beach of the great, irregular sea, and count whether the thunder of it is not out of time. One—two—here comes a well-formed wave at last, trembling a little at the top, but, on the whole, orderly. So, crash among the shingle, and up as far as this grey pebble; now stand by and watch! Another! Ah, careless wave! why couldn't you have kept your crest on? It is all gone away into spray. striking up against the cliffs there. I thought as much—missed the mark by a couple of feet! Another! How now, impatient one! couldn't you have waited till your friend's reflux was done with, instead of rolling yourself up with it in that unseemly manner? You go for nothing. A fourth, and a goodly one at last. What think we of yonder slow rise and crystalline hollow, without a flaw? Steady, good wave; not so fast, not so fast: Where are you coming to? By our architectural word, this is too bad; two yards over the mark, and ever so much of you in our face besides; and a wave which we had some hope of, behind there, broken all to pieces out at sea, and laying a great white table-cloth of foam all the way to the shore, as if the marine gods were to dine off it! Alas! for these unhappy arrow-shots of Nature; she will never hit her mark with those unruly waves of hers, nor get one of them into the ideal shape, if we wait for her a thousand years. . . . . But the sea was meant to be irregular! Yes, and were not also the leaves and the blades of grass; and, in a sort, as far as may be without mark of sin, even the countenance of man? Or would it be pleasanter and better to have us all alike, and numbered on our foreheads, that we might be known one from the other?—*Ruskin.*

The sun comes forth. And first I perceive the chick-weed blossoming, almost inconspicuous. It is born again of the sun, and shows the sun's power. Just beyond there is a clump of violets. They are born again out of death into life by the power of the sun. Further on are bulbs of various kinds. And each developes in its own way. One has one style of leaf or bloom, and another another. And they multiply as the sun grows warmer, till the woods and fields swarm with myriads of growths, some purple, some red, some white, some blue, some green, all shades, and combinations, and forms being represented. They are all born of the sun, and brought into their life and power; and yet they are widely different in their structure and appearance. Would you reduce them all to one, and have nothing but daisies, nothing but tulips, or nothing but violets? Are not God's abundant riches in this, that when He creates life from death in so many ways there are presented such variations of beauty and amiableness? So it is with the truths of the Gospel. God does not make those truths the same to any two minds. If men had the subtle power of analysis, so as to seize just what they feel, and put their feelings exactly into words, I believe it would be found that no two persons on the face of the earth ever stated, or could state, their views of a fact alike. God, that never made two faces alike; God, that never made two leaves alike; God, that makes unity with infinite diversity—He does not mean that men shall feel just alike. The amplitude of being is expressed by variations of being, that go back to essential unity, and take hold of a common root. And the attempt to bring the glowing and fervid Orientals, the staid and practical Occidentals, the mediæval minds, the artist minds, the sombre and unirradiating natures, and the light and gay natures, all to one statement of speculative truth, is as wild and preposterous as the boy's race after the rainbow. It cannot be done.—*H. W. Beecher.*

MAN IN RELATION TO ORDER, HOME, AND GOD.

(*Verse 2.*)

Let us inquire what God would teach by this.

I. The importance of Order in everything.

God here insists upon method in all their movements. Each was to be in his own place. He was thus teaching His people, and, through them, the world. The sojourn in the wilderness was their school-time; hence we have so much of it. In the lessons God taught them we find principles that are to guide us. God loves order in everything: He is not the author of confusion. Satan brought discord into the world. There was not a jarring note in the universe till sin came into existence. God loves order. You can see this in all His works; there is no confusion or waste in anything; nothing is neglected or left out; nothing can be improved upon. In all there is completeness and harmony. God is our pattern in this. The highest art is the best copying of nature. So in human life, the noblest, the highest is the one that follows most closely in the footprints of God. To live well is of vast importance to us, and it is impossible with disorder and confusion. In business, if there is no method, failure must be the result. In the home life, if there is no order, there must be misery. So order is essential to success in the religious life. "Let all things be done decently and in order," said Paul. The reference is to the regularity and discipline of an army: the order is as perfect as possible; and it is this which makes all the difference between an army and a rabble. Order is the essence of beauty, strength, comfort, and usefulness.

II. The sacredness of family life.

Each was to be "with the ensign of his father's house;" his place was to be with his family. The people had been slaves; and slavery saps the foundation of family life. God has to teach them the sacredness of the family circle. There can be no real national life unless the family life be pure and sacred. *Men only* live in families. The brutes dwell in herds. God has given man the family instinct; and the Bible and religion ever tend to strengthen, purify, and ennoble it. The higher a man rises in the scale of being, the deeper is his interest in his family. The more we love God, the more we love one another. Divine love sanctifies and elevates the human. God taught the people here to respect their families. Many parents seem to be anxious only to feed, clothe, and help their children for this life. Are their children brutes? Are they to perish like the beasts? Or, have they a soul? Parents, strive to make your homes abodes of peace and blessedness, centres of attraction and holy influence, so that your children may gather round the ensign, etc. God's eye is on our family life.

III. The right way to feel and to act towards Himself.

They were to be "far off about the tabernacle." True life is impossible apart from right esteem of God. He is the centre, the pivot of all true life. As amongst this people, so in His Church, God is the attracting power, etc. He is in the midst to rule, protect, and guide. As there is no circle without a centre, so the Church falls to pieces unless God be in the midst. Love to Him brings His people together, and binds them together. The earth is made of particles: gravitation, as it attracts each particle to itself, binds them together so as to form the earth. Thus God attracting each soul to Himself, binds them together as a Church. We are to turn around Him as the planets around the sun, receiving our light, our beauty, our influence from Him.

"Truth is dual." The above is only half the truth; the other half is involved in the expression, "far off." In nature there are two great forces at work—the centripetal and the centrifugal. If either of these were to fail, the earth would be wrecked. In religion we have two similar forces. God must attract us; He is the centre of our soul. But we must also keep our distance; we must be "far off." There is no religion without reverence. God is great and holy. The people were to be "far off" as well as "about the tabernacle." Divine things are to be treated with respect and handled with reverence. There is no true religion without awe; no true love without fear. While we lovingly trust God as our Father, let us give Him the respect due to His name.

Learn.

1. *The deep interest God takes in His people.* He wants them to be the very best possible—to be perfect.

2. *How religion affects the whole of man and His life.* It teaches us how to act in all things. There is nothing above or beneath its notice that affects us. It is then our best Friend. If it is not yours, seek it without delay.—*David Lloyd.*

THE CAMP.

(*Verse 2.*)

When Balaam looks down upon the outstretched camp of Israel, his very soul expands. It must break forth into praise. The beauty captivates. The order charms. (See chap. xxiv. 5-9.) Let us, too, view this favoured camp.

I. The Tents.

Not splendid palaces; poor tents. They are the pilgrim-dwellings of a pilgrim-troop—the short-lived homes of short-lived sojourners. Reminds of mortal state. These frames have one original—the dust. Is it not folly, then, to pamper and admire the flesh? At best these bodies are a tent. How soon they crumble! The tents must fall; but when? Perchance this very hour. Is he not then the fool of fools, who boasts him of to-morrow's dawn? Learn how fleeting is life's day. When I go hence, is an abiding mansion mine? Flesh is a mean abode. This thought commends the grace of Jesus. He scorned not to assume it. No man was ever man more thoroughly than Jesus. He thus descended that He might bear the curse. He sought a lowly tent to do a godlike work. But soon the degradation passed. The cross was triumph's car. Manhood now shines in Him arrayed in light of Deity. And all, whom faith makes one with Him, shall soon behold and share this lustre. Weakness and frailty shall put on unfading freshness.

II. The Order.

Let Israel's camp be now more closely scanned. What perfect regularity appears! Arrangement is complete, etc. Our God delights in order. Where He presides, confusion vanishes. Is it not so in every Christian's heart? When Jesus takes the throne, wise rule prevails, disturbing lusts lie down, etc. Is it not so in Christian life? Each duty occupies its stated post. The home, the closet, the public, the world, in turn have claims, in turn are served. How different is the worldling's day! It seems an upset hive, etc.

But in Israel's camp each tribe has its place. . . . God fixes all the bounds, and all the bounds are gladly kept. The same all-ruling mind disposes now each member of Christ's body. Each enters on the stage of life, as God is pleased to call. Each runs a pre-ordained course. Each disappears, when the allotted task is done. We see this clear arrangement throughout the Church's history. . . Bow humbly before this ordering mind, then discontent will not arise; no murmurings will mourn an obscure lot, a grievous burden, a lengthened pilgrimage, or an early grave.

III. The Position.

"About the tabernacle of the congregation shall they pitch." As the planets circle the sun, so these surround the sanctuary. God is the centre; they form the wide circumference.

Is there no meaning here? God in Christ Jesus is the centre, the heart, the life, the strength, the shield, the joy of His believing flock.

Is there no warning here? Let Christians ponder this Camp's plan when called to fix their dwellings upon earth. When weighing the advantages of place, the foremost thought should be, Is God known here? Are His pure truths here clearly taught? Was Lot a gainer, when his eye only coveted the fertile plains? Can fairer fields, or sweeter prospects, make amends for a cold blank within? Can air-salubrity repay for inward sickness and a spiritual decline?

IV. The Standard.

A standard floats above each tribe. Beneath the well-known sign they rest, and by its side they march. Believers have an ensign too. The banner over them is Jesu's love. (Song, ii. 4.) The standard is a pledge of safety. Mighty foes hate and assail, plot and rage, etc.; but they must fail. Beneath it there is sweet repose. The weary spirit and the worn-out flesh can often watch no more. But as is the vineyard of the Lord, so is His camp. "I the Lord do keep it," etc. (Isa. xxvii. 3.)

Beside it there is victory. Many have fought beneath the Gospel-banner, and all have triumphed. They who go boldly forward, looking unto Jesus, assuredly prevail. (2 Cor. ii. 14.) Happy camp, where Jesus is salvation's Captain; His cross, salvation's ensign; His heaven, salvation's rest!

Believer, glory in your standard, and be steadfast. Cling constantly to Christ. Let every company, moment, place, witness your firm resolves. Wave now and ever the glorious ensign—"Christ is all." Thus dwell within the camp, and you will reign upon the throne.—*Henry Law, D.D.*

ASPECTS OF HONOUR.

(*Verses* 3–9.)

"It seems to us," says Dr. Cumming, "an uninteresting and unprofitable exercise to read the list of the tribes and their names, the camps and their numbers, the captains and their names, who together composed the mighty host that took their exodus from Egypt, through the desert, to the land of Canaan; but surely it was important in the circumstances in which they were placed that each and all should be recorded—it was important with reference to the separate and distinct maintenance of the tribes—that the promise of the Messiah from a specific tribe might be vindicated and established in the fulness of the times. In the next place, this mighty crowd, numbering six hundred thousand men, able to bear arms—and that must have amounted, with camp followers, to nearly two millions—a vast population in the desert—must of necessity be reduced to some order of regiments or companies, in order that authority might be exercised where it was needed; that the means of defence might be had recourse to most speedily and effectually where they were required; and that each loving his own company, each individual loving by preference his own tribe best, might yet, as a tribe mingled with the rest, have that wider feeling, which recognised an Israelite under whatever standard he was, in the great army of which they formed a part. For these and other reasons, God commanded Moses and Aaron to make the arrangements here specified; and what God saw useful to command, it cannot have been useless to record, and it may not be altogether unprofitable to read. We must not think that the chapter that does not personally benefit us spiritually is therefore of no use. It is possible for true Christians often to be somewhat selfish, and to think that that cannot be useful which does not benefit the individual, or that that cannot play a part important in the whole which does not produce a deep, a spiritual, and profitable impression upon each. We must learn to look wider, to extend our horizon, and to learn that there are parts in the Bible which may not bring personal instruction to us, but which nevertheless may have a force in relation to the whole book that vindicates it from the assaults of the sceptic; sets out its great truths in bolder relief and in clearer light; and even those parts which we cannot see or comprehend the use, the place, and the necessity of now, if we can only exercise a little patience we shall know, and understand, and see the usefulness of more clearly hereafter. There are many parts in this globe that we cannot understand the end of; we cannot see the use perhaps of so much water; we cannot see the necessity of those large wasted and blasted deserts. But yet I have no doubt they have a use, and are subserving a purpose; and we must not deny that God made this or made that because we cannot see the purpose that it subserves in the great economy of the universe. I believe that with the exception of what sin has done, there is not a star in the sky, however tiny it looks to us, that is not necessary to the balance of the universe; and that if one star were to fall from its socket, or one orb to be shattered in its march, a shock might be felt that would influence injuriously at least the whole solar system. And it may be that in this blessed Book, which is God's inspired Book, some of those dull and dry passages, as they must appear to us personally, are probably subserving great and ultimate purposes, which we may not see now, but shall see hereafter."

Our text gives us the account of the composition of the first camp, which was situated on the east side, toward the rising of the sun. This post of honour was conferred upon Judah. To him was given the first standard. With him were Issachar and Zebulun. These three tribes were descended from the three younger sons of Leah; and their union under one standard was, therefore, an appropriate arrangement. To each tribe a captain was appointed; these captains being the "princes of the tribes of their fathers," who assisted Moses and Aaron in the numbering. Here, then, are differences of rank ordered by God. One tribe has the most distinguished position of all. Three other tribes are placed each at the head of a camp; and in each tribe one person was appointed by God as captain, or prince, or commander-in-chief. Leaders and rulers are essential to society. "To have neither superiors nor inferiors would be to breathe a stifling atmosphere of mediocrity. Natural leadership is the soul of common action." Inasmuch as the most distinguished place was assigned to the tribe of Judah we take as our subject: *Aspects of Honour.*

We see here—

1. **Honour wisely conferred.**

The tribe of Judah was the most numerous and powerful of all the tribes. This was a good reason for placing it in the most prominent and illustrious position. Honours of title and place are not always wisely conferred. They are sometimes bestowed upon those who are neither distinguished in their abilities, exalted in their character, nor exemplary in their conduct. This is a sad perversion of things. *(a)* But the truest and highest honours are those of character and conduct, and these are attainable through the grace of God unto all men.

"Trust me, Clara Vere de Vere,
   From yon blue heavens above us bent,
The grand old gardener and his wife
   Smile at the claims of long descent.
Howe'er it be, it seems to me,
   'Tis only noble to be good.
Kind hearts are more than coronets,
And simple faith than Norman blood."
   Tennyson

The honour of being children of the Most High, "heirs of God and joint heirs with Christ," of being made "kings and priests unto God," of sharing in the spirit and service of Christ, we may all attain through Him. But in these honours there are differences of degree. There are some to whom will be given "an abundant entrance," while others will "be saved yet so as by fire."

II. Honour in relation with duty and responsibility.

The tribe of Judah in being appointed to the place of honour in the Israelitish host had also the place of peril. Being at the head of the camp, if there were dangers to be met or foes to be encountered, they must first enter the lists against them. In their case rank and risk, distinction and duty, were united. The places of distinction should ever be for those who render the most and best service. And the highest places in both the Church and the State involve gravest responsibilities and most arduous duties. He who treads the path of duty faithfully and bravely will find in due time that it leads to the most unfading honours. (See notes and illustrations on ch. i. 4-16.) *(b)*

III. Honour as connected with parental influence.

Judah was the first of the sons of Jacob who was blessed by the venerable patriarch "when he was a-dying." Reuben, Simeon, and Levi were censured by him. The parental blessing in the case of Judah has not been in vain. And in the honour now put upon the tribe the influence of that blessing is still further manifest (see Gen. xlix. 8-12). It is in the power of every parent instrumentally to bless his children. By wise teaching, holy example, and believing prayer, parents may confer the greatest advantages on their offspring, and aid them to reach the highest honours. Let parents seek thus to bless their children. *(c)*

Let the children of godly parents appreciate their privileges in this respect. *(d)*

IV. Honour as related to future greatness.

The dying patriarch had predicted that Judah should be the ruling tribe; he promised to Judah a kingdom and sovereignty. Many years have since passed away; and still Judah has neither lawgiver nor sceptre. But here are two things to encourage faith in the patriarchal prediction—viz., the numerical superiority of the tribe, and the post of honour assigned to it. Ages more were to pass away before the prediction was fulfilled; but the honour now conferred on the tribe would encourage faith in its predicted destiny. Its natural tendency would be to stimulate them to—

1. *Believe in their destiny.*
2. *Work for their destiny.*
3. *Wait for their destiny.*

In like manner let every blessing which we receive from God be to us a pledge of our full and final salvation. Let every privilege conferred upon us increase our assurance of the splendid honours which await us hereafter. "Henceforth there is laid up for me a crown of righteousness," etc. "To him that overcometh will I grant to sit with Me in My Throne," etc. "Now are we the sons of God, and it doth not yet appear what we shall be," etc.

ILLUSTRATIONS.

(a)　　　　　Let none presume
To wear an undeserved dignity.
O, that estates, degrees, and offices,
Were not derived corruptly! and that clear honour
Were purchased by the merit of the wearer!
How many then should cover, that stand bare!
How many be commanded, that command!
How much low peasantry would then be gleaned
From the true seed of honour! and how much honour
Pick'd from the chaff and ruin of the times,
To be new varnish'd!—*Shakespeare.*
"The Merchant of Venice," ii. 8.

(b) Not once or twice in our rough island-story
The path of duty was the way to glory:
He that walks it, only thirsting
For the right, and learns to deaden
Love of self, before his journey closes,
He shall find the stubborn thistle bursting
Into glossy purples, which outredden
All voluptuous garden roses.

Not once or twice in our fair island-story
The path of duty was the way to glory:
He, that ever following her commands,
On with toil of heart and knees and hands,
Thro' the long gorge to the far light has won
His path upward, and prevail'd,
Shall find the toppling crags of duty scaled
Are close upon the shining table-lands
To which our God Himself is moon and sun.
　　　　　　　　　　　　　Tennyson.

(c) The voice of parents is the voice of gods,
For to their children they are Heaven's lieutenants,
Made fathers not for common uses merely
Of procreation (beasts and birds would be
As noble then as we are); but to steer
The wanton freight of youth through storms and dangers,
Which with full sails they bear upon, and straighten
The mortal line of life they bend so often.
For these are we made fathers; and for these
May challenge duty on our children's part.
Obedience is the sacrifice of angels,
Whose form you carry.
　　　　　　　　　　　　　Shakespeare.

Mr. Irving, in his "Life of Washington," brings to the knowledge of the public, we believe for the first time, a beautiful incident in the religious training of the youthful George when left to the sole care of his widowed mother. Of her general course, Mr. Irving remarks, with fine discrimination: "Endowed with plain, direct good sense, thorough conscientiousness, and prompt decision, she governed her family strictly, but kindly, exacting deference while she inspired affection. George, being her eldest son, was thought to be her favourite, yet she never gave him undue preference, and the implicit deference exacted from him in childhood continued to be habitually observed by him to the day of her death. He inherited from her a high temper and a spirit of command, but her early precepts and example taught him to restrain and govern that temper, and to square his conduct on the exact principles of equity and justice." No Maternal Association has ever devised a better principle to be observed in training children than this of Mary Washington—'*exacting deference while she inspired affection.*' How rarely do we see these two essential elements in family government justly combined in either parent! From this general view Mr. Irving passes to the following incident: "Tradition gives an interesting picture of the widow with her little flock gathered round her, as was her daily wont, reading to them lessons of religion and morality out of some standard work. Her favourite volume was Sir Matthew Hale's ' Contemplations, Moral and Divine.' The admirable maxims therein contained, for outward action as well as self-government, sank deep into the mind of George, and doubtless had a great influence in forming his character. They certainly were exemplified in his conduct through life. This mother's manual, bearing his mother's name, Mary Washington, written with her own hand, was ever preserved by him with filial care, and may still be seen in the archives of Mount Vernon. A precious document! Let those who wish to know the moral foundation of his character consult its pages." Would that the minds and hearts of all our youth might be trained after such a model!—*New York Independent.*

(d) Hold fast to home influences and remembrances; and recollect that he who tries to shame you out of a father's and a mother's fear, and out of obedience to them, tries to steal the most precious treasure you have. He that is trying to destroy the influence of your parents upon you is trying to take from you the most faithful love you ever knew. You shall lie down in the grave when you shall have traversed forty or eighty years of life, without having found another friend who has borne as much for you, or done as much for you, as your father or your mother.—*H. W. Beecher.*

The Mercy of God in Relation to the Consequences of Sin.

(Verses 10-16.)

We have here the account of the composition of the second camp. Its place was south of the tabernacle. At its head was placed the tribe of Reuben, the eldest son of Jacob and Leah, and with it were associated the tribe of

Simeon, the second son of Leah, and that of Gad, the eldest son of Leah's handmaid, Zilpah.

Reuel, in verse 14, is doubtless an error of some copyist, and should be *Deuel*, as in chap. i. 14. Several MSS. and Versions read Deuel in this place.

In this section we have—

I. **An example of the continuance of the consequences of sin.**

How is it that Reuben, being the first-born, does not take the first place? Why was Judah, the fourth son, preferred before him? Because Reuben had been guilty of the most shocking incest. (See Gen. xxxv. 22; xlix. 4; 1 Chron. v. 1.) He sinned grievously, and now his posterity suffer loss thereby. Sin when it is done is not done with. It lives in its results in the person of the sinner, and in the persons of others who are related to the sinner. Sin may be repented of, confessed, forgiven; and yet many of its consequences may remain, and that for many generations. *(a)*

1. *The Sacred Scriptures declare this.* (See Exod. xx. 5; Lev. xxvi. 39; Lam. v. 7; Luke, xi. 49-51.)

2. *The connexion between one generation and another necessitates this.* The consequences of the vices of parents are transmitted to their offspring.

3. *Our social relationships necessitate this.* We are ever exerting an influence upon others, and being influenced by others. One corrupt character corrupts others. One holy character tends to purify and exalt others.

4. *The facts of human life attest this.* The drunkard may forsake his drunkenness, may seek and obtain the Divine forgiveness, may lead a new life, yet many of the results of his sinful indulgences will remain in himself, and if he be a parent will be transmitted to his children. The spendthrift may abandon his reckless courses; but it requires many years, perhaps more than one generation, to repair the shattered fortunes and restore the family estate to its ancient prosperity. Man may turn to God late in life, may be pardoned, accepted, saved; but he cannot recover the years spent in the service of sin, or undo the evil which he has wrought. The guilt is taken away; but the loss, and much more than the loss, remains. God is just. His laws are immutable. They cannot be set at nought, or disregarded, without incurring stern and certain penalties. Let these solemn facts restrain us from sin. Let parents especially lay them to heart; and for the sake of their offspring, let them eschew evil, and cultivate virtue.

"Parents bequeath not to your children's lot
The shame that from them no device can take,
The blemish that will never be forgot."

II. **An example of the exercise of the Divine mercy in mitigating the consequences of sin.**

Notwithstanding the horrible sin of Reuben, he was not altogether cut off from his father's house. Though he forfeited his birthright he was not exiled from the family. His posterity was not cast out of the chosen people. His tribe was not degraded to the lowest rank among the tribes, but placed in an inferior position to that of Judah only. "So then," says Attersoll, "albeit he was punished justly, he was punished gently. Thus God dealeth evermore. He correcteth both moderately and mercifully; and as the physician allayeth the bitterness of the potion with some sweetness, so God assuageth the greatness of His punishment with some mildness and favour that He mingleth with it." We have illustrations of this in the case of Miriam (ch. xii.) and that of David (2 Sam. xxiv. 10-16). (Comp. Psa. lxxxix. 30-33; Isa. liv. 7, 8; Lam. iii. 31-33.) In further elucidation and confirmation of our position, let the following points be noted:—

1. *God delighteth not in judgment, but in mercy.* "The Lord is merciful and gracious, slow to anger, and plenteous in mercy," etc. (Psa. ciii. 8-11.) Mark the tenderness of His appeal to His faithless and rebellious people, "Why will ye be stricken any more?" (Isa. i. 5.) "He delighteth in mercy." *(b)*

2. *He is our Father, and deals with us as a Father.* He is not simply our Creator, Sustainer, and Sovereign, but our Father. When He punishes, He

does so as a Father. "Consider in thine heart, that as a man chasteneth his son, so the Lord thy God chasteneth thee" (comp. 2 Sam. vii. 14, 15).

3. *In His dealings with us He duly considers our weakness, our exposedness to temptation,* etc. Our temperament, tendencies, temptations, trials, etc., are all known to Him. In His judgments all these things are taken into consideration. He never judges harshly. "Like as a father pitieth his children, so the Lord pitieth them that fear Him: for He knoweth our frame," etc. (Psa. ciii. 13-18.)

His mercy is ever in exercise mitigating the severity of the consequences of sin, and tempering the sternness of the woes of life.

Conclusion:

1. *Let the mercy of God deter us from sin.* Shall we be so base as to sin against so much kindness?

2. *Let the mercy of God encourage our confidence in Him.* In sorrow let us seek Him; for he pities, etc. In guilt let us seek Him; for He forgives, etc.

3. *Let this example of the mercy of God lead us to be patient under life's trials.* Like those of Reuben, our trials are not so severe as we have deserved, and they are tempered by the rich mercy of God. He is ever evolving good out of them, making them by His grace the occasion of strength and blessing to us.

4. *Let this example of the mercy of God encourage the wicked to forsake sin and seek salvation.* "Let the wicked forsake his way," etc. (Isa. lv. 6, 7.)

ILLUSTRATIONS.

(*a*) If sin were mortal, then thirty years would swing the world over into the millenium; we should bury it with the next generation. But it is not mortal. It is not barren, but prolific; it propagates itself; it has paternal functions, and sends its children out in swarms to possess the earth. I wish you all to understand that whatever evil you are tolerating in your lives, will live after you are gone; you will pass away, but this shall not pass away. One immortality you will take with you at death; another you will leave behind. It shall stand above your grave when the mound is fashioned and the mourners depart; and shake itself as a strong man rejoiceth in his strength, and go forth as one of the forces of the world. It will be impersonal; it will have no name; it will show no face; and yet it will be you, your worse half unchecked, unrestrained by the good that was once mated with it, and that kept it within bounds. It is in the moral and spiritual as it is in the material world. It is said that one cannot stir the air with a sound so soft and slight that it will ever cease to be a sound. The words we speak, whether of love or hate, whether pure or vile, start pulsations in the air that will never cease to throb. You cannot open your lips and start a motion in the atmosphere, which shall not, like a wave on a shoreless sea, whose forces are within itself and adequate, roll on and on for ever. An oath once spoken sounds for ever in the universe as an oath; it is an explosion whose reverberations can never die. They roll around all continents; they crash against the sides of all mountains; they beat discordantly in and upon the atmosphere of all worlds; the devils hear them, and rejoice; the holy, and fly in dismay. And, at the Judgment, why may we not suppose that these sounds shall all come back to us—the good in soothing music, and the evil in torturing discord, and every man shall be judged according to the word of his mouth? Indeed, it seems to me that everything in man that is of the mind and soul is immortal.—*W. H. H. Murray.*

(*b*) Man having destroyed that which God delighted in, the beauty of his soul, fell into an evil portion, and, being seized on by the Divine justice, grew miserable, and condemned to an incurable sorrow.

In the midst of these sadnesses God remembered His own creature, and pitied it; and, by His mercy, rescued him from the hands of His power, and the sword of His justice, and the guilt of His punishment, and the disorder of his sin, and placed him in that order of good things where he ought to have stood. It was mercy that preserved the noblest of God's creatures here below; he who stood condemned and undone under all the other attributes of God, was saved and rescued by His mercy; that it may be evident that God's mercy is above all His works, and above all ours, greater than the creation, and greater than our sins. As is His majesty, so is His mercy, that is, without measures and without rules, sitting in heaven and filling all the world, calling for a duty that He may give a blessing, making man that He may save him, punishing him that He may preserve him. And God's justice bowed down to His mercy, and all His power passed into mercy, and His omniscience converted into care and watchfulness, into providence and observation for man's avail; and heaven gave its influence for man, and rained showers for our food and drink; and the attributes and acts of God sat at the foot of mercy, and all that mercy descended upon the head of man. . . . . For, ever since the fall of Adam, who, like an unfortunate man, spent all that a wretched man could need, or a happy man could have, our life is repentance, and forgiveness is all our portion; and though angels were objects of God's bounty, yet man only is, in proper speaking, the object of His mercy; and the mercy which dwelt in an infinite circle became confined to a little ring, and dwelt here below; and here shall dwell below, till it hath carried all God's portion up to heaven, where it shall reign and glory upon our crowned heads for ever and ever! . . . I must tell concerning God's mercy as we do concerning God Himself, that He is that great fountain of which we all drink, and the great rock of which we all eat, and on which we all dwell, and under whose shadow we are all refreshed. God's mercy is all this; and we can only draw the great lines of it, and reckon the constellations of our hemisphere, instead of telling the number of the stars; we only can reckon what we feel and what we live by; and though there be, in every one of these lines of life, enough to engage us for ever to do God service, and to give Him praises, yet it is certain there are very many mercies of God on us, and toward us, and concerning us, which we neither feel, nor see, nor understand as yet; but yet we are blessed by them, and are preserved and secure, and we shall then know them, when we come to give God thanks in the festivities of an eternal Sabbath.—*Jeremy Taylor.*

The Tabernacle in the Midst of the Host.

(Verse 17.)

We have spoken of two of the standards, and two other remain to be spoken of. In this verse, Moses interlaceth the placing and situation of the tabernacle, which was so environed with the Levites, and they flanked and fortified with the whole host, that it remained in the midst, in a place of the greatest safety, fittest for access in regard of the people, and hardest for access in regard of their enemies.

I. **The Reasons for placing the Tabernacle after this manner.**

1. God doth hereby admonish them, that they should always have Him before their eyes, lest they should forget His worship or offend Him with their sins (comp. Lev. xxvi. 11, 12).

2. He had respect indifferently unto all the tribes. If any others had pitched their tents farther than from the Tabernacle, they would have quarrelled and complained that they had been contemned and despised.

3. The Levites were hereby put in mind of their duty, and therefore are lodged about it.

II. **The Uses of placing the Tabernacle after this manner.**

1. It assureth us that God will ever be in the midst of us, and settle His rest and residence among us (comp. Lev. xxvi. 11, 12; Ezek. xxvii. 27). We must know how God is said to dwell among us. Difference between His general presence and His special presence. His general presence is in all places; His special presence is in His Church. His general presence is of His power; His special presence is of His grace and favour. There is a common manner of God's being everywhere, and in all things, by His essence: there is a special way of God's being present, as that which is loved is present in him that loveth (comp. John xiv. 23). (1) God is joined unto us in the person of His own only Son *Emmanuel*—*i.e., God with us.* We are made members of His body (see Matt. xxviii. 20). (2). We have with Him the preaching of the Gospel, whereby God is, as it were, brought down to reside and remain among us. (3) We have the promise of His presence and the seals thereof in His Sacraments, whereby we are at one with Him, and He with us (see Gal. iii. 27; John vi. 54-56; 1 Cor. x. 16, 17). (4) When we come together in the Church to call upon His name, He is near unto us, and most familiar with us (see Matt. xviii. 20). (5) He dwelleth among us whensoever He preserveth us from evil, and delivereth us from our enemies. . . . Let us take heed to walk in fear before Him, etc. (see Deut. vi. 12-15; 2 Cor. vi. 16-18). We ought to walk always as in God's presence, and to consider evermore that His eye is upon us.

2. It serveth to teach us to what end God hath instituted Civil States and

Commonwealths in this world—to wit, to be stays and props to the Church, that the people of God may assemble together in peace and quietness. (1) Let all persons, princes, and people, high and low, do good to the Church of God, and employ their best endeavours to promote the glory of God and the safety of the Church (see Pss. cxxii. 6, 7; cxxxii. 1-5). (2) It is the duty of all persons to assemble together to hear His word. . . . . If we would dwell with God, let us repair to His house; if we would see Him, we shall see Him there; if we would hear Him, we shall hear Him there; if we would know Him, we shall know Him there, for His face is to be seen there, His voice is to be heard there, His presence is to be found there (see Pss. xxvii. 4; xlii. 1; lxxxiv. 2). (3) Let us not stand in fear of any enemies, as if they would bear and beat down the Church before them; neither let us forsake our mother, for fear of troubles that may come upon her. . . . . The Church is set in a safe place; they shall not be able to hurt it: it hath a safe Keeper, that neither slumbereth nor sleepeth; they shall not be able to destroy it: the gates of hell and the power of the devil are set against it, but they shall never have victory over it (see Deut. vii. 21, 22).

3. It serveth to conclude the full and final happiness of the faithful, which is begun in this life, but shall be consummated in the end of this world. Then will God dwell with us, and we shall dwell with Him; then we shall be admitted into His presence, and never be cast out; then no evil shall touch us, or come near us, and no good thing shall be wanting unto us that we can desire (see Rev. xxi. 3, 4; 2 Pet. iii. 13; Rev. vii. 15-17; xxi. 22-27).—*W. Attersoll.*

The Camp of Ephraim, and its Suggestions.

(Verses 18-24.)

In these verses we have an account of the third camp, which was posted to the west of the Tabernacle. It consisted of the tribes of Ephraim, Manasseh, and Benjamin, all descendants of Rachel. Looking at this camp homiletically we discover in it—

I. An illustration of the Divine Sovereignty.

Ephraim and Manasseh were sons of Joseph by his wife Asenath. Though Manasseh was the elder, yet Ephraim was placed at the head of this camp. "The first indication we have of the ascendancy of Ephraim over Manasseh is in the blessing of the children by Jacob (Gen. xlviii.). The intention of Joseph was evidently that the right hand of Jacob should convey the ampler blessing to the head of Manasseh, his first-born, and he had so arranged the young men. But the result was otherwise ordained."

Jacob persisted in setting Ephraim before Manasseh. "God chose from the beginning," says Bishop Patrick, "in several instances, to prefer the younger before the elder, as Abel before Cain; Shem before Japheth; Isaac before Ishmael; Jacob before Esau; Judah and Joseph before Reuben; and here Ephraim before Manasseh; and Moses before Aaron; and David, the youngest of all, before his elder brethren—to show that the Divine benefits were not limited to the order of nature, but dispensed freely, according to God's most wise goodness." God bestows all His gifts freely, according to His own good pleasure, both when He will, and where He will, and to whom He will. Our salvation from beginning to end is owing to His sovereign favour. We have nothing of our own. "For who maketh thee to differ? and what hast thou that thou didst not receive?" etc. God is debtor to no man. We have no claim upon His bounty. If He should withhold His blessing from any of us, we should have no just ground of complaint against Him. We, however, do well ever to bear in mind that His is *the sovereignty of a Being of infinite wisdom, righteousness, and love.* It is the sovereignty of GOD, the Supremely Good. *(a)* Though we know not the reasons of many of His decisions and doings, yet we know that in them all He is actuated by motives and seeks the accomplishment of ends which are worthy of Himself. Let us then, like the Hebrew poets, rejoice in God's sovereignty, and celebrate it in reverent and hearty songs.

II. An illustration of the sacredness of family ties

These three tribes which constitute this camp were all descended from Rachel, and were the whole of her descendants. We may fairly conclude that this was one reason, and a chief one, why they were grouped together. To the eye of God family ties are sacred things. Jesus our Lord "was subject unto" His parents. On the cross, amidst His own fierce agonies of both body and soul, He was mindful of His mother, spake to her, and committed her to the care of His beloved disciple. The ties of kinship are of the closest, tenderest, strongest, holiest nature; and should be so regarded. In our families let us cultivate mutual forbearance, and helpfulness, and holy love; "for without hearts there is no home." Let us make our houses *homes;* the scenes of confidence, peace, affection, and worship. "It is just as possible to keep a calm house as a clean house, a cheerful house, an orderly house, as a furnished house, if the heads set themselves to do so. Where is the difficulty of consulting each other's weakness, as well as each other's wants; each other's tempers, as well as each other's health; each other's comfort, as well as each other's character? Oh! it is by leaving the peace at home to chance, instead of pursuing it by system, that so many houses are unhappy." *(b)*

III. An illustration of the Divine regard for the weak.

This was the least numerous of the four great divisions, and therefore by direction of God it was appointed to that position in which there was the last danger. Tenderly God cares for the feeble. "He shall gather the lambs with His arm, and carry them in His bosom, and shall gently lead those that are with young." "A bruised reed shall He not break, and the smoking flax shall He not quench." What a rich fund of comfort and encouragement there is here—

1. *For those who are physically afflicted.*
2. *For those whose faith is feeble.*
3. *For those who are sorely tried.*

He is acquainted with us altogether; and in our great need He will bestow upon us the tenderest care and the richest grace. *(c)*

Conclusion:

Let us unfalteringly trust in God. Let us rejoice in the sovereignty of so wise and kind a Being.

" He everywhere hath sway,
And all things serve His might,
His every act pure blessing is;
His path unsullied light.

Leave to His sovereign sway,
To choose and to command:
So shalt thou wondering own His way,
How wise, how strong His hand!

Thou comprehend'st Him not;
Yet earth and heaven tell
God sits as Sovereign on the throne;
He ruleth all things well.

Thou seest our weakness, Lord,
Our hearts are known to Thee;
O lift Thou up the sinking hand,
Confirm the feeble knee.

Let us in life and death,
Boldly Thy truth declare;
And publish with our latest breath,
Thy love and guardian care."

P. Gerhard.

ILLUSTRATIONS.

(a) The sovereignty of God naturally ariseth from the relation of all things to Himself as their entire Creator, and their natural and inseparable dependence upon Him in regard of their being and well-being. The first cause of everything hath an unquestionable dominion of propriety in it upon the score of justice. By the law of nations, the first finder of a country is esteemed the rightful possessor and lord of that country, and the first inventor of an art hath a right of exercising it. If a man hath a just claim of

dominion over that thing whose materials were not of his framing, but form only the addition of a new figure from his skill; as a limner over his picture, the cloth whereof he never made, nor the colours wherewith he draws it were never endued by him with their distinct qualities, but only he applies them by his art to compose such a figure; much more hath God a rightful claim of dominion over His creatures, whose entire being, both in matter and form, and every particle of their excellency, was breathed out by the word of His mouth. He did not only give the matter a form, but bestowed upon the matter itself a being; it was formed by none to His hand, as the matter is on which an artist works. He had the being of all things in His own power, and it was at His choice whether He would impart it or no; there can be no juster and stronger ground of a claim than this. A man hath a right to a piece of brass or gold by his purchase, but when by his engraving he hath formed it into an excellent statue, there results an increase of his right upon the account of his artifice. God's creation of the matter of man gave Him a right over man; but His creation of him in so eminent an excellency, with reason to guide him, a clear eye of understanding to discern light from darkness, and truth from falsehood, a freedom of will to act accordingly, and an original righteousness as the varnish and beauty of all; here is the strongest foundation for a claim of authority over man, and the strongest obligation on man for subjection to God.—*Charnocke.*

(*b*) Families are not isolated individuals, but the descendants of their fathers, and therefore essentially members one of another; God himself being the Father of all the families of the universe. What can be more interesting than to contemplate the intelligent universe, as consisting of endlessly multiplied bonds of fatherhood and childhood; and all these held in the strong unity of one Divine Fatherhood and one Divine Sonship?

Family relationship is therefore a very sacred thing. Its root being not in the creation, but in God. And though we shall not find on earth any development worthy of its holy root, nevertheless, the flower which fills the world with choicest fragrance is family affection. It is capable of becoming most heavenly, since the Eternal Father is Himself the spring of parental, as His Eternal Son is of filial love. Therefore, also, family affections are capable of ceaseless cultivation. There is nothing to hinder family love from becoming evermore deeper, stronger, and lovelier. If it be so strong and so precious among fallen creatures, what must it be among the perfect? If family life on the earth gives rise, as it often does, to a very paradise of courtesies and tender sanctities, what must family life be in the immediate Presence, and under the direct influence, of the Infinite Father and His Only Begotten Son? Christian parents and their children should know therefore, that in their families they have not a little world, but a little heaven to cultivate.

What a *solace to our hearts* is the assurance, that we shall never cease to be members of a family! The perfection of the great heavenly household is that it is a Household of households. We are born into a family, we grow up in a family, we die in a family, and after death, we shall not simply go into the great heaven, but to our own family, in our Father's House. "Abraham gave up the ghost, and was gathered *to his people.*" "Thou shalt go to *thy fathers* in peace," God had said to him. All in heaven will not know us, but *our own people* will know us. We shall go to them.— *J. Pulsford.*

(*c*) "A bruised reed I will not break." Is there anything that grows so high, carrying up so little strength of stem, as the reed that rises twenty or thirty feet in the air, and has a stalk not larger than my finger? Now, a beast striking through the thicket, eager, with his unquenched thirst, for the cooling draught, strikes against a joint of the slender reed, shattering it so that it has but just strength to bear its own weight. So weak is it, that if there be so much wind as to lift one of its leaves, or to bend it in the least degree in either direction, it must surely break. But God says, "My gentleness is such that when I go down among men whose condition is like that of a bruised reed, I will do nothing to complete their overthrow, but will deal with them in such a way that they shall gather strength till I have sent forth judgment unto victory."

"And smoking flax I will not quench." If the flame is just dying out in a lamp it is not in danger of being suddenly extinguished, for the old warmth in the wick seems for a time to nourish and sustain it; but immediately after the wick is lighted, and before any warmth is communicated to it, the least movement is sufficient to extinguish it. Now God says, "Wherever there is a spark of grace lighted in the soul, if it flickers so that the least breath of the person who carries it, or the least motion of his hand is in danger of putting it out, I will deal so gently with him as not to quench that spark. I will treat it with such infinite tenderness that it shall grow into a flame which shall burn on for ever." And these are the symbols by which God measures His wonderful gentleness.— *H. W. Beecher.*

THE CAMP OF DAN: ASPECTS OF DIVINE SERVICE.

(Verses 25-31.)

This is the fourth great division which encamped north of the tabernacle, and brought up the rear on the march. The powerful tribe of Dan was placed at the head of it, and with it the remaining tribes, Asher and Naphtali. Dan was the fifth son of Jacob, and the first of Bilhah, Rachel's maid. Asher was the eighth son of Jacob, and the second of Zilpah, Leah's handmaid. Naphtali was own brother to Dan, being the sixth son of Jacob, and the second of Bilhah. The composition and station of this camp suggest certain homiletic points concerning the Divine service.

I. Persons of every kind and degree of faculty may find employment in the Divine service.

Each of the tribes had its position and duties in one of the four great divisions, or in the interior near to the tabernacle. Whatever its number or its peculiar characteristics, every one had its allotted place and work. It would appear that Judah was strong and courageous, while Dan was secret and subtle (see Gen. xlix. 8-12, 17); yet for Dan, as well as for Judah, there is a place in the great army of Israel. In the great work of God amongst men there is room for workers of every kind and degree of ability. And God lays claim to the services of every one. There is work suited to every one, as St. Paul clearly shows in 1 Cor. xii. Eloquence, scholarship, teaching power, courage, patience, tact, administrative ability, aptitude for the details of business, etc., may each find its appropriate sphere in the great work and warfare of the Church of Jesus Christ. Even the patient sufferer has a place in His service.

"They also serve who only stand and wait."

Let this serve as—
1. *An encouragement to the feeble.*
2. *A rebuke to the slothful.* (a)

II. It is essential that even the lowest position in the Divine service should be faithfully filled.

It may appear to some that the place allotted to the camp of Dan was an inferior and obscure one. "They shall go hindmost with their standards." But it was essential that some of the tribes should occupy this position, and discharge its duties. There must be a rearguard as well as a vanguard. In building the temple the services of the hewers of wood are as indispensable as those of the skilled workmen. The blower of the organ-bellows is as necessary to secure its grand aid in worship as the accomplished musician.

"Small service is true service while it lasts;
  Of friends, however humble, scorn not one:
The daisy, by the shadow that it casts,
  Protects the ling'ring dewdrop from the sun."
                                    Wordsworth.

Moreover, great achievements are impossible apart from faithful attention to the details of the enterprise. The strength of the whole chain is not greater than that of its weakest link. The efficiency of the entire body is affected by the condition of its obscurist and feeblest member. Faithfulness in littles is imperatively demanded as a condition of success in all true and noble work. (b)

III. Even the lowest position in the Divine service is one of privilege and honour.

If the position of Dan and the two associated tribes be regarded as the lowest in the great host, yet it was a distinguished and advantageous position. They were as truly a part of the people chosen of God as those in the first camp. The privileges which those of the other camps enjoyed, they enjoyed also. The promises and prospects which encouraged the others, encouraged them also. The Lord was their God, etc. The feeblest and obscurist member of God's spiritual Israel occupies a place and sustains relationships of highest honour and richest privilege. "We are the children of God: and if children, then heirs; heirs of God," etc. In calling us to any work, even the most menial, in His service, God confers upon us the most exalted distinction. It is a call to co-operation with Himself, etc. " We are workers together with Christ."

"Our Master all the work hath done
He asks of us to-day;
Sharing His service every one,
Share too His sonship may:
Lord, I would serve and be a son,
Dismiss me not, I pray."
—*T. T. Lynch.*

IV. **Seemingly obscure positions in the Divine service are in many instances positions of great importance and responsibility.**

It was so in this case. There was danger of attack in the rear. With the exception of the camp of Judah, which led the way, the camp of Dan was in a position which required the greatest strength. And, being numerically inferior only to Judah, the wisdom of its appointment to that position is obvious. Though their position was "hindmost," yet in importance it was second only to that of the camp of Judah. An illustration of spiritual work. The services of the quiet and comparatively obscure scholar, thinker, and writer are, at the very least, quite as important as those of the popular preacher. The wise and faithful pastor, who is almost unknown beyond his own sphere of service, is doing as worthy and as needful a work as the evangelist whose fame is world-wide. The quiet members of the Church, who are influential in the family and in the prayer meetings, are perhaps more necessary to the existence and prosperity of the Church than the men who are prominent in committees and on public platforms. (*c*)

Conclusion:

1. *Have we any place in the spiritual Israel?*
2. *Are we endeavouring faithfully to discharge its duties?*

ILLUSTRATIONS.

(*a*) *The feeblest power may be beneficially exerted.* Are there any who are flattering themselves that if they possessed *gigantic talents* they would employ them on behalf of human freedom and human progress? I pronounce such self-consolation a deadly error. Man's business is to employ the talents with which Almighty Wisdom has endowed him, and by their employment to multiply them. Deposit the acorn in a cabinet, and time will turn it to corruption; but plant that acorn where the light and the dew of heaven can exert upon it their fructifying influence, and time will develope the majestic oak. So with talents; bury them in disuse, and they will become morally pestilential; but give them free and beneficent exercise, and they will breathe new life into the social constitution. Young man! employ thy one talent diligently, and thou shalt be promoted to the rulership of larger empire: wait not for time that may never advene; sigh not for golden opportunities and felicitous coincidences; the true man makes every opportunity golden by turning it to a golden use, and the robust soul conquers the infelicities of unpropitious circumstances. That will be a glorious day in human history on which all Christians, the feeblest and mightiest, will be working for the advancement of Christ's Kingdom;—the orator swaying the multitude, the writer sending forth his richly laden page, the widow giving her two mites, and the child of poverty bestowing "a cup of cold water." When the whole Church is at work the kingdom of darkness will be shaken to its centre.—*J. Parker, D.D.*

(*b*) Napoleon was the most effective man in modern times—some will say of all times. The secret of his character was, that while his plans were more vast, more various, and, of course, more difficult than those of other men, he had the talent, at the same time, to fill them up with perfect promptness and precision, in every particular of execution. His vast and daring plans would have been visionary in any other man: but with him every vision flew out of his brain a chariot of iron, because it was filled up, in all the particulars of execution, to be a solid and compact framework in every part. His armies were together only one great engine of desolation, of which he was the head or brain. Numbers, spaces, times, were all distinct in his eye. The wheeling of every legion, however remote, was mentally present to him. The tramp of every foot sounded in his ear. The numbers were always supplied, the spaces passed over, the times met, and so the work was done. . . . . There must be detail in every great work. It is an element of effectiveness, which no reach of plan, no enthusiasm of purpose, can dispense with. Thus, if a man conceives the idea of becoming eminent in learning, but cannot toil through the million of little drudgeries necessary to carry him on, his learning will be soon told. Or, if a man undertakes to become rich, but despises the small and gradual advances by which wealth is ordinarily accumulated, his expectations will, of course, be the sum of his riches. Accurate and careful detail, the minding of common occasions and small things, combined with general scope and vigour, is the secret of all the efficiency and success in the world.—*H Bushnell, D.D.*

(c) *Slight services may be invaluable services.* What can be a more trivial image than "a cup of cold water?" Less trivial, unquestionably, in the hot East than in our well-watered England; but a trivial image even there. And yet I have read of cases in which a cup of water would have fetched more than its weight in gold. Look into the despairing eyes of that boat-load of ship-wrecked sailors, tossing hour after hour on the ocean in the heat of the sun: the briny water glancing and flashing all around them as if in mockery, and not a drop anywhere of that which might slake their wild human thirst. What would not those men give for a draught of fresh water a-piece? Look at the caravan in the desert, when the last camel, "the ship of the desert," lies stranded and doomed upon the sand; when no hope remains to the travellers of reaching in time the spot where the cool palm-trees draw their life from the hidden spring. How much of his rich merchandize would not that dying trader be content to part with in exchange for "a cup of cold water?" Or traverse the battle-field when the fight is ended, and one poor wounded soldier, whose courage had carried him too far has been overlooked. The sun goes down, the stars appear, but dewy night fails to alleviate the burning thirst which always follows gun-shot wounds. Yet if some comrade shall venture out to look for the wounded man, shall find him groaning under the silent stars, and shall bring him, though it were from the nearest puddle, the draught he craves, they two shall know for ever what a blessing there may be in "a cup of cold water." And have we not all heard of the generous Sidney, as he was borne dying from the field of Zutphen, how he had just put the cup to his lips, when a poor fellow was carried by, who looked as he went at the richer Sidney's draught with the longing eyes of despair,—and how the dying rich man withdrew his lips before he drank, and gave the cup to the dying poor man with the words, "Thy necessity is yet greater than mine!" Beside the noble Sidney's name is that simple story still inscribed upon the immortal page. Of such and of so great a value may even "a cup of cold water" be. And I often think of HIM who sat once by Jacob's well in the heat of the day, asking for a drink of water from the Samaritan woman. *He* accepted all the conditions of human weakness and human want. *He* knew by experience, even whilst he used this image to indicate the slight nature of such an offering as this, what a precious offering it might really be, and that it might be employed, and that without exaggeration, to denote all the difference between life and death.—*J. G. Pigg, B.A.*

CONTENTMENT AND OBEDIENCE.

(Verses 32-34.)

These verses present to us two topics on which we may reflect with profit.

I. Contentment with the Divine appointment.

We have seen that God in His infinite and sovereign wisdom allotted to each tribe its place and duty as it pleased Him. And it appears from the text that each tribe freely accepted the Divine appointment, and fell into its allotted position. There is not even a hint that any one of the tribes was guilty of any murmuring against the arrangements. This is the more remarkable when we take into account how prone the people were to complain and fret upon the very slightest pretext. Let us learn to be content cheerfully to occupy the position, and diligently to do the work allotted to us by God. "My times are in Thy hand." "He shall choose our inheritance for us." "Thou shalt guide me with Thy counsel." The most cogent reasons urge us to be content with the appointments of God concerning us.

1. *We are incompetent to determine our own place and duty.* This will at once appear if we consider—(1). *Our ignorance.* How ignorant we are *(a)* of *ourselves.* Possibilities of both good and evil are latent within us which only God knows. If the determination of our lot were with us, we might choose such an one as would tend to kill any germs of truth and goodness which are within us, and to stimulate the germs of evil into awfully rapid and ruinous development. God alone is thoroughly acquainted with us. How ignorant we are *(b)* of the *future.* The particular character and circumstances of the coming minute are veiled from us. The choice which now seems wise and good, amid the altered circumstances and conditions of the morrow, may appear foolish and evil. To God only is the entire future clearly visible. Our

incompetence to determine our own lot will appear further if we consider—(2) *Our proneness to self-indulgence.* In choosing for ourselves, we should select the pleasant rather than the painful, the sweet rather than the bitter. And yet for us the bitter may be the more wholesome, and the painful may be indispensable to our well-being. We are incapable of choosing our own place and work.

2. *We have ample grounds for confidence in the determinations of God for us.* We discover these in—(1) *His knowledge.* He knows all things. He knows the whole future perfectly. He knows us individually and thoroughly (see Ps. cxxxix. 1-4). (2) *His wisdom.* "Wisdom and might are His: He giveth wisdom unto the wise," etc.; "O the depth of the riches both of the wisdom and knowledge of God!" etc.; "The only wise God." (3) *His kindness.* He is as gracious as He is wise. "God is love" (see Ps. cxlv. 8, 9). Surely, in considerations like these we have most powerful reasons for contentment with the place and work to which we are appointed by God. *(a)* These considerations should—

First—*Silence our murmurings because of our particular circumstances and condition.*

Second—*Deter us from seeking to alter our condition and circumstances by any unrighteous or unworthy methods. (b)*

II. Obedience to the Divine commands.

The obedience of Israel upon this occasion seems to have been most exemplary, "And the children of Israel did according to all that the Lord commanded Moses: so they pitched by their standards," etc. Without murmuring or disputing, without abatement or omission, they did as they were directed. Their obedience was prompt and complete. Let us note this to their credit, and as an example to us. Entire obedience is required of us also.

1. *All God's commands are binding, because they are all right.* He requires of us nothing but what is just and true. We cannot break the least of His commandments without sin. "The law is holy, and the commandment holy, and just, and good."

2. *All God's commands are benevolent.* "In keeping of them there is great reward." Obedience is blessed as well as binding. *(c)*

Conclusion:

Let us seek Divine aid that we may render full and hearty obedience to all the commands of God.

"O let Thy sacred will
   All Thy delight in me fulfil!
Let me not think an action mine own way,
   But as Thy love shall sway,
Resigning up the rudder to Thy skill."
                                Geo. Herbert.

ILLUSTRATIONS.

(a) There are two forms of discontent: one laborious, the other indolent and complaining. We respect the man of laborious desire, but let us not suppose that his restlessness is peace, or his ambition meekness. It is because of the special connection of meekness with contentment that it is promised that the meek shall "inherit the earth." Neither covetous men, nor the grave, can inherit anything; they can but consume. Only contentment can possess. The most helpful and sacred work, therefore, which can at present be done for humanity, is to teach people (chiefly by example, as all best teaching must be done) not how to "better themselves," but how to "satisfy themselves." It is the curse of every evil nation and evil creature to eat, and *not* be satisfied. The words of blessing are, that they shall eat and be satisfied. And as there is only one kind of water which quenches all thirst, so there is only one kind of bread which satisfies all hunger, the bread of justice or righteousness; which hungering after, men shall always be filled, that being the bread of Heaven; but hungering after the bread, or wages, of unrighteousness, shall not be filled, that being the bread of Sodom. And, in order to teach men how to be satisfied, it is necessary fully to understand the art and joy of humble life,—this, at present, of all arts or sciences being the one most needing study. Humble life,—that is to say, proposing to itself no future exaltation, but only a sweet continuance; not excluding the idea of foresight, but wholly of fore-sorrow, and taking no troublous thought of coming days: so, also, not excluding the idea of providence, or provision, but wholly of accumulation; the life of domestic affection and domestic peace, full of sensitiveness to all elements of costless and kind

pleasure;—therefore, chiefly to the loveliness of the natural world.—*J. Ruskin.*

(*b*) But that Thou art my wisdom, **Lord**,
    And both mine eyes are Thine,
My mind would be extremely stirr'd
    For missing my design.

Were it not better to bestow
    Some place and power on me?
Then should Thy praises with me grow,
    And share in my degree.

But when I thus dispute and grieve,
    I do resume my sight;
And pilf'ring what I once did give,
    Disseize Thee of Thy right.

How know I, if Thou should'st me raise,
    That I should then raise Thee?
Perhaps great places and Thy praise
    Do not so well agree.

Wherefore unto my gift I stand;
    I will no more advise:
Only do Thou lend me a hand
    Since Thou hast both mine eyes.
                  Geo. Herbert.

(*c*) That principle to which Polity owes its stability, Life its happiness, Faith its acceptance, and Creation its continuance, is Obedience. . . . How false is the conception, how frantic the pursuit, of that treacherous phantom which men call Liberty! most treacherous, indeed, of all phantoms; for the feeblest ray of reason might surely show us, that not only its attainment, but its being, was impossible. There is no such thing in the universe. There can never be. The stars have it not; the earth has it not; the sea has it not; and we men have the mockery and semblance of it only for our heaviest punishment. . . . If there be any one principle more widely than another confessed by every utterance, or more sternly than another imprinted on every atom of the visible creation, that principle is not Liberty, but Law.

The enthusiast would reply that by Liberty he meant the Law of Liberty. Then why use the single and misunderstood word? If by liberty you mean chastisement of the passions, discipline of the intellect, subjection of the will; if you mean the fear of inflicting, the shame of committing, a wrong; if you mean respect for all who are in authority, and consideration for all who are in dependence; veneration for the good, mercy to the evil, sympathy to the weak; if you mean watchfulness over all thoughts, temperance in all pleasures, and perseverance in all toils; if you mean, in a word, that Service which is defined in the liturgy of the English Church to be perfect Freedom, why do you name that by the same word by which the luxurious mean licence, and the reckless mean change; by which the rogue means rapine, and the fool equality, by which the proud mean anarchy, and the malignant mean violence? Call it by any name rather than this, but its best and truest is Obedience. Obedience is, indeed, founded on a kind of freedom, else it would become mere subjugation, but that freedom is only granted that obedience may be more perfect; and thus, while a measure of licence is necessary to exhibit the individual energy of things, the fairness and pleasantness and perfection of them all consist in their Restraint. Compare a river that has burst its banks with one that is bound by them, and the clouds that are scattered over the face of the whole heaven, with those that are marshalled into ranks and orders by its winds. So that though restraint, utter and unrelaxing, can never be comely, this is not because it is in itself an evil, but only because, when too great, it overpowers the nature of the thing restrained, and so counteracts the other laws of which that nature is itself composed.—*J. Ruskin.*

CHAPTER III.

Critical Notes.—"Muster of the Tribe of Levi. As Jacob had adopted the two sons of Joseph as his own sons, and thus promoted them to the rank of heads of tribes, the tribe of Levi founded, strictly speaking, the thirteenth tribe of the whole nation, and was excepted from the muster of the twelve tribes who were destined to form the army of Jehovah, because God had chosen it for the service of the sanctuary. Out of this tribe God had not only called Moses to be the deliverer, lawgiver, and leader of His people, but Moses' brother Aaron, with the sons of the latter, to be the custodians of the sanctuary. And now, lastly, the whole tribe was chosen, in the place of the first-born of all the tribes, to assist the priests in performing the duties of the sanctuary, and was numbered and mustered for this its special calling."—*Keil and Del.*

Ver. 1. *Generations.* "The term 'generations' is strictly a technical word (cf. Gen. ii. 4; v. 1, vi. 9, etc.; Ruth iv. 18). It does not point to birth and origin so much as to downward history and development." The "generations" here are not merely the descendants of Moses and Aaron, but of the Levites generally. "Aaron is placed before Moses here" (see at Ex. vi. 26 *sqq.*), "not merely as being the elder of the two, but because his sons received the priesthood, whilst the sons of Moses, on the contrary, were classed among the rest of the Levitical families" (cf. 1 Chron. xxiii. 14).

Ver. 3. *Whom he consecrated:* lit. as marg., "whose hand he filled," by setting them apart to the office of priests.

Ver. 4. *In the sight of Aaron, their father*—*i.e.*, during his lifetime.

AARON AND HIS SONS: PARENTS AND CHILDREN.

(Verses 1-4.)

In these verses we have—

1. An incidental illustration of the exalted personal character and the Divine mission of Moses.

Aaron was the ancestor of a regular succession of priests. But Moses seeks nothing for himself or for his descendants. He does not use his high position or his great power for the attainment of any selfish end. He "passes by his own family, or immediate descendants; he gave no rank or privilege to them during his life, and left nothing to them at his death. They became incorporated with the Levites, from or amongst whom they are never distinguished." An illustration of *the nobility of his character and the utter unselfishness of his aims.* Other eminent men seek to advance the interests of their descendants; but it was not so with him. In this we have also a confirmation of *the Divinity of his vocation*—that he was called of God to his great enterprise. Had it been otherwise, we should have seen him aim at the gratification of avarice, or the acquisition of power, or the attainment of honours for himself and his successors. The disinterestedness of his conduct witnesses to the Divinity of his calling.

II. An intimation that the duties of the ministers of religion demand for their faithful discharge their entire consecration thereto.

It seems to us that the striking expression used in the third verse may fairly be regarded as suggesting this truth, "Whose hands he filled to minister in the priest's office." The apostles soon found this entire consecration of their time and powers to the work to be necessary. "We will give ourselves continually to prayer, and to the ministry of the word" (see Acts vi. 1-4). And St. Paul, in writing to Timothy, says: "Give thyself wholly to them" (see 1 Tim. iv. 13-16, and remarks on this point in our notes on ch. i. 47-54).

III. An example of wicked sons descending from a godly parent.

Aaron, though far from being so great or so holy a man as his brother, was without doubt a good man; yet Nadab, his eldest son, and Abihu, his second son, were consumed by God because of their sin. "Nadab and Abihu died before the Lord, when they offered strange fire before the Lord, in the wilderness of Sinai." Their sin was that they kindled the incense in their censers with fire not taken from that which burned perpetually on the altar, and probably that they did this while in a state of intoxication (Lev. x. 1-11). *God will be served as He pleases and directs.* There is peril even in the slightest infringement of Divine directions. In sacred services the least deviations from the clearly revealed will of God are displeasing unto Him. For their sin Nadab and Abihu were devoured by "fire from the Lord." They were degenerate and depraved sons of a pious father. Generation is not regeneration. Personal character is not hereditary as personal possessions often are. Our Lord represents one "in hell" and "in torments" as addressing Abraham as "Father," and Abraham in reply addressing him as "Son." The children of godly parents may at last find their own place in hell. Salvation is not transmissible. It is a personal concern. Repentance, faith, self-consecration, are acts which cannot be done by proxy. The general rule undoubtedly is that the children of pious parents, who have been well and wisely trained by them, will themselves become pious. It is also true that moral tendencies are transmissible from parent to child. Still there are exceptions to this rule. Yet we think if we knew all the particulars of the home-life and the parental training and example, we should find such exceptions to be very rare indeed. Many parents of undoubted piety fail sadly in the training of their children: some through over-severity, others by undue indulgence, etc. Did not Eli fail in this respect? (1 Sam. iii. 13.) Do not the troubles which arose to Jacob by reason of the sins of his sons look like the natural retribution of his own sins, in deceiving his aged father and in wronging his brother? Were not the troubles in the later life of David, because of the wickedness of some of his sons, connected with his own sins? (2 Sam. xii. 10-12.) Let pious parents take heed to themselves and to their duties. (*a*)

IV. An example of the widest difference of character and destiny in children of the same parents.

While Nadab and Abihu were sadly depraved and suddenly destroyed, their younger brethren Eleazar and Ithamar faithfully "ministered in the priest's office in the sight of Aaron their father," and upon his death, Eleazar succeeded him as high priest. The children of the same parents frequently differ widely from each other in features, in disposition, and, as amongst the sons of Aaron, in character. The freedom of the human will to a very great extent explains this. The things which to one man are the very bread of life, another man will pervert into deadly poison. The ministry of the Divine Gospel to some is "the savour of life unto life," to others "the savour of death unto death." (*b*)

Conclusion:

Our subject utters earnest counsels—
1. *To the children of godly parents.* Trust not in the character and prayers of your parents for salvation. These are of priceless value, yet they will not avail to your salvation apart from your own faith and obedience. (See Ezek. xviii.) (*c*)
2. *To parents.* Be diligent and faithful in the discharge of your duty to your children. (1) Let your own life be right, and so set them a good *example*. (*d*) (2) Give them wise religious *instruction* and training. (*e*) (3) Commend them often and earnestly to God in *prayer*. (*f*) (4) Afford them *encouragement* in every manifestation of pious feeling and conduct. (*g*)

ILLUSTRATIONS.

(*a*) I do not overlook the dreadful possibility, that, in the stress of temptation, and a depraved inclination, the child, even when all this has been done for him, may wander off and be a prodigal. He may viciously disown the covenant made in his behalf. He may plunge into sin, in despite of all. Then his only way back into the Church of Christ must be by conversion, as with the children of unbelievers. All I say is, that such instances ought to be prevented or diminished by wiser and more Christian notions and practices. Let the Christian parents continually speak to the young child of Church privileges, of the joy and the duty of his Christian heritage and home. Let that child have the doctrines and life of Christ faithfully instilled into his soul, by domestic instruction and family prayer. Let him be reminded of his baptismal dedication, and taught to live worthily of it. No magical, talismanic effect is thus to be wrought upon him, but a perfectly natural and simple one, standing in harmony with all other educational influences, and guaranteed also a peculiar blessing. This Christian child, like others, must have a spiritual nature and life formed upon him, in addition to his natural life. Only, this blessed boon of a new and holy heart steals in upon him gradually, by way of his parents' eyes and voice and prayers, from the very dawn of his consciousness, grows with his growth, hardens with his muscles, expands with his understanding, and matures in him as gently and regularly as any of the growths of the forest or the field; so that there shall be no period in his remembrance, when he was not moving straight on towards a ripe Christian character, and full communion in the Church. All this I place in contrast with our strange and savage habit of turning off our little ones to feed on the husks and chaff of the senses, till some dreadful wrench of sorrow, after they have grown up, possibly wakens a few of them to conviction, and drives them back, broken-spirited, from the far country where they had wandered, to their Father's house.—*F. D. Huntington, D.D.*

(*b*) So from the heights of will
Life's parting stream descends,
And, as a moment turns its slender rill,
Each widening torrent bends.
From the same cradle's side,
From the same mother's knee,
One to long darkness and the frozen tide,
One to the peaceful sea!
O. W. Holmes.

(*c*) The child of a very godly father, notwithstanding all the instructions given him, the good education he has had, and the needful rebukes that have been given him, and the restraints he has been laid under, after all the pains taken with him and prayers put up for him, may yet prove wicked and vile, the grief of his father, the shame of his family, and the curse and plague of his generation. This wicked man shall perish for ever in his iniquity, notwithstanding his being the son of a good father. He is his own destroyer; and his relation to a good father will be so far from standing him in stead that it will aggravate his sin and his condemnation, and will make his misery hereafter the more intolerable.—*M. Henry.*

(*d*) Truth must be lived into meaning before it can be truly known. Examples are the only sufficient commentaries; living epistles the only fit expounders of written epistles. When the truly Christian father and mother teach as being taught of God, when their prayers go into their lives, and their lives into their doctrine; when their goodness melts into the memory, and heaven, too, breathes into the associated thoughts and sentiments, to make a kind of blessed memory for all they teach, then we see the beautiful office they are in fulfilled.—*H. Bushnell, D.D.*

(*e*) There must be regular Biblical teaching. Somewhere and somehow, not by chance, not at interrupted and infrequent seasons, but patiently and humbly, and week by week, that wonderful, most ancient and Eternal Book must be opened before him. Its sublime yet simple truths, plain to the child's understanding; its holy personages, its grand Prophets and ardent Apostles; its venerable patriarchs and its inspired children, must all pass, in their robes of light and forms of singular majesty and beauty before him. Its psalms must be sung into his soul. Its beatitudes and commandments must be fixed in his remembrance. Its parables must engage his fancy. Its miracles must awe his wonder. Its cross, and ark, and all its sacred emblems, must people his imagination. Without that Bible, no child born among us can come to Him whom only the Bible reveals.—*F. D. Huntington, D.D.*

(*f*) There must be prayer. Your child must know, he must see, he must feel, that between your parent-heart and Him who is the Infinite Father of all alike there is open and conscious communion. Till there is established, in all simplicity, this confiding and daily intercourse between the soul and Heaven, you have not received your child in the name of Christ. What was testified by one of the strong statesmen of early American history might be declared, in spirit, probably by nearly all the best men that have lived in Christendom. "I believe," he said, "that I should have been swept away by the flood of French infidelity if it had not been for one thing—the remembrance of the time when my sainted mother used to make me kneel by her bedside, taking my little hands folded in hers, and causing me to repeat the Lord's Prayer."—*Ibid.*

(*g*) Piety is very commonly discouraged in children by giving them tests of character that are inappropriate to their age. The child, for example, loses his temper in some matter in which he is crossed; and the conclusion is forthwith sprung upon him that he has a bad heart, and is certainly no Christian child. It is only necessary to ask how the father, how the mother, would themselves fare tested by the same rule? . . . It is never to be assumed by us that they are without piety because they falter in some things. The child must be judged or tested in the same general way as the adult. If he is wholly perverse, has no spirit of duty, turns away from all religious things, it will not encourage anything good in him to tell him that he is without piety; but if he loves religious things, wants to be in them, tries after a good and obedient life, he is to be shown how tenderly God regards him, how ready He is to forgive him, and when he stumbles or falls, how kindly He will raise him up, how graciously help him to stand!—*H. Bushnell, D.D.*

The Dedication of the Levites—Church Work and Workers.

(*Verses* 5-10.)

These verses suggest the following observations:—

I. That the offices of the Church are Divinely instituted.

The Lord here institutes the Levitical order with its duties, the priestly order with its duties, and places both under the high priest, who also had his duties. In the Christian Church the office of the Ministry was instituted by our Lord Himself. (See Matt. xxviii. 18-20; Mark xvi. 15, 16; Luke xxiv. 45-49.) The deacon's office was instituted by the inspired apostles with solemn prayer to God, and was ratified by the signal blessing of God which followed. (See Acts vi. 1-8.) Apostles, prophets, evangelists, pastors and teachers, are spoken of by St. Paul as the gifts of Christ to the Church, "for the perfecting of the saints, for the work of the ministry, for the edifying of the body of Christ." These offices are not human inventions. They are Divine in their origin, and in their authority. (*a*)

II. There are different ranks in the offices of the Church as instituted by God.

The Levites were given to the priests for the performance of those religious duties which were of an inferior kind. The priests ranked higher than the Levites. They were granted a nearer access to God in the Holy of holies. The high priest held the highest office in the tribe, and ranked as the head of both the priests and the Levites. With respect to the Levites this is clearly indicated in the text. Thus, in verse 6, "the expression עָמַד לִפְנֵי is frequently met with in connection with the position of a servant, as standing before his master to receive his commands."—*Keil and Del.* And Fuerst: "*To stand before one* in a respectful, submissive, ministering position before the great, hence *to serve, to wait upon.* Deut. i. 38; Dan. i. 5." The ninth verse also expresses their "complete surrender" to him. We must be careful in applying this to the Christian Church; for, as Dr. Stoughton observes, "the Jewish Church was in certain respects, and those the most characteristic and striking, so utterly different from the Churches instituted by the Apostles, that a combination of the principles of the first, with the principles of the second, is simply impossible." But in the offices of the Christian Church there are grades or ranks. Various ranks are *necessary* for the maintenance of the order, and the performance of the various duties of the Church. Various ranks are *inevitable.* While there are differences of mental capacity and spiritual power amongst the members of the Church, differences of rank there must be. Thus we find that ministers were rulers in the Churches in the Apostolic age. St. Paul writes, "We beseech you, brethren, to know them which labour among you, and are over you in the Lord, and admonish you," etc. (1 Thess. v. 12, 13. And the writer of the Epistle to the Hebrews says, "Remember them which have the rule over you, who have spoken unto you the Word of God." "They ruled in the name of their Divine Master, administering *His* laws, not enacting any of their own."

III. The lowliest labour in the service of God is sacred and blessed.

The Levites were to perform the most common and laborious duties. They were the servants of the priests. They had to keep guard round the tabernacle, to keep the sacred vessels pertaining to it, to remove it from place to place during their wanderings and journeyings, to prepare supplies for the sanctuary, such as incense, wine, oil, etc., and to keep all pertaining to the tabernacle clean and in order. Yet they were dedicated to this work, and taught to regard the work itself as sacred. The most menial labour in connection with the cause of God should still be regarded as sacred.

Its high and holy associations and ends exalt and hallow it. "I had rather be a doorkeeper in the house of my God, than," etc. Indeed, all work which is faithfully done is sacred. Duty is ever divine and ennobling. "One thing I will remind you of," says Mr. Carlyle, "that the essence and outcome of all religions, creeds, and liturgies whatsoever is, to do one's work in a faithful manner. Unhappy caitiff, what to you is the use of orthodoxy, if with every stroke of your hammer you are breaking all the Ten Commandments,—operating upon Devil's dust, and endeavouring to reap where you have not sown?" (*b*)

IV. God also appoints the persons to fill the various offices in His Church.

Here He appoints the tribe of Levi to the service of the tabernacle, and the sons of Aaron to the priesthood; and He called Aaron to be the high priest. "And no man taketh this honour unto himself, but he that is called of God, as was Aaron." True ministers are creations of God, not the manufacture either of university or college professors, or of consecrating bishops, or of both united. He alone is able to qualify men for the office, and He alone is competent to utter the authoritative call to it. (*c*)

V. Intrusion into sacred places and duties awakened the stern displeasure of the Lord.

"Aaron and his sons shall wait on their priest's office; and the stranger that cometh nigh shall be put to death." Any one who was not a son of Aaron, even though he were a Levite, that should draw nigh to perform any of the duties pertaining to the office of the priest was to be put to death. "Let this be thought upon by our over-bold intruders into the work of the ministry." God will have sacred things reverently regarded, and sacred duties reverently performed.

Conclusion:

The subject affords.—1. *Encouragement to those who are called of God to Christian work.* He who has called you to your work will sustain you in it, make it efficient by His blessing, and confer upon you rich rewards. 2. *Admonition as to our estimate of the ministers of the Lord.* They "are ambassadors for Christ." God Himself speaks through them to men. They are called and commissioned by Jesus Christ. And He says, "He that receiveth whomsoever I send receiveth Me, and he that receiveth Me receiveth Him that sent Me;" "Despise not prophesyings." "Know them which labour among you, and are over you in the Lord, and admonish you; and esteem them very highly in love for their work's sake."

ILLUSTRATIONS.

(*a*) All men cannot work in the same way: "There are diversities of operation." Upon the face of a watch you may see an illustration of my meaning. On that small space you have three workers: there is the *second*-pointer performing rapid revolutions; there is the *minute*-pointer going at a greatly reduced speed; and there is the *hour*-pointer tardier still. Now any one unacquainted with the mechanism of a watch would conclude that the busy little second-pointer was doing all the work—it is clicking away at sixty times the speed of the minute-pointer; and as for the hour-hand *that* seems to be doing no work at all. You can see in a moment that the first is busy, and in a short time you'll see the second stir, but you must wait still longer to assure yourself of the motion of the third. So is it in the Church. There are active, fussy men who appear to be doing the work of the whole community, and others who go at less speed, and others slower still. But can we do without the minute and the hour-pointers? The noisy second-hand might go round its little circle for ever, without telling the world the true time. We should be thankful for all kinds of workers. The silent, steady hour-hand need not envy its noisy little colleague. Each man must fill the measure of his capacity. Your business is to do your allotted work, so as to meet the approbation of the Master.—*Jos. Parker, D.D.*

(*b*) There is a perennial nobleness, and even sacredness, in work. Were he never so benighted, forgetful of his high calling, there is always hope in a man that actually and earnestly works; in idleness alone is there perpetual despair. . . . . It has been written, "an endless significance lies in work" —as man perfects himself by writing. Foul jungles are cleared away, fair seed-fields rise instead, and stately cities; and withal, the man himself first ceases to be a jungle and foul, unwholesome desert thereby. Consider how, even in the meanest sorts of Labour, the whole soul of a man is composed into a kind of real harmony, the instant he sets himself to work! Doubt, Desire, Sorrow, Remorse, Indignation, Despair itself, all these, like hell-dogs, lie beleaguering the soul of the poor day-worker, as of every man; but as he bends himself with free valour against his task, all these are stilled, all these shrink murmuring far off into their caves. The man is now a man. The blessed glow of Labour in him, is it not a purifying fire, wherein all poison is burnt up? and of sour smoke itself there is made bright, blessed flame! . . . . Work is of a religious nature; work is of a *brave* nature, which it is the aim of all religion to be. . . . Admirable was that of the old monks, "*Laborare est orare:* Work is Worship." . . . . All true Work is sacred: in all true Work, were it but true hand-labour, there is something of divineness. Labour, wide as the Earth, has its summit in Heaven. Sweat of the brow; and up from that to sweat of the brain, sweat of the heart: which includes all Kepler calculations, Newton meditations, all Sciences, all spoken Epics, all acted Heroisms, Martyrdoms—up to that "Agony of bloody sweat," which all men have called divine! O brother! if this is not "worship," then I say the more pity for worship, for this is the noblest thing yet discovered under God's sky! Who art thou that complainest of thy life of toil? Complain not. Look up, my wearied brother; see thy fellow-Workmen there, in God's Eternity; surviving there, they alone surviving: sacred band of the Immortals, celestial Body-guard of the Empire of Mankind! Even in the weak Human Memory they survive so long, as saints, as heroes, as gods; they alone surviving; peopling, they alone, the immeasured solitudes of Time! To thee, Heaven, though severe, is *not* unkind; Heaven is kind—as a noble Mother; as that Spartan Mother, saying, while she gave her son his shield, "With it, my son, or upon it!" Thou too shalt return *home*, in honour to thy far-distant Home, in honour; doubt it not—if in the battle thou keep thy shield! Thou, in the Eternities and deepest Death-kingdoms, art not an alien; thou everywhere art a denizen! Complain not; the very Spartans did not *complain.—Thos. Carlyle.*

(*c*) The man who has adopted the church as a profession, as other men adopt the law, or the army, or the navy, and goes through the routine of its duties with the coldness of a mere official—filled by him, the pulpit seems filled by the ghastly form of a skeleton, that, in its cold and bony fingers, holds a burning lamp.—*Thos. Guthrie, D.D.*

GOD'S CLAIMS UPON MAN'S SERVICE.

(*Verses* 11-13.)

These verses suggest the following observations:—

I. That God's claims upon man's service are incontestable.

Upon what are they grounded?

1. *Upon what He is in Himself.* "The Levites shall be Mine . . . Mine shall they be. I am the Lord." The concluding words of verse 13 are better thus expressed: "Mine shall they be, Mine, the Lord's." He is the Proprietor of all things. All things and all persons were created by Him, and are sustained by Him. He is over all. He is the greatest, the best Being. And as such His claim upon man is complete and indisputable. The inventor has a right to his invention; the maker to the thing made. So God, etc. The Supremely Great and Good has a right to the admiration, the worship, and the service of all intelligent beings.

2. *Upon what He does for man.* "All the firstborn are mine; for on the day that I smote all the firstborn in the land of Egypt I hallowed unto me all the firstborn in Israel," etc. The preservation of the firstborn of the Israelites on the dread night when all the firstborn of the Egyptians were slain is here put forth by the Lord as a ground of claim upon them. Their preservation was an exercise of the Divine mercy. He spared them that they might devote themselves unreservedly to His service. God spares the sinful race of man, and constantly confers upon the ill-deserving many choice gifts. He has redeemed us at a great cost,—"not with corruptible things, as silver and gold; but with the precious blood of Christ." His claims upon us are not only incontrovertible, but most heart-constraining also. (*a*)

Such being the character of His claims upon us, we cannot withhold from Him our loyal and hearty service without incurring the guilt of manifest fraud and basest ingratitude.

II. There is a correspondence between the gifts and the claims of God.

His demands are proportioned to His bestowments. He had spared the lives of the firstborn of Israel, and He claims the firstborn. "Unto whomsoever much is given of him shall be much required: and to whom men have committed much, of him they will ask the more." "Freely ye have received, freely give." All our possessions and powers involve corresponding responsibilities. (*b*)

1. *This is righteous.* No one can truthfully complain that the requirements of God are unreasonable or excessive.

2. *This is beneficent.* By the operation of this principle the weak are aided by the strong, the great and gifted render much and noble service, etc. Let no one boast of the greatness of his powers or possessions, as though they were his own, etc. "For who maketh thee to differ? and what hast thou that thou didst not receive?" etc. Let us rather be humble, and faithful in the use of all our gifts in God's service.

III. The Divine arrangements are ever marked by infinite wisdom and kindness.

In the substitution of the tribe of Levi for the firstborn of all the tribes, we have an illustration of this. "And I, behold, I have taken the Levites from among the children of Israel instead of all the firstborn," etc.

1. By assigning the sacred duties of the service of the tabernacle to the one tribe *they would be likely to be more faithfully and efficiently performed* The undivided interest of the tribe would be devoted to this holy calling.

2. By this arrangement *the convenience of the nation was undoubtedly consulted.* The Divine requirements in this respect would be the more easily complied with by this arrangement than by that for which it was substituted.

3. *The tribe of Levi was numerically the most fitted for these duties.* "This was the *smallest* tribe, and they were quite enough for the service. To have had a more numerous tribe at this time would have been very inconvenient."

4. *The tribe of Levi had manifested its moral fitness for these duties.* By their faithful and courageous defence of the honour of the Lord, by slaying the worshippers of the golden calf, the children of Levi had shown themselves to be the most suitable of all the tribes for this service. So we are able to trace the wisdom and kindness of God in this arrangement. And all His plans and doings are perfectly wise and kind. We may not always be able to discover this wisdom and kindness. But the limitation of our powers should never be regarded as a reason for questioning the Divine perfections. Let every additional illustration of His wisdom and goodness that we discover lead us to cherish increased gratitude to Him, and to repose increased confidence in Him.

ILLUSTRATIONS.

(*a*) A gentleman, visiting a slave-mart, was deeply moved by the agony of a slave-girl, who had been delicately reared, and feared that she should fall into the hands of a rough master. The gentleman inquired her price, paid it to the slave-trader, then placed the bill of sale in her own hands, telling her she was free, and could now go home. The slave-girl could not realise the change at first, but, running after her redeemer, cried, "He has redeemed me! he has redeemed me! Will you let me be your servant?" How much more should we serve Him who has redeemed us from sin, death, and hell?—*Dict. of Illust.*

(*b*) Thyself and thy belongings
Are not thine own so proper, as to waste
Thyself upon thy virtues, them on thee.
Heaven doth with us, as we with torches do;
Not light them for themselves: for if our virtues
Did not go forth of us, 'twere all alike
As if we had them not. Spirits are not finely touch'd,
But to fine issues: nor nature never lends
The smallest scruple of her excellence,
But, like a thrifty goddess, she determines
Herself the glory of a creditor,
Both thanks and use.—*Shakespeare.*
"Measure for Measure," i. 1.

The earth that in her genial breast
Makes for the down a kindly nest,
Where wafted by the warm south-west
   It floats at pleasure,
Yields, thankful, of her very best,
   To nurse her treasure:

True to her trust, tree, herb, or reed,
She renders for each scatter'd seed,
And to her Lord with duteous heed
   Gives large increase:
Thus year by year she works unfeed,
   And will not cease.

Woe worth these barren hearts of ours,
Where Thou has set celestial flowers,
And water'd with more balmy showers
   Than e'er distill'd
In Eden, on th' ambrosial bowers—
   Yet nought we yield.

Largely Thou givest, gracious Lord,
Largely Thy gifts should be restor'd,
Freely Thou givest, and Thy word
   Is, "Freely give."
He only, who forgets to hoard,
   Has learn'd to live.   *Keble.*

THE MEASURE OF THE DIVINE DEMANDS UPON MAN.

(*Verses* 12, 13.)

In the text God calls attention to the reason he had for selecting a tribe for the service of the sanctuary. It was to be in lieu of the firstborn, who were specially His because He smote the firstborn of Egypt to effect the deliverance of Israel. He had a right to the firstborn in the sense that all are His; but, in addition to that, they are now His, as redeemed by Him. It is the same with us now. While all things and all men are God's, the Christian is especially His—he is His child. God is said to be the father of us all; and so He is. But then we have sinned, and have thereby forfeited all our rights. We are the prisoners of Justice. The parent of the criminal cannot exercise his fatherly functions: practically his child has ceased to be his, for the State claims him. So with us and God. Although as Creator He is the Father of us all, yet, through our sin, we are practically not His children. He cannot exercise the paternal functions towards us till we are ransomed from the curse of the law and become free, which we only do in and through Christ. It is then, by redemption, that we become His dear children, and enjoy all the privileges of sonship. Thus Christians, like the firstborn, specially belong to God; for he has not only given them being, but he has ransomed them.

The text further contains a principle of deep importance to us. As God smote the firstborn of Egypt, He demanded the firstborn of Israel. The measure of their redemption became the measure of His demands from them. He expected them, and He expects us to do in our way what He has done in His way for us. He calls upon us to give to Him what He has given to us. We find the same principle in the New Testament. Christ is more than the sacrifice for sin: He is our Pattern. As He made Himself of no reputation, we are to have the mind that was in Him. We are to crucify self, to die to sin, and to rise again in newness of life.

We shall now take two comprehensive points.

I. God gave the best He had to effect our salvation.

He withheld not His only begotten, His well-beloved Son. A parent's love to his child is the deepest and tenderest. Such was God's love to Christ. The sacrifice was the greatest that the Father could make. We feel sure that if man could have been saved in any other way the Son would have been spared the ignominy, the bitterness, and the pain He endured through His life and in His death. God gave *Him*, the best, the chiefest treasure that He had, for our ransom. In this we have a significant hint of what He expects from us. We must give Him the very best of all we are and of all we have. As there was no salvation without God giving His best for us, so there is no religion unless we are prepared to give our best to Him. There is no hardship in this. It really means no more than this, that we are to love Him supremely. He asks nothing of us that He has not done for us first Himself. In the life of Christ this is conspicuous. He lived all His sermons. He taught much that was new, that was hard to do, and was against the practice of the world; but He did it all first Himself. God has given us His best in giving His Son; let us then give our best of everything to Him.

II. The Son gave Himself.

On the part of Christ there was the sacrifice of His own life as the ransom for our sin. Redemption is more than doctrine—it is the Son of God giving Himself for man. Just so, religion is more than creed—it is man giving Himself to God. Christ might have given many things; but nothing would do for our salvation but the consecration of Himself. This is the extent of God's demand on us. "My son, give me thine heart." We have to yield ourselves to Him. Not merely to die for Him, but to give up ourselves to live for Him—to burn out in His work —to be faithful unto death—which is often harder to do than to die for Him. Many are willing to give time, talents, money. But Christ wants us. He knows that if we give Him our heart we shall give Him all; and if we withhold this from Him, we give Him nothing at all. Consecrate yourselves to Him as He did Himself for you. This is the great principle of the text. And it is the principle which governs God's demands of us at the present day. Let us sacrifice ourselves to God as He sacrificed His Son for us. I urge this because—

1. *Thus only can we attain to a high ideal in religion.* Be the best possible Christian: be not content with mediocrity: aim high.

2. *This is the best way to be useful.* The power of Christianity is in the fact of Christ giving Himself. Our influence for good is in proportion to our self-sacrifice.

3. *This is the way to enjoy religion.* The more we give of self to God, the more will He give of Himself to us.

Let all think of what God has done for them, and consider what returns they have made to Him.

David Lloyd.

THE NUMBERING OF THE LEVITES: COMMAND AND OBEDIENCE.

(*Verses* 14-16.)

In these verses we have the command of the Lord to Moses to number the Levites, and the record of the obedience of Moses. In dealing with the command we shall notice only such suggestions as arise out of that part of it in which it differs most from the command to number the other tribes. In the other tribes "every male from twenty years old and upward, all that were able to go forth to war" were numbered. But concerning the tribe of Levi, Moses is directed to number 'every male from a month old and upward." This command is suggestive of—

I. The interest of God in childhood.

The tribe of Levi was not appointed to the same service as the other tribes; and, consequently, they are not numbered by the same rule. "Number the children of Levi,—every male from a month old and upward shalt thou number them." The Levites "were to be sanctified to Jehovah in the place of the firstborn; and it was at the age of a month that the latter were either to be given up or redeemed" (compare verses 40 and 43 with chap. xviii. 16). The children of the Levites were to be taught that from their infancy they belonged to the Lord, and were dedicated to His service. Only 8,580 out of 22,000 were regarded as fit to be employed in the service of the tabernacle, yet all were numbered as belonging to the Lord. God is profoundly and tenderly interested in childhood. In His spiritual Kingdom, in which all His loyal subjects are priests, He claims for His service every child even from the very dawn of its existence. His interest in little children is strikingly illustrated in the presentation of the little child by the Lord to His disciples as the picture of the "greatest in the kingdom of heaven." (Matt. xviii. 1-6.) And perhaps even more strikingly in the blessing which He bestowed upon the infants that were brought to Him for that purpose. (Matt. xix. 13-15.) It is the duty of Christian parents to recognise God's claim upon their offspring, and to dedicate them to Him. That dedication cannot take place too early, since from their very birth they are His by the divinest rights. It is also their duty to train their children for Him. "Ye fathers, provoke not your children to wrath; but bring them up in the nurture and admonition of the Lord." Let parents be encouraged in the performance of their duty by the interest of God in their offspring. He will approve and bless their devout efforts. (*a*)

The command here given to Moses suggests,—

II. The generosity of God's dealings with man.

He here accepts even infants, who must live many years before they can actively engage in His service, in exchange for able-bodied men. "Observe we again with comfort," saith Bishop Babington, "what exchanges God maketh with men. He taketh a child of a month old, and foregoeth a firstborn of ripe years. Such is His manner and most gracious goodness; He giveth more than He wanteth, and gainers ever are His children by Him. Job had a bitter trial and a heavy loss, yet mark the end, and the Lord made him greater than ever he was—the Lord blessing the last days of Job, as the text saith, more than the first, etc. David's child was taken away, but a far better was given again, even Solomon, the wisest son that ever father had. A cake was taken of the poor widow of Sarepta for His prophet, but what a requital made God unto her? The meal in the barrel and the oil in the cruse decayed not till other comfort grew. Another kindness done by the Shunamite, was it not recompensed by that blessing that was so vehemently wished—even a son; first given, and after revived from death to life again? Think of the saying in the Gospel concerning this point: 'Verily I say unto you, there is no man that hath forsaken house, or brethren, or sisters, or father, or mother, or wife, or children, or lands for My sake and the Gospel's, but he shall receive an hundred-fold now at this present, houses, and brethren, and sisters, and mothers, and children, and lands with persecutions, and in the world to come life everlasting.' See the change, and mark the gain for your exceeding comfort. Such a God is our God, that not a cup of cold water can be given, but He will yield a far greater gift for it. We cannot visit Him, feed Him, clothe Him, etc., in His poor members, but He will acknowledge it before the host of heaven, and give that which passeth ten thousand worlds—eternal joy in heaven."

Let us notice,—

III. The obedience of God's servant.

"And Moses numbered them according to the word of the Lord, as he was commanded." The point to which prominence is here given is the completeness of the obedience. It was not merely general, but particular. He conformed to the directions which he had received from the Lord in detail. Herein he is an example to us. Nothing which God directs can be trifling or unimportant. What Infinite Wisdom commands minutely, it must be both our duty and our interest minutely to do. "General obedience," says Dr. Parker, "is only *so far* good: we must be minute and exhaustive, or we shall incur Divine displeasure. Learn that *Divine language never exceeds Divine meaning.* There is significance in every word; you cannot amputate a single syllable without doing violence to the Divine idea." Let us strive to render complete and hearty obedience to all the commands of God. *(b)*

ILLUSTRATIONS.

(*a*) God's interest in human life begins at the earliest possible period. This is an argument for infant baptism which I have never known to be touched, much less shaken. The narrow critics who have taken upon themselves to settle that question, have been fighting each other with Greek derivatives and grammatical inflexions, as if *any* moral question could be settled by such means! I make this question one of *life*, not one of grammar; and I put this direct and urgent inquiry—namely, When does God's interest in human life *begin?* When does Christ's heart begin to yearn in pity over all human creatures? *When* does compassion's tear well into the Redeemer's eyes? *When* does He feel the kindling of love towards human beings? Is it when they are five years old, or ten—does He shut up His love until they are twenty-one? The question may appear quaint, but I press it; I urge a distinct answer— When does Christ's interest in human life begin? I contend that His interest relates to life, not to age; to birth, not to birth-*days*. As soon as a child is born, that great redeeming heart yearns with pitying love. What has Christ to do with what we call *age?* What is *age?* It may be useful for us to keep a record of anniversaries, to tabulate for statistical purposes, to call one man twenty and another forty, though forty, in reality, may be less than twenty; but will you presume to reduce Christ to a commercial agent, who deals with men according to their age? No! I hold to it as a sweet joy, a most delicious and enrapturing thought, that Jesus Christ interests Himself in me, that my name was written in His heart ere it fell from my mother's lips, and that before a father knows the mystery and pride of parental life, Jesus experiences the travail of the soul which yearns to make the child an heir of immortality.—*Jos. Parker, D.D.*

(*b*) Nothing is more certain or clear than that human souls are made for law, and so for the abode of God. Without law therefore, without God, they must even freeze and die. Hence even Christ Himself must needs establish and sanctify the law; for the deliverance and liberty He comes to bring are still to be sought only in obedience. Henceforth duty is the brother of liberty, and both rejoice in the common motherhood of law. And just here, my friends, is the secret of a great part of your misery and of the darkness that envelopes your life. Without obligation you have no light, save what little may prick through your eyelids. Only he that keeps God's commandments walks in the light. The moment you can make a very simple discovery, viz., that obligation to God is your privilege, and is not imposed as a burden, your experience will teach you many things—that duty is liberty, that repentance is a release from sorrow, that sacrifice is gain, that humility is dignity, that the truth from which you hide is a healing element that bathes your disordered life, and that even the penalties and terrors of God are the artillery only of protection to His realm. —*H. Bushnell, D.D.*

It ought to be the great care of every one of us to follow the Lord fully. We must, in a course of obedience to God's will, and service to His honour, follow Him universally, without dividing; uprightly, without dissembling; cheerfully, without disputing; and constantly, without declining: and this is following Him fully.—*M. Henry.*

SACRED THINGS AND DUTIES.

(*Verses* 17–39.)

Critical Notes.

Verse 36. *The custody and charge.* Margin: "Hebrew, the office of the charge."

Verse 38. *Keeping the charge of the sanctuary for the charge of the children of Israel,* "*i.e.*, to attend to everything that was binding upon the children of Israel in relation to the care of the sanctuary, as no stranger was allowed to approach it on pain of death."—*Keil and Del.*

Verse 39. The number of the Levites as stated in this verse is 22,000; but as stated in verses 22, 28, and 34, it is 22,300. Various attempts have been made to reconcile the two. That of Dr. Kennicott, given by Dr. A. Clarke, *in loco*, seems to us the most reasonable. " Formerly, the numbers of the Hebrew Bible were expressed by *letters*, and not by *words of full length;* and if two nearly similar letters were mistaken for each other, many errors in the number must be the consequence. Now it is probable that an error has crept into the number of the Gershonites, verse 22, where instead of 7,500 we should read 7,200 as ך *caph*, 500, might have been easily mistaken for ר *resh*, 200, especially if the down stroke of the *caph* had been a little shorter than ordinary, which is often the case in MSS." Keil and Del. regard the discrepancy as arising from "a copyist's error in the number of one of the Levitical families; possibly in verse 28 we should read שלש for שש (8,300 for 8,600)."

In these verses we have the record of the numbering of the Levites, with the names of the chiefs who had the oversight of them, the places assigned to them about the tabernacle, and the duties as distributed amongst them. They suggest the following *homiletic points.* Notice—

I. The Divine directions for insuring order.

By Divine direction the whole tribe is arranged in four divisions, the families composing each division are clearly distinguished, the station of each division is appointed, a chief is set over each division, and Eleazar the son of Aaron is appointed chief over the chiefs. In this we clearly discover a Divine recognition of—

1. *The importance of arrangement and order.* (See our notes and illustration on chap. ii., verses 1 and 2, on this point.)

2. *The importance of supervision and authority for the maintenance of order.* (On this point see our notes and illustrations on *Society's need of leaders,* ch. i. 4–16.)

II. The Divine distribution of duty.

1. *The duties were distributed amongst the whole.* No family was exempted; nor was any individual of the prescribed age, etc. There was work for all, and for every one. So in our day there is most urgent need for the services of every true man and woman. The greatest need of both the Church and the world is true-hearted labourers.

"There's something for us all to do
　In this great world of ours;
There's work for me; there's work for you,
　Heaven sends no idle hours:
We have a mission to perform,
　A post of trust to fill,
Then rouse the soul, and nerve the arm,
　And lend the lofty will." (*a*)

2. *The duties distributed to each division were different from those distributed to the other divisions.* Moses, and Aaron and his sons, were appointed to the position of the highest honour and the weightiest **responsibility.** The duties which rank second in honour were allotted to the Kohathites. To the Merarites, which, though the smallest of the families of Levi, yet contained the largest number of able-bodied men (compare vers. 22, 28, 34, and ch. iv. vers. 36, 40, 44), were allotted the most heavy and laborious duties. All men cannot work at the same tasks or in the same way. Division of duty is (1) *necessary,* because of the differences in the kind and degree of ability amongst men. (*b*) It is also (2) *advantageous.* By means of it more work may be accomplished and better. The advantage will be found both in the quantity and in the quality of the results. Contrast the ancient and the modern method of pin manufacture in illustration of this point.

3. *The duties of all were Divine.* All were engaged in the service of God; all were appointed by God. The duties were assigned to each division and to all as a "charge" from God—a sacred trust. So now, all duty, even the lowliest and most menial, when rightly regarded and faithfully discharged, is holy. The highest duties can never of themselves exalt the hireling or the unfaithful worker; but the spirit of the faithful and devoted worker will dignify and hallow the meanest labours. (*c*)

III. The Divine recognition of the sacredness of things associated with religious worship.

Not only the ark and the altars, but the hangings, the coverings, the cords, the boards, the bars, the sockets, the pins, etc., connected with the tabernacle were given in solemn charge to the Levites. All these things were to be held as sacred. And if any stranger came nigh to the sanctuary itself he was to be put to death. And still there are sacred places and sacred things. They have been made sacred neither by the "consecration" of pope or cardinal, of archbishop or bishop, nor by the "dedication" of any minister or ministers; but by the memories which gather round them, or by the uses to which they are set apart. To reverent spirits the commonest things are hallowed by sacred uses, and even the plainest places are consecrated by pure and precious associations. The spiritual history of every godly man has its sacred places. And have we not each things which are profoundly sacred to us personally? (*d*)

Conclusion:
Let us endeavour to be true and tender in sentiment, pure and reverent in feeling, and hearty and faithful in duty.

ILLUSTRATIONS.

(*a*) There is something for all to do, but by different instruments—one by his organ, another by his piano, another by his paint-brush, another by his sculptor's chisel, another by his plough, another by his carpenter's tools, another by his trowel—every man by that to which he is called in the providence of God, that he may give some expression to the inwardness that is waked up in him. There are rude workmen who have, back of their hand, back of their skill, a soul that is trying to express itself in the realities of life. This is the ordination which makes true manhood and true genius. — *H. W. Beecher.*

(*b*) See the illustration on verses 5–10, by Dr. Parker.

(*c*) Teach me, my God and King,
In all things Thee to see,
And what I do in any thing,
To do it as for Thee:

Not rudely, as a beast,
To run into an action;
But still to make Thee prepossest,
And give it his perfection.

A man that looks on glass,
On it may stay his eye;
Or, if he pleaseth, through it pass,
And then the heav'n espie.

All may of Thee partake:
Nothing can be so mean,
Which with his tincture (for Thy sake)
Will not grow bright and clean.

A servant with this clause
Makes drudgery divine:
Who sweeps a room, as for Thy laws,
Makes that and th' action fine.

This is the famous stone
That turneth all to gold:
For that which God doth touch and own
Cannot for less be told.
George Herbert.

See also the illustration by Carlyle given under verses 5–10.

(*d*) It is given us to transfer our own mental and moral nature to the objects of our sight or of our conception. One man, who has never read the Sacred History, and whose mind is wholly uninformed as to its wonderful facts, might visit the Holy Land and make himself familiar with its existing scenery, and as his foot impressed its hallowed soil, and his eye rested on its mountains and its vales, on its rivers and its lakes, and on all its natural phenomena, he might betray no more emotion than would be awakened by the contemplation of similar phenomena in any other part of the world; while another man, who had imbibed the spirit and the inspiration of the Bible, and whose faith reposed in its simple, yet sublime narratives, would everywhere find the most extraordinary appearances, and feel that he was in a land teeming with miracles. To him, "every name commemorates a mystery—every grotto announces a prediction—every hill echoes the accent of a prophet." He cannot get away from the impression that "God Himself has spoken in those regions—dried up rivers—rent the rocks—and opened the graves." To him "the desert still appears mute with terror;" and he imagines that it can never have "presumed to interrupt the silence, since it heard the awful voice of the Eternal!" He feels that he is on holy ground; and his very step is reverent. He approaches every object with deepening awe, and like Moses at the burning-bush, sees everything glowing with Divine glory. The natural scenery of Palestine may not be superior to that which is to be found in other parts of the world; but where can we find a country so rich in associations, or with what other place can we connect associations so hallowed and so unique! It is our remembrances and our memories which give to the outward phenomena such transcendent interest. We throw the whole living flame of our holiest feeling upon everthing without us and around us, and everywhere we see beauty, and magnificence and glory—everywhere we trace the footsteps of Divinity, and everywhere we hear the voice of God.—*R. Ferguson, LL.D.*

ALLOTED DUTIES.

(*Verses 21–38.*)

I. They differed in importance, yet there was no vain ambition.

II. They differed in labour, yet there was no complaining.

III. They differed in nature, yet were all undertaken with equal cheerfulness.

IV. They differed according to the wise will of God.—*The Biblical Museum*

The Responsibility of each and the Co-operation of all in the Service of God.

(Verses 25, 26, 31, 36, 37.)

Having chosen the Levites for His service, God portions out their work to them. The priesthood was conferred upon Aaron and his family, and the rest of the tribe were to assist them in the service of the tabernacle. In making these arrangements the character of Moses stands out strikingly prominent. He does not demur because his tribe has no inheritance, neither do we find him seeking any special honour for his own family. Few men there are who are not injured by prosperity and power, and who take no advantage of their position to further the interests of their families. Nepotism is common in Church and State. Moses was above that, and was ready to acquiesce in God's way, thinking it great honour to his family to be engaged in His service, though in the humble position of Levites.

God divides the tribe of Levi, having selected from it the family of Aaron for the priesthood, into three distinct families; and, in the text, He gives to each his own work to do in connection with the tabernacle. Their duty in the wilderness was to carry it and its furniture from place to place, etc. Each had his work to do, and all had to co-operate. Thus the tabernacle and its services were ever attended to, and God's work among the people was constantly carried on. Looking thus at the verses which constitute our text, they suggest to us the subject of *personal responsibility and co-operation in the service of God.*

I. God has a work for every one of His children to do, and He expects each one to do it.

He holds each responsible for it. We are to be His servants; we are to be useful. He brings up none of His children in luxurious idleness. God hates idleness. Amongst the countless forms and varieties of life in the universe, there is not one that has not some purpose to answer—something given it to do by its Creator. To show how He hates idleness He has linked poverty to it. It is so in religion too. The spiritual idler is ever a spiritual pauper, and can never possess the riches of religion. We must work before we can possess them. The hand of the diligent God blesses. There is much need of calling attention to this truth at the present day. The age is a luxurious one; ease and comfort seem to be the ends of life. This spirit is creeping into our churches. It is difficult to get people to realize their responsibility, and to work for God. They guage everything by the amount of pleasure it gives, and not by the good it is calculated to do them. *Men* ought to have a higher ideal. God saves us that we might be His fellow-workers. God makes us soldiers before He makes us saints. The highest test of religion is not enjoyment, but usefulness. There is joy in religion. It is the most joyous thing in the world; but then the joy is associated with work. There is no real pleasure in idleness. It is the working man, and not the skulking idler, that has the most physical enjoyment. So in spiritual things. There is no luxury like that of doing good. If any Christian lacks joy in religion, let him work more for God. He expects us all to be workers. None are exempt. There is not one without a "talent;" and God expects it with usury. He exempts none on the ground of youth or age, of inability or weakness, etc. If you are poor, you can show how religion can support in poverty. If you are old, you can "bring forth fruit in old age." Sometimes a Christian is laid by through affliction, and feels that he is of no use whatever. But the sick bed of a child of God is of great profit to the world and to the Church by showing how religion can support the mind and comfort the heart in trial. Moreover, the afflicted Christian can benefit others by intercession with God. We all know how the suffering child prevails with his parent, and none can tell what the world and the Church owe to the prayers of God's suffering children. All can do something for God. He has given it them to do, and He holds them responsible for it.

II. Not only does God expect each one to work for Him, but He expects all to co-operate in His service.

Each Levite had his own work to perform, but the three divisions were to move together and to halt together. Without their co-operation the tabernacle could not have been erected, and God would not have appeared on the Mercy-seat. We are not to be isolated workers, but fellow-labourers. While it is true that each one is accountable only for himself, it is also true that no one liveth to himself. If we are units, we are parts of a whole. Paul takes the different parts of the human body as an illustration of the body of Christ, which is the Church. Co-operation is the secret of success. The Church and the Sunday-school, the pulpit and the pew, each must do its own work, and all must work together, if the work of God is to prosper amongst us. It ought to be so between various Churches—the different sections of the one Church of the living God. The work of God suffers for the want of co-operation. Often jealousy and rivalry creep in amongst us; we watch one another instead of our common foe, and prosperity becomes impossible. Are we not all soldiers of the same Christ? Different regiments in one and the same army? The dress may differ, but we all bear the coat-of-arms of our King. Surely, then, there ought to be no jealousy amongst us, and we ought to band together to fight against His enemies. The Church of God must come closer together, and co-operate more heartily, before the world is won for Christ. No opposition can stand before the united Church of God.—*David Lloyd.*

THE COMPLETENESS OF GOD'S CLAIMS, AND THE DIGNITY OF HIS SERVICE.

(*Verses* 40-51.)

In this section of the history we have the account of the numbering of the firstborn males throughout the twelve tribes in order to effect the exchange of the Levites for them, which God had commanded. Three enquiries claim our attention.

1. *How are we to account for so large a number of firstborn in so short a time?* The command for the sanctification of the firstborn, recorded in Exod. xiii. 1, 2, was not retrospective, but was meant to apply to all that should be born from that time forward. "Hence the difficulty is to explain how the firstborn sons, amongst two millions of persons in a single year, could have been so many as is stated in the text; and it must be admitted, notwithstanding the well-known and often remarkable fluctuations in statistics of this sort, that some unusual causes must have been concerned. Such, not to mention the Divine Blessing, may be found in the sudden development of national energies which would immediately ensue on the exodus. Before that event, the miserable estate of the people, and especially the inhuman order for the destruction of their first-born, would check very seriously the ratio of marriages and births; and this ratio would naturally, when the check was removed, exhibit a sudden and striking increase."—*Speaker's Comm.* As additional arguments, the great fruitfulness of the Israelitish women, and the fact that amongst them the proportion of male births is unusually large, are adduced. (See Keil and Del. *in loco.*)

2. *What is the value of* "*the shekel of the sanctuary?*" "Here the shekel is evidently a weight, and of a special system of which the standard examples were probably kept by the priests." At this time silver, and not gold, was used

as the standard of value. It is impossible to determine exactly what was the value of the "sacred shekel" as compared with our English money of to-day, but probably it would be about two shillings and sixpence.

3. *Who paid the redemption money for the 273 firstborn who were in excess of the number of the Levites?* "The redemption money," says *The Speaker's Comm.*, "would perhaps be exacted from the parents of the *youngest* children of the 22,273, they being in the case most nearly approaching that of those who would pay the tax for the redemption of the first-born in future." But the opinion of Attersoll, A. Clarke, and others, seems to us the most probable. Was the money paid " by the firstborn that were last numbered, or by the people? I answer," says Attersoll, " by the people, to Moses, for the priests: for so doth common equity require, that one might not be eased, and another burdened. But if these firstborn had borne the burden, and others been freed from the payment of this sum appointed and enjoined, there had been no equity nor equality observed, which the dignity of holy things seemeth to require."

The command for substituting the Levites for the firstborn (vers. 11-13) we have already considered, and endeavoured to show the reason of the substitution. In considering this portion of the history we confine our attention to two main homiletic points. Notice,—

I. **The completeness of God's claims.**

We see this here in two things:

1. *He claims not only the firstborn of Israel, but also the firstlings of their cattle.* (See verses 41 and 45.) All were His by right of creation. "Every beast of the forest is Mine, and the cattle upon a thousand hills." Moreover, the cattle of Israel were spared on that night when "all the firstborn of cattle" belonging to the Egyptians were slain. So that His claim upon the firstborn of cattle, both as having created and as having spared them, rested on the same ground as His claim upon the firstborn sons. (See our notes on vers. 11-13.) "The cattle of the Levites were doubtless taken in the gross as an equivalent for the firstborn cattle of the other tribes, which of course, no less than the firstborn of men, belonged to the Lord; and in future would have to be redeemed." (See Exod. xiii. 11-15; Num. xviii. 15; Deut. xv. 19.)

God claims ours as well as us; what we have as well as what we are; first ourselves, then our possessions. (Comp. Matt. x. 37-39, xix. 21-24.) When we have truly given ourselves to the Lord we shall withhold nothing else from Him. And apart from this self-consecration to Him, the consecration of even our most costly and treasured possessions is not acceptable to Him. Without our supreme love all other gifts are worthless in His sight. (Comp. Psa. l. 7-14, and Isa. i. 11-14.)

2. *He claims that the 273 firstborn in excess of the Levites shall be redeemed by money.* He does not accept the Levites as a whole for the firstborn as a whole, taking no account of their relative numbers. The Levites must be numbered, and the firstborn must be numbered, and as there is an excess in the number of the firstborn, every one of these must be redeemed. Every one is His; and He is not willing to lose any one. May we not regard this as exhibiting His high estimate of men? We are so precious in His sight that He will not lose one of us if He can prevent it. His heart yearns in unutterable love towards every prodigal wanderer from His service, His home, and His heart. "Turn, O backsliding children, saith the Lord; for I am married unto you. . . . How shall I put thee among the children, and give thee a pleasant land, a goodly heritage of the hosts of nations? and I said, Thou shalt call Me, My Father; and shalt not turn away from Me." "When Israel was a child, then I loved him," etc. "How shall I give thee up Ephraim?" etc. God is so exact in His claims upon us, because His love toward us is so great. His demands are always characterised by (1) *generosity*. We have seen (in considering verses 11-13) that the substitution of the Levites was for the advantage of the

people. All His requirements are unspeakably kind in their intention, and beneficent in their operation. (2) *Exactness.* There is no exaggeration in His claims, nor anything unreasonable. He means what He says. He really requires what He demands. He claims from us the unreserved consecration of ourselves and our possessions,—that all shall be used in accordance with His will, etc. Have we duly considered His claims? Are we complying with them? "I beseech you, brethren, by the mercies of God, that ye present," etc. Rom. xii. 1.

II. The dignity of God's service.

It was instead of the firstborn that the tribe of Levi was chosen for the service of the tabernacle, or the ministry of religion. Now amongst the Jews the firstborn son ranked higher than the other members of the family, and enjoyed special privileges and honours. He received a double portion of the estate; he exercised an authority over the younger members of the family similar to that of a father; and he was the priest of the entire family. "The birthright of Esau and of Reuben, set aside by authority or forfeited by misconduct, prove a general privilege as well as quasi-sacredness of primogeniture (Gen. xxv. 23, 31, 34; xlix. 3; 1 Chron. v. 1; Heb. xii. 16), and a precedence which obviously existed, and is alluded to in several passages (as Psa. lxxxix. 27; Job xviii. 13; Rom. viii. 29; Col. i. 15; Heb. xii. 23)." Now inasmuch as the religious functions of the firstborn were given to the Levites, is not the inference warranted that their service as the ministers of religion was especially honourable? This is true of the Christian minister, because of—

1. *The position which He occupies.* He is the messenger of God to men. He stands before man instead of Jesus Christ. "We are ambassadors for Christ, as though God did beseech by us: we pray you in Christ's stead," etc. "Verily, verily," said our Lord, "He that receiveth whomsoever I send receiveth Me; and he that receiveth Me, receiveth Him that sent Me."

2. *The Work in which he is engaged.* It is his business to expound and illustrate the saving truth of God, and to apply that truth to the souls of men with their many and deep needs; to lead men in their approaches to the throne of the Highest in public worship; and by every possible means to promote the divine culture of human spirits. There can be no work more responsible and honourable than this.

3. *The object for which he labours.* The grand aim of the Christian ministry is the salvation of the souls of men. How transcendently great and important is this aim! (1) Think of the *soul*—its powers, preciousness, etc. How great are its possibilities of progress, usefulness, enjoyment; or of degradation, mischief, misery! Unlimited are the possibilities of every human soul. Consider the Divine estimate of it. We see this in the stupendous price paid for its redemption. "He gave His only begotten Son," etc. "Redeemed with the precious blood of Christ," etc. We see the Divine estimate of its worth also in the means and agencies which God employs for its salvation. (2) Think what its *salvation* means. Not merely deliverance from punishment, etc. But restoration to the Divine image. "To be conformed to the image of his Son," etc. "That ye might be partakers of the Divine nature," etc. How grand then is the object of the Christian ministry! And how exalted the honour of those who are called to its sacred services!

A service so important and honourable:

First: *Demands for its faithful discharge, great gifts, great godliness, and great devotion.* (*a*)

Second: *Should be highly esteemed by men and especially by Christians.* To this high and holy service let Christian parents consecrate with gladness their best and most gifted sons. Let Christian young men not shrink from it by reason of any of the sacrifices which it involves; but if called thereto, count it the highest honour, etc. (*b*) Let all esteem the true minister of Christ highly because of the work in which he is engaged, and the Divine Being whom he represents. (*c*)

ILLUSTRATIONS.

(a) Your work is not lightened by the extraordinary development of education and literature within the last few years, nor by the certainty that it will take huge strides in advance before you have reached middle life. In a few years every village will swarm with men and women who will have gone through, in one form or another, more mental training and competitive examination in some departments of literature, science, or art, than was the lot of four-fifths of the professional men of half a century ago. Those who have nothing to say, and who obviously have no mental culture, will soon be scoffed out of the position of public teachers in every department. The love of luxury, the passion for the sensuous and the comfortable, the desire for amusement, for strong sensation, for pleasing *spectacle*, for fresh effects, which have impregnated every department of modern life and duty, have entered into the house of God, so that all the wisdom of the serpent must be joined with the harmlessness of the dove to do successful battle with the spirit of the world within the sanctuary of God. The beautiful building, the well-trained choir, the comfortable pew, the gorgeous effect, have not infrequently been the ghastly sepulchre of a dead church. Unchristlike passions are not charmed by sweet music, nor subtle speculation; nor are unspiritual men sanctified by sentimental eloquence, or moral essays, or stained windows. And believe me the great tide of human suffering and wrong doing, of hopeless toil, of grievous sickness and poverty, of boundless avarice and greed, is hardly touched by all the work of all our preachers, teachers, and philanthropists of every school. The knell is always ringing, and the spirits of men are always passing away in dread procession to the silent land . . . It appears to me that another great desideratum is what some might call enthusiasm; some, intensity of conviction; some would call it life. I prefer to speak of it as *reality*. My brethren, the one thing we want is absorbing realisation of the end of preaching; such a treatment of truth, and such a dealing with souls, that those who hear must at least know that the preacher believes what he says, and is putting forth every available power to make others see it with his eyes. If men speak of the Father God, it should be because they know what it is to be His child, and have found peace in His house, and have laid their head on His bosom. If they dare to lift the veil of the supernatural darkness which shrouds Gethsemane and Calvary, will it not be with sore amaze and eyes filled with tears? Yet is this the tone of our ordinary preaching?—*H. R. Reynolds, D.D.* From an Address to Students for the Ministry.

(b) Gentlemen, yours is a noble vocation. To be the ally of Christ in His great endeavour to save the world,—with Him to assert the authority of the throne and law of God; with Him to support human weakness in its vacillating endeavours to do the Divine will; to inspire the sinful with trust in the Divine mercy; to console sorrow; to awaken in the hearts of the poor, the weak, the desolate, the consciousness of their relations to the Infinite and Eternal God; to exalt and dignify the lives of old men and maidens, young men and children, by revealing to them things unseen and eternal which surround them now, and the mysterious, awful, glorious life which lies beyond death—this is a great work. There is nothing on earth comparable to it.—*R. W. Dale, D.D.*

(c) As Paul shows the Thessalonians how the preachers of the Word should be honoured, so he teaches the Philippians how to honour their teacher, saying:—"Receive him in the Lord with great gladness, and make much of such" (ii. 29); that is, show yourselves glad of him, that he may be glad of you. Have you any need to be taught why Paul would have you make much of such? Because they are like lamps which consume themselves to give light to others; so they consume themselves to give light to you. Because they are like a hen which clucks her chickens together from the kyte; so they cluck you together from the serpent. Because they are like the great shouts which beat down the walls of Jericho; so they beat down the walls of sin. Because they are like the fiery pillar which went before the Israelites to the Land of Promise, so they go before you to the Land of Promise. Because they are like good Andrew, who called his brother to see the Messias; so they call you to see the Messias; and therefore make much of such.—*Henry Smith.*

He's Christ's ambassador that man of God,
Steward of God's own mysteries! From on high
His warrant is: his charge, aloud to cry,
And spread his Master's attributes abroad,
His works, His ark of mercy, and His rod
Of justice: *his* to sinners to supply
The means of grace, and point how they may fly
Hell-flames, and how Heaven's pathway must be trod.
Hold him in honour on his works' account,
And on his Master's! Though a man he be,
And with his flock partake corruption's fount,
Holy and reverend is his ministry:
And, hark! a voice sounds from the heavenly mount,
"He that despiseth *you*, despiseth ME!"
Bishop Mant.

CHAPTER IV.

Critical Notes.—Ver. 3. צָבָא, *host*, " signifies military service, and is used here with special reference to the service of the Levites as the *militia sacra* of Jehovah."—*Keil and Del.*

Ver. 4. " Omit the word *about*, which is unnecessarily supplied. The sense is, 'this is the charge of the sons of Kohath, the most holy things:' *i.e.*, the Ark of the Covenant, the Table of Shewbread, the Candlestick, and the Golden Altar, as appears from the verses following, together with the furniture pertaining thereto."—*Speaker's Comm.*

Ver. 6. *Put in the staves.* " Rather probably, 'put the staves thereof in order.' These were never taken out of the golden rings by which the Ark was to be borne (see Exod. xxv. 14, 15), but would need adjustment after the process described in vers. 5 and 6, which would be likely to disturb them."—*Ibid.*

Vers. 10 and 12. חֲמוֹט, *a bar*, a bearing frame, or as in ch. xiii. 23, a pole for bearing on the shoulder.

Ver. 20. *When the holy things are covered.* " Literally, בְּבַלַּע *Keballa*, when they are *swallowed down;* which shows the promptitude with which everything belonging to the holy of holies was put out of sight, for these mysteries must ever be treated with the deepest reverence."—*A. Clarke.* " Render: *to see the holy things for an instant.* The expression means literally, 'as a gulp,' *i.e.*, for the instant it takes to swallow."—*Speaker's Comm.*

The numbering in this chapter differs from that recorded in the preceding chapter. In that every male from a month old and upward of the tribe of Levi was numbered, in order that they might take the place of the firstborn of all the tribes. In this only those who were fitted by their age for the service of the tabernacle, " from thirty years old and upward even until fifty years old," were numbered for that service.

The first main division of this chapter (vers. 1-20) we shall take as suggesting for homiletic treatment the following subject:—

ASPECTS OF THE CHRISTIAN MINISTRY.

(Verses 1-20.)

Looking at these verses in this light, the following points are suggested. The Christian ministry is,—

I. An arduous service.

The Levites were here numbered " from thirty years old and upward even until fifty years old, to do the work in the tabernacle of the congregation." The men selected for service were in the full maturity of their physical powers. Such men were needed, for the labour of the Levites was very severe during the journeyings of the Israelites. " When we consider," says A. Clarke, " that there was not less than 10 *tons* 13 *cwt.* 24 *lbs.* 14 *oz.*, *i.e.*, almost *ten tons* and fourteen hundred pounds' weight of *metal* employed in the tabernacle, besides the immense weight of the *skins, hangings, cords, boards,* and *posts,* we shall find it was no very easy matter to transport this moveable temple from place to place." " The work of the ministry," says Trapp, " is not an idle man's occupation, but a labouring even to lassitude; compared therefore to harvest work, and to that of cleaving wood, digging in mine-pits, rowing with oars, etc. All the comfort is, that God that helped the Levites to bear the Ark of the Covenant (1 Chron. xv. 26), will not be wanting to His weak, but willing servants, ' that labour in the Word and doctrine' (1 Tim. v. 17)."

II. A Holy Warfare.

The service of the Levites is regarded in this aspect in the third verse, where all who engage in it are said to "enter into the host." This is expressed more fully and clearly in verse 23 : " all that enter in to perform the service." Margin : " to war the warfare." Fuerst : "to do military service " In the New Testament the ministry of the Word is called a warfare, and faithful ministers of the Gospel good soldiers of Christ, and their doctrines weapons of war. Compare 2 Cor. x. 3, 4 ; 1 Tim. i. 18 ; 2 Tim. ii. 3 ; iv. 7. "Every faithful minister," says Burkitt, "is a spiritual soldier, warring under Jesus Christ, his captain and chief commander : must the soldier be called and do all by commission ? So must the minister. Must the soldier be armed, trained up, and disciplined, and made fit for service ? So must the minister. Must the soldier shun no dangers, stick at no difficulties, pass through thick and thin ? must he use allowed weapons, approved armour of his general's directing, not of his own inventing ? All this must the minister be and do . . . . He must also please his Captain, not please himself, his appetite, his pride, his covetousness, much less must he please the enemies he is to fight against —the devil, the world, and the flesh."

III. A Sacred Charge.

The Levites had to do with consecrated things ; the Kohathites with " the most holy things." They are most solemnly enjoined to exercise the most reverent care in the performance of their duties. They were to carry the most holy things, but not to touch them or curiously pry into them upon pain of death (verses 15, 17-20). The ministry of the Gospel is a charge still more sacred. He who is called to its high and holy duties is under the most solemn obligations to expound the revealed will of God, to break the bread of life to men, to labour diligently for the salvation of souls, and to seek in all things the glory of God. He is solemnly charged to " preach the word, convict, rebuke, exhort in all long suffering and teaching ; " to " feed the flock of God, . . . being ensamples to the flock." "They watch for souls, as they that must give account."

Our text suggests further, that the Christian ministry,—

IV. Demands the exercise of the highest faculties of those who are called to it.

It demands—

1. *Their mature powers.* Of the Levites numbered for active service none were to be under thirty or over fifty years old : they were to be in the very zenith of physical strength. And the duties of the Christian ministry challenge the utmost energies of those who undertake them. The design of this arrangement was probably twofold : (1) *That the service might be satisfactorily performed.* The Levitical duties in the wilderness could be properly discharged only by strong men. It is noteworthy that Joseph was thirty years old when he stood before Pharaoh, and David when he began to reign, and John the Baptist when he entered upon his mission, and Jesus Christ when He commenced His ministry. But is this a rule binding the Church of Christ ? Certainly not ; for a man may be young in years, yet old in gifts, and in the graces of character which are necessary to this calling. And, on the other hand, a man may be old in years, yet a mere babe as regards the gifts and graces requisite for this sacred office. " Such as execute this holy calling," says Attersoll, " ought to be qualified with judgment, gravity, sobriety, integrity, diligence, yea with power, courage, strength, and to have agility and ability in mind and body, that they may do all things wisely, exactly, studiously, and constantly." (*a*)

2. *That the servants might not be overburdened.* That this end was contemplated in this arrangement appears from this, that the young men were taken into training when they were twenty-five years of age, and into laborious service when they were thirty, and the aged did not cease from service at fifty, but only from severe labours (see ch. viii. 23-26). And it is important that the energies of the young Christian minister be not over-taxed, lest both the

quality and duration of his service be diminished thereby. And as for the aged, as M. Henry remarks, "twenty years' good service was thought pretty well for one man."

2. *Their acquaintance with their duties.* The duties of the priests and of the Levites of each division are particularly set forth in this chapter. Each one must become acquainted with his own. The Christian minister must learn his Master's will, study his Master's Word, thoughtfully consider the needs of those amongst whom he labours, etc.

3. *A reverent spirit.* Reverently were the sacred vessels to be borne and regarded. Prying curiosity was utterly and sternly prohibited. "Note the great care," says Babington, "God hath to maintain reverence of holy things in men's hearts, knowing the corruption of man in soon despising that which is common. And when He so wisheth reverence, shall man be careless of it?" And Attersoll: "We must do nothing that may make our ministry fruitless and bring it into contempt, but seek to adorn it and beautify it by all reverent carriage of ourselves in it, and in the discharge of the duties of it." (*b*)

4. *A faithful and dutiful spirit.* Each one was required to do his own duty, not meddling with those of others. Their well-being, and even their very life, depended upon the faithful performance by each one of his own service (verses 15, 17-20). The progress, health, even the stability of human society are inseparable from a faithful discharge of the duties of the Christian ministry. Upon this point the testimony of history is unequivocal. (See remarks on this point on ch. i. 47-54.)

ILLUSTRATIONS.

(*a*) We all see and must confess, that an aged man, ripe in judgment and experience, is more fit for government than a younger, destitute of such mature wisdom and knowledge, be the place ecclesiastical or civil. Whereupon Silla said of *Marius* the younger, *Debere juvenem prius remo quam gubernaculo admoveri.* That a young man was first to be appointed to the oar and then to the stern. Fruit that is not ripe will serve so well neither for use nor store as ripe fruit will. The untimely fruit of a woman is a cause of grief, and not of comfort. The young fowls that are not fledged cannot fly, and green walls of any building should have no weight laid upon them till they were settled and sound. *Non difficulter delectabit oratio magis ornata quam solida,* etc. *Sed difficillime ute oportet, docebit,* etc. Easily may a speech that hath more beauty than substance please, but never so well teach as that which hath matter and substance in it. The one usually is the speech of young men, the other of elder. Look, saith Plutarch, how a dart differeth in his piercing, according to the strength of the arm that cast it, so differeth the word of a young and old man. The one cometh from a weaker strength, and so pierceth less; the other from a strong ability, and so entereth even through and through. The old man's speech, saith the same author again, is like to a strong and sweet ointment, that filleth all the room with his sweetness.—*Bishop Babington.*

Ministers have oftentimes given unto them in the Scripture the name of *Elders.* Many titles are given unto them, and every one of them carrieth some instruction and admonition with it unto the conscience. They have not their names in vain, they are not idle sounds of vain words, but they offer the signification of some duty to be performed, and lead to the consideration of something to be practised, as shepherds call to their remembrance to be busied in feeding; watchmen, to prove to them that they ought to have a vigilant care of the City of God; messengers, that they must not do their own business, but His that sent them. So they are called Elders. 1 Tim. v. 17, 19; 1 Pet. v. 1; Acts xiv. 23, xv. 2. xvi. 4, and xx. 17, to imprint and engrave in their hearts, the cogitation and consideration of the care, wisdom, sobriety, and stayedness that ought to be in men of that calling; all which gifts are for the most part proper to men of that age, for "days shall speak, and the multitude of years teach wisdom," Job xxxii. 7. And therefore they are resembled unto them, not because they are so always in age, but because they should be like unto them, and have the properties and qualities of them.—*W. Attersoll.*

(*b*) Would I describe a preacher, such as Paul,
Were he on earth, would hear, approve, and own—
Paul should himself direct me. I would trace
His master strokes, and draw from his design.
I would express him simple, grave, sincere;
In doctrine uncorrupt; in language plain,
And plain in manner; decent, solemn, chaste
And natural in gesture; much impressed
Himself, as conscious of His awful charge,
And anxious mainly that the flock he feeds
May feel it too; affectionate in look
And tender in address, as well becomes
A messenger of grace to guilty men.—*Cowper.*

DIVINE SECRETS AND HUMAN CURIOSITY.

(Verse 20.)

I. There are certain things in the universe which are hidden from man.

The vessels of the sanctuary were concealed from the Levites. To the priests themselves the Holy of holies was a secret place, into which they dare not enter. And even the high priest might enter therein only once a year, and that after careful and significant preparation. In these arrangements we have an illustration of the truths that there are certain realms in the universe which are accessible only to God, and certain things which are concealed from man. This is the case,

1. *In the material universe.* Nature has secrets the existence of which is not even conjectured by her most enthusiastic students, and mysterious provinces into which neither the most daring nor the most reverent enquirer can enter. (*a*)

2. *In the arrangements of Providence.* In the dealings of God with nations and with the race as a whole, there are inscrutable mysteries to us. In His dealings with us as families and as individuals, there are things the wisdom and love and righteousness of which we cannot discover—things which perplex, and sometimes confound and distress us. "Clouds and darkness are round about Him." "Thy way is in the sea, and Thy path in the great waters, and Thy footsteps are not known." "How unsearchable are His judgments, and His ways past finding out!"

3. *In the economy of redemption.* There are deepest, closest secrets here. We ask question after question, to which, at present, we receive no reply. "Great is the mystery of godliness," etc., "Which things the angels desire to look into."

4. *In the character and contents of the future.* "Thou knowest not what a day may bring forth." "Ye know not what shall be on the morrow." Let us notice concerning these secrets that,

First: They are *inevitable*. "We are but of yesterday and know nothing, because our days upon the earth are as a shadow." It is utterly unreasonable to suppose that we, with our limited faculties and brief existence, should comprehend the works and ways, the thoughts and utterances of the Infinite and Eternal. "Canst thou by searching find out God? canst thou find out the Almighty to perfection?" Comp. Job xxxviii.—xli.

Second: They are *merciful*. The intense light of a fuller and clearer revelation might, were it given, smite us with spiritual blindness. As cloud and shadow and darkness in nature are good for us, so the Divine reserve is good for us spiritually. What man is there of us who could bear the revelation of the scenes and events which await him and his dear friends in the future? (*b*)

Third: They are *educational*. Mysteries provoke enquiry; and reverent enquiry conduces to intellectual and spiritual growth. Wonderful are the discoveries of wisdom, and power, of righteousness, and love which God will make to His children in the endless hereafter. Let us be thankful for the Divine reserve. "We do amiss," says Dr. Parker, "to stand before these sublime mysteries as we would stand before a vizored army of bloodthirsty foes. We should stand before them as before the veiled images of Love. They are Wisdom in disguise. They are Affection in shadow. They are Royalty in its royalest pomp."

II. Men are prone to curiously pry into hidden things.

This is clearly implied in the careful and minute directions for covering the sacred furniture of the sanctuary, in the prohibition of the text, and in the stern penalty annexed to any breach of this prohibition. There is a sad tendency in human nature, as it now is, to curious enquiry concerning forbidden things. It has been well said by Monro: "Curiosity is a languid principle, where access is easy, and gratification immediate; remoteness and difficulty are powerful incentives to its vigorous and lasting operations." In proportion as the secret things are regarded as mysterious, important, or sacred, will the strength of curiosity be in relation to them.

III. Irreverent prying into hidden things may lead to the most terrible results.

"They shall not go in to see when the holy things are covered" (or, "for an instant," see *Critical Notes*), "lest they die."

The curiosity of Eve concerning the fruit of "the tree of the knowledge of good and evil" led to the spiritual death of our first parents and their countless posterity. All curious enquiries as to sacred things, and irreverent pryings into Divine mysteries, tend to utterly destroy spirituality of mind and faith in the great Christian verities. "Curiosity," says Fuller, "is a kernel of the forbidden fruit, which still sticketh in the throat of a natural man, sometimes to the danger of his choking." Nor is it less perilous to the spiritually renewed man, leading, as it does, to the death of some of the highest and divinest things of the spirit. (c)

Conclusion:

1. *Guard against curiously enquiring into Divine secrets.* It may be that some of these secrets are part of that ineffable glory into which no man can enter and live.

2. *Be humble, seeing that we are surrounded by mysteries, countless and deep.* Humility becometh the ignorant.

3. *Be reverent in all our enquiries into Divine things.* "The secret of the Lord is with them that fear Him," &c. "The meek will He guide in judgment," &c. "Thou hast hid these things from the wise and prudent, and hast revealed them unto babes."

4. *Let us be diligent in the performance of our manifest duty.* "If any man will do His will, He shall know of the doctrine, whether it be of God," etc.

ILLUSTRATIONS.

(*a*) The eye can alight on no spot free from the presence of mystery. Questions may be asked concerning a grass-blade or an insect, which no intellect could answer. Men know much about the *outside* of things, but of the interior organism of the universe, its fine balances, adaptations, springs, impulses, relationships, and purposes, they understand little or nothing. No intelligent being can observe the universe without knowing that it is a magnificent mystery. God has imposed silence upon it. In the thunder-roar of the ocean we never hear the revelation of its mysteries. The whirlwind gives no account of its hidden way and unknown tabernacle. The glorious stars, in their nocturnal vigils ever shine, but never speak the mystery of their birth. Mysterious, indeed, are all things. Worlds suspended upon nothing, the calm, majestic roll of countless orbs, the dew of the morning, the glare of the lightning, the riven strata of the earth, the pulsation of unnumbered millions upon millions of hearts, the chequered history of life, the complicated workings and evolutions of intellect, *all* bespeak the power of a Mysterious, Dread Being, whose ways are unsearchable.—*Joseph Parker, D.D.*

(*b*) O heaven! that one might read the book of fate;
And see the revolution of the times
Make mountains level, and the continent
(Weary of solid firmness) melt itself
Into the sea! and, other times, to see
The beachy girdle of the ocean,
Too wide for Neptune's hips; how chances mock
And changes fill the cup of alteration
With divers liquors! O, if this were seen,
The happiest youth, viewing his progress through,
What perils past, what crosses to ensue,
Would shut the book, and sit him down and die.

Shakespeare. Second part of King Henry IV. III., I.

Were the time of our death foreseen, what a melancholy character would it impart to the pursuits and occupations of the human race! If every man saw the moment of his death continually before him, how would his thoughts be fixed to the fatal spot; and, upon its near approach, the consideration of it would probably absorb every other. With respect to our fellow-creatures, how would it poison the springs of enjoyment, were parents and children, husbands and wives, brothers and sisters, able to calculate with certainty the period of each others' lives! We should seem to be walking among the victims of death; the scenes of human existence would lose all cheerfulness, animation, and beauty. The interests of society would also sustain most serious injury. Many great and noble enterprises would never have been begun could the persons who, in the hope of life, engaged in them have foreseen that before they could be concluded, they themselves would be snatched away by the hand of death. Many discoveries, by which great benefit has been conferred on the world would not have been elicited. Few efforts probably would be made to attain any object, the consequences of which terminate with the life of the party, if he foresaw that they would be intercepted by death. Who would venture to engage in any lucrative employment if he certainly knew that the benefit would not be even partially realized during the time of his mortal existence? But, happily for mankind, events are concealed—duties only are made known.—*Rob. Hall, A.M.*

(*c.*) How notably again doth this commandment of hiding and folding them up, teach us to beware of curiosity in things not revealed. What God is pleased we should know, that safely we may search for and seek to know, but further we may not go. We must not have an ear to hear when God hath not a mouth to speak. *To eat much honey,* saith Solomon, *is not good;* and to search out curiously God's Majesty is to endanger myself to be oppressed with His glory. *Seek not out things which are too hard for thee, neither search the things rashly which are too mighty for thee,* saith wise Sirach. But what God hath commanded thee, think of that with reverence, be not curious in many of His works: for it is not needful for thee to see with thine eyes the things that be secret. Be not curious in superfluous things, for many things are showed unto thee above the capacity of men. The meddling with such hath beguiled many, and an evil opinion hath deceived their judgment. Thou canst not see without eyes, profess not therefore the knowledge that thou hast not. Thales the philosopher gazed so upon the stars, that he fell into the ditch before him, and his maid mocked him. Seneca wisely complained, that a great part of our life was spent in doing nothing, a greater part in doing ill, and the greatest part of all in doing that which appertains not to us. This is curiosity in other men's business, and foolish meddling with needless things. Socrates was wise, and said it wisely: "*Quæ super nos, nihil ad nos;* Matters that are above us, belong not to us." David, a man indeed with another light than Socrates had, professeth we know, as he was not high minded, neither had any proud looks; so he did not exercise himself in matters that were too high for him. But he did wean his soul, and keep it under even as a young child, &c. Bernard taxeth this foul fault in these words, "*Multi student magis alta quam apta proferre:* Many study to utter rather high matters than fit matters." Let us avoid this fault.—*Bishop Babington.*

THE BURDENS OF LIFE.

(*Verses 21-33.*)

In these verses we have the Divine directions as to the service of the Gershonites and the Merarites. They present an instructive illustration of the burdens of human life. Regarding them in this light, they suggest concerning these burdens that they are—

I. Distributed to all men.

The Kohathites, Gershonites, and Merarites each had their service and burden. (See verses 19, 27, 32.) And "from thirty years old and upward until fifty years old" no man of either of these families was exempted from duty. "Aaron and his sons shall appoint them every one to his service and to his burden." And now there is no human life in this world without its burden of some kind and degree. It is not simply those who are manifestly oppressed, or afflicted, or sorely tried, that have a burden to bear. Could we read the inner history of those whose life seems most pleasant and prosperous and favoured, we should doubtless find some secret sorrow, or wearing anxiety, or life-long disappointment. There is no sunshine without its shadow, no happy family without its trial or sorrow, and no individual life without its burden of some kind or other. "Every individual experience," says Dr. Huntington, "has, soon or late, its painful side, its crucial hours, when there is darkness over all the land, and we cry out to know if God has forsaken us. For the time, longer or shorter, we taste only the bitter, and feel only the thorns. The separations of death, the distance between our aspiration and performance, unsatisfied ambition, labouring year after year in vain, affection returned by indifference, the symptoms of fatal disease, former energy prostrate, a friend alienated, a child depraved, an effort to do good construed into an impertinence, —unconquerable obstacles that we cannot measure and can scarcely speak of, heaped up against our best designs—these are some of the most frequent shapes of the misery; but no list is full. The one essential thing is that the will is crossed, crucified. Character is everywhere put into this school of suffering." (a)

II. Distributed variously.

All men are burdened, but all are not alike burdened. The burdens of human life—

1. *Differ in kind.*—The burden of the Kohathites consisted of "the most holy things," the furniture of the sanctuary; that of the Gershonites, of the hanging, curtains, and coverings of the tabernacle, with "their cords, and all the instruments of their service;" and that of the Merarites, of the pillars, boards, bars, sockets, and the more solid parts of the tabernacle. So the burdens of human life are of various kinds. Some labour under a great load of temporal poverty, others suffer more or less throughout their entire life by reason of bodily afflictions, the burden of others is some crushing family trial, of others some sore and secret sorrow, and of others some profound and painful longing which finds no satisfaction, &c.

2. *Differ in degree.* The burden of the Merarites was much heavier than that of either the Kohathites or Gershonites. And the burdens of men now are not alike in weight. Some are much more heavily laden than others. All good men are not tried so severely as Job was. The Lord Jesus Himself bore the heaviest burden of all. As compared with His, our heaviest load is light. And comparing the burdens of men one with another, some appear almost free, while others labour under a heavy load.

III.—Distributed Divinely.

By Divine direction Aaron and his sons were to appoint to each one his burden. (See verses 19, 27, 32.) In the case of the Merarites the direction as to this appointment was very explicit: "By name ye shall reckon the instruments of the charge of their burden." "This direction, which occurs only in reference to the charge of the Merarites, imports apparently that 'the instruments' were to be assigned, no doubt, by Ithamar and his immediate assistants, to their bearers singly, and nominatim. These instruments comprised the heavier parts of the Tabernacle; and the order seems intended to prevent individual Merarites choosing their own burden, and so throwing more than the proper share on others." — *Speaker's Comm.* The burdens of human life do not fall by chance or accident. God is not the Author of the burdens which oppress human life. Pain and poverty, sorrow and trial, are the offspring of sin. But God *regulates* the burdens of men. No trial befalls us without His permission, and He determines the extent and severity of every trial. (Comp. Job i. 12, ii. 6.) "Thou art my God. My times are in Thy hand." "He shall choose our inheritance for us." The Divine regulation of trial affords a guarantee that no man shall be overburdened; for the Lord knoweth how much we can bear; He knoweth us altogether, and He has promised to bestow grace adequate to our need. "As thy days so shall thy strength be." "My grace is sufficient for thee," &c. "There hath no temptation taken you but such as is common to man: but God is faithful, who will not suffer you to be tempted above that ye are able," &c.

"God will keep his own anointed;
Nought shall harm them, none condemn;
All their trials are appointed;
All must work for good to them:
All shall help them
To their heavenly diadem."—*Lyte.*

Our text further suggests that the Burdens of Life should be—

IV. Patiently borne.

We do not read of any murmuring amongst the Levites because of the duties assigned to any of them. Each one appears to have accepted his allotted service, and performed its duties. Let each one of us learn to bear his life-burden without murmuring, to accept his lot in life cheerfully, to do his duty faithfully.

1. *God regulates our burden, let us therefore be content under it.* (b)
2. *God sanctifies our burden to most blessed ends, let us therefore be thankful.* "We glory in tribulation also: knowing that tribulation worketh patience," &c. "Count it all joy when ye fall into divers temptations; knowing that the trying of your faith worketh patience," etc. (c)
3. *God will soon deliver us from our burden, let us therefore be hopeful.* "The time will come," says Babington, "that our God will free us, and then we shall receive an eternal reward. Remember what you read: *The Lord God of Israel,* saith David, *hath given rest unto His people, that they may dwell in Jerusalem for ever, and the Levites shall no more bear the Tabernacle, and all the vessels for the service thereof.* So shall it be said one day of you, of me, of all the members of the Lord's body. The Lord hath given rest, and we shall no more carry our burdens and portions of woe in this world, but live in the heavenly Jerusalem for ever. O, wished rest, and ten thousand times welcome when God is pleased! Do men fear a safe harbour in a mighty storm? Do men grieve to come home to their own houses after a long and painful journey? No, no, we know; and no more should we shrink to find heavenly rest."

ILLUSTRATIONS.

(a) What is included in the term *burden*? Whatever makes right living, according to the law of God, difficult to a sincere man *that* is a burden. Whatever thing within or without a man, in his nature, in his habits, or in his circumstances, makes it hard for him to live purely and rightly—that is included in this term *burden*. It may be in his mental constitution; it may be in his bodily health; it may be in the habits of his education; it may be in his relation to worldly affairs; it may be in his domestic circumstances; it may be in his peculiar liabilities to temptation and sin. It includes the whole catalogue of conditions, and influences, and causes, that weigh men down, and hinder them, when they are endeavouring to live lives of rectitude.—*H. W. Beecher.*

To-day I had a long and strange interview with a lady who has recently become a member of the congregation. . . . She asked me if I had ever known a case of trial so severe as hers. "Yes," I replied, "numbers; it is the case of all. Suffering is very common, so is disappointment." "Are our affections to be all withered?" "Very often, I believe." "Then why were they given me?" "I am sure I cannot tell you that, but I suppose it would not have been very good for you to have had it all your own way?" "Then do you think I am better for this blighting succession of griefs?" "I do not know, but I know you ought to be." 'Wordsworth' was lying open on the table, and I pointed to her these lines:—

"Then was the truth received into my heart,
That under heaviest sorrow earth can bring,
If from the affliction somewhere do not grow,
Honour, which could not else have been a faith,
An elevation and a sanctity;
If new strength be not given nor old restored,
The blame is ours, not nature's."

The deep undertone of this world is sadness. a solemn bass occurring at measured intervals, and heard through all other tones. Ultimately, all the strains of this world's music resolve themselves into that tone; and I believe that, rightly felt, the Cross, and the Cross alone, interprets the mournful mystery of life—the sorrow of the Highest, the Lord of Life; the result of error and sin, but ultimately remedial, purifying, and exalting.—*F. W. Robertson, M.A., Life and Letters.*

(b) Contentation (*i.e.* contentment) is a ready and approved medicine for all miseries and maladies whatsoever. No man is troubled with any grief or disease, but he is most willing to hear of a salve for it. This is sovereign for this purpose. It easieth the burden of all afflictions, it taketh away the smart of all sores; it poureth oil and wine into our wounds, and of half dead it maketh us alive again; it maketh a rough way plain and crooked things straight. It casteth down high hills, and maketh the path easy before us. It turneth outward wants into inward comforts. It maketh the bond to be free, the poor to be rich, the sick to be whole, the miserable to be happy, and such as are owners of nothing to be lords of all things. Give an hearty draught of this strong drink to him that is ready to perish, and a cup of this wine to him that hath an heavy heart, it will make him forget his poverty, and remember his misery no more. This we see in the Apostle Paul, he had drunk of the wine of contentation, (2 Cor. vi. 9. 10) and therefore saith, "As unknown, and yet well known; as dying, and, behold, we live; as chastened, and not killed; as sorrowful, yet always rejoicing; as poor, yet making many rich; as having nothing, and yet possessing all things."—*W. Attersoll.*

(c) "I know," is all the mourner saith,
"Knowledge by suffering entereth,
And life is perfected by death;
"I am content to touch the brink
Of pain's dark goblet, and I think
My bitter drink a wholesome drink.
"I am content to be so weak;
Put strength into the words I speak,
For I am strong in what I seek.
"I am content to be so bare
Before the archers; everywhere
My wounds being stroked by heavenly air.
"Glory to God—to God," he saith;
"Knowledge by suffering entereth,
And life is perfected by death."

Burdens are not pleasant; yet they are profitable. They develop strength. The only way to make strong men is to impose burdens that require strength; then if they have the substance in them, it will come out. We know a man who has been struggling for years to escape from business cares yet they have accumulated upon him. Every measure of relief has brought additional work and sometimes extreme trial. But he has risen in power as the load was increased, and he has grown to be a man of might. Those who run flinch, dodge, faint, as crushing cares increase, are broken and suffer loss; but those who stand, fight, tug, hold on and cry to God, grow strong. It is a misfortune always to have an easy time, a blessing to have work to do which taxes all our powers and then taxes more and more.—*The Study.*

The Importance of Little Things.

(*Verses* 31–32.)

In the charge of Merari we find not only the heaviest things and most cumbersome, but also some little things which are specially mentioned. "Their pins, and their cords, with all their instruments, and with all their service; and by name ye shall reckon the instruments of the charge of their burden." It is upon these little things that we would fix attention. From the fact that we have here Divine directions concerning such small things as "pins and cords," we infer *the importance of little things.* The following considerations will help us to realise this.

I. **The completeness and perfection of great things is impossible apart from due attention to little things.**

These "pins and cords" were essential to the completeness of the tabernacle. By tiny and delicate touches the enchanting beauty of the painting is achieved. By scrupulous attention to details the greatest inventions have been brought to successful issues. A wise economy in small expenses has had no little to do in many instances in the accumulation of great wealth. "An onlooker, observing the slight taps given to a statue by Canova, spoke as if he thought the artist to be trifling, but was rebuked by this reply: "The touches which you ignorantly hold in such small esteem are the very things which make the difference between the failure of a bungler and the *chef d'œuvre* of a master."

II. **The most important issues sometimes depend upon what seem to us slight circumstances.**

Trivial incidents sometimes appear to constitute the great turning points in life. How often in the life of Joseph, as we view it to-day, events of incalculable importance depended upon what men call "the merest chance," or the most trivial incident! What stupendous issues depend upon the preservation of the imperilled life of that goodly child in his frail ark of bulrushes on the Nile! A remarkable illustration of our point occurs in the life of the distinguished F. W. Robertson. He had a passionate enthusiasm for military life, had chosen the army as his profession, and was studying for it, and application had been made to the Horse Guards for a commission for him. "To two great objects," says his biographer—"the profession of arms which he had chosen, and the service of Christ in that profession—he now devoted himself wholly." The circumstances which led him to abandon that profession for the calling of the Christian minister are remarkable. This result was brought about by the influence of the Rev. Mr. Davies, who thus relates the origin of their friendship:—"The daughter of Lady French, at whose house I met my friend, had been seriously ill. She was prevented from sleeping by the barking of a dog in one of the adjoining houses. This house was Captain Robertson's. A letter was written to ask that the dog might be removed; and so kind and acquiescent a reply was returned, that Lady French called to express her thanks. She was muck struck at that visit by the manner and bearing of the eldest son, and, in consequence, an intimacy grew up between the families." Mr. Robertson himself thus refers to this matter:—"If I had not met a certain person, I should not have changed my profession; if I had not known a certain lady, I should not probably have met this person; if that lady had not had a delicate daughter who was disturbed by the barking of my dog; if my dog had not barked that night, I should now have been in the dragoons, or fertilising the soil of India. Who can say that these things were not ordered, and that, apparently, the merest trifle did not produce failure and a marred existence?" ("Failure and a marred existence"—so it seemed to him then. But how very different it really was! How different must it appear to him now!) Such slight circumstances, apparently, led to his entering upon the career of a Christian minister—a career so rich in the highest results. *(a)*

III. Life itself is composed almost entirely of little things.

Great events and noteworthy experiences are very rare things in life. Day after day we live in the performance of small duties, amidst ordinary circumstances and events. With the exception of a very few remarkable events, our life is made up of the most ordinary and common-place, and apparently, unimportant things. And yet life itself, as a whole, is a thing of utterly unspeakable importance, most momentous in its character, its influence, its capabilities, &c.

IV. Character, which to each of us is the most important thing, is formed almost entirely of littles.

"Character," says Beecher, "is not a massive unit; it is a fabric rather. It is an artificial whole made up by the interply of ten thousand threads. Every faculty is a spinner, spinning every day its threads, and almost every day threads of a different colour. Myriads and myriads of webbed products proceed from the many active faculties of the human soul, and character is made up by the weaving together of all these innumerable threads of daily life. Its strength is not merely in the strength of some simple unit, but in the strength of numerous elements." The great Williams of Wern, when preaching at Bala, where many women are employed in knitting stockings, inquired, "How is character formed?" "*Gradually*," he replied, "just as you Bala women knit stockings—*a stitch at a time.*" *(b)*

Conclusion:

1. *Be careful as to the little things of personal character and conduct.* "Let us not neglect little duties, let us not allow ourselves in little faults. Whatever we may like to think, nothing is really of small importance that affects the soul. All diseases are small at the beginning. Many a death-bed begins with a 'little cold.' Nothing that can grow is large all at once; the greatest sin must have a beginning. Nothing that is great comes to perfection in a day; characters and habits are all the result of little actions. Little strokes made the ark which saved Noah. Little pins held firm the tabernacle which was the glory of Israel. We, too, are travelling through a wilderness. Let us be like the family of Merari, and be careful not to leave *the pins* behind."

Let us beware of small sins. *(c)*
Let us be faithful in small duties. *(d)*

2. *Be careful as to the little things of church life and work.* Let the most feeble member of the Church do the work for which he is fitted faithfully. Let not the least or lowliest duty be neglected, or the welfare and prosperity of the whole will be thereby injured. When all the members of the Church

—the least gifted and the most gifted — are faithful in life and work; and when every duty—the least as well as the greatest—is faithfully performed, great will be her prosperity and her power.

ILLUSTRATIONS.

(a) Where God in generous fulness dwells,
Nor small nor great is known;
He paints the tiniest floweret-cells
O'er emerald meadows strewn;
And sees, but not with kinder eyes,
The heavens grow rich with sunset dyes;
Both ministrant to beauty's sense,
Both signs of one Omnipotence.

He comes not forth with pageant grand
His marvels to perform.
A cloud "the bigness of a hand"
Can blacken heaven with storm.
A grain of dust, if he arrange,
The fortunes of a planet change.
An insect reef can overwhelm
The stately navies of a realm.

There are no trifles. Arks as frail
As bore God's prince of old,
On many a buoyant Nile stream sail
The age's heirs to hold.
From Jacob's love on Joseph shed,
Came Egypt's wealth and Israel's bread;
From Ruth's chance gleaning in the corn,
The Psalmist sang,—the Christ was born.
W. M. Punshon.

(b) Have you ever watched an icicle as it formed? You noticed how it froze one drop at a time, until it was a foot long or more. If the water was clear, the icicle remained clear, and sparkled brightly in the sun; but if the water was but slightly muddy, the icicle looked foul, and its beauty was spoiled. Just so our characters are forming: one little thought or feeling at a time adds its influence. If each thought be pure and right, the soul will be lovely, and sparkle with happiness; but if impure and wrong, there will be deformity and wretchedness.—*Temperance Anecdotes, in Dict. of Illust.*

(c) Little things are seeds of great ones. Little cruelties are gems of great ones. Little treacheries are like small holes in raiment, the beginning of large ones. Little dishonesties are like the drops that work through the bank of the river; a drop is an engineer: it tunnels a way for its fellows, and they, rusting, prepare for all behind them. A worm in a ship's plank proves, in time, worse than a cannon-ball.—*H. W. Beecher.*

(d) Let us be content to work,
To do the thing we can, and not presume
To fret because it's little. 'Twill employ
Seven men, they say, to make a perfect pin.
Who makes the head consents to miss the point;
Who makes the point agrees to leave the head;
And if a man should cry, "I want a pin,
And I must make it straightway, head and point,"
His wisdom is not worth the pin he wants.
Elizabeth B. Browning.

PROPORTION BETWEEN NUMBER AND SERVICE.

(*Verses 34—49.*)

In these verses we have the account of the numbering of the Levites for active service, according to the command given unto Moses and Aaron in verses 1-3. The result here recorded is this: Of males from thirty years old and upward even unto fifty years old, there were of Kohathites 2,750; of Gershonites, 2,630; and of Merarites, 3,200, making a total of 8,580. This number bears a just proportion to that of all the males of the Levites from a month old and upward, which was 22,000. "But the number of Merarites available for the sacred service bears an unusually large proportion to the total number of males of that family, which is (iii. 34) 6,200. Looking at the relation of the numbers to the service required of them we discover illustrations of—

I. The Wisdom of God.

"By this diversity of numbers among the Levite families," saith Trapp, "God showeth His wisdom, saith an interpreter, in fitting men for the work, whereunto He hath appointed them, whether it requireth multitude or gifts. 'For to one is given by the Spirit the word of wisdom,' etc. (1 Cor. xii. 8-12). It is reported that in Luther's house was found written, '*Res et verba Phillipus, res sine verbis Lutherus, verba sine re Erasmus,* Melancthon hath both matter and words; Luther hath matter but wants words; Erasmus hath words, but wants matter.' Every one hath his own share; all are not alike gifted." M. Henry: "The Merarites were but 6,200 in all, and yet of these there were 3,200 serviceable men, that is, more than half. The greatest burden lay upon that family, the boards and pillars and sockets; and God so ordered it that, though they were the fewest in number, yet they should have the most able men among them; for whatever service God calls men to He will furnish them for it, and give strength in proportion to the work, grace sufficient." God's appointments to service are ever made in perfect wisdom. There are ever a fitness and proportion between the workers and the work. (a)

II. The reasonableness of the Divine requirements.

"Though the sum total of effective Levites," says Greenfield, "was very small compared with that of the other tribes; yet they would be far more than could be employed at once in this service. But they might carry by turns and ease one another, and thus do the whole expeditiously and cheerfully. They would also have their own tents to remove, and their own families to take care of." There was an ample number for the performance of the work; and its distribution amongst so many would render it comparatively easy to everyone. God's claims upon us and our service are in the highest degree reasonable. He is a kind and gracious Master. "His yoke is easy and His burden is light." And if He summon us to difficult tasks, He will increase our wisdom and strength, so we shall not be overmatched. "As thy days so shall thy strength be." "My grace is sufficient for thee." "I can do all things through Christ which strengtheneth me." (b)

We have also in this section of the history an illustration of—

III. The exemplary obedience of the servants of the Lord.

We see how carefully and faithfully Moses and Aaron carried out the directions which they received from Him. In this they are an example to us. (See notes and illustrations bearing on this point given on chaps. ii. 34, iii. 16.)

ILLUSTRATIONS.

(a) God's wisdom appears in the various inclinations and conditions of men. As there is a distinction of several creatures, and several qualities in them, for the common good of the world, so among men there are several inclinations and several abilities, as donatives from God, for the common advantage of human society; as several channels cut out from the same river run several ways, and refresh several soils, one man is qualified for one employment, another marked out by God for a different work, yet all of them fruitful to bring in a revenue of glory to God, and a harvest of profit to the rest of mankind. How unuseful would the body be if it had but "one member" (1 Cor. xii. 19)! How unprovided would a house be if it had not vessels of dishonour as well as of honour! The corporation of mankind would be as much a chaos as the matter of the heavens and the earth was before it was distinguished by several forms breathed into it at the creation. Some are inspired with a particular genius for one art, some for another; every man hath a distinct talent. If all were husbandmen where would be the instruments to plough and reap? If all were artificers where would they have corn to nourish themselves? All men are like vessels, and parts in the body, designed for distinct offices and functions for the good of the whole. As the variety of gifts in the Church is a fruit of the wisdom of God for the preservation and increase of the Church, so the variety of inclinations and employments in the world is a fruit of the wisdom of God for the preservation and subsistence of the world by mutual commerce.—*Charnocke.*

(b) Power is the measure of obligation. It is the circumference that bounds every line, starting from the centre of duty. What we cannot do, we are not bound to attempt. The command that outstrips our capacity is no law to us. Why is religion not binding on brutes? God is as truly their Creator and Sustainer as He is ours—they have not the power. Our faculties are adequate to the Divine will respecting us. They are made *for* it—made *to* it. The sun is not more nicely adjusted to the work of lighting the planets—the rolling atmosphere to the purposes of life—these bodies to all the laws, influences, and sceneries of this material universe—than are all the powers of the soul adjusted to the work of worship. To trace effects to causes, to discern moral distinctions, to reverence greatness, to love excellence, to praise goodness—these are the sacred functions of religion; and whilst that seraph, glowing with rapture in the full sunlight of the Eternal, can perform nothing higher, that human babe, gazing for the first time with wonder at the stars, has ample powers to do the same.—*D. Thomas, D.D.*

The whole relation of discipleship is a relation of liberty. No one goes to his duty because he must, but only because his heart is in it. His inclinations are that way, for his heart is in the Master's love, and he follows Him gladly. It, no doubt, seems to you when you look on, only as strangers to Christ, that this must be a hard and dry service, for you see no attraction in it. But the reason is that your heart is not in it. With a new heart, quickened by the grace of Christ, all this would be changed. It will then seem wholly attractive. All the currents of your love will run that way, and the freest freedom of your nature will be to go after Christ. No sacrifice will be hard—no service a burden. The wonder now will be that all men do not rush in after Christ to be His eager followers.—*H. Bushnell, D.D.*

"In service which Thy love appoints,
There are no bonds for me;
My secret heart is taught the truth
That makes Thy children free.
A life of self-renouncing love
Is one of liberty."—*Waring.*

CHAPTER V.

THE EXCLUSION OF THE UNCLEAN.

(*Verse* 1-4.)

" Now that the nation was regularly organised, the sacred tribe dedicated, and the sanctuary with the tokens of God's more immediate Presence provided with its proper place and attendants in the camp, it remained to attest and to vindicate, by modes in harmony with the spirit of the theocratical law, the sanctity of the people of God. This accordingly is the general purpose of the directions given in this and the next chapter. Thus the congregation of Israel was made to typify the Church of God, within which, in its perfection, nothing that offends can be allowed to remain" (*cf.* Matt. viii. 22; Rev. xxi. 27.)—*Speaker's Comm.*

In the verses now before us we have the directions for the expulsion of unclean persons out of the camp. The laws as to ceremonial uncleanness are given with considerable minuteness in Lev. xi., xv., xxi., xxii., and Num. xix. But it appears that they are now carried out for the first time.

We shall look at our text in two aspects.

I. As a Sanitary Measure.

A number of rules and regulations for securing the cleanliness and health of the people were promulgated and enforced. Some of the sanitary regulations "seem minute and indelicate to modern ideas, but were, doubtless, intended to correct unseemly or unhealthful practices, either of the Hebrew people or of neighbouring tribes." Some have asserted that the reason for the expulsion of every leper from the camp was that the disease was contagious. So scholarly and well-informed a writer as Dr. Milman says that "the disease was highly infectious." But this is extremely doubtful. "All who have looked closest into the matter," says Archbishop Trench, " agree that the sickness was incommunicable by ordinary contact from one person to another. A leper might transmit it to his children, or the mother of a leper's children might take it from him; but it was by no ordinary contact communicable from one person to another. . . . . Naaman, the leper, commanded the armies of Syria (2 Kings v. 1); Gehazi, with his leprosy that never should be cleansed (2 Kings v. 27), talked familiarly with the king of apostate Israel (2 Kings viii 5). And even where the law of Moses was in force, the stranger and the sojourner were expressly exempted from the ordinances relating to leprosy; which could not have been, had the

75

disease been contagious. How, moreover, should the Levitical priests, had the disease been this creeping infection, have ever themselves escaped it, obliged as they were by their very office to submit the leper to actual handling and closest examination?" It seems to us indisputable "that, if the disease is contagious, a very rare and critical concurrence of circumstances is required to develop the contagion." There were special reasons for selecting this disease from all others for exclusion from the camp. "The Egyptian and Syrian climates, but especially the rainless atmosphere of the former, are very prolific in skin diseases. . . . The Egyptian bondage, with its studied degradations and privations, and especially the work of the kiln under the Egyptian sun, must have had a frightful tendency to generate this class of disorders; hence Manetho (*Joseph. cont., Ap.* I. 26) asserts that the Egyptians drove out the Israelites as infected with leprosy—a strange reflex, perhaps, of the Mosaic narrative of the 'plagues' of Egypt, yet also probably containing a germ of truth. The sudden and total change of food, air, dwelling, and mode of life, caused by the Exodus, to this nation of newly emancipated slaves may possibly have had a further tendency to skin disorders, and novel and severe repressive measures may have been required in the desert-moving camp to secure the public health, or to allay the panic of infection. . . . In the contact of a dead body there was no notion of contagion, for the body the moment life was extinct was as much ceremonially unclean as in a state of decay. Why, then, in leprosy must we have recourse to a theory of contagion? It would perhaps be nearer the truth to say that uncleanness was imputed, rather to inspire the dread of contagion, than in order to check contamination as an actual process. . . . On the whole, though we decline to rest leprous defilement merely on popular notions of abhorrence, dread of contagion, and the like; yet a deference to them may be admitted to have been shown, especially at the time when the people were, from previous habits and associations, up to the moment of the actual Exodus, most strongly imbued with the scrupulous purity and refined ceremonial example of the Egyptians on these subjects."—*Smith's Dict. of the Bible.*

In each case mentioned in the text, "every leper, and every one that hath an issue, and whosoever is defiled by the dead,"—the person was put without the camp because of ceremonial pollution, not because of contagion. It was the will of God that the people should cultivate the most scrupulous physical cleanliness. In a camp composed of more than two millions of persons cleanliness was of the utmost importance. Dirt is the prolific parent of disease. Wise sanitary measures are the most certain means of insuring bodily strength and safety. *(a)* Two things in the text show that this sanitary measure was regarded as of great importance by the Lord.

1. *The universal application of the rule.* "*Every* leper, and *every* one that hath an issue, and *whosoever* is defiled by the dead: *both male and female* shall ye put out." No one whatever was exempted from its application. When Miriam, the prophetess, and sister of Moses and Aaron, was smitten with leprosy, she "was shut out from the camp seven days." With strict impartiality the rule was carried out.

2. *The sacred reason by which it was enforced.* "That they defile not their camps, in the midst whereof I dwell." The Lord is the God of cleanliness and health. All impurity is an abomination to Him. Purity of body, of home, of towns and cities, is well-pleasing to Him. As a condition of the Divine Presence, let us cultivate comprehensive and scrupulous cleanliness. Impurity separates from Him.

II. As a spiritual parable.

Ceremonial uncleanness was intended to illustrate spiritual uncleanness. The ceremonial purity which was insisted upon in the camp of Israel was typical of the spiritual purity which God requires of His people. By enacting that any one who had anything to do with the dead should be regarded as unclean, and put out of the camp, the Lord teaches that sin and death are not from Him, and cannot dwell with Him. And the loathsome and terrible disease of "leprosy was the outward and visible sign of the innermost spiritual corruption, the sacrament of death." The leper "was himself a dreadful parable of death,"—"a walking grave." Thus, parabolically, the text represents sin—

1. *As a defiling thing.* The sinner is morally unclean. Deeply did David feel this when he cried, "Wash me throughly from mine iniquity, and cleanse me from my sin. Purge me with hyssop, and I shall be clean; wash me, and I shall be whiter than snow. Create in me a clean heart, O God." Every sin proceeds from the corruption of the human heart, and tends to increase that corruption.

2. *As a deadly thing.* "The soul that sinneth it shall die." "The wages of sin is death." "Sin, when it is finished, bringeth forth death." Every sinful act tends to kill some element or power of the spiritual life. The life of the soul consists in truth and trust, righteousness and love, reverence and obedience, etc. Every lie spoken or acted is a blow aimed at the very life of truth in us. Every infidelity of which we are guilty tends to destroy our trust. So in relation to every element of the soul's life. Sin is deadly in its character and influence.

3. *As a separating thing.* The unclean were to be put out of the camp. Ceremonial uncleanness involved forfeiture of social privileges and of citizenship among the people of God for a time. "The man that shall be unclean, and shall not purify himself, that soul shall be cut off from among the congregation, because he hath defiled the sanctuary of the Lord." Where sin is cherished God will not dwell. (1) *The openly and persistently wicked should be expelled from the Church on earth.* (a) Because of their corrupt influence. "Know ye not that a little leaven leaveneth the whole lump?" 1 Cor. v. 6-13. (b) Because of the dishonour to God which their presence in the Church involves. He has promised to dwell in His Church, and to manifest Himself to His people as He does not unto the world. Matt. xviii. 20; John xiv. 21-23. And He demands that His people shall follow after entire holiness. He demands our entire consecration. "Know ye not that your body is the temple of the Holy Ghost which is in you, which ye have of God, and ye are not your own?" &c. "Know ye not that ye are the temple of God, and that the Spirit of God dwelleth in you? If any man defile the temple of God, him shall God destroy; for the temple of God is holy, which temple are ye." Our Lord "gave Himself for us, that He might redeem us from all iniquity, and purify unto Himself a peculiar people, zealous of good works." "A chosen generation, a royal priesthood, an holy nation, a peculiar people," etc. Such is the Divine pattern of the Church and people of God: and He is dishonoured when the openly and persistently wicked are allowed to remain in His Church. With such a church HE will not dwell. (b) (2) *The wicked will be excluded from the city of God above.* "There shall in no wise enter into it anything that defileth," etc. Rev. xxi. 27. All the citizens of that glorious realm "have washed their robes, and made them white in the blood of the Lamb." (c)

Conclusion.

1. *He who demands this purity has provided the means whereby we may attain unto it.* "The blood of Jesus Christ His Son cleanseth us from all sin."

2. *Let us diligently use the means which He has provided.* "Wash you, make you clean," etc. Isa. i. 16, 18. "Purifying their hearts by faith." "Let us cleanse ourselves from all filthiness of the flesh and spirit, perfecting holiness in the fear of God."

ILLUSTRATIONS.

(*a*) Cleanliness may be defined to be the emblem of purity of mind, and may be recommended under the three following heads; as it is a mark of politeness, as it produces affection, and as it bears analogy to chastity of sentiment. First, it is a mark of politeness, for it is universally agreed upon, that no one unadorned with this virtue can go into company without giving a manifold offence; the different nations of the world are as much distinguished by their cleanliness as by their arts and sciences; the more they are advanced in civilization the more they consult this part of politeness. Secondly, cleanliness may be said to be the foster-mother of affection. Beauty commonly produces love, but cleanliness preserves it. Age itself is not unamiable while it is preserved clean and unsullied; like a piece of metal constantly kept smooth and bright, we look on it with more pleasure than on a new vessel cankered with rust. I might further observe, that as cleanliness renders us agreeable to others, it makes us easy to ourselves, that it is an excellent preservative of health; and that several vices, both of mind and body, are inconsistent with the habit of it. In the third place, it bears a great analogy with chastity of sentiment, and naturally inspires refined feelings and passions; we find from experience, that through the prevalence of custom, the most vicious actions lose their horror by being made familiar to us. On the contrary, those who live in the neighbourhood of good examples fly from the first appearance of what is shocking; and thus pure and unsullied thoughts are naturally suggested to the mind by those objects that perpetually encompass us when they are beautiful and elegant in their kind. —*Addison.*

It is wonderful how views of life depend upon exercise and right management of the physical constitution. Nor is this, rightly looked at, any cause for perplexity, though it seems so at first; for though you might be inclined to view it as a degradation of our higher nature to find it so dependent on the lower, and hope and faith and energy resultant from a walk or early hours—yet, in fact, it is only a proof that all the laws of our manifold being are sacred, and that disobedience to them is punished by God. And the punishment in one department of our nature of the transgressions committed in the other—as, for instance, when mental gloom comes from uncleanliness or physical inertia, and, on the other hand, where ill-health ensues from envy or protracted doubt—is but one of many instances of the law of vicarious suffering. We are, as it were, two, and one suffers by what the other does.—*F. W. Robertson, M.A., Life and Letters.*

(*b*) They are deceived that think it is not necessary to purge out the great and gross offenders. The Church is the City of God, excommunication is the sword; it is the school of Christ, this is the rod, as the Apostle calleth it; it is the Temple of God, this is, as it were, the whip, to scourge out such as abuse it and themselves; it is the body of Christ, this is as a medicine to cure the diseases of it; it is the vine and sheepfold, this serveth to keep the foxes and wolves from it.— *W. Attersoll.*

(*c*) How real is that description of sin— "it defileth, it worketh abomination, it maketh a lie!" It is uncleanness, unloveliness, untruth! But it shall "in no wise enter" heaven. There "shall be nothing to hurt and to destroy." Moral evil cannot for a moment dwell in it. As though the leprosy of sin had struck too inextricably into the abode of man, had even contaminated the habitation of angels, we anticipate a scene purer than earth could afford however it were changed, purer than the heavens from which the angels fell. And when we can conceive of such a state, that which gives to law all its power of sway and yet debars its curse, that is heaven, the highest heaven, the heaven of heavens! We know it by this, we desire it for this, "wherein dwelleth righteousness!"—*R. W. Hamilton, LL.D., D.D.*

WHERE GOD DWELLS THERE MUST BE PURITY.

(*Verse 2.*)

"Put out of the camp every leper." God gave the people moral, civil, and sanitary laws. These in the context were partly sanitary. He would teach the people habits of cleanliness, which were essential to the health of the camp. Filth is a child of sin, and the fruitful parent of diseases which decimate mankind. But the text is something more than a sanitary precaution; for it is probable that leprosy was not contagious, and the ordinances respecting it did not apply to the sojourner and the stranger. Why then the injunction of the text? No doubt the great object was to enforce the ideas of purity and holiness, and to teach them that God cannot dwell among the sinful and impure.

Leprosy has ever been considered *a striking illustration of sin*. For instance,—1. *Sin, like leprosy, is a transgression of law*. All evils, physical as well as moral, arise from disregard of some law. Natural laws have their penalties; they cannot be broken with impunity. Cholera, fevers, and other terrible scourges that visit us, are penalties. We call them "visitations from God," and such they are in the sense of being penalties for breaking the laws that He has imposed on us. Intemperance, vice, etc., breed disease, poison the blood, ruin the body, and become curses to posterity. Leprosy was caused through disregard of the laws of health, and the Bible definition of sin is "the transgression of the law." 2. *Sin, like leprosy, is very loathsome and defiling*. Leprosy spreads over the whole body, destroying its beauty and vitality, and rendering it most repulsive in appearance. In this it is a meet emblem of sin, which corrupts, degrades, and defiles the soul of man. 3. *Sin, like leprosy, is incurable by man.* No human skill could help the leper. "Am I God to kill and to make alive?" cried the king of Israel when Naaman came to him. Only God could cure the disease. Sin, in like manner, baffles human skill. God alone can remove this curse and blight from the soul. No human priest, no work of merit, can affect the malady. The stain is too deep for anything but the blood of Christ to wash away. "God can save, and God alone." Other points might be mentioned; but the above are enough to show that leprosy is a striking type of sin, and to suggest the reason why God should select this "sickness of sicknesses," as Archbishop Trench calls it, "to testify against that out of which it and all other sicknesses grew, against sin, as not from Him and as grievous in His sight." We shall take the text as teaching the great fact that *where God dwells there must be purity*. "Put out of the camp every leper. . . . in the midst whereof I dwell." That God insists on purity as the condition of dwelling with us is the emphatic teaching of the whole Bible. What care was manifested to have clean and perfect animals for sacrifice! The Psalmist asks: "Who shall ascend into the hill of the Lord?" He replies: "He that hath clean hands and a pure heart," *i.e.*, whose life within and without is holy. His prayer is: "Create within me a clear heart." The teaching of the New Testament is the same: "Blessed are the pure in heart; for they shall see God." "Holiness, without which no man shall see the Lord.' "The wisdom that is from above is first pure." "Be ye holy; for I am holy." The grand design of the atonement is described as being "to redeem us from all iniquity, and purify unto Himself a peculiar people, zealous of good works." God insists on purity. Why?

I. **God Himself is pure, and cannot associate with the impure.**

Sin is hateful to Him. His very nature prohibits Him from being on terms of intimacy with any one living in sin. "God is light, and in Him is no darkness at all." The God of the Bible is *the only pure God*. This being His character, purity must distinguish those with whom He associates. Character divides the world—unites or separates men. So it does with God and man. He can only dwell with the pure. Purity attracts Him to us. If discipline is lax, if sin is tolerated by the Church, or by the individual Christian, God departs. It is not the large Church, or the intelligent or the wealthy one, that attracts Him, but the pure one. As the lightning passes by the polished marble and the carved wood to touch the iron or steel, because there it finds something akin to itself, so God passes by those to visit and to dwell with the pure, because in them He finds a character akin to His own.

II. **God will not, because He cannot, do any good to the impure.**

It would answer no good purpose for Him to dwell with them. The essence of impurity is to love sin; to love sin is to hate God; hating God shuts the door against the possibility of improvement in character. God will not dwell with man unless He can do him good. God with us is always equivalent to God blessing us. He wants us to be perfect as He Himself is perfect. This is His end in dwelling with us. Any one tolerating or living in sin would not appreciate the design of God and accept His blessing; and where He cannot bless, He will not come to dwell. Let us then "put out of the the camp every leper," everything that defileth; for the presence of God in our midst is of the utmost importance to us as His Church and people. *His presence is essential.*

1. *To our comfort as Churches and Christians.* What the shining sun is in nature His presence is with us—our brighness, our joy, etc.

2. *To our prosperity.* Without God in the midst the camp would have been helpless, would soon have become a prey to its enemies, and been broken up and scattered. God with His Church has been in all ages the secret of its power and success. His presence is the life of the ministry and of all Christian work. Without Him we are, and we can do, nothing. How to secure His presence ought to be the all-absorbing problem. He tells us how : " Put out of the camp every leper." Let us put from the Church and from our hearts all that is offensive to Him, and let us do His commands, and He will come. He has said so, and He is waiting to bless. God is not with us as we should like : let us search and see if there be any leper in the camp, any sin tolerated, and by His help let us put it out.

If to tolerate the leper was so bad to the camp, what must it have been to be the leper himself! If sin in the Christian is so terrible, what must it be to the altogether sinful! Let us think of it, and seek pardon at once through Christ.—*David Lloyd.*

GOD DWELLING WITH HIS PEOPLE.

(Verse 3.)

"In the midst whereof I dwell."

I. God is present with His people.

He was with Israel as He was not with the neighbouring nations. The Tabernacle—the Shekinah, etc. He led, supported, defended them, etc. He is everywhere present *influentially.* See Psa. cxxxix. 1-10. " He giveth to all life, and breath, and all things. He is not far from every one of us ; for in Him we live, and move, and have our being." " By Him all things consist." He is also present with His people *sympathetically.* They realise His presence, have fellowship with Him, etc. See Gen. xxviii. 16-17 ; Matt. xviii. 20; John xiv. 15-26 ; Ephes. iii. 16, 17 ; 1 John i. 3.

II. God is present "in the midst" of His people.

The Tabernacle was " in the midst " of the camp. Our Lord Jesus Christ is " in the midst " of His Church (Matt. xviii. 20). Like the sun in the midst of the planets.

1. *As the Centre of union.* The true union of the Church is not in oneness of doctrinal system or ecclesiastical polity, but in the vital fellowship of its members with the Lord.

2. *As the Source of blessing.* Life, light, growth, power, joy, beauty—all good flows from Him.

III. God's presence in the midst of His people should exert a great and blessed influence upon them.

It should prove :—

1. *A restraint from sin.* "The subject will do nothing unseemly in the presence of His prince, nor the child in the sight of his father. We are always in God's eye ; He beholdeth all things that are done of us."

2. *An incentive to holiness.* It is thus that it is brought forward in this place. Because the Lord dwelt in the camp it was to be kept pure. See also Deut. xxiii. 14; Ezek. xliii. 7-9.

3 *An encouragement to duty.* The

presence of so gracious a Master should cheer and strengthen us.

4. *An assurance of support in the trials of life.* He marks the strain which the spirit feels, and he will either temper its severity, or increase the spiritual strength. "I will fear no evil; for Thou art with me."

5. *An assurance of victory in the conflicts of life.* "Through God we shall do valiantly; for He shall tread down our enemies." See Psa. cxviii. 6-16; Rom. viii. 31-37.

6. *An assurance of perfect salvation.* "The Lord is in the midst of thee: thou shalt not see evil any more. The Lord thy God in the midst of thee is mighty; He will save, He will rejoice over thee with joy; He will rest in His love, He will joy over thee with singing."

Fraud and Forgiveness.

(*Verses* 5-8.)

In these verses we have another measure which was instituted to secure the sanctity of the congregation. Wrong done by one man against another is here legislated for in a spirit of just severity. Consider—

I. The sin of fraud.

"When a man or woman shall commit any sin that men commit," etc. *Lit.*—"Commit one of all the transgressions of man." *Keil* and *Del.* "Do one of the sins of men,"—one of the sins occurring amongst men. The reference is to sins of dishonesty or fraud. Fraud is here represented—

1. *As assuming many forms.* "Any sin that men commit." "One of all the transgressions of man." Our text is supplementary to the law on this matter as stated in Leviticus vi. 2, 3, and there various forms of this sin are stated. (1) Fraud in the matter of goods entrusted to the keeping of another. (2) In business transactions. (3) In seizing by force that which belongs to another. (4) In wronging another by means of deceit. (5) In the finder of lost property injuring the loser by falsehood. And in our own age fraud assumes many forms, and is widely prevalent. The employer who does not pay just wages to those in his service is guilty of it. (Prov. xxii. 16; Isa. iii. 14, 15: Colos. iv. 1; Isa. v. 4.) So also is the servant or workman who squanders the time for which his employer pays him; in so doing he defrauds his employer. The trader who takes an unfair advantage of his customer, which he calls by some specious name, *e.g.*, "practice of the trade," etc.; the broker or speculator or manager who induces persons to invest their money in unreliable or doubtful enterprizes; the person who contracts a debt without the sincere intention and reasonable prospect of paying it—all these, and others, are guilty of fraud. (*a*)

2. *As a wrong done to God.* "To do a trespass against the Lord." *Keil* and *Del.*: "To commit unfaithfulness against Jehovah." He who is guilty of any act of fraud against his neighbour commits sin against God. All sin is against Him. When Joseph was tempted to sin against Potiphar, his master, he said, "How can I do this great wickedness, and sin against God?" And David after he had committed the blackest injuries against Uriah the Hittite and others, when brought to repentance cried, "Against Thee, Thee only, have I sinned; and done evil in Thy sight." As viewed in their social relations, he was deeply sensible of the greatness of his crimes; but so overwhelming was his sense of their enormity as committed against God, as to render the former view of them comparatively unimportant. (*b*) How grievous a thing, then, is dishonesty of any kind! Let us strive to be utterly free from it. (1 Thess. iv. 6.) Let us cultivate the most thorough uprightness in all our relations and dealings with each other.

II. The conditions of its forgiveness.

1. *Consciousness of guilt.* "The

expression, 'that person be guilty,' does not merely refer to his actual criminality; but to his consciousness of guilt respecting it: for this case must be distinguished from that of a person detected in dishonesty which he attempted to conceal."—*Scott.* Without the consciousness of guilt the other conditions of forgiveness could not be truly complied with.

2. *Confession.* "Then they shall confess their sin which they have done." This is an essential condition of forgiveness. (Psa. xxxii. 5; Prov. xxviii. 13; 1 John i. 9.) To be of any avail confession must be sincere, must proceed from the heart. It is the natural expression of penitence. Where true penitence is, hearty confession will be welcomed as a relief, not shunned as a burden or regarded as an exaction. And without true penitence forgiveness of sin is a crime, an injury to society and even to the offender himself. Sincere penitence must utter itself in confession. Such confession is not the wail of despair, but the cry of sorrow and of hope. In itself it relieves the burdened and troubled soul, and it leads to the joy and peace of forgiveness. *(c)*

3. *Restitution.* "And He shall recompense his trespass with the principal thereof, and add unto it the fifth part thereof, and give it unto him against whom he hath trespassed. But if the man have no kinsman to recompense the trespass unto, let the trespass be recompensed unto the Lord, to the priest." Restitution is an act of justice by which we restore to another that of which we have deprived him, or make him adequate compensation for the same. In this law it is enacted that the sum of which any one has been defrauded shall be restored, with the addition of one-fifth of its value. Restitution is essential to remission of sin; for where restitution is not made it is evident that sincere repentance is absent. See Ezek. xviii. 7, 9, 12, 13. xxxiii. 15. The true penitent will find it an unspeakable relief if he is able in any degree to repair the wrong which he has done. There was no exemption or escape from this law. If the person defrauded were deceased, restitution must be made to his kinsman (Heb. Goël); and if there were no kinsman, to the priest as the representative of Jehovah. The priests were the Lord's receivers. In every case the property which was dishonestly acquired must be given up, restitution must be made, or the sin would not be forgiven. And this is still true. If we have acquired anything by dishonest means let us make full and speedy restitution for the same, even if by so doing we should be reduced to utter penury. Better extreme poverty in our circumstances with a clear conscience and an approving God, than the greatest wealth with a guilty conscience and a condemning God. "What is not our property will never be our profit." And restitution should be made promptly. Every minute of unnecessary delay increases the guilt of the wrong-doer. *(d)*

4. *Sacrifice.* In addition to making restitution the offender was commanded to offer "the ram of the atonement, whereby an atonement shall be made for him." He who was guilty of fraud wronged not only his fellow-man, but God also; and therefore, in order that he might be forgiven, he must draw near to God with a sacrifice, and so make atonement for his sin. The ram was for the "trespass-offering," which differed from the sin-offering. In each offering the victim was a ram; but "the sin-offering looked more to the guilt of the sin done, irrespective of its consequences, while the trespass-offering looked to the evil consequences of sin, either against the service of God or against man, and to the duty of atonement, as far as atonement was possible." This arrangement would tend to set forth the great evil of sin as an offence to God Himself. It would also meet a great need of the penitent heart, which cries out for atonement for its sin. When all these things were accomplished the offender was held to be cleared from the guilt of his offence, as is stated in ver. 8—

"whereby an atonement shall be made for him," Lit. " which shall clear him of guilt as to it," *i.e.*, as to the trespass. For us the One Offering has been made which perfects all others. And if we have wronged or defrauded any one, and are conscious of our guilt, we have but to make confession and restitution for the same, with faith in the merits and mediation of Jesus Christ, and full forgiveness will be ours.

Conclusion.
1. *Let those who have injured others make speedy and full confession and restitution.*
2. *Let us all cultivate the most thorough integrity and uprightness in our whole life and conduct.* " All things whatsoever ye would that men should do to you, do ye even so to them: for this is the law and the prophets."

ILLUSTRATIONS.

(*a*) The rules which God has given us forbid every wish, much more every attempt, to defraud, or deceive our neighbour. They render it highly criminal for the seller to take the smallest advantage of the ignorance, inexperience, or simplicity of his customers; or to conceal any defect which he may have discovered in the article of which he wishes to dispose. They render it equally criminal for the buyer to wish or attempt to take any advantage of the seller, either by exaggerating the defects of his merchandise, or by falsely pretending that he does not wish to purchase. They render it highly criminal for any one to contract debts, when he has no sufficient reason to believe that he shall be able to discharge them; or to persuade another to become responsible for his debts, when he has reason to suspect that his sponsor will in consequence suffer loss. In a word, they require us to put ourselves in the place of our neighbour, to be as willing to defraud him as to be defrauded ourselves; to be as careful of his property and interest, as of our own; to think no more of enriching ourselves at his expense, than we should think of robbing our left hand with our right. They require us, in all our transactions, to act as we should do if our fellow creatures could see our hearts; for though they cannot see them, yet God can, and does see them; He is both witness and judge between us and our neighbour in every transation, and surely His eye ought to be as effectual in regulating our conduct as would the eye of our fellow creatures, could they, like Him, search the heart. . . . . These rules evidently forbid us to take any advantage of the necessities or imprudence of those whom we employ, and require us to give them a prompt and adequate compensation for their services; and on the other hand, they make it the duty of all who are employed, to be as faithful to the interests of their employers as to their own, and to avoid defrauding them of any portion of their time by idleness, or of their property by negligence, as they would avoid theft or robbery.—*E. Payson, D.D.*

(*b*) All sin is against *God.* There are some sins which are exclusively against God; there are others which are against man, but no sin can be exclusively against man. This point is fraught with the most profound significance. Let us put it in this form: *Whoever sins against man sins against God.* Then how *sacred* are all human interests! How solemn are all human relations! You cannot harm a widow's child without sinning against God; you cannot sneer at a good man without touching the sensibilities of your heavenly Father; you cannot injure your wife or husband or friend without, in the degree of that injury, insulting Him who is the Creator and Redeemer of human kind. Let it be known then, in all the breadth and force of its significance, that every blow struck against humanity is a blow struck against God! It will be a token of solid progress when man has more respect for man. We have held manhood too cheaply. We have not sufficiently pondered the great fact that every man sustains a vital relation to the great Creator of all life, and that everything which appertains to man has also an immediate relation to God. Would that we could thunder these doctrines into the ear of all despotism; they would make the throne of tyranny tremble at its foundations; they would blanch every tyrant's cheek, and wither the power of every despot. This they will assuredly attain. As Christianity is developed, the true feeling of Christianity will be more and more understood; and they who once saw no image higher than human on the countenance of mankind, shall on that same countenance see the image and super-cription of Him who is infinite in pity and infinite in love.—*Jos. Parker, D.D.*

(*c*) The *confession* of sin against a brother is a reasonable condition of receiving a brother's forgiveness. The confession of sin to God is of the essence of repentance and faith, and this does not interfere with the grand truth that a man is justified by faith only. It is a sign that momentous spiritual changes are going on in a man when he can bring his sin into the presence of the Holy God, and see it in the light of perfect law and perfect sacrifice. The effort to do so tears up the roots of evil desire, and crucifies the world with its affections. It is the sublime peculiarity of Christianity that a sinner can take his sins to God and find mercy, even amid the burning light of that most Holy Presence. More than this, one man may help another to make this confession, to see himself and judge of himself more accurately than he would do, in the solation and awfulness of his own repentance. The danger of self-deceit and self-flattery is great. The experience of the devout and impartial Christian who knows something of human nature, and has realised the full assurance of faith, may be found of the greatest avail in the struggle of the soul heavenwards. All Churches and all Christians admit this great advantage.—*H. R. Reynolds, D.D.*

(*d*) He must bring forth fruits meet for repentance. In other words, he must make restitution to every one whom he has injured, or defrauded, so far as he can recollect who they are—this is indispensable. There is no repentance, and, of course, no forgiveness without it. How can a man repent of iniquity, who still retains the wages of iniquity? It is impossible. If he feels any sorrow, it is occasioned, not by hatred of his sin, but by fear of the consequences. Restitution, then, must be made, or the offender must perish. If thou bring thy gift to the altar, says our Saviour, and there rememberest that thy brother has aught against thee, that is, any reason to complain of thee, go thy way, first be reconciled to thy brother, and then come and offer thy gift. The altar was then the place to which the worshippers of God brought their thank-offerings, gifts, and sacrifices for sin. Christ, we are told, is now our altar, and to this altar we must bring our prayers, our praises, our services. But he plainly intimates that he will accept no gift of us, receive no thanks from us, listen to none of our prayers, so long as we neglect to make satisfaction to those whom we have injured. And in vain shall we attempt to atone for neglecting this duty, by performing others, by contributing to the promotion of religious objects, or by liberality to the poor; for God has said, I hate robbery for burnt offering; that is, I hate, I will not receive an offering, which was unjustly acquired. There is, then, no way but to make restitution; and this every real Christian will make to the utmost of his ability. Agreeably, we hear Zaccheus, the publican, saying as soon as he became a Christian, "If I have wronged any man, I restore him fourfold." I am aware that this is a most disagreeable duty. Nothing can be harder, or more painful to our proud hearts. But it will be far easier to perform it, than to suffer the consequences of neglecting it. If it is not performed, our souls must perish, as sure as the Word of God is true; and in consequence of indulging a false shame, we shall be overwhelmed with shame and everlasting contempt. Even as it respects our interest in this world only, we had better, far better, put a blazing fire-brand into the midst of our possessions, than retain among them the smallest particle of gain, which was not fairly obtained; for it will bring the curse of God upon us, and upon all the works of our hands.—*E. Payson, D.D.*

The Maintenance of the Ministry.

(*Verses* 9, 10.)

In the preceding verses it was enacted that, in case of fraud, restitution should be made to the injured person, and, if he were deceased, to his Goël, and, if there were no Goël, to the priest, who should offer the trespass offering for the wrong-doer. The restitution in this case belonged to the priest. And in these verses other perquisites of the officiating priests are mentioned. In this and other ways provision was made for their temporal support. It was of the first importance that such provision should be made; for the proper discharge of their duties precluded them from engaging in the ordinary activities of life. "At first," says Professor Plumtre, "the small number of the priests must have made the work almost unintermittent, and even when the system of rotation had been adopted, the periodical absences from home could not fail to be disturbing and injurious, had they been dependent on their own labours. The serenity of the priestly character would have been disturbed had they had to look for support to the lower industries. It may have been intended that their time, when not liturgically employed, should be given to the study of the Law, or to instructing others in it. On these grounds, therefore, a distinct provision was made for them. This consisted (1) Of one-tenth of the tithes which the people paid to the Levites, one per cent., *i.e.*, on the whole produce of the country (Numb. xviii. 26-28). (2) Of a special tithe every third year (Deut. xiv. 28, xxvi. 12). (3) Of the redemption money paid at the fixed rate of five shekels a head, for the first-born of man or beast (Num. xviii. 14-19). (4) Of the redemption money paid in like manner for men or things specially dedicated to the Lord (Lev. xxvii). (5) Of spoil, captives, cattle, and the like, taken in war (Num. xxxi. 25-47). (6) Of what may be described as the perquisites of their sacrificial functions, the shew-bread, the flesh of the burnt-offerings, peace-offerings, trespass-offerings (Num. xviii. 8-14 ; Lev. vi. 26, 29 ; vii. 6-10), and, in particular, the heave-shoulder and wave-breast (Lev. x. 12-15). (7) Of an undefined amount of the first-fruits of corn, wine, and oil (Ex. xxiii. 19 ; Lev. ii. 14 ; Deut. xxvi. 1-10). (8) On their settlement in Canaan the priestly families had thirteen cities assigned them, with "suburbs" or pasture grounds for their flocks (Josh. xxi. 13-19). These provisions were obviously intended to secure the religion of Israel against the dangers of a caste of pauper priests, needy and dependent, and unable to bear their witness to the true faith. They were, on the other hand, as far as possible removed from the condition of a wealthy order." In the foregoing sources of emolument, only the chief ones are given. The "offering" mentioned in the text is given in the margin as "heave-offering." The Hebrew is תְּרוּמָה an *oblation*, used here, says Fuerst, " of holy gifts generally." " The reference is to dedicatory offerings, first-fruits, and such like."—*Keil and Del*. These were to be the property of the officiating priests. These arrangements suggest *the obligation of the Church to adequately support its ministry*. We rest this obligation—

I. On the ground of honesty.

The physician and the solicitor are paid, and that handsomely, for their attention and counsel, as a matter of duty. The Christian minister has equally a claim that his services shall be remunerated by those who have the benefit of them. Yet professedly Christian people are far less conscientious in paying for ministerial than they are for legal and medical services. The testimony of our Lord and of His apostles as to this obligation is unmistakeably clear. (See Matt. x. 9, 10; Luke x. 7 ; 1 Cor. ix. 7-14; Gal. vi. 6 ; 1 Tim. v. 17, 18.) *(a)*

II. On the ground of interest.

The Christian congregation that does not adequately support its minister is not wisely mindful of its own best interests.

1. *The services of the true minister of Christ are of the greatest benefit to the Church and to the world.* His ministry tends to quicken thought on the most important and sublime subjects, to educate the conscience aright, to arouse the will to true and earnest action, and to lead the soul to the great Source of life and light.

2. *The adequate maintenance of the ministry is indispensable to its efficiency.* When his mind is harassed with temporal anxieties, or when much of his time is occupied with matters not pertaining to his ministry, in order to provide for the wants of his family, the minister is prevented from rendering the highest service of which he is capable. The ministry should be the great business of his life, and his mind should be free to prosecute it. Hence—

3. *If Christians consult their own interests they will see to it that their ministers are adequately maintained.* The money which is so spent will prove a most remunerative investment. *(b)*

Conclusion.

1. *Let Churches recognise their interest and heartily do their duty in this respect.*

2. *Let ministers recognise the importance of their duties, and endeavour to faithfully perform them.* "It is great reason that he which looketh for his hire should do his work ; and that he which intendeth to live of the Gospel of Christ, should preach to others the Gospel of Christ." Let us strive to be "scribes instructed unto the kingdom of heaven," etc. (Matt. xiii. 52). "Study to show thyself approved unto God," etc. (2 Tim. ii. 15).

ILLUSTRATIONS.

(a) No true minister will ever preach with an eye to secular results. All mercenary considerations will be borne down and engulfed by the ever-deepening current of spiritual sympathies and aims. His main purpose will be not to acquire wealth, but to win souls. Still, in common with all men, he has his physical and domestic wants. Food, raiment, and a home, are as necessary to his existence as to that of any man; and according to the present arrangements of society, these are only supplied by money. Whence is he to receive this? As a general rule, it comes only as the reward of labour. He labours. The office of a true minister is no sinecure; there is no work so arduous as his; it is the labour, not of limbs, but of brain and heart; it is a constant draw upon the very fountains of nervous energy. Nor is there any work so useful to society. In the reason of things, therefore, has any worker a stronger claim to secular support than he? If his labour is the most arduous and the most useful, ought it not to secure the most ample secular returns? Paul recognises and enforces this natural and common-sense claim. (1 Cor. ix. 7, 9, 11, 14.)

There are men who receive and expect large services from their minister, and who make little or no return. For a paltry pound or two per annum, he must preach to them thrice per week, pay them frequent pastoral visits, or else they set up their complaints against him, and seek to spread a spirit of dissatisfaction through his sphere. There are families in connection with congregations who spend more on perfumery, or on toys for their children, than to support the man who is giving the best energies of his cultivated mind to save their souls. A man takes a pew in a church, pays his five or six pounds per annum,—a less sum than he pays his scullery-maid,—and for that he expects twelve months' preaching, and great pastoral attention. What is still worse—still more unreasonable, he regards the paltry sum he subscribes rather as a *charity* than a debt. Charity, indeed! Call the money you pay to your grocer, draper, physician, or landlord, charity; but in the name of all that is true in reason and justice, don't call what you tender to the man to whom you owe your best ideas, your holiest impressions—who gives to you the choicest products of his educated and sanctified intellect, *charity*. It is he that shows charity, not you; your gold is a miserable compensation for the results of his sweating brain and ever-anxious heart.—*D. Thomas, D.D.*

(b) As the Church dependeth upon them for their allowance, so they depend upon her for their maintenance. Thus the Pastor and the people do feed one another, as a flock of sheep nourisheth the shepherd, who eateth the milk of them, and clotheth himself with the wool of them; and again the shepherd coucheth them into green pastures, and leadeth them by the still waters. The people feed him with the bread of this life; he feedeth them with the bread of everlasting life. They minister to him in carnal things; he to them in spiritual things. They cannot lack him in regard of their souls; he cannot be without them in regard of his body. Thus then they do feed one another, or at least ought to do. If he receive food of them, and give none unto them again, he robbeth them of their goods, and murdereth their souls. If they on the other side receive food of him, so that they be taught of him, and yet make him not partaker of a part of their goods, they rob him, and cause him to depart from them, and so become murderers of their own souls, as if they did lay violent hands upon themselves, or rather as if they did famish themselves by refusing bread provided for them; inasmuch as "where vision ceaseth, there people perish." (Prov. xxix. 18.)—*W. Attersoll.*

The Trial of the Suspected Wife

(*Verses* 11-31.)

We have here another law intended to secure the sanctity of the Israelites, by maintaining fidelity in conjugal relations, and removing even the suspicion of adultery from amongst them. "The chastity of females," says Dean Milman, "was guarded by statutes, which, however severe and cruel according to modern notions, were wise and merciful in that state of society. Poems and travels have familiarised us with the horrible atrocities committed by the blind jealousy of Eastern husbands. By substituting a judicial process for the wild and hurried justice of the offended party, the guilty suffered a death, probably, less inhuman; the innocent might escape. The convicted adulterer and adulteress were stoned to death. Even the incontinence of a female before marriage, if detected at the time of her nuptials, which was almost inevitable, underwent the same penalty with that of the adulteress. Where the case was not clear, the female suspected of infidelity might be summoned to a most awful ordeal. She was to be acquitted or condemned by God Himself, whose actual interposition was promised by His daring law-giver. . . . What guilty woman, if she had courage to confront, would have the command of countenance, firmness and resolution, to go through all this slow, searching, and terrific the process, and finally expose herself to shame and agony, far worse than death? No doubt, cases where this trial was undergone were rare; yet the confidence of the legislator in the Divine interference can hardly be questioned; for had such an institution fallen into contempt by its failure in any one instance, his whole law and religion would have been shaken to its foundation." "We do not read of any instance in which this ordeal was resorted to; a fact which may be explained either (with the Jews) as a proof of its efficacy, since the guilty could not be brought to face its terrors at all, and avoided them by confession; or more probably by the licence of divorce tolerated by the law of Moses. Since a husband could put away his wife at pleasure, a jealous man would naturally prefer to take this course with a suspected wife rather than to call public attention to his own shame by having recourse to the trial of jealousy. The Talmud states that the trial lapsed into disuse forty years before the destruction of Jerusalem; and that because the crime of adultery was so common amongst men that God would no longer inflict the curses here named upon women (cf. Hos. iv. 14).—*Speaker's Commentary.*

A critical examination and exposition of the details of the process of trial will be found in Keil and Del., *in loco.* Let us consider the principal moral truths which are here illustrated.

I. Confidence in conjugal relations is of great importance.

This awful ordeal was instituted for cases where this confidence was lost, and the proof of guilt was lacking. Suspicion and jealousy are terrible evils. "Suspicion," says Babington, "is the cut-throat and poison of all love and friendship." And in proportion to the intensity of the love will be the anguish of suspicion in respect to the object of the love.

"Where love is great, the littlest doubts are fear;
Where little fear grows great, great love is there." *Shakespeare.*

"Jealousy, each other passion's calm,
To thee, thou conflagration of the soul!
Thou king of torments! thou grand counterpoise
For all the transports beauty can inspire." *Young.*

And Hannah More:
"O, jealousy,
Thou ugliest fiend of hell! thy deadly venom
Preys on my vitals, turns the healthful hue
Of my fresh cheek to haggard sallowness,
And drinks my spirit up." (*a*)

"Jealousy," says Solomon, "is the rage of a man." "Jealousy is cruel as the grave; the coals thereof are coals of fire, a most vehement flame." This dread ordeal was intended as a remedy for suspicion and jealousy. And no one can examine it without perceiving that, if it was severe, it was also calculated to be thoroughly effective. See how searching, solemn, and stern it is.

1. *The whole trial was to take place in the sight of God* (ver. 16).

2. *The dread appeal was made to the Omniscient and Almighty* (ver. 21).

3. *The appeal was weighted by the most terrible imprecations* (vers. 21, 22).

4. *It was solemnly declared in the law that if the woman were guilty these imprecations would be fulfilled* (ver. 27).

5. *The appeal was to be solemnly ratified by the suspected woman.* "The woman shall say, Amen, Amen." "Twice," says Trapp; "to show the fervency of her zeal, the innocency of her cause, the uprightness of her conscience, and the purity of her heart." Surely, if any suspected wife went through so solemn and terrible an ordeal, the effect would be completely to clear the mind of her husband from the least taint of suspicion, and to restore the brightness of her reputation. The sternness of this ordeal for the removal of suspicion impressively sets forth the importance of con-

fidence between husband and wife. Destroy this confidence; and what ought to be one of the holiest and most lasting bonds is snapped asunder, the helpfulness and peace of the family are banished for ever, and, if the evil prevail to any considerable extent, the foundations of the civil commonwealth will be gradually but certainly undermined.

II. Adultery is a sin of the greatest enormity.

This dreadful ordeal, which was intended to prevent it, shows how great was its heinousness in the Divine estimation. This is expressed—

1. *In the abasement of the suspected woman.* The "barley meal" of which the offering was composed, the "earthen vessel" which contained the water, and "the dust" that was put into the water, indicate a state of deep humiliation and disgrace. The absence from the offering of oil, the symbol of the gifts and graces of the Holy Spirit, and of frankincense, the symbol of prayer, also proclaimed her questionable repute and the suspicion with which she was regarded. In like manner the "uncovering of the woman's head" was indicative of the loss of woman's best ornament, chastity and fidelity in the marriage relation.

2. *In the terrible punishment which came upon the guilty.* "If she be defiled, and have done trespass against her husband, the water that causeth the curse shall enter into her, and become bitter, and her belly shall swell, and her thigh shall rot: and the woman shall be a curse among her people."— Keil and Del. translate, "her hip vanish." And Adam Clarke: "her thigh fall." This ordeal was made so terrible that the dread of it might effectually prevent the wives in Israel from the least violation of their fidelity to their husbands. It remains as an impressive proclamation of the utter abhorence with which God regards the sin of adultery. It is a sin against God; it inflicts the most grievous and intolerable injury upon the husband; it is an unmitigated blight and bane upon the family; and it is a wrong to society generally. The most terrible condemnations are pronounced upon it in the Sacred Word. (See Lev. xx. 10; Mal. iii. 5; 1 Cor. vi. 9, 10; Heb. xiii. 4.)

III. The punishment of sin is closely related to the sin itself.

"It cannot be determined with any certainty what was the nature of the disease threatened in this curse. . . . At any rate, the idea of the curse is this: Δἰ ὧν γὰρ ἡ ἁμαρτία διὰ τούτων ἡ τιμωρία ('the punishment shall come from the same source as the sin,' *Theodoret*). The punishment was to answer exactly to the crime, and to fall upon those bodily organs which had been the instruments of the woman's sin, viz., the organs of child-bearing."— *Keil and Del.* The punishment came in those portions of her body which she had abused. "David sinned in committing adultery with the wife of Uriah, his faithful servant, and destroyed him with the sword of the Ammonites; he is paid home, and punished in his own kind; for God, by way of rewarding him and serving him as he had served others, as a just judge, doth raise up evil against him out of his own house. His own sons break out into the same sins, and he kindleth such a fire in his own family, that they rise up against him, and one against another. Absalom spreadeth a tent, and lieth with his father's concubines, in the sight of all Israel. Ammon deflowereth his sister Tamar; to revenge this, Absalom killeth his own brother."—*Attersoll.* (See Judg. i. 6-7; Esth. vii. 10; Matt. vii. 1-2.) "Whatsoever a man soweth that shall he also reap. For he that soweth to his flesh shall of the flesh reap corruption." (*b*)

IV. God will bring to light the secret sins of men.

If the suspected woman were guilty, after this ordeal her guilt would be made manifest. All sins are known unto Him. "For His eyes are upon the ways of man, and He seeth all his goings. There is no darkness, nor shadow of death, where the workers of iniquity may hide themselves." "Thou hast set our iniquities before Thee, our secret sins in the light of Thy countenance." Sometimes hidden sins are strangely discovered in this life and world. (c). The great day will reveal all. "For God shall bring every work into judgment, with every secret thing, whether it be good, or whether it be evil." "The day when God shall judge the secrets of men by Jesus Christ." In that day the dark secrets of evil will be all brought to light.

V. God will assuredly vindicate the innocent who have suffered from suspicion or slander.

In this case the vindication was most complete. "If the woman be not defiled, but be clean : then she shall be free, and shall conceive seed." "If not guilty after such a trial," says Adam Clarke, "she had great honour ; and, according to the rabbins, became strong, healthy, and fruitful ; for if she was before barren, she now began to bear children ; if before she had only daughters, she now began to have sons; if before she had hard travail, she now had easy ; in a word, she was blessed in her body, her soul, and her substance." Thus to the innocent there was no terror in this stern ordeal. It was rather a blessing to them, if by any means they had come to be regarded with suspicion by their husbands; for by means of it such suspicions would be removed, and their fidelity and honour vindicated and exalted. And God will, sooner or later, splendidly vindicate all who suffer from misrepresentation, slander, or false accusation.

Conclusion.

"We must all appear before the judgment seat of Christ," etc. Let us seek by the grace of God to be ready for that great and awful tribunal.

ILLUSTRATIONS.

(a) Jealousy is the bane and poison of marriage, and maketh that sociable life to be uncomfortable, and mingleth it with worse than gall and wormwood. Jealousy, therefore, is a grief of mind, arising from hence, that another is judged to enjoy that which we desire to have wholly and properly as our own, and none beside us to possess any part with us. Here, then, we cannot abide any community, but hate it as our enemy and the right cause of this jealousy. Or we may describe it otherwise on this manner : It is an affection proceeding from fear to have that communicated to another, which we challenge and covet to retain as peculiar and proper to ourselves alone. From hence it appeareth, farther, what the nature of jealousy is, to wit, that it is mixed and compounded, partly of love, partly of fear, and partly of anger. Of love, which admitteth no fellow-partner in the thing he loveth : for as the king will suffer no companion to be equal unto him, or partaker with him in his kingdom, so will the husband suffer no co-rival to mate him in his love. Of fear, lest another enjoy the use of that which we cannot abide or suffer he should enjoy. Of anger, whereby it cometh to pass, that he is ready to break out to seek revenge and punishment upon him that hath offended him that way.—*W. Attersoll.*

Yet is there one more cursed than they all,
That canker worm, that monster, Jealousy,
Which eats the heart and feeds upon the gall,
Turning all love's delight to misery,
Through fear of losing his felicity.

Nor ever is he wont on aught to feed
But toads and frogs (his pasture poisonous),
Which, in his cold complexion, do breed
A filthy blood, or humour rancorous,
Matter of doubt and dread suspicious,
That doth with cureless care consume the heart,
Corrupt the stomach with gall vicious,
Cross-cuts the liver with eternal smart,
And doth transfix the soul with death's eternal dart.
—*Edmund Spenser.*

(b) The punishment of sin is not an arbitrary infliction, but it is a necessary law. Penalty is not a direct interference, but a genuine child of the transgression. We receive the things that we have done. There is a dreadful coercion in our own iniquities. There is an inevitable congruity between the deed and its consequences. There is an awful germ of identity in the seed and in the fruit. We recognise the sown wind when we are reaping the harvest whirlwind. We feel that it is we who have winged the very arrows that eat into our hearts like fire. It needs no gathered lightnings—no Divine intervention—no miraculous messenger to avenge in us God's violated laws; they avenge themselves. . . . . Take disease as one form of the working of this inevitable law—not always, of course, the direct result of sin ; yet how much of disease is directly due to dirt, neglect, folly, ignorance —the infected blood, the inherited instincts of this sad world. But are there not some diseases, and those the most terrible which I have known, which do spring directly, immediately, exclusively, solely, from violence of God's law? Is not madness very often such a disease? Is there not at this moment many a degraded lunatic who never would have been such but for repeated transgressions of God's known will? Is there not in the very life-blood of millions, a hereditary taint blighting the healthy, poisoning, as with a fury's breath, the flower of their happiness, and breaking out afresh in new generations, which has its sole source and origin in uncleanliness? Is there not, too, an executioner of justice which God has told off to wait upon drunkenness, which would cease if drunkenness ceased to exist? It is God's warning against that fearful intemperance against which senates will not fight, and against which they who love their fellows fight as yet in vain.—*F. W. Farrer, D.D.*

(*c*) When Dr. Donne, afterwards Dean of St. Paul's, took possession of the first living he ever had, he walked into the churchyard as the sexton was digging a grave; and on his throwing up a skull, the doctor took it into his hands to indulge in serious contemplation. On looking at it, he found a headless nail sticking in the temple, which he secretly drew out, and wrapped in the corner of his handkerchief. He then asked the grave-digger, whether he knew whose skull it was? He said he did; adding, it had been a man's who kept a brandy shop; a drunken fellow, who, one night, having taken two quarts of ardent spirits, was found dead in his bed the next morning. "Had he a wife?" "Yes." "Is she living?" "Yes." "What character does she bear?" "A very good one; only her neighbours reflect on her because she married the day after her husband was buried." This was enough for the doctor, who, in the course of visiting his parishioners, called on her; he asked her several questions, and, among others, of what sickness her husband died. She giving him the same account, he suddenly opened the handkerchief, and cried, in an authoritative voice, "Woman, do you know this nail?" She was struck with horror at the unexpected question, instantly acknowledged that she had murdered her husband; and was afterwards tried and executed.—*Biblical Museum.*

HINTS ON THE LAW OF JEALOUSIES.
(*Verse 29.*)

Describe trial by ordeal. This existed among all primitive nations, and modern ones that are yet in a primitive state. Nations have their infancy; this belongs to that state in their existence. Israel had seen this in Egypt. God permits them to use it; only stipulating that water only should be used, so that no innocent one should suffer, and that all should see that the guilty was detected by Him. Why should He permit this?

1. To show the importance He attaches to domestic morality.

2. To teach them that He was looking on and knowing their most secret sins.

3. To train them to cultivate a tender conscience, and to acknowledge its authority.

4. To restore confidence between husband and wife where it was wrongly shaken.

5. Though this custom is done away with, God is still the same, and will bring all secret sin into the light.—*David Lloyd.*

CHAPTER VI.

THE VOW OF THE NAZARITE, OR ACCEPTABLE CONSECRATION TO GOD.
(*Verses 1-8.*)

"The previous chapter has provided for the exclusion from the pale of God's people of certain forms of guilt and defilement. The present one offers an opening to that zeal for God which, not content with observing what is obligatory, seeks for higher and stricter modes of self-dedication. Thus the law of the Nazarite is appropriately added to other enactments which concern the sanctity of the holy nation. That sanctity found its highest expression in the Nazarite vow, which was the voluntary adoption for a time of obligations resembling, and indeed in some particulars exceeding, those under which the priests were placed."—*Speaker's Comm.*

Nazarite, or more properly, Nazirite (Heb. נָזִיר from נָזַר *to separate*), signifies a separated one, then ; one consecrated, especially by a vow.

From the mode in which the law is introduced in ver. 2, it is evident that Nazaritism was not a new institution, but was already familiar to the people. Moses "appears to have done no more than ordain such regulations for the vow of the Nazarite of days, as brought it under the cognizance of the priest, and into harmony with the general system of religious observance. It is doubted, in regard to Nazaritism in general, whether it was of native or foreign origin. . . . Winer justly observes that the points of resemblance between the Nazarite vow and heathen customs are too fragmentary and indefinite to furnish a safe foundation for an argument in favour of a foreign origin for the former."

Nazarites were of two kinds, and were styled respectively, "Nazarites of days," and "perpetual Nazarites." The former took the vow only for a limited and specified time. The Sacred Scriptures are silent as to the length of time for which the vow was taken. "According to *Nazir*, the usual time was thirty days, but double vows for sixty days, and treble vows for a hundred days, were sometimes made." Of perpetual Nazarites, three are mentioned in the Scriptures : Sampson, Samuel, and John the Baptist. The laws which are laid down in this chapter apply to those who were Nazarites for a limited period only, not to those who were Nazarites for life.

On the moral significance of Nazaritism we cannot do better than transcribe the remarks of the Rev. S. Clark, M.A., in Smith's *Dict. of the Bible*. "The meaning of the Nazarite vow has been regarded in different lights. Some consider it as a symbolical expression of the Divine nature working in man, and deny that it involved anything of a strictly ascetic character ; others see in it the principle of stoicism, and imagine that it was intended to cultivate, and bear witness for, the sovereignty of the will over the lower tendencies of human nature : while some regard it wholly in the light of the sacrifice of the person to God . . . Philo has taken the deeper view of the subject. According to him the Nazarite did not sacrifice merely his possessions, but his person, and the act of sacrifice was to be performed in the completest manner. The outward observances enjoined upon him were to be the genuine expressions of his spiritual devotion. To represent spotless purity within, he was to shun defilement from the dead, at the expense even of the obligation of the closest family ties. As no spiritual state or act can be signified by any single symbol, he was to identify himself with each one of the three victims which he had to offer as often as he broke his vow by accidental pollution, or when the period of his vow came to an end. He was to realise in himself the ideas of the whole burnt-offering, the sin-offering, and the peace-offering. That no mistake might be made in regard to the three sacrifices being shadows of one and the same substance, it was ordained that the victims should be individuals of one and the same species of animal. The shorn hair was put on the fire of the altar in order that, although the Divine law did not permit the offering of human blood, something might be offered up actually a portion of his own person . . . . That the Nazarite vow was essentially a sacrifice of the person to the Lord is obviously in accordance with the terms of the Law (Num. vi. 2). In the old dispensation it may have answered to that 'living sacrifice, holy, acceptable unto God,' which the believer is now called upon to make. As the Nazarite was a witness for the straitness of the Law, as distinguished from the freedom of the Gospel, his sacrifice of himself was submission to the letter of a rule. Its outward manifestations were restraints and eccentricities. The man was separated from his brethren that he might be peculiarly devoted to the Lord. This was consistent with the purpose of Divine wisdom for the time for which it was ordained. Wisdom, we are told, was justified of her child in the life of the great Nazarite who preached the baptism of repentance when the Law was about to give way to the Gospel. Amongst those born of women, no greater than he had arisen, 'but he that is least in the kingdom of heaven is greater than he.' The sacrifice which the believer now makes of himself is not to cut him off from his brethren, but to unite him more closely with them; not to subject him to an outward bond, but to confirm him in the liberty with which Christ has made him free. It is not without significance that wine under the Law was strictly forbidden to the priest who was engaged in the service of the sanctuary, and to the few whom the Nazarite vow bound to the special service of the Lord; while in the Church of Christ it is consecrated for the use of every believer to whom the command has come, 'drink ye all of this.'" Confining our attention to the first eight verses, we have in them an illustration of acceptable consecration to God. *Acceptable personal consecration to God is characterised by*—

I. **Voluntariness.**

The self-consecration of the Nazarite was entirely spontaneous. It is true that Samson, Samuel, and John the Baptist, were dedicated to the Lord as perpetual Nazarites by their parents previous to their birth. But as a rule, the vow was voluntarily assumed. In the legislation recorded in this chapter it is regarded as the free act of the individual. Our self-consecration to God must be willing and hearty, or it will not be accepted by Him. The strictest obedience, which is begotten of fear; the most careful performance of religious duties, which is not hearty; the most diligent service, which is not free, is regarded as worthless in the sight of God. To be accepted by God, we must "serve Him with a perfect heart and with a willing mind." The service of the slave or of the hireling, He rejects; but the free consecration of the heart and life to Him is an offering with which He is well pleased (*a*).

II. **Completeness.**

The Nazarite dedicated himself wholly to God. This is symbolised especially by the uncut hair, which is spoken of in verse 7 as "the diadem of God upon his head." "The consecration of the Nazarite culminated in his uncut hair. The free growth of the hair, unhindered by the hand of man, was 'the symbol of strength and abundant vitality' (cf. 2 Sam. xvi. 25, 26)." Hence in the Nazarite it proclaimed the fact that he had dedicated himself wholly, with all his powers, to the service of God. Our consecration to God must be unreserved to be acceptable. Divided allegiance is no allegiance. "Ye cannot serve God and mammon." Whole-heartedness is indispensable to true allegiance to any person or to any cause. Divided service God rejects. He claims us entirely. He requires our supreme affection. The throne of our being must be freely given to Him, or our consecration will not be accepted by Him. When our whole self is given to God, we shall keep back nothing else from Him. "May the God of peace Himself sanctify you wholly," etc. (1 Thess. v. 23). (*b*)

III. **Subordination of sensual enjoyments.**

The Nazarite was to abstain entirely from wine and intoxicating drink. He was neither to eat nor to drink of anything prepared from the vine, "from the kernel even to the husk." This was to represent his abstinence from every gratification of the senses, which would in any way impair the holiness of his soul. This entire abstinence from the products of the vine is not a law for Christians. It is never represented as such in the Sacred Scriptures. The Nazarite was free to "drink wine" when the period of his separation was ended. But it *is* a law of the Christian life, that the sensual must ever and in all things be subordinated to the spiritual. Sensual appetites must not lord it over spiritual aspirations. Our animal passions must be controlled by moral principles. Everything which tends to weaken or becloud our soul's vision, to blunt our susceptibility to spiritual impressions and impulses, to interrupt our conscious communion with God, or to deprive us of spiritual purity and power, we are bound to abstain from. "Abstain from fleshly lusts, which war against the soul." "Walk in the Spirit, and ye shall not fulfil the lust of the flesh." (c)

IV. Separation from all moral evil.

"Because the Nazarite was holy to the Lord during the whole period of his consecration, he was to approach no dead person during that time, not even to defile himself for his parents, or his brothers and sisters, when they died, according to the law laid down for the high priest in Lev. xxi. 11. Consequently, as a matter of course, he was to guard most scrupulously against other defilements, not only like ordinary Israelites, but also like the priests."—*Keil and Del.* The people of God must "abstain from every form of evil." Jesus Christ was "holy, harmless, undefiled, separate from sinners," even while he received sinners and ate with them. A similar separation is required from His followers. "I pray not that Thou shouldst take them out of the world, but that Thou shouldest keep them from the evil." "Come out from among them, and be ye separate, saith the Lord, and touch not anything unclean, and I will receive you," etc. "Ye that love the Lord hate evil." By your consecration you are "holy unto the Lord," therefore shun utterly all sin whatsoever. (d)

Do these characteristics of acceptable personal consecration to God mark our lives?

ILLUSTRATIONS.

(a) Personal devotion to the Lord Jesus Christ has distinguished the saints of all churches, and of all countries. They have acknowledged that they were not their own, but His. They have renounced, for His sake, all private interests, and all personal aims. They have lived, and worked, and suffered, and died for Him. They have been the slaves of Christ—His slaves, not because their spirit was crushed by a tyrannical authority which they had no power or courage to resist, but because His Divine majesty, His infinite love for them, and the glory of His personal perfection kindled their imagination, commanded the homage of their conscience, and won their hearts. They were His slaves, but they found in His service a larger freedom than they had known before they accepted the Lord Jesus Christ as their Master; and, with the larger freedom, there came a fuller life and a nobler joy.

The act of consecration is an act of the will. It is a voluntary surrender of the life to Christ, a yielding to His claims as our rightful Owner. But His Ownership belongs to the moral and spiritual order, and is ultimately asserted in His personal ascendancy over the whole moral and spiritual life of those who are His. Consecration is an indispensable condition of holiness, for it is a free consent to belong to Christ, and not to ourselves; but where there is personal devotion to Christ, Christ is not merely accepted by the will as the Lord and Owner of life, He is enthroned over all the forces of our moral and spiritual nature.—*R. W. Dale, D.D.*

(b) It is related of the missionary, Henry Martyn, that, when at college, "he never lost an hour;" but then every moment was spent in seeking honour for himself. When, however, he had obtained the highest honours, he was disappointed in finding that he had grasped a shadow. A friend told him one day that he ought to attend to his studies not to obtain the praise of men, but that he might be better fitted to promote the glory of God. He thought such a demand very strange, and when his sister spoke to him on the subject, and begged him to give his heart to God, he did not like to listen to her, because he felt that he would have to give up many things if he became religious. At length, however, a great change came over him—a change of heart; and he resolved to "seek first the kingdom of God." His prospects were every day becoming brighter and brighter; but the love of God had entered his heart, and he was enabled to conquer his ambition and love of fame. He became a minister of the Gospel, and was greatly esteemed for his learning and amiable manners. He began now, more than ever, to feel that he was not his own, and therefore that he must not live to himself; and although he might have risen to posts of distinction in his native land, he chose rather to be a missionary to the heathen. He sacrificed home, friendship, worldly comfort, health, earthly love, and last of all, life itself, that he might tell the heathen of the true God, and of the Lord Jesus Christ, who died to save sinners; for, as he said, "he could not endure life if Jesus were not glorified." He left all that he might follow Jesus. He felt that it was what God required of him, and he acted in the spirit of his Divine Master, who gave Himself for the sins of the world.—*Sunday School Teacher.*

(*c*) Stimulants, like wine, inflame the senses, and through them set the imagination and feelings on fire; and the law of our spiritual being is that which begins with the flesh, sensualizes the spirit—whereas that which commences in the region of the spirit, spiritualizes the senses, in which it subsequently stirs emotiom. But the misfortune is that men mistake this law of their emotions; and the fatal error is, when having found spiritual feelings existing in connection, and associated with fleshly sensations, men expect by the mere irritation of the emotions of the frame to reproduce those high and glorious feelings. . . The worst case of all occurs in the department of the affections. That which begins in the heart ennobles the whole animal being, but that which begins in the inferior departments of our beings is the most entire degradation and sensualizing of the soul. Wine is but a specimen of a class of stimulants. All that begins from *without* belongs to the same class. The stimulus may be afforded by almost any enjoyment of the senses. Drunkenness may come from anything wherein is excess; from over-indulgence in society, in pleasure, in music, and in the delight of listening to oratory, nay, even from the excitement of sermons and religious meetings. The prophet tells us of those who are drunken, and not with wine. . . . This is what we want: we want the vision of a calmer and simpler Beauty, to tranquillize us in the midst of artificial tastes—we want the draught of a purer spring to cool the flame of our excited life; we want, in other words the Spirit of the Life of Christ, simple, natural, with power to calm and soothe the feelings which it rouses: the fulness of the Spirit which can never intoxicate.—*F. W. Robertson, M.A.*

(*d*) Christ had His power in the fact that He carried the impression of His separateness from the world and His superiority to it. He was no ascetic, His separation no contrived and prescribed separation, but was only the more real and radical that it was the very instinct or first impulse of His character. He could say, "The prince of this world cometh, and hath nothing in Me;" counting the bad kingdom to be only a paste-board affair, whose laws and ways were but a vain show, that He could not even so much as feel. This, now, is what we want, such a fulness of Divine participation, that we shall not require to be always shutting off the world by prescribed denials, but shall draw off from it naturally, because we are not of it. A true Christian, one who is deep enough in the godly life to have his affinities with God, will infallibly become a separated being. The instinct of holiness will draw him apart into a singular, superior, hidden life with God.

It is not conformity that we want; it is not being able to beat the world in its own way, but it is to stand apart from it, and produce the impression of a separated life; this it is, and this only, that yields any proper sense of the true Christian power. It is not the being popular that makes one a help to religion, no holy man was ever truly a popular character. Even Christ Himself, bringing the Divine beauty into the world, profoundly disturbed the quiet of men by His very perfections. All really bad men, adhering to their sin, hated Him, and their animosity was finally raised to such a pitch, that they crucified Him. And what does He say, turning to His disciples but this very thing, "The servant is not greater than his lord; if they have persecuted me, they will persecute you. I have chosen you out of the world, *therefore* the world hateth you." We are certainly not to make a merit of being hated, for the worst and most wicked men can do that; as little are we to make a merit of popularity and being ever with the world in its ways. There is no just mode of life, no true holiness, or fruit of holy living, if we do not carry the conviction, by our self-denial, our sobriety in the matter of show, and our withholding from all that indicates being under the world, that we are in a life separated to God. Therefore His great call is —" Come out from among them, and be ye separate, and touch not the unclean thing, and ye shall be my sons and daughters, saith the Lord Almighty." And there is a most profound philosophy in this. If we are to impress the world we must be separate from sinners, even as Christ our Master was, or at least, according to our human degree, as being in His Spirit. The great difficulty is, that we think to impress the world, standing on the world's own level and asking its approbation. We conform too easily and with too much appetite. We are all the while touching the unclean thing—bowing down to it, accepting its law, eager to be found approved in it. God therefore calls us away. Oh, that we could take our lesson here, and plan our life, order our pursuits, choose our relaxations, prepare our families, so as to be truly with Christ, and so, in fact, that we ourselves can say, each for himself, "The prince of this world cometh, and hath nothing in me."—*H. Bushnell, D.D.*

The Involuntary Defilement of the Nazarite, or Sin in the Consecrated.

(*Verses* 9-12.)

Provision is here made for cases in which the Nazarite involuntarily contracted defilement, by reason of a person dying suddenly by him. He was to go through the ordinary process of purification commanded for others ; he was also to offer a trespass-offering as having "sinned through ignorance, in the holy things of the Lord ;" his head was to be shaved, and he was to begin the days of his separation over again. We have, then, in this section—

First : *A recognition of the fact that man may die suddenly and unexpectedly.* "If any man die very suddenly by him." It is here implied that death may seize a man so quickly and so entirely without any sign of his approach, that the most zealous and watchful Nazarite may be unable to avoid defilement from the dead body. While death sometimes approaches his victims with measured steps and slow, at other times he smites them with the suddenness and rapidity of a lightning-flash. He arrests not only the aged and the weak, but the young and the strong also. In the case even of the healthy and vigorous, and apparently secure, frequently there is but a step between them and death. Wise and blessed are they to whom even sudden death is great gain ! (*a*)

Second : *An illustration of the truth that a good man may fall into sin, and of the consequences of such sin.* The case which is here legislated for is that of defilement which is quite involuntary, and, as we should say, accidental. It is a figure of the involuntary sins of good men, sins of infirmity, sins into which they are suddenly surprised, faults by which they are overtaken. In our present state we are exposed to subtle Satanic temptations ; currents of evil influence, which are both insidious and strong, bear frequently upon us ; we are in danger of being taken in an unguarded moment, and surprised into sin. "We have heard how suddenly the storm sweeps down upon certain lakes. One moment all is calm, and in another the loosened wind lashes the slumbering waters into waves and billows, as if the storm-spirit had been looking on from some rift of the hills, and watching for an opportunity of plaguing the unsuspecting lake. So is it with men who are overtaken in a fault. They are apt to imagine that momentary quiet means permanent rest, and when they resign their weapons, the enemy leaps upon them fiercely." "You were going quietly on your way, thinking no evil, suddenly temptation, for which you were not prepared, presented itself, and before you knew where you were, you were in the dust, fallen." It is sins of this class, class in men of sincere piety, which are illustrated in the text. It is here suggested—

I. That such sins defile and dishonour good men.

"If any man die very suddenly by him, and he hath defiled the head of his consecration : then he shall shave his head in the day of his cleansing, on the seventh day shall he shave it." The head is mentioned as defiled not because uncleanness was specially retained in the hair ; but because "the consecration of his God was upon his head." His unshorn hair was the mark of his self-dedication to God. He himself, as a person thus consecrated, was regarded as impure by reason of his nearness to the dead. If a good man be ensnared by temptation and commit sin, that sin will leave its mark upon his being. We cannot sin under any circumstances without contracting some measure of defilement. Nor can any good man sin without dishonour. even his involuntary sins tarnish and soil the lustre of "the diadem of his God upon his head." When Abram sinned through fear, by telling only a half-truth with an intention to deceive Pharaoh, how mean and dishonoured he appeared! As we look upon Pharaoh, the man of the world, rebuking Abram, the man of God, we feel how painfully the latter has humiliated and degraded himself. When the godly man is even suddenly surprised into sin by subtle and strong temptation, he incurs impurity and sad reproach.

II. That such sins require atonement on the part of good men.

The Nazarite who had unintentionally contracted ceremonial uncleanness was required to bring to the priest a sin-offering and a burnt-offering, as in the case of those who had unclean issues (comp. vers. 10, 11, with Lev. xv. 14, 15). He was also required to bring a trespass-offering, as one who had "sinned, through ignorance, in the holy things of the Lord" (comp. ver. 12 with Lev. v. 15, 16). For us in this gospel age the grand offering, which consummates and crowns all previous offerings, has been made: "Once in the end of the world hath He appeared to put away sin by the sacrifice of Himself." And if a good man sin by reason of infirmity, or be tripped up and overthrown by temptation almost ere he is aware of it, he must penitently approach unto God through that great sacrifice,—must repent of his sin, humbly confess it unto God, and seek forgiveness from Him. (See 1 John i. 9; ii. 1, 2.)

III. That such sins involve loss to good men.

The Nazarite who involuntarily was defiled lost time. The former days of his separation were not reckoned unto him: "the days that were before shall be lost, because his separation was defiled." He was put back, and required to begin afresh: "he shall consecrate unto the Lord the days of his separation." In this we have a striking illustration of a very solemn spiritual truth: a godly man cannot sin under any circumstances without suffering sad loss—loss not only of progress, but of spiritual purity, peace, and power. This will account for the very slow progress of many in the Christian course. In an unguarded moment we are led astray, and wander from God and light into sin and darkness. In great mercy "He restoreth our soul;" but the journey home is sad and sorrowful, and we have lost much of good and gained bitter experience and painful memories. (*b*)

IV. That such sin will be followed by new efforts on the part of good men.

The Nazarite who had unintentionally incurred defilement began again the term of separation which he had vowed unto the Lord. "And he shall consecrate unto the Lord the days of his separation." The godly man may fall into sin, but he will not continue therein. He will "remember from whence he has fallen, and repent, and do the first works." "Though he fall, he shall not be utterly cast down; for the Lord upholdeth him with his hand." "A just man falleth seven times, and riseth up again." "Rejoice not against me, O mine enemy: when I fall I shall arise; when I sit in darkness the Lord shall be a light unto me." "There are ever," says Archbishop Trench, "goads in the recollection of a better and a nobler past, goading him who has taken up with meaner things and lower, and urging him to reclaim and recover what he has lost; as, to take an extreme instance, it is the Prodigal's recollection of the bread enough and to spare in his father's house, which makes the swine's husks, and the famine even among them, so intolerable to him" (Luke xv. 17; cf. Heb. x. 32). And Robertson: "In the darkest, wildest, wanderings, a man to whom God has shown His love in Christ is conscious still of the better way. In the very gloom of his remorse, there is an instinctive turning back to God."

Conclusion.

1. *Let godly men watch and pray lest they be ensnared by temptation and fall into sin.* "Be sober, be vigilant," etc.

2. *Let those who, in an unguarded hour, have fallen into sin be encouraged to return penitently unto God through Jesus*

Christ. "Return, thou backsliding Israel, saith the Lord," etc. (Jer. iii. 12-15). "O Israel, return unto the Lord thy God," etc. (Hos. xiv. 1-7).

ILLUSTRATIONS.

(a) "In the midst of life we are in death." Ha is the interjection of laughter. Ah is an interjection of sorrow; the difference betwixt them is very small, consisting only in the transposition of what is no substantial letter, but a bare aspiration. How quickly, in one minute, in the very turning of a breath, is our mirth changed into mourning! Thus it was with upwards of seventy (mostly females) who were burned to death in the sudden conflagration of the theatre at Richmond, in Virginia. "Ah!" said the narrator of the dreadful catastrophe, "how little thought the fair one, whose curls were adjusted, whose garments, costly and elegant, were disposed so as to produce on the spectator the most impressive effect, that those curls were that same night to be crisped with the devouring flame, and those garments to be denied the service of a winding sheet!"—*Gleanings.*

I was meditating yesterday upon death, till I was amazed that it is almost the only subject which is never treated of in conversation further than as a mere uninteresting fact. Were any number of persons intending to embark for a distant, unknown country, of whom some might be called to-morrow, and all must be called soon, would they not, whenever they met as friends and fellow-travellers, be enquiring amongst themselves how each was provided for the journey; what accounts each had heard of the place; the terms of reception; what interest and hopes each had secured, what treasures remitted, what protection insured; and would they not excite each other to despatch what was yet possible to be done, and might to-morrow be irretrievably too late? I think it would sit pleasingly on the mind when a friend was vanished out of this visible world to have such conversations to reflect upon. What astonishing scenes are now opened to the minds of many with whom, a few months ago, we used familiarly and triflingly to converse; with whom we have wasted many an inestimable hour! What clear views have they now of those great and important truths, for which the foolish bustle of this world leaves scarcely any place in the immortal mind.—*Talbot.*

(b) A young man was for several months in a backsliding state, which manifested itself in the usual way—of conformity to a fashionable and unholy course of life, and a neglect of the ordinances and institutions of the house of God. During this time he called on a deacon of the church, who was a watchmaker, and asked him to repair his watch. "What is the difficulty with your watch?" said he. "It has lost time lately," said the young man. The deacon looked up to him with a steady and significant eye, and said, "*Havn't you lost time lately?*" These few words brought the backslider to repentance, to the Church, and to duty.—*Christian Treasury.*

How a single sin tends to modify the history, to check the progress, and to impair the happiness and honour of even a child of God! This was eminently the case with Aaron and Moses. They had "spoken unadvisedly with their lips" at Massah and Meribah, and therefore God had "sworn in His wrath that they should not enter into His rest," that, namely, of the earthly Canaan. One reason why God is more apt to punish His people on earth for sin is, that they are not to be punished for it hereafter. Hence, for the sake of justice and impartiality, He often inflicts upon them severe rebukes even here, while taking little cognizance, seemingly, of the sins of some of His enemies, for whom the wrath of the future is reserved. He forgives His people and yet He "takes vengeance on their inventions." Thus Noah's drunkenness was punished by Canaan's contempt and Ham's unnatural conduct. Thus David's sin, in the matter of Uriah, was punished by the death of the child of guilt. Thus Lot's sin, in choosing to dwell in Sodom, was punished by the vexation he met with there, and by the sins of his family. Thus Peter's denial of his Master was punished by that look of Christ which sent a dart of remorse through his soul, and wrung from his eyes those bitter penitential tears. And thus Aaron and Moses, might be said, in a sense, to expiate their sins by a premature and public death. There can be little doubt that God still visits His "people's faults with rods and their sins with chastisements;" now by permitting a remorse even greater than their iniquities had deserved; now by allowing their subjection to abuse and calumny fiercer than they are entitled to; now by hiding His countenance from them; now by visiting them with the loss of friends and other painful bereavements; now by breaking their own health, and abridging their days; and now by clouding their death-beds, and depriving them there of all sensible comfort and hope. Many a one wonders how a great, sincere, and Christian man like Dr. Johnson, should have been so gloomy in his feelings, so terribly afraid of death, so void of peace and joy in believing; but his biographer, Boswell, has, with characteristic honesty and imprudence, explained one cause at least of this, by mentioning a certain sin which did easily beset the philosopher on even to old age, although he struggled against it energetically, and most bitterly deplored its power over him; and were the biographers of other sad-hearted Christians, whose dark diaries are printed, acting with the same downrightness, they might account for much that is at present mysterious in their misery. God will by no means "clear the guilty" even among His own people; and although all their sins are laid on Christ, and pardoned for His sake at last, it is quite consistent with this that they should be punished here. This dispensation is a merciful, as well as a just one. It tends to check men in courses that might otherwise become habitual and hopeless. And it shows what a fatherly interest God takes in His people, administering to them salutary discipline, and bringing them back to Him by the rod. "If ye be without chastisement, whereof all are partakers, then are ye bastards, and not sons." How happy those who receive all their "evil things" here!—*George Gilfillan, M.A.*

The Offering of the Nazarite, or the Sacrifice of the Consecrated.

(*Verses* 13-21).

In these verses we have the ceremonies to be observed by the Nazarite when the days of his separation were ended. "The directions as to the release from consecration are called '*the law of the Nazarite*' (verse 13), because the idea of the Nazarite's vows culminated in the sacrificial festival which terminated the consecration, and it was in this that it attained to its fullest manifestation." In these ceremonies we discover illustrations of certain important truths of universal application; to these truths let us direct our attention.

I. That the lives even of the best of men in the present state are imperfect.

When the Nazarite had successfully fulfilled the days of his separation he could not approach God without a sin-offering. He was required to "offer one ewe lamb of the first year without blemish," as an expiation for sins involuntarily committed during the period of consecration. This, though mentioned second in the text, was offered first. "Though he had fulfilled the vow of his separation without any pollution, yet he must bring a sacrifice for sin; for there is guilt insensibly contracted by the best of men, even in their best works—some good omitted, some ill admitted, which, if we were dealt with in strict justice, would be our ruin, and in consequence of which it is necessary for us to receive the atonement, and plead it as our righteousness before God." "When ye shall have done all those things which are commanded you, say, We are unprofitable servants; we have done that which was our duty to do." When we have done our uttermost and best, we still need an interest in the great sacrifice of the Lord Jesus Christ. (*a*)

II. That our services are acceptable to God only as we give ourselves to Him.

After the sin-offering, the Nazarite was to "offer unto the Lord one he lamb of the first year without blemish for a burnt offering." The burnt-offering was an acknowledgment of God's sovereign claims upon the Nazarite, and a symbol of his surrender of himself, body and soul, to the Lord. So, also, the hair of his head, which had been worn in honour of God, he was to cut off at the door of the tabernacle, and put it into the altar fire which was under the sacrifice of the peace-offerings, thus offering up a portion of his own person in sacrifice to the Lord. The grand meaning and end of all sacrifice is the surrender of ourselves to God. Our most treasured possessions we must give to Him; we must worship Him with our best. Apart from this self-sacrifice all other sacrifices and services are worthless in the sight of God. The worth and efficacy of the death of Jesus Christ as a sacrifice for sin consisted in the entire surrender of Himself to the will of God. And the grand object of that death as set forth by St. Paul on one occasion is, that every man should sacrifice himself to God. "He died for all, that they which live should not henceforth live unto themselves, but unto Him which died for them and rose again." "We are Christ's 'slaves,'

He purchased us, not to set us free and to make us our own masters, but that we might belong to Him. The rights of a master over a slave appeared to the Apostle to represent the rights of Christ over us. . . The slave has no personal independence. He has to do his master's will. His master determines where he shall live and what he shall do. He works to increase, not his own wealth, but his master's. He has to live for his master, not for himself. The renunciation of all personal objects in the presence of Christ is the precise characteristic of Christian living." Without this self-renunciation all other services and sacrifices are vain in the sight of God. (*b*)

III. **That all that is good both in ourselves and in our services is attributable to God.**

The Nazarite was also required to "offer unto the Lord one ram without blemish for peace-offerings, and a basket of unleavened bread, cakes of fine flour mingled with oil, and wafers of unleavened bread anointed with oil, and their meat-offering and their drink-offerings." By reference to Lev. vii. 11-12, it will be seen that this was offered "for a thanksgiving." The Nazarite presented the sacrifice of peace-offerings unto the Lord as an expression of thankfulness to Him for the grace by which he had been enabled to fulfil his vow. Whatever of good there is in us is the result of Divine grace. All holy desires are quickened by Him. Every worthy resolution which we form He inspires within us by His Spirit. The strength for holy living, and diligent working, and patient suffering, He imparts. "Every good gift, and every perfect gift, is from above," etc. "By the grace of God I am what I am." "For who maketh thee to differ? and what hast thou that thou didst not receive? now if thou didst receive it, why dost thou glory as if thou hadst not received it?" "Not unto us, O Lord, not unto us, but unto Thy name give glory, for Thy mercy, and for Thy truth's sake."

IV. **That the good man when he has complied with the express requirements of the Divine law will seek for other opportunities of expressing his devotion.**

"This is the law of the Nazarite who hath vowed his offering unto the Lord for his separation, beside that which his hand shall get, according to the vow which he vowed, so he must do after the law of his separation;" that is, says Keil and Del., "he had to offer the sacrifices previously mentioned on the ground of his consecration vow. Beyond that he was free to vow anything else according to his ability, to present other sacrificial gifts to the Lord for His sanctuary and His servants, which did not necessarily belong to the vow of the Nazarite, but were frequently added." The fulfilment of even the largest requirements of the Divine law cannot exhaust the devotion of the truly godly soul. He who has truly given himself to the Lord can never give Him enough to satisfy his own desire; where he has given his utmost he would fain give more. "Love never puts its own name upon anything. Love has some object, *must* have some object, on whose shrine it lays its every possession. Love, warm, intelligent, growing Love, keeps back nothing from God. Its beaming eyes look upon every treasure with a view of ascertaining its proper relation to the King. Love has endless resources, because it has endless sacrifices. We make a grievous mistake when we say, 'Such a man must be *rich* because he *gives* so much to the cause of God;' he may not be rich in material possessions, but he must be rich in *the spirit of self-sacrifice*. He has a wealthy *heart*, and *that* explains the bounty which astonishes and confounds those who have a prince's gold, but a beggar's spirit." (*c*)

V. **That the good man through the sacrifices by which He approaches God has communion with Him.**

Such seems to be the meaning symbolized in that part of the ceremonial, for which directions are given in verses 19 and 20. We quote the note of Keil and Del.: "When this had been done the priest took the boiled shoulder of the ram, with an unleavened cake and wafer out of the basket, and placed these pieces in the hands of the Nazarite, and waved them before Jehovah. They then became the portion of the priest, in addition to the wave-breast and heave-leg which fell to the priest in the case of every peace-offering (Lev. vii. 32-34), to set forth the participation of the Lord in the sacrificial meal. But the fact that, in addition to these, the boiled shoulder was given up symbolically to the Lord through the process of waving, together with a cake and wafer, was intended to indicate that the table-fellowship with the Lord, shadowed forth in the sacrificial meal of the peace-offering, took place here in a higher degree; inasmuch as the Lord directed a portion of the Nazarite's meal to be handed over to His representatives and servants for them to eat, that he might thus enjoy the blessedness of having fellowship with his God, in accordance with that condition of priestly sanctity into which the Nazarite had entered through the vow that he had made." Through the sacrifice of Jesus Christ, the good man may have the most intimate and blessed communion with God. "Jesus saith, I am the way, the truth, and the life: no man cometh unto the Father, but by me." "Through Him we have access by one Spirit unto the Father." "Having therefore, brethren, boldness to enter into the holiest by the blood of Jesus," etc. (Heb. x. 19-22.) "Our fellowship is with the Father, and with His Son Jesus Christ."

Conclusion.

1. *Let us give ourselves unreservedly and heartily to God.* "I beseech you, brethren, by the mercies of God, that ye present your bodies a living sacrifice," etc.

2. *Let us seek through God to realize close and constant communion with Him.*

"I would commune with Thee, my God,
  E'en to Thy seat I come;
I leave my joys, I leave my sins,
  And seek in Thee my home.
I stand upon the mount of God,
  With sunlight in my soul;
I hear the storms in vales beneath,
  I hear the thunders roll;
But I am calm with Thee, my God,
  Beneath these glorious skies;
And to the height of Thine abode,
  Nor storms nor clouds can rise.
O this is life, and peace, and joy,
  My God, to find Thee so—
Thy face to see, Thy voice to hear,
  And all Thy love to know."
—*G. B. Bubier.*

ILLUSTRATIONS.

(*a*) When, because we have accomplished some little work, we count that we may straightway take our ease, and esteem our "Well done" as already gained, very profitable will be then the warning of the parable (Luke xvii. 7-10); the example of the hind, who having laboured all day in the field, resumes his labours in the house, and only looks to rest and refresh himself when his master has no further need of his service; good for us that, in the words of the son of Sirach, we learn to "wax old in our work" (xi. 20), and, so long as we are here, to see in one task completed but a stepping-stone to another which shall be begun; ever as we have surmounted one hill of labour, perceiving a new one rising above it, and girding ourselves for the surmounting of that as well. Well for us, too, is it to know and to confess that we are not doing God a favour in serving Him, but He the highest favour to us in enabling us to this service; and that He, graciously accepting our work and rewarding it, does this solely out of the freedom and riches of His grace; adding to it a worth which of itself it does not possess; that there is another footing, that namely of the parable, upon which He might have put all—yea, upon which, though *He* does not, yet *we* must evermore put it, so far as is necessary for subduing every motion of pride and vain-glory, every temptation to bring in God as our debtor—which we evermore are doing, or are on the point of doing.—*Archbishop Trench.*

There is an anecdote of the saintly and learned Archbishop Usher, not unfamiliar to religious readers, which is meant to illustrate his spiritual modesty. It relates how a friend frequently urged him to write his thoughts on Sanctification, which at length he engaged to do; but, a considerable time elapsing, the performance of his promise was importunately claimed. The Archbishop replied to this purpose: "I have not written, and yet I cannot charge myself with a breach of promise, for I began to write; but when I came to treat of the new creature which God formeth by His own Spirit in every regenerate soul, I found so little of it wrought in myself that I could speak of it only as parrots, or by rote, but without the knowledge of what I might have expressed; and, therefore, I durst not presume to proceed any further upon it." Upon this his friend stood amazed to hear such a confession from so grave, holy, and eminent a person. The Archbishop then added: "I must tell you, we do not well understand what Sanctification and the new creature are. It is no less than for a man to be brought to an entire resignation of his own will to the will of God; and to live in the offering up of his soul continually in the flames of love, as a whole burnt-offering to Christ; and oh, how many who profess Christianity are unacquainted, experimentally, with this work upon their souls!"—*F. D. Huntington, D.D.*

(*b*) It is very possible for Christian men to miss the real extent of the devotion to Himself which is claimed by our Lord, and which, throughout the New Testament, is assumed and implied as the true Christian life. A Christian man may consider that he is at liberty to determine for himself the objects for which he will live, provided he seeks those objects in ways which the ethics of the New Testament do not condemn. He may suppose, for instance, that if he likes he may determine to accumulate a hundred thousand pounds or a quarter of a million, and that the law of Christ simply requires him to carry on his business or profession in a just and honourable manner, and to give a fair proportion of his wealth to the relief of the poor, and the maintenance of various religious societies. Or he may suppose that having set his heart upon rising to a certain social rank, or winning a certain political position, he is quite at liberty to concentrate all his strength on this object, so long as there is nothing dishonest or ignoble in the means which he adopts to secure it. But if there be any truth at all in the Apostle's description of us, if in any sense we are the "slaves" of Christ, there is obviously a fundamental mistake in this conception of the limits of our duty. Our first question must be whether Christ wants us to accumulate a hundred thousand pounds or a quarter of a million; and whether He wants us to win the social rank, or the political power which we have resolved to make our own. A master may often trust his servants to determine for themselves *how* they will get a certain work done, but whether the work shall be done at all or not, is a question which must in all cases be referred to his decision. And when we are choosing an object to live for—an object which it may take us many years to achieve—it certainly shows a curious conception of the kind of relationship in which we stand to Christ, to imagine that we need not consult Him about the *end* for which we are to live, though we must be careful to employ only those means which He approves. Our life, on this theory, is not given to Christ. We keep it for ourselves. We are not really His. We choose the objects to which it shall be devoted. The renunciation of self which He imperatively requires of us is altogether evaded. The Lord Jesus Christ is the Lord of our life in such a sense that it is for Him to determine the objects for which our life shall be spent, as well as the way in which these objects shall be sought. We are in such a sense His servants, that we have no right to do any work but His. If we desire that He should say to us at last, "Well done, good and faithful servants," it is clear that whatever we do must be done for Him.—*R. W. Dale, M.A., D.D.*

(*c*) David wanted to make an offering himself, wanted to give vent to the sorrow, dependence, and gratitude of his soul; and a costless sacrifice would not have met this want. It would have been useless to suggest that such a sacrifice would be as good as any other; in itself it might be, but not to him. He felt that the occasion demanded something more, that something more was due both to God and to himself: the offering must be the fruit and form of deep and holy emotions, and to give a gift would be to mock rather than to manifest these emotions. An illustration may be taken from some of the old sacred buildings. You will find them "finished with the most circumstantial elegance and minuteness in those concealed portions which are excluded from public view, and which can only be inspected by laborious climbing or groping," a fact explained by saying, "that the whole carving and execution was considered as an act of solemn worship and adoration, in which the artist offered up his best faculties to the praise of the Creator." These men of "the dark ages," as we love in the pride of our compassion to call them, had in this a true and grand idea: what would they say of our veneered and gilded modern life, in which everything is for show and nothing from reality, everything for a purpose and nothing from a principle? As these men builded, so David sacrificed. They builde not for man, and hence the secret and distant parts of their work were just as accurately conceived and finely finished as those exposed to the public gaze; their object was not to do something as cheaply and easily as possible, but something as well as possible; they wished to raise structures worthy of the Lord; they had a zeal for His glory and the glory of His worship which spurned meanness and imperfection however hidden; and the same spirit in David rendered needful to him what was needless in itself, and made it "more blessed to give" an offering of his own than one received from Araunah.

It is the end and essence of all religion to turn the mind from self to God; to give it absorbing views of the Divine beauty and glory; to fill it with Divine love and zeal; to make it feel honoured in honouring God, blessed in blessing Him; to make it feel that nothing is good enough or great enough for

Him; and when the mind is thus affected and thus possessed, it will understand and share the spirit of David's resolve, not to offer burnt-offerings unto the Lord God of that which doth cost nothing.—*A. J. Morris.*

THE NAZARITE.

(*Verse* 21.)

"This is the law of the Nazarite."

Here a new ordinance appears. Israel's whole race was severed from the world. But the wide circumference was girdle to a narrower circle. Where all were separate, the Nazarites occupied special separation. They bound themselves by voluntary vows. The vow might be the act of men weighed down by consciousness of sin, appalled by sight of inborn evil, or penitent by grievous falls. It might be gratitude for signal mercies. It might be zeal to arouse others to think more of God. The Nazarites' motives are unknown. But Nazarite rules are rigidly prescribed.

I. No juice of grape, no produce of the vine, from kernel unto husk, may touch the consecrated lips.

Believer, this principle is broad and deep. You openly avow that you are not your own. Your body, spirit, mind, and soul, are purchased by redeeming blood. They all are bound a living sacrifice to the one altar—Christ. Hence you must keep them pure, clean, bright, strong, vigorous for His work. They should stand as servants, with loins girt, ready at all times to discharge His will. Then sedulously flee whatever may tend to weaken the firm energy, or to stir up the sleeping brood of sensual and ungodly lusts.

II. No razor approaches the Nazarite's hair. His flowing locks openly announce his separate state.

The dedication must not be a secret act, known only to the conscience and the Lord. Religion is not for the closet or the knees alone. It is not a lily, growing only in the shade. It must be conspicuous, as locks pendent from the head. Like the standard, it must proclaim the country to which the ship belongs. Pure religion shines as the sun, without one cloud. Thus others profit by its rays.

III. He must avoid all contact with the dead. (Verse 6, 7.)

Wherefore is death to be thus shunned? It is the penalty of sin. Therefore it is emblem of what holy men should holily abhor. Life, too, is God's inseparable essence. Therefore, to intermix with death, denotes a separation from God. He who is Christ's must flee the touch of everything allied to sin. The Spirit's temple must be pure. Believer, rigidly apply this maxim. It drives you from the contagion of ungodly scenes. How many crowds are nothing but a crowded charnel house! How many books are deathful! This rule brands many a pulpit as a plague-spot. A lifeless teacher often guides in paths of death. Here, too, we see the misery of those who by dead works expect to buy soul-life. All works are dead which grow not on the stem of faith. How can they purchase life?

But no precautionary care can always keep men from the dying scene. Death has an unrestricted range. Thus the most watchful Nazarite might most unwillingly stand by the dead. If so, pollution has polluted him; his vow is broken. Therefore, atonement must be made. He is required to place a whole burnt-offering on the blazing altar. He must then add a sacrifice for sin. Moreover, as a debtor, he must buy remission by a trespass-offering. Thus the chief types which shadowed out Christ's blood must all be brought. This is not all. The former period of his Nazarate is cancelled; he must commence afresh his dedicated walk. Beware of sudden evil. Satan is a lurking foe; where least suspected, nets are spread. But there is hope for suddenly-contracted guilt. There is a Saviour waiting to obliterate; there is no stain which He removes not. Pardon found must be the starting-point of new devotedness. The cleansed hands fight with more vigour.

But what if deliberate transgression be indulged? The ordinance is silent here, and thus warns solemnly. Where shall he turn who turns presumptuously from God? Grieve not the Spirit's gentle mind.

The Nazarite continued only for a fixed time; but grand solemnities attested the completion of this hallowed state. No rite is absent which confesses need of remission, and trust in reconciling blood. (Verses 13-21.) What is the purport of this multitude of rites? They all seek expiation. They graphically show that holiest deeds of holiest men can only find acceptance through the dying Jesus. Believer, is not this the conscious feeling of your humbled soul? Behold the cross. There is your only help; cleanse there the stains of your most holy hours. Live under vows, as a strict Nazarite; but wrestle for forgiveness as a sad short-comer.—*Henry Law, D.D.*

The Priestly Blessing.

(Verses 22-27.)

"The spiritual character of the congregation of Israel culminated in the blessing with which the priests were to bless the people. The directions as to this blessing, therefore, impressed the seal of perfection upon the whole order and organization of the people of God, inasmuch as Israel was first truly formed into a congregation of Jehovah by the fact that God not only bestowed His blessing upon it, but placed the communication of this blessing in the hands of the priests, the chosen and constant mediators of the blessings of His grace, and imposed it upon them as one portion of their official duty. The blessing which the priests were to impart to the people, consisted of a triple blessing of two members each, which stood related to each other thus. The second in each case contained a special application of the first to the people, and the three gradations unfolded the substance of the blessing step by step with ever-increasing emphasis."
—*Keil and Del.*

Let us notice—

I. The Divine Direction.

"And the Lord spake unto Moses, saying, Speak unto Aaron and to his sons, saying, On this wise ye shall bless the children of Israel." It was the duty of the priests ministerially to bless the people by prayer to God on their behalf; they were to entreat Him to bless them. But in this place they are commanded to pronounce His blessing upon them: speaking in His name, and as His representative, they were to declare the people blessed. The blessing which is pronounced in accordance with the Divine direction cannot be a mere form; it must accord with reality. The command to pronounce the blessing may be regarded as an assurance that, when it was pronounced, the blessing itself would be given. The command to the priest to pronounce the blessing is equivalent to the promise of God to bestow that blessing. The Christian minister is required both to pray for the blessing of God upon the people of His charge, and with confidence to pronounce that blessing upon all who sincerely seek God.

II. The Divine Benediction.

"Saying unto them, The Lord bless thee, and keep thee: The Lord make His face shine upon thee, and be gracious unto thee: The Lord lift up His countenance upon thee, and give thee peace."

Let us notice here—

1. *The significant form of the Benediction.* (1) *The triple use of the sacred Name is significant.* "The Priestly

Blessing prescribed for ritual usage in the Book of Numbers," says Canon Liddon, "is spoken of as putting the *Name* of God, that is to say, a symbol unveiling His nature upon the children of Israel. Here, then, we discover a distinct limit to the number of the Persons Who are internal to the Unity of God. The priest is to repeat the Most Holy Name Three times. The Hebrew accentuation, whatever be its date, shows that the Jews themselves saw in this repetition the declaration of a mystery in the Divine Nature. Unless such a repetition had been designed to secure the assertion of some important truth, a single mention of the Sacred Name would have been natural in a system, the object of which was to impress belief in the Divine Unity upon an entire people. This significant repetition, suggesting, without distinctly asserting, a Trinity in the Being of God, did its work in the mind of Israel." The same thing has been argued from a consideration of the several members of the Benediction. Thus Richard Watson says, "If the three members of this form of benediction be attentively considered, they will be found to agree respectively with the three Persons taken in the usual order of the Father, the Son, and the Holy Ghost. The Father is the Author of blessing and preservation; illumination and grace are from the Son; illumination and peace from the Spirit, the Teacher of truth, and the Comforter." And while in the triple mention of the sacred Name and the threefold blessing, we have suggestions of the Trinity of Persons in the Godhead, in the great assurance, "I will bless them," we have a revelation of the Divine Unity—that God is One. (2) *The use of the singular number in reference to the subjects of the blessing is significant.* "The Lord bless thee, and keep thee," etc. Six times we have the pronoun in the singular number—"thee." According to the *Speaker's Comm.*, the singular number indicates that the blessing is conferred on Israel *collectively.* May we not view it also as indicating the regard of God for the individual? "If we take the law to ourselves, we may take the blessing to ourselves, as if our names were inserted." So the Christian believer may say, "The son of God loved *me,* and gave Himself for *me.*"

2. *The Divine fulness of the Benediction.* "As the threefold repetition of a word or sentence serves to express the thought as strongly as possible (cf. Jer. vii. 4, xxii. 29), the triple blessing expressed in the most unconditional manner the thought, that God would bestow upon His congregation the whole fulness of the blessing enfolded in His Divine Being which was manifested as Jehovah." Man's need of God's blessing is implied. That need arises from his condition as a creature dependent on God for "life, and breath, and all things;" and as a sinful creature, who merits no good from God. Apart from the blessing of God man is utterly undone. First, the blessing of God in general is pronounced, "The Lord bless thee;" and then that blessing is pronounced in some of its particular forms (*a*). The second clause in each verse of the Benediction defines more closely the general tenor of the preceding one. The blessing includes—(1) *The preservation of God.* "The Lord bless thee, and keep thee." Danger is implied. We are weak, inexperienced, prone to sin, exposed to temptation. God is our only sufficient and all-sufficient Guardian. What subtlety can surprise Him who is infinite in intelligence? What strength can stand against Omnipotence? "Kept by the power of God, through faith unto salvation" (*b*). (2) *The favour of God.* "The Lord make His face shine upon thee, and be gracious unto thee." When the Divine face is dark with frowns, distress and death ensue; when it is bright with favours, life and joy flow to man. "They perish at the rebuke of Thy countenance." "Cause Thy face to shine, and we shall be saved." There seems to be an allusion to the shining of the sun. It gives life, light, heat, beauty, power, joy. "In His favour is life." "The light of

the Divine countenance is the sum of all delight." (See our notes on Psa. lxxx. 3; *Hom. Comm. on Psalms,* pp. 466-468). (3) *The peace of God.* "The Lord lift up His countenance upon thee, and give thee peace." שָׁלוֹם *peace,* "the sum of all the good which God sets, prepares, or establishes for His people." M. Henry: "Peace, including all that good which goes to make up a complete happiness." This great blessing is viewed as flowing from the gracious regard of God for man. Pardon, preservation, peace, an unspeakable wealth of blessing flows to man from the sovereign favour of our gracious God.

III. **The Divine Ratification.**

"And they shall put my name upon the children of Israel, and I will bless them." The Benediction was not to be the mere utterance of a pious wish; but God would give effect to it. The people were to be blessed in the Sacred Name, and as the people of God; and God promises to make good the blessing pronounced by the priests. "A Divine blessing goes along with Divine institutions, and puts virtue and efficacy into them." God will certainly bless His own ordinances unto all those who believe.

Conclusion.

Let us firmly believe in the great willingness of God to bless us, and let us heartily seek for "the fulness of the blessing of the Gospel of Christ."

ILLUSTRATIONS.

(*a*) When we ask God's blessing, we pray that first He would bless us with all spiritual blessings in heavenly places in Christ Jesus. We pray that He would bless us with the pardon of every sin, with the healing of every moral disease, with fitness for the world to come, with victory over the trials of the world that now is. We pray that He would stamp upon our hearts that Divine and inexhaustible blessing which will turn our trials into elements of sanctification, our griefs and our tears into a ministry of grace and progress, and education for glory; and all the assaults of Satan and the obstructions of sin into means of ripening and maturing us as the sons of God for a kingdom that fadeth not away. It is God's blessing laid upon the heart within that alters to a Christian the whole world without. If the world were now to be turned into Paradise by God's breath coming over it again,—yet, if unconverted men were left to tread that Paradise, they would soon reduce it to the desert, polluting, blasting, and destroying all. No outer change for the better will ever do without an inner one. There must not only be a pure and beautiful Paradise, but there must be a holy man and a holy woman to live in it; and it would be in vain that the millennium were to burst upon our world if we had not first a little millennium within to melt into the great millennium without, making the outer world and the inner world in harmony, at peace with God, and therefore at peace with one another. Our constant idea is, that what man wants is something done to his outer circumstances; the real and the Divine one is that something should be done for man in his inner heart. Man is sick and dying; it will be of very little, or of very transient use to change his bed; what he wants is to be cured of his disease. The great mischief is, not what sin has done to the outer world, but what sin has done to the inner world; and if the inner world can be made right, then all the outer will seem to be altered. If you go forth with a sad, a grieved, and a bruised spirit into the loveliest scenes of nature, they will all lose their charms to you. To a man who is sorrowful, his own fireside will only reflect sorrow; to a heart that is ill at ease, the fairest landscape will communicate no ecstasy. But on the other hand, let a man's heart be overflowing with joy—let the first light of Eden that is to be, shine into his mind, and the very desert itself to that man's eye will grow beautiful, and the blackest scenes of the world will shine bright, and all nature will reflect a joy that is first in his own heart, and repeats itself by a law as beneficent as it is true, wherever he sets his foot, or in whatever path of the world he walks. What we need therefore is, first the blessing pronounced on the heart, and then we shall hear it in multiplying echoes, and reflected in sweet music from every point of the horizon around and without us.—*John Cumming, D.D.*

(*b*) Christians are kept by the supreme love of their omnipotent Saviour (John x. 28, 29; Jude i.). The Lord Jesus not only *redeemed* His people; He is at this hour *interceding* for them; and His intercession *keeps* the saints. As Peter was kept (Luke xxii. 31) by the Saviour's mediation, so all the good of all lands, in every age, are supported in temptation and brought through to the praise and glory of God. Sublime is the realization of the thought that our LIVING AND DIVINE LORD is standing before the Throne promoting the well-being of His struggling and oftentimes dispirited Church. He knows that we are still in the wilderness as "strangers and pilgrims"—still exposed to the attacks of a relentless antagonist—and still possessors of a depraved nature; hence. He "ever liveth to make intercession" for His Church. Would it not comfort our hearts in seasons of distress to ponder the fact of our Saviour's intercession? No longer would we be oppressed with a sense of loneliness, for no spirit can be desolate for which the Son of God is interceding. Am I addressing a faint-hearted disciple of the Lord—one who is ever on the stormy lake of Galilee? Cheer thee! though human sympathy may flow scantily, Divine sympathy is unlimited in abundance. The Saviour, though unseen, is not inaccessible; and though no longer on the CROSS, He stands as the great High priest in the Holy of Holies. He will "keep" His people as the apple of His eye. He has "all power" to curb the rage of the whirlwind, and to pacify the roar of the storm, and to bring His Israel to their "desired haven"! "Kept by the power of God." What more can we need to assure our hearts and to transfuse them with peace? "The power of God" is the stay of the universe—it is the hope of all creation animate and inanimate. Blessed God! they are well kept whom Thou keepest; do Thou in Thy abounding goodness comfort our hearts with the assurance that Thou wilt keep us unto the end! We cannot keep ourselves: we are blind and weak, and ignorant, but Thou art full of help; teach us, therefore, by Thy Spirit, to feel that "our help is in the Name of the Lord, who made heaven and earth."—*Jos. Parker, D.D.*

THE PREACHER'S BLESSING; OR THE HAPPY NEW YEAR.

(*Verses* 22-26.)

New Year's Day so seldom falls on a Sunday, that, when it does, it would be a pity to let it slip, without wishing you all a happy new year, according to the good old English custom. But the world's notion of happiness, and the Gospel notion of happiness, are very different; and therefore the world's wishes for your happiness, and the preacher's wishes for your happiness must be very different also. The world's good wishes are like itself, worldly: they look chiefly to the body: they reach not beyond earth, and the things of earth. Whereas the good wishes of the preacher are chiefly for your souls: he looks, and by his office is bound to look, first to the one thing needful; his desires for your welfare are guided by the Gospel, and, like that, would raise you up to heaven. Even with regard to this world, the preacher knows full well, that the greatest happiness we can any of us enjoy is a peaceful mind, a quiet conscience, the feeling that God is reconciled to us, and loves us, and cares for us, and watches over us, and will so order and arrange whatever may befall us, that all things shall work together for our good. These are the very best gifts which any man can have in this life; and they are all contained in the text. Therefore, to every one of you I say, "The Lord bless thee, and keep thee," etc. But let us look at the text a little in detail; and let us keep in mind that this solemn blessing was of God's own appointment; so that we may expect to find mention of all those things which He knows to be best for His people.

"The Lord bless thee"! that is, the Lord give thee every good gift, and pour down on thee in due abundance whatever is wholesome and profitable, for thy soul first, and also for thy body. "The Lord keep thee!" that is, the Lord watch over thee for good, and shield thee from every kind of evil.

"The Lord make His face shine upon thee, and be gracious unto thee." You all know the difference of feel between a sunshiny and a cloudy day. The real heat may be the same—nay, the cloudy may be warmer than the sunshiny—for we often have bright sunshine in the clear frosty days of winter, and heavy clouds in the middle of summer. But though the real heat may be the same—though the thermometer may tell us that the cloudy day is the warmer of the two—yet to our feelings it may be quite the contrary. There is something so enlivening in the sun, that I have often known persons come in from a walk on a bright winter's day, and speak of it as very pleasant; while the same persons on a damp, cloudy evening in July, would be the first to shiver, and to wish for a fire. Now, the same difference does it make to a man's soul, whether God's face is shining on him or no. Let God's face shine on the soul, it walks in the brightest sunshine; let God veil His face and cloud it over, the soul feels chilled and is discomforted. (Psa. xxx. 7.) Do we not see many a man disquieted and ill at ease in the midst of riches and luxuries; while his poor neighbour, who lives in a sorry hovel, may look always cheerful and contented? What is this difference owing to? Not to the health and strength of the poor man; for he may be old, and often a sufferer from cold and wet, and he cannot afford to buy himself the little comforts suited to his years and infirmities. The rich man, on the other hand, may still be young; his disease, if it can be called one, is more of the mind than of the body; he can consult the best physicians; he can travel from place to place in search of pleasure; he is not forced to deny himself any one earthly thing that may tend to his ease and enjoyment. Yet with all this, in spite of his youth and riches, in spite of his having no outward ailment, and possessing every comfort and luxury that heart could wish for, he may be always growling and grumbling; while the dweller in the old hovel, with the pinching frost of poverty and age, and sometimes sickness to boot, sharp upon him, may be ever making the best of his condition, and finding out something in it to thank God for. What, then, is this difference owing to? The cause is simply this, that the poor man has led a Christian life, or at least has turned to God in earnest, and repented of his sins betimes; and so God has allowed His face to shine upon him and to cheer him; while his rich neighbour has been led astray by the deceitfulness of riches, and has been so taken up with his pleasures, or with the cares which riches bring with them, that he could not spare time to think about God. He has turned his face away from God; therefore God has turned away His face from him, and left him in clouds and heaviness. Oh, that you might but know and feel the joy and gladness which the light of God's face can shed on the soul of the Christian!

"The Lord be gracious to thee!" that is, the Lord receive thy prayers, as a kind and merciful king hearkens to the petitions of his subjects (comp. Exod. xxii. 27; Neh. ix. 17; Jonah iv. 2; Psa. lxxvii. 7-9). To pray, then, that God will be gracious to His people, is to pray that He will listen to your supplications, and grant your requests, that He will be slow to mark what you have done amiss, and ready to take you into favour when you forsake your sins and cry to Him for pardon.

"The Lord lift up His countenance upon thee!" that is, the Lord show forth His favour and love toward you. We may suppose this expression taken from a king sitting on his throne, and looking with eyes of such goodwill on the petitioners who come before him that the by-standers perceive, and the petitioners themselves feel, that he is their friend: they feel that they have the happiness of being esteemed and loved by him, and that they can reckon with certainty on his protection. To be countenanced thus by the King of kings is the highest privilege a son of Adam can enjoy. If the king had looked favourably upon us, we should expect to receive some honour or preferment; or at least we should feel certain that, so far as he could hinder, he would not suffer anyone to hurt us. So is it with those who have God's countenance, but in a far, far higher degree. For the king, great as he is, is only a man. His power is cut short in a thousand ways, and, at the best, can only follow us to the grave. But God is the King of kings: His power has no bounds, except His own wisdom and goodness and will: in the grave, where human rule is at an end, His rule and sovereignty are doubled etc.

"The Lord give thee peace!" Peace is the fruit of God's favour. "The effect of righteousness is peace." If we know we are forgiven for Christ's sake, we are at peace. If, out of gratitude and love to our Master and Saviour, we are living in obedience to His holy laws, then too we have every ground and reason to be at peace (1 Pet. iii. 13).

There is a false peace, a peace arising out of recklessness and carelessness, and the never thinking about God. Would you say that Samson was at peace when he lay sleeping in the lap of Delilah? So dangerous, so deadly is the false security of the self-righteous and the careless. Rouse yourselves, I beseech you, from such fatal slumbers, if any of you have hitherto been sinking beneath them. Awake! behold, the face of the Lord does not shine, but frown upon you. Let this be the first day of a new year of godly fear and hope.

The Lord bless you this year, and keep you! etc.—*A. W. Hare, A.M.*

God will Bless His own Ordinances.
(*Verses 23-27.*)

The exercise of benevolence is that which every child of God should cultivate to the uttermost; but ministers above all should consider it as the distinguishing badge of their office; they are compelled indeed sometimes to "use sharpness;" but whether they rebuke, or whether they exhort, they should be actuated by nothing but a principle of love. Under the Law it was a very important part of the priestly office to bless the people, and God prescribed a form of words to be used by Aaron and his sons in the discharge of that duty. Nor can any words better express the scope and end of the Christian ministry. If the people be brought to receive abundant communications of grace and peace, and to surrender up themselves entirely to God, a minister can desire nothing more in this world; his labours are well repaid. To promote this blessed end, we shall—

I. **Explain the words before us.**

God is here making known His will to Moses, and directing him what orders to give to Aaron and his sons respecting the execution of their priestly office; and there are two duties which He assigns to them:—

1. *To bless the people in God's name.* This was repeatedly declared to be their office (Deut. xxi. 5), and the constant practice of the Apostles shows that it was to be continued under the Christian dispensation. In conformity to their example, the Christian Church has universally retained the custom of closing the service with a pastoral benediction. We are not indeed to suppose that ministers can, by any power or authority of their own, convey a blessing (Acts iii. 12); they can neither select the persons who shall be blessed, nor fix the time, the manner, or the degree in which any shall receive a blessing; but, as stewards of the mysteries of God, they dispense the bread of life, assuredly expecting that their Divine Master will give a salutary effect to the ordinances of His own appointment. The direction in the text was confirmed with an express promise, that what they spake on earth should be ratified in heaven; and every faithful minister may take encouragement from it in the discharge of his own duty, and may consider God as saying to him, Bless *thou* the congregation, "*and I will bless them*" (Luke x. 5-6; John xx. 23).

2. *To claim the people as God's property.* To "put the name of God upon them" is to challenge them as His portion, the lot of His inheritance (Deut. xxxii. 9). This every minister must do in most authoritative terms; and not only claim them as His property, but excite them with all earnestness to surrender up themselves to His service. Nor shall their exhortations be lost, for God will accompany them "with the Holy Ghost sent down from heaven;"

and the people, constrained by the Divine impulse, shall say, "I am the Lord's" (Isa. xliv. 3-5). Moreover, in their intercession for the people, they are also to urge this plea with God on their behalf (Jer. xiv. 9; Dan. ix. 17-19). Thus are they to strengthen the connection between God and them, and to promote that fellowship with God, which is the end, as well as the means, of all spiritual communications.

II. Notice some truths contained in them.

Amidst the many profitable observations that may be deduced from the text there are some deserving of peculiar attention.

1. *The priests under the Law, while they blessed the people, typically represented the office of Christ Himself.* Christ as our great High Priest performs every part of the priestly office; and it is remarkable that He was in the very act of blessing His disciples when He was taken up from them into heaven (Luke xxiv. 50, 51). Nor did He then cease, but rather began, as it were, to execute that office, which He has been fulfilling from that time to the present hour. St. Peter, preaching afterwards to a vast concourse of people, declared to them that to bless them was the great end for which Jesus had ascended, and that He was ready, both as a Prince and a Saviour, to give them repentance and remission of sins (Acts iii. 26; v. 31). Let us then conceive the Lord Jesus standing now in the midst of us, and, with uplifted hands, pronouncing the benediction in the text; is there one amongst us that would not cordially add, "Amen, Amen"? Nor let this be thought a vain and fanciful idea, since He has promised to be wherever two or three are gathered together in His name, and *that* too for the very purpose which is here expressed. (Compare Matt. xviii. 20, with Exod. xx. 24.)

2. *The ministers are used as instruments to convey blessings; God Himself is the only Author and Giver of them.* The very words which the priests were commanded to use, directed the attention of all to God Himself; nor could the frequent repetition of Jehovah's name fail to impress the most careless auditor with a conviction, that the blessing could come from God alone. We ought indeed to reverence God's ministers as the authorised dispensers of His blessings (1 Thess. v. 13); but we must look for the blessings themselves to God alone; and endeavour to exercise faith on the Father as the Fountain of them, on Christ as the Channel in which they flow, and on the Holy Spirit as the Agent by whose Divine energy they are imparted to the soul (Rev. i. 4, 5). At the same time we should remember the obligations which these mercies lay us under to devote ourselves entirely to the service of our gracious and adorable Benefactor.

3. *However weak the ordinances be in themselves, yet shall they, if attended in faith, be available for our greatest good.* Nothing can be conceived more simple in itself than a priestly benediction; yet, most undoubtedly it brought down many blessings upon the people. And can we suppose that God will put less honour upon His ordinances under the Gospel dispensation? Shall not "*grace, mercy and peace* flow down from God the Father and from the Lord Jesus Christ," in answer to the fervent intercessions of His ministers? (2 Tim. i. 2). Though ministers be but earthen vessels, yet shall they impart unto the people the richest treasures (2 Cor. iv. 7). Their word shall not be in vain, but shall accomplish God's good pleasure, etc. (Isa. lv. 10, 11). Let not then the benediction be so often slighted, as though it were only a signal to depart: but while it is delivered with solemnity in the name of God, let every heart be expanded to receive the benefit. Let every one consider *himself in particular* as the person addressed ("*thee*" was repeated six times); and may the experience of all attest at this time that God is ready to "grant us above all that we can ask or think."—*C. Simeon, M.A.*

CHAPTER VII.

CRITICAL AND EXPLANATORY NOTES.

In this chapter we have the narrative of the presentation of gifts by the princes of the tribes at the dedication of the altar. "This presentation took place at the time (יוֹם) when Moses, after having completed the erection of the tabernacle, anointed and sanctified the dwelling and the altar, together with their furniture (Lev. viii. 10, 11). Chronologically considered, this ought to have been noticed after Lev. viii. 10. But in order to avoid interrupting the connection of the Sinaitic laws, it is introduced for the first time at this point, and placed at the head of the events which immediately preceded the departure of the people from Sinai, because these gifts consisted in part of materials that were indispensably necessary for the transport of the tabernacle during the march through the desert. Moreover, there was only an interval of at the most forty days between the anointing of the tabernacle, which commenced after the first day of the first month (cf. Exod. xl. 16, and Lev. viii. 10), and lasted eight days, and the departure from Sinai, on the twentieth day of the second month (chap. x. ii), and from this we have to deduct six days for the Passover, which took place before their departure (chap. ix. 1 sqq.); and it was within this period that the laws and ordinances from Lev. xi. to Num. vi. had to be published, and the dedicatory offerings to be presented. Now, as the presentation itself was distributed, according to vers. 11 sqq., over twelve or thirteen days, we may very well assume that it did not entirely precede the publication of the laws referred to, but was carried on in part contemporaneously with it. The presentation of the dedicatory gifts of one tribe-prince might possibly occupy only a few hours of the day appointed for the purpose, and the rest of the day, therefore, might very conveniently be made use of by Moses for publishing the laws. In this case the short space of a month and a few days would be amply sufficient for everything that took place."—*Keil* and *Del.*

Ver. 2. *The princes of the tribes, and were over them,* etc. Margin : *Who stood over,* etc. Keil and Del : " *Those who stood over those that were numbered, i.e.,* who were their leaders or rulers " (see chap. i. 4-16).

Ver. 3. *Covered wagons.* Gesenius and De Wette translate : " *litter wagons ;*" but their rendering " can neither be defended etymologically, nor based upon צָבִים in Isa. lxvi. 20."—*Keil* and *Del.* The rendering of the LXX is ἁμάξας λαμπηνίκας, which, according to Euseb. Emis. signifies two-wheeled vehicles. Dr. A. Clarke renders : "*tilted wagons.*" And Dr. H. E. J. Howard : "*tilted wains.*" They use the word tilted in the sense of tented, or, as in the A. V., covered ; and this seems to be the meaning of the original.

The service of the sanctuary. Heb. lit., "the holy," *i.e.,* the holy things (see chap. iv. 5-20).

Ver. 10, *In the day.* Keil and Del., " That is, at the time 'that they anointed it.' 'Day,' as in Gen. ii. 4."

Ver. 13. *One silver charger.* A dish, or deep bowl. (See Exod. xxv. 29.) |*One silver bowl.* A basin to receive the blood of the sacrifice in.

Ver. 14. *One spoon.* A censer, on which they placed the incense, as in Exod. xxv. 29.

Ver. 84-86. Attersol (1618) reckons the whole of the dishes, basins, and censers to be worth about £420. Dr. A. Clarke (1836), *in loco,* gives his calculation in detail, and makes the total £627 1s. 11¼d. The *Speaker's Comm.* (1871): " If a silver shekel be taken roughly as weighing 2·5 of a shilling, and a golden shekel 1·15 of a sovereign, the intrinsic worth, by weight of each silver charger, will be 325s., of each bowl 175s., of each golden spoon 230s. Consequently the aggregate worth, by weight, of the whole of the offerings will be £438. But the real worth of such a sum, when measured by the prices of clothing and food at that time, must have been vastly greater. It must not be forgotten, too, that the tabernacle itself had been recently constructed at a vast cost."

Ver. 89. *The tabernacle of the congregation.* Heb., "The tent of meeting." *To speak with Him, i.e.,* with God, as in the margin ; for "the name Jehovah, though not expressly mentioned before, is contained *implicite* in *ohel moēd.* 'the tent of meeting.'" *He heard the voice of one speaking.* Rather, "he heard the voice speaking," or "conversing."

Proceeding to our Homiletical treatment of the chapter, we have in the first paragraph—

An Ancient Offering, and its Modern Lessons.
(*Verses* 1-9.)

These verses suggest the following lessons—

1. That they who hold the most honourable positons should be most liberal in contributions to worthy objects.

The princes of the tribes of Israel are here prominent in bringing their offering for the service of the Tabernacle. They present an example well worthy the imitation of those who are exalted in rank, rich in possessions, or great in power. Such persons are under all the ordinary obligations to help forward every good work. They, in common with all men, are required to use their talents, means, and opportunities so as to accomplish the greatest amount of good. They are also under special obligations to advance every true and good cause amongst men, because of the conspicuousness of their position, and the extent of their influence. The extent of our obligations is determined by our opportunities. Privilege is the measure of responsibility. "For unto whomsoever much is given, of him shall be much required: and to whom men have committed much, of him will they ask the more."

1. *Great honours should incite to great efforts to do good.* Those upon whom God has bestowed great wealth, or whom He has raised to exalted stations, should manifest their thankfulness by generously promoting those objects which accord with the Divine will. "The more any are advanced, the more is expected from them, on account of the greater opportunity they have of serving God and their generation. What are wealth and authority good for, but as they enable a man to do so much the more good in the world?"

2. *Great influence involves great obligation.* The example of persons in high station is extensively observed; their exalted position gives conspicuousness to their life and conduct. Their example is also very effective, for persons are generally prone to copy it, when that of persons in lowly stations would be disregarded. So their influence is very great; and the possession of great influence is a sacred and solemn trust. So "superior rank demands superior worth." They who are exalted in station should cultivate the exalted in character and conduct ; and so their great influence will be a great blessing.

"Since by your greatness you
Are nearer Heaven in place, be nearer it
In goodness. Rich men should transcend the poor,
As clouds the earth; raised by the comfort of
The sun, to water dry and barren grounds."
— *Tourneive.* (*a*)

II. That they who are not entirely engaged in religious ministries should seek to help those who are so engaged.

111

These princes of the tribes were not set apart for religious duties; but by this offering of wagons and oxen for the service of the tabernacle, they evinced their desire to assist the Levites in discharging their sacred duties. "You know," says Babington, "how the Levites were to carry upon their shoulders the things belonging to the tabernacle when they removed, but now they shall be eased by these chariots and oxen. So the laity careth for the clergy, to help them, to ease them, to comfort them in their duties belonging to God. And O! how could I dwell in the meditation of it a whole day, it is so sweet. Will you note it and think of it? I trust you will, and so I commit it to you." There are still many ways in which Christian men and women may, and in which some of them do, assist their ministers. It is the privilege and duty of every disciple of Christ Jesus to engage in some work for the good of others; and when every one is so engaged, the labours of the ministers of the Gospel, which in some instances are very arduous and continuous, will be much lightened, and from many things, which by reason of the sloth or unreasonableness of the churches they now have to do, though they pertain not to their work, they will then be entirely free. The offering of the princes of the tribes manifests a thoughtfulness and appropriateness, which are well worthy of commendation and imitation. They gave with wise judgment such things as proved most useful in the service of the tabernacle.

(b)

III. That God is graciously pleased to accept of man's offerings.

"And the Lord spake unto Moses, saying, Take it of them, that they may be to do the service of the tabernacle of the congregation; and thou shalt give them unto the Levites, to every man according to his service." Thus God signifies his acceptance of their offering. Surely it is a great honour which God confers upon us in accepting our gifts in His service. If our heart be sincere the offering of even the smallest gift, or the feeblest effort in His cause, He accepts, approves, and, in His great grace, will reward. "Whosoever shall give to drink unto one of these little ones a cup of cold water only in the name of a disciple, verily I say unto you, he shall in no wise lose his reward." Let this be to us an incentive to liberal and hearty giving, and faithful and diligent working in His cause.

IV. That gifts for religious purposes should be used in accordance with the will of God.

"Thou shalt give them unto the Levites, to every man according to his service. And Moses took the wagons and the oxen, and gave them unto the Levites. Two wagons and four oxen he gave unto the sons of Gershom, according to their service," etc. The offering was faithfully applied by Moses in such a way as to gratify the wishes of the givers, serve the interests of the people, and comply with the directions of the Lord. Here is a lesson which is very wide in its applications, and which is urgently needed in some quarters to-day. The offerings which are contributed to the cause of God, should be used not for the mere increase and aggrandisement of a sect or party, not for the mere advocacy and spread of any pet notions, favourite theories, or sectarian creeds, but for the promotion of the cause and glory of God in the well-being of humanity. This is attained by doing the largest amount of good in the most Christlike spirit. The money or property, which in past ages, was left for purposes which were then useful and worthy, but which, in the altered circumstances of this age, have very much ceased to be so, should be applied to such purposes as shall be at once productive of the most good to the community, and most nearly in accord with the wishes of the giver, as far as they can be ascertained. To attempt to monopolise such gifts, or restrict the benefits which might be attained by them, on the ground of the wishes of the "pious donor," or

112

"founder," is, to say the least, utterly unworthy of Christian men.

V. That in the Divine arrangements help is granted unto men according to their respective needs.

"Thou shalt give them unto the Levites, to every man according to his service. And Moses took the waggons and the oxen, and gave them unto the Levites," etc., vers. 5-9. The principle of distribution which Moses adopted, was laid down by God Himself; "Give to every man according to his service." In harmony with this principle, the Merarites, to whom was assigned the most burdensome part of the service (chap. iv. 29-33), received four wagons and eight oxen; the Gershonites, whose service was less burdensome (chap. iv. 21-26), received two wagons and four oxen; while the Kohathites, who had to carry the most holy things upon their shoulders, and were provided with poles for that purpose (chap. iv. 4-20), received neither wagon nor oxen. There is a proportion between the burden imposed and the strength imparted. "God proportions the burden to the back," says Trapp. But it is both more correct and more inspiring to say, God proportions the back to the burden. (Comp. 1 Cor. x. 13, with 2 Cor. xii. 9.) God will not suffer us to be tempted above that we are able, because as the power of temptation increases, He will increase our power of resistance. As our need increases He increases the communications of His grace; and the infinitude of His resources must ever immeasurably surpass our utmost need. And as His knowledge of us and kindness toward us are infinite, we may rest assured that He will not fail to proportion His assistance to our necessities. What an encouragement is this as we look on to the future, with its unknown experiences, its possibilities of sore trial, of insuperably difficult labour, etc. Infinite resources of patience and power, grace and courage, are pledged to us. Apart from Christ we can do nothing; but with the help of the Holy one of Israel even a "worm shall thresh the mountains, and beat them small, and make the hills as chaff." (See Isa. xli. 13-16.) "God is able to make all grace abound toward you; that ye, always having all sufficiency in all things, may abound to every good work." "When I am weak, then am I strong;" for Christ's strength is made perfect in His people's weakness. "I can do all things through Christ which strengtheneth me." (c)

ILLUSTRATIONS.

(a) They that are great, and worthy to be so,
Hide not their rays from meanest plants that grow.
Why is the sun set on a throne so high,
But to give light to each inferior eye?
His radiant eyes distribute lively grace
To all according to their worth and place;
And from the humble ground these vapours drain,
Which are sent down in fruitful drops of rain.—*Beaumont.*

(b) We want labourers; persons who can distribute tracts silently, and persons who can speak a word in season; we want rich men who can go in carriages, and poor men who can only walk; we want ladies who are muffled and furred with all the armour of a luxurious civilization, and poor women whose hearts are warm with a glowing love to the Saviour: we want persons who can teach ragged children, and persons who can address ragged men: *Who will come?* Don't oppress those who are working too much already. There is a vast amount of non-productive energy in the Church. There are men and women voluntarily dumb, *they* must speak; there are Christians who have an enormous talent for sleeping, *they* must be awakened; there are disciples who imagine that their Christian duties are discharged when they have criticised other people, *they* must be persuaded or provoked into activity; as with the body, so with the soul—we cannot do our duty with mere empty words;—"if a brother or a sister be naked, and destitute of daily food, and one of you say unto them, Depart in peace, and be ye warmed and filled; notwithstanding ye give them not those things which are needful for the body; what doth it profit?" So with the soul. It is not enough to erect your buildings, you must go out, and with all the gentle violence of love "*compel* men to come in." . . . . You can bring in the millennium when you please; God is waiting; the Redeemer is at hand; "Prove me now herewith, saith the Lord, if I will not open the windows of heaven, and pour you out a blessing, until there shall not be room enough to contain it." That is the challenge; who will accept it? God says He *waits* to be gracious; then let *us* wait patiently upon God! The rain will come if we pray for it. The battle will be given to Israel if we hold up the hands of His servant.—*Jos. Parker, D.D.*

(*c*) Christianity boldly, undisguisedly declares to every human being under sin, that he has no complete power beforehand, as in reference to anything really good. And then it calls him to be good, on the express condition always that he is to have powers, stimulants, increments, accruing as he wants them; that on these, or the promise of them, he may rest his faith, and so go forward. It says to the struggling and misgiving penitent, "Let him take hold of My strength, that he may make peace with Me, and he shall make peace with Me." It calls every man to earnest and hopeful endeavour, by the consideration of an all-supporting grace that cannot fail; "Work out your salvation with fear and trembling, for it is God that worketh in you." It shows the Christian testifying in sublimity of confidence, "When I am weak, then am I strong; I can do all things through Christ, which strengtheneth me." It promises the faithful man all the support needed for his exigencies as they arise, "They that wait upon the Lord shall renew their strength; they shall mount up with wings as eagles; they shall run, and not be weary; they shall walk, and not faint." It also establishes, in a manner to comprehend everything, a doctrine of Divine concourse by the Holy Spirit, which carries in it the pledge of all-accruing grace, and light, and might, and holy impulsion; "Ask, and ye shall receive; seek, and ye shall find; knock, and it shall be opened." Indeed, the doctrine or fact of the Holy Spirit is only another way of generalizing the truth that God will co-work invigoratively, correctively, and directively in all the good struggles of believing souls; and so will bring in, at all times and junctures, those increments of power that are necessary to success.

All the simplest, most living, and most genuine Christians of our own time are such as rest their souls, day by day, on this confidence and promise of accruing power, and make themselves responsible, not for what they have in some inherent ability, but for what they can have in their times of stress and peril, and in the continual raising of their own personal quantity and power. They throw themselves on works wholly above their ability, and get accruing power in their works for others still higher and greater. Instead of gathering in their souls timorously beforehand upon the little sufficiency they find in possession, they look upon the great world God has made, and all the greater world of the Saviour's kingdom in it, as being friendly and tributary, ready to pour in help, minister light, and strengthen them to victory, just according to their faith. And so they grow in courage, confidence, personal volume, efficiency of every kind, and instead of slinking into their graves out of impotent lives, they lie down in the honours of heroes.

Go to your duty, every man, and trust yourselves to Christ; for He will give you all supply just as fast as you need it. You will have just as much power as you believe you can have. Be a Christian, throw yourself upon God's work, and get the ability you want in it.—*H. Bushnell, D.D.*

THE OFFERINGS FOR DEDICATING THE ALTAR, AND THEIR MORAL SUGGESTIONS.

(*Verses* 10-88.)

Two introductory points are suggested:

First: *The obligation of man to honour God with his possessions.* The princes of the tribes liberally contributed to the erection and furnishing of the tabernacle, that the Lord might be honoured amongst the people. And all men are under the most solemn obligations to employ their possessions in such a way as to honour God thereby. He is the sole proprietor of all things. "Every beast of the forest is Mine, and the cattle upon a thousand hills." "The silver is Mine, and the gold is Mine, saith the Lord of hosts." "The earth is the Lord's, and the fulness thereof; the world, and they that dwell therein." The wealthiest man has nothing that he can really call his own; his relation to his temporal possessions is not that of ownership but of stewardship. In giving to the cause of God, or to the needs of man, we only give God His own. Well did king David say, "All things come of Thee, and of Thine own have we given Thee." To the "rich in this world" it is a charge from God, "that they do good, that they be rich in good works, ready to distribute, willing to communicate." And according to his ability every man is required to communicate unto others, and so to distribute his worldly goods, that God shall be honoured thereby. Our business is not to selfishly hoard, but to generously dispense ; not vainly to accumulate, but wisely to use the goods with which God has entrusted us. He will one day call us to give account of our stewardship. What account will the selfish and useless be able to render unto Him ? (*a*)

Second : *The obligation of man to continue in a right and good course.* These princes of the tribes had already liberally contributed to the construction of the tabernacle (Exod. xxxv. 27, 28*)*; they had also presented the wagons and the oxen for its removal from place to place ; and now they are offering their gifts for the dedication of the altar. Having begun this good work, they continued therein until it was brought to perfection. As man accustoms himself to give for the promotion of worthy objects, both his *disposition* to give and his *power* to give are increased. His disposition to give is increased ; for he learns the joy of giving ; he increasingly proves that " it is more blessed to give than to receive." His power to give is also increased ; for " there is that scattereth, and yet increaseth ; and there is that withholdeth more than is meet, but it tendeth to poverty. The liberal soul shall be made fat ; and he that watereth shall be watered also himself."

" There was a man,—some men did count him mad—
The more he gave away the more he had."

Good beginnings must be carried onward to perfect endings. Continuance and progress in duty and service are required from us. Having given much, let us endeavour to give more. Having done well, let us try to do better. " Forgetting those things which are behind," etc. (Phil. iii. 13, 14). " Let us go on unto perfection."

Let us now proceed to consider—

I. The Significance of the Offerings for the Dedication of the Altar.

1. *Their offerings express the sense of of equality of obligation.* Every tribe, by its prince, presents the same kind of offering, and in the same quantity, as an expression of their equal indebtedness to God. By Him they all alike had been emancipated from slavery and cruelty in Egypt ; by Him they were all alike protected, provisioned and led ; and it was fitting that each should thus testify to their equality of obligation. There are certain mercies which all men have in common ; certain Divine gifts which are bestowed upon all men ; Christ " died for all " men ; and there are certain obligations to God in which all men share. " He died for all, that they which live should not henceforth live unto themselves," etc.

2. *Their offerings express symbolically the Divine calling of the nation to be holy unto the Lord.* All the vessels presented were for sacrificial uses, all the animals were ceremonially clean and such as were proper for sacrifices ; all the other gifts were of the best quality and were to be used in the worship of God. By these things it was indicated that the people were to be a separate people, entirely dedicated to God, and that God was to dwell in their midst. The lesson for us is, that God is to be worshipped with our highest and best. The best of our affections, of our thoughts, of our actions, of our possessions, we should cheerfully consecrate to Him. Beautifully was this illustrated by Mary of Bethany, when, with glowing gratitude and reverent and rapturous love she poured the precious ointment on the head and feet of her adored Lord. (*b*)

3. *Their offerings express symbolically the great truths taught by the different sacrifices.* They brought a " kid of the goats for a *sin-offering.*" The sin-offering expressed the consciousness of sin on the part of the offerer, the need of forgiveness and taonement with God, and the belief that these were to be obtained through the sacrifice of the appointed victim. They offered " one young bullock, one ram, one lamb of the first year, for a *burnt-offering.*" The burnt-offering was wholly consumed upon the altar to the honour of God ; and its main idea is that it represents the entire devotion of the offerer to God, that he

gives himself wholly and for ever to Him. Canon Barry well says that "the best comment upon it is the exhortation in Rom. xii. 1, to 'present our bodies a living sacrifice, holy and acceptable to God.'" They also brought "for a sacrifice of *peace-offerings*, two oxen, five rams, five he-goats, and five lambs of the first year." The peace-offerings were expressions of the gratitude of the worshipper to God; they "were simply offerings to God of His own best gifts, as a sign of thankful homage, and as a means of maintaining His service and His servants." All these ideas and feelings, therefore, which these sacrifices represent, were expressed in the offerings which the princes, each one representing his respective tribe, presented to the Lord. And should not the ideas and feelings which these offerings were intended to express be ours? Do not we need forgiveness? Let us seek it in faith through the One great Sin-Offering. Are not we under the most sacred and binding obligations to consecrate ourselves entirely unto God? "Know ye not that ye are not your own? For ye are bought with a price; therefore glorify God in your body, and in your spirit, which are God's." "I beseech you therefore, brethren, by the mercies of God, that ye present your bodies a living sacrifice," etc. Have not we many and moving reasons, for most fervent gratitude to God? "What shall I render unto the Lord for all His benefits toward me?" Let us present to Him the offering of sincere and ardent praise. "Bless the Lord, O my soul; and all that is within me, bless His holy name." (*c*)

II. The Significance of the Record of the Offerings for the Dedication of the Altar.

It is remarkable that the particulars are given of each offering, in the case of each one of the princes, though each of the offerings was exactly similar to the others. The repetition seems uninteresting, tedious, wearisome. But is there not some reason for this minuteness of statement? In a Book where subjects of deep interest are mentioned and dismissed sometimes in a few words, a Book moreover which is inspired by God—is there not significance in this wearisome repetition of uninteresting details? What does it mean? It seems to us to suggest—

1. *The pleasure of God in the gifts of His people.* "That everything is so particularly noted," says Babington, "and the weight so precisely mentioned, may teach us to our comfort, what an observation there is in God of the gifts we bestow on Him in promoting His glory, advancing his service, maintaining His ministers in a liberal manner, relieving the poor, and doing such good things as with God and man are praiseworthy. Surely the number, the measure, with all circumstances, are observed; and the Lord is a plenteous Rewarder of all love to Him." "Man may pass hastily or carelessly over gifts and offerings; but God never can, never does, and never will. He delights to record every little act of service, every little loving gift. He never forgets the smallest thing; and not only does He not forget it Himself, but He takes special pains that untold millions shall read the record. How little did those twelve princes imagine that their names and their offerings were to be handed down, from age to age, to be read by countless generations! Yet so it was, for God would have it so." They who honour Him with their offerings, He will honour with His expressed approbation. Mary's offering of her precious ointment is known in all the world where the Gospel is preached (Matt. xxvi. 13). And the widow who cast into the treasury of the temple "all that she had," though that "all" was only "two mites," has been crowned by Christ with similar immortality and fame (Mark xii. 41-44). "God is not unrighteous to forget your work and labour of love," etc. (Heb. vi. 10).

2. *The permanence of good works.* When any one does a kind or noble deed, or bestows a generous gift from worthy motives, he does a permanent, an imperishable thing. The breath of

an immortal life is in such deeds. God remembers and will reward them. The grateful heart will for ever cherish the memory of the kind service or generous gift. "The righteous shall be in everlasting remembrance." The noble deed shall live, and bring forth fruit. And the doer himself by his deed has gained somewhat of nobility and strength as a permanent acquisition in his own being. *(d)*

Conclusion.

Our subject is most fruitful of encouragement to—

1. *Liberality of giving to promote worthy objects.*
2. *Diligence in working to promote worthy objects.*

ILLUSTRATIONS.

(*a*) There is nothing made for itself, nothing whose powers and influences are entirely circumscribed to self. Whatever a creature receives it gives out, with the modification and increase of its own force. The clouds borrow water of the ocean, but they pour it forth again in refreshing showers upon the thirsty hills, which, in their turn, send them amongst the valleys. Planets borrow light of their centres, and forthwith fling their rays abroad upon the dark regions of space through which they roll. The tree borrows from every part of the world in order to build up itself, but it gives out, in return, beauty, fragrance, and fruit. Thus all things give what they appropriate. The material is but the emblem of the spiritual, and thus all nature typifies man's distributive function. Is not he who appropriates and does not give an anomaly in the universe?—*David Thomas, D.D.*

There is a popular but unfounded axiom respecting the use of wealth, namely, that "a man may do what he will with his own." Christianity denies this assertion. Every man has indeed a legal right to the disposal of his own property; but religion interdicts his right to spend it in vanity or vice; or if he be exempt from these grosser temptations, she still abridges his right to monopolize it. Christianity expects that the deserving and the distressed shall come in for such a proportion of his wealth as an enlightened conscience shall dictate. The Divine Person who refused, in a legal sense, to be *a divider or a judge* over a contested property, did not fail to graft on the question He avoided answering, the imperative caution, *Take heed, and beware of covetousness.—Gleanings.*

It has been found, by persons disposed to distribute of their substance, that they have supposed themselves more liberal than has really been the case. They have seemed to give frequently, and perhaps have done so; and have at times feared that they were exceeding proper bounds, when at last, resolving to set apart a certain portion of their income for the specific object, they have been surprised at the end of the year to find their funds not exhausted, even though their applications had seemed as numerous, as urgent, and as liberally attended to as before.

Let it be remembered that the sums which some give, however large, may be given without the self-privation of a single worldly comfort, or even of the luxurious enjoyment of the good things of this life, and thence be as *sacrifices that cost nothing*. The Christian had need to enquire in his closet concerning the faithful discharge of his stewardship.—*Ibid.*

(*b*) The act once taken as an homage to the Saviour, recommends itself to us by the sentiments which appear to have inspired it. That homage is agreeable to Jesus Christ, not only because it is addressed to Him, but because it is worthy of Him. That homage, whatever may be said as to its form, expresses all that a Christian soul must feel for Jesus Christ. What ought we, in truth, to say to that God-man, and what ought we to find in our hearts when we render Him homage? What? Admiration? Respect? An estimation of Him above all sages, all heroes, all men? No! but that as He has given Himself for us, we, in our turn, give ourselves to Him; that we exist for Him; that everything we have is held not for ourselves, but for Him; that no sacrifice on our part appears to bear any proportion to that which He has made for us? and that we are ready to abandon everything for His service and for His glory. Now what is the language of the act of Mary, but all this at once? See her search amongst her whole possessions for the most precious and the most valued thing, that she may consume it in honour of Jesus Christ—for it is truly a loss or waste which she intended to make,—and the objection of the disciples, To what purpose is this *waste?* expresses the true meaning of the act better than they imagined. It was not enough to employ this perfume if she did not expend it wholly. And since it is to lose or waste it to pour it all out at once over the head of Jesus Christ, she resolves to waste it. She is better pleased to waste it by consecrating it directly to the honour of Jesus Christ than to employ it more usefully, perhaps, in another way. Ah! this perfume was doubtless the most precious thing she could find in her stores! Doubtless if she had possessed a single thing more precious, she would have preferred to sacrifice it, since, not content with having in a moment bestowed so valuable an object, she broke (needless sacrifice) the alabaster vase in which the ointment was contained. It was then that Judas might cry out with displeasure, "To what purpose is this waste?" since the perfume spread around might minister gratification, but not the broken box. But in this the character of the first of these acts might be misapprehended. Mary had in view in pouring out like water this perfumed ointment, not to afford pleasure, but to subject herself to a loss. She wished at once to express and to prove her feeling that nothing was so dear to her as her Saviour, that she was prepared for all sacrifices for His sake, and that, not having it in her power to make all sacrifices at once, she made that the opportunity of which presented itself, that which was at once a sacrifice and an act of homage. She united in one act the reality and the symbol—she gave and she adored. It was with this view she poured out the ointment, it was with this view she broke the box. And has she no other sacrifice to make for the sake of Him who for her gave up everything, sacrificed everything? Cannot she devote herself? She did so, my brethren, she did this at the moment when the perfumed ointment flowed in streams over the blessed forehead of her Master. She broke another vase whence issued odours still more sweet. She broke her own penitent heart; and grief, love, and hope, perfumes more exquisite than spikenard, myrrh, and incense, spread themselves around and filled the house. You perceived nothing of this, O, intolerant disciples! in vain is this perfume spread around you; but your Master has breathed it; He has understood an action incomprehensible by your proud hearts; He has seen the sorrow of heart of that poor Mary; He has discerned the tears of her repentance, which perhaps could not get outward vent, roll drop by drop from her heart; He knows the secret of that mute grief;—the Saviour and the sinner understand each other, and there passes between them, silently, something sublime, something ineffable, which you will not be able to comprehend unless you, yourselves, come, transported with sorrow and love, to pour perfumes also on the head of Jesus, to shed tears at His feet, and to break your hearts before Him.—*Alex. Vinet, D.D.*

(c) Let us offer the sacrifice of praise to God continually, that is, the fruit of our lips, giving thanks to His name. Had not David a most heavenly spirit, who was so much in this heavenly work? Doth it not sometimes raise our hearts, when we only read the Song of Moses, and the Psalms of David? How much more would it raise and refresh us to be skilful and frequent in the work ourselves! Oh, the loss to many of the saints who drench their spirits in continual sadness, and waste their days in complaints and groans, and so make themselves, both in body and mind, unfit for this sweet and heavenly work! Instead of being employed in the praises of God, they are questioning their worthiness, and studying their miseries, and so rob God of His glory, and themselves of their consolation.—*Gleanings.*

(d) There is nothing, no, nothing innocent or good, that dies, and is forgotten: let us hold to that faith, or none. An infant, a prattling child, dying in its cradle, will live again in the better thoughts of those who loved it; and play its part, through them, in the redeeming actions of the world, though its body be burnt to ashes, or drowned in the deepest sea. There is not an angel added to the host of heaven but does its blessed work on earth in those that loved it here. Forgotten! oh, if the good deeds of human creatures could be traced to their source, how beautiful would even death appear; for how much charity, mercy, and purfied affection would be seen to have their growth in dusty graves.—*Charles Dickens.*

Thousands of men breathe, move, and live, pass off the stage of life, and are heard of no more. Why? They do not partake of good in the world, and none were blessed by them; none could point to them as the means of their redemption; not a line they wrote, not a word they spake, could be recalled; and so they perished; their light went out in darkness, and they were not remembered more than insects of yesterday. Will you thus live and die, O man immortal? Live for something. Do good, and leave behind you a monument of virtue that the storm of time can never destroy. Write your name in kindness, love, and mercy, on the hearts of thousands you come in contact with year by year; you will never be forgotten. No, your name, your deeds will be as legible on the hearts you leave behind as the stars on the brow of evening. Good deeds will shine as the stars of heaven.—*Chalmers.*

THE SUPPORT OF RELIGIOUS INSTITUTIONS.

(*Verse* 88.)

"This was the dedication of the altar, after that it was anointed."

In this chapter we see how the altar was dedicated; and we learn that God expects His people to provide for and to carry on His work. This dedication of the altar

I. Suggests to us some of the responsibilities of the wealthy.

Wealth is a talent. God will demand

an account of it. He holds the wealthy responsible—

1. *To give of their wealth to carry on His work.* God claims a share of all we get; how much that shall be He leaves to our conscience. He looks not so much at the amount as at the motive. He measures our gifts by our hearts. To Christ the "two mites" was the greatest offering in the Treasury of the Temple for that reason. God expects us to take care of His house and work; not to do so is a sin. David was in distress because he lived in a better house than the Ark of God had; that is the right feeling. Surely we ought to take as good care of God's house as of our own. Were it so, the treasury of God's house would never be empty.

2. *To take the lead in doing good—to be examples in giving.* The wealthy are looked up to; if they fail to do their duty, not only do they fail to do good, but they also check and prevent others from doing so.

II. **Is a striking illustration of the voluntary principle.**

It teaches us the true method of giving for the support of religious institutions.

1. *God has left His work to be carried on by His people.*
2. *The voluntary principle is the most effective for doing this.* (1) Because conscience is brought into action by it: giving becomes an act of worship. (2) Because man is then on his honour. (3) As a matter of fact it has never failed. See how much it produced here in the wilderness. The Church in the present age supplies ample proof of its success. (a)
3. *God is greatly pleased with it.* He approves of it. Read ver. 89 with the text. He approves—(1) Because voluntary giving evinces real interest in His work—shows that it is done from love. The free-will offering is a good guage of the people's hearts and interest. (2) He will accept nothing that is done from constraint. (3) He testifies to His pleasure, in His Word and by blessing those who so help His work. "Every man according as he purposeth in his heart; not grudgingly, or of necessity; for God loveth a cheerful giver." Those who give to God are ever blessed by Him. Our Master pays well; we never lose by serving Him faithfully. "He which soweth bountifully shall reap also bountifully."—David Lloyd.

ILLUSTRATION.

(a) In Scotland, during the last seventeen years (1861), an experiment has been made on a large scale of the power of the voluntary principle, and made, too, by men who had but little faith in it at first. Of course, I now refer to the "Free Church of Scotland." The alternative was placed before the Church of Scotland, to give up their rights of self-government or to give up State pay. And **478** ministers and professors said, We will give up the pay, we will be free, whatever may be the result. They left their homes, and the churches in which their fathers had worshipped, trusting in God to provide for them. And what the results have been I am now about to lay before you. Let us first look at what they have done, in sixteen years, in the way of providing accommodation for religious worship. They have built—

	£	s.	d.		£	s.	d.
800 Churches at an average cost of	918	6	0	total 734,641	1	2
565 Manses, ditto	600	0	0	„ 339,000	0	0
620 Schools, ditto	335	0	0	„ 207,700	0	0
Carried forward				1,281,341	1	2

	£	s.	d.
Brought forward	128,341	1	2
Edinburgh College, total cost	33,879	5	1
Glasgow College, „ „	11,220	0	0
Aberdeen College „ „	2,360	0	0
Edinburgh and Glasgow Normal Schools	22,564	9	6
Assembly Hall and site, Edinburgh	8,500	0	0
Church Offices in Mound-place	7,500	0	0
Churches, Manses, Schools, erected at the expense of individuals, not appearing in the public accounts	50,000	0	0
Aggregate cost of buildings	£1,422,364	15	9

From this large amount of money spent in buildings, there are two small deductions to be made. First, the existing debt upon them is estimated at £90,000; and second, towards the erection of the schools they have received £20,000 from the Government. Deducting these there is the noble sum of £1,312,364 15s. 9d. left, which in sixteen years the Free Church of Scotland has invested in lime, stone, and land! Let us now look at the ministry of the Free Church. There were **478** ministers who left their emoluments and status in the Established Church. In the first year of the Free Church each of these received a stipend from £105 and upwards. In the year 1859 the number of ministers had increased to 784, and the lowest stipend was then £138. Besides which, 565 of them had a pleasant manse, built by the free-will offerings of the people.

But perhaps it may be thought that all the energies of the Free Church have been confined to building churches and schools, and providing for their own wants at home; but this has not been the case. They have been doing much for others in various ways, and in many lands. Allow me to read you the income for the year 1859, for various religious objects:—

Building Fund, General and Local ...	£50,519 16 0½
Sustentation Fund	126,282 14 6
Congregational Fund	94,481 19 6
Education Fund	17,764 15 3
College Fund	9,000 8 5
General Trustees and Miscellaneous...	36,619 4 7½
Carried forward	334,668 18 4

Brought forward	£334,668 18 4
Glasgow Evangelisation	2,539 11 1
Missions to the Highlands	1,314 3 2
Missions to the Colonies	4,487 15 9
Missions to the Continent	2,456 19 8
Foreign Missions	13,210 2 6
Missions to the Jews	7,673 13 3
Making a total income for 1859 of	£342,723 12 4½

You will see from these figures that the zeal of the Free Church is expansive. If they begin at home they do not stay there. From the year 1843 to 1859, a period of sixteen years, the Free Church raised for all purposes £4,883,132 12s. 6¾d. And after sixteen years' experience the income of the Free Church still increases. "Leaving out of view the building funds which are temporary, the aggregate of all the other funds has been steadily, year by year, increasing; so that the yearly average of the last five years is twenty-five per cent. above the yearly average of the first five years."—*Marmaduke Miller.*

THE CONDESCENSION OF GOD AND THE PRIVILEGES OF MAN.

(*Verse* 89.)

Already the Lord had promised Moses that He would meet with him, and commune with him from above the mercy-seat (Exod. xxv. 22); and now He fulfils that promise. The tribes had cheerfully contributed everything necessary for the tabernacle and its sacred services! and now the Most High acknowledges His acceptance of their offerings by manifesting His Presence in thus speaking to Moses in the holy of holies. Let us consider,—

1. The great condescension of God. "When Moses was gone into the tabernacle of the congregation to speak with Him, then he heard the Voice of One speaking unto him," etc. Moses heard the Voice conversing with him. Great is the condescension of the Lord in thus speaking with Moses, and through Moses to the people. Let us notice here—

1. *The sacred place in which He speaks.* It was in the holy of holies in "the tabernacle of meeting." It was in this place that he had promised to meet with His servant. "There I will meet with thee, and I will commune with thee," etc. He is represented as dwelling in this place, and as enthroned between **the cherubim.** It was the place of His special self-manifestation. God is everywhere present.

"Earth's crammed with heaven,
And every common bush afire with God;
But only he who sees takes off his shoes;
The rest sit round and gather blackberries."

The thoughtful and reverent mind beholds signs of the presence and activity of God on every hand. We see his glory in the countless orbs of heaven, and in the exquisite pencillings and perfumes of the flowers of earth, etc. But still He specially manifests Himself to man in His house. In the proclamation of the glorious Gospel, in the administration of the holy sacraments, and in the presentation of reverent worship to Him, man most often and fully realses the presence and hears the Voice of God (compare Exod. xx. 24; 2 Chron. vi. 18; and Matt. xviii. 20).

2. *The grand medium through which He speaks.* "Speaking unto him from off the mercy-seat that was upon the ark of testimony, from between the two cherubims." The mercy-seat was "the massive golden cover of the ark of the covenant, on which the glory of Jehovah appeared between the cherubim. It was that upon which especially the

blood of the propitiatory sacrifice was sprinkled on the day of atonement (Lev. xvi. 15), and from this circumstance apparently, the propitiation taking place on it, it obtained its name of ἱλαστήριον. It was the footstool of God (1 Chron. xxviii. 2 ; Psa. xcix. 5). The spot where He, the God of the covenant, met with Israel, the people of the covenant." It is also called "the oracle" (1 Kings vi. 19, 20, 23). Now the mercy-seat is an illustration, perhaps a type, of the Lord Jesus Christ. He is the true Mercy-seat, the Divine ἱλαστήριον (Rom. iii. 25). By the shedding of His blood, the great atonement for the sins of the world was made. In Him God draws near to man, and communes with him. He is the true Divine Oracle ; through Him the most precious revelations of God have been made ; in Him we hear the voice of God most clearly and graciously (Heb. i. 1-3).

3. *The gracious purpose for which He speaks.* In this instance, the voice from between the cherubim doubtless announced to Moses the gracious acceptance by Jehovah of the cheerful offerings of the princes of the tribes ; and intimated that He had taken up His abode in their midst. All the utterances of God are for the benefit of man. Even the proclamation of His law is an expression of His benevolence to our race. "Law is love defined." "The law is holy, and the commandment holy and just, and good." But how gracious are His utterances to us by Christ Jesus ! "All wondered at the gracious words which proceeded out of His mouth." "Never man spake like this Man." "The words that I speak unto you are spirit, and are life." "Thou hast the words of eternal life." The grand purpose for which God speaks to us through Christ is that we might be saved from sin, and restored to the perfect likeness and the intimate fellowship of Himself. Jesus Christ is preeminently the Word of God ; He is the fullest, grandest, most eloquent expression of the Divine love ; and the great object of His incarnation was the redemption of man from evil, and the conference upon him of eternal and blessed life. How great is the condescension of God in all this. (*a*)

II. **The great privileges of man.**

Moses went into the tabernacle of meeting to speak with Jehovah, and he heard the voice conversing with him : and he spake unto Him. Here is a twofold privilege which through Jesus Christ every man may enjoy :—

1. *We may speak unto God.* He invites us to do so, and promises us a gracious audience. "Offer unto God thanksgiving, and pay thy vows unto the Most High ; and call upon Me in the day of trouble : I will deliver thee, and thou shalt glorify Me." "In everything by prayer and supplication with thanksgiving, let your requests be made known unto God." (See Isa. lxv. 24 ; Dan. ix. 20-23 ; Mal. iii. 16, 17 ; Matt. xviii. 19, 20 ; John xvi. 23-27.) In all ages godly souls have proved the reality and the preciousness of this privilege. In time of grief or gladness, of perplexity or penitence, of doubt or dread, of triumph or tribulation, we may speak unto God in praise or prayer, or in the silent language of the heart, which He perfectly comprehends, assured that He will hear us graciously, and bless us generously. Blessed privilege ! (*b*)

2. *We may receive communications from God.* The soul which, through the mediation of Jesus Christ, is brought into sympathy with Him, receives communications from Him through many voices. In the melodies and minstrelsies of nature such a soul hears with reverent delight the Divine music of the Father's voice. We receive messages from Him through the sacred Scriptures, through the operations of His providence, and through the mysterious and gracious ministry of His Spirit. And how precious and helpful are His communications ! Pardon to the guilty, peace to the penitent, joy to the sorrowful, direction to the perplexed, hope to the despondent, etc. Unspeakably great and blessed are our privileges. (*c*)

121

III. The consequent duty of man.

The possession of privileges always involves corresponding obligations. Since man possesses these privileges, it becomes his duty—

1. *To wait upon God in His house.* No one can neglect public worship without sinning against his own soul and God.

2. *To address God in His house.* Since He invites us to do so, we cannot neglect the privilege of uniting in praise and prayer without sin.

3. *To listen for the Voice of God in His house.* The wise and godly soul resorts to the temple of God not to be charmed with the eloquence, or stimulated by the reasoning, or moved by the pathos of the preacher; not to be gratified by the spectacles of a gorgeous ritualism, or delighted by the musical performances of professional choirs; but with humble reverence to speak to God, and with devout attention to listen to His voice. (*d*)

ILLUSTRATIONS.

(*a*) A king might have the whole of his reign crowded with the enterprises of his glory; and by the might of his arms, and the wisdom of his counsels, might win the first reputation among the potentates of the world, and be idolized throughout all his provinces for the wealth and the security that he had spread around them—and still it is conceivable, that by the act of a single day in behalf of a single family; by some soothing visitation of tenderness to a poor and solitary cottage; by some deed of compassion, which conferred enlargement and relief on one despairing sufferer; by some graceful movement of sensibility at a tale of wretchedness; by some noble effort of self-denial, in virtue of which he subdued his every purpose of revenge, and spread the mantle of a generous oblivion over the fault of the man who had insulted and aggrieved him; above all, by an exercise of pardon so skilfully administered, as that, instead of bringing him down to a state of defencelessness against the provocation of future injuries, it threw a deeper sacredness over him, and stamped a more inviolable dignity than ever on his person and character:—why, on the strength of one such performance, done in a single hour, and reaching no farther in its immediate effects than to one house or one individual, it is a most possible thing, that the highest monarch upon earth might draw such a lustre around him, as would eclipse the renown of all his public achievements—and that such a display of magnanimity, or of worth, beaming from the secrecy of his familiar movements, might awaken a more cordial veneration in every bosom, than all the splendour of his conspicuous history—ay, and that it might pass down to posterity as a more enduring monument of greatness, and raise him farther, by its moral elevation, above the level of ordinary praise; and when he passes in review before the men of distant ages, may this deed of modest, gentle, unobtrusive virtue, be at all times appealed to as the most sublime and touching memorial of his name.

In like manner did the King eternal, immortal, and invisible, surrounded as He is with the splendours of a wide and everlasting monarchy, turn Him to our humble habitation; and the footsteps of God manifest in the flesh, have been on the narrow spot of ground we occupy; and small though our mansion be amid the orbs and the systems of immensity, hither hath the King of glory bent His mysterious way, and entered the tabernacle of men, and in the disguise of a servant did He sojourn for years under the roof which canopies our obscure and solitary world. Yes, it is but a twinkling atom in the peopled infinity of worlds that are around it—but look to the moral grandeur of the transaction, and not to the material extent of the field upon which it was executed—and from the retirement of our dwelling-place, there may issue forth such a display of the Godhead, as will circulate the glories of His name amongst all His worshippers. Here sin entered. Here was the kind and universal beneficence of a Father repaid by the ingratitude of a whole family. Here the law of God was dishonoured, and that too in the face of its proclaimed and unalterable sanctions. Here the mighty contest of the attributes was ended—and when justice put forth its demands, and truth called for the fulfilment of its warnings, and the immutability of God would not recede by a single iota from any one of its positions, and all the severities He had ever uttered against the children of iniquity, seemed to gather into one cloud of threatening vengeance on the tenement that held us—did the visit of the only begotten Son chase away all these obstacles to the triumph of mercy—and humble as the tenement may be, deeply shaded in the obscurity of insignificance as it is, among the statelier mansions which are on every side of it—yet will the recall of its exiled family never be forgotten, and the illustration that has been given here of the mingled grace and majesty of God will never lose its place among the themes and the acclamations of eternity.—*Thomas Chalmers, D.D., LL.D.*

(*b*) **Prayer is not asking for something.** I have nothing to ask for since I have known what God's fatherhood meant. I have but one petition, and that is, "Thy will be done." It is not for me to wake the sun. It is not for me to call the summer. It is not for me to ask for colours in the heavens. All these things are abundantly provided. The earth is the Lord's, and the fulness thereof, and I am God's beloved. He died for me by His Son Jesus Christ. He thinks of me. Do I ever forget my children? Shall a mother forget her baby, cradled in her arms, by day or by night? And shall God forget us in that great rolling sea of His thoughts, in that everlasting fecundity of His love, in the infinite bound of the Divine tenderness and mercy for man? Is there anything left to ask for? When I am tired I carry my weariness there, and lay it down. When I am in sorrow, I am glad when I think of the Sorrowing One. The God of all comfort is my God. When my burden is heavy, it is not so heavy as was His cross. Ten thousand thoughts of this kind that spring from every side of human experience and touch human life in every part—these are elements of prayer. So that when I pray, I rejoice; as the Apostle would say, "Giving thanks in prayer." Prayer is cheerful to me. Prayer is sweet to me; it is not ascetic. I know that I am wicked; I know that I grieve God; I know that there are times when I am glad to say, "God, be merciful to me a sinner!" So there are times for the majesty of storms in summer. But thunderstorms do not march in procession all the way across the bosom of the summer. There is more brightness than darkness, more tranquil fruitfulness than agitation and thunder.—*H. W. Beecher.*

(*c*) What we want in this English land, and down in the midst of this busy nineteenth century—want as a gain that would be to us as life from the dead, is a firm persuasion of God's presence with our human affairs, and of His influence, not only about us, but within us. If He be not thus present with us, where can be the object—the rationality of prayer? Religious men of all creeds have been praying men—must pray. In fact, the Light of the World is ever knocking at the door, now by frustrating our fond earthly schemes, now by bringing us face to face with the judgment-seat through disease or accident; now summoning us to look upon our loved ones dead—in a thousand ways like these does the Incarnate One appeal to our susceptibilities of religious life, and we hearken to His voice, and bid Him welcome, or we heed Him not, and bid Him go His way until some more convenient season. We have to do with a living God. We are in the midst of a living universe. Influences between heaven and earth, like the figures seen on the mystic ladder, are constantly descending and ascending, and spirits have been passing through all time, like an ever-widening stream of light, from this lower world to the higher, where the Highest Himself receives them as His own.—*Robert Vaughan, D.D.*

(*d*) Hear the Word with constant *self-application*. Hear not for others, but for yourselves. What should we think of a person who, after accepting an invitation to a feast, and taking his place at the table, instead of partaking of the repast, amused himself with speculating on the nature of the provisions, or the manner in which they were prepared, and their adaptation to the temperament of the several guests, without tasting a single article? Such, however, is the conduct of those who hear the Word without applying it to themselves, or considering the aspect it bears on their individual character. Go to the house of God with a serious expectation and desire of meeting with something suited to your particular state; something that shall lay the axe to the root of your corruptions; mortify your easily-besetting sin, and confirm the graces in which you are most deficient. A little attention will be sufficient to give you that insight into your character, which will teach what you need; what the peculiar temptations to which you are exposed, and on what account you feel most shame and humiliation before God. Every one may know, if he pleases, the *plague* of his own heart. Keep your eye upon it while you are hearing, and eagerly lay hold upon what is best adapted to heal and correct it. Remember that religion is a personal thing, an individual concern; for every one of us must give an account of *himself* to God, and every man bear his own burden.

Receive with meekness the engrafted Word, which is able to save your souls. If you choose to converse with your fellow-Christians on what you have been hearing, a practice which, if rightly conducted, may be very edifying, let your conversation turn more upon the tendency, the spiritual beauty and glory, of these great things of God which have engaged your attention, than on the merit of the preacher. We may readily suppose that Cornelius and his friends, after hearing Peter, employed very few words in discussing the oratorical talents of that great Apostle; any more than the three thousand, who at the day of Pentecost were pricked to the heart; their minds were too much occupied by the momentous truths they had been listening to, to leave room for such reflections. Yet this is the only kind of religious conversation (if it deserves the application) in which too many professors engage. "Give me," says the incomparable Fenelon, "the preacher who imbues my mind with such a love of the Word of God, as makes me desirous of hearing it from any mouth."—*Robert Hall, A.M.*

Man's Access to God, and God's Word to Man.

(Verse 89.)

The high priest alone had access to the holy of holies; he alone could approach the mercy-seat, and there enjoy the immediate and special presence of God. But Moses seems to have been an exceptional case; a privileged person; for he was permitted to approach God in a way, and to an extent, which was the peculiar privilege of the high priest alone. This may be explained by the fact that Moses was a subordinate mediator between God and Israel in the desert; he is called a mediator in one of the epistles of the New Testament. And that would show that he had an office, an elevation, and a relationship to God, which none else had in that economy, and which gave him, therefore, privileges which none else were permitted to enjoy. But now every Christian has all the right that Moses had. The humblest believer in the house of God is a priest in the truest and only existing sense of the word; and has access as a priest into the immediate presence of God (comp. Eph ii. 18).

What was this way of access by which Moses drew near to God, and by which we draw near? There never was but one, there never will be but one way by which fallen man can draw near to God—Christ the way, the truth, and the life. The mode of revealing it has differed, but the way itself has always been the same. Moses did not see it as clearly as we do, but he trod the same path, nevertheless.

When Moses approached to God, what was the object that he had first in view? Moses drew near to Him to speak to Him. But to speak how? No doubt about it, to pray. And to speak in what manner? No doubt in the name of Jesus, with all freedom (see Heb. iv.14-16). Moses went into the presence of God to tell Him what the wants, the sorrows, the sufferings, the fears, the difficulties of Israel were. We, too, are welcome to go into the very chancel of the universe, into the very presence of Deity, and to tell God our least and our worst cares; for there is no trouble so trivial that God will refuse to listen to it, and there is no trouble so bitter and so burdensome that God will not either remove or give strength to bear.

Not only did Moses go to speak to God, but we read that God spoke to him. I know not which is most precious; that we may speak to God, or that God has spoken to us (Heb. i. 1, 2). Many persons think it strange that God should give a revelation of Himself to us. It would seem, on the contrary, that it would be strange if God did not give us a revelation of Himself. If it be true that we have lost Him, that we cannot by any searching find Him, is it not reasonable—is it not probable that the Father of us all should tell us where He is, what He is, who we are, and whither we are going? Does not the father instruct the children? Does not ripe age warn and teach unripe youth? The Great Father will teach His children, etc.

But how and by whom has God spoken to us? Moses says it was from the mercy-seat, and from between the cherubim. What was that the symbol of? The Apostle tells us, in his epistle to the Romans (iii. 25), "Propitiation," literally, "Mercy-seat." When God, therefore, spoke from the mercy-seat, and from between the cherubim, where the *Shecinah* or the glory shone, it was speaking then, translated into New Testament language, by Christ, the Mediator between God and us. All that can be known of God, He has made known; all that can be seen of God, He is; all that can be heard of God, He speaks. Christ thus is the medium of this communication.

The Book that the Spirit inspired—the Bible—is the depository of what

God said from between the cherubim; or, translated into our language, what God spoke by Jesus Christ. "Holy men of God spake as they were moved by the Holy Ghost." Whatever is not in the Bible, however true, is not essential to salvation; whatever contradicts the Bible, however popular, is not true. But all that is in the Bible is profitable for instruction, for correction in righteousness; for all Scripture is given by inspiration of God. It is the Word perpetuated in ceaseless echoes along the centuries as God spake it in and by Christ Jesus.

We may presume that the Book thus inspired is at least an intelligible Book. There is not a more intelligible book than the Bible. It is not asserted that every word of the Book is plain; but if there be darkness, it is because of the infinitude of the subject, and our imperfection; not because of the inadequacy of the writer or the Inspirer of it. Finite minds cannot comprehend all-infinite truth. We must, therefore, expect that there will be some pages difficult, because the subjects are infinite; but we do find that the passages that relate to our personal well-being are so plain, that he who reads may run while he reads.

The preacher, or the minister, is simply the expositor of this Book. He is not to add to it, nor is he to subtract from it; but he is simply to set it forth, to explain allusions to customs that have passed away; to set its truths in clear light, applying them to modern circumstances, and to the varying phases of every social system.

We have reason to believe that this revelation is God's last communication to man in this dispensation (Heb. i. 1, 2). We cannot add to it; it is not a *discovery* which man has made, and man can mend; but a *revelation* which God has given, and which man, therefore, cannot improve.

God spoke "from between the cherubim." Angels desire to look into these things. They are hearers; we are actors. They can afford to look; but we cannot afford to be passive spectators. It is to us it is spoken; it is about us that God speaks; our responsibility is increased by hearing it.

And what God has put in this Book is of infinite importance. God has not bowed the heavens to make known an idle or a useless tale. It is of infinite value, unspeakably precious. If so, let us be thankful we have heard it, that we have the Word uncorrupted, a lamp to our feet, a light to our path. And if we are thankful for it, how diligently, how devoutly should we study it! And, appreciating this blessed Book ourselves, we ought to circulate and spread it among all mankind.—*John Cumming, D.D.*

THE CHERUBIM AND THE MERCY-SEAT.

(Verse 89.)

Surely there was some design in bringing together all these different objects into one great symbol or type;—the tables of the law, the covering of the mercy-seat, the representation of the cherubim, and the glory of God, the cloud of the Divine presence surmounting them. They teach us that betwixt law and grace; betwixt the administration of grace to man and the heavenly world; and betwixt the whole of this dispensation and arrangement, and the glorious manifested presence of Jehovah, there is a close and interesting connexion.

I. There is now a relation betwixt law and grace.

Why are the tables of the law, which were "a witness against" the people (Deut. xxxi. 26), placed in the sanctuary where everything spake of mercy? (1 Kings viii. 9).

1. *Because the law is eternal, and must therefore harmonise with every dispensation of religion to man.* The whole Gospel is founded upon the eternity of

the law; for if its authority did not continue, we could not sin against it, and should therefore need no mercy. The very nature of the law bears with it internal evidence that it must endure for ever; it is holy, and just, and good. Wherever, then, you look for the Gospel you will find the law.

2. *Because it was the violation of the law by which the dispensation of mercy was rendered necessary.* If man had never sinned, there would have been no need of sacrifice, no need of mediation. The very Gospel implies our guilt. The tables are put into the ark to teach us, that if they were not there, we could expect nothing but the law's malediction, and the execution of its sentence.

3. *To intimate to us that the grand end of the administration of grace to man is the re-establishment of the law's dominion over him.* The grand end of this dispensation is certainly, in the first instance, to deliver us from the guilt and penalty of sin; and then, in the next place, by the almighty grace of Christ, to implant within us principles which the influences of the Spirit shall carry on to maturity, that we may be filled with all the fruits of righteousness for ever.

4. *To indicate that the administration of grace is in every part consistent with law.* The mercy-seat was God's throne of grace founded upon law. It was sprinkled with the blood of atonement (comp. Rom. iii. 25, 26; Heb. ix. 13, 14; 1 Pet. ii. 24; Isa. liii. 5). . . . . Wherever these three principles unite— that the righteous character of the Governor is upheld; that men are deterred from offences; that the authority of the law is maintained, and its purity and excellence declared;— there is a righteous government; and such is the government of God, even while He is abundant in mercy, waiteth to be gracious, and is ever ready to forgive.

II. **There is an harmonious relation betwixt the dispensation of grace to man and the heavenly world.**

Over the mercy-seat the cherubim were placed. Cherubim are placed before us in Scripture under two views. First, they are presented to us as the ministers of Divine vegeance (Gen. iii. 24). But in the tabernacle, from the very position in which they were placed, hiding the ark with their wings, "shadowing the mercy-seat," bending, as if looking down upon it, they are represented as interested spectators of the administration of the grace of God to men, through the atonement and sacrifice of the Saviour.

1. *Angelic powers have an intellectual interest in this great subject.* (Comp. 1 Peter i. 12.)

2. *The connexion of the angelic world with the Christian system is likewise one of large and important moral benefit.* We may fairly infer this from Eph. iii. 10. If to any being already pure, brighter views of God, more important degrees of moral knowledge be communicated, such communications of knowledge must always be the instrument of an increase both of holiness and felicity. And there must be great subjects with which the angels must become better acquainted than they ever could have been, but for the occurrences and history of our redemption. We may see this in relation to the evil of sin, the love of God, the power of God, the power of grace in man, etc.

3. *Angelic beings are ministers to the Church and ministers to individuals* (see Colos. i. 20; Heb. i. 14.) God Himself is the Friend of those who are reconciled to Him through Jesus Christ; and all His agents, whether angels or men, are ministers to do them good (Rom. viii. 28.)

III. **There was the presence of God crowning the whole.**

In the sanctuary was the visible symbol of the Divine presence. Thus are we shown that all things are of Him, and by Him, and for Him (2 Chron. vi. 41). As creation is from the will of God, so is redemption. All is the result of His benevolence (2 Cor. v. 18).

This indicates, too, the necessity of Divine agency. As He originated the whole scheme of redemption, so must He be present with it to give it power and efficacy. This was felt under the law (comp. Ps. lxxx. 1, 2; cxxxii. 8, 9). As the most beautiful arrangements of the temple would have been insufficient without the cloud of the Divine presence, so, unless God be especially present, even with Christianity, it cannot profit.

The whole points out the everlasting presence of God with His Church (comp. Isa. xii. 6; Psa. cxxxii. 13-16).

The people of God dwell already in the outer courts; but they are waiting till they shall be permitted to pass "within the vail, whither the Forerunner is for them entered." There God Himself shall be with them, and be their God for ever and ever.—*Richard Watson.*

CHAPTER VIII.

Critical and Explanatory Notes.

Verses 1-4. (Compare Exod. xxv. 31-40; xxvii. 20, 21; xxxvii. 17-24; xl. 24, 25). Here we have the command to actually light the lamps, and the statement of its fulfilment. "When Aaron is commanded to attend to the lighting of the candlestick, so that it may light up the dwelling, in these special instructions the entire fulfilment of the service in the dwelling is enforced upon him as a duty. In this respect the instructions themselves, coupled with the statement of the fact that Aaron had fulfilled them, stand quite appropriately between the account of what the tribe-princes had done for the consecration of the altar service as representatives of the congregation, and the account of the solemn inauguration of the Levites in their service in the sanctuary."—*Keil and Del.*

Verses 5-22. Before entering upon their duties the Levites were to be consecrated to the office, and then formerly handed over to the priests.

Verse 6. *Cleanse them,* טַהֵר; not קַדֵּשׁ, to *hallow* or *sanctify,* used of the consecration of the priests (Exod. xxix. 1; Lev. viii. 12).

Verse 7. *Water of purifying.* Lit., "sin-water." The water used for the cleansing of persons cured of leprosy (Lev. xiv. 5), and the "water of separation" (chap. xix. 9), were both of them prepared with peculiar and significant ingredients. The "sin-water;" *i.e.,* water designed to cleanse from sin, was doubtless taken from the water in the laver of the sanctuary, which was provided for the purification of the priests before they entered upon the performance of their duties (Exod. xxx. 17-21).

Let them shave all their flesh. Margin: "Let them cause a razor to pass over," etc. Keil and Del.: "'They shall cause the razor to pass over their whole body, הֶעֱבִיר תַּעַר is to be distinguished from גִּלָּה. The latter signified to make bald or shave the hair entirely off (Lev. xiv. 8, 9); the former signifies merely cutting the hair, which was part of the regular mode of adorning the body."

Verse 10. *The children of Israel shall put their hands upon the Levites.* The princes of the tribes would do this as the representatives of their respective tribes. By this act they represented the transfer to the Levites of the sacred duties which were previously obligatory upon the whole nation in the persons of its first-born sons.

Verse 11. *And Aaron shall offer the Levites before the Lord for an offering.* Lit., as in margin: "Shall wave the Levites before the Lord (as) a wave-offering." "How this was to be done is not determined. Most likely, Aaron pointed to the Levites, and then waved his hands, as in ordinary cases of making this offering. The multitude of the Levites seems to preclude the other modes suggested, *e.g.,* causing them to march backwards and forwards before the altar, or taking them round it. The ceremony of waving indicated (cf. Lev. vii. 30) that the offering was dedicated to God, and again, by grant from Him, withdrawn for the use of the priests. It was therefore aptly used at the inauguration of the Levites."—*Speaker's Comm.*

Verse 12. *The Levites shall lay their hands,* etc. "By this imposition of hands, they made the sacrificial animals their representatives, in which they presented their own bodies to the Lord as a living sacrifice, well pleasing to Him."—*Keil and Del.*

Verse 16. *The firstborn of all the children of Israel.* Heb.: "The firstborn of every one of the," etc.

Verse 19. *To make an atonement for the children of Israel.* "*I.e.,* by performing those services which were due from the children of Israel; the omission of which by the children of Israel would, but for the interposition of the Levites, have called down wrath from God."—*Speaker's Comm.*

That there be no plague among the children of Israel, etc., by reason of any irreverent, or otherwise improper performance of sacred duties, or any trifling with sacred things. (Compare chapter i. 53.)

Verse 21. *And the Levites were purified.* More correctly: "Purified themselves."

Verse 24. *To wait upon the service of,* etc. Heb., as in margin: "To war the warfare of," etc. Keil and Del.: "To do service at the work of," etc.

Verse 25. *Shall cease waiting upon the service.* Heb., as in margin: "Return from the warfare of the service." Keil and Del.: "Return from the service of the work, and not work any further."

Verse 26. *To keep the charge, and shall do no service.* "*Charge,* as distinguished from *work,* signified the oversight of all the furniture of the tabernacle (see chap. iii.); *work* (service) applied to laborious service, *e.g.,* the taking down and the setting up of the tabernacle, and cleaning it, carrying wood and water for the sacrificial worship, slaying the animals for the daily and festal sacrifices of the congregation," etc.—*Keil and Del.*

Proceeding to view the chapter *homiletically,* in the first paragraph we have:

THE GOLDEN CANDLESTICK, AN EMBLEM OF THE CHURCH OF GOD.

(*Verses* 1-4.)

The Golden Candlestick was part of the furniture of the Holy place, and was placed on the South side of that apartment. The full description of the candlestick is given in Exod. xxv. 31-40; xxxvii. 17-24. According to the Rabbins, the height of it was five feet, and the breadth of it, or the distance between the outer branches, three and a half feet. During the night the whole of the seven lamps were kept burning, but in the day there were only three. The weight of the entire candlestick was a talent, or one hundred and twenty-five pounds. It has been calculated to have been worth £5,076. Regarding the candlestick as an emblem of the Church, the text suggests—

I. The Preciousness and Sacredness of the Church of God.

The candlestick was of pure beaten gold, so also were the snuffers and snuff dishes. Much of the furniture of the sanctuary was made of pure gold—the mercy-seat, the cherubim, the dishes, spoons, covers, bowls, the pot which contained the manna; and many of the larger things were overlaid with gold (Exod. xxv. 10-39). In so large a use of this, the costliest and most perfect of all metals, we have an intimation of the preciousness of the Church of God, and all its belongings. The people of God are highly esteemed by Him. "The precious sons of Zion, comparable to fine gold." "The Lord taketh pleasure in His people.") See

Isa. xlix. 15, 16; Mal. iii. 16, 17; Acts xx. 28; 2 Tim. ii. 19.) "But the mere costliness of gold," says Archbishop Trench, "that it was of all metals the rarest, and therefore the dearest, this was not the only motive for the predominant employment of it. Throughout all the ancient East there was a sense of sacredness attached to this metal, which still to a great extent survives. Thus 'golden' in the Zend-Avesta is throughout synonymous with heavenly or divine. So also in many Eastern lands while silver might be degraded to profane and every-day uses of common life, might as money pass from hand to hand, 'the pale and common drudge 'twixt man and man,' it was not permitted to employ gold in any services except only royal and divine." The Church of God is a sacred institution. "Ye are a chosen generation, a royal priesthood, an holy nation, a peculiar people," etc. "Know ye not that ye are the temple of God, and that the Spirit of God dwelleth in you? . . . The temple of God is holy, which temple ye are."

II. **The Light of the Church of God.**

The light in the holy place is an emblem of the Word of God in His Church. His Word, His truth, including in this all which He has declared of Himself in revealed religion, is the light of the Church. "Thy Word is a lamp unto my feet, and a light unto my path." "For the commandment is a lamp; and the law is light; and reproofs of instruction are the way of life." Like its Divine Author, the Word of God is light in itself. "God has ordained His Gospel," says Milton, "to be the revelation of His power and wisdom in Christ Jesus. Let others, therefore, dread and shun the Scriptures for their darkness; I shall wish I may deserve to be reckoned amongst those who admire and dwell upon them for their clearness. There are no songs comparable to the songs of Zion, no orations equal to those of the prophets, and no politics like those which the Scriptures teach." The Word of God gives light to others, as the lamps on the candlestick gave light to the priests in the holy place. "It is a book full of light and wisdom," says Sir Matthew Hale, "will make you wise to eternal life, and furnish you with directions and principles to guide and order your life safely and prudently. There is no book like the Bible for excellent learning, wisdom, and use." The *perfection* of this light is shadowed forth by the Golden Candlestick, with its seven lamps. Seven is the number of mystical completeness; and the seven lamps set forth the full perfection of the Sacred Scriptures. *(a)*

III. **The Ministers of the Church of God**, and their Function.

Aaron and his sons, the priests, were to light the lamps in the Holy Place. It is the duty of ministers to expound and apply the teachings of the Word of God: not to use that Word to illustrate and confirm their own theories or the systems of other men; but reverently and earnestly to strive to ascertain its meaning and message, and to make that meaning and message clear and convincing to others. It is their sacred function to bring the light of the Divine Scriptures to bear upon the duties and experiences, the problems and perplexities, the sins and struggles of human life. It has been suggested that "the lighting of one lamp from another showed the opening of one text by another." This work of the Gospel ministry, if it is to be well done, demands careful and suitable education, diligent and devout study, and the gracious help of the Divine Spirit. *(b)*

It is also necessary that the Christian minister should live well. His life should be luminous as well as his ministry. It was well said by Thomas Adams: "He that preaches well in his pulpit, but lives disorderly out of it, is like a young scribbler; what he writes fair with his hand, his sleeve comes after and blots."

IV. **The Function of the Church of God.**

Like the Golden Candlestick, the

Church is to be a light-bearer. The Church is not the light, but it is the bearer of light, that which holds it forth and causes it widely to spread abroad its rays. It has no light of its own, but it diffuses that which it receives from its Saviour and Lord. Every Christian is "light in the Lord," and should show forth this light in the darkness of this world. He is called to this: "Ye shine as lights in the world, holding forth the Word of Life." "Ye are the light of the world," etc. (Matt. v. 14-16.) "I would not give much for your religion," says Mr. Spurgeon, "unless it can been seen. Lamps do not talk; but they do shine. A lighthouse sounds no drum, it beats no gong; and yet far over the waters its friendly spark is seen by the mariner. So let your actions shine out your religion. Let the main sermon of your life be illustrated by all your conduct, and it shall not fail to be illustrious." (c).

Application.

1. *To individuals:* Are our lives luminous in the light of the Lord Jesus Christ?
2. *To Churches:* Are we making good our claim to a place in "the Church of the living God" by taking our part in performing the Divine function of that Church? Are we diffusing the light of God in Christ in this dark world?

ILLUSTRATIONS.

(*a*). How large a space does a candle occupy? Just a little hole in the candlestick. But when it shines out to the poor traveller that has lost his way in the morass at midnight, how far it reaches! And to him how much it means, when it guides him to a highway, and to a hospitable place of residence! And how much it means on a rocky shore, when it gives light to a thousand ships with their imperilled mariners! It means safety. It does an important office-work, although it requires but a small space to stand in. And although the Word of God does not cover much ground, the ground that it does cover is so vital, and it stands so connected with man's life here and hereafter, that it shines with a clear light. And he that takes heed to it will certainly find the harbour, the shore, the haven. It is transcendently important; in present and temporal, and human respects, not so important as men have supposed; but in future, and eternal, and spiritual respects, a great deal more important than men have supposed.—*H. W. Beecher.*

Whatever else may be said about the Bible, I am sure no man can deny that it is the best book to guide men toward practical virtue and true holiness that has ever appeared in the world. Whatever may be the disputes about its origin, whatever may be the controversies and the doubts upon the various theories of inspiration, as a practical book, as a light to a man's feet, and a lamp to his path, it has proved itself to be, and can, by investigation, be shown to be the wisest book to follow that is known.—*Ibid.*

(*b*) Learning, as well as office, is requisite for a minister. An unlearned scribe, without his treasure of old and new, is unfit to interpret God's oracles. The priest's lips shall preserve knowledge, is no less a precept to the minister than a promise to the people; we are unfit to be seers if we cannot distinguish between Hagar and Sarah. A minister without learning is a mere cypher, which fills up a place and increaseth the number, but signifies nothing. There have been some niggardly affected to learning, calling it man's wisdom. If the moral saying of a poet or a philosopher, or, perhaps, some golden sentence of a father, drop from us, it is straight called poisoned eloquence, as if all these were not the spoils of the Gentiles, and mere handmaids unto divinity. They wrong us: we make not the pulpit a philosophy, logic, poetry-school; but all these are so many stairs to the pulpit. Will you have it? The fox dispraiseth the grapes he cannot reach. If they could beat down learning, they might escape censure for their own ignorance. For shame! Let none that have born a book dispraise learning. She hath enemies enough abroad. She should be justified of her own children. Let Barbary disgrace arts, not Athens.—*Thomas Adams.*

(*c*) This world, with all its darkened societies, is but God's large house, in which so many of His children cry in the night, but never see or find their father; and as housewives do not kindle the household lamp at evening only to turn over it the big wheat measure to hide it or to quench it, but set it uncovered on its lamp-stand, that it may shed a cheerful gleam through all the room, so has our Heavenly House-Father, in mercy to His still darkened children, placed His saints on their conspicuous elevation of church-membership, that their clear light of Gospel knowledge and their reflected radiance of holy affections and Christlike deeds might spread abroad by open professsion and unconcealed well-doing, a blessed illumination. It is not that the Christian need pant after notoriety, or vaingloriously flash his little spark where he has no business. The House-Master who kindles us must place us, one on a loftier and one on a lower lamp-stand as it pleaseth Him. For us it is enough that we be content with the height or conspicuousness of our place, and cheerfully let such light as we have be seen as it may be, neither ambitiously envious nor timorously unfaithful. We are not free to descend from the stand on which He has put us, nor to hide our Christianity because we are looked at, any more than we are free to cease from shining because there are few to see us, or to flare the higher when many applaud. . . . As I have seen the glow-worm at late evening, by the silent side of an empty English lane, mount some tall spike of grass, and turn up its tiny lamp, content to hang head downwards, itself unseen, so that the exquisite soft green light which God had given it might be visible in its loveliness, so may one find in this world's lowly and unfrequented paths Christ's light-bearers, who shed each his own sweet love-light round a narrow circle of the dark, that the wayfarer who sees may praise, not his unsightly, and, sooth to say, concealed self, but that great Father in heaven who lit this faint taper upon earth, even as He lit the nobler fires which burn far up in heaven. But just as I have shut the poor glow-worm in a box or under an inverted dish, yet found that it spent all its radiance there unseen, only for sake of love and because shine it must, so will the true soul, whom his Lord shall chance to imprison from shedding light on any human eye, rejoice no less to let his devout affections and gracious deeds be seen of Him who looks through the densest cover, and knows how to bestow an open reward.

Since, then, Jesus hath taught us that to be visible is no accident in Christian life, but the very condition of its usefulness, let us each with patient tendance trim our inward lamp, that in our hearts there may be the light of a sevenfold blessed grace; then let us not be ashamed with modest faithfulness to let that silent efficacious light of Christian character tell of us, that we have been shone upon by the face of Jesus; and of your Lord, that He is Light, and that in Him there is no darkness at all.—*J. O. Dykes, M.A., D.D.*

THE CONSECRATION OF THE LEVITES; OR, ASPECTS OF ACCEPTABLE CONSECRATION TO GOD.

(*Verses* 5-22.)

Several of the homiletic suggestions arising out of these verses have already been noticed by us in our notes on the preceding chapters. Repetition of them is undesirable. They will be found on pp. 21-23; 48-53; 61-65. In this section of the history we have the account of the ordination of the Levites to the duties already assigned to them in chapters iii. and iv. They have been exchanged for the firstborn; and now they are consecrated to the work of their sacred calling. The order and ceremonies of their consecration were appointed by God; we shall regard that consecration as setting forth several aspects of acceptable consecration to God.

I. **In acceptable consecration to God there is a practical recognition of the necessity of moral purity.**

"Take the Levites from among the children of Israel, and cleanse them," etc. (verses 6 and 7). Human nature is defiled by sin. Its springs of thought and feeling are corrupt. Heart and hands are both stained by evil in thought and deed. If we would approach unto God acceptably, we must seek spiritual cleansing. The offerings that are presented to God must be pure, and before man can offer himself to God, he must cleanse himself from sin (See Exod. iii. 5; Isa. i. 11-18; 1 Tim. ii. 8). Ministers of the Gospel are specially required to cultivate and exhibit moral purity in their life. They must translate the doctrine of their sermons into the practice of their life; they must be sound in doctrine and sincere in life. "Be ye clean that bear the vessels of the Lord." "A bishop must be blameless," etc. (1 Tim. iii. 2-7). "In all things shewing thyself a pattern of good works," etc. (Titus ii. 7, 8). "Being ensamples to the flock." Let all Christians, and all ministers especially, cultivate this moral purity. But how may it be attained?

1. *By personal effort.* "Let them shave all their flesh, and let them wash their clothes, and so make themselves clean." The cleansing elements provided by God in the Gospel are of no

avail unless they are personally applied. "Wash you, make you clean," etc. The innumerable white-robed multitude, before the throne and before the Lamb, "have washed their robes, and made them white in the blood of the Lamb." "Purifying their hearts by faith."

2. *By Divine influence.* Moses was commanded to cleanse the Levites: "And thus thou shalt do unto them to cleanse them: Sprinkle water of purifying upon them." "Then will I sprinkle clean water upon you, and ye shall be clean: from all your filthiness, and from all your idols, will I cleanse you." "The blood of Jesus Christ His Son cleanseth us from all sin," &c. (1 John i. 7-9). God both provides the cleansing element and blesses man's cleansing efforts. "It is our duty to cleanse ourselves, and God's promise that He will cleanse us."

II. **In acceptable consecration to God there is a practical recognition of the necessity of atonement for sin.**

A young bullock was, by the Divine direction, offered to God as a sin-offering for the Levites (ver. 8, 12). In this, two truths of vital importance were symbolically expressed.

1. *That man needs forgiveness of sin and reconciliation with God.* Man cannot truly serve God or commune with Him until these are attained by him.

2. *That forgiveness of sin and reconciliation to God are to be attained through sacrifice.* Christ Jesus came into the world "to put away sin by the sacrifice of Himself . . . . Christ was offered to bear the sins of many." "In whom we have redemption through His blood, the forgiveness of sins, according to the riches of His grace." (See remarks on the sin-offering in our exposition of chaps. vi. 13-21, and vii. 10-88). (*a*)

III. **Acceptable consecration to God must be unreserved and full.**

"A young bullock with his meat-offering of fine flour mingled with oil" was to be offered to God for the Levites as a burnt-offering; which symbolically expressed the entire surrender of the offerer unto God. As the offering was entirely consumed upon the altar to the honour of God, so the offerer gave himself wholly to God. (On this point see our exposition of chaps. vi. 13-21, and vii. 10-88). Notice two points:—

1. *God demands this entire consecration.* "The Levites are wholly given unto Me from among the children of Israel," etc., verses 16-18. (See pp. 50-53.)

2. *Gratitude urges to this entire consecration.* We have an intimation of this in this ceremony of consecration. The young bullock that was offered for a burnt-offering was to be presented to the Lord "with his meat-offering." This meat-offering of fine flour mingled with oil was an appendage to the devotion implied in the burnt-offering: it was eucharistic—a symbolical expression of man's gratitude for God's goodness. The Apostle besought the Roman Christians "by the mercies of God" to present their bodies a living sacrifice, holy, acceptable unto God, as their reasonable service. "What shall I render unto the Lord for all His benefits toward me? I will offer to Thee the sacrifice of thanksgiving," etc. Let us through Jesus Christ offer ourselves wholly and for ever unto God. (*b*)

IV. **Acceptable consecration to God must be open.**

The Levites were consecrated to the service of the Lord in the presence of all the congregation. "Thou shalt bring the Levites before the tabernacle of the congregation; and thou shalt gather the whole assembly of the children of Israel together" etc. (verses 9-12). "Whosoever shall confess Me before men, him will I confess also before my Father which is in heaven." "If thou shalt confess with thy mouth the Lord Jesus," etc. (Rom. x. 9, 10.) "Every tongue shall confess that Jesus Christ is Lord, to the glory of God the Father." Avoiding parade and ostentation on the one hand, and secrecy and undue reserve on the other, the true Christian both by word and deed acknowledges Christ as his Saviour and Lord. See Psa. lxvi. 15, 16 ; Mark v. 19, 20 ; Matt. v. 14-16. (c)

V. Acceptable consecration to God is followed by religious service.

"And after that shall the Levites go in to do the service of the tabernacle of the congregation. . . . And after that went the Levites in to do," etc. They were consecrated for this purpose, that they might "do the service of the children of Israel in the tabernacle of the congregation." The consecration to God which is only a thing of profession and sentiment is worse than worthless ; it is offensive in the sight of God, and baneful in its influence upon men. The true consecration is for service according to the will of God. In a special sense Christian ministers are the servants of God in the work of His Church ; but every true Christian is also a servant of God. "We can serve God anywhere and everywhere, as well as in the pulpit or in the congregation. You may glorify God behind a counter just as in a cathedral ; you may serve God sweeping a street as well as being a bishop." In respect to the service of the Levites two things are indicated :—

1. *In religious services there are different grades, and even the lowest grade is sacred and honourable.* " I have given the Levites as a gift to Aaron and to his sons. . . . The Levites went in to do their service in the tabernacle of the congregation before Aaron and before his sons." See pp. 48-50.

2. *The faithful performance of religious services is of the greatest importance to society.* "I have given the Levites to do the service of the children of Israel in the tabernacle of the congregation, and to make an atonement for the children of Israel : that there be no plague among the children of Israel, when the children of Israel come nigh unto the sanctuary." (See explanatory notes on ver. 19. and pp. 22, 23).

But the true and acceptable Christian consecration extends to all our life and work : he who is truly devoted to God will do all things as for Him. *(d)*

"If on our daily course our mind
Be set to hallow all we find,
New treasures still, of countless price,
God will provide for sacrifice.

As for some dear familiar strain
Untir'd we ask, and ask again,
Ever, in its melodious store,
Finding a spell unheard before ;

Such is the bliss of souls serene,
When they have sworn, and stedfast mean,
Counting the cost in all t' espy
Their God, in all themselves deny.

O could we learn that sacrifice,
What lights would all around us rise !
How would our hearts with wisdom talk
Along Life's dullest, dreariest walk !

We need not bid, for cloister'd cell,
Our neighbour and our work farewell,
Nor strive to wind ourselves too high
For sinful man beneath the sky :

The trivial round, the common task,
Would furnish all we ought to ask :
Room to deny ourselves ; a road
To bring us, daily, nearer God."—*Keble.*

ILLUSTRATIONS.

(a) The Lord did not study attractive æsthetics. He did not prepare a tabernacle that should delight men's tastes ; it was rich indeed, but so blood-stained as to be by no means beautiful. No staining of glass to charm the eye, but instead thereof the inwards of slaughtered bullocks. Such sights would disgust the delicate tastes of the fops of this present age. Blood, blood on every side ; death, fire, smoke, and ashes, varied with the bellowings of dying beasts, and the active exertions of men whose white garments were all crimson with the blood of victims. How clearly did the worshippers see the sternness and severity of the justice of God against human sin, and the intensity of the agony of the great Son of God who was in the fulness of time by His own death to put away all the sins and transgressions of His people ! By faith come ye, my brethren, and walk round that blood-stained altar, and as you mark its four-square form and its horns of strength, and see the sacrifices smoking thereon acceptable to God, look down and mark the blood with which its foundations are so completely saturated, and understand how all salvation and all acceptance rests on the atonement of the dying Son of God.— *C. H. Spurgeon.*

(b) If you could know regrets in the realm of blessedness, would not these be the regrets, that you have not served Christ better, loved Him more, spoke of Him oftener, given more generously to His cause, and more uniformly proved yourselves to be consecrated to Him? I am afraid that such would be the form of the regrets of Paradise, if any could intrude within those gates of pearl. Come, let us live while we live! Let us live up to the utmost stretch of our manhood! Let us ask the Lord to brace our nerves, to string our sinews, and make us true crusaders, knights of the blood-red cross, consecrated men and women, who, for the love we bear Christ's name, will count labour to be ease, and suffering to be joy, and reproach to be honour, and loss to be gain! If we have never yet given ourselves wholly up to Christ as His disciples, now hard by His cross, where we see His wounds still bleeding afresh, and Himself quivering in pain for us, let us pledge ourselves in His strength, that we give ourselves wholly to Him without reserve, and so may He help us by His Spirit, that the vow may be redeemed and the resolve may be carried out, that we may live to Christ, and dying may find it gain.—*Ibid.*

(*c*) It is in all cases the instinct of a new heart, in its experience of God, to acknowledge Him. No one ever thinks it a matter of delicacy or genuine modesty entirely to suppress any reasonable joy, least of all any fit testimony of gratitude toward a deliverer and for a deliverance. In such a case no one ever asks, what is the use? where is the propriety? for it is the simple instinct of his nature to speak, and he speaks. Thus, if one of you had been rescued in a shipwreck on a foreign shore, by some common sailor who had risked his life to save you, and you should discover him across the street in some great city, you would rush to his side, seize his hand, and begin at once, with a choking utterance, to testify your gratitude to him for so great a deliverance. Or, if you should pass restrainedly on, making no sign, pretending to yourself that you might be wanting in delicacy or modesty to publish your private feelings by any such eager acknowledgment of your deliverer, or that you ought first to be more sure of the genuineness of your gratitude, what opinion must we have in such a case of your heartlessness and falseness to nature! In the same simple way, all ambition apart, all conceit of self forgot, all artificial and mock modesty excluded, it will be the instinct of every one that loves God to acknowledge Him. He will say with our Psalmist, "Come and hear, all ye that fear God, and I will declare what He hath done for my soul." —*H. Bushnell, D.D.*

(*d*) Holiness is the attribute of persons, places, times, or things, set apart by the will of God from common uses, and devoted to Himself. But by God's own appointment, those who were thus consecrated to His service in Jewish times spent a great part of their life in work which *in itself* was of quite a secular character. The Levites, for instance, were not always praying, or preaching, or reading the scriptures, or offering sacrifices. When the nation was in the desert, the Levites had to take down the Tabernacle and set it up, and to carry the furniture from one camping-ground to another, just as the rest of the people had to take down their own tents and set them up again, and to carry their own goods from place to place. The work of the Levites was as hard as the work of the common people; but the work of the Levites was holy, because the Tabernacle was the Tent of God. They swept the courts of the Tabernacle, and when the Temple was built they swept the larger courts of the Temple; they kindled fires; they made incense; they stored wine and oil; they drew water; they killed animals; they learnt to play musical instruments; but there was nothing profane in their most menial occupations, for whatever they did, they did as God's servants. They had charge of large revenues; but the revenues consisted of what the people offered to God. They acted as magistrates and administered the law; but the law which they administered was Divine. Even the priests had to change the shew-bred, to burn incense, and to tend fires.

A great part of the work that was done by Priests and Levites was *in itself* mere secular work; but they and their work were "holy," because they were set apart to God's service, and because their work was done for God, and in obedience to God's commandments. A great part of the work that must be done by Christian people in our times is *in itself* mere secular work. It has to be done at the carpenter's bench, at the blacksmith's anvil, in the kitchen, behind a draper's counter, at the desk in a merchant's office, on the box of an omnibus, on the platform of a locomotive, in the van of a railway guard, in cotton mills, in bank parlours, in the private rooms of newspaper editors, in political committees, at School Boards, in Government offices, in Parliament;—and if there is hearty, unreserved consecration to God, if God's will is the law by which all the work is controlled, if God's honour is the end to which all the work is devoted, the "secular" work, however earnestly it is done, is no more inconsistent with saintliness than were the menial duties of Priests with their "consecration" to the duties of their priesthood. The Priests would have been unfaithful to the solemnities with which they were set apart to their holy office if, in the conceit and fastidiousness of priestly pride, they had neglected their menial duties under the pretence of maintaining their sanctity. Christian men are equally unfaithful to their nobler calling if, under the influence of a similar conceit and fastidiousness, they regard what they call secular work as "common and unclean," and refuse to discharge obvious duties under the pretence of keeping their holiness untainted.

But holiness is something more than a faultless morality. The difference between a holy man and a moral man is the difference between a Temple or a Church and a house. You may erect a very noble building; the design may be stately; the proportions magnificent; there may be plenty of space, and air, and light; the walls may be of pure white marble like the walls of Italian palaces; the decorations may be perfectly beautiful; but if you build it for yourself it is a House, and not a Temple. It was not the splendour of the building on Mount Moriah that made it a Temple, but the Divine uses to which by Divine appointment it was consecrated. Nor does Holiness consist in fidelity to certain ecclesiastical traditions. You may build a House in the style of a Church; there may be nave and transepts and chancel; there may be clustered columns, and the windows may be glorious with crimson and purple and gold; but if the building is for yourself and for your private uses, it is no Church, but a mere House. And, on the other hand, no matter how poor and mean our life may look to common eyes, it is sacred—every part is sacred—if we have consecrated ourselves to God. The tent which was God's Tabernacle in the wilderness was more awful and august than the palaces of kings. Everything depends on the law which we are trying to obey, and the Master whom we are trying to serve. Holiness is the result of the consecration of our whole life to God. It requires that we should make God's will our supreme law, and that we should do God's will for God's glory. —*R. W. Dale, M.A., D.D.*

The Divine Master and His Human Servants.

(*Verses* 23-26).

We have here the Divine directions as to the period of the Service of the Levites. The manner in which these directions are introduced—" And the Lord spake unto Moses, saying;" the words which immediately follow these directions—" Thus shalt thou do unto the Levites touching their charge;" and their position in the history, immediately after the ordination of the Levites to their sacred duties, show that they are intended to be the fixed law for the service of the Levites at the sanctuary. In chap. iv. ver. 3, Moses was commanded to number the Levites "from thirty years old and upward even until fifty years old, all that enter into the host, to do the work in the tabernacle of the congregation," while in the text the period of service is fixed from twenty-five years old and upward until fifty years old. That numbering had reference especially to the carriage of the tabernacle from place to place during the wanderings in the wilderness, a laborious service requiring the strength of mature manhood: whereas the directions of the text refer to the entire service of the tabernacle, which, when it was stationary, could be performed without difficulty by persons of twenty-five years of age. At a subsequent period the age at which the Levites began their service was fixed at twenty years, because the tabernacle being permanently placed upon Mount Zion, they were no longer required to "carry the tabernacle, nor any vessels of it for the service thereof" (1 Chron. xxiii. 24-32).

The text suggests the following Homiletic points:—

I. **The necessity of fitness for the Divine service.**

Though the Levites entered upon their service at the age of twenty-five years, they took no part in its heaviest duties until they had attained thirty years, and thorough physical fitness; and when at fifty years that fitness began to fail, they were released from the severe duties, and employed only in such as would not try their physical powers. God requires fit instruments for His work. He can use any instrumentality whatsoever, or He can accomplish His purpose without any instrumentality; but His rule is to use those instruments who are best adapted for the accomplishment of His purposes. The arrangement of the service of the Levites shows this. The calling and career of such men as Joseph, Moses, David, John the Baptist, Paul, show this. In learning any handicraft or trade, years are spent under instructors: for the practice of law or medicine men must have special and careful training: and is it not important that they who engage in religious services should be qualified for such services? Let all religious workers do their utmost to prepare themselves for their important and sacred duties: let them study, pray, &c. (*a*)

Let Christian ministers especially be conscientious and painstaking in this respect. (*b*)

II. **The variety of employment in the Divine service.**

In their life in the wilderness there was Levitical service suited to young men of twenty-five years of age, there was severe labour for men from thirty to fifty years of age, and there was honourable and easy service for those who were fifty years old and upward. (See explanatory notes on these verses). The aged Levites had the oversight of the furniture of the tabernacle, and were probably engaged in instructing the young men, and in guarding the tabernacle against the approach of any prohibited persons. In the service of God to-day there is room for workers of every kind and degree of faculty; there is ample scope for the enthusiasm of youth, the strength of manhood, and the ripe experience of age. The able reasoner, the eloquent orator, the skilful manager of affairs, the patient plodding worker, the sympathetic visitor of the sick and sorrowful, the gifted and loving teacher, the prevailing intercessor at the Throne of Grace, the unobtrusive and kindly tract distributor, even the worn and weary sufferer, calm, and sweetly submissive to the Divine will, each and all have their sphere and their mission in the service of God. In this we have—

1. *An encouragement to persons of feeble powers and narrow opportunities to try to do good.* (*c*)

2. *A rebuke to those who plead inability as an excuse for their indolence in religious service.* Use the ability you have, however small it may be; and by so doing you will increase it. God holds us responsible only for the ability we have or may have, not for that we have not and cannot obtain. (See pp. 40, 41).

III. **The care of the Great Master for His servants.**

He will not have His servants overburdened; His youthful servants He will not prematurely call to posts of severe labour or solemn responsibility, and for those who "have borne the burden and heat of the day" He arranges an eventide of honourable and restful service. He calls men to work for which they are adapted; and if in their work any severe strain be imposed upon them, He giveth unto them more grace. His yoke is easy and His burden is light. He graciously sustains every worker in his toil, gives to every worker sweetest joy in his toil, and will gloriously reward even the smallest service of the feeblest worker. (*d*)

"How blessed from the bonds of sin,
  And earthly fetters free,
In singleness of heart and aim,
  Thy servant, Lord, to be!
The hardest toil to undertake
  With joy at Thy command,
The meanest office to receive
  With meekness at Thy hand!

How happily the working days
  In this dear service fly,
How rapidly the closing hour,
  The time of rest draws nigh!
When all the faithful gather home,
  A joyful company,
And ever where the Master is,
  Shall His blest servants be."—*Spitta*.

Conclusion.

This subject supplies—

1. *Encouragement to enter into this service.* "Come thou with us," etc.

2. *Encouragement to persevere in this service.* A glorious reward awaits those who patiently continue in well doing.

ILLUSTRATIONS.

(*a*) You have read in history of that hero who, when an overwhelming force was in full pursuit, and all his followers were urging him to more rapid flight, coolly dismounted to repair a flaw in his horse's harness. While busied with the broken buckle, the distant crowd swept down in nearer thunder; but, just as the prancing hoofs and eager spears were ready to dash upon him, the flaw was mended, and, like a swooping falcon, he had vanished from their view. The broken buckle would have left him on the field a dismounted and inglorious prisoner; the timely delay sent him in safety back to his comrades. There is in daily life the same luckless precipitancy, and the same profitable delay. The man who, from his prayerless awakening, bounces into the business of the day, however good his talents and great his diligence, is only galloping upon a steed harnessed with a broken buckle, and must not marvel if, in his hottest haste or most hazardous leap, he be left ingloriously in the dust; and though it may occasion some little delay beforehand, his neighbour is wiser who sets out all in order before the march begins.—*James Hamilton, D.D.*

(b) I believe that at bottom most people think it an uncommonly easy thing to preach, and that they could do it amazingly well themselves. Every donkey thinks itself worthy to stand with the king's horses; every girl thinks that she could keep house better than her mother; but thoughts are not facts, for the sprat thought itself a herring, but the fisherman knew better. I daresay those who can whistle fancy that they can plough; but there's more than whistling in a good ploughman; and so let me tell you there's more in good preaching than taking a text, and saying firstly, secondly, and thirdly. I try my hand at preaching myself, and in my poor way I find it no very easy thing to give the folks something worth hearing; and if the fine critics, who reckon us up on their thumbs, would but try their own hands at it, they might be a little more quiet. Dogs, however, always will bark, and what is worse, some of them will bite, too; but let decent people do all they can, if not to muzzle them, yet to prevent their doing any great mischief.—*C. H. Spurgeon.*

(c) In order to serve Christ acceptably, we have not to revolutionize our lot, nor to seek other conditions than those Providence supplies. The place is nothing; the heart is all. Chambers of patient invalids, beds of submissive sickness, obscurity, weakness, baffled plans,—a thousand nameless limitations of faculty, of opportunity, of property,—all these are witnesses of silent but victorious faith. In all of them God is glorified, for in all of them His will is done. Out of all of them gates open into heaven and the joy of the Lord. Mercifully the Father has appointed many ways in which we may walk toward His face, and run on His errands. Work is the way for strength; lying still is the way for infirmity. If only there are trust and prayer in both, there is some instruction in a picture I have read of, which represents the lives of twin brothers diverging from the cradle. One, by study, becomes a learned and skilful physician, reaching great riches and honour by administering to the sick. The other has no talent for books, and no memory, and no science; he becomes a poor strolling musician, but spends his days in consoling, by his late, sufferings that are beyond all medicine. The brothers are shown meeting at the close of their career. The vagrant is sick and worn out, and the brother prescribes for him out of his learning, and gathers ingenious compounds for his relief; but, meantime, he to whom God gave another gift touches his instrument for the solace of the great man's shattered nerves, and heals his benefactor's disordered spirit.—*F. D. Huntington, D.D.*

Out of this whole structure of the human body, every little muscle, every single cell has its own secretion and its own work; and though some physicians have said this and that organ might be spared, I believe there is not a single thread in the whole embroidery of human nature that could be well spared—the whole of the fabric is required. So in the mystical body, the Church, the least member is necessary; the most uncomely member of the Christian Church is needful for its growth. Find out, then, what your sphere is, and occupy it. Ask God to tell you what is your niche, and stand in it, occupying the place till Jesus Christ shall come and give you your reward. Use what ability you have, and use it at once.—*C. H Spurgeon.*

(d) I know your gifts to His Church, and His poor, are necessarily but little, for yours is the poor widow's portion perhaps, and you can give only your two mites; but I know that, as they fall into the treasury, Jesus sits over against the treasury and hears sweet sounds in the dropping of your gifts. I know your life is such that you mourn over it every day, but still you do serve God in it, and you long to serve Him more, and that love of yours is written in the books of the King's record, and you shall be His in the day when He makes up His jewels; and your works shall be His too, for your works shall follow you to the skies when you rise in Jesus, and your reward even for a cup of cold water shall be as sure as it will be gracious, and your entrance into the joy of your Lord shall certainly be bestowed upon you according to the grace which is in Christ Jesus, by which he has accepted you.—*Ibid.*

SERVICE.
(*Verse* 24.)

The Levitical service in the wilderness was very severe; it required strong, able-bodied men. There were, in addition to the ministrations in the tabernacle, many heavy weights to carry. (It is computed by some that the metal of the tabernacle alone weighed 10 tons, 13 cwts., 24 lbs., 14 ozs., beside skins, hangings, cords, boards, and posts). In David's time we read they began at twenty years of age; but in the wilderness they did not fully engage in the more laborious service until thirty, although the time for their assisting was fixed at twenty-five.

I. **The service God demands of all Levites.**

Every Christian should be a priest, ever ministering in His temple.

1. *Burden-bearing.* How often Christians murmur about their burdens, as though they were not honoured in being permitted to bear anything for God.

2. *Singing.* The Levites sang and played on instruments. Sing the song of gratitude and contentment.

3. *Studying of the law.* "Search the Scriptures."

4. *Attendance on the ordinances of the sanctuary.* There is a special blessing for those who worship in God's house.

II. **God demands the service in our prime.**

"From twenty and five." We must give God the best we have. The lamb must be without blemish; the fruit the first and choicest, to show our love and gratitude.

III. **God demands this service when it can be most easily rendered.**

God did not ask of the Levites, nor does He of us, impossibilities. The very young and the old were exempt from the bearing of the heavier burdens. God suits the burden to the back. All he asks is that we shall do what we can.—*R. A. Griffin.*

CHAPTER IX.

Critical and explanatory notes.

Verses 1-5. This Passover, having been kept in the first month of the second year, preceded the numbering and the other events recorded in this book. For this reason some writers have said that verses 1-14 should be transposed to an earlier portion of the narrative. But the observance of the supplementary Passover (verses 6-14) was one of the last events before the departure from Sinai; and the ordinance of it is very properly placed here; and the account of the observance of the ordinary Passover which gave rise to it is not unnaturally placed before it.

From Exod. xii. 24, 25, the Israelites might have concluded that they were not to keep the Passover until they came to Canaan; but, inasmuch as the Anniversary of the Feast occurred while they were still in the desert of Sinai, a special command is given to them to keep it. And had it not been for the subsequent unbelief and rebellion of the people, before the anniversary returned again they would have been possessors of the land promised unto them.

Verse 3. *According to all the rights of it, and according to all the ceremonies thereof.* See Exod. xii. 3-28, 43-51, xiii. 3-11.

Verse 6. *There were certain men,* etc. "Probably Mishael and Elizaphan, who buried their cousins, Nadab and Abihu, within a week of this Passover (Lev. x. 4, 5). None would be more likely to make this inquiry of Moses than his kinsmen, who had defiled themselves by his express direction."—*Speaker's Commentary.*

Verse 15. *The tent of the testimony,* or, *witness,* denotes the whole of the tabernacle, comprising the holy of holies and the holy place, and not merely the holy of holies. The phrase seems to indicate the same portion of the structure as *ohel moëd,* "tent of meeting."

Verse 20. *And so it was, when,* etc. Rather, "And there was also when," etc.

Verse 21. *And so it was, when,* etc. Rather, "And there was also when the cloud abode from even unto morning, and the cloud was taken up in the morning, and they journeyed."

Verse 22. *A year.* Heb., "days," *i.e.,* a space of time not precisely determined.

As long as the cloud rested upon the tabernacle, whether it was for one day, a few days, or many days, they continued their encampment; and when it arose from the tabernacle they broke up their encampment and resumed their march. The movements of the cloud were to them the commands of the Lord God. For the numerous Homiletic suggestions connected with the institution and observation of the Passover we must refer the reader to *The Homiletical Commentary* on Exod. xii. and xiii. where the directions for keeping the ordinance are given in detail. To attempt anything like an exhaustive treatment of the ordinance would be out of place here.

The Feast of the Passover, a Memorial and a Type.

(Verses 1-5.)

The Passover, the celebration of which is here commanded by God, was—

I. A Memorial of a great Deliverance.

1. *Deliverance from the most terrible evils.* (1) From a *miserable slavery.* The Israelites in Egypt were held in most degrading and cruel bondage. (2) From a *terrible visitation of Divine judgment.* When the firstborn of the Egyptians, both of man and of beast, were all destroyed, the firstborn of the Israelites were exempted from the destruction. Primarily and essentially the Passover was a memorial of this great historical fact. Exod. xii. 26, 27. (*a*)

2. *Deliverance from the most terrible evils associated with the sacrifice of life.* A lamb of the first year, without blemish, and a male, was to be slain for every family (unless the family were too small to consume the lamb, in which case they were to unite with their nearest neighbour in the matter), and the blood sprinkled upon the posts of the door, and the flesh entirely eaten after having been roasted with fire. Such were the explicit commands of God by His servants Moses and Aaron. Exod. xii. 3-10.

3. *Deliverance from the most terrible evils through the sovereign grace of God.* Their exemption from the stroke of the destroying angel, and their emancipation from their bitter slavery in Egypt, were due to the sovereign favour of the Lord God. The gracious purpose and the grand performance were alike owing to Him. "Thou hast with Thine arm redeemed Thy people, the sons of Jacob and Joseph."

4. *Deliverance from terrible evils by means of faith and obedience.* The sprinkling of the blood upon the doorposts was an act of faith and obedience, which God required as a condition of their exemption from the stroke of the destroying angel, and which, when performed, He graciously accepted. However ill-adapted the means might have seemed to the end, they employed them as they were directed,

and so secured their safety (Heb. xi. 28).

So great and marvellous a deliverance demanded a fitting memorial.

II. **A type of a greater deliverance.** This portion of the history of Israel typifies—

1. *The morally enslaved and perilous state of man.* Sinful men are in a far more terrible state of bondage than that of Israel in Egypt. Their slavery was *physical*; that of the sinner is *spiritual*. His soul is the slave of animal appetites, and turbulent passions, and evil habits. Their slavery was a *calamity*; that of the sinner is a *crime*. The Lord God pitied them because of their bondage; He condemns man because of his. To be the slaves of sin is to be guilty of grievous moral wrong in the sight of God. Their slavery, at the farthest, would *end at death*; but *death has no power to terminate the slavery of the sinner*. The death of the body cannot free the soul from the bondage of evil passions or tyrannical habits. The peril also of the sinner is greater than was that of the ancient Israelites. They were delivered from the stroke of the destroying angel. But the destruction of physical life is a small evil as compared with the destruction of all that constitutes the life of the soul. In many cases the death of the body is the great gain of the man. But what tongue or pen can describe the awfulness and the painfulness of the destruction by sin of the moral purity, the power, the reverence, the aspiration, the hope, the peace of the soul? Such is the destruction of which the sinner is in danger.

2. *The Divine method of deliverance.* The Lamb of the Passover exhibits the closest type of the atoning Sacrifice who died for us and has made our peace with God. Our Lord is spoken of in the Bible as a lamb. "Behold the Lamb of God," &c. The Passover lamb was to be "without blemish." St. Peter speaks of Jesus Christ as "a Lamb without blemish and without spot." He was "holy, harmless, undefiled, separate from sinners." The Passover lamb was to be slain, and its blood upon the door-posts was the sign by which the houses of the Israelites were distinguished, and so exempted from the power of the destroyer. Jesus Christ was crucified for us. By His death we have life. "We have redemption through His blood." "Ye were not redeemed with corruptible things, as silver and gold, but with the precious blood of Christ." "The blood of Jesus Christ cleanseth us from all sin." "Christ our passover is sacrificed for us." God delivers us from sin through the self-sacrifice of Christ for us. "Neither is there salvation in any other: for there is none other name under heaven given among men whereby we must be saved." (*b*)

3. *The Divine Author of deliverance.* The Lord God spared the first-born of Israel when the first-born of Egypt were destroyed. He also delivered them from their cruel bondage in Egypt. He only can emancipate the soul from the thraldom of sin, and deliver it from that death which is the wages of sin. He originated the method of deliverance; and His is the power by which the deliverance is accomplished. Neither of these things could man have done. Education, science, philosophy, means and efforts of social reform and amelioration, may do much for man; but they cannot free him from the dominion of sin, or deliver him from spiritual death—they cannot save him. God alone can do this; and He is "mighty to save," "He is able to save them to the uttermost," etc.

4. *The human appropriation of deliverance.* The Israelites were to "strike the lintel and the two side-posts with the blood" of the slain lamb as a condition of their deliverance. If they would be saved from the visit of the destroyer, they must believe the word of the Lord by Moses and obey it. If the death of Jesus Christ is to be of any real benefit to us personally, we must personally believe in Him as our Saviour. "Whosoever believeth in Him shall not perish, but have eternal life." (*c*)

Conclusion:
Sentence of death has gone forth against all sinners. "The wages of sin is death." "The soul that sinneth it shall die." God in Christ is the only One who can deliver from this death. Faith in Him is the only condition by which we can avail ourselves of His deliverance. Believe in Him, at once and fully, and life eternal is yours.

ILLUSTRATIONS.

(*a*) Such a night as never darkened from heaven before or since in Egypt, now descends upon her in the mysterious providence of God. It is "a night much to be remembered." The children of Israel are all up and ready for departure, their loins girt, and their lamps burning, the Paschal lamb, the unleavened bread, and the bitter herbs with which it was to be eaten, in their hands and mouths; the blood from the basins sprinkled on the lintel and the two door-posts, and all awaiting the moment when the shriek of the victims of the angel of death shall act as the blast of God's trumpet to tell them to depart! Such a feast! without one song of gladness or word of converse; ate in absolute silence and in a standing posture, and with every ear erect to listen to the sounds of wrath and woe which are expected. Do they hear the wings of the destroying angel without their dwellings, first sweeping near, then pausing (what a moment of suspense, for may not some have forgotten to stamp the stain upon the door, or stamped it too feebly?), and then hurrying onward? And do not, by-and-bye, faintly-heard and distant shrieks arise, swelling soon into one desperate and universal "cry," proclaiming that there is "not an house where there is not one dead"? It is at midnight that this fell-stroke lights on guilty Egypt, and the darkness contributes to the confusion, the horror, and the despair. "All the firstborn are smitten, from the firstborn of Pharaoh that sate on the throne to the firstborn of the captive that was in the dungeon." In one house, a child has been newly born to those who had been long married without the usual fruits of wedlock, and the parents are, perhaps, with a fond and foolish joy, exulting over the recent birth, when a sharp short cry from the cradle tells them their child is dead. In another, all the family have been cut off previously, except their firstborn, a boy who has become more the delight of their parents that he is their little all, as if he had absorbed the interest and life of the rest, but he, too, on his small couch is smitten, and their hope and joy die with him. In a third house, the firstborn is a fair female, and to-morrow is her wedding day, but death anticipates the bridegroom, and claps his cold ring upon her shrinking finger. In a fourth, a heroic youth who had projected a journey to the lands of Ethiopia and the sources of the Nile, and is dreaming that he has set out on his way, awakes for a moment to feel the death-pang summoning him to a farther and more adventurous exploration. In another house, one lies down who is on the morrow to be initiated into the higher mysteries of priestdom, but death says to him, "Understand this my mystery first, deeper infinitely than they." In another, the firstborn son is to rise next day to bury his father, but long ere morning he is laid cold by his side. How impartial this terrible angel! Here one firstborn has been condemned to die a public and a shameful death on the approaching day; but at midnight there is a corpse in the prison cell, and the law is disappointed of its prey. And there another, it is Pharaoh's own eldest son, whose birthday, he is come of age, is to be celebrated to-morrow, expires at the very moment of midnight, and his father rises and begins that wild wail which is echoed by every homestead in the land of Ham—*G. Gilfillan, M.A.*

(*b*) Here is the firstborn, the unblemished beauty, the chaste Lamb of God; never came to mortal eyes any such perfect one before. And the expense He makes, under His great love-struggle and heavy burden of feeling, His Gethsemane, where the burden presses Him down into agony; His Calvary, where, in His unprotesting and lamb-like submission, He allows Himself to be immolated by the world's wrath; what will any one, seeing all this, so naturally or inevitably call it, as His sacrifice for the sins of the world? His blood, too, the blood of the incarnate Son of God, blood of the upper world half as truly as of this—when it touches and stains the defiled earth of the planet, what so sacred blood on the horns of the altar and the lid of the mercy-seat did any devoutest worshipper at the altar ever see sprinkled for his cleansing? There his sin he hoped could be dissolved away, and it comforted his conscience that, by the offering of something sacred as blood, he could fitly own his defilement, and by such tender argument win the needed cleansing. But the blood of Christ, He that was born of the Holy Ghost, He that was Immanuel—when this sprinkles Calvary, it is to him as if some touch of cleansing were in it for the matter itself of the world! In short, there is so much in this analogy, and it is so affecting, so profoundly real, that no worshipper most devout before the altar having once seen Christ, who He is, what He has done by His cross, and the glorious offering He has made of Himself in His ministry of good, faithful unto death—who will not turn away instinctively to Him, saying, "No more altars, goats, or lambs; these were shadows I see; now has come the substance. This is my sacrifice, and here is my peace—the blood that was shed for the remission of sins—this I take and want no other."—*H. Bushnell. D.D.*

(c) Let me suppose that you profoundly long to know what you must do, on what you must lay hold, in order that you may appropriate to yourself the benefits of Christ's death, that you may be saved by His sacrifice, that you may be reconciled to God by His atonement. You come to me and ask, "What must I do? do first? How am I to set about this great quest and task?"

With much sympathy, as of one who has himself had to solve your problem as best he could, I reply, Fix your thoughts first and chiefly on the fact on which both St. Paul and St. John lay such extraordinary emphasis, viz., that the death, the cross, the blood, the sacrifice of Christ—take which term you will—is a manifestation of the eternal and inexhaustible love of God for sinful men, for all sinful men; a manifestation of the resolve and intention of that Love to take away the sin of the whole world, and to redeem you personally from all your iniquities. You see at once how great, how voluntary, how unmerited, how intense and Divine that Love is. It shrinks from nothing—from no effort, from no sacrifice, from no pang whether of body or of spirit, from no contact with evil, from no experience whether of the ingratitude and insolent wickedness of man or of the pain of self-limitation to any form of life or of death. So much you cannot fail to see with the story of the Gospel in your hand. And *your first duty* is to believe in that almost incredible Love, a Love that would be absolutely incredible but for its manifestation and proof in the history of Jesus Christ the Lord. You are to trust in that Love, to be sure that a love which extends to all the world *must* extend to you. You are to commit yourself to it—your soul as well as your body; commit yourself to it in life, in death, after death; and to sincerely believe that all must go well with you because that Love is over you and upon you. *This* is what you are to do and believe. It is *this* on which specifically you are to lay hold. It is *thus* that you are to appropriate the benefits of Christ's death.

And, then, if you take this first step, what will be your second? What will be the inevitable result and consequence of having taken the first? Obviously, if you do sincerely and heartily believe in such a Love as that, your own love will spring up and run out to meet it. You will love Him who first loved you. And your love will be, or will come to be as God's love takes effect upon you, of the same quality with His—an unselfish love, a love capable of living and dying for others, a love pure and righteous, strong and enduring; a love that will gradually transform you into His likeness, and make you of one will with Him . . . . You are to lay hold of the Cross of Christ as at once a manifestation of God's righteous anger against the sins with which you, too, are angry, and from which you seek to be delivered, and a revelation of the Love which is bent on conquering sin and redeeming you from all evil. You are to so appreciate and trust that Love as that it shall quicken a corresponding affection, and make it the ruling affection, in your own soul.—*Samuel Cox.*

ORDINANCE OF THE PASSOVER.

(*Verses* 1-5.)

The design of God in instituting this remarkable ordinance, the Passover, was to explain to us, as well as to prefigure to the Jews, the method of salvation through the blood of Christ. He is the One great Sacrifice for sin; and here, the application to Him in His mediatorial work is most comprehensive. Behold the analogy. It holds—

I. With regard to the victim which was chosen.

Was it a lamb? Christ is often so called on account of His innocence, meekness, and resignation (Isa. liii. 7; John i. 29; 1 Peter i. 19; Rev. v. 6.) Was it chosen from the flock? Christ was taken from among His brethren (Acts iii. 22). Was it a male of the first year? Christ suffered in the prime of His days. Was it without blemish? Christ was altogether perfect (Heb. vii. 26; 1 Peter i 19).

II. With regard to the oblation which was made.

As the lamb was slain, so was Jesus (Rev. v. 9). As the lamb was slain before the whole assembly (Exod. xii. 6), so Jesus was publicly put to death. As the lamb was slain between the two evenings, so Jesus was offered between three o'clock and six (Matt. xxvii. 45). As the lamb was set apart four days before it was slain (Exod. xii. 3, 6), so Christ entered the city four days before His crucifixion (Matt. xxi. 1 *sqq*).

III. With regard to the blood which was sprinkled.

The blood was sprinkled with a bunch of hyssop (Exod. xii. 22, dipt into the bason; so the blood of Christ is the blood of the everlasting covenant, the deposit of privileges, which all become ours by the exercise of faith. The blood was sprinkled upon the door-posts of their dwellings. So the blood of Christ is to be applied to the hearts and consciences of believers (Heb. ix. 13, 14; x. 22). The blood was sprinkled upon the lintel and the side posts; but not behind nor below the door. So the blood of Christ is not to be trodden under foot (Heb. x. 29). The blood secured every family where it was sprinkled, it being within the limits of the Divine protection, so that the destroying angel was forbidden to hurt them. So the blood of Jesus is the only refuge for the guilty.

IV. With regard to the flesh which was eaten.

The flesh of the lamb was eaten roasted with fire, strikingly exhibiting the severity of our Saviour's sufferings. (Isa. 1. 6; lii. 14, 15; Psa. xxii. 14, 15.) It was eaten whole, and not a bone broken, which was amazingly fulfilled in reference to Christ. (John xix. 31-36.) It was eaten in haste, with the staff in their hands, to intimate that Christ is to be received immediately without delay. It was eaten with bitter herbs, importing our looking to Christ with sorrow of heart, in remembrance of sin, as expressed in Zech. xii. 10. It was eaten with the loins girded, implying that we must be prepared for His coming. (Eph. vi. 14.) It was eaten with the feet shod, to remind us of the freedom and happiness which Christ imparts to the believing Israelites. (compare Isa. xx. 2-4 with Rom. v. 11.) It was eaten with unleavened bread, because we are to receive and profess Christ with unfeigned sincerity. (1 Cor. v. 7, 8; John i. 47.)

Upon the whole, we learn from the subject the happy state of believers, who, though once afar off, are now made nigh by the blood of Christ; and likewise the unhappy state of unbelievers, who, rejecting the atonement, must inevitably perish. — *William Sleigh.*

UNWILLING EXCLUSION FROM RELIGIOUS ORDINANCES.

(Verses 6-12, 14.)

In these verses we have the following homiletic points, which we may profitably consider :—

I. The Divine recognition of the need of personal fitness for an acceptable observance of religious ordinances.

A person who was ceremonially unclean was prohibited from taking part in the Passover; for only those who were clean could participate in any sacrificial meal, or offer any sacrifice. (Lev. vii. 20, 21.) So "there were certain men, who were defiled by the dead body of a man who could not keep the Passover on that day." A certain moral fitness is essential to an acceptable approach unto God. Our Lord taught that a man cannot present an acceptable offering to God who is not in right relations with his fellow-men. (Matt. v. 23, 24.) And St. Paul exhorted the Corinthian Christians to examine themselves before partaking of the Supper of the Lord. (1 Cor. xi. 28.) Two things at least appear to us as indispensable to an acceptable approach to God in public religious ordinances:

1. *Faith in the mediation of the Lord Jesus Christ.* (John xiv. 6.; Rom. v. 1, 2; Eph. ii. 18; Heb. iv. 15, 16; x. 19-22.)

2. *Devout preparation of the heart.* There are many persons who derive no benefit from the public means of grace because they enter upon them with minds engrossed by worldly engagements or anxieties, or with thoughless, frivolous minds, &c. Such mental

states preclude communion with God. (*a*)

II. **The unwilling exclusion of men from religious ordinances.**

Here are certain men who were excluded from keeping the Passover through no fault of their own. Their defilement was not moral, but ceremonial; and this was contracted not of their own free choice, but of inevitable necessity; not by association with the morally depraved, but by the needful work of the burial of the dead; yet they were prohibited from observing the Passover. There are many to-day who are unwillingly deprived from taking part in public religious ordinances,—some by reason of severe bodily afflictions; others by the pressure of the infirmities of age; others by their ministry to the afflicted; and others by legitimate domestic duties, *e.g.*, the care of infants and little children, &c. Every Lord's day there are very many persons who would esteem it a privilege and joy to unite in the engagements of public worship, but they cannot do so. Let us learn to prize the opportunities of doing so while we have them.

III. **A commendable enquiry concerning the reason of such exclusion from religious ordinances.**

The men who were so excluded "came before Moses and before Aaron on that day;" &c. Their enquiry was commendable—

1. *As regards its spirit.* It implied (1) *Faith in the reasonableness of the Divine requirements.* "Wherefore are we kept back"? &c. It is as though they had said, "There must be a reason for this prohibition; may we know that reason? can you explain it to us? or can you meet in some way what seems to us the hardship of our case?" All the Divine arrangements are in the highest degree reasonable; they are expressions of infinite wisdom. (2) *Affection for Divine ordinances.* The deprivation was painful to them. It is a grief to the godly soul to be deprived of the public means of grace. "Lord I have loved the habitation of Thy house, and the place where Thine honour dwelleth." "How amiable are Thy tabernacles, O Lord of hosts! My soul longeth," &c. There is good ground for this affection. In Divine ordinances God manifests Himself graciously to His people (Exod. xx. 24; Matt. xviii. 19, 20), and makes unto them rich communications of grace and truth.

2. *As regards its direction.* "They came before Moses and before Aaron," and enquired of them. The leader and lawgiver, and the high priest, both of whom were appointed by God, were the proper persons to consult on the difficulty which had arisen. Let those who are religiously perplexed seek help from those who by reason of their character and attainments are qualified to render the same.

The solicitude of these men for participation in this religious ordinance is a rebuke to many who, in our own day, disregard the public worship of God and the ministry and the sacraments of the Gospel.

IV. **The exemplary conduct of religious teachers in answering the enquiries of their charge.**

"And Moses said unto them, Stand still," &c. In the conduct of Moses we see,—

1. *Exemplary humility.* He tacitly admits his inability to answer their enquiry of himself. It is only ignorance and conceit that assumes the airs of infallibility. The minister of spiritual intelligence and power is ever humble. (*b*)

2. *Exemplary enquiry.* "I will hear what the Lord will command concerning you," said Moses. That he might answer these enquiries, he himself enquires of the Lord. So should the Christian minister in instructing others. We have, (1) The teaching of the sacred Scriptures: we should search them. We have (2) The promised guidance of the Holy Spirit: we should seek it by prayer. (*c*)

3. *Exemplary efficiency.* Guided by God, Moses was enabled to deal with the difficulty satisfactorily,—practically to do away with it. Christian ministers should be able efficiently to counsel the people of their charge. Those who

humbly acknowledge their ignorance, search the Scriptures, and seek help of God, will be able to do so. Let all religious instructors copy the example of Moses in this matter.

V. **A Divine arrangement for the compensation of those who are unwillingly excluded from religious ordinances.**

"And the Lord spake unto Moses, saying, Speak unto the children of Israel," &c. (verses 9, 12, 14.) Provision is here made for three distinct classes—for the defiled, for the traveller far from home, and for the stranger. For the two former a supplementary Passover is instituted; and for the latter who desired to unite in the observance of the ordinance, liberty to do so is granted. In the directions given to Moses by the Lord, two things are clear and conspicuous—

1. *No one was to be unwillingly deprived of religious ordinances without compensation.*

2. *All must faithfully fulfil the Divine directions in the keeping of such ordinances as they had access to* (verses 11, 12, 14). The three leading points of the original institution are here repeated—that they were to eat the lamb with unleavened bread and bitter herbs, they were to leave none of it till the next day, and they were not to break a bone of it. The foreigner, also, who kept the feast was to do so with minute accuracy as to the directions concerning it. Compare verse 14 with Exod. xii. 48, 49. And still when any one is involuntarily detained from religious ordinances, God will supply unto him precious and abundant compensations. To the patient sufferer on his bed, to the attentive nurse as she ministers to the afflicted, and to the loving mother at home with her babe, if only the spirit of true worship be theirs, God will graciously reveal Himself, and enrich them with the treasures of His grace. He will be with them; and the chamber of sickness, or the nursery of infancy, shall become a Bethel, "a little sanctuary," sacred with His presence and radiant with His glory. (*d*)

ILLUSTRATIONS.

(*a*) Previous to your entering into the house of God, seek *a prepared heart,* and implore the blessing of God on the ministry of the Word. It may be presumed that no real Christian will neglect to preface his attendance on social worship with secret prayer. But let the acquisition of a devout and serious frame, freed from the cares, vanities, and pollutions of the world, accompanied with earnest desires after God, and the communications of His grace, form a principal subject of your private devotions. Forget not to implore a blessing on the public ministry, that it may accomplish in yourselves, and to others, the great purposes it is designed to answer; and that those measures of assistance may be afforded to your ministers which shall replenish them with light, love, and liberty, that they may speak the mystery of the Gospel as it ought to be spoken. Pastors and people would both derive eminent advantages from such a practice; they, in their capacity of exhibiting, you, in your preparation for receiving, the mysteries of the Gospel. As the duties of the closet have the happiest tendency, by solemnizing and elevating the mind, to prepare for those of the sanctuary, so the conviction of your having borne your minister on your heart before the throne of grace would, apart from every other consideration, dispose him to address you with augmented zeal and tenderness. We should consider it as such a token for good, as well as such an unequivocal proof of your attachment, as would greatly animate and support us under all our discouragements.—*Robert Hall, A.M.*

(*b*) A more despicable character I know not than the poor mortal who proclaims his opinions as if they were the very Gospel of God; who denounces all who adopt them not as heretics. I pity the mental serfs, who, instead of drinking at the crystal river of truth, that rolls majestically by, consent to sip at the puddled cisterns of the would-be theological dictators. While around us have been flung, with God-like profusion, the fruits and beauties of a Paradise, shall we consent to confine ourselves to the scanty provisions of a petty kitchen garden? To all the dogmatists who would bind us to their own narrow creed we would say with Pope:—

"Go, wondrous creature! mount where science guides;
Go, measure earth, weigh air, and stem the tides;
Instruct the planets in what orbs to run,
Correct old time and regulate the sun.
Go, teach eternal Wisdom how to rule,
Then drop into thyself, and be a fool."

It is the duty of every man to get convictions of Divine truth for himself, to hold those convictions with firmness, and to promote them with earnestness; but at the same time with a due consciousness of his own fallibility, and with a becoming deference to the judgment of others. Sure am I that he who has penetrated farthest into the realms of truth, wrestled most earnestly with its questions, will be the most free from all bigotry and dogmatism in the proclamation of his views. The more knowledge the more humility. True wisdom is ever modest. Those who live most in the light are the most ready to veil their faces.—*David Thomas, D.D.*

(*c*) Among all the formative influences which go to make up a man honoured of God in the ministry, I know of none more mighty than his own familiarity with the mercy-seat. All that a college course can do for a student is coarse and external compared with the spiritual and clear refinement obtained by communion with God. While the unformed minister is revolving upon the wheel of preparation, prayer is the tool of the Great Potter by which He moulds the vessel. All our libraries and studies are mere emptiness compared with our closets. We grow, we wax mighty, we prevail in private prayer. That we may be strong to labour, tender to sympathise, and wise to direct, let us pray. If study makes men of us, prayer will make saints of us. Our sacred furniture for our holy office can only be found in the arsenal of supplication; and after we have entered upon our consecrated warfare, prayer alone can keep our armour bright.— *C. H. Spurgeon.*

Moses was but the echo of God's voice; John Baptist "the voice of one crying in the wilderness;" St. Paul "received of the Lord" what he delivered to the Church (1 Cor. xi. 23), and took care that the faith of his hearers "might not be in the wisdom of man, but in the power of God" (1 Cor. ii. 4, 5). Unwarranted doctrines come not *cum gratia et privilegio.*—*John Trapp, M A.*

(*d*) Do not think for a moment that by frequenting places that have an odour of peculiar sanctity you can alone acceptably worship God.

Have you got a contrite heart? That can consecrate the meanest place on earth. It does not matter where the congregation may gather, only let them be a congregation of faithful men, yearning for truth, ready to make any sacrifice to obtain it, and that God who is everywhere present will reveal Himself in blessings wherever they may choose to assemble. They may crowd into the solemn Minster, and while the organ peals out its alternate wail and psalm, to them it may be a spiritual service, and their hearts may glow in purer light than streams through painted windows. They may draw around the hearth of the farmer's homestead, and while the frost king reigns outside, their spirits may burn with a warmth that may defy the keenness of the sternest winter. For them there may be a spiritual harvest more plentiful than the garnered store in the barn that has been lent for worship; or a season of refreshing beneath the thatch through which the penitent soul can filter up its sighs for heaven. On the gallant vessel's deck, with no witnesses of the service but the sky and sea, there may be the sound of many waters as the Lord of hosts comes down. And in the Alpine solitudes, where the spirit, alone with God mid murmuring streams, and bowing pines, and summits of eternal snow, uplifts its adoration, there may be a whisper stiller, and sweeter, and more comforting than that of nature, saying, "Peace, peace be unto you." Oh! it is a beautiful thought, that in this, the last of the dispensations, the contrite heart can hallow its own temple! Wherever the emigrant wanders—wherever the exile pines—in the dreariest Sahara, rarely tracked save by the Bedouin on his camel—on the banks of rivers yet unknown to song—in the dense woodlands where no axe has yet struck against the trees—in the dark ruin—in the foul cell—in the narrow street—on the swift rail—there where business tramps and rattles—there where sickness gasps and pines—anywhere—anywhere in this wide, wide world, if there is a soul that wants to worship, there can be a hallowed altar and a present God.—*W. M. Punshon, LL.D.*

THE WILFUL NEGLECT OF RELIGIOUS ORDINANCES.
(*Verse* 13.)

In this verse we have set before us a case of,—

I. The wilful neglect of religious ordinances.

"The man that is clean, and is not in a journey, and forbeareth to keep the Passover." The Passover was instituted by command of God; neither ceremonial uncleanness nor absence from home prevented his observing it; yet he fails to do so—such is the case which is set before us in the text. In our day the wilful neglect of religious ordinances is painfully prevalent. Churches, chapels, mission halls, and religious services abound; yet in this nominally Christian country there are hundreds of thousands who are in a position to attend public worship, who live in the habitual neglect of it. (*a*)

II. The wilful neglect of religious ordinances is sinful.

It is said in the text that the man who wilfully forbeareth to keep the Passover "shall bear his sin." The worship of God is not optional, but obligatory upon man; it is our duty. He who wilfully neglects religious ordinances by such neglect sins, because he,—

1. *Withholds from God that which is His due.* God has an indefeasible right to our homage. His greatness should excite our awe; His kindness should enkindle our gratitude; His skill should awaken our admiration; His holiness should inspire our adoring love.

2. *Despises the gifts which God bestows.* Worship is a privilege as well as a duty. It is a great kindness on the part of God that He has instituted the ordinances of worship, and great condescension that He graciously accepts our worship. To neglect public worship is to despise the ordinance and reject the gift of God.

3. *Neglects the culture and development of the highest faculties of his being.* Worship is a necessity of our nature. We have religious tendencies and aspirations which seek expression and satisfaction in worship. We cannot neglect worship without the deepest and most deplorable self-injury. (*b*) Wilfully to neglect religious ordinances, then, is to sin—to sin against our own nature and against God.

III. The wilful neglect of religious ordinances will be punished.

"The man that is clean and is not in a journey, and forbeareth to keep the Passover, even the same soul shall be cut off from among his people," &c. The expression "cut off from among his people" denotes either capital punishment, or exclusion from the society and privileges of the chosen people. The latter seems to us the more probable. No one can neglect religious ordinances without incurring punishment—a punishment which grows directly out of the sin. By his wilful neglect he brings the punishment upon himself.

1. *He foregoes the highest joys of life.*
2. *He dwarfs and degrades his soul.*
3. *He excludes himself from the highest fellowship on earth.*
4. *He renders himself unfit for the fellowship of heaven.* The worship of God here is a natural and necessary preparation for uniting in His worship in the innumerable company of the glorified.

ILLUSTRATIONS.

(*a*) The need of more effort to induce persons who never attend a place of worship to do so seems very great. Thus there are 2,500 people living in one block of buildings in the South of London, of whom not more than 130 frequent public worship. This is a sad fact, and needs the consideration of Christian people.—"*The Christian World,*" May 10, 1878.

A very large proportion of the outside world is voluntarily irreligious or indifferent. A very large proportion of those who are not church-goers, who connect themselves with no religious society, and make no profession of religion, reside in the midst of those who do. Intelligent, educated, surrounded by religious influences, it is not through ignorance they remain where they are. Had they the longing for that peace which Christianity gives, they know in general where to find it. Their indifference and irreligion are in a great measure their own choice. No special mission is needed to them, as it is to those who have not their knowledge or their opportunities. They may be reached by the quiet, unobtrusive influence, and by the steady growth of vital religion among their neighbours; by the appeal of a Christian friend in sickness; by the perusal of a book; by the voice of some distinguished preacher whom they are led to hear. This class is very large; it is hindered by causes within rather than without.—*Joseph Mullens, D.D.*

That the religion of the working man is at a low ebb is a fact there can be no disputing. Our churches are for the rich, our chapels for the lower half of the middle class; the working man seldom finds his way to either. The Sunday morning is mostly spent in bed, the afternoon in an indolent and half apathetic condition, lolling on chairs or sofa, if he has one, nodding and slumbering over *Lloyd's,* or the *Weekly Times*; it is only during the few hours of evening that he begins to show any signs of active life. On the Monday he feels more tired, and imagines the day to have been very considerably longer than any other. This is how the majority of London working men, at least, spend their Sunday, half sad to see it come, and wholly glad when it is over. This is a state of things to be lamented; who can doubt it is only in the degree in which families are happy (to rise to which there must be love, sympathy, confidence, and mutual esteem), that a nation becomes truly great; and this happiness is not possible without religion. We trust the day is not far distant when almost every working man will not only think it a duty to attend public worship, but will feel it a pleasure likewise.—*Eclectic Review.*

(*b*) Worship is the instinctive act and necessity of the religious consciousness. Its root lies in our recognition of God, and of our personal relationship to Him, its eucharistic element in our sense of His transcendent excellencies, and its supplicatory element in our consciousness of absolute dependence upon Him. We do not, that is, worship in mere compliance with a Divine injunction, nor in conformity with a conventional cultus, nor as a means of religious benefit. We worship under the impulse of our own religious instincts, because the constitution of our nature being what it is, we cannot without violence to it help doing so. Worship, therefore, has its ultimate reason neither in the sense of obligation, nor in considerations of utility; it is the simple necessity of the religious soul. Hence, in the severest persecutions of the Church, no considerations of personal peril have ever been sufficient to deter Christian men from assembling for social worship. Although there is no direct injunction of public worship, and although the spiritual relationships of the soul are so personal, and find their full expression in acts of personal and private devotion, yet the consecrating impulse of social worship has led men for the sake of it to dare and sacrifice life itself.— H. Allon, D.D.

The Manifestation of the Divine Presence.

(*Verses* 15, 16.)

I. The Sphere of the Manifestation of the Divine Presence.

"And on the day that the tabernacle was reared up the cloud covered the tabernacle, namely, the tent of the testimony." Previously the cloud had hung up on high over the camp; but now that the tabernacle is finished it descended and rested upon it. In the tabernacle and in the ordinances of religion God specially manifested Himself. He is everywhere present. The thoughtful mind discovers evidences of His power and skill everywhere. To the religious heart the whole world is a temple resplendent with His glory and resounding with His praise. But still He is specially present in His Church:

1. *By the ministry of the Word.* He speaks to men by His servants as they expound and apply the teachings of His Book.

2. *By the observance of the Sacraments.* To the believer Christ is really and blessedly present in the Sacraments which He instituted.

3. *By the presence and power of the Holy Spirit.* By His Spirit the Lord Jesus abides with His Church. In His material works we see Him as the God of nature; in His Church we see him as the God of grace and salvation, we realize His helpful and hallowing presence, and hold delightful communion with Him. Comp. Pss. xxvii. 4; cxxxii. 13-16; Matt. xviii. 20. (*a*)

II. The Aspects of the Manifestation of the Divine Presence.

"The cloud covered the tabernacle, namely, the tent of testimony; and at even there was upon the tabernacle, as it were the appearance of fire, until the morning."

1. *The aspect of the manifestation of the Divine Presence was varied.* In the day He appeared in cloud; in the night in the appearance of fire. The Divine Being does not present the same aspects to different minds; nor does He always appear in the same aspects to the same persons. *He* changes not, "with Him is no variableness;" but the forms of His manifestation to His creatures change. Moreover, our vision of Him varies with our varying spiritual conditions and moods.

2. The aspect of the manifestation of the Divine Presence *was varied according to the need of the people.* The diversity of the Divine manifestation was perfectly adapted to the diversity of human need. The cloud by day and

148

the appearance of fire by night were easily discernible. Mark the precious truth of universal application which is here shadowed forth : God manifests Himself to His people according to their need. To the soul seeking Him in penitence He reveals Himself as a gracious Sovereign or a kind Father waiting to forgive ; to the distressed mourner, as the great and tender-hearted Comforter ; to the perplexed student of the Divine will and work, as the wise and kind Guide ; to the lonely and sad by reason of the bereavements of death, as "the Resurrection and the Life ;" &c. With infinite wisdom and goodness He adapts the revelations of His presence and the communications of His grace to our varying circumstances, conditions, and needs. (b)

III. The Permanence of the Manifestations of the Divine Presence.

"So it was alway : the cloud covered it by day, and the appearance of fire by night." Through the whole of their wanderings the blessed Presence never forsook them. God has never left His Church. The light of His Presence has varied, sometimes burning more brightly than at others ; but it has never been extinguished or withdrawn. The light of the Church has waned in one place, but it has shone the more brightly in another. "I am with you alway, even unto the end of the world." In the abiding presence of our Lord and Saviour with us we have *the guarantee of the continuance, the progress, and the ultimate triumph of His Church over all enemies.* (c)

Conclusion.

1. *Here is admonition for Christians.* The Lord is with us ever, His eye is ever upon us ; let us, then, walk circumspectly, &c.

2. *Here is encouragement for Christians.* The Lord is ever present to guide us in our way, to sustain us in difficulty and trial, to defend us from harm, and to conduct us in safety and in triumph to our rest and home with God. Wherefore, let us be of good cheer.

"In thy presence we are happy ;
In Thy presence we're secure ;
In Thy presence all afflictions
We will easily endure ;
In Thy presence we can conquer,
We can suffer, we can die ;
Far from Thee, we faint and languish :
Lord, our Saviour, keep us nigh."

W. Williams.

ILLUSTRATIONS.

(a) If Louis Napoleon could call a senate of all the potentates in the world in Paris, and hold a congress there, the whole of them put together would not be worth the snap of a finger compared with half-a-dozen godly old women who meet together in the name of Christ as a Church, in obedience to the Lord's command ; for God would not be there with the potentates—what cares He for them ?—but He would be with the most poor and despised of His people who meet together as a church in Jesus Christ's name. "Lo, I am with you always, even unto the end of the world," is more glorious than ermine, or purple, or crown. Constitute a church in the name of Christ, and meet together as such, and there is no assembly upon the face of the earth that can be compared with it, and even the assembly of the first-born in heaven is but a branch of the grand whole of which the assemblies of the Church on earth make up an essential part.—*C. H. Spurgeon.*

(b) There are in the Bible many allusions to this cloud ; all of them indicating its remarkable and peculiar and significant character. Several times we find allusions to it in the book of Psalms. See Pss. lxxviii. 14, cv. 39. We also find it mentioned in Nehemiah ix, 19. And we have a very beautiful allusion, assuming the shape of a cheering promise, in Isaiah iv. 5, 6. We find in all these passages very plain and unmistakeable allusions to this symbol. Now what does it seem to have been ? First a luminous fire, in the midst of the darkness of the night ; supposed to extend to a mile in height into the sky, as if a great pillar, majestic in appearance, but phosphorescent or luminous and shining. Then in the daytime, when the splendour of a fire would be lost in the greater splendour of the sun, and could not necessarily be a guide to those that sought to follow it, the fire, or the luminous portion of it, retreated into the innermost recesses of the cloud, and a dark pillar, as if made of smoke or of cloud, stretched from the place where the tabernacle rested, a mile upward into the sky. And when God meant that the children of Israel should proceed forward, it marched before them, or moved before them, their signal, their director, and their guide. It was adapted exactly to the circumstances of their journey ; a beautiful proof in its being cloud by day, and in its being fire by night, that God adapts the manifestations of Himself, the supplies of His wisdom, His grace, and His bounty to the peculiar circumstances, necessities, and condition of His believing people. Now, this symbol, as we gather from all the allusions to it scattered through the Scriptures, was a type of Christ, God manifest in the flesh. It was God's mode of revealing Himself to that people in the midst of the desert ; and was to them the perpetual pledge of His favourable and gracious presence.—*John Cumming. D.D.*

God rises upon the sight of some Christians as the sun comes right up against a clear sky, and over a sharp-cut horizon, and upon others as the sun comes up behind clouds, which it is his first work to wear out and disperse with His bright beams. I have seen men that never realized God till they were dying. Some never see Him till the midday of their life. Others see Him early in the morning. Some see Him during sickness ; some after sickness ; some on the occurrence of some special providence. Sometimes Christians are lifted up, through the susceptibility of their imagination, their affections, and their reason, all conjoined, into such an extraordinary sense of God's glory that it seems as though their soul could not abide in the body, and they think, " Praise God ! At last He has had mercy on me, and revealed Himself to me "—supposing that He had not before cast the light of His countenance upon them.—*H W. Beecher.*

(c) It was enough for the army of Cromwell to know that he was there, the ever-victorious, the irresistible, to lead on his Ironsides to the fray. Many a time the presence of an old Roman general was equal to another legion ; as soon as the cohorts perceived that he was come whose eagle eye watched every motion of the enemy, and whose practised hand led his battalions upon the most salient points of attack, each man's blood leaped within him, and he grasped his sword and rushed forward sure of success. My brethren, our King is in the midst of us, and our faith should be in active exercise—" The shout of a King is in the midst of us," it is said, for where the King is there the people shout for joy, and because of confidence of victory. The preacher may preach, but what is that ? but if the King be there, then it is a preaching in very deed. The congregations may have met, and they may have gone again. " The panoramic view which has dissolved," you say. Ah, so it may seem to you, but if the Spirit of God was there, all that has been done will abide, and remain even to that day of judgment, when the fire shall try every man's work of what sort it is. " Nothing but a simple girl sitting down to talk to a few little children about their souls." Just so, but if the Lord be there, what awe gathers round that spot ! If the King Himself sit in that class, what deeds are done that sha'l make the angels of heaven sing anew for joy ! " Nothing but a humble man, unlettered, earnest, but not eloquent, standing at the corner of a street addressing a few hundred people. His talk will soon be forgotten." The footprints of every true servant of the Lord shall not be in the sand, but in the enduring brass, the record of which shall outlast the wreck of matter.—*C. H. Spurgeon.*

The Pillar of Cloud and Fire.
(Verse 16.)

One of the most extraordinary things associated with the journey of God's ancient people was the pillar of cloud and fire. The fame of this wonderful phenomenon was spread abroad among the nations of the earth. There were several miraculous things connected with it that made it differ from other clouds. Its form was never changed. It always maintained its station over the tabernacle, unlike other clouds, that are carried about with the wind and tempest. It preserved its consistency and shape for forty years ; while other clouds are either exhaled in the sun, dissipated by the wind, or dissolved in rain or dew, and in a very short time blotted out of the firmament. It moved in a peculiar direction. And, above all, it was brighter at night than by day. We cannot be mistaken in the typical meaning of this cloud. It must be viewed as *a symbol of the presence and glory of God in the midst of His people* (see Exod. xvi. 10 ; xix. 9 ; xxxiv. 5 ; 1 Kings viii. 10). Notice two things in reference to the presence of God :

I. **The Advantages of its Possession.**

Let us select some of the advantages to be derived from it by believers on earth :

1. *The distinction it maintains.* The pillar of cloud and fire among the Israelites may be viewed as a token of their being a separate people from other nations. This distinguished them:

they were the only nation that were so privileged. It was a complete division of their forces one from the other (see Exod. xiv. 19, 20). Christians, you are a peculiar people—your origin is peculiar—your character is peculiar—your spirit—your desires and affections—the objects of your pursuit. You have peculiar privileges and honours conferred on you. There is to be a marked difference between you and the world. "No man can serve two masters," etc.

2. *The guidance it ensures.* All the movements of the Israelites were under the direction of this cloud. God's presence now goes with His people for their guidance, and shall conduct them safely home. "My presence shall go with you, and I will give you rest." Jesus is now the guide of His people. He leads in the way of truth and wisdom. How? By His *example.* He has gone before us in the path of duty, temptation, and sorrow. By His *Word.* This is our rule. By His *ordinances.* He sends His ministers as your guides. By His *Spirit,* effectually. By the leadings of His *providence.* As the Israelites watched the motion of the cloud, so must we the movements of His providence.

3. *The protection it affords.* This was remarkably the case with the Israelites when pursued by their enemies, the Egyptians. . . . . (Psa. lxxvii. 16-20.) How admirably does this apply to the protecting presence of God with His people now. They have their enemies, who thirst for their destruction. How numerous, crafty, and powerful they are! But God is their hiding-place, etc.

4. *The joy it inspires.* God is the source of happiness, the fountain of life. His presence gives joy even in sorrow, and makes us glory in tribulation.

5. *The glory it confers.* What a wondrous, glorious sight must have been the exit of the Israelites out of Egypt, and their encampment in the wilderness. Balaam viewing them from a neighbouring mountain, cried out in admiration, etc. (See Ch. xxiii. 9, 10). The presence of God is our highest, best, only real glory. But what is all that God confers here to what is in reserve! The partial enjoyment of God's presence affords some particles of glory; but the full enjoyment of Him shall constitute a weight of glory.

II. **The perpetuity of its enjoyment.** "So it was alway." Notwithstanding all the sins and provocations of the Israelites, the cloud did not leave them till they arrived in Canaan. Will not this apply to Christians now in their enjoyment of God's presence? Observe two things:

1. *Its necessity.* It was indispensably necessary to the Israelites, for the purposes to which we have alluded; and is it less so now? We always need the Divine presence. We are dependent on Him for every thing. We need His providential presence and agency to continue us in being and supply our numerous wants; and we require His gracious presence for the maintenance of spiritual life, and for the reception of spiritual blessings. We need His presence for the duties of life, for consolation in sorrow, for support in temptation, peace in death, and happiness in glory. If we have His presence, we have everything; if we want it, we have nothing.

2. *The manner in which it is ensured.* This may be seen three ways. From what He has done—is doing—and has promised to do. (1) *A retrospect of the past.* May not we say of God's presence with His Church, "So it was alway?" Was not His presence with Abraham? and Moses? and David? and Daniel? And in the New Testament times, was He not with Peter? and Paul? He has never left His Church to the will of her enemies. But come to individual experience. Has He not been with *you?* Recall past scenes, deliverances, comforts, joys. (2) *A view of the present.* Is He not near at hand? always accessible? (3) *A glance at the future.* So it shall be always. How is it ensured? His past

dealings with us would be enough; but we have more. Look at His *promises.* "I will never leave you," etc. Look at *the mediation of His Son.* The death and intercession of Christ ensure it. Look at *the influences of His Spirit.* All combine to testify His continual care and watchfulness over you.
Conclusion :—
1. *What a privileged character is the Christian.* How many peculiar mercies.
2. *The misery of the ungodly.* Without God. How deplorable !—*Ebenezer Temple.*

The Cloudy Pillar.

(*Verses* 15-19).

The cloudy pillar may be regarded—
I. As an emblem of Divine truth.
1. *Supernatural as to origin.*
2. *Stable :* only a cloud, yet not dispersed.
3. *Adapted to both night and day.*
4. *Reliable.*
5. *Intolerant : "This* is the way," and no other.
II. As a symbol of Divine Providence.
1. *Different appearance to different characters.*
2. *Presented alternations of aspect to the same people.*
3. *Mysterious in its movements.*
4. *Aims at the good of all who follow its guidance.*
II. As a type of the Divine Saviour.
1. *Mysterious nature.*
2. *Challenges attention.*
3. *His purpose beneficent.*
4. *The source of great comfort.*
5. *Constant in His attachment.*
Learn,—
(1) Seek to be on the right side of the cloud.
(2) To seek it in the right place—over the tabernacle.
(3) To follow its guidance.—*Biblical Museum.*

The Pilgrimage of the Good.

(*Verses* 17-23).

We propose to use these verses as illustrating the Pilgrimage of the People of God. So regarding them they present three main homiletical points for consideration :
I. The infallible Guide in the Pilgrimage of the Good.
In journeying through the desert the Israelites needed constant direction. There were no well-defined roads along which they could travel ; there were no beaten tracks of travellers for their guidance ; it was customary for travellers to steer their course as mariners at sea do, by a mathematical chart. But the Israelites went by a better direction." The Lord Himself led them by means of "the fiery, cloudy pillar." "In the daytime he led them with a cloud, and all the night with a light of fire." The movement of the cloud was to them "the commandment of the Lord ;" its ascent from the tabernacle was the signal of departure ; its descent upon the tabernacle was the signal for halting. Thus Infinite Wisdom was their Guide. In the pilgrimage of our life we also need guidance. There are perils to be avoided, misleading and evil ways to be shunned ; and we have not the experience, the skill, or the wisdom to shun these ways and avoid these perils. "The way of man is not in himself ; it is not in man that walketh to direct his steps." God is still the Guide of all who acknowledge Him. Compare Psalms xxxii. 8 ; lxxiii. 24 ; Prov. iii. 6.
In what way is this guidance now exercised ?
1. *By the indications of Providence.* Circumstances sometimes become to us

a guiding pillar, sometimes summoning us to arise and depart, or to pitch our tent and rest awhile. The good man in the combinations of circumstances frequently reads the directions of God.

2. *By the teachings of the Bible, and especially by the example of Jesus Christ as it is there set forth.* "Thy Word is a lamp unto my feet, and a light unto my path." "When thou goest it shall lead thee . . . . For the commandment is a lamp; and the law is light; and reproofs of instruction are the way of life." "I have given you an example, that ye should do as I have done to you." "Christ also suffered for us, leaving us an example, that ye should follow His steps." "I am the Light of the world: he that followeth Me shall not walk in darkness, but shall have the light of life."

3. *By the influences of the Holy Spirit.* He enters into our being, and mysteriously and mightily influences our intellect and heart and will, and works within us deep convictions which lead to corresponding actions. Thus the Divine guidance, though no longer outward and visible, but inward and spiritual, is as real as when He led His people through the wilderness. *(a)*

II. **The perfect Protector in the Pilgrimage of the Good.**

The pillar of cloud and of fire was not only a guide, but a protection also to the Israelites. In the passage of the Red Sea it was an impenetrable barrier between them and their Egyptian pursuers. During the scorching heat of the daytime in the desert, like a veil it sheltered them from the fierce rays of the sun. And during the night its brightness shielded them from the attacks of wild beasts. It is a beautiful symbol of the Divine protection of the people of God in their pilgrimage.

1. *This protection was constant.* Night and day, during all their life in the desert, it was never withdrawn. (Comp. Pss. xci. 1-13; cxxi.; John x. 27, 28; 1 Pet. i. 5.)

2. *This protection was adapted to the varying circumstances of the people.* By day it assumed the aspect of a cloud, and by night that of fire. God is perfectly acquainted with us and with our circumstances, and with infinite skill He adapts His defence to our danger. He renders His faithful servants, and their very garments, utterly insensible to the heat of the furnace, even when it is heated "seven times more than it is wont to be heated." He shuts the mouths of the hungry lions; and to His servant, tried and true, makes their den a place not only of perfect safety, but of angelic fellowship also.

3. *This protection was inviolable.* When this cloud was their shield, not even the mightiest and most malignant force could penetrate it to their hurt. (Comp. Pss. xxvii. 1-3; cxviii. 6; Rom. viii. 31; 1 Pet. iii. 13. *(b)*

III. **The true Spirit in the Pilgrimage of the Good.**

The spirit of the Israelites in their wanderings in the desert had two characteristics which are worthy of imitation:

1. *Dependence upon God.* They were uncertain as to the duration of their sojourn in any place; when the cloud came down upon the tabernacle, they did not know whether it would continue there for a few hours, "or two days, or a month, or a year." And with respect to the time of their departure, they did not know "whether by day or by night the cloud" would be taken up. They were entirely dependent upon the will of God in these matters; and, believing that the Divine Presence was in the cloud, they trusted God, and waited and watched for its movements as for His orders. We, too, are dependent upon God in our pilgrimage. Let us endeavour to realize our dependence; let us trust in Him; let us watch the movements of His providence, etc. *(c)*

2. *Obedience to God.* "The children of Israel kept the charge of the Lord," as indicated by the rising and resting of the cloud. Disobedient and rebellious in many things, yet in this they obeyed the commandment of the Lord. In this let us imitate them; let us make God's "statutes our songs in the

house of our pilgrimage;" let our prayer be, "Teach me, O Lord, the way of Thy statutes, and I shall keep it unto the end." When God commands let us promptly and cheerfully obey; so shall our pilgrimage end in the rest and refreshment, the sanctity and society, the gladness and glory of Home.

Conclusion.

Life here is a pilgrimage in the case of every one. Be it ours to realise the fact; to seek the infallible guidance and inviolable protection of the Shepherd of Israel in our pilgrimage; and to maintain and manifest the true spirit of pilgrims; so shall our pilgrimage be secure, and our rest glorious. (d)

ILLUSTRATIONS.

(a)
Lead, kindly Light, amid th' encircling gloom,
    Lead Thou me on;
The night is dark, and I am far from home;
    Lead Thou me on;
Keep Thou my feet; I do not ask to see
The distant scene; one step enough for me.

I was not ever thus, nor prayed that Thou
    Shouldst lead me on;
I loved to choose and see my path; but now
    Lead Thou me on.
I loved the garish day, and spite of fears,
Pride ruled my will: remember not past years.

So long Thy power has blest me, sure it still
    Will lead me on
O'er moor and fen, o'er crag and torrent, till
    The night is gone,
And with the morn those angel faces smile
Which I have loved long since and lost awhile.

        J. H. Newman.

(b) The utmost degree of personal *security* that can be enjoyed under any form of civil power, is a most imperfect shadow of the *safety* which Jesus Christ bestows upon the subjects of His *spiritual* reign. Until a man submits to *His* mediatorial authority, he remains exposed to unutterable evils. He *ought* to feel perpetual anxiety and alarm; for, in the declared judgment of God, he is in a state of *condemnation* and *death*:—" he that believeth not in the Son of God is condemned *already*"; he that is not " quickened together with Christ Jesus" is " *dead* in trespasses and sins;" he is a criminal under sentence of execution, and only respited for a brief and uncertain period; the sword of Divine justice, suspended over him, may fall at any moment, and he is lost for ever. This is certainly the condition of every unconverted sinner—every one that has not yielded himself a willing subject to Jesus Christ his Lord. But " Kiss the Son;" yield yourself as such a subject to *Him*; and from that moment, you are placed in a state of perfect *security*; you are *saved with a great salvation* —protected from the wrath of God, from the dread of eternity, from the misery of sin; according to the prophet's beautiful description of our Saviour—" In that day a King shall reign in righteousness; and a man shall be as a covert from the storm, as the shadow of a great rock in a weary land." The subjects of Jesus Christ, justified by faith, have *peace* with God. The last donation He promised His disciples was peace:—"Peace I leave with you; *My* peace I give unto you: not as the world giveth give I unto you." " *My* peace !" —the same peace which filled the bosom of the eternal Son of God, when, having finished His work, He was acknowledged by the Father as His " Beloved Son, in whom he was well pleased." For, " because ye are sons, God hath sent forth the Spirit of His Son into your hearts "—of His Son, the First-born of many *brethren*. And (as the Apostle argues) "if *God* be for us, who shall be against us? Who shall lay anything to the charge of God's elect? Shall *God* that justifieth? Who is he that condemneth? *Christ* that *died*, yea, rather that is *risen* for us? Who shall separate us from the love of God which is in Christ Jesus our Lord?" The *Church* of Christ, as a collective society, is invested with absolute security; it is a city on whose walls is engraven the name, JEHOVAH SHAMMAH, THE LORD IS THERE! it stands fast "like Mount Zion that *cannot be moved*;" it is founded on a *Rock*, and that Rock is Christ: He has "all power in heaven and earth" for its preservation; and not " the gates of hell shall prevail against it." But a *portion* of this general security of the body belongs to every member of it: every believer in Christ enjoys the same; and, as he grows in grace and knowledge, he *feels* himself at peace with God; this peace *keeps* and justifies his heart and mind against every assailing trouble; and, on the most trying occasions, he learns to say with humble confidence, "I will go forth in the *strength* of the Lord."—*Robert Hall, A.M.*

(c) Everything in their experience taught them their dependence upon God. They were led throught a region that no adventurer had ever explored, or foot had ever trod. When they pitched their tents at eventide, they knew not at what hour they should strike them, nor whether they should strike them at all; there might be forced years of encampment in that one spot; there might be forced marches and rapid progress; but they had no control over it: as the pillar went, and wherever the pillar went, they went; and as they sounded forth their matin song of praise there was not a man in the whole congregation that could tell through what rocky clifts or woody defiles the echoes of the vesper hymn would sound. Their supply was as miraculous as their guidance. No plough had turned up the soil, no river murmured by their side; they never gazed for forty years upon one solitary blossom of the spring time, nor the golden grain ever once in their sight bent gracefully to the sickle of the reaper; they were fed with manna which they knew not.

"When faint they were and parched with drought,
Water at His word gushed out."

Oh! it is the world's grandest illustration of man's absolute feebleness and of God's eternal power. 600,000 fighting men, besides women and children, led by Divine leadership, and fed by Divine bounty, for the space of forty years. Brethren, the dealings of Providence with ourselves are intended to show us our dependence upon God, and to humble us in the dust under His mighty hand. We are very proud sometimes, and we talk about our endowments, and we boast largely of what we have done, and what we intend to do; but we can do absolutely nothing. The athletic frame—how soon can He bring it down! The well-endowed heritage—how soon can He scatter it! The mental glance, keen and piercing—how soon can He bring upon it the dimness and bewilderment of years! We cannot any one of us, bring ourselves into being; we cannot, any one of us, sustain ourselves in being for a moment. Alas! who of us can stay the spirit when the summons has gone forth that it must die?—*W. M. Punshon, LL.D.*

(*d*) We are all upon a journey. We are walking either by faith or by sight. We have either committed our destiny to God, or we have taken it under our own care. Can you order your own destiny as well as God? Would you rather trust your own eye than the eye of Omniscience? I address some who have no other care than to walk with God. With firm hold of His hand they wander on, knowing that He will lead them by a path they have not known. Happy the people that are in such a case! They are what they are by the grace of God,—that grace which stands for ever revealed and honoured in the Person and work of JESUS. And now we are going on: the road is often mountainous, and many a wild beast prowls upon it; but we are obeying God, and obedience ensures perpetual joy. It is God's to lead; it is man's to follow. We are going to a land of which Canaan was but a poor emblem,—we advance toward a city which hath foundations whose builder and maker is God! If the road is sometimes dreary, the Guide is ever safe. God hath not permitted imagination to conceive the end. Fancy's mighty wing cannot soar to the altitude of such sublimity. It remains a mystery till our eyes are closed in death. Be it ours to move our tent and erect our altar as God may direct. We shall in due time exchange the tent for an ever-during mansion, and our prayer shall burst into praise. Our journey hath an end,—its name is HEAVEN. But what is involved in that term "heaven," we can never know on earth. Loiter not in the way. The shadows deepen. One star more venturous than others is already twinkling, and telling of the coming night. *Up!* my brethren,— FORWARD, ye hosts of God!

"Here in the body pent,
Absent from Him we roam,
Yet nightly pitch our moving tent
A day's march nearer home."

Joseph Parker, D.D.

THE CLOUD TARRYING.

(*Verse 22.*)

The Israelites were favoured by God with the pillar of fire and cloud. Hereby they were reminded of His special presence, and instructed as to His will. If it moved, they must journey; if it tarried, they must encamp. Let us describe these seasons, when the cloud tarried. Remembering although we have no visible symbol of the Divine will, yet we are not ignorant of His mind. If Israel of old had the cloud, we have the Word of God, and the Holy Spirit to teach us

I. A word of description.

The time "the cloud tarried" was:

1. *One of rest.* Such times in our experience. Blessed tranquillity. Sweetest fellowships with each other.

2. *One of spiritual activity.* Then they worshipped in the tabernacle, etc. Use your opportunities. Go while you can to the means of grace.

3. *Peculiarly a time of temptation.* Remember Taberah and the consuming fire, Num. xi. 1; Hazeroth and Miriam's leprosy, Num. xii. 10; remember the fiery serpents, and the blasphemy of Sinai. In these haltings the people sinned most grievously.

II. A word of exhortation.

1. *Be more anxious to keep the cloud in sight than to see it tarry.* We are responsible for the one, but not for the other. We must strive to delight more in God's will, than in what we desire.

2. *Be more anxious to improve than enjoy these refreshing times.* Times like these are for holy labour as well as for peaceful quiet and contemplation. Think not that Nathanael was always sitting beneath the fig tree.

3. *Be more anxious to improve than prolong these periods.* Seek not so much a protracted as a useful life. Strive to use seasons of rest and prosperity, rather than marring them by over anxiety about the morrow.

III. A word of caution.

1. *If the cloud tarry long, think not it will never move.* The Church, the home, the soul must have vicissitudes. Activity is necessary to every form of life. Rest should be the preparation time for exertion.

2. *Be not impatient if it tarry when you wish to journey.* It does rest sometimes over a desert land. Such is life to some of you aged ones. There were most arid deserts in the confines of Canaan.

3. *Be ready, that whenever the cloud moves you may be ready to journey.* Whether it be to go forward to the fight, to the Elim of plenty, or the land of promise.—*R. A. Griffin.*

CHAPTER X.

CRITICAL AND EXPLANATORY NOTES.

Verses 1-10. Instructions for signalling the movements of the camp are properly inserted here as one of the necessary preliminaries for the march which was about to commence.

Verse 2. *Two trumpets.* "The trumpet (*khatsotserah*) was a straight instrument, differing in this respect from the curved horn or cornet (*keren, shophar*); yet the latter is frequently rendered 'trumpet' in the A. V., when the two instruments are not mentioned together. The Jewish trumpet is described (Joseph. 'Ant.' iii. 12.6) as 'a little less than a cubit in length; the tube narrow, a little thicker than a flute, and just wide enough to permit the performer to blow it; while it terminated, like other trumpets, in the form of a bell.'"—*Speaker's Comm.*

At this time only two trumpets were ordered. Two only were required, inasmuch as they were to be used only by the priests, of which at this time there were only two. When there were more priests there were also more trumpets. Comp. 1 Chron. xv. 24; 2 Chron. v. 12.

Verse 3. The blowing of both the trumpets was the signal for convening the great assembly, composed of all the representatives of the entire congregation, viz., the heads of families, the princes of the tribes, the elders, judges, *et al.*

Verse 4. The blowing of one trumpet only was the signal for a more select assembly, composed merely of the heads of the clans and the princes of the tribes.

Verse 7. Expositors are not agreed as to the difference between the signal for assembly and the signal of alarm. Henry, Trapp, *et al,* hold that the alarm was a broken, quavering, interrupted sound; and the signal for assembly a continued equal sound. Keil and Del. and the Speaker's Comm. propound the opposite view: that for an alarm a long continuous peal was to be blown, and for an assembly short sharp notes. Dr. A. Clarke suggests that the alarm consisted of *short, broken, sharp tones,* terminating with *long* ones, blown with both the trumpets at once. It is perhaps impossible to determine which of these interpretations is correct.

Verse 9. The trumpets were blown

by the priests in war as an expression of the dependence of Israel on the help of God. (Comp. ch. xxxi. 6; 2 Chron. xiii. 12, 14.)

Verse 11. This verse is the beginning of the second great division of the book. The preparations for the march being completed, the camp is broken up, and they set out on their march to Canaan.

Verse 12. *The cloud rested in the wilderness of Paran.* This statement seems to be made by anticipation, as we find that the desert of Paran was the third station: Kibroth-Hattaavah being the first, and Hazeroth, the second (ch. xi. 35; xii. 16). Notes on "the wilderness of Paran" will be more suitable on ch. xii. 16, than in this place.

And here, at the beginning of the journeyings, we may as well mention the difficulties of tracing them accurately, especially after the arrival in the desert of Paran. For, as Mr. Hayman observes, "we have not merely to contend with the fact that time has changed the desert's face in many parts, and obliterated old names for new; but we have beyond this, great obscurity and perplexity in the narrative. The task is, first, to adjust the uncertainties of the record *inter se*, and then to try and make the resultant probability square with the main historical and physical facts, so long as the latter can be supposed to remain unaltered. Besides the more or less discontinuous form in which the sacred narrative meets us in Exodus, a small portion of Leviticus, and the greater part of Numbers, we have in Num. xxxiii. what purports at first sight to be a complete skeleton route so far as regards nomenclature; and we further find in Deuteronomy a review of the leading events of the wandering—or some of them—without following the order of occurrence, and chiefly in the way of allusion expanded and dwelt upon. Thus the authority is of a three-fold character. And as, in the main narrative, whole years are often sunk as uneventful, so in the itinerary of Num. xxxiii., on a near view great chasms occur, which require, where all else bespeaks a severe uniformity of method, to be somehow accounted for. But, beyond the questions opened by either authority in itself, we have difficulties of apparent incongruity between them; such as the omission in Exodus of Dophka and Alush, and of the encampment by the Red Sea; and, incomparably greater, that of the fact of a visit to Kadesh being recorded in Num. xiii. 26, and again in xx. 1, while the itinerary mentions the name of Kadesh only once."

We shall endeavour to offer some hints on these difficulties as they arise in our course; but it seemed desirable to call attention to their existence at the beginning of the march from Sinai.

Verse 13. *And they first took their journey, etc.* "Rather, 'And they journeyed' (or set forth) 'in the order of precedence according to (*i.e.*, established by) the commandment of the Lord,' etc. The meaning of the Hebrew word for 'first' seems determined by its use in the following verse, where it applies to the camp of Judah going before the rest. This order of precedence is described in verses 14-28."—*Speaker's Commentary.*

Verse 14. *According to their armies.* "Cf. I. 3. There were three tribal hosts in each camp; and each tribe had, of course, its sub-divisions."—*Ibid.*

Verse 17. When the tabernacle was taken down the Gershonites and the Merarites set forward with the materials of which it was composed, so that at the place of the next encampment they might set it up again, before the arrival of the Kohathites (who followed after, verse 21) with the sacred vessels, etc. So that during the march, the place of the tabernacle, in the midst of the host, was represented by the sacred furniture of the sanctuary, in charge of the Kohathites.

Verse 29. *Hobab, the son of Raguel, etc.* There is some uncertainty as to the relation of Hobab to Moses. Here he would seem to be the son of Moses' father-in-law. But in Judg. iv. 11, he is spoken of as "the father-in-law of Moses." The preponderance of evidence seems in favour of his being the brother-in-law of Moses. The Hebrew word translated "father-in-law" may be used to express any relation by marriage. Raguel, or Reuel, who was also named Jethro, was the father-in-law of Moses (Exod. ii. 18; iii. 1). He had departed from the camp of Israel previous to their arrival at Sinai (Exod. xviii. 27); whereas Hobab obtained a settlement with them in the land of Canaan (compare Judg. i. 16: iv. 11). Moreover the request of Moses that he would accompany them as their guide seems to imply that he was a younger man than the father-in-law of Moses must have been at this time. We conclude that Hobab was the son of Reuel or Jethro, and consequently the brother-in-law of Moses.

Verse 31. *Thou mayest be to us instead of eyes.* "Hobab may have been of great use to the Israelites, with respect both to guiding their parties to wells and springs in the desert, and to giving them notice where they might find fuel. But besides this, the sacred history expressly mentions several journeys undertaken by detachments of the Israelites, while the main body remained still: so in chap. xiii. we read of a party sent out to reconnoitre the land of Canaan; in chap. xx. of the messengers sent from Kadesh to the King of Edom; in chap. xxxi. of an expedition against the idolatrous Midianites; of some little expeditions in the close of chap. xxxii.; and more journeys of the like kind were, without doubt, undertaken, though they are not particularly recounted. Moses, foreseeing this, might well beg Hobab to accompany him, not as a single Arab, but as the prince of a clan to supply conductors for these detached parties, while the body of the people, and the cloud of the Lord continued stationary."—*Harmer.*

THE SILVER TRUMPETS, OR THE RELATION OF THE GOSPEL MINISTRY TO THE SEASONS AND SERVICES OF THE CHRISTIAN LIFE.

(Verses 1-10.)

Let us notice the following preliminary points:

First: *The trumpets and their use were commanded by God.* He enjoins their use as means to secure order and progress. He blesses men, saves men by the use of the means which He has appointed.

Second: *The trumpets were to be blown by the priests.* Every Christian is now a priest; but the ministers of the Gospel are especially the heralds of the Divine messages: it is especially incumbent upon them to blow the silver trumpet of the Gospel.

Third: *The trumpets were to be blown in accordance with clear and well-understood instructions.* When they were to blow one trumpet only, and when they were to blow both; when the short, sharp, broken notes, and when the long and continuous peal—these things were clearly explained and enjoined. There was to be no uncertainty as to the meaning of the signals. The meaning of the sounds of the Gospel trumpet should be equally and unmistakeably clear. (Comp. 1 Cor. xiv. 7, 8.)

Fourth: *The trumpets were to be blown at different seasons and for different purposes*—for conventions, for journeyings, for battles, for festivals, etc. In this we have an illustration of *the Relation of the Gospel Ministry to the seasons and services of the Christian life.* We proceed to offer some hints on the analogy. The silver trumpets were used—

I. For the calling of assemblies.

"Use them for the calling of the assembly. And when they shall blow with them," etc., verses 3, 4. In the assemblies of the Church of Jesus Christ for conference, or instruction, or worship, the ministry of the Gospel should be heard. The Word of God has a clear and precious relation to the peaceful engagements of holy worship. In such seasons the Christian minister should lead the people into the green pastures of spiritual instruction, and by the still waters of pure refreshment. The ministry of the Gospel should draw men together, even as the silver trumpets convened the assemblies of Israel. (*a*)

II. For summoning the people to advance.

"Use them for the journeying of the camps. When ye blow an alarm, then the camps," etc. (Vers. 5, 6.) The Christian minister is required to summon the people to arise and "go forward" in their upward pilgrimage. He summons them to advance—

1. *In personal holiness.* He exhorts them to "follow on to know the Lord," to "grow in grace," to "forget those things which are behind," etc. (Phil. iii. 13, 14.) It is his to

"Allure to brighter worlds, and lead the way."
(*b*)

2. *In personal and collective usefulness.* He should incite both individuals and churches to more diligent and devoted services in the cause of Christ. The true Gospel ministry will never allow the Church to sink into an inglorious and indolent rest; but as with the blast of a trumpet will rouse it to continuous effort and to interminable progress.

III. For encouraging the people in battle.

"And if you go to war in your land against the enemy," etc., verse 9. "Great force is in the sound of instruments, of any sort, to stir up both courage and cheerfulness in the hearers of them." But these trumpets were blown to express their dependence upon God, and to inspire their faith in Him. Like the priests with the silver trumpets the minister of the Gospel should—

1. *Encourage Christians to battle against evil.* Many are the motives which he may employ for this purpose, *e.g.*, the righteousness of the warfare, the glory of the great Leader, the certainty of victory, etc. (*c*)

But, as the priests with the silver trumpets, so the Christian minister is to encourage Christians in their battle against evil—

2. *By inciting them to trust in God.* He gives the victory. We conquer through Him. "The God of peace shall bruise Satan under your feet shortly." "We are more than conquerors through Him that loved us." "Above all taking the shield of faith," etc. "Fight the good fight of faith," etc.

"The world cannot withstand
Its ancient Conqueror;
The world must sink beneath the hand,
That arms as for the war:
This is our victory!
Before our faith they fall;
Jesus hath died for you and me;
Believe, and conquer all."
C. Wesley.

IV. For suitably observing seasons of special interest.

"Also in the day of your gladness," etc. (verse 10). Here are three seasons specified at which the trumpets were to be blown, and to which Christianity has a relation and a ministry.

1. *Seasons of joy.* "In the days of your gladness ye shall blow with the trumpets," etc. The Gospel aims at the consecration and promotion of human gladness. "That My joy might remain in you, and your joy might be full." "Rejoice in the Lord alway." "The kingdom of God is not meat and drink; but righteousness, and peace, and joy in the Holy Ghost." "Believing, ye rejoice with joy unspeakable and full of glory." The Gospel forbids no pure delight, but hallows and increases it.

2. *Seasons of solemnity.* "In your solemn days ye shall blow with the trumpets," etc. There are many solemn days in life—days of mental conflict, of spiritual darkness, of social bereavement, etc. In such days the hopeful and helpful sounds of the Gospel trumpet are peculiarly precious.

3. *Closing and commencing seasons.* "And in the beginnings of your months ye shall blow," etc. "The return of the new moons was announced by the sounding of the silver trumpets; and in this way provision was made for

keeping up a knowledge of the end and commencement of each month." And as one period of time comes to an end, and we look back upon its opportunities and privileges gone for ever, and gone when we, alas, how often! have made but little use of them, that Gospel which tells of free and full forgiveness is very precious. And as we look forward to periods of time which are yet in the future, with their manifold and serious possibilities, the voice of that trumpet which announces "Grace to help in time of need," and strength proportioned to our day, is most gladly welcomed by us.

To all the varying scenes and circumstances of life the Gospel ministry, like the silver trumpets, has an important and beneficent relation.

And we have a twofold intimation that God would bless this institution of the blowing of the silver trumpets. "Ye shall be remembered before the Lord your God, and ye shall be saved from your enemies. . . . That they may be to you for a memorial before your God: I am the Lord your God."

If He blessed even the blowing of trumpets, when performed in obedience to Him, will He not much more bless the ministry of the Gospel of His Son?

ILLUSTRATIONS.

(a) The trumpet was the sacred joyful sound in old Palestine, the silver trumpets blown by the priests of the sons of Aaron. The trumpet proclaimed the opening of the year, the trumpet proclaimed the commencement of the sabbatical year, the trumpet proclaimed the year of Jubilee that was kept by the Israelites, the feast of trumpets, and the tone of the trumpet mingled with their most solemn feasts and domestic scenes:

"Then rose the choral hymn of praise,
The trump and timbrel answered keen,
And Judah's daughters poured their lays,
The priests' and warriors' voice between."

Conceive such an evening as this in that delightful land; it is the evening of the sixth day, our Friday; the sky is peaceful, it is the wilderness; among those crags are the foes of Israel's race; there is the tabernacle; there is the cloud about to yield to the fire; a star or two has already appeared; reverently waiting and expecting, the labourers are reposing from their day's toil; the sun is setting, and darkness approaching. Hark! hark! this is the peal of the silver trumpet over the waste, and the tool is dropped; instantly all labour ceases—and it is more, it is the commencement of the sabbatical year! Yonder Philistines may put their own interpretation on it, and say, Their sabbath is begun; but we can say "Blessed is the people that know the joyful sound."—*E. P. Hood.*

Amazing is the power of sound; it searches the soul more than vision; it vibrates and reverberates—sound more immediately and more deeply penetrates. Nothing presented to the eye tingles along the blood like things presented to the ear. Sound thrills in a wood at night, in loneliness and darkness; the fall of leaves, the stir of creatures in the grass, and a thousand nameless sounds, stir the feeling of mystic awe. Sight is finite; the imagination plays more freely among sounds—the forms are unshaped—the powers are more abiding. Memory—attention—seems to take a deeper hold upon the things presented in sound than in sight. And hence, the preacher is a trumpet. The birth of the Society of Friends was in this wise: George Fox was one of the most stirring trumpets of the Church; in the power he possessed by his holy earnestness to rouse men he shows in an eminent manner what "the voice of one crying in the wilderness" may be. And Whitefield was such a trumpet. Men heard and trembled. A mysterious fearfulness shook the souls of listeners; it must have been as when the prophet stood on the mount, and the Lord passed by in the wind, and the earthquake, and the fire, and broke in pieces the rocks; they were the announcements of danger, and wreck, and death. . . . .

There are trumpets—they startle and surprise, indeed; but even the trumpet has another purpose; it marshals into order, it becomes motive, beneath its inspiring strains men fall into ranks and march, and it becomes not merely a blast—a breath—its tones fall into the harmonies and melodies of other instruments. *Ibid.*

(b) If a man would be a Christian after Christ's type of Christianity, he must aim at making progress continually. His life must be a continual endeavour from the well to the better, from the better to the best. The summit of his attainment of yesterday must be the starting-point for his venture of to-morrow. He must not go to his rest upon the reputation of old victories, or beneath laurels won so long ago that they have absolutely faded from their greenness by the lapse of time. Every morning of his life must light him to a fresh battle-field; every evening of his life must set upon some vanquished lust or slain desire He must fix his eye on Jesus, and long and strive to be like him. He must trample upon every sin, and he must exhibit every grace which was formerly lacking, until he stands out as the new creature in Christ Jesus the Lord. Brethren, this must of necessity be the aim of every Christian's life. He must grow if he would live. If he would ascertain his sense of the Divine favour, he must constantly aim at conformity to the Divine image. Nothing short of perfection must be the ideal standard after which we aim. In the world around us the selectest models are uniformly chosen. The young sculptor, and the embryo poet, are thrilled with high exultation; but it is to wield a Phidias's mallet, or to sweep a Homer's lyre. The young soldier gazes at reverent distance upon some hero of a hundred fights; but it is that he may be brave and honoured as he. Visions of fame and fortune flit before the young aspirant's eye, only to be embodied in some renowned statesman, or some wealthy millionaire. And why are all these models chosen, but that each, in his own sphere, may reach or approximate perfection? Worldlings would scorn to aim at a mark less high, or to set before them a standard inferior to themselves. Let them shame you, Christians, into a holier ambition to-day.—*W. M. Punshon, LL.D.*

(c) Give me to feel that the strongest will win; that he who has most arm will have most wealth and most enjoyment generally in life; give me to feel that the weakest must go to the wall, however good he be, and I cease to be a man; I lose many of the qualities which redeem men from the utmost vulgarity and bestiality! But tell me that the highest strength is spiritual, that the noblest power is the power of ideas, the power of love; give me to feel that God is watching the battle, and that eventually He will make right victorious, and instantly I start my life from new centres, I am controlled by new and higher considerations.—*Joseph Parker, D.D.*

THE SILVER TRUMPETS.

(*Verse 2.*)

"Make thee two trumpets of silver."

We see God's all-pervading care. He directs all things for His people's weal. Their least arrangements are arranged in heaven. Each little matter on the earthly stage is offspring of decree. There are no trifles in a soul's career. Make conscience of each trivial event. It has an influence on eternity. When God appears to order two Silver Trumpets for the camp, surely He stamps all little things with magnitude.

The material must be silver. Emblem of rare purity. Compare Psalms xii. 6. xciii. 5. Ministers should precede with silver brightness. The flock should follow, as silver without alloy.

Draw nearer to the camp. Two priests are seen. Each blows a Silver Trumpet. Light falls hence on the office of God's ministers. Their voice should sound with trumpet-clearness through the flock. They are entrusted with God's message to a fallen world. . . . The Silver Trumpets sent a piercing note. So should the Gospel-herald utter aloud the Gospel news. Let statements be clear, as the sun without one cloud—pellucid as the crystal stream—distinct as the unmuffled trumpet's voice.

The Trumpets were of one piece. So is the Gospel-message. It is not partly works. Christ is All. No diverse metal soiled these Trumpets. No intermingling error should soil pulpits.

The type, moreover, fixes attention on the Christian as a worshipper—a pilgrim—a warrior—a son of joy. For let the occasions on which these Trumpets sounded be now more closely marked.

I. **They call the people to God's sanctuary.**

It is a Gospel-ordinance, that worshippers should throng the holy courts —that public prayer and praise should reverence the glorious name. A saintly congregation is an antepast of heaven. The faithful meet to honour God. They honour and are honoured. They come in faith, and they depart in peace. Think not that such assemblage is superfluous. Doubtless God is not linked to means. He can bless in solitude, and hear in the secluded closet. But it has pleased Him to order public worship. His commands are always gain. Faith hears, obeys, and finds obedience to be wealth.

II. **They give command to march.**

Christians are portion of a marching host. Earth is not our rest. We live a stranger-life. We hold a pilgrim-staff. Our home is far away. Let all be ready for departure. Death should not find a Christian unprepared. When it appears let there be no tremor—no surprise—no work unfinished. The Gospel's Silver Trumpets ever cry, Arise, Depart. Come up hither.

III. They sound for war.

The life of faith is one incessant fight. Beneath the Cross a sword is drawn, of which the scabbard is cast far away. The foes are many—mighty—wily—restless. They are without—around—within. Count, if you can, the hateful legions who compose hell's hosts: they all rush at the soul. Survey the world—its snares, etc. Behold the heart, and all its brood of lusts and raging passions. The Gospel-trumpet ever cries, Battle is near. Stand firm. Resist. But when the Gospel calls, it promises sure triumph. It gives an armour wrought of God. It points to a Captain, beneath whose banner no warrior was ever slain. Believer, hear, and go forth in hope, etc.

IV. In the grand feasts they cheer the worshippers around the bleeding victims.

The precept is obeyed; "Sing aloud," etc. (Psa. lxxxi. 1.) Believer, thus, too, the Gospel teaches you to joy, when you in faith contemplate, and in worship plead the meritorious death of Christ. My soul, obey, remember Calvary, and pour forth music of delight.

The Gospel-trumpet is now within your hearing. But it is prelude of another clang (1 Thess. iv. 16). Are you prepared? If you heed now the Gospel-trumpet calling you to Him, you will hear then the last-day trumpet calling you to glory.

It is faith's happiest hour when it goes forth in spirit to intermingle in the fast-coming scene (1 Cor. xv. 51-55).

This trumpet soon will sound. Bless Jesus—and fear not.—*Henry Law, D.D*

The Resting and the Rising of the Good.

(*Verses* 11, 12.)

These verses suggest—

I. That the people of God are sometimes called to remain, as it were, stationary for a time in this life.

For nearly twelve months Israel remained in the desert of Sinai, without making any advance, as regards locality, to the Promised Land. In our individual lives there are sometimes seasons of quiet and rest, in which we live our life and work our work without any apparent change: no sickness seizes us reminding us of our mortality; no great loss or sharp sorrow shakes our tabernacle or tells us of our pilgrim state; no disturbing influence reaches us, crying, "Arise ye, and depart; for this is not your rest." In our family life occasionally there are similar occasions; when there is a long exemption from the visitations of death, and the strokes of affliction and grief seem far removed, and no great change takes place in the home circle. And in the larger circle of our friends, events sometimes move on serenely for months without any shock; and our pleasant intercourse is not interrupted by any trumpet-call to march onward. These are seasons of quiet rest and precious privileges. And even as the sojourn at Sinai was for wise and most important ends, so these seasons of rest have their sacred uses and obligations: in them we have lessons to learn for ourselves and services to render to others, which cannot well be accomplished in anxious and laborious times. (*a*)

II. Though the people of God may appear to remain stationary for a time, yet there is no permanent settlement in this world.

The Israelites made a long halt in the desert of Sinai; but it was only a halt; it was not a settlement. Pauses in the march have their use; and when that use is accomplished, orders to resume the march are at once given. Abiding rest is not in this world. The home of the soul is not here. The longest season of tranquillity and repose is at length broken. The most protracted life has its end. We are "strangers and pilgrims on the earth." (*b*)

III. That both the restings and the risings of the people of God are ordered by Him.

"The cloud was taken up from off the tabernacle of the testimony. And the children of Israel took their journeys," etc. The rising of the cloud was the Divine signal for their departure; the resting of the cloud, for their encampment. "Thou leddest Thy people like a flock by the hand of Moses and Aaron." "And guided them in the wilderness like a flock." And God is still the Guide of His people. "The steps of a good man are ordered by the Lord." (See our notes on chapter ix. 17-23). (*c*)

IV. That the people of God, whether resting or marching, are protected by Him.

In the cloud which preceded them on the march, and overshadowed them in their encampments, the Lord was present for their protection. God is the Guardian of His people. "God our shield." "In the time of trouble He shall hide me in His pavilion," etc. "Kept by the power of God through faith unto salvation." Compare Psalms xci. 1-13; cxxi. (See our notes on chap. ix. 17-23.) (*d*)

Learn, in conclusion, to—

1. *Gratefully appreciate and diligently use the seasons of quiet rest in life.*
2. *Remember that, however long and grateful a rest may be granted unto us, we are only pilgrims here.* Be ready to arise and depart when the cloud arises.
3. *Follow the guidance of God.*
4. *Trust the protection of God.*

ILLUSTRATIONS.

(*a*) "Rest a while!" Why, it is a *mother's* word; she says to her little weary child who has toddled itself out of breath, "Rest a while." It is the word of a great, generous, noble-hearted leader of men. He says, "My company must have rest. I know I am sent to gain victories and conquests, and to work great programmes; but in the meantime my over-worked men must have *rest*." It is a gentle word. Where do you find such gentleness as you find in Jesus Christ? *Joseph Parker, D.D.*

Rest time is not waste time. It is economy to gather fresh strength. Look at the mower on the summer's day, with so much to cut down ere the sun sets. He pauses in his labour—is he a sluggard? He looks for his stone, and begins to draw it up and down his scythe, with rink-a-tink, rink-a-tink, rink-a-tink—Is that idle music? Is he wasting precious moments? How much he might have mown while he has been ringing out those notes on his scythe! But he is sharpening his tool, and he will do far more when once again he gives his strength to those long sweeps which lay the grass prostrate in rows before him. Even thus a little pause prepares the mind for greater service in the good cause. Fishermen must mend their nets, and we must every now and then repair our mental waste and set our machinery in order for future service. To tug the oar from day to day, like a galley-slave who knows no holidays, suits not mortal men. Mill streams go on and on for ever, but we must have our pauses and our intervals. Who can help being out of breath when the race is continued without intermission? Even beasts of burden must be turned out to grass occasionally; the very sea pauses at ebb and flow; earth keeps the Sabbath of the wintry months; and man, even when exalted to be God's ambassador, must rest or faint; must trim his lamp or let it burn low; must recruit his vigour or grow prematurely old. It is wisdom to take occasional furlough. In the long run we shall do more by sometimes doing less.—*C. H. Spurgeon.*

(*b*) "Strangers and pilgrims." That is the Christian view of life. Christians are all travellers, through a country they cannot stay in; travellers, blessed be God, towards a home, but all travellers; some seemingly going through swiftly, buoyantly, with a high head and an open eye; some foot-sore, jaded, sleepy; some with a chariot of fire, as if the horses of God were whirling them onwards before the eyes of an admiring Church; splendid saints, the tune of whose worship goes manly. Some heavy-hearted, heavy-limbed, but still crawling onwards, feeling, perhaps, no less than the others that here they have no continuing city, but that they seek one to come. Limping by the wayside, but still creeping humbly and bravely on.—*Harry Jones, M.A.*

(c) A journey may be the outcome of an inspiration. "There's a Divinity that shapes our ends, rough hew them as we will." I feel life to be most solemn when I think that inside of it all there is a Spirit that lays out one's day's work, that points out when the road is on the left, and when it is on the right, and that tells one what words will best express one's thought. Then is God nigh at hand and not afar off. "The steps of a good man are ordered by the Lord." And thus, too, men are misunderstood: they are called enthusiastic, and are said to be impulsive; they are not "safe" men; they are here to-day and gone to-morrow, and no proper register of their life can be made. Of course, we are to distinguish between inspiration and delusion, and not to think that every noise is thunder. We are not to call a "maggot" a "revelation." What we are to do is this: We are to live and move and have our being in God; to expect His coming and long for it; to be patient and watchful; to keep our heart according to His word; and then we shall know His voice from the voice of a stranger, for "the secret of the Lord is with them that fear Him." If God be our supreme consciousness He will reveal His providence without cloud or doubtfulness. I think it can be proved that the men who have done things apparently against all reason have often been acting in the most reasonable manner, and that inspiration has often been mistaken for madness. I feel that all the while you are asking me to give you tests by which you may know what is inspiration, you have little or nothing to do with such tests,—you have to *be* right and then you will be sure to *do* right.—*Joseph Parker, D.D.*

(d) I do not think of the pillar of cloud as being simply a column of smoke arising from the centre of the Tabernacle; it was such, but besides that it covered the whole camp as a vast canopy or pavilion, so that in the great and terrible wilderness they fainted not under the burning heat of the sun, but this pillar of cloud interposed a friendly shade, so that they passed through the wilderness beneath the wings of God. At night their encampment would have been like a great city wrapped in darkness, but the pillar of fire supplied them a light far superior to that which glows in London or in Paris through the art of man; that great flaming pillar lit up every habitation, so that in point of fact there was no night there. They were always sheltered by God, both by day and by night. If they strayed away from the camp for a little time in the heat of the sun, they had only to come flying back, and there that emblem of the present God became their shelter; or at night, if they wandered for awhile, that vast blazing lampion conducted them back again to their place of rest. So it is with us. In nights of trouble and grief, the fire of Divine comfort glows within us, the precious promises are round about us, and we rejoice in the Holy Ghost, the Comforter; and when by day we travel over this burning wilderness to the rest appointed, God interposes perpetually the sweet presence of His love to screen us from the sharper sorrows of the world, that we may still, while walking onward to heaven, behold the shield of heaven uplifted above our heads.—*C. H. Spurgeon.*

Aspects of Human Pilgrimage.

(*Verses* 13-28.)

These verses suggest the following remarks:

I. That human pilgrimage should be prosecuted in accordance with Divine directions.

"And they first took their journey according to the commandment of the Lord by the hand of Moses." The march proceeded in the order prescribed in chap. ii. In the pilgrimage of life the directions of God should be faithfully followed. This will appear if we consider—

1. *The infinity of the knowledge of God.* He knows us altogether and perfectly; He knows the road which we have to travel, and the events which await us, and the circumstances through which we must pass in the future. The minutest circumstances cannot be hidden from Him, and the greatest event He fully comprehends. He has the knowledge which is necessary for efficiently directing our path through life.

2. *The depth and tenderness of God's interest in man.* He exercises the kindest care towards every man. There is not a creature in the world but is cared for by Him. And man, who is at the head of His creations in this world, is the object of His special regard. Comp. Matt. vi. 25-34. His kind interest in us affords a guarantee that in directing our path through life He will

ever aim at the realization of our best interests.

3. *The supremacy of God's authority over man.* He has a right to issue commands for our guidance. As our Creator and Sustainer, and especially as our wise and kind Father, His authority over us is most absolute and sacred. When they were condemning Socrates for teaching the people their duties to God, he replied, "O ye Athenians, I will obey God rather than you; and if you would dismiss me and spare my life on condition that I would cease to teach my fellow-citizens, I would rather die a thousand times than accept the proposal." How much more should we recognise and bow loyally to His authority! "He shall choose our inheritance for us." "Thou shalt guide me with Thy counsel." His appointments concerning us are always infinitely wise and kind. (*a*)

II. **In human pilgrimage the arrangements and provisions for Divine worship should be matters of primary concern.**

"And the Tabernacle was taken down, and the sons of Gershon and the sons of Merari set forward, bearing the tabernacle. . . . And the Kohathites set forward, bearing the sanctuary : and" (the Gershonites and Merarites) "did set up the tabernacle against they came." Thus it was arranged that the Tabernacle should in every encampment be erected in readiness to receive the Ark and the most holy things. The arrangements for the worship of the Lord were regarded as of the first importance. In like manner we find that wherever Abraham pitched his tent, "there he builded an altar unto the Lord" (see Gen. xii. 7, 8; xiii. 4, 18). The conduct of these ancient saints in this respect is—

1. *A rebuke to many nominal Christians*, who in their changes of residence make the arrangements and provisions for worship a very inferior consideration. (*b*)

2. *An example to all Christians* who contemplate a change of residence. (*c*)

III. **In human pilgrimage the most reverent care should be exercised in relation to sacred things.**

"And the Kohathites set forward bearing the sanctuary." Their station was in the midst of the host : thus the most holy things, of which they had charge, were in the place of the greatest safety and the highest honour during the march. Here is an example for us. Let things around which tender and precious memories cluster be highly esteemed and jealously guarded; let things dedicated to sacred uses be reverently regarded and piously cared for.

IV. **In human pilgrimage the weak and the wandering should be tenderly cared for.**

"And the standard of the camp of Dan set forward, the rearward of all the camps," etc. The squadron of Dan came last, and was called the rearward or gathering host (Josh. vi. 9, margin) because they gathered up those who lagged behind—the lame, the faint, and the feeble—and took care that none were lost or left behind. God is solicitous for the salvation of the weak and the wandering. Our Lord is careful to lose none of His followers (John xvii. 12). "He gathers the lambs with His arm, and carries them in His bosom, and gently leads those that are with young." "He has compassion on the ignorant, and on them that are out of the way." In like manner "we that are strong ought to bear the infirmities of the weak," and to strive to restore the erring. "Brethren, if a man be overtaken in a fault, ye which are spiritual restore such an one," etc.

Conclusion :

In our pilgrimage let us diligently cultivate this spirit of loyal obedience and reverent worship towards God, and of kind ministries towards our fellow men.

ILLUSTRATIONS.

(*a*) You are to consider that the position which you occupy is, all things considered, the most advantageous that you could possibly have occupied for doing the utmost that you are capable of doing for the glory of God. Suppose the mole should cry, "How could I have honoured the great Creator if I could have been allowed to fly!" it would have been very foolish, for a mole flying would have been a very ridiculous object, while a mole fashioning its tunnels and casting up its castles is viewed with admiring wonder by the naturalist, who perceives its remarkable suitability to its sphere. The fish of the sea might say, "How could I display the wisdom of God if I could sing or mount a tree like a bird!" but you know a fish in a tree would be a very grotesque affair, and there would be no wisdom of God to admire in fishes climbing trees; but when the fish cuts the wave with agile fin, all who have observed it say how wonderfully it is adapted to its habitat, how exactly its every bone is fitted to its mode of life. Brother, it is just so with you. If you begin to say, "I cannot glorify God where I am, and as I am," I answer, Neither could you anywhere if not where you are. Providence, which arranged your surroundings, appointed them so that, all things considered, you are in the position in which you can best display the wisdom and the grace of God.—*C. H. Spurgeon.*

(*b*) Men make choice of a home without making any inquiry as to the religious state of the neighbourhood. They do not care how poor the church is if the farm be good. They will give up the most inspiring ministry in the world for ten feet more garden, or a paddock to feed an ass in. They will tell you that the house is roomy, the garden is large, the air is balmy, the district is genteel, and if you ask them what religious teaching they will have there, they will tell you they really do not know, but must inquire! They will take away six children into a moral desert for the sake of a garden to play in; they will leave Paul or Apollos for six feet of greenhouse! Others, again, fix their tent where they can get the best food for the heart's life; and they sacrifice a summer house that they may now and again get a peep of heaven.—*Joseph Parker, D.D.*

(*c*) The good man's Tent and Altar go together. You might summarise much of a good man's life in this brief sentence,—" He pitched his tent, and built an altar." As the one was necessary for the body, so was the other necessary for his soul. There are, however, many tents now which are unaccompanied by an altar. Man is oftentimes more anxious about his tent than about his altar. Not so with the good man. His altar is his chief joy. He communes there with God. Across the altar he catches glimpses of heaven. Upon his altar angels drop blessings from their wings of light. When he is stained with guilt or weary with sorrow, he draweth nigh to his altar, and rises forgiven and strong. It is a poor life that has no altar. Nay, 'tis not a *life*, it is mere *existence*. The altar is the link which connects the human worshipper with the adoring seraphim. The whole of the reverent intelligences of the universe meet around the altar. All our Graces are strengthened and beautified by worship. Faith inhales new life, hope gains clearer vision, joy learns some new song to cheer the hours of pilgrimage and toil. If *you* take care of the altar, *God* will take care of the tent. "Seek ye first the kingdom of God and His righteousness, and all these things shall be added unto you."—*Ibid.*

AN EXEMPLARY INVITATION.

(*Verses* 29-32).

Let us consider:

I. The Journey.

"We are journeying unto the place of which the Lord said, I will give it you." It was—

1. *A journey to a glorious destiny.* Canaan was a goodly and a glorious land (Deut. viii. 7-9). To this land the Israelites were advancing. All men are journeying; but it is to be feared that many are travelling on a dreary road with a dreadful ending. Not so the Christian: he is travelling to the spiritual Canaan. Frequently Canaan is regarded as a type of heaven; but it is rather a type of the spiritual privileges and high calling of the Christian. We are journeying to *perfection of character*. We go forward to the rest, not of outward security, but of inward harmony. We advance not to any material inheritance, but to the inheritance of spiritual perfection—to love, holiness, peace, joy, etc. This is the surest guarantee of heaven; this *is* heaven. (*a*)

2. *A journey to an assured destiny.* "The Lord said, I will give it you."

God hath promised us the inheritance. True, there are many foes to be cast out before we can enter upon it; base lusts, evil passions, besetting sins, have to be conquered before we attain our high calling; but God hath assured us of victory. "Ye shall be holy, for I am holy." "A glorious Church not having spot, or wrinkle, or any such thing," etc. "Exceeding great and precious promises are given unto us; that by these ye might be partakers of the Divine nature." Perfection of character is perfect blessedness. Holiness, the heaven of the soul, is the gift of God, and is promised by Him to all who believe in His Son Jesus Christ. He cannot deny Himself; His word cannot pass away. "All the promises of God in Jesus Christ are yea, and in Him Amen, unto the glory of God by us."

II. The Invitation.

"And Moses said unto Hobab, the son of Raguel the Midianite, Moses' father-in-law, We are journeying unto the place of which the Lord said, I will give it you: come thou with us."

1. *The spirit of true religion is social and benevolent.* The child of God is not content to travel alone to the place which God promised to give him; but invites others to accompany him, saying, "Come thou with us." I cannot understand the piety of the man who possesses the grace of God himself, and believes that they who do not possess it will be lost, and yet makes no effort to save them. Such conduct is inconsistent, selfish, utterly unchristian. The true Christian knows that God has declared that He "will have all men to be saved;" and He longs, prays, and works for the salvation of others. Godliness enkindles in the soul the most kind and generous emotions. *(b)*

2. *The exercise of this spirit should be first directed to those who are most closely related to us.* Moses invited Hobab, his brother-in-law. Next to our own spiritual well-being we should seek that of our own kindred,—parents that of their children, the husband that of his wife, etc. The principle is clearly taught by our Lord and His Apostles (see Mark v. 19; Luke viii. 38, 39; xxiv, 47; 1 Tim. v. 4). *(c)*

III. The Inducements.

Moses holds out to Hobab two inducements to accompany them,—

1. *The benefits he would receive.* "We will do thee good: for the Lord hath spoken good concerning Israel. . . . . And it shall be if thou go with us, yea, it shall be, that what goodness the Lord shall do unto us, the same will we do unto thee." We have here,— (1) *An Assurance*—(a) *That they would do him good.* The Christian pilgrim can do good to his fellow-pilgrims by *kindly companionship.* Brotherly sympathy and fellowship are helpful. By presenting a *good example* we can also do good. How great is the influence of example! And, when it is good, how strong it is to correct the imperfect and the wrong! and to stimulate and strengthen to the doing of the right! By *prayer* also we can do good to our fellow-travellers. The prayers of a truly Christian man are perhaps the greatest boon that one man can confer upon another. "Come thou with us, and we will do thee good." (β) *That he should share in the goodness of God to them.* "What goodness the Lord shall do unto us, the same will we do unto thee." And what great goodness the Lord had led them to expect He would do for them! He leads us to expect even higher and richer blessings. He promises to *supply our needs.* "Bread shall be given him; his waters shall be sure." "No good thing will He withhold," etc. "Your heavenly Father knoweth that ye have need," etc. In our journey the manna will not fail, etc. He will *guide and protect us.* "I will instruct thee and teach thee in the way which thou shalt go; I will guide thee with Mine eye." "In all thy ways acknowledge Him, and He shall direct thy paths." "God is our refuge and strength," etc. He will *accompany and sustain us all the way.* "My presence shall go with thee," etc. "Lo, I am with you always," etc. "I will never leave thee, nor forsake thee." "My grace is sufficient for thee," etc.

167

"As thy days, so shall thy strength be." He leads us to expect *a glorious future*. He calls us to a higher standard of character than that to which the Israelites attained, and to a more glorious inheritance than theirs. They had only a very faint hope beyond Canaan and the present life; but we look for "an inheritance, incorruptible, and undefiled," etc. Wherefore, "Come thou with us," &c. We have here—
(2). *The ground of this assurance.* "For the Lord hath spoken good concerning Israel." Our faith and hope rest in the sure promises of the faithful and unchangeable God. Are we not warranted then in saying as an inducement to others to join us, "We will do thee good"? *(d)*

2. *The benefits he would confer.* The hope of deriving benefit did not prevail with Hobab: he said unto Moses, "I will not go; but I will depart to mine own land, and to my kindred." Then Moses tried to persuade him with this inducement, that his presence would be a benefit to them: "he said, Leave us not I pray thee; forasmuch as thou knowest how we are to encamp in the wilderness, and thou mayest be to us instead of eyes." Hobab appears to have been an "experienced Bedouin sheikh, to whom Moses looked for the safety of his cumbrous caravan in the new and difficult ground before them. The tracks and passes of that 'waste howling wilderness' were all familiar to him, and his practised sight should be to them 'instead of eyes' in discerning the distant clumps of verdure which betokened the wells or springs for the daily encampment, and in giving timely warning of the approach of the Amalekites or other spoilers of the desert."

What a vast amount of good many who are outside the pale of the Church, yet not out of sympathy with the Christian religion, might do, if they would but "heartily come with us"! As wise counsellors in the business affairs of the Church; as visitors of the sick, the ignorant, and the spiritually destitute; as Sunday-school teachers, and in many other ways, they could render invaluable service to the cause of Jesus Christ among men. Apply this motive to *the young,* to *the undecided,* to *the almost persuaded.*

Conclusion:

With what company are you prosecuting your life-journey? To what destiny are you advancing? "Come with us, and we will do thee good;" &c. In our own name, in the name of the Church, and in the name of our gracious Lord, we heartily invite you, "Come with us," &c.

ILLUSTRATIONS.

(*a*) Man must go. It is not a question of whether we will go or not go, that is determined for us—we *must* go. Every man is accomplishing a journey, going through a process. No man is standing still. The infant is going on towards youth; youth is advancing towards the stature and strength of manhood; and man, in the summer of his prosperity and honour, is going on towards the sere leaf, and towards a land of darkness as darkness itself. Men must go on, then. The only question is—*How?* Man may either with God or without Him.—*Joseph Parker, D.D.*

(*b*) These happy disciples were now united in conversion, and each one was made the instrument of blessing the other. Philip and Nathanael, Andrew, Peter, and John co-operated with Christ, and with the work of the Holy Spirit. It was a most delightful, simple, thorough, hearty work of Christian love. Friends began with friends, relatives with relatives. Presently we see the circle enlarging, but here it is small and distinctly visible. Each rising wave is apparent, and we see how it spreads, each circling ripple on the lake of love, before there are so many of them, and so vast and deep and widening, that we can no more trace them but as one common impulse, one grand heaving and waving in the mighty sea. In this simple early life of Christianity, every infant missionary impulse of sympathy and love is visible, and can be counted. First come John, Andrew, and Peter, then Philip, then Nathanael; and then the wave that starts at Bethabara from the person of Christ, spreads all over Galilee and Judea, and then over the world. It is a missionary wave, and here is the very life of Christianity, the very essence of discipleship, and the very way of the world's evangelization. Nothing can be more beautiful than the working of this principle of the socialism of grace, the social principle and power of Christianity. It is a sympathising, impulsive, progressive, diffusive life. It is the leaven of the world, which will work till the whole is leavened. And it works, where it works at all, with an accumulating, accelerating tendency and power.—*G. B. Cheever, D.D.*

(c) In their first coming to Christ themselves, they brought others with them (John i. 40-46). It was a delightful example of the practical, social, sympathizing, working power and tendency of true piety, and of the direction and manner in which it works. . . . .

Return to thine own house, and tell thy friends and relatives how great things the Lord hath done for thee, and hath had mercy on thee. It seems there was no need of this command of Christ in the case of Andrew; his own heart led him in that very way, and it was a lovely development of character in him. No doubt he was thinking of his brother all the way to the dwelling of Jesus, and no sooner had he and John arrived with Christ, and entered the house, to abide with Him that day, than he thought within himself, I must go and find Peter first, and we will be here together.—*Ibid.*

(d) Where I am, there shall My servant be. They are great words, words of infinite weight of meaning, words of transcendent inconceivable glory, words covering up an eternal and exceeding weight of glory. Where Christ is, there God is, and God's infinite love and happiness are revealed in Christ. Where Christ is, there heaven is, and the source and fountain of heaven's light and glory. Where Christ is, there all good things are, all the holy, loving beings of the universe, concentrated and circled in adoring ranks around Him, the visible Centre of their bliss, the Author of their holiness. Now of all this glory Christ says, in the midst of it, To him that overcometh will I grant to sit with Me in My throne, even as I also overcame, and am set down with My Father in His throne. He speaks also of His disciples and servants as partakers of His own joy; and the welcome of His servants is even this: Well done, good and faithful servant, enter thou into the joy of thy Lord! The joy of thy Lord! What a heaven of glory and blessedness is contained in that one expression! The joy of thy Lord! Who can measure its degree, who can conceive or fathom the infinite depth of its greatness, the infinite intensity of its bliss? And yet that is the joy that awaits every faithful follower and servant of the glorious Redeemer; the Redeemer's own joy, a thing no more to be measured or fathomed than the actual infinitude of God. They shall be with Him where He is, they shall behold His glory, they shall enter into His joy. For that joy, set before Him, He endured the cross, despising the shame, and is set down for ever at the right hand of the throne of God. There the saints shall walk with Him in glory, heirs of God, and joint-heirs with Christ, received to the possession of an inheritance incorruptible, undefiled, and that fadeth not away, reserved in heaven for those who are faithful unto death, who are kept by the power of God through faith unto salvation. . . . .

Now let it be remembered that all this consummation is connected indissolubly with every thought and effort of the saint's life. Every victory that through Divine grace the Christian gains over sin and temptation, every labour done for Christ, every prayer of faith, every patient bearing of Christ's cross, is a pledge that the soul is advancing to that consummation in glory. Every co-operation of the children of God with Christ, is a pledge that Christ is working in them and with them, preparing them for this mighty revelation, when they are to shine out like the sun in the firmament, at His coming, His appearing, His kingdom. O, what an inducement to a life of holiness is here, what animating encouragement to every effort, and what infinite obligation for such effort laid upon the soul.—*Ibid.*

A GENEROUS PROPOSAL.

(*Verse 29.*)

"Come thou with us, and we will do thee good."

The people of Israel in the wilderness were a type of the Church of Christ. The invitation here given was such as may be given to those who are proper subjects for communion with the Christian Church.

I. **What are the characteristics of a true church as it is pictured by Israel in the wilderness?**

1. The people in the wilderness were a redeemed people. They had been redeemed by blood and redeemed by power. All the true members of God's Church understand what the blood of sprinkling means. They have been redeemed by blood; and the Holy Spirit has entered into their hearts, and made them hate their former sins, has delivered them from the dominant power of their inward corruptions, has set them free and brought them out of the bondage of sin.

2. The Israelites were *a people who were passing through a land wherein they found no rest, neither did they desire any, for they were journeying to another country, the promised land, the Canaan.* Now, here is another description of the true Church of God. They are not of the world, even as Christ is not of the world. Here they have no continuing city.

3. Israel was a people *walking by faith as to the future.* "They were going to the place of which the Lord said, I will give it you." They had never seen it; no one had come from it to tell them of it (1 Cor. ii. 9, 10). We walk by faith as Israel did of old.

4. These people, also, *as to their present circumstances were walking by faith.* Faith told them of the manna which fell day by day, and the water which flowed from the rock, which stream followed them in their journeyings. In this world the Christian man has to live by faith upon God as to present things. As to temporal necessities he must cast all his care on Him who careth for us : but especially as to all spiritual supplies the Christian has no stock of grace. He has no minor spring within himself in his old nature. He has to look for everything that can sustain his new life to God, even the Father, who hath promised not to forsake him.

5. These people found, wherever they went, *that they were surrounded by foes.* In the wilderness the Amalekites were against them. When they crossed into the Promised Land all the inhabitants of Canaan were up in arms against them. So, I think, will you find it if you are a child of God. You will have to fight continually. Till the last step you take it will be a conflict, and you will never be able to sheathe your sword until you are in the bosom of Christ.

II. It is the duty of the Christian Church to invite suitable persons to join with it.

1. As you read, "*Come thou with us,* and we will do *thee* good," say if these are not the terms in which any church should invite *a suitable pastor* to unite with it. I have always felt that they have a better application to a pastor than they have to the people; for it is said of Hobab, "Thou knowest how we are to encamp in the wilderness, and thou mayest be to us instead of eyes." It was inviting a really efficient helper, who would be of great service to the Israelites, to come and cast in his lot with them. So should a church expect to find in its pastor one who may guide them, etc. Their invitation should come in this way, not only, "Come thou with us, that we may get good out of thee"—that is one design —but it should also be, "Come with us, that we may do thee good, that we may hold up thy hands," etc.

2. The words are significant of the manner in which churches should invite *suitable persons to come among them as private members.* It is the duty of every child of God to be associated with the Christian Church, and surely it is part of our duty to instruct others to do what the Lord would approve of. Do not, therefore, hesitate to say to such as serve and fear the Lord, "How is it that you remain outside of the visible Church? Come thou with us," etc.

Let it be spoken *persuasively.* Use such reasoning as you can to prove that it is at once their duty and their privilege.

Do it heartily. Give a hearty, loving, warm invitation to those whom you believe to be your brethren and sisters in Christ.

Do it repeatedly, if once will not suffice. Hobab said he thought he would depart to his own land and his kindred, but Moses returned to the charge, and says, "Leave us not, I pray thee."

3. Let me call your attention to *a certain sense in which Christian men may address this invitation to all that they meet with.* "Come thou with us," etc. Not "come and join our church," etc. You cannot say that to any but to those in whom you see the fruits of the Spirit, but you may say, and you

ought to say, to all persons of all classes on all sides, "Come away from the seed of evil doers, cast in your lot with the people of God; leave the world," etc.

III. The main argument—the most powerful incentive we can ever use is —that association with the Church of Christ will do those who enter into it good.

1. The Church of God may say this, *because she can offer to those who join with her good company.* "We will do thee good," for we will introduce you to the goodly fellowship of the saints, to a section of the general assembly and Church of the firstborn whose names are written in heaven, and whose work of faith, patience of hope, and labours of love are so spread abroad throughout the world, even where their memory is forgot, that we need not to speak anything.

2. "Come thou with us," and you shall have *good instruction.* The teaching of the Church shall do thee good; thou shalt hear those glorious doctrines which shall build thee up in thy most holy faith.

3. "We will do the good" *in the best sense, for thou shalt feel in our midst the good presence of God* (see Matt. xviii. 20).

4. "Come with us," *for you shall participate in the good offices of the Church.* If there be *prayer* thou shalt have thy share in it. In the true Church of God there is *sympathy.* If there be anything to be found in *ordinances,* thou shalt have a share of that good thing. If our *fellowship* be *with Christ,* thou shalt have a share in it. We invite thee to a pure brotherly fellowship, etc.

5. But the good that Hobab was to get *was not only on the road.* He must have got a good deal of good on the road, etc. You shall get good on the road. But *Hobab went into the Promised Land with God's people* (Judges. i. 16; iv. 11). So, the main blessing that you get from being united with the invisible Church of Christ *is reserved for the hereafter.*

IV. Let all of us who belong to Christ's Church take care to make this argument true.

How have you carried out this silent compact which has been made with the friends of Christ? "Come thou with us, and we," etc.

1. You say this to *the poor members of the Church.* Has God prospered you? If thou knowest a brother in Christ whose need is pressing, open thine hand wide unto him; do him good in this respect.

2. You old members of the Church have virtually promised to do good *to the young* members; will you not try to do so?

3. Some of your fellow Christians *are faint-hearted;* they always look on the black side, etc. Do them good (Isa. xxxv. 3, 4).

4. Some amongst your number will be *backsliders.* Watch over them (Gal. vi. 1).

5. Some in the Church may be *ignorant.* Hide his shortcomings and help his progress.

6. There may be some *who are in a good deal of trouble.* If you never owned him a friend before, be to him a friend now.

God grant us to be one with Christ, and to be one with His people, in time and in eternity.—*C. H. Spurgeon.*

"COME THOU WITH US, AND WE WILL DO THEE GOOD."

(*Verse* 29.)

"Come thou with us, and we will do thee good."

This passage expresses the essential spirit of Judaism. There are those in the Church who believe that God's express aim in Judaism was to keep the Jewish people as separate from the world as possible; to keep them, like Noah, in an ark, while He plagued and punished the world at His will. But I maintain, on the contrary, that Judaism was always genial to the stranger who would adopt its belief, and accept its blessings. From the evil which was in the world God was minded to keep the Jewish people free at any cost. From idolatry and its attendant pollutions He sought to deliver them, inasmuch as idolatry in the long run inevitably leads to national decline and death. To the stranger, the foreign person, or nation, who would dishonour its beliefs and trample on its blessings, Judaism was stern as Fate, and pitiless as Death. There was no weak pity for nations which had become so corrupt as to become inevitably corruptive, just as there is no weak pity in society for abandoned criminals now. How utterly, hopelessly, awfully profligate the Canaanitish nations were is narrated in Lev. xviii. 24-30. The Jews were simply God's executioners here, and the same doom, they are plainly warned, awaited them if they suffered themselves to be tempted into the same sins. . . . I am persuaded that the more carefully the spirit of the dispensation is studied, the more plainly will it appear that it is expressed in our text. From Moses to Zechariah, it is a cry to the nations, not to rot in their own corruption, "COME THOU WITH US, AND WE WILL DO YOU GOOD."

1. And this leads me to lay down this general principle—

God's privileges, the gifts which He bestows, and the advantages which He confers on some, are never intended to be exclusive.

God calls all, He calls you. The banquet is spread for all, it is spread for you. The message is pressed on all, it is pressed on you.

It is a condition of high privilege—of great, eminent, glorious joy and hope. But if any man say, "these privileges and hopes are mine, because I am happy enough to belong to a sealed number, to which poor sinners are not called, who are not privileged like me," he wrongs God, he wrongs God's great Love, in his thoughts. If God gives to one man advantages which He denies to another, it is that the first may be His minister to bring that other to share in His joy. Unless a Church or a Christian be attracting men, ever saying to them by look, voice, manner, hand, "Come with us and we will do thee good," it is simply doing what the Jews did, causing the name of God to be blasphemed.

II. The invitation, "Come with us and we will do thee good."

1. *Come with us to the house of God.* I believe that God never gave to man a more blessed boon than the day of rest. But like all God's other gifts, just in proportion to its preciousness is it despised and profaned by those to whom its ministries are most important, and its benediction most large and complete. It is not a *law* of the Sabbath which you are breaking, but something which it is yet more terrible to sin against, God's loving and gracious counsel, in creating for you a day of rest, and guarding it as man cannot guard it by the most elaborate positive laws. I want you to feel how good the ordinance is, and to love it for its goodness, and to love the Lord who gave it, and who guards it by His Spirit in the Church.

Read Gen. ii. 1-3. From what did God rest? From activity? Surely not; but simply from creation; from what under human conditions is conceived of as the toil of production. Comp. John v. 16, 17. God rested; but His rest was the sustaining of the Creation, the upholding of the order, beauty, and fruitfulness of the world. And man is to rest in his measure like God—a rest of joyful, holy activity; the activity of that which is highest and most God-like in him; not the rest of a brute sleeping lazily before a fire. Man is a spirit, and man's spirit rests only in communing with God, and doing the Father's mission.

A God-fearing man, who gathers his household around him for prayer, and goes up with them to the house of God to worship and get fresh strength for the work of life, belongs at once to a higher class. Life means more to him and to his. Work means more, and

produces more. Higher faculties are in play within him, higher joys and ends are within his reach. . . . .
Come with us to the house of God. Learn with us wherein the true rest of a man's spirit consists, what it is which lightens life's burdens, soothes its sorrows, sanctifies its discipline, and crowns its labours.

2. *Come with us to the word of truth.* I will suppose that sickness has entered your home. There is a fair young child, the darling of your heart, the little thing whose voice always welcomed you home at night, whose prattle never failed to cheer you as she sat on your knee by your fireside at tea. Death has marked her. Day after day you come home, and miss the familiar welcome; you steal up to the bedside, and watch with an agony, whose measure none can *guess* at, the swift progress of the destroyer. At length the moment of the last struggle comes. One choking gasp—perhaps the word "Father," "Mother," seemed to form on her lips, and it is over. She lies there, fair as a lily, and as perishing; soon you have to bury her out of your sight. Tell me, will it hurt you then to open your Bible and read there that the glorious King of Heaven, the King who reigns in the world into which your darling has passed—said once when a man upon earth, "Suffer little children to come unto Me," etc.? Would it be a dark thought, that He who took them in His arms and blessed them, has there gathered your little lamb in His arms, and folded her in His bosom, with a tenderness which casts even yours into the shade?

Or, let us say you have fallen into trouble. All around you is dark, and the prospect darker still; will it hurt or help you to open your Bible, and read the words of a man whose case was still darker, and, to a human eye, more hopeless than yours (Psa. xlii. 7-11)? Or those words of the great Apostle on the meaning and end of the discipline we endure (Heb. xii. 3-11)? Or, it may be that the dear companion of your pilgrimage, the sharer of all your joys and sorrows through long and faithful years, lies dead at length; and you must write "There I buried Rachel," in your way-book of life, and go sadly, tearfully, through the rest of your journey alone. I think that if she died in faith, in the faith and hope of the Gospel, in sure and certain hope of a joyful resurrection, these words will come home to your spirit with a strange grandeur and power as you stand by her new-made grave (1 Cor. xv. 20-23, 50-58). Or when you yourself grow old and weary, and see the form of the angel of death advancing, will it depress and distress you to read, "The Lord is my shepherd," etc. (Psa. xxiii.)? There is no condition, there are no circumstances, for which blessed words are not to be found in that Book—words such as no mere man could speak to you. Come with us to the word of truth.

3. *Come with us to the living Saviour.* . . . One who can cure the disease of sin, renew the heart, reform the nature, kindle within the spirit the love of God, of truth, of purity, and inspire the hope of heavenly glory. For this the Lord came, wrestled, suffered, died, etc. (Heb. vii. 24, 25). Come with us to the living Saviour; come and listen to His message of mercy; come, stand before the cross on Calvary, look on Him, whom you, too, have pierced, and mourn, and hear for yourself the blessed words, "Thy faith hath saved thee, go in peace."

4. *Come with us to our Father's home on high.* The life struggle will soon be ended. It will soon seem but a slight matter to you how you struggled through. It is said of Paul's companions, "Some on boards, some on broken pieces of the ship . . . they all escaped safe to land." It is a picture of the life-course of how many noble and faithful ones. . . Oh! the rapture of the moments when the feet first feel the touch of that blissful shore! The peril, the darkness, the battle, the anguish behind us for ever; before us, etc.

Come with us to Him who is "The

Way." No man cometh unto the Father, or to His love, but by Him. Come with us to the Cross—no Cross, no Crown. Come with us to the battle—no battle, no victory. Come with us to the school of discipline—no suffering, no glory. "Come with us and we will do you good," etc.—*J. Baldwin Brown, B.A.*

ON THE MARCH.

(*Verses* 33-36.)

The Israelites are departing from Sinai, and are marching on towards the Promised Land.
Consider:
I. The immense number on the march.

Moses speaks of them as "the many thousands of Israel." Margin, as in Heb.: "ten thousand thousands." In all there were about two-and-a-half millions of persons: an immense multitude to be marching through the desert. The greatness of the number of this pilgrim host illustrates the countless multitude of the redeemed of the Lord. Some men of small souls and narrow creeds have represented the number of the saved as comparatively small, an elect few only, and that of the lost as terribly large. Very different is the representation of the Sacred Scriptures. "God so loved the world," etc. Christ "died for all." "Many shall come from the east and west," etc. "In My Father's house are many mansions." "A great multitude, which no man could number," etc. (*a*)

II. The bitter opposers of the march.

The Israelites had powerful foes to encounter and vanquish before they could possess the Promised Land. Of these enemies Moses speaks in our text: "Rise up, Lord, and let thine enemies be scattered," etc.

1. *The enemies of this marching host are also the enemies of the God of the host.* Moses in his prayer says, "Thine enemies." When Saul persecuted the early Christian Church, our Lord appearing to him, demanded, Saul, Saul, why persecutest thou Me? "He that toucheth you toucheth the apple of His eye." The Church is confronted and opposed by enemies to-day,—"the devil and his angels;" the world which is led by him; and the lusts and passions of our carnal nature, oppose our heavenward march. Conflict is a condition of progress. We must fight if we would advance. The Lord accounts our enemies as His; combats them as His; and aids us that we may successfully meet and battle with them.

2. *That the opposition of the enemies arises from deep-rooted aversion to God.* Moses speaks of them as "them that hate" God. The spirit of Satan and the spirit of the world is still hostile to God, and to His people also in proportion to their loyal devotedness to Him. "If the world hate you," said our Lord, "ye know that it hated me," etc. (John xvi. 18, 19). "The world hath hated them, because they are not of the world." "Marvel not, my brethren, if the world hate you." Mark the awful depravity which is involved in this. How unspeakably terrible to hate truth, righteousness, and love! How much more terrible to hate Him who is infinite Truth and Righteousness, and Love! to hate the Supremely Holy and Kind! The Church of Christ is opposed now by enemies who are inveterate in their hatred to God, and to the people of God. (*b*)

III. The victorious Leader of the march.

1. *Their Leader was Divine.* "The Ark of the covenant of the Lord went before them." Keil and Del.: "Jehovah still did as He had already done on the way to Sinai (Exod. xiii. 21, 22): He went before them in the pillar of cloud, according to His promise (Exod. xxxiii. 13, 14), on their journey from Sinai to Canaan, with this simple difference,

however, that henceforth the cloud that embodied the presence of Jehovah was connected with the Ark of the covenant, as the visible throne of His gracious presence, which had been appointed by Jehovah Himself. To this end the Ark of the covenant was carried separately from the rest of the sacred things, in front of the whole army; so that the cloud which went before them floated above the Ark, leading the procession, and regulating its movements and the direction it took in such a manner that the permanent connection between the cloud and the sanctuary might be visibly manifested even during their march." The Lord Himself led them in all their journeyings. He is still the infallible and gracious Leader of His people.

2. *Their leader was victorious.* He had, as it were, but to arise and the enemies were scattered, and fled in dismay. The enemies of the Church are unable to stand before "the Captain of our salvation." When He leads us onward we march to certain victory. "We are more than conquerors through Him that loved us." (*c*)

3. *His lead was earnestly desired.* Moses prayed for it: "Rise up, Lord, and let thine enemies be scattered," &c. The prayer implies the consciousness of weakness and inability. Moses and the hosts of Israel were not sufficient of themselves to cope with their enemies. And as we look upon our foes to-day we may adopt the language of Jehoshaphat: "We have no might against this great company that cometh against us, neither know we what to do; but our eyes are upon Thee."

IV. **The abiding Presence of God on the march.**

"And when it rested, he said, Return, O Lord, unto the many thousands of Israel." On the march the Lord in the symbol of His Presence went before them, and when they encamped He abode with them. The presence of the Lord continued with them.

1. *The welfare of the Church of God depends upon His presence in their midst.* "Apart from Me," said Christ, "ye can do nothing."

2. *The continuous Presence of God is promised to His Church.* "Lo, I am with you alway, even unto the end of the world." "He shall give you another Comforter, that He may abide with you for ever." (*d*)

3. *The continuous presence of God should be sought by the Church in earnest prayer.* The promise of His presence should prove a basis of confidence and an encouragement to prayer.

Conclusion:

1. *Let the enemies of the Lord submit themselves to Him.* "Kiss the Son, lest He be angry," etc.

2. *Let every member of the pilgrim-host seek to realize constantly the victorious and blessed Presence of the Lord.*

ILLUSTRATIONS.

(*a*) When these words are set before us as descriptive of the heavenly state, it can hardly fail but that the first thing on which the mind shall fasten will be the expression—"a great multitude, which no man could number." It is so in regard of parallel sayings—"In My Father's house are many mansions;" and, "many shall come from the east and from the west, and shall sit down with Abraham, and Isaac, and Jacob, in the kingdom of heaven." "A great multitude"!—"many mansions"!—"many shall come"! But what are many in the Divine arithmetic? Doubtless, thousands, and tens of thousands—yea, an innumerable company. Many are the worlds scattered through immensity—who shall reckon them? Many are the leaves of the earth's forests—who shall compute them? Many are the grains of sand on the sea shore—who shall count them up? Neither may we think to compass the multitude that St. John saw before the throne and before the Lamb. Indeed, he tells us this, when he adds, "which no man could number." But it is a comforting thing to be told that "a great multitude"—not great on a mere human estimate, but great on a Divine—shall press into the inheritance purchased by Christ's blood. Then, not only is heaven no narrow, no contracted spot; but, on the contrary, spacious enough for myriads upon myriads of happy beings. But these myriads upon myriads shall be there; the vast expanse shall not stand empty, but shall be occupied by a rejoicing and adequate assembly! It is a refreshing thing to look away for a moment from the strife and uncharitableness of human systems and conclusions, each disposed to narrow heaven within its own pale and party, to behold a multitude such as no man could number, entering by the gate into the everlasting city. There is something unspeakably cheering in the contrast between the representation furnished in our text, and that derived from the exclusive systems of miscalled theology. If heaven were to be peopled according to the estimate of self-opiniated sects; if human judgments were to settle who shall be privileged to find place within its precincts; not "many," but few; it may be very few would constitute the celestial assembly. . . . . I kindle at the thought of there being a great multitude in heaven. A *great* multitude! There is room for us! A *great* multitude! There will be no deficiency without us. We can be spared. The loss will be ours! but, O! what a loss!—*Henry Melville, B.D.*

(b) Our field of conflict is different from that on which men oppose each other. It comprises the whole unseen realm. All the secret roads, and paths, and avenues, in which spirits dwell, are filled with a great invisible host. These are our adversaries. And they are all the more dangerous because they are invisible. Subtle are they. We are unconscious of their presence. They come, they go; they assail, they retreat; they plan, they attack, they withdraw; they carry on all the processes by which they mean to suborn or destroy us, without the possibility of our seeing them. When, in physical warfare, the enemy that is over against us establishes the line of a new redoubt, we can see that; and when a new battery is discovered, a battery may be planted opposite to it; but no engineering can trace these invisible engineers or their work. And there is something very august in the thought that the most transcendent powers in the universe, that fill time and space, are removed from the ordinary sight and inspection of men.—*H. W. Beecher.*

(c) Just when the battle was about to turn with the Ironsides, and the Cavaliers were coming on with one of Rupert's hot charges, ready to break the line, and the brave old Ironsides were half inclined to turn, up came the General, old Noll, riding on his horse, and they passed the word along, " 'Tis he, boys! here he comes!" and every man grew into a giant at once; they stood like iron columns, like walls of granite, and the Cavaliers as they came on broke like waves against rocks, and dashed away, and were heard of no more. It was the presence of the man that fired each soldier. And so it is now with us. We believe in Jesus Christ. We know that He is with His Church. He was dead, but rose again. He has gone to heaven, but His Spirit is with us,—King of kings and Lord of lords is He. If He seems to sleep in the midst of our ship, yet He sleeps with His hand on the helm, and He will steer the vessel rightly; and now the love that we bear His name steers our souls to holiness, to self-denial, to seek after God, to make full proof of the faith and fellowship of the Gospel, to seek to become like God, and to be absorbed into God that He may be all in all. This is what was wanted—a stimulus potent enough, under God's grace, to break through the barriers of sin.—*C. H Spurgeon.*

Is the strife long and hard? Long and hard it would be, to be ever defeated. But Christ shall lighten it for *thee*. He will bear it in *thee;* He will bear thee over it, as He will bear thee over the molten surges of this burning world. Christ will go before thee. He saith unto *thee*, "Follow Me; and where I am, there shall *thou* be with Me." "Follow *thou* Me." "Be of good cheer; I have overcome the world." "If Christ be for us, who shall be against us"? Safely mayest thou fight, who art secure of victory. And thou *art* safe, if thou fight for Christ, and with Christ. Only give not way. If defeated, be the humbler, and rise again; begin again, and pray to persevere. If thou succeed, give "thanks to Him who giveth us the victory, through Jesus Christ our Lord." And He will, by His Blood, intercede *for* thee; He will, by His grace, fight *in* thee; He will keep thee unto the end, who Himself crowneth, and is crowned, in all who are faithful to His grace. —*Dr. Pusey.*

(d) It is one of the fundamental things in godliness to know and realize the continual presence with us of the great Unseen Spirit. A thousand foes beleaguer my soul, and lie in wait, and assault it through the gates of sense. A thousand fears rise up in my path to terrify me, and a thousand smiling joys to seduce and allure me. But to be *as seeing Him who is invisible*—what a defence against fear! What a perennial, full-flowing spring of joy and strength and calmness and purity! How it sustains the soul in trouble, whether in the fierce, tumultuous storm-blast, or in the slow years of weary sorrow, creeping on with sluggish pace! There is a little garret-room—I recall what I have seen — with a single window looking out to the smoke and chimneys of a great city. The marks of poverty are abundant in its worn and scanty furniture. A few sickly flowers are in the window, testifying to the longing which never deserts even the most afflicted, to have but a glimpse of Nature's sweet face, or but the edge of her smile. There is a rough couch in the room, and a thin, pale, wasted woman lies upon it. For years she has scarcely risen from that bed. For years she has been subject to wasting pain. Her friends are seldom with her; they are poor, and cannot afford the luxury of constantly attending her. But her long trouble has not soured her. Her room is perhaps the happiest and lightsomest in the whole city. Go in upon her when you may, you find the same calm contentment, the same sweet, chastened look, the same quiet, all but celestial peace. Poor caged bird, she sings to God as gladly as the lark at heaven-gates. If one could take down the words she utters, and the tone in which they are uttered—if one could tell the heavenly thoughts that are unspoken, and that give the celestial calmness to that marble brow, the world might learn the blessed joy and power of a sense of God's constant nearness. "Nevertheless I am continually with Thee; Thou hast holden me by my right hand."—*James Culross, A.M., D.D.*

THE MARCH.

(*Verse* 35.)

I think I shall be warranted in using the text in three ways:

I. This has been the watchword of the Church of God in all ages.

The people of God in the wilderness were the picture of God's Church upon earth. We are strangers and foreigners upon earth; we are pilgrims and sojourners as all our fathers were. Here we have no abiding city. "We seek a city that hath foundations," etc.

Albeit that they had no habitation except their tents, yet is it true of Israel in the wilderness that they always had an habitation. (Comp. Psa. xc. 1.) Wherever they were, God was their dwelling place. God's wings were always over them; He carried them all the days of old, and they did really rest and dwell in Him. This, too, is true of the entire Church; always wandering, yet never far from home; unhoused, yet always in palaces, etc.

In another point the people of God in the wilderness were the picture of the Church of Christ. Wherever they marched, when God went before them, they marched to victory. Even so hath it been with the Church of God in all ages; her march has been that of one who is fair as the moon, clear as the sun, and terrible as an army with banners. Her path is the pathway of a conqueror; her march has been a procession of triumph. Let me show how this war-cry has really been heard of God and has been fulfilled to all His people. . . . . Shall not this be our song to-day? Let but God go forth with our armies; let Him but speak through our ministers; let Him but dwell in our elders; let Him but make the bodies of our Church members His temples, and His enemies must be scattered, and they must consume away.

Quietly, for the edification of each Christian, let me remark that this prayer will suit your personal difficulties. Have you been in conflict lately? Can you not deliver yourself? Pray, "Rise up, *Lord*," etc. Do your doubts prevail? Has your faith suffered an eclipse? Say, "Rise up Lord." All that is wanted in the darkest night to clear it away is for the sun to rise. Are you serving God in some particular work where many are seeking to undo all that you can accomplish? Has the Lord commanded you to some special work, and do friends discourage and enemies abuse? This prayer may suit you, "*Rise up Lord*." His uprising is enough, etc.

II. We shall now take the text in its reference to Christ.

Scripture is the best expounder of Scripture. The diamond is not to be cut except with a diamond. The sixty-eighth Psalm informs us that the moving of the Ark, from the lower place to the city of David, was typical of the ascending of Christ into heaven. How dense must have been the gloom over the fearing hearts of the Church when they saw their King, their Head dragged away, and nailed ignominiously to the tree, and how dead must all their hopes have been when at last He bowed His head and gave up the ghost! Was it not the day of hell's triumph, the hour of earth's despair, the moment of heaven's defeat? No; it was the reverse of all this. That moment when Christ died, He gave the death-blow to all His enemies. If the Church had had faith, they might have come early on the dawn of the first day in the week, and standing outside the tomb, they might have begun to sing, "Rise up, Lord," etc.

He rises, and in that moment *sin* dies. The resurrection of Christ was God's acceptance of Christ's sacrifice. "He rose again for our justification." Nor was sin alone that day scattered. Did not all the hosts of *hell* flee before Him? When He rose, blank despair sat on the face of every fiend. Where was that day the boast of *death?* Had Christ remained in the jaws of death, then had the redeemed remained the bond slaves of death too; but He lives. Blessed are they that sleep, for they shall rise too.

Nor was this all. After Christ had thus risen you will remember that He rose again. He rose from the grave to earth—He next rose from earth to heaven. (Comp. Psa. xxiv. 7-10.) On, on He rides; having scattered for ever all His enemies; having put all things under His feet, and being crowned King of kings, and Lord of lords.

III. What message has this text for us, and how may we use it?

* * * * * * *

C. H. Spurgeon.

THE CHURCH AND ITS ENEMIES.
(*Verses* 35, 36.)

The Almighty is here represented under two very different characters; as a God of terror, and as a God of grace.

I. That the Church of God has had enemies in every age.

This is accounted for in three ways:

1. *The favours they received.* God has set His heart upon His people; He bestows much on them, and expects much from them. This creates envy. Joseph's brethren hated him because he was the favourite. This evil principle soon grows into opposition and mischief.

2. *The principles they professed.* They were the only true principles; they worshipped the only true God, and therefore their conduct condemned all other modes of worship—all idolatry, and those sins which the nations committed.

3. *The expectations which they cherished.* These were deemed vain. Are these to become universal conquerors? Come, let us rise up against them, and destroy them. And does not this bear a resemblance to the good in the present age? Have they not enemies? Are they not a chosen people? Are not their principles peculiar, and their expectations large? The Church not only has outward enemies, but she has civil discords, **inward commotions, secret foes.**

II. That the enemies of the Church are considered the enemies of God.

The Church is intimately connected with God's dealings in a providential and merciful way, for He is near to His people (Deut. xxxii. 10; Isa. lxiii. 9). He sustains tender and intimate relations to the Church, hence her foes become His.

III. That when God rises up to judgment the destruction of His enemies is easy, terrible, and complete.

The Divine Being is here spoken of as rising up to judgment; this is figurative language, but indicates peril and alarm. But let us consider the second part of the prayer.

1. *That when God is represented as proceeding to acts of justice, it intimates that He is departing from the ordinary course of His dispensations.* Judgment is His strange work. He is said to come out of His place to punish the inhabitants of the earth. He takes no pleasure in the death of a sinner.

2. *That the aggregate number of the Lord's people is by no means inconsiderable.* I have no sympathy with that spirit which would straiten the gate already straight. Some unduly limit the number of Israel: (1) Because the limits of their observation are contracted. (2) Because the people of

God are widely dispersed and scattered. (3) Because their own prejudices often un-Christianize those whom God designs we should encourage. (4) Because we do not know how many Christians are concealed in the grave.

IV. **That the constant abode of God with His Church is an object of their supreme desire.**
"*Return, O Lord.*"
1. Let us learn from this passage the condescension and grace of God in that He will dwell with us.
2. Let each of us inquire whether we are amongst the many thousands of Israel.
3. What comfort should this give to the Church amidst her many trials.
4. This subject affords to the enemies of the Church a motive for seeking reconciliation with God.—*George Clayton. From "The Homiletic Quarterly."*

CHAPTER XI.

CRITICAL AND EXPLANATORY NOTES.

Verse 1. "*And when the people complained,*" etc. Margin: "the people were, as it were, complainers." *Speaker's Comm.*: "And the people were as those that complain of evil in the ears of the Lord."
Fire of Jehovah: "a fire sent by Jehovah, but not proceeding directly from Him, or bursting forth from the cloud, as in Lev. x. 2. Whether it was kindled through a flash of lightning, or in some other such way, cannot be more exactly determined."—*Keil and Del.*
And consumed in the uttermost parts of the camp. The words supplied by the translators of the A.V. are unnecessary. Keil and Del.: "And ate at the end of the camp." The fire did not proceed far into the camp.

Verse 3. *Taberah, i.e.,* burning or place of burning. Not the name of a station; but the local name given to that part of the camp where the fire broke out. The station was called Kibroth-Hattaavah, because of the more dreadful judgment which the people incurred by their renewed murmurings.

Verse 4. *The mixt multitude.* Heb., *Hasaphsuph,* "a number of people gathered together from all quarters: rabble."—*Fuerst.* "The word resembles our 'riff-raff,' and denotes a mob of people scraped together."—*Speaker's Comm.* See Exod. xii. 38. "The words '*they wept again*' point back to the former complaints of the people respecting the absence of flesh in the desert of Sin (Exod. xvi. 2 sqq.), although there is nothing said about their weeping there. By the flesh which they missed, we are not to understand either the fish which they expressly mention in the following verse (as in Lev. xi. 11), or merely oxen, sheep, and goats; but the word בָּשָׂר signifies flesh generally, as being a better kind of food than the bread-like manna."—*Keil and Del.*

Verse 5. *We remember the fish, which we did eat in Egypt freely.* Instead of "freely," Keil and Del. translate, "for nothing." Fish were so abundant in the Nile and neighbouring waters that they could be purchased at very low prices.

The cucumbers of Egypt are abundant and distinguished for softness and sweet flavour.

The melons: By the Hebrew word *abatichim,* we are probably to understand both melons and water-melons. They are largely cultivated in Egypt, and are sold so cheaply that they are used both by rich and poor, and much appreciated for their refreshing juice. The water-melon is said to "serve the Egyptians for meat, drink, and physic."

The leeks were from the earliest times a very favourite vegetable with the Egyptians, as both a nourishing and savoury food.

The onions from time immemorial have been a favourite article of food amongst the Egyptians. They flourish greatly in Egypt, are mild and pleasant in flavour, and are unsurpassed as to their quality.

Garlick, an important article of food amongst Egyptian workmen. All these things were refreshing and pleasant, and were plentiful and cheap in Egypt.

Verse 6. *There is nought at all,* etc. "Heb., 'Nought at all have we except that our eyes are unto this manna;' *i.e.,* 'Nought else have we to expect beside this manna.' Cf. on the phrase, 'to have the eyes towards,' Ps. xxv. 15."—*Speaker's Comm.*

Verses 7-9. On the *manna* see Exod. xvi. The description of it seems to be inserted parenthetically in this place to show the unreasonableness of the people in murmuring because of it.

Verse 10. *Weep throughout their families;* the weeping prevailed amongst the entire people.

Every man in the door of his tent; the weeping was unconcealed and open.

Verse 17. *I will take of the spirit which is upon thee.* "Render rather *separate from the spirit,* etc.; *i. e.,* they shall have their portion in the same Divine gift which thou hast."—*Speaker's Comm.*

Verse 25. *The Lord came down in a cloud; i.e.,* the cloud of the Divine presence, which soared on high above the Tabernacle, came down to the door of it. (Comp. chap. xii. 5; Exod. xxxiii. 9.)

They prophesied, does not mean that they foretold future events, but that inspired by the Holy Spirit, in an exalted state of mind, they poured forth the praise of God or declared His will.

And did not cease, is incorrect. It should be, *and did not add; i.e.,* they prophesied at this time only. This sign was given as a proof that God had called them to assist Moses, and had given them authority in their office.

Verse 26. Eldad and Medad were enrolled amongst the seventy, but for some reason they remained in the camp, and did not come to the Tabernacle.

Verse 31. *A wind from the Lord; i.e.,* an extraordinary wind, not the effect of a natural cause. The wind was from the south-east (Psa. lxxviii. 26).

Quails. The common quails. "The whole description answers to the well-known habits of these birds, and the Arabic name for them is even now *Salwa.* In the spring they migrate northwards from Africa, and flying low, especially when wearied, are taken or come to ground in immense multitudes."—*Alford.*

As it were two cubits high upon, etc. The lxx., the Vulgate, and Josephus, explain this as referring to the height at which the quails flew above the ground, in their exhausted condition from their long flight. Vulg.: *Volabant in aere duobus cubitibus altitudine super terram.* But that this interpretation is correct is very questionable: "for נָמָשׁ עַל הַמַּחֲנֶה does not mean to cause to fly or spread out over the camp, but to throw over or upon the camp. The words cannot therefore be understood in any other way than in Psa. lxxviii., 27, 28, viz., that the wind threw them about over the camp, so that they fell upon the ground a day's journey on either side of it, and that in such numbers that they lay, of course not for the whole distance mentioned, but in places about the camp, as much as two cubits deep."—*Keil and Del.*

Verse 32. *Ten homers.* The homer was ten ephahs. But there is considerable uncertainty as to the absolute capacity of these measures. The *Speaker's Comm.* says, "The homer must have been something above five-and-a-half bushels."

And they spread them all abroad, etc., for the purpose of drying them, as the Egyptians are said to dry both quails and fish (see Herod. ii. 77).

Verse 33. *The Lord smote the people,*

etc. "The plague with which God smote the people is to be regarded, as are miracles in many other cases, as a Divine interference enhancing a pre-existing cause. The surfeit in which the people indulged, of itself disposed them to sickness. God's wrath, visiting the gluttonous through their gluttony, aggravated natural consequences into a supernatural visitation."—*Speaker's Comm.*

Verse 34. *Kibroth-Hattaavah*; i.e., the graves of lust, or graves of greediness. "From there being no change of spot mentioned between it and Taberah in verse 3, it is probably like the latter about three days' journey from Sinai (x. 33.); and from the sea being twice mentioned in the course of the narrative (verses 22, 31), a maritime proximity may perhaps be inferred. If the conjecture of Hudhera as a site for Hazeroth be adopted, then the 'graves of lust' may be perhaps within a day's journey thence in the direction of Sinai, and would lie within fifteen miles of the Gulf of Akabah."—*Smith's Dict. of the Bible*.

Verse 35. *Hazeroth*. The word means simply the *enclosures*. But "topographically it is a *village*; generally a Bedouin village, such as are formed of tent-cloths, spread over stone walls."—*Stanley, S. and P.* Fuerst gives its meaning in this place as *hamlets*. The difficulty of identifying the locality is increased by the fact that the names of many places are compounded with חָצֵר. Perhaps Hazeroth is identical with Hudhera, which lies about eighteen hours' distance from Sinai on the road to the Akabah (see Stanley, *S. and P.*, pp. 81, 82). Keil and Del. say concerning Kibroth-Hattaavah and Hazeroth: "The situation of these two places of encampment is altogether unknown."

TABERAH AND ITS TEACHINGS.

(*Verses* 1-3).

In this brief record of the sin of Israel and the judgment of God at Taberah, the following points claim consideration.

I. Man sinning against the goodness of God.

"And the people complained," etc. Or, "And the people were as those that complain of evil in the ears of the Lord." No particular ground or reason of complaint is mentioned by the historian. It is probable that they murmured because of the privations of the march through the wilderness. Or it may have been, as Matthew Henry suggests, "that those who complained did not all agree in the cause. Some perhaps complained that they were removed from Mount Sinai, where they had been at rest so long; others that they did not remove sooner; some complained of the weather, others of the ways; some perhaps thought three days journey was too long a march, others thought it not long enough, because it did not bring them into Canaan." In so doing they sinned against the great goodness of God. He had emancipated them from a miserable bondage by marvellous and mighty deeds; He had given to them most excellent laws; He was graciously supplying their wants, guiding their movements and guarding their interests; and He had promised them a glorious land as their inheritance. Fervent thanksgiving should have engaged their hearts and voices, and not mean murmuring. Their complaining was a sin against the great kindness of the Lord. Base was their ingratitude. Amidst present inconveniences we are all too prone to overlook past and present mercies, and to complain as though we were receiving ill-treatment at the hands of the Lord. This is a great evil; it comprises ingratitude, unbelief, rebellion against God. (*a*)

II. God recognising the sin of man.

"And the Lord heard, and his anger was kindled," &c.

1. *He knew the sin.* They "complained in the ears of the Lord." "And the Lord heard." There is no voice of man that escapes His ear. Every cry of blasphemy, every murmur of unbelief, every mutter of rebellion against Him every whisper of evil conspiracy, is distinctly audible to Him. Words and thoughts, deeds and purposes, are all known to Him.

2. *He was angry because of the sin.* "And His anger was kindled." To the Lord sin is the abominable thing which He hates. His anger burns like an intense and unquenchable fire against sin.

3. *He manifested His anger because of the sin.* "And the fire of the Lord burnt among them, and consumed in the uttermost parts of the camp." Or, "So that fire of Jehovah burned against them, and ate at the end of the camp." (1.) The manifestation of His anger was *unmistakeable.* In whatsoever way the fire was kindled, there was no doubt in the minds of the people as to its being an expression of the wrath of God because of their sin. Their appeal to Moses is evidence of this. God has not left us in any uncertainty as to His hatred of evil. The stern penalties which are annexed to transgression, and the clear testimony of history as to the connexion of sin with suffering, loss, and ruin, are conclusive on the matter. (2.) The manifestation of his anger was *restrained.* The fire of Jehovah burnt only in "the end of the camp." In wrath He remembered mercy.

III. **Suffering men seeking the intercession of the good.**

"And the people cried unto Moses."

1. *This is very common.* It was common with the Israelites. "When He slew them, then they sought Him; and they returned and enquired early after God." "Those that slight God's friends when they are in prosperity would be glad to make them their friends when they are in distress. 'Father Abraham, send Lazarus.'"

2. *This is sometimes very mean.* It was so with the Israelites in the wilderness. They were painfully, terribly prone to the most shameful rebellion; and then when the consequences of their sin came upon them, like base slaves, they hastened to entreat Moses to intercede with God for them. Pharaoh is a notable example of this mean spirit and conduct (see Exod. viii. 8; ix. 27-35; x. 16, 17).

"When men in health against physicians rail
They should consider that their nerves may fail;
Nay, when the world can nothing more produce,
The priest, the insulted priest, may have his use."
Crabbe.

IV. **The intercession of the good resulting in blessing to men.**

"And when Moses prayed unto the Lord, the fire was quenched." See here—

1. *The great mercy of God.* "Thou, Lord, art good, and ready to forgive, and plenteous in mercy," etc. "He is gracious and merciful, slow to anger, and of great kindness, and repenteth Him of the evil."

2. *The great efficacy of prayer.* In answer to the prayer of Moses the fire of Jehovah was quenched. Comp. Jas. v. 16-18. Tennyson says beautifully—

. . . . "Prayer,
A breath that fleets beyond this iron world
And touches Him that made it." (*b*)

3. *The distinguishing power of a good man to benefit his race.* We may approach God in prayer on behalf of others. The power of intercession with God is the greatest power conferred on the good man; and by its exercise he may confer the richest blessings upon mankind. Comp. Gen. xviii, 23-33; Job viii. 20; Heb. vii. 25. (*c*)

V. **The employment of a transient judgment as a permanent warning.**

"And he called the name of the place Taberah, because the fire of the Lord burnt among them." The new name was a memorial of the sin and shame of the people, and of the judgment and mercy of the Lord; it has been a monitor to all succeeding ages, uttering its solemn warning against sin, and especially against the sin of ungratefully and unbelievingly complaining against the arrangements of God. Comp. 1 Cor. x. 10, 11.

Let us heed the warning, and shun the sin.

ILLUSTRATIONS.

(a) I think we are too ready with complaint
In this fair world of God's. Had we no hope,
Indeed beyond the zenith and the slope
Of yon grey bank of sky, we might grow faint
To muse upon eternity's constraint
Round our aspirant souls. But since the scope
Must widen early, is it well to droop
For a few days consumed in loss and taint ?
O pusillanimous heart! be comforted,
And, like a cheerful traveller, take the road,
Singing beside the hedge. What if the bread
Be bitter in thine inn, and thou unshod
To meet the flints?—At least it may be said,
"Because the way is short, I thank Thee, God." *Elizabeth B. Browning.*

As it frequently happens that many persons in easy circumstances, or who have many comfortable things, are notwithstanding very discontented; it would be well for some friend thus to reason with them: "Have you ever compared your situation with those who hardly ever see the sun, but live confined in tin mines, stone quarries, and coal-pits? Before you think yourself miserable, walk through the wards of an hospital; think of the galley slave, and the day labourer; reflect upon the condition of many large, poor families who have continued distress or sickness. Many are often witnesses to scenes even more wretched than these, where to poverty, cold, and nakedness, are added the languors of lingering and loathsome diseases and the torments of excruciating pain." Now let those who are miserable among many mercies, return as it were from these sad scenes to their closets, gratefully acknowledge the goodness of God in exempting them from so many *real* ills, which so many labour under, and instead of spending their hours brooding over their own imaginary evils, let them be continually cheerful, happy, and thankful.—*Gleanings.*

(b) What has prayer done? According to its history as given in this Book, it has conquered the elements, it has healed the diseased, it has put armies to flight, it has restored life, it has sent back the angel of death when he has shown his face in the dwelling, it has brought down angels, and it has changed the hearts of men, even hearts the most stubborn. Prayer ! It does move the fingers which create, and which have created, and doubtless still creates. Prayer ! It does move the hand, as is often said, which moves the world.—*Samuel Martin.*

(c) O priceless grace ! if thou, O believer, knowest how to ask by faith, thou mayest hand out to thy brethren wealth more precious than the gold of Ophir; for intercession is the key to the ivory palaces wherein are contained the boundless treasures of God. Saints in intercession reach a place where angels cannot stand. Those holy beings rejoice over penitent sinners, but we do not read of their being admitted as suppliants for the saints. Yet we, imperfect as we are, have this favour, we are permitted to open our mouth before the Lord for the sick and for the tried, for the troubled and for the downcast, with the assurance that whatsoever we shall ask in prayer believing we shall receive.—*C. H. Spurgeon.*

Our power to help and bless each other is, primarily and pre-eminently, *the power of prayer.* We can aid each other by gifts of our worldly goods; we can aid each other by words of instruction, correction, and consolation; we can help each other by the influence of good example, and by services so numerous and various that it is almost impossible to classify and describe them; but above all these ministrations is the intercession of a true Christian. Prayer, brethren, directs and impels to other services of love. Prayer secures the efficiency and success of all other ministrations, while prayer is independent of time, independent of place, independent of temporal circumstances, independent of a man's bodily condition, and independent of a man's worldly estate. Prayer, too, appeals to the fountain of good, and to the Father of mercies; and if God be true (and let God be true, and every man a liar) it fills the channel of blessing sometimes even to overflowing. Let Christians say to each other, "Brother, whatever you withold from me, deny me not your prayers; whatever you may give to me, crown all your gifts by your prayers."—*Samuel Martin.*

THE SUPREMACY OF THE SENSES OVER THE SOUL.

(*Verses* 4-6.)

This portion of the history of Israel is clearly stated by Krummacher in a passage given in the *Illustrations.* (a)

Four preliminary remarks are suggested :

First : *There is in unrenewed human*

nature an amazing and saddening proneness to sin. The fire of Jehovah, which had burnt amongst them as a judgment because of former sin, was scarcely quenched when they broke out afresh into sin. Only a very little time previously they were in their distress crying to Moses for mercy, and now they are again crying in rebellion against God. "No sooner is one murmuring ended," says Babington, "but another begins. *Obsta principiis*, Stay beginnings, for then is sin weakest, and may best be snubbed and overcome. Let it enter in at the door, and get a little footing it will foil us, and we shall hardly get it out again. First will enter a bare cogitation, then a vehement imagination, after that a wicked delectation, and lastly a killing and damning consent, if God recover us not."

Second: *The cries for mercy which are made under the pressure of suffering are seldom followed by reformation of life.* While the fire was consuming them they cried earnestly to Moses; but as soon as the fire was extinguished they returned to the sins which kindled it. Vows begotten of pain are generally ignored in ease and health. (*b*)

Third: *We may be associated with the people of God without possessing a godly spirit.*

"The mixed multitute," with whom the lusting and murmuring commenced, were not Israelites, but had joined themselves to them when they left Egypt, probably from selfish motives. They were utterly destitute of the true Israelitish spirit. Membership in the visible Church of Christ, and union with His true and spiritual Church, are by no means identical. Mere outward profession is spiritually worthless: nay, it is a lying semblance. Religious profession is valuable only as it is joined with holiness of heart and life. Comp. Rom. ii. 28, 29; ix. 6–8; Gal. iii. 7, 9; Tit. i. 16.

Fourth: *Sin is terribly contagious.* The sin in this case began with the mixed multitude, but it speedily spread to the children of Israel. One evil character corrupts another. "Evil communications corrupt good manners." "Observe," says Trapp, "the danger of ill company. To converse with the ungodly, and not to learn their manners, is marvellously rare and difficult. A man may pass through Ethiopia unchanged; but he cannot dwell there and not be discoloured." Wherefore, shun the society of the wicked. (*c*)

But it appears to us that the most conspicuous feature in this sad scene is *the Supremacy of the Senses over the Soul.* Let us glance at the characteristics of this supremacy which are here exhibited :

I. **Unsatisfied Cravings.**

"And the mixed multitude that was among them fell a lusting." Margin, as in Heb., "lusted a lust." They were not satisfied with the provision which God had made for them. Where animal appetites are supreme, satisfaction is unattainable. Man will ever remain restless and unsatisfied until his animal appetites are controlled by spiritual principles. The senses must be governed by the soul, the lower nature by the higher, before man can find satisfaction and rest. While the senses are supreme in man they are never satisfied; soon as one lust is gratified, another grows clamorous for gratification. "The eye is not satisfied with seeing, nor the ear filled with hearing." "All the labour of man is for his mouth, and yet the appetite is not filled."

II. **Humiliating effeminacy.**

"And the children of Israel wept again."

Tears are of various kinds, and of these kinds many are beautiful and blessed.

"Tears! what are tears? The babe weeps
   in its cot,
The mother singing; at her marriage bell
The bride weeps; and before the oracle
Of high-faned hills, the poet hath forgot
That moisture on his cheeks. Commend
   the grace,
Mourners who weep! Albeit, as some
   have done,
To grope, tear-blinded, in a desert-place,
And touch but tombs—look up! These
   tears will run
Soon, in long rivers, down the lifted face,
And leave the vision clear for stars and
   sun." *Elizabeth B. Browning.*

But who shall commend these tears of the children of Israel in the desert? Men and women generally weeping openly, because they could not obtain the particular kind of food which they desired! Weeping openly for cucumbers, melons, etc.! Pitiable spectacle! Such tears will never clear the vision for either stars or sun. Tears are revealers of character. Here they surely indicate the most deplorable weakness and waywardness of soul. We have spoken of "men and women weeping." The expression is inaccurate; for this weeping host was composed of those who were men and women in body only, in soul they were pusillanimous children. A host of weeping weaklings and cowards! The supremacy of the senses in man is destructive of strength and heroism of spirit. Patience under privations, persistence in duty despite of difficulty, calm endurance of present suffering for the attainment of great good in the future—these are incompatible with the sovereignty of man's lower nature. Such sovereignty is destructive of the noblest attributes of manhood. (d)

III. Daring unbelief.

"And said, who shall give us flesh to eat?" Cowards in the face of any difficulty or privation, yet they have the hardihood wickedly to challenge the ability of God. Thus the poet Asaph describes their conduct, "They tempted God in their heart by asking meat for their lust. Yea, they spake against God; they said, Can God furnish a table in the wilderness? Behold, He smote the rock, that the waters gushed out, and the streams overflowed; can He give bread also? can He provide flesh for His people?" Their unbelief was the more inexcusable, the more guilty, because of the illustrious displays of the power of God which they had witnessed; and not of His power only, but also of His goodness to them. The supremacy of the senses tends to close the eye of the soul to the great verities of the spiritual universe, destroys the power of the soul for grasping those verities, leads to the conviction that the things which are apprehensible by the senses are the only real, trustworthy things. Carnality of mind tends directly first to the prostration and then to the destruction of the faith-faculty.

IV. Deplorable degradation.

"We remember the fish which we did eat in Egypt freely," etc. Their degradation appears,—

1. *In what they remembered.* "The fish, the cucumbers, the melons, the leeks," etc. To what a dreadful depth must human nature have fallen or sunk when its most vivid and treasured memories are of savoury dainties for the gratification of the palate! How inexpressibly mournful when to any one the meat is more than the life!

2. *In what they forgot.* The unspeakable degradation of their slavery in Egypt appears to be forgotten by them. The servitude at the brick-kilns, the severe oppressions of their cruel taskmasters, the intolerable insult and injury of slavery, are all lost sight of now that the gratification of their carnal appetite is denied them. Freedom seemed a poor thing in their eyes to be purchased at the cost of the denial of their senses. Alas, how sad is all this! But far more sad is it that this is a picture of what is widely prevalent in our own land and age. Education, books, music, religion, and even manhood, are regarded by immense numbers as utterly inferior to the animal pleasures of eating and drinking. The soul is engulfed in the stomach.

V. Decided Contempt of Divine Blessings.

"But now our soul is dried away: there is nothing at all, beside this manna, before our eyes." Moses describes the nature, form, and taste of the manna, and the mode of its preparation, to show the unreasonableness of the people in despising it. The manna was (1) Wholesome for health; (2) Pleasant to the palate; (3) Abundant in quantity; and (4) Free of cost. "But the sweet bread of heaven wanted 'the sharp and sour, which are required to give a stimulating flavour to the food of man, on account of his sinful, restless desires, and the incessant changes of his earthly life.' In this respect the manna resembled the spiritual food supplied by the Word of God, of which the sinful heart of man may also speedily become weary, and turn to the more piquant productions of the spirit of the world." When the senses are supreme, spiritual and divine things are rejected, while carnal and earthly things are eagerly pursued and heartily cherished.

Conclusion:

"The mind of the flesh is death; but the mind of the spirit is life and peace." Submit not to the rule of the senses and passions of your nature. Let your spirit be the sovereign of your fleshly nature, and let God be supreme in your spirit. "Seek ye first the Kingdom of God and His righteousness."

ILLUSTRATIONS.

(*a*) The people were now in a waste-howling wilderness. Nothing presented itself in the way of food, but that which descended from heaven, which lasted only for a day, and they had water only by a miracle from the rock that followed them. The eye was tired of resting upon the horrible uniformity of the boundless waste around it, which produced only here and there a solitary thorn or brier. Not a trace of any previous traveller. No pleasing sound delighted the ear. No turtle-dove cooed its melancholy note, no lark soared warbling aloft, as if to point the way to the repenting mind. Nothing but an occasional howl was heard. Sometimes a solitary pelican sounded its harsh and grating note, or the roar of hungry lions and the growls of bloodthirsty tigers and hyenas struck the ear from a distance, and excited a feeling of horror. The Israelites had been accustomed to something very different. In the pleasant land of Goshen the case had been otherwise—fruitfulness and pleasing scenery, fields, gardens, and meadows, rivers, and pools, abounded everywhere. Unhappily, they began to draw comparisons, and by these, an evil or a good is either made greater or less. If a great good is compared with one still greater, it loses in our estimation; and so it is with an evil. If we reflect that it might be much worse, it becomes more tolerable. But when the evil is compared with the opposite good, it becomes more grievous, even as black laid upon white appears still blacker. In hell, the rich glutton thought a drop of water a good blessing, who previously would not have esteemed the most costly wine as much. If the sight of the misery of Lazarus had contributed to increase his enjoyment when on earth, by comparing his own health and ease with it—so the sight of the glory he enjoyed in heaven must have increased his torment.

The children of Israel also drew a comparison. In the burning desert, they call to mind the cooling cucumbers, and the juicy, pleasant, and well-flavoured water-melons. The thought of these things, it must be confessed, may well make the mouth water whilst traversing the burning sand. The Egyptian fish came also unfortunately to mind, as well as the savoury leeks, onions, and garlic. There they had them for nought—here nothing of the kind was to be had, even for its weight in gold.

Let us not be unjust towards them, but confess that the temptation was not a small one to flesh and blood. In one respect there was nothing sinful in the idea that they would gladly now have gathered up the melons which perhaps in Egypt they had trampled under foot, and have considered the fish as a dainty which there they disregarded. But this became sin to them, because they desired them in an inordinate, violent manner, and out of, nay, even in opposition to, the Divine order. What did they not lose sight of in doing so? Was not Canaan promised them, where they should have these things in abundance? Should they therefore refuse to wait a little longer, since in the course of a few days or weeks they might arrive there, seeing that they were travelling towards it, and had already accomplished more than half the distance—not considering that they were the people from whom was to come salvation, and out of whom a seed should rise up, in whom all the nations of the earth should be blessed—not considering that what they endured and were deprived of, would be to their own advantage, and that of the whole world—not reflecting that they were really not in want of any thing necessary. Did God, His guidance, His promise, and His will appear to them of so little value; and melons, onions, and garlic all to them? Was everything forgotten which had been done to them and for them? How disgustingly does their gloomy, earthly and carnal-mindedness manifest itself! They imagine themselves in extreme misery.—*G. D. Krummacher.*

(*b*) How often do we find such whom God hath beleaguered with an affliction, or planted His battery against by a disease, whom He seemed to have marked out for death, make covenants and promises for a future reformation, and of putting away their sin; whom yet, when He withdraws His terrors, and puts up His arrows, those ties do no more bind than the withes did Samson; but they arise, and go out, and do as at other times. While their backs smart under the rod, and they sit on the brink of the grave, their spirits stoop, their passions are broken, and the heat of them assuaged; their thoughts are humbled to sobriety. Then to be liberal of promises is an easy bounty; but when the storm is over, and they return to their former freedom and delight, in sensible converses, then are they restrained in performance, and rescind former engagements. The sighs of their sick bed, which they turned into penitent groans, are now vanished into air, and forgotten; the sad reflections on their former vanities, the serious recollection of their ways which they were reduced to, when the flesh sat uneasy upon them, and dwelt in sorrow, are now as little thought upon as the dolorous accents of their grief. When they are newly come out of the furnace, while the smell of fire is yet on them, they are scrupulous and tender. But it is as those who come out of a hot stove, that shrink from cold at first, but by degrees are brought to their former hardiness of temper. If the *soul* be not changed, though there may for a while some *religious colour* appear in the man's face, he will at last return to his former habit. —*Spiritual Bee.*

(*c*) Sin is like the bale of goods which came from the east to this city in the olden time, which brought the pest in it. Probably it was but a small bale, but yet it contained in it the deaths of hundreds of the inhabitants of London. In those days one piece of rag carried the infection into a whole town. So, if you permit one sin or false doctrine in a church knowingly and wittingly, none can tell the extent to which that evil may ultimately go. The church, therefore, is to be purged of practical and doctrinal evil as diligently as possible. That sour and corrupting thing which God abhors must be purged out, and it is to be the business of the Christian minister and of all his fellow-helpers, to keep the church free from it.—*C. H. Spurgeon.*

(*d*) The most terrible scourges with which the east is afflicted in the way of disease are the fruits of gross living—eating as well as drinking—perhaps the first most. Men in those climates cannot bear it; students cannot in this. To keep a clear eye, a firm hand, a steady brain were more to Daniel than pleasures of the palate. I venture to say that no man has ever greatly distinguished himself whose body was not in firm control. It is not enough to follow nature and never be excessive; nature wants curbing, and unless young men take their bodies in hand, and compel them sometimes to abstain, and obey the mastery of the will, it is impossible to keep the body in due subjection, and make it the eager and rapid handmaid of the soul. Fasts are good things in youth, simply as a moral discipline; as a man training for a race abstains from all which might imperil his hope of a prize. The Romanists abuse them to superstitious ends, and the peril of doing so is great; therefore the Protestant churches, wisely, I think, leave them alone. But you *must* master the body; you *must* make its limbs to move to the music of temperance and chastity; and there are times when pulse and water will be the fittest nourishment, and leave the spirit free for aspiration, and the mind clear and strong for work.—*J. Baldwin Brown.*

PARTIAL MEMORIES.

(*Verses* 4-6.)

I. Observe what they ought to have remembered:
1. *What they had suffered.*
2. *What God had done for them.*
3. *What He then was doing.*
4. *What He had promised to do.*

II. Observe what they chiefly dwelt upon:
1. *Creature comforts, not spiritual deprivations.*
2. *Personal satisfaction, not national freedom.*

III. Observe the effects of this partial memory of the past:
1. *It led to discontent.*
2. *It resulted in Divine anger.*
3. *It prolonged their stay in the wilderness.*—*Biblical Museum.*

THE MANNA AN ILLUSTRATION OF THE DIVINE PROVISION FOR THE SPIRITUAL NEEDS OF MAN.

(*Verses* 7-9.)

The subject of the Manna has been treated at length in *The Hom. Comm.* on Exod. xvi.

This paragraph is introduced parenthetically to show the unreasonableness of the people in murmuring and speaking contemptuously of the Manna. The historian speaks of it as being like coriander seed. "The coriander seed is that of the *coriandrum sativum*, cultivated in England for confectionery, and wild in Egypt and Palestine. The seed is globular, grayish-coloured, and hollow, the surface marked with fine stripes. It has a pleasant spicy flavour."—*Alford*. The colour of the manna is said to be "as the colour of bdellium." בְּדֹלַח, which is translated bdellium, has been variously interpreted. The theory of Bochart, which is adopted by Gesenius and seems to us the most probable, is that it signifies *pearls*, which are found in great abundance on the shores of the Persian Gulf. Fuerst also gives this as the meaning in this place—"*pearl*, with the shining of which the grains of manna were compared, Num. xi. 7."

But it is our purpose to regard the gift of the manna as an illustration of the Provision which God has made for the spiritual needs of our race in Jesus Christ. We have warrant for so regarding it in the Scriptures of the New Testament, John xi. 31-58 ; 1 Cor. x. 3, 4. We discover the following points of analogy :

I. **Both are of Divine Origin.**

It seems to us utterly unreasonable to question the miraculous nature of the supply of manna. As Dr. Kitto remarks, " If any human infatuation could surprise a thoughtful and observant mind—and especially if any folly of those who deem themselves wiser than their Bible could astonish—it might excite strong wonder to see grave and reverend men set forth the strange proposition that two or three millions of people were fed from day to day, during forty years," with the gum of the tamarisk tree. "A very small quantity—and that only at a particular time of the year, which is not the time when the manna first fell—is now afforded by all the trees of the Sinai peninsula ; and it would be safe to say, that if all the trees of this kind then or now growing in the world had been assembled in this part of Arabia Petræa, and had covered it wholly, they would not have yielded a tithe of the quantity of gum required for the subsistence of so vast a multitude." (*a*)

And all spiritual provision for man's needs proceeds from God. The idea, the agencies, and the means of human salvation are all of Divine origin. All inspiring and strengthening influences are from above. "The bread of God is He which cometh down from heaven, and giveth life unto the world. . . . . Jesus said unto them, I am the bread of life," etc. (*b*)

II. **Both are unmerited Gifts.**

Just before the first bestowal of the manna the people were guilty of the most grievous murmurings and rebellion against God (Exod. xvi. 1-12) ; they could not therefore advance the slightest pretence of meriting any good from Him. The blessings of Divine grace also are entirely owing to the free favour of our heavenly Father. Man merited nothing but pain and punishment from God. Rebels against His authority, we had forfeited all claim to His favour. "But God commendeth His love towards us," etc. (Rom. v. 8, 20). "For by grace are ye saved," etc. Eph. ii. 8 ; 1 John, iv. 9, 10. (*c*)

III. **Both are wholesome.**

The manna, which they despised, "was highly nutritive and wholesome food, as nearly as possible analogous to what forms the staff of life, be it rice or corn, to the present inhabitants of the desert, who rarely taste meat or vegetables, and are but too happy if they can get enough of their customary food." The provisions of Divine grace for our spiritual needs are compared in the Scriptures to those great essentials of life and health, bread and water. Comp. John iv. 13, 14 ; vi. 35, 50, 51. Spiritual life and health are unattainable save through the provisions of the Gospel. Only Jesus Christ can satisfy the cravings of the immortal soul of man. His salvation is new life to the spiritually dead, health to the sin-sick soul, strength to the morally weak.

IV. **Both are pleasant.**

The manna was very agreeable to the palate. "Eaten as gathered, it tasted like cakes made of meal and honey (Exod. xvi. 31); but when dressed, it acquired the taste of fresh oil, a flavour highly agreeable to the Israelites" (ver. 8). The provisions of Christianity are pleasant as well as wholesome. One of the favourite images of the prophets to set forth the blessings of the Gospel age is that of a great and bounteous festival (Cant. v. 1; Isa. xxv. 6; lxv. 13, 14). Our Lord also uses the same figure for the same purpose (Matt. xxii. 1-14; Luke xiv. 15-24). God in the Gospel provides a delightful feast of spiritual experiences, exercises, and services—a feast of peace, hope, love, joy, service, fellowship, worship.

V. Both are Abundant.

There was no scarcity of manna. For forty years the Lord caused it to fall with unfailing regularity, so that there was an omer (*i.e.* nearly three English quarts) for every person in the vast host every day. The supplies of Christianity are abundant. Like the air and the light, they are inexhaustible. They are like a river deep and broad, which is fed by perennial springs. "The unsearchable riches of Christ." "God is able to make all grace abound toward you," etc.

VI. Both are Free.

All the Israelites might avail themselves of the manna; no restriction was placed upon them in this respect. Gloriously free are the blessings of salvation. "Ho, every one that thirsteth, come ye to the waters, and he that hath no money," etc. "God so loved the world, that He gave His only begotten Son," etc. "I will give unto him that is athirst of the fountain of the water of life freely." "Let him that is athirst come. And whosoever will, let him take the water of life freely." (*d*)

VII. Both require personal Appropriation.

The Israelites were required to gather the manna in the early morning; they then prepared it for eating by grinding or pounding it, and baking it in cakes. The blessings of the Divine Gospel will profit us nothing unless we personally appropriate them. We must believe the Christ of the Gospel (John iii. 36; vi. 47-58); we must meditate upon the teachings of the Gospel; we must practise the precepts of the Gospel; we must live the Gospel, if we would enjoy the rich provisions which it contains for our spiritual needs. Without this personal appropriation we shall perish even in the midst of the banquet-house of Christ, and in presence of the choicest, most abundant, and freest provisions of the grace of the heavenly King. (*e*)

Conclusion:

1. *Take heed that ye despise not the spiritual provisions of the Divine grace.*
2. *Gratefully and gladly accept these provisions.* (*f*)

ILLUSTRATIONS.

(*a*) The natural products of the Arabian deserts and other Oriental regions, which bear the name of manna, have not the qualities or uses ascribed to the manna of Scripture. They are all condiments or medicines rather than food, stimulating or purgative rather than nutritious; they are produced only three or four months in the year, from May to August, and not all the year round; they come only in small quantities, never affording anything like 15,000,000 of pounds a-week, which must have been requisite for the subsistence of the whole Israelitish camp, since each man had an omer (or three English quarts) a day, and that for forty years; they can be kept for a long time, and do not become useless in a day or two; they are just as liable to deteriorate on the Sabbath as on any other day; nor does a double quantity fall on the day preceding the Sabbath; nor would natural products cease at once and for ever, as the manna is represented as ceasing in the book of Joshua. The manna of Scripture we therefore regard as wholly miraculous, and not in any respect a product of nature.—*C. E. Stowe, D.D.*

(*b*) If it would be marvellous to see one river leap up from the earth full-grown, what would it be to gaze upon a vast spring from which all the rivers of the earth should at once come bubbling up, a thousand of them born at a birth! What a vision would it be! Who can conceive it? And yet the love of God is that fountain from which all the rivers of mercy which have ever gladdened our race —all the rivers of grace in time and of glory hereafter—take their rise. My soul, stand thou at that sacred fountain-head, and adore and magnify for ever and ever "God, even our Father, who hath loved us."—*C. H. Spurgeon.*

(c) The love which God has for us, did not, does not, spring from moral excellence in us; and still less does its depth and breadth answer to the loveableness of our dispositions. No man can ponder for a moment the facts in our case without being obliged to say that God loves man, not so much from the adaptation of human nature and disposition to produce love, as from a Divine nature that overflows from the necessity of its own richness and fulness. The reasons must needs be in God, and not in us.—*H. W. Beecher.*

(d) I walked over a long sandy road one day, when the weather was sultry, and the heat, far beyond our common experience in this country, was almost tropical; I saw a little stream of cool water, and being parched with thirst I stooped down and drank. Do you think I asked anybody's leave, or enquired whether I might drink or not? I did not know who it belonged to, and I did not care. There it was, and I felt if it was there it was enough for me. I was thirsty, and there was the water. I noticed after I had drank that there were two poor tramps came along, and they went down and drank too. I did not find anybody marching them off to prison. There was the stream. The stream being there, and the thirsty men being there, the supply was suited to their need, and they promptly partook of it. How strange it is that when God has provided the Gospel, and men want it, they should require somebody to call out to them, "Ho! ho! ho!" and then they will not come after all. Oh! if they were a little more thirsty, if they did but know their need more, if they were convinced more of their sin, then they would scarcely want an invitation, but the mere fact of a supply would be sufficient for them and they would come and drink, and satisfy the burning thirst within.—*C. H. Spurgeon.*

(e) What a wonderful deal is made of faith in God's Book! We are justified by faith and not by works. . . . There is nothing arbitrary in this. It is not an arbitrary appointment of God that man should be justified and receive all blessedness when he believes on the Lord Jesus Christ. It arises from the nature of things. I should like to give you an illustration of this. There are many beautiful trees in yonder park; take one of them. Now, in order to grow and bring forth fruit, the tree must have its roots in the earth, and its branches spread out to the air and the sun. It is no arbitrary appointment. It arises from the nature of the tree and earth. It cannot be otherwise. Would man be blessed? Then he must be united to Christ. He must believe on the Lord Jesus Christ. He must appropriate Christ. Now, in one respect I almost tire of saying, Believe on the Lord Jesus Christ. Such words as, Come to Christ, and Come to Jesus have been used in such a poor, meaningless, parrot-like way that they have almost been spoiled. But there is deep meaning, brethren, in coming to Christ. It is the passing through a cloud of doubts, fears, sins, right up to Him, and not only as the poor woman did, taking hold of the hem of His garment, but taking hold on Him and saying, "Lord, I perish; do Thou save me." And mark: the moment I am united to Christ, the moment I am in Him, all good is possible to my nature. There is no limitation but the limitation of my powers. All the blessedness possible to man is mine the moment I am united to Him.—*Thomas Jones.*

(f) Come then quickly. All is in vain if you do not come. See, the Gospel feast is spread, and the springs of life are all open; and Jesus stands in view of all the world, and cries that all the world may hear, and names no man by name and yet names every man that lives, each and all being contained in His invitation when He says, "If ANY man thirst, let *him* come to Me and drink." "Any man." Why that is *you!* That is *you!* He waits for you. He has happiness for you; He has righteousness for you, and love untold for you, and life, life evermore, for you. And what have you for Him? What have you to give Him? Surely now, at length, a willing heart—surely now an open trusting hand. Have you not had enough of life without Him? Will you attempt the wilderness once more, and perhaps perish of thirst? Will you go again to hew out a broken cistern, or a cistern that will be broken some time or other, and, perhaps, one day be found dead by its side? Are you so in love with misery? Is the covenant with death so dear? Come, thirsty soul and drink. "The Spirit and the bride say, 'Come;' and let him that heareth say, 'Come;' and let him that is athirst come. And whosoever will let him come and take of the water of life freely."—*Alex. Raleigh, D.D.*

THE BURDENS OF LEADERSHIP.

(*Verses* 10-15).

Sorely was Moses tried by the unbelief, the cowardice, the complainings, and the rebellions of the Israelites. Pre-eminent was he for patience and meekness, yet there were times when the strain and burden of the perverse people that he was called to lead were too great for his endurance. Such a time was that with which we are now dealing. (a)

This impassioned appeal to God suggests—

I. That the position of Leader or Governor of men is a very trying one.

1. *Because of the responsible nature of the duties of leadership.* The guidance and direction of a large number of men, even under the most favourable circumstances, involve a great weight of responsibility. And the government of a large number of men, even when the governor is most able and the governed most reasonable, is a thing of enormous difficulty.

2. *Because of the interest which the true leader takes in his charge.* The true leader, like Moses, is so deeply interested in those over whom he is placed as to be afflicted in all their afflictions; their privations and sufferings sorely pain him; their meannesses and sins cause him to blush with shame, or to weep in penitence. A great interest involves, almost invariably, a great burden.

3. *Because of the intractableness of men.* It was this which made the burden of Moses so heavy and grievous to bear at this time. "Antoninus the Emperor said often, *Imperium oceanum esse malorum*, that to be a governor of others is to be plunged into an ocean of miseries. Pope Adrian caused to be engraven upon his own tomb, *Felix si non imperitasset*. Melancthon said, the three sorest labours of all were *Docentis, imperantis, parturientis*, the labours of ministers, magistrates, and of travailing women. . . . . Crowns have their cares; high seats are uneasy; many a cumber attends honour. *Beatus ille qui procul negotiis*. —*John Trapp*.

II. The true leader of men must often be painfully conscious of his insufficiency.

Moses felt it at this time and cried to the Lord, "I am not able to bear all this people alone, because it is too heavy for me." The difficult demands of changing circumstances and situations, the perplexing problems which arise in questions of government, the perverse dispositions and practices of men, these and other things at times, give rise to such demands upon the personal powers of leaders of men as to fill and almost prostrate them with a sense of their insufficiency. Christian ministers have felt this, and cried, "Who is sufficient for these things?" Kings have felt it, and exclaimed :—

"Uneasy lies the head that wears a crown."

Statesmen have felt it, &c.

III. The ablest and holiest leaders of men sometimes fail under the burdens of their position.

Moses was unquestionably one of the most distinguished of men—distinguished for mental power, and for elevation, strength, and holiness of character; but that he erred at this time is very clearly manifest from his appeal to the Lord. He erred—

1. *In exaggerating the extent of his responsibility.* It appears that when the discontent of the people became deep and clamorous, God did not at once interpose, "but withdrew with His help, and let the whole storm of the infuriated people burst upon him." This accounts for the language of verses 11-15. But it was an exaggeration to say that "the burden of all this people" was cast upon him alone. The Lord was constantly assisting him both by direction and by all-sufficient help. When our anxieties and cares obtain the mastery of our faith and patience, they at once assume most exaggerated dimensions and gravity.

2. *In overlooking the history of God's dealings with them, and the promises which He had made to them.* For a time Moses seems to forget the glorious deeds of the high Hand and the outstretched Arm which had brought them forth out of Egypt, the marvellous and mighty works at the Red Sea, the miracles of the quails and the manna at Sin, and that of the water from the rock at Rephidim. He forgot the gracious and all-inclusive promise, "My Presence shall go with thee, and I will give thee rest." What Moses did, we are all more or less prone to do when

life's burdens press severely and its sorrows are most sore.

3. *In passionately appealing to God for deliverance or death.* "And if Thou deal thus with me, kill me, I pray Thee out of hand," etc. "This is the language of the discontent of despair," says Keil and Del., "which differs from the murmuring of unbelief, in the fact that it is addressed to God, for the purpose of entreating help and deliverance from Him; whereas unbelief complains of the ways of God, but while complaining of its troubles, does not pray to the Lord its God. . . There was good ground for his complaint. The burden of the office laid upon the shoulders of Moses was really too heavy for one man; and even the discontent which broke out in the complaint was nothing more than an outpouring of zeal for the office assigned him by God, under the burden of which his strength would eventually break down, unless he received some support. He was not tired of the office, but would stake his life for it if God did not relieve him in some way, as office and life were really one in him. Jehovah therefore relieved him in the distress of which he complained, without blaming the words of His servant, which bordered on despair." Still it appears to us that Moses was presumptuous in presenting to the Lord the alternative that He would either deliver him or kill him, and that he was impatient and passionate in his appeal to the Lord. But if even he failed under the heavy burden, how terribly complete and unutterably mournful would our failure have been had we been subjected to such a trial!

Conclusion:

1. *Great honours involve great obligations.*

2. *A man may fail even in the strongest point of his character.* Moses was pre-eminently meek, yet here he is petulant, etc. Therefore, "Watch thou in all things," etc.

3. *It is the duty of men not to increase, but if possible to lessen the difficulties and trials of leadership.*

ILLUSTRATIONS.

(a) Up to the hour of his mysterious departure, he devoted himself to his people with an earnestness and an energy which no combination of words can express. For their sakes he gave up his own will, while in the fulfilling of the Infinite Will he made the most costly sacrifices, and suffered the severest penalties. His very first act on behalf of his oppressed nation was misunderstood and misinterpreted, and drove him into solitude and exile. Scarcely had the ambassador of Heaven, with the Divine credentials of his mission in his hands, left the presence of Pharaoh, where he had asserted the rights of his people to spiritual freedom and privilege, than they assailed him with the most bitter invective, and accused him of aggravating the evils under which they were doomed to suffer. Only a few hours had run their round since he had finished those stupendous deeds of might and mercy, which had resulted in setting them free—he had but just sundered the link of the chain which chafed and fettered their inmost soul, when the mere sight of the Egyptians following them in their flight, led them to chide their illustrious leader by charging him with subjecting them to a worse calamity than bondage, and to protest even that they would rather have found a grave in Egypt than fall into the hand of the enemy; and this in direct opposition to the assurance given them from on high, that their deliverance was part of the plan and purpose of Him who is of one mind, and to whose powers and resources there is no limit. No sooner had they passed through the Red Sea, whose waters they had seen to part and stand as a wall of adamant on either hand, in whose depth they had beheld the horse and the rider sink as a stone to the bottom, and on whose hither bank they had given voice and volume to their joy in a song of triumph and gratitude, than they murmured and repined, because the water which was offered to them in their thirst was neither so sweet nor so living as the current of the Nile, or as Goshen's springs and streams. Scarcely had the bitter been extracted from the waters of Marah; scarcely had they amid the solitude and the scantiness of the desert found themselves free to enjoy their rest and quiet—their recreation and refreshment—when their thoughts went back to Egypt, and their soul lusted after its provisions. Hence on reaching the wilderness of Sin, which lay between Elim and Sinai, and finding that they could not indulge their sensuous appetites as they did before their emancipation, they lost sight for the moment of the higher good involved in their deliverance, and charged Moses with the fixed design of bringing them into the wilderness to compass their death by hunger. How crushing to his big and generous heart must have been their complaint—"Would to God we had died by the hand of the Lord in the land of Egypt, when we sat by the flesh-pots, and when we did eat bread to the full"! Was it their dream that life is made up of bodily ease and fleshly indulgence? Had they no faith in the matchless Power which had so often travelled forth on their behalf, and whose mighty deeds had all been in their favour? Or were they resolved to break the heart of the Man who, in the spirit of the most self-denying love and devotedness, was prepared to give up all that he had—not excepting life itself—for their wider freedom and higher good?—*Robert Ferguson, LL.D.*

(*b*) If Moses is ever to be held as one of the greatest men of olden times, and of all times, then it must be confessed that no man ever paid a heavier penalty for his greatness. Never did human being stand so completely solitary and alone; never were motives and actions so misconstrued or misunderstood; never were noble and generous deeds so requited; never were charges and criminations so unfounded; never were labour and suffering so depreciated; never was heart so afflicted, or life so embittered, or death so isolated; and all this in the prosecution of an object which involved a nation's freedom and a world's weal. Though his soul was filled with one of Heaven's sublimest purposes, his heart was all but broken by the ingratitude and rebellion—the selfishness and the sensuousness of those whose cause he had made his own. So continued was the crucifixion of thought and feeling to which he was subject—such was the total immolation of self to which he was called, that his life was more than a martyr's death. His mental anguish threw all physical suffering into the distance, and the outward privation was as nothing in comparison with the inward affliction. But under the crushing pressure of all that was laid upon him, he still stood erect—manly in his attitude and heroic in his mien.—*Ibid.*

It is a gallant thing to fight with the free and the brave in defence of our country, our shrines, our hearthstones, and our fathers' sepulchres—action animates and prevents the spirit drooping; companions in arms, though they be few, invite us on: we fling fear, doubt, irresolution to the winds—and death is indifferent to us, for we know that glory decks the hero's bier if it does not bind his brow. But *to bear witness!*—

To bear witness! what a world of meaning is hidden in these few words: how many of the grandest elements of human nature it requires to mould a character like this. Every man values the honest hearty good word of his neighbours; and there are associations gathered round the heart of each of us which it is impossible to efface. To be estranged from those we have lived with and loved from infancy—to pass from under the shadow of the faith that has fostered us—to look upon old sights, old haunts, familiar scenes, and find they are but fiends to mock us with a memory of what once was—to see contempt and scorn assume the place where love was wont to reign—to know that the affections we prized more than life are changed to wormwood—to watch our tried and trusted friends deliberately range themselves in the foemen's ranks—to have the harrowing conviction burned in upon the soul that we must go on now alone—go along the path we have chosen, and forego all the pleasures on which we counted to render existence endurable—these, *these* things try the temper and the tone of spirit—these constitute a frightful and a fiery ordeal at which human nature shudders. And yet all this must frequently be undergone for the cause of truth. The alternative is a terrible one and many waver; but such have not the elements of real greatness in them, the qualities which constitute one who must bear witness. The world has its laws and customs, its usages and ordinances, and woe to the man who sets himself in opposition to these. The world has its idols, its creed, its rule of faith —woe to the man who rises and declares its worship blasphemy—its creed a falsehood— its rule of faith a damnable delusion. Woe! truly; but unutterable woe would it be if these men did not rise up ever and anon, to smite the lazy blood into the cheeks of humanity; to exorcise the demon that directs the rabid multitude; to breathe a holier feeling through a land defaced by blood and crime. They are the pioneers of freedom, the vanguard of the hosts of truth. And their fate is to be reviled and ridiculed—blasphemed and buffeted—tortured body and soul with all the ingenuity of cruelty. Well, so it is, and so it will be; they have counted the cost; their death-smile is the calm of conquest; and—

"They flee far
To a sunnier strand;
And follow Love's folding star
To the evening land."—*J. W. Lester, D.D.*

The Sufferings of the Good in the Path of Duty.

(*Verse* 11.)

"And Moses said unto the Lord, Wherefore hast Thou afflicted Thy servant?" Keil and Del. translate, "Why hast Thou done evil to Thy servant?"

We propose to look at *the afflictions of godly men in the path of duty*—

I. As a Fact.

1. *Good men suffer afflictions.* Our text is the utterance of a distinguished servant of the Most High. "Moses was learned in all the wisdom of the Egyptians, and was mighty in words and in deeds;" he was a man of extraordinary abilities, and of extraordinary excellence—wise, meek, courageous, prayerful, self-denying, &c. One would have thought that such a man would have been unmolested by suffering, and free from affliction. But our thinking would have been erroneous; for out of sharp suffering Moses is here appealing to God. God's servants suffer. Job, David, Asaph, Jeremiah, John the Baptist, the Sisters of Bethany, the Apostles of Jesus Christ, were all sufferers; some of them very severe sufferers. The Lord Christ, the Supreme Servant of God, was the Supreme Sufferer.

2. *Good men suffer afflictions in the path of duty.* It does not seem strange when the storm pursues and overtakes a disobedient prophet trying to escape from duty (Jonah i.); but it does seem strange that it should overtake the disciples of our Lord while they are engaged in carrying out His commands (Mark iv. 35-39). So the afflictions of Moses arose in the fulfilment of the duty which God had appointed him. The same is true of Jeremiah, John the Baptist, the Apostles of Jesus Christ, and a great host of others in subsequent times. It is pre-eminently true of our Divine Lord. It is true of very many in our own age.

II. As a Problem.

"Wherefore hast Thou afflicted Thy servant?" This inquiry implies—

1. *A difficulty.* Moses could not understand why the Lord had called him to a task, involving so much annoyance and pain. He is the servant of the Lord, engaged in the work of the Lord, and that a most arduous work; yet he is crossed, opposed, reviled, and the affliction is allowed by God, unrelieved by God, indeed, for a time God appears not to heed either his sorely tried servant, or the rebellious and provoking people, over whom He had placed him. The painful obstructions which impede the course of the good, and the heavy burdens which oppress them, and the bitter enemies which assail them, and which are allowed by God, even while they tread the path of duty, are a source of sore perplexity to their mind and sharp pain to their heart. It is supremely difficult, in the time of trial, to discover how these things can be under the rule of a wise and kind and holy Being.

2. *Faith in the power of God to remove the difficulty.* "Wherefore hast Thou afflicted Thy servant?" "Why hast Thou done evil to Thy servant?" Clearly Moses believed that there were sufficient reasons for the sore trials which he met with while fulfilling his vocation; that these reasons were known unto the Lord; and that the revelation of them would relieve his perplexed brain and his troubled heart. When the tried servants of God appeal to Him as Moses did, we may regard their appeals as expressions of faith in Him, and as precursors of relief and rest from Him.

III. Offer some Hints towards the Solution of the Problem.

The afflictions of the good in the path of duty, under the blessing of God, tend—

1. *To test their faith.* "Character," says Dr. Huntington, "depends on inward strength. But this strength has two conditions: it is increased only by being put forth, and it is tested only by some resistance. So, if the spiritual force, or character, in you is to be strong, it must be measured against some competition. It must enter into conflict with an antagonist. It must stand in comparison with something formidable enough to be a standard of its power.... Suffering, then, in some of its forms, must be introduced, the appointed minister, the great assayist, to put the genuineness of faith to the proof, and purify it of its dross." (*a*)

2. *To promote their perfection.* "As

the Perfect One reached His perfectness through suffering," says Dr. Ferguson, "so it was with His servant. It was through the fire and the flame that the law of separation and refinement acted on the whole nature, and gave to it higher worth and glory. Trial ripened his manly spirit, and made it patient to endure.

'Useless and badly-tempered is the steel
If it refuse to bend; but the goodly blade—
The true Toledo—circleth on itself
Uninjured.'

He had learned to suffer as well as to do; and but for suffering, and his character, could never have reached that matchless height and perfection which belong to it." Comp. Acts xiv. 22; Rom. v. 3-5; James i. 2-4, 12. (b)

3. *To enhance their joy hereafter.* Comp. Matt. v. 10-12; Rom. viii. 17, 18; 2 Cor. iv. 17, 18. (c)

4. *To promote the good of the race.* In fulfilling the Divine calling, which caused him so much trial and suffering, Moses carried forward the purposes of God, and conferred unspeakable benefits on our race. By the travail and sorrow of the good, God is saving humanity from its sins and miseries. The Christian is called to "know the fellowship of Christ's sufferings;" to suffer vicariously with Him, that others may be benefited and blessed. In the privilege of this high fellowship, the sharpest sufferings become sacred and exalting services. (d)

Conclusion:
1. *Severe afflictions in the path of duty are in full accord with the character of God.*
2. *Such sufferings are quite compatible with the favour of God towards us.* Comp. Heb. xii. 5-11.
3. *When severe suffering leads to sore perplexity, let us seek help of God.* Comp. Psa. lxxiii. 16, 17.

ILLUSTRATIONS.

(a) Some time ago I heard a party of friends singing the same piece of music. For a while their voices blended very sweetly, and I, not being able to offer a scientific criticism upon the performance, thought that they were all about equal. But presently they came to a passage of very high notes, very lofty music: and in that moment they all ceased but *one*, and that one voice went aloft alone, and thrilled me by the perfectness of its ease! If they had stopped before that, I should have said, "I give you common applause; one is as good as another, and I thank you all." But there was a time of trial, and in that time of trial the masterly voice rose where other voices could not follow it. It is so in the greater concerns and trials of life. For days together we seem to be tolerably equal, but there come special hours, critical trials, and in those moments—which are condensed lifetimes—we show the stuff we are made of and the capacity we represent. It is *then* that the religious man—if deeply and truly intelligent and earnest—shows himself a man.—*Joseph Parker, D.D.*

(b) Tribulations are treasures; and if we were wise, we should reckon our afflictions among our rarest jewels. The caverns of sorrow are mines of diamonds. Our earthly possessions may be silver, but temporal trials are, to the saints, invariably gold. We may grow in grace through what we enjoy, but we probably make the greatest progress through what we suffer. Soft gales may be pleasant for heaven-bound vessels, but rough winds are better. The calm is our way, but God hath His way in the whirlwind, and He rides on the wings of the wind. Saints gain more by their losses than by their profits. Health cometh out of their sicknesses, and wealth floweth out of their poverties.—*C. H. Spurgeon.*

(c) The contrast between suffering on earth and its fruits in heaven, is wonderful. They ought to be kept constantly together, so that the darkness of the one shall be interpreted by the light of the other; that we shall not feel that sorrows have ended their course when aching ceases; that we shall not for a moment be left to believe that all the fruit of suffering is that which we pluck hitherward. We should know that sufferings produce their final results only after we are disembodied, and stand on the heavenly plain in the glorious fellowship of the redeemed. Then it will be made known to us that these and all of them came out of great tribulation, and washed their robes, and made them white in the blood of the Lamb, by the maintenance of their faith, by their endeavours to live according to God's commandments, by undergoing pain, and self-denial, and hardness as good soldiers; by accepting providential afflictions, by cleansing their dispositions and purifying their hearts, by suffering death itself. The marvellous economy of earthly suffering, rightly understood, is an economy of cleansing and beautifying. It is a lustration, and is preliminary to a state of glorification.—*H. W. Beecher.*

(d) We see no good done in this world that somebody does not suffer. There can be no education of children without there is somebody to suffer for them. A child with no mother or with no nurse, the mother having been taken away, or worse yet, with a mother or nurse that is heartless and inhuman, grows up so much less than a human being as it lacks the training which its helplessness demands. And if a child is sweet, and pure, and aspiring, and noble, somebody must have practised self-denial, or suffered for it; somebody must have agonised to save the child from agony; somebody's conscience must have been crucified that the child's conscience might be saved from the thorn. And wretched is the child that has had nobody to suffer for it, to think for it, to feel for it, to live for it—for substituted life is the law of the development of life. My soul is the yeast of my children's souls; and I mix my being into theirs, and theirs are raised and brought to vitality by it. And if there is to be a Bible that is true to life, there must be somewhere in that Bible a recognition of the Christian principle of vicarious suffering, the suffering of one for another. For it is in nature, it is in the household, it is in the Church, and it is in the whole realm of benevolence outside of the Church. And when we find the Bible teaching it, everybody says, "It ought to teach it, it is but the echo of fact."—*Ibid.*

THE ANSWER OF GOD TO THE APPEALS OF MEN.

(*Verses* 16-20.)

In these verses we have—

I. **The Lord's Answer to the Appeal of his much-tried Servant.**

"And the Lord said unto Moses, Gather unto me seventy men," &c. (verses 16, 17). The Lord here arranges to lighten the burden of which Moses had complained as too heavy for him, by appointing seventy elders who should bear the burden of the people with him. Notice—

1. *The number of these assistants.* "Gather unto me seventy men of the elders of Israel." The number seventy probably has a backward reference to the number of persons that went down into Egypt (Gen. xlvi. 26, 27). The same number of elders were called to accompany Moses to Mount Sinai (Exod. xxiv. 1); but their calling seems to have been for that one occasion only, while these were called to permanent service. This number was continued in the Sanhedrim, or great council of the Jews. And our Lord probably had reference to it when He appointed seventy disciples, and sent them forth as assistants to the apostles. But the point for us to seize concerning this number is, that it would afford adequate relief to Moses; the answer of the Lord to his appeal was sufficient and satisfactory.

2. *The selection of these assistants.* "And the Lord said unto Moses, Gather unto me seventy men of the elders of Israel, whom thou knowest to be," &c. The choice of the seventy was assigned to Moses. The people being so unstable and wayward were not fit to be entrusted with the choice. Moses was to select persons who were elders not merely in respect of years, but also in ability and character, and influence with the people for good. If Moses made the selection himself, he would have no ground for complaint afterwards.

3. *The qualification imparted to these assistants.* "And I will come down and talk with thee there: and I will take of the spirit which is upon thee," &c. This does not imply any diminution of the Divine grace and power to Moses. Unto them was to be granted a measure of the spirit which had been given in such great fulness to him; truth, wisdom, courage, piety, power, were to be bestowed upon them to fit them for their duties and responsibilities. "We do not find that Moses was less fit for government than he was before: rather his gifts were derived to others, as one candle lighteth another, and yet the light is not diminished." God never calls any one to the discharge of any duty without granting him ability for the same. When we are clear as to the Divine call we may be confident as to the Divine qualification.

Such was God's gracious answer to the appeal of Moses. That appeal was somewhat imperfect and faulty; it was impetuous, and, to a certain extent, expressive of discontent and passion; but it was the utterance of a true and noble spirit, of one whose zeal in the work assigned him by God was most ardent, and who was sublimely forgetful of self in his solicitude for the glory of God. So the Lord answers him by granting him relief.

II. **The Lord's Answer to the Appeal of His Perverse People.**

"And say thou unto the people, Sanctify yourselves against to-morrow," &c. This answer—

1. *Recognises the sinful character of their appeal.* "Ye have wept in the ears of the Lord, saying," &c. "Tears, of what sort soever, have a voice in them (Psa. xxxix. 12), as blood hath (Gen. iv. 10)." Their sin is manifest (1) In the lowness of their supreme desire. "Who shall give us flesh to eat?" Their highest and most eager longing was for the gratification of their animal appetites. (2) In their depreciation of the Divine blessings. "It was well with us in Egypt . . . Why came we forth out of Egypt?" Their emancipation from slavery with its cruelty and unutterable degradation, the provisions with which they were so bounteously supplied, the glorious inheritance which was promised to them, these things they disparaged as unworthy of comparison with the dainties of Egypt which they had sacrificed. They preferred cucumbers to freedom, &c. (3) In their contempt of the Divine Presence. "Ye have despised the Lord which is among you." The unbelief expressed in the enquiry, "Who will give us flesh to eat?" was a despising of the Lord. It was a questioning, if not a denial, of His power, and that after the extraordinary displays of His power which they had witnessed. God marks the feelings which find utterance in our cries to Him, or to His servants.

2. *Demands preparation for the granting of their appeal.* "Sanctify yourselves against to-morrow, and ye shall eat flesh." Keil and Del. explain " sanctify yourselves:" " to prepare themselves by purifications for the revelation of the glory of God in the miraculous gift of flesh." The interpretation of Fuerst is in substantial agreement with this. They had sinned grievously against God; and now they must prepare themselves by ablutions and by humbling of themselves, for the extraordinary manifestation of the Divine power.

3. *Promises the most abundant bestowment of that which they had so passionately and sinfully desired.* "The Lord will give you flesh, and ye shall eat. Ye shall not eat one day, nor two days, nor five days, neither ten days, nor twenty days; but even a month of days," &c. Inordinately they had craved flesh; generally and openly they had wept for it; and God determines to bestow it upon them in super-abundance. Their clamorous demand shall be granted; and the granting of it shall be their punishment. "He gave them their request; but sent leanness into their soul." No punishment can be more terrible than to grant the desires of a soul in which carnal appetites are supreme. Let our desires be subject in all things to the wise and gracious will of God. (*a*)

Conclusion. Mark well—

1. *The disgusting nature of the sins of gluttony and drunkenness.*

2. *The necessity of firmly controlling carnal desires.* Even those animal appetites which are lawful must be kept subordinate to higher things.

3. *The necessity of submissiveness in prayer.*

"We, ignorant of ourselves
Beg often our own harms, which the wise powers,
Deny us for our good; so find we profit,
By losing of our prayers."—*Shakespeare.*

Let us pray in the spirit of Him who in His most intense agony said, " Nevertheless, not My will, but Thine, be done."

ILLUSTRATIONS.

(a) Mr. Edmund Calamy relates, in his Life, that some persons of the name of Mart, in whose family he resided for some time, had a son who discovered the most wicked and impious disposition. When confined in prison, he wrote letters professing penitence; but as soon as he had an opportunity he returned to his former sins.

This young man had been the darling of both his father and mother; and the latter had set her affections upon him to so great a degree that when she saw him a monster of wickedness, she became deranged, and attempted to destroy herself, which she at length effected. So far from being suitably impressed with this awful event, her son now proceeded to greater lengths in wickedness. At length he professed to be sorry for his depraved course, and applied to the Rev. Samuel Pomfret to intercede for him with his father. He was made ready for sea, but, unhappily, became connected with a gang of villains, and, on the very night before he was to set sail, he robbed Mr. Pomfret, was pursued, tried, and condemned to die.

On the Sabbath preceding the Wednesday on which he was condemned to die, his father entreated Dr. Calamy to accompany him that evening to his cell in Newgate, to converse with his unhappy son, and to give his opinion as to the propriety of seeking to obtain his pardon. The doctor went, and found him in a very awful state of mind, resenting different things which he conceived his father had done wrong, and saying that he might obtain a pardon for him, if he would but part with some of his money. In vain did the doctor expostulate with him on the improper feelings he manifested, and entreat him to humble himself before God on account of his sins, as the only way of engaging his friends to obtain for him a reprieve. His reply was, "Sir, I scorn anything of that nature; and would rather die with my company." The doctor reasoned with him on the existence of a hereafter, charged him with the death of his mother, taxed him with the murder of some persons abroad, whose blood he had actually shed, and showed him the heavy punishment he must endure in an eternal world, unless he turned to God, repented of his sins, and prayed for pardon through the atonement of the Lord Jesus. He admitted the truth of all these things, but was filled with trifling unconcern. He frankly said that he had no hope of being better in his character, and that, on the contrary, he was satisfied he should grow worse. The next morning he was visited by Dr. Jekyl, who asked him whether, during the whole time he had been confined in Newgate, he had once bowed his knees to the great God, making it his earnest request to Him to give him a sense of his sins, and to create in him a tender heart; he admitted that he had not, nor did he think it of any use. He was promised that if he would agree to pray morning and evening for the grace of God, an effort should be made with every probability of success, for a reprieve, and subsequently a pardon. But he would make no engagement, and was hung on the day appointed.

On the day of his execution, the father of this unhappy young man told Dr. Calamy that when the culprit was a very young child, he was exceedingly ill with a fever, and that both his wife and himself, thinking their lives were bound up in the life of the child, were exceedingly importunate with God in prayer that his life might be spared. A pious mother expostulated with him on the vehemence he manifested, and said she dreaded the consequence of his praying in such a way, and that it became him to leave the matter to an infinitely wise God. At length the father said, "Let him prove what he will, so he is but spared, I shall be satisfied." The old man added, "This I now see to have been my folly. For, through the just hand of God, I have lived to see this wretched son of mine a heart-breaking cross to them that loved him with the greatest tenderness, a disgrace to my whole family, and likely to bring my grey hairs with sorrow to my grave. I read my sin very distinctly in my punishment; but must own that God is righteous in all His ways, and holy in all His works."—*R. Arvine, A.M.*

It is of great importance that we should entreat the Spirit of God to enable us to pray as we ought. It is quite possible to ask for what may appear to us good things, but which, if we had them, would prove evil. Rachel, indulging a petulant disposition, said, "Give me children, or I die;" her desire was granted, and as the result, she died.

The late Mr. Kilpin, of Exeter, writes, "I knew a case in which the minister, praying over a child, apparently dying, said: 'If it be Thy will, spare —' The poor mother's soul yearning for her beloved, exclaimed: 'It must be His will! I cannot bear *ifs*.' The minister stopped. To the surprise of many the child recovered; and the mother, after almost suffering martyrdom by him while a stripling, lived to see him hanged before he was two-and-twenty! Oh, it is good to say, 'Not my will, but Thine be done.'"—*Ibid.*

The Unbelief of Good Men, and its Divine Antidote.

(*Verses* 21-23.)

This incident in the history leads us to consider—

I. **The proneness of even the best of men to unbelief.**

When we think of the character of Moses, and the experiences of his past life, it seems almost incredible that he should "stagger at the promise of God through unbelief." He was one of the great heroes of faith (Heb. xi. 24-28); he had witnessed the most marvellous manifestations of the Divine power; he had himself been the instrument of some of its most extraordinary achievements; yet for a little time his faith in the promise and power of God fails. The error of Moses consisted in his arraying the conclusions of human reason against the promise of God. (*a*) To his judgment the thing promised seemed impossible. Moses considered (1) The number to be supplied. "And Moses said, The people among whom I am are six hundred thousand footmen." The whole population could not have been less than two millions, and was probably more numerous. (2) The time for which the supply was to be continued. "And Thou hast said, I will give them flesh, that they may eat a whole month." (3) The inadequacy of their resources. "Shall the flocks and the herds be slain for them to suffice them? or shall all the fish of the sea be gathered together for them, to suffice them?" Of the flocks and herds some were needed for the sacrifices, and some would be required when they settled in the Promised Land. The result of the consideration of the case by Moses was, that he could not see how the promise could be fulfilled; and not seeing this, he failed to believe the promise. Even the most distinguished servants of the Lord amongst men have their infirmities. (*b*) "We need not to labour too curiously," says Attersoll, "to clear the faithful of the remnants of sin and other infirmities, forasmuch as he and other the best of God's servants have their failings in faith and obedience, as we see in the examples of Abraham, Lot, Noah, Isaac, Jacob, David, Peter, Thomas, Zacharias, and which of them not? (2 Chron. xv. 17; xvi. 12; Rom. vii. 17-19) because we know in part, and we prophesy in part; we are yet in our journey, and walk in our way, and run in a race, we are not yet attained to our journey's end, we have not yet obtained the crown. Again, we proceed all from an unclean fountain (Job xiv. 4). There is a combat remaining in us between the flesh and the Spirit (Rom. vii. 23; Gal. v. 17), and these are contrary the one to the other, and can never be reconciled." Two inferences should be heeded:—

1. *The most eminent saints continually need the grace of God.* "Hold Thou me up, and I shall be safe," is an appropriate aspiration for even the holiest of men. And this, too, "Lord, increase our faith."

2. *It behoves us to be slow to censure men.* We should rather take heed to ourselves, that we fail not.

> "Search thine own heart. What paineth thee
> In others, in thyself may be;
> All dust is frail, all flesh is weak;
> Be thou the true man thou dost seek."
> *Whittier.*

II. **The Divine Antidote for unbelief in the good.**

1. *Consideration of the past deeds of the Lord.* "And the Lord said unto Moses, Is the Lord's hand waxed short?" What He has done is an example of what, under similar circumstances and conditions, we may expect Him to do again. "The power that is *unlimited* can never be *diminished.*" Faith argues from the past to the present and the future. David did so, with the grandest results (1 Sam. xvii. 34-37; Psa. lxiii. 7). So also did Paul (2 Cor. i. 8-10; 2 Tim. iv. 17, 18). (*c*).

2. *Consideration of the unchangeableness of the Lord.* "Is the Lord's hand waxed short?" "With whom is no variableness, neither shadow of turning." He is "the same yesterday, and to-day, and for ever." "Thou art the same, and Thy years shall have no end." "I am the Lord, I change not." The consideration of the immutability of God should inspire confidence in His promises.

3. *Consideration of the faithfulness of God.* "Thou shalt see now whether My word shall come to pass unto thee or not." "God is not a man, that He should lie; neither the son of man, that He should repent: hath He said, and shall He not do? or hath He spoken, and shall He not make it good?" "Heaven and earth shall pass away, but My words shall not pass away." Here, then, in the consideration of these great themes is Heaven's antidote for the proneness to unbelief in godly men.

Conclusion:

The subject suggests the inspiring fact that *history is an argument for faith in God of ever-increasing power.* Incalculably greater to-day than when it was addressed to Moses is the force of the Divine demand, "Is the Lord's hand waxed short?" as a rebuke of unbelief and an encouragement of faith.

ILLUSTRATIONS.

(*a*) I like to reason; I like to search out results from causes; but it is sweet also, in the midst of the turmoils and troubles of life, to rest in faith in God. It is sweet to be able to say, "I do not care for to-morrow. I do not fear what shall befall me. I will trust in God." To understand the philosophy of a Divine command, where I can, affords me satisfaction; but where a command comes from such an authority, and with such variety of illustration in nature, I do not care whether I understand the philosophy of it or not. My soul is hungry for it, and I accept it because my God has given it. I trust and rest in God simply because He has said, "You may, and you must." That is ground enough.—*H. W. Beecher.*

(*b*) All these four reflective men are in some way *unbelievers.* Nathanael cultivates inward piety, but *he cannot believe* that the holy heaven and the common world shall ever be one, as if angels came and went between them. Matthew earnestly desires, and promotes as he can, the rule of justice among men; but *he cannot believe* that the law of Truth will ever be the law of outward religious and political society. Philip is a student of the Scriptures, and can see much of the God of Israel in them and in the world, but not enough anywhere; and *he cannot believe* that God will show Himself to man so as thoroughly to content the pious as the world seems to satisfy the worldly. Thomas has chosen the "better part;" he is determined to know the truth and not to trust to deceits. He, for one, will examine the pretensions and the evidences of things. He *has* examined, and is quite convinced that Jesus has no mere pretensions. Jesus, at least, is a real man, if there be no other and never should be. And yet Thomas *cannot believe* that "the way" Jesus takes is a safe successful way. Excellent men these four! reflective men; yet all in some degree, each in his own manner, unbelievers!—*Thomas T. Lynch.*

(*c*) Is God all-mighty? Then have no fears about the realization of His promises. Oftentimes it is difficult to see how certain promises are to be realized. We have nothing to do with that whatever. God keeps our hands off His promises quite as surely as He keeps them off His stars, and if He won't let us intermeddle with His planets, and do our little scrubbing and burnishing upon those great lights, He will not ask us to have anything to do with the outworking and realization of His promises. He asks that their fulfilment be left to Him, and afterwards he will challenge our own life as the witness, and answer, and confirmation of all that is gracious and all that is sure in the outworking of His words of promise.—*Joseph Parker, D.D.*

THE GLORIOUS RIGHT HAND OF THE LORD.

(*Verse 23.*)

For Introduction see the Illustrations. (*a*)

I shall try to mention some four or five cases in which men act as if they really believed that God's hand had waxed short.

I. With regard to the Church as a whole, how often is it true that she so behaveth herself as if she had a question in her mind as to whether the Lord's hand had waxed short?

She believes that the Divine hand was once mighty enough to bring in three thousand in one day by the simple preaching of Peter. She believes that her God was with her in olden times so mightily that her poor illiterate preachers were more than a match for the scholars of Socrates and Solon, and were able to overturn the gods of the heathen, though they had both poetry and philosophy to be their bulwarks. She believes all this, and yet how often doth she act as though the Gospel had become effete and outworn, and the Spirit of God had been utterly withdrawn from her! . . . The doubts, the fears, the calculations, the policies, the judicious advices of too many Christians prove my point, that often the Church acts as if she thought the Lord's hand were waxed short. O Zion! get thee up! Come thou forth in simple confidence in His promise, and thou shalt see whether He will not do according to His Word.

II. **When believers doubt their God with regard to Providence**, the question might well be asked of them, "Is the Lord's hand waxed short?"

Some have had many losses and crosses in their business. Instead of getting forward, they are going back, and perhaps even bankruptcy stares them in the face. Or possibly, being hard-working men, they may have been long out of employment, and nothing seems to be before their eyes but the starvation of themselves and their little ones. It is hard to bear this . . . But dost thou doubt, O believer, as to whether God will fulfil His promise, wherein He said, "His place of defence"? &c (Isa. xxxiii. 16). Wouldst thou question the advice of thy Master: "Therefore take no thought"? &c. (Matt. vi. 25-32). When not a sparrow falls to the ground without your Father, and the very hairs of your head are all numbered, yet you must mistrust and doubt Him! (*b*)

III. This question might be very naturally suggested **when a man who has faith in Christ is exercised with doubts and fears with regard to his own final perseverance or his own present acceptance in Christ.**

Doubt not, I pray you; believe your God, and you shall prosper. The joy of the Lord is our strength, not the melancholy of our hearts.

IV. "Is the Lord's hand waxed short?" is a question which I may well ask of any who are **convinced of sin**, but are afraid to trust their souls now, at this very hour, in the hand of a loving Saviour.

"Oh, He cannot save me, I am so guilty, so callous! Could I repent as I ought, could I but feel as I ought, then He could save me; but I am naked, and poor, and miserable. I have grieved away His Spirit; I have sinned against light and knowledge—against mercy—against constant grace received. He cannot save me." "Is the Lord's hand waxed short?" Did He not save the chief of sinners, Saul of Tarsus? Why, then, can he not save you? Is it not written, "The blood of Jesus Christ His Son, cleanseth us from all sin?" Has that blood lost its efficacy? Wouldst thou add to thy sin? Then doubt Christ's power to save thee. But wouldst thou be saved? Then dare, in the teeth of all thy sins, to trust my Master.

"He is able,
He is willing: doubt no more."

He is able, for He is God. He is willing, for He that died for us cannot be unwilling. Christ did not make any exception; He said, "*Him that cometh,*" and that means any "him" in all the world who comes. Come, then, I pray thee: trust Him, &c.

V. You say, do you, that God will not avenge your sins upon you, that ye may go on in your iniquities, and yet meet with no punishment; that ye may reject Christ, and do it safely; trample on His blood, and yet God is so calm, that His anger will never flame forth against you? Well, soul, "thou shalt see whether His word shall come to pass or not." But let me tell thee His hand is not waxed short; He is as strong to punish as when He bade the floods cover the earth; as powerful to avenge as when He rained hail out of heaven upon the cities of the plain. Thou shalt see whether He will keep His word or not.—*C. H. Spurgeon.*

ILLUSTRATIONS.

(*a*) It is a singular thing that such a question as this should ever be asked at all: "Is the Lord's hand waxed short?" If we look anywhere and everywhere, apart from the conduct of man, there is nothing to suggest the suspicion. Look at God's *creation!* Is there anything there which would make you say, "Is the Lord's hand waxed short?" What pillar of the heavens hath begun to reel? What curtain of the sky hath been rent or moth-eaten? Have the foundations of the earth begun to start? Do they not abide as the Lord hath settled them? Hath the sun grown dim with age? or have the starry lamps flickered or gone out in darkness? Are there signs of decay to-day upon the face of God's creation? Have not howling tempests, the yawning ocean, and death-bearing hurricanes, asserted but yesterday their undiminished might? Say, is not the green earth as full of vitality, as ready to yield us harvests now, as it ever hath been? Do the showers fall less frequently? Hath the sun ceased to warm? Are there any signs and tokens that God's creation is tottering to its decay? No, journey where you will, you will see God is potent upon the face of the earth, and in the very bowels of the globe, as He was when He first said, "Let there be light, and there was light." There is nothing which would tempt us to the surmise or the suspicion that the Lord's hand hath waxed short. And look ye too in *Providence;* is there aught there that would suggest the question? Are not His prophecies still fulfilled? Doth He not cause all things to work together for good? Do the cattle on a thousand hills low out to Him for hunger? Do you meet with the skeletons of birds that have fallen to the ground from famine? Doth He neglect to give to the fish their food, or do the sea-monsters die? Doth not God still open His hand and supply the want of every living thing? Is He less bounteous to-day than He was in the time of Adam? Is not His cornucopia still as full? Doth He not still scatter mercies with both His hands right lavishly? Are there any tokens in Providence any more than in Nature, that God's arm hath waxed short? And look ye too in the matter of *Grace*: is there any token in the work of grace that God's power is failing? Are not sinners still saved? Are not profligates still reclaimed? Are not drunkards still uplifted from their sties to sit upon the throne with princes? Are not harlots as truly reclaimed as were those in the days of Christ? Is not the Word of God still quick and powerful, sharper than any two-edged sword? Which of His arrows hath been blunted? Where have ye seen the sword of the Lord snapped in twain? When hath God assayed to melt a heart and failed in the attempt? Which of His people has found the riches of His grace drained dry? Which of His children has had to mourn that the unsearchable riches of Christ had failed to supply his need? In Grace, as well as in Providence and Nature, the unanimous verdict is that God is still Almighty, that He doeth as He wills, and fulfilleth all His promises and His counsels. How is it, then, that such a question as this ever came from the lips of God Himself? Who suggested it? What suggested it? What could there have been that should lead Him or any of His creatures to say, "Is the Lord's hand waxed short?" We answer, there is but one creature that God has made that ever doubts Him. . . . . It was left for *man*, the most favoured of all creatures, to mistrust his God.—*C. H Spurgeon.*

(*b*) And now, O true believer, what sayest thou to this picture? In the cold, cold winter, when the snows have fallen thick on every tree, and the ground is hard and crisp, ye have sometimes seen the charitable man open wide the window of his house, and scatter crumbs along the white snow, and ye have seen the birds come from all the trees around, and there they ate and were satisfied. A slanderer who lives next door tells you that that man starves his children. Do you believe him? Feed the sparrows and neglect the offspring of his loins—give crumbs to birds, and not feed his sons and daughters? You feel instinctively that the kind heart which remembers the fowls of heaven must yet more remember his own offspring. But what sayest thou to this picture concerning thyself? Thy God heareth the young ravens when they cry, and giveth liberally to all the creatures that His hands hath made, and will He forget His sons and His daughters—His people bought with blood, His own peculiar heritage? No; dare to believe Him *now*. His hand has not waxed short. Dare to trust Him *now*.—*Ibid.*

The Question Concerning the Lord's Hand.

(*Verse* 23.)

"Is the Lord's hand waxed short?" Let us apply this question—

I. **To the Subject of Creative Manifestations.** We are in the midst of a marvellous universe. Full of the wisdom and power of God. Now, some suppose Creation was finished, as related in Genesis. But that relates to this world only. Creation glorifies God. He can continue to create, &c. He may do so for His own glory. Myriads of worlds may rise in magnificent succession. Worlds now get old, may decay, and fall into ruin; and He may supply their place. As in the revivifications of the seasons. New harvests, new forms, &c.

II. **To Divine Providences for His Church and People.**

1. *The Preservation of His Church.* Its extension, prosperity, glory.

2. *The destruction to the enemies of the Church.* In the past He did it. Egypt, Babylon, &c.

3. *The good of His individual servants.* He can keep, deliver, bless. However dark, &c. Overrule; turn crosses into blessings, &c.

III. **To the Salvation of the most guilty and obstinate sinners.**

1. *Cannot His hand reach them in the lowest pit of guilt?*

2. *Break the heart of the flinty rock?*

3. *Humble and save the proudest and worst?* Manasseh, the thief, Saul, the Corinthians. We need despair of none.

IV. **To the fulfilment of the Divine prophecies and promises.**

1. *The glory of the Lord filling the earth.* Psa. lxxii. 17-19.

2. *The spread of universal holiness.*

3. *Universal worship.* Psa. lxvii.

4. *The salvation of the world to Christ.* Phil. ii. 9-11. The world filled with righteousness, peace, and blessedness. The discouragements may be great and numerous; but the text answers them all.

Application.

1. *The text should lead us to Divine reliance.* Trust in the Lord, &c. This will cheer and strengthen us.

2. *To joyous hope.* No need of doubts and fears.

3. *To more earnest effort.*

4. *To profound humility.* God's hand alone can do His work.—*Jabez Burns, D.D.*

Helpful Thoughts for the Lord's Servants.

(*Verses* 24-30.)

This section of the history presents several topics on which we may meditate with advantage:

I. **The Obedience of Moses, an example for the Lord's Servants.**

"And Moses went out, and told the people," &c. (verse 24). Very recently Moses had doubted the word of the Lord, and questioned His ability to fulfil His promises; but now he obeys His commands, trusting in Him to fulfil His promises. Doubt is not the normal state of a good man, but an exceptional thing in his life. It is ours, not to question the Lord concerning the reason of His commands, or the way in which He will fulfil His promises; but trusting His promises, we should obey His commands. Faith and duty are ours; reasons and results are God's.

II. **The Bestowment of the Spirit upon the seventy Elders, Encouragement for the Lord's Servants.**

"And the Lord came down in a cloud, and spake unto him, and took of the Spirit that was upon him, and gave unto the seventy elders." Notice:—

1. *The Lord's care of His servants.* By granting to him the aid of these elders, He relieves Moses of the op-

pression of the burden of which he had complained. When the duties and responsibilities of His servants become too heavy, He lightens them either by diminishing their burdens, or by increasing their strength. He is a gracious Master, &c.

2. *The Lord's qualification of His servants.* When the elders were assembled about the tabernacle, the cloud of the Divine Presence, which had soared on high above it, came down, and the Lord spake unto Moses, and gave of His Spirit to the seventy elders (See notes on ver. 17). Those whom God calls to duty He also qualifies for it.

3. *The Lord's authentication of His servants.* "And it came to pass, when the spirit rested upon them, they prophesied, and did not add. But there remained two," &c. Under the impulse and inspiration of the Spirit of God they spoke to the people with such "admirable clearness and fulness, and readiness, and aptness of expression," and wisdom, that all who heard them were convinced that God was with them. By this sign the Lord accredited them to their office; this was their credential to the people, the Divine warrant for the exercise of their calling. God still authenticates His servants. In the holiness of their lives, in their qualifications for their work, and in the usefulness of their work, we mark the Divine credentials of the servants of the Lord.

III. **The error of Joshua, Admonition to the Lord's Servants.**

Two of the persons who were called to the eldership did not go up to the tabernacle, but remained in the camp; and the Spirit came upon them there, and they prophesied. This caused some excitement, and a boy went and told the matter to Moses. "And Joshua the son of Nun, the servant of Moses, one of his young men, answered and said, My lord Moses, forbid them." The prophesying of Eldad and Medad seemed to him an irregular and unauthorised thing. They were not in the company of the others; they had not received the gift through the mediation of Moses; and Joshua fears that if they are not restrained, the honour and authority of Moses will be diminished. So he proposes to Moses to prohibit it. I discover no sufficient reason for supposing that Joshua was jealous of this prophesying on his own account. He was rather jealous for the honour of Moses, as the disciples of John the Baptist were for the honour of their Master (John iii. 26). Still the counsel of Joshua was unwise and rash. Let us take warning from his mistake. The Spirit of God is not limited by our poor notions and narrow parties. The streams of Divine influence are much too plenteous to be confined in the strait and shallow channels which we have scooped out for them. The true way of regarding new and seemingly irregular manifestations of religious feeling and effort is indicated by Jesus Christ in Mark ix. 38-40, and by the Apostle Paul in Phil. i. 14-18. *(a)*

IV. **The Magnanimity of Moses, an Example for the Lord's Servants.**

"And Moses said unto him, Enviest thou for my sake? would God that," &c. So far from being displeased with Eldad and Medad, Moses, who sought not his own honour, but the glory of God, rejoiced in the gifts bestowed upon them, and "gave expressions to the large-hearted wish, that the whole people of the Lord might prophesy. And most assuredly there can be no such thing now, under the grace of the New Testament, which works at large and unconstrained, as a confining of the Spirit of the Lord to this or to that place, to the communion of this or of that party. The Spirit bloweth where He listeth; where is the man who will or can hinder Him? Whenever devils are cast out there is the Spirit of God (Matt. xii. 27, 28); wherever the name of Jesus is confessed, the confessor of that name is accepted before God, whether he stand in our roll or not." —*Stier.* *(b)*

ILLUSTRATIONS.

(*a*) I do dislike narrow churches, I do dislike little, *little* self-enclosing, self-subsisting clubs of so-called Christian professors. I find nothing narrow in Christianity. I find Christianity the broadest system, either of religion or of thought, or of philanthropy, that I can find in the world. If there are persons that wrap their sectarian garments about them, and say, "We are the people of God, and there is no other people that belong to Him," then are they liars, and the truth is not in them. Little people that live in a nutshell, which they mistake for the universe, that have their own little Bethel, and their own little hymn book, and their own little sectarian movements, and their own little heaven, I do not know anything about them, except that, having heard about them, I do not wish to prosecute inquiry further. If there are such people—no, I would alter that grammar, and say if there *be* such people, hoping that their existence is quite contingent and future—if there be such people they know nothing about the Divine, catholic, universal liberty of Jesus Christ's teaching. I trust that we all belong to the Broad Church, that we hail a brother, whatever be the temporary name by which he is known in ecclesiastical life; and that we allow heart to speak to heart, and know something of the intercourse of brotherly unity in Christ Jesus.—*Joseph Parker, D.D.*

(*b*) If ever you can say a good word of a fellow-minister, I charge it upon your honour to say it, and if you *cannot* speak a good word you *need* not speak a bad one. Don't set up your own style of preaching as the standard by which to try the preaching of all other men. Try (hard lesson!) to be thankful for *another man's success*. When you can heartily thank God for another minister's prosperity (*and that minister in your own neighbourhood*), you will have taken an eminent position in the temple of Christian magnanimity. It is easy to thank God for the success of a man who is fifty miles distant from your own ministerial orbit; but to give thanks for the success of a man who preaches within an hour's walk of your own pulpit, *that* is what I mean by *magnanimity*. Men who do not profess Christianity, are not expected to conform to its requirements, but surely its expounders and defenders should merge their little selfishness in the all-absorbing importance of winning the world back to filial love and reverent loyalty.—*Ibid.*

The truth is, that it is natural to all of us to envy the growing reputation of others; and to be jealous where it seems likely to trench upon our own. We may speak very justly of the littleness of mind which is displayed by the envious and the jealous; nevertheless, this littleness of mind belongs naturally to most, if not all of us. And he wins a fine triumph, or displays great command over himself, who can be content with inferiority, provided the cause of God and truth be advanced. Now, this is precisely the case in which both Moses and John showed greatness of soul. And though it be one in which we have most reason to look for a forgetfulness of self, experience shows that the expectation is but too often disappointed. In other cases we can hardly wonder that men should be mortified by the superiority of their rivals; that is, look with dislike and bitterness on those who eclipse them in the respects in which they most wish to shine. The courtier, for example, who has long sought to stand high in the favour of his sovereign; and who perceives that a younger candidate, who has just entered the field, is fast outstripping him, so that the probability is that he will soon be widely distanced,—we cannot marvel if he regard the youthful competitor with irritated feelings in place of generously rejoicing in his rapid success. It would be a very fine instance of magnanimity if this courtier were to cede gracefully the place to his rival, and offer him, with marks of sincerity which could not be mistaken, his congratulations on having passed him in the race. But we could not look for such magnanimity. The occasion, if we may venture to say so, scarcely warrants it; the whole business is of so worldly, so ignoble a character, that the high principles of religion can scarcely be supposed to be brought into exercise; yet the loftiness of spirit is such as that these principles alone can be considered adequate to produce or effect. The case, however, is widely different when it is in the service of God, and not of an earthly king, that the two men engage. Here by the very nature of the service, the grand thing aimed at is the glory of God and not personal distinction or aggrandisement; and there is, therefore, ground for expecting that if God's glory be promoted, there will be gladness of heart in all Christians, whoever the agent who has been specially honoured. But, alas! for the infirmity of human nature; there is room for questioning that even Christians can be jealous of each other, and feel it a sore trial when they are distanced and eclipsed in being instrumental in promoting Christianity. I can imagine to myself a missionary settlement, where a devoted servant of God has striven many years with idolatry, but has made but little way in winning heathens to the faith. Here and there he can point to a convert from superstition, but, for the most part, he seems to have laboured in vain; and is forced to exclaim with the prophet, "Who hath believed our report, and to whom hath the arm of the Lord been revealed?" And then there arrives in that missionary settlement, another and a younger preacher of truth, and God has endowed him with higher powers, and honours him with greater success, so that there is a rapid demolition of the whole system of heathenism—savages renouncing by hordes ancestral superstitions; forming themselves into peaceful communities, and embracing, with delight, the Religion of Jesus Christ. It is very easy to say that the elder missionary ought to feel nothing but exultation and thankfulness, as he witnesses the glorious results which follows the labours of youth. The object that he had nearest his heart was the conversion of Pagans; what should he do but rejoice in the accomplishment of his object, though effected through the instrumentality of another? And we do not say that the elder missionary would have other feelings than those which he is bound by his profession to entertain; nevertheless, there will have been a great deal to try that missionary, and we can hardly doubt—for as much as his having been a Christian will not have destroyed his being a man—that his breast must have been the scene of no inconsiderable struggle; that there must have been earnest prayer, and earnest resistance to natural feelings, ere he could bring himself to survey, with composure, the distinguished honours which God is putting on another. We are far enough from regarding it as a matter of course, that a veteran in the missionary work would feel contented and pleased at seeing that work which had gone on so slowly with himself, progress with amazing rapidity when undertaken by a younger labourer; on the contrary, arguing from the known tendencies of our nature, we assume that he must have had a hard battle with himself before he could really rejoice in the sudden advance of Christianity; and we should regard him as having won, through the assistance of Divine grace, a noble victory over some of the strongest cravings of the heart when he frankly bid the stripling God speed! and rejoiced as he saw the idols fall prostrate before him.

Here you have very nearly the case of Moses and John.—*Henry Melville, B.D.*

Envy.

(*Verse 29.*)

"And Moses said unto him, Enviest thou for my sake?"

To envy is "to grieve at another's good; to fret or hate another on account of his superiority." Envy "is an affection," says Attersoll, "compounded of sorrow and malice. For such persons are malicious, always repining and grudging at the gifts of God bestowed upon others, and as it were look asquint at them, as Gen. xxvi. 12, 13, 14, 27; xxx. 1; xxxi. 1; Mark ix. 38; John iii. 26, 27."

"Envy," says Jeremy Collier, "is an ill-natured vice, and is made up of meanness and malice. It wishes the force of goodness to be strained, and the measure of happiness abated. It laments over prosperity, and sickens at the sight of health. It oftentimes wants spirit as well as good nature." (*a*)

Concerning this vice we call attention to three facts:—

I. It is sadly common.

It is almost invariably present and active in mean souls; and it has been discovered in souls which in other respects were noble. Here it is in Joshua, a man of brave and beautiful character. True, he was not envious on his own account; but he was for the sake of his master. Great men are not free from littlenesses. Strong men are generally weak in some point. Good men, on earth, are not without their imperfections, and are liable to fall into sin. Even excellencies, if not properly regulated, like Joshua's zeal for the honour of Moses, may lead to error and sin. Wherefore it behoves us to be on our guard against envy. Endeavour to rejoice in the prosperity of others, &c. (*b*)

II. It is extremely foolish.

"Envy," says Attersoll, "is a very torment to the envious, who envying at others, do plague and punish themselves. For as envy hurteth not him at all that is envied, so the envious man carrieth about within his own bosom an inward and home-bred tormentor that never suffereth him to be quiet. Such a monster is spite and envy, that if he see, or hear, or think another to have more or as much, to go beyond him or be equal unto him, it is a quotidian, nay, a continual fever without any intermission, it paineth him day and night (Psa. cxii. 9, 10)." "Every other sin," says Burton, "hath some pleasure annexed to it, or will admit of some excuse; but envy wants both: we should strive against it, for if indulged in, it will be to us a foretaste of hell upon earth." "Envy," says Solomon, "is the rottenness of the bones." (c)

III. **It is heinously sinful.**

The sin of Joshua, in envying for Moses' sake, because of the exercise of the prophetic gift by Eldad and Medad, is seen in that—

1. *The gift was bestowed by God.* He bestoweth His gifts as it pleaseth Him; and to envy those who receive them is to call into question His wisdom or righteousness in bestowing them. Comp. Matt. xx. 15. Many of the things which excite envy in our day are gifts of God.

2. *The gift was for the benefit of all the people.* The eldership of Eldad and Medad was for the good of all Israel, and by this gift of prophecy the Lord accredited them to their office in the eyes of the people. The spiritual gifts of every Christian are for the advantage of the entire Church. How sinful then to envy them their possession!

3. *Joshua's envy was a violation of the law of brotherly kindness.* To envy is always to outrage Christian charity. "Charity envieth not." Mark the evil features of this vice as it is pourtrayed by Socrates: "An envious man waxeth lean with the fatness of his neighbours. Envy is the daughter of pride, the author of murder and revenge, the beginner of secret sedition, and the perpetual tormentor of virtue. Envy is the filthy slime of the soul; a venom, a poison, or quicksilver which consumeth the flesh, and drieth up the marrow of the bones." How much more loathsome should it appear to us, who should view it in the light of the teaching and spirit of Jesus Christ!

Conclusion:
1. *Cultivate Christian contentment.*
2. *"Follow after charity."*
3. *Rejoice in the gifts of God in whomsoever we discover them.*

ILLUSTRATIONS.

(a) In some unlucky dispositions, there is such an envious kind of pride, that they cannot endure that any but themselves should be set forth for excellent; so when they hear one justly praised, they will either seek to discount his virtues, or, if they be like a clear night, eminent, they will stab him with a *but* of detraction, as if there were something yet so foul, as did obnubilate even his brightest glory. Thus when their tongue cannot justly condemn him, they will leave him in suspected ill, by silence. Surely, if we considered detraction to be bred of envy, nested only in deficient minds, we should find that the applauding of virtue would win us far more honour than the seeking slyly to disparage it. That would show we loved what we commended, while this tells the world we grudge at what we want in ourselves.—*Feltham.*

We shall find it in Cain, the proto-murderer, who slew his brother at the instigation of envy. We shall find it in the dark and gloomy and revengeful spirit of Saul, who, under the influence of envy, plotted for years the slaughter of David. We shall find it in the King of Israel, when he pined for the vineyard of Naboth, and shed his blood to gain it. Yea, it was envy that perpetrated that most atrocious crime ever planned in hell or executed on earth, on which the sun refused to look, and at which Nature gave signs of abhorrence by the rending of the rocks: I mean the crucifixion of Christ; for the evangelist tells us, that for envy, the Jews delivered our Lord.—*J. A. James.*

(b) Envy is a weed that grows in all soils and climates, and is no less luxuriant in the country than in the court; is not confined to any rank of men or extent of fortune, but rages in the breasts of all degrees, Alexander was not prouder than Diogenes; and it may be, if we would endeavour to surprise it in its most gaudy dress and attire, and in the exercise of its full empire and tyranny, we should find it in schoolmasters and scholars, or in some country lady, or the knight, her husband; all which ranks of people more despise their neighbours than all the degrees of honour in which courts abound; and it rages as much in a sordid affected dress as in all the silks and embroideries which the excess of the age and the folly of youth delight to be adorned with. Since then it keeps all sorts of company, and wriggles itself into the liking of the most contrary natures and dispositions, and yet carries so much poison and venom with it, that it alienates the affections from heaven, and raises rebellion against God Himself; it is worth our utmost care to watch it in all its disguises and approaches, that we may discover it on its first entrance, and dislodge it before it procures a shelter or retiring place to lodge and conceal itself.—*Lord Clarendon.*

(c)
Of all antagonists, most charity
I find in envious men, for they do
Sooner hurt themselves, than hurt or me or
Him that raised me up. An envious man is
Made of thoughts; to ruminate much doth
melt

The brain, and make the heart grow lean. Such men
As these, that in opposing, waste their proper
Strength; that sacrifice themselves in silly
Hope to butcher us; save revenge a labour;
And die to make experiment of wrath.
Sir. W. Davenant.

KIBROTH-HATTAAVAH: STRIKING ILLUSTRATIONS OF SOLEMN TRUTHS.

(*Verses* 31-35.)

In these verses we have illustrations of several important truths—

I. **The Sovereignty of God.**

"And there went forth a wind from the Lord, and brought quails," &c. This wind does not appear to have been an ordinary one, the simple effect of a natural cause. It was Divinely ordered for this special purpose. In this great quantity of quails, bestowed in accordance with the promise of the Lord, the Divine Hand is equally manifest. The wind and the quails are both illustrations of the power and dominion of the Lord. His sovereignty is universal. The mightiest and the meanest of creatures are subject unto Him. This fact should minister,—

1. *Encouragement to those who trust Him.* He can never want means or instruments to help them; He can make all things to promote their interests. He can use the ravens as the dispensers of His bounty, as He did for Elijah, &c.

2. *Warning to those who rebel against Him.* He can marshal all ranks of creatures, and all the forces of nature against you, if it please Him so to do. "Hast thou an arm like God?" "Who may stand in Thy sight when once Thou art angry?" "Kiss the Son, lest He be angry," &c.

II. **The eagerness with which men toil in the pursuit of temporal and material good.**

"And the people stood up all that day, and all night," &c. (verse 32). See with what zeal and diligence they gather and preserve the quails. They forego their ordinary sleep and rest, &c. It is an illustration of the way in which men pursue pleasure, and scheme and toil for money, &c. Tens of thousands to-day are as eager in the pursuit of the perishable things of earth and time as the Israelites were in gathering quails. And like the Israelites, many are laboriously accumulating what they will never live to enjoy. Death shall cut them down in the midst of their possessions, just as they are composing themselves to take their "ease, eat, drink, and be merry." How great is the contrast between the eagerness with which men pursue these earthly and temporal things and their lukewarmness and indolence as to the things which are eternal and divine! "Labour not for the meat which perisheth," &c. (John vi. 27); "Lay not up for yourselves treasures upon earth," &c. (Matt. vi. 19-21.) (*a*)

III. **The gratification of the desires of men resulting in their ruin.**

"And while the flesh was yet between their teeth, ere it was chewed," &c. (verse 33). Their passionate lust was gratified, and the gratification killed them.

"Heaven is most just, and of our pleasant vices
Makes instruments to scourge us."
Shakespeare.

The thing we have eagerly coveted often proves when attained—

1. *Unsatisfactory in possession.* The realization is a painful contrast to the anticipation; it disappoints us, it saddens us, &c. (*b*)

2. *The occasion of spiritual loss and harm.* Gratified appetites often lead to crushed aspirations; carnal luxuries to spiritual famine; temporal riches to eternal destitution, &c. (*c*)

IV. **A sin, which on its first commission was mercifully passed over, if repeated may call forth the judgment of God.**

They had murmured aforetime, and the Lord gave them quails, and did not punish them (Exod. xvi. 2-13). But now, after additional proofs of His power and goodness, they murmur again and more wickedly, and He sends them quails and smites them in anger. Persistence in wickedness must lead to perdition. (Prov. xxviii. 14; xxix. 1). "Relapses are desperate, where the sickness itself is not."

V. **The sins and punishments of one generation should be remembered as a warning to future generations.**

"And he called the name of that place Kibroth-Hattaavah; because there they buried the people that lusted." So Moses endeavours to perpetuate, as a warning to others, the memory of their sin, and the judgment of God which it called forth. Comp. 1 Cor. x. 5, 6.

ILLUSTRATIONS.

(*a*) Oh, what tears have strong men shed in this city, tears which fell not outside the cheek, these had been harmless; but they dropped within the soul, to scald and sear it with ever-abiding melancholy! That which cheered and comforted them, the gain of wealth, has gone, and the busy merchants have been ready for the lunatic asylum or for suicide. How these golden bellows will cease to blow when men come to die! Ah, how little will wealth stimulate the joys of the last moment! Fool, thou hast only bought thyself a marble tomb, and what is that to thy poor dust and ashes? Thou art now to leave all thou hast; thou art as the partridge that sitteth on the eggs, but hatcheth them not; thy joys are all for another, and not for thee. Oh, how often do men that have been happy enough in the accumulation of riches, die in utter misery, with all their gold and silver about them, because their bellows of avaricious acquisition have been burned by their very success, and the flame of hope and ambition has hopelessly died out!—*C. H. Spurgeon.*

(*b*) Persons in the midst of pleasure know more of its emptiness than any minister who preaches of the worthlessness of this world. The votaries of pleasure are the least satisfied with it. He who inveighs against immoralities and vices has not half so strong a conviction of their rottenness as they who commit them. No man has such a sense of the mischief and misery of intemperance as the very drunkard himself, when for a moment he staggers back from his bowl and has one of those lucid intervals in which his better nature returns, and he is led to loathe himself as other men loathe him. No man knows how heavy care is, and how weak human strength is under it, so well as the elect children of sorrow. No man ever counts riches at their true value, as measured by the other world, so truly as business men who have been the most industrious, the most avaricious, the most greedy, and are after all the most unsatisfied.—*H. W. Beecher.*

(*c*) Upon such a wretched creature, who in life thought nothing of death, nothing of God, nothing of man, and who took God's treasures and prosperities as pirates take jewels and coin, to hide them in the cave of his own selfishness—upon such a one there was an eye beaming steadily down, and, unheard by him, a voice went forth in heaven, which should ere long put all his arrogance and selfishness to shame. For, while men were calling him rich, and making him honourable; while his relations flattered him, and his dependents fawned upon him; while men stood out of his path, and turned to look back admiringly after him, and to say to the stranger newly come to town, "Knowest thou who that is? That is the great and wealthy Mr. Fat-soul!"—amid all these congratulations and admirations, and human praises, there were others looking at him, and expressing opinions about him not quite so complimentary. For God and holy angels looked down upon his gross abundance, upon his fat and dozing ease, and upon his arrogant self-congratulations; and God calmly said to this man, who stood so large, who was so prospered, and who very likely was the topmost man of the whole circle in which he moved, "Thou fool, this night thy soul shall be required of thee."—*Ibid.*

KIBROTH-HATTAAVAH: THE GRAVES OF LUST.

(*Verses* 31-34).

We will stand by those graves, and listen to their teachings: they may save us from standing by the graves of the idols of our own hearts. I shall endeavour to illustrate this subject by dwelling on three principles.

I. *There are perpetual resurrections of easily besetting sins.*

This lusting was no novelty in their experience; it was the besetting temptation of the desert, and the besetting sin of their hearts. But they ought to have viewed the first rising of its ghastly shape with horror; there were graves enough in the path from Egypt, to remind them of its deadly work. God had been at great pains to teach them the lesson of dependence, that "man doth not live by bread alone," &c. (Exod. xiv. 10-16; xvi. 1-5: xvii. 1-17). And now with firmer assurance than ever that God was in the midst of them, to bring them into the place which He had prepared, they resumed their march through the unknown desert paths. The tabernacle, the ark, the order of the camp, the pillar of cloud and flame, were all among them, the pledge of His presence. But all in vain. They must have flesh, or they would give up the enterprise, and die in despair. And they had flesh; they were fed, were crammed with it to nauseation, and with it "God sent leanness into their souls." I dwell on two points of large importance for the understanding of this history.

1. *The side from which the temptation came to them* (verses 4-6). This mixed multitude corresponds to the troop of disorderly passions and appetites with which we suffer ourselves to march through the desert of life. The mixed multitude was but loosely attached to them. They were a loose, coarse, common company, with nothing to dignify, elevate, inspire. No wonder they fainted, murmured, lusted; and thought flesh for to-day was better than Canaan to-morrow, and heaven beyond. The question was not one of sustenance. Enough for appetite was there; enough for all the uses of life, guaranteed by God; "but they wept again, saying, who shall give us flesh to eat;" &c. Lust was strong in them, the love of the satisfaction of the bodily appetites for the sake of the momentary pleasure they bring. And appetite runs swiftly into lust in every one of us; each act of indulgence opens a fresh mouth which craves to be fed. The moment you take pleasure in the indulgence of appetite beyond the use for which it was ordained by God, you take an element into your life which will humble it, and drag its glory in the dust. It is the grand battle of life, to teach lust the limits of Divine law.

2. *The special season when the easily-besetting sin rose up and again made them its slave.* Look at this orderly and gallant host. They had been baptised as God's soldiers by the splendours of the Mount of the Law. Full of Divine joy, zeal, courage, hope, they set forward, &c. "Scant fare, hard marching, fierce battles, but exhilarate us. The flesh-pots, the melons, the garlic, they belong to the days of our bondage; we are free men now, and their power to tempt us is gone." And so many a gallant young spirit, having heard the trumpet call of the Gospel, and joined the glorious company of the soldiers of the Cross, feels in the first pride of strength and flush of joy, that the flesh is so bruised, as to be broken and crushed for ever. But dread the hour when the glow begins to die down; when the practical burdens, pains, trials, which you still meet with, prove to you that the Divine life on earth is no paradise regained; when you find your strength barely equal to the demands made upon it, and see stretching on through long years a path of struggle, denial and mortification of the flesh, the end of which is not yet in sight.

Beware of your best moments, as well as of your worst; or rather the moments which succeed the best. They are the most perilous of all. Just when the consciousness of triumph seems to permit and justify disarmament for a moment, the subtle foe with whom you have to deal will steal in on you, and win a treacherous victory. Never relax the strain. Never allow temptation within arm's length. Never believe that the devil is asleep; that a besetting sin is eradicated, &c. "Lay aside every weight," &c.

II. *There comes a point in the*

history of the indulgence of besetting sins, when God ceases to strive with us and for us against them, and lets them have their way.

1. *God has great patience with the weaknesses and sins of the flesh.* But it is a dreadful mistake to suppose that therefore He thinks lightly of them. He regards them as sins that must be conquered, and no matter by what sharp discipline, extirpated and killed.

2. *Hence all the severer discipline by which the Lord seeks to purge them, the various agencies by which He fights with us and for us against their tyrannous power.* What is life but one long discipline of God for the cleansing of the flesh? Are not the after-pains of departed sensual joys among its chief stings and thorns? God has made a sure link of connexion between such sins and their penalties. The body itself is made the index of its indulgence, &c. Does He not give us the bread of heaven, that He may waken within us a taste for purer pleasures, and lead us out of the coils of the fleshly tempters, by giving us the food of a Diviner life? It is only when a man *will* not enter into his Father's counsel in this; *will* not suffer the higher tastes to develope themselves, and the higher appetites to indulge their craving with the bread of God; *will* grovel when God gives him wings to soar; *will* clamour for flesh when the bread of God is in his very hand: it is only then, when the evil becomes deadly, that God stays His hand, withdraws His guardian angel, and leaves the will to itself.

3. *Let alone by God.* "Ephraim is joined to his idols, let him alone!" is to any mind among the most awful sentences in the word of God. It is very wonderful to see how often, if a man is bent on an end which is not God's end, God gives it him, and it becomes his curse. God does not curse; He leaves us to ourselves; that is curse enough, and from that curse, what arm can save us? We *will* have it, and we shall have it.

III. The end of that way is, inevitably and speedily, a grave.

The grave of lust is one of the most awful of the inscriptions on the headstones of the great cemetery, the world. The words in Psa. cvi. 13-15, cast much light on this passage. There the lust is spoken of as the grave of the soul. And I believe that it is the common form of God's judgment. Where He buries one in the wilderness, He suffers a thousand to bury themselves in their lust. It is the inevitable end of all wanton self-indulgence; either a sharp judgment, or that slow pining of soul which makes the body its grave. . . Where are the graves? I need only look on that sensual face, that bloated form, that dull and glassy eye, that brazen brow, to tell. . . How many have learnt now to laugh at emotions which once had a holy beauty in their sight; to fence skilfully with appeals which once would have thrilled to the very core of their hearts; to grasp at advantages which once they would have passed with a scornful anathema, and to clutch at the gold which was once the glad instrument of diffusing benefits around! Yes! there are graves enough around us—graves of passion, graves of self-will, graves of lust.

Beware! young men; young women, beware! The grave-diggers began their work far back in those wretched histories. The first step was the really fatal one: the first flying, in sorrow and heart-ache, to any refuge but God. Beware! Each act of indulgence makes the grave wider and deeper, where the whole breadth of God-like faculty will at length lie buried; and it fixes in the brain a memory which will one day turn tyrant, and be the dread avenger of a murdered hope. — *J. Baldwin Brown, B.A.*

The Graves of Lust.

(Verse 34.)

The circumstances leading to the fact of the text are full of instruction to us. The mischief originated with "the mixed multitude." These were the rabble that had followed the Israelites out of Egypt; who having seen what God had done for His people in Egypt, thought it was a good chance to better themselves by so doing. They soon found out the mistake they had made, and began to murmur and to excite the people to discontent. Their connection with the history suggests—

1. *That those who join themselves to God's Church from worldly motives are ever disappointed.*
2. *That such characters ever do harm to the Church.*

The events which gave rise to the text show *how easily God can provide for our necessities, and punish us for our sins!* To Moses it seemed impossible to feed this vast multitude with flesh. God said, "I will do it for a month, until they are surfeited with it." How easily He keeps His promise It is never a difficult matter to Him to help us. Let us trust Him. *How easily He can punish!* The very blessing owing to their conduct, became their curse. They were wayward, and God let them have their own way, than which no greater curse can befall man. God can punish by plenty as well as by scarcity. What people have lusted after often becomes their torment.

I. **It is the tendency of lust to shorten life and to bring men to an untimely grave.**

The word *lust* in the Bible has, for the most part, its general meaning of inordinate desire—man's corrupt nature ruling instead of being ruled, and held in check. The finger of God has written on all gluttony, intemperance, debauchery—"This is the pathway to the grave." There is nothing exceptional in the death of these Israelites. There is no fact better attested than this, that all living for the animal in man destroys the body as well as the soul. When intellect becomes the slave of passion, and man is ruled by his lusts, he transgresses the laws of health, undermines his constitution, and soon sinks into the grave. Our animal desires are good servants; but, when they gain the mastery, they are fearful tyrants, loading the conscience with guilt and the body with disease, ruining life, and making eternity a hell. The Romans, it is said, held their funerals at the Gate of Venus, to teach that lust shortens life. The pleasures of sin are dearly bought. There are pleasures in sin, which have great attraction to our sinful nature. Folly's house, as Solomon tells us, is full of forbidden sweets; there is the pleasure of the sensualist, the vanities of the giddy and the gay, and the fatal cup which has such deadly hold on our land; they are there to attract, and they do attract corrupt hearts; but over the portal is written—"The dead are there—her guests are in the depths of hell."

II. **Let us record some of our feelings as we contemplate "the graves of lust."**

These graves made a deep impression on the mind of Moses, as we see from his giving the name to the encampment. It was, indeed, a sad, sad funeral, &c. The grave ever suggests sober thoughts. But all by the grave is not sad. Gospel light paints the rainbow of hope in our tears, as we place there the dead in Christ, with the assurance that we shall be re-united in the "home over there." But graves like these of the text—how sad! As we stand by them there are two feelings prominent—

1. The one is of *intense pity*, that man should be so foolish as to live in sin when he knew how it would end; that life should be so wasted, and opportunities lost, &c.

2. The other is of *awful solemnity.* He is gone! but whither? He has given up the ghost; but where is he? He is somewhere, &c. We cannot but think of his future.

> "Wrapp'd in a Christless shroud,
> He sleeps the Christless sleep;
> Above him, the eternal cloud,
> Beneath, the fiery deep.
>
> Laid in a Christless tomb,
> There, bound with felon-chain,
> He waits the terror of his doom,
> The judgment and the pain.
>
> O Christless shroud, how cold!
> How dark, O Christless tomb!
> O grief that never can grow old!
> O endless, hopeless doom!
>
> O Christless sleep, how sad!
> What waking shalt thou know?
> For thee no star, no dawning glad,
> Only the lasting woe!
>
> To rocks and hills in vain
> Shall be the sinner's call;
> O day of wrath and death and **pain,**
> The lost soul's funeral!
>
> O Christless soul, awake
> Ere thy last sleep begin!
> O Christ, the sleeper's slumbers break,
> Burst Thou the bands of sin."
>
> *Bonar.*

Thank God, this is possible now. While we are on earth we may obtain salvation, &c.

Let us all—

1. *Ascertain whether or no we are on the way to this grave.*
2. *Resolve through the help of God that we will not be there.*

Seek Jesus Christ. He, and He only, can rescue us from the power, the curse, and the consequences of sin.— *David Lloyd.*

CHAPTER XII.

CRITICAL AND EXPLANATORY NOTES.

Verse 1. *The Ethiopian woman, &c.* Heb.: "The woman, the Cushite." This could not have been Zipporah, who was a Midianite, not a Cushite. And even if it be supposed that Miriam called her a Cushite from feelings of contempt and bitterness, yet the historian would not have confirmed the epithet by adding, "for he had taken a Cushite woman." Moreover it is exceedingly improbable that Miriam should have reproached Moses with a marriage made many years previously, and long before he received the call to his great mission. The probability is that Zipporah had died, and Moses had entered into "marriage with a Cushite woman, who either sprang from the Cushites, dwelling in Arabia, or from the foreigners who had come out of Egypt along with the Israelites." Such a marriage was perfectly allowable, so long as the woman was not a daughter of Canaan. Exod. xxxiv. 11-16.

Verse 2. *Hath He not spoken also by us?* Aaron, as the high-priest, was the spiritual head of the whole nation, and as a prophetess Miriam was distinguished above all the women of Israel. Having received a measure of the prophetic spirit (Exod. iv. 15; xv. 20), they aspired to a share in the authority of Moses.

Verse 3. *Now the man Moses was very meek, &c.* It has been objected that Moses, being a humble and modest man, would not have written this verse. Hence Dr. A. Clarke translates, "Now this man Moses was *depressed* or *afflicted* more than any man of that land."

Fuerst renders עָנָו, in this place, "a humble one." Sept.: πραΰς. Vulg.: *mitis.* Keil and Del.: "meek." This seems to us the best rendering. The objections which have been raised against it are not valid. The statement "is not an expression of vain self-display, or a glorification of his own gifts and excellencies, which he prided himself upon possessing above all others. It is simply a statement which was indispensible to a full and correct interpretation of all the circumstances." When we regard these words "as uttered by Moses, not *proprio motu*, but under the direction of the Holy Spirit which was upon him (cf. xi. 17), they exhibit a certain 'objectivity,' which is a witness at once to their genuineness and also to their inspiration. There is about these words, as also about the passages in which Moses no less unequivocally records his own faults (cf. xx. 12 sqq.; Exod. iv. 24 sqq.; Deut. i. 37), the simplicity of one who bare witness of himself, but not to himself (cf. St. Matt. xi. 28, 29). The words are inserted to explain how it was that Moses took no steps to vindicate himself, and why consequently the Lord so promptly intervened."—*Speaker's Comm.*

Verses 6-8. *If there be a prophet among you*, &c. Keil and Del.: "If there is a prophet of Jehovah to you (*i.e.* if you have one), I make myself known to him in a vision; I speak to him in a dream (בוֹ, lit. 'in him,' inasmuch as a revelation in a dream fell within the inner sphere of the soul-life). Not so my servant Moses: he is approved in My whole house; mouth to mouth I speak to him, and as an appearance, and that not in enigmas; and he sees the form of Jehovah. Why are ye not afraid to speak against My servant, against Moses?

"Through this utterance on the part of Jehovah, Moses is placed above all the prophets, in relation to God and also to the whole nation. The Divine revelation to the prophets is thereby restricted to the two forms of inward intuition (vision and dream) . . . The prophets were consequently simply organs, through whom Jehovah made known His counsel and will at certain times, and in relation to special circumstances and features in the development of His kingdom. It was not so with Moses. Jehovah had placed him over all His house, had called him to be the founder and organizer of the kingdom established in Israel through his mediatorial service, and had found him faithful in His service. With this servant ($\theta\epsilon\rho\alpha\pi\omega\nu$, LXX.) of His, He spake mouth to mouth, without a figure or figurative cloak, with the distinctness of a human interchange of thought; so that at any time he could inquire of God and wait for the Divine reply. Hence Moses was not a prophet of Jehovah, like many others, not even merely the first and highest prophet, *primus inter pares*, but stood above all the prophets, as the founder of the theocracy, and mediator of the Old Covenant . . . The prophets subsequent to Moses simply continued to build upon the foundation which Moses laid. And if Moses stood in this unparalleled relation to the Lord, Miriam and Aaron sinned grievously against him, when speaking as they did."

Verse 7. *My servant Moses*, &c. Comp. Heb. iii. 1-6.

Verse 10. *Leprous.* See pp. 75-77.

Verse 12. *Let her not be as one dead*, &c., "*i.e.*, like a still-born child, which comes into the world half decomposed. His reason for making this comparison was, that leprosy produces decomposition in the living body."—*Keil and Del.*

Verse 14. *If her father had but spit*, &c. To spit in the face was a mark of extreme contempt. See Deut. xxv. 9; Job xxx. 10; Isa. l. 6; Mark xiv. 65. When a parent did this to his child, it is said the child was banished from his presence for seven days. How much more, then, should Miriam, who had sinned so grievously and whom God had smitten with leprosy, be exiled from the people and presence of God for seven days!

Verse 16. *The wilderness of Paran* "was the great tract south of Palestine, commencing soon after Sinai, as the people advanced northwards,—that perhaps now known as the desert *Et-Tih*," or the desert of the Wandering. "Between the wilderness of Paran and that of Zin no strict demarcation exists in the narrative, nor do the natural features of the region, so far as yet ascertained, yield a well-defined boundary." (See *The Speaker's Comm.*, and Keil and Del on Chap. x. 12; Smith's *Dict. of Bible*, Arts. *Kadesh, Paran*, and *Wilderness of the Wandering;* and the maps of *Egypt* and the *Peninsula of Sinai*, in Stanley's *Sinai and Pal.*).

The Sin of Miriam and Aaron: Evil Speaking, Divine Hearing, and Saintly Silence.

(Verses 1-3.)

Consider:

I. **The Sin of Miriam and Aaron.** "And Miriam and Aaron spake against Moses," &c. In considering this sin, let us notice—

1. *Its root.* The source of this evil speaking was (so we infer from verse 2) jealousy on the part of Miriam and Aaron at the authority exercised, and the powers assumed by Moses. They were envious of his position and power, and ambitious for the exercise of equal authority. As Dr. Kitto has pointed out, the position assigned to Aaron "in the commonwealth was in some respects superior to that of Moses. The function of Moses was temporary, and would pass away with his life; whereas Aaron's was permanent in himself and his heirs, and would leave him and them the foremost and most important persons in the state. He might not therefore always regard with patience the degree in which his own high office was superseded by the existing authority of Moses." The fact that he was the elder brother, probably contributed further to his discontent and jealousy. Miriam also was jealous and ambitious. It seemed to her, that being a prophetess, she ought to have a more eminent position and greater power. Here in their mean jealousy and "vaulting ambition" we have the root of their sin. (*a*).

2. *Its occasion.* It is probable that the fact that Aaron and Miriam had not been consulted in the choice of the seventy elders awakened their discontent. But that which they put forth as the occasion of their reproaches was the marriage which Moses had contracted with the Cushite woman. This seems to have annoyed Miriam, and led her to engage Aaron in envious and evil speeches. That Miriam was the instigator of the open rebellion appears from three things: (1) That she is named before Aaron. (2) From the use of the feminine verb וַתְּדַבֵּר in ver. 1; and (3) from the fact that the punishment fell upon her only, and not upon Aaron. It appears that Aaron was deficient in firmness, and was too easily persuaded by others. Weakly and wickedly he yielded to the desire of the people for a golden idol (Exod. xxxii); and now at the instigation of his sister he unites in rebellion against the leader whom God had appointed. It is natural that the wife of Moses would be regarded with feelings of respect and honour in the camp. Miriam was jealous of these honours; she wished to occupy the rank of chief lady in the camp; hence she instigated this mean and sinful rebellion.

3. *Its expression.* They "spake against Moses," &c. Evil speaking is a grievous offence in the sight of God. But when, as in this case, the evil speeches are directed against His chosen servants, the sin is greatly aggravated. "Jealousy, the green-eyed monster," discovers flaws in and heaps reproaches upon its object, even though his character and conduct be most faultless and beautiful. The bitter feeling goes forth in unjust and bitter speech. (*b*.)

II. **The Divine Cognizance of their Sin.**

"And the Lord heard." No one utterance of all the myriads of voices in

His universe ever escapes His ear. There is a Divine Hearer of every human speech. This is clear from—

1. *His omnipresence.* See Psa. cxxxix. 7-12. He who is everywhere present sees all things, hears all things.

2. *His infinite intelligence.* He to whom all things are known cannot be ignorant of the evil speeches of men.

3. *His interest in His servants.* God is deeply concerned in the honour and welfare of His servants. Their reputation is a sacred thing in His sight. Therefore He notes all the evil which is spoken against them.

Let all evil speakers and slanderers ponder the solemn truth that every whisper is distinctly audible to the Divine ear.

III. **The commendable conduct of Moses under the provocation of their sin.**

1. *He was sorely tried.* Under any circumstances it is a severe trial to be reproached without cause, or to be falsely accused; but the trial of Moses was embittered by the source from whence it sprung. Comp. Psa. lv. 12-15.

2. *He bore his sore trial most nobly.* Under extreme provocation he maintained a saintly silence. He did not resent the attack made upon him, or attempt in any way to vindicate himself, for he was " meek and lowly in heart." " Now the man Moses was very meek, above all the men which were upon the face of the earth." We have here a hint as to—(1) *The nature of meekness.* "Meekness," says Attersoll, "is a gift of the Spirit, which moderateth anger and desire of revenge, forgiving offences and pardoning injuries for peace and quietness sake: so that albeit a man be provoked by injuries received, yet he doth not intend nor enterprize to requite it, but bridleth all hatred and impatience." (*c*) (2) *The occasions of its manifestation.* When we are injured personally, like Moses, we must be meek. But when the honour of God is impeached, like Moses in the matter of the golden calf (Exod. xxxii. 19-29), we must be zealous and determined. He was "as bold as a lion in the cause of God, but as mild as a lamb in his own cause."

Conclusion:

1. *In the conduct of Miriam and Aaron we have a beacon.* Let us shun their sin, &c.

2. *In the conduct of Moses we have a pattern.* Let us imitate his meekness.

ILLUSTRATIONS.

(*a*) Ambition threw Adam out of the garden of God: it quickly crept into the family of Christ, and infected his disciples, and, therefore, being a subtle and secret evil, it is to be looked unto that it steal not suddenly upon us. If any man ask what it is, I answer, It is an immoderate desire after dignity, it is a thirst that never can be quenched; for as the covetous person hath never enough money, so the ambitious hath never enough honour; it is a secret poison, a hidden plague, the mistress of craft, the mother of hypocrisy, the father of envy, the fountain of vices, the moth of piety, a blind guide and leader of the hearts of men; finally, we may say of the love of it as Paul doth of the love of money, "It is the root of all evil" (1 Tim. vi. 10). The farther we think ourselves from it, the nearer commonly it cometh unto us; and, therefore, "let nothing be done through strife and vainglory, but in lowliness of mind let each esteem other better than themselves" (Phil. ii. 3).—*W. Attersoll.*

(*b*) Sweetness is lost if you pour in bitterness to it. And certainly, if otherwise you have many sweet qualities and virtues, if you have an ill tongue to speak against Moses, the bitterness of it will mar them all. The little bee hath but a little sting, and, therefore, the wound is not mortal that she can make; yet little as it is, it procureth usually her death if she be caught. So will your stinging tongue, assure yourself, kill you, although it little hurt him or her whom you have stung. The foul frog lieth all day in the mud and mire, at night putting up the head and croaking with a foul noise; and such foul creatures are they said to be that have croaking tongues against Moses. Put a swine into the sweetest garden you can make, and what will he do? Smell to the pleasant rose or any other delightful flower there? No; but straight he will fall to rooting, and with his foul mouth turn up both moor and mould of every good thing. Such foul swine are they said to be, that have foul tongues, ever passing by that which is good, and rooting up the good names of them, whose virtues, how sweet soever to God and men, yet to them are ever hateful. I will go no further, but pray you to mark him that toppeth a candle, and taketh not good heed, doth he not usually black his fingers, and sometimes also burn them, although he make the candle more bright? So do such persons as will be meddling with their neighbours' lives. Well may their prattling make them burn and shine more bright, whom they meddle withal; but their own fingers carry a mark—nay, their souls receive such a blot as all the water in the sea will not wash off, but only the saving blood of Christ Jesus, upon repentance and amendment. Follow we not, then, Miriam and Aaron speaking against Moses, but pray for His grace to guide our tongues in a holy course, and so, clean tongues being the outward tokens of our clean souls, our life shall be godly and our end happy.—*Bishop Babington.*

(c) All genuine meekness among men—all, I mean, which is more than mere easiness of disposition—may be defined to be that bearing of a man towards the things of time and of this world, which springs from having the heart broken by religious penitence, and the will put humbly into the hand of God. Do we call him "meek" who gives way in silence before noisy pretension, will rather give up his due than wrangle for it, and is so far from pushing himself into foremost places, that he yields before the force or "importunity of earthly-minded" men, nor murmurs at the "usurpation of the unjust"? Is it not because his natural self-importance has been humbled into "poverty of spirit," that he is prepared thus to accept the lowest place? Or is it "meekness," as some older expositors defined it, to be "undesirous of revenge" (non cupidus vindictæ)—"not easily provoked," slow to take offence, and, though stung deep, betraying no personal bitterness, but hiding oneself beneath the wing of God, who is the promised "avenger of all such"? Surely he forbears and forgives best who knows by the depth of his contrition for personal guilt how deeply he has been forgiven. Or shall we say he is the "meek" man, who, resting in the quiet and peaceable enjoyment of so much as God has been pleased to give, can meet each turn of fortune's wheel with an equal mind, quarrelling neither with injurious providence, nor with more successful rivals; in prosperity unassuming, undesponding in adversity? Show me a will made pliable to the Heavenly Father under the experience of grace and forgiven sin, and I will show you equanimity above the philosophers—the equanimity of the Christian child! Yes, we must be converted to become meek.—*J. O. Dykes, M.A., D.D.*

The Modern Application of an Ancient Incident.

(*Verses* 1-3.)

The incident recorded in these verses warrants the following practical observations:—

I. **The possession of the greatest gifts does not exempt men from the liability to meanness and sin.**

Miriam, a prophetess and poet, and Aaron an eloquent man (Exod. iv. 14), in a measure inspired by God (Exod. iv. 15), and appointed by God the religious head of the nation (Exod. xxviii.), are here guilty of extreme meanness and great sin. The possession of great gifts does not necessarily involve the possession of great grace also. Balaam was a highly gifted man; but he was covetous, unprincipled, &c. A man may hold high office in the Church, and yet sin grievously. Let persons of great abilities and influence remember their great responsibilities. Let those who occupy prominent positions in religion look well to their own spiritual life and health. *(a)*

II. **The most excellent and eminent servants of God are not exempt from the reproaches of men.**

Even Moses, so distinguished for piety as he was, was spoken against.

"No might nor greatness in mortality
Can censure 'scape; back-wounding calumny
The whitest virtue strikes: What king so strong,
Can tie the gall up in the slanderous tongue?"
Shakespeare.

"Be thou as chaste as ice, as pure as snow
Thou shalt not escape calumny."—*Ibid*

"The worthiest people are the most injured by slander," said Swift, "as we usually find that to be the best fruit which the birds have been pecking at." It was said of our Holy Lord, "He hath a devil and is mad." "If they called the Master of the house Beelzebub, how much more them of His household?" (*b*)

III. **Our greatest trials sometimes arise from the most unlikely quarters.**

It was remarkably so in the present trial of Moses. It arose from—

1. *Persons in eminent positions.* One would have thought that they would have sympathised with and endeavoured to sustain Moses in the duties and burdens of his office; but, &c.

2. *Persons of excellent character.* Aaron and Miriam were undoubtedly, in the main, good and worthy persons. Many of the trials of ministers and other religious leaders in our own day come from religious and well-meaning men; from their unreasonable complaints, their ignorant criticism, their conceited censures, &c.

3. *Persons in near relationship.* The present trial of Moses arose from his own brother and sister. David suffered sorely in this way from Absalom, Ahithophel, *et al.* Comp. Psa. xli. 9; lv. 12-14. When trials arise in this way they cause great *disappointment.* We expect such different things from kinsfolk and friends. They also cause sore distress. They wound the tenderest feelings, &c.

IV. **The Lord takes cognizance of the reproaches which are cast upon His servants.**

When "Miriam and Aaron spake against Moses, . . . the Lord heard."

1. *He is perfectly acquainted with all things.* "The Lord is a God of knowledge." "His understanding is infinite." "God knoweth all things."

2. *He is deeply interested in all that concerns His servants.* This interest is set forth in most expressive forms in the Scriptures (Deut. xxxii. 9, 10; Isa. xlix. 15, 16: Zech. ii. 8). The reputation of His servants is sacred and precious in His sight.

V. **The servants of the Lord do well in bearing patiently the reproaches which are cast upon them.**

Moses did not attempt to vindicate himself against the reproaches of Miriam and Aaron. The good man in similar circumstances may well follow his example in this. If we are thoroughly devoted to God's service, we may safely leave it to Him to vindicate us against the reproaches of man. Comp. Job xvi. 19; Psa. xxxvii. 5-6. (*c*)

ILLUSTRATIONS.

(*a*) Years ago Hamburg was nearly half of it burned down, and among the incidents that happened there was this one. A large house had connected with it a yard, in which there was a great black dog, and this black dog in the middle of the night barked and howled most furiously. It was only by his barking that the family were awakened just in time to escape from the flames, and their lives were spared; but the poor dog was chained to his kennel, and though he barked and thus saved the lives of others, he was burned himself. Oh! do not you, who work for God in this church, perish in that fashion. Do not permit your sins to enchain you, so that while you warn others you become lost yourselves. Do see that you have the godliness which has the promise of the life to come.—*C. H. Spurgeon.*

(*b*) I think there is no Christian, but sooner or later, first or last, shall have cause to say with David, "False witnesses did rise up, they laid to my charge things that I knew not" (Psa. xxv. 11). They charged me with such things whereof I was both innocent and ignorant. It was the saying of one, that there was nothing so intolerable as accusation, because there was no punishment ordained by law for accusers, as there was for thieves, although they stole friendship from men, which is the goodliest riches men have. Well, Christians, seeing it has been the lot of the dearest saints to be falsely accused, and to have their names and reputes in the world reproached, do you hold your peace, seeing it is no worse with you than it was with them, of whom this world was not worthy.—*Brooks.*

(*c*) The celebrated Boerhaave, who had many enemies, used to say that he never thought it necessary to repeat their calumnies. "They are sparks," said he, "which, if you do not blow them, will go out of themselves. The surest method against scandal is to live it down by perseverance in well-doing, and by prayer to God, that He would cure the distempered mind of those who traduce and injure us." It was a good remark of another, that "the malice of ill tongues cast upon a good man is only like a mouthful of smoke blown upon a diamond, which, though it clouds its beauty for the present, yet it is easily rubbed off, and the gem restored, with little trouble to its own lustre."—*Dict. of Illust.*

Rowland Hill, when once scurrilously attacked in one of the public journals, was urged by a zealous friend to bring a legal action in defence; to this he replied with calm, unruffled dignity,—"I shall neither answer the libel, nor prosecute the writer, and that for two reasons: first, because, in attempting the former, I should probably be betrayed into unbecoming violence of temper and expression, to my own grief, and the wounding of my friends; and in the next place, I have learned by experience, *that no man's character can be eventually injured but by his own acts.*"—*Gleanings.*

THE INQUEST OF THE LORD INTO THE SIN OF MIRIAM AND AARON.

(*Verses* 4-9.)

We now come to the second scene in this painful chapter of Israelitish history. Consider—

I. The solemn convocation.

"And the Lord spake suddenly unto Moses, and unto Aaron, and unto Miriam, Come out," &c. (verses 4, 5). We have here the solemn summons of the Divine Voice to Moses and to the two offenders, the majestic descent of the cloud of the Divine Presence, &c. Two great truths appear to be set forth in all this:

1. *The timeliness of the Divine interposition.* "The Lord spake suddenly." His interposition was not delayed. In due season, at the earliest fitting opportunity, He appears for the vindication of His reproached servants.

2. *The righteousness of the Divine judgment.* This seems to be taught by the summoning of the offenders and of the person wronged before Him, and by the descent of the cloud of His presence. He knows all things, yet, He makes inquiry, &c. There is no haste in the Divine judgments; but patient and thorough examination precedes them. Comp. Gen. iii. 8-13; vi. 12; xi. 5; xviii. 21; Zeph i. 12. (*a*)

The unimpeachable righteousness of the judgments of God should prove—

1. *A comfort to the upright when unjustly reproached.*

2. *A warning to the wicked.*

II. The splendid vindication.

"And he said, Hear now my words: If there is a prophet of Jehovah to you," &c. (verses 6-8). Miriam and Aaron had aspired to equality with Moses, and disputed his claim to superior authority, and now Jehovah splendidly vindicates his pre-eminent character, and privileges, and consequent authority. He asserts that Moses was—

1. *Pre-eminent in the intimacy of his communion with God.* In the revelations which God made to men there were different degrees of clearness. To prophets He spake in visions and dreams; He revealed His will to them in "the inner sphere of the soul-life." But He spake to Moses "mouth to mouth," "*i.e.,* without any mediation or reserve, but with the same closeness and freedom with which friends converse together" (Exod. xxxiii. 11). He spake to Moses "as an appearance, and that not in enigmas," *i.e.,* His communications were made to him directly and in the plainest and most intelligible manner. And of Moses He says further, "the similitude of the Lord shall he behold." By "the similitude" we are not to understand the unveiled essence of the Deity (John i. 18 1 Tim. vi. 16) nor any representation of God in the form of man or in the form of the angel of Jehovah (Ezek. i. 26-28; Dan. vii. 9, 13; Gen. xvi. 7). "It was the Deity Himself manifesting Himself so as to be cognizable to mortal eye." Thus Moses was exalted far above all the other prophets. (See *explanatory notes* on verses 6-8.)

2. *Pre-eminent in his faithfulness in the charge which he received of the Lord.* "My servant Moses is approved in My whole house." The "house" of Jehovah in this place does not signify the Tabernacle, but the covenant people, who were to be instructed and regulated by

Moses. In all his duties to the people of God, Moses is declared faithful; in all he was approved by God. "He said and did everything in the management of that great affair, as became an honest good man, that aimed at nothing else but the honour of God and welfare of Israel." How completely does the Lord vindicate His servant, and how highly does He honour him! Well does Trapp say, "God had never so much magnified Moses to them, but for their envy. We cannot devise to pleasure God's servants so much as by despiting them. *Quisquis volens detrahit famœ meœ, nolens addit mercedi meœ*, saith Augustine; He that willingly detracteth from mine honour, doth, though against his will, add to my reward."

III. **The unanswerable interrogation.**

"Wherefore, then, were ye not afraid to speak against My servant, against Moses?" This inquiry implies that their speech against Moses was—

1. *Unreasonable.* "Wherefore, then," &c. Their reproaches were groundless. The Divine "Wherefore?" reveals the utter absence of any true cause for them.

2. *Profane.* "Were ye not afraid to speak against MY *servant?*" In reproaching the *servant*, they had dishonoured the MASTER. "The rule is, *Injuria illata legato redundat in legantem*, Wrong done to a messenger reflects on him that sent him."

3. *Daring.* "Why were ye not afraid?" If they had considered, they would have discovered strong reasons to dread the result of their conduct. "We have reason," says Matthew Henry, "to be afraid of saying or doing anything against the servants of God; it is at our peril if we do so, for God will plead their cause, and reckon that what 'touches them touches the apple of His eye.' It is a dangerous thing to 'offend one of Christ's little ones' (Matt. xviii. 6). Those are presumptuous, indeed, that 'are not afraid to speak evil of dignities' (2 Pet. ii. 10)." Interrogated thus by the Lord, Aaron and Miriam were "speechless," like the man at the marriage feast who had not on a wedding garment (Matt. xxii. 12). Their conduct was utterly indefensible.

IV. **The Divine anger.**

"And the anger of the Lord was kindled against them, and He departed." There are here two considerations concerning the anger of the Lord:

1. *Its righteousness.* It was kindled by sin—the sin of Aaron and Miriam. The anger of God is a perfectly holy principle which hates and antagonises sin. (*b*)

2. *Its manifestation.* "And He departed." "The removal of God's presence from us," says Matthew Henry, "is the surest and saddest token of God's displeasure against us. Woe unto us if He depart; and He never departs till we by our sin and folly drive Him from us." "The final absence of God is hell itself." (*c*)

Conclusion:

The time approaches when God will summon all men to give account of themselves and their lives to Him. "Prepare to meet thy God."

ILLUSTRATIONS.

(*a*) There are many ways of representing perfect justice. The Thebans represented her as having neither hands nor eyes, for the judge should neither receive bribes nor respect persons. We, for similar reasons, picture her with a sword in one hand, scales in the other, and bandaged eyes. Whatever doubt there may be as to the justice of the earthly judge, as to that of the Heavenly there can be none. Now, His ways may sometimes appear to be "unequal." We see the wicked in prosperity and the righteous in adversity. Like David, we are troubled at it. But when with David we "enter into the tabernacle of God, then understand we their end;" for God "hath appointed a day in which He will judge the world in righteousness by that Man whom He hath ordained."—*J. G. Pilkington.*

(*b*) There is a deep wrath-principle in God, as in all moral natures, that puts Him down upon wrong, and girds Him in avenging majesty for the infliction of suffering upon wrong. Just as we speak of our felt indignations, and tell how we are made to burn against the person, or even the life of the wrong-doer, so God has His heavier indignations, and burns with His more consuming fire. This combustion of right anger is that girding power of justice that puts Him on the work of redress, and that armature of strength upon His feeling, that enables Him to inflict pain without shrinking.—*H. Bushnell, D.D.*

Say you that God is love? Oh! but look round this world. The aspect of things is stern—very stern. If they be ruled by love, it is a love which does not shrink from human agony. There is a law of infinite mercy here, but there is a law of boundless rigour, too. Sin, and you will suffer—that law is not reversed. The young, and the gentle, and the tender, are inexorably subjected to it. We would shield them if we could; but there is that which says they shall not be shielded.

They shall weep, and fade, and taste of mortal anguish, even as others. Carry that out into the next world, and you have "wrath to come."—*F. W. Robertson, M.A.*

(c) Think of God sending a famine upon the soul—of minds pining and dying because Divine messages have been withdrawn! We know what the effect would be if God were to withhold the dew, or to trouble the air with a plague, or to avert the beams of the sun; the garden would be a desert, the fruitful field a sandy plain, the wind a bearer of death, summer a stormy night, and life itself a cruel variation of death, so penetrating, so boundless is the influence of God in nature. Is it conceivable that the withdrawment of God's influence would be less disastrous upon the spirit of man?—*Joseph Parker, D.D.*

HONOUR TO MOSES; GREATER HONOUR TO CHRIST.

(*Verse* 7.)

We have an inspired comment in the New Testament on these words (Heb. iii. 1-6). Paul, reasoning with the Jews, tries to divert their minds from giving to Moses a glory that was in excess; and to show that all the honour they gave to Moses, the early servant, belonged in a far richer degree to Jesus, their rejected Lord. It is said that Moses, in all his offices, as priest, as prophet, as ruler, as teacher, as guide, was faithful in all his house.

What was his house? "Whose house," says the Apostle, "are we."

What does faithfulness mean? Whatever be the function assigned to you, that you honestly, impartially, earnestly, and fully discharge. Moses was in the midst of the people of God faithful. He finished the tabernacle; and you remember how specific are the injunctions laid down, and how minutely Moses fulfilled them all. So Jesus, the antitype, dimly foreshadowed by Moses, has been faithful in all the arrangements of His house. He has furnished it with precious sacraments; He has appointed it a teaching and a preaching ministry; He has redeemed it by His precious blood; He has bequeathed to it the ceaseless presence of His Holy Spirit, &c.

The Apostle justly says, that this *Moses, who was faithful in all his house, is counted worthy of glory; though One is counted worthy of greater glory.* The very comparison indicates that Moses was counted worthy of honour. We need not disparage the servant in order to exalt the Master. Moses was a servant in the house; as a servant to be honoured; Jesus, the Builder of the house, as the Builder of the house to have the great and the lasting glory. Comp. John v. 23.

We see what is *the true definition of the Church.* The definition of Scripture of the Church is not the size of an edifice, or the splendour of its architecture; but the regenerated men that meet together in the name of Christ, &c. The orator may collect a crowd, but that is not a Church. The architect may build a cathedral, but that is not a Church. It is living stones, knit together by living love, not dead stones fastened together by dead mortar, that constitute a Church of the Lord Jesus Christ.

We see also the *true oneness of the Church of Christ in all ages.* There was, says the Apostle, but one house. "Moses was faithful in all his house; ... whose house," says the Apostle, "are we." Then the Church that was in the days of Moses is the Church that

221

exists now. There never has been but one Church; there never has been but one religion—I mean true religion; there never has been but one Saviour. The formula has differed, the circumstances have varied, the degree of spirituality or conformity to Christ has differed; but the substance has been everywhere and always essentially the same.

Now the argument of the Apostle (Heb. iii. 1-6) is most logical; a building infers and suggests a builder; an effect throws you back upon a cause; a creation leads you back or upwards to a Creator; and if Christ be the builder of all, and peculiarly the builder of that edifice of living stones which is called the Church; to build which requires more of God than to build the universe; then, says the Apostle, of how great honour ought He to be the inheritor who is thus God, the Builder and the Maker of all? If it required God to make a world; it requires God to regenerate sinners; nay, if possible more so. Omnipotence has but to mould the obedient dust into all its forms of beauty, of symmetry and order; and no resisting element, from first to last, will intrude to disturb the perfection, or to mar the beauty of the product. But in dealing with sinners there is not simply dead material to be moulded into its varied forms of loveliness and symmetry, but resistant passions, rebellious feelings, reluctant appetites, diverging tendencies; a thousand things to obstruct, to resist and to mar. And hence, if it required God to build the outer world, it requires no less a God to build that inner house, &c. Now then, argues the Apostle, if the servant Moses is counted by every Jew worthy of honour, what language shall express the honour due to Him who built all things? Comp. Heb. i. And thus he shows that Christ is superior to Moses; that He is superior to angels; he proves by comparison that he is God; and therefore, that the glory, and the honour, and the thanksgiving, and the praise are exclusively due to Him, who redeemed us by His blood, and has made us what we are.

We infer from the whole—

1. The greater glory of the New Testament economy. The figures are removed because their reality has come.

2. The greater responsibility of all who live under so clear, so simple, so spiritual an economy. Comp. Heb. x. 28, 29.

3. Paul shows us also the secret of our safety (Heb. iii. 6).

4. If Christ was faithful in His house, and Moses faithful in his, let us be faithful in ours (Matt. xxiv. 45-50).

Are we living stones, laid upon Christ the rock?—*Arranged from "Sabbath Morning Readings," by John Cumming, D.D.*

THE PUNISHMENT OF MIRIAM AND AARON.

(*Verses* 10-16.)

Consider:

I. The Divine judgment because of the sin of Miriam and Aaron.

"And the cloud departed from off the tabernacle; and, behold, Miriam became leprous," &c. (ver. 10).

1. *The punishment was inflicted by the Lord.* "Leprosy," says Archbishop Trench, "was often the punishment of sins committed against the Divine government. Miriam, Gehazi, Uzziah, are all cases in point; and when Moses says to the people, 'Take heed of the plague of leprosy' (Deut. xxiv. 8), this is no admonition diligently to observe the laws about leprosy, but a warning lest any disobedience of theirs should provoke God to visit them with this plague. The Jews themselves called it 'the finger of God,' and emphatically, 'the stroke.' It attacked, they said, first a man's house; and then, if he refused to turn, his clothing; and lastly, should he persist in sin, himself —a

fine parable, let the fact have been as it might, of the manner in which God's judgments, if a man refuse to listen to them, reach ever nearer to the centre of his life. So, too, they said that a man's true repentance was the one condition of his leprosy leaving him." The leprosy of Miriam was certainly "the stroke" of Divine punishment because of her sin.

2. *The punishment was appropriate to the sin.* "Her foul tongue," says Bishop Hall, "is justly punished with a foul face, and her folly in pretending to be a rival with Moses is made manifest to all men, for every one sees his face to be glorious, and hers to be leprous. While Moses needs a veil to hide his glory, Miriam needs one to hide her shame." Not content with her exalted position, she aspired to the highest place of all, and for seven days she was not allowed even the lowest place in the camp, but was completely exiled from it.

3. *The punishment fell most severely upon Miriam.* Aaron was not struck with leprosy. (1) She was the instigator of the sin. The Lord visits her greater guilt with a severer punishment. (2) Aaron's office of High Priest also probably helped to shield him. Had he been smitten with leprosy he would have been deeply disgraced in the eyes of the people, and his holy office would probably have been brought into disesteem amongst them. (3) Yet Aaron was not altogether exempted from punishment. As priest he had to examine Miriam and pronounce her leprous. Again he had to examine her and pronounce her clean before she was readmitted to the camp. That he deeply realized his painful position is evident from the narrative (verses 10-12). Let us remember that there is judgment with God, He punishes men for their sins. If His chosen and distinguished servants sin against Him, He "will visit their transgression with the rod, and their iniquity with stripes." (a)

II. **The Divine judgment leading to personal humiliation.**

"And Aaron said unto Moses, Alas! my lord, I beseech thee," &c. (verses 11, 12). We see here—

1. *Humble acknowledgment to Moses.* A short time since Aaron had spoken against Moses; but mark the humility with which he now approaches him, and the respect with which he now addresses him—"Alas! my lord, I beseech thee," &c. When the Lord takes up the cause of His servants He speedily humbles their detractors.

2. *Confession of sin.* "Lay not the sin upon us, wherein we have done foolishly, and wherein we have sinned." Though he was not himself smitten with leprosy, yet Aaron deeply feels and penitently acknowledges his sin.

3. *Entreaty for the removal of the severe judgment from Miriam.* "Let her not be as one dead," &c. "Leprosy," says Archbishop Trench, "was nothing short of a living death, a corrupting of all the humours, a poisoning of the very springs of life; a dissolution little by little of the whole body, so that one limb after another actually decayed and fell away. Aaron exactly describes the appearance which the leper presented to the eyes of the beholders, when, pleading for Miriam, he says, 'Let her not be as one dead, of whom,'" &c. Thus he invokes the aid of Moses in intercession for the removal of the dreadful punishment. How speedily God by His judgments can humble men! Even the greatest and the mightiest are utterly unable to sustain His strokes.

III. **The remarkable acknowledgment of the eminence of Moses, the servant of the Lord.**

In Aaron's confession and appeal to Moses we have a splendid tribute to the character and power with God of the latter.

1. *In the manner in which he was addressed by Aaron.* "And Aaron said unto Moses, Alas! my lord, I beseech thee," &c.

2. *In the appeal which was made to him by Aaron.* "Let her not be as one dead," &c. This appeal implies on the part of Aaron—(1) Faith in the

magnanimity of Moses—that he would not retaliate upon them for their attack upon him; that he was forgiving and generous. (2) Faith in the influence which Moses had with God. Aaron does not dare to present his prayer directly to God, but he seeks the mediation and intercession of Moses. Thus out of the evil speaking of Aaron and Miriam against Moses, God brings a splendid tribute to the magnanimity, the holiness, and the spiritual power of His servant. Men in prosperity may reproach the servants of the Lord, but in adversity they will eagerly seek their sympathies and services.

IV. The distinguished magnanimity and grace of Moses.

"And Moses cried unto the Lord, saying, Heal her now, O God, I beseech Thee." There was no resentment in his heart towards the brother and sister who had injured him; but fullest forgiveness for both, and sincerest pity for his smitten sister. His prayer for Miriam is an anticipation of the precept of our Lord, "Pray for them which despitefully use you, and persecute you" (Matt. v. 44). We have another beautiful example of this forgiving and gracious spirit in the "man of God out of Judah," who prayed that the withered hand of Jeroboam, which had been stretched out against him, might be healed (1 Kings xiii. 1-6). This spirit found its supreme and perfect expression in the Lord Jesus Christ. For those who crucified Him, when He was enduring the anguish of the cross, He prayed, "Father, forgive them; for they know not what they do" (Luke xxiii. 34). Let us imitate Him.

V. The great power of the intercession of good.

In answer to the prayer of Moses Miriam was healed of her leprosy, and, after an exclusion lasting seven days, was restored to her place in the camp and congregation of the Lord. "Pray one for another, that ye may be healed. The effectual fervent prayer of a righteous man availeth much." (*b*)

VI. The justice and mercy of God as manifested in His treatment of Miriam.

1. *He manifests His justice.* To mark His abhorrence of her sin He commands that Miriam shall be shut out of the camp seven days. "To deal lightly with sin is actually to commit sin." God punishes sin in whomsoever He finds it. "There is no respect of persons with God in punishing, for none shall escape His hand. He doth not strike the poor and spare the rich; wink at the noble and honourable, and strike down the unnoble and baser sort; but He respecteth every one as He findeth him, and punisheth sin wheresoever sin reigneth, that all should fear."

2. *He manifests His mercy.* He does not deal with Miriam and Aaron as they deserve, but mingles His judgment with mercy. We see His mercy in healing Miriam, and in sentencing her to only seven days banishment from the camp. He does not execute the fierceness of His anger. In wrath He remembers mercy. "He delighteth in mercy." (*c*)

VII. The sin of one person checking the progress of an entire nation.

"The people journeyed not till Miriam was brought in." For seven days the advance of the entire people was arrested by reason of the sin of Miriam. In consequence of the sin of Achan the Israelites were smitten at the battle of Ai, and ignominiously defeated. How often have we seen since those days the current of the progress of a nation, or of nations, arrested and turned back by some unprincipled and ambitious monarch, or by some unrighteous and powerful statesman! "None of us liveth to himself." The sin of one person of high position and great influence may result in deepest injury to thousands.

Conclusion:

The history supplies materials for a strong argument against sinning. By the heinousness of sin, by the Divine judgment upon sin, and by the injury which sin inflicts upon others, we are urged to "abstain from every form of evil."

ILLUSTRATIONS.

(*a*) Let us all learn this fact—that the consequences of sin are inevitable ; in fact, that punishment is the extreme consequence of sin going on unchecked. There is in human nature an element of the gambler. There is a willingness to take the chances of things—a willingness to run a risk, however uncertain. There is no such element here. The punishment of sin is certain. All Scripture tells us so. "The soul that sinneth it shall die." "Be sure your sin will find you out." "Though hand join in hand, the wicked shall not go unpunished." "The way of transgressors is hard." All the world's proverbs tell us so. "A reckless youth: rueful age." "As he has made his bed, so he must lie in it." "He who will not be ruled by the rudder, must be ruled by the rock." Even Satan himself tells us so. In the old legend of Dr. Faustus, when he bids the devil lay aside his propensity for lying, and tell the truth, the devil answers, "The world does me injustice to tax me with lies. Let me ask their own conscience if I have ever deceived a single man into believing that a bad deed was a good one." Even wicked men admit it. . . . God is no respecter of persons.

Fire burns and water drowns, whether the sufferer be a worthless villain or whether it be a fair and gentle child. And so the moral law works, whether the sinner be a David or a Judas, whether he be a publican or a priest. In the physical world there is no forgiveness of sins. Sin and punishment, as Plato said, walk this world with their hands tied together, and the rivet by which they are linked is as a link of adamant. A writer has said that a man who cannot swim might as well walk into a river and hope that it is not a river, and will not drown, as a man, seeing judgment and not mercy, denounced upon willing sin, hope that it will turn out to be mercy, and not judgment, and so defy God's law. Will he escape? No. He who chooses sin must meet with retribution; must experience in his own individual person the *lex talionis* of offended nature—eye for eye, tooth for tooth, hand for hand, burning for burning, wound for wound, stripe for stripe.—*F. W. Farrar, D D.*

(*b*) I wish we did believe in prayer: I am afraid most of us do not. People will say, "What a wonderful thing it is that God hears George Müller's prayers!" But is it not a sad thing that we should think it wonderful for God to hear prayer? We are come to a pretty pass certainly when we think it wonderful that God is true! Much better faith was that of a little boy in one of the schools at Edinburgh, who had attended the prayer-meetings, and at last said to his teacher who conducted the prayer-meeting, "Teacher, I wish my sister could be got to read the Bible; she never reads it." "Why, Johnny, should your sister read the Bible?" "Because if she once could read it, I am sure it would do her good, and she would be converted and be saved." "Do you think so, Johnny?" "Yes, I do, sir, and I wish the next time there's a prayer-meeting you would ask the people to pray for my sister, that she may begin to read the Bible." "Well, well, it shall be done, John." So the teacher gave out that a little boy was very anxious that prayers should be offered that his sister might begin to read the Bible. John was observed to get up and go out. The teacher thought it very unkind of the boy to disturb the people in a crowded room and go out like that, and so the next day when the lad came, he said, "John, I thought that was very rude of you to get up in the prayer meeting and go out. You ought not to have done it." "Oh! sir," said the boy, "I did not mean to be rude, but I thought I should just like to go home and see my sister read her Bible for the first time." That is how we ought to believe, and wait with expectation to see the answer to prayer. The girl was reading the Bible when the boy went home. God had been pleased to hear the prayer; and if we could but trust God after that fashion we should often see similar things accomplished.—*C. H. Spurgeon.*

Frail art thou, O man, as a bubble on the breaker,
Weak, and governed by externals, like a poor
  bird caught in the storm;
Yet thy momentary breath can still the raging
  waters,
Thy hand can touch a lever that may move
  the world.
O Merciful! we strike eternal covenant with
  Thee,
For man may take for his ally the King who
  ruleth kings;
How strong, yet how most weak, in utter
  poverty how rich,
What possible omnipotence to good is dormant
  in a man;
Prayer is a creature's strength, his very breath
  and being;
Prayer is the golden key which can open the
  wicket of mercy;
Prayer is the magical sound that saith to Fate,
  So be it;
Prayer is the slender nerve that moveth the
  muscles of Omnipotence.—*M. F. Tupper.*

(*c*) Mercy is God's Benjamin, and He delighteth most of all in it. It is the son of His right hand, though, alas! in bringing it forth, it might well have been called the son of sorrow, too, for mercy came into this world through the sorrows of the only-begotten Son of God. He delights in mercy, just as some men delight in trade, some in the arts, some in professions; and each man, according to his delight, becomes proficient in pursuing a work for the very love thereof. So God is proficient in mercy. He addicts Himself to it. He is most God-like, most happy, if such a thing may be said of Him, when He is stretching out His right hand with his golden sceptre in it, and saying to the guilty, "Come to Me, touch this sceptre, and you shall live." —*C. H. Spurgeon.*

Miriam smitten with Leprosy: Transfiguration through Transgression.

(*Verse* 10.)

I. This transfiguration was brought to pass on account of the jealousy of Miriam of Moses, and the jealousy of God for Moses.

"Hath the Lord indeed spoken only by Moses?" (ver. 2). "Were ye not afraid to speak against My servant Moses?" (ver. 8).

Thoughts that contain the venom of jealousy, when expressed, form the character and pass judgment upon it. (Comp. Matt. xii. 37.) Miriam's jealousy of her brother came out in her speech, and her speech brought miraculous judgment upon her. God was jealous of the honour of His servant, and *His* jealousy manifested itself in words of reproof. So a righteous and sinful jealousy led to this transforming judgment. God's words justified Him; Miriam's condemned her.

II. The transformation was in keeping with the expressed jealousy of God and of Miriam.

The narrative leads us to think that Miriam's feelings broke forth like sudden fire. While she was "musing, the fire burned," and she spake bitter and angry words. And we are told that the Lord likewise spake suddenly (ver. 4) in words of authority and reproof. And the punishment came suddenly. "The cloud departed, and behold Miriam became leprous." So, we are told, shall "the coming of the Son of Man be" (Matt. xxiv. 27). The indignation of the Lord was great, the bitter feeling of Miriam was intense, and the disease which was the consequence of both was of the most malignant kind.

Lessons.

I. That inequalities of position in the Church of God have their origin in the will of God. Vessels belonging to the same owner vary in the amount of cargo they carry because they vary in their capacity. One is 1,000 tons burthen, another 500, and so on. But why do they differ in tonnage? This must be referred to the will of the owner who built each one. The forest trees are all free to grow, but the willow cannot attain to the dimensions of the oak, or the ash to the strength of the cedar of Lebanon. It has not been given to them to do so. So there are intellectual inequalities among God's servants (Comp. Matt. xxv. 15). Why not give to each one the same number of talents? Why does not the shipbuilder build each vessel of the same size? or the Creator make each tree exactly like its fellow? Because they are destined for different service, and this destiny must be referred to the will of their owners. Neither Miriam nor Aaron could grow into a Moses.

II. That God is, from a *blessed necessity,* a respecter of persons in relation to *character.*

Some of God's children command more affection and respect than others, because they deserve more. We find ourselves under the necessity of esteeming some more highly than others, and God is, so to speak, under the same blessed necessity. He did esteem Moses more highly than He esteemed Aaron or Miriam, and the reason is found, not in his mental superiority, but because he "was very meek, above all the men which were upon the face of the earth" (ver. 3).

III. That the abstract devil of jealousy *within* the Church of God hinders its progress more than a legion of personal devils *without*. "The people journeyed not," &c., (ver. 15). When leaders of an army become jealous of each other's reputation, they let loose an enemy which will soon take the wheels off the artillery, and ham-string the horses; and the same devil in the Church of God has often made the chariot wheels go heavily.

IV. The practice and precept of the New Testament were anticipated by some Old Testament saints. The river at its well-head may be narrow, but the water is the same in quality as it is when it flows into the ocean. The channel was not so broad, but the spirit was the same. "Heal her now, O God, I beseech Thee" (ver. 13), anticipates Acts vii. 60; Luke xxiii. 34; Matt. v. 44.—*From "Outlines of Sermons on the Miracles and Parables of the Old Testament."*

The Prayer of Moses for Miriam.

(*Verses* 13-15.)

A man's foes too often are those of his own house. The sister and brother of Moses spake against him; his marriage displeased them; their resentment led them beyond the mere expression of discontent; they question his authority, envy his power, are jealous of his position. They have much influence—the one a prophetess, the other a high priest. But for Divine interposition the whole of Israel might have been led to revolt against Moses' authority. "The Lord heard it." They are summoned to His presence. He applauds Moses; Miriam becomes a leper; Aaron also was punished. *For the lips that sinned with Miriam must pronounce her leprous.* And now Moses turns to God, and prays for Miriam's recovery.

I. **The prayer.** How conclusively does it attest the excellency of the character of Moses! How worthy of power is one so large-hearted and forgiving! How much of resemblance is there between the behaviour of Moses and the law of Christ! "Pray for them which despitefully use you."

1. *The prayer was explicit.* Nothing vague. He prays not for wrong doers in the mass, but for one in particular, and that one who had wronged him. Many will pray general prayers heartily enough. Lips willing to say, "Have mercy on us miserable sinners," refuse to say, "Lord, be merciful to *me* a sinner."

2. *The prayer was earnest.* "I beseech Thee." Did he see the Shekinah receding (ver. 10), and would have God return at once? God's withdrawals excite prayer.

3. *The prayer was generous.* "Heal her now." Not make her penitent, or cause her to beg forgiveness, and then heal her, or remove the disease after a certain time, but, "Heal her now." This is how *true brothers* always pray. Sympathy produces generosity and earnestness.

4. *The prayer was well-timed.* He waited not till the memory of her sin and her wrong were fainter; at once his cry goes up, as Miriam's departing foot-fall is heard. "Love one another." We are not to "give place unto wrath." *He gives* Place *who gives* Time.

II. **The answer.** ver. 14.

1. *It was most gracious.* He condescended to return and speak to Moses. Intimates she shall be healed at the expiration of seven days.

2. *It was most wise.* Seven days she must suffer for her own good, for Aaron's good, for all Israel's good, to show that an exalted position in His service does not exempt from the punishment of sin.

3. *It was most speedy.* He answered at once. Why so speedy? Because He desired the innocent should not be afflicted with the guilty. Read ver. 14, how God sets forth the

case to Moses, so that he, seeing the wisdom of the punishment, and God's grace in curtailing it, may be at rest.

Think, brethren, of the Miriams without the camp, think of the time when, timbrel in hand, they joined with you; now kneel with Moses to pray, "Heal them now, O God."—*R. A. Griffin.*

CHAPTER XIII.

CRITICAL AND EXPLANATORY NOTES.

Verses 1, 2. *And the Lord spake unto Moses,* &c.

It appears from Deut. i. 22, 23, that the sending of the spies to search out the land was suggested by the people and approved by Moses; and here it is permitted by the Lord. God had commanded them to go and take possession of the land; and the motion to send the spies was an expression of their unbelief.

Everyone a ruler among them. By a comparison of the names of these "rulers" with those of "the princes of the tribes" (chap. i. 5-16), we see that they were not the same in any one case. These now sent forth were doubtless selected from the chiefs of each tribe for their fitness for the work entrusted to them. In verse 3 they are spoken of as "heads of the children of Israel;" *i.e.,* heads of families.

Verse 16. *And Moses called Oshea . . . . Jehoshua.* Oshea, Hoshea, or Hosea signifies help or deliverance. To this Moses added a syllable of the sacred Name, and made it Jehoshua, contracted into Joshua, which signifies Jehovah is help, or deliverance; or, "whose help is Jehovah." This verse does not imply that the alteration in the name was made at this time. It was probably made at the time of, and in consequence of his victory over the Amalekites (Exod. xvii. 8-16).

Verse 17. *Get you up this way southward.* Or, "Get you up there in the south country." *The Negeb* (south country) primarily signifies a dry, parched district, from *nagab,* to be dried up, to be withered. This name was applied to the southern and least fertile district of Canaan, which "extended northward from Kadesh to within a few miles of Hebron, and from the Dead Sea westward to the Mediterranean (cf. especially Josh. xv. 21-32)."

And go up into the mountain. The hill-country of Palestine, including the mountains of Judah and Ephraim or Israel. The expressions "the south country" and "the mountain" seem intended to set forth the whole land of Canaan.

Verse 19. *In tents,* or camps, *i.e.,* in open or unwalled villages.

Verse 20. *The time of the first-ripe grapes.* The first grapes ripen in Palestine as early as August, and sometimes even in July; and the vintage takes place in September and October. It appears to us most probable that the spies were despatched early in August. Dr. Kitto, however, conjectures that "probably they set out early in September, and returned about the middle of October."

Verse 21. *The wilderness of Zin.* The north-eastern portion of the great desert of Paran, and part of the southern border of the Promised Land (chap. xxxiv. 4; Josh. xv. 1-3). (See notes on "The wilderness of Paran," chap. xii. 16).

Rehob as men come to Hamath, or "at the entrance of Hamath," *i.e.,* at the commencement of the territory of that name, on the northern boundary of Canaan. Rehob was probably the Bethrehob of Judg. xviii. 28, near to Dan-Laish, the modern *Tell el Kady.*

Hamath, the principal city of Upper Syria, from the time of the Exodus to that of the prophet Amos. It is situated on the Orontes. Antiochus

Epiphanes changed its name to Epiphaneia. Hamah is its present name.

The spies went through the whole land from the southern to the northern frontier.

Verse 22. *Came unto Hebron.* Hebron signifies an associate or friend. A most ancient city, situated amongst the mountains (Josh. xx. 7), 20 Roman miles south of Jerusalem, and the same distance north of Beersheba. It was a well known place, when Abram entered Canaan about 3800 years ago (Gen. xiii. 18). Trapp points out that at Hebron "lay buried those three reverend couples: Abraham and Sarah, Isaac and Rebekah, Jacob and Leah (Gen. xlix. 31). Here David began his reign over Israel (2 Sam. ii. 1), and hither came Mary to visit Elizabeth (Luke i. 39)."

The original name of Hebron was Kirjath-Arba, the city of Arba, so called from Arba, the father of Anak and progenitor of the Anakim (Josh. xv. 13, 14; xxi. 11).

Ahiman, Sheshai, and Talmai, the children of Anak. Probably the names not of individuals, but of tribes of Anakim; for we meet with them again fifty years or more after this time (Josh. xv. 14).

Anak, the name of the ancestor of the Anakim, signifies long-necked.

Now Hebron was built seven years before Zoan in Egypt. "Some think," says Dr. A. Clarke, "it was to humble the pride of the Egyptians, who boasted the highest antiquity, that this note concerning the higher antiquity of Hebron was introduced by Moses."

Zoan, an ancient city situated near the eastern border of Lower Egypt, and called by the Greeks and Romans *Tanis.* At the time of the Exodus the Pharaoh dwelt at Zoan (Psa. lxxviii. 43).

Verse 23. *The brook of Eshcol,* or, The valley of the cluster, or bunch; a fertile *wady,* probably about two miles north of Hebron, where the largest and best grapes in the whole of Palestine are grown, besides apricots, figs, pomegranates, &c., in abundance.

One cluster of grapes and they bare it, &c. Not simply because of the size of the cluster did they carry it in this way, but chiefly to prevent its being bruised. Clusters of grapes of great size are found in Palestine. "Pliny mentions," says Dr. A. Clarke, "bunches of grapes in Africa each of which was larger than an infant. Paul Lucas mentions some bunches which he saw at Damascus that weighed above forty-five pounds. I myself once cut down a bunch of grapes nearly twenty pounds in weight. Those who live in cold climates can scarcely have any conception to what perfection both grapes and other fruits grow in climates that are warm, and where the soil is suitable to them."

Verse 26. *Kadesh* signifies the Holy Place or Sanctuary. Great uncertainty exists as to the situation of Kadesh. Dr. Robinson identified it with Ain el-Weibeh, on the western side of the Arabah; and this identification has been generally accepted by English geographers as the most probable. Dean Stanley (*Sinai and Pal.,* pp. 93-96) identifies Kadesh with Petra. But Petra was in the heart of Edom, while Kadesh is said to be "in the uttermost border" of that land (chap. xx. 16). And in chap. xxxiii. 37 an encampment at Mount Hor is mentioned as quite distinct from the encampment at Kadesh, and Mount Hor is situated close to Edom. Moreover, in chap. xxxiv. 4, and Josh. xv. 3, Kadesh is reckoned as part of the land of Canaan. Keil and Del. are of the opinion that "the name Kadesh embraces a large district of the desert of Zin, and is not confined to one particular spot." The conclusion of Mr. Hayman (Smith's *Bible Dict.,* arts. "Kadesh" and "Wilderness of the Wandering") seems to us satisfactory: "It seems that Kadesh probably means, firstly, a region of the desert spoken of as having a relation, sometimes with the wilderness of Paran, and sometimes with that of Zin (comp. vers. 21, 26); and secondly, a distinct city within that desert limit."

Ver. 32. *A land that eateth up the*

inhabitants thereof does not mean "that it was so barren and unfruitful that it did not produce food sufficient for the inhabitants of it." Keil and Del. give what we regard as the correct interpretation: "The land was an apple of discord, because of its fruitfulness and situation; and as the different nations strove for its possession, its inhabitants wasted away."

The Sending forth of the Spies.

(*Verses* 1-20.)

The people have now arrived at the border of the Promised Land; and there seems to be no reason why they may not, if they will, speedily enter and take possession of it. But instead of this, they propose to send spies into the land to investigate it, and bring back a report to them. The results of this in the subsequent history were both great and disastrous.

Consider :—

I. The Origin of this Expedition.

"And the Lord spake unto Moses, saying, send thou men," &c. (vers. 1, 2). But we find, from the history as given in Deut. i. 20-25, that the proposal to search the land originated with the people themselves, and was an expression of their unbelief, and, at the least, a failure to render prompt obedience to the command of the Lord. Let us see how the case stood at this time. (1) God had Himself declared to them the excellence of the land (Exod. iii. 8; xxxiii. 3). (2) He had promised to guide them to the land (Exod. xxxii. 34; xxxiii. 2, 14). Moreover, He was visibly present with them in the mysterious and majestic pillar of cloud and fire. (3) He had promised to drive out the heathen nations and give them possession of the land (Exod. xxiii. 20-33; Deut. i. 8). (4) He commanded them to "go up and possess" the land (Deut. i, 8, 21). (5) Yet their answer was, "We will send men before us, and they shall search us out the land," &c. (Deut. i. 22). Clearly their duty was not to send men to search out the land, but trusting in God, to obey His voice and go and take possession of the land. Their proposition involved a sinful distrust of the presence of God with them and of His promises to them; it also involved a failure in their obedience to Him. Moses did not suspect the unbelief which had suggested their proposal; and approving it himself, he asked counsel of the Lord, who permitted it. God may allow us to carry out our unbelieving plans to our own confusion. If we will "lean unto our own understanding," He will let us take our way until we find what utter folly our fancied wisdom is. (*a*). In this way in after years when they demanded a king, God directed Samuel to "hearken unto their voice, and make them a king" (1 Sam. viii. 5-22). Our business is not to suggest alterations in or additions to the Divine plans, but heartily to trust and promptly to obey the Divine Word.

II. The Agents in this Expedition.

"Of every tribe of their fathers shall ye send a man, every one a ruler among them," &c. (vers. 2-16). Three points here require notice:

1. *The wisdom of this arrangement.* (1) In sending one man from each tribe. By this arrangement every tribe was represented, and would have a witness of its own. (2) In sending a leading man from each tribe. They were approved men, men of influence, and therefore their testimony would be the more likely to be received and credited.

2. *The scarcity of worthy leaders.* We see here that a large proportion of even these leading men, these "rulers" and "heads of the children of Israel," were inferior men and unworthy of the position which they occupied. Here are the names of twelve men, and ten of them seem to have been feeble and common-place men, and (as we shall

hereafter see) deficient in faith, in enterprise, and in courage. How many of the world's heroes and leaders are mentally weak and morally inferior, or even corrupt men! The true hero and the worthy leader often fail of recognition except by a superior few. Hitherto in the world's history the majority of the leaders of men have been feeble and cowardly, and very often base and corrupt. (*b*)

3. *The diversity of human fame.* The names of these twelve men have been handed down from generation to generation, and at the present time the record which contains them is to be found throughout the whole of the known world; but how different are the positions which they occupy! Two of them, Joshua and Caleb, are in the foremost rank of saints and heroes: while the other ten are known as the chief agents in arresting the progress of the nation for more than thirty-eight years. History perpetuates the memory of Nero as well as of St. Paul, of Judas Iscariot as well as of Jesus Christ. We are making our posthumous reputation now; let us take heed that it be of a worthy character. (*c*)

III. **The Aims of this Expedition.**

"And Moses sent them to spy out the land of Canaan, and said unto them, Get you up," &c. (vers. 17-20). They were to examine and report as to the condition of—

1. *The land,* whether it was fertile or barren, whether it was wooded or bare, &c.
2. *The towns,* whether they were walled and fortified or open and unprotected, &c.
3. *The people,* whether they were strong or weak, whether they were few or many, &c.

Their investigation was to be *thorough.* " Get you up there in the south country, and go up into the mountain." They were to search the whole land of Canaan. Partial investigations are apt to prove misleading.

Their report was to be *verified.* " And bring of the fruit of the land." They were charged to bring of the fruit as a confirmation of their testimony.

IV. **The Spirit appropriate to this Expedition.**

"And be ye of good courage." The mission with which they were entrusted would require firm and fearless hearts; for if the object of their journey had been discovered by the Canaanites, it would have fared ill with them. They needed courage, too, in order that they might view things hopefully, and bring back an inspiring report. Want of courage in its leaders is a sore hindrance and calamity to any people. The courage they needed could spring only from faith in God, and could be sustained only by faith in Him. Faith in Him is the soul of all true heroism. (*d*)

ILLUSTRATIONS.

(*a*) A man sets his mind on standing on some high place; he points to a pillar and says that if he could ascend to its summit he would see from that lofty elevation glimpses of heaven, and he determines that he will stand upon that summit, whatever hazards he may incur. At length God grants him his request, and when the man has ascended to the eminence which he coveted, what does he find? Sand, sand, sand! Mile on mile of sand—sand for mile on mile! And now he wishes to descend; but how to get down is his great difficulty. There may be no way down but that which involves suicide. Yet the man was determined to reach that elevation; nothing could stand between him and his wish; he urged God to grant him his request; with importunate desire he besought that he might have his way; and there is no punishment heavier than that which falls upon any man when God allows him to take his own course.—*Joseph Parker, D.D.*

(*b*) The servile *imitancy* of mankind might be illustrated under the figure, itself nowise *original,* of a Flock of Sheep. Sheep go in flocks for three reasons: First, because they are of a gregarious temper, and *love* to be together: Secondly, because of their cowardice; they are afraid to be left alone: Thirdly, because the common run of them are dull of sight, to a proverb, and can have no choice in roads; sheep can in fact see nothing; in a celestial Luminary, and a scoured pewter Tankard, they would discern only that both dazzled them, and were of unspeakable glory. How like their fellow-creatures of the human species! Men, too, are gregarious; then surely faint-hearted enough, trembling to be left by themselves; above all, dull-sighted, down to the verge of utter blindness. Thus are we seen ever running in torrents, and mobs, if we run at all; and after what foolish scoured Tankards, mistaking them for Suns! Foolish Turnip-lanterns likewise, to all appearance supernatural, keep whole nations quaking, their hair on end. Neither know we, except by blind habit, where the good pastures lie: solely when the sweet grass is between our teeth, we know it, and chew it; also when grass is bitter and scant, we know it,—and bleat and butt: these last two facts we know of a truth and in very deed. Thus do Men and Sheep play their parts on this nether Earth; wandering restlessly in large masses, they know not whither; for most part, each following his neighbour, and his own nose.—*Thomas Carlyle.*

(*c*) Posthumous influence invests life with enhanced dignity. While Bunyan lived he was but as a mustard-seed; now he is as a great cathedral tree, in which ten thousand voices are lifted up in laudatory and grateful song! "Thou fool! that which thou sowest is not quickened except it die." No living man is complete. While your heart beats you are undergoing a process. Time will mellow you; age will tone your character. Do not urge society to give you a verdict just now. Society is too heated and confused to pronounce upon you with the accuracy of deliberation and the dignity of repose. Death will befriend you. A most solemn and righteous estimation of character is often introduced by death. The green hillock in the yard of the dead is a judgment-seat which might appal an unjust judge. Your appeal, then, under all misapprehension and misrepresentation, must be to the new hours which Time has yet to strike from her bell, and which shall chime out many a reversal of condemnation, and many a fulfilment of expectation long deferred.—*Joseph Parker. D.D.*

(*d*) The courage that can go forth, once and away, to Chalk-Farm, and have itself shot, and snuffed out, with decency, is nowise wholly what we mean here. Such courage we indeed esteem an exceeding small matter; capable of co-existing with a life full of falsehood, feebleness, poltroonery, and despicability. Nay, oftener it is cowardice rather that produces the result: for consider, Is the Chalk-Farm pistoleer inspired with any reasonable Belief and Determination; or is he hounded on by haggard indefinable Fear,—how he will be *cut* at public places, and "plucked geese of the neighbourhood" will wag their tongues at him a plucked goose? If he go, then, and be shot without shrieking or audible uproar, it is well for him: nevertheless there is nothing amazing in it. Courage to manage all this has not perhaps been denied to any man, or to any woman. Thus, do not recruiting sergeants drum through the streets of manufacturing towns, and collect ragged losels enough; every one of whom, if once dressed in red, and trained a little, will receive fire cheerfully for the small sum of one shilling *per diem*, and have the soul blown out of him at last, with perfect propriety. The Courage that dares only *die*, is on the whole no sublime affair; necessary, indeed, yet universal; pitiful when it begins to parade itself. On this Globe of ours, there are some thirty-six persons that manifest it, seldom with the smallest failure, during every second of time. Nay, look at Newgate: do not the offscourings of creation, when condemned to the gallows as if they were not men but vermin, walk thither with decency, and even to the scowls and hootings of the whole universe give their stern good-night in silence? What is to be undergone only once, we may undergo; what must be, comes almost of its own accord. Considered as Duellist, what a poor figure does the fiercest Irish Whiskerando make, compared with any English Game-cock, such as you may buy for fifteen pence!

The Courage we desire and prize is not the courage to die decently, but to live manfully. This, when by God's grace it has been given, lies deep in the soul; like genial heat, fosters all other virtues and gifts; without it they could not live. In spite of our innumerable Waterloos and Peterloos, and such campaigning as there has been, this Courage we allude to, and call the only true one, is perhaps rarer in these last ages, than it has been in any other since the Saxon Invasion under Hengist. Altogether extinct it can never be among men; otherwise the species Man were no longer for this world: here and there, in all times, under various guises, men are sent hither not only to demonstrate but exhibit it, and testify, as from heart to heart, that it is still possible, still practicable.—*Thomas Carlyle.*

GLIMPSES OF THE BETTER LAND.

(*Verses* 1, 2.)

I. The search.
II. The retreat.
III. An emblem of God's dealings with His people.
  1. The children of Israel were sent back to the wilderness on account of their sin.
  2. While they are sent in judgment, they go back of their own accord.
  3. Though the fruit of sin, and the

token of God's righteous displeasure, all was overruled for their good.

4. Though chastened and afflicted they are not cast off. (1) They are Divinely delivered. (2) They are Divinely sustained. (3) They are Divinely guided. (4) They are Divinely chastened.

IV. Improvement.

1. Let young believers be not high-minded, but fear.
2. Let backsliders remember and weep.
3. Let tried and troubled saints take fresh courage.—*J. Burns.*

THE EXPLORATION OF THE PROMISED LAND BY THE SPIES, AN ILLUSTRATION OF HUMAN INQUIRIES INTO DIVINE REALMS.

(*Verses* 21-25.)

I. **The exploration of the Promised Land by the Spies was thorough.**

"So they went up, and searched the land from the wilderness of Zin unto Rehob, at the entrance of Hamath." They went quite through the land from the *Negeb* in the south to Rehob on the northern border. In this they are worthy of imitation by inquirers into Divine realms. It is the shallow and superficial students of *Nature*, of *Providence*, and of the *Bible* who carp and cavil at the discoveries which they make; for such investigators can only make obscure, partial, one-sided discoveries. If man would be admitted into the secrets of Nature, of Providence, or of the Bible; if he would discover the power, the wisdom, and the grace which are enshrined in them; if he would be brought into communion with the mind and spirit of their Divine Author, he must investigate them thoroughly, patiently, and reverently. (*a*)

II. **The exploration of the Promised Land by the spies led to the discovery of difficulties.**

1. *They discovered formidable enemies to their taking possession of the land.* "And they came unto Hebron; where Ahiman, Sheshai, and Talmai, the children of Anak, were." Before they entered upon the Promised Land the Israelites would have to conquer these mighty tribes. We cannot attain unto a large and correct acquaintance with the revelation of God in Nature, Providence, or the Bible, without battling with and overcoming many and grave difficulties. We cannot attain unto self-conquest, self-possession, without patient, persistent, and courageous warfare. We cannot inherit the Promised Land of Divine privileges without determined struggles with powerful foes. Our own unbelief, carnality, worldliness, and selfishness; the corrupt influences of society; and the temptations of the devil,—these are the Anakim with which we must contend, and which we must conquer if we would enter into full possession of our Promised Land. No true kingdom is ever entered except "through much tribulation." (*b*)

2. *They discovered these formidable enemies where they least expected them.* It was at Hebron that they found the Anakim. Now Hebron was sacred in the annals of the greatest of their ancestors. Abraham and Sarah, Isaac and Rebekah, Jacob and Leah all found their last resting place there (Gen. xxiii. 19, 20; xlix. 31); yet there they find the tribes that are likely to offer the stoutest resistance to their taking the land. "In that place where they expected the greatest encouragements they met with the greatest discouragements. Where the bodies of their ancestors kept possession for them the giants kept possession against them." So with us in Christian life and enterprise, it is not where we feel there is danger and are guarding against it that our real foes and grave perils are; but in places and in circumstances where we least expect them. How often have godly men failed where they seemed most strong! Abraham was preëminent for faith; yet he fell into sin more than once through the failure of his

233

faith in little trials. Peter deemed his courage unquestionable and invincible; yet it was his courage that gave way in the hour of trial.

III. **The exploration of the Promised Land by the spies led to the discovery of rich treasures.**

"And they came unto the brook of Eshcol, and cut down from thence," &c. (23-25).

1. *The discovered treasures were rich.* The valley of Eshcol was celebrated for its abundant and choice fruits. One very large and rich bunch of grapes they cut and conveyed from thence to the people. "They cut down from thence a branch with one cluster, and they bare it between two upon a staff," &c. (c)

How rich are the fruits of that inheritance of Divine privilege to which God calls us! What satisfaction, peace, hope, joy! &c.

2. *The discovered treasures were various.* "Grapes, pomegranates, and figs." How various are the treasures and delights God bestows upon His people! They have joy in the new discoveries of truth; joy in high and holy fellowships; joy in Christ-like service; joy in loving and being loved, &c.

3. *Specimens of the discovered treasures were carried to the people by the explorers.* "They cut down a branch with one cluster," &c. The probability is that Caleb and Joshua brought this cluster; for the other explorers were not disposed to encourage the people to attempt to to take possession of the land. The knowledge and enjoyments we now have of Divine things are but specimens and foretastes of what is reserved in heaven for us. The "fulness of joy," and the "far more exceeding and eternal weight of glory," await us in the hereafter.

4. *The discovered treasures deeply impressed the mind of the explorers and of those who saw the specimens.* We see this from the fact that the valley from which the bunch of grapes was cut was henceforth called, "the valley of the cluster." "The place was called the brook Eshcol, because of the cluster of grapes which the children of Israel cut down from thence." Were we not blinded and prejudiced by sin, the rich treasures of Gospel grace would so impress our hearts that we should eagerly seek Him in whom they are stored and through whom they are bestowed.

ILLUSTRATIONS.

(a) Only those who wait upon the Bible through a life-time of prayer, study, and patience, can be rewarded with an intelligent and beautiful reverence for it, as for "the Wisdom of God in a mystery." Think! it is not simply Wisdom, but the Wisdom *of God*, and not simply the Wisdom of God, but the Wisdom of God *in a mystery.*

Very notable is the agreement between the Book, and every man's *deep* nature. "Deep calleth unto deep." The Bible is the only *profoundly* human thing in the world. The world, and all that is in the world, are in agreement only with our shallow nature. When conscience awakes from its sensual slumbers, there is a marvellous agreement between its suspicions, its fears, its dark utterances, and the Old Testament. The true Mount Sinai is in the human soul. But there are also deep and far-reaching longings in man, as well as conscience, and the New Testament is a complete answer to all these longings.

The Bible seems to be the law of my own being outwritten. It meets every difficulty, it throws light on every mystery, it supplies every want, it leaves nothing to be desired.

There is much in the Book to exercise both patience and hope; and I need both. I need patience, under the present dark and corrupt condition of nature, and I need hope, that the mystery of God will be finished. It is finished in our Lord Jesus Christ. When all the redeemed shall have the Spirit of Christ for their spirit, and when all matter shall be like unto His glorious Body, then the mystery of God will be finished also in the universe.—*John Pulsford.*

(b) Any service for God, if it be done at all, should be hard work. If you want to be feather-bed soldiers, go and enlist somewhere else; but Christ's soldiers must fight, and they will find the battle rough and stern. We, of the Church militant, are engaged in no mimic manœuvres and grand parades; our life is real and earnest; our battle, though not with flesh and blood, is with spiritual wickedness in high places, and it involves hard blows and keen anguish. You must look for real fighting if you become a soldier of Christ, and O, Sir, if the excuse for fainting be that the work is toilsome, that it is too much a drag upon you, why did you begin it? You ought to have known this at the first. You should have counted the cost. But, ah, let me add, the work was not toilsome when your heart was loving, neither would it now be so hard if your soul were right with God. This is but an unworthy excuse. Ardent spirits love difficulties; fervent love delights in making sacrifices; they would not wish to swim for ever in smooth seas of pleasure; they know that manhood's truest glory lies in contending with and overcoming that which is hard. Give to the child the easy task, but let the man have something worth the doing to perform. Instead of shrinking because the work is tedious, we ought to gird up our loins and push on the enterprise with all the greater force.—*C. H. Spurgeon.*

(c) In conformity with the text before us, the size and richness of the *clusters* of the grapes in many parts of Palestine excite more astonishment than even the size and richness of the grapes. An Italian traveller, Mariti, avers, that in different parts of Syria he saw clusters that would be a sufficient burden for one man. A German traveller, Neitzschutz, declares, with some solemnity of assertion, that in the mountains of Israel he had seen and eaten from vine clusters that were half an ell long, and the grapes of which were equal to two finger joints in length. A very intelligent French traveller, Nau, is still more particular. He declares that one who had seen the vine only in the vine countries of France and Italy, could form no just conception of the size to which the clusters attain in Syria. He had himself seen clusters weighing ten or twelve pounds; and he had reason to believe that in the Archipelago clusters of thirty or forty pounds were not uncommon. A still older traveller of the same nation, Doubdan, tells us that, travelling near Bethlehem, he found himself in a delightful valley, replete with rose-trees and aromatic plants, and planted with vines. This was that which tradition regards as the valley of Eshcol, from which the spies obtained their cluster. Not being there in the season, he did not see the fruit himself; but he was assured that clusters of ten and twelve pounds were not seldom gathered from these vines. We share the doubt, however, that this was the vale of Eshcol, which seems rather to have been near to Hebron. It was in this neighbourhood that Nau saw the large vine-clusters of which he makes mention. In this quarter the hill-sides are still thickly planted with vineyards, the vines of which are laden with large clusters of delicious grapes. It is beyond a doubt that the cluster in question was gathered in the south of Palestine; for as the spies had seen these grapes in their outward way, it would have been absurd for them to gather any but at the last available point towards their own encampment. As striking an instance as any that we have quoted, has occurred in our own country, in regard to the produce of a *Syrian* vine at Welbeck, the seat of the Duke of Portland. A bunch from this vine was sent, in 1819, as a present to the Marquis of Buckingham, which weighed nineteen pounds. It was conveyed to its destination, more than twenty miles distant, on a staff, by four labourers, two of whom bore it in rotation; thus affording a striking illustration of the means adopted by the explorers in transporting the Eshcol cluster. The greatest diameter of this Welbeck cluster was nineteen inches and a half; its circumference four feet and a half; and its length nearly twenty-three inches.—*John Kitto, D.D., F.S.A.*

ESHCOL.

(*Verse* 23.)

"They came unto the brook of Eshcol, and cut down from thence a branch with one cluster of grapes."

We reach the brook of Eshcol through a humbling path. When Sinai is left the march of Israel advances prosperously. There is no check. And now a few more steps will plant the pilgrim-host in Canaan.

Surely courage will now brace each nerve, &c. But is it so? Alas! they pause. The unworthy thought creeps in—perchance the nations are too strong for us, &c. Thus they distrust: and tremblingly propose to search the country by spies. They follow sight—not faith. And unbelief is not dead. It lurks in corners of each heart, &c. Beware—look inward . . . . He is the fool of fools, who tests Divine assurances in the scales of mortal vision.

The spies are named. They are sent forth to ascertain whether their God be true, &c.

Contemplate that cluster which they bear—that earnest of rich fields. These grapes are proof of Canaan's exuberant fertility. So, too, there is a heavenly Eshcol before faith's eye. It shows delicious clusters. The joy before

Christ cheered His heart. The joy before us should gird up our loins. The racer bounds when he discerns the goal just won. Come, then, in Eshcol's grapes read faith's amazing prize.

Heaven! It is the palace of the great Eternal. Salvation for its walls—its gates are praise. Its atmosphere is perfect love It is the home prepared of God before the worlds were made, for His redeemed children. It is the mansion which the ascended Jesus still labours to make fit. It is so fair that all Jehovah's skill cannot increase the beauty. . . .

This cluster was the vine's perfection. So, too, perfection is the essence of our heaven. Nothing can enter there to stain, &c. Oh! what a contrast to our present state! . . . But our high home is barricaded against sin.

Here the foul tempter all day long is spreading nets. There is no saint too saintly for his vile approach. In Eden he approached the innocent. To Jesus he said, Worship me. . . . . But in heaven this misery has ceased. Satan is without—far off—the bottomless pit has shut its mouth upon him.

Here fears rush in. The ground is slippery. A precipice is near. We tremble on the brink . . . . May I not, after all, fail of salvation! But fear dies at heaven's gate. The happy company realize that they are lofty above injury.

Earth is affliction's home. A troop of sorrows compass us about. Death tears away the much-loved friend.

Sickness invades the frame . . . . But heaven is a wide sea of bliss without a ripple. All tears are wiped away. We bathe in oceans of delight.

Here unbelief oft gathers, as a chilly cloud. It mantles the soul in darkness . . . . But in heaven a present God is always everywhere. We cannot move beyond the sunshine of His love.

Here we thirst for knowledge, but we reach it not. How much concerning God is utterly beyond our grasp. Blindness curtails our prospect. Clouds narrow our circumference. But heaven is a realm without horizon. We know God, as we are known. We love intelligently, &c.

In the true Eshcol's cluster there is this richer fruit; Jesus is seen. This is the crown of heaven. The rising of the sun makes day. The presence of the king constitutes the court. The revelation of the Lord, without one intervening cloud, is the grand glory of the endless kingdom.

Believer, what will it be to gaze on the manifested beauty of Him, who is altogether lovely! What, to comprehend all that Jesus is! What, never to lose sight of Him!

Are you a traveller towards this heaven? When you behold the grapes of Eshcol, do you know that the vineyard is your sure heritage? The kingdom is for the subjects of the King. Are you His by faith? This is that Spirit-implanted confidence, which looks to Eshcol, and claims all Canaan as a promised home.—*Henry Law, D.D.*

THE REPORTS OF THE SPIES, AND THE LESSONS THESE REPORTS TEACH US.

(*Verses* 26-33.)

I. **Examine the Reports of the Spies.**

First: *The report of the majority.* The impression produced upon ten of the explorers from their survey differed from that produced upon the other two. We will first attend to the testimony of the ten.

1. *They testify to the fertility of the land.* "Surely it floweth with milk and honey; and this is the fruit of it" (See remarks on verses 23-25, and comp. Deut. viii. 7-9).

2. *They set forth the difficulties in the way of taking the land.* Speedily they pass from the cheering announcement of the fertility of the country to a gloomy and discouraging representation of the grave difficulties which opposed

their possession of it. "Nevertheless, the people be strong that dwell in the land," &c. (verses 28, 29, 32, 33). These obstacles which seemed to them insuperable were of two classes:—(1) The defences of the cities. "The cities are walled and very great." In their eyes every town was an impregnable stronghold. (2) The strength and stature of the inhabitants. "Moreover, we saw the children of Anak there," &c. "All the people that we saw in it are men of great stature," &c.

3. *They declare their inability to take the land.* "We be not able to go up against the people, for they are stronger than we." And yet the army of Israel numbered 600,000 able men, and was well organized.

4. *They suggest the difficulty of maintaining possession of the land.* "It is a land that eateth up the inhabitants thereof." According to their representation, by reason of the fertility of its soil and the importance of its situation, different nations contended for its possession; so that they who held it must needs be armed and watchful, and frequently suffer loss in battle.

5. *They exhibit the most despicable cowardice.* Surely the tone of their report is utterly unworthy of men who knew that the army of Israel was 600,000 strong. Alas! they were almost destitute of the higher attributes of manhood. If we would estimate the cowardice of their conduct aright we have but to compare, or rather contrast it with the conduct of Caleb (verse 30), or with that of David (1 Sam. xvii. 32-37). (*a*)

6. *They manifest the most deplorable and sinful unbelief.* In framing their conclusions and delivering their report they utterly ignored the Lord God. Faith in Him was entirely absent. Unbelief was supreme. Their unbelief was aggravated in its sinfulness by reason of—(1) The promises which He had repeatedly made to them. Had He not assured them again and again that he would give them the land? (2) The mighty works which He had wrought for them. Is it possible that they have forgotten the wonders wrought for them in Egypt and at the Red Sea? Could they discover no significance or feel no inspiration to faith in the daily miracle of the manna? (3) The visible symbol of His presence with them. The miraculous and majestic Pillar of His Presence was visible to every eye. Yet despite all these things unbelief held undisputed supremacy within them.

Second: *The Report of the minority.* Caleb and Joshua seem to have agreed with the report of the ten other spies in some particulars; but in two most important matters they differed from them. (1) Their impression of their relative power was different; they held that they were "well able to overcome" the inhabitants of the land. (2) Their advice as to their practical action was different; they counselled that they should "go up at once and possess" the land. In considering the conduct of Caleb, who was supported by Joshua, let us notice—

1. *The exhortation which he addressed to the people.* "Let us go up at once, and possess it." He exhorts to (1) *Mutual action.* "Let us go up." There is far more inspiration in, "Let us go," than in Let them go, or than in Go ye. (2) *Prompt action.* "Let us go up at once." He would lose no time in debating what they could do, or what they should do; but urges immediate and bold action. (3) *Confident action.* "Let us go up at once, and possess it." "He does not say, 'Let us go up, and conquer it;' he looks upon that to be as good as done already; but, 'Let us go up, and possess it; there is nothing to be done but to enter, and take the possession which God our great Lord is ready to give us.'"

2. *The assurance by which he enforced this exhortation.* "For we are well able to overcome it." The fortified cities and the giant peoples did not appal Caleb and Joshua. They were confident that Israel could vanquish the Canaanites and take the land.

3. *The faith in God which inspired this assurance.* The confidence of these two brave men was neither in the strength and courage of their army, nor in the skill and spirit of their leaders; but in the Lord their God. This is made abundantly clear in verses 8 and 9 of the following chapter. This faith of theirs had sure and splendid warranty in—(1) The divine promises to Israel. (2) The divine performances for Israel. (3) The Divine Presence with Israel. Their faith was profoundly *reasonable.* Can walled cities or armies of giants withstand the Almighty? (*b*) Their faith was thoroughly *religious.* It rested in God; it honoured Him.

II. Deduce the Lessons arising from these reports.

1. *A statement may be true as to matters of fact, yet false and evil in its spirit and influence.* The report of the ten spies was true as to actual facts; but the balance or proportion of its statements was false, the spirit which breathed in it was mean and cowardly, and its influence was extremely pernicious. A man may be guilty of lying while speaking the truth in words. You may lie by an accent, by disproportion of the respective branches of a narrative, by undue warmth in one thing and coldness in another, by the drapery in which bare facts are clothed. Truthfulness is a thing not merely of words, but first and chiefly of spirit.

2. *The cause of God has never been left without some true witnesses.* Here there were ten faithless cowards, but there were two brave believers; ten who brought an evil report, but two who brought a good report. "Thou hast a few names even in Sardis which have not defiled their garments."

3. *Majorities are not trustworthy criteria of truth and right.* Of the twelve explorers "only two deal faithfully and truly, the rest were treacherous and hollow-hearted hypocrites." "*Vox populi vox Dei,* is true only in a community of holy beings—true only in heaven. In a corrupt world like ours it is impossible for language to embody a greater falsehood. As the devil leads the world captive at his will, *Vox populi vox diaboli,* is the truth here." The popularity of a doctrine, or a cause, or a party, is no guarantee of its truth or righteousness. Because the many tread the wrong path our obligation to tread the right path is in no wise diminished. "Error does not become truth because majorities accept it, and truth does not become falsehood because a minority only accept it." Let us follow those things which are right and true whether they be popular or not.

4. *To judge by appearances only is foolish, sinful, and perilous.* The report of the ten spies was based solely upon what they saw through their bodily eyes! it does not take any account whatever of the presence, or power, or promise of God. In ordinary every-day purposes and duties he is a foolish man who trusts solely to bodily sight for guidance. To walk by sight alone instead of by faith; to accept the testimony of the senses, and reject the testimony of the soul; to trust our own reasonings rather than the Word of God, is egregious folly and heinous sin. Well does Mr. Carlyle say, "There is but one thing without honour; smitten with eternal barrenness, inability to do or to be: insincerity, unbelief. He who believes no *thing,* who believes only the shows of things, is not in relation with nature and fact at all." (*c*)

NOTE.—The points suggested in the preceding article are too numerous and important for one discourse. Three sermons may without difficulty be arranged on this section,— one, on *a discouraging report;* another, on *an encouraging exhortation;* and a third, on *modern lessons from ancient reports.*

ILLUSTRATIONS.

(*a*) Moral cowardice is the source of every mean and pitiful thing, renders a man afraid of duty, afraid of death; so that when the moment for action arrives, he equivocates, intreats, fears. Moral courage is religion in action; moral cowardice is religion in defeat. Oh, brother, exclaims a strenuous thinker, never strike sail to a fear, come gently into port or sail with God over the seas. Without courage, the courage of the heart, no one can be truly great. This is a courage that does not depend on thews or sinews, but on the soul. It animated the patriots and martyrs of old, as it animates the patriots and martyrs of to-day. Moral courage makes the man, the absence of it the knave, the driveller, and the fool. It is to the age's dishonour that its intellectual tendencies are marked with the characters of fear. Yet courage must be guided by purity and truth; since divested of these, it is shorn of half its strength.—*H. McCormac.*

(*b*) He who walks by sight only, walks in a blind alley. He who does not know the freedom and joy of reverent, loving speculation, wastes his life in a gloomy cell of the mouldiest of prisons. Even in matters that are not distinctively religious, faith will be found to be the inspiration and strength of the most useful life. It is faith that does the great work of the world. It is faith that sends men in search of unknown coasts. It is faith that retrims the lamp of inquiry, when sight is weary of the flame. It is faith that unfastens the cable and gives men the liberty of the seas. It is faith that inspires the greatest works in civilization. So we cannot get rid of religion unless we first get rid of faith, and when we get rid of faith we give up our birthright and go into slavery for ever.—*Joseph Parker, D.D.*

(*c*) Imagine a man who disbelieves everything he cannot see with his naked eye. Suppose that it should come to pass to-morrow that everything shall be taken away which cannot be read by the naked eye, or that has not been discovered by the naked eye. What will come? Shut up the heavens, for astronomy must go; and cover over the fields, for botany shall tell little to the naked eye. All science, indeed, would be impoverished, insulted, degraded. Yet the man who cannot read his own mother's letter without the aid of an eyeglass, insists upon reading the infinite and eternal God by his own unassisted powers; says, that whatsoever is too mysterious for his natural understanding is but worthy of insult, degradation, and contempt. I charge him, before God's face, with insulting his own common sense, and contradicting the highest experiences of mankind.—*Ibid.*

Walking by sight is just this—"I believe in myself;" whereas walking by faith is—"I believe in God." If I walk by sight, I walk by myself; if I walk by faith, then there are two of us, and the second One—ah! how great, how glorious, how mighty is He—the Great All-in-all—God-all-sufficient! Sight goes a warfare at its own charges, and becomes a bankrupt, and is defeated. Faith goes a warfare at the charges of the King's Exchequer, and there is no fear that Faith's bank shall ever be broken. Sight builds the house from its own quarry, and on its own foundation, but it begins to build and is never able to finish, and what it does build rests on the sand and falls. But faith builds on the foundation laid in eternity, in the fair colours of the Saviour's blood, in the covenant of grace. It goes to God for every stone to be used in the building, and brings forth the top-stone with shouting of "Grace, grace unto it."—*C. H. Spurgeon.*

Where men are called of God to go forth, it should be theirs instantly and gladly to obey, how dark soever or stormy the night into which they move. Life is a discipline. Shrewd men say they want to know whither they are going before they set out on a journey; but men of higher shrewdness, men of Christian faith, often go out into enterprise and difficulty without being able to see one step before them. The watchword of the noblest, truest souls is, "to walk by faith, not by sight;" faith has a wider dominion and a more splendid future.—*Joseph Parker, D.D.*

The Ancient Canaan, a Type of Heaven.

(*Verse* 30.)

I. In what respects the ancient Canaan was a type of heaven.

1. It was a promised land, and the right of possession was founded on the promise.

2. It was a land in which God was peculiarly present.

3. It was a land of fruition.

4. It was a free gift.

II. As the Israelites had dangers, difficulties, and discouragements on their way to Canaan, so have Christians in their progress to heaven.

1. There are formidable foes to be encountered.

2. There are adversaries in timid and faint hearted associates.

3. The Israelites in their progress were made dependent on the Lord for all things.

III. Consider the resolution: "Let us go up at once and possess it."

1. The title to it is sure.
2. We have means and ordinances by which needed strength is supplied.

3. Here we have many foretastes of the good land.—*The Evangelical Preacher*, *quoted in "The Biblical Museum."*

CALEB.—A CALL TO INQUIRY AND COURAGE.

(*Verse* 30.)

Glance at the history. This incident sets forth vividly some of the difficulties which lie in the way of the higher kingdom, the kingdom of Jesus Christ, and it is in this view that I intend to regard the graphic narrative.

I. **The kingdom of heaven challenges the inquiry of all men.** It addresses an appeal to human reason and to human trust. Though itself a revelation, and therefore not to be handled as a common thing, nor to be tested by common instruments, yet Christianity invites the most careful inquest. It does not seek to rest upon the human intellect as a burden, but to shine upon it as a light; it does not fasten itself upon the human heart as an excrescence, but blesses and enriches it with a new and mightier life. If Christianity may be represented under the image of a land such as ancient Canaan, then it is fair to say of it, that it offers right of way over its hills and through its valleys, that its fruits and flowers are placed at the disposal of all travellers, and that he who complains that the land is shut against him speaks not only ungratefully, but most falsely.

There are not wanting men who say that Christianity forbids inquiry.

The kingdom of heaven is the highest revelation of the mind of God to the mind of man. The mind must be at its highest possible point of energy in order to lay hold of the doctrines which constitute that revelation. To get the mind to the point requires the excitement of the *heart*; for mind is never fully alive whilst the moral powers are dormant. When the heart is moved in its deepest passions, and the mind is set in its highest key, the man is prepared to enter upon the great studies to which he is invited by the Gospel.

It is certainly true, and ought to be taken account of in this connection, that some people have peculiar notions of what is meant by inquiry. In the first instance, they dismiss everything like reverence; in the next place, they make themselves the standard and measure of all truth; and in the third place, they seek to materialize and debase everything that is spiritual and heavenly. This is not inquiry, it is insolent self-sufficiency: it is not the spirit of a student seeking light, it is the spirit of a braggart who thinks the sun inferior to his spark. The tone of mind must be in harmony with the subject considered; in every department of intellectual life it is required that a student be self-controlled, patient, docile; that his temper be subdued, and that his conclusions be reached through long and earnest watching of processes. This is required in all sciences; why not in the science of sciences—the knowledge and worship of the true God?

II. **Different reports will of course be brought by the inquirers.** It was so in the case of the spies—it will be so in all inquiry. The result of the survey will be according to the peculiarities of the surveyors. As streams are impregnated by the soils over which they flow, so subjects are affected by the individualism of the minds through which they pass. Thus Christianity may be said to be different things to different minds. To the speculative man it is a great attempt to solve deep problems in theology; to the controversialist it is a challenge to debate profound subjects on new ground; to the poet it is a dream, a wondrous vision many-coloured as the rainbow, a revelation many-voiced as the tunes of the wind or the harmonies of the sea. Each inquirer will have his own way of reporting the result of his inquiry. Christian testimony is not of one unchanging sort. One Christian will report his experience in highly intellectual phraseology, as if God had entered his heart through the shining chambers of his mind; another will show that he has reached peace through many a stormy conflict with doubt; another will speak the language of music as though he had been taught it in intercourse with the angels; another will stammer by reason of sobs and tears. Yet the subject is the same, the result is the same—this is the diversity that is unity—

"Ten thousand thousand are their tongues,
But all their joys are one."

1. Some inquirers will see *all the hindrances*. 2. All will confess that there is *something good* in the land. 3. Those who hold back by reason of the difficulties will come to a miserable end. (*a*) We don't escape by *false reasoning*. (*b*) We don't escape by *fear*.

Application: 1. Some have shown the spirit of Caleb—*what is your testimony?* 2. Will any resolve now, in Divine strength, to follow the Lord fully?

Observe that it is the *spirit* of Caleb which is commended.—*Joseph Parker, D.D.*

The Spies.

(*Verse* 32, *and chap.* xiv. 6, 7.)

The land of Canaan is a very excellent picture of religion. The children of Israel must stand as the representatives of the great mass of mankind. The great mass of mankind never try for themselves what religion is; they neither search our sacred books, nor taste and try our religion. But this is what they do; they consider those who make a profession of religion as spies who have entered the land, and they look upon our character and our conduct as the message we bring back to them. And if they find that our report is a gloomy one or an unholy one, they turn aside and they say, "It is not a good land; we will not enter into it, for its difficulties are great, but its enjoyments are few."

I. The ungodly world are not to be excused for that instead of investigating religion for themselves, they usually trust to the representation of others.

The worldly man looks at a Christian to see whether his religion be *joyful*. "By this," says he, "shall I know whether there is that in religion which will make a man glad. If I see the professor of it with a joyous countenance, then I will believe it to be a good thing." But hast thou any right to put it to that test? Is not God to be counted true, even before we have proved Him? Would you not know from Scripture, if you were to take the Bible and read it, that everywhere the Christian is commanded to rejoice, because it is comely for him? Psa. xxxii. 11; 1 Thess. v. 16; Phil. iv. 4. Again, you say you will test the *holiness* of Christ's religion by the holiness of Christ's people. The proper test that you ought to use is to try it yourselves —to "taste and see that the Lord is good." Your business is yourselves to enter into its valleys and pluck its grapes; yourselves to climb its hills and see its inhabitants. Inasmuch as God has given you a Bible, He intended you to read it, and not to be content with reading men. You have no right to judge religion from anything extra or external from itself.

It will be in vain for you to say at the day of Judgment, "Such and such a man was inconsistent, therefore I despised religion." In business, &c., you were independent enough. You are asked to follow Christ Himself.

241

Until, then, you can find a flaw in *His* character, a mistake in *His* conduct, you have no right to fling the inconsistency of His followers in the teeth of Christ, nor to turn from Him because His disciples forsake Him and flee. "Every man shall bear his own burden."

II. Bring forth the bad spies.

These spies are to be judged, not by what they say, but by *what they do;* for to a worldling, words are nothing—*acts* are everything.

1. I produce a man who brings up an evil report of the land, for *he is of a dull and heavy spirit*. If he preaches, he takes this text—"Through much tribulation we must enter into the kingdom." He never mentions God's people, without calling them, "God's *tried* children." He is always in the valley, &c. See him at home. . . . . Hear him pray. . . . These men are evil spies. . . . Permit me to bear my testimony. "Her ways are ways of pleasantness," &c. It is a land that floweth with milk and honey, &c.

2. The next one *makes very boastful pretensions to piety*. Everybody says when they see him in his good frames in chapel or elsewhere, "What a dear good man he is!" Follow him to business. He will not swear, but he will lie. He won't out-and-out rob, but he will cheat. . . . What does the world say of religion when they see these people? They say at once, "Well, if this be religion, we had better have none of it." . . . . But while you have met with hypocrites, you have met with men whom you could not doubt. Do not believe the ill report of the hypocrite and the unholy man.

3. *The Christian man, ... there are times when his witness is not consistent.* When you see an angry Christian—and such a thing may be seen; and when you meet with a Christian who is proud—and such a thing has been known; when you catch a Christian overtaken in a fault, as you may sometimes do, then his testimony is not consistent. He contradicts then what he has at other times declared by his acts. . . . If sometimes you see a Christian man betrayed into a hasty or a wrong expression, do not set it down to our religion, set it down to our poor fallen humanity.

III. Now we have some good spies.

1. *An aged Christian.* "Fifty and six years have I served Him, and I have never found Him once unfaithful."

2. *The sufferer.* "He has made my bed in all my sickness; He has given me joy in my sorrows," &c.

3. *A Christian merchant;* he is immersed in the cares of this life, and yet he always finds time to prepare for a world that is to come. Men said of him in the Exchange and in the Market, "If there is a Christian, it is that man." Such a man brings up a good report of the land.

4. *My sisters, it is possible for you, too, to bring up a good report.* We have known an ungodly husband converted by a godly wife. When you have done what you can for Christ, by holy, patient, quiet meekness, you are good spies; you have brought a good report of the land.

5. *And you, servants, can do the same.* A religious servant girl ought to be the best servant anywhere.

IV. The great necessity of bringing out a uniformly good testimony concerning religion.

1. *Every unguarded word you use, every inconsistent act, puts a slur on Christ.* Do not suffer His escutcheon to be tarnished; do not permit His banner to be trampled in the dust.

2. *If you do wrong, the world will be quite sure to notice you.* Remember, too, that the world always wears magnifying glasses to look at Christians' faults. If we have more privileges, and more culture, and make more profession, we ought to live up to them, and the world is quite right in expecting us to do so.

3. *If you do not bring a good testimony for your religion, an evil testimony will defeat a great deal of good.* The Christian may flow on in a steady course of life, unseen, unheard; but you are sure

to hear of him if he makes a fall. Be watchful, therefore, &c.

As for you who fear not God, remember, if Christians do sin, that shall not be an excuse for you.— *C. H. Spurgeon.*

CHAPTER XIV

CRITICAL AND EXPLANATORY NOTES.

Verse 4. *Let us make a captain.* It appears from Neh. ix. 17, that they actually appointed another leader.

Verse 5. *Fell on their faces,* &c. In solemn prayer to God, and in the presence of all the people, in the hope of changing their minds.

Verse 9. *They are bread for us; i.e.,* we can easily destroy them, and all their possessions, and their land with all its productions shall become ours.

Their defence is departed. Heb. lit., "their shadow." A very expressive metaphor for shelter and protection in the sultry east. Comp. Ps. xci. 1; cxxi. 5; Isa. xxx. 2; xxxii. 2; xlix. 2; li. 16.

Verse 13, 14. Keil and Del. translate, "'Not only have the Egyptians heard that thou hast brought out this people from among them with Thy might; they have also told it to the inhabitants of this land. They (the Egyptians and other nations) have heard that Thou, Jehovah, art in the midst of this people—that Thou, Jehovah, appearest eye to eye,' &c. The inhabitants of this land (verse 13) were not merely the Arabians, but, according to Exod. xv. 14, sqq., the tribes dwelling in and around Arabia, the Philistines, Edomites, Moabites, and Canaanites, to whom the tidings had been brought of the miracles of God in Egypt and at the Red Sea."

Verse 15. *As one man;* equivalent to "with a stroke" (Judg. vi. 16).

Verse 18. Comp. Exod. xxxiv. 6, 7.

Verses 21-23. Translate, "But as truly as I live, and as all the earth shall be filled with the glory of Jehovah, all those men . . . . shall not see the land," &c. The Hebrew particle כִּי in verse 22 (incorrectly rendered "because" in the A.V.) introduces the apodosis of the sentence and the substance of the oath; and, according to the ordinary form of an oath, the particle אִם, in the beginning of verse 23, merely signifies "not."

Verse 22. *These ten times.* Ten is used here as the number of completeness (Comp. Gen. xxxi. 7). They had now filled up the measure of their iniquities.

Verse 24. *Hath followed me fully.* Lit., "Fulfilled after Me." He had manifested unwavering fidelity in the Divine service. Caleb only is mentioned here because of the conspicuous part he took in opposing the exaggerated account of the evil spies, and in urging the people to a true and courageous course of conduct. And "this first revelation of God to Moses is restricted to the main fact; the particulars are given afterwards in the sentence of God, as intended for communication to the people (verses 26-38)."

Verse 25. *Now the Amalekites and the Canaanites dwelt in the valley.* "These words are best understood as the continuation of the answer of God to Moses: 'And now the Amalekites and the Canaanites are dwelling (or abiding) in the valley: wherefore, turn you,' &c. (that so ye be not smitten before them). Some difficulty has been occasioned by the fact that in verses 43-45 these tribes are represented rather as dwelling on the hill. The Syriac version alters the passage before us accordingly; but such procedure is unnecessary. What was in one respect a valley, or rather, as the Hebrew term *emek* implies, a broad sweep between hills, might in another respect be itself a hill, as lying on top of the mountain-plateau. Such was precisely the case with the elevated plain on which the conflict of the disobedient Israelites with the Amalekites and Canaanites eventually ensued."—*Speaker's Comm.*

Verse 27. "This announcement commences in a tone of anger, with an *aposiopesis*, 'How long this evil congregation' (sc., 'shall I forgive it,' the simplest plan being to supply אֶשָּׂא, as Rosenmüller suggests, from verse 18) '*that they murmur against me?*'"—*Keil and Del.*

Verse 32. *But as for you, your carcases,* &c. "Rather, 'But your carcases, even yours, shall fall,'" &c.— *Speaker's Comm.*

Verse 33. *Your children shall wander,* &c. Margin: "shall feed." Keil and Del: "'will be pasturing,' *i.e.*, will lead a restless shepherd's life."

Your whoredoms. Their many faithless departures from the Lord.

Verse 34. *My breach of promise.* Margin: "altering of Thy purpose." תְּנוּאָה, from נוּא, *removal, alienation, i.e.,* the withdrawal of oneself from a person or thing, and so metaphor. *enmity.—Fuerst.* The word is used only in this place and in Job xxxiii. 10. Keil and Del.: "'My turning away from you,' or *abalienatio.*"

Verse 45. *Hormah.* Keil and Del. say the word means, "the ban-place"; but Fuerst: "fortress, mountain fastness; from הָרַם, to be high, to be prominent." The name is used here by anticipation. Its earlier name was Zephath (Judg. i. 17). The circumstances which led to the change of the name are given in chap. xxi. 1-3. It was a royal city of a Canaanitish tribe on the southern frontier of Palestine. Its precise situation is uncertain.

THE REBELLION OF ISRAEL UPON RECEIVING THE REPORT OF THE SPIES.

(*Verses 1-5.*)

In this chapter we have the consequences of the evil report which the ten unbelieving explorers gave to the people; and in the section now before us we see its immediate effect upon the people.

I. **Grievous mental distress.**

"And all the congregation lifted up their voice, and cried; and the people wept that night."

1. *The distress was general—almost universal.* "All the congregation" were disheartened by the gloomy report which they had heard. The whole nation, with very few and distinguished exceptions, was stricken with dismay and grief, and spent the night in lamentation and weeping.

2. *The distress was unrestrained in its expression.* They "lifted up their voice, and cried." "The word crying," says Babington, "noteth out the manner of their weeping, even with vociferation or roaring, howling and yelling, that is, in most impatient and grievous manner." In the most childish and pusillanimous manner they utterly give way to their feelings. (*a*)

3. *The distress was sinful.* It sprang from their unbelief of God's assurances to them. The reports of the spies were opposed to the word of God to them, yet they receive those reports rather than that word. They even accept the cowardly opinions of the faithless spies rather than the inspiring declarations of the Lord God. Their cries and tears are the expression of their cowardly fears; and their cowardly fears arose from their unbelief towards God. Their cries and tears proclaim their sin and shame.

II. **Unreasonable and unjust murmuring.**

"And all the children of Israel murmured against Moses and against Aaron," &c. (ver. 2). Their murmuring was—

1. *Unreasonable.* They cry out because they dread death by the sword of the Canaanites, and yet they wish that they had died in Egypt or in the wilder-

ness. "Surely it had been at least as eligible to have fallen, soldier-like, sword in hand, in attempting to conquer Canaan, as to have died slaves in Egypt, or by famine or pestilence in the wilderness!" "They wish to die, for fear of dying." There is neither reason nor nobility in their conduct. (*b*)

2. *Unjust.* (1) To Moses and Aaron, who had dared and done and borne so much for them. (2) Their murmuring was still more unjust to God, who had done and was still doing such great and gracious things for them. All His mercies are forgotten, all His glorious purposes towards them disregarded, all His precious promises disbelieved, and base and bitter murmuring openly indulged in, because ten cowards have magnified the difficulties in the way of their enterprise. (*c*)

III. Shocking blasphemy.

"And wherefore hath the Lord brought us unto this land, to fall by the sword, that our wives and our children should be a prey?" As Matthew Henry expresses it, "Here is a most wicked blasphemous reflection upon God Himself, as if He had brought them hither on purpose that they might fall by the sword, and that their wives and children, those poor innocents, should be a prey. Thus do they in effect charge that God, who is Love itself, with the worst of malice, and eternal Truth with the basest hypocrisy, suggesting that all the kind things He had said to them, and done for them, hitherto, were intended only to decoy them into a snare, and to cover a secret design carried on all along to ruin them. Daring impudence! But what will not that tongue speak against Heaven that is set on fire of hell?" Their blasphemy involved—

1. *Unbelief of the Divine Word.* It expresses the complete rejection of God's declared purposes concerning them and His promises to them, and the unqualified acceptance of the worst suggestions of the faithless explorers.

2. *Base ingratitude to the Divine Being.* To all His great and undeserved kindness to them, and for all His mighty and merciful deeds on their behalf, this is their response, "Wherefore hath the Lord brought us unto this land?" &c. How applicable to them are the words of Rowe—

"To break thy faith,
And turn a rebel to so good a master,
Is an ingratitude unmatched on earth.
The first revolting angel's pride could only
Do more than thou hast done; thou copiest well,
And keep'st the black original in view!" (*d*)

IV. Foolish and wicked rebellion.

"Were it not better for us to return into Egypt? And they said one to another: Let us make a captain, and let us return into Egypt."

Consider:

1. *The folly of this rebellion.* (1) How could they get back into Egypt? Could they expect that the Lord would lead them, defend them, and provide for them in a journey which was directly and entirely opposed to His will? Yet without this, how was it possible for them to "return into Egypt"? (2) If they could have returned into Egypt, what kind of reception were they likely to meet with there? Their folly was utter and egregious.

2. *The baseness of this rebellion.* To return into Egypt was to go back into bondage. If the nobler attributes of manhood had not been crushed out of them by their former slavery, they would have preferred to die a thousand deaths fighting for the maintenance of their freedom than to be again subjected to the deep degradation of serfdom. But though free in body, they were, alas! mean and cowardly slaves in spirit.

3. *The wickedness of this rebellion.* Rebellion against an oppressive and cruel despotism is justifiable under certain circumstances; but they were under a most righteous and beneficent government. Their rebellion was not against even an excellent human government: blacker than this was their guilt; for they rebelled against the government of the Lord their God.

V. The noble conduct of Moses and Aaron in these painful circumstances.

245

Consider:

1. *Their exhortation to the people.* From the narrative of the rebellion which Moses gave to the people more than thirty-eight years afterwards, it appears that he endeavoured to calm and encourage the people (Deut. i. 29-31). This appeal to them was (1) *Manly.* "Dread not, neither be afraid of them." (2) *Inspiring.* "The Lord your God which goeth before you, He shall fight for you." (3) *Religious.* He bases his assurance of Divine aid on the wondrous and glorious works which God had done for them. "According to all that He did for you in Egypt before your eyes, and in the wilderness," &c. But he appeals to them in vain. "Wise and true," says Babington, "was that inscription in Plato his seal, '*Facilius est movere quieta, quam quietare mota.*'"

2. *Their prayer to God.* "Then Moses and Aaron fell on their faces before all the assembly of the congregation of the children of Israel." (1) They thus manifest their deep distress and shame because of the rebellion of the people. (2) By thus publicly prostrating themselves they probably hoped to move the people for good. (3) They prayed for the interposition of God. "In such distress, nothing remained but to pour out their desires before God." When human strength and wisdom are of no avail; when all other resources fail, and every other hope expires, the good man still hopes in God, and in prayer to Him has an unfailing resource.

NOTE.—In preaching from this portion of the history, it may perhaps be well to take *the noble conduct of Moses and Aaron in the rebellion of the people*, as the subject of a separate discourse; taking Deut. i. 29-31, and ver. 5 of this chap. as the text.

ILLUSTRATIONS.

(*a*) Shallow judges of human nature are they who think that tears in themselves ever misbecome a man. Sooner mayest thou trust thy purse to a professional pickpocket than give loyal friendship to a man who boasts of eyes to which the heart never mounts in dew. Only when man weeps he should be alone,—not because tears are weak, but because they should be sacred. Tears are akin to prayers. Pharisees parade prayers; impostors parade tears.—*Lord Lytton.*

Tears are not always fruitful ; their hot drops
   Sometimes but scorch the cheek and dim the eye;
Despairing murmurs over blackened hopes,
   Not the meek spirit's calm and chastened cry.

Oh! better not to grieve than waste our woe,
   To fling away the spirit's finest gold,
To lose, not gain, by sorrow; to overflow
   The sacred channels which true sadness hold.

Weep not too fondly, lest the cherished grief
   Should into vain, self-pitying weakness turn;
Weep not too long, but seek Divine relief;
   Weep not too fiercely, lest the fierceness burn.

It is not tears but teaching we should seek;
   The tears we need are genial as the shower;
They mould the being while they stain the cheek,
   Freshening the spirit into life and power.
                                H. Bonar, D.D.

(*b*) When these ten spies brought back the disastrous account, it spread depression amid the sensitive crowd. And it is singular enough, that if each individual of a crowd were alone, he would think rationally, weigh fairly, and act with some common sense. But of all things upon earth, a crowd, when once excited, seems to become the most tumultuous, and to defy every prescription of precedent and common sense. The excitement runs through the ranks, accumulating at each step till the whole presents one of those anomalous spectacles that make us sometimes wonder at the insanity and infatuation of mankind. We have in this chapter a specimen of a genuine mob, frightened by false fears, acting with all that indiscretion, imprudence, inconsistency, by which mobs, in most countries and in most ages, have been branded or characterised. When they heard the news, they forgot that God was with His people; they forgot that His promises were committed to their success, and sinking into the very depths of despair they "lifted up their voice and wept" a whole night; and gave utterance to their tumultuous feelings in language the most disgraceful to them as men, the most discreditable to them as professing Christians.—*John Cumming, D.D.*

(*c*) Consider that murmuring is a mercy-embittering sin, a mercy-souring sin. As the sweetest things put into a sour vessel become sour, or put into a bitter vessel bitter; so murmuring puts gall and wormwood into every cup of mercy that God gives into our hands. The murmurer writes "Marah," that is bitterness, upon all his mercies; and he reads and tastes bitterness in them all. As "to the hungry soul every bitter thing is sweet," so to the murmuring soul every sweet thing is bitter.—*Brooks.*

(*d*) Blow, blow, thou winter wind,
Thou art not so unkind
   As man's ingratitude;
Thy tooth is not so keen,
Because thou art not seen,
   Although thy breath be rude.

Freeze, freeze, thou bitter sky,
Thou dost not bite so nigh
   As benefits forgot:
Though thou the waters warp,
Thy sting is not so sharp
   As friend remember'd not.
Shakespeare. "*As you Like it.*" ii. 7.

JOSHUA AND CALEB: A NOBLE EFFORT TO ARREST A NATION'S REBELLION.

(*Verses* 6-10.)

I. Joshua and Caleb were deeply grieved by reason of the rebellion of the nation.

"And Joshua the son of Nun, and Caleb the son of Jephunneh, of them that searched the land, rent their clothes." They did this as a sign of their deep distress at the rebellious attitude of the people. The sins of men are ever a cause of deep grief to holy souls. They who are faithful cannot but mourn over the unfaithfulness of others when they see it. "Rivers of waters," said the Psalmist, "run down mine eyes, because they keep not Thy law." "I beheld the transgressors, and was grieved, because," &c. And Jeremiah cried, "Oh that my head were waters, and mine eyes a fountain of tears," &c.

II. Joshua and Caleb nobly endeavoured to arrest the rebellion of the nation.

"They spake unto all the company of the children of Israel, saying," &c. (verses 7-9). In this address—

1. *They re-assert the excellence of the land.* "The land, which we passed through to search it, is an exceeding good land, . . . a land which floweth with milk and honey" (see notes on chap. xiii. 23, 24).

2. *They declare the attainableness of the land.* "If the Lord delight in us, then He will bring us into this land, and give it us." (1) It was attainable as a Divine gift. "He will give it us." God had repeatedly promised to lead them in and to give them possession of the land. See Gen. xvii. 8; xviii. 4; Exod. iii. 8; vi. 4, 8; and comp. Psa. xliv. 3. (2) This gift would certainly be bestowed unless they alienated from them the Divine favour. "If the Lord delight in us," &c. If they did not by their sin cause Him to withdraw His good pleasure from them the land would certainly be theirs.

3. *They exhort the people not to violate the conditions of its attainment* (1) By rebelling against the Lord. "Only rebel not ye against the Lord." Rebellion against God deprives man of every worthy spiritual inheritance, excludes him from every heaven of the soul. (2) By dreading the people of the land. "Neither fear ye the people of the land; for they are bread for us," &c. To dread the people of the land was to dishonour God by distrusting Him. He was not with the people of the land. "Their shadow is departed from them." When God gives up a people, as He had given up the idolatrous and corrupt Canaanites, their defence is gone. When a people have sunk so deeply in sin as to compel God to abandon them, the strongest walls are but a miserable and worthless defence to them. But the Lord was with

Israel. "The Lord is with us: fear them not." "If God be for us, who can be against us?" While God is with us, we may confidently say, even in the presence of the most numerous and mighty foes, "Fear not; for they that be with us are more than they that be with them." To dread our enemies is to distrust, and, by distrusting, to dishonour God. So Joshua and Caleb wisely and bravely tried to crush the rebellion, and to awaken a worthy spirit in the people. But their excellent effort was in vain. The excited multitude was utterly impervious to reason. Still, honour to Joshua and Caleb for their brave effort! (a)

III. **Joshua and Caleb were in danger by reason of their effort to arrest the rebellion of the nation.**

"All the congregation bade stone them with stones." See here—

1. *The tactics of an excited mob when defeated in argument.* This mad multitude could not gainsay or controvert the statement of Joshua and Caleb; but having on its side some six hundred thousand men and on the other side only four (including Moses and Aaron), it was an easy thing to propose to stone them; and as cowardly as it was easy. That must be a bad cause that needs to be supported by persecution. Reasons must be very scarce when men resort to stones.

2. *The folly of an excited mob.* This proposal to stone Joshua and Caleb was quite insane. (1) Stoning would not disprove the testimony, or take away the wisdom from the counsel of the two true and brave explorers. (2) Stoning would involve the nation in deeper guilt and disgrace. Utterly and sometimes outrageously unreasonable is an excited multitude, and ready to propose and to perform things not only extremely foolish but terribly wicked, as in this case.

3. *The perils of faithfulness.* Because of their loyalty to truth and duty Joshua and Caleb are in danger of being stoned to death. It has always been a perilous thing for a man to bear witness to an unpopular truth, or to advocate an unpopular cause, or to oppose a popular movement. He who would do any of these things must not count it a strange thing if he is reviled, slandered, and sorely persecuted. But, rightly regarded, it is unspeakably more perilous if man from fear, or any other motive, prove unfaithful to truth and recreant to duty. A destiny of eternal shame awaits such.

> "They are slaves who will not choose
> Hatred, scoffing, and abuse,
> Rather than in silence shrink
> From the truth they needs must think;
> They are slaves who dare not be
> In the right with two or three." (b)

IV. **Joshua and Caleb rescued from danger by the interposition of God.**

"And the glory of the Lord appeared in the tabernacle of the congregation before all the children of Israel." Keil and Del.: "Jehovah interposed with His judgment, . . . the majesty of God flashed out before the eyes of the people in a light which suddenly burst forth from the tabernacle (see Exod. xvi. 10)." A revelation like this would strike that cowardly host with instant confusion and alarm. "Those who faithfully expose themselves for God," says M. Henry, "are sure to be taken under His special protection, and shall be hidden from the rage of men, either under heaven or in heaven."

ILLUSTRATIONS.

(a) On the whole, honour to small minorities, when they are genuine ones. Severe is their battle sometimes, but it is victorious always like that of gods. Tancred of Hauteville's sons, some eight centuries ago, conquered all Italy; bound it up into organic masses, of vital order after a sort; founded thrones and principalities upon the same which have not yet entirely vanished,—which, the last dying wrecks of which, still wait for some worthier successor it would appear. The Tancred Normans were some Four Thousand strong; the Italy they conquered in open fight, and bound up into masses at their ordering will, might count Eight Millions, all as large of bone, as eupeptic and black whiskered as they. How came the small minority of Normans to prevail in this so hopeless-looking debate? Intrinsically, doubt it not, because they were in the right; because in a dim, instinctive, but most genuine manner, they were doing the commandment of Heaven, and so Heaven had decided that they were to prevail. But extrinsically also, I can see, it was because the Normans were not afraid to have their skins scratched; and were prepared to die in their quarrel where needful. One man of that humour among a thousand of the other, consider it! Let the small minority, backed by the whole Universe, and looked on by such a cloud of invisible witnesses, fall into no despair.—*Thos. Carlyle*.

(*b*) An English officer, Colonel Wheeler, used to preach in the bazaar of the great city of Delhi. A Mohammedan, Wilayat Ali, was persuaded to give up the false prophet, and to believe in the true Saviour. He was baptised, and, in spite of the sufferings he had to endure in consequence, became a preacher in the bazaars. At last he came to live at Delhi, where he often preached, and thousands flocked to hear him. A great prince, Mirza Hajee, used to creep like Nicodemus, in the dark evenings, to Wilayat's house, to hear in secret about Jesus. One Monday morning a friend rushed into the house, crying, "The sepoys! the sepoys! They are murdering the Christians!" Wilayat called Fatima, his wife, and his seven children around him, and prayed, "O Lord, we have fallen into the fiery trial! Oh, help us to confess our dear Lord, that if we die we may obtain a crown of glory." He then kissed his wife and children, and said, "Whatever comes, don't deny Christ. If you confess Him, you will have a crown of glory." His wife crying bitterly, he said all he could to comfort her. "Oh, remember, my dear wife, if you die you will go to Jesus, and if you live Jesus will be with you. If any of the missionaries are alive, they will take care of you after my death; but if the missionaries should all die, Christ lives for ever. Even if the children are killed before your eyes, do not deny Christ." While Wilayat was yet speaking, a number of sepoys on horseback rode up to his house, and knowing him to be a Christian, said, "Repeat the Mohammedan creed, or we will shoot you." But he would not deny his Lord. "Tell us what you are," said one. "I am a Christian, and a Christian I will live and die." They dragged him along the ground, beating him about the head and face with their shoes. Not being soldiers, they had no swords. "Now preach Christ to us," some cried out in mocking tones. Others said, "Turn to Mohammed, and we will let you go." "No, I never, never will!" the faithful martyr cried; "my Saviour took up His cross and went to God, and I will lay down my life and go to Him." The scorching rays of the sun were beating on the poor sufferer's head. With a laugh one of the wretches exclaimed, "I suppose you would like some water." "I do not want water," replied the martyr. "When my Saviour was dying, He had nothing but vinegar mingled with gall. But do not keep me in this pain. If you mean to kill me, do so at once." Another sepoy coming up lifted his sword, the martyr called aloud, "Jesus receive my spirit!" and with one stroke his head was nearly cut off. Fatima, standing under a tree, beheld the stroke; she shrieked with agony, and ran back to her house. But she found it on fire and surrounded by people who were plundering it. Then she fled to Prince Mirza Hajee's house, where she discovered her fatherless children. At the end of three days Mirza Hajee came to Fatima, and said, "I dare not keep you any longer, but if you will become a Mohammedan, you will be safe, and I will give you a house, and three pounds a month for your support." But Fatima would not give up her Saviour. No one attempted to kill her, for very few knew she was a Christian. After ten days she escaped with her children out of the town of Delhi; and went to a village forty miles off. After three months, hearing that the English had taken Delhi, she returned thither. But soon her little baby died. Fatima wept much. She now began to inquire about the missionaries, but found they had all been killed. But remembering the missionaries at Agra, her native town, she sent to one of them. What was her joy when an answer arrived, inviting her to go to Agra! She cried for joy, thanked God, and went to her native city with all her surviving children.—"*The Sunday School Teacher.*"

JOSHUA AND CALEB'S ENCOURAGING DECLARATION.

(*Verse* 8.)

Let us lose sight of the Israelites, and direct our thoughts to the universal family of God; and look beyond Canaan to the heavenly land. Our text contains,—

I. **A Supposition.**

"If the Lord delight in us." Prov. viii. 30. God delights in His Son, &c. He delights in His holy angels, &c. But have we reason to suppose that He delights in His saints?

1. *We might conclude, indeed, that He could not delight in them*, when we reflect, (1) On their nothingness and vanity.

"Man at his best estate," &c. (2) On their guilt and rebellion. Not one but is a sinner. (3) On their pollution and want of conformity to His likeness. (4) And more especially when we reflect on His greatness, independence and purity.

2. *But there are the most satisfactory evidences that He does delight in His people.* (1) Observe the names by which He distinguishes them. He calls them His "jewels"—"inheritance"—"treasure"—"diadem"—"crown" and "portion." See the very term in the text. And Prov. xi. 20. (2) Observe the declarations He has made respecting them. "He that toucheth you, toucheth the apple of Mine eye." He has engaged His constant presence—His unremitting care—His ceaseless goodness—His tender mercy—His gracious interpositions—His richest gifts—His greatest blessings. (3) Observe what He has done for them. Favoured them —sustained them—redeemed them—given His Son—Spirit—promises. (4) What He has provided for them. All needful grace. "The Lord God is a sun," &c. "My God shall supply," &c. "Eye hath not seen," &c. (5) Eternal life and unceasing glory.

"His saints are precious in His sight,
He views His children with delight,"

II. An inference.

"Then He will bring us into this land," &c. Observe here,—

1. *The land specified.* It is "the land afar off." The good land. The heavenly Canaan. The region of immortality. We shall not live here always. Need this rest, &c.

"There is a land of pure delight," &c.

2. *This land is God's gift.* Not the result of merit—free gift of God. It is given in promise—given in Christ. Purchased inheritance.

3. *To this land God must bring His saints.* Difficulties, enemies, and dangers intervene. He will guide to it. Keep—safely conduct, and at length put people into it, as He did Israel. "Fear not, little flock," &c. "Let not your hearts be troubled," &c. Rev. ii. 10, 26; iii. 5, 12. O, yes; the inference is satisfactory, and most conclusive. Let,—

1. *Christians expect it, and live in reference to it.*

2. *Invite others to go with you to the better land.*—Jabez Burns, D.D.

The Divine Declaration of Judgment because of the Rebellion of Israel.

(*Verses* 11, 12.)

In the eleventh verse the Lord remonstrates with Moses on the sin of the rebellious people, and in the twelfth He announces His judgment because of their sin. Let us notice :—

I. The Divine view of Israel's sin.

"And the Lord said unto Moses, How long will this people provoke Me?" &c. (ver. 11). This remonstrance sets forth—

1. *The nature of their sin.* They distrusted God. The very root of their rebellion was their unbelief. "How long will it be ere they believe Me?" They did not believe His promises to them, or His power to fulfil His word. They distrusted both His truth and His strength. (1) Unbelief is a terribly prolific sin: it gives birth to many other sins. (2) Unbelief is a terribly fatal sin: it involves the soul in condemnation and death (John iii. 18, 36).

2. *The reproach which their sin cast upon God.* "The Lord said unto Moses, How long will this people provoke Me?" "Provoke" is not a good rendering of נָאַץ; to scorn, to despise, to contemn, to reject, would better express the meaning of the word (See Fuerst's *Lex.*).

Keil and Del. clearly and truly express the meaning of the interrogation: "Jehovah resented the conduct of the people as base contempt of His Deity, and as utter mistrust of Him, notwithstanding all the signs which He had wrought in the midst of the nation." Unbelief is an insult to God. "He that believeth not God hath made Him a liar." (*a*)

3. *The long continuance of their sin.* "How long will this people despise Me? and how long will it be ere they believe Me?" Protracted, indeed, must have been their unbelief, when the infinitely Patient One cries out concerning it, "How long?" God notes how long we continue in evil. Solemn reflection this. He has marked some of you persisting in evil through many years; and He cries concerning you, "How long?" Let the young see to it that the longsuffering God shall not have to make such an inquiry concerning them.

4. *The aggravation of their sin.* "How long will it be ere they believe Me, for all the signs which I have shewed among them?" Many and marvellous were the manifestations of the Divine power, which they had seen working on their behalf; these should have destroyed their unbelief, and confirmed their faith. Man's unbelief is aggravated in proportion to the number and power of the aids to faith which God has granted to him.

II. **The Divine judgment for Israel's sin.**

"I will smite them with the pestilence, and disinherit them."

1. *The nature of the judgment.* "I will disinherit them." God proposes to deprive them of the inheritance to which He had called them. They had despised their destiny, and they shall forfeit it. "Let us therefore fear, lest a promise," &c. (Heb. iv. 1-11.)

2. *The instrument of the judgment.* "I will smite them with the pestilence." In God's armoury there is no deficiency of weapons. Fire and hail, storm and tempest, plague and pestilence, famine and war, are all His instruments, &c. (*b*)

3. *The righteousness of the judgment.* They had despised the good land, and they shall not inherit it. They wished that they had died in Egypt or in the wilderness, and they shall have their wish—in the wilderness they shall die. They had shown themselves utterly unworthy of their inheritance, and it shall not be theirs. The rigteousness of such a judgment is unquestionable. "The Lord is righteous in all His ways," &c. "All His ways are judgment: a God of truth and without iniquity, just and right is He."

III. **The Divine regard for His covenant.**

"I will make of thee a greater nation and mightier than they."

In these words we see:

1. *God's regard for His covenant.* "My covenant will I not break, nor alter the thing that is gone out of My lips." "My counsel shall stand, and I will do all My pleasure." He may cut off Israel, but He will not fail to carry out His plans. By sin we may violate our interest in the purposes of His grace; but we cannot frustrate their fulfilment.

2. *God's independence of man.* He could accomplish His designs without the aid of Israel. He needs not the support of any of His creatures. He Himself is the great sustainer of all creatures, and of all worlds. He can do without any of us, or without all of us. "Who hath known the mind of the Lord? or who hath been His counsellor? or who hath first given to Him?" &c. (Rom. xi. 34-36).

3. *God's regard for His faithful servant.* See the honour which the Lord here puts upon Moses. (1) In announcing to him His purposes. He would not destroy this rebellious race until He had communicated with His faithful servant. Comp. Gen. xviii. 17-19: "And the Lord said, Shall I hide from Abraham that thing which I do?" &c. "The secret of the Lord is with them that fear Him," &c. (2) In offering to him this extraordinary honour. "I will make of thee a greater nation and mightier than they." "If

any man serve Me, him will My Father honour."

Conclusion.

Impress such considerations as these:—

1. *The heinousness of unbelief;*—shun it.

2. *The large number and convincing character of the evidence of Christianity;* —remember that our faith should bear a proportion to them. "For unto whomsoever much is given, of him shall be much required," &c.

3. *God takes our conduct as evidence of our belief or unbelief;*—let us show our faith by our works. "Faith without works is dead," worthless, unreal. "Faith worketh by love," &c.

4. *Take heed lest we be disinherited because of unbelief.* Rom. xi. 20, 21; Heb. iii. 12—iv. 11.

ILLUSTRATIONS.

(*a*) The goodness of God is contemned by a distrust of His Providence. As all trust in Him supposeth Him good, so all distrust of Him supposeth Him evil; either without goodness to exert His power, or without power to display His goodness. Job seems to have a spice of this in His complaint (Job xxx. 20), "I cry unto Thee and Thou dost not hear me; I stand up, and Thou regardest me not." It is a fume of the serpent's venom, first breathed into man to suspect Him of cruelty, severity, regardlessness, even under the daily evidences of His good disposition: and it is ordinary not to believe Him when He speaks, nor credit Him when He acts; to question the goodness of His precepts, and misinterpret the kindness of His providence, as if they were designed for the supports of a tyranny and the deceit of the miserable. Thus the Israelites thought their miraculous deliverance from Egypt, and the placing them in security in the wilderness, was intended only to pound them up for a slaughter (Num. xiv. 3); thus they defiled the lustre of Divine goodness which they had so highly experimented, and placed not that confidence in Him which was due to so frequent a Benefactor, and thereby crucified the rich kindness of God, as Genebrard translates the word "limited" (Psa. lxxviii. 41). It is also a jealousy of Divine goodness, when we seek to deliver ourselves from our straits by unlawful ways, as though God had not kindness enough to deliver us without committing evil. What! did God make a world and all creatures in it, to think of them no more, not to concern Himself in their affairs? If He be good, He is diffusive, and delights to communicate Himself; and what subjects should there be for it but those that seek Him and implore His assistance? It is an indignity to Divine bounty to have such mean thoughts of it, that it should be of a nature contrary to that of His works, which, the better they are, the more diffusive they are. Doth a man distrust that the sun will not shine any more, or the earth not bring forth its fruit? Doth he distrust the goodness of an approved medicine for the expelling of his distemper? If we distrust those things, should we not render ourselves ridiculous and sottish? And if we distrust the Creator of those things, do we not make ourselves contemners of His goodness? If His caring for us be a continual argument to move us to cast our care upon Him as it is (1 Pet. v. 7); then, if we cast not our care upon Him, it is a denial of His gracious care of us, as if He regarded not what becomes of us.—*Charnocke.*

A very tender parent had a son, who from his earliest years proved headstrong and dissolute. Conscious of the extent of his demerits, he dreaded and hated his parent. Meanwhile every means were used to disarm him of these suspicions, so unworthy of the tenderness and love which yearned in his father's bosom, and of all the kindness and forbearance which were lavished upon him. Eventually, the means appeared to be successful, and confidence, in a great degree, took the place of his ungenerous suspicions. Entertained in the family as one who had never trespassed, he now left his home to embark in mercantile affairs, and was assured that if in any extremity he would apply to his parent, he should find his application kindly received. In the course of years it fell out that he was reduced to extremity; but instead of communicating his case to his parent, his base suspicion and disbelief of his tenderness and care again occupied him, and he neglected to apply to him. Who can tell how deeply that father's heart was rent at such depravity of feeling? Yet this is the case of the believer, who, pardoned and accepted, and made partaker of a Father's love and covenant promises, when under distress refuses to trust his heavenly and almighty Parent, throws away his filial confidence, and with his old suspicions stands aloof in sullen distrust. O! how is God dishonoured by this sinful unbelief.—*Salter.*

(*b*) By His sovereign authority God can make any creature the instrument of His vengeance. He hath all the creatures at His beck, and can commission any of them to be a dreadful scourge. Strong winds and tempests fulfil His word (Psa. cxlviii. 8); the lightnings answer Him at His call, and cry aloud, "Here are we" (Job xxxviii. 35). By

His sovereign authority He can render locusts as mischievous as lions, forge the meanest creatures into swords and arrows, and commission the most despicable to be His executioners. He can cut off joy from our spirits, and make our own hearts to be our tormentors, our most confident friends our persecutors, our nearest relations to be His avengers; they are more His, who is their Sovereign, than ours, who place a vain confidence in them. Rather than Abraham shall want children, He can raise up stones, and adopt them into His family; and rather than not execute His vengeance, He can array the stones in the streets, and make them His armed subjects against us. If He speak the word, a hair shall drop from our heads to choke us, or a vapour, congealed into rheum in our heads, shall drop down and putrefy our vitals. He can never want weapons, who is Sovereign over the thunders of heaven and stones of the earth, over every creature; and can, by a sovereign word, turn our greatest comforts into curses.—*Charnocke.*

THE INTERCESSION OF MOSES FOR THE DOOMED NATION.

(*Verses* 13-19.)

Moses does not appear to have entertained for a moment the proposal that a people greater and mightier than Israel, and arising from him, should take the place of Israel. He sought not his own honour, but the glory of God. And at once in broken speech, indicating a spirit deeply moved, he earnestly intercedes with God for the guilty and condemned people. His simple and earnest intercession requires very little explanation. Let us consider :—

I. **The petition which he presented.**
"Pardon, I beseech Thee, the iniquity of this people." "The pardon of a national sin, as such, consists in the turning away of the national punishment; and that is it for which Moses is here so earnest." His prayer is that God would not disinherit the guilty nation; that he would not kill all this people at a stroke; but that he would manifest His mercy in mitigating their doom.

II. **The pleas by which he urged his petition.**

1. *The honour of the Divine Name amongst the heathen.* "And Moses said unto the Lord: Then the Egyptians shall hear," &c. Verses 13-16. (See *Critical and Explanatory Notes.*) The main points of this plea seem to be these: (1) The relations of God with Israel and His doings for Israel were well known amongst neighbouring nations. (2) If God should destroy Israel at a stroke, that also would be known amongst these nations. (3) The interpretation of such destruction by the nations would be such as would reflect on the honour of God. They would conclude that His resources were exhausted; that His power had failed to sustain and lead Israel onward; and thus His glory would be tarnished. (4) That this might not be the case Moses entreats the Lord not to disinherit the rebellious people. This plea of the Divine honour in the eyes of the nations should afford both encouragement and exhortation to the Church of God. *Encouragement,* inasmuch as it implies that the glory of God amongst men is bound up with the prosperity of His Church. And *exhortation,* since it implies that it is the duty of every member of the Church to seek in all things the glory of His Name. (*a*)

2. *The Divine character as revealed to Moses.* "And now, I beseech Thee, let the power of my Lord be great," &c. (Verses 17, 18); Comp. Exod. xxxiv. 6, 7. Keil and Del. : "The words: Let the power be great, equivalent to show Thyself great in power, are not to be connected with what precedes, but with what follows; viz. 'show Thyself mighty by verifying Thy word, Jehovah, long suffering and great in mercy,' &c." For a ruler to forgive on a large scale and wisely, and at the same time to uphold the authority of the law and the dignity of the throne, demands much *power,* and that of the highest kind. Excellent is Matthew

253

Henry's note on this point: "If He should destroy them God's power would be questioned; if He should continue and complete their salvation, notwithstanding the difficulties that arose, not only from the strength of their enemies, but from their own provocations, this would greatly magnify the Divine power; what cannot He do who could make so weak a people conquerors, and such an unworthy people favourites?" The servant of God pleads especially *the great mercy of God as manifested in His forbearance with sinners and His forgiveness of sin.* "The Lord is longsuffering and of great mercy, forgiving iniquity and transgression." And his plea is strengthened by the fact that God has revealed Himself as exercising this mercy in such a way as to *afford no encouragement to evil.* "By no means clearing the guilty, visiting the iniquity of the fathers upon the children unto the third and fourth generation." The Psalmist celebrates the same aspect of God's dealings with Israel in the wilderness: "Thou wast a God that forgavest them, and Thou tookest vengeance of their inventions." How powerful is this plea! (*b*)

3. *The truth of the Divine word.* "Let the power of my Lord be great, according as Thou hast spoken." God had Himself proclaimed to Moses those attributes of His character which he pleads. So the man of God appeals to the Divine faithfulness. Surely God will maintain the character which He had Himself proclaimed! (*c*)

All the pleas which we have mentioned are based upon the doings and character and honour of God. No plea is based upon anything in the people. Moses does not even urge their great need. But, like David, he entreats God to forgive for His own sake. "For Thy Name's sake, O Lord, pardon mine iniquity." "The reason of our forgiveness is not in ourselves, but in God. The least sinner has no more right to the forgiveness of the least sin, than the greatest sinner has to the forgiveness of the greatest sin. Both must seek mercy, not because of any extenuating elements in themselves, but wholly and solely because God is 'the Lord God, merciful and gracious, forgiving iniquity, transgression, and sin.' God's sovereign love originated salvation; God's sovereign love must get the glory of that salvation."

3. *The forgiveness which God had already bestowed.*

"Pardon, I beseech Thee, the iniquity of this people, . . . as Thou hast forgiven this people from Egypt even until now." This is bold pleading; but it puts great honour upon God. It would not do to make this a plea in asking anything of man. But "God makes past favours precedents for new ones."

"Man's plea to man is that he never more
Will beg; and that he never begged before.
Man's plea to God is that he did obtain
A former suit, and therefore sues again.
How good a God we serve, who, when we sue,
Makes His old gifts the examples of the new!"
(*d*)

Conclusion.

From this intercession of Moses let us learn—

1. *How to plead with God for ourselves.*
2. *How to plead with God for others, and especially for His people.*

ILLUSTRATIONS.

(*a*) The zeal of many rises and falls like a barometer. They are hot as fire, and cold as ice, in the shortest space; their fervour is as transient as the flame of thorns, and hence it is very hard to turn it to any practical account. Oh, for more of the deeply-seated principle of intense love to God's salvation, steady and abiding, which shall make a man say continually, "Let God be magnified!" We would desire to wake up in the morning with this on our lips. We would begin with the enquiry, "What can I do to magnify God this day?" We would be in business in the middle of the day, and yet never lose the one desire to magnify God. We would return to our family at night, urged by the same impulse, "How can I magnify God in my household?" If I lie sick, I would feel that I must magnify God by patience; if I rise from that bed, I would feel the sweet obligation to magnify Him by gratitude; if I take a prominent position, I am doubly bound to magnify Him who makes me a leader to His flock; and, if I be unknown and obscure in the Church, I must with equal zeal magnify Him by a conscientious discharge of the duties of my position. Oh, to have one end always before us, and to press forward towards it, neither turning to the right hand nor to the left! As though we were balls shot out of a rifled cannon, we would rush on, never hesitating or turning aside, but flying with all speed towards the centre of the target. May our spirits be impelled by a Divine energy towards this one only thing. The Lord be magnified! whether I live or die, may God be glorified in me!—*C. H. Spurgeon.*

(*b*) Consider what it is for God to be glorious. It is the glory of pity unfathomable. He considers glory to lie in longsuffering love. It is not that He shoots the light of His countenance far as the sun shoots its beams, that makes God proud. It is because He knows how to work for men that are ungrateful, that His heart swells with consciousness of its power. It is not because He is able, as it were, by His hands to span easily the orbs that fill immensity. It is the glory of magnanimity; it is the glory of waiting upon imperfection and weakness; it is the glory of pardoning and healing, and pardoning again and healing again, and still continuing to pardon and heal to the uttermost and to the end—it is this that makes Divine glory. It is the power of God's heart to be magnanimous that makes Him think well of Himself. There lies His glory.—*H. W. Beecher.*

(*c*) Moses takes what God had said, next to what God is, as the ground and warrant of his plea and cry to Him for mercy and for forgiveness. What God has promised is given to us to be returned to Him in prayer. The meaning of promises is to suggest and be the language of prayer. Wherever you find a promise in the Bible, there you find the substance, the element, the words of prayer. "All the promises of God in Jesus Christ are Yea and Amen." They wait for you—dead in themselves on the sacred page—to seize them, translate them into prayer, and return them in that shape to Him who spake them, pleading with Him,—"O Lord, remember Thy power, as Thou hast promised us, saying, The Lord, the Lord God, merciful and gracious." You can never need a prayer-book as long as you have a Bible. You can never plead that you cannot pray as long as you can open the book of Psalms, and see what God has promised; take those beautiful Psalms, which Martin Luther called "A little Bible," and as you read them, turn their promises into prayer. "The Lord is my shepherd, I shall not want . . . . Yea, though I walk through the valley of the shadow of death, I will fear no evil: for Thou art with me; Thy rod and Thy staff they comfort me." Turn that into prayer; and plead with God, that He will never let you want—that He will never forsake you and leave you—that He will be your rod and your staff —that He will furnish your table in the presence of your enemies—that He will let mercy and goodness follow you all the days of your life—and that you may dwell in His house for ever. Take promises so frequent, so full of power in all that can cheer, comfort, and sustain, scattered through every page of this blessed Book, and transmit them back to God in prayer, in the name of Christ Jesus.— *John Cumming, D.D.*

(*d*) It is a strange thing in human nature, that if anybody does you a kindness, you may forget him, and be ungrateful; but if you bestow a kindness on a person you will love him and remember him. It is not the receiver generally that is certain to give the love, it is the giver of kindness who binds himself to the other. A mother must love her child because she has done so much for it; she has suffered and she has cared so much, that she must love it. The more you have done for a person the better you love him. Now, Jesus does not love us because of any good in us, but to-day He loves us because He has done so much for us. He has taken the yoke from our necks, He has laid meat to us, He has drawn us with bands of love and cords of a man, and having spent so much love on us, He loves us dearly. Jesus, who suffered so much, is bound to us by new bonds. Calvary is not only the fruit of His love, but the root of fresh love. Another stream of love springs up at the cross' foot " I," saith the Redeemer, " can see My groans and agonies in them." He loves us because He has loved us. This thought ought to cheer us—God has done too much for us to let us perish.

"And can He have taught me
To trust in His name,
And thus far have brought me
To put me to shame?"
C. H. Spurgeon.

The Rev. Philip Henry, after praying for two of his children who were dangerously ill, said, "If the Lord will be pleased to grant me this my request concerning my children, I will not say as the beggars at our door used to do, 'I'll never ask anything of Him again;' but, on the contrary, he shall hear oftener from me than ever; and I will love God the better as long as I live."—*Dict. of Illust.*

GOD'S PARDONING GRACE IN THE PAST AN ENCOURAGEMENT TO SEEK FOR THE SAME IN THE PRESENT.

(Verse 19).

"Pardon, I beseech Thee, the iniquity of this people . . . . as Thou hast forgiven this people, from Egypt even until now."

The narrative from which the text is taken shews,—

2. *How apt we are to look at the dark side of things and to believe the bad before the good.*

3. *How unreasonable people are when angry.* "The children of Israel murmured against Moses and against Aaron," when they knew that it was Jehovah who was leading them.

3. *How fearful it is to give way to and to nurse evil temper.* Here, having spent the night fostering bitter feeling, we find the people proposing to murder Joshua and Caleb. Man in a passion has for the time his reason dethroned, &c. The Bible condemns anger, shews it to be of the essence of murder.

The text teaches, *That God's merciful dealings with us in the past, are encouragements for us to ask and to hope for the same in the present.* God does not change as we do; what He has done, He does now, and will do. His past treatment of us is an index to His future. History is a revelation of His character. God ever has forgiven, and He does so now. In this lies our only hope as sinners. We deserve not to be forgiven; we dare not hope for it time after time, were it not that God has forgiven until now, and that with Him there "is no variableness, neither shadow of turning." This thought helped Moses to pray for the people. He had nothing to offer as an excuse for them; his only hope was in the known character of God. He had forgiven them again and again, and because of that Moses had faith to ask Him still to do so. We could not use this argument with any one but God. With our fellow-man we should feel,—"he has done it so often, I have no heart to ask him again." But God gives that we might still ask; every gift of His is an "earnest." No sinner need despair. Let him only think of the character of God, and he cannot sink. Is the sin great? God has "forgiven until now," and we have His word that "Whosoever will" may come to Him. It is more certain that God will forgive the penitent than that the sun and moon will rise in their appointed time. They have done so; we therefore conclude that they will continue to do so. God has forgiven in all ages; and in addition to that we have His Word. Let those who under a deep sense of guilt are trembling on the verge of despair, take heart. Go to God as you are, seek Him in Christ: He has "forgiven until now," and He will forgive. We argue this because,—

I. **God is as able and as willing to forgive now as ever He has been.**

"The Lord's hand is not shortened," &c. (Isa. lix. 1). His mercy is not exhausted. He has been giving to numberless ages; but he has lost nothing in imparting to others. Notice how the word *power* is associated with pardon and salvation. "Mighty to save;" "able to save;" "power of God unto salvation;" and here in verse 17, "Let the power," &c. It is not a trifling thing to save man. It is only the strong that can afford to forgive the rebel. God is great enough and strong enough to offer a free and full pardon to all who will accept it. Not only has He the power to forgive, but He is now as full of compassion as ever He has been. His heart is as tender as His arm is strong. None need fear to come to Him. If sin abounds, grace abounds much more. As the tide covers the rock as well as the grains of sand, so Divine mercy covers the sins of every penitent.

II. **Man is now, as much as ever he has been, the object of God's compassion.**

There has been no change in man's condition or deserts. We are no better or worse than others who have been forgiven. We, in this enlightened age, have not in any way ceased to need the mercy of God. We are helpless, full of sin, in great danger, &c. God knows this, and yearns for our salvation.

III. God's purpose with regard to the human race is now what it ever has been.

His purpose has been, and is, our salvation. This is near to His heart, &c. He gave His Son, &c. He has the same motives and the same desire to pardon now as ever He has had.

Well, then, we can confidently invite *all*, ALL to Him. " Him that cometh to Me I will in no wise cast out." Let none despair. He has forgiven through Christ "until now."

"*Until now*"! Let there be no misunderstanding. " Now is the accepted time." None of us have to-morrow; that belongs to God. All we have is this moment. Let it not be misused. Mercy is within reach. God forgives "until now."—*David Lloyd.*

THE ANSWER OF THE LORD TO THE INTERCESSION OF MOSES.

(*Verses* 20-25.)

In this reply we have—

I. Pardon in answer to prayer.

"And the Lord said, I have pardoned according to thy word." Moses had prayed that God would not cut off all the people at a stroke, but that He would pardon them; and God grants him his requests. " The answer of God," says Attersoll, "is to be referred to the prayer of Moses, and is proportioned out according to his request. He desired that God would not utterly root out that whole people as one man, according as He had threatened : his prayer is granted, and God declareth that He had pardoned them, not absolutely, but according to His word : he requested they might not utterly be destroyed, he receiveth answer, they shall not utterly be destroyed." Observe here :

1. *The great power of prayer.* " Pray one for another .... The effectual fervent prayer," &c.

2. *The great mercy of God.* " He hath not dealt with us after our sins," &c. " Thy mercy is great unto the heavens." (*a*)

II. Punishment for aggravated sins.

1. *Their sin, and its aggravations.* (1) They tempted God by their unbelief and disobedience. " Have tempted me now these ten times, and have not hearkened to My voice." With a perversity which is almost incredible, they questioned His power to provide for them and give them possession of the land, His goodness in His dealings with them, and His faithfulness as to the promises which He had made to them. They " tempted " and " provoked " Him by demanding signs and wonders as a proof of His power. Comp. Psa. lxxviii. 17-20. (2) They thus tempted God by their unbelief notwithstanding many and mighty encouragements to faith. " These men have seen My glory and My miracles, which I did in Egypt and in the wilderness." This was the great aggravation of their sin. (See notes on ver. 11). (3) They had been guilty of this sin many times. " These ten times." Some expositors enumerate ten occasions on which they had tempted God since their emancipation from Egypt. But we take it that " ten " is used here as the number of completeness, as in Gen. xxxi. 7. They had filled up the measure of their provocations; and now God will visit and punish them.

2. *Their punishment and its certainty.* " As truly as I live, and as all the earth shall be filled with the glory of Jehovah, all those men . . . shall not see the land which I sware unto their fathers, neither shall any of them that provoked Me see it." (1) The nature of their punishment. They had despised the good land, and they shall not

inherit it; they had distrusted His promise, and its blessings shall not be to them. "They shall not see the land," &c. Comp. Psa. xcv. 11. (2) The certainty of their punishment. God declares it with an oath. "As truly as I live," &c. He swears by His own existence, and by the certainty of the accomplishment of His purposes, that they shall not see the good land. Sure as He lives, and sure as, "notwithstanding the sin and opposition of these men, He would still carry out His work of salvation to a glorious victory," these men shall not enter into the Promised Land. Thus they were pardoned, but they were punished. "Thou wast a God that forgavest them, and Thou tookest vengeance of their inventions." Many of the consequences of sin are not annulled, cannot be annulled by forgiveness. (b)

III. Reward for eminent service.

"But my servant Caleb, because he had another spirit," &c. Caleb is here distinguished from the rest (Joshua is honourably named hereafter) in three respects :

1. *As to his spirit.* "He had another spirit with him," and a different one. His was a believing spirit, theirs an unbelieving one; his was courageous, theirs cowardly; his was obedient, theirs rebellious.

2. *As to his conduct.* "And hath followed Me fully." He had manifested unfaltering fidelity to God. (c)

3. *As to his destiny.* "Him will I bring into the land whereinto he went; and his seed shall possess it." Comp. Josh. xiv. 6-15.

IV. Judgment for cowardice.

"And now the Amalekites and the Canaanites are dwelling in the valley; wherefore, to-morrow turn you, and get you into the wilderness by the way of the Red Sea." They had taken alarm when they heard of the Amalekites and the Canaanites (chap. xiii. 29), and shown themselves utterly unfit to encounter them: and now when they must advance to meet them or retreat into the wilderness, most naturally they are commanded to retreat. The life of struggle and enterprize and glory is not for cowards: it is for them to turn back from these things, and to wander ingloriously, ignobly, in the desert. Unto these cowards is awarded a coward's doom. "The backslider in heart shall be filled with his own ways."

ILLUSTRATIONS.

(a) Say not that any crime of man
   Was e'er too great to be forgiven;
Can we within our little span,
   Engrasp the viewless mind of Heav'n?
Shall we attempt with puny force
   To lash back ocean with a rod?
Arrest the planets in their course?
   Or weigh the mercies of a God?

Our mercies, like ourselves, may be
   Small, finite, and ungracious ever;
May spurn a brother's bended knee—
   But God forsakes the contrite, never!
Vast as Himself they shine above,
   To eyes that look through sorrow's tear;
Great though the crime, great is the love,
   If those who seek it are sincere.
                              Mackay.

(b) Men's sins carry with them a punishment in this life. Different sins are differently punished. The degrees of punishment are not always according to our estimate of the culpability. Many sins against a man's body go on in the body, reproducing their penalties from year to year, and from ten years to ten years. And the ignorant crime, or the knowing crime, committed when one is yet in his minority, may repeat itself and repeat its bitterness and its penalty when one is hoary with age. Mere repenting of sin does not dispossess the power of all sins. There are transgressions that throw persons out of the pale of society. There are single acts, the penalties of which never fail to reassert themselves. There are single wrongs that are never healed. This great transgression that seemed in the commission without any threat and without any danger, pursued this man through all his early life, and clear down until he was an old man and returned from his exile. And now then he was quit of it only by one of those great critical transitions that take place, or may take place, in the life of a man, without which he would have gone on, doubtless, expiating still his great wrong.—*H. W. Beecher.*

Gay, dissolute man, there is that poor girl ruined body and soul through you in years gone by, and nothing you can ever do can undo that mischief. Could your tears for ever flow, you can never unwrite the past nor restore the lost one. Could you bring that wandering soul back by Divine grace, even then the bitter past could not be unwritten, for she, too, has spread the poison. All that accursed past of sin must live on. God forgives sin, but much of the consequences of sin God Himself does not avert. If you light the fire it will burn on to the lowest hell; God may forgive your incendiarism, but the fire itself still continues. You spoke a word against the Lord Jesus in the ears of some youngster years gone by, which turned him aside from the right path. You cannot unsay it, and that youngster's infidelity and unbelief you cannot now destroy. The perpetual mischief which you have done to others might fitly be a reason with the Most High why He should not forgive you, but yet He says, "My thoughts are not your thoughts." With all this before Him, with all the consequences of your sin before Him, He forgives you freely if you rest on Jesus.—*C H. Spurgeon.*

(*c*) Is there anything we value amongst ourselves more than faithfulness, honesty, constancy—punctual, critical, scrupulous virtue? Do we not trust the faithful one? Do we not praise faithfulness above all other virtues when we are talking about relationships which subsist between us and amongst us? It is faithfulness that God values; not brilliance, not greatness, not astonishing, dazzling splendour, but reality, honour, honesty, diligence. Herein it is that the appeal of the Gospel comes to every man—to the man of great powers, and the man of the feeblest influence; to the man of the highest honour, and to the man of the remotest obscurity.—*Joseph Parker, D.D.*

The Earth filled with the Glory of the Lord.

(*Verses* 20, 21.)

I. The import of the promise before us.
"As I live, saith the Lord, all the earth shall be filled with the glory of the Lord." Glory is the manifestation of excellence. The glory of God is that display of His most blessed character and will which opens the way for His intelligent creatures to know, to love, and to obey Him. This glory is exhibited in various ways. It shines in all the works of *creation*; .... is manifested by the works of His *providence*; .... above all, in His works of REDEMPTION. Here all His perfections unite and harmonize, and shine with transcendent glory. Now, when the Gospel shall be preached and received throughout the world; when every kindred, and people, and nation, and tongue shall not only be instructed in its sublime doctrines, but also brought under its benign and sanctifying power, then, with emphatic propriety, may it be said that "the earth is filled with the glory of the Lord." As the highest glory of which an individual creature is capable is to bear the image of his Maker, so the highest glory of which our world at large is capable is to be filled with the holy and benevolent Spirit of Him who is the brightness of the Father's glory, and the express image of His person,—is to have the knowledge and love of the Saviour reigning over all the populations of our globe, "from the rising of the sun even unto the going down of the same." Such appears to be the import of the promise before us.

II. What reason have we for believing that these scenes will be one day realized?

1. *Our hope is founded on Jehovah's faithful and unerring promise* (Num. xxiii. 19; Matt. xxiv. 35). Take the following as a small specimen of the "exceeding great and precious" catalogue found in the inspired volume,—Ps. ii. 8; lxvii. 2; lxxii. 17; Isa. xl. 5; Hab. ii. 14; Zech ix. 10; Mal. i. 11; Phil. ii. 10, 11; Rev. xi. 15.

2. *Our confidence is confirmed by the consideration that this religion is, in its nature, adapted above all others to be a universal religion.* Its doctrines, its worship, and its system of moral duty are all equally adapted to universality. Acts x. 34, 35; xvii. 26. It teaches that He is alike related to the children of men as their Creator, Preserver, and Benefactor; and that the high and the low, the rich and the poor, the monarch and the slave, all stand upon a level in His sight, and have all equal access, if penitent and believing, to the throne of His heavenly grace.

3. *The present aspect of the world furnishes much reason to hope that the accomplishment of this promise is drawing nigh.* I know not that there is at this hour a single portion of the globe to which the enlightened and prudent missionary may not obtain some degree of access. He who "sits as Governor among the nations" seems to be spreading a natural preparation around the world for the preaching of the Gospel among all nations.

Contemplate, further, the singular progress of various forms of improvement throughout the civilized world, all of which may be considered as bearing on the great promise contained in the text. The intercourse between different parts of the globe increasing every day with a rapidity and to an extent beyond all former precedent; the endless improvements in the means of conveyance from one part of the world to another; the wonderful improvements in the art of printing; and the many indications that the English language—the language of those parts of the world which are most favoured with Gospel light— will probably, ere long, become the prevailing language of the whole world.

III. **What is our present duty in relation to the promise before us?**

1. *To believe the promise.* Unbelief cuts the nerves of all spiritual exertion, and tends to discouragement and despondency.

2. *To labour and pray without ceasing for its accomplishment.* There is no piety in the confidence which neglects prayer, and which does not add to prayer diligent effort to attain that for which it prays. God's Kingdom is a Kingdom of means.

3. *In labouring for the spread of the Gospel no adverse occurrence, however painful, ought to discourage us, or at all to weaken either our confidence or our efforts.* With that promise we may meet the most distressing difficulties without fear.

4. *To pray without ceasing for the power of the Holy Spirit to render all the means which are employed for its accomplishment effectual.* It is "not by might nor by power, but by My Spirit, saith Jehovah," that means are attended with a saving energy.

5. *If so great a work as evangelizing the whole world is promised, and is certainly to be accomplished, then our plans and efforts for promoting this object ought to bear a corresponding character; that is, they ought to be large, liberal, and ever expanding.* We ought to consider it as our duty to devote to this object our utmost resources, and to engage the co-operation of all over whom we exert an influence.—*Sam. Miller.*

CALEB—THE MAN FOR THE TIMES.

(*Verse* 24.)

There are three things about Caleb worthy of consideration:—

I. **His faithful following of his God.**

Perceive, *he never went before his God.* That is presumption. The highest point to which the true believer ever comes is to walk *with* God, but never to walk *before* Him. We ought to *follow* the Lord. The sheep follow the shepherd (John x. 4). They follow as the soldier follows the captain. . . . . as the disciple follows the master. Caleb followed the Lord "*fully,*" says one text, "*wholly,*" says another. And here I shall follow the explanation of good Matthew Henry.

1. He followed Him *universally, without dividing.* He did not wish to divide the commands; what God had joined together he did not desire to put asunder. Caleb was quite as ready to fight the giants as he was to carry the clusters. If you say concerning the Lord's will, "I will do this and I will not do that," you do in fact make yourself the master, the spirit of rebellion is in you. Some excuse themselves for neglecting duties on the ground that

they are non-essential—as if all duty was not essential to the perfect follower of Christ. "They are unimportant," says the man, "they involve nothing;" whereas it often happens that the apparently unimportant duty is really the most important of all. Many a great lord, in the olden times, has given up his land on copyhold to his tenant, and perhaps the fee which was to be annually paid was to bring a small bird or a peppercorn to the lord of the manor—in some cases it has been the bringing of a turf or a green leaf. Now, if the tenant should on the annual day refuse to do his homage, and say it was too trifling a thing to bring a peppercorn to the lord of the manor in fee, would he not have forfeited his estate, for he would have been setting himself up as a superior owner, and asserting a right which his feudal lord would at once resist?

Brother, is there not some command which as yet you have not obeyed?

2. Caleb followed the Lord *sincerely, without dissembling.* One of the safest tests of sincerity is found in a willingness to suffer for the cause. How courageous was that man, who had only numbered forty summers, to put himself in opposition to the other ten princes, and declare in flat contradiction to them—"Let us go up; we are able to possess the land." When the people took up stones, and Joshua was forced to speak with Caleb, it was with no small peril, and required no little mental courage to stand up amidst the insults and jeers of the crowd, and still to bring up a good report of the land. . . . . How many profess to follow God who follow Him without their hearts!

3. Caleb followed the Lord *cheerfully, without disputing.* God requires no slaves to grace His throne; He is the Lord of the empire of love. God loveth to have the joyful obedience of His creatures. That obedience which is not cheerful is disobedience, for the Lord looketh at the heart of a thing, and if He seeth that we serve Him from force, and not because we love Him, He will reject our offerings at our hands. The service which is coupled with cheerfulness is hearty service, and therefore true. Cheerfulnesss, again, makes a man strong in service. It is to our service what oil is to the wheels of a railway carriage.

Brother, do you serve the Lord cheerfully?

4. He followed the Lord *constantly, without declining.* Forty-five years he lived in the camp of Israel, but all that time he followed the Lord and never once consorted with murmuring rebels; and when his time came to claim his heritage at the age of eighty-five, the good old man is following the Lord fully; he shows a constant heart. How many professors fail in this respect! They follow the Lord by fits and starts, &c. But, to use the metaphor of Gotthold, we may compare Caleb to a tree. The wind had been blowing—it was a dreadful hurricane, and Gotthold walked into a forest and saw many trees torn up by the roots; he marvelled much at one tree which stood alone and yet had been unmoved in the tempest. He said, "How is this? The trees that were together have fallen, and this alone stands fast!" He observed that when the trees grow too closely they cannot send their roots into the earth; they lean too much upon each other; but this tree, standing alone, had space to thrust its roots into the earth, and lay hold on the rocks and stones, and so when the wind came it fell not. Caleb was constant, because he was a rooted man. He had a firm hold upon his God.

II. **Caleb's favoured portion.**

In reward for his faithful following of his Master,—

1. *His life was preserved in the hour of judgment.* The ten fell, smitten with plague, but Caleb lived. If he follows God fully, God will fully take care of him. Caleb is willing to give his life for his Master, and therefore his Master gives him his life.

2. Caleb was also comforted with *a long life of vigour.* At eighty-five he was as strong as at forty, and still able to face the giants. If there be a Christ-

ian man who shall have in his old age a vigour of faith and courage, it is the man who follows the Lord fully.

3. Caleb received *great honour among his brethren*. He was at least twenty years older than any other man in the camp except Joshua. At their council he would be regarded with as much reverence as Nestor in the assemblies of the Greeks; in their camps he would stand like another Achilles in the midst of the armies of Lacaedaemon. As king and sire he dwelt among men. If we honour God, He will honour us (1 Sam. ii. 30).

4. Caleb was *put upon the hardest service*. That is always the lot of the most faithful servant of God. Caleb had the distinguished honour of being permitted to lead the van against the gigantic Anakim (Josh. xiv. 12; xv. 13, 14). Get your soul right, and you may defy the sharpest arrow of the adversary.

5. He had *the honour of enjoying what he had once seen*. He had only seen the land when he said, "We are able to take it." He lived not only to take it, but to enjoy it for himself. God does reward those who dare to do hard things in confidence in His name.

6. Caleb *left a blessing to his children*. If there is any man who shall be able to leave his children the blessing of the upper and nether springs, it is the man who follows the Lord fully (Josh. xv. 13-19).

III. Caleb's secret character.

"He had another spirit with him," —not only a bold, generous, noble, and heroic spirit, but the Spirit and influence of God which thus raised him above human inquietudes and earthly fears. Everything acts according to the spirit which is in it. The real way to make a new life is to receive a new spirit. The distinguishing mark of a right spirit is *faith*. Then a faithful spirit always begets a *meek* spirit, and a meek spirit always begets a *brave* spirit. The true believer has also a *loving* spirit . . . . a *zealous* spirit . . . . a *heavenly* spirit. Such a spirit had good Caleb. O that His Holy Spirit would lead us to go to Jesus just as we are, and look up to Him and beseech Him to fulfil that great covenant promise—"A new heart also will I give them, a right *spirit* will I put within them."—*C. H. Spurgeon.*

HOLY SINGULARITY DIVINELY HONOURED.

(*Verse* 24.)

In considering what is here recorded concerning Caleb, we may notice—

I. The relation he bore.

He was God's servant—a relation denoting that he acknowleged no other master, Matt. vi. 24; that he had his allotted work, Matt. xxi. 28; that he was not at liberty to govern himself, Deut. xii. 8; that he was to do all for God and His service, Rom. xiv. 8; that his employment was highly honourable, Psa. lxxxiv. 10.

II. The disposition he possessed.

"He had another spirit with him;" —a spirit altogether different from that of the rest of the spies,—the one being base, mean, sneaking, and cowardly; whilst the other inspired with courage and undaunted resolution (ver. 2-10; Josh. xiv. 7, 8; 2 Cor. iv. 13). We may learn hence that all men must unavoidably be actuated by one spirit or another, in their different ways; that God perfectly knows what spirit is with us; and that a right spirit is of great and essential importance if we would secure the Divine approval.

III. The course he pursued.

He followed the Lord fully. To follow the Lord fully is to follow Him sincerely, without dissimulation; alone, without dividing; universally, without reserve; openly, without shame; fixedly, without instability; constantly, without weariness; submissively, without dictating; and confidently, without doubting.

IV. The recompense he obtained.

God brought him into the land of Canaan;—typical of heaven, the *better country* which God's people have ever sought, having earnest desires after its possession, as the dwelling-place of all their brethren, and as their Father's house.—*William Sleigh.*

I. Real Christians are actuated by a different spirit from that of the world.

II. Those who possess a right spirit will follow the Lord fully.

III. Those who follow the Lord fully shall be honourably distinguished by Him.—*G. Burder.*

THE SENTENCE OF GOD UPON THE SINFUL PEOPLE.

(*Verses* 26-39.)

The Divine judgment upon the rebellious people has already been declared in general terms to Moses (vers. 21-25). In this paragraph that judgment is pronounced in full to Moses and Aaron, for announcement to the people. We have spoken of the sin and punishment of the people in our notes on vers. 20-25; the additional suggestions introduced in this paragraph we will now endeavour to indicate, taking as our subject, *The sentence of God upon the sinful people.*

I. **The sentence was conspicuously just.**

Its justice is manifest—

1. *In the correspondence between the nature of the sin and the nature of the punishment.* They had disbelieved God's solemn and repeated promise to give them the land; they had shrunk as utter cowards from attempting to take possession of it; and God sentences them to exclusion from it. They had cried, "Would God that we had died in the wilderness!" and God takes them at their word; in the wilderness they shall die. The Divine punishment of sin ever answers in its nature to the sin itself. "Of what kind the sin is, of the same kind is the punishment (Gen. xlii. 21). David sinned greatly in numbering of the people, through the pride of his heart, and vain glory in his own greatness: God could have punished him many other ways, but He meeteth with him in the same kind, He diminisheth the number of his people exceedingly by the pestilence, in whose strength he much trusted." Comp. Judg. i. 6, 7; Jer. li. 56. The punishment of sin generally grows out of the sin itself. "Whatsoever a man soweth, that shall he also reap," etc. (*a*)

2. *In the correspondence between the duration of the unbelieving exploration and the duration of the punishment.* "After the number of the days in which ye searched the land, even forty days, each day for a year, shall ye bear your iniquities, even forty years." M. Henry: "They were content to wait forty days for the testimony of men, because they could not take God's word; and therefore justly are they kept forty years waiting for the performance of God's promise." Attersoll: 'A year for a day. A dram of sin hath a pound of sorrow. A day of pleasure hath a year of pain."

3. *In the correspondence between the different degrees of guilt and the different severities of punishment.* The heaviest and sternest doom fell upon the ten unbelieving explorers, who were the greatest sinners. "The men which Moses sent to search the land, who returned, and made all the congregation to murmur against him, by bringing up a slander upon the land, even those men that did bring up the evil report upon the land, died by the plague before the Lord." They were smitten by a sudden death which manifestly proceeded from Jehovah Himself. When God ariseth to judgment He distributeth punishment in proportion to the guilt of the offenders. Those who not only sin themselves but lead others into sin will have the sorest punishment. (*b*) Here is warning to those who tempt others to evil, and to those whose example leads others astray.

Repent; or you will be "beaten with many stripes" (Luke xii. 47, 48; Heb. x. 28, 29). (*c*)

4. *In the exemption from punishment of those who had not shared in the guilt.* When the ten faithless explorers were smitten with sudden death by the Lord, Caleb and Joshua were spared. "Joshua the son of Nun, and Caleb the son of Jephunneh, of the men who went to search the land, lived." In like manner, those who had not joined in the murmuring and the rebellion were not excluded from the Promised Land. "Your little ones which ye said should be a prey, them will I bring in, and they shall know the land which ye have despised." Caleb and Joshua also were to enter and possess the good land. In His judgments God discriminates between the righteous and the wicked. Comp. Gen. xviii. 25.

But the innocent, though exempt from the punishment of the guilty, suffered privation and loss on account of their sins. "Your children shall wander in the wilderness forty years, and bear your whoredoms until your carcases be wasted in the wilderness." So closely are we related to each other by national, social, and family ties, that the good cannot altogether escape the consequences of the sins of the wicked. "None of us liveth to himself." "We are members one of another." No one can sin without inflicting loss and injury upon others. "One sinner destroyeth much good." The innocent suffer with the guilty. Children still bear the sins of their parents. Very clearly is this the case with the children of the extravagant and wasteful, the drunken and the unchaste. Here is solemn admonition to parents. "If they love their sons, they must leave their sins, and walk in a careful obedience to the law of God. Wicked parents are the greatest enemies to their children."

II. The sentence was utterly irreversible.

"Say unto them, As I live, saith the Lord, as ye have spoken in mine ears, so will I do to you . . . . I the Lord have said, I will surely do it unto all this evil congregation, that are gathered together against Me: in this wilderness shall they be consumed, and there they shall die." God forgives the sinners, but pronounces irreversible judgment against their sin. He pardons the rebels; but they shall not enter the Promised Land. The penalties of sin are certain. "The soul that sinneth it shall die." "Be sure your sin will find you out." "Though hand join in hand, the wicked shall not go unpunished." The punishment of sin is inevitable. Let no one go on presumptuously in wickedness imagining that he shall escape the penalties of his course. "Because sentence against an evil work is not executed speedily, therefore the heart of the sons of men is fully set in them to do evil." This is the extreme of folly; for though the execution of the sentence be delayed, nevertheless it is infallibly certain. What God hath said He will surely do. (*d*)

III. The sentence caused great sorrow.

"And Moses told these sayings unto all the children of Israel, and the people mourned greatly."

1. *Their sorrow had a real and sufficient cause.* Only a little time previously they had mourned without any true reason (verse 1); but now they have sadly real and abundant reason for grief and tears.

2. *Their sorrow was not that of repentance, but of selfishness.* They mourned because of the punishment of sin, not because of the sin itself. "In the sorrow of the world," says F. W. Robertson, "the obliquity of the heart towards evil is not cured; it seems as if nothing cured it; heartache and trials come in vain; the history of life at last is what it was at first. The man is found erring where he erred before. The same course, begun with the certainty of the same desperate end which has taken place so often before. They have reaped the whirlwind, but they will again sow the wind." Such was the sorrow of the people at this time. Such mourning is never blessed; never issues in blessing.

ILLUSTRATIONS.

(*a*) It pleaseth God to make His punishments answerable, and carrying a likeness with the sin for which it is inflicted; so that they are punished by that thing by which they have sinned against God. Covetous persons which get their goods by fraud and oppression, are themselves or their heirs many times oppressed and deceived, and brought to beggary. Gluttony, surfeiting, and drunkenness, are oftentimes punished with dropsies, and many gross and corrupt humours, distempering their bodies, and bringing them with speed to their graves. But these judgments belong only to the body, and do not stretch to the soul and conscience: nevertheless, the Lord ceaseth not to repay us even in this kind also, according to our sin. Hence it is, that He threateneth to send strong delusions upon men to believe lies, which will not receive and believe the truth (2 Thess. ii. 11); and they which will not believe wholesome doctrine, but having itching ears, get them an heap of teachers, shall turn their ears from the truth, and be turned unto fables, and believe lies (2 Tim. iv. 3, 4).—*Attersoll.*

(*b*) The makers of criminals are more guilty than the criminals that they make. They who lay the foundations for the destruction of men by inciting them to evil through their appetites and passions, are the architects of damnation in the world, and are the wickedest of men. Not the man that drinks, but the man who puts the cup to his neighbour's lips, is the most wicked. Not the man that steals, but the man who makes a haunt for the production of thieves, rears them, nourishes them, and insures them, is the culprit—the arch-demon.—*H. W. Beecher.*

(*c*) The legend of St. Macarius of Alexandria, runs thus :—" One day, as Macarius wandered among those ancient Egyptian tombs wherein he had made himself a dwelling-place, he found the skull of a mummy, and, turning it over with his crutch, he inquired to whom it belonged; and it replied, 'To a pagan.' And Macarius, looking into the empty eyes, said, 'Where, then, is thy soul?' And the head replied, 'In hell.' Macarius asked, 'How deep?' And the head replied, 'The depth is greater than the distance from heaven to earth.' Then Macarius asked, 'Are there any deeper than thou art?' The skull replied, 'Yes; the Jews are deeper still.' And Macarius asked, 'Are there any deeper than the Jews?' To which the head replied, 'Yes, in sooth! for the Christians whom Jesus Christ hath redeemed, and who show in their actions that they despise His doctrine, are deeper still.'"—*Dict. of Illust.*

(*d*) The pea contains the vine and flower and the pod in embryo; and I am sure, when I plant it, that it will produce them, and nothing else. Now, every action of our lives is embryonic, and, according as it is right or wrong, it will surely bring forth the sweet flowers of joy, or the poison fruits of sorrow. Such is the constitution of this world; and the Bible assures us that the next world only carries it forward. Here and hereafter, "whatsoever a man soweth, that shall he also reap."—*H. W. Beecher.*

For additional illustrations of the certainty of the punishment of sin, see pp. 89, 225, 258.

BASE MURMURING.

(*Verse 27.*)

No sin stands alone. Every sin is related to other sins, and frequently involves other sins. Such is the case with the sin of murmuring. It is not a simple sin, but involves—

1. *Presumption.* The murmurer regards his view as to how things ought to be, as superior to the Divine arrangements. Man murmuring, is folly arraigning infinite wisdom; it is like a glowworm grumbling at the sun.

2. *Ingratitude.* Blessings are depreciated and inconveniencies are exaggerated by the murmurer: in present difficulties he quite ignores past kindnesses. "Murmuring persons," says Dyer, "think everything done by themselves too much, and everything done for them too little."

3. *Rebellion.* The will of the murmurer is in a state of active antagonism to the holy will of God.

We have a mournful, but by no means a solitary example of murmuring mentioned in the text. Let us mark its conspicuous features as they are here indicated.

I. **Murmuring without any cause.**

The Israelites had much reason for thankfulness and praise; but none for complaint. They had been emancipated from Egyptian bondage by God; they were being graciously led, provisioned, and protected by Him; they were on the borders of that excellent land which He had promised to give them; yet because of the false report of the cowardly spies they break forth into unrestrained murmuring against God, and against the leaders whom He had appointed.

Psalms of grateful praise would have been becoming in them; but ungrateful murmurings were utterly unbecoming and base. And still men murmur without any cause, except the ingratitude and discontent of their own souls. (*a*)

II. **Murmuring against the Best Being.**

"This evil congregation which murmur against Me." In vers. 2 it is said, "All the children of Israel murmured against Moses and against Aaron." The Lord says, "They murmur against Me." Complaints made against the servants of God in the fulfilment of their appointed duties He regards as against Himself.

1. *Think who and what He is,*—the Supremely Wise and Good, &c.

2. *Think of what He had done for the Israelites, and what He has done for us,*—redeemed, guarded, sustained, &c.

3. *Think of what He had promised to them, and what He has promised to us,*—the continuance of His presence and support, victory over our enemies, the possession of a glorious inheritance, &c. How heinously base, then, is it to murmur against Him! to murmur against Him who in Himself is perfect, and who is our great Benefactor! Yet all our complaints as to our circumstances, our duties, our lot in life, are murmurings against Him.

III. **Murmuring of long continuance.**

"How long shall I bear with this evil congregation, which murmur against Me?" Murmuring had become chronic with this generation of the Israelites. There are many to-day who are habitual grumblers; murmuring is not an occasional and infrequent thing with them, but a constant mood which is more or less manifest in all their speech. (*b*) How great is their sin! How great also is the patience of God with them!

IV. **Murmuring known to God.**

"I have heard the murmurings of the children of Israel, which they murmur against Me." God hears every bitter complaint, whether uttered in loud wailings or soft whispers; He perceives every unthankful and rebellious mood of the spirit. Consider this, ye murmurers, and be shamed, and be warned!

V. **Murmuring punished by God.**

These Israelite murmurers were excluded from the Promised Land. The murmurer excludes himself from the Canaan of joy and peace and contentment. Murmuring is a self-punishing sin. God has made it so. Murmuring is misery. The murmurer is his own tormentor. (*c*)

Let us endeavour to conquer and avoid this evil by cultivating a spirit of thankfulness and contentment.

"Some murmur when their sky is clear
And wholly bright to view,
If one small speck of dark appear
In their great heaven of blue;
And some with thankful love are filled
If but one streak of light,
One ray of God's good mercy, gild
The darkness of their night.

In palaces are hearts that ask,
In discontent and pride,
Why life is such a dreary task,
And all good things denied?
And hearts in poorest huts admire
How love has in their aid
(Love that not ever seems to tire)
Such rich provision made."

Archbishop Trench.

ILLUSTRATIONS.

(*a*) In a love-feast in Yorkshire, a good man had been drawing out a long complaining strain of experiences about his difficulties and trials on the way to heaven. Another, of a different spirit, followed, who said, "I see our brother who has just sat down lives in Grumbling Street. I lived there myself for some time, and never enjoyed good health. The air was bad, the house bad, the water bad; the birds never came and sung in the street; and I was gloomy and sad enough. But I 'flitted.' I got into Thanksgiving Street;

and ever since then I have had good health, and so have my family. The air is pure, the water pure, the house good; the sun shines on it all day; the birds are always singing; and I am as happy as I can live. Now, I recommend our brother to 'flit.' There are plenty of houses to let in Thanksgiving Street; and I am sure he will find himself a new man if he will only come; and I will be right glad to have him for a neighbour."—*Dict. of Illust.*

(*b*) Some people are always "out of sorts." The weather is always just what they don't want. I met one of these men a while ago, a farmer, who raised all manner of crops. It was a wet day, and I said, "Mr. Nayling, this rain will be fine for your grass crop."—"Yes, perhaps; but it is bad for the corn, and will keep it back. I don't believe we shall have a crop." A few days after this when the sun was shining hot, I said, "Fine sun for your corn, sir."—"Yes, pretty fair; but it's awful for the rye. Rye wants cold weather." Again: on a cold morning I met my neighbour, and said, "This must be capital for your rye, Mr. Nayling."—"Yes; but it is the very worst weather for the corn and grass. They want heat to bring them forward."—*Dr. Todd.*

(*c*) For an illustration of this point see p. 247.

A Presumptuous Enterprise and its Disastrous Termination.

(*Verses* 40-45.)

We have in these verses an illustration of—

First: *The sad perversity of sinful human nature.* The children of Israel seemed determined to walk contrary to God. When He said, "Go, and possess the land," they disobeyed, saying, "Let us return into Egypt." And now that He says, "Ye shall not come into the land," they say, "Lo, we will go up unto the place which the Lord hath promised." "When they should go forward," says Attersoll, "then they will go backward and make them a captain to conduct them into Egypt. When they should go backward, then they will go forward, though they perish for it. This is our corrupt nature. That which God willeth us to do, we will not do; and that which He willeth us not to do, that we will do; whereby we see that the lusts of the flesh are enmity against God."

Second: *The confession of sin and persistence in sin.* "We have sinned," said the Israelites, and in the same breath they propose to sin again. They were not penitent for their sin; they do not seem at all conscious of that unbelief which was their great sin, and the prolific parent of so many other sins. When God said that He would give them the land, they did not believe Him; and now He says that they shall not enter the land, they do not believe Him. Then they sinned by their unbelieving despair; now they sin by their presumptuous self-confidence. "Man is ever supposing," says Dr. A. Clarke, "he can either *do all things*, or *do nothing;* he is therefore sometimes *presumptuous,* and at other times in *despair.*" The people cried. "We have sinned," and at once proceeded to sin again in another form. How many of us bear a close resemblance to them in this respect! (*a*)

Third: *The great difficulty of walking humbly and patiently in the path which our sins has rendered necessary for us.* The unbelief of the Israelites had rendered it necessary that they should be ordered back into the wilderness, and against this they rebelled; they would go forward, not backward. So with us. We rebel against God, or fail to enter into His purposes concerning us; and when suffering and loss follow, we fail to see in them the just and natural consequences of our sin; and, instead of humbly submitting to them, we blame circumstances or find fault with Providence, and presumptuously rebel against the Divine order.

Now let us turn to the main subject of this paragraph, and consider—

I. The presumptuous enterprise.

In the narrative as given both here and in Deut. i. 41-45, their presumption is mentioned. Their presumption is seen in that they went forth—

1. *In opposition to the command of the Lord.* "And the Lord said, To-morrow turn you and get you into the wilder-

ness by the way of the Red Sea. Doubtless ye shall not come into the land," &c. "And they rose up early in the morning, and got them up into the top of the mountain, saying, Lo, we be here, and we will go up into the place which the Lord hath promised." The enterprise which is forbidden by God cannot possibly under any circumstances be either wise or right.

2. *Despite the remonstrance of Moses.* Being acquainted with their purpose, Moses points out to them (1) The sin of their proposal. "And Moses said, Wherefore now do ye transgress the commandment of the Lord?" (2) The peril of their proposal. "It shall not prosper. Go not up, for the Lord is not among you; that ye be not smitten before your enemies. For the Amalekites and the Canaanites are there before you, and ye shall fall by the sword." To firm believers in God, the taking of the land would have been a question between the Lord and the heathen nations of Canaan. But by their unbelief the Israelites had made it a question between themselves and the Canaanites; and, without the Divine Presence, the Israelites were not a match for the Canaanites. (3) The reason of their peril. "The Lord is not among you .... Because ye are turned away from the Lord, therefore the Lord will not be with you." The presence of God with His people is the secret of their strength and victory. Comp. 2 Chron. xx. 15, 17. But sin strips us of the consciousness of His Presence, despoils us of calmness and courage, withdraws from us our defence, and leaves us an easy prey to our enemies. Thus Moses remonstrated with them; "but they presumed to go up unto the hill top."

3. *Without the symbol of the Divine Presence and the presence of the Divinely-appointed leader.* "Nevertheless the Ark of the covenant of the Lord, and Moses departed not out of the camp." Moses would not countenance their enterprise in any way or in any degree whatsoever. But they despised all remonstrances and counsels and expressions of disapproval; and they set out to "go up unto the place which the Lord had promised."

II. **The disastrous termination of this presumptuous enterprise.** "Then the Amalekites came down, and the Canaanites which dwelt in that hill, and smote them, and discomfited them, unto Hormah." Their presumptuous enterprise ends in—

1. *Disgraceful defeat.* They had said, "We will go up and fight; .... We will go up unto the place which the Lord hath promised." And they went out; but returned more quickly than they went; for the Canaanites which dwelt in that mountain, came out against them, and chased them, as bees do, unto Hormah (Deut. i. 44). They did not fight like men; but fled like cowards. Their defeat was ignominious. (*b*)

2. *Sore slaughter.* The Canaanites "smote them and discomfited them;" ... "and destroyed them in Seir." They were defeated with severe loss of men. Already they are beginning to bring about the fulfilment of the Divine sentence, that their carcases should fall in the wilderness.

3. *Bitter sorrow.* "And ye returned and wept before the Lord." How prone these people were to weep. Shallow hearts perhaps weep most. There was nothing noble or commendable in these tears. They were the expressions of disappointment and cowardice, and were as fruitless as they were bitter; for "the Lord would not hearken to their voice, nor give ear unto them."

Conclusion.

From the whole let us *learn the sin and the folly of entering upon any enterprises, and especially difficult ones, in our own strength.* "Apart from me," said Christ, "ye can do nothing." This is applicable to—

1. *Spiritual life in its origin and progress.* The attempt in our own strength to lead a religious, godly life, is sure to end in sad disappointment and utter failure. (*c*)

2. *Spiritual conflict.* Unless we take to ourselves "the whole armour of God," our spiritual foes will be too

many and too mighty for us. We can conquer only through Christ.

3. *Spiritual service.* Our efforts to benefit our fellow men will succeed only as they are made in reliance upon the blessing of God. We can bless others only as He blesses us. Comp. 1 Cor. iii. 5-7.

ILLUSTRATIONS.

(*a*) How many a hardened rebel on shipboard, when the timbers are strained and creaking, when the mast is broken, and the ship is drifting before the gale, when the hungry waves are opening their mouths to swallow up the ship alive and quick as those that go into the pit—how many an hardened sailor has then bowed his knee, with tears in his eyes, and cried, "I have sinned!" But of what avail and of what value was his confession? The repentance that was born in the storm died in the calm; that repentance of his that was begotten amidst the thunder and the lightning, ceased so soon as all was hushed in quiet, and the man who was a pious mariner when on board ship, became the most wicked and abominable of sailors when he placed his foot on *terra firma*. How often, too, have we seen this in a storm of thunder and lightning! Many a man's cheek is blanched when he hears the thunder rolling; and the tears start to his eyes, and he cries, "O God, I have sinned!" while the rafters of his house are shaking, and the very ground beneath him reeling at the voice of God which is full of majesty. But alas, for such a repentance! When the sun again shines, and the black clouds are withdrawn, sin comes again upon the man, and he becomes worse than before. How many of the same sort of confessions, too, have we seen in times of cholera, and fever, and pestilence! Then our churches have been crammed with hearers, who, because so many funerals have passed their doors, or so many have died in the street, could not refrain from going up to God's house to confess their sins. And under that visitation, when one, two, and three have been lying dead in the house, or next door, how many have thought they would really turn to God! But, alas! when the pestilence had done its work, conviction ceased; and when the bell had tolled the last time for a death caused by cholera, then their hearts ceased to beat with penitence, and their tears did flow no more. . . . It is of no use for you to say, "I have sinned," merely under the influence of terror, and then to forget it afterwards.—*C. H. Spurgeon.*

(*b*) A noble ship was bearing into port. It was the evening hour, and too late to enter without a pilot. There were two passages into the harbour; one a dangerous narrow channel, the other a wide and safe one. The captain determined to pilot himself by the narrow passage. A storm was coming up; and the passengers, with fear and consternation, begged him to take the wider channel. He laughed at their cowardice, and swore he would do as he pleased. As the night advanced, the gale increased. Soon rose a cry, "*Breakers ahead, breakers ahead!*" The captain flew to the wheel; the sails were struck; the wind had the mastery; and the captain found a will that could defy his own. The vessel made a fearful plunge, struck the foreship deep into the sand, to be shattered by the wild waves' pleasure. Few survived the terrors of that fearful night; but among the dead thrown up by the rising tide was the body of the wilful and presumptuous captain.—*Dict. of Illust.*

(*c*) There is not a daisy that was not organised to be a daisy, but I should like to see one that did not have the sun to help it up from the seed; there is not an aster that was not organised to be an aster, but where is there one that grew independent of the sun? What the sun is to flowers, that the Holy Ghost must be to our hearts, if we would be Christians. If there is a man who can be a Christian without the help of God, he has a heart such as I never knew a person to have. I never seek to put down wicked thoughts and incite good ones without feeling that if God does not help me I shall not succeed. And here we come to the very bosom of the truth I am enforcing, for what God commands us to be, that He is Himself, and when we need help in our Christian course, He stands ready, of all others, to help us, working in us both to will and to do of His good pleasure.—*H. W. Beecher.*

CHAPTER XV.

CRITICAL AND EXPLANATORY NOTES.

In this and the next four chapters we have a narrative of certain occurrences and enactments during the penal wandering in the desert, which lasted for nearly thirty-eight years. The relation of these chapters to the history is well expressed by Keil and Del. in this note: "After the unhappy issue of the attempt to penetrate into Canaan, in opposition to the will of God and the advice of Moses, the Israelites remained 'many days' in Kadesh, as the Lord did not hearken to their lamentations concerning the defeat which they had suffered at the hands of the Canaanites and Amalekites. Then they turned, and took their journey, as the Lord had commanded (chap. xiv. 25), into the wilderness, in the direction towards the Red Sea (Deut. i. 45; ii. 1); and in the first month of the fortieth year they came again into the desert of Zin, to Kadesh (chap. xx. 1). All that we know respecting this journeying from Kadesh into the wilderness in the direction towards the Red Sea, and up to the time of their return to the desert of Zin, is limited to a number of names of places of encampment given in the list of journeying stages in chap. xxxiii. 19-30, out of which, as the situation of the majority of them is altogether unknown, or at all events has not yet been determined, no connected account of the journeys of Israel during this interval of thirty-seven years can possibly be drawn. The most important event related in connection with this period is the rebellion of the company of Korah against Moses and Aaron, and the re-establishment of the Aaronic priesthood and confirmation of their rights, which this occasioned (chaps. xvi.-xviii). The rebellion probably occurred in the first portion of the period in question. In addition to this there are only a few laws recorded, which were issued during this long time of punishment, and furnished a practical proof of the continuance of the covenant which the Lord had made with the nation of Israel at Sinai. There was nothing more to record in connection with these thirty-seven years, which formed the *second* stage in the guidance of Israel through the desert. For, as *Baumgarten* has well observed, the fighting men of Israel had fallen under the judgment of Jehovah, and the sacred history, therefore, was no longer concerned with them; whilst the youth, in whom the life and hope of Israel were preserved, had as yet no history at all."

In this chapter certain regulations concerning certain offerings and observances are laid down.

Verse 4. On the *meat offering* comp. Lev. ii.

Verse 14. *A stranger.* "There were two sorts of strangers among the Israelites; some that entirely embraced and professed the Jewish religion, into which they were admitted by circumcision, &c; others that lived among them by permission, having renounced all idolatry, but did not submit to their whole religion. The former sort are understood to be meant here.—*Bp. Patrick.*

Verse 15. *One ordinance,* &c. Keil and Del. translate: "'As for the assembly, there shall be one law for the Israelite and the stranger, ... an eternal ordinance .... before Jehovah.' הַקָּהָל, which is construed absolutely, refers to the assembling of the nation before Jehovah, or to the congregation viewed in its attitude with regard to God."

As ye are, so shall the stranger be, &c. "The meaning is, 'as with you, so shall it be with the stranger,' &c."—*Speaker's Comm.*

Verses 17-21. The ordinances here prescribed are based upon the general principle stated in Exod. xxii. 29; xxiii. 19.

Verse 20. *Dough.* עֲרִיסֹת, is only used in Neh. x. 37; Ezek. xliv. 30, and in both places the reference is to this ordinance. Keil and Del. say that the word "signifies most probably groats, or meal coarsely bruised." Fuerst, however, regards the old interpretation, *dough* or *mixed dough,* as the more probable.

Verse 24. *By ignorance without the knowledge,* &c. Lit., as in margin, "By ignorance from the eyes of," &c. Keil and Del.: "If it occur away from the eyes of the congregation through error."

According to the manner. Margin: "According to the ordinance." H. E. J. Howard: "According to the appointment."

Verse 26. *Seeing all the people were in ignorance.* Keil and Del.: "'For' (sc. it has happened) 'to the whole nation in mistake.'" Howard: "For to all the people (it was) unintentional."

Verse 30. *Presumptuously.* Margin: "With an high hand." Fuerst: "With a raised hand;" raised "as a sign of presumption."

Reproacheth the Lord. Translate, "Blasphemeth the Lord." Keil and Del.: "Whoever committeth a sin 'with a high hand,'—*i.e.*, so that he raised his hand, as it were, against Jehovah, or acted in open rebellion against Him,—blasphemed God, and was to be cut off (see Gen. xvii. 14); for he had despised the word of Jehovah, and broken His commandment, and was to atone for it with his life"

Verse 31. *His iniquity shall be upon him.* Howard: "Its sin (is) in it." Keil and Del.: "'Its crime upon it;' *i.e.*, it shall come upon such a soul in the punishment which it shall endure."

Verse 34. *Because it was not declared,* &c. It had already been determined that Sabbath-breaking should be punished by death (Exod. xxxi. 14, 15); but the mode of death was not declared.

Verse 35. *The man shall be surely put to death.* "For as no fire was to be made throughout their habitations on a Sabbath day (Exod. xxxv. 2, 3), gathering sticks for such a purpose was a work that was a violation of the Sabbath, punishable with death."—*Dr. Gill.*

Verse 38. The outer garment of the Hebrews was a quadrangular piece of cloth. They are here commanded to wear fringes or tassels at the corners of this garment, and to fasten the tassels to the edge of the garment by a riband or thread of a deep blue colour. This riband or thread of blue was designed to remind them of the commandments of the Lord, and of their obligation to keep them.

Verse 39. *That ye seek not.* Speaker's Comm.: "That ye wander not." Keil and Del.: "And ye shall not stray after," &c.

Propriety in Worship.

(Verses 1-16.)

In this paragraph we have certain instructions as to the offering of sacrifices, when the people had entered into the Promised Land. These instructions are supplementary to the laws concerning sacrifices which had already been promulgated. Let us consider—

I. **The gracious intimation.**

"When ye be come into the land of your habitations, which I give unto you."

We know not at what time during their long wanderings, these directions were given unto them; but the place which they occupy in the history is significant and suggestive. Immediately after the record of the sentence of death in the wilderness, which was passed upon the generation of rebels, these instructions are inserted which graciously intimate that another generation should possess the good land. This intimation was eminently calculated to promote their—

1. *Encouragement.* It assures them that, notwithstanding the sin of the parents, their children should not be disinherited; and this assurance would be to them a pledge of the renewal of the favour of God to them. These would animate and cheer them in their tedious wanderings in the desert.

2. *Instruction.* Here they are taught that, notwithstanding all the unfaithfulness and rebellion of man, God "abideth faithful: He cannot deny Himself." We may by our sin exclude ourselves from the enjoyment of the privileges promised to the people of God; but we cannot prevent the fulfil-

ment of those promises, or frustrate the Divine purposes. "My counsel shall stand, and I will do all My pleasure."

II. **The directions concerning the worship of God.** (Vers. 3-12).

1. *The perpetual obligation of worship is here implied.* These instructions concerning worship are spoken of as "an ordinance for ever in your generations." (1) Man's need of worship is permanent. Human nature can never outgrow its need of worship. The higher man rises in the scale of being, the more reverently he adores the Holy One. (2) God's worthiness to receive worship is permanent. He is eternally and unchangeably the Supremely and Infinitely Perfect, the Supremely and Infinitely Beautiful. Hence the perpetual obligation of worship.

2. *That man must approach God through sacrifice* is also implied in the text. Man's consciousness of sin is the reason of this need. Feeling our guiltiness, we are afraid to approach unto the Being of perfect holiness against whom we have sinned. We draw near to God through the mediation of Jesus Christ, the great Sin Offering (John xiv. 6). He removes our suspicions concerning God, and banishes our guilty fears, and brings us near to Him. "God hath reconciled us to Himself by Jesus Christ," &c. (2 Cor. v. 18, 19). But the chief teaching of these directions is this—

3. *In the offerings which we present to God, proper proportions should be observed.* These proportions are stated in the text. "If the sacrifice was a lamb or a kid, then the meat offering must be a tenth-deal of flour, that is an omer, which contained about five pints; this must be mingled with oil, the fourth part of a hin (a hin contained about five quarts), and the drink offering must be the same quantity of wine, about a quart and half a pint," (vers. 3-5). If it was a ram, the meat offering was doubled, two tenth-deals of flour, about five quarts, and a third part of a hin of oil (which was to them as butter is to us) mingled with it; and the same quantity of wine for a drink offering (vers. 6, 7.) If the sacrifice was a bullock, the meat-offering was to be trebled, three omers, with five pints of oil, and the same quantity of wine for a drink-offering (vers. 8-10). And thus for each sacrifice, whether offered by a particular person or at the common charge." The principle seems to be this, that there should be order and congruity in the services which we offer to God; everything connected with the worship of God should be appropriate and harmonious. This principle may be applied to (1) The edifices for Divine worship. (*a*). (2) The exercises of Divine worship. (*b*). (3) The great sacrifice for us and our offerings to God. "God gave His only begotten Son." "He spared not His Own Son, but delivered Him up for us all." Then we should give ourselves unreservedly to Him. Comp. Rom. xii. 1.

III. **The pleasure of God in the worship of His people.**

Five times in this paragraph we meet with the words, "A sweet savour unto the Lord" (vers. 3, 7, 10, 13, 14). The words express the pleasure which God takes in the true worship of His people. For what reasons does God delight in His people's worship?

1. *Because the feelings which find expression in true worship are good and beautiful.* The sin-offering was designed to express the penitence, the meat-offering the gratitude, and the burnt-offering the self-consecration of the worshippers; and penitence, gratitude, and consecration of self to God are good and becoming in us, beneficial to us, and well-pleasing to God.

2. *Because worship is essential to the education and progress of His creatures.* Without worship the noblest capacities and faculties of our nature remain undeveloped. Gratitude, humility, admiration, adoration, aspiration, these are worship; and without these our spirits cannot grow, cannot even live in any worthy sense. True worship transforms the worshipper into the image of the object worshipped. Hence the worship of the Lord God exalts, purifies, enriches, strengthens the worshipper. "It is

good to give thanks unto the Lord," &c. (c)

3. *Because these sacrifices were types of the perfect Sacrifice of Jesus Christ.* The sacrifices offered under the ceremonial law pointed onward to Christ Jesus, and found their consummation in His glorious self-sacrifice. In the sublime self-devotion of that sacrifice, in the unspeakable love which it so eloquently expresses, and in the hearty obedience even unto death, we have the highest worship. As Thomas Carlyle says, "O brother, if this is not 'worship,' then I say, the more pity for worship; for this is the noblest thing yet discovered under God's sky." For these reasons the offerings of His people are "a sweet savour unto the Lord," and in their worship He takes delight.

IV. **The directions concerning the stranger sojourning with the Israelites.** "All that are born of the country shall do these things after this manner," &c. (vers. 13-16). Before the Lord and in the exercises of worship, the Israelite had no advantage over the stranger; there was one law for both, and one ordinance. This arrangement would tend—

1. *To check exclusiveness and pride among the Israelites.* It was eminently calculated to suppress the risings of spiritual pride and pride of race to which they were so prone (John viii. 33, 39).

2. *To encourage the Israelites in the humane treatment of foreigners.* They are here taught that if the foreigner were willing to adopt their religion, they were to receive him with kindness, &c.

3. *To encourage the Gentiles to unite in the worship and service of the Lord God.*

4. *To foreshadow the universality of the Christian Church.* Comp. John iii. 14-17; Acts x. 34, 35; xvii. 26-28; Gal. iii. 7-9, 14, 22, 26-29; Rev. xxii. 17.

ILLUSTRATIONS.

(*a*) Excess of material circumstance in spiritual worship, whether of architectural adornment, ritual ceremony, musical elaboration, or even intellectual fastidiousness, is as injurious to it as is over-cumbrous machinery in manufacture, excess of ceremonial in social life, superfluous raiment to personal activity, or gaudy ornamentation to personal grace. It is both injurious to life and offensive to taste. But equally so, on the other hand, is penuriousness and nakedness. If we may not overlay spiritual life, neither may we denude it. The true law of life is that its energies be developed in all the force and with all the beauty of which they are capable, and that it worship with such cultured adornment as in the highest degree may appeal to and express its own spiritual emotions. This is the simple law and the sufficient test of all artistic appliances. Is any particular culture conducive to the worshipping heart of the congregation? If not, and still more if it be injurious to it, then no matter how beautiful in itself it may be—how conducive to the profit and joy of other congregations—however sanctioned by history and contemporary use—let it be rejected, and, if needful, let it be dealt with as the serpent of brass which Hezekiah destroyed and pronounced to be "Nehushtan."—*H. Allon, D.D.*

(*b*) In the Temple service there was not only the Holy Sacrifice and the fragrant incense, but the golden altar, and the richly-robed priest—not only the holy song, but the rich poetry of David's psalms, and the cultured music of the sons of Asaph and Korah. In every allusion of the psalmists, as well as in every record of the historian, we feel the implications of an earnest reverential manner. What special spirituality can there be in the pious doggrel of hymns, or in the rude incongruities of tunes? Why should it be necessary to abjure all culture and excruciate all taste, in order that piety may have its supreme enjoyment? It is true that worship does not consist in artistic song, but neither does it in inharmonious doggrel. While the essence of all worship must ever lie in the true and fervent expression of spiritual feeling, the reverence which constitutes the perfection of such feeling demands that worship be clothed with every beauty that can adorn, with every appliance that can enhance it, so that in God's sanctuary there may be beauty as well as strength; for beauty is the comely costume of strength. Strength bedizened is not beauty, neither is strength denuded, but strength clothed in rich but yet unobtrusive garments. It is surely a careless if not a scornful disparagement of the service of the Church, to be contented with rude, inharmonious song in it, while we bestow upon our drawing-room song and our music-hall concerts our highest artistic culture and care. No genuine piety can excuse negligence; by its very negligence it will testify to its own defects. Everything pertaining to worship should surely indicate a reverent solicitude to bring to God the best that we can proffer—an offering perfect in every appliance that can give emphasis to its adoration; intensify its rapture, or beautify its love. Hence the devoutest worshippers will provide for their praise hymns of the highest poetry, and music of the richest harmony.—*Ibid.*

(*c*) He who worships the God and Father of our Lord Jesus Christ, must, in all the qualities of his soul, in all the relations of his life, be a *better* man than the atheist, than the man who denies the existence of God. The man who worships a stone is a better man than he who worships nothing. The man who falls down before carven wood, or worships the beasts of the field, is a grander nature than he who never bows his head in prayer, and never lifts up his heart in aspiration and religious desire. The tendency of worship is to elevate our nature. He who worships sincerely, however ignorantly, is the better for his worship; he is enlarged in his nature, his outlook upon things is widened, he is led away from self-trust, and is taught to depend upon a power, not lower, but higher, and in his estimation better, than his own.—*Joseph Parker, D.D.*

The worship of praise is the supreme act of intercourse between God and the creature. We gather into it all the elements of our complex nature, our intellect, conscience, religious emotion and physical faculty,—and engage them in a great religious service; and thus we realize the noblest fellowship with the Creator that is possible to a creature. In other ways also we have fellowship with God; in prayer, when we come to Him to ask the supply of our need; in meditation, when we muse upon His excellencies, or rest in the quiet assurance of His love; and in service, when we enter into His purposes, and as "workers together with God" consecrate ourselves to the accomplishment of them; but in praise, our fellowship with God is far higher than in any other; the personal want that prompts prayer is forgotten; the anxious thought that ponders Divine mysteries is banished; the strenuous toil that wearies even the consecrated hand is suspended; and we lift up the face of our worship to the light and glory of God's great love. Absorbed and blessed in the sense of His Divine excellencies, we stand before Him as the angels do; our reverence and love are quickened into adoring rapture, and we utter our reverent estimate of what He is, in the largest and most rapturous words that we can find. Such worship God graciously accepts; all natures that love crave love, and the loving God supremely craves the love of His creatures. Else would our worship be chilled and driven back into our own hearts. We speak to Him our admiration and praise because He graciously listens to it and joyously accepts it. We look up with gladness into the face of our Father in Heaven, because He responds to our loving rapture with His,— His Divine heart answers the love of our poor human hearts,—" God is love," and He *seeketh* loving souls to worship Him.—*H. Allon, D.D.*

AIMS AT PERFECTION.

(*Verse* 12.)

Here we have the doctrine enforced, that what is done should be well done.

I. Attention to the greater does not excuse neglect of the less (Matt. xxiii. 23; Luke xi. 42).

II. Obedience in the greater matters tested, as to sincerity, by obedience in the lesser details of ceremonial observance (Matt. xxv. 21; Luke xvi. 10.)

III. The offering up of the great sacrifice for sin does not liberate us from the duty of offering, on our part, the lesser sacrifice of faith, &c. (2 Cor. v. 15; Rom. xii. 1.)

IV. The offering of the less manifests our appreciation of the greater.— *Biblical Museum.*

THE OFFERING OF THE FIRST OF THE DOUGH.

(*Verses* 17-21.)

We have here an application of the law of the firstfruits, which is laid down in Exod. xxii. 29; xxiii. 19. Other applications of the law we find in Lev. ii. 12-14; xxiii. 10, 11, 14, 17. At a later period other directions were given concerning the observance of this law (Deut. xxvi. 1-11).

The command here is that of the first dough made of the first corn that was threshed, winnowed, and ground, they were to take to the priest a cake as a heave-offering unto the Lord. The size of the cake is not specified, but was left to the generosity of the offerer. In this offering we have—

I. **An expression of gratitude.**

In presenting the firstfruits to the Lord the Israelites acknowledged that they owed everything to Him. Very clearly this is brought out in the confession of the offerer of the basket of firstfruits (Deut. xxvi. 1-11). The offering was an expression of gratitude to Him for His bounty and beneficence. All the good that we possess we have received from Him. "He giveth to all life, and breath, and all things." "Every good gift and every perfect gift is from above," &c. We have received countless and priceless benefits from Him. Seeing that all good comes from God two conclusions are irresistible:

1. *That all good should be accepted and enjoyed gratefully.* "Bless the Lord, O my soul, and forget not all His benefits." "What shall I render unto the Lord for all His benefits toward me?" Very great should be our gratitude to Him. (*a*)

2. *That all good should be employed in accordance with His holy will.* We must guard against the abuse of any of His gifts; for He will require of us an account of them. Gratitude for our blessings urges us to use them in such a way as shall please Him—to use them for His glory.

II. **An acknowledgment of dependence.**

In offering the first of their dough after they entered the Promised Land they confessed their continued dependence upon Him. Very clearly and impressively Moses enjoined upon the Israelites that they should reverently remember the Lord their God, and humbly acknowledge their dependence upon Him after they entered the good Land (Deut. viii. 10-20). We too are constantly dependent upon God for all things. He is the one great Fountain of all physical, mental, and spiritual good. "All our springs are in Him." (*b*)

Seeing that we are thus absolutely dependent, it becometh us to be—

1. *Humble.* "What hast thou that thou didst not receive?" &c. "Shall the axe boast itself against him that heweth therewith?" &c. (*c*)

2. *Prayerful.* Surely it behoves us to acknowledge our dependence, and seek support. "Give us this day our daily bread;" "Uphold me with Thy free Spirit;" "Leave me not, neither forsake me, O God of my salvation;"— such petitions are ever appropriate on the lips of dependent creatures.

III. **A consecration of common things.**

To the offerer of the basket of firstfruits all his goods were sacred; all were blessed to him (Deut. xxvi. 11; and comp. Ezek. xliv. 30; 1 Tim. iv. 4, 5). Blessings are most enjoyed by us when we receive them with gratitude, and with practical acknowledgment of our obligation to God for them. The practical recognition of God's goodness to us in the mercies of every-day life, by heartily contributing to the cause of God amongst men, sanctifies all our mercies. So St. Paul affirms in the Epistle to the Romans (xi. 16), referring to this offering of the first dough, "If the firstfruit be holy, so also is the lump." After the cake of the first of their dough was offered unto the Lord the whole mass was consecrated to the use of man. (*d*)

IV. **A provision for the maintenance of the ministry and of the worship of God.**

This offering of the first of the dough, being an heave-offering, was the perquisite of the priests. Comp. chap. xviii. 24; Neh. x. 37. The meat offerings were designed by the Lord to be means of maintaining His service and His servants.

(For remarks and illustrations on this topic see pp. 84-86).

ILLUSTRATIONS.

(*a*) A gentleman of very considerable fortune, but a stranger to both personal and family religion, one evening took a solitary walk through part of his grounds. He happened to come near a mean hut, where a poor man lived with a numerous family, who earned their bread by daily labour. He heard a continued and pretty loud voice. Not knowing what it was, curiosity prompted him to listen. The man, who was piously disposed, happened to be at prayer with his family. So soon as he could distinguish the words, he heard him giving thanks, with great affection, to God, for the goodness of His providence, in giving them food to eat and raiment to put on, and in supplying them with what was necessary and comfortable in the present life. He was immediately struck with astonishment and confusion, and said to himself, "Does this poor man, who has nothing but the meanest fare, and that purchased by severe labour, give thanks to God for His goodness to himself and family; and I, who enjoy ease and honour, and everything that is pleasant and desirable, have hardly ever bent my knee, or made any acknowledgment to my Maker and Preserver!" It pleased God to make this providential occurrence the means of bringing him to a real and lasting sense of religion.—*The Sunday School Teachers' Treasury.*

(*b*) We stand to God in the relation of *dependents*. That is our actual position in life. "What hast thou that thou hast not received?" Let a man begin his studies there, and he will become correspondingly reverent. Have you genius? *Who lighted the lamp?* Have you health? *Who gave you your constitution?* Do you find the earth productive? "Yes." *Who made it productive?* "I did. I till it, I supply all the elements of nourishment needful; I did." *Did* you? Can you make it rain? Can you make the sun shine? Come, I will set you a little task, mighty man, potentate! This: *Change the quarter of the wind!* Now, come, that is a very little thing for a great man like you. "Well," you say, "that is the sort of thing that I really cannot do." Then, *clear a fog off the hill.* You can do *that.* Look what a port you have, and what infinite impudence. Come, *clear a fog!* Where would your tilling, and your manuring, and your subsoiling, and your harrowing and rolling all be, and what would they come to, if God were to say to the wind, "Never leave the east;" if God were to say to the clouds, "Stand still;" if God were to say to the sun, "Don't shew thyself for a year"? All these things shew us that we are, notwithstanding our resources, which are undoubtedly numerous and great, *dependents.*—Joseph Parker, D.D.

(*c*) How often have we aimed at building for ourselves tabernacles of remembrance and of rest, and we have gazed joyfully as it progressed to completion, and then the breath of the Lord has blown upon it, and it has been scattered, and we have been turned adrift and shelterless; and, lo! dwellings already provided for us, of firmer materials and of more excellent beauty, upon which we bestowed no labour nor thought. And so it is with all the matters of human glory. The strong man rejoiceth in his strength, and magnifieth himself in the might of his arms, but the Lord hath made him strong; the wise man glorieth himself in his intellect, but the clear perception, and the brilliant fancy, and the fluent utterance, these are God's gifts; the rich man rejoiceth in his riches, but the prudence to plan, and the sagacity to foresee, and the industry to gather, these are the bestowments of God.

Ah! why will men sacrifice to their own net, and burn incense to their own drag, when they have absolutely nothing which they have not received; and when every gift "cometh from the Father of lights, with whom is no variableness, neither shadow of turning"? And in the realm of morals, and in the spiritual life, our feebleness is the same. A conscience void of offence, a good report of those that are without, a heavenly purpose or a holy resolve, the inner purification or the comely outgrowth of a beneficent life—we are poor to compass them. We acquire them only by our dependence upon God. Have you learned this lesson, this deep hard lesson of humility? Forty years' sins you have committed! have they humbled you in the presence of God? Forty years' chastenings have corrected you! have they humbled your pride or fretted you into greater audacity of rebellion? Forty years' mercies have blessed you! have they excited your gratitude or inflated your vanity? Brethren, we must be humbled if we would be happy. It was in the valley of Humiliation, you remember, that the lad that had the herb heart's-ease in his bosom kept his serene and his rejoicing home. —*W. M. Punshon, LL.D.*

(*d*) Between the element of evil and the Christian elements there can be but one relation—that of war and struggle. They are antagonistic—the strength of the one is the weakness of the other. The evil must be wrestled with and overcome and exterminated, if it is to be well with the religious life. There is no such opposition between the Christian and the non-Christian elements of our existence. They become assimilated; the Christian absorbs the non-Christian elements of good. The ordinary duties of life—the every day virtues which form so large a portion of our being—have thus a Christian direction given them; they are elevated to a higher region than that which they naturally occupy. They become idealized; for just as the poetical spirit elevates and idealizes the most ordinary scenes, so does the religious spirit elevate and idealize the most ordinary ongoings of life. Religion is like poetry, an elevation and consecration of common things. You have seen a landscape which, while under the shadow, looked cold and bleak and forbidding, burst forth into life and beauty when the sun's rays fell upon it; so are the most ordinary affairs —the weary plodding, the dreary sameness, the dull routine—of our daily existence irradiated with a Divine glory by the light which comes from God.—*C. K. Watt, M.A.*

Sins of Omission and Ignorance.

(*Verses* 22-29.)

This paragraph suggests the following observations:—

I. Omissions of duty are accounted sinful by God.

"If ye have erred, and not observed all these commandments, which the Lord hath spoken unto Moses," &c. We sin not only when we break the commandments of God, but also when we fail to keep any of them. How many are our sins of omission! We are conscious of very many. And how many are there which have eluded our observation, and are known only to God! "Sins of commission," says Bulwer Lytton, "may not, perhaps, shock the retrospect of conscience. Large and obtrusive to view, we have confessed, mourned, repented, possibly atoned them. Sins of omission, so veiled amidst our hourly emotions—blent, confused, unseen in the conventional routine of existence;—Alas! could these suddenly emerge from their shadow, group together in serried mass and accusing order, would not the best of us then start in dismay, and would not the proudest humble himself at the Throne of Mercy!" (*a*)

II. Omissions of duty, even when arising from ignorance, are accounted sinful by God.

"If ought be committed by ignorance without the knowledge of the congregation," &c. (verse 24). "And if any soul sin through ignorance," &c. (verse 27). So David prays, "Who can understand his errors? Cleanse Thou me from secret faults." The reference is to unintentional sins; to sins not only unobserved by men, but not even known to the person himself at the time; unintentional sins of omission. (*b*) But let it be noticed in this connection, that—

1. *Ignorance of the Divine requirements is itself sinful in the case of most persons.* If a person can ascertain the will of God concerning him, he is bound to do so. That will is revealed to us in Nature and in the Bible: it is proclaimed and expounded regularly and freely and frequently by Christian teachers and preachers. We may know it if we will; we ought to know it. Spiritual ignorance is frequently not a misfortune, but a sin; not to be pitied, but to be condemned. (*c*)

2. *It is to be feared that in many cases where ignorance is urged as an excuse for sin, the real cause is indifference.* When men make no effort to know the will of God, and are but little concerned to do it, it is not ingenuous on their part to plead ignorance as an excuse for their sins.

III. A whole nation may be guilty of sins of omission and ignorance as well as an individual.

The legislation laid down in verses 22-26, is with a view to the whole nation being guilty of such sins. "This 'not doing all the commandments of Jehovah,' of which the congregation is supposed to incur the guilt without perceiving it, might consist either in the fact that, in particular instances, whether from oversight or negligence, the whole congregation omitted to fulfil the commandments of God, *i.e.* certain precepts of the law, *sc.* in the fact that they neglected the true and proper fulfilment of the whole law, either, as *Outram* supposes, 'by retaining to a certain extent the national rites, and following the worship of the true God, and yet at the same time acting unconsciously in opposition to the law, through having been led astray by some common errors,' or by allowing the evil example of godless rulers to seduce them to neglect their religious duties, or to adopt and join in certain customs and usages of the heathen, which appeared to be reconcilable with the law of Jehovah, though they really led to contempt and neglect of the commandments of the Lord."—*Keil and Del.* As illustrations of the sins here legislated, for Outram refers to the apostate kings, "when the people neglected their hereditary rites, and, forgetting the sacred laws, fell by a common sin into the observance of the religious rites of other nations." This view is confirmed by the offerings which Hezekiah made as an atonement for the sins of his father's reign (2 Chron. xxix. 21-36); and by the offerings made by the Israelites upon their return from their captivity (Ezra viii. 35).

It is, alas! not difficult to discover sins which may be truly called national even in our own enlightened country and age; but it would be difficult honestly to allege that they are sins of ignorance. Is not drunkenness a national sin? Are we as a nation guiltless in relation to the opium traffic? Are there not other sins of which this British nation is greatly guilty?

IV. **Sins of omission and ignorance may be forgiven.**

There is a sin for which there is no forgiveness; but sins of ignorance and omission may be forgiven upon certain conditions. Our Lord pleaded that His crucifiers might be forgiven because of their ignorance of the **true** character of their deed (Luke xxiii. 34). And St. Paul writes, "I obtained mercy, because I did it ignorantly in unbelief."

1. *In every case sacrifice was a condition of forgiveness.* When the congregation or the individual became aware of the sinfulness of their omissions, they were to offer a sin-offering as an acknowledgment of guilt and a condition of forgiveness. Whether the case were that of the whole congregation, or one member of the congregation; whether the individual were an Israelite, or a foreigner, sacrifice must be offered when the sin became known. The great truth here set forth is that the sinner needs atonement. Every sin tends to estrange the sinner from God. We are forgiven through the sacrifice of Jesus Christ, which strikingly exhibits the heinousness of sin, God's abhorrence of it also, and His infinite love for the sinner. (*d*). Our need of the merit of the Saviour's sacrifice, and the aid of His intercession, is continual.

2. *The extent of the sacrifice required varied in different cases.* When the sin was national, "all the congregation shall offer one young bullock for a burnt-offering, for a sweet savour unto the Lord, with his meat-offering, according to the ordinance, and one kid of the goats for a sin offering;" but when the sin was personal, "then he shall bring a she-goat of the first year for a sin-offering." The law of proportion is observed in the sacrifices which God demands. His requirements are ever "reasonable." Comp. Rom. xii. **1.**

Conclusion.

1. *Let us heartily loathe sin, whether of omission or commission* (Jer. xliv. 4).

2. *Let us faithfully examine ourselves in the light of God's holy Word.* Let no sin hide itself from our view, if we can prevent it (2 Cor. xiii. 5).

3. *Let us earnestly seek forgiveness for all sins through the mediation of Jesus Christ our Lord* (Eph. i. 7; 1 John i. 9).

ILLUSTRATIONS.

(*a*) Omissions cannot be trivial, if we only reflect what an influence they would have upon an ordinary commonwealth, if they were perpetrated there as they are in God's commonwealth. Think a minute, if one person has a right to omit his duty, another has, and all have. Then the watchman would omit to guard the house, the policeman would omit to arrest the thief, the judge would omit to sentence the offender, the sheriff would omit to punish the culprit, the government would omit to carry out its laws; then every occupation would cease, and the world would die of stagnation; the merchant would omit to attend to his calling, the husbandman would omit to plough the land: where would the commonwealth be? The kingdom would be out of joint; the machine would break down, for no cog of the wheels would act upon its fellow. How would societies of men exist at all? And surely if this is not to be tolerated in a society of men, much less in that great commonwealth of which God is the King, in which angels and glorified spirits are the peers, and all creatures citizens! How can the Lord tolerate that here there should be an omission, and there an omission, in defiance of His authority? As the Judge of all the earth, He must bring down His strong right hand upon these omissions, and crush out for ever the spirit that would thus revolt against His will.—*C. H. Spurgeon.*

(*b*) The perfection and spirituality of God's law render it almost impossible for a fallen son of Adam ever to know all the innumerable instances of his transgressing it. Add to which, that false principles and inveterate prejudices make us regard many things as innocent, and some things as laudable, which, in the eye of Heaven, are far otherwise. Self-examination is a duty which few practise as they ought to do: and he who practises it best will always have reason to conclude his particular confession with this general petition, "Cleanse Thou me from secret faults."—*George Horne.*

Many books have a few lines of *errata* at the end, but our *errata* might well be as large as the volume if we could but have sense enough to see them. Augustine wrote in his older days a series of Retractations; ours might make a library if we had enough grace to be convinced of our mistakes, and to confess them. If we had eyes like those of God we should think very differently of ourselves. The transgressions which we see and confess are but like the farmer's small samples which he brings to market, when he has left his granary full at home.—*C. H. Spurgeon.*

(*c*) The things revealed belong to us and our children to do them; and to be ignorant of any of these is a sin in the sight of God. We have the light of the truth shining in our faces, but we shut our eyes against it, lest it should shine in our hearts. We have the Word, we may read it, or hear it read, we have it preached, and other means of knowledge offered to us, therefore all such are left without excuse. It shall not excuse a subject when he hath broken some penal statute, to say, "Alas! I knew not the law, I was utterly ignorant of it, I never heard in all my life of any such matter." For the law is passed, printed, and published, and thou must take knowledge of it. Every man at his own peril must look to it, and if he run in danger of it, it is his own fault: so we may say of the law of God. He hath set it forth to the view of all, and all must make inquiry after it at their uttermost peril.—*Attersoll.*

(*d*) Sinners are saved not simply because so much pain and grief have been endured in their stead, but because Christ has performed a great spiritual work on their behalf, and has performed it in the full foresight of all the suffering that would be inseparable from His so doing. It is monstrous to suppose that the Deity could be pleased with mere suffering. It is the spiritual essence in the Atonement that makes it to be what it is to us. It may be accepted as certain, that in the gift of the Son of God we have the brightest manifestation of the love of the Father; and that in the willing humiliation and grief of the Redeemer we have the tenderest revelation of pity towards the evil and unthankful, and at the same time the noblest act of worship ever rendered to the good and the holy. In this sense, it is truly by the sorrows, the death, the cross of Christ that we have salvation. It has been His will to become thus acquainted with grief, and to die—to die the death of the cross—that we might be saved.—*Robert Vaughan, D.D.*

The Nature and Punishment of Presumptuous Sins.

(*Verses* 30, 31.)

A very marked difference is recognised between sins of omission and ignorance and sins of presumption; the heinousness of the latter is much greater than of the former. "All unrighteousness is sin;" and all sin is essentially evil; but all sins are not alike evil; the evil of some sins is greater than the evil of others. Moreover the guilt of the same sin may differ greatly when committed by different persons under different circumstances and influences, and with different motives. Attersoll says truly, "There is great difference in the manner of sinning; some sin ignorantly, some willingly (Psa. xix. 12, 13; 1 Tim. i. 13). Some are principal and ringleaders in the sin, others are only accessories; some are only in thought, others in deed; some offend of malice, some offend of weakness; some commit sin, others, besides this, have pleasure in them that do them (Rom. i. 32)." (*a*) We have now to consider the worst of sins. Notice:—

I. The nature of presumptuous sins.

279

"But the soul that doeth ought presumptuously," &c. The marginal rendering, which is correct, gives us an insight into the nature of these sins. "The soul that doeth with an high hand." To sin "with a high hand" is to sin in a daring spirit and defying manner. Comp. Job xv. 25. Presumptuous sins are here represented as involving—

1. *Positive breach of the law of God.* "He hath broken His commandment." Very great is the difference between sins of omission unwittingly committed, and sins of commission wilfully committed. The guilt of the latter is very dark.

2. *Contempt of the word of God.* "He hath despised the word of the Lord." He despised God's word of command by disregarding its authority; His word of promise by disregarding its encouragements to obedience; and His word of threatening by setting at nought its design and power to deter from sin.

3. *Blasphemy against God Himself.* "The same reproacheth" (revileth, or blasphemeth) "the Lord." "Yes, reproacheth Him: reproacheth His omniscience as if He did not know; reproacheth His holiness as if He did not care; reproacheth His truth as if, having spoken, yet He would not do it; reproacheth His power as if His arm were shortened, and He could not strike! Are we prepared for this cluster of impieties? 'Lord, keep back Thy servant from presumptuous sins.'" (*b*)

II. **The punishment of presumptuous sins.**

1. *Death.* "That soul shall be cut off from among his people; .... that soul shall utterly be cut off." We conclude that these words point to the punishment of death, and not simply to exclusion from the political and religious privileges of the nation, because of—(1) The solemn force and emphasis of the words themselves; and (2) The illustration of the operation of the law given in the next paragraph (verses 32-36). Presumptuous sinners were put to death, in some instances by public execution, and in others by the immediate judgment of God. Persistence in sin leads to worse than bodily death. "The soul that sinneth it shall die." "Sin, when it is finished, bringeth forth death." (*c*)

2. *Confirmed sinfulness.* "His iniquity shall be upon him." The natural tendency of wilful and daring sin is to harden the heart in its rebellion against God beyond all hope of repentance. Comp. Heb. x. 26-29. (*d*)

Conclusion.

1. *As the guilt of sin differs so also does the punishment.* Comp. Matt. xi. 22-24; xxiii. 14; Luke xii. 47, 48; Heb. x. 28, 29.

2. *Let those who have already advanced far in sin turn from their evil ways ere it be too late.* You cannot remain stationary. You must either turn from sin to the Saviour, or go on in sin until you become a daring and defiant and hopeless rebel against God. Be warned in time.

3. *If we would keep clear of presumptuous sins let us guard against sins of every kind and degree.* "Cultivate a holy shrinking from sin in its most unobserved beginnings, and in its least degrees. Sensitiveness to the smallest degree of offending is the true and only security of the Christian. Sin shall never have dominion over him who resists the first putting on of its chains."

ILLUSTRATIONS.

(*a*) Two persons may commit the same identical crime, yet the guilt may be inconceivably greater in the one case than the other. The one may have had no instruction—no benefit from parental culture—no faithful warnings and admonitions—no holy example to direct and regulate—no warning to restrain—no encouragement to animate in the right path. The other may have been surrounded by all the helps and inducements to right consideration—to holy fear—to correct conduct; and therefore his sin is marked with a far higher degree of aggravation than the other; and thus, in the sight of God, the judge on the bench often may be far more guilty than the criminal at the bar.—*Joseph Fletcher, D.D.*

(*b*) The final stage of presumptuous sinning

is reached when, to the clearest knowledge of the greatness of our sin, and to the most elaborate and carefully-contrived schemes for effecting it, there is added the resoluteness of obstinacy—a dogged and persevering stubbornness in getting our own way, even though, in addition to all the remonstrances of conscience and the Holy Spirit of God, all the aspects of God's Providence are against us—frowning us back every step we take. A striking illustration of this form of presumption we have in the history of Balaam. We see there a man intent on a scheme for his own aggrandisement. God opposed that scheme. The man keeps tampering with his conscience to get leave to do a wrong thing, till at last God in anger gives him leave. But no sooner does this bad man set out than the frown of God meets him. A mysterious power drives him back. His foot is crushed. His ass falls. Before his opened eyes stands the angel of God, telling him his way is a perverse way, and yet, after a few hollow professions of contrition, he determines to go on. So it is that the transgressor "holdeth fast his iniquity," and will not let it go. He would break a lance even with an angel in the path of the vineyards. Oh! how often does God make it difficult for us to find opportunities for our besetting sin. The farther we go the more we find our way hedged up with thorns. The difficulties grow upon us like a waking nightmare. And yet with a madness that knows no control, and a hardihood that braves all consequences, we rush upon the thick bosses of the Almighty, and, in an attitude of defiant presumption, stretch out our hands against God.—*Daniel Moore, M.A.*

(*c*) The tale of the goblet which the genius of a heathen fashioned was true, and taught a moral of which many a death-bed furnishes the melancholy illustration. Having made the model of a serpent, he fixed it in the bottom of the cup. Coiled for the spring, a pair of gleaming eyes in its head, and in its open mouth fangs raised to strike, it lay beneath the ruby wine. Nor did he who raised the golden cup to quench his thirst, and quaff the delicious draught, suspect what lay below, till, as he reached the dregs, that dreadful head rose up, and glistened before his eyes. So, when life's cup is nearly emptied, and sin's last pleasure quaffed, and unwilling lips are draining the bitter dregs, shall rise the ghastly terrors of remorse and death and judgment upon the despairing soul. Be assured, a serpent lurks at the bottom of guilt's sweetest pleasure.—*Thomas Guthrie, D.D.*

(*d*) There is a gravitating power about sins of presumption from which the soul rarely ever rises. Every wilful sin hardens the heart and renders it less accessible to converting influences than it was before. One conquest over the conscience makes way for another, and that for a third, till at length this inward monitor becomes "seared as with a hot iron." It has neither voice to speak, nor authority to restrain, nor sensibility to feel. Sceptreless, deaf, stifled, gagged, it dies and makes no sign. Thus evil men and wilful sinners wax worse and worse ; because the habit of presumptuous sinning, of tampering with conscience, and resisting the Holy Ghost, forecloses against them all the means of their ever getting better . . . . From transgression to transgression, from lower depth to lower depth, neither heaven nor earth, neither angels nor men have it in charge to interfere : —"Ephraim is joined to his idols : let him alone."—*Daniel Moore, M.A.*

SINS DANGEROUS AND SINS DEADLY.

(*Verses 27 and 30.*)

In the text God seeks to impress on all that no sin can be trifled with, because every sin must be atoned for, and then to warn that constant trifling with sin must harden the soul and place it beyond the limits of pardon. The text suggests two thoughts—

I. That there are degrees in sin.

The Lord distinguishes here between sins of ignorance, which might be atoned for, and sins of presumption, for which there could be no atonement. There are degrees in guilt. The same act of sin in two different persons, or in the same person at different times, varies as to guilt. Take any sin—the mere deed is the same in the professing Christian and the man that has been brought up in ignorance and vice, but the degrees of guilt are very different. Guilt is not to be measured by the mere act of the sin ; but by the mind that gives birth to it, by the circumstances under which it is done, by the results which follow, &c.

Sins of ignorance are those which are not intentional and deliberate ; those resulting from human frailty and thoughtlessness, from lack of watchfulness or courage, &c.

Presumptuous sins are those committed "with a high hand," deliberately, daringly, against light and conviction and the known commands of God.

Between these two God made a distinction. He did not and could not deal with them alike. He weighs actions; He estimates conduct. His knowledge, wisdom and justice are such that He cannot err, and that no one shall be wronged. There are then degrees in sin; and it is of the utmost importance for all to know and realise this. It will act as a great check on sin. People sometimes say, as an excuse for their sin, that as they have gone wrong they might as well suffer for much as for little. No! it is false. With every sin the man gets worse; sinfulness increases. Sin grows; there is development in it. Every step in sin is a step into greater danger, and leaves less hope of reclamation. Sins of ignorance through trifling and neglect may grow to be those of presumption.

II. **That while all sins are dangerous some are deadly.**

The text shows that all sin is dangerous by the fact that an atonement had to be made for sins of ignorance; none could be forgiven without. In sinning we trifle with our best interests, and expose ourselves to the greatest danger. While ignorance may excuse, nothing can justify any sin. The text further tells us of sins for which the doer was cut off from among the people. These sins were murder, adultery, swearing, Sabbath-breaking, *et al.* For these there was no pardon. Why? Not because God was not merciful enough to forgive; but because the sinner knew these things to be wrong, and did them in defiance of God. The text gives the reason, "The same reproacheth the Lord," treats Him with contempt and scorn, and despises His law. And when man gets into that state penitence is impossible, and that being so God will not and cannot forgive. The New Testament teaches the same. We find there that sin was so dangerous as to need the sacrifice of Christ, and it tells us of "a sin which is unto death," and of "the blasphemy against the Holy Ghost, which shall not be forgiven unto men." We think that this is not any one sin so much as a state of mind that opposes God,—a malicious contempt and wilful rejection of the Gospel. For such the Bible tells us there is no hope; that the "day of grace has closed with them before the day of life." How is this? Not because God is not ready to pardon, or the sin too great to be forgiven. There is no sin beyond the merits of Christ's atonement. His blood " cleanseth from all sin." Why, then? The reason is in the man himself. God forgives only the penitent; it would be neither right nor safe to forgive without penitence. But this man is *im*penitent; he resists and hates God; he "reproacheth the Lord." To such a man pardon becomes impossible because penitence has become impossible. God leaves him! What a doom! Let hearers of the Gospel think of it. This doom is possible; and it is possible only in Christian lands, &c. Learn :—

1. *That God is merciful.* He sent His Son to die that He might put away sin, and restore us unto Himself.

2. *That there is a limit to His mercy.* What cost Him so much He will let no one despise. Let the sinning one take care. The door of mercy will be closed, and it may be against him.

Are you afraid that you have committed the "sin unto death"? The fear proves that, so far, you have not. If there is pain in the injured limb, it is certain that mortification has not set in; &c. Hasten to Christ at once, while there is hope. Out of Him man is ever in danger.—*David Lloyd.*

PRESUMPTION.

(Verse 30.)

We desire to warn you against *presumption*. The Psalmist prays to be cleansed from secret faults, and kept back from presumptuous sins. Our text and the context indicate the heinousness and fearful consequences of this kind of evil. Yet we fear that sins of this kind are awfully prevalent. Let us notice—

I. **What presumption includes.** It signifies—

1. *Boldness in evil.* Sinning without fear. Hardihood, daring, recklessness.

2. *Arrogance in evil.* Setting ourselves up against God. Pride of heart and spirit and tongue. Ps. lxxiii. 6; ix. 2; Acts ii. 18.

3. *Irreverence towards God.* All profanity. Blasphemies of the Divine name, &c. All cursing and defying God. As in the case of Pharaoh :— "Who is the Lord?" &c.

4. *Confidence of escape from the threatenings of God.* This is one of the chief elements of presumption. Not dreading nor caring for consequences, &c.

II. **The chief causes of presumption.**

1. *Spiritual ignorance.* Blindness of mind, &c. Ignorance of self and God. It is the offspring of darkness.

2. *Recklessness and inconsideration.* Do not reflect. Do not consider the claims of God or man. The grandeur of Jehovah, and the guilty worm. The holy law, and man's criminality.

3. *Confirmed unbelief*, giving no credit to the Word. Its revelations, or threatenings, &c.

4. *Hardness of heart.* This is both a cause and a result. It makes men presumptuous. Presumption increases it.

III. **The terrible results of presumptuousness.**

1. *God, defied, will vindicate His authority.* He cannot let it pass. His majesty and law concerned, &c.

2. *Threatening despised, He will terribly execute.* Not one jot fail. There may be delay, waiting, longsuffering, but the execution of vengeance is certain.

3. *Mercy despised will involve in fearful retribution.* Hear God,—Prov. i. 24; Ps. ii. 4, &c. The instances of this, how numerous! The old world, Pharaoh, Sodom, &c., nations of Canaan, Jerusalem. (See Luke xix. 41-44).

Application.

1. How needful is consideration.
2. Repentance, how imperative!
3. To seek mercy. The Gospel publishes it in Christ, and offers it to every sinner.—*Jabez Burns, D.D.*

THE SIN AND PUNISHMENT OF THE SABBATH-BREAKER.

(Verses 32-36.)

This event is recorded here as an illustration of presumptuous sin and its punishment. Notice :—

I. **The sin committed.**

This man violated the law of the Sabbath (Exod. xx. 8-11) by gathering sticks on that day. Looking at the mere act it seems a very small sin indeed, and the punishment seems utterly disproportioned to the sin; but in estimating the moral quality of an action much has to be taken into account in addition to the mere act. Thus in the present case, in order to form a correct judgment it is necessary to consider—

1. *The solemn urgency with which the violated command is enforced in the Sacred Scriptures.* See Exod. xvi. 22-30; xx. 8-11; xxxi. 13-17; xxxv. 1-3; Lev. xxiii. 3; xxvi. 2; Deut. v. 12-15. The first incontrovertible institution of the Sabbath amongst the Israelites is

recorded in Exod. xvi. 23-29. Shortly afterwards, at the giving of the Law, " it was re-enacted in the Fourth Commandment, which," as Mr. Garden points out, "gave it a rank above that of an ordinary law, making it one of the signs of the Covenant. As such it remained together with the Passover, the two forming the most solemn and distinctive features of Hebrew religious life. Its neglect or profanation ranked foremost among national sins; the renewed observance of it was sure to accompany national reformation." The importance attached to the keeping of the Sabbath in subsequent times appears from Isa. lviii. 13, 14; Jer. xvii. 21-27; Ezek. xx. 12-24; Neh. x. 31; xiii. 15-22.

2. *The relation of the violated command to the Lord God.* (1) The day was consecrated to God; it was dedicated to His honour; its violation, therefore, involved reproach to Him. "The holy Sabbath unto the Lord;" "the Sabbath of rest holy to the Lord;" "the seventh day is the Sabbath of the Lord thy God;" thus the observance of the day is bound up with His honour. (2) The day was a memorial of their emancipation from Egypt; its violation, therefore, involved ingratitude to God, their Emancipator (Deut. v. 15). So that he who wilfully broke the Sabbath reproached the Lord.

3. *The beneficence of the violated command.* The beneficent character of the institution is unmistakably clear in the version of it given in Deut. v. 12-15. Its design and tendency are to promote human well-being, by securing to man a regularly recurring season of bodily rest and opportunity of spiritual culture. The day of rest has been well compared to "the green oasis, the little grassy meadow in the wilderness, where after the week-days' journey the pilgrim halts for refreshment and repose; where he rests beneath the shade of the lofty palm trees, and dips his vessel in the waters of the calm, clear stream, and recovers his strength to go forth again upon his pilgrimage in the desert with renewed vigour and cheerfulness."

4. *The wilfulness of the violation of the command.* This man certainly knew the law; the manner in which the manna was bestowed was a regular reminder of it; he could not have been ignorant of the penalty of breaking the law (Exod xxxi. 14, 15); yet he breaks it. He sins knowingly, wilfully, " with a high hand ; " and in accordance with the law which he had broken, he is put to death for his sin. So we see that his sin was not a small or slight one, but one of great heinousness.

II. The punishment inflicted upon the sinner.

He was stoned to death. Three points deserve notice :—

1. *The case was dealt with in an orderly and becoming manner.* The man was taken in the very act of gathering sticks, he was then brought before Moses and Aaron and the whole congregation, *i.e.,* "the college of elders, as the judicial authorities of the congregation" (Exod. xviii. 25, 26). Death had been assigned as the penalty of the transgression (Exod. xxxi. 14, 15; xxxv. 2); but it had not been determined by what mode the transgressor should be put to death; he was therefore kept in custody until the next day, in order that Moses might consult the Lord on that point. Comp. Lev. xxiv. 12. There was nothing rash or disorderly in the procedure in the case.

2. *The punishment was ordered by God.* "And the Lord said unto Moses, The man shall be surely put to death;" &c. Both the penalty itself and the mode of inflicting it were declared by the Lord to Moses.

3. *The punishment was calculated to deter others from the sin.* This was probably the design in calling upon the people to stone him : "All the congregation shall stone him with stones without the camp. And all the congregation brought him," &c. This would be likely to impress them deeply with the enormity of the sin and the severity of the punishment, and to awaken within them a wholesome fear of the offence.

Conclusion.

1. *Here is solemn warning to those who attend to moral duties, but neglect religion.* There are some who strive to obey the commands of the second table of the Law, but disregard those of the first. The violations of the commands of the first table are directly against God Himself, and they will not go unpunished. The man who neglects worship dwarfs and degrades his own soul, &c.

2. *The essential element in the law of the Sabbath is of perpetual obligation.* Several non-essentials have been altered, or have passed away; *e.g.*, instead of observing the seventh, we observe the first day of the week; instead of reckoning the day from sunset to sunset, we reckon it from midnight to midnight; and many things as to the mode of its observance have passed away. But the spirit and substance of the law is as binding now as ever it was. Worship for the soul and rest for the body are two of the deepest needs of man. The institution of the Sabbath is designed to meet these needs. "The Sabbath was made for man," and man cannot do without it. "Eternal as the constitution of the soul of man, is the necessity for the existence of a day of rest." The proportion also, one day in seven, is of perpetual obligation. "One day in ten, prescribed by revolutionary France, was actually pronounced by physiologists insufficient." No man can set at nought this ordinance of God without inflicting upon himself sore loss and injury.

ILLUSTRATIONS.

Whatever Divine commands Moses gave the Israelites, he communicated to them their grounds. When he gave them the law of the Jewish Sabbath he gave them along with it its basis, that is, the revelation of God's Sabbath. At the time of the Israelitish captivity in Egypt we find not a trace of the Sabbath. It was a new thing when Moses gave it by God's command as a law unto the Israelites; and he made it the seal of a covenant which marked them out from other nations. On what did it rest? It rested upon something greater than mere human will, or even Divine will, and that something was an eternal necessity of man's nature, derived from a similar necessity in the nature of his Maker. And this is the only ground on which *our* obligation to keep the Sabbath day can rest. We cannot place it on the ground of the Mosaic law.

We have abrogated almost all that belonged to the Sabbath day. We have taken away "every manner of work." We have changed many other important particulars. From sunset to sunset we have altered to from midnight to midnight. And then instead of "the seventh day," we have left only this "one day in seven;" and the sceptical mind requires some proof of the moral obligation of keeping one day without work when we have admitted all the rest of the covenant to be ceremonial. We must take higher ground, and tell the doubter that there is an eternal necessity for the recurring Sabbath. It is just on this, only on this perpetual necessity of a Sabbath, that our observance of the Sabbath must be founded, in this requirement of physical rest by our nature, in the fact also that it is only by means of these stated returns of particular seasons that man can, in rest from temporal concerns, fix his attention on his Maker.

There is a further necessity for a similar outward form in the mode of worship on the Sabbath, which illustrates the primal necessity of having a day set apart. Thoughtful men have often asked why they cannot go out and have their worship in the great temple of the universe. The man who argues so knows not his own nature. There is a temple of God's universe, and those who deny it forget a grand spiritual truth; but the feeling gained in this temple of God is one thing, that gained in the church of God is another. We may in like manner worship God all the week, but the emotion of worship on the Sabbath when we lay aside work is different from the emotions felt towards God in the midst of work.—*F. W. Robertson, M.A.*

Although I think that the whole law is done away with, so far as it is the law given on Mount Sinai, yet as far as it is the law of the Spirit I hold it to be all binding; and believing that our need of a Lord's-day is as great as ever it was, and that, therefore, its observance is God's will, and is likely as far as we can see, to be so to the end of time, I should think it mischievous to weaken the respect paid to it.—*Dr. Arnold.*

Religion has been the basis, the mother, the nurse of the English day of rest. It has sprung out of deep convictions of the sacredness of life, the holiness of law, the certainty of judgment, and the prospect of heaven. . . . . The English Sunday will not be preserved without the continued operation of this religious principle. The love of money will be stronger than the love of rest. Competition can wage successful battles with anything short of conscience; God knows that it often avails to conquer this. But religious convictions are stronger, more widely spread, more deeply penetrating than any notion of conventional right, than any laws of a shallow expediency. If you try, if the nation tries, if a few noisy talkers try, to found the sanctity of the Sabbath on the advantage of recreation, —rational or irrational,—there will be very soon an end of its sacredness altogether. Let Sunday become the day on which ordinary travelling for recreation takes place,—and it will occupy tens of thousands of hands, who will find that day, as many do on the continent of Europe, the hardest and most laborious of the seven. Let recreation and amusement be the main reasons upon which you ask for the preservation of this day of rest, and you will have it invaded at every point. Let us be distinctly forewarned, that if the great use of a Sunday is a holiday; if we have no deeper reason than the relaxation of our physical energies; no other attraction than that which music, or fresh air, or public amusement may afford; we are destroying the great safeguard of the day, we are running in danger of being robbed altogether of a sacred and invaluable right. To reduce our English Sunday to the level of a Continental or pleasure-taking Sunday, would be to deprive the people of England of their birthright, to hand labour, more than ever, into the power of capital, and to open the door along which all kinds of toil must, as in other countries, infallibly follow. . . . .

In the name of your own rights, by reason of your own need, out of regard to the obvious necessities of the case, and in view of the experience of all Europe, beware how you trifle with the conscience, the religious spirit, the Christian consecration, the holy safeguards, of what, even in spite of yourselves, is blessing you.—*H. R. Reynolds, D.D.*

Experience tells us, after a trial, that those Sundays are the happiest, the purest, the most rich in blessing, in which the spiritual part has been most attended to;—those in which the business letter was put aside till evening, and the profane literature not opened, and the ordinary occupations entirely suspended;—those in which as in the temple of Solomon, the sound of the earthly hammer has not been heard in the temple of the soul: for this is, in fact, the very distinction between the spirit of the Jewish Sabbath and the spirit of the Christian Lord's-day. The one is chiefly for the body—"Thou shalt do no manner of work." The other is principally for the soul —"I was in the spirit on the Lord's-day."—*F. W. Robertson, M.A.*

THE SABBATH-BREAKER AND HIS DOOM.

(*Verses* 32-36.)

Here is another arrangement for the exposition of this paragraph:—

I. The sin.

1. *The transgression of a moral law, which was enforced by the most solemn commands and by the severest penalty.*

2. *The transgression of this law wilfully.*

II. The arrest.

The offender was seized in the act of transgression, and taken before the judicial authorities.

III. The consultation.

The direction of the Lord is sought as to the mode by which the sentence of death is to be executed upon him.

IV. The sentence.

This was determined by the Lord. The transgressor must be put to death (Exod. xxxi. 14, 15); he must be put to death by stoning (ver. 35).

V. The execution.

"And all the congregation brought him without," &c. (ver. 36). The people were the executioners. This would increase the force of the warning which the event gave to the nation.

Conclusion.

1. *The moral element in the Law of the Sabbath is of perpetual obligation.* We still need rest for body and mind; we still need worship for the spirit.

2. *The neglecters of religious duties and privileges will do well to take warning.* If any man fails to observe religiously the Lord's day, he does so at his own loss and peril.

The Ordinance of the Fringes: Gracious Reminders of Divine Commands.

(Verses 37, 41.)

In previous paragraphs we have had legislation concerning sins of ignorance and of presumption; in this paragraph we have an institution designed to prevent sins of ignorance—sins committed unwittingly—by keeping before the eyes of the people reminders of the commands of God, and of their duty in relation to them. The Israelites are commanded to wear fringes or tassels, &c. (*See Explanatory Notes* on ver. 38). This institution is not binding upon us, but it contains important instruction for us. Consider—

I. The proneness of man to forget "the commandments of the Lord."

This is clearly implied in this ordinance. The counteraction of this proneness is the design of the ordinance. This tendency to lose sight of the commands of God arises from—

1. *The sinfulness of human nature.* Unless we are renewed by the Spirit of God we naturally "wander after our own heart and our own eyes." The commandments of the Lord are opposed to many of the desires and purposes of the human heart; and we are not anxious to bear in mind that which clashes with our wishes, and rebukes us for much of our life and conduct. Men do not remember the commands of God *because they do not want to remember them.* Comp. Psa. lxxvii. 10, 11; cvi. 13; Rom. i. 28.

2. *The wordly spirit which so largely prevails in human society.* In the conduct of trade, as a rule we fear, men do not ask if their practices accord with the laws of God, but if they accord with the usages of trade or profession. In social relations to a very large extent men are not governed by the commands of God, but by the requirements of the society in which they move. The first and the supreme inquiry is not, Is this right? but, Is this expedient? or, popular? or, Will it pay? In this way "the commandments of the Lord" are overlooked, or cast aside. "Our memories," says Trapp, "are like strainers, nets, grates, that let the pure water run away, but retain mud, trash, &c. It is with us as with those in Psa. cvi. 13, 'they soon forgat His works,' &c., and therefore we have need of all good helps."

II. The arrangements which God has made to remind man of His commandments.

"Speak unto the children of Israel, and bid them that they make them fringes," &c. These fringes "were not appointed for the trimming and adorning of their clothes, but to 'stir up their pure minds by way of remembrance' (2 Pet. iii. 1), that they might look upon the fringe and remember the commandments.... If they were tempted to sin, the fringe would be a monitor to them not to break God's commandments; if a duty was forgotten to be done in its season, the fringe would remind them of it." Notice—

1. *The means which God employs to remind us of His commandments.* (1) The Bible. In this He not only reveals His will concerning us, but illustrates and enforces it in various ways so that we might not forget it. (2) The Holy Spirit. He influences our spirits; speaks in us by means of conscience, &c. (3) Holy examples. In these the will of God is "drawn out in living characters." (4) Warning examples of the evil consequences of overlooking His commands. These witness to us that it is perilous to forget the Divine will, and admonish us against doing so. (*a*)

2. *The design of God in reminding us of His commandments.* "That ye wander not after your own heart and your own eyes, after which ye use to go a whoring; that ye may remember and do all My commandments, and be holy unto your God." Recollection of the will of God must be followed by obe-

dience to that will, or it will be worse than useless. The grand end of God's dealings with us is that we may be holy unto Him. He seeks to bind us to Himself in hearty loyalty. (*b*)

III. **The grounds upon which God requires from us this recollection of, and obedience to His commands.**

"I am the Lord your God, which brought you out of the land of Egypt to be your God; I am the Lord your God." Here are two reasons for His claims upon us:

1. *His personal relation to us.* He is the Lord our God. He alone is the rightful Sovereign of our being. He is our Creator, the Supremely Great, the Supremely Good, and His claim upon our loyal obedience is incontrovertible.

2. *His gracious doings for us.* "I brought you out of the land of Egypt to be your God." What has He not done for us? He has redeemed us from a captivity immeasurably worse than that of Israel in Egypt; and that at an immense cost (1 Pet. i. 18, 19). He sustains us in being, enriches our life with many blessings, and opens out to us the most inviting and inspiring prospects. We cannot overlook His claims upon us without base ingratitude.

Be it ours with diligence and prayerfulness to endeavour to do all God's commandments, and to be holy unto Him. (*c*)

ILLUSTRATIONS.

(*a*) The gracious provisions of the Christian dispensation do not encourage, but discourage sinning. . . . We often sin through ignorance—the Christian dispensation enlightens us as to sin; shows us what God thinks of our transgressions; what God feels about them; what an evil and a bitter thing it is to sin against God. We sin through carelessness—the Christian dispensation makes us serious concerning sin. Who can look at the cross of Christ, and believe that He who is suspended on that cross is dying there on account of sin, and not be serious about sin? We sin through moral deadness—the Christian dispensation inspires us with life. It is a ministration by which the living God seeks to restore life to us. We sin on sometimes through despair—the Christian dispensation fills us with hope. Men say sometimes, when they have sunk very low, It is of no use trying to rise up out of this horrible pit, and to extricate myself from this miry clay. But, looking at redemption, we see that no man need ever sin through despair; on the contrary the Christian dispensation fills us with hope. We sin often through feverishness and through restlessness of spirit—the Christian dispensation imparts peace, restores quiet to our distracted nature, and keeps the heart and mind in that holy quiet. We sin through weakness—the Christian dispensation imparts power. We sin by the force of evil motives—the Christian dispensation changes our motives; so that if any man be in Christ he is a new creature; old things have passed away, and all things have become new. The Christian dispensation does not encourage sin, but discourages it.—*Samuel Martin.*

(*b*) Throughout the Old Testament the holiness of God is made a sufficient, yea, the highest reason, why those who recognised this fact and this perfection of His nature should be holy too. God had revealed His holiness to Israel; and He wished them to consider it the "beauty" of His nature . . . . We have the sublime, the supernatural spectacle of an obscure tribe of men, who recognised no other God than their "Holy One," who were distinguished from all other nations by being separated from sin, and who felt that nothing short of holiness befitted "the house of their God." "The High and Lofty One who inhabited eternity" bore in their creed a mighty name: it was no other than this, "Holy;" and no worship could be acceptable in His sight, no rites could lift the soul heavenwards, which were not holy. As their God was distinguished from all other gods by the dazzling holiness of His nature, so they were to be distinguished from all other people by their purity, their moral excellence, their resemblance to Him. The new relation in which they found that they were standing to the Holy God, the obligations under which He had placed them, the gratitude that He could claim from their hearts, the attraction of His love, the human cords, the loving hands by which He drew them to Himself, all insisted upon their holiness; and so we find it written in the Law of Moses, "I am the Lord your God; therefore shall ye sanctify yourselves;" and, "Ye shall be holy, for I am holy;" "I am the Lord your God, that brought you up out of the land of Egypt, to be your God: ye shall therefore be holy, for I am holy." And again, "Sanctify yourselves, and be ye holy, for I am the Lord your God, and ye shall keep My statutes and do them; I am the Lord that doth sanctify you." Again we find it written, "Ye shall be holy unto Me, for I the Lord am holy, and have severed you from other people, that ye should be Mine." Israel was taught to "Give thanks at the remembrance of his holiness," to "Glory in His holy name, to exalt the Lord God, and worship at His holy hill," because "The Lord God was holy." The Psalmist and the prophets, like the pillars in the temple of their God, all palpitate with the light of His holiness, and are moved with the voice of the seraphs' song; they are dark with this excessive brightness, and by the holy service that they rendered shed on mankind the luminous principle, that the holiness of God is the chief reason for the holiness of man.—*H. R. Reynolds, D.D.*

(c) Much of the beauty of holiness lies in little things. Microscopic holiness is the perfection of excellence: if a life will bear examination in each hour of it, it is pure indeed. Those who are not careful about their words, and even their thoughts, will soon grow careless concerning their more notable actions. Those who tolerate sin in what they think to be little things, will soon indulge it in greater matters. To live by the day and to watch each step, is the true pilgrimage method. More lies in the careful noting of every single act than careless minds can well imagine. Be this then your prayer: "Lord, direct my morning thoughts, that the step out of my chamber into the world may be taken in Thy fear. At my table keep me in Thy presence; behind my counter, or in my field, or wherever else I may be, suffer me not to grieve Thy Spirit by any evil; and when I come to lie down at night, let the action (which seemeth so indifferent) of casting myself upon my pillow, be performed with a neart that loveth Thee; so that I shall be prepared to be with Thee, if wakeful during the night." This brief prayer, "Order my steps," teaches us attention to the minutiæ of life; may we have grace to learn the lesson.—*C. H. Spurgeon.*

END OF VOLUME III.